D1524555

Congress and the Nation

Sara Miller McCune founded SAGE Publishing in 1965 to support the dissemination of usable knowledge and educate a global community. SAGE publishes more than 1000 journals and over 800 new books each year, spanning a wide range of subject areas. Our growing selection of library products includes archives, data, case studies and video. SAGE remains majority owned by our founder and after her lifetime will become owned by a charitable trust that secures the company's continued independence.

Los Angeles | London | New Delhi | Singapore | Washington DC | Melbourne

Congress and the Nation

VOLUME XV   •   2017–2020

POLITICS AND POLICY IN THE
115TH AND 116TH CONGRESSES

S Sage Reference | CQPRESS

FOR INFORMATION:

CQ Press

An Imprint of SAGE Publications, Inc.

2455 Teller Road

Thousand Oaks, California 91320

E-mail: order@sagepub.com

SAGE Publications Ltd.

1 Oliver's Yard

55 City Road

London, EC1Y 1SP

United Kingdom

SAGE Publications India Pvt Ltd

Unit No 323-333, Third Floor, F-Block

International Trade Tower Nehru Place

New Delhi - 110 019

India

SAGE Publications Asia-Pacific Pte. Ltd.

18 Cross Street #10-10/11/12

China Square Central

Singapore 048423

Acquisitions Editor: Laura McEwan

Editorial Assistant: Elizabeth Hernandez

Production Editor: Aparajita Srivastava

Copy Editor: Diane DiMura

Typesetter: Hurix Digital

Cover Designer: Candice Harman

Marketing Manager: Gabrielle Perretta

Printed in the United States of America

ISBN: 9781071855218

This book is printed on acid-free paper.

23 24 25 26 27 10 9 8 7 6 5 4 3 2 1

Brief Contents

Contents

Chapter 3   Homeland Security Policy

Chapter 4   Foreign Policy

Chapter 5   Defense Policy

Chapter 6   Transportation, Commerce, and Communications

Tables, Figures, and Boxes

Introduction

The four-year period of President Donald Trump's presidential term saw the United States veer from relative prosperity and peace to the economic and societal havoc caused by the coronavirus pandemic. Even before the pandemic struck in 2020, however, the nation's social fabric seemed to be unraveling as Americans hunkered down into partisan and demographic divides, fueled at times by angry and false narratives on social media platforms and compounded by a resurgence of racial tensions.

Towering over this period was the figure of Trump himself. His populist leanings and open contempt for longstanding political norms won the unswerving approval of millions of followers and persuaded many Republicans in Congress to ally themselves with him even as they sometimes kept a distance from his rhetoric and policies. Democrats and a number of traditional Republicans, however, viewed the president as corrupt, racist, and, eventually, an existential threat to democracy. Besieged by multiple investigations into allegations of wrongdoing, including questions over Russian efforts to aid his 2016 election, Trump became the first president in U.S. history to be impeached twice—the second time in the final week of his presidency over his role in the storming of the U.S. Capitol. Yet he was acquitted both times by the Senate and remained a polarizing figure even as his successor, Joseph R. Biden Jr., took office.

The first three years of Trump's presidency saw steady but slow economic growth, low inflation, and an unemployment rate that dipped below 4 percent—the lowest level since the 1960s. Although this occurred alongside fast-growing annual deficits and a national debt that reached $22 trillion in January 2020, the overall economic picture appeared favorable by traditional metrics. Even before the coronavirus pandemic hit, however, household wealth had failed to return to the level prior to the 2008–2009 recession, and economic inequality, measured by discrepancies in income and wealth between richer and poorer households, continued a multidecadal trend of widening.

In the final year of Trump's presidency, the pandemic severely disrupted the economy. As businesses laid off millions of workers in response to state and local quarantines, the unemployment rate shot up to nearly 15 percent in the spring of 2020 before declining to less than 7 percent by the end of the year. The economy in 2020 contracted by 3.5 percent, which was the worst performance for U.S. economic growth since 1946. The Federal Reserve took steps to keep credit flowing and Congress softened the economic blow by clearing about $3.5 trillion in COVID-related legislation, signed by Trump, to help low-income families, the unemployed, small businesses, and local governments. These actions generally had bipartisan support, but they sent the annual deficit soaring to a record $3.1 trillion.

Regardless of the state of the economy, Americans expressed deep unease over the country. During the first three years of Trump's presidency, Gallup polling consistently found that fewer than 40 percent of respondents expressed satisfaction with the direction of the United States, extending a trend that dated back more than a decade (in contrast, Gallup's first poll of 2000 found that nearly 70 percent of Americans were satisfied with the nation's direction). As the U.S. population continued to diversify, anti-immigration views hardened and racial tensions repeatedly surfaced. The nation was rocked by large-scale demonstrations and violence, including a 2017 rally by armed white supremacists in Charlottesville, Virginia, that left one dead and dozens injured and spurred questions about Trump's own racial views when he initially failed to condemn right-wing militias. Three years later, massive and sometimes violent protests erupted in cities across the country in response to the death of George Floyd, a Black man who was murdered by a Minneapolis police officer. Repeated mass shootings dominated the headlines, one of which—a 2017 massacre at a country music festival in Las Vegas that left sixty dead and hundreds wounded—was the deadliest mass shooting in recent American history. The violence even reached Congress: a gunman seriously wounded House GOP whip Steve Scalise of Louisiana and wounded others while they practiced for a congressional baseball game.

Throughout the Trump years, lawmakers who represented deeply divided constituencies could not come to terms over such charged issues as immigration and policing, let alone must-pass annual spending bills. Tensions between the president and Congress hit a new low at the midpoint of Trump's term with the longest government

shutdown in history. Societal fractures affected policymaking at every level, with state and local officials in 2020 clashing over mask mandates and lockdowns intended to stop the spread of the coronavirus. Such disagreements, along with inconsistent guidance by the administration and misinformation on social media channels, contributed to the United States suffering the world's worst death rate from COVID-19, with nearly 400,000 Americans dying in 2020.

Trump embodied the anger and havoc of the era. His sparring with Congress extended to repeatedly insulting powerful lawmakers in both parties, calling House Speaker Paul Ryan of Wisconsin a "baby" and referring to Senate Democratic Leader Chuck Schumer of New York as "cryin' Chuck." His incendiary rhetoric and crude insults on Twitter targeted everyone from NFL players to Canadian Prime Minister Justin Trudeau, whom he called "very dishonest & weak" in a June 2018 tweet. He told so many falsehoods, beginning with a demonstrably untrue statement at the beginning of the presidency that the inauguration crowd stretched to the Washington Monument, that he spawned something of a cottage industry for fact-checkers. Trump fired several cabinet secretaries via tweets and often replaced them with acting secretaries, leaving departments with uncertain leadership while frustrating lawmakers who wanted to hold confirmation hearings.

Election results during Trump's term highlighted the splintered political leanings of the public. The Democrats in 2018 clawed back the House and then, in 2020, toppled Trump and won both chambers by razor-thin margins. At the same time, however, Republicans kept their hold on most state legislatures while rolling up larger margins in rural areas.

These historic events and the political debates they spawned are the subject of this book. *Congress and the Nation, Vol. XV*, like its predecessor volumes, is framed by a presidential term, but its content is deeply informed by national and world affairs. In the case of the period from 2017 to 2020, many of the events are unique, reflecting the unorthodox style of Trump himself—a prominent New York businessman who became the first U.S. president to have never held political office or served in the military prior to becoming the nation's chief executive. His impulsive style and disregard for precedence enabled him to score impressive political victories while, at the same time, exposing him to repeated investigations and, eventually, electoral defeat.

POLITICAL RECORD

On both domestic and foreign issues, Trump put his stamp on U.S. policy and executed a complete break from the priorities of the administration of Barack Obama. The new president made his presence known quickly, aided by Republicans who controlled both chambers of Congress during his first two years of office. Lawmakers used the 1996 Congressional Review Act to send a flurry of measures to Trump's desk that rescinded more than a dozen Obama-era regulations, including those that governed certain environmental protections and education policies. Trump also signed sweeping legislation that restructured the U.S. tax code and reduced taxes, as well as measures that scaled back requirements on financial institutions.

These achievements, passed over Democratic opposition, fulfilled two of Trump's campaign pledges to reduce tax and regulatory burdens on Americans in order to strengthen the economy. Democrats, however, warned that the regulatory rollbacks would degrade environmental, health, and consumer protections, while the tax cuts would worsen the deficit.

Even more momentous than such legislation, Trump worked with Senate Majority Leader Mitch McConnell of Kentucky to reshape the federal judiciary. Senate Democrats in 2013 had scaled back the filibuster to enable confirmation of circuit and district judges by a simple majority vote. Republicans in 2017 went one step further, applying the rule change to Supreme Court nominations as well. This helped Trump shift the federal courts decisively to the right, especially with three Supreme Court appointments that established a 6–3 conservative majority on the nation's highest tribunal.

Although such actions sparked sharp partisan debate, Trump also worked across party lines on several important issues. These included the 2018 First Step Act, which sought to curb the nation's soaring incarceration rate and provide more support for prisoners upon their release. The bill, which had been years in the making, won the backing of a rare alliance of influential conservative and liberal organizations.

Once the coronavirus pandemic hit, the White House worked with Republican and Democratic leaders in Congress to enact a series of sweeping measures to help shore up the nation's economy. The most important of

---

HOW TO USE THIS BOOK

Readers can access information in several ways. The sixteen chapters are listed in the Brief Contents (**page v**). An outline of each chapter, including boxes, tables, graphs, and other related material, is provided in the detailed Table of Contents (**page vi**). For specific topics, turn to the complete index at the end of the volume (**page 793**). Throughout the book, page references to related subjects in other chapters are provided. These page "flags" are designed to speed research across an array of subjects. The Introduction provides an overview of political and legislative activity and a thumbnail description of each chapter's content.

these was the CARES ACT, which appropriated $2.1 trillion to help individuals, small businesses, and others, while protecting renters from being evicted. Although Trump faced searing criticism from public health experts for an erratic and risky approach to the pandemic, such as trumpeting unproven remedies for the virus and casting doubt on the efficacy of facial coverings, the administration spent billions on Operation Warp Speed, a public-private partnership that helped spur the development of lifesaving vaccines.

Trump, however, fell short on several of his key priorities. Perhaps most notably, he failed to persuade Congress to appropriate sufficient funds to build a wall along the U.S.–Mexican border or pass legislation restricting immigration. Instead, he relied on highly controversial executive actions to reduce the number of immigrants. These included restricting immigration from certain Muslim-majority countries and, for a brief period, instituting a zero-tolerance approach that separated infants and children from parents or guardians after entering the United States from Mexico, often with no measures to reunite the families.

The administration also fell short in efforts to make major investments to upgrade the nation's aging infrastructure. Such a priority had the backing of Democrats as well as business leaders. But it foundered because of differences between the White House and Democrats over how much private money, as opposed to federal funding, to tap for the effort. Another major setback, both for Trump and Republican leaders in Congress, was the failure to repeal and replace the Affordable Care Act—a central target of conservatives since its enactment during the Obama administration.

When it came to foreign policy, Trump espoused an "America First" policy that marked an abrupt shift from the internationalism that had been pursued by presidents since World War II. He pulled the nation out of several international pacts that had been negotiated by Obama but never ratified by the Senate. Frustrated with long-running military conflicts, he withdrew troops from Afghanistan and Syria, sometimes to the dismay of Republican congressional leaders. He often seemed more comfortable with dictators than with democratically elected allies, threatening to pull out of the North Atlantic Treaty Organization while praising Russian president Vladimir Putin and saying that North Korean leader Kim Jong Un wrote him "beautiful letters." He imposed tariffs on billions of dollars of goods from China, Mexico, and Canada to try to shore up the nation's economy, igniting trade wars and enduring criticism from both international leaders and free trade advocates in Congress. But he scored a notable triumph by renegotiating key provisions of the North American Free Trade Agreement with Canada and Mexico.

CONGRESSIONAL DIVISIONS

The 115th and 116th Congresses continued a multi-decadal trend toward more partisanship and increasing polarization, sometimes encouraged by Trump. *CQ Roll Call's* analyses of party unity voting showed that Senate Republicans backed the president, and Senate Democrats opposed him, far more often than had been the case during the administration of the previous Republican president, George W. Bush. In the House, Democrats set records for how often they voted together once they took control of the chamber. With both parties vying for advantage, Senate Republican leader Mitch McConnell of Kentucky used a rare parliamentary tactic known as the "nuclear option" to enable Senate Republicans to confirm Supreme Court justices with a simple majority vote, even though some senators worried about the continuing erosion of the filibuster. Trying to bridge the partisan divide, moderate lawmakers in the 115th Congress created a new group, The Problem Solvers Caucus, to foster more bipartisan cooperation.

The differences sometimes caused fissures within the parties. After tangling repeatedly with Trump, House speaker Paul Ryan of Wisconsin opted against running for reelection in 2018. He was replaced as Republican House leader by a Trump ally, Kevin McCarthy of California. On the other side of the aisle, the Democratic gains in the 2018 midterm elections enabled 78-year-old Nancy Pelosi of California to regain the speakership that she had lost when Republicans won control of the House eight years earlier. But with many members wanting younger leadership, she had to pledge to serve no more than four years—and even then lost the votes of 15 Democrats.

Partisan divisions were further inflamed during the COVID-19 pandemic, which led to a significant overhaul in congressional operations and the closing of the Capitol to the public. When the House began requiring lawmakers to wear protective face coverings, a number of Republicans objected. On a party line vote, the House subsequently adopted rules allowing members to vote remotely via proxy, ending the chamber's longstanding tradition of casting votes in person. Republicans, many of whom represented districts that had led the push to reopen schools and businesses, castigated the change and filed a lawsuit in federal court in a vain effort to reverse it. The GOP-controlled Senate did not require facial coverings or allow proxy voting, although it permitted senators and witnesses to participate in committee hearings remotely. Dozens of lawmakers would contract the virus or go into quarantine during 2020.

The final and most serious disruption to hit Congress during the Trump years occurred with the storming of the Capitol on January 6, 2021, as lawmakers were certifying the Electoral College vote showing that Biden had won the election. The insurrection was the Capitol's most serious security breach since invading British troops burned the building during the War of 1812, and it represented the last-ditch effort by Trump supporters to overturn the election after weeks of false claims by Trump that his loss was due to widespread fraud. As the rioters approached the House chamber where Vice President Mike Pence was overseeing the certification, both houses of Congress adjourned and evacuated. With the building overrun,

lawmakers hid in offices and donned gas masks after being advised that tear gas was being used in the Rotunda. More than two hours passed before Trump summoned the National Guard, which worked with police to finally clear the mob, eventually allowing the electoral vote count to resume.

PRESIDENTIAL IMPEACHMENTS

The Trump years were marked by almost continuous investigations of the president. Trump became only the third president in history to be impeached (after Andrew Johnson and Bill Clinton) and the only one to be impeached twice. He was acquitted both times by the Senate, where a two-thirds majority was required for conviction.

As a businessman with extensive financial holdings, Trump faced a wave of lawsuits during his presidency that threatened to expose many of his private dealings. But one of the most serious threats began in the spring of 2017, when the Justice Department appointed a special counsel, Robert S. Mueller III, to look into Russian interference in the 2016 election. Mueller's team would eventually indict or obtain guilty pleas from 34 people, including a half-dozen former Trump advisors and a number of Russian nationals. The Mueller report, issued in March 2019, found Russian interference in the 2016 election, but it did not establish that the Trump campaign conspired with the Russian government. It also stopped short of accusing the president of committing obstruction of justice by interfering with the special counsel's investigation. Instead, it stated, "While this report does not conclude that the President committed a crime, it also does not exonerate him."

Undaunted, House Democrats who had gained investigatory powers after the midterm elections examined a range of other alleged abuses by Trump. They were making limited progress until, in September 2019, revelations surfaced that Trump appeared to use military aid to Ukraine as leverage to persuade that nation to announce an investigation into Biden.

The allegations that Trump had solicited foreign interference in the 2020 presidential election riveted Washington and jolted the Democrats into launching a full-scale investigation. In the face of intense resistance by the White House and opposition from Republican lawmakers who asserted that the president had not violated the law, Democrats took depositions from senior administration officials. The House on October 31 voted along party lines to adopt a resolution establishing a formal impeachment inquiry.

Following a series of public hearings, the House Judiciary Committee on December 13 approved two articles of impeachment on separate 23–17 party line votes. The first count alleged that Trump abused his power by seeking help from Ukraine with his 2020 reelection bid. The second count alleged that Trump obstructed Congress. Five days later, the House passed both counts on near party line votes.

With polls showing the public divided over impeachment and Republicans asserting that Trump had not violated the law, a Senate acquittal seemed preordained. Senate Majority Leader Mitch McConnell of Kentucky laid the groundwork for a brief trial and relatively quick vote. On February 5, senators fell far short of the two-thirds majority needed for conviction, voting 48–52 to reject the House's abuse of power charge and 47–53 to reject the obstruction of Congress charge. A single Republican, Mitt Romney of Utah, joined all Democrats in voting for conviction on the first count. After Trump's acquittal, he claimed vindication.

The House impeached Trump again on January 13, 2021. The 232–197 vote charged the president with inciting the January 6 insurrection. Ten Republicans, including Rep. Liz Cheney of Wyoming, the head of the House Republican Conference, joined Democrats in impeaching Trump.

At the Senate trial, which occurred after Trump left office, his lawyers argued that he could not be held responsible for the actions of the mob. The Senate on February 13, 2021, acquitted Trump on a vote of 57 to 43, falling 10 votes short of the two-thirds majority needed for conviction. Seven Republicans joined all Democrats in voting to convict the former president, making it the most bipartisan vote in history for the conviction of the chief executive.

LEGISLATION AND POLITICS

This book continues a series begun in 1965 with the publication of *Congress and the Nation, Vol. I*, which covered national government and politics from 1945 to 1964. Subsequent volumes, published every four years, covered the same subjects over the two congresses of each succeeding administration. As with the preceding volumes, this edition is divided into chapters focusing on various substantive subjects such as economic and regulatory policy, commerce, law and law enforcement, and foreign policy. This volume, as with recent ones, contains sixteen chapters, an extensive appendix, and a comprehensive index. Following are brief summaries of the chapters and the highlights of events described in them.

Chapter 1: Politics and National Issues

This chapter is an overview of the four-year period from 2017 to 2020, which encompassed Trump's presidential administration and the 115th and 116th Congresses. It discusses the bitter and sometimes chaotic political climate that undermined efforts in Congress to bridge partisan and ideological divides. In the midterm elections, a polarized and closely divided electorate voted for a House Democratic majority while leaving the Senate in Republican hands. Amid the coronavirus pandemic of 2020, however, voters backed Joseph R. Biden Jr. over Trump and gave Democrats full, if narrow, control of Congress. The major legislative events highlighted

in this chapter are covered in more detail in subsequent chapters.

Chapter 2: Economic Policy

This chapter, in four parts, summarizes the national economy from 2017 to 2020 and then describes congressional action on economic and financial regulation, budget and tax policy, and trade issues.

National economy. In the first three years of Trump's presidency, the economy grew slowly but steadily. Although Trump predicted that a combination of tax cuts and tariffs would help eliminate the budget deficit and enable the government to start paying down the national debt, the opposite occurred: annual deficits ballooned even before the government increased spending in response to the COVID-19 pandemic, and the national debt grew. On the plus side, unemployment rates dropped to below 4 percent and inflation remained low. In 2020, the pandemic delivered a body blow to the economy, with the unemployment rate spiking at nearly 15 percent in the spring before the economy began a strong recovery.

Economic and financial regulation. Republicans fell short in efforts to repeal or completely overhaul the 2010 Dodd-Frank Wall Street Reform and Protection Act, a long-time target of conservatives who said it excessively regulated the financial sector. But the 115th Congress cleared a significant package of revisions to ease restrictions on small- and medium-size financial institutions. For their part, House Democrats in the 116th Congress tried unsuccessfully to reverse regulatory changes that the administration made at the Consumer Financial Protection Bureau, which had been created by the Dodd-Frank law.

Budget and tax policy. The Republicans scored a major success in 2017 when Trump signed the first tax code overhaul since 1986. The measure, which was projected to add $1.5 trillion to the nation's debt over 10 years, made changes to income tax brackets, reduced rates for higher earners, and cut corporate taxes.

Democrats and Republicans battled incessantly over the twelve appropriations bills that fund most government agencies. The biggest clash occurred at the end of the 115th Congress and the beginning of the 116th, when a dispute over funding for a border wall on the Mexican border—a top Trump priority—resulted in a record, 35-day partial government shutdown. Trump and congressional leaders, however, worked together on a series of bipartisan spending measures in response to the COVID-19 pandemic in 2020, including the massive the $2.1 trillion CARES Act to help individuals, small businesses, hospitals, and state governments.

Trade policy. More protectionist than traditional Republicans, Trump launched a global trade war that involved China, the European Union, and other countries. He wanted to protect domestic manufacturing industries and national security interests while boosting the U.S. balance of trade. While many members of Congress shared the president's concerns about unfair trade practices, especially those involving China, Republicans and Democrats alike worried over his unileral actions on tariffs. Congress, however, had limited power to restrict the administration's actions. Trump also pulled the nation out of the Trans-Pacific Partnership Agreement and spoke of withdrawing from other treaties as well as the World Trade Organization. After threatening to pull out of the North American Free Trade Agreement, he agreed to renegotiate the pact with Mexico and Canada, ultimately signing a revised agreement in 2018.

Chapter 3: Homeland Security

Trump's nationalistic and isolationist views on immigration sparked a number of controversies over homeland security issues, especially when it came to his insistence on building a wall along the U.S.–Mexico border. Although Trump initially claimed Mexico would pay for the wall, such an idea gained little traction, and the White House and Congress instead clashed over appropriating funds for the project, setting the stage for the unprecedented thirty-five-day partial government shutdown. Amid concerns over the administration using military construction funds for the border wall, the 116th Congress voted to block the practice but failed to override Trump's veto.

Additional tensions were generated over congressional investigations into Russian interference with the 2016 presidential election. Although Trump denounced such investigations as "witch hunts" and a number of Republicans had little interest in looking into the matter, the Senate Intelligence Committee provided a rare example of bipartisanship as Republicans and Democrats joined forces to determine what had happened.

Congress passed several notable homeland security measures. These included extending key provisions of the Foreign Intelligence Surveillance Act (FISA), a voluntary registry for firefighters affected by cancer, a fiscal 2021 intelligence authorization bill that was included in a larger piece of legislation, and a reauthorization of a September 11 victims' compensation fund.

Chapter 4: Foreign Policy

Protracted conflicts in the Middle East, U.S.–Russia relations, and the administration's pursuit of a so-called trade war with China were key areas of focus for foreign policy. In the Middle East, Trump disengaged from the protracted Syrian civil war after ordering missile strikes, and he pulled out troops from northeastern Syria in 2019, engendering criticism for exposing Syrian Kurds to attacks from Turkey. The administration also stood by Saudi Arabia despite mounting concerns over that nation's

airstrikes against Yemen and the murder of a Saudi journalist, Jamal Khashoggi, who was an outspoken critic of the Saudi royal family. Trump also criticized a deal that Obama had negotiated with Iran, which lifted certain U.S. sanctions in exchange for Iran limiting its nuclear activities.

U.S.–Russia relations drew considerable attention, due to the U.S. intelligence community's assessment that Russia tried to use cyberattacks and disinformation to bolster Trump's chances of winning the 2016 election. The president claimed vindication after the Mueller report cleared his campaign of colluding with Russia. But Trump continued to stir controversy by speaking warmly of Russian president Vladimir Putin, saying in a joint press conference with the Russian leader on July 16, 2018, that Putin was "extremely strong and powerful in his denial" that Russia meddled in the 2016 election. Lawmakers remained concerned about Russian influence, and they proposed various measures seeking either to prevent the easing of sanctions or impose new sanctions, as well as bolstering U.S. cybersecurity.

As Trump targeted China with a series of tariffs and other trade barriers for what he perceived as unfair trade practices, lawmakers in Congress followed his lead and began taking a tougher approach to China. Hundreds of China-related bills and resolutions were introduced during the 116th Congress. Many focused on trade and commerce, but several measures specifically targeted China's alleged human rights violations, including the unlawful detention and forced labor of ethnic and Muslim minorities.

The Republican-controlled 115th Congress generally supported the administration's foreign policy initiatives. But House and Senate appropriators repeatedly rejected Trump's proposed cuts to U.S. foreign assistance and contributions to the United Nations, and they also pressed for sanctions against Russia, Saudi Arabia, and North Korea, which engaged in repeated weapons testing. The change in House leadership in the 116th Congress did not have a significant impact on foreign policy legislation, other than proposals for more extensive state-foreign operations spending.

Chapter 5: Defense Policy

The Trump administration scored several notable successes on defense issues. These included a 20-percent increase in the Pentagon's budget and the creation of a new military branch focused on space. However, the president frequently clashed with traditional U.S. allies and faced a growing threat from the Islamic State in Iraq and Syria.

The administration, which inherited the nearly two-decades-long war in Afghanistan, signed a deal with the Taliban in 2020 that aimed to end U.S. involvement in the country the following year. Trump touted the fragile agreement as fulfilling his campaign promise to bring the country's longest-running war to a conclusion. But it was based on several conditions, such as the Taliban severing its ties with al Qaeda and not attacking Afghan cities. In the end,

while the president removed about 11,000 troops from Afghanistan, the Taliban failed to meet the conditions of the peace agreement.

In the Middle East, a number of administration actions—including the engagement of U.S. forces in Yemen's civil war, airstrikes targeting terrorist networks in Syria, and troop withdrawals in Iraq and Somalia—raised questions in Congress. Many lawmakers pressed for either repealing or replacing the 2001 and 2002 Authorization for Use of Military Force (AUMF), which had been passed in the wake of September 11, 2001, to give the president authority to root out terrorist networks and those who had perpetrated the attacks. Calls for their repeal peaked after a U.S. airstrike in January 2021 killed a leading Iranian military figure, provoking an Iranian airstrike on two military installations in Iraq. Lawmakers proposed multiple bills and amendments to overturn the AUMFs and restrict the president from engaging U.S. forces in combat with Iran. None succeeded, and the situation cooled when Trump focused on sanctions instead of military force.

Amid concerns over medical care at the Department of Veterans Affairs (VA), Congress passed the MISSION Act in 2018. This consolidated a number of private care programs for veterans, lifted restrictions on veterans seeking covered care from non-VA providers, and provided a $5.2 billion cash infusion. However, the legislation moved funding from mandatory to discretionary, making it subject to spending caps and creating challenges for lawmakers who wanted to fund the new Veterans Community Care Program within statutory budget limitations.

Chapter 6: Transportation, Commerce, and Communications

One of the administration's major priorities was to modernize and upgrade the nation's aging infrastructure. Although lawmakers in both parties shared such a goal, the initiative fell victim to uncertainty over how to pay for infrastructure upgrades and the extent to which the private sector should play a role. Instead, lawmakers in the 115th Congress focused on a five-year reauthorization measure for the Federal Aviation Administration (FAA). In the 116th Congress, they cleared legislation to reform the FAA's certification process for aircraft, engines, and other components after two Boeing 737 Max airplanes crashed in 2018 and 2019, killing 246 people. After the start of the coronavirus pandemic in 2020, Congress cleared several measures to provide payroll support for airlines and transit agencies, which had suffered a severe drop in ridership.

Congress also advanced legislation on communications issues, reauthorizing the Federal Communications Commission for the first time in twenty-five years. The White House and congressional Republicans reversed a series of Obama-era communications rules, including one that had required internet providers to treat customers the same in terms of price and connection speeds and another

that would have required internet service providers to tell consumers what information they were collecting. Despite extensive discussions, Congress did not take action to end civil liability protections for social media companies that permitted the distribution of disinformation, fake news, hate speech, or violence.

Congress cleared a measure that granted new protections from copyright infringement lawsuits to companies that streamed music online, as well as a measure that made it easier for the blind and physically impaired to obtain access to foreign works of music and literature. However lawmakers failed to move the U.S. Copyright Office under Congress's control.

Chapter 7: Energy and Environment

Trump's top priorities included promoting domestic energy production and achieving independence from foreign imports. He used his executive authority to approve the Keystone XL pipeline and the Dakota Access pipeline, breaking with the Obama administration. He withdrew from the Paris Accord on climate change, scrapped Obama's Clean Power Plan to reduce emissions from coal-fired power plants, and did away with regulations governing the waters of the United States. He faced legal battles in his efforts to scale back Obama's creation of national monuments in Utah.

During the 115th Congress, the administration worked with GOP lawmakers to overturn four Obama-era regulations under the 1996 Congressional Review Act, including a rule governing stream pollution from mining. The energy industry scored a major victory when Congress voted to permit oil and gas development in the Arctic National Wildlife Refuge, and it also gained more access to offshore oil and gas reserves. After Democrats took charge of the House, they tried unsuccessfully to advance a Green New Deal to curb climate change.

Despite the antagonism over energy and environmental issues, lawmakers came together on a few key issues. Congress cleared a permanent authorization for the contentious Land and Water Conservation Fund. It also passed two water resource development laws and conservation legislation for land and animals.

Chapter 8: Agricultural Policy

Although agriculture was not a major focus during Trump's term, Congress in 2018 passed a multiyear, multibillion-dollar farm bill. The measure sparked considerable debate between Democrats and Republicans over the Supplemental Nutrition Assistance (SNAP) program, previously known as food stamps, with Democrats successfully protecting it from Republican-proposed cuts. The farm bill legalized domestic industrial hemp production and enabled hemp growers to access crop insurance.

Congress weighed a number of more minor pieces of agriculture-related legislation but did not pass them. They included measures to ease pesticide regulations, encourage the participation of women and underrepresented minorities from rural areas in science and technology, update rules pertaining to migrant farmworkers, and make it easier for farmers and forestry workers to participate in carbon credit markets.

Chapter 9: Health and Human Services

Republicans in 2017 sought to fulfill a central campaign promise by taking aim at Obama's signature piece of legislation, the 2010 Patient Protection and Affordable Care Act (ACA). That effort narrowly failed because a handful of Senate Republicans broke party ranks even after House Republicans voted to repeal and replace the law. Although a major setback for conservatives, Republicans instead chipped away at ACA provisions, successfully delaying or eliminating a number of the law's most unpopular pieces. After Democrats assumed control of the House during the 2018 midterms, the focus shifted to strengthening key provisions of the ACA and bolstering funding for other health programs, especially with the beginning of the COVID-19 pandemic in 2020.

Despite political differences, Congress made headway on several bipartisan priorities. The 115th Congress sought to rein in the rising cost of prescription medications through two measures that Trump signed into law that banned the use of gag clauses, which prohibited pharmacists from alerting consumers when a certain medication would cost less if purchased out-of-pocket than with insurance. The 116th Congress weighed a number of proposals to reduce prescription drug costs, such as streamlining the process for bringing over-the-counter medications to market and requiring the Department of Health and Human Services to negotiate with drug makers on the prices of some of the most expensive prescriptions covered by Medicare. None, however, made it to Trump's desk.

Amid concerns over addictions to opioid-based medications and the mounting death toll of the drugs—exceeding 47,000 in 2017 alone—the 115th Congress cleared an omnibus package that included dozens of measures to help stem the opioid crisis. Highlights included additional funding for public health campaigns and outreach, new tools for community organizations to deploy against the epidemic, and changes to regulations that would help make it easier for some individuals to access and pay for the treatment they need. The law also encouraged multiple federal agencies, including the Department of Health and Human Services (HHS) and the Food and Drug Administration, to study alternative treatments for pain management. The measure included a variety of offsets to cover the cost of the legislation, estimated at $44 million over ten years.

Chapter 10: Education Policy

Although education was not a major focus for Trump during his presidential campaign, he promised to limit the

amount of income that people had to spend on college loans and fund a school choice program to provide vouchers for low-income parents to send children to any school they chose. Several bills in the 115th and 116th Congress, which would have made changes to student loans or expanded school choice, failed to advance. However, the president's keystone tax legislation, the Tax Cuts and Jobs Act of 2017, included a provision allowing people to use funds from 529 savings accounts to pay for tuition for students attending private K–12 schools, although the accounts were originally designed to be used only for college expenses.

Another spending bill, the fiscal 2021 omnibus spending bill and coronavirus relief package, also contained significant education provisions. It reinstated Pell Grants for incarcerated students, restored Pell Grant eligibility for students defrauded by their institutions, and increased the maximum grant. It simplified the Free Application for Federal Student Aid (FAFSA) application and forgave $1.3 billion in loans to historically black colleges and universities.

Republicans made other policy changes to education by rolling back controversial regulations that had been promulgated under Obama. One had to do with how states would rate schools and deal with parents who removed their children from testing; another focused on regulating teacher preparation programs. The administration also revoked the so-called gainful employment regulation, which attempted to hold colleges and universities accountable if students who earned degrees failed to make enough money to repay their student loans. The administration argued the regulation unfairly targeted for-profit institutions.

Trump set off a storm of controversy even before he was inaugurated by announcing he would nominate billionaire school-choice advocate and philanthropist Betsy DeVos to run the Department of Education. The nomination was heatedly opposed by teacher unions and others in the education community who argued that DeVos lacked the needed educational experience and credentials and was too closely linked to Republican politics. The confirmation ended with a historic first for a cabinet nominee: the vote by a vice president, in this case Mike Pence, was needed to break a tie and put DeVos in charge of the education department.

Chapter 11: Housing and Urban Aid

For most of the Trump presidency, housing and urban aid issues took a back seat to other concerns. The 115th Congress enacted a few elements of the Trump administration's housing and urban aid agenda as pieces of larger, more prominent pieces of legislation. That included creation of investment "opportunity zones" aimed for low-income neighborhoods and easing lending requirements for some small banks.

After Democrats took control of the House in the midterm elections, they attempted to focus on affordable housing. In 2020, however, the COVID-19 pandemic dominated the agenda. Congress passed measures to provide assistance to renters and impose a moratorium on evictions.

Chapter 12: Labor and Pensions

Amid unusually low unemployment during the early years of the administration, the president initially pushed to reduce funding for worker training and education programs overseen by the Labor Department while expanding industry apprenticeship programs. Trump backed off the funding cuts amid backlash from both Democrats and Republicans who wanted to protect programs in their districts, but he called on the Labor Department to reduce red tape and allow industries to initiate and oversee new apprenticeship programs. Republicans in the 115th Congress also wanted to increase work or job training requirements for welfare recipients in order to reduce spending on such entitlement programs that contributed to the federal deficit. But such efforts failed and Congress authorized several short-term authorizations to continue to provide for low-income and unemployed Americans.

Democrats who took over the House in the 2018 tried to strengthen worker protections, boost the minimum wage, expand overtime pay, and provide pay equity for female workers. Such efforts failed to gain traction in the Republican-controlled Senate. After the coronavirus pandemic began, Congress and the White House turned their attention to providing expanded unemployment and welfare benefits to Americans as businesses closed and the unemployment rate soared.

Chapter 13: Law and Justice

One of Trump's greatest triumphs was the reshaping of the federal judiciary, especially the Supreme Court. He successfully won confirmation of all three of his Supreme Court nominees, cementing a conservative majority on the nation's highest tribunal and raising expectations that the justices would roll back government regulations, bolster gun rights, and possibly overturn the 1973 *Roe v. Wade* decision that legalized abortion. Each nomination seemed to create even more partisan bitterness than the last, raising questions about how a divided Senate would approach future Supreme Court vacancies.

Trump also scored a victory at the end of 2018 when lawmakers succeeded in making substantial changes to the criminal justice system with legislation known as the First Step Act. The bill, which resulted from years of negotiations, aimed to lower the number of federal inmates by scaling back certain tough-on-crime policies and to provide more assistance to prisoners upon release to lower the rate of recidivism. It gave judges more discretion over some sentencing, scaled back requirements for some mandatory minimum sentences in certain cases, and expanded early-release programs. It also created more job training and drug treatment programs for prison inmates.

Congress, however, fell short in fulfilling a top Trump priority to overhaul the nation's immigration system. Continuing a pattern that had persisted for many years, lawmakers could not find a balance between tightening security, cracking down on illegal immigration, and deciding whether to provide a path to citizenship for many of the estimated 10 to 11 million undocumented immigrants living in the United States. They also failed to reach agreement on regulating police practices or take major steps to curb gun violence, despite a spate of mass shootings. However, Congress lifted the longstanding prohibition of federally funded research into gun violence, and it provided funding to boost student safety in schools and strengthen the FBI background check system.

The impeachment of Trump in 2019 provided further confirmation of raw partisan divisions. Democratic investigations into the administration were turbocharged by revelations that the president had sought to use military aid to Ukraine as leverage to persuade that nation to announce an investigation into his presidential rival, former vice president Joseph R. Biden. The House subsequently passed two articles of impeachment at the end of 2019 for abuse of power and obstruction of justice. But Democrats failed to win Republican support, and the Senate easily acquitted Trump in February 2020. In the final days of the Trump administration, the House would take the unprecedented action of impeaching him again, this time over his actions on January 6, 2021, when he encouraged the storming of the Capitol.

Chapter 14: General Government

Trump and his congressional allies in Congress initially focused on two general government issues: regulatory reform and the federal workforce. The 115th Congress succeeded in repealing fourteen regulations promulgated under Obama. But lawmakers failed to pass legislation that would have taken a more overarching approach to the regulatory process. The House approved measures that would have constrained the ability of agencies to enact new regulations, but the Senate did not take them up.

Although Republicans were unified in targeting regulations, Congress often found itself at odds with the White House when it came to provisions dealing with the civilian workforce. Those differences became readily apparent in late 2018 when Trump signed an executive order freezing worker pay at the same time as the two chambers were negotiating a fiscal year 2019 appropriations bill that included a 1.9 percent pay raise. Congress ultimately won enactment of the pay raise, but only after a 35-day government shutdown triggered by the president's demand for billions of dollars to fund a wall along the U.S.–Mexico border.

In the final year of the Trump administration, the Postal Service took center stage. After years of trying to address the Postal Service's long-running funding shortfall, Congress turned to the issue of maintaining operations during the COVID-19 pandemic. But political sparks flew when the Postal Service Board of Governors—all of whom had been selected by Trump—tapped the fundraising chair of the Republican National Committee, Louis DeJoy, to be the next postmaster general. Democrats fiercely criticized the pick, noting he was the first postmaster general since 1992 without experience in Postal Service operations, but they could not block his appointment.

Chapter 15: Inside Congress

Even before the storming of the Capitol on January 6, 2021, Congress faced considerable upheaval during the Trump years. These events included a shooting at a congressional baseball practice that seriously wounded House Majority Whip Steve Scalise of Louisiana and others, the toppling of several lawmakers over allegations of sexual harassment, and the use of remote hearings and proxy voting when the COVID-19 pandemic began.

Trump's unabashedly partisan style and willingness to violate political norms contributed to more turmoil, with House Speaker Paul Ryan choosing not to run for reelection in part over his frustration that the president had made the normal process of legislating more difficult. California's Kevin McCarthy, who subsequently became the House minority leader, was a vocal Trump booster. In the Senate, Majority Leader Mitch McConnell of Kentucky focused on installing Republican judicial nominees on the federal bench, even to the extent of engineering a change in Senate rules that enabled Republicans to confirm a Supreme Court justice with a simple majority vote. Democrats bitterly opposed the move, but it mirrored their own decision in 2013 to allow a simple majority to approve lower court judges and other administration nominees.

Congress displayed ample evidence of increased polarization, with party unity voting reaching new highs. Part of the reason may have been the inability of rank-and-file members to offer floor amendments. But the hardening of partisanship and increase in polarization mirrored shifts among Congress's constituents. Polls showed that Republicans and Democrats in the public held increasingly negative views of each other. After the January 6 insurrection, some Democrats said they had even less inclination to work with Republicans.

Chapter 16: The Trump Presidency

Trump entered the White House with no experience in elective politics and upended Washington with a norm-shattering style and unorthodox policies that did not always track with the longstanding priorities of his own party or the Democrats. He scored signature successes, including a significant tax cut his first year in office, a roll-back of regulations throughout his term, and the confirmation of three Supreme Court justices. But he broke with

Republican orthodoxy by imposing trade tariffs, withdrawing troops from Syria and Afghanistan, quarreling with longstanding U.S. allies while speaking highly of such strongmen as Russian president Vladimir Putin, and advocating high levels of spending for such priorities as infrastructure and pandemic aid. He failed to deliver on some of his biggest priorities, including constructing a wall on the U.S.–Mexican border.

The president was hounded by allegations of wrongdoing throughout his term. He faced years of wide-ranging investigations of his finances and his dealings with foreign countries, among other issues. His own Justice Department appointed Special Counsel Robert S. Mueller III, a former FBI director, to investigate Russian interference in the 2016 election, which led to convictions of short-lived national security adviser Michael Flynn and several political aides. Trump became the first president in history to be impeached twice—first on charges of improper dealings with Ukraine and then for inciting an insurrection against the peaceful transfer of power to his successor. He was acquitted both times by the Senate.

Trump's final year in office was dominated by the worst pandemic in a century, which killed nearly 400,000 Americans during that year. The administration spent billions spurring the development of several vaccines completed for distribution in less than a year. But stay-at-home orders to curb the spread of the virus devastated the economy. Trump's mixed messages on health recommendations for wearing masks and practicing social distancing resulted in confusion about how to combat the deadly virus, and he eventually got sick himself. He narrowly lost reelection to former vice president Joseph R. Biden. But his refusal to admit defeat divided the nation even more and set the stage for the insurrection at the Capitol.

Appendix

The appendix contains a variety of supplemental materials, including a glossary of congressional terms, an explanation of how a bill becomes a law, information about House and Senate committees, Senate cloture votes, and presidential vetoes. In addition, the appendix includes extensive political charts, including presidential, House, Senate, and gubernatorial election returns for the period of Trump's term.

CONTRIBUTORS

This volume has been prepared under the direction of editors at CQ Press, an imprint of SAGE Publications Inc. The chapters were prepared and edited by a group of veteran reporters and freelance writers, several of whom covered Congress for Congressional Quarterly Inc. and other Washington, D.C., news organizations. The principal contributors were Linda Grimm, Bart Jansen, Ken Jost, Deborah Kalb, Heather Kerrigan, Christina Lyons, David Mark, William Theobald, and David Hosansky, who also served as volume editor.

MAJOR LEGISLATION PASSED BY CONGRESS DURING TRUMP'S TERM

This chart highlights some of the major bills that law-makers passed during the 115th and 116th Congresses. In addition to the legislation listed here, lawmakers debated controversial measures that did not make it to Trump's desk, including proposed changes to immigration, the Affordable Care Act, and gun regulations. Those debates are covered in the relevant chapters of this volume.

Congressional action on annual budget and appropriations bills is summarized in the Economic Policy chapter and covered in more detail in the relevant subject chapters. Trump's executive orders on such issues as immigration, agreements with other nations, and environmental and education regulations, as well as his cabinet appointments, are also covered in the relevant subject chapters.

Economy and Financial Regulation

Tax Cuts and Jobs Act (2017). The largest tax overhaul in more than three decades, it cut the corporate income tax rate and repealed the corporate alternative minimum tax.

Dodd-Frank financial regulation (2018). Republicans made a number of revisions to the 2010 Dodd-Frank Wall Street Reform and Protection Act that removed thousands of smaller banks from some of the Federal Reserve's toughest rules, although they failed to fully overhaul the financial services law.

Coronavirus Aid, Relief, and Economic Security Act, or CARES (2020). The CARES Act provided relief for families, workers, and businesses during the COVID-19 pandemic, including relief checks for individuals and forgivable loans for small businesses. Congress also passed other bills in 2020 that allocated billions of dollars for the Department of Health and Human Services and other federal agencies for coronavirus relief.

Trade

USMCA (2020). Congress ratified the United States–Mexico–Canada Agreement, which included major revisions to the North American Free Trade Agreement, or NAFTA, including provisions to address digital trade, open access to the Canadian dairy market, and strengthen labor and environmental rules for the trading partners.

Defense and Foreign Policy

Countering America's Adversaries Through Sanctions Act (2017). Lawmakers combined three bills into a single, bipartisan measure requiring the president to impose new sanctions on certain individuals and entities in Russia, North Korea, and Iran. Trump reluctantly signed the bill despite concerns that it would restrict his ability to negotiate.

Veterans Community Care Program (2018). In the wake of a nationwide scandal over care delays at the Department of Veterans Affairs (VA), lawmakers in 2018 created the Veterans Community Care Program, a permanent entity within the VA that consolidated various programs and gave veterans the option to seek care outside VA facilities.

Transportation

Federal Aviation Administration Reauthorization (2018). Congress cleared a five-year reauthorization of the FAA that included such consumer protections as directing the agency to set minimum requirements for passengers' legroom and to prohibit airlines from bumping passengers from a flight after they had boarded the plane.

Harbor Maintenance Trust Fund (2019). Congress cleared a measure to free up money in the Harbor Maintenance Trust Fund to be spent on harbor maintenance projects, particularly dredging projects, responding to reports that channels at the nation's busiest ports were frequently unavailable because of maintenance work.

FAA Certification Process (2020). In the wake of two fatal crashes of Boeing's 737 Max airplane, Congress cleared legislation to reform the FAA's certification process of aircraft and aircraft engines and components, in part to reduce the influence of manufacturers and to boost FAA training and oversight for certification.

Commerce

Online Platforms (2018). Lawmakers cleared a measure aimed at ensuring Microsoft Corp. and other online platforms would comply with U.S. search warrants seeking emails stored on offshore networks without violating foreign data privacy laws.

Energy and Environment

Arctic National Wildlife Refuge (2017). A controversial provision in the Tax Cuts and Jobs Act opened Alaska's Arctic National Wildlife Refuge to oil and gas drilling, overcoming decades of staunch opposition by environmentalists.

Water Resources Development Act (2018). Lawmakers agreed to a bipartisan measure providing $6.1 billion for 15 Army Corps of Engineers projects, as well as $4.4 billion for the state drinking water revolving loan fund program, which provides federal financing for states and utilities to provide drinking water infrastructure.

(Continued)

MAJOR LEGISLATION PASSED BY CONGRESS DURING TRUMP'S TERM (Continued)

Land and Water Conservation Fund (2019). After months of negotiations and compromises, Congress agreed to protect millions of acres of federal lands and permanently reauthorize the Land and Water Conservation Fund. The measure included sweeping protections for federal lands, the creation of four national monuments, and 1.3 million acres of federal wilderness designations.

Agriculture

Farm Bill (2018). Congress passed a major, five-year reauthorization of agriculture and nutrition programs after rejecting Republican proposals to reduce the Supplemental Nutrition Assistance (SNAP) program.

Health and Human Services

FDA Reauthorization (2017). Congress passed a bipartisan reauthorization of the Food and Drug Administration (FDA) authority to collect nearly $1.4 billion in annual fees for prescription medications, medical devices, generic medications, and biosimilar biological products.

Individual Mandate (2017). Congress, as part of the Tax Cuts and Jobs Act, cancelled the penalty enforcing the individual mandate of the Patient Protection and Affordable Care Act.

Children's Health Insurance Program (2018). After allowing the popular program to lapse for two months, lawmakers agreed to a four-year reauthorization as part of the Bipartisan Budget Act of 2018.

Tobacco (2019). Antismoking advocates won a partial victory with the enactment of legislation raising the minimum age for purchasing tobacco products from 18 to 21, although they failed to ban flavored tobacco products.

Education

529 Savings Accounts (2017). The 2017 tax cut legislation included a provision allowing people to use funds from 529 savings accounts, which were originally designed to be used only for college expenses, to pay for tuition for students attending private K–12 schools.

Pell Grants (2020). The fiscal 2021 omnibus spending bill reinstated Pell Grants for incarcerated students, restored Pell Grant eligibility for students defrauded by their institutions, and increased the maximum grant, among other provisions.

Housing

Opportunity zones (2017). A bill to provide tax breaks for investments by businesses in low-income communities was incorporated into the Tax Cuts and Jobs Act of 2017, with the goal of helping parts of the country that did not particularly benefit from the recovery following the 2008–2009 economic crash.

Law and Justice

First Step Act (2018). Amid concerns that the criminal justice system was overly expensive and unfair, Congress passed a sweeping overhaul that aimed to lower the number of federal inmates by scaling back certain tough-on-crime policies and provide more assistance to prisoners upon release to lower the rate of recidivism.

CHAPTER 1

Politics and National Issues

Politics and National Issues

D onald Trump's surprise win in the 2016 presidential election and Republican majorities in the House and Senate at the beginning of his term created an environment in which bitter partisanship became the order of the day in Congress. While Republicans used their trifecta of control to push through a number of top policy priorities, including an extensive rollback of rules and regulations implemented by the administration of Barack Obama and sweeping tax code reform, cracks soon began to show in the party's façade. Disagreements between party factions on signature Republican issues, such as the drive to repeal and replace Obamacare, combined with partisan bickering over everything from annual appropriations to parliamentary procedure, limited the GOP's legislative successes.

A slight drop in partisanship during the second session of the 115th Congress dissipated the following year, as Democrats regained control of the House of Representatives in the 116th Congress and used their majority power to bring forward dozens of bills that had no hope of passing the Senate but helped establish the party's agenda heading into the 2020 election cycle. Much of the 116th Congress was consumed by House Democrat-led impeachment proceedings against President Trump that summarily died in the Republican-controlled Senate. The emergence of the COVID-19 pandemic early in 2020 also had historic implications, both in terms of congressional procedure—as the House approved, for the first time in history, remote voting by proxy—and the trillions of dollars in economic stimulus and other aid allocated by

---

CONGRESSIONAL LEADERSHIP, 2017–2020

115th Congress

Senate

President Pro Tempore: Orrin Hatch, R-Utah
Majority Leader: Mitch McConnell, R-Ky.
Majority Whip: John Cornyn, R-Texas
Republican Conference Chair: John Thune, R-S.D.
Republican Policy Committee Chair: John Barrasso, R-Wyo.
Minority Leader: Charles Schumer, D-N.Y.
Minority Whip: Richard Durbin, R-Ill.
Assistant Democratic Leader: Patty Murray, D-Wash.

House

Speaker of the House: Paul Ryan, R-Ohio
Majority Leader: Kevin McCarthy, R-Calif.
Majority Whip: Steve Scalise, R-La.
Republican Conference Chair: Cathy McMorris Rodgers, R-Wash.
Minority Leader: Nancy Pelosi, D-Calif.
Minority Whip: Steny Hoyer, D-Md.
Assistant Minority Leader: James Clyburn, D-S.C.

116th Congress

Senate

President Pro Tempore: Chuck Grassley, R-Iowa
Majority Leader: Mitch McConnell, R-Ky.
Majority Whip: John Thune, R-S.D.
Republican Conference Chair: John Barrasso, R-Wyo.
Republican Policy Committee Chair: Roy Blunt, R-Mo.
Minority Leader: Charles Schumer, D-N.Y.
Minority Whip: Richard Durbin, R-Ill.
Assistant Democratic Leader: Patty Murray, D-Wash.

House

Speaker of the House: Nancy Pelosi, D-Calif.
Majority Leader: Steny Hoyer, D-Md.
Majority Whip: James Clyburn, D-S.C.
Democratic Caucus Chair: Hakeem Jeffries, D-N.Y.
Minority Leader: Kevin McCarthy, R-Calif.
Minority Whip: Steve Scalise, R-La.
Republican Conference Chair: Elizabeth Cheney, R-Wyo.

lawmakers to support the federal response to the public health crisis.

By the end of the 116th Congress, the major parties' fortunes had effectively reversed. Thanks to key victories in the 2020 election cycle, Democrats were set to control the White House and both chambers of Congress, although their grip on the Senate was razor thin and relied on vice president–elect Kamala Harris to be their tiebreaker.

2017

The Legislative Year

With a Republican in the White House and Republican majorities in both the House and Senate, the 115th Congress appeared poised to greenlight a number of conservative policy priorities, with little to no buy-in from Democratic members. A *Congressional Quarterly* analysis of votes during the 115th Congress' first year in session underscored how closely the parties closed ranks, finding a record-setting level of partisanship in both chambers in 2017. Three out of every four votes in the House were decided along party lines, as were about two of every three Senate votes. Senate Republicans voted together 97 percent of the time, while Democrats in that chamber voted with each other 92 percent of the time. Both set records for party unity votes. House Republicans and Democrats were also closely aligned, voting with their parties 92 percent and 93 percent of the time, respectively.

On the Republican side, much of the party's unity, at least early in the session, appeared linked to President Trump's demand for loyalty from his GOP colleagues. Those who did not line up behind the president's rhetoric or policy positions—or who went a step farther, by publicly expressing a criticism or opposition—could find themselves the subject of an angry Twitter tirade. Or, they might face a Trump-supported primary challenger when their term was up. Such tactics were on full display in two high-profile Republican defections during the year. Sen. Jeff Flake, R-Ariz., did not support Trump as a candidate and frequently clashed with the president during his first months in office. Flake was uncomfortable with what some analysts characterized as Trump's reshaping of what it meant to be a Republican—an embrace of nationalism, populism, and partisanship—as well as the president's use of bombastic rhetoric. Flake took particular issue with Trump's disparaging comments about immigrants and openly disagreed with the president's positions on trade and immigration policy. For his part, Trump repeatedly called Flake weak and ineffective, becoming increasingly hostile toward the senator in a series of tweets and public comments. He also endorsed one of Flake's primary challengers ahead of the 2018 midterms. Flake announced in October that he would not seek reelection. In floor remarks following his decision, Flake warned his Senate colleagues that a "flagrant disregard of truth and decency" was threatening to undermine U.S. democracy. "There is an undeniable potency to a populist appeal by mischaracterizing or misunderstanding our problems and giving in to the impulse to scapegoat and belittle," Flake said, adding that such an impulse "threatens to turn us into a fearful backward-looking people" and the GOP "into a fearful, backward-looking minority party."

Sen. Bob Corker, R-Tenn., also feuded with Trump before announcing in September that he would not seek another term. Unlike Flake, Corker supported Trump's campaign and had shown an appreciation for some of the president's language and positions on foreign policy issues, such as North Korea's pursuit of nuclear weapons. But tensions between the two began to emerge when Corker, who chaired the Senate Committee on Foreign Relations at the time, dismissed Trump's proposed foreign operations budget as a "waste of time" and grew increasingly focused on keeping federal deficits in check. The conflict escalated when Corker slammed the president's response to clashes between neo-Nazis and counter protesters in Charlottesville, Virginia, saying Trump had not "demonstrated he understands the character of this nation." He also spoke of a "lack of discipline" and "chaos" at the White House amid reports that Trump had shared sensitive intelligence with two Russian officials. Trump responded with a bevy of critical tweets and comments, including a claim that Corker begged him for a midterm endorsement and had done nothing in Congress except pass the Iran nuclear deal, which Trump loathed. Corker fired back that the White House had become "an adult day care center." The feud continued throughout the year, even after Corker announced his retirement. Some of Corker's Republican colleagues, including McConnell, expressed frustration with the president's actions, implying that it was unwise to pick a fight with an influential senator who remained an important part of the party and would be a critical vote on tax reform legislation, as well as fiscal 2019 funding.

Even though Trump's overall voter approval rating had fallen below 40 percent by the spring of 2017, he remained popular with Republicans, who consistently gave him an approval rating at or above 80 percent. Eager to please—or at least appease—the president, Republicans across the House and Senate voted with Trump on nearly 99 percent of the bills and issues he publicly supported.

OBAMA REGULATION ROLLBACK

One area in which Republicans marched in lockstep with Trump was his push to reduce the federal bureaucracy and eliminate red tape, including by repealing numerous rules and regulations approved in the waning days of the Obama administration. Republicans leveraged the Congressional Review Act of 1996 (CRA) to reverse fifteen such measures. The CRA allows Congress to overturn recently issued federal department and agency rules with a simple majority vote. This not only nullifies the rule in question, but also prevents the authoring agency from pursuing a similar measure in the future. The CRA had only been used once prior to the 115th Congress: to rescind a Department of Labor rule issued at the end of the Clinton administration.

Obama-era regulations targeted by the Republican rollback included an Office of Surface Mining Reclamation

and Enforcement rule that sought to limit runoff pollution from open pit coal mines by requiring mining operations to avoid disturbing streams and the land around them. Republicans argued the rule was unnecessary and had been designed to regulate coal mining out of business; they were joined by several Democrats from coal-rich states in voting to repeal this rule.

Republicans also moved to rescind a Social Security Administration rule requiring benefit recipients with mental illness to be listed in the National Instant Criminal Background Check System, and thereby be prevented from buying firearms at licensed gun shops. The rule had been opposed by a wide variety of groups when it was first announced, ranging from the National Rifle Association to the American Civil Liberties Union and other groups who were concerned it could add to the stigma surrounding mental illness. The push to overturn this rule later exposed Republicans to some criticism, following mass shootings in Las Vegas, Nevada, and at a high school in Parkland, Florida.

Another regulation that drew Republican ire had only been finalized on July 10 of 2017. This was possible because an Obama appointee, Richard Cordray, remained head of the Consumer Financial Protection Bureau (CFPB). The CFPB had pursued a rule prohibiting companies from including mandatory arbitration clauses in their consumer contracts. Congress repealed the rule fifteen days after it took effect.

Many of these CRA-backed reversals were achieved using closed rules, meaning members did not have an opportunity to propose or debate amendments on the House or Senate floor; only amendments reported by the committee of jurisdiction can be considered. In fact, while House Republicans generally followed regular order to

Table 1.1 Partisanship in Congress, 2013–2020

The table shows the percentage of times that the majority of one party voted against the majority of the other during President Donald Trump's first term. In the 115th and 116th Congresses, more than two-thirds votes split the two parties in the House. Even in the Senate, with a more bipartisan tradition, the two parties differed on a little more than half of votes during most of the Trump administration. These were among some the highest percentages of party unity votes since *Congressional Quarterly* began this study in 1953. Note: (Section has yet to be revised)

	2017	2018	2019	2020
Party Unity (% of votes in which majority of party voted together)				
House Democrats	93	89	89	95
House Republicans	92	91	95	87
Senate Democrats	92	87	84	88
Senate Republicans	97	92	94	93
Partisan votes (% of total)				
House	76.1	58.6	68.0	69.8
Senate	68.9	49.6	54.0	64.4

pass legislation—that is, the standard process of moving bills from committee or subcommittee through to holding floor votes—they set a new record for closed rules, using this procedural maneuver fifty-eight times in 2017.

TAX REFORM PASSED WITHOUT A SINGLE DEMOCRATIC VOTE

Republicans also worked with the president to deliver the Tax Cuts and Jobs Act (PL 115-97), Trump's signature legislative achievement. Packaged as a budget reconciliation measure, the bill cut the corporate tax rate from 35 percent to 21 percent, reduced individual income tax rates, limited itemized deductions, doubled the standard deduction, and increased the refundable portion of the child tax credit. It also sought to encourage domestic business investment by creating a new territorial international tax system for U.S. companies with overseas operations, and it provided new tax breaks for owners of pass-through entities who pay taxes on their individual returns. Lawmakers added a few loosely related provisions, as well, such as language eliminating the tax penalty imposed by Obamacare's individual mandate and a measure permitting oil and gas drilling in the Arctic National Wildlife Refuge.

The first version of the bill proposed in the House met with some Republican resistance, specifically from lawmakers representing high-tax coastal states such as California and those in the Northeast. These Republicans opposed the bill's elimination of state and local income tax deductions, limit on mortgage interest deductions, and $10,000 cap on property tax deductions. However, because there were few Republicans representing these constituencies, the bill still had plenty of support to pass the House, which it did without any Democrats voting in its favor. In the Senate, Democrats mounted a procedural challenge to the bill, claiming that chamber rules prevent the Senate from considering "extraneous matters" in budget reconciliation measures. The Senate parliamentarian responded by removing provisions pertaining to the use of 529 savings accounts and excise taxes on small, private universities' investment income. Several other changes were made to ensure the bill's approval. The cap on mortgage interest deductions was raised, for example, and the individual tax rate cuts were set to expire in 2025. The Senate passed the bill on party lines on December 20, 2017, with Sen. Bob Corker, R-Tenn., casting the only dissenting Republican vote. Due to the changes made in the Senate, the House had to reapprove the bill, which it did the same day.

REPUBLICAN FISSURES IMPERIL PARTY AGENDA

Even though Republicans presented a mostly united front, Congress struggled to pass several major initiatives during the year due to internal policy disagreements between different factions of the party. Also, a thin margin

Table 1.2 Age Structure of Congress, 1949–2019

Year	House	Senate	Congress
1949	51.0	58.5	53.8
1951	52.0	56.6	53.0
1953	52.0	56.6	53.0
1955	51.4	57.2	52.2
1957	52.9	57.9	53.8
1959	51.7	57.1	52.7
1961	52.2	57.0	53.2
1963	51.7	56.8	52.7
1965	50.5	57.7	51.9
1967	50.8	57.7	52.1
1969	52.2	56.6	53.0
1971	51.9	56.4	52.7
1973	51.1	55.3	52.0
1975	49.8	55.5	50.9
1977	49.3	54.7	50.3
1979	48.8	52.7	49.5
1981	48.4	52.5	49.2
1983	45.5	53.4	47.0
1985	49.7	54.2	50.5
1987	50.7	54.4	52.5
1989	52.1	55.6	52.8
1991	52.8	57.2	53.6
1993	51.7	58.0	52.9
1995	50.9	58.4	52.2
1997	51.6	57.5	52.7
1999	52.6	58.3	53.7
2001	55.4	59.8	54.4
2003	54.0	59.7	55.5
2005	55.0	60.4	56.0
2007	56.0	61.2	57.1
2009	57.2	63.1	58.2
2011	56.7	62.2	59.5
2013	57.0	62.0	59.5
2015	57.0	61.0	59.0
2017	57.8	61.8	59.8
2019	57.6	62.9	60.3

SOURCE: Congressional Research Service, *Membership of the 115th Congress*, R44762 (Washington, DC: Congressional Research Service, 2018); *Membership of the 116th Congress*, R45583 (Washington, DC: Congressional Research Service, 2018).

NOTE: The table shows average age of members at the beginning of each Congress.

of control in the Senate meant that just a few defectors could derail a bill with their votes.

Both scenarios came into play as Republicans tried to seize their first real opportunity to make good on their promise to repeal and replace the Patient Protection and Affordable Care Act, otherwise known as Obamacare. Almost as soon as the bill was signed into law in 2010, Republicans were pledging to change it, but they were unable to mount a significant challenge to its popular provisions. Their efforts were stymied in part by a coordinated push from Democrats, activists, and medical professionals to keep the negative ramifications of a prospective repeal in the spotlight. Congressional Budget Office (CBO) estimates that showed millions of Americans could lose their health insurance also proved damaging to Republicans' arguments against the program. But Trump made no secret of his desire to do away with Obamacare once and for all, telling Republicans in his first few days in office that he wanted them to repeal

the ACA within weeks. This quickly became one of the major focus points for Congress in 2017.

In the House, leadership called at least seventeen votes during the year on a host of measures intended to either repeal the whole bill or reverse parts of it. The first major attempt to repeal Obamacare came in March 2017, when Republican leadership unveiled the American Health Care Act (AHCA). The bill generally sought to replace the ACA's health insurance mandates and subsidies with a variety of tax credits, but this was opposed by conservatives who did not want to replace one type of subsidy with another. Moderate Republicans were concerned by a CBO estimate that the bill would cause more than 20 million Americans to drop their health insurance. That same estimate showed that while the bill would reduce the federal deficit, it would do so mostly by cutting Medicaid coverage, which was another concern for the moderates. House Speaker Paul Ryan, R-Ohio, ultimately pulled the bill from consideration before it came to a vote on the House floor and sent it back to committee for further discussion.

The House tried again in May, bringing forward a revised version of the AHCA that gave states a greater say in which benefits health insurance providers would be required to offer. It also allowed insurance providers to charge people with preexisting conditions more money while granting larger subsidies to help those individuals pay for their coverage. By this time, Trump had grown increasingly frustrated that Congress had yet to repeal Obamacare and began threatening lawmakers who had opposed the earlier version of the AHCA that if they did not vote for the revised bill, he would support primary challengers in their next reelection campaign. In the end, House moderates remained opposed to the bill, but conservatives supported it, and it passed the full House by a three-vote margin.

Despite this narrow victory, Republican leaders in the Senate said they would draft their own bill for consideration, instead of taking up the AHCA. In June, leadership introduced the Better Care Reconciliation Act, which repealed the individual mandate, cut federal support for Medicaid, and eliminated taxes for wealthy Americans and health insurance providers. But moderate Republicans opposed the Medicaid cuts and called for more funding for women's health and insurance subsidies. Conservatives were dissatisfied with anything less than full repeal. Leadership pulled the bill five days later and attempted to bring up a slightly revised version in July, but conservatives claimed it still did not go far enough and pledged to block a vote. The Senate tried twice more in July to tackle this issue, first with the Obamacare Repeal and Reconciliation Act, which eliminated the individual mandate and Medicaid expansion, but left other reforms intact. However, the CBO estimated on July 19 that this would leave 32 million Americans uninsured—the highest number yet for a Republican proposal. Days later, Senate Majority Leader Mitch McConnell, R-Ky., proposed a

so-called "skinny repeal" eliminating the ACA's individual mandate and insurance regulations, but not affecting Medicaid funding or coverage. Republican leadership expressed confidence that this measure could pass, even though Sens. Lisa Murkowski, R-Alaska, and Susan Collins, R-Maine, said they would not vote for it. Sen. John McCain, R-Ariz., ended up casting the deciding vote, with a dramatic thumbs down. This failure, combined with the president's waning interest in the health care debate, effectively put an end to Republican efforts to repeal Obamacare. Lawmakers were successful, however, in adding language to a tax reform bill that eliminated the tax penalty for individuals without health insurance.

BIPARTISAN VICTORIES

Despite the sharp divisions in both chambers, and sometimes within parties, lawmakers did succeed in passing several significant pieces of bipartisan legislation during the year. One such bill was proposed in response to ongoing concerns about the quality of veterans' health care, sparked by the 2014 complaint of a VA doctor about patients' excessive wait times and other allegations. The bill made it easier for the VA to fire, demote, or suspend employees for misconduct or poor performance, and it created a whistleblower office to receive and investigate related disclosures. Some opponents of the bill expressed concerns that it could weaken worker protections for federal employees across the government, but it still received strong support from both parties and became law in June.

Republicans and Democrats also joined together to challenge Trump's push for warmer relations with Russia, approving new sanctions aimed at the Kremlin and preventing the president from easing any existing sanctions without prior congressional approval. The bill also imposed sanctions on North Korea and Iran. It passed the House and Senate with near unanimous support in both chambers. Corker led the Senate push to pass the bill, in a further indication of his split with Trump, whose approach to foreign policy would put the United States "on the path to World War III," according to the senator. Trump reluctantly signed the bill into law after briefly raising the possibility of a veto.

Another of the 115th Congress' successes actually started with a deal between Trump and Democratic leadership. In early September, Trump announced a tentative agreement to raise the debt limit, provide emergency disaster relief to help those affected by Hurricane Harvey, and provide government funding through the end of fiscal 2017. The deal caught Republican leaders by surprise, as they had rejected a similar Democratic proposal hours before the president's announcement. At first, the House approved by a near unanimous vote a bill providing $7.85 billion in emergency relief, plus fiscal 2017 funding; it did not include the debt limit. But the next day, the Senate passed a companion bill that included a debt limit suspension through early December and nearly doubled the

amount of disaster relief funds. Deficit hawks were not happy with the bill because they wanted to include spending offsets, but efforts to cover the increased disaster relief costs and separate the debt limit from the rest of the package failed. When the bill went back to the House, conservative Republicans initially expressed opposition to the revised package because they wanted to address the debt ceiling and government funding separately, but many relented and voted for the bill in order to expedite assistance to those struggling from the storms.

SENATE CONSIDERS PRESIDENTIAL NOMINEES

In 2013, frustrated by Republicans' refusal to allow votes on President Obama's nominees, Senate Democrats changed chamber procedural rules to eliminate the use of the filibuster to block certain presidential nominees. The changes required only a simple majority, rather than the traditional sixty votes, to end debate and vote on most executive and judicial branch nominees. This, combined with Republican control of the Senate, helped Trump to win all ninety-four of the confirmation votes that came up in 2017.

Not all of these votes proceeded smoothly, however. Perhaps the most contentious of Trump's early nominees was Betsy DeVos, his pick for education secretary. A wealthy philanthropist and prominent Republican donor, DeVos had no real experience in education, leading to Democratic criticisms that she was "uniquely unqualified" for the position. Her vocal support of charter schools, school vouchers, and alternatives to public schools also made her unpopular with Democrats. Many outside groups were also opposed to DeVos' nomination, and protestors attended her confirmation hearing at the end of January. In the run up to her confirmation vote, Senate Democrats held the chamber floor for twenty-four hours, using the time to underscore DeVos' lack of qualifications and highlight red flags from her confirmation hearing, such as her apparent confusion over whether state officials or the federal government had jurisdiction on certain issues. Sens. Susan Collins, R-Maine, and Lisa Murkowski, R-Alaska, joined with Democrats to vote against DeVos, prompting Vice President Mike Pence to cast a historic tie-breaking vote to ensure her confirmation.

Trump's nomination of Rep. Tom Price, R-Ga., to head the Department of Health and Human Services was also controversial. For at least part of the time that Price had been in Congress, he traded medical industry stocks whose price was affected in part by legislative activity. Senate Democrats used Price's confirmation hearings to probe his stock trades, with some suggesting he may have received or profited from insider information about them. Price denied these allegations and agreed to divest his holdings in more than forty companies. The Senate ultimately voted along party lines to confirm him, but a scandal involving Price's use of private planes for official business cut his tenure short: Price resigned seven months into his term after

the Department of Health and Human Services (HHS) inspector general announced an investigation into the matter. Price was succeeded by Alex Azar, a former pharmaceutical company executive. Although Democrats questioned Azar about the company's drug price increases while he was in leadership, his nomination was not as contentious as Price's, and six Democrats joined with Republicans to confirm him early in 2018.

Another cabinet-level nominee did not make it through the confirmation process. Andrew Puzder, the CEO of a restaurant group that owns the popular Hardee's and Carl's Jr. chains, was chosen by Trump to become the next secretary of labor. However, Puzder withdrew his name from consideration in February 2017, roughly two months after his nomination was announced, after Republican senators advised the White House that he did not have enough votes to be confirmed. A series of revelations—ranging from Puzder's acknowledgement that he did not pay the required taxes on an undocumented immigrant employee's services to his ex-wife's accusing him of abuse—prompted the GOP lawmakers to pull their support for his nomination. Alexander Acosta, a lawyer and former member of the National Labor Relations Board, was put forward instead; he was easily confirmed by the Senate in April.

SENATE REPUBLICANS EXERCISE NUCLEAR OPTION

McConnell had promised in 2013 that Democrats would come to regret exercising the so-called "nuclear option"—that is, requiring a simple majority for confirmation votes. That appeared to be a prescient prediction in 2017. Republicans employed the same procedural tactic to eliminate the use of the filibuster during consideration of U.S. Supreme Court nominees. Supreme Court justices had been excluded from the Democrats' rule change. With the Republicans' change, the filibuster could only be used moving forward to block or delay votes on legislation.

McConnell moved quickly to orchestrate the rules change amid Senate consideration of Neil Gorsuch, Trump's nominee to fill the Supreme Court seat left empty since Justice Antonin Scalia's death in February 2016. Republicans had refused to consider Obama's nominee to replace Scalia, D.C. Circuit Court of Appeals judge Merrick Garland, because it was an election year and they claimed the next president should choose Scalia's replacement. With Gorsuch, Republicans moved quickly toward confirmation. Gorsuch's qualifications included a stint on the U.S. Court of Appeals for the Tenth Circuit, service as a principal deputy associate attorney general, and a clerkship for Justice Anthony Kennedy. While all Senate Republicans were ready to vote in Gorsuch's favor, Democrats signaled they may filibuster his nomination, and McConnell did not have enough votes to break it. Thus, he exercised the same nuclear option the Democrats had four years prior. Gorsuch was confirmed by a 54–45 vote, with three moderate Democrats joining the Republicans.

CONGRESS IN 2017

The first session of the 115th Congress began on January 3, 2017. Both chambers adjourned on January 3, 2018. The House was in session on 192 days while the Senate was in session on 195 days.

House members introduced 5,619 bills and resolutions during the year, compared to the Senate's 2,713. Of these bills, Congress cleared 117 to become public law. President Donald Trump did not veto any bills during the first session of the 115th Congress.

The House took 708 roll call votes in 2017, eighty-seven more than in 2016. The Senate took 325 recorded votes during the year, or roughly twice as many votes as that chamber took in 2016.

The Political Year

TRUMP APPOINTMENTS PROMPT MULTIPLE SPECIAL ELECTIONS

A total of seven special elections were called in 2017. Five of these were to fill seats vacated by President Trump's nominees for several cabinet-level positions: Sen. Jeff Sessions, R-Ala., nominated to become U.S. attorney general; Rep. Mick Mulvaney, R-S.C., selected as director of the Office of Management and Budget; Rep. Ryan Zinke, R-Mont., chosen to become secretary of the interior; Rep. Tom Price, R-Ga., nominated as Health and Human Services secretary; and Rep. Mike Pompeo, R-Ga., appointed director of the Central Intelligence Agency. Only one of the contested seats—that of outgoing Sen. Sessions—changed parties.

On December 12, Alabama voters selected former U.S. attorney Doug Jones to fill Sessions's Senate seat. Alabama Gov. Bob Bentley appointed Luther Strange to fill Sessions's seat until the special election was held, but Strange was defeated by former Alabama Supreme Court chief justice Roy Moore in the Republican primary. The race became a difficult one for the Republicans as Moore came under fire for comments he had made about women's health, Russia, and whether Muslims could hold office in the United States. Several women also accused Moore of sexually assaulting them or making unwanted sexual advances in the 1970s, when they were teenagers and Moore was in his thirties. The controversy prompted the Republican National Committee to withdraw funding for Moore's campaign, and some of Moore's would-be colleagues in the Senate called for him to exit the race. Jones was declared the winner the evening of the vote, but Moore refused to concede and filed a lawsuit seeking to block certification of the results. His suit was rejected on December 28, allowing Jones to be certified as the winner.

In South Carolina, Republican Ralph Norman defeated Democrat Archie Parnell in a special election to replace Mulvaney. Norman won the June 20 poll by less than 3,000 votes, after narrowly defeating state representative Tommy Pope in the Republican primary. Norman was a former state representative himself, having served in the South Carolina House of Representatives from 2008 to February 2017.

Karen Handel, a former Georgia secretary of state, successfully kept the seat of outgoing House member Tom Price under Republican control. The Democratic Party mounted a significant effort to flip the seat. They considered the race to be competitive since Trump won the district by less than 2 percent during the 2016 presidential election, and viewed it as one of several opportunities to reduce the Republican majority in the House. Combined spending for the campaign was more than $50 million, with Handel's challenger Jon Ossoff, a journalist and former Capitol Hill staffer, raising more than any Democrat had in the district's recent history. In the end, Handel won by nearly 10,000 votes.

In the race to fill Zinke's House seat in Montana, Republican Greg Gianforte, an entrepreneur who founded a technology company, defeated Democratic candidate Rob Quist, a musician and small business owner. Gianforte was widely expected to win the race, since Zinke's seat had been held by a Republican since 1997. He won a comfortable victory despite being charged with misdemeanor assault against a reporter the day before the vote.

Initially considered to be a safely Republican seat, the race to replace Pompeo in the House ended up closer than expected, due largely to the flagging popularity of Republican Gov. Sam Brownback. However, fellow Kansas Republican Ron Estes—a farmer, consultant, and engineer—defeated Democratic challenger James Thompson, an attorney, by roughly 7 percent. Libertarian candidate Chris Rockhold received less than 2 percent of the vote.

The other two special elections of 2017 took place in Utah and California. Provo City, Utah, mayor John Curtis easily won the House seat of fellow Republican Jason Chaffetz, who resigned from office on June 30, 2017, saying he wanted to spend more time with his family and return to the private sector. In a crowded field of twenty-two candidates, including thirteen Republicans, Curtis emerged as the frontrunner early in the race, benefitting from the endorsement of Utah Gov. Gary Herbert and strong public support. California State Assemblymember Jimmy Gomez was elected to replace fellow Democrat Xavier Becerra, who gave up his House seat in January 2017 to become California's attorney general. Gomez faced another Democrat, attorney and former Los Angeles City planning commissioner Robert Lee Ahn, in the June 6 vote. Gomez and Ahn were the top two vote-getters in the April primary, which featured twenty-three candidates from across the political spectrum. Gomez won Becerra's seat by a comfortable margin of nearly 9 percent.

Table 1.3 Presidential Vote by Region

Democrat Barack Obama in 2012 won reelection by a comfortable margin, taking 65.9 million votes to former governor Mitt Romney's 60.9 million for a margin of just under 5 million votes, or 3.9 percentage points. The regional vote shows Republican Romney dominating the southern states, and Democrat Obama in full command of the eastern and western regions and splitting the midwestern region but winning the vote-heavy states of Michigan, Ohio, Illinois, Minnesota, and Wisconsin.

In 2016, Democrat Hillary Clinton won the popular vote against Republican Donald J. Trump by 2,868,686 votes, but was projected to receive fewer electoral votes. In a major upset in December, the Electoral College gave the election to Trump, 304–227 votes, the second time in fifteen years the candidate with the popular vote lost the presidential election. *(National vote breakdown by state).*

In 2020, Democrat Joe Biden won both the popular and electoral vote against incumbent President Donald J. Trump. Biden secured many key battleground states, including Arizona, Georgia, Michigan, Minnesota, Nevada, New Hampshire, Pennsylvania, and Wisconsin.

| | *2012* | | | |
| | *Popular Votes* | | *Electoral Votes* | |
Region	*Obama*	*Romney*	*Obama*	*Romney*
East	59%	21%	112	5
Midwest	51	38	80	38
South	44	54	42	133
West	54	43	98	30
National	51	47	332	206

| | *2016* | | | |
| | *Popular Votes* | | *Electoral Votes* | |
Region	*Trump*	*Clinton*	*Trump*	*Clinton*
East	40%	55%	26	91
Midwest	49	45	88	30
South	53	43	160	13
West	38	53	30	93
National	46	48	304	227

| | *2020* | | | |
| | *Popular Votes* | | *Electoral Votes* | |
Region	*Biden*	*Trump*	*Biden*	*Trump*
East	58%	41%	111	6
Midwest	48	50	57	61
South	45	53	29	146
West	57	40	109	19
National	51	47	306	232

DEMOCRATS WIN TWO GUBERNATORIAL SPECIAL ELECTIONS

Democrats notched two important gubernatorial victories in 2017, including in Virginia, which had been a key battleground state in the 2016 presidential election. There, the race to replace term-limited Democratic Gov. Terry McAuliffe was seen as an early test of Trump's messaging and policies ahead of the 2018 midterms. The campaign pitted Ralph Northam, the state's Democratic lieutenant governor and a former pediatrician, against former Republican National Committee Chair Ed Gillespie. Northam adopted

a low-key approach to campaigning, seeming to embrace a strategy that relied on the Democratic Party's turnout efforts and voter disaffection with Republican lawmakers and their rhetoric. Gillespie's campaign emphasized law-and-order messaging similar to that of the president, but simultaneously sought to create distance from Trump, who lost the state to Hillary Clinton by about 5 points. Another challenge for Gillespie was the refusal of his primary opponent, Corey Stewart, to endorse him as the party's nominee. This cost Gillespie support from rural Republican voters, with whom Stewart was more popular due to his Trump-like positioning. Gillespie ultimately began echoing Trump on more issues as Election Day approached, including by trying to link illegal immigration to crime rates and opposing efforts to remove or replace Confederate monuments. Virginia voters turned out in higher numbers for this poll than they had in any gubernatorial election held in the previous twenty years, with much of that increase comprised by Democrats and liberals. Republicans reported a record-low turnout. Northam defeated Gillespie by more than 8 points—a decisive win that Northam and party leadership positioned as an indication that voters were turned off by Trump's divisive politics and that public sentiment was shifting away from Republicans' favor.

Table 1.4 Incumbents Reelected, Defeated, or Retired, 1946–2020

Year	Retired	Total Seeking Reelection	Defeated in Primaries	Defeated in General Election	Total Reelected	Percentage of those seeking Reelection	Year	Retired	Total Seeking Reelection	Defeated in Primaries	Defeated in General Election	Total Reelected	Percentage of those seeking Reelection
House							Senate						
1946	32	398	18	52	328	82.4	1946	9	30	6	7	17	56.7
1948	29	400	15	68	317	79.3	1948	8	25	2	8	15	60.0
1950	29	400	6	32	362	90.5	1950	4	32	5	5	22	68.8
1952	42	389	9	26	354	91.0	1952	4	31	2	9	20	64.5
1954	24	407	6	22	379	93.1	1954	6	32	2	6	24	75.0
1956	21	411	6	16	389	94.6	1956	6	29	0	4	25	86.2
1958	33	396	3	37	356	89.9	1958	6	28	0	10	18	64.3
1960	27	405	5	25	375	92.6	1960	4	29	0	1	28	96.6
1962	24	402	12	22	368	91.5	1962	4	35	1	5	29	82.9
1964	33	397	8	45	344	86.6	1964	2	33	1	4	28	84.8
1966	23	411	8	41	362	88.1	1966	3	32	3	1	28	87.5
1968	24	408	4	9	395	96.8	1968	6	28	4	4	20	71.4
1970	30	401	10	12	379	94.5	1970	4	31	1	6	24	77.4
1972	40	392	14	13	366	93.4	1972	6	27	2	5	20	74.1
1974	43	391	8	40	343	87.7	1974	7	27	2	2	23	85.2
1976	47	384	3	13	368	95.8	1976	8	25	0	9	16	64.0
1978	49	382	5	19	358	93.7	1978	10	25	3	7	15	60.0
1980	34	398	6	31	361	90.7	1980	5	29	4	9	16	55.2
1982	31	387	4	29	354	91.5	1982	3	30	0	2	28	93.3
1984	22	409	3	16	390	95.4	1984	4	29	0	3	26	89.7
1986	38	393	2	6	385	98.0	1986	6	28	0	7	21	75.0
1988	23	408	1	6	401	98.3	1988	6	27	0	4	23	85.2
1990	27	407	1	15	391	96.1	1990	3	32	0	1	31	96.9
1992	65	368	19	24	325	88.3	1992	7	28	1	4	23	82.1
1994	48	387	4	34	349	90.2	1994	9	26	0	2	24	92.3
1996	49	384	2	21	361	94.0	1996	13	21	1	1	19	90.5
1998	33	402	1	6	395	98.3	1998	4	30	0	3	27	90.0
2000	32	405	3	6	396	97.8	2000	5	29	0	6	23	79.3
2002	35	398	8	8	382	96.0	2002	5	28	1	3	24	85.7
2004	29	404	2	7	395	97.8	2004	8	26	0	1	25	96.2
2006	27	404	2	22	380	94.1	2006	4	29	1	6	23	79.3
2008	32	403	4	19	380	94.3	2008	5	30	0	5	25	83.3
2010	36	397	4	54	339	85.4	2010	12	25	3	2	21	84.0
2012	39	391	13	27	351	89.8	2012	10	23	1	1	21	91.2
2014	41	392	4	14	374	95.4	2014	7	28	0	5	23	82.1
2016	42	380	6	7	367	96.6	2016	5	29	0	2	27	93.1
2018	55	376	4	37	337	89.7	2018	3	32	0	5	27	84.4
2020	36	395	8	13	374	94.7	2020	4	31	0	5	26	83.9

SOURCE: Norman J. Ornstein, Thomas E. Mann, and Michael J. Malbin, *Vital Statistics on Congress 2001–2002* (Washington, DC: American Enterprise Institute, 2002); *CQ Weekly*, selected issues; Richard M. Scammon, Alice McGillivray, and Rhodes Cook, *America Votes 2001* (Washington, DC: CQ Press, 2001) various editions; Howard W. Stanley and Richard G. Niemi, *Vital Statistics on American Politics 2013–2014* (Washington, DC: CQ Press, 2013); *Vital Statistics on American Politics 2015–2016* (Washington, DC: CQ Press, 2016); Jeffrey L. Bernstein and Amanda C. Shannon (2022). "Elections and Political Parties." In *Vital Statistics on American Politics: 2017–2020* (pp. 1-86). CQ Press, https://dx.doi.org/10.4135/9781071836903.n4

NOTE: The column titled Retired does not include persons who died or resigned before the election except in the case of deaths, for candidates whose name remained on the ballot. Some numbers in the table involved incumbents defeated in primaries but who won as independents in the general election. For details on these and other special cases, consult footnotes in Stanley and Niemi, *Vital Statistics on American Politics 2015–2016*.

Democrats also celebrated a return to the governor's mansion in New Jersey, where Republican Gov. Chris Christie had been serving since 2010. Although New Jersey has long been considered a solidly Democratic state, Christie's bipartisan approach to governing had earned him strong support and he easily won reelection in 2013. However, his alignment with Trump and his involvement in the "Bridgegate" scandal (involving allegations over a deliberate traffic jam) that spanned his second term eroded his popularity and hampered the campaign of his would-be successor, Lt. Gov. Kim Guadagno. Guadagno's opponent was former U.S. ambassador to Germany and Democratic National Committee finance chair Phil Murphy, whom she sought to portray as soft on crime and illegal immigration, using some of the president's divisive rhetoric on these issues. Murphy outraised Guadagno three-to-one and secured the governorship with 56 percent of the vote. Unlike in Virginia, the New Jersey race was not considered an indicator of Trump's or Republicans' popularity. Its importance instead came from its potential to narrow Republicans' majority in the Senate. At the time, Sen. Robert Menendez, R-N.J., was facing federal corruption and bribery charges. If he were removed from office or decided to step down, the governor would appoint his replacement.

2018

The Legislative Year

The second session of the 115th Congress was unique in that it started and ended with a government shutdown. Protracted negotiations over the fiscal 2018 budget, which began in the summer of 2017, spilled over into the new session of Congress, and a brief lapse in funding caused a three-day shutdown in January. This would be followed by a record-setting, thirty-five-day shutdown that started days before Christmas and lasted until late January 2019. Both were presaged by major disagreements on immigration policy, either between the leading parties or between Congress and the president.

These disagreements occurred in a year that was otherwise marked by a drop in partisanship. Party line votes were less common in both chambers, according to a *Congressional Quarterly* analysis. In the House, the number of party unity votes fell from 76 percent of all roll call votes in 2017 to 56 percent in 2018. In the Senate, these numbers were 69 percent and 50 percent, respectively.

Table 1.5 Number of Public Laws Enacted, 1975–2020

Year	Public Laws	Year	Public Laws	Year	Public Laws
1975	205	1996	245	2017	98
1976	383	1997	153	2018	313
1977	223	1998	241	2019	137
1978	410	1999	170	2020	177
1979	187	2000	410		
1980	426	2001	136		
1981	145	2002	241		
1982	328	2003	198		
1983	215	2004	300		
1984	408	2005	169		
1985	240	2006	248		
1986	424	2007	161		
1987	242	2008	321		
1988	471	2009	125		
1989	240	2010	258		
1990	410	2011	90		
1991	243	2012	193		
1992	347	2013	72		
1993	210	2014	224		
1994	255	2015	115		
1995	88	2016	214		

Table 1.6 Recorded Vote Totals

Following are the recorded vote totals between 1955 and 2020. The figures do not include quorum calls or two House roll calls in 2011 and 2012 that were vitiated. The numbers, while high during President Donald Trump's first term, did not set records. The highest total for the Senate was 688 recorded votes in 1976. The highest number in the House was 1,177 in 2007. Also in 2007 Congress set a new record for the highest number of recorded votes ever taken in a single year: 1,619. But the 95th Congress (1977–1979) still held the record for the most votes taken in a single Congress: 2,691.

Year	House	Senate	Total	Year	House	Senate	Total	Year	House	Senate	Total
1955	76	87	163	1986	451	354	805	2017	709	325	1034
1956	73	130	203	1987	488	420	908	2018	498	274	772
1957	100	107	207	1988	451	379	830	2019	700	428	1128
1958	93	200	293	1989	368	312	680	2020	252	292	544
1959	87	215	302	1990	510	326	836				
1960	93	207	300	1991	428	280	708				
1961	116	204	320	1992	473	270	743				
1962	124	224	348	1993	597	395	992				
1963	119	229	348	1994	497	329	826				
1964	113	305	418	1995	867	613	1,480				
1965	201	258	459	1996	454	306	760				
1966	193	235	428	1997	633	298	931				
1967	245	315	560	1998	533	314	847				
1968	233	281	514	1999	609	374	983				
1969	177	245	422	2000	600	298	898				
1970	266	422	688	2001	507	380	887				
1971	320	423	743	2002	483	253	736				
1972	329	532	861	2003	675	459	1,134				
1973	541	594	1,135	2004	543	216	759				
1974	537	544	1,081	2005	669	366	1,035				
1975	612	602	1,214	2006	540	279	819				
1976	661	688	1,349	2007	1,177	442	1,619				
1977	706	635	1,341	2008	688	215	903				
1978	834	516	1,350	2009	987	397	1,384				
1979	672	497	1,169	2010	660	299	959				
1980	604	531	1,135	2011	945	235	1,180				
1981	353	483	836	2012	656	251	907				
1982	459	465	924	2013	640	291	931				
1983	498	371	869	2014	563	366	929				
1984	408	275	683	2015	703	339	1,042				
1985	439	381	820	2016	621	163	784				

SOURCE: "Résumé of Congressional Activity," *Congressional Record—Daily Digest*, various issues, Eightieth Congress (1947) through 114th Congress (2016); *Votes*. United States Senate. (n.d.). https://www.senate.gov/legislative/votes_new.htm

Party loyalty remained strong but also decreased from 2017. House Republicans voted with their party 91 percent of the time, compared to Democrats' 89 percent. Senate Republicans aligned 92 percent of the time, while Democrats voted together 87 percent of the time.

Republicans in the Senate had at least one reason to collaborate more with their Democratic peers: Doug Jones's special election victory in Alabama had reduced their already narrow majority by one seat. Additionally, Sen. John McCain, R-Ariz., was absent for part of the year, as he underwent brain cancer treatment in his home state. McCain succumbed to his illness in August; his seat was not filled until December. In this environment, Republicans and Democrats worked together on major bills addressing financial regulations, the nation's opioid crisis, and an overhaul of the overwhelmed criminal justice system.

Interestingly, Trump's influence on GOP lawmakers remained strong, despite their periodic criticisms of the president, several high-profile members' defections, and Trump's role in the fiscal 2018 funding debacle. Republican leadership continued to hold back many bills they did not believe would have the president's support, and 93 percent of the time Congress voted with Trump on legislation he supported. The threat of facing a Trump-supported primary challenger in the midterms appeared to be an effective deterrent for many lawmakers, particularly more moderate Republicans.

IMMIGRATION BATTLE LEADS TO GOVERNMENT SHUTDOWNS

Immigration was by far the biggest issue facing Congress in 2018. Lawmakers repeatedly failed to draft immigration legislation that could both secure enough votes to pass Congress and gain the president's support, and efforts to address—or ignore—controversial measures in annual funding bills caused both of the year's government shutdowns.

The most prominent aspect of the immigration debate was Trump's repeated call to build a solid wall along the United States' southern border. Trump pledged to make Mexico pay for the wall during his campaign, but it refused to do so, leaving the president to request funding from Congress. He included $1.6 billion for border wall construction in the fiscal 2018 proposal he submitted to lawmakers, but Republicans and Democrats disagreed on whether to grant his request. Amid their negotiations, Trump announced in September 2017 that he was ending the Deferred Action for Childhood Arrival (DACA) program, which prevented the government from deporting unauthorized immigrants who arrived in the United States as children and met certain other criteria, and giving Congress until March 2018 to come up with a replacement. Democrats and other critics accused the president of using DACA participants, otherwise known as "Dreamers," as pawns in the budget debate, hoping that Democrats would agree to border wall funding in exchange for Dreamers' protection.

Meanwhile, lawmakers passed and Trump signed three continuing resolutions to extend government funding past the start of the new fiscal year and into 2018. When the time came to pass a fourth continuing resolution, Senate Democrats sought to force Trump's hand on DACA by including language that would preserve existing protections for the Dreamers, but Republicans opposed this approach. Senate Minority Leader Chuck Schumer, D-N.Y., tried to negotiate a deal with the president that would provide border wall funding in exchange for a path to legalization for Dreamers, but the White House ultimately rejected the offer. Senate Democrats responded by joining with several Republican colleagues to oppose the continuing resolution and the government shut down from January 20 to January 23, with more than 690,000 federal workers furloughed. The shutdown ended when Senate Majority Leader Mitch McConnell, R-Ky., agreed to hold a vote on an immigration bill addressing Dreamer status, and Democrats agreed to approve another stopgap spending measure. The final omnibus spending bill passed in March 2018 included neither DACA language nor Trump's requested border wall funds.

Lawmakers in both chambers subsequently tried to draft comprehensive, bipartisan immigration legislation. In the Senate, at least four separate bills were considered and rejected. The bill that came the closest to gaining approval was crafted by Sens. Angus King, I-Maine, and Mike Rounds, R-S.D. It provided $25 billion over eight years for border security, including "physical barriers." It prohibited the deportation of DACA recipients and provided a ten- to twelve-year path to citizenship. It also reduced the cap on family-sponsored visas, continued the visa lottery, and stipulated enforcement priorities for the Department of Homeland Security. Trump opposed the bill's promise of eventual citizenship for Dreamers, prompting most Republicans to vote against and ultimately defeat the bill. In the House, Republicans drafted a bill without Democrats' input. Their proposal offered $23.4 billion for border security, including $16.6 billion for a border wall system. It allowed DACA recipients to renew their non-immigrant legal status for six years; after five years, they could apply for a Green Card. The bill was unpopular with both parties. Not a single Democrat voted for the proposal, refusing to support legislation that did not extend Dreamers' protections. Conservative Republicans wanted the program eliminated entirely.

With no stand-alone immigration measure addressing the president's border wall demands, the barrier once again became a sticking point in budget negotiations. This time, Congress was struggling to finalize funding for fiscal 2019. Lawmakers passed two minibus spending bills in late September, covering several agencies, and two short-term continuing resolutions to keep the rest of the government funded through December 21. The Senate attempted to pass a third continuing resolution to keep the government open through February 8, 2019, but Trump refused to sign

it unless Congress added $5.7 billion for border wall funding. House Republicans, upon receiving the Senate bill, added Trump's requested funds, but this revised bill failed to pass the Senate. A partial government shutdown ensued.

Extending from December 22 through January 25, 2019, the shutdown was the longest in U.S. history. An estimated 380,000 federal employees were furloughed; another 420,000 were required to work without knowing whether they would receive backpay. When the 116th Congress began on January 3, 2020, lawmakers quickly set to work trying to resolve the impasse. At least four separate measures were considered in the House and Senate, but all of them failed. Facing a public relations crisis, lawmakers managed to pass a three-week continuing resolution on January 25. Trump signed it, even though it did not include border wall funding, following assurances by both parties that they would dedicate the three weeks to negotiating DHS and border wall funding. In the end, Congress appropriated only $1.37 billion for steel fencing along a designated portion of the border. Trump responded by declaring a national emergency at the border and shifting funds from the Departments of Defense and Treasury to pay for wall construction.

FISA REAUTHORIZED

Outside of the immigration battle, lawmakers came together to pass several significant pieces of bipartisan legislation, beginning with Foreign Intelligence Surveillance Act (FISA) reauthorization in January. The debate surrounding FISA reauthorization centered on the bill's controversial Section 702, which allows the National Security Agency (NSA) to collect from U.S. companies, emails, phone calls, and other communications of foreigners abroad without a warrant, supporting the surveillance of foreign terrorism suspects. That program became the focus of intense national debate over privacy and security in 2013, after former intelligence contractor Edward Snowden leaked information showing that Americans' communications were getting swept up by the NSA as well, specifically when they were communicating with foreigners or if their emails were routed through overseas servers. Since FISA had last been reauthorized for six years in 2012, Congress had its first post-leak opportunity to review the bill's provisions in 2018. Civil libertarians in the Senate took the opportunity to push for amendments that would require the NSA to obtain warrants prior to collecting communications, and would establish greater oversight of the agency's surveillance activities. But these efforts failed, as undecided senators came under great pressure from their colleagues to reauthorize the act without amendment. Trump had also made it clear that he wanted a clean bill, without the changes advocated by some senators.

BANKING REGULATIONS EASED

A compromise between Republicans and moderates in the Senate facilitated passage of a package of changes to the Dodd-Frank Act of 2010. That bill became law in the wake of the 2008 financial crisis, and combined new consumer protections—such as the establishment of the Consumer Financial Protection Bureau—with stricter banking regulations to stave off a future financial collapse. Many Republicans wanted to repeal the bill outright, claiming the rules it set for banks were too burdensome, but Democrats argued that repeal would allow lenders to engage in discriminatory mortgage practices and put taxpayers at risk for more bank failures, all while lining the pockets of bank executives. In lieu of full repeal, Banking, Housing and Urban Affairs Committee Chair Michael Crapo, R-Idaho, made a deal with moderate Democrats—many of whom expected to face tough electoral challenges in the 2018 midterm—to roll back regulations for the largest banks. Their compromise changed the requirement that banks with assets between $50 billion and $100 billion automatically be subject to enhanced oversight by the Federal Reserve, applying this rule instead to banks with assets over $100 billion. It exempted small and midsize banks from the regulatory stress tests designed to ensure they had enough capital to weather a recession. It also reduced reporting requirements for small banks and created new criteria to help them comply with qualified mortgage rules, among other provisions. When the bill came up for floor votes, most Democrats in both chambers remained opposed and voted against the changes, but there were enough moderates who supported the deal to ensure its passage.

CONGRESS SEEKS SOLUTION TO OPIOID CRISIS

The nation's continued opioid addiction crisis also prompted bipartisan action in 2018. As a follow-up to Congress' inclusion of about $8.5 billion in fiscal 2018 funding to help address this crisis, lawmakers spent months negotiating a resolution that would support the ongoing fight. Their negotiations culminated in a measure that expanded Medicare and Medicaid to cover medication-assisted treatment for substance use disorders, and outlined new Medicaid drug review and utilization requirements for states. It allocated $15 million annually, over five fiscal years, to help public health laboratories detect synthetic opioids, and supported research to develop nonaddictive painkillers. It also provided grants for substance abuse prevention programs and included a measure to prevent opioids from being shipped to the United States via international mail. A Congressional Budget Office (CBO) estimate that the resolution would increase the federal deficit by $44 million over the next ten years raised some concerns, but lawmakers responded by adding spending offsets, such as a provision allowing Medicaid to cover inpatient treatment at larger—and likely less expensive—substance abuse facilities. The bill passed the House by an overwhelming margin in September, followed days later by a near-unanimous Senate vote.

CRIMINAL JUSTICE OVERHAUL

Perhaps the biggest legislative victory of the year—both for Congress and the president—was the end-of-year passage of the First Step Act, a sweeping package of criminal justice system reforms. The bill represented a marked shift in Republicans' law-and-order rhetoric, which had emphasized tough sentencing rules and enforcement measures as a crime deterrent since the 1980s. The First Step Act placed a greater focus on inmates' rehabilitation and reintegration into society. This change in strategy was characterized as a necessary response to a major strain on federal prison resources. The number of federal inmates grew from about 25,000 in 1980 to more than 205,000 in 2015, leading to double- and triple-bunking of prisoners, higher inmate-to-staff ratios, waiting lists for education and drug treatment, and limited work opportunities for prisoners. A Government Accountability Office report identified these factors as causes of reduced prison safety and increased recidivism.

The bill's centerpiece was arguably its reduction of mandatory minimum sentences for certain crimes, including the "three strikes" penalty for drug felonies, which dropped from a life sentence to twenty-five years in prison. It also included changes that limited the disparity in sentencing for crack versus powder cocaine offenses. The bill created more job training and drug treatment programs for inmates and provided more funding for these programs. It also directed the Department of Justice to evaluate prisoners' recidivism risks so they could earn time in prerelease custody at the end of their sentence. Other notable measures prohibited the use of restraints against pregnant inmates and the use of solitary conferment for most juvenile prisoners.

Bipartisan support for the bill was bolstered by a CBO estimate that it would trim federal inmates' sentences by a total of about 53,000 years. It easily passed the Senate on December 18 and the House two days later. The timing of this significant legislative achievement meant that it was largely overshadowed by the second government shutdown of the year, which began one day after Trump signed the First Step Act into law.

HOUSE REPUBLICAN INDICTED

While numerous ethics investigations were initiated during the 115th Congress, Rep. Duncan Hunter, R-Calif., was the only member to face criminal charges in 2018. Hunter was elected to Congress in 2008, filling the former seat of his father, Rep. Duncan L. Hunter. He was also a respected veteran, having served several tours of duty in Iraq and Afghanistan as a U.S. Marine. But Hunter also faced allegations that his campaign committee had reported expenses that were not "legitimate and verifiable campaign expenditures," prompting the Office of Congressional Ethics to launch an investigation in August 2016 to probe claims that Hunter may have spent tens of thousands of campaign dollars on personal items in travel.

In March 2017, the House Ethics Committee announced that it was deferring its investigation at the request of the Department of Justice, which had launched a criminal investigation into Hunter's campaign spending. The Federal Bureau of Investigation reportedly raided the office of Hunter's campaign treasurer the month before. Meanwhile, Hunter maintained his innocence, stating that he knew and followed the rules for campaign spending and that any use of campaign funds for personal reasons was an accident. He also made several payments to his campaign to cover what he said were mistaken, personal, or insufficiently documented expenses. As of November 2017, Hunter had repaid more than $60,000, selling his family's home in California to help cover these costs.

On August 12, 2018, Hunter was indicted on dozens of federal charges, including misuse of campaign contributions, falsifying campaign finance records, wire fraud, and making false statements to investigators. The indictment stated that the Hunters stole more than $250,000 from his campaigns to cover various personal expenses at a time when their family was deeply in debt. It cited instances of the Hunters using campaign funds to pay for items ranging from fast food, movie tickets, and toys, to luxury hotels and family vacations. Hunter allegedly gave his wife a campaign credit card to use for personal spending, and made her his paid campaign manager on two separate occasions, while knowing that she was misusing campaign funds. The indictment further stated that Hunter reported these personal expenses to his campaign treasurer as being campaign related.

Hunter initially dismissed the charges and claimed the investigation was politically motivated, as the indictment was released shortly before the 2018 midterm election. One of Hunter's attorneys also questioned prosecutors' credibility in the case, claiming that two of them had supported Hillary Clinton's failed bid for the presidency in 2016. Both Hunter and his wife pled not guilty to the charges. House Speaker Paul Ryan, R-Wisc., moved to strip Hunter of his committee assignments, though some Republicans continued to defend the congressman. Hunter also won reelection despite the indictment.

In June 2019, Hunter's wife pled guilty to corruption and named him as a co-conspirator. Hunter continued to insist the case was a politically motivated witch hunt, up until December 3, when he pled guilty to one count of conspiring to misuse campaign funds. In the plea agreement, Hunter admitted to using more than $150,000 of campaign funds for personal expenditures between 2010 and 2016. Hunter resigned from Congress in January 2020 and was sentenced to eleven months in prison in March. His wife was later sentenced to eight months home confinement followed by three years of probation. However, both Hunters were pardoned by President Trump in December 2020, before their sentences began.

SUPREME COURT NOMINEE DIVIDES CONGRESS AND THE NATION

U.S. Supreme Court Justice Anthony Kennedy's retirement in July 2018 created a second opportunity for Trump

to appoint another conservative justice to the nation's highest court. Kennedy had long been a swing vote on the Court, offering balance to his more liberal and conservative colleagues, and the confirmation of his replacement was expected to be a battle in the Senate.

Trump selected D.C. Circuit Court Judge Brett Kavanaugh to fill Kennedy's seat and called for the Senate to quickly confirm him. Kavanaugh had clerked for Kennedy before becoming involved in some of the most contentious legal proceedings of the 1990s and early 2000s. He had worked for independent counsel Kenneth W. Starr to impeach President Bill Clinton, for example, and for George W. Bush in the *Bush v. Gore* case.

Although Republicans' elimination of the filibuster for Supreme Court nominees meant Kavanaugh could be confirmed without any Democratic votes, Senate Democrats used his confirmation hearings to grill Kavanaugh on hot-button issues, such as abortion and LGBTQ+ rights, as well as his views on judicial precedent and presidential power. Kavanaugh comported himself well and generally avoided answering tough questions. He appeared poised for confirmation when the hearings concluded in early September.

A few days later, however, various news reports indicated that Sen. Dianne Feinstein, D-Calif., the ranking member on the Judiciary Committee, had received a letter from a constituent who claimed Kavanaugh sexually assaulted her when they were in high school together. Feinstein acknowledged that she had received such a letter and referred it to the Federal Bureau of Investigation (FBI), noting that she had not said anything publicly because the author requested privacy. The woman, Dr. Christine Blasey Ford, made her identity known shortly thereafter, detailing her allegations in an interview with *The Washington Post*. A second accuser, this time a college peer of Kavanaugh's, came forward the next week, followed by two other women (one of whom later recanted her allegations). Kavanaugh denied all the allegations, but Democrats demanded that his nomination be withdrawn. Ultimately, after negotiations between the two parties, the Senate Judiciary Committee scheduled a special session to hear testimony from both Ford and Kavanaugh.

What unfolded next was unprecedented. The session began with four hours of testimony from Dr. Ford, who calmy provided her account of the alleged assault and answered senators' questions, despite sharing that she was terrified to be there. Kavanaugh presented a stark contrast to his accuser as he began his testimony. Kavanaugh spent the first forty-five minutes yelling a rambling opening statement at the senators, in which he decried the entire confirmation process and claimed Democrats were seeking "revenge on behalf of the Clintons." At several points, he became emotional to the point of tears. He remained angry and combative during the question and answer period of the session.

Kavanaugh's critics, Democrats among them, claimed his performance showed he lacked the character required

---

CONGRESS IN 2018

The second session of the 115th Congress began on January 3, 2018. The House was in session on 174 days. The Senate was in session on 191 days. Both chambers adjourned on January 3, 2019.

In the House, members introduced 3,257 bills and resolutions during the year. Senators introduced 1,967. Congress sent 325 of these measures to President Trump to become public law. The president did not issue any vetoes. Altogether, the 115th Congress passed a total of 442 public laws, the most of any Congress since the 110th.

The number of roll call votes decreased in both chambers in 2018. The House took 497 roll call votes, compared to 708 in 2017, while the Senate recorded 274 floor votes, compared to 325 votes during the first session.

---

of a Supreme Court justice and maintained that his nomination should be rescinded. Republicans, including Sen. Lindsey Graham, R-S.C., argued that Democrats were trying to use Kavanaugh and Dr. Ford's allegations to drum up support for their midterm campaigns. Amid this divisive bickering, the Judiciary Committee voted to advance Kavanaugh's nomination. Yet in another twist, Sen. Jeff Flake, R-Ariz., requested that a confirmation vote be delayed so the FBI could investigate Dr. Ford's allegations. Republicans and the White House acceded to this request, because Flake's vote was necessary to confirming Kavanaugh, but Trump strictly limited the investigation's length and scope. It produced no new information.

In the end, Sen. Lisa Murkowski, R-Alaska, was the only Republican to vote against Kavanaugh. However, Sen. Joe Manchin, D-W.V., who was facing a tough reelection challenge in the fall, voted for Kavanaugh's confirmation. The final vote was 50–48 in Kavanaugh's favor, the narrowest margin by which a Supreme Court justice had been confirmed in more than 130 years.

The Political Year

SPECIAL ELECTIONS

A spate of lawmaker resignations and retirements prompted the calling of ten special elections in 2018. Three of the contested House seats flipped from Republican to Democratic control. While this had no impact on Republicans' House majority during the 115th session, Democrats' ability to win in Pennsylvania's eighteenth congressional district—a district President Trump won by nearly twenty points in 2016—was considered a major

Table 1.7   Black Members of Congress, 1947–2020

Congress	Senate	House
80th (1947–1949)	0	2
81st (1949–1951)	0	2
82nd (1951–1953)	0	2
83rd (1953–1955)	0	2
84th (1955–1957)	0	3
85th (1957–1959)	0	4
86th (1959–1961)	0	4
87th (1961–1963)	0	4
88th (1963–1965)	0	5
89th (1965–1967)	0	6
90th (1967–1969)	1	5
91st (1969–1971)	1	9
92nd (1971–1973)	1	12
93rd (1973–1975)	1	15
94th (1975–1977)	1	16
95th (1977–1979)	1	16
96th (1979–1981)	0	16
97th (1981–1983)	0	17
98th (1983–1985)	0	20
99th (1985–1987)	0	20
100th (1987–1989)	0	22
101st (1989–1991)	0	24
102nd (1991–1993)	0	26
103rd (1993–1995)	1	39
104th (1995–1997)	1	38
105th (1997–1999)	1	37
106th (1999–2001)	0	37
107th (2001–2003)	0	36
108th (2003–2005)	0	39
109th (2005–2007)	1	40
110th (2007–2009)	1	40
111th (2009–2011)*	0	39
112th (2011–2013)	0	42
113th (2013–2014)	2	41
114th (2015–2016)	2	44
115th (2017–2018)	3	49
116th (2019–2020)	3	52

SOURCE: Congressional Research Service, *Membership of the 115th Congress*, R44762 (Washington, DC: Congressional Research Service, 2018); *Membership of the 116th Congress*, R45583 (Washington, DC: Congressional Research Service, 2018).

NOTE: House totals reflect the number of members at the start of each Congress and exclude nonvoting delegates.

*President-elect Barack Obama of Illinois resigned his Senate seat in November 2008. African American Roland W. Burris assumed the seat on January 15, 2009.

warning sign that the GOP could lose control of the chamber in the 2018 midterms. Democrats' victory in this race caused election strategists and analysts to revise their estimates of the number of Republican-held House seats that would be competitive in 2018 to as many as 119.

Two Senate Special Elections

Minnesota Gov. Mark Dayton appointed Lt. Gov. Tina Smith to fill the Senate seat vacated by fellow Democrat Al Franken in January 2018, as he faced numerous allegations of sexual misconduct. The seat was expected to remain Democratic, as Minnesota had not elected a Republican senator since 2002. Indeed, Smith defeated her Republican challenger, State Sen. Karin Housley, by a margin of roughly 10 percent.

In Mississippi, the race to fill the Senate seat vacated by Thad Cochran went to a runoff after neither the Republican nor Democratic candidate received more than 50 percent of the vote. Cochran resigned from the Senate in April 2018 due to health concerns. Republican candidate Cindy Hyde-Smith had been appointed by Gov. Phil Bryant to fill Cochran's seat on an interim basis; her main challenger was Democrat Mike Espy, a former U.S. secretary of agriculture. Both candidates received about 41 percent of the vote in the first-round election held on November 6. Hyde-Smith was the victor in the runoff election held on November 27, winning nearly 54 percent of votes cast.

Eight House Special Elections

All three of the House seats that changed parties during 2018 special elections represented Pennsylvania districts. The first of these special elections was seen as a potential bellwether for the 2018 midterms, and pitted Democratic candidate Conor Lamb, an attorney, against Republican State Rep. Rick Saccone. The election was called to replace Republican Tim Murphy, who resigned in October 2017 following allegations that he had an extramarital affair with a woman and encouraged her to get an abortion. Trump won the district by a large margin in the 2016 election, but polling data showed that Lamb had unexpectedly strong support, and he outraised Saccone. The race drew considerable investments from the national political parties, as well as leading politicians from both sides of the aisle, including Trump and former vice president Joe Biden. The election was held on March 13, 2018. Results were initially considered too close to call, but Saccone conceded to Lamb about one week later. The final tally showed Lamb led Saccone with less than 1,000 votes.

Mary Gay Scanlon was another Pennsylvania Democrat who succeeded in flipping a formerly Republican seat. Scanlon was elected to replace Republican Patrick Meehan, who resigned amid a sexual misconduct scandal. Scanlon defeated Republican challenger Pearl Kim in both the special election and a concurrent regular election, both held on November 6, 2018. Notably, the map for the 7th district was redrawn by the Pennsylvania Supreme Court after justices ruled that the original district map constituted an illegal partisan gerrymander. The original district map was used for the special election; the new map was used for the regular election.

In the third Pennsylvania special election, Democrat Susan Wild was elected to succeed Republican Charlie Dent, narrowly beating Marty Nothstein, another Republican, to win the House seat. Dent had retired from office in May 2018. As in Pennsylvania's 7th district, the special election was held concurrently with the regular 2018 election on November 6. Wild won both elections, even though the regular election used a different district map. The original map had also been declared an illegal partisan gerrymander by the Pennsylvania Supreme Court.

Table 1.8 Women in Congress, 1947–2020

Congress	Senate	House
80th (1947–1949)	1	7
81st (1949–1951)	1	9
82nd (1951–1953)	1	10
83rd (1953–1955)	1	12
84th (1955–1957)	1	17
85th (1957–1959)	1	15
86th (1959–1961)	1	17
87th (1961–1963)	2	18
88th (1963–1965)	2	12
89th (1965–1967)	2	11
90th (1967–1969)	1	10
91st (1969–1971)	1	10
92nd (1971–1973)	1	13
93rd (1973–1975)	1	16
94th (1975–1977)	0	17
95th (1977–1979)	2	18
96th (1979–1981)	1	16
97th (1981–1983)	2	19
98th (1983–1985)	2	22
99th (1985–1987)	2	22
100th (1987–1989)	2	23
101st (1989–1991)	2	28
102nd (1991–1993)	3	29
103rd (1993–1995)	7	48
104th (1995–1997)	8	48
105th (1997–1999)	9	51
106th (1999–2001)	9	56
107th (2001–2003)	13	59
108th (2003–2005)	14	59
109th (2005–2007)	14	64
110th (2007–2009)	16	71
111th (2009–2011)	17	75
112th (2011–2013)	17	72
113th (2013–2014)	20	80
114th (2015–2016)	20	84
115th (2017–2018)	23	87
116th (2019–2020)	25	101

SOURCE: Congressional Research Service, *Membership of the 115th Congress*, R44762 (Washington, DC: Congressional Research Service, 2018); *Membership of the 116th Congress*, R45583 (Washington, DC: Congressional Research Service, 2018).

NOTE: House totals reflect the number of members at the start of each Congress and exclude nonvoting delegates.

Republican Debbie Lesko won the special election to succeed fellow Republican Trent Franks of Arizona, who resigned from the House in April 2018 amid sexual misconduct allegations. The recent victory of Conor Lamb in Pennsylvania prompted increased Republican spending in this campaign, even though the district is generally considered Republican leaning and had voted for Republican presidential candidates by wide margins in the previous three election cycles. Lesko, a former state senator, ultimately defeated Democratic challenger Hiral Tipirneni, a physician, by about 9,000 votes.

Republicans eked out a victory in Ohio's 12th congressional district in a vote considered too close to call for nearly three weeks. State Sen. Troy Balderson was elected to succeed fellow Republican Patrick Tiberi, who resigned his House seat in October 2017 to lead the Ohio Business Roundtable, by a margin of less than 1 percent. Balderson's main challenger was Franklin County Recorder Danny O'Connor, a Democrat with hopes of flipping a swing state seat. Both parties' congressional campaign committees were active in the race, and Trump made a campaign appearance to help drum up support for Balderson. The counting of absentee and provisional ballots proved critical in determining the race's razor-thin margin.

Brenda Jones won an overwhelming victory in the special election to fill the House seat vacated by fellow Democrat John Conyers of Michigan. Conyers resigned in December 2017 as he faced allegations of sexual misconduct from several staffers. At the time, Jones was serving as the Detroit City Council president. She took nearly 87 percent of the vote in the November poll, which occurred alongside the regular 2018 election. No Republican filed to contest the seat. Jones served the remainder of Conyers' term, which ended in January 2019. At that point she was succeeded by former state representative Rashida Tlaib, who won the regular 2018 election.

Democrat Joseph Morelle was elected to succeed the late Louise Slaughter of New York in the House on November 6, 2018. Morelle previously served in the New York State Assembly for roughly seventeen years, including stints as majority leader and Assembly speaker. He defeated Republican challenger James Maxwell by roughly 40,000 votes.

RECORD-SETTING MIDTERM ELECTION

On November 6, 2018, Americans turned out in droves to vote in a midterm election in which every seat in the House of Representatives, thirty-five seats in the Senate, and thirty-six governors' mansions were on the ballot, in addition to thousands of state and local races. Approximately 49 percent of eligible voters cast their ballots in 2018. According to data compiled by the United States Elections Project, this was the highest level of voter turnout in a midterm election since 1914, when 50.4 percent of eligible voters went to the polls. U.S. Census Bureau data showed the largest increase in turnout among 18- to 29-year-olds, 36 percent of whom cast a vote in 2018, compared to just 20 percent in the previous midterm. Asian, Hispanic, and Black voter turnout all increased by double digits as well. These increases appeared to be facilitated in part by alternative voting methods, such as voting by mail. About 40 percent of voters used these methods, according to the U.S. Census Bureau, with multiple news outlets reporting a historic surge in early voting.

The primary factor driving this record-setting turnout appeared to be a sharp divide between President Trump's enthusiastically supportive Republican base and Democrats who were deeply dissatisfied with his administration and wanted to oust his allies in Congress. In fact, sixty percent of respondents in a Gallup poll said they planned to use their vote to "send a message" of either support or opposition to the president. Multiple other factors cited by analysts included anti-incumbent sentiment, frustration with partisan gridlock, support for the record

Table 1.9 Hispanic Members of Congress, 1947–2020

Congress	Senate	House
80th (1947–1949)	1	1
81st (1949–1951)	1	1
82nd (1951–1953)	1	1
83rd (1953–1955)	1	1
84th (1955–1957)	1	1
85th (1957–1959)	2	0
86th (1959–1961)	2	0
87th (1961–1963)	2	1
88th (1963–1965)	1	3
89th (1965–1967)	1	4
90th (1967–1969)	1	4
91st (1969–1971)	1	5
92nd (1971–1973)	1	6
93rd (1973–1975)	1	6
94th (1975–1977)	1	6
95th (1977–1979)	0	5
96th (1979–1981)	0	6
97th (1981–1983)	0	7
98th (1983–1985)	0	10
99th (1985–1987)	0	11
100th (1987–1989)	0	11
101st (1989–1991)	0	11
102nd (1991–1993)	0	11
103rd (1993–1995)	0	17
104th (1995–1997)	0	17
105th (1997–1999)	0	18
106th (1999–2001)	0	18
107th (2001–2003)	0	19
108th (2003–2005)	0	24
109th (2005–2007)	2	23
110th (2007–2009)	3	23
111th (2009–2011)*	3	24
112th (2011–2013)	2	24
113th (2013–2015)	4	33
114th (2015–2017)	3	34
115th (2018–2019)	5	39
116th (2019–2020)	5	43

SOURCE: Congressional Research Service, *Membership of the 115th Congress*, R44762 (Washington, DC: Congressional Research Service, 2018); *Membership of the 116th Congress*, R45583 (Washington, DC: Congressional Research Service, 2018).

NOTE: Totals reflect the number of members at the start of each Congress and exclude nonvoting delegates.

*Democrat Ken Salazar of Colorado, a member of the Senate when the 111th Congress convened, resigned on January 21, 2009, to become secretary of the Interior. His replacement, appointed by the Colorado governor, was not Hispanic.

number of female House candidates, and highly competitive Senate races. Some also speculated that the Kavanaugh confirmation battle—and the potential for Trump to appoint additional Supreme Court justices—helped energize both Democrats and the Republican base.

Beyond voter turnout, the 2018 midterm also set a record for the number of women elected to the House of Representatives—a total of 116. The growth in female representation, which also included fifteen women in the Senate, helped make the 116th Congress the most diverse in history. Reps. Deb Haaland, D-N.M., and Sharice Davids, D-Ks., were the first Native American women elected to Congress, while Reps. Ilhan Omar, D-Minn., and Rashida Tlaib, D-Mich., were the first Muslim women

to serve. The Black and Hispanic caucuses set new records for delegation size, as well, at thirty-nine and fifty-five members, respectively. Additionally, the average age of incoming lawmakers was forty-seven—at least ten years younger than the average age in the 115th Congress.

DEMOCRATS WIN CONTROL OF THE HOUSE

Republicans were widely expected to lose their House majority, and these predictions proved correct: Democrats won 235 seats in the House to Republicans' 199—a net loss of forty seats. Nearly 60 million people voted for House Democratic candidates, according to an analysis by the website FiveThirtyEight, which is almost as many votes as presidential candidates had received in recent general elections.

One of the year's most prominent House races, and one in which anti-incumbent sentiment was on display, was in New York's 14th Congressional District. There, twenty-nine-year-old activist Alexandria Ocasio-Cortez first defeated Democratic Caucus Chair and ten-term congressman Joe Crowley in the party primary, then easily beat her Republican challenger. Her victory made Ocasio-Cortez the youngest woman ever elected to Congress.

Another notable vote took place in North Carolina's 9th Congressional District. Republican Mark Harris, a pastor, was chosen to fill the vacant House seat on November 6. However, the North Carolina State Board of Elections declined to certify the results amid allegations of voter fraud. A Harris campaign operative was later accused of collecting absentee ballots from voters in violation of state election law, which stipulates that only the voter or a close relative may submit an absentee ballot. A special election was subsequently held in February 2019, when Republican State Sen. Dan Bishop defeated Democrat Dan McCready, by less than 4,000 votes.

Speaking to reporters on November 7, House Minority Leader Nancy Pelosi, D-Calif., claimed that Democrats' focus on health care was critical to their Election Day victories, and that the shift in chamber control should be a sign to Republicans that the American people did not support their push to repeal Obamacare. But Pelosi also called for greater collaboration between the two parties, noting that Democratic majorities had successfully worked with Republican presidents on a number of economic and other issues in the past.

Democrats were expected to leverage their new majority to launch a series of investigations into the Trump administration, such as the president's potential conflicts of interest and his personal and business taxes. Pelosi warned her party colleagues against congressional overreach and continued to emphasize passing legislation over pursuing wide-ranging probes and some Democrats' calls to impeach the president. The presumed speaker instead preferred to focus on making major changes on health care, immigration, gun control, voting laws, and infrastructure projects.

REPUBLICANS HOLD THE SENATE

The Democrats had no such wins to celebrate in the Senate, where Republicans picked up two seats, bolstering their thin majority. One of those seats previously belonged to Heidi Heitkamp of North Dakota, a moderate who was frequently targeted by Republican leadership as a potential Democratic supporter in tight votes, because they knew she had a tough reelection battle ahead. Heitkamp, who won election in 2021 by less than a percentage point, faced popular House Republican Kevin Cramer in a heavily conservative state where 63 percent of voters supported Trump for president. Heitkamp did not poll well in the run-up to the election, but it was widely agreed that her vote against Kavanaugh's confirmation ended her chances of remaining in the Senate. She lost by more than 10 percent.

Another closely watched race occurred in Texas, where Democratic Rep. Beto O'Rourke mounted a surprisingly strong challenge to the incumbent Republican Sen. Ted Cruz. The charismatic O'Rourke was often compared to President Obama, drawing huge crowds at events across the state and raising tens of millions of dollars while focusing on pushing young people to the polls. Cruz relied on Trump's support and his record in Congress to win over voters, which he ultimately did. O'Rourke lost the vote by about 3 percent, but the enthusiasm for his candidacy did drive turnout and helped Democrats win several state House and Senate races, in addition to picking up two U.S. House seats in the state.

Trump focused on Republicans' Senate victories in his post-Election Day remarks, declaring it to be the biggest gain for a president's party in the Senate during a first-term midterm election in more than fifty years. He also claimed the Senate pickup was due both to voters' repudiation of how Democrats handled the Kavanaugh confirmation proceedings and to their embrace of his administration's messages on everything from taxes to immigration. However, he did echo Pelosi's call for unity, expressing optimism that members of Congress would work together on infrastructure, trade, and other issues in the next session.

In the days after the election, McConnell signaled that the Senate would continue efforts to reform the health care system and address prescription drug prices. Confirmation of judicial nominees and immigration legislation were also expected to be priorities for the chamber.

GUBERNATORIAL RACES

Nationwide, gubernatorial elections were held in thirty-six states. Republicans were defending twenty-six of those seats, compared to nine Democratic seats that were up for election. The GOP had a net loss of six seats, all of which were won by Democratic candidates. These Democratic pickups occurred in Illinois, Kansas, Maine, Michigan, Nevada, New Mexico, and Wisconsin. Illinois and Wisconsin were the only states in which Democrats defeated a sitting Republican governor. The four other

races did not feature an incumbent candidate. In Alaska, Republican Mike Dunleavey won a seat previously held by Independent Bill Walker.

The most-watched gubernatorial votes included the Illinois race, in which Republican Gov. Bruce Rauner faced Democratic challenger and businessman J. B. Pritzker. Outside of the change in party control, this race was noteworthy for the candidates' unprecedented fundraising. Both Rauner and Pritzker contributed more than $50 million to their own campaigns. When combined with outside contributions, the two campaigns raised more money than in any other gubernatorial election in U.S. history. Pritzker's win also cemented Democratic control of the state, as the party held majorities in both the state house and senate.

The Georgia race was also closely watched. Democrat Stacey Abrams, a former state house minority leader, was vying to become the first Black female governor in the United States. Republicans, represented in this race by Secretary of State Brian Kemp, sought to maintain their political trifecta—control of the governorship, state house, and state senate. The stakes in this race were also high because the incoming governor would have the power to approve or veto new congressional and state district maps following the 2020 Census. In the end, Kemp narrowly avoided a runoff, winning 50.2 percent of the vote to Abrams' 48.8 percent.

STATE BALLOT INITIATIVES

A total of 167 ballot measures were considered by voters in thirty-eight states in 2018. Twelve of those were decided during polls held earlier in the year, leaving 155 measures on November ballots. Although this was a lower total number of ballot initiatives than seen in recent years, the number of initiatives brought by citizens remained high—sixty-eight compared to 2016's record of seventy-six. More than $1.18 billion was raised by supporters and opponents of the various ballot measures, with about $1.16 billion spent by initiative-related campaigns. Among the most popular issues on the ballot were elections policy, marijuana, taxes, the Obamacare Medicaid expansion, and a template crime victim's rights measure known as Marsy's Law.

Elections Policy

Sixteen states featured twenty-one measures on election-related policies, including redistricting, voting requirements, and campaign finance rules. Redistricting was the most popular issue in this category, with six measures approved in five states. Colorado, Michigan, and Utah all considered and adopted measures creating independent redistricting commissions to draw up congressional or state legislative district maps. The Utah initiative was later amended by state lawmakers to allow the state legislature to establish a redistricting committee, which could draw and recommend its own version of district maps for consideration alongside those created by the commission. Voters in

Ohio adopted a change requiring a bipartisan vote by the state legislature to approve redistricting maps, rather than a simple majority. And in Missouri, voters approved a measure creating the position of state demographer, who would be charged with drawing recommended maps for state legislative districts, subject to approval by the state's bipartisan redistricting commissions.

Nine states had ballot measures proposing a variety of changes to their voting requirements and election systems. This included Maine, where voters affirmed their support for a ranked-choice voting system, in which voters rank candidates in order of preference instead of selecting one candidate to win, first approved via ballot initiative in 2016. The state legislature had passed in 2017 a bill to delay, and potentially repeal, the system's implementation, but the 2018 initiative's approval meant ranked-choice voting would be used for the first time in the 2018 election. In Florida, a citizens initiative put a measure on the ballot to automatically restore convicted felons' right to vote upon completion of their sentences. People convicted of murder or felony sexual offenses were excluded from this provision, which was approved by voters. In Arkansas and North Carolina, voters approved measures requiring people to show photo identification before casting nonprovisional or in-person ballots, respectively. Another five states—Colorado, Massachusetts, Missouri, North Dakota, and South Dakota—featured ballot initiatives related to campaign finance limits, restrictions on lobbying activities, and other election-related ethics issues.

Marijuana

The legalization of medical marijuana continued to be a popular issue in 2018, with five states considering seven such measures. Voters in Michigan and North Dakota approved legalization for recreational uses, while Oklahoma and Missouri voters approved legal medical uses. Missouri actually had three separate and competing ballot measures that proposed medical marijuana's legalization; the one that passed also imposed a 4 percent tax on marijuana sales, with revenues dedicated to paying for health care services for veterans. In Colorado, voters approved a measure requiring the state to use the same definition of industrial hemp, a substance used in products ranging from textiles to nutritional supplements, as federal law. The change was expected to allow the state to expand hemp cultivation and provide more regulatory flexibility.

Taxes

Various tax-related proposals appeared on ballots in Arizona, California, Florida, North Carolina, Oregon, and Washington. Arizona voters approved an initiative preventing state and local governments from implementing new, or raising existing, taxes on services. In California, voters rejected a proposal to require their approval before state lawmakers imposed, increased, or extended fuel taxes or vehicle fees. The same measure would also have repealed

a gas tax increase passed in 2017. Oregon voters turned down a proposed ban on grocery taxes, while their neighbors in Washington agreed to implement such a ban. Oregon voters also opposed an initiative requiring supermajorities in the state legislature to increase taxes; Florida voters approved a similar measure. Both Florida and North Carolina approved measures capping certain tax rates.

Medicaid and Health Care

Montana, Idaho, Nebraska, and Utah were among the states considering measures related to expanded Medicaid coverage under the Affordable Care Act. Voters in Idaho, Nebraska, and Utah further expanded Medicaid coverage to 138 percent of the federal poverty line, with Utah also implementing a new sales tax to help pay for the expansion. In Montana, voters rejected a proposal to increase tobacco taxes to cover Medicaid expansion, and to eliminate the automatic June 2019 expiration date for expanded coverage. Earlier in the year, Oregon voters said the state should uphold 2017 legislation that taxes health care insurance and the revenue of some hospitals to pay for expanded Medicaid coverage.

Other notable health care initiatives included Nevada voters' approval of a measure exempting certain types of medical equipment, the use of which had been prescribed by a licensed health care provider, from sales and use tax. California voters approved a measure authorizing $1.5 billion in bonds for construction and equipment for children's hospitals, but they rejected a measure requiring dialysis clinics to refund revenue above 115 percent of the costs of direct patient care and health care improvements. In Massachusetts, voters rejected a proposal to establish limits on the maximum number of patients assigned to registered nurses working in hospitals.

Marsy's Law

Florida, Georgia, Kentucky, Nevada, North Carolina, and Oklahoma all featured a bill known as Marsy's Law on their ballots in 2018. Marsy's Law is a crime victims' rights bill that passed in California in 2008 and has since provided something of a template for other states seeking to adopt similar protections. The law's specific provisions typically vary by state, but they commonly include a crime victim's right to be notified about and present at legal proceedings, to be protected from the accused, to be notified about the release or escape of the accused, and to receive restitution from the person who committed the crime. Voters in all six states supported the adoption of Marsy's Law, although a circuit court judge in Kentucky blocked that state's votes from being certified. The ruling followed a challenge by the Kentucky Association of Criminal Defense Lawyers, whose members claimed that the ballot question's language failed to fairly and fully inform voters about the measure's substance. The lower court ruling was later upheld by the State Supreme Court.

Abortion

Abortion continued to be a contentious issue, with some conservative-leaning states seeking to approve measures restricting funding or access to the procedure. Alabama voters, for example, approved a measure making it state policy to "recognize and support the sanctity of unborn life and the rights of unborn children, including the right to life" and declaring that nothing in the state's constitution provided a right to abortion or required funding for abortions. West Virginia voters agreed to add similar language to their state's constitution. In Oregon, a proposal to prohibit the use of public funds from being spent on abortions, except in cases where the procedure was deemed medically necessary or when it was required by federal law, was rejected by voters.

Energy

Initiatives aimed at reducing greenhouse gas emissions and encouraging the use of renewable energy were on the ballot in Arizona, Nevada, and Washington. Voters in both Arizona and Nevada were asked to consider requiring electric utilities to obtain 50 percent of their power from renewable sources. Arizona voters rejected the proposal, while Nevadans approved it. Nevada voters also considered a separate measure ending energy monopolies and requiring an open and competitive electricity market. This was rejected. Finally, in Washington, a proposal to impose a fee on carbon emissions from power plants, refineries, and other greenhouse gas emitters—with funds generated by the fee allocated to environmental programs and projects—failed.

Minimum Wage

In Arkansas, voters agreed to raise the state's minimum wage incrementally from $8.50 per hour to $11 an hour by 2021. Missouri voters approved a similar, graduated increase, agreeing to raise the state's minimum wage from $7.85 at the time of the vote to $12 by 2023.

2019

The Legislative Year

A newly minted Democratic majority and a spate of reelection losses by moderate House Republicans in the House, combined with stronger Republican control of the Senate, heralded the start of a particularly acrimonious year in Congress. While intrachamber disputes still occurred, more focus was placed on the House–Senate divide. Democrats used their majority to push hundreds of bills through the House in 2019, but few pieces of legislation made it through the Senate. According to a *Congressional Quarterly* analysis, the Senate held 107 votes on legislation in 2019, including on procedural measures, such as motions to invoke cloture. In the previous twenty years, the Senate averaged 249 such votes per year. This slowdown served as a key messaging point for both parties: Democrats applauded their own productivity while criticizing Senate Republicans as obstructionists; Senate Majority Leader Mitch McConnell, R-Ky., positioned himself and the chamber as defending the country against the "radical, half-baked, socialist" legislation produced by the House.

Democrats knew much of what they approved would never be brought up for a vote in the Senate, but major House bills still passed with near-unanimous party support. Analysts surmised that in this way, Democrats were effectively using destined-to-fail bills to highlight their 2020 platform. Meanwhile, McConnell's refusal to bring bills to the floor that did not have the president's support was seen as an effort to protect GOP members from tough votes. It also enabled him to save floor time for consideration of judicial nominations, which McConnell had pledged to prioritize early in the 116th Congress. McConnell also moved to change another Senate procedural rule that reduced the maximum debate time allowed for most nominations from thirty hours to two hours. This allowed him to further speed the process for confirming Trump's judicial nominees.

TRUMP ADMINISTRATION INVESTIGATED

The divisiveness of the first session of the 116th Congress was also fueled by numerous ongoing investigations of the Trump administration—both within and outside Congress. Emboldened by their House majority and resultant committee leadership, Democrats launched dozens of inquiries into issues ranging from the president's potential conflicts of interest; contentious policies, such as the separation of unauthorized immigrant families arriving at the southern border; cabinet secretary actions; regulatory rollbacks; and the administration's relationship with Russia. According to an analysis by *The New York Times*, at least twelve of these investigations were focused on the president.

One such inquiry was announced on March 4 by Rep. Jerry Nadler, D-N.Y., head of the House Judiciary Committee. The committee would investigate "alleged obstruction of justice, public corruption, and other abuses of power by President Trump, his associates, and members of his Administration," Nadler said. In the days preceding this announcement, lawmakers had heard public and closed-door testimony from Michael Cohen, the president's former lawyer. Republicans challenged Cohen's credibility, but his statements and the documents he provided convinced Democrats that further investigation was necessary. While Cohen said he did not have evidence that Trump colluded with the Russian government to influence the 2016 election—the crux of the separate investigation being led by special counsel Robert Mueller—he said the president did know about a meeting between his campaign staff and Russians who claimed to have damaging information about his opponent, Hillary Clinton. Cohen also claimed that Trump had authorized hush-money payments to a woman with whom he allegedly had an affair, misrepresented his assets during business dealings, and committed other misdeeds. Cohen further alleged that Trump and his personal lawyer had pressured Cohen into lying to Congress when he offered testimony on the Trump–Russia link in 2017. (Cohen pled guilty to lying to Congress in 2018 and was two months away from beginning his prison sentence when he appeared before lawmakers in 2019.)

Cohen's testimony and Nadler's announcement of the Democrats' latest probe prompted fresh speculation that the House would push to impeach the president. Such speculation intensified a few weeks later, when Special Counsel Mueller provided the Department of Justice with the final report from his twenty-one-month investigation. That probe had been announced by Deputy Attorney General Rod Rosenstein in May 2017 and was directed to investigate "any links and/or coordination between the Russian government and individuals associated with the campaign of President Donald Trump" and to "prosecute federal crimes arising from investigations of these matters." The inquiry involved hundreds of interviews and the review of thousands of documents, and Mueller's team issued indictments for thirty-four people and three companies as the work progressed.

The final report concluded that the investigation "did not establish that members of the Trump campaign conspired or coordinated with the Russian government in its election interference activities." It did find that Russian operatives had interacted with campaign members on numerous occasions, but it was unclear if Trump campaign personnel knew they were with Russian officials who had criminal intent. The report also considered

whether a series of actions taken by Trump and his associates—such as Trump's request that White House Counsel Don McGahn fire Mueller—constituted an attempt to obstruct the investigation, but essentially declined to make a determination on this matter. Notably, the document stated that, "while this report does not conclude that the president committed a crime, it also does not exonerate him."

While Trump and Vice President Mike Pence celebrated the report as clearing the president's name, Republicans in Congress generally adopted a more measured tone in their response to Mueller's conclusions. Some, including Sen. Marco Rubio, R-Fla., focused on the report's discussion of Russian efforts to influence the American public, expressing alarm at how effective these actions had been and warning they may be repeated in the future. Others acknowledged that Trump had acted inappropriately, if not criminally. Sen. Mitt Romney, R-Utah, was one of the few vocal critics within the party, declaring himself "sickened" by the "pervasiveness of dishonesty and misdirection" in the administration. By contrast, Democrats seized on the report as an indication that Trump and his associates must be held accountable, and left open the possibility that the president could be found guilty of obstruction of justice. Several members of the party's liberal wing called for impeachment, with Rep. Rashida Tlaib, D-Mich., circulating a petition to drum up her colleagues' support. Nadler, Pelosi, and others, however, largely avoided talk of impeachment by saying they needed to review the full report and gather further information. Pelosi, in particular, remained reluctant to impeach, despite months of lobbying by some of her colleagues.

HOUSE LAUNCHES IMPEACHMENT INQUIRY

Interestingly, while the House did launch impeachment proceedings in the fall, it was not because of the Mueller report, but a whistleblower complaint alleging that Trump had used his office to curry political favor. The complaint had been filed with the intelligence community inspector general's office in August and became known to Congress in mid-September. It alleged that Trump had attempted to condition the provision of foreign aid to Ukraine on that government's launch of an investigation into former vice president Joe Biden and his son, Hunter. While in office, the elder Biden had urged the Ukrainian government to improve its anticorruption efforts and fire an unpopular prosecutor general. Trump and his associates have long claimed that by doing so, Biden was trying to protect Hunter, who at the time was serving on the board of a Ukrainian energy company owned by a man facing money laundering and other criminal charges. According to the whistleblower complaint, Ukraine's president-elect, Volodymyr Zelenskyy requested additional U.S. aid to help counter Russian aggressions in the region while on a

phone call with Trump in July. Trump, in turn, repeatedly pressed Zelenskyy to begin investigating Biden.

Trump denied doing anything wrong and said there was no "quid pro quo," as Democrats and others alleged, and the White House released a rough transcript of the conversation to support his claims. In Congress, many Republicans rallied to the president's defense, citing the transcript as evidence that the phone call had been above board and claiming he and two leaders had simply discussed the need to continue fighting corruption in Ukraine. However, a few raised concerns that the conversation had been inappropriate, even if it was not an impeachable offense.

Democrats viewed the complaint and call transcript quite differently. The same day the transcript was released, Pelosi announced impeachment proceedings against the president, declaring that "the actions taken to date by the president have seriously violated the Constitution." The first subpoenas were issued three days later. Initially, the House Intelligence Committee began its investigation of the president behind closed doors, but this met with considerable resistance from Republicans, who argued that proceedings should be public for the sake of transparency. They also noted that past presidential impeachments had been authorized by a vote of the full House before investigations began and claimed that without such a vote, the committee's work would be invalid. Democrats agreed to the Republicans' demand: On October 31, the House voted on a bill to formalize the impeachment inquiry and establish rules for the remainder of the investigation. The bill was approved mostly along party lines, and the impeachment proceedings were allowed to continue.

The House Intelligence Committee conducted public and closed-door hearings for two weeks before issuing a report on its findings to the House Judiciary Committee, which conducted two public hearings to discuss the investigation findings and whether they presented constitutional grounds to impeach Trump. Legal experts called to testify by the Judiciary Committee were divided by party: The five witnesses called by Democrats agreed that Trump's actions represented an impeachable offense; the two called by Republicans disagreed. The White House declined the committee's invitation to participate in the hearings, and Trump continued to decry the proceedings as a witch hunt.

At the conclusion of all these hearings, Democrats wrote two draft articles of impeachment. One accused Trump of abusing the power of his office; the other claimed he had obstructed justice by directing White House officials to defy congressional subpoenas. After a highly charged, and at times personal, two-day markup, the Judiciary Committee voted 23–17, along party lines, to send the articles of impeachment to the full House for consideration. The next step was for the House Rules Committee to establish parameters for the floor vote. The committee agreed to allow six hours of debate, with three hours allocated to each party, with no amendments allowed and a vote taking place immediately after the debate.

The debate began on December 18. Democrats largely used their floor time to defend their investigation of the president and to urge their colleagues to protect American democracy by supporting impeachment. Republicans continued to dismiss the proceedings as politically motivated, noting that Democrats had been looking for a way to push Trump out of office since the 2016 election. Ultimately, both articles of impeachment passed the House without a single Republican vote. Two Democrats voted against article one, while three voted against article two.

Contrary to historical precedent, Pelosi delayed sending the approved articles of impeachment to the Senate for trial until January 15, 2020. In previous impeachment proceedings, the approved articles were immediately sent to the Senate. Pelosi claimed she was concerned Republicans would not hold a fair trial and so wanted to delay the articles' submission. The Senate trial began on January 21 and was presided over by U.S. Supreme Court Justice John Roberts. Both the House impeachment managers and Trump's legal team had an opportunity to present their case, then answered questions submitted by senators. A final vote on the articles was held on February 5, with a two-thirds majority necessary to remove Trump from office. The Senate rejected both articles on party lines. Mitt Romney was the only Republican to break ranks and join the Democrats in voting to impeach.

U.S.–MEXICO–CANADA AGREEMENT

Amid these impeachment proceedings, Democratic leaders in the House were also pushing the administration for policy concessions in the recently negotiated U.S.–Mexico–Canada Agreement (USMCA). This new trade agreement was a top priority for Trump and was intended to replace the twenty-five-year-old North American Free Trade Agreement (NAFTA), which the president had repeatedly described as one of the worst trade deals in history. Negotiations between U.S., Canadian, and Mexican officials began back in August 2017 but proceeded slowly due to key disagreements between the parties on issues such as steel and aluminum tariffs, farmers' access to markets, and automotive exports. The parties signed a draft agreement in November 2018 that retained many of NAFTA's original provisions, but with a series of updates, including those that reflected the increasingly digital nature of the economy. It also included new labor protections, encouraged more auto manufacturing in North America, and expanded markets for U.S. farmers, especially dairy producers.

The USMCA then had to be approved by each government. In the United States, Congress must approve trade agreements, but lawmakers do not vote on the text of the agreement itself. Instead, the administration is responsible for writing and submitting an implementing bill, which includes all the changes to U.S. law necessary to allow the agreement to take effect. Consideration of this implementing legislation is where Congress can exercise its power: If

members are opposed to certain provisions of a deal, House leadership can delay consideration until changes are made. Pelosi, for example, delayed consideration of the U.S.–Colombia Free Trade Agreement for nearly four years, until parts of the deal were renegotiated to meet Democrats' demands. Understanding this dynamic, Trump sought to pressure Congress into quick action by threatening in December 2018 to begin the six-month process for withdrawing the United States from NAFTA. Had the president acted on this threat, Congress would have needed to approve the USMCA by May 2019 or otherwise face the consequences of not having an agreement in place to provide a framework for trade with Mexico and Canada.

As 2019 began, however, the administration largely backed off this threat, and instead began conducting a series of meetings with House Ways and Means Committee members and lawmakers and staff from various congressional caucuses to help drum up support for the deal on both sides of the aisle. Throughout this process, lawmakers successfully pushed for a number of changes.

Among Republicans, the primary objection to the USMCA appeared to involve language included by Canada that protected pregnant and LGBTQ+ workers from employment discrimination. Approximately forty GOP members wrote to the president urging him not to sign the USMCA unless that language was removed. The administration was able to address these concerns by adding language that simply committed countries to implementing antidiscrimination policies that they considered "appropriate" and that indicated the United States would not be required to introduce new laws in this area.

Democrats were more vocal in expressing concerns about, or opposition to, various aspects of the agreement. Some called for the pact to be renegotiated entirely, but the administration refused to consider that option. Much of the Democratic resistance was generated by doubts that the deal's labor and environmental rules would be enforceable. Mexican workers' rights were of primary concern here, because of the country's issues with forced labor, violence against workers, and low wages that undercut American competitors. The administration responded by adding provisions that created an independent panel empowered to investigate factories accused of labor rights violations and to stop shipments of goods from those factories from crossing borders. Another change established an interagency committee to monitor Mexican labor laws and reforms.

Democrats also took issue with provisions pertaining to prescription drug pricing, particularly a measure extending intellectual property protections for biologics, an advanced and expensive class of drugs, for ten years. Democrats argued this and other deal components would lock in high drug prices. Here, the administration again conceded. Officials rolled back these protections from competition created by cheaper alternatives. They also removed the process by which drug companies can seek

extended patent protections for products that have new uses identified.

Another point of contention, for both Democrats and Republicans, was a proposed system of arbitration that companies could use to sue the participating governments for unfair treatment under the agreement. Republicans claimed this would encourage outsourcing, while Democrats argued it would enable corporations to challenge important environmental and consumer regulations. The final USMCA limited the scope of this system so that it could not be used in disputes between the United States and Canada, and would only be applied to limited types of disagreements between the United States and Mexico.

These negotiations lasted through the fall, with Democratic leadership announcing on December 10 they had struck a deal with the White House to take up implementing legislation. Pelosi and other senior Democrats hailed the revised agreement as a major win for their party's agenda. Some Republicans complained that the administration had conceded too much to the Democrats, and that the deal was too liberal. However, the implementing bill still received significant bipartisan support in both chambers. It was approved by the House on December 19 with a vote of 295–41. The Senate followed on January 16, approving the bill by a vote of 89–10. Democrats continued to highlight their negotiating success as Trump readied to sign the bill into law. "What the president will be signing is quite different from what the president sent us," Pelosi said during a press conference on January 29, shortly before Trump signed the bill.

CONGRESS CHALLENGES BORDER EMERGENCY DECLARATION

The House and Senate also united in a rare bipartisan rebuke of the president. After failing to persuade Congress to grant his request for border wall funding in the fiscal 2019 omnibus, Trump declared a national emergency at the U.S.–Mexico border. His mid-February announcement enabled him to reallocate more than $6 billion, that Congress had appropriated for military construction, the Defense Department's anti-drug activities, and the Treasury Department's drug-asset forfeiture program, to border wall construction.

Democrats decried the move as executive overreach, emphasizing that only Congress had the power to appropriate funds. Republicans expressed concerns that Trump's announcement would set a potentially damaging precedent, opening the door for future presidents to leverage national emergency declarations to advance their policy preferences. In the House, Democrats pushed to adopt a joint resolution to overturn the emergency declaration. Thirteen Republicans joined all Democrats in approving the resolution on February 26, less than two weeks after Trump's announcement. The Senate also approved the resolution, on March 14. Twelve Republicans joined their Democratic colleagues in supporting the resolution, despite an intense lobbying effort by the White House that sought to cast the vote as a show of loyalty to the president and the party ahead of the 2020 election. However, even with some Republican support, neither chamber had enough votes to overturn Trump's subsequent veto—the first of his presidency.

CONSERVATION OF PUBLIC LANDS SIGNIFICANTLY EXPANDED

The 116th Congress' other major accomplishments included passage of sweeping land conservation legislation, which passed both the House and Senate with overwhelming margins. The bill began in the Senate and easily gained bipartisan support, as it provided nearly every member with a home-state win they could promote to their constituents. The bill's passage was also preceded by years of negotiations that began at the local level among diverse communities, advocacy groups, and conservationists seeking to build broad-based support for the package. It was originally slated to come up for a vote before the 115th Congress, late in 2018, but it was sidelined by the fraught budget negotiations that ended in a government shutdown. The bill's congressional champions, including Sen. Lisa Murkowski, R-Alaska, pushed for its revival in 2019 and secured a promise from McConnell to bring it up for consideration early in the year.

Widely characterized as the most significant conservation legislation in at least a decade, the bill contained more than 120 proposals. Among its main provisions was the extension of wilderness protections to 1.3 million acres of land, the permanent withdrawal of mining claims around Yellowstone National Park and North Cascades National Park, the creation of four new national monuments, and the expansion of five national parks. The bill also permanently authorized the federal Land and Water Conservation Fund, which allocates offshore drilling revenue to conservation efforts ranging from preservation of wildlife habitats to maintenance of local recreational facilities. Other popular provisions opened all federal lands to hunting, fishing, and recreational shooting, and allowed bow hunters to carry their weapons through national parks enroute to designated hunting areas.

The most significant challenge to the bill's passage was raised by Sen. Mike Lee, R-Utah, who argued that wilderness protections were too restrictive and that the bill would make it easier for the federal government to take control of private land. Lee also introduced an amendment to limit the bill's extension or establishment of national monuments in Utah, but more than a dozen of his Republican colleagues joined with Democrats to table his proposal and prevent it from receiving a floor vote. The bill passed the Senate with a 92–8 vote and easily gained approval in the House two weeks later, with a vote of 363–62. Trump signed the bill into law in March, despite his administration's prior efforts to limit the size of national monuments and open more public lands to oil and gas operations.

The first session of the 116th Congress began January 3, 2019. Both chambers adjourned on January 3, 2020. The Senate was in session for 168 days, whereas the House was in session on 193 days.

Members in the House introduced 6,467 bills and resolutions in 2019, while senators introduced 3,703 bills and resolutions. Congress cleared 108 bills that were enacted into law. President Donald Trump issued six vetoes during this session. None was overturned by Congress.

The House took 701 roll call votes in 2019, a significant increase over the 497 roll call votes taken in 2018. The Senate took 428 recorded votes, compared to 274 floor votes in 2018.

The Political Year

REPUBLICANS KEEP SEATS IN SPECIAL ELECTIONS

Only three special elections were held in 2019, all of which were to fill vacant House seats. The first special election of the year took place on May 21 in Pennsylvania's 12th congressional district. Republican State Rep. Fred Keller faced Democrat Marc Friedenberg, a Pennsylvania State University professor, in the race to fill the House seat vacated by fellow Republican Tom Marino. Marino left Congress in January to take a job in the private sector. The race was not considered to be competitive given the district's solidly Republican leanings. Also, Friedenberg had challenged Marino in 2018 and lost to the incumbent congressman by more than thirty points. His second bid for Marino's seat was similarly unsuccessful: Keller easily beat him by a margin of roughly 36 percent.

Special elections in North Carolina's 3rd and 9th congressional districts came next. In the 3rd district, candidates sought to fill the seat of the late Republican congressman Walter Jones, who died on February 10, 2019. Republican State Rep. Greg Murphy won a comfortable victory with a margin of roughly 28 points over Democratic candidate Allen Thomas, a former mayor of Greenville, during the election on September 10. By comparison, the outcome of the 9th congressional district's special election was much closer. The House seat representing this district had been vacant since the beginning of the 116th Congress. Republican Mark Harris, a pastor, was elected to fill the seat during the 2018 midterm, but the North Carolina State Board of Elections refused to certify the election results due to allegations of vote tampering and mishandling of absentee ballots. Harris declined to run in the 2019 special election. Ultimately, Republican State Sen.

Dan Bishop defeated Democrat Dan McCready, founder of a solar energy company, by less than 4,000 votes. Analysts attributed the closer vote count in part to the district's inclusion of three pivot counties (i.e., those that Obama won in 2008 and 2012, but that Trump won in 2016). Bishop won two of those three counties in the special election, while McCready won the third.

MEMBERS OF CONGRESS VIE FOR PRESIDENTIAL NOMINATION

Eleven Independent and Democratic members of Congress announced their intent to run for president in 2020 and officially launched their campaigns in 2019. Seven candidates held seats in the Senate; the other four were House members. By the close of the year, four of the declared senators—Bernie Sanders of Vermont, Elizabeth Warren of Massachusetts, Amy Klobuchar of Minnesota, Cory Booker of New Jersey—and Hawaii Representative Tulsi Gabbard remained in the running.

Bernie Sanders

Sanders declared his candidacy on February 19, 2019, officially launching his second bid for the presidency. "Our campaign is about transforming our country and creating a government based on the principles of economic, social, racial and environmental justice," Sanders said in an email to supporters. The senator, who identifies as a democratic socialist, went on to emphasize economic issues and income inequality throughout his campaign, proposing policy solutions such as a $15 federal minimum wage, tuition-free college, and Medicare for All.

Sanders got his start in politics in the 1970s, when he founded the Liberty Union Party in Vermont. With that organization, Sanders sought to advance independent candidates who did not have a connection to corporate backers. He ran for a variety of local and state-level offices before winning his first victory and becoming the mayor of Burlington in 1980. Sanders was elected to the House of Representatives in 1990 and held that seat until 2007, when he was elected senator.

Sanders gained an unexpectedly large following during his first campaign for president in 2016. His embrace of far-left policy positions, disdain for corporate influence in politics, and emphasis on addressing income inequality made him popular with more progressive elements of the Democratic Party, particularly younger votes who considered themselves to be both liberal and independent. Though initially viewed as a long-shot candidate in 2016, Sanders' campaign persisted throughout the primary season and the senator pledged to remain in the race through the Democratic convention to ensure that progressive voters had a voice during the formal nominating process.

Sanders' 2020 campaign got off to a strong start thanks to his enthusiastic supporters and an online donor network that enabled him to repeatedly outraise his competitors. He emerged as the party's front-runner in February 2020

after winning the Iowa Democratic caucuses and New Hampshire Democratic primary and opening up a double-digit lead over his rivals in national opinion polls. However, former vice president Joe Biden soon catapulted into the lead after a critical victory in the South Carolina Democratic primary, receiving multiple endorsements from primary competitors who had since dropped out of the race, and winning ten of the fourteen Democratic primaries held on Super Tuesday. Biden's decisive victory in the Michigan Democratic primary one week later was the final blow to Sanders' campaign. Acknowledging in a live-streamed speech that "the path toward victory is virtually impossible," the senator ended his bid for the presidency on April 8, 2020.

Elizabeth Warren

Massachusetts Senator Elizabeth Warren announced the formation of an exploratory committee in December 2018 and made her candidacy official on February 9, 2019. Like Sanders, Warren proved a popular candidate with progressives in the party, thanks in part to her embrace of Medicare for All, the Green New Deal, tougher financial regulations, and new taxes on wealthy Americans.

A former teacher and law professor with expertise in commercial and bankruptcy law, Warren was repeatedly tapped to advise federal lawmakers on related issues and served on the Congressional Oversight Panel that oversaw implementation of the Emergency Economic Stabilization Act following the 2008 financial crisis. Warren is also credited with being a main architect of the Consumer Financial Protection Bureau (CFPB), established in 2010 by the Dodd-Frank Act. Warren was expected to be named director of the CFPB, but strong Republican opposition to her nomination prompted then-president Barack Obama to select a more moderate leader. Warren was elected to the U.S. Senate in 2012.

Warren consistently polled at the top of the pack of Democratic candidates early in the 2020 campaign, but her support waned as states began to hold their respective caucuses and primaries. She finished fourth in the Iowa Democratic caucuses and third in the New Hampshire Democratic primary. She did not win any states on Super Tuesday, including her home state of Massachusetts. Two days later, Warren ended her campaign.

Amy Klobuchar

Amy Klobuchar, the senior senator from Minnesota, announced her candidacy one day after Warren. While a strong supporter of several key liberal policies and positions—including Obamacare, protections for LGBTQ+ rights, and a woman's right to choose—Klobuchar was generally considered among the party's more moderate candidates. She was critical of the Green New Deal and Medicare for All proposals promoted by Sanders and Warren, for example, and focused more on voting rights, affordable health care, and climate protections.

Klobuchar was in the midst of her third term in the Senate, having been first elected in 2006. Her reelection in 2018 was particularly noteworthy because she won a number of rural districts that had voted for Trump in 2016. Before she became a senator, Klobuchar was a partner in two private law practices and had served as the elected attorney for Hennepin County. She often said she was motivated to enter politics following the birth of her daughter. Klobuchar was forced to leave the hospital twenty-four hours later, even though her daughter had a condition that left her unable to swallow. This experience prompted Klobuchar to lobby state lawmakers to guarantee new mothers and their babies a two-day hospital stay.

Klobuchar's support in early polls was low, but it was enough for her to earn a spot in every Democratic debate. Her debate performance was widely credited with sustaining her candidacy, and her poll numbers improved dramatically between the Iowa Democratic caucuses, where she finished fifth, and the New Hampshire primary, where she made a surprisingly strong showing and came in third. However, her sixth-place finishes in the Nevada and South Carolina primaries signaled that the surge in her popularity could not be sustained. Klobuchar ended her campaign on March 2, 2020, the day before Super Tuesday. Upon withdrawing from the race, she endorsed Biden, saying she believed he could bring the country together and "win big."

Michael Bennet

Colorado Senator Michael Bennet declared his candidacy for president on May 2, 2019. "We cannot be the first generation to leave less to our kids, not more," Bennet said during his announcement. "Let's build opportunity for every American and restore integrity to our government." Bennet sought to distinguish himself from the other centrist candidates by highlighting his record of working with Republicans in Congress. He was also more critical of the liberal wings of the party, though he did support a single-payer option for health care. Bennet was known for his support of comprehensive immigration reform, since he had cosponsored the Dream Act of 2017, as well as his advocacy for increased education funding.

Bennet worked as the director of the Anschutz Investment Company for several years before shifting to a career in public service. His first public position was as chief of staff to former Denver mayor John Hickenlooper, after which he became the superintendent of the Denver School System. Gov. Bill Ritter appointed Bennet to fill the Senate seat vacated by fellow Democrat Ken Salazar in 2009. He won reelection in 2010 and again in 2016.

Bennet failed to gain traction with Democratic voters from the beginning, and he did not meet the polling thresholds to participate in the third or subsequent party debates. Acknowledging he was unlikely to perform well in the Iowa caucuses, Bennet focused nearly all his campaign efforts on New Hampshire. However, he still finished in last place, with some write-in candidates receiving more votes.

Bennet announced his withdrawal from the race on February 11. He said he would support the party's eventual nominee, but did not endorse a specific competitor.

Cory Booker

Cory Booker, a charismatic senator from New Jersey who at times drew comparisons to former president Barack Obama, officially announced his candidacy on February 1, 2019. Booker told supporters he was running to restore "civic grace in America," and his campaign largely focused on issues related to criminal justice reform, the legalization of marijuana, and environmental protections.

Booker's political star began rising during his tenure as mayor of Newark, New Jersey, from 2006 to 2013. He had been serving in the Senate since 2013. Booker was one of the main authors of the First Step Act of 2018, having pushed for an end to mandatory minimum sentencing laws and increased funding for inmate rehabilitation since assuming his Senate seat. Booker was also vocal on issues related to race, which included his cosponsorship of a proposal to make lynching a federal hate crime.

Booker was another candidate whose poll numbers remained in the single digits for months. Although he participated in the party's first five debates, he did not qualify for the sixth debate due to flagging support for his candidacy. Booker ended his campaign on January 13, prior to the Iowa caucuses, saying he did not have enough campaign funding to continue. Fundraising had been difficult, he said, because he was not able to participate in additional debates, and impeachment proceedings in the Senate prevented him from campaigning as actively as possible.

Kamala Harris

When she announced her candidacy on January 21, 2019, California Senator Kamala Harris became the third Black woman in U.S. history to seek the Democratic nomination. Her candidacy represented a number of potential firsts: If she were elected, Harris would be the country's first Asian American, first Black female, and first Indian American to serve as president.

Announcing her campaign, Harris emphasized her "unique experience of having been a leader in local government, state government, and federal government," and said she was prepared to be a "fighter" for the American people. Criminal justice reform was a central component of Harris' platform, due in large part to her service as California's attorney general. In that role, Harris had developed a program designed to reduce recidivism rates among first-time drug offenders. Harris also advocated for immigration reform, pay raises for teachers, and tax cuts for low-income and middle-class families. She had been elected to the Senate in 2016.

Although she was initially considered to be a frontrunner for the nomination, Harris struggled with fundraising and her early, promising poll numbers dropped quickly. Her campaign also announced widespread layoffs in November, which came amid reports of internal turmoil and disagreements among her staff. With her campaign sputtering, Harris withdrew her candidacy on December 3. "I've taken stock and looked at this from every angle, and over the last few days have come to one of the hardest decisions of my life," she wrote in an email to her supporters.

Kristen Gillibrand

Kristen Gillibrand, a senator from New York, announced her candidacy on late night television on March 17, 2019. "I'm going to run for president of the United States because as a young mom I am going to fight for other people's kids as hard as I would fight for my own," she said. Women's issues formed the centerpiece of Gillibrand's campaign, and she repeatedly challenged her competitors over their positions on abortion rights and the child tax credit, among other issues.

Gillibrand had been serving in Congress since 2006, when she was elected to the House. She was tapped to fill Hillary Clinton's Senate seat in 2009 when Clinton became Obama's first secretary of state. A former corporate lawyer, Gillibrand had positioned herself as a moderate House member with some liberal and some conservative stances on certain issues, but she moved toward the left when she joined the Senate. She gained prominence as a vocal abortion rights supporter and an advocate for sexual abuse survivors, particularly U.S. service members who were victims of sexual assault.

Gillibrand's campaign was short-lived. Her poll numbers hovered at or below 1 percent, and she did not qualify to participate in the third Democratic debate. Calling this a fatal blow to her campaign, Gillibrand withdrew from the race in August.

Tulsi Gabbard

Among the House members seeking the Democratic nomination, Tulsi Gabbard of Hawaii remained in the race the longest. Gabbard announced her candidacy on January 11, 2019.

Gabbard became the first Hindu member of Congress when she was elected to the House in 2012. She briefly served as a vice chair of the Democratic National Committee, but resigned this post in 2016 so she could endorse Sanders' candidacy in that year's presidential election. An officer in the Army National Guard, Gabbard was active on defense and foreign policy matters, and as a presidential candidate, she said "war and peace" was her main issue. She also supported universal health care, tuition-free community college education, and raising the federal minimum wage.

Gabbard ended her campaign on March 19, 2020, after poor showings in the early Democratic primaries. She endorsed Biden, saying that after Super Tuesday, it was "clear that Democratic Primary voters have chosen Vice President Joe Biden to be the person who will take on President Trump."

Tim Ryan

Ohio congressman Tim Ryan declared his candidacy on April 4, 2019. Elected to Congress in 2002, Ryan was perhaps most known for trying to replace Pelosi as minority leader in 2016. He was also a vocal critic of Trump's immigration policies. Among other issues, Ryan campaigned on revitalizing Rust Belt economies, spurring electric automobile manufacturing, and reforming health care. He ended his presidential campaign in late October after he failed to meet the fundraising and polling thresholds for debate participation, but he successfully ran for reelection to the House.

Seth Moulton

Seth Moulton, a member of the Massachusetts House delegation, also had a short-lived campaign. Announcing his candidacy on April 22, 2019, Moulton, an Iraq War veteran, highlighted his military service, declaring himself to be "a patriot" who "never wanted to sit on the sidelines." Moulton was elected to Congress in 2014 and established himself as a moderate who supported legalizing marijuana, same-sex marriage, and abortion rights. He also focused on encouraging young people to consider public service. Moulton withdrew from the race in August to run for reelection to the House.

Eric Swalwell

Of all the members of Congress who decided to run for president, Eric Swalwell of California had the shortest campaign. Swalwell announced his candidacy on April 8; three months later, he withdrew to focus on winning reelection to the House. Swalwell had earned a reputation as one of Trump's most vocal critics in the House. He had promised to make gun control a centerpiece of his campaign.

2020

The Legislative Year

Congressional productivity dropped decisively during the second session of the 116th Congress, with most of its activity occurring in the last two months of the year. According to one analysis by Pew Research, more than 40 percent of bills that became law during the 116th Congress were passed in November and December 2020. This was the highest share of lame duck action in Congress since at least the early 1970s.

Much of this low productivity could be explained by a number of significant and competing priorities that occupied lawmakers' time. The COVID-19 pandemic's arrival in the United States and its tremendous impact on the American economy and society prompted months of wrangling over proposed relief packages and stimulus funding. The House also approved, for the first time in history, remote proceedings and the use of vote by proxy—actions intended to help keep lawmakers safe amid the coronavirus' spread, but that also limited the chamber's productivity during the year. Additionally, lawmakers were concluding impeachment proceedings against President Trump, preparing for a divisive election season, and contending with the usual partisan breakdown in budget negotiations. The session also ended in dramatic fashion, as Trump supporters who believed the president's false claims about vote fraud stormed the Capitol building as lawmakers sought to certify the 2020 election results.

CONGRESS APPROVES CORONAVIRUS RELIEF

The mounting public health crisis spurred by the COVID-19 pandemic dominated legislative negotiations in Congress for much of the year. As case counts rose, hospitals became overwhelmed with patients, straining the U.S. health care system and prompting many states to institute various lockdown orders to encourage Americans to stay at home and stop the virus' spread. With local economies suffering and concerns about job loss mounting, lawmakers recognized a need for stimulus funding and congressional support for the development of vaccines and other treatments.

In early March, Congress began passing a series of bills in response to the pandemic. The first piece of legislation that was approved, the Coronavirus Preparedness and Response Supplemental Appropriations Act, cleared Congress in the first week of March. Since COVID-19 cases were not yet widespread in the United States and the pandemic's full economic impact had yet to be felt, this bill focused on allocating funds for vaccine development and public health programs. The bill was approved by nearly unanimous votes in both the House and Senate, although some House Republicans complained that the bill's funding total—$8.3 billion—was too high, without a clear plan of how it would be spent.

Less than two weeks later, Congress passed the Families First Coronavirus Response Act. By this time, states had begun shutting down their economies and President Trump had declared a national emergency. Accordingly, this bill extended unemployment benefits and paid sick leave to help American workers facing financial uncertainty. The bill also required private health insurance plans and Medicare to cover COVID-19 testing. Although approved by overwhelming margins in both chambers, this bill encountered more Republican resistance than the supplemental appropriations act. In the House, forty Republicans voted against the measure; eight Republicans voted against it in the Senate. Their primary arguments against the bill were that workers would be better off claiming workers compensation because that income is non-taxable, versus receiving additional paid leave, which is taxable. Some also expressed concerns about establishing mandates for business' paid sick and family leave.

These dissenters signaled a tougher road ahead for future COVID-19 relief packages, and indeed, the debate surrounding the next stimulus bill was more contentious. The Coronavirus Aid, Relief, and Economic Security Act (CARES) was the biggest relief bill Congress passed during the year. It provided more than $2 trillion in aid for hospitals, small businesses, individuals, and state and local governments, making it the largest financial relief package in U.S. history. Its major provisions included one-time cash payments to most Americans, of either $1,200 for individuals or $2,400 for married couples, plus $500 per child. It established the Paycheck Protection Program, which provided forgivable government loans to small businesses that kept their staff on the payroll, even during temporary closures. It also increased unemployment benefits by $600 per week; provided billions of additional dollars for food stamps, school meals, and childcare funding; and allocated funds for the Department of Defense to manufacture and stockpile personal protective equipment. The bill hit several stumbling blocks in the Senate, as Democrats blocked cloture votes to move the bill forward due to concerns over business-focused provisions that leadership claimed could amount to a corporate bailout with little oversight at taxpayer expense. After several days of further negotiations, Republicans and Democrats reached a compromise, and the bill passed unanimously. The House also approved the bill, and Trump signed it on March 27.

Lawmakers implied a fourth COVID-19 bill was on the horizon in the summer or fall of 2020. However, the two parties struggled to agree on what should be included, and the presidential election and its aftermath pushed negotiations into December. One of the most contentious issues

was whether to provide another round of direct payments to Americans and in what amount. Republicans ultimately supported a provision authorizing $600 checks, which came with income restrictions, while blocking several efforts by Democrats—and a surprising, last-minute call from President Trump—to increase the check amounts to $2,000. Outside of this specific issue, disagreements over the package largely centered on its total price tag. Republicans had initially proposed a smaller, $500 billion investment, while Democrats sought $2.2 trillion in funding. Senate Republicans argued that the reopening of state economies made such a large package unnecessary; Democrats countered that Republicans' proposal did not go far enough to help struggling Americans. Democrats also took issue with a Republican-supported provision imposing a moratorium on pandemic-related lawsuits, while Republicans opposed a Democrat-favored provision offering aid to state and local governments.

A compromise measure negotiated by a bipartisan group of lawmakers and members of the Problem Solvers Caucus removed both of these contentious provisions and capped the total relief package at $900 billion. In the end, many lawmakers decided to support the compromise negotiated by leadership despite their lingering concerns, because they knew Americans were in dire need of assistance. The final package was incorporated into the fiscal 2021 appropriations omnibus. In addition to the cash payments, the bill's major provisions also extended unemployment benefits, a moratorium on rent payments, and the Paycheck Protection Program. It also provided additional funding for food stamps, vaccine development, and testing and contact tracing.

Pandemic Prompts Rules Change in the House

The emphasis on social distancing as key to slowing the coronavirus' spread prompted some lawmakers to call on congressional leadership to close the House and Senate. Both chambers adjourned in late March as case counts rose around the country, but leaders took distinct approaches to addressing member concerns that reflected their parties' respective stances on appropriate COVID-19 response measures overall.

In the House, Democrats worked to establish new procedures permitting virtual committee hearings and markups, and allowing representatives to both vote remotely and vote by proxy. Under the vote by proxy plan, one member could vote on the floor for as many as ten other representatives. Republicans were largely opposed to the procedures, claiming it could limit debate preceding votes and would preclude lawmakers who were not on the floor from changing their minds or being able to respond quickly to amendments or other proposals. Not a single Republican voted in favor of the bill implementing the new procedures, but three of them voted with Democrats to approve it, and the House resumed its work under the new protocols in mid-May.

Senate leadership opted to call lawmakers back for in-person legislating at the beginning of May, despite the objections of some members. Announcing the Senate's return, Majority Leader Mitch McConnell also outlined new health guidelines that would be in place to prevent the spread of COVID-19 among members and their staff. The guidelines generally directed senators to avoid gatherings, wear masks, practice social distancing, and limit the number of staff and visitors in their offices. None of these measures were mandatory, however, and testing was not widespread in Congress, prompting further concerns from lawmakers and public health experts that members may be at increased risk for infection.

PUSH FOR POLICE REFORM FAILS IN CONGRESS

The May killing of George Floyd, a Black man who died while being pinned down by a white Minneapolis police officer, sparked protests against police brutality across the country and reignited a debate over race relations and police reforms that reverberated in state houses and the halls of Congress. On Capitol Hill, both the House and Senate took up proposals to implement policing reforms in response to this crisis, with debate surrounding measures to strengthen police accountability, improve training, and restrict officers' use of force.

In the House, Democrats advanced a measure establishing new reporting and oversight requirements for data related to policing practices. It also banned the use of chokeholds and no-knock warrants and ended police officers' immunity from civil suits. The bill passed along party lines over the objections of Republicans, who supported a less stringent approach, but it was destined to fail in the Senate. In that chamber, South Carolina Republican Tim Scott introduced a measure that would have created new requirements for law enforcement agencies to report data on use of force, no-knock warrants, and police misconduct; retained and publicized officers' disciplinary records; and prohibited the use of chokeholds except in situations where deadly force was authorized. It would also have made it more difficult for a fired police officer to be hired by another agency. Nearly all Democrats opposed the bill, however, calling for measures to eliminate legal protections for officers from civil lawsuits and tougher language barring aggressive policing tactics. The bill failed to pass a cloture vote in that chamber.

FIRST VETO OVERRIDE OF TRUMP PRESIDENCY

In the summer, Congress found itself facing an unexpected battle with the president over the annual national defense authorization bill, also known as the NDAA. For any given fiscal year, the NDAA outlines U.S. national security policies and priorities and authorizes funding for everything from military pay to engagements abroad. The bill has become unique among annual appropriations

measures in that it generally receives broad bipartisan support in Congress and is quickly signed into law by the sitting president. In 2020, however, Trump took issue with several provisions of the NDAA for fiscal 2021.

Chief among these concerns was his objection to a provision requiring the removal of any names, symbols, or monuments that honored Confederate leaders or soldiers from military property. Although the measure was aligned with a national movement to take down such monuments and rename public buildings, Trump refused to sign the NDAA unless it was taken out. This generated a mixed reaction among Republicans, some of whom sided with the president and blamed Democrats for trying to create political theater. But others suggested the provision had merit, and did not believe defense funding should be held up over it.

The president also objected to lawmakers' inclusion of measures restricting his ability to withdraw U.S. troops from Afghanistan and Germany. In Afghanistan, a drawdown had been agreed to as part of the U.S.–Taliban peace agreement, but lawmakers were concerned both by the possibility of a hasty withdrawal—as Trump pushed to bring as many troops home before the 2020 election as possible—and reports that Russia had paid the Taliban bounties for any U.S. soldier killed in the country. As such, House Democrats sponsored an amendment requiring the administration to assess whether any other country had offered such bounties as well as the potential risks of a continued drawdown to U.S. personnel and counterterrorism efforts before more troops could be brought home. In the Senate, Utah Republican Mitt Romney led a push to add language to the NDAA preventing Trump from withdrawing troops from Germany—a move widely opposed in Congress—until the Defense Department provided lawmakers with an analysis of potential costs and impacts of the drawdown.

A third issue involved Trump's call for repeal of Section 230 of the Communications Decency Act, which protects websites and tech companies such as Facebook and Twitter from being held liable for their users' content. Congress had begun considering this issue, particularly as misinformation about the COVID-19 pandemic and the 2020 election increasingly spread online, but lawmakers generally agreed that the NDAA was not the place to address the issue, and the final bill did not include Trump's desired language.

As in prior years, the NDAA easily cleared Congress with wide margins in both chambers. Trump waited twelve days before making good on his promise to veto the bill, offering sharp criticisms of both the NDAA's provisions and members of Congress as he announced his decision. But support for the bill remained strong in Congress, and the House and Senate moved quickly to overturn the president's veto. Both chambers approved the override by overwhelming margins, and the NDAA became law on January 1, 2021.

SENATE CONFIRMS SCOTUS NOMINEE

Senate Republicans had a third opportunity to confirm a Trump nominee to the U.S. Supreme Court in the fall of 2020, following the September death of Justice Ruth Bader Ginsburg from complications related to pancreatic cancer. To fill her seat on the Court, Trump nominated Amy Coney Barrett, a judge on the U.S. Court of Appeals for the Seventh Circuit. Barrett was a graduate and former faculty of Notre Dame Law School who served as a judge for three years before Trump appointed her to the Seventh Circuit in 2017. Barrett was known as a textualist, interpreting the Constitution strictly as it was written, who followed in the mold of the late conservative Justice Antonin Scalia. Barrett's family life was also a focus of media attention: As a mother of seven children, she would be the first mother of school-age children to sit on the Court if confirmed.

McConnell's move to schedule Barrett's confirmation hearing a month later sparked Democratic claims of hypocrisy. McConnell had blocked consideration of an Obama Court nominee in 2016 because it was an election year. McConnell had argued that the voters should have a say in the matter, by picking the next president who would select a new justice. Barrett's nomination came little over a month before the 2020 presidential election, and yet McConnell raised no concerns about proceeding with her confirmation. He declared that the situation in 2020 was different because the president was up for reelection—whereas Obama was term-limited in 2016—and the president's party controlled the Senate.

Barrett's religion and her personal views were a focus of her Senate confirmation hearing, with Democrats particularly concerned about the Court's potential to overturn *Roe v. Wade* if Barrett filled the vacant seat. Barrett affirmed the importance of her faith but told lawmakers it would not influence "the discharge of my duties as a judge." Democrats also tried to press Barrett on whether she

---

CONGRESS IN 2020

The second session of the 116th Congress began on January 2, 2019. Both chambers adjourned on January 3, 2020. The Senate met on 168 days, compared to the House's 163 days in session.

In the House, members introduced 4,106 bills and resolutions in 2019. Senators introduced 2,325 bills and resolutions. Congress cleared 236 bills that were signed into public law. President Donald Trump issued four vetoes, one of which Congress overturned.

The House took 253 roll call votes in 2020, far fewer than the 701 votes held in 2019. The Senate took 292 recorded votes during the year, compared to 428 such votes in 2019.

MONEY IN ELECTIONS

The 2019–2020 election cycle ran from January 1, 2019, through December 31, 2020. According to a report from the Federal Election Commission (FEC), approximately $24.5 billion was raised for presidential and congressional elections occurring within that timeframe. Nearly all of that total was spent. Presidential candidates spent $4.1 billion, congressional candidates spent roughly $3.8 billion, political parties spent about $3 billion, and outside political action committees (PACs) spent $12.9 billion.

At the national level, the Republican National Committee (RNC) both raised and spent significantly more campaign funds than the Democratic National Committee (DNC). The RNC raised about $890 million, of which it spent approximately $833 million. By contrast, the DNC raised roughly $492 million and spent about $462 million. The two parties' congressional and senatorial campaign committees reported much smaller differences in their funding amounts. The Democratic Congressional Campaign Committee raised $346 million and spent $330 million; its Republican counterpart brought in $281 million and spent $285 million. On the Senate side, the Democratic committee raised $304 million, of which it spent $300 million. The Republican Senatorial Campaign Committee raised about $338 million and spent about $331 million.

Presidential Race

Biden outraised Trump during the 2020 election cycle, taking in a little more than $1 billion. Of that total, more than $823 million came from individual contributions. Trump raised approximately $812 million, $487 million of which came from individual contributions.

Neither Trump nor Biden accepted public financing for their primary or general election campaigns. As major party nominees, each candidate was eligible for about $103 million in public funds. However, if a candidate accepts such funds, they must also agree not to raise private contributions or spend their own money, with a few exceptions.

Super PACs continued to play a significant role in providing indirect campaign support in 2020. These groups raised approximately $3.4 billion during the election cycle and spent about $2.1 billion.

Congressional Races

According to the Federal Election Commission, House and Senate candidates running in 2020—including special elections to fill vacant seats in both chambers—raised $4 billion and spent $3.8 billion. This marked a significant increase over campaign receipts and disbursements in the 2016 general election, during which candidates for the House and Senate raised about $1.7 billion and spent about $1.6 billion. As is typically the case in a given election cycle, incumbents in both chambers raised significantly more money than their challengers—an average of $28.6 million per incumbent compared to $5.2 million per challenger—thanks largely to greater name recognition and an established supporter base.

Of the 289 candidates running for the Senate, $2 billion were raised and spent. The 2020 election cycle featured nine of the ten most expensive Senate races in history, with the North Carolina race between incumbent Republican Thom Tillis and Democratic challenger Cal Cunningham reporting a record-breaking expenditure of more than $298 million. About $220 million of that amount came from outside groups.

On the House side, the 2,082 candidates raised another $2 billion and spent about $1.8 billion. Four House races topped more than $30 million in spending by candidates and outside groups, earning them a spot on the list of most expensive House races of all time. Those campaigns occurred in New Mexico's 2nd District, Texas' 22nd District, Louisiana's 1st District, and New York's 14th District.

would support the administration's repeated efforts to repeal Obamacare. Barrett largely avoided giving direct answers to questions about specific legal issues. As the Judiciary Committee neared a vote, Democrats tried to leverage a procedural rule to keep Barrett's nomination from moving forward. Committee rules require at least two members of the minority party to be present; as such, all committee Democrats except Dick Durbin of Illinois waited outside the committee room while the vote took place. However, the committee chair, Lindsey Graham of South Carolina, called the vote anyway, and Barrett's nomination was sent to the Senate floor. Only one Republican—Susan Collins of Maine—voted with Democrats to oppose Barrett's nomination, stating she believed the winner of the 2020 election should fill the seat, but the party still had enough votes to confirm the new justice.

The Political Year

Outside of the COVID-19 pandemic and response, much of 2020 was consumed by the presidential race between President Trump and his Democratic challenger, former vice president Joe Biden. Election Day 2020 also saw voters cast their ballots in 435 House races, thirty-five Senate races, and eleven gubernatorial races, in addition to dozens of state and local elections.

COVID-19 IMPACTS CAMPAIGN

The pandemic had an outsized impact on the presidential campaign season. U.S. presidential candidates typically crisscross the country during their lengthy campaigns, holding countless rallies, town halls, and fundraisers and hearing from voters in person. Much of this activity was not possible in 2020, as many states announced shutdowns and governors asked residents to stay home. All leading presidential candidates had suspended in-person campaigning by late March, opting to conduct virtual forums and fundraisers to drum up support. The pandemic also prompted some states to postpone their primaries, while others encouraged the public to vote by mail.

For Democratic candidates, these decisions were as much about the party's messaging as they were public health. Biden and other federal-level candidates made Trump's poor handling of the COVID-19 pandemic and his degradation of medical experts and scientists a central campaign message. In this context, it was seen as important for Democrats to follow the Centers for Disease Control and Prevention's COVID-19 guidelines and carefully observe state and local restrictions related to the pandemic. State Democratic parties stopped their door-to-door canvasing efforts in favor of online outreach, for example, which analysts said likely hampered their local voter registration and mobilization efforts, particularly as Republicans continued to downplay the pandemic's severity. In August, the Trump campaign claimed to be knocking on one million doors per week. By September, some down-ballot Democrats facing tougher election battles had resumed door-to-door canvasing, but the Biden campaign did not.

POSTAL SERVICE REFORMS CAUSE BALLOT DELAYS

The COVID-19 pandemic was also one of several factors impacting election-related operations of the United States Postal Service (USPS). In July, USPS officials notified forty-six states that the agency may not be able to meet postage and delivery deadlines for voters to receive and submit mail-in ballots in a timely manner. These delays were attributed to the significant increase in demand for mail-in voting and staffing challenges caused by the pandemic, but it was also linked to reforms implemented by the recently appointed postmaster general, Louis DeJoy. DeJoy's selection had been controversial because he had no experience in USPS operations; his credentials largely seemed to be his fundraising chairmanship of the Republican National Convention and status as a Trump megadonor. From his first day in office, DeJoy had pushed an ambitious agenda of operational reforms in an effort to cover a $160 billion budget shortfall. Those changes included removing underutilized mail collection boxes, shutting down hundreds of sorting machines, cutting back overtime, and cancelling extra delivery runs. While DeJoy maintained these changes were necessary to the postal

service's sustainability, Democrats cried foul, accusing the president and DeJoy of a coordinated effort to suppress voter turnout. Amid lawmakers concerns and a widespread public backlash, DeJoy suspended implementation of his reforms until after the election.

BIDEN, TRUMP ACCEPT NOMINATIONS

Additionally, public health concerns pushed both parties to shift to a mostly virtual format for their official nominating conventions. Democrats postponed their convention, initially scheduled to take place in Milwaukee, Wisconsin, in mid-July, for a full month after the governor banned large gatherings. Party officials hoped that conditions would change by mid-August, but with the pandemic still raging, they opted for remote speeches by party luminaries in New York City, Los Angeles, Milwaukee, and Wilmington. Convention delegates were also asked to cast their votes virtually.

Due to the sheer number of Democratic candidates at the beginning of the election cycle—a total of twenty-eight—there was some speculation that the convention may be contested, meaning that more than one round of voting would be required to choose the official nominee. However, the vast majority of candidates withdrew from the race after poor primary showings and Biden's decisive victories in several states, and many endorsed the former vice president before the convention, effectively clearing his way to the nomination. Notably, Sanders remained on the convention ballot and received 1,151 votes during the delegates' roll call. Biden received 3,558 votes.

Biden announced California Senator Kamala Harris as his running mate on August 11, six days before the convention began. In tweeting the news, Biden described Harris as "a fearless fighter for the little guy, and one of the country's finest public servants." Biden officially became the party's nominee on August 18. "The current president has cloaked America in darkness for far too long. Too much anger, too much fear, too much division," he said during his acceptance speech. "We can and will overcome this season of darkness."

The Republican Party did not delay their convention, but they did change locations several times due to pandemic-related restrictions. The event was originally scheduled for August 24 through 27 in Charlotte, North Carolina, but the city's limits on large gatherings made a new venue necessary. The major speeches would take place in Jacksonville, Florida, party leaders announced, but this plan was revised again after Jacksonville officials called for the implementation of specific health precautions at the convention site. The convention was moved back to Charlotte, with a plan to scale back in-person events in favor of more virtual options.

Although four Republicans had declared themselves as challengers to the president, none of them gained traction, and Trump easily won the party's nomination. Trump cast the choice ahead of voters in stark terms as he accepted

the nomination. "This election will decide whether we will defend the American way of life, or whether we allow a radical movement to completely dismantle and destroy it," he said.

TRUMP REJECTS BIDEN VICTORY

The divisive campaign, combined with the pandemic-induced proliferation of alternative voting options, spurred record-level voter turnout, with about 70 percent of eligible Americans casting an in-person or mail-in ballot. This was the highest recorded percentage of voting since 1900.

Although Election Day took place on November 3, the high volume of mail-in ballots delayed the announcement of final results until November 7. This was due primarily to rules in some states that prevent officials from opening and counting ballots until Election Day, even if they were received well in advance. Battleground states such as Arizona, Georgia, Michigan, Nevada, North Carolina, Pennsylvania, and Wisconsin were all delayed in reporting final vote tallies, which meant that by the end of Election Day, neither candidate had received the 270 electoral votes necessary to claim victory.

This gave Trump additional time to raise the specter of voter fraud, which had become a key part of his campaign strategy. Trump had been sending a message of potential voter fraud for months, claiming that it was impossible for him to lose reelection unless there was massive fraud. He falsely claimed that mail-in ballots were more likely to be fraudulent—an assertion Republican Party officials appeared to support by blocking states' use of ballot drop boxes and filing various legal challenges to various mail-in voting procedures. On November 4, Trump declared himself the winner and demanded that vote counting stop because anything tallied after the polls closed must be fraudulent. Trump continued to decry mail-in ballots and make false claims about the election process as the vote counts plodded on, suggesting during a White House press briefing on November 5 that the Biden campaign may try to "steal the election from us." He observed on several occasions that a higher number of mail-in ballots were cast for Democrats versus Republicans. Trump used this data to imply fraudulent activity, but election experts noted that this discrepancy was logical, given that many Democratic candidates had urged supporters to stay home and vote by mail, whereas Republicans had favored in-person voting.

In the end, Biden was declared the winner, with a projected total of 306 electoral votes to Trump's 232. The former vice president had received a total of 81.3 million votes compared to Trump's 74.2 million. In his victory speech on November 8, Biden promised to "be a President who seeks not to divide, but to unify." He acknowledged that he "ran as a proud Democrat," but would "be an American president. I will work as hard for those who didn't vote for me—as those who did."

For Trump, who refused to concede, the election was not over. Joined by his legal team and congressional Republicans, the president filed more than eighty lawsuits seeking to overturn election results, most of which were thrown out or had their allegations of voter fraud debunked. At the state and local levels, Trump and his associates tried to pressure officials into recounting or throwing out votes, and even threatened to seize voting machines. In some cases, the president urged state officials to replace their Electoral College members with individuals who would cast their votes for him. Despite the president's efforts, the process by which electors met in each state to cast their Electoral College votes proceeded without incident on December 14. The electors voted in line with their states' respective outcomes, cementing Biden's win with 306 votes.

Trump still refused to concede and persisted in making false claims that Biden had stolen the election, although many Republican leaders and members of Congress, including McConnell, congratulated Biden on his win. Trump's continued denial of the election results fueled the anger of his staunchest supporters, several thousand of whom converged on Capitol Hill on January 6, 2021, as Congress met to certify the outcome. The mob later stormed the building, forcing lawmakers and their staff off the House floor in search of shelter, attacking Capitol Police officers, and vandalizing the building. The rioters were cleared from the building roughly four hours later, and Congress reconvened in the early morning hours of January 7 to complete their certification of Biden as the next president.

The insurrection and lawmakers' response to it set the political stage for much of 2021, as the House initiated fresh impeachment proceedings against the president and efforts by Congress to investigate the siege and Trump's role in it contributed to the further fracturing of the Republican Party.

DEMOCRATS CLAIM NARROW CONTROL OF SENATE

Of the Senate seats up for grabs in 2020, thirty-three appeared on the regular ballot and two were decided by special election. At least sixteen of these races were considered by analysts to be battlegrounds, and Democrats poured a massive amount of money into these races in pursuit of a Senate majority. Efforts to unseat incumbent Republican senators Thom Tillis in North Carolina, Lindsey Graham in South Carolina, and Susan Collins in Maine were unsuccessful, despite significant campaign spends in these areas. Democrats were able to flip a Senate seat in Colorado, however, when former governor John Hickenlooper defeated the Republican incumbent Cory Gardner by nearly ten points.

Democrats also claimed victories in the year's two special Senate elections. In Arizona, Mark Kelly won the Senate seat formerly held by Republican John McCain, who passed away in August 2018 following a battle with brain cancer. Underscoring the importance of this race,

Federal Election Commission filings showed that it was the third most expensive Senate race in the country in 2020, with the two lead candidates raising more than $145 million. Kelly, a retired NASA astronaut and husband to former Arizona congresswoman Gabrielle Giffords, challenged Republican Martha McSally, who was tapped to temporarily fill McCain's seat in December 2018. McSally was the second appointee to fill the seat; Gov. Doug Ducey originally appointed Sen. Jon Kyl to replace McCain, but Kyl resigned as the 115th Congress was drawing to a close. Some Republicans questioned Ducey's selection of McSally because she lost her 2018 Senate bid to Democrat Kyrsten Sinema. Reports also suggested there were tensions between the McCain family and McSally in part because she adopted similar rhetoric and positioning as President Trump, instead of the late senator's more moderate legacy. In the end, Kelly beat McSally by a margin of less than 3 percentage points. Kelly's victory was attributed both to his significant financial edge—he raised twice as much as McSally—and his ability to flip Maricopa County, which comprises more than 60 percent of the state's population.

In Georgia, the special election to choose a successor to Republican Johnny Isakson, who resigned his Senate seat at the end of 2019 due to health concerns, was another closely contested race. Fellow Republican Kelly Loeffler, CEO of a digital asset management company, was appointed by Gov. Brian Kemp to fill Isakson's seat temporarily. Loeffler was sworn into office on January 6, 2020. Loeffler had two main challengers in the race. The first was Democratic candidate Raphael Warnock, the pastor of Ebenezer Baptist Church, Martin Luther King Jr.'s former church, and chair of the New Georgia Project, a nonpartisan initiative to help Georgians register to vote and become civically engaged. Her other main challenger was fellow Republican Doug Collins, who was representing Georgia's 9th district in the House at the time. Per Georgia election law, there are no primaries for special elections; all candidates, regardless of party, are placed on the same ballot. Collins and Loeffler battled each other for positioning as the dominant Republican ahead of the vote, scheduled for November 3. Polls released shortly before voting began indicated that support for Loeffler and Collins was about equal. As results were tallied, however, Collins withdrew from the race and endorsed Loeffler. A total of twenty candidates ran in the special election. None of them received more than 50 percent of the vote, meaning that the top two candidates were headed to a runoff. In this case, that was Loeffler, who received about 26 percent of the vote, and Warnock, who got roughly 33 percent. The runoff was scheduled for January 5, 2021. Although the vote was close, media outlets began calling the race for Warnock early on January 6. Loeffler initially said she would challenge the results but changed course and conceded to Warnock on January 7. The final vote tally put Warnock about 2 percentage points ahead of Loeffler. Most election analyses attributed his win to significant turnout among Black voters. With his victory, Warnock became the first Black senator from Georgia and the first southern Black Democrat elected to the Senate.

Democrats eked out a second Senate victory in Georgia, as well. In the regular election, Democrat John Ossoff, a former investigative journalist and documentarian, challenged incumbent Republican senator David Purdue. Although the race was considered competitive, Ossoff fell behind Purdue in the polls shortly before Election Day, leading few analysts to project he would pull off a win. However, neither Purdue nor Ossoff received 50 percent of the vote on November 3. The two faced each other again in a runoff vote on January 5. In the end, Ossoff claimed a narrow victory, defeating Purdue by little more than 1 percent. Like Warnock, Ossoff's win made history, as he became the youngest ever member of the Senate and Georgia's first Jewish senator.

These victories in Arizona, Colorado, and Georgia—minus an expected loss in Alabama, where incumbent Doug Jones was defeated by Republican challenger Tommy Tuberville—gave Democrats a net gain of three Senate seats. In the run up to Election Day, Republicans held a fifty-three seat Senate majority, compared to Democrats' forty-five seats, plus the two Independent senators—Sanders and Maine Senator Angus King—who caucused with the party. The Democrats' victories meant the Senate of the 117th Congress would have a fifty-fifty party split, with vice president-elect Harris providing the tie breaking vote and effectively giving Democrats majority control of the chamber.

DEMOCRATS RETAIN HOUSE MAJORITY

Democrats were not as successful in winning House races, despite widespread projections by political analysts that the party would capitalize on Trump's dwindling popularity in certain parts of the country to increase its majority. As of Election Day, Democrats held 232 seats in the House, compared to Republicans' 197. When all votes had been tallied, Democrats had a net loss of ten House seats, bringing this margin down to 222–213. Every incumbent House Republican won reelection, but thirteen incumbent Democrats lost to their Republican challengers. Democrats won three vacant seats that had previously been filled by Republicans; GOP candidates won two such seats. Many of the Republican Party's gains came from rural areas where Trump's approval ratings were higher, suggesting those candidates benefited from voter support at the top of the ticket. Democrats did not appear to benefit from a similar coattail effect, however, as Biden outperformed many of the party's House candidates. Analysts speculated that some of this discrepancy may be due to Republicans' success portraying their Democratic rivals as radical socialists. Observers also pointed to some Democrats' advocacy for controversial policing reforms following the death of George Floyd in May 2020 as a factor in their poor electoral performance. Although a reduced majority meant

Democrats could have more difficulty advancing their legislative priorities in the 117th Congress, party leaders still celebrated their control of the House. "We have the gavel," Pelosi said during a post-election news conference on November 6. "We've lost some battles, but we won the war."

HOUSE SPECIAL ELECTIONS

In addition to the Senate special elections in Arizona and Georgia, five special elections were called to fill vacant House seats. In Maryland, Democrat Kweisi Mfume secured an overwhelming victory in the special election to fill the House seat vacated by the late Elijah Cummings, also a Democrat. Mfume had previously represented the district from 1987 to 1996 and had served as a Baltimore City Council member for eight years. He beat out Republican candidate Kim Klacik, founder of a nonprofit that supported professional development opportunities for underserved women. Due to the COVID-19 pandemic, election officials allowed all voters to submit their ballots by mail and limited in-person voting to three locations in the district.

No Republican candidates contested the Georgia special election to fill the House seat of Democrat John Lewis, who passed away on July 17, 2020. Seven candidates—five of whom were Democrats—registered for the election held on September 29. No candidate received more than 50 percent of the vote, and a runoff was scheduled for December 1. Kwanza Hall, a former Atlanta City Council and School Board member, and Robert Franklin, a professor at Emory University, received the highest number of votes in the September poll, meaning they would face each other in the runoff. Hall won with 54 percent of the vote to Franklin's 46 percent. Hall only served in Congress for about a month, completing Lewis' term. Nikema Williams, also a Democrat, won the regular election for Lewis' seat in November, and was sworn in at the beginning of the 117th Congress.

Republican Tom Tiffany was chosen to succeed fellow Republican Sean Duffy of Wisconsin during a special election held on May 12. Duffy resigned from the House on September 23, 2019, to be with his family after learning that his soon-to-be-born child was likely to have health complications. Tiffany, a state senator, defeated Democratic candidate Tricia Zunker, a Wausau School Board member and associate justice on the Ho-Chunk Nation Supreme Court, by approximately fourteen points. Voters chose New York State Sen. Christopher Jacobs to replace fellow Republican Chris Collins in June 2020. Collins resigned from the House in October 2019 after pleading guilty to charges of conspiracy to commit securities fraud and making false statements to investigators in an insider trading case. The special election to replace Collins was originally scheduled for April, but was postponed by Gov. Andrew Cuomo due to COVID-19 concerns. Jacobs received roughly 8,000 more votes than Democratic candidate Nate McMurray, the town supervisor of Grand Island and former businessman. Jacobs also beat McMurray to win reelection to a full House term in November 2020.

The only House seat to change party affiliation was in California, where Republican Mike Garcia was elected to replace Democrat Katie Hill. Hill resigned in November 2019 while facing allegations that she had extramarital affairs with a campaign staffer and a member of her congressional staff. Garcia, a Raytheon Company executive, defeated Democratic California Assemblymember Christy Smith by roughly ten points. As in Maryland, state officials allowed all-mail voting for the May 12 election due to the COVID-19 pandemic, and both candidates conducted much of their campaigning virtually.

GUBERNATORIAL RACES

There were far fewer gubernatorial races on the 2020 ballot than there had been in 2018. Eleven states held elections for governor, with incumbents winning nine of those seats. Incumbent Republican governors won reelection in Indiana, Missouri, New Hampshire, North Dakota, Vermont, and West Virginia. Democratic incumbents retained their seats in Delaware, North Carolina, and Washington. In Utah, Republican Spencer Cox was elected to replace outgoing Gov. Gary Herbert, who had decided not to run for reelection. The only governor's seat to change parties was in Montana, where the Democratic incumbent, Gov. Steve Bullock, was term-limited. Republican Rep. Greg Gianforte—who Bullock defeated in 2016—beat Democratic Lt. Gov. Mike Cooney by more than thirteen points.

STATE BALLOT MEASURES

Voters in thirty-four states considered a total of 129 ballot initiatives in 2020. This represented the lowest number of ballot measures recorded since 1980. There was also a precipitous drop in the number of citizen-initiated proposals; forty-two such measures appeared on ballots in 2020, compared to sixty-eight in 2018. A total of $1.24 billion was raised by ballot initiative campaigns, of which a reported $1.22 billion was spent to sway voters. Major issues included changes to elections policy, taxes, and the continued push to legalize marijuana.

Taxes

Taxes were by far the most dominant issue among ballot initiatives in 2020. A total of twenty-six ballot measures concerning tax-related policies were considered in fourteen states. Ten of these measures proposed changes to states' property tax laws. In California, voters approved one measure that allowed property tax assessments to be transferred from an individual's former home to their new home while requiring inherited residences to be reassessed at market value when their ownership changed. They rejected a separate measure requiring commercial and industrial properties to be assessed based on their market value, instead of their

Table 1.10 House of Representatives Vote by Region

Republicans held on their House majority at the end of President Obama's term and the beginning of President Trump's. However, Democrats quickly regained control in 2018 for the duration of President Trump's first and only term.

	South			West		Midwest		East			Total House		
	R	D	I	R	D	R	D	R	D	I	R	D	I
2000	81	55	1	43	50	57	48	40	59	1	221	212	2
2002	85	57	0	46	52	61	39	37	57	1	229	205	1
2004	91	51	0	45	53	60	40	36	58	1	232	202	1
2006	85	57	0	41	57	51	49	25	70	0	202	233	0
2008	80	62	0	35	63	45	55	18	77	0	178	257	0
2010	102	40	0	43	55	65	35	32	63	0	242	193	0
2012	108	41	0	39	63	59	35	28	62	0	234	201	0
2014	109	40	0	41	61	57	36	34	56	0	241	194	0
2016	109	40	0	39	63	61	33	31	59	0	240	195	0
2018	99	50	0	27	75	54	40	20	70	0	200	235	0
2020	100	49	0	33	69	57	37	23	67	0	213	222	0

SOURCE: Compiled from Rhodes Cook, *America Votes 30 and America Votes 31* (Washington, DC: CQ Press, 2013 and 2017). Rhodes Cook, *America Votes 32* and *American 33* and *America Votes 34* (Washington, DC: CQ Press, 2018 and 2020 and 2021)

NOTES: R: Republican, D: Democrat, I: Independent. The following groups of states make up the four regions. South: Alabama, Arkansas, Florida, Georgia, Kentucky, Louisiana, Mississippi, North Carolina, Oklahoma, South Carolina, Tennessee, Texas, and Virginia. West: Alaska, Arizona, California, Colorado, Hawaii, Idaho, Montana, Nevada, New Mexico, Oregon, Utah, Washington, and Wyoming. Midwest: Illinois, Indiana, Iowa, Kansas, Michigan, Minnesota, Missouri, Nebraska, North Dakota, Ohio, South Dakota, and Wisconsin. East: Connecticut, Delaware, Maine, Maryland, Massachusetts, New Hampshire, New Jersey, New York, Pennsylvania, Rhode Island, Vermont, and West Virginia.

purchase price, which is what state law stipulated at the time. Had the measure passed, the revenue it generated—an estimated $6.5 billion to $11.5 billion—would have been allocated to local governments and school districts. Florida voters approved two separate measures extending the state's homestead property tax discounts and exemptions. Coloradans voted to repeal a 1982 law setting residential and nonresidential property tax rates and to allow the state legislature to freeze the current property tax assessment rates. In New Jersey, voters approved a new property tax deduction for veterans, while in Virginia, voters supported a property tax exemption for certain vehicles belonging to disabled veterans. Two of the three property tax-related measures on the ballot in Louisiana were approved. The first called for the value of oil and gas production to be included in tax assessments of oil and gas wells. The second raised the income threshold to qualify for property tax freezes. Voters rejected a proposal to allow manufacturers to make payments to local tax authorities in lieu of paying property taxes.

Other notable tax initiatives included Nebraska voters' adoption of three separate measures that allowed for increased regulation and taxation of gambling in the state, with an emphasis on licensed racetracks. In Arizona and Colorado, voters approved changes to state income tax levels, while an initiative authorizing enactment of a graduated income tax failed in Illinois. Measures that increased cigarette taxes and imposed new taxes on e-cigarettes and other nicotine products were adopted in Colorado and Oregon.

Elections Policy

Eighteen measures on the ballots in fourteen states related to election systems, campaign finance rules, redistricting, and the right to vote. Five of the ballot measures in this category proposed changes to states' election systems. Voters in Alaska and Florida considered initiatives to move their states from closed primary to open primary systems, meaning all candidates from all parties run in the same primary election. In Alaska's proposal, the top four primary vote getters would move on to the general election; Florida proposed that the top two candidates move forward. Alaska's measure also sought to establish ranked-choice voting for general elections, as well as new requirements for campaign finance disclosures. The Alaska measure was approved by voters, but Floridians rejected the move to an open primary. Massachusetts voters also considered establishing a ranked-choice voting system, for both primary and general elections, but this proposal was rejected. In Colorado, voters were asked if lawmakers should repeal a 2019 bill adding Colorado to the National Popular Vote Interstate Compact (NPVIC), an agreement by participating states to assign their electoral college votes to the presidential candidate who wins the national popular vote. The pledge does not take effect until NPVIC has enough member states to represent 270 electoral votes. Fifteen states and the District of Columbia, with a total of 195 electoral college votes, have joined the NPVIC since it was first adopted by Maryland in 2007. Voters decided the law should be upheld. The final election system change of 2020 was on the ballot in Mississippi. There, voters considered a proposal to repeal the state's requirement that the winning candidate for governor or other state elected office receive the most votes in a majority of Mississippi's 122 districts. This requirement would be replaced with a measure stipulating that a candidate receive a majority of votes to be declared the winner. If no candidate received a majority, a runoff election would be held between the top two vote getters. Mississippi voters agreed to make this change.

Suffrage was another top electoral issue on state ballots, with five measures presented to voters in Alabama, California, Colorado, and Florida. Alabama, Colorado, and Florida voters approved initiatives amending their state's constitution to state that "only a citizen" of the United States had the right to vote, rather than "every citizen." Republicans and some conservative interest groups in these states argued the changes were needed to protect election integrity and ensure that noncitizens were not allowed to vote. Opponents of these measures—including

Democratic lawmakers, immigrant groups, and civil liberties organizations—claimed the ballot initiatives were designed to tap into anti-immigrant sentiment and suppress voter turnout. California voters considered two separate voting rights measures. The first, which was approved, allowed convicted felons who had completed their prison sentences and were on parole to vote. The second measure sought to allow seventeen-year-olds who would be eighteen by the next general election to vote in primary and special elections. Voters rejected this proposal.

Three measures on state ballots in 2020 were related to redistricting procedures. In Missouri, voters reversed course from a 2018 ballot initiative that created the position of state demographer and charged this individual with developing and recommending district maps. Voters in 2020 decided to return this responsibility to bipartisan redistricting commissions. In Virginia, voters approved a measure that stripped the state's General Assembly of its redistricting authority and reassigned the responsibility for drawing congressional and legislative district maps to a redistricting commission. The commission is to be comprised of eight lawmakers from the General Assembly's two largest parties and eight citizens, to be nominated by legislative leaders and confirmed by a panel of former circuit court judges. New Jersey voters adopted a ballot measure extending the deadline for the state redistricting commission to approve a redistricting plan. The extension was prompted by an anticipated delay in receiving updated demographic data from the U.S. Census Bureau, whose data compilation had been hampered by the COVID-19 pandemic.

Other notable ballot measure in the elections category included Arkansas voters' approval of increased term limits for state lawmakers, Kentucky voters' rejection of longer term limits for attorneys and judges, and Missourians' decision not to impose term limits on select state offices. In New Mexico, voters granted the state legislature the authority to adjust the dates of elections for state and county offices. Additionally, Oregon voters approved a measure allowing state and local officials to set the state's first-ever limits on campaign contributions and establish related disclosure requirements.

Legalization of Marijuana

Continuing the nationwide trend, voters in Arizona, Montana, New Jersey, and South Dakota approved ballot measures legalizing the recreational use of marijuana. South Dakotans also adopted a separate measure allowing the use of medical marijuana by individuals with debilitating illnesses. South Dakota's recreational measure was later overturned by a circuit court judge who said that it violated the state's single-subject rule for ballot initiatives. The officials who filed the suit had claimed the measure comprised five different subjects—legalization of marijuana, regulation of recreational marijuana, regulation of medical

marijuana, marijuana licensing, and regulation of hemp products. The plaintiffs also alleged, and the judge concurred, that the measure should be considered a revision to the state's constitution rather than an amendment. This rendered the measure invalid, because it had been put on the ballot by citizen initiative; constitutional revisions can only be placed on the ballot by the state legislature.

The Gig Economy, Mushrooms, and a Flag

Several states became the first to enact unique proposals via ballot initiative in 2020. In California, voters approved a measure, Proposition 22, that classified rideshare and delivery drivers as independent contractors, rather than employees of the companies for which they drove. It also set specific wage and labor policies for rideshare drivers and companies, including limits on the number of hours that could be worked per week. Voters' adoption of Proposition 22 marked the first time so-called gig economy policies appeared on a statewide ballot. The measure had been sponsored by Uber, Lyft, and DoorDash in response to lawmakers' 2019 passage of California Assembly Bill 5 (AB 5). That controversial bill established a three-factor test to determine whether a worker could be classified as an independent contractor, in which case, state wage and labor laws would not apply to them. Prior to passage of AB 5, the rideshare companies had classified their drivers as independent contractors, and company executives declined to reclassify workers following the law's implementation. The Superior Court of San Francisco ruled in August 2020 that Uber and Lyft had violated the law because their drivers were employees. This decision was upheld by California's First District Court of Appeal in October 2020, which further ruled that the companies had to make changes to comply with AB 5 unless voters approved Proposition 22. The ballot initiative was subsequently challenged in court by the Service Employees International Union and four rideshare drivers, who claimed the proposition was both unconstitutional and unenforceable. A superior court judge ruled in favor of the plaintiffs in August 2021, thereby overturning the measure.

In Colorado, voters approved a measure requiring the Colorado Parks and Wildlife Commission to develop and implement a plan to reintroduce the endangered gray wolf on designated state lands. Mississippi voters approved a new design for the state's flag. The previous state flag had become controversial during the national push to remove or replace Confederate monuments and symbols, because it featured the Confederate Battle Cross in its upper left corner. The new flag was approved by an overwhelming margin of roughly 73 percent to 27 percent. Additionally, the use of psychedelic mushrooms was legalized for the first time by Oregon voters. The ballot measure approved in 2020 permitted the administration of psilocybin products, including mushrooms and fungi that produce this substance, at approved psilocybin service centers.

Economic Policy

Economic Policy

President Donald Trump entered the White House in 2017 seeking a more protectionist yet hands-off approach to the American economy, pledging to pull the United States out of free-trade deals, ease taxes and regulations for corporations, and reduce spending on social safety net programs while beefing up the nation's industrial defense base. He said his plans would drive up the economy, revive U.S. manufacturing, create jobs, and decrease the deficit.

With Republican control of both chambers of Congress in 2017 and 2018, Trump's administration did push through a long-desired overhaul of the U.S. tax code and tweaked regulations governing the financial services industry. Trump also used his own presidential authority to launch a global tariff war. But the president failed to gain wide support in the Republican party for many of his drastic domestic spending cuts, and his team's economic forecasts ultimately proved wrong.

Initially, unemployment continued its steady decline of previous years, but the nation's debt continued to rise and by 2019 the federal deficit reached nearly $1 trillion. In 2020, the coronavirus pandemic further complicated the U.S. economic situation and the administration's plans. Still, by the end of Trump's administration in January 2021, the stock market was reporting near record highs, having rebounded from a steep plunge the previous spring. But the nation was still grappling with the effects of the continuing coronavirus pandemic and economists questioned how to gain control over the nation's rising debt.

PRESIDENT TRUMP'S ECONOMIC RECORD

In the initial years of Trump's presidency, the economy saw continued growth but not to the extent he had predicted would happen as a result of the Republicans' 2017 tax overhaul that provided $1.5 trillion in tax cuts. The real gross domestic product (GDP) increased 2.2 percent in 2017 and 2.9 percent in 2018, missing Trump's 3 percent target. In 2019, the GDP increased just 2.3 percent.

Trump had predicted that economic growth from the tax cuts combined with proceeds from stiff tariffs on a range of goods would help eliminate the budget deficit and enable the government to begin to pay down the national debt, which was about $19 trillion when he took office. By 2019, the debt was $22 trillion, and by late January 2020, before the coronavirus pandemic hit, the national debt was about $23 trillion. Meanwhile, the federal deficit grew from $587 billion in fiscal 2016 to $984 billion in 2019.

Nevertheless, unemployment rates dropped to below 4 percent. Phillip Swagel, Congressional Budget Office (CBO) director, said in January 2020 that the agency was projecting deficit levels the country had not seen during times of low unemployment since World War II.

Many economists and other observers blamed a lack of government spending restraint as well as the 2017 tax overhaul, particularly the law's sharp decrease in the corporate tax rate, for reducing federal revenues. Trump in 2018 began imposing hefty tariffs on steel, aluminum, and a range of other imports, nearly doubling tariff revenues. But in 2018 and 2019, the administration also paid out $28 billion to farmers who had been negatively impacted by the trade wars through 2019. Businesses that were struggling as a result of the tariffs also received a tax break.

In 2020, the coronavirus pandemic also was to blame for an even sharper rise in the deficit and debt. State and local governments put in mandatory quarantine orders, which ultimately forced businesses to lay off millions of workers and many companies to completely shut down. Businesses in the service industry particularly suffered as most Americans remained home. The Federal Reserve, however, took several actions to keep credit flowing to limit economic damage. For instance, it made large purchases of federal government and mortgage-backed securities and provided lending support to households, employers, participants in the financial market, and local and state governments. And Congress cleared about $3.5 trillion in COVID-related funding to help low-income families, the unemployed, small businesses, and local governments.

In 2020, the worst year for U.S. economic growth since World War II, the economy contracted 3.5 percent. The nation lost 9.4 million jobs in 2020 as the unemployment rate reached a peak of 14.8 percent in April before declining to 6.7 percent by the end of the year. The national debt increased to $27.75 trillion (exceeding 100 percent of

GDP) by December 31, 2020—an increase of 39 percent or nearly $7.8 trillion since Trump had taken office. The federal deficit reached $3.1 trillion, equal to 14.9 percent of GDP, in 2020.

During Trump's tenure, the Consumer Price index rose an average of 1.9 percent each year, or 7.6 percent overall, indicating a continued period of low inflation. But average weekly earnings rose 8.7 percent for workers in the private sector. Among rank-and-file production and nonsupervisory workers in the private sector, wages rose 9.8 percent during Trump's four-year term.

Revising Dodd-Frank

President Trump's team and conservative Republicans could not move through Congress a complete overhaul or outright repeal of the Dodd-Frank Wall Street Reform and Protection Act (PL 111-203), which had created new regulations and oversight agencies in the wake of the 2008 economic crises. But the 115th Congress did clear a package of revisions to Dodd-Frank and other financial laws which Republicans said would ease restrictions on small and medium-size financial institutions. During negotiations, Democrats fought to keep in place protections for consumers and investors.

Budget Negotiations

The Trump administration waged a series of battles with Congress over government spending which typically resulted in the government operating under a series of stop-gap funding measures while negotiations continued. From December 2018 to January 2019, however, the government shut down for a record thirty-five days, primarily due to disagreement over Trump's demand for more than $5 billion for a wall along the U.S.–Mexico border.

Republicans and the administration repeatedly pushed for increased defense spending at the expense of domestic spending. But Trump failed to get support from the GOP, particularly the most conservative members, to sharply reduce funding for the social safety net, including Medicare and food stamps. Trump also pushed to reduce or eliminate spending for climate change programs, job training initiatives, and other domestic programming, but lawmakers were not willing to go along with his budget proposals.

Congress exceeded Trump's requests for disaster aid funding as states and local communities suffered from a series of record hurricanes, wildfires, flooding, and more. In 2020, debates over restricting domestic spending ceased as the administration and lawmakers addressed the economic and health effects of the coronavirus pandemic, approving about $3.5 trillion in supplementary spending to help the unemployed, low-income people, businesses, and communities stay afloat during the government-mandated quarantines.

Tariff War

In 2018, Trump launched a global trade war when he imposed tariffs of up to 25 percent on steel and aluminum. He eventually imposed hefty duties on more than $230 billion worth of Chinese imports as well as imports from the European Union, the United Kingdom, and other countries. Each round of tariff announcements by the administration sparked retaliatory tariffs on billions of dollars' worth of U.S. exports. Industry observers said the tariffs increased uncertainty for businesses and put a damper on investment. The tariff war particularly hurt U.S. agricultural trade with China. In December 2019, U.S. and Chinese leaders reached an agreement on a number of trade issues that halted the escalating trade war but left in place most of the tariffs.

ECONOMIC LEADERSHIP

Treasury Secretary

Steven Mnuchin, a former investment banker for the Goldman Sachs Group, served as secretary of the treasury during the Trump administration.

President-elect Trump nominated Mnuchin for treasury secretary on November 30, 2016. During Mnuchin's confirmation hearing before the Senate Finance Committee on January 19, Democrats harshly criticized him for not disclosing nearly $100 million of his assets on disclosure documents. When the committee scheduled a vote on the nomination on January 31, Democrats boycotted the meeting, saying they had unanswered questions about Mnuchin and the foreclosure practices at OneWest Bank that he once owned. Mnuchin defended the foreclosure practices of the bank.

On February 1, 2017, committee Republicans voted 14–0 to advance Mnuchin's nomination. Committee rules required the presence of at least one member of each party, but the Republican majority on the panel turned to a parliamentary rule that allows the panel to suspend its own rules for any reason.

The Senate on February 14, 2017, voted 53–47 to confirm the nomination. One Democrat, Joe Manchin III of West Virginia, joined Republicans in voting for the confirmation.

Mnuchin played a role in drafting the tax reform proposal that Trump signed into law (PL 115-97) in December 2017. Mnuchin said the plan would pay for itself through economic growth. He did not submit a full economic analysis of the plan, but did release a one-page summary that showed that the 2017 tax cut law would not pay for itself through economic growth alone.

During his tenure, Mnuchin refused Democrats' requests to turn over six years' worth of federal tax returns for President Trump and his companies. Mnuchin faced criticism often from liberals as well as conservatives. But in 2020, he was praised by many observers for helping steer a $2.2 trillion government rescue package to aid workers, families, small businesses, and large companies during the pandemic, which many observers said helped stabilize the economy.

Federal Reserve Chair

Janet Yellen, who was appointed chair of the Board of Governors of the Federal Reserve System (the Fed) by President Obama in February 2014, remained on with the Trump administration until her term ended in February 2018. The first woman to lead the board, Yellen had previously been vice chair of the Federal Reserve and had served as president and chief executive officer of the Federal Reserve

Bank of San Francisco and as chair of the White House Council of Economic Advisers under President Clinton.

On December 16, 2015, Yellen oversaw the Fed as it increased its key interest rate for the first time since 2006. The Fed increased rates four more times under her tenure, leaving its key rate in a range of 1.25 percent to 1.5 percent, low according to historical standards.

After President-elect Trump announced his plans to revise the Dodd-Frank Financial Reform and Consumer Protection Act (PL 111-203), financial overhaul legislation passed in the wake of the 2008 economic crisis, Yellen defended the law before the Joint Economic Committee. On Yellen's last day as chair, she enforced sanctions against Wells Fargo following a series of reports of consumer abuses. The sanctions restricted the firm's growth until it revamped its governance and put in place more risk management controls and processes.

Trump did not renominate Yellen for another term, instead picking Federal Reserve Governor Jerome Powell, a Republican, to take her place when her term ended in February 2018. The decision not to renominate Yellen was considered an unprecedented, political move by a president. Many observers considered Yellen to be among the most successful Federal Reserve chairs because, during her term, unemployment fell steadily and inflation remained checked.

President Obama had appointed Powell, an attorney and investment banker, to the Federal Reserve Board of Governors in 2012. During his confirmation hearing in November 2017, Powell pledged to continue Yellen's policies, aiming to push inflation toward 2 percent, to shrink the Fed's balance sheet (reducing its securities holdings), and bring more transparency to the operations of the central bank. The Senate Banking Committee's ranking Democrat, Sherrod Brown of Ohio, said he was concerned about Trump's suggestions he wanted to weaken the Federal Reserve's independence.

On December 5, 2017, the committee voted 22–1 to approve Powell's nomination. Sen. Elizabeth Warren, D-Mass., voted against the nomination. Warren had supported Powell's renomination to the Fed board in 2014. But during consideration of his nomination as chair, Warren said she was concerned the Fed would roll back financial regulations, particularly since Powell had testified and stated in public that he believed the financial rules were too strict.

Chairman Michael D. Crapo, R-Idaho, had voted against Powell's renomination to the Fed board in 2014, but voted for his nomination as chair, saying his expertise would be a continued asset for the board.

(Continued)

The Senate confirmed Powell's nomination by a vote of 84–13. Independent Bernie Sanders of Vermont, along with four Republicans and eight Democrats voted no. The Republicans included Ted Cruz of Texas, Mike Lee of Utah, Rand Paul of Kentucky, and Marco Rubio of Florida. The Democrats included Richard Blumenthal of Connecticut, Cory Booker of New Jersey, Dianne Feinstein and Kamala Harris of California, Kirsten Gillibrand of New York, Edward J. Markey and Warren of Massachusetts, and Jeff Merkley of Oregon. Republicans Bob Corker of Tennessee, John McCain of Arizona, and Tim Scott of South Carolina did not vote.

Over the next three years, Powell received bipartisan praise, particularly for his leadership of the Fed's response to the economic crisis during the COVID-19 pandemic. Powell advocated more spending to protect low- and middle-income workers amid the government shutdowns and cutting interest rates, for example. But he also received criticism for injecting more money into the corporate credit market to prop up the business sector during the pandemic.

Office of Management and Budget Director

Former Republican Rep. Mick Mulvaney of South Carolina served as the first director of the Office of Management and Budget during the Trump administration. President-elect Trump nominated the four-term congressman, a prominent member of the conservative House Freedom Caucus, on December 17, 2016. In January, Mulvaney said he would divest from certain stock holdings and relinquish leadership roles in several real estate entities if he was confirmed.

Mulvaney faced controversy during confirmation hearings before the Senate Homeland Security and Governmental Affairs Committee and the Budget Committee. Sen. John McCain, R-Ariz., challenged Mulvaney on his votes in Congress related to defense spending and the withdrawal of troops from abroad, saying he believed Mulvaney did not support the military.

Mulvaney sparked objections from Vermont Independent Sen. Bernie Sanders when he told the Senate Budget Committee that, in order to reduce the federal deficit, the administration may need to make cuts to entitlement programs such as Medicare and Social Security—contrary to Trump's campaign pledge to protect such programs.

On February 2, 2017, Republicans on the two committees with jurisdiction voted to approve the nomination. The Senate Homeland Security Committee voted 8–7, along party lines, to approve Mulvaney's nomination. McCain voted to send the nomination to the floor but did not indicate how he would vote on final confirmation. The Senate

Budget Committee voted along party lines, 12–11, to approve the nomination.

On February 16, the Senate voted 51–49 to confirm Mulvaney's nomination. All 46 Democrats, the two independents who caucused with them, and McCain voted against the nomination.

In January 2019, amid a thirty-five-day government shutdown, Trump made Mulvaney his acting White House chief of staff, a position he held until March 2020, when he was replaced by Rep. Mark Meadows, R-N.C. (Mulvaney was subsequently appointed special U.S. envoy to Northern Ireland, and resigned on January 7, 2021, saying he objected to Trump's behavior during the riot at the U.S. Capitol on January 6.)

After tapping Mulvaney as chief of staff, Trump appointed Russell Vought to be acting director of the Office of Management and Budget (OMB). The Senate had confirmed Vought as deputy director in February 2018. Trump formally nominated him in March 2020 to the position as director.

The Senate confirmed his nomination by a vote of 51–45 on July 20. But Vought faced criticism from both sides of the aisle—from Democrats for stonewalling congressional oversight and ignoring subpoenas for testimony, and from Republicans who opposed two unsuccessful attempts by the OMB to cuts millions of dollars in the federal budget for foreign aid.

In September 2020, Vought authored a memo to federal agencies instructing them to list all contracts related to training sessions that address "white privilege" or "critical race theory" and to cancel those contracts. In December, during the transition of President-elect Biden's team, Vought said he would not help officials of the transition team draft policies that would unravel the Trump administration's work. Biden's team said the OMB was withholding information critical to national security.

Council of Economic Advisers Chair

Kevin A. Hassett, a former economics professor and consultant to two previous administrations, served as chair of the Council of Economic Advisers (CEA) in the Trump administration for two years, advocating corporate tax cuts and other policies he said would boost the nation's economic growth rate. Trump nominated Hassett to the CEA on April 7, 2017. Hassett was a former Columbia Business School professor and a former economist in the Division of Research and Statistics at the Federal Reserve Board of Governors. He had served as consultant to the Treasury Department during the administrations of George H.W. Bush and Bill Clinton, and was resident scholar at the American Enterprise Institute, a conservative think tank in Washington.

The CEA chair leads a team of economists that develops economic forecasts for the president's budget. During his confirmation hearing on June 6, 2017, Hassett told the Senate

Banking, Housing, and Urban Affairs Committee that he believed the United States could see a 3 percent annual economic growth rate, up from 2 percent, if the administration implemented policies that encouraged growth in the labor force, capital stock, and technological innovation. The committee on June 14 approved Hassett's nomination by voice vote, although Sen. Elizabeth Warren, D-Mass., asked that her vote be recorded as "nay."

On September 12, 2017, the Senate voted 81–16 to confirm Hassett. The nomination was opposed by independent Bernie Sanders of Vermont and 15 Democrats, including: Richard Blumenthal of Connecticut, Cory Booker of New Jersey, Catherine Cortez Masto of Nevada, Tammy Duckworth of Illinois, Kirsten Gillibrand and Charles E. Schumer of New York, Kamala Harris of California, Martin Heinrich and Tom Udall of New Mexico, Mazie K. Hirono and Brian Schatz of Hawaii, Edward J. Markey and Warren of Massachusetts, and Ron Wyden and Jeff Merkley of Oregon.

Senate Banking ranking Democrat Sherrod Brown of Ohio said he supported Hassett's nomination, but added that he was concerned about the White House's projections of high economic growth in a tax overhaul proposal, a plan that he said favored the wealthy.

Hassett's research during his career had focused on the potential to expand economic growth by cutting corporate tax rates, and he was a strong proponent of the tax overhaul plan that Trump signed into law (PL 115-97) on December 22, 2017. The tax reform law included Hassett's plan for opportunity zones to create tax incentives for investment in distressed parts of the country.

Hassett, however, cautioned for a more conservative approach to open foreign trade markets and opposed Trump's reliance on increasing and expanding tariffs. In April 2019, Hassett reportedly refused to endorse Trump's requests to the Federal Reserve to cut interest rates to help spur economic growth. Hassett said his role was not to give the Fed advice because it was an independent agency. On June 4, 2019, Hassett resigned his position. (He returned in March 2020 to advise Trump on economic policy during the COVID-19 pandemic, staying for three months.)

On June 30, 2019, Trump named Tomas Philipson as acting chair of the council. Trump had appointed Philipson, a University of Chicago public professor and economist, to the council in August 2017, where he served as one of three members. Philipson previously had served as a senior economic adviser to the directors of the Food and Drug Administration and the Centers for Medicare and Medicaid Services during the George W. Bush administration.

As acting chair, Philipson played down the economic threat of the COVID-19 pandemic. He served until June 2020 and was succeeded by Tyler Goodspeed as acting chair. Goodspeed had served the council since 2017, first as a senior economist, then as chief economist for macroeconomic policy and then as a member. Goodspeed had previously taught economics at University of Oxford and lectured at King's College in London. Goodspeed remained in the position as acting chair until the end of Trump's term in January 2021.

National Economic Council Director

Gary Cohn, president and chief operating officer of Goldman Sachs Group Inc., served for a little more than a year as director of the National Economic Council (NEC) during the Trump administration.

Trump in December 2016 selected Cohn for the position, drawing Cohn away from the Wall Street firm for which he had worked for more than twenty-five years. On January 20, 2017, Cohn took office as director of the council, which former President Clinton had established to coordinate White House economic policies. Cohn operated nearly single-handedly pending the confirmation of Steven Mnuchin as Treasury Secretary.

The president tapped Cohn to play a leading role in tax reform, help create an infrastructure plan, address financial regulation, and replace the 2010 health care law. *The Wall Street Journal* said Cohn was becoming an "economic-policy powerhouse" in the White House. Cohn, however, considered resigning following an August 2017 rally by white supremacists and neo-Nazis in Charlottesville, Virginia. He decided not to resign, but he told *The Financial Times* that the administration should more strongly condemn hate groups.

Cohn did resign in early 2018 after President Trump announced he would impose hefty tariffs on steel and aluminum imports. Cohn had argued against the tariffs, warning that they would result in price increases for steel and aluminum products.

Trump immediately chose Larry Kudlow, a prominent conservative writer and commentator, to replace Cohn. Trump in 2016 had reportedly considered Kudlow to head the Council of Economic Advisors before he chose Hassett.

Kudlow, named assistant to the president for economic policy as well as director of the NEC, had worked for Office of Management and Budget Director David Stockman in the Reagan administration. He also had openly criticized Trump's announcement to impose high steel and aluminum tariffs, but Trump said Kudlow had since learned the tariffs could be a valuable negotiating tool.

Kudlow had long supported tax cuts, and in 2018 said the Congressional Budget Office was wrong when it projected the 2017 tax law would raise the annual federal deficit to more than $1 trillion. He later falsely asserted that the tax cut was generating extensive economic growth. He also countered warnings from the Centers for Disease Control and Prevention in February 2020 about a domestic coronavirus

(Continued)

ECONOMIC LEADERSHIP (Continued)

outbreak, saying the threat had been contained. Kudlow served as NEC director for the remainder of Trump's term.

Comptroller of the Currency

Trump's Comptroller of the Currency Joseph Otting, a longtime executive in the banking industry, sought to reduce the regulatory burden on national banks and savings associations while he was in the position. The president nominated Otting as comptroller in June 2017. The Senate Banking, Housing, and Urban Affairs Committee on September 7 approved the nomination by a 13–10 vote, with just one Democrat, Heidi Heitkamp of North Dakota, voting yes.

The committee's ranking Democrat, Sherrod Brown of Ohio, questioned Otting's tenure as president and chief executive officer of OneWest Bank, the successor to IndyMac Bank that was purchased in 2009 by an investor group led by Steven Mnuchin, who became Trump's Treasury secretary. Brown, along with other Democrats, criticized Otting for his bank's foreclosure of thousands of mortgages during the financial crisis.

On November 16, 2017, the Senate voted 54–43 to confirm Otting's nomination. Just two Democrats supported him: Heitkamp and Joe Manchin III of West Virginia.

Otting took over from Keith A. Noreika, who had been acting comptroller since May 2017. He led a rewrite of long-standing 1977 Community Reinvestment Act rules that aimed to bar banks from a practice known as "redlining" under which they would not issue loans for borrowers in lower-income areas in the communities.

On May 21, 2020, one day after releasing the new, finalized rules, Otting announced he would step down as comptroller. Brian P. Brooks, Otting's former colleague at OneWest Bank who had joined the Office of the Comptroller of the Currency (OCC) in April as deputy comptroller and chief operating officer, stepped in as acting comptroller. On November 27, the president nominated Brooks to a five-year term, but his nomination was returned to the White House when the new Congress was sworn in on January 3.

Brooks resigned as acting comptroller on January 14 and was replaced by Blake Paulson, who had joined the office in 1986 and was serving as senior deputy comptroller and chief operating officer.

Federal Deposit Insurance Corporation Chair

On May 24, 2018, the Senate voted 69–24 to confirm the nomination of Jelena McWilliams to be chair of the Federal Deposit Insurance Corporation, which regulates American banks and insures deposits. As such, she helped negotiate on legislation to rewrite the 2010 Dodd-Frank financial law (PL 111-203).

McWilliams briefly had been executive vice president at Fifth Third Bank, a regional bank holding company that had $142 billion in assets. She also previously served as chief counsel and deputy staff director for the Senate Banking Committee under former GOP chairmen Richard C. Shelby of Alabama and Michael D. Crapo of Idaho.

She replaced Martin Gruenberg, who had been chairman since November 2012. Her term as chair would be for five years. The Senate also voted by voice vote to confirm her to a six-year term on the FDIC board.

In 2020, she abstained from joining the Office of the Comptroller of the Currency's effort to rewrite the Community Reinvestment Act anti-redlining rules for banks. The FDIC had been part of a proposed rule that would alter how banks are assessed on their lending to low- and moderate-income neighborhoods in their communities, but did not sign off on the final version. McWilliams told Bloomberg Law in June that a rewrite of the rules should wait until after the pandemic. Instead, McWilliams said, the FDIC was reviewing its regulations to seek ways to better address discriminatory lending practices.

However, under her leadership the FDIC continued to loosen regulations. In December 2020, for instance, it adopted two new rules to help financial technology companies expand partnerships with banks or to start up their own banks.

A LOOK AT THE ECONOMY 2004–2020

Economic Growth
Annual Percentage Change

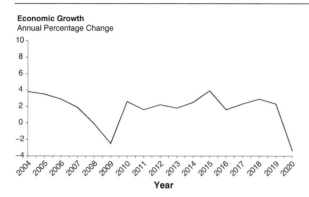

Year

Growth: Annual changes in real GDP, measured in chained 2012 dollars.

SOURCE: Commerce Department, Bureau of Economic Analysis; "GDP growth (Annual %)—United States," The World Bank.

Economic growth sagged during President George W. Bush's first term (2001–2005), which was marked by a mild recession followed by a mild recovery. Economic growth in his second term (2005–2009) slowed gradually until December 2007, when the country entered a deep recession. By 2010, the economy was growing again, albeit slowly, under the stewardship of President Barack Obama. Annual growth did not return to the level of 3 percent or higher that the nation had sometimes achieved in the first decade of the century.

Inflation
Annual Percentage Change

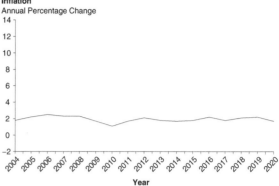

Year

Inflation: Annual change in the consumer price index for all urban consumers, expressed as an annual average rate.

SOURCE: Labor Department, Bureau of Labor Statistics.

Inflation stayed relatively consistent and tame during the first years of the 2000s. It rose somewhat before the 2008 recession but never approached the double-digit levels of 1979–1980. During President Obama's first term, the aftershocks of the sharp economic downturn meant that deflation was at times a larger concern than inflation. Prices rose annually during Obama's second term but at a mild rate.

Unemployment
Annual Percentage Average

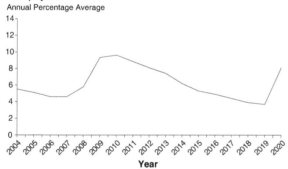

Year

Unemployment: Annual rate of unemployment for all civilian workers (does not include the military)..

SOURCE: Labor Department, Bureau of Labor Statistics.

Unemployment experienced a slight uptick in the early 2000s before settling at about 5 percent. As a deep recession took hold in 2008, unemployment began to rise, reaching a high point of 10.6 percent in January 2010 before steadily falling during the rest of the Obama presidency. By Obama's last year in office, it had dropped to less than 5 percent.

Iterest Rates
Annual Percentage Average

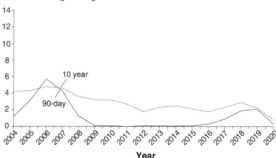

Year

Interest Rates: Annual average for ninety-day Treasury bills and ten-year Treasury notes, adjusted for constant maturities.

SOURCE: Federal Reserve; Federal Reserve Bank of St. Louis.

Interest rates on short- and long-term Treasury securities fell in 2003 to their lowest levels in almost thirty years then rose slightly as the Fed tried to engineer a "soft landing" for the booming housing market. In late 2008, interest rates fell again and remained low as the Fed intervened in an effort to stimulate the slumping economy. They remained low through the Obama presidency.

Chronology of Action on Economic and Regulatory Policy

As a presidential candidate, Donald Trump had pledged to dismantle federal regulations governing the financial sector, and within a month of taking office in January 2017 he began filling various agencies with Wall Street executives and attorneys who had long challenged such regulations or government efforts to prosecute financial crimes. Those officials and appointees then moved to relax the government's stiffest rules on the financial industry, including those imposed by the Democratic Congress in 2010.

House and Senate Republicans supported the efforts, saying that financial regulatory restrictions were constraining economic growth because they overburdened companies, particularly small and midsize financial institutions seeking to expand operations and create jobs. Consumer advocates and Democrats, however, contended that deregulating the financial sector threatened to return the U.S. economy to an environment similar to the high-risk environment that led to the 2008 financial crisis.

GOP leaders in the 115th Congress helped the Trump administration achieve its goal to rework the Dodd-Frank Wall Street Reform and Protection Act, the 2010 law cleared by a Democratic Congress and signed by President Obama in the wake of the 2008 crisis. The final measure was not a complete overhaul of the law, as many conservatives had hoped, but instead left much of the law in place while making a number of small changes to regulations that lawmakers said would ease the regulatory burden on financial institutions and help spur economic growth.

House Financial Services Chair Jeb Hensarling, R-Texas, hoped to make further regulatory changes and pushed through the House dozens of measures that he said could further spur investment and growth. With the support of Financial Services ranking Democrat Maxine Waters of California and other lawmakers from both parties, he pushed through the House in 2018 a thirty-two-bill package that aimed to ease regulatory burdens on smaller companies seeking capital and to create jobs. The effort was stymied in the Senate.

Meanwhile, Congress again failed to reauthorize the charter for the Commodity Futures Trading Commission (CFTC), the commodities and swaps regulator whose previous authorization had expired in 2013. During the 115th and 116th congresses, however, the Senate did confirm a series of nominations to the CFTC, returning it to a full five-member board.

When Democrats retook control of the House in 2019, they sought to block or reverse several of the Trump administration's efforts to weaken certain regulatory agencies, such as the Consumer Financial Protection Bureau. They also sought to halt the administration moves to unravel regulations, such as a Community Investment Act rule that aimed to encourage banks to provide loans to low-income and middle-income neighborhoods. The rule was designed to avoid a decades-old practice known as "redlining" that discriminated against African American and other minority individuals and families. The GOP-controlled Senate blocked most of the Democrats' efforts to reverse the administration's actions, including its weakening of the redlining rule.

The 116th Congress did reach bipartisan agreement to clear a seven-year reauthorization of the Terrorism Risk Insurance Program, which helps large companies, colleges, stadiums, and other businesses cover the risk of a foreign or domestic terrorism attack. Lawmakers also cleared legislation aimed at forcing securities exchanges to delist certain Chinese companies that refused to cooperate with U.S. regulators, and a measure aimed at shutting down so-called shell companies that hide illicit financial activities of unnamed operators. The chambers did not reach agreement on a measure aimed at clearly defining and targeting "insider trading."

2017-2018

During the 115th Congress, Republicans claimed a long-awaited victory when the Trump administration signed legislation making revisions to the 2010 Dodd-Frank Wall Street Reform and Protection Act. The measure did not fully overhaul the financial services law or undo the toughest regulations on the nation's biggest banks, as many conservatives had hoped, but made a number of changes that aimed to free thousands of smaller banks from the Federal Reserve's toughest rules.

The House moved dozens of other smaller bills aimed at easing more financial regulations and helping small companies find capital and create jobs, but most of the measures failed to move in the Senate. Likewise, the House passed a reauthorization of the Commodity Futures Trading Commission, but the legislation stalled in the Senate.

Dodd-Frank Revision

The 115th Congress cleared a package of tweaks and small revisions to the 2010 financial services law that conservatives for years had sought to dismantle. The Economic Growth, Regulatory Relief, and Consumer Protection Act (S 2155) left in place much of the Dodd-Frank Wall Street Reform and Protection Act (PL 111-203) that Congress had cleared after the financial crisis of 2008. Instead the measure, which had some Democratic support, made a number of changes that many lawmakers said would ease regulations on small and medium-size banks. Trump signed the measure into law (PL 115-174) on May 24, 2018.

BACKGROUND

In 2010, the Democrat-led Congress cleared the Dodd-Frank Wall Street Reform and Protection Act (PL 111-203) in response to the financial crisis of 2008. The law was intended to boost regulatory oversight of financial firms in order to bar future crises. Democrats said the law had helped ensure the safety and stability of financial institutions and markets, and provided more protections for consumers and investors from institutions' predatory lending practices, for instance.

Republicans complained about many of the law's regulatory requirements, saying it created barriers to economic growth because it restricted lending, subjected small financial institutions to hefty and unnecessary compliance burdens and stifled innovation in the financial sector. They also complained about the structure and funding of the Consumer Financial Protection Bureau and about the Financial Stability Oversight Council's authority to impose heightened regulations on certain institutions, among other provisions of the law.

In the years after Republicans regained control of the House in 2011, they tried repeatedly to roll back provisions of the law. They did include language in an omnibus appropriations measure (PL 113-235) in late 2014 that repealed a provision of the law which had required banks to drop their derivatives swaps activities from any part of a bank holding company that was federally insured.

President Trump also was critical of the 2010 law and in 2017 ordered Treasury Secretary Steven Mnuchin to conduct a broad review of financial regulations.

House Action

The House passed sweeping financial services legislation in June 2017. The measure (HR 10) had been introduced by House Financial Services Chair Jeb Hensarling, R-Texas, on April 26, 2017, to repeal major portions of the Dodd-Frank law and to grant relief from heightened Federal Reserve scrutiny for banks that maintain a 10 percent capital ratio. The bill would overhaul the Consumer Financial Protection Bureau, lift regulatory requirements for large banks, and repeal a rule, called the Volcker rule, that restricted trading by federally insured commercial banks. Hensarling said the 2010 financial services law was to blame for the nation's slow recovery from the 2008 financial crisis, but many banks and retailers opposed his measure.

On May 4, the House Financial Services Committee voted 34–26, along party lines, to approve the bill after rejecting 19 Democratic amendments. Eight of the amendments would have maintained the Consumer Financial Protection Bureau's financial independence and enforcement authority.

The House on June 8, 2017, voted 233–186 to pass the measure. No Democrats voted for the bill, and just one Republican, Walter B. Jones of North Carolina, crossed party lines to vote against it.

Senate Action

The Senate did not act on the House-passed measure (HR 10). Instead, it passed alternative legislation in 2018 after the Senate Banking, Housing, and Urban Affairs Committee worked on drafting a compromise measure with members of the administration.

On November 16, 2017, Banking Committee Chair Michael D. Crapo, R-Idaho, introduced a financial deregulation measure (S 2155) that would increase, from $50billion to $250 billion, the threshold for more stringent regulation of banks. The measure, which five committee Democrats cosponsored, also would exempt small banks from having to prohibit proprietary trading and would require credit reporting firms to allow unlimited, free credit freezes to consumers. Most of the changes would make revisions to the 2010 financial overhaul law, but other financial laws were tweaked as well. Federal Reserve

Governor Jerome Powell, who Trump later nominated as chair of the Fed, had testified in June that he would support increasing the $50 billion threshold, among other changes.

On December 5, 2017, the Banking Committee voted 16–7 to approve the measure, with four Democrats joining the twelve Republicans in favor. The panel rejected thirty-two Democratic amendments, mostly by votes of 7 to 16. Among those rejected were the following:

- An amendment by Sen. Catherine Cortez Masto of Nevada which would have reinstituted a Consumer Financial Protection Bureau arbitration rule that had been finalized in July and repealed by Congress in a resolution under the Congressional Review Act that the president signed in November (HJ Res 111—PL 115-74). The rule had barred financial companies from including in contracts clauses requiring consumers to use arbitration rather than class-action lawsuits to resolve complaints.
- An amendment by Sen. Elizabeth Warren of Massachusetts which would have barred credit reporting companies from selling information about consumers who froze their credit reports. The underlying measure would allow an unlimited number of credit freezes, but would allow the companies to continue selling information.
- An amendment by Sen. Robert Menendez of New Jersey which would have denied the bill's regulatory relief to large banks that had adopted sales incentives that led to the creation of fraudulent consumer accounts. The measure was in response to reports that Wells Fargo had fraudulently established millions of customer accounts.

On January 30, 2018, Treasury Secretary Steven Mnuchin endorsed the bill and urged Congress to clear it. On March 1, Powell, the Federal Reserve's new chair, said he endorsed the main provisions of the bill, particularly the higher threshold for the Fed to impose stringent regulation on banks. The bill's higher threshold would reduce from forty-four to thirteen the number of banks subject to the Fed's strict scrutiny.

On March 14, the Senate voted 67–31 to pass the measure (S 2155). Sixteen Democrats and independent Sen. Angus King of Maine joined fifty Republicans to vote for the legislation. Democrats who opposed the bill argued that it would weaken the 2010 law, which had stabilized the financial system and made Wall Street more accountable.

The Senate passed the legislation after adopting a substitute amendment by Banking Chair Crapo that included provisions similar to language in a series of financial measures, many of them advanced by House and Senate committees and several passed by the full House. Crapo said he selected provisions that had sufficient bipartisan support

so as not to impede final passage by the Senate. Many of those measures were intended to make it easier for companies to raise capital, including increasing from 100 to 250 the number of investors a company could have and still be exempt from registering with the Securities and Exchange Commission.

According to the Congressional Research Service, the bills with provisions similar to those of the Senate-passed bill (S 2155) included the House-passed measure, HR 10, as well as

- HR 2226, passed by the House by voice vote on March 6, 2018, addressing additional criteria for a mortgage to be considered a "qualified mortgage"
- HR 2255, passed by the House by voice vote on March 6, addressed charitable donations of home appraisals
- HR 3221, approved by the House Financial Services Committee in 32–26 vote on March 8, addressing exemptions from appraisal requirements for rural or low-value mortgages
- HR 2954, passed by the House, 243–184, on January 18, addressed exemptions from certain reporting requirements of the Home Mortgage Disclosure Act
- HR 2121, approved by the House Financial Services Committee, 60–0, on April 26, to exempt certain custodial banks from the Statutory Liquidity Ratio, a mandatory reserve requirement
- HR 1624, passed by the House by voice vote on October 3, 2017, to address treatment of municipal debt under Loan-to-Deposit Ratio (the ratio of a bank's total loans to its total deposits)
- HR 4656, approved by the House Financial Services Committee on January 25, 2018, and HR 3978, passed by the House, 271–145, on February 14, to exempt from state registration securities qualified for national trading by the SEC and listed on a national exchange, and a provision addressing a loan original grace period during license changes
- HR 1219, passed by the House on a 417–3 vote on April 6, 2017, to exempt some venture capital funds from registration and disclosure requirements
- HR 1257, approved by the House Financial Services Committee in a 59–0 vote on August 15, 2017, to require the Securities and Exchange Commission (SEC) to offset futures fees and assessments due from a national securities exchange that has previously overpaid such fees
- HR 1366, passed by the House by voice vote on May 1, 2017, to address certain securities requirements for funds operating in U.S. territories
- HR 1343, passed by the House, 331–87 on April 4, 2017, to increase from $5 million to $10 million the one-year sales threshold beyond which an issuer of securities must disclose to investors further details about compensatory benefit plans

- HR 2864, passed by the House in a 403–3 on September 5, 2017, to streamline the SEC review for securities offerings by certain small public companies
- HR 4279, passed by the House in a 418–2 vote on January 17, 2018, requiring the SEC to streamline communications or closed-end companies with investors
- HR 1699, passed by the House, 256–163, on December 1, 2017, providing mortgage rule exemptions for certain manufactured homes retailers
- HR 3971, passed by the House, 294–129, on December 12, 2017, setting escrow requirements for mortgage exemptions from the Real Estate Settlement Procedures Act of 1974
- HR 2133, considered in hearings, addressing rules for exemptions from mortgage waiting period requirements and reciprocal deposit restrictions, and other provisions
- HR 4771, passed by the House, 280–139, to require the Federal Reserve to amend its Small Bank Holding Company Policy Statement to raise the asset threshold at which the statement would apply
- HR 4790, passed by the House, 300–104, on April 13, 2018, and HR 3093, passed by House by voice vote on December 11, 2017, providing exemptions from the Volker rule
- HR 4725, to shorten the required "call report" that details a bank's financial health, passed by the House by voice vote on March 6, 2018
- HR 1426, passed by the House by voice vote on January 29, 2018, addressing an alternative to charter changes for federal thrifts seeking to increase certain types of loans
- HR 5076, approved by the Financial Services Committee 60–1 on April 26, to reduce examination frequency for certain small banks
- HR 4537, addressing international insurance standards oversight
- HR 1457, passed by the House in a 397–8 vote on January 29, about scanned images of ID cards and online banking
- HR 2148, passed by the House by voice vote on November 7, 2017, addressing high-volatility commercial real estate exposures in capital requirements
- HR 2683, addressing the waiting period before including veterans' medical debt in credit reports
- HR 2255, which passed the House by voice vote on January 29, and HR 3758, approved by House Financial Services on November 28, 2017, to enhance whistleblower protection for those who identify cases of defrauding seniors
- HR 4258, which passed the House by a 412–5 vote on January 17, was intended to address changes to the Family Self-Sufficiency Program, which helps families increase their income and reduce dependency on welfare and rental assistance from Housing and Urban Development

- Provisions similar to three bills to improve prudential regulation regime changes:
- HR 3312, passed by the House on December 19; HR 4292, passed January 30; and HR 4293, passed April 11

Final House Action

The House cleared S 2155 in May 2018. House Financial Services Chairman Jeb Hensarling, R-Texas, said he wanted to add to the measure as many as twenty-nine more banking, financial services, and securities bills the committee had approved. Senate Democrats who had supported the measure on the Senate floor warned they might drop their support if the bill was drastically altered.

On March 21, 2018, the Financial Services Committee approved eight more financial deregulation bills, which Hensarling also pushed as candidates to add to the Senate bill. On May 8, House Speaker Paul D. Ryan, R-Wisc., and Majority Leader Kevin McCarthy, D-Calif., said they intended to move the banking bill to a vote separately from the other financial regulation bills the committee had passed. Hensarling later said that Ryan agreed to hold off a vote until the Senate considered more than thirty bills that his committee had approved. But members agreed that the House would not amend the Senate bill.

The House on May 22 voted 258–159 to clear the Senate's banking deregulation bill (S 2155). Financial Services committee member Blaine Luetkemeyer, R-Mo., said the bill would provide banks regulatory relief. But Financial Services Committee ranking member Maxine Waters, D-Calif., said the measure aimed to help banks that were already reporting record profits.

One Republican, Walter B. Jones of North Carolina, voted against the measure, while thirty-three Democrats crossed party lines to support the legislation.

HIGHLIGHTS OF THE LAW

The following are some highlights of the changes the law made in financial regulations. The law

- No longer automatically imposed higher regulation on larger banks with $50 billion to $250 billion in assets, allowing the Federal Reserve to decide whether to impose further regulation on such banks
- Eased filing requirements to help small and medium businesses raise up to $50 million a year through the sale of securities
- Allowed private companies to provide larger stock payments to employees without triggering disclosure requirements
- Allowed certain closed-end investment companies to issue securities with reduced requirements for SEC filing
- Reduced reporting requirements, simplified capitalization standards, and lengthened the time interval between regulators' examinations for smaller community banks. It also provided new criteria to help

small banks comply with qualified mortgage lender rules, and exempted small lenders from some disclosure requirements

- Reduced the regulatory burden for mortgage lending to help ease the burden on smaller institutions
- Allowed consumers to freeze their credit reports, at will and without cost
- Allowed veterans to have certain medical debt excluded from their credit reports
- Permanently extended foreclosure relief for veterans when they leave the military
- Provided some protections to student loan borrowers
- Required financial institutions to train employees about financial abuse of senior citizens, and exempted those institutions and employees from liability for potential exploitation of a senior citizen

Financial Stability Oversight Council

Congress in 2017 cleared a bill (HR 3110) that would modify the membership rules for the Financial Stability Oversight Council (FSOC) to extend the term of its independent member, S. Roy Woodall. The FSOC, created by the Dodd-Frank law to identify risks to the financial system, had ten voting members, including one independent member appointed by the president and confirmed by the Senate. The bill would allow the independent member to serve up to eighteen months beyond the end of a six-year term if a successor had not been named. The term of S. Roy Woodall Jr., the independent member, was to expire at the end of September.

Woodall, confirmed to the council in 2018, had previously served as the Kentucky insurance commissioner, president of the National Association of Life Companies, and chief counsel for state relations at the American Council of Life Insurers.

The measure, authored by Rep. Randy Hultgren, R-Ill., aimed to correct what both Republicans and Democrats called a technical flaw in the 2010 Dodd-Frank law.

The House on September 5 passed HR 3110 by a vote of 407–1. The Senate passed the measure by unanimous consent on September 19. President Trump signed the bill into law (PL 115-61) on September 27, 2017.

On February 8, 2018, the Senate Banking Committee gave voice vote approval to the nomination of Thomas E. Workman to replace Woodall. In March, the Senate confirmed the nomination of Workman, who previously had served as president and chief executive officer of the Life Insurance Council of New York, Inc.

JOBS Package

House Financial Services Committee Chairman Jeb Hensarling, R-Texas, and the panel's ranking Democrat, Maxine Waters of California, worked together during the 115th Congress to advance a package of bills that would tweak financial and securities regulations and aim to help businesses raise capital and create jobs. A similar but narrower effort was made by members of both parties on the Senate Banking, Housing, and Urban Affairs Committee as well. While the House ultimately passed a massive, thirty-two-bill package, dubbed the JOBS and Investor Confidence Act of 2018 or JOBS 3.0, the Senate did not act on it. However, several provisions of the same bills passed by House and Senate committees were included in the package of Dodd-Frank revisions (see above).

Senate Action

On March 9, 2017, the Senate Banking, Housing, and Urban Affairs Committee approved by voice vote five bipartisan bills, including

- S 488, introduced by Sens. Patrick J. Toomey, R-Pa., and Mark Warner, D-Va., that would raise from $5 million to $10 million the twelve-month sales limit to trigger a requirement that issuers make additional disclosures to investors, such as on risk factors, and the limit would be indexed to inflation and updated every five years
- S 327, introduced by Sens. Dean Heller, R-Nev., with Gary Peters, D-Mich., which stated that research covering Exchange Traded Funds would not have to be considered as a securities offering under Securities and Exchange Commission (SEC) rules
- S 444, introduced by Sens. Heidi Heitkamp, D-N.D., and Heller, would increase from 100 to 250 the number of investors that venture capital funds could have and still remain exempt from registering under the Investment Company Act. The measure also would limit any qualifying venture capital fund to $10 million in securities purchases from one issuer
- S 462, introduced by Sens. Heller, Heitkamp, Toomey, and Joe Donnelly, D-Ind., which would require the SEC to credit national securities exchanges or national securities associations that have overpaid fees and assessments
- S 484, introduced by Sen. Robert Menendez, D-N.J., and cosponsored by Sens. Catherine Cortez Masto, D-Nev., and Orrin G. Hatch, R-Utah. The bill would end an exemption for investment companies in U.S. territories from the Investment Company Act

The Senate passed the five bills on September 11, 2017, by unanimous consent.

House Action

On March 9, 2017, the House Financial Services Committee approved five bipartisan bills which were all companion measures to the bills that the Senate had passed earlier in the day. The measures included

- HR 1343, a companion measure to S 488, which was adopted by a vote of 48–11. The measure was introduced by Reps. Hultgren, MacArthur, John Delaney, D-Md., Brian Higgins, D-N.Y., Kyrsten Sinema, D-Arizona, and Steve Stivers, R-Ohio
- HR 910, a companion measure to S 327 which was introduced by Reps. French Hill, R-Ark., and Bill Foster, D-Ill., and adopted in a 56–2 vote
- HR 1219, a companion measure to S 444 which was introduced by Reps. Patrick T. McHenry, R-N.C., and Nydia M. Velazquez, D-N.Y., and adopted in a 54–2 vote
- HR 1257, a companion to S 462, which was introduced by Reps. Gregory W. Meeks, D-N.Y. and Hultgren, and adopted in a 59–0 vote
- HR 1366, a companion measure to S 484, which was introduced by Reps. Velazquez, Sean P. Duffy, R-Wisc., Jose E. Serrano, D-N.Y., and Tom MacArthur, R-N.J. The committee adopted the bill by a 58–0 vote

On July 17, 2018, the House voted 406–4 to pass an amended version of the Senate's bill (S 488) to ease company reporting requirements on employee stock option plans, building it into a package of thirty-two measures aimed at making it easier to raise capital and loosen security regulations. The measure was called the Jobs and Investor Confidence Act of 2018 or JOBS Act 3.0.

Most of the bills had been passed by the House previously.

Among the bills included in the package were

- HR 1645 to amend the Sarbanes-Oxley Act of 2002 (PL 107-204) to extend an exemption from the law for certain low-revenue emerging growth companies
- HR 4281, to require the SEC to issue a report on unique challenges for rural area small businesses in securing access to capital
- HR 79 to allow business startups to raise capital to make presentations before angel investor groups
- HR 477 to simplify the securities registration system to alleviate costs for small business owners
- HR 1585 to change the definition of accredited investors, allowing professionals such as accountants and bankers to invest in private offerings without triggering registration requirements
- HR 2364 to amend the Small Business Investment Act (PL 85-699) to increase the percentage a financial institution could invest in a small business investment company
- HR 3972, to clarify that family offices and family clients are accredited investors under SEC rules
- HR 4292 that would alter a requirement that banks annually submit plans on how they would be liquidated in case of a bankruptcy

- HR 4294 to set criminal penalties for unauthorized disclosure of an individual's identifiable information by federal officials
- HR 4768 to require the administration to craft a national strategy to combat financial networks of transnational criminal organizations
- HR 5953 to tweak financial laws to allow simpler disclosure forms for nonprofit organizations that make residential mortgage loans charging zero percent interest

The Senate did not consider the House's amended version of S 488. On September 27, the House cleared the Senate bill (S 327) that would ensure that research reports covering Exchange Traded Funds would not have to be considered as a securities offering under SEC rules. The president signed that measure into law (PL 115-66) on October 6.

Meanwhile, provisions of several of the measures that the House Financial Services Committee approved on March 9 were included in the package of Dodd-Frank provisions, which President Trump signed into law (PL 115-174) in May 2018. Those measures included HR 1343, HR 1219, HR 1257, and HR 1366, mentioned above.

Commodity Futures Trading Commission

The House in January 2017 passed legislation to reauthorize the Commodity Futures Trading Commission (CFTC), nearly four years after legislative authority had expired for the regulator of the futures trading and derivatives market. Legislation failed to move in the Senate, however. Meanwhile, the Senate did confirm nominees to fill all seats on the five-member commission, which had been operating without a full slate for several years.

BACKGROUND

Congress called for the creation of the independent agency under the Commodity Futures Trading Commission Act of 1974 (PL 93-264) to replace the Commodity Exchange Authority. While its predecessor regulated only agricultural commodities, the CFTC was granted jurisdiction over futures trading in all commodities and later its charter was expanded to encompass derivatives.

The Dodd-Frank Financial Reform and Consumer Protection Act (PL 111-203) expanded CFTC's oversight of over-the-counter derivatives known as swaps. The commission also oversees industry regulatory groups and the registration of futures commission brokers, floor traders, commodity pool operators, and commodity training advisers.

Congress had last reauthorized the agency's charter in 2008. Since that reauthorization expired at the end of fiscal 2013, Congress had tried but failed to clear another reau-

thorization measure. The CFTC continued to operate under expired authorization and received annual funding through the appropriations process.

House Action

On January 12, 2017, the House voted 239–182 to pass a measure (HR 238) that would reauthorize the Commodity Futures Trading Commission through fiscal 2021 and to make changes to the 2010 financial services law to clarify the CFTC's authority to regulate derivatives and swaps. The measure was not taken up by the Senate.

One Republican, Walter B. Jones of North Carolina, crossed party lines to vote against the bill, while seven Democrats joined the GOP in voting for the measure. The Democrats included Sanford D. Bishop Jr. of Georgia, Henry Cuellar of Texas, Josh Gottheimer of New Jersey, Scott Peters of California, David Scott of Georgia, Kyrsten Sinema of Arizona, and Tom Suozzi of New York. Libertarian Justin Amash and independent Paul Mitchell of Michigan also voted for the measure.

Republicans said the bill aimed to ensure that the CFTC did not impose burdensome rules on some "end users" of derivatives, treating farmers and utilities, for instance, as if they were swap dealers. The bill also would require the CFTC to complete cost-benefit analyses of proposed rules. Democrats, including House Agriculture ranking member Collin C. Peterson of Minnesota, said the measure was part of the Republicans' effort to weaken the 2010 financial overhaul law.

Before passing the bill, the chamber rejected, in a 190–235 vote, a Democratic motion to recommit the bill. Democrats in both chambers raised concerns about a proposed flat, multiyear funding level for the commission and exemptions for some regulations. The measure set annual CFTC funding at $250 million a year through fiscal 2021, level with the amount provided in fiscal 2015 and fiscal 2016 and included in the fiscal 2017 continuing resolution (PL 114-100).

The House voted 236–191 to adopt an amendment by Agriculture Chairman K. Michael Conaway of Texas that would rescind provisions in existing law that detailed how the CFTC could limit excessive speculation. Conaway said the amendment aimed to clarify that the commission could impose position limits if the commission determined, before changing requirements, that the new limits were necessary.

The House adopted several other amendments by voice vote, including a proposal by Rep. Austin Scott, R-Ga., that would limit funding for CFTC's Customer Protection Fund to no more than $50 million per year. Members also gave voice vote approval to an amendment by Sean P. Duffy, R-Wisc., that would require the agency to obtain a subpoena before compelling companies or individuals to give the agency algorithmic trading source codes or other intellectual property.

Confirmation

On June 29, 2017, the Senate Agricultural Committee voted 16–5 to approve the nomination of Christopher Giancarlo as chair of the CFTC. Giancarlo, a former executive vice president of the financial services firm GFI Group Inc., had been serving as acting chairman since former Chair Timothy Massad left in January.

On August 2, 2017, the committee approved Dawn DeBerry Stump, Rostin (Russ) Behnam, and Brian D. Quintenz to serve on the board. Behnam, a Democratic nominee, had served as senior counselor and aid to ranking member Sen. Debbie Stabenow, D-Mich., for six years. Quintenz, a Republican nominee, had won committee approval in September 2016 but the full Senate did not act on the nomination before the end of the session. Quintenz previously had operated his own commodity hedge firm, Saeculum Capital Management LLC, and served as a senior policy advisor for then-Rep. Deborah Pryce, R-Ohio. Stump, a Republican nominee for CFTC, was a former executive director of the Americas Advisory Board for the Futures Industry Association and had served as a staff member for the Senate Agriculture Committee.

The Senate on August 3 unanimously confirmed the nominations of Quintenz and Behnam, as well as the nomination of Giancarlo to serve as chair. Stump's nomination, however, was held until Trump put forward another Democratic nominee.

On July 31, 2018, the Senate Agriculture Committee approved, by voice vote, the nomination of Dan M. Berkovitz to serve on CFTC. The former general counsel for CFTC had left the commission in 2013 to become a partner and cochair of the futures and derivatives practice at Wilmer Cutler Pickering Hale and Dorr. On August 28, the Senate confirmed the nominations of Stump and Berkovitz, filling the final seats on the five-member panel.

2019–2020

The Democratic House during the 116th Congress passed a measure to reverse regulatory changes made at the Consumer Financial Protection Bureau while it was under the control of Office of Management and Budget Director Mick Mulvaney, as well as his successor at the bureau. The GOP Senate did not act on the measure.

House and Senate leaders, however, found agreement in a few other areas. Congress cleared a seven-year reauthorization of the Terrorism Risk Insurance Program, sending the measure to the president's desk one year before the existing authorization was set to expire. Lawmakers also cleared for the president's signature a measure that would force securities exchanges to delist companies that refuse to provide annual audits to U.S. regulators. The measure was an effort by lawmakers to delist many Chinese companies.

Congress also cleared legislation that was intended to bar the creation of anonymous shell companies that hide illicit financial activities, such as those of tax evaders, traffickers, and counterfeiters. The Senate, however, did not take up a House-passed measure that aimed to clearly define "insider trading," or a House-passed resolution that would have reversed the administration's easing of Community Reinvestment Act rules that barred a discriminatory lending practice among banks known as "redlining."

Consumer Financial Protection Bureau

The House in 2019 passed a bill (HR 1500), which the Senate did not take up, that aimed to reverse many regulatory changes made at the Consumer Financial Protection Bureau (CFPB) under Mick Mulvaney, the director of the Office of Management and Budget who took over the CFPB as acting director in November 2017 after the departure of the bureau's first director. Kathy Kraninger, the associate director for general government at OMB, became CFPB director in 2018 and made further changes. The Supreme Court subsequently ruled that the bureau's structure, with a single director who could only be removed "for cause" and not at the president's discretion, violated the constitutional doctrine of separation of powers.

Since the CFPB was created by the Dodd-Frank law (PL 111-203), financial industry representatives and conservatives had complained about its stiff regulatory oversight and criticized its former chair, Richard Cordray, as overzealous. Democrats complained when Mulvaney unraveled several CFPB rules and charged that morale at the agency had dropped. In the year after Mulvaney took over as acting director in November 2017, the bureau had lost more than 100 employees and enforcement actions had declined 75 percent, according to *The Washington Post*.

House Financial Services Chair Maxine Waters, D-Calif., introduced the bill on March 6, 2019. Among its provisions, the bill would

- Require that data on consumer complaints be made public, reversing changes by Mulvaney that had reduced the scope of public reports
- Reinstitute memoranda of understanding, which had been terminated in 2017, between CFPB and the Department of Education on data sharing and collaboration on complaint response
- Reestablish the Office of Students and Young Consumers, which Mulvaney had combined with the Office of Financial Education
- Restore the enforcement powers of the Office of Fair Lending and Equal Opportunity, which Mulvaney had eliminated
- Limit cost-benefit analyses of proposed rules to exclude the enforcement costs from the equation, which Mulvaney required be included
- Limit political appointees to a number equivalent to that of other federal agencies

The bill would leave untouched some other changes at CFPB, including a move by Kraninger to suspend a finalized rule that would have required payday lenders to prove that their customers could repay a loan before issuance.

While Democrats said the measure would reverse anti-consumer changes made at CFPB by Mulvaney, Republicans said it was a political attempt to undercut efforts to increase agency transparency. On March 28, the House Financial Services Committee voted 34–26, along party lines, to approve the bill. The House on May 22 passed the measure by a party line vote of 231–191.

Before passing the measure, the House, by a vote of 235–193, approved an amendment by Rep. Al Green, D-Texas, that would require the bureau to reissue the 2017 rule barring financial companies, such as credit card companies, from including in contracts clauses that require consumers to use arbitration rather than class-action lawsuits to resolve complaints. The House also adopted, by voice vote, an amendment by Rep. Rashida Tlaib, D-Mich., that would require the bureau to report quarterly to Congress on payday loans and car-title loans, including the number of investigations and enforcement actions. The chamber voted 190–234 to reject an amendment by Bryan Steil, R-Wisc., that would have required the Government Accountability Office to study the CFPB's effectiveness in meetings its statutory mandates.

CFPB DIRECTOR

Trump had appointed Mulvaney as CFPB acting director in November 2017 to temporarily replace the agency's first director, Richard Cordray, who had been appointed by

President Obama. Cordray resigned under intense criticism from conservatives and Trump allies. Mulvaney subsequently slowed regulatory initiatives at the bureau and halted several enforcement actions. Democrats said Mulvaney's appointment was against the law, as the CFPB's deputy director should have been named acting director until the Senate approved a nominee.

On June 18, 2018, Trump nominated Kraninger as director of the agency. On August 23, the Senate Banking Committee approved her nomination to a five-year term on a party line vote. The Senate confirmed her nomination in a party line, 50–49 vote on December 6, 2018. Republicans said Kraninger's OMB experience qualified her for the job, but Democrats complained that she had no financial industry regulation experience.

SUPREME COURT CASE

On October 18, 2019, the Supreme Court said it would hear a case, *Seila Law LLC v. Consumer Financial Protection Bureau*, challenging how Congress structured the CFPB and whether its statute unconstitutionally impedes the president's authority because the independent agency has a single director who can only be fired for cause.

The Supreme Court said it also would decide if it could strike down the section of the Dodd-Frank law that bars the president from firing the director at will. Seila Law LLC, a law firm that was under CFPB investigation, issued the challenge. The firm said the president's ability to remove federal officers helps keep them accountable. The House filed a brief in the case asking to defend the law.

On June 29, 2020, the court ruled, in a 5–4 decision, that the bureau's structure, with a single director who could only be removed from office for cause, violated the separation of powers doctrine of the U.S. Constitution.

Republicans had long desired to replace the independent director of CFPB with either a five-member board like the SEC or with an administration official serving at the president's will. In 2017, the House had passed such a bill, but it stalled in the Senate.

Terrorism Risk Insurance Program

Congress in December 2019 cleared a measure providing a seven-year reauthorization of the Terrorism Risk Insurance Program (TRIP), which helps large companies, colleges, stadiums, and other businesses cover the risk of a foreign or domestic terrorism attack. The program's previous authorization (PL 114-1) was set to expire the following year, December 2020. The latest measure would extend the authorization through 2027.

BACKGROUND

Congress created the Terrorism Risk Insurance Program (PL 107-297) in 2002, shortly after the September 11, 2001, terrorist attacks, to address concerns that insurers might stop providing property and casualty insurance without government protection for potential costs related to such attacks. Some observers said affordable terrorism risk insurance was needed to ensure large real estate development deals moved forward.

Subsequent reauthorizations of the program reduced the government's potential share of losses, although in 2007 lawmakers increased the program's scope to include domestic terrorism.

House Action

The House Financial Services Committee approved a reauthorization bill (HR 4634) for TRIP in a 55–0 vote on October 31, 2019. The bill would reauthorize the program for seven years.

Chair Maxine Waters, D-Calif., initially proposed a ten-year reauthorization, but later agreed to reduce the term to seven years. Ranking member Patrick McHenry, R-N.C., said he wanted to update the deal to cover cyber terrorism attacks. Waters included in the measure a provision requiring the Government Accountability Office (GAO) to study whether the program adequately covered such risks. On November 18, the House passed the measure by a vote of 385–22.

Senate Action

The Senate Banking Committee on November 20, 2019, gave voice vote approval to a measure (S 2877) to reauthorize TRIP for seven years. The measure was authored by Sens. Thom Tillis, R-N.C., and Tina Smith, D-Minn.

Sen. Jack Reed, D-R.I., offered but later withdrew an amendment that would have called on GAO to study how well the insurance program addressed nuclear, biological, chemical, or radiological attacks, none of which are explicitly identified in the statute.

Final Action

House and Senate conferees on a fiscal 2020 omnibus spending bill (HR 1865) agreed to include provisions from Waters' seven-year reauthorization bill (HR 4624). The House passed the omnibus bill on December 17, 2019, in a 297–120 vote. The Senate cleared the bill by a 71–23 vote on December 19. President Trump signed the measure into law (PL 116-94) on December 20.

Accountability of Foreign Companies

On December 3, 2020, the House, by voice vote, cleared legislation (S 945) that would force securities exchanges to delist companies that refuse to provide annual audits to U.S. regulators. The measure targeted many Chinese companies.

U.S. regulators had long been concerned about certain Chinese companies that refused to allow access to their audits for the Public Company Accounting Oversight Board, which was created by the Sarbanes-Oxley Act (PL 107-204) to audit public companies whose shares are

traded in the United States. The law came in the wake of high-profile accounting fraud scandals, such as those involving Enron Corporation, an energy company based in Houston that subsequently declared bankruptcy in 2001, and WorldCom, a long-distance telephone company, in 2002.

At the time, more than 200 Chinese companies—thirteen of them state owned—were listed on U.S. exchanges and had market value totaling $2.2 trillion.

The bill, authored by Sen. John Kennedy, R-La., did not specify Chinese companies. But the measure would require securities exchanges to delist public companies if they had denied regulators access to audits for three consecutive years and if they do not certify to the Securities and Exchange Commission that they are not owned by a foreign government. Chinese companies, even if they were not subject to an audit inspection, would have to report the percentage of shares owned by government entities, information about board members who are officials in the Chinese Communist Party, and other information about government connections.

The Senate had passed the measure by unanimous consent on May 20. The president signed the bill into law (PL 116-222) on December 18, 2020.

EXECUTIVE ORDER

Trump took the additional action, on November 20, 2020, of issuing an executive order banning U.S. investments in companies with ties to the Chinese military. The order would be effective January 11, 2021, and applied to thirty-one companies and their subsidiaries that the Department of Defense had already identified.

SHELL COMPANIES

Congress in December 2020 cleared legislation aimed at putting an end to anonymous shell companies that can hide the financial activities of tax evaders, traffickers, and counterfeiters.

For years, members of both parties had sought to crack down on money laundering, particularly after a report by the United Nations, which was confirmed by the Department of the Treasury, that about $300 billion in illicit proceeds had flowed through the U.S. financial system in 2010. Much of the money flowed through corporate entities, which could be easily created in some states and could allow for the creation of foreign-held subsidiaries without revealing their owners. Federal regulators and investigators had difficulty tracking owners and executives of such subsidiaries.

During the 116th Congress, leaders of both parties in the House and Senate negotiated for months on a potential measure. Each chamber began moving measures with bipartisan support, but attentions were diverted with the coronavirus pandemic and related economic issues in 2020. Proponents of the measure then looked for a vehicle on which to attach language addressing shell companies.

In December, House and Senate negotiators on a fiscal 2021 defense authorization measure (HR 6396) agreed to include provisions that would create a corporate ownership reporting regime and make changes to various anti-money laundering laws.

The measure would require new entities to provide the Treasury Departments Financial Crimes Enforcement Network (FinCEN) with names, birthdates, addresses, and passport or driver's license numbers of anyone owning more than 25 percent of a company or exercising control. Any changes in ownership would have to be reported within a year. The measure would not affect highly regulated companies or those with more than twenty employees and more than $5 million in revenue. The measure also would increase staffing at FinCEN and encourage collaboration between FinCEN and the Justice Department.

The House passed the measure (HR 6396) on December 8 by a 335–78 vote. The Senate cleared the measure on December 11 by an 84–13 vote. The president vetoed the defense authorization measure—in a political maneuver focused on economic relief checks during the coronavirus pandemic—on December 23. The House on December 28 voted 322–87 to override the president's veto. The Senate voted 81–13 on January 1, 2021, to enact the measure into law (PL 116-283).

Insider Trading

The House in 2019 passed a measure, authored by Connecticut Democrat Jim Himes, that aimed to create a clear standard for courts and markets to identify "insider trading." The Republican-controlled Senate did not take up the measure.

Congress had never formally defined *insider trading*, a practice of using non-public information when trading stocks or other securities. No statute bars corporate insiders from using nonpublic information to gain an advantage when trading securities. Instead, the term is a judicial concept that was developed from decades of legal rulings and derived from the Securities and Exchange Commission's general rule barring fraud.

Himes' measure (HR 2534) was similar to a bill he had introduced in 2015 after a U.S. Court of Appeals for the 2nd Circuit issued a decision that narrowed the applicability of the insider trading concept. Insider trading generally was barred when applied only to information that was misappropriated, such as when an employee used company secrets to buy stocks or tip off another trader. The 2014 decision said the government had to prove that the individual supplying the information was gaining a personal benefit. But the ruling did not clarify "personal benefit." The decision, in effect, made it harder to prove insider trading, according to experts.

Himes said the bill's new test would reflect the Supreme Court's holding in *Salman v. US. Supreme Court* that the person who provided the tip did not necessarily have to be

paid. The court also said that the receiver of the information did not have to be limited to friends or family.

Himes' bill, as it was introduced, would bar trading when "in possession" of insider information, that is, non-public information. On May 8, 2019, the House Financial Services Committee adopted the bill by voice vote. Debate, however, revealed a split between Himes and the Republicans. Himes agreed to continue negotiations with the committee's ranking member, Patrick T. McHenry, R-N.C., before the bill was put on the floor.

Just before the House Rules Committee considered rules for floor debate, Himes said he had negotiated some language changes with McHenry. Among other changes, Himes agreed to tweak the bill so that it would bar trading while an individual is "aware" of insider information, rather than "in possession" of insider information. To appease Republicans, Himes also included a provision to give safe harbor for trades pursuant to prewritten, automatic trading plans.

On December 5, the House passed the bill by a vote of 410–13, with independent Justin Amash of Michigan and twelve Republicans voting against it.

Commodity Futures Trading Commission

On October 30, 2019, the House Agriculture Committee approved a bill (HR 4895) to reauthorize the Commodity Futures Trading Commission through 2025. However, the measure was not considered on the floor and the independent agency, which oversees trading of futures and derivatives, continued to operate under an authorization that expired in 2018.

Meanwhile, the Senate on June 5, 2019, in an 85–9 vote, confirmed the nomination of Heath P. Tarbert to be a member and chair of the CFTC.

The Senate Agriculture Committee on April 1 gave voice vote approval to the nomination of Tarbert, who was serving as Treasury Department assistant secretary for international markets. Tarbert, a lawyer, previously had served as special counsel to the Senate Banking Committee, as associate counsel to President George W. Bush and as a clerk for Supreme Court Justice Clarence Thomas. Tarbert, whose term would expire April 13, 2024, would replace J. Christopher Giancarlo as chair. Giancarlo's term ended in April.

Community Reinvestment Act Rule

Democrats pushed through the House in 2020 a resolution to reverse the Trump administration's rewrite of rules for evaluating banks' lending and investment practices in low- and moderate-income communities which had been in place since 1995. However, the effort failed in the Senate.

Under the Community Reinvestment Act (CRA) of 1977 (PL 95-128), federal regulators can monitor banks' lending and investment in such communities and can halt mergers and other expansion plans if the banks receive low grades in that regard. The Comptroller of the Currency Joseph Otting released revised rules in May 2020 to make it easier for banks to prove they are making such investments, allowing the banks to use simplified, quantitative tests.

BACKGROUND

The CRA required federal regulators to evaluate how well banks meet the credit needs of the entire community—including low- and moderate-income neighborhoods—where they are located. Congress enacted the law with the aim to end a decades-old practice known as "redlining," in which banks would refuse to insure mortgages in certain lower-income neighborhoods that they would outline in red on maps. The practice in effect favored white families and discriminated against African Americans and other people of color, leaving them out of new suburban communities.

Regulators could not take enforcement actions against a bank for not complying with the rules, but they could consider the bank's practices when it applied for approval to expand its operations. Banks had often complained the rules were difficult to comply with and were subjective. Other critics said the emphasis on investing in lower-income areas had inadvertently encouraged "gentrification" of areas. Further, the rules were written before the growth of online and mobile banking, which increasingly resulted in no geographic link between a bank's offices and the communities they served.

In December 2019, Otting's office released a proposed rule that would ease the burden on banks by requiring them to only show a "significant portion" of their assessment area received a satisfactory rating for its lending and investment practices. Otting said that under the proposal, bank examiners would review all of a bank's assessment areas, not just a sampling. He said that, given a higher burden, banks should have leeway for underperforming in certain areas.

The rule also would create a new compliance assessment area for digital banks with few or no branches. Otting said the revised rules would encourage banks and savings associations to invest and provide more services in the communities that they serve, including distressed neighborhoods. But community groups said the revised rules would weaken the CRA and its intent.

On May 20, 2020, the OCC issued a final rule that would be phased in, beginning October 1, 2020, before it took full effect on January 1, 2023, for large banks, and on January 1, 2024, for small and medium-size banks. The final rule said a bank would have to receive a satisfactory rating in 50 to 80 percent of its assessment areas. The percentage differed based on the number of assessment areas for the bank.

The rules were finalized over the objections of community banks and without the approval of the Federal Reserve

for the Federal Deposit Insurance Corporation (FDIC). The FDIC had initially joined in the proposal, but indicated on May 20 it was not ready to proceed with the finalized rule. Therefore, the rule would apply to national banks and savings associations, which the OCC oversees. The FDIC oversees state-chartered banks that are not part of the Federal Reserve system.

CONGRESSIONAL ACTION

House Financial Services Chair Maxine Waters, D-Calif., on June 11 introduced a resolution (HJ Res 90) that would block the new community reinvestment rules for the banks. Under the 1996 Congressional Review Act (PL 104-121), Congress can vote to rescind agency rules within sixty legislative days.

On June 29, 2020, the House voted 230–179, along party lines, to pass the resolution. The president threatened to veto the measure if Congress cleared it. On October 19, the Senate rejected the joint resolution (HJ Res 90) in a 43–48 vote that fell almost entirely along party lines. Susan Collins of Maine was the only Republican to vote for the measure.

LAWSUIT

On June 25, 2020, the National Community Reinvestment Coalition and the California Reinvestment Coalition filed a lawsuit against the Comptroller of the Currency for unlawfully changing the anti-redlining rules created under the Community Reinvestment Act. The lawsuit said the rule "guts the Act and eviscerates the backing it provides to the low- and moderate income . . . communities and communities of color that have long suffered from discrimination by financial institutions."

On August 31, the Trump administration filed a motion to dismiss the lawsuit. On January 29, 2021, the U.S. District Court in the Northern District of California denied the petition.

Chronology of Action on Budget and Tax Policy

The 2016 election of Republican Donald Trump and continued GOP control of both the chambers during the 115th Congress gave Republicans an opportunity to try to alter priorities in federal spending and overhaul the U.S. income tax code. As in previous years, however, Democrats and Republicans repeatedly fought about the budget and delayed passage of appropriations measures, keeping the government running through stopgap funding bills or allowing the government to shut down entirely. Republicans and the administration pushed for increased defense spending, but most conservatives were not willing to go along with drastic funding cuts that President Trump proposed for the social safety net, including Medicare and food stamps, as well as for education funding and other areas of the budget.

When the 115th Congress started, a major portion of the government was being funded by a continuing resolution because lawmakers the previous year had not wrapped up fiscal 2017 appropriations. But first the GOP-led House and Senate adopted a budget resolution to pave the way to fast-track a bill to repeal the 2010 health care law—an effort that ultimately failed. They were more successful in 2017 in clearing a tax overhaul package, another long-term goal of Republicans and a top item on President Trump's agenda.

Congress also approved bills to raise the discretionary spending caps and avoid the across-the-board federal spending cuts that would have been imposed as the result of a 2011 deficit reduction law. That allowed lawmakers to reject many of the spending cuts Trump requested, but negotiations still became tangled by the president's mandate for billions in funding for a new wall along the U.S.–Mexico border, Democrats' request to provide continued protection from deportation for immigrants brought to the United States as children by their parents,

and a series of other policy issues. For fiscal 2017 and 2018 appropriations, lawmakers ultimately resorted to clearing omnibus spending bills after keeping the government running via a series of stop-gap spending measures.

For fiscal 2019, leaders hoped for a return to a regular appropriations process, by which the chambers would approve individual spending bills for government departments and agencies. But disagreements, again over the border wall funding and other issues, impeded completion of seven of the bills and led to a partial government shutdown that lasted into January 2019.

Shortly after Congress cleared two minibus spending measures to fund the government in fiscal 2020, lawmakers had to grapple with how to help citizens and businesses amid the COVID-19 pandemic. Deaths resulting from the coronavirus began to increase, unemployment rose, schools and businesses closed their doors amid local and state government mandates that people remain home and quarantine. Congress began clearing billions in funding for health care services, research, unemployment, small business loans, and more.

The fiscal 2021 appropriations process was significantly delayed as Congress focused on clearing the series of COVID-relief packages. Once work began on the spending measures, controversies over the president's funding requests as well as over Democratic policy riders to address police reform, social justice, and other issues further complicated the process. Lawmakers ultimately cleared a series of five stopgap-funding measures to keep the government running beyond the 2020 presidential and congressional elections. In December, Congress cleared a $1.4 billion omnibus spending package encompassing all twelve appropriations bills as well as another package of COVID-relief measures.

Table 2.1 Federal Budget, Fiscal 1964–Fiscal 2020 (Millions of Dollars)

Year	Revenues	Outlays	On-Budget Surplus or Deficit	Social Security	Total Surplus or Deficit	Public Debt
1964	112.6	118.5	−6.5	0.6	−5.9	256.8
1965	116.8	118.2	−1.6	0.2	−1.4	260.8
1966	130.8	134.5	−3.1	−0.6	−3.7	263.7
1967	148.8	157.5	−12.6	4.0	−8.6	266.6
1968	153.0	178.1	−27.7	2.6	−25.2	289.5
1969	186.9	183.6	−507	3.7	3.2	278.1
1970	192.8	195.6	−8.7	5.9	−2.8	283.2
1971	187.1	210.2	−26.1	3.0	−23	303.0
1972	207.3	230.7	−26.1	2.7	−23.4	322.4
1973	230.8	245.7	−15.2	0.3	−14.9	340.9
1974	263.2	269.4	−7.2	1.1	−6.1	343.7
1975	279.1	332.3	−54.1	0.9	−53.2	394.7
1976	298.1	371.8	−69.4	−4.3	−73.7	477.4
1977	355.6	409.2	−49.9	−3.7	−53.7	549.1
1978	399.6	458.7	−55.4	−3.8	−59.2	607.1
1979	463.3	504.1	−39.6	−1.1	−40.7	640.3
1980	517.1	590.9	−73.1	−0.7	−73.8	711.9
1981	599.3	678.2	−73.9	−5.1	−79.1	789.4
1982	617.8	745.7	−120.6	−7.4	−128.1	924.6
1983	600.6	808.4	−207.7	−0.1	−207.8	1,137.3
1984	666.4	851.9	−185.3	−0.1	−185.4	1,307.1
1985	734.0	946.4	−221.5	9.2	−212.3	1,507.3
1986	769.2	990.4	−237.9	16.7	−221.2	1,740.6
1987	854.3	1,004.1	−168.4	18.6	−149.7	1,889.8
1988	909.2	1,064.5	−192.3	37.1	−155.2	2,051.6
1989	991.1	1,143.8	−205.4	52.8	−152.6	2,190.7
1990	1,032.0	1,253.0	−277.6	56.6	−221.0	2,411.6
1991	1,055.0	1,324.2	−321.4	52.2	−269.2	2,689.1
1992	1,091.2	1,381.6	−340.4	50.1	−290.3	2,999.7
1993	1,154.3	1,409.4	−300.4	45.3	−255.1	3,248.4
1994	1,258.6	1,461.8	−258.8	55.7	−203.2	3,433.1
1995	1,351.8	1,515.7	−226.4	62.4	−164	3,604.4
1996	1,453.1	1,560.5	−174.0	66.6	−107.4	3,734.1
1997	1,579.2	1,601.1	−103.2	81.4	−21.9	3,772.3
1998	1,721.7	1,652.5	−29.9	99.2	69.3	3,721.1
1999	1,827.5	1,701.8	1.9	123.7	125.6	3,632.4
2000	2,025.2	1,789.0	86.4	149.8	236.2	3,409.8
2001	1,991.1	1,862.8	−32.4	160.7	128.2	3,319.6
2002	1,853.1	2,010.9	−317.4	159.7	−157.8	3,540.4
2003	1,782.3	2,159.9	−538.4	160.8	−377.6	3,913.4
2004	1,880.1	2,292.8	−568.0	155.2	−412.7	4,295.5
2005	2,153.6	2,472.0	−493.6	175.3	−318.3	4,592.2
2006	2,406.9	2,655.1	−434.5	186.3	−248.2	4,829.0
2007	2,568.0	2,728.9	−342.2	181.5	−160.7	5,035.1
2008	2,524.0	2,982.5	−641.8	183.3	−454.6	5,803.1
2009	2,105.0	3,517.7	−1549.7	137.0	−1412.7	7,544.7
2010	2,162.7	3,457.1	−1371.4	77.0	−1294.4	9,018.9
2011	2,303.5	3,603.1	−1366.8	67.2	−1299.6	10,128.2
2012	2,450.2	3,537.1	−1148.9	61.9	−1087.0	11,281.1
2013	2,775.1	3,454.6	−719.0	39.5	−679.5	11,982.7
2014	3,021.5	3,506.1	−514.1	29.5	−484.6	12,779.9
2015	3,250.0	3,688.4	−465.8	27.3	−438.5	13,116.7
2016	3,268.0	3,852.6	−620.2	35.5	−584.7	14,167.7
2017	3,316.2	3,981.6	−714.9	44.1	−665.4	14,665.4
2018	3,329.9	4,109.0	−785.3	3.1	−779.1	15,749.6
2019	3,464.2	4,448.3	−991.8	2.5	−984.2	16,800.8
2020*	3,706.3	4,789.7	−1090.7	10.9	−1083.4	17,881.2

SOURCE: Executive Office of the President: Office of Management and Budget. Budget of the United States Government, Fiscal Year 2018, Historical Tables (Washington, DC: US Government Printing Office, 2018), Table 1.1; Social Security Administration. Old-Age, Survivors, and Disability Insurance Trust Funds, 1957–2021 (2022).

Table 2.2 Deficit History, 1929–2020 (Fiscal Years in billions of Dollars)

Fiscal Year	Receipts	Outlays	Surplus or Deficit (−)	Surplus/ Deficit as % of GDP
1929	$3.9	$3.1	$0.7	—
1933	2.0	4.6	−2.6	−4.5%
1939	6.3	9.1	−2.8	−3.2
1940	6.5	9.5	−2.9	−3.0
1945	45.2	92.7	−47.6	0.5
1950	39.4	42.6	−3.1	−1.1
1955	65.5	68.4	−3.0	−0.8
1960	92.5	92.2	0.3	−0.1
1965	116.8	118.2	−1.4	−0.2
1969	186.9	183.6	3.2	−0.3
1970	192.8	195.6	−2.8	−0.3
1975	279.1	332.3	−53.2	−3.4
1980	517.1	590.9	−73.8	−2.7
1981	599.3	678.2	−79.0	−2.6
1982	617.8	745.7	−128.0	−4.0
1983	600.6	808.4	−207.8	−6.0
1984	666.4	851.9	−185.4	−4.8
1985	734.0	946.4	−212.3	−5.1
1986	769.2	990.4	−221.2	−5.0
1987	854.3	1,004.1	−149.7	−3.2
1988	909.2	1,064.5	−155.2	−3.1
1989	991.1	1,143.8	−152.6	−2.8
1990	1,032.0	1,253.0	−221.0	−3.9
1991	1,055.0	1,324.2	−269.2	−4.5
1992	1,091.2	1,381.6	−290.3	−4.7
1993	1,154.3	1,409.4	−255.1	−3.9
1994	1,258.6	1,461.8	−203.2	−2.9
1995	1,351.8	1,515.7	−164.0	−2.2
1996	1,453.1	1,560.5	−107.4	−1.4
1997	1,579.2	1,601.1	−21.9	−0.3
1998	1,721.7	1,652.5	69.3	0.8
1999	1,827.5	1,701.8	125.6	1.4
2000	2,025.2	1,789.0	236.2	2.4
2001	1,991.1	1,862.8	128.2	1.3
2002	1,853.1	2,010.9	−157.8	−1.5
2003	1,782.3	2,159.9	−377.6	−3.4
2004	1,880.1	2,292.8	−412.7	−3.5
2005	2,153.6	2,472.0	−318.3	−2.6
2006	2,406.9	2,655.1	−248.2	−1.9
2007	2,568.0	2,728.9	−160.7	−1.2
2008	2,524.0	2,982.5	−458.6	−3.2
2009	2,105.0	3,517.7	−1412.7	−10.1
2010	2,162.7	3,457.1	−1294.4	−9.0
2011	2,303.5	3,603.1	−1299.6	−8.7
2012	2,450.2	3,537.1	−1087.0	−7.0
2013	2,775.1	3,454.6	−679.5	−4.1
2014	3,021.5	3,506.1	−484.6	−2.8
2015	3,250.0	3,688.4	−438.5	−2.4
2016	3,268.0	3,852.6	−584.7	−3.2
2017	3,316.2	3,981.6	−665.5	−3.5
2018	3,329.9	4,109.4	−779.1	−3.8
2019	3,464.2	4,448.3	−984.2	−4.6
2020*	3,706.3	4,789.7	−1083.4	−4.9

SOURCE: Executive Office of the President: Office of Management and Budget. Budget of the United States Government., Fiscal Year 2021, Historical Tables (Washington, DC: US Government Printing Office, 2020). Table 1.1, 1.3, 2.1, 2.2.

NOTE: GDP: Gross domestic product. *Estimate

Figure 2.1 Federal Budget Receipts

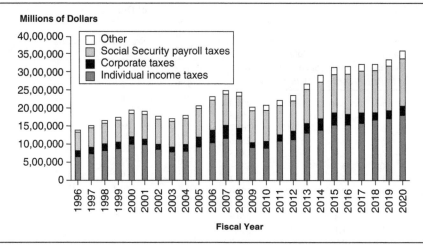

SOURCE: Office of Management and Budget: Historical Tables, Budget of the United States Government, Fiscal Year 2021 (Washington, DC: U.S. Government Printing Office, 2020), Table 2.1.

NOTE: * indicates estimate

2017–2018

When Congress opened in January 2017, the government was being funded under a continuing resolution developed by a lame-duck Congress after Trump's election as president.

As soon as the new Congress stepped into office, and before Trump was inaugurated, House and Senate Republicans adopted a fiscal 2017 budget resolution that paved the way, via the reconciliation process, to fast-track a measure to repeal President Obama's signature health care law of 2010. The repeal effort failed, however. Subsequently, Congress cleared a $1.07 trillion omnibus spending package, which the president signed into law even though the measure did not include his requested cuts to domestic programming, nor did it include funding for his promised wall along the U.S. border with Mexico.

The delay in fiscal 2017 funding measures contributed to a delay in considering fiscal 2018 appropriations bills, necessitating another series of stopgap funding measures to keep the government running. In October 2017, GOP leaders adopted a fiscal 2018 budget resolution, but only to activate the budget reconciliation process to enable them to fast-track a measure to overhaul the tax code as well as open the Arctic National Wildlife Refuge in Alaska to oil and gas drilling. That resulted in the first tax overhaul law since 1986 and the end of more than 60 years of federal protection for parts of the refuge.

Meanwhile, Congress in the second half of 2017 also cleared three supplemental funding measures to provide relief and recovery funds for communities damaged by hurricanes, wildfires, flooding, or other natural disasters. In February 2018, Congress cleared a two-year budget agreement that set new discretionary spending caps for fiscal years 2018 and 2019. The president had sought massive spending cuts to welfare programs and low-income assistance, but the new spending caps allowed Congress to reject most of his requests as it cleared a fiscal 2018 omnibus spending measure in March.

Lawmakers then hoped to get back on track and enact individual spending bills for fiscal 2019, but they had limited time for negotiations. Disagreements on the president's requested border wall funding and other issues again hampered progress. Failing to reach a deal on seven of the twelve spending bills, lawmakers and the president delayed completion of the appropriations process until the next Congress and allowed much of the government to shut down.

Fiscal Year 2017 Budget

The Republican-led House and Senate in January agreed to a fiscal 2017 budget resolution (S Con Res 3) that was primarily intended to pave the way to fast-track a measure to repeal the Affordable Health Care Act of 2010

Table 2.3 Growing Public Debt

The public debt is the amount owed to the public, American or foreign, through individual or institutional purchase of government securities such as bonds. The remainder of the federal debt is the amount the government has borrowed from government trust funds such as Social Security. The latter is an intragovernmental transaction but is still an obligation that must be paid someday and carries interest the same as debt owed to the general public.

		Public Debt (Millions of Dollars)		
Fiscal Year	Total Public Debt	As a % of GDP	Total Federal Debt	As a % of GDP
1990	$2,411.6	40.8%	$3,206.3	54.2%
1991	2,689.0	44.0	3,598.2	58.9
1992	2,999.7	46.6	4,001.8	62.2
1993	3,248.4	47.8	4,351.0	64.0
1994	3,433.1	47.7	4,643.3	64.5
1995	3,604.4	47.5	4,920.6	64.9
1996	3,734.1	46.8	5,181.5	64.9
1997	3,772.3	44.5	5,369.2	63.3
1998	3,721.1	41.6	5,478.2	61.2
1999	3,632.4	38.2	5,605.5	58.9
2000	3,409.8	33.6	5,628.7	55.5
2001	3,319.6	31.4	5,769.9	54.6
2002	3,540.4	32.5	6,198.4	57.0
2003	3,913.4	34.5	6,760.0	59.7
2004	4,295.5	35.5	7,354.7	60.8
2005	4,592.2	35.6	7,905.3	61.3
2006	4,829.0	35.3	8,451.4	61.8
2007	5,035.1	35.2	8,950.7	62.5
2008	5,803.1	39.3	9,986.1	67.7
2009	7,544.7	52.3	11,875.9	82.4
2010	9,018.9	60.9	13,528.8	91.4
2011	10,128.2	65.9	14,764.2	96.0
2012	11,281.1	70.4	16,050.9	100.1
2013	11,982.7	72.6	16,719.4	101.2
2014	12,779.9	74.2	17,794.5	103.3
2015	13,116.7	73.3	18,120.1	101.2
2016	14,167.7	77.0	19,539.4	106.1
2017	14,665.4	76.0	20,205.7	104.8
2018	15,749.6	77.4	21,462.3	105.5
2019	16,800.7	79.2	22,699.5	106.9
2020*	23,900.2	80.5	26,945.4	107.6

SOURCE: Executive Office of the President: Office of Management and Budget. *Budget of the United States Government, Fiscal Year 2021, Historical Tables* (Washington, DC: U.S. Government Printing Office, 2020), Table 7.1.

NOTE: GDP: Gross domestic product. * indicates estimate

(PL 111-148, PL 111-152). Measures to repeal the health care law, however, failed to clear Congress.

BACKGROUND

In February 2016, President Obama had released a $4.23 trillion budget request for fiscal 2017 which would be partly funded by an expected $3.64 trillion in revenue. White House officials estimated actual spending would total $4.15 trillion, resulting in an estimated deficit of

$503 billion. His ten-year budget was projected to cost $52.63 trillion between 2017 and 2026.

Congress, however, had been unable to complete its annual appropriations process, in part due to disagreements on discretionary spending caps. Lawmakers in 2015 had enacted a bipartisan two-year deal to partially roll back defense and non-defense sequestration cuts that had been required under the 2011 Budget Control Act (PL 112-25), but conservatives opposed the budget agreement's higher domestic spending caps for fiscal 2017 and Democrats opposed Republican efforts to hike defense spending. Lawmakers also disagreed on several policy riders attached to several appropriations bills.

BUDGET RESOLUTION

Immediately after the start of the 115th Congress, and before President-elect Donald Trump was sworn into office, House and Senate Republicans passed a fiscal 2017 budget resolution (S Con Res 3). Unlike typical budget resolutions, however, the blueprint for fiscal 2017 was moved only to activate the budget reconciliation process to repeal the 2010 health care law. GOP leaders planned to later develop a budget resolution for fiscal 2018.

Senate Action

Wyoming Republican Michael B. Enzi, chairman of the Senate Budget Committee, released a fifty-four-page fiscal 2017 budget blueprint (S Con Res 3) on the first day of the 115th Congress, January 3, 2017. The resolution, which recommended budget funding levels for fiscal years 2017 through 2026, was primarily a vehicle for Republicans to repeal Obama's 2010 signature health care law, the Affordable Care Act (PL 111-148, PL 111-152).

Republicans blamed the health care law for rising health care costs, a lack of choice for consumers, and high costs for small businesses. Democrats countered that the law had helped expand health care coverage and slow the increase in health care costs.

Under the fiscal 2017 resolution, two reserve funds would be created to preserve savings from the repeal, which Republicans leaders said would be used later to help cover the cost of replacement legislation. About $2 billion from the savings would be reserved for deficit reduction.

The measure's projected spending, revenue, and debt and deficit levels reflected existing baselines. The measure set budget authority for fiscal 2017 at $3.3 billion and fiscal 2018 at $3.35 billion, rising each year to $4.96 billion in fiscal 2026. Under the measure, deficits would rise to more than $1 trillion by fiscal 2026, and total federal debt would increase by more than $9 trillion to $29.1 trillion in fiscal 2026. The Obama White House criticized the GOP budget for sharply increasing the federal debt and making it easier to pass legislation that would increase the deficit.

The resolution's reconciliation instructions called for two committees in the House (the Ways and Means Committee and the Energy and Commerce Committee) and two in the Senate (the Finance Committee and the Health, Energy, Labor, and Pensions Committee) to write legislation by January 27 to repeal the 2010 health care law. The reconciliation process, permitted under the Congressional Budget Act of 1974, would allow for expedited consideration of budget-related legislation by barring the use of a Senate filibuster, limiting debate to twenty hours, and requiring a fifty-one-vote majority in the Senate for passage (rather than sixty votes). The legislation also asked each committee to find a way to reduce the deficit by at least $1 billion over ten years.

The Senate on January 11 voted 51–48 to adopt the budget resolution (S Con Res 3). Democrats opposed to repealing the health care reform law stood firm against the measure. Sen. Rand Paul of Kentucky was the only Republican to vote against the measure. Paul objected that the blueprint did not show a balanced budget at the end of ten years and that Republicans had not yet prepared a replacement for the 2010 health care law.

The chamber considered, and defeated, nineteen amendments before the final vote. Among the rejected amendments was a proposal by Sen. Joe Manchin, III, D-W.Va., that would have barred legislation aimed at reducing federal funding for rural hospitals or reducing insurance coverage in rural communities. The amendment was blocked by a 51–47 procedural vote that required sixty votes for approval. In a similar procedural vote of 48–50, senators barred an amendment by Wisconsin Democrat Tammy Baldwin that aimed to protect a provision in the health care law that allowed children to stay on their parents' health plan until age twenty-six.

Senators also voted 49–49 not to waive a budget point of order against an amendment by Sen. Bernie Sanders, I-Vt. Sanders said his proposal would have barred the Senate from breaking Trump's promise not to cut Social Security, Medicare, or Medicaid.

House Action

In the House, some conservative and moderate Republicans worried about repealing the 2010 health care law without a plan for a replacement. Leaders worked to assure them they would draft a replacement plan immediately.

On January 13, the House adopted the budget resolution (S Con Res 3) by a vote of 227–198. Eight Republicans voted against the resolution: Charlie Dent and Brian Fitzpatrick of Pennsylvania, Walter B. Jones of North Carolina, John Katko of New York, Raúl R. Labrador of Idaho; Tom MacArthur of New Jersey; Thomas Massie of Kentucky; and Tom McClintock of California. Libertarian Justin Amash of Michigan also voted against the resolution. Amash and several of the Republicans said they did not like that the blueprint projected rising deficits over the next ten years. Dent and other moderates wanted an alternative ready before Congress repealed the existing health care law.

Four members, all of whom had been tapped for positions in President-elect Trump's administration, did not

vote: Republicans Mike Pompeo of Kansas, Tom Price of Georgia, Ryan Zinke of Montana, and Mick Mulvaney of South Carolina.

President's Budget Request

President Trump, who was sworn into office on January 20, 2017, on March 16 proposed a $1.8 trillion budget for fiscal 2017. His proposal included several changes to President Obama's request, such as the following:

- Increasing defense spending by $30 billion to boost the fight against the Islamic State and begin replenishing Pentagon war accounts
- Increasing Department of Homeland Security spending by $3 billion, including $1.4 billion to begin construction on Trump's proposed U.S.–Mexico border wall
- Making $18 billion in unspecified reductions to non-defense discretionary spending, to offset the funding boosts.

The administration's ten-year plan would reduce spending by $5.6 trillion by cutting funding for Medicaid and welfare programs and assuming a planned tax overhaul would spur strong economic growth. The budget would add $3.2 trillion to the national debt over a decade, although the administration forecast a balanced budget by fiscal 2027.

Health Care Repeal

On May 4, 2017, the House passed, in a 217–213 vote, legislation (HR 1628) that would reduce federal Medicaid funding for states by $880 billion over ten years and change the 2010 health care law's protections for people who buy coverage on their own. The bill would make available about $115 billion for states to create "high risk" pools to mitigate high premiums. A Congressional Budget Office analysis concluded the underlying measure would cause 24 million Americans to lose insurance.

House Speaker Paul D. Ryan, R-Wisc., had pulled an earlier version from the floor on March 24 when leaders realized it did not have sufficient support. On July 28, 2017, the Senate rejected a repeal measure in a 49–51 vote. The measure had been offered as a substitute to the House-passed bill (HR 1628) to repeal the health care law. Senate Parliamentarian Elizabeth MacDonough determined that the reconciliation instructions expired September 30, which barred Republican leaders from attempting to move another measure aimed at repealing the health care law.

FISCAL 2017 APPROPRIATIONS

Continuing Resolution

When Congress opened in January 2017, the government was being funded under a continuing resolution (PL 114-254) developed by the Republican leadership of the previous Congress and cleared on December 5, 2016, after Trump's election as president. That measure, set to expire on April 28, 2017, was intended to provide time for the new president to set his mark on government spending.

Full-year appropriations for military construction and the Department of Veterans Affairs (PL 114-223) had been enacted in September 2016. The continuing resolution provided continuing appropriations for the rest of the government, totaling $1.163 trillion in discretionary spending. The measure also provided $10.1 billion in supplemental Overseas Contingency Operations (OCO) funding, considered war funding, for the Pentagon and other security-related accounts, and $4.1 billion in emergency supplemental funding for hurricane and flooding response efforts.

In addition, the measure provided $170 million to help the city of Flint, Michigan, whose drinking water had been contaminated by lead; $872 million for medical research and other activities under the Cures Act (PL 114-255), a 2016 law that aimed to accelerate the development of medical drugs and devices; and $45 million to enable coal miners' health plans to pay out their benefits.

Negotiations on the fiscal 2017 spending bills bogged down again in spring 2017 when the Trump administration pushed for funding to begin building a wall on the U.S.–Mexico border and Democrats requested funding for cost-reduction payments under the 2010 health care law, which they said were needed to help stabilize the insurance market for individuals. With government funding under the previous continuing resolution set to expire April 28, Congress cleared, and the president signed, another continuing resolution (HJ Res 99–PL 115-30) that extended funding through May 5.

Fiscal 2017 Omnibus

In May, Congress cleared and the president signed a $1.07 trillion fiscal 2017 omnibus spending package (HR 244, PL 115-31) to finance government operations through September 30, 2017. The final agreement did not include the president's proposed cuts to domestic programs, funding for the president's promised U.S.–Mexico border wall, or Democrats' requested funds to help stabilize the health insurance market for individuals.

The omnibus included $608 million for health benefits for retired coal miners, $296 million for Medicaid payments to Puerto Rico, and $298 million for veterans and military construction programs. The measure encompassed eleven annual spending measures (full-year appropriations for the Military Construction–Veterans Affairs bill had been enacted the previous September). The final measure also included an agreement reached on the fiscal 2017 intelligence authorization.

The House passed the omnibus spending bill (HR 244) by a vote of 309–118 on May 3. The vehicle for the omnibus spending measure was an unrelated Labor Department bill.

The Senate cleared the bill on May 4 by a vote of 79–18. Trump signed the measure into law on May 5.

Highlights. The spending measures in the package were consistent with the budget caps set in the two-year budget deal in November 2015. The omnibus provided about $1.16 trillion in discretionary spending, with $1.07 trillion subject to spending caps, $93.5 billion designated as OCO funds, and $8.2 billion for disaster and emergency spending. The omnibus included $15 billion more in defense spending and $1.5 billion more in border security spending than was included in a $30 billion supplementary budget request that Trump had submitted in March.

The following are highlights of the fiscal 2017 omnibus measure:

Agriculture. The measure provided $153.4 billion for the Department of Agriculture and the Food and Drug Administration (FDA), $13.5 billion more than in fiscal 2016. The measure included $38.4 billion for agriculture programs (a boost of $15.3 billion from 2016), almost all of which was for mandatory price support funding. Appropriators provided $108.1 billion for domestic food assistance programs. The FDA was provided $4.7 billion, a $22-million reduction from the previous fiscal year.

Commerce-Justice-State. Appropriators provided $56.6 billion—$2 million more than requested and $883 million above the fiscal 2016 level—for the portion of the omnibus covering the Commerce, Justice, and State department programs. The measure decreased funding for the Commerce and Justice departments while increasing funding for the National Science Foundation and NASA. The measure also included a provision barring the Justice Department from enforcing federal laws against marijuana in states that permit medical uses of the drug.

Defense. The omnibus boosted defense spending by $19.9 billion above the fiscal 2016 level to $593 billion, which was $16.3 billion more than former President Obama had requested. It included $516.1 billion in discretionary funding and $76.6 billion for OCO spending associated with the war in Afghanistan and other counterterrorism operations.

Energy-Water. The Energy Department and related agencies were allocated $37.8 billion in discretionary spending, $586 million more than in fiscal 2016. The agreement included $6 billion for the Army Corps of Engineers and $30.7 billion for the Energy Department, including $1.9 billion for Defense nuclear nonproliferation activities.

Financial Services. The financial services portion of the omnibus provided $42.9 billion for the Treasury and related financial agencies, including $21.5 billion in discretionary funding. The agreement maintained the fiscal 2016 funding for the IRS and included a provision

barring the IRS from targeting groups based on ideological beliefs, a response to two federal lawsuits filed by dozens of conservative groups that accused the IRS of targeting organizations whose names included such words as "Tea Party" or "patriots" when they applied for tax-exempt status. (The Justice Department reached a settlement with the groups in October 2017.)

Homeland Security. Appropriators provided the Department of Homeland Security $42.4 billion in discretionary funding subject to spending caps ($1.5 billion more than in fiscal 2016) and $7.3 billion for disaster recovery. The measure boosted funding for U.S. Customs and Border Protection by 8 percent, Immigration and Customs Enforcement by 10 percent, and the Transportation Security Administration by 7 percent, but reduced funding for the Coast Guard by 4 percent.

Interior-Environment. The omnibus included $32.2 billion in discretionary funding for the Department of Interior and the Environmental Protection Agency (EPA), including $12.3 billion for the Interior Department and $8.1 billion for the EPA. Funding for the EPA was 21 percent less than in 2010. The measure provided the National Park Service $2.9 billion, including funds to build the Dwight D. Eisenhower memorial near the National Mall in Washington, D.C.

Labor-HHS-Education. The measure included $161 billion in discretionary funding and $750.2 billion in mandatory funding for labor, health, and education programs and services. The Department of Health and Human Services received $780.2 billion, including a $2 billion increase for the National Institutes of Health. Congress provided $71.6 billion for the Department of Education and $13.7 billion for the Labor Department. The funding included about $801 million to fight opioid addiction, $650 million more than in fiscal 2016.

Legislative Branch. Appropriators included $4.4 billion for legislative branch operations, $77 million more than fiscal 2016 but $219 million less than offices and agencies requested. The measure continued a salary freeze for members of Congress.

State-Foreign Operations. The fiscal 2017 measure included $53.1 billion for foreign programs, including $36.6 billion in discretionary funding and $16.5 billion for programs related to the wars in Afghanistan, Syria, and Iraq and for such expenses as humanitarian aid for Syrian refugees in Jordan and Lebanon. The total included $8.7 billion for global health programs, $3.2 billion for military assistance for Israel, $1.4 billion in assistance for Egypt, $1.3 billion for Jordan, and $410 million for Ukraine.

Transportation-HUD. The omnibus included $57.7 billion in discretionary funding for the departments of Transportation and Housing and Urban Development

programs, $350 million more than in fiscal 2016 but $5.5 billion less than Obama's request. The measure also provided for the release of $57.7 billion from the highway and aviation trust funds for federal highway and aviation projects.

Fiscal Year 2018 Budget

PRESIDENT'S BUDGET REQUEST

President Trump on May 23, 2017, sent Congress a $4.1 trillion fiscal 2018 budget request. It would maintain discretionary spending at the cap of $1.065 trillion, set by the Budget Control Act (PL 112-25), by increasing defense spending by $54 billion and cutting nondefense spending by the same amount. The White House forecast balancing the budget in ten years, in part by assuming economic growth would increase, reaching 3 percent in fiscal 2021 and continuing with a steady increase through fiscal 2027.

White House Budget Director Mick Mulvaney said the budget would trim unnecessary spending and boost the economy with tax cuts and deregulation, reducing the deficit by $5.6 trillion over ten years. The budget proposed reducing base nondefense spending by $1.5 trillion over ten years.

The measure included billions in funding cuts to Medicaid; the Children's Health Insurance Program; Temporary Assistance for Needy Families, a basic welfare program; and the Supplemental Nutrition Assistance Program known as the food stamp program. Meanwhile, the budget proposed increasing mandatory spending by $25 billion over ten years to extend paid family leave, which would include six weeks of paid family leave for new parents. The program would require congressional approval.

The president also proposed requiring a Social Security Number to receive the earned income tax credit or child tax credit, and requested funding to build a wall along the U.S.–Mexico border.

The administration's proposal purported to balance the budget in ten years. The budget assumed more than $40 billion in deficit reduction would occur by repealing the 2010 financial services overhaul, known as the Dodd-Frank Financial Reform and Consumer Protection Act (PL 111-203), and restructuring the Consumer Financial Protection bureau, created by that law. Both were goals of conservative Republicans.

Democrats quickly criticized the plan for gouging domestic discretionary spending, cutting social safety net programs such as foods stamps and health care for children, and not detailing the president's tax plans. Republicans mostly praised the budget but were wary of political effects of cutting popular domestic programs.

Highlights of the President's Request

Highlights of the White House budget request for each department and agency included the following.

Agriculture. The administration requested about $21 billion in discretionary funding and $114 billion in mandatory funding for the Agriculture Department. The request was an $18.5 billion or 14 percent drop in mandatory funding from the fiscal 2017 level.

The request included $73.6 billion for the Supplemental Nutrition Assistance Program (SNAP), down from the $78.5 billion provided in fiscal 2017. SNAP provided food stamps for about 43 million low-income people. The White House proposed requiring states to pay about 25 percent of food stamp benefits to reduce the federal share for SNAP.

The administration also proposed capping crop insurance premium subsidies at $40,000 per farmer; limiting eligibility for commodity crop payments and federally subsidized crop insurance to producers who bring in $500,000 or less in adjusted gross income; and ending subsidies for the harvest price option for crop insurance.

Army Corps of Engineers. The president's budget would reduce funding for the Army Corps of Engineers by $976 million from the $6 billion funding level in fiscal 2017. The budget proposed a new annual fee for commercial barge operators on inland waterways to raise more than $1 billion over ten years, and proposed selling the Washington Aqueduct that supplies water for the District of Columbia and Northern Virginia.

The budget proposed spending $993 million from the Harbor Maintenance Trust Fund, down from annualized spending of $1.3 billion, even though the administration projected a $9 billion surplus in the fund at the beginning of fiscal 2018.

Defense. The administration proposed $603 billion in base defense spending and $65 billion for war accounts, for a total of $668 billion, exceeding defense base budget caps by $54 billion.

The request aimed to improve the U.S. military's readiness by providing $10.8 billion to purchase seventy F-35 Joint Strike Fighters for the Air Force, Navy, and Marine Corps and $1.3 billion to purchase fourteen F/A-18E/F Super Hornets for the Navy, $3.1 billion for fifteen KC-46 aerial refueling tankers, $1.4 billion for sixty-one AH-64 Apache attack helicopters, $1.1 billion for forty-eight UH-60 utility helicopters, and $1.6 billion for seven P-8 Poseidon anti-submarine aircraft. Other big program requests included $1.9 billion for the Evolved Expendable Launch Vehicle and $1.4 billion for the Space-Based Infrared System, among other equipment. The request also provided for a 2.1 percent pay raise for military personnel and funds to expand military strength by 56,400 troops.

Energy. The administration requested $28 billion for the Department of Energy, an estimated $2.8 billion cut from fiscal 2017. The Office of Energy Efficiency and Renewable Energy was targeted for a 70 percent budget

cut from 2017, to $636 million, and the budget for the Office of Science—which conducts a variety of research, from supercomputing to nuclear fusion—would see a $900 million cut to $4.5 billion. The budget proposed eliminating several programs, including the Advanced Research Projects Agency–Energy, the Department of Energy (DOE) Loan Program, the Weatherization Assistance Program, and the State Energy Program that helped low-income families reduce their heating bills.

The budget would provide an 8 percent funding increase, from $12.9 billion in fiscal 2017 to $13.9 billion, for nuclear weapons programs. The administration also planned to resurrect plans for the Yucca Mountain site in Nevada for nuclear waste storage, seeking $120 million for licensing the site while calling on Congress to allow DOE to move forward on an interim storage facility.

Education. Under the request, the Department of Education's discretionary funding would be reduced by 13.5 percent, from $68.2 billion to $59 billion. The proposal also included changes to mandatory higher education spending, eliminating subsidized student loans and public service loan forgiveness. The proposal called for the creation of a single income-driven student loan repayment plan and for some mandatory Pell funding to be reallocated to support year-round discretionary Pell Grants. The administration suggested the changes would reduce the federal deficit by just over $4 billion. The administration also proposed eliminating two Federal TRIO Programs (TRIO) higher education programs, programs that began with the Johnson administration's War on Poverty in the 1960s with the aim to help low-income individuals, first-generation college students, and students with disabilities succeed in education.

Environmental Protection Agency. The administration proposed $5.7 billion for the EPA in fiscal 2018 funding, $2.4 billion or 30 percent below the fiscal 2017 level of $8.1 billion. The budget would cut more than 50 EPA programs, zero-out funding for most programs addressing climate change, and eliminate nearly about 23,800 positions, about a quarter of the EPA workforce.

The budget also would eliminate funding for the Great Lakes Restoration Initiative, a program founded in 2010 to protect Lakes Superior, Michigan, Huron, Erie, and Ontario. The deep cuts proposed for the EPA angered Democrats as well as many Republicans.

Health and Human Services (HHS). The White House requested $69 billion for HHS, a $15.1 billion or 17.9 percent decrease from the 2017 level provided in the continuing resolution. The request included a $500 million increase above fiscal 2016 levels to address opioid abuse. The budget would decrease National Institutes of Health funding by $5.8 billion to $25.9 billion, and would eliminate $403 million in health professional and nursing training programs.

The president proposed to cut Medicaid funding by about 25 percent by 2027, reducing spending by an estimated $839 billion over a decade. The nonpartisan Congressional Budget Office, however, said such cuts would make another 14 million low-income Americans ineligible for Medicaid by 2016.

The president also proposed to cut the Supplemental Nutrition Assistance Program, or food stamps, by $193 billion over ten years, and to cut spending for the Children's Health Insurance Program by more than $5.8 billion over ten years. Trump's budget also would eliminate discretionary programs within the Office of Community Services, including the Low-Income Home Energy Assistance Program and the Community Services Block Grant, which cost $4.2 billion in fiscal 2017.

The budget assumed a savings of $250 billion over ten years through the repeal of the 2010 health care law (which Congress did not pass). In addition, the budget proposed wiping out the Social Services Block Grant to save $16.7 billion and the Temporary Assistance for Needy Families Contingency Fund to save $6 billion in ten years.

Federal spending on Medicare would be cut by $6 billion, or 1 percent, to $587 billion in fiscal 2018. Federal Medicaid spending would rise by $25.3 billion, or more than 6 percent to almost $404 billion in fiscal 2018.

Homeland Security. The budget would provide $44.1 billion for the Department of Homeland Security, a 4-percent increase from the $42.4 billion in the fiscal 2017 level. Customs and Border Protection would receive a 22 percent increase over fiscal 2017, to $13.9 billion, while Immigration and Customs Enforcement (ICE) would see a 19 percent boost, to $7.6 billion. The budget request also included $197 million for border surveillance technology and $100 million to hire and support 500 new agents for a Border Patrol force of 20,258 officers.

The budget request also included $1.5 billion for ICE to maintain 51,379 detention beds for immigrant detainees, a sharp increase from the existing 34,000. That total included $164 million for transportation costs expected from detaining more immigrants and $57 million more for ICE's Alternatives to Detention Program, which used technology and other tools to oversee immigrants' compliance with conditions for release.

The department budget request also included $1.6 billion to begin building a new U.S.–Mexico border wall envisioned by Trump. The funds would cover thirty-two miles of the new wall and twenty-eight miles of a new levee wall in the Rio Grande Valley of Texas, plus fourteen miles of replacement walls. Initially

Trump considered cutting Coast Guard funding to pay for the border wall and to hire more border agents, but dropped the idea in the face of congressional opposition. (The request called for a slight boost for the Coast Guard, to $8.75 billion from $8.63 billion in discretionary funds.)

The budget also would boost by $15 million, to $131.5 million, funding for E-Verify, a voluntary program that helps U.S. employers check applicants' or workers' immigration status. Trump requested another $90.6 million to finalize implementation of a biometric system to record the entry and exit of all foreign visitors.

The president's request would maintain the fiscal 2017 funding level of $7.32 billion for the Transportation Security Administration while dropping spending for the Federal Emergency Management Agency by 14 percent, to $10.5 billion in 2018. The president proposed a $50 million decrease in Secret Service funding, to $1.95 billion.

Housing and Urban Development. The budget would provide $40.7 billion for the Department of Housing and Urban Development in fiscal 2018, about 13.2 percent below the fiscal 2017 level of $46.9 billion. The White House proposal included requests to eliminate funding for the Community Development Block Grant program, the HOME Investment Partnerships Program (HOME), Choice Neighborhoods, and the Self-Help and Assisted Homeownership Opportunity Program. Combined, those programs received about $4.1 billion in fiscal 2017. The White House also proposed to reduce funding for rental assistance programs by $1.9 billion, to $35.2 billion for fiscal 2018. The request proposed to reduce funding for the Native American Housing Block Grant program from $654 million to $600 million and to eliminate the Indian Community Development Block Grant program.

Judiciary. The budget would provide the federal courts and staff about $7.2 billion in discretionary funds, up from $6.8 billion in fiscal 2017, in part to boost pay for personnel at courts and the federal public defender program. Salaries for court clerks and other support personnel would be funded at $5.2 billion, a $259 million increase. The Supreme Court would receive about $2 million more than the $76 million budgeted for fiscal 2017.

Labor. The budget proposal included $9.7 billion in discretionary funds for the Department of Labor, $2.4 billion less than in fiscal 2017. The proposal included the reduction or elimination of various worker training programs, reducing funding for adult training activities by $324 million or 40 percent, from $814 million to $490 million, and for youth training and employment programs by $392 million or nearly 40 percent, from $1 billion to $608 million.

For example, the administration proposed closing certain underperforming Job Corp centers and ending a program to help low-income senior citizens find work. Meanwhile, the administration said it would prioritize apprenticeships. The White House also said it would request $20 billion over ten years in mandatory spending to allow parents six weeks of paid leave after the birth or adoption of a child.

State. The budget would provide $37.6 billion for the State Department and foreign operations, $15.5 billion or 29 percent less than the fiscal 2017 level. Trump proposed to eliminate the Food for Peace Program, which had been budgeted at more than $1.7 billion for the first seven months of fiscal 2017; and about an 80 percent cut to the Migration and Refugee Assistance account, bringing that funding to $715 million.

The administration said it was "streamlining" spending for nutritional assistance by funding all emergency food aid through the International Disaster Assistance account. However, just $1.5 billion would be targeted for food aid. The administration also proposed eliminating international development assistance, which had been budgeted at $2.5 billion in the latest continuing appropriations measure (PL 114-254).

The budget proposed to eliminate about $1.6 billion in annualized funding for the Green Climate Fund and Global Climate Change Initiative, Obama-era funds created to help developing countries address the effects of global warming. The administration also sought to reduce funding by $2.2 billion or 89 percent for international peacekeeping activities connected to the United Nations (dropping the budget from $2.5 billion to $269 million). The White House sought $2 billion less for global health programs, which were funded at about $8.5 billion. The request included $5.6 billion for State and USAID to respond to threats from terrorist groups, and $1.1 billion to help shut down transnational criminal organizations.

Transportation. The budget request included $16.2 billion in discretionary spending for the Department of Transportation, 12.4 percent less than in fiscal 2017. The proposal included plans to cancel the $500 million Transportation Investment Generating Economic Recovery (TIGER) grant program, which was intended to help states and localities fund highways, bridges, transit programs, and other surface transportation infrastructure. The administration also proposed to cancel the $150 million Essential Air Service program, and to reduce by about 50 percent funding for grants to Amtrak from $1.4 billion to $774 million.

The request also reflected the president's support for a proposal by House Transportation and Infrastructure Chairman Bill Shuster, R-Pa., to remove air traffic control from the Federal Aviation Administration (FAA)

and spin it off to a private nonprofit. *(See Transportation chapter.)*

The administration's budget assumed taxes on airfares would end, thereby reducing aviation taxes by $115.6 billion from fiscal 2021 to 2027, but the blueprint did not indicate a replacement for those funds. The plan also projected to save $72.8 billion in Federal Aviation Administration (FAA) spending between 2021 and 2027. Additionally, the budget included $200 billion, to be spent between fiscal 2018 and 2026, to fund the president's infrastructure initiative aimed at incentivizing private investments in new highways, bridges, rail lines, and other transportation projects.

Treasury. Trump's proposal included $12.1 billion for the Treasury, a $600 million decrease from fiscal 2017. The president requested nearly $11 billion for the IRS in fiscal 2018, $260 million less than in fiscal 2017. The reduction reflected his proposal to cut more than 5,000 jobs at the agency. The agency's budget had become controversial since conservative groups alleged biased targeting in 2013.

Veterans Affairs. The White House requested $82.1 billion in discretionary funding for the Department of Veterans Affairs (VA), an increase of $4.3 billion or 6 percent from fiscal 2017. Total spending, including mandatory spending, would be $186.5 billion, with $75.2 billion provided for health care, according to the VA. Of that health care funding, $13.2 billion would be dedicated for the Veterans Choice Program, a program created by Congress in 2014 (PL 113-146) to help some veterans access private medical care for certain services.

The administration would cut back on a program that provides checks for disabled veterans who are considered unemployable, including barring checks to veterans once they reach retirement age. The White House estimated it would save about $40 billion from the change, another $2.7 billion by rounding down to the nearest dollar veterans' disability compensation checks, and another $500 million over ten years by capping GI Bill payments for flight school.

BUDGET RESOLUTION

In October 2017, the House and Senate agreed to a budget resolution (H Con Res 71) that was primarily intended to activate the budget reconciliation process to enable Republicans to fast-track a measure to overhaul the tax code—a priority of the Trump administration. The resolution allowed for a tax overhaul to result in a net tax cut that would add $1.5 trillion to the debt over ten years.

The measure also included reconciliation instructions to enable Republicans to move legislation to open the Arctic National Wildlife Refuge to oil and gas drilling. The resolution assumed $549 billion in defense discretionary spending, $516 billion in nondefense discretionary spending, and $2.5 million in mandatory spending in fiscal 2018. In

February 2018, the president signed a two-year budget deal (HR 1892 — PL 115-123) that raised the spending caps.

House Action

The House Budget Committee approved its version of the fiscal 2018 budget (H Con Res 71—H Rep 115-240) by a party line vote of 22–14 on July 19, 2017. The committee's blueprint capped discretionary spending at $621.5 billion for defense programs and $511 billion for non-defense programs. It also allowed for up to $75 billion in war funding for the military and $12 billion for the State Department and other civilian agencies. The budget provided reconciliation instruction for eleven authorizing committees to draft legislation to reduce the deficit by at least $203 billion over ten years. The measure was seen as a vehicle for advancing a major tax overhaul through reconciliation.

During the committee markup, Republicans rejected twenty-eight Democratic amendments, including an amendment by Barbara Lee of California that would have reduced the war funding to $65 billion to match the president's request. The amendment was defeated by a 16–19 vote.

The full House voted 219–206 to adopt the budget resolution on October 5, five days after the start of fiscal 2018. No Democrats voted for the plan, while eighteen Republicans opposed it.

The final measure called for a deficit-neutral tax bill.

Senate Action

The Senate Budget Committee on October 5 approved its fiscal 2018 budget resolution (S Con Res 25—S Rep 115-20) on a 12–11, party line vote, hours after the House approved its version. The resolution included reconciliation instructions for committees to craft tax overhaul legislation with no more than $1.5 trillion in revenue loss over ten years.

During the markup, members rejected an amendment by Rep. Angus King, I-Maine, that would have reinstated a 2007 rule, named for former Senate Budget Chairman Kent Conrad, D-N.D., that barred reconciliation legislation that would increase the deficit. The Senate GOP majority in 2015 had repealed the rule. Members also rejected an amendment by Democrats Tim Kaine of Virginia and Kamala Harris of California that would have reinstated a rule that required a Congressional Budget Office score on committee-reported legislation twenty-eight hours before members voted on it. The underlying budget resolution included a provision repealing the two-year-old rule.

The committee approved, 12–11, an amendment by Kaine that would specify that a tax bill would have to be "revenue-neutral" rather than "deficit-neutral," meaning that all cuts would have to be offset by eliminating other tax breaks. The committee approved an amendment by Rep. John Kennedy, R-La., to establish a deficit-neutral reserve fund that would help implement work requirements for certain recipients of welfare programs, not

including Social Security, Medicare, unemployment insurance, and workers' compensation.

The Senate on October 19, 2017, adopted the budget resolution in a 51–49 vote after amending it to satisfy House Republicans and avoid a conference negotiation. The amendment by Budget Chairman Mike Enzi, R-Wyo., eliminated reconciliation instructions for $203 billion in mandatory spending cuts and replaced the House's language calling for a deficit-neutral tax cut with language calling for a tax cut that could add up to $1.5 trillion to the deficit over ten years. The amendment was approved by a vote of 52–48. The change would enable the Ways and Means Committee to send a tax overhaul bill directly to the floor, bypassing the House Budget Committee.

The Senate-adopted budget was approved as an amendment to the House-passed resolution (H Con Res 71). The budget included reconciliation instructions for the House Energy and Natural Resources Committee to craft legislation to reduce the deficit by $1 billion, paving the way for a measure to sell oil and gas leases in the Arctic Wildlife Refuge Area in Alaska, which had been under federal protection for more than sixty years. The resolution also duplicated language in the House measure that would allow for an appropriations deal to raise the discretionary spending caps without their additional cost being offset.

GOP senators acknowledged the purpose of the budget was to set a path for a tax cut package through reconciliation, which would enable a tax measure to be approved by a simple majority in the Senate. The Senate rejected two amendments by Sen. Rand Paul, R-Ky. One amendment, rejected 5–95, would have cut $43 billion in discretionary spending in fiscal 2018 to match the estimated $43 billion in fiscal 2018 outlays for war funds. Senators also rejected, 4–94, Rand's amendment that would have added reconciliation instructions for nine committees to reduce the deficit or cut spending by $97.9 billion in fiscal 2018.

Final Action

On October 26, the House concurred with the Senate's changes to its resolution (H Con Res 71) in a 216–212 vote.

Major Provisions

Spending levels. The resolution assumed $2.5 trillion in mandatory spending in fiscal 2018, rising to $3.5 trillion in fiscal 2027 and totaling $29.6 trillion over the ten-year period. Interest on the debt would total another $5.2 trillion. Discretionary spending was set at $549 billion for defense spending and $516 billion for nondefense spending. The measure would allow another $77 billion for Overseas Contingency Operations funding and $7 billion for disaster relief.

Deficit and Debt Reduction. The resolution outlined $5.1 trillion in deficit reduction by reducing spending over ten years—including $4.3 trillion in savings from mandatory programs, $534 billion from nondefense discretionary spending, and $259 billion in reduced payments for interest on the debt. It assumed a $472 billion reduction in Medicare spending over ten years, as well as a $1.3 trillion reduction in spending for Medicaid and other health programs over the same time period.

The resolution also included instructions for a reserve fund that would be used to offset the cost of any legislation Congress cleared to repeal the 2020 health care law. In addition to the $5.1 trillion in spending reductions, the resolution said the deficit would be reduced another estimated $1.24 trillion as a result of "positive macroeconomic" policies. The budget assumed total debt would rise from $21.28 trillion at the end of fiscal 2018 to $26 trillion by the end of fiscal 2027. Debt held by the public would rise from $15.6 trillion to $20.78 trillion over those ten years, according to the blueprint.

Reconciliation and Tax Reform. The resolution instructed the House Ways and Means and Senate Finance committees to craft tax overhaul legislation that would add no more than $1.5 trillion to the deficit over a ten-year period. The resolution also called on the Senate Energy and Natural Resources Committee to craft a measure to reduce the deficit by at least $1 billion.

Disaster Relief

Congress in 2017 cleared three supplemental spending bills that provided more than $136.1 billion in disaster relief for states and communities impacted by hurricanes, wildfires, flooding, and more. Lawmakers exceeded the Trump administration's request by $54.4 billion or nearly 67 percent.

The first measure (HR 601—PL 115-56), cleared in September, provided $15.3 billion in fiscal 2017 supplementary funds. The second measure (HR 4008—PL 115-72), cleared in October, provided $36.5 billion in fiscal 2018 supplementary funds. The final measure (HR 1892—PL 115-123), cleared in February 2018, provided another $84.2 billion in fiscal 2018 funds.

BACKGROUND

The National Oceanographic and Atmospheric Administration declared 57 major disasters in 2017, including several damaging hurricanes and wildfires. Hurricane Harvey made landfall on August 25 on San José Island in the Gulf of Mexico along Texas as a Category 4 hurricane and remained over southeast Texas for several days and then hit Louisiana.

Hurricane Irma, which the National Weather Service said was the strongest hurricane ever observed in the open Atlantic Ocean, arrived in September with winds of 185 miles per hour. Irma passed north of the U.S. Virgin Islands and Puerto Rico on September 6 as a Category 5 hurricane, then made its way up the coast of Florida on September 10 and 11. Storms reached into the panhandle and into southern Georgia and Alabama.

Hurricane Maria became a Category 5 storm on September 18 and two days later struck the U.S. Virgin Islands and Puerto Rico. Meanwhile, California faced forty-two wildfires in the last months of 2017, which burned more than 700,000 acres and more than 9,000 structures.

FIRST DISASTER RELIEF

Hurricane Harvey in late August devastated a swath of communities from Houston into Louisiana. Rain topped fifty inches in some areas, causing catastrophic flooding, more than 100 deaths, and an estimated $125 billion in damage, primarily in the Houston area and Southeast Texas.

On September 1, the Trump administration requested $7.85 billion in supplemental funding, including $7.4 billion for the Disaster Relief Fund and $450 million for Small Business Administration disaster loans. After more hurricanes ravaged Puerto Rico, Texas, and the southern panhandle, among other regions, Congress ultimately cleared a measure (HR 601—PL 115-56) that provided $15.3 billion in fiscal 2017 funds. That measure also extended a suspension of the debt limit, included a three-month stopgap government funding measure to keep the government running until December 8, and provided a three-month extension of the National Flood Insurance Program that was set to expire September 30.

House Action

On September 6, the House voted 419–3 to pass an emergency $7.85 billion measure (HR 601) for hurricane relief. The vote was on a resolution (H Res 502) to concur with the expected Senate changes to the House bill, which would ease final passage of the measure through that chamber. The House had further amended the bill by inserting the text of an aid bill (HR 3672), introduced September 5 by Rep. Rodney Frelinghuysen, R-N.J., which included $7.4 billion for FEMA's Disaster Relief Fund and $450 million for the Small Business Administration's disaster loan program.

Republicans Andy Biggs of Arizona and Thomas Massie of Kentucky and independent Justin Amash of Michigan opposed the measure, but Sen. Majority Leader Mitch McConnell, R-Ky., said it would be impossible to clear the measure without raising the debt ceiling. He also wanted to attach a measure to continue fiscal 2017 funding to keep the government running as lawmakers continued to debate fiscal 2018 spending measures. Several conservative Republicans, however, said they opposed increasing the debt limit without a commitment to cut future spending. Senate Democratic Leader Charles E. Schumer and House Democratic Leader Nancy Pelosi proposed a short-term debt limit increase of three months, giving lawmakers time to work out a long-term agreement on the debt limit.

Senate Action

With Hurricane Irma heading for the coast of Florida on September 7, the Senate approved the House bill (HR 601) in an 80–17 vote after almost doubling the aid package to nearly $15.3 billion and adding a suspension of the debt limit, a three-month stopgap government funding measure to keep the government running, and a three-month extension of the National Flood Insurance Program that was set to expire September 30.

The measure also included a provision to cover a $300 million shortfall in the U.S. Forest Service's wildfire suppression efforts for fiscal 2017. At the time, nine western states were facing seventy-six active, large wildfires affecting nearly 1.5 million acres of land, according to the National Interagency Fire Center. The Forest Service had already spent about $1.7 billion that year on fighting wildfires.

Treasury Secretary Steven Mnuchin said he might not have funds to spend on hurricane aid without increasing borrowing authority. Sen. Rand Paul, R-Ky., unsuccessfully pushed an amendment that would have required Congress to pay for the hurricane aid by cutting foreign aid rather than increasing the debt limit. Senators tabled that proposal, 87–10. Republican conservatives said they opposed increasing the debt limit without reducing future spending.

The "nay" votes on the amendment included Republican Sens. Bob Corker of Tennessee, Steve Daines of Montana, Michael B. Enzi of Wyoming, Joni Ernst and Charles E. Grassley of Iowa, Deb Fischer and Ben Sasse of Nebraska, Jeff Flake and John McCain of Arizona, Lindsey Graham of South Carolina, Ron Johnson of Wisconsin, James Lankford of Oklahoma, Mike Lee of Utah, Jerry Moran of Kansas, Rand Paul of Kentucky, Jim Risch of Idaho, and Patrick J. Toomey of Pennsylvania.

Final Action

The House on September 8, 2017, voted 316–90 to clear the disaster aid bill (HR 601). Ninety Republicans opposed the bill. The president signed the measure into law (PL 115-56) the same day.

SECOND DISASTER RELIEF

The Trump administration on October 4, 2017, requested another $12.7 billion for the Disaster Relief Fund, as well as $16 billion in debt cancellation for the flood insurance fund as federal and state officials continued to struggle to provide relief and recovery support following a heavy hurricane season in parts of the United States and Puerto Rico. Congress ultimately cleared a measure (HR 4008—PL 115-72) that provided $36.5 billion in fiscal 2018 disaster aid supplemental spending.

House Action

The House in October took up a $36.5 billion disaster aid supplemental spending bill (HR 4008) that included $16 billion to partially cover the flood insurance program's debt collections; $18.7 billion for FEMA's Disaster Relief Fund, including $4.9 billion for the agency's Community

Disaster Loan Program to help Puerto Rico; and almost $1.3 billion in additional SNAP funds to help low-income Puerto Ricans affected by hurricanes.

In advance of a scheduled vote, conservative House members and activist groups tried to stir up opposition to the bill's provision to cancel the $16 billion in flood insurance debt and raised concerns about loans to Puerto Rico that they said might not be repaid. On October 12, the House passed the measure in a 353–69 vote. House leaders secured the necessary two-thirds support to pass the bill under suspension of the rules, with 164 Republicans and all Democrats voting yes.

The House vote came on a resolution (H Res 569) that allowed approval of the aid package (HR 4008) as an amendment to unrelated House- and Senate-passed legislation (HR 2266) to authorize bankruptcy judgeships. The move would allow Senate leaders to bypass a potential filibuster to bring the measure to the Senate floor.

Senate Action

Senators from hurricane-damaged states such as Texas and Florida threatened to block the measure unless additional relief funds were added. The White House promised more aid down the road. Meanwhile, Sen. Mike Lee, R-Utah, wanted to open debate about the provisions cancelling flood insurance debt relief.

On October 23, 2017, the Senate voted 79–16 to cut off debate and proceed to vote on the bill. On October 24, the Senate cleared the measure in an 82–17 vote. Robert Menendez, D-N.J., did not vote as he was attending his trial on bribery and corruption charges.

Before passing the measure, the Senate voted 80–19 to waive a point of order by Kentucky's Rand Paul, who wanted to remove the bill's emergency designations that allowed funds to be allocated without regard to statutory spending caps.

Final Action

The president signed the measure into law (PL 115-72) on October 26, 2017.

THIRD DISASTER RELIEF

On November 17, the Trump Administration requested about $44 billion in additional disaster aid funding. Congress ultimately, in February 2018, approved $84.3 billion in supplementary fiscal 2018 funding (HR 1892 — PL 115-123). The relief was packaged with a stopgap funding bill to keep the government running, the two-year budget deal that set defense and non-defense discretionary caps, a temporary suspension of the debt limit, and some tax-break extensions.

House Action

Rep. Rodney Frelinghuysen, R-N.J., on December 18 introduced a measure (HR 4667) that would provide about $81 billion in hurricane and wildfire disaster relief, including disaster recovery reform, agriculture assistance, and nutrition aid. The bill would provide about $37 billion more than Trump requested.

The bill included $27.6 billion for FEMA; $26.1 billion for Community Development Block Grants; $12.1 billion for the Army Corps of Engineers, $3.8 billion for agriculture recovery, $2.9 billion to help schools rebuild; $1.6 billion for the Small Business Administration disaster loan program, $1.5 billion to repair military facilities, $1.4 billion for damaged federal highways, and $600 million in economic development grants.

The bill included provisions to allow people whose property was damaged by wildfires to make tax deductions for the costs, to remove penalties for withdrawing from retirement accounts, and to incentivize donations to people and communities rebuilding after fires. On December 21, 2017, the House passed the measure by a vote of 251–169.

Rep. Mike Thompson, D-Calif., said the package was a first step in helping his state recover from wildfires that had decimated many communities. But Rep. Jose E. Serrano, D-N.Y., was among those who opposed the measure. He said he did not like that it gave Puerto Rico's oversight board authority over disaster recovery on the island, and he wanted more support for hurricane victims in New York and New Jersey.

Senate Action

Senate Minority Leader Charles E. Schumer, D-N.Y., criticized the House measure for not including additional funds for Medicaid, drinking water and infrastructure, and for not extending the earned-income tax credit for Puerto Rico. The measure languished while lawmakers returned to their districts in late December for the holiday recess. While the bill failed to move in the Senate, FEMA said the Disaster Relief Fund had a large enough balance to make it to January.

On February 7, 2018, the Senate took up an unrelated, House-passed measure (HR 1892) that included fiscal 2018 defense funding and stopgap funding to keep the government open while negotiations continued on the regular appropriations measures. Senators agreed to amend the measure to include a two-year bipartisan budget deal and more than $89.3 billion in supplementary disaster relief funding, as well as a temporary suspension of the debt limit and some tax-break extensions.

The disaster aid portion of the bill included $23.5 billion for the Disaster Relief Fund, $28 billion for the Community Development Block Grant Program, and $17.4 billion for the Army Corps of Engineers to repair infrastructure and complete dredging and other activities. The measure also included $3.7 billion in Medicaid funding for Puerto Rico. The Senate on February 9 passed the measure (HR 1892) by a vote of 71–28, with sixteen Republicans, eleven Democrats and independent Bernie Sanders of Vermont opposing the bill.

Final Action

The House cleared the Senate's amended measure (HR 1892) on February 9, 2018, and the president signed it into law (PL 115-123) on the same day.

Tax Overhaul

In December 2017, Congress cleared and the president signed the first tax code overhaul since 1986. The Tax Cuts and Jobs Act (PL 115-97) was the GOP's first major legislative victory under a unified Republican government and fulfilled one of President Trump's promises.

Republicans had long pressed for federal income tax cuts, arguing they would spur economic growth. The measure reformed the income tax brackets in the federal code, reducing rates for high earners, and reduced taxes for corporations.

It also included a provision to remove the individual mandate in the 2010 health care law, essentially ending a penalty for Americans who do not carry health insurance. The CBO estimated the repeal of the mandate would reduce the federal deficit by about $338 billion between 2018 and 2027. But the CBO reasoned that the number of people with health insurance would decrease by 4 million in 2019 and 13 million in 2027 and the average premiums in the nongroup market would increase by about 10 percent in the next decade, primarily because healthier people would be less likely to obtain insurance and the resulting premium increases would dissuade others not to purchase insurance.

The final tax bill also repealed a law that for decades had permitted churches and charities to endorse political candidates.

Democrats contended the bill would primarily benefit corporations, corporate executives, and the wealthy while hiking the deficit and the debt and ultimately would spur Republicans to cut federal entitlement programs. Republicans argued that the bill would spur economic growth that would more than offset the bill's expected impact on the federal deficit. They also said that all Americans would benefit from reduced taxes and that U.S. companies would repatriate profits, investment, and jobs back to the United States.

BACKGROUND

Lawmakers last cleared a rewrite of the federal tax code in 1986 (The Tax Reform Act of 1986, PL 99-514), lowering individual income tax rates. Before that, in 1981, President Reagan signed the Economic Recovery Tax Act of 1981 (PL 97-34), which provided an across-the-board 25 percent tax cut in individual tax rates.

The Tax Reform Act of 1986 (PL 99-514), which was revenue neutral, collapsed the existing fourteen tax brackets to two brackets, with an individual top tax rate of 28 percent and a second rate of 15 percent, which would affect about 85 percent of taxpayers. It dropped many spe-

cial tax breaks and shifted $120 billion in tax liability from individual taxpayers to corporations. Additional tax rates were added back in during the Bush and Clinton administrations. A 1990 law (PL 101-508) established a 31 percent tax rate for the wealthiest taxpayers, and a 1993 law (Pl 103-66) established two new tax brackets, including a top bracket rate of 39.6 percent.

With a booming economy and growing budget surpluses, Congress in 2001 and 2003 enacted measures (PL 107-16, PL 108-27) that temporarily cut taxes. In 2012, Congress cleared the American Taxpayer Relief Act (PL 112-240) that made all but the top tax rate permanent beginning in 2013.

Even before the 115th Congress, Republicans had pushed for an overhaul of the corporate and business tax code, arguing that the U.S. corporate rate of 35 percent was much higher than that of most other industrialized nations and thereby encouraged companies to move their operations overseas. A Department of Treasury Office of Tax Analysis working paper from January 2017 recommended tax changes affecting the "pass-through" business sector—sole proprietorships, partnerships, and S corporations that are not subject to the corporate income tax—and changes to ease the burden of the tax system on corporations.

Passage of the fiscal 2018 budget resolution (H Con Res 71) paved the way for the House and Senate tax-writing committees to begin working on tax overhaul legislation that the Senate would be permitted to pass with a simple majority vote and avoid a filibuster, as permitted in the so-called budget reconciliation process. Under the House Republican's budget blueprint, the tax legislation could add no more than $1.5 trillion to the deficit over ten years. The Senate's reconciliation rules said the tax measure could not add to the deficit outside the ten-year budget window, meaning costs would have to be fully offset. Ultimately, both the House and Senate tax plans, and the final conference agreement, were negotiated by Republicans.

House Action

The House passed a sweeping tax measure in November 2017 on a mostly party line vote. House Republican leaders on November 2, 2017, released the proposed tax measure (HR 1) that would collapse seven individual tax brackets into four, keeping the top individual rate at 39.6 percent for high-income earners. GOP leaders said the bill would provide an estimated tax cut of $1,182 for the average middle-income American. The legislation included provisions to eliminate a variety of tax deductions and credits.

Provisions for families and individuals included the following:

- Four tax rates would be created: 12 percent (for joint filers earning $24,000 to $90,000), 25 percent (those earning up to $260,000), 35 percent (earners up to $1 million), and 39.6 percent (over $1 million). The amounts for individuals would be half of those assessed on joint filers, except for the 25 percent

bracket, which would apply to individuals earning up to $200,000.

- The child tax credit would be boosted from $1,000 to $1,600 per qualifying child.
- A new family credit would be created, including a $300 credit for each parent and non-child dependent.
- A mortgage interest deduction would continue to be permitted for existing mortgages, but future home purchases and refinancings would be eligible to claim only the deduction for interest paid on the first $500,000 of the total cost of their mortgage.
- Retirement incentives for 401(k)s and individual retirement accounts would be continued.
- The estate tax would be repealed in 2022.
- The itemized deduction for state property taxes would be capped at $10,000.
- Deductions for state and local income taxes (known as the SALT deduction) would be eliminated.

The measure also would cut the corporate tax rate from 35 percent to 20 percent. A new 25 percent tax rate would apply to "pass-through" businesses such as partnerships, limited liability companies, and subchapter S corporations whose owners' profits are taxed at the individual's level.

The bill would assess a one-time repatriation tax on corporations' profits stored overseas if they are returned to the United States. That one-time tax rate would be 5 percent for brick-and-mortar businesses overseas and 12 percent for liquid assets or cash, according to the top tax writer for the House. In addition, the measure would impose a new global minimum tax on foreign profits equal to 10 percent.

For the forty banks in the United States with more than $50 billion in assets, the measure would eliminate the deduction for Federal Deposit Insurance Corporation assessments. The deduction would be reduced on a sliding scale for banks with $10 billion to $50 billion in assets—100 percent at $50 billion, and 0 percent cut at $10 billion. The change would raise an estimated $137 billion through fiscal 2027, according to the Joint Committee on Taxation.

Many members and interest groups indicated concerns about how the package addressed deductions for state and local income taxes, the provisions on "pass-through" tax rates for small businesses, and mortgage interest deductions, among other provisions. Democrats raised concerns that, as detailed in a report from the nonpartisan Joint Committee on Taxation, lower-income taxpayers could see a high tax increase after several years under the tax reform plan.

The House Ways and Means Committee on November 9, 2017, approved the tax plan (HR 1) in a party line, 24–16 vote after making several changes to the package during a four-day markup. The Joint Committee on Taxation estimated the bill would cost $1.437 trillion over ten years, below the $1.5 trillion threshold set in the Republicans' budget blueprint (H Con Res 71).

Most of the changes to the measure were included in a manager's amendment introduced by Chairman Kevin Brady, R-Texas. That amendment, approved 24–16, would change the tax rates on corporate assets brought back from overseas to the United States, raising the rates for nonliquid assets from 5 percent in the original bill to 7 percent, and for cash from 12 percent to 14 percent. The Joint Committee on Taxation estimated the change would add more than $70 billion in revenue over ten years, which would help pay to restore other tax breaks in the manager's amendment, including the adoption tax credit.

Another provision would require amortization of business research expenses over five years, beginning in 2023, rather than immediate deductions, to produce an estimated revenue of $108 billion. For research conducted outside the country, the amortization period would be fifteen years.

The manager's amendment also changed a section of the bill that would impose excise taxes on corporations' payments to offshore affiliates, which would raise an estimated $88 billion over ten years.

In addition, Brady's amendment adjusted the 25 percent rate on pass-through income on businesses. His amendment would set a 9 percent tax rate for the first $75,000 in net business taxable income for the pass-through businesses. That rate would be phased in, beginning with an 11 percent rate in 2018 and 2019 and 10 percent in 2020 and 2021, and dropping to 9 percent in 2022. The new rate would apply to all pass-through business sectors, including those of doctors, lawyers, accountants, engineers, and other service providers.

The amendment did not include a provision to repeal the individual mandate in the 2010 health care law, as many Republicans had hoped.

The amendment included a provision exempting businesses engaged in so-called floor plan financing—common among auto dealers—from a limit on net interest expense deductibility. The amendment also would preserve deductions for moving expenses for military families.

In addition, Brady's amendment repealed a so-called Johnson Amendment, a provision included in the 1954 tax law and authored by then-Sen. Lyndon B. Johnson, R-Texas, that bars churches and charities from engaging in political activity. The repeal would thereby allow churches or other 501c3 organizations to endorse political candidates.

The committee, meanwhile, rejected a series of Democratic amendments by party line votes, including

- An amendment by Rep. Earl Blumenauer of Oregon, rejected 15–22, that would have removed language in Brady's amendment that would modify or eliminate tax credits for electricity produced from renewable resources
- A proposal by Judy Chu of California, rejected 14–24, that would have reinstated the estate tax on estates valued at about $5.5 million

- An amendment by Rep. Ron Kind of Wisconsin, rejected 16–24, that would have increased the corporate tax rate to an amount that would offset the reduction in revenues resulting from Brady's amendment
- An amendment by Rep. Bill Pascrell, Jr., of New Jersey, rejected 16–24, that would have delayed implementation of the tax bill until the Department of Treasury provided the committee with President Trump's tax returns for years 2007 through 2016

On November 14, the House Rules Committee adopted, in an 8–3 party line vote, a closed rule for floor debate, meaning no amendments could be considered on the floor. That barred another opportunity for Republicans to try to repeal the individual mandate in the health care law.

On November 16, the full House voted 227–205 to pass the $1.5 trillion tax overhaul package (HR 1). No Democrats supported the bill, and thirteen Republicans opposed it: Appropriations Chairman Rodney Frelinghuysen, Leonard Lance, Frank A. LoBiondo, and Christopher H. Smith of New Jersey; Dan Donovan, Peter T. King, Lee Zeldin, John J. Faso, and Elise Stefanik of New York; Darrell Issa, Tom McClintock, and Dana Rohrabacher of California; and Walter B. Jones of North Carolina.

Republicans, particularly those from New York and New Jersey, said they opposed a new $10,000 cap on property tax deductions and the SALT deductions repeal, as well as a lower cap on mortgage interest deductions.

Senate Committee Action

Weeks after the House passed HR 1, the Senate narrowly passed its own tax overhaul legislation. Senate Republicans unveiled their tax plan on November 9, 2017. Like the House plan, the measure would provide tax cuts for all income levels, reduce the corporate tax rate from 35 percent to 20 percent, and expand benefits for families with children. The corporate tax cut, however, would be delayed for one year and the deduction for state and local taxes (SALT) would be fully repealed under the Senate plan. Only the House bill would allow a property tax deduction up to $10,000.

Both chambers' plans would keep the adoption tax credit. The Senate bill would retain the student loan interest deduction and the estate tax, but would double the estate tax exemption limit for money left to heirs.

However, the Senate plan would retain seven tax brackets for individuals (compared to four brackets in the House bill), adjusting the rates for those brackets to

- 38.5 percent for individuals making $500,000 (or $1 million for joint filers)
- 35 percent for $200,000 (single) and $390,000 (joint)
- 32.5 percent for $170,000 (single) and $290,000 (joint)
- 25 percent for income above $60,000 (single) or $120,000 (joint)
- 22.5 percent for $38,700 (single) and $77,400 (joint)

- 12 percent for income above $9,525 (single) and $19,050 (joint)
- 10 percent for income up to $9,525 (joint) and $19,050 (joint)

The Senate plan also would keep an existing mortgage interest deduction for debt up to $1 million and would boost the child tax credit from $1,000 to $1,650 per child. The plan would create a 17.4 percent deduction for qualified pass-through income earned by noncorporate businesses, whose owners pay taxes on their profits as individuals.

Hours after the House passed its tax plan on November 16, the Senate Finance Committee approved its draft tax plan in a 14–12 vote along party lines. The panel adopted, by a vote of 14–12, a manager's amendment by Chairman Orrin Hatch, R-Utah, to make several changes to the underlying draft, including provisions that would

- Lower the fourth income tax bracket further, from 25 percent to 24 percent, and the fifth income bracket from 22.5 percent to 22 percent
- Sunset all income tax rate reductions after December 21, 2025
- Increase the maximum child tax credit to $2,000 per child
- Restore certain cuts to the historic rehabilitation tax credit
- Bar expense deductions for government lobbying
- Exempt mutual funds from proposed rules that require stock sales to be valued based on the oldest holdings for capital gains purposes
- Postpone to 2026 the start date for denial of business meal deductions
- Move up to 2023 the start date for tighter limits on deductions for companies' net operating losses
- Alter the IRS whistleblower program and tax treatment of certain whistleblower awards
- Raise from 15 percent to 20 percent the excise tax on stock compensation for officers of inverted corporations
- Extend the IRS free-file program
- Provide more tax relief for victims of the Mississippi River Delta flood between May and June 2017
- Set at 27.5 percent the "orphan drug" credit rate and remove a cap on the credit
- Require a three-year holding period for investment fund managers' "carried interest" income to qualify as long-term capital gains
- Require corporations to report the dividends paid to shareholders annually and during the two-and-a-half months of the following year

The manager's amendment also included a provision to repeal the individual health insurance mandate under the 2010 Affordable Care Act. The amendment did not address some Republicans' concerns about pass-through businesses.

Committee Republicans rejected a series of Democratic amendments, including one by Sen. Claire McCaskill of

Missouri that aimed to restrict how business owners making at least $1 million a year could benefit from the 17.4 percent deduction for certain pass-through income.

Other Democratic proposals that Republicans rejected included

- An amendment by Sen. Ron Wyden of Oregon which would have sunset the corporate tax cuts to pay for permanent individual tax cuts
- An amendment by Sen. Debbie Stabenow of Michigan which would have eliminated provisions providing tax cuts for households making more than $1 million a year, and used the savings to send taxpayers annual rebate checks
- An amendment by Sen. Thomas R. Carper of Delaware which would have maintained the top individual tax rate at 39.6 percent, rather than cut it to 38.5 percent
- An amendment by Sen. Bob Casey of Pennsylvania which would have rolled back the proposed corporate tax rate and the rest of the tax package if median household income did not rise by at least $4,000 over a certain period

Senate Floor Action

Early on December 2, the Senate voted 51–49 to pass its tax overhaul plan, which the Congressional Budget Office estimated would cost $1.45 trillion over ten years. All forty-six Democrats and two independents voted against the bill, as did Republican Sen. Corker, who said he was concerned about the trillion-dollar spike expected in the deficit. (Corker was planning to retire after that Congress.) Republicans hailed the bill for taking a major step toward rewriting the tax code, while Democrats criticized it as a giveaway to wealthy Americans and corporations.

Republicans passed the measure after making several major changes. Most of the changes were adopted as part of a manager's amendment by Majority Leader Mitch McConnell, R-Ky., which was adopted by unanimous consent. Among the changes, the amendment would match the House proposal to maintain the property tax deduction with a $10,000 cap; expand the plan's deduction for pass-through business income from 17.4 percent to 23 percent; and scale down, rather than cut, the alternative minimum tax (AMT) for individuals and maintain the existing corporate AMT.

The amendment also would increase repatriation tax rates to 14 percent for liquid assets and 7 percent for non-cash assets; provide a tax break for domestic companies that export to foreign customers; and expand for two years an existing itemized deduction for medical expenses, lowering the threshold to claim the deduction to expenses exceeding 7.5 percent of adjusted gross income—down from 10 percent in existing law.

Among the other amendments adopted was a proposal by Sen. Ted Cruz, R-Texas, that would allow 529 education savings accounts, typically used for college expenses, to be used to fund elementary and secondary school expenses, including private and religious schools. That amendment was adopted 50–50, with Vice President Mike Pence breaking the tie.

By a 52–48 vote, senators adopted one Democratic amendment, by Sen. Jeff Merkley of Oregon, to remove from the bill language that would have exempted from a new excise tax on endowment funds those colleges and universities that opt out of federal funding. In a procedural move, Democrats turned back an amendment by Republican Sens. Marco Rubio of Florida and Mike Lee of Utah that would have made the child tax credit fully refundable against payroll taxes and raised the proposed corporate tax rate to nearly 21 percent, rather than 20 percent.

Final Action

Congress cleared the measure in December. Negotiations between the House and Senate focused on, among other provisions, the individual health care mandate included in the 2010 health law, which would be repealed in the Senate bill; provisions in the House bill that would eliminate a deduction for people with high medical costs; and language in the House measure that would eliminate an orphan drug tax credit, designed to incentivize development of treatments for rare diseases. The Senate measure would cut the orphan tax credit to 27.5 percent of the costs of preapproved research, down from 50 percent.

House and Senate conferees, who also consulted with the White House, agreed to a final package that was unveiled on December 15, 2017. The Congressional Budget Office estimated the measure would reduce revenues by about $1.65 trillion and reduce outlays by $194 billion over ten years, leading to a rise in the deficit of $1.455 trillion over a decade.

The conference agreement included provisions to allow oil and gas drilling in a portion of the Arctic National Wildlife Refuge in Alaska and to repeal the 2010 health care law's individual mandate. Both of those provisions had been included in the Senate package.

The final package did not include several provisions in the House bill, including language that would have allowed churches and other 501c3 nonprofits to be politically active. Negotiators also agreed to allow taxpayers who itemize to continue deducting a limited amount of state and local income taxes, further reduce the top tax rate for individuals to 21 percent, and to set the corporate tax rate at 21 percent rather than 20 percent. They also increased the refundable portion of the child tax credit.

On December 19, 2017, the House voted 227–203 to adopt the conference report. A dozen House Republicans joined Democrats to oppose the bill: Reps. Dan Donovan, John J. Faso, Peter T. King, Elise Stefanik, and Lee Zeldin of New York; Rodney Frelinghuysen, Leonard Lance, Frank A. LoBiondo, and Christopher H. Smith of New Jersey; Darrell Issa and Dana Rohrabacher of California; and Walter B. Jones of North Carolina.

Early on December 20, the Senate voted 51–48, along party lines, to adopt the conference report on the tax overhaul measure (HR 1) after Democrats removed several provisions that violated a budget reconciliation rule. The Byrd rule, named for the late Sen. Robert Byrd, D-W.Va., (Section 313 of the Congressional Budget Act of 1974) bars extraneous provisions in reconciliation legislation. Democrats challenged and successfully removed three parts of the measure that were related to an excise tax on endowments of small private universities, 529 savings accounts for homeschooling expenses, and the bill's shorthand title, "Tax Cuts and Jobs Act."

Later that day, the House cleared the final plan in a 224–201 vote. The same dozen House Republicans joined Democrats to oppose the bill. President Trump on December 22, 2017, signed the measure into law (PL 115-97).

HIGHLIGHTS OF TAX LAW

Individual and family tax rates

The final measure reduced federal individual income tax rates, as well as the threshold income levels, to

- 10 percent on taxable income up to $9,525 for single filers and $19,050 for joint
- 12 percent for up to $38,700 for single filers and $77,400 for joint
- 22 percent for up to $82,500 for single filers and $165,000 for joint
- 24 percent for up to $157,500 for single filers and $315,000 for joint
- 32 percent for up to $2,000 for single filers and $400,000 for joint
- 35 percent for up to $500,000 for single filers and $600,000 for couples
- 37 percent for more than $500,000 for individuals and more than $600,000 for couples.

(Previously, a top 39.6 percent tax rate applied to income above $418,400 for individuals and $470,000 for joint filers).

The final measure also eliminated several personal exemptions but doubled the standard deduction. It permitted a mortgage interest deduction on up to $750,000 of a home loan, and up to $10,000 in state and local income and property taxes. It raised the child tax credit from $1,000 to $2,000 with $1,400 refundable. The law increased exemptions for the estate tax and alternative minimum tax.

Corporate taxes

The law cut the corporate tax rate from 35 percent to 21 percent. It also allowed businesses to write off as an expense 100 percent (up from 50 percent) of the cost of assets that are acquired and put into service, and repealed the corporate alternative minimum tax. The law encouraged companies to bring stockpiled foreign earnings and assets back into the United States, offering a one-time, 15.5 percent tax rate on those cash funds. The law limited business deductions for net interest expenses to 30 percent of adjusted taxable income.

Other business taxes

The law permitted pass-through businesses that pay taxes at the individual tax rate to deduct 20 percent of business income, subject to certain limits. The law imposed a 1.4-percent excise tax on endowments of certain private colleges and universities, repealed exceptions to the $1 million deduction limit for corporate executives' commissions and compensation, and ended a tax deduction for deposit insurance premiums for large banks. For two years, the law reduced certain federal excise tax on beer, wine, and liquor.

Other provisions

The law permitted the Gulf Coast states to receive an increased share of revenues from oil and gas royalties related to Gulf of Mexico offshore drilling for two years. It also required the sale of oil from the Strategic Petroleum Reserve to produce revenue to meet reconciliation requirements. The final measure barred individuals or entities from deducting settlement fees related to sexual harassment or abuse claims if the payments were subject to a nondisclosure agreement.

Debt Limit

Throughout the 115th Congress, lawmakers continued to suspend the debt limit, although twice they raised it slightly in accordance with rules of the Bipartisan Budget Act of 2015 (PL 114-74). The debt limit previously had been suspended at $18.113 trillion under the Budget Act of 2015, which was enacted February 2, 2015. That suspension expired March 15, 2017, and the 2015 law directed that the amount of borrowing that occurred during the suspension of the debt limit would be added to the previous debt ceiling. So the Treasury Department reset the debt limit at $19.809 trillion. But to avoid breaching the limit, the department had to use extraordinary measures to borrow more for a limited time or delay payments.

In June, the Treasury Department warned the Trump administration that the government might hit its legal limit on borrowing sooner than expected. In early August, Trump asked Congress to raise the debt limit by the end of September.

On September 8, the president signed a stopgap spending measure (HR 601—PL 115-56) that suspended the debt limit at $20.456 billion through December 8, 2017, and the Treasury Secretary again used extraordinary measures to avoid crossing that limit when the suspension lapsed after December 9. The Bipartisan Budget Act of 2018 (PL 115-123), enacted February 9, 2018, suspended the debt limit through March 1, 2019.

FISCAL 2018 APPROPRIATIONS

Congress in March 2018 cleared a $1.3 trillion omnibus spending measure for fiscal 2018 (HR 1625—PL 115-141) after months of protracted debate over spending caps and other issues. During negotiations on the package, the House and Senate passed several continuing resolutions to keep the government open.

Enactment of fiscal 2018 appropriations bills had been heavily delayed for several reasons: The fiscal 2017 process was not complete until May 2017, the Trump administration did not release a detailed budget proposal until late that May, and the GOP leaders of both chambers that spring were primarily focused on trying to repeal the 2010 health care law. At the start of the process, Congress also did not have a bipartisan budget deal on discretionary spending for fiscal 2018, nor a deal to raise spending limits, without which defense programs would be hit with cuts, known as sequestration, of about 13 percent, as required under the 2011 Budget Control Act (PL 112-25). But to reach agreement on a defense spending cap, Republicans knew Democrats would insist on increases for nondefense programs too.

President Trump proposed increasing the fiscal 2018 defense cap by $54 billion and reducing the nondefense cap by the same amount. House Republicans, when first drafting their appropriations bills, called for higher levels of defense spending in light of growing global threats. They proposed a defense spending cap of $621.5 billion ($72.5 billion more than the cap set by the 2011 Budget Control Act) and a $511 billion nondefense cap ($5 billion below the BCA cap).

House appropriators moved individual bills, then the chamber passed a four-bill minibus which it later added to an eight-bill package. The measures were all set under the fiscal 2017 caps since no new budget agreement had been reached. But Senate GOP leaders did not move on the House's combined measure as they were not certain they had sufficient support to overcome a potential filibuster.

In February 2018, Congress cleared a two-year budget agreement (HR 1892—PL 115-123), which promulgated final negotiations on the fiscal 2018 omnibus measure.

FISCAL 2018 MINIBUS

The House Appropriations Committee approved all twelve of its fiscal 2018 spending bills by mid-July 2017. With time then running out to pass all the bills before October 1, the beginning of fiscal 2018, some House Republicans pushed to combine the bills into one omnibus spending measure, but GOP leaders feared they could not win enough support to pass such a package. Instead, appropriations leaders crafted a nearly $790 billion "minibus" for fiscal 2018 that included four appropriations bills: defense (HR 3219), energy and water (HR 3266), military construction–VA (HR 2998), and legislative branch (HR 3162). The measure included

- $658.1 billion for the Defense department, including $584.2 billion in discretionary funding, $18.4 billion more than Trump requested
- $37.6 billion for energy and water projects, which was $3.7 billion more than Trump requested
- $88.8 billion for military construction and veterans affairs, including $78.2 billion in discretionary funding for the Department of Veterans Affairs, about $500 million less than the White House requested
- $3.58 billion for the legislative branch

GOP leaders also announced that, during floor debate, they would add $1.6 billion to begin construction on Trump's promised U.S.–Mexico border wall. Democrats balked. The Appropriations Committee's ranking Democrat, Nita M. Lowey of New York, also complained that the minibus would breach the cap on defense spending set in the deficit reduction law cleared in 2011 (PL 112-25). That law set a cap on defense spending at $549 billion, beyond which across-the-board cuts—known as sequestration—would be triggered for all defense programs. To raise the limit on defense spending, Congress would have to amend the deficit reduction law.

On July 27, the House voted 235–192 to pass the minibus, using the defense bill as the underlying measure (HR 3219). Five Democrats supported the bill, and five Republicans opposed it. Before passing the bill, House members considered more than 120 amendments. Among those adopted on July 26 were amendments that would bar the Veterans Affairs Department from conducting dog experiments that cause "significant pain or distress" and bar the VA from beginning a new round of base realignments and closures.

Lawmakers rejected, by a vote of 107–314, an amendment by Rep. Scott Perry, R-Pa., that would have reduced the budget for the Congressional Budget Office by 50.4 percent. They also rejected, 116–309, an amendment by Rep. Morgan Griffith, R-Va., that would have eliminated eighty-nine positions from CBO's budget analysis division.

FISCAL 2018 OMNIBUS

In September 2017, as the end of fiscal 2017 neared a close, House Republican leaders brought to the floor another minibus that contained the eight remaining appropriations bills which would fund programs and activities at the Department of Agriculture (HR 3268); Departments of Commerce, Justice, and Science (HR 3267); financial services agencies (HR 3280); Department of Homeland Security (HR 3355); the Department of Interior and the Environmental Protection Agency (HR 3354); the departments of Labor, Health and Human Services, and Education (HR 3358); the State Department and other foreign operations agencies (HR 3362); and the departments of Transportation and Housing and Urban Development (HR 3353). The House approved a rule (H Res 500) that added the text of the four-bill minibus to

the measure to create a $1.23 trillion omnibus spending package (HR 3354) for fiscal 2018.

The House on September 14 passed the measure in a 211–198 vote after considering 342 amendments during two weeks of floor debate. Fourteen Republicans joined 184 Democrats to oppose the bill, while one Democrat, Collin C. Peterson of Michigan, voted for the measure.

The bill included $621.5 billion for defense discretionary spending and $511 billion for nondefense discretionary spending, including the nearly $1.6 billion for Trump's promised border wall. The bill violated the caps set in the 2011 budget law.

House Speaker Paul D. Ryan, R-Wisc., said it was the first time since 2009 that the House had passed all twelve spending bills before the start of the fiscal year. However, Senate GOP leaders did not have sufficient support to overcome a potential Democratic filibuster on the bill, and did not move on the measure. Meanwhile, Congress turned its focus to enacting a tax-cut package as called for in the budget resolution's reconciliation instructions. As a result, with the start of fiscal 2018, the government began operating under a series of continuing resolutions.

STOPGAP FUNDING BILLS

Lawmakers cleared five stop-gap funding measures to keep the government running while negotiations continued on fiscal 2018 appropriations. Congress cleared and the president signed on September 8, 2017, a stopgap spending measure (HR 601, PL 115-56) that continued government funding through December 8, as well as provided hurricane relief funds and suspended the debt limit.

Another stopgap spending measure (H J Res 123), which the president signed into law (PL 115-90) on December 8, continued government funding another two weeks. House Democrats overwhelmingly opposed the measure in response to President Trump's decision in early September to terminate President Obama's Deferred Action for Childhood Arrivals (DACA) program, under which undocumented immigrants who as children were brought to the United States illegally by their parents could register with the government and obtain a work permit that protected them from deportation. Trump gave Congress until March 2018 to come up with a legislative fix, and Democrats pledged to block government funding until protections were enacted.

A third stopgap measure (HR 1370), which the president signed into law (PL 115-96) on December 22, continued government funding through January 19, 2018. The measure also included funding for the Children's Health Insurance Program and community health centers through March 2018 and $2.1 billion for a private care access program for veterans.

House Republicans and a majority of Senate Democrats had opposed the measure in response to a lack of action on legislation to revive DACA. To ensure sufficient GOP support for the measure, Republican leaders included $4 billion in emergency funding for additional missile defense activities and $674 million to repair two Navy vessels, fulfilling requests the president had made in November.

The stopgap measure also temporarily extended, until January 19, 2018, Section 702 of the Foreign Intelligence Surveillance Act (PL 110-261), a law that allowed U.S. intelligence agencies to conduct targeted surveillance of foreigners and their communications outside the United States, even if the agencies picked up private information on Americans. The law would have expired December 31 and lawmakers had considered various versions of reauthorization legislation. The temporary extension bought them time to iron out those differences.

Disagreement over a fourth resolution to continue funding the government caused a partial government shutdown until Congress cleared, and the president signed, a three-week stopgap measure (HR 195—PL 115-120) on January 24, 2018. All but five Senate Democrats had opposed the bill in response to Trump's rejection of a bipartisan immigration proposal, which triggered a three-day shutdown until Senate Majority Leader McConnell, R-Ky., promised to bring an immigration measure to the Senate floor.

A fifth stopgap measure (HR 1892—PL 115-123), which the president signed on February 9, 2018, bought lawmakers another six weeks, through March 23, to agree on a full spending package. That measure, the Bipartisan Budget Act, also included a two-year budget agreement that increased caps on defense and nondefense discretionary spending.

TWO-YEAR BUDGET DEAL

The bipartisan budget deal (HR 1892—PL 115-123), cleared in February 2018, raised the discretionary caps for both defense and nondefense spending for fiscal years 2018 and 2019 to increase spending by $296 billion over those two years ($165 billion for defense, $131 billion for non-defense). Specifically, the measure

- Increased the defense discretionary spending cap by $80 billion to $629 billion, and the nondefense cap by $63 billion to $579 billion, for fiscal 2018
- Suspended the limit on public debt through march 1, 2019
- Provided $89.3 billion more in disaster aid
- Retroactively extended several expired tax breaks
- Extended and modified dozens of family and health programs

On February 9, 2018, the Senate passed the bill in a 71–28 vote, and the House cleared the measure, 240–186. The president signed the measure into law on February 9.

FINAL FISCAL 2018 OMNIBUS

On March 21, 2018, House Republicans released a new $1.3 trillion omnibus spending bill (HR 1625) after appropriators had developed detailed, full-year fiscal 2018

spending measures under the recently enacted budget deal. Debate ensued, without resolution, over Democrats' push to extend authorization of the DACA program, Trump's demand for $25 billion to fully fund a border wall, and Republicans' desire to boost immigration enforcement, among other issues.

The new GOP spending bill for fiscal 2018 included $1.6 billion for the construction of more than ninety-five miles of barriers along the border. Leaders agreed to include provisions aimed at boosting enforcement of the existing National Instant Criminal Background Check System, used when individuals sought to purchase guns, and to allow federal research of gun violence. Republican leaders conceded to President Trump's mandate that the measure not include funding for a project to build a new tunnel between New Jersey and New York City.

Another provision modified the Low-Income Housing Tax Credit to adjust for the impact of the new tax law (PL 115-97) on the housing credit. That provision also fixed a so-called grain glitch in the tax law which did not extend to farming cooperatives a generous tax deduction for the income they generate from nonmember sources. The measure did not include any provisions to address DACA.

The House approved the measure, 256–167, on March 22. The Senate voted 65–32 to clear the measure on March 23. On March 23, 2018, Trump signed the measure into law (HR 1625, PL 115-141). The measure provided $138 billion more in funding compared to the fiscal 2017 level.

Highlights

The measure provided $1.3 trillion in discretionary spending, with $78.1 billion designated for Overseas Contingency Operation funds, or war spending.

Highlights of the law include the following:

Agriculture. The measure provided $146 billion for agricultural programs, $7.6 billion less than in fiscal 2017. But the $23.3 billion total in discretionary spending for agriculture programs was $2.1 billion more than provided for fiscal 2017. The measure included $104.9 billion for domestic food programs.

Included in the total was $74 billion in mandatory funding for the food stamp program (SNAP), $4.5 billion or 6 percent less than fiscal 2017 but $401 million more than Trump requested. The measure also provided "such sums as may be necessary" for the federal crop insurance program, an estimated $8.9 billion. That amount was $246 million, or 3 percent more than fiscal 2017, and $668 million, or 8 percent more, than Trump requested.

Commerce, Justice, and State. The measure included $59.6 billion for programs under the departments of Commerce, Justice, and State—$3 billion more than in fiscal 2017. Increased funds were directed to national security, including cybercrime, counterterrorism, and countering espionage and election-related threats, and to increase federal law enforcement on illegal immigration, violent crime, gangs, and opioid trafficking.

Defense. The bill included $654.6 billion in discretionary funding for the Department of Defense, providing funding increases to purchase more planes, ships, and other equipment.

It met the president's request of $1.8 billion for Iraqi, Kurdish and other forces engaged in the fight against ISIS, and $4.7 billion to train and equip Afghanistan's national army and other security forces. It included about $4.8 billion for various initiatives in Europe in response to Russia's actions in Ukraine and Crimea, including $200 million for weapons for Ukraine. It also provided large increases for missile defense programs, including more funding for Ground-Based Midcourse Defense (GMD), European missile defense, and cooperative programs with Israel. It provided $23.8 billion for fourteen major Navy vessels (five more than the administration requested), $10.2 billion for ninety F-35 fighter aircraft, and $1.1 billion to upgrade eighty-five Abrams heavy tanks. It also funded an average 2.4 percent pay increase for military personnel.

Energy and water. Congress provided $43.2 billion for the Energy Department and related agencies, including $6.8 billion for the Army Corps of Engineers and $34.5 billion for the Department of Energy. The measure included $2.3 billion for the Office of Energy Efficiency and Renewable Energy, $232 million or 11 percent more than fiscal 2017. The president had requested a 70 percent cut for the office's funding.

The measure also provided funding for several programs the president had requested to terminate, including: $353 million for the Advanced Research Projects Agency–Energy (ARPA-E), $248 million for the Weatherization Assistance Program (up from $225 million in fiscal 2017), and $55 million for State Energy Program grants (up from $50 million). The agreement provided $10.6 billion for nuclear weapons programs, an increase of $1.4 billion or 15 percent from fiscal 2017 level. The president had sought $13.9 billion. The measure did not include the administration's request to resurrect plans for the Yucca Mountain nuclear waste storage site in Nevada.

About $1.4 billion of the Corps of Engineers' activities would be covered by the Harbor Maintenance Trust Fund, up $100 million from 2017. Congress did not call for the sale of the Washington Aqueduct, as Trump requested, and did not include his proposal for a new annual fee for commercial barge operators on inland waterways.

Financial Services. Lawmakers agreed to $23.4 billion in discretionary funding for government financial services, $1.9 billion more than in fiscal 2017. The total included $11.4 billion for the IRS, 2 percent more than

in fiscal 2017, including 16 percent increased funding for taxpayer services. The president had requested $10.98 billion for the IRS.

Homeland Security. The measure included $47.7 billion in discretionary funding for the Department of Homeland Security—$5.3 billion more than in fiscal 2017—and $7.4 billion in disaster relief funding. Funding for U.S. Customs and Border Protection was boosted 15 percent, ICE increased by 11 percent, the Transportation Security Administration (TSA) by 7 percent, and the Coast Guard by 16 percent. It also provided $163 million in OCO spending, $7.4 billion in disaster relief, and $1.7 billion in mandatory funding.

Congress included $1.6 billion to construct ninety-five miles of physical barriers along the U.S.–Mexico border. The measure also boosted funding for ICE for removal operations by 11 percent, and for 65 more ICE agents and officers and 70 attorneys and staff, and added 1,196 detention beds. It did not extend protections for children of illegal immigrants under DACA, as the Democrats had desired.

Rather than decreasing spending for FEMA as the president requested, Congress provided the agency $12.5 billion, including $7.4 billion for the Disaster Relief Fund. It also boosted funding by $1.6 billion for the Coast Guard, rather than decreasing funding as Trump requested. In addition, Congress increased funding for TSA, which the president requested remain level, and increased funding for the Secret Service, as the president desired.

Interior and Environment. Under the bill, $35.2 billion for discretionary funding was allocated for Interior and Environment department programs, including $13.1 billion for the Interior Department and $8.1 billion for the EPA. The bill provided $3.2 billion for the National Park Service.

Congress generally disregarded cuts and reductions Trump had sought in the EPA budget, keeping funding at 2017 levels, including the Great Lakes Restoration Initiative and similar programs to restore Puget Sound and the Chesapeake Bay. Lawmakers increased funding by 50 percent for programs for the Long Island Sound and the Gulf of Mexico.

Labor, Health and Human Services, and Education. The bill included $13.8 billion for the Labor Department, $847.6 billion for the Health and Human Services (HHS) Department, and $74.3 billion for the Education Department. The measure included $1 billion in new funding to fight opioid addiction through a variety of programs.

The appropriations for the Department of Labor included $10 billion for Employment and Training Administration programs, $4 million more than in 2017 and $2.4 billion or 31 percent more than requested. The measure provided $1.7 billion for Job Corps, $15 million more than in fiscal 2017 and $270 million more than requested, but assumed the closure of selected Job Corps centers as the president requested.

The appropriations for HHS included a $3 billion increase for the National Institutes of Health for a total of $37.1 billion. The measure included $384.6 billion—$30.4 billion or 9 percent more than in fiscal 2017—for the federal share of Medicaid costs. It also included $410 billion (including advance funds from the previous fiscal year) for state grants for Medicaid, and $134.8 billion in advance funding for fiscal 2019.

Congress rejected the administration's request to end the Low-Income Home Energy Assistance Program and provided $3.6 billion, $250 million more than in fiscal 2017, as well as the request to terminate the community services block grant program, providing $783 million, a slight increase. The Bipartisan Budget Act of 2018 extended the Children's Health Insurance Program (CHIP) funding for another four years through September 30, 2023, with annual allotments of $21.5 billion in fiscal 2018 and $25.9 billion by fiscal 2023.

The measure allocated $70.8 billion in discretionary spending for fiscal 2017 for the Department of Education, $2.7 billion more than in fiscal 2017 and $8 billion more than requested. The measure designated $1 billion for TRIO programs that help low-income and first-generation college students prepare for and succeed in college—6 percent more than in fiscal 2017. Congress rejected several administration proposals such as terminating funding for Native Hawaiian and Alaska Native education programs, instead providing each an increase of $3 million to reach $36 million and $35 million, respectively. Congress also included $2.1 billion for state grants to support instruction, equal to those of 2017, even though the administration requested zeroing out the account.

Legislative Branch. The measure provided $4.7 billion for operations of the House and Senate, the Library of Congress, the Capitol Police, the Government Accountability Office, the Government Printing Office, and other congressional offices. It maintained a pay freeze on congressional members' salaries.

Military Construction and Veterans Affairs. The measure provided $92 billion in discretionary spending (a 9.5 percent boost) and $103.9 billion in mandatory spending for veterans' pensions and other benefits, and $750 million in OCO funding for the Department of Veterans Affairs and military construction. The bill included $10.1 billion for military construction funding, a 31 percent increase from fiscal 2017.

State Department and Foreign Operations. The bill allocated $54.2 billion for State programs, including $42.2 billion in discretionary spending and $12 billion for Overseas Contingency Operations to fund programs related to the war in Afghanistan, Syria, Iraq and other

expenses, such as humanitarian relief for Syrian refugees in Jordan and Lebanon. It rejected the president's request to eliminate the Food for Peace Program or the McGovern-Dole International Food for Education Program, boosting funding for both.

Transportation and Housing and Urban Development. The bill provided $129.2 billion in spending authority for Transportation and HUD, including $70.3 billion in discretionary spending—$12.6 billion more than in fiscal 2017. The bill did not spin off air traffic control to a nonprofit entity, as the president requested. It also did not include Trump's request for an infusion of infrastructure spending, that he said would then spark private investment to overhaul the nation's roads, bridges, schools, and other infrastructure.

Lawmakers allocated $1.5 billion for TIGER funding, a boost of $1 billion from 2017, even though the president had sought to terminate the program. The administration also asked to cancel the Essential Air Service Program, which subsidized airline carriers for service to smaller communities, but Congress included $189 million for the program—a $12 million increase from 2017.

The measure also provided $3.1 billion for the Federal Railroad Administration, $1.2 billion or 67 percent more than in fiscal 2017 and $1.9 billion more than requested. Unlike with previous transportation spending measures, lawmakers did not bar funds from being used for high-speed rail in California. *(See Transportation chapter).*

The measure designated $1.9 billion for Amtrak, $447 million or 30 percent more than the fiscal 2017 level and $1.2 billion more than requested. The measure also allowed for the release of $58.9 billion from the highway and aviation trust funds for federal highway and aviation projects.

Congress rejected the administration's proposal to wipe out the Community Development Block Grant (CDBG) program and the HOME Investments Partnership Program, which provides state and local grants to help communities fund affordable housing projects or provide rental assistance for low-income individuals. The measure funded CDBG at $3.4 billion and HOME at $1.4 billion. Lawmakers also provided $150 million for Choice Neighborhoods, $13 million more than in fiscal 2017. The president had sought to terminate that program, as well as the Self-Help and Assisted Homeownership Program, which lawmakers funded with $54 million, level with the fiscal 2017 funding. They also provided the Native American Housing Block Grants Program with $755 million, $101 million more than in 2017, although the president had requested to cut the program's funding to $600 million.

Spending Cuts Request

President Trump on May 8, 2018, asked Congress to rescind $15.19 billion in budget authority between 2018 and 2028, essentially cancelling those funds that had previously been authorized. In accordance with The Congressional Budget and Impoundment Control Act of 1974, Congress had 45 days after the president's request to pass recission legislation, otherwise the money would remain available. Although the House ultimate passed a measure, the Senate failed to take action before the deadline.

House Action

House Majority Leader Kevin McCarthy, R-Calif., on May 9 introduced a rescissions bill (HR 3). The Congressional Budget Office estimated on May 11 that the proposed cuts would reduce the deficit by $1.26 billion over eleven years. However, the CBO added that the cuts would achieve much lower actual budget savings: $64 million in fiscal 2018, $380 million in fiscal 2019, then declining through 2028. The CBO explained that most of the funding was not going to be spent under existing law and included funding that was no longer necessary for agencies to fulfill the purposes for which Congress had originally appropriated the funds.

The Agriculture Department would see the highest cuts, totaling $259 million over eleven years and affecting programs from conservation assistance to wastewater disposal grants. Authorized funding for the Department of Health and Human Services would be reduced by $198 million.

About $8.8 billion of the nearly $15.2 billion in cuts requested would come from mandatory programs, funded outside the annual appropriations process, the CBO said. Known as "changes in mandatory programs" or CHIMPS, the cuts would include $7 billion from the Children's Health Insurance Program, which at the time covered about 9 million children of low-income families, and $800 million from the Center for Medicare and Medicaid Innovation.

Many rank-and-file Republicans were concerned about the president's requested cuts to social programs so close to the 2018 mid-term election, particularly as Democrats criticized them for being ready to cut funds for low-income children. Both Republicans and Democrats were particularly wary of cutting the funding for the Children's Health Insurance Program. Even though the funds were not going to be spent on the CHIP, often appropriators would use that fund to cover shortfalls in other programs. Democrats also wanted to use the funds in case offsets were needed in other programs, but Republican leaders did not want to allow them to be spent on other nondefense programs. Smaller cuts would be made to the Justice Department's assets forfeiture account; the Treasury Department's Capital Magnet Fund, which finances affordable-housing projects; the Railroad Retirement Board's extended unemployment benefits program; and the Agriculture Department's conservation funds.

Trump's proposal also included a request to cancel $4.3 billion in unspent funds for the Energy Department's Advanced Technology Vehicles Manufacturing Program,

which had not made new loans since 2011. Budget watch-dog groups supported the cut, as did GOP lawmakers. The measure also would rescind $252 million in funding to combat the Ebola virus in developing countries, money the CBO said would not be used.

Mick Mulvaney, director of the Office of Management and Budget, talked with House conservatives to persuade them to support the package, but leaders decided to postpone a decision until June. Meanwhile, Sen. Mike Lee, R-Utah, introduced a counterpart rescissions measure (S 2979) in the Senate but Majority Leader McConnell, R-Ky., would not commit to a vote on that bill.

Revised Request

On June 5, 2018, the Trump administration submitted a revised rescissions request that would reduce the cuts by $515 million to about $14.7 billion. The revision did not alter his request to cut funds in the CHIP program, but did drop his request to cut $252 million in unspent funds to combat Ebola overseas, leftover funds from a 2013 supplemental spending law (PL 113-2) for recovery from Superstorm Sandy that had battered the East Coast in late 2012, and $10 million in EPA water quality research grants. The revised request also left in place $134 million in cuts for two Transportation Department highway funding accounts, which the Government Accountability Office ruled in May could not be rescinded by the administration.

Other funds that would be left in place, as compared to Trump's original request, included $2.1 million in cuts from unspent Housing and Urban Development public housing capital funds and $151.3 million in cuts to unspent Treasury Department balances made available by a 2008 housing law (PL 110-289). Trump reduced by $9.6 million his proposed cuts to Treasury's Capital Magnet Fund.

Final Action

On June 7, 2018, the House passed the $14.7 billion spending cuts package (HR 3) by a vote of 210–206, after approving a rule that incorporated the White House's changes. All Democrats opposed the measure, as did nineteen Republicans. In the Senate, many Republican appropriators objected that the White House was invading appropriators' jurisdiction. Senate leaders proceeded to consider the House-passed measure, but on June 20, senators rejected, by a vote of 48–50, a motion to discharge the bill and send it directly to the floor, bypassing the Appropriations Committee.

Sens. Susan Collins, R-Maine, and Richard M. Burr, R-N.C., opposed the motion. Collins said budget cuts were the purview of appropriators, not the White House. Burr, according to an aide, opposed the measure's proposed $16 million cut to unspent balances in the Land and Water Conservation Fund, which distributes royalties from federal offshore oil and gas leases to states and communities to develop outdoor recreation areas. The measure effectively died before the June 22 deadline.

Fiscal Year 2019 Budget

PRESIDENT'S BUDGET REQUEST

The White House on February 12, 2018, proposed a $4.4 trillion fiscal 2019 budget and proposed cutting $1.5 trillion over the next ten years in nondefense discretionary spending as well as $1.66 trillion in mandatory spending, including about $675 billion from the repeal of the 2010 health care law, $554 billion in Medicare reductions, and $1.4 trillion in reductions to Medicaid.

President Trump submitted his fiscal 2019 budget request before Congress had completed the appropriations process for fiscal 2018. The government at that point was operating under a continuing resolution (PL 115-123). That law, called the Bipartisan Budget Act of 2018, also set discretionary and mandatory spending caps for fiscal years 2018 and 2019, raising defense caps by $165 billion over those years and nondefense caps by $131 billion.

Under the administration's ten-year blueprint, mandatory spending would increase by $10 billion in fiscal 2019 but drop by $30 billion in fiscal 2020, with increasing reductions each year and reaching $419 billion by fiscal 2028. Meanwhile, discretionary spending would see an $11 billion increase in fiscal 2019, but then drop by $16 billion in fiscal 2020, with reductions increasing each year to a $313 billion decrease in 2028.

The budget plan forecast a deficit of $984 billion in fiscal 2019, dropping to $363 billion in fiscal 2028. The federal debt was set at slightly more than in fiscal 2019 and was predicted to increase to $32.5 billion in fiscal 2028.

The White House said it aimed to end what it called wasteful spending, pointing to a steep drop in the unemployment rate and the creation of more jobs, and said its budget would put the American economy on a path toward 3 percent growth. The plan proposed a number of changes to welfare that the administration said would encourage more Americans to return to work. The budget proposal also would fund Trump's proposed border wall, increase border enforcement and immigration judges, and increase funding to fight gangs such as MS-13. The budget also reflected the president's goal of a new infrastructure program. Additionally, the White House budget document said the administration also aimed to lessen the burden of regulation on businesses and citizens.

Under Trump's proposed budget, Social Security would face a $25 billion cut over ten years, but overall mandatory spending would drop by almost 5 percent over a decade, while the administration would dedicate nearly $200 billion in mandatory spending into an infrastructure initiative, and $19 billion into a paid parental leave program for federal employees which was promoted by Ivanka Trump, the president's daughter who was acting as a White House advisor. Other savings were proposed by reforming the Postal Service (for a savings of $39.5 billion), changing crop insurance programs ($26 billion), streamlining conservation programs ($13 billion), creat-

ing a single income-driven student loan repayment plan ($128.4 billion), and overhauling the Supplemental Nutrition Assistance Program (SNAP), known as the food stamp program (to save $213.5 billion). Another $72 billion in savings were proposed by making changes to the Supplemental Security Income benefits and Disability Insurance program.

Highlights of the Budget Request

Agriculture. The president sought $19.2 billion in discretionary funding, 15 percent less than fiscal 2017 enacted levels, the last year of enacted appropriations at that time. The budget aimed to cut $938 million in discretionary spending by eliminating several programs: the McGovern-Dole International Food for Education program; rural business and cooperative service; rural water and wastewater grants; direct loans for single family housing; a U.S. Forest Service program for purchasing land; Food for Progress, an international food aid program; and the Rural Economic Development program. The budget also would rely on state and local governments to finance a greater share of salaries for the Animal and Plant Health Inspection Service. Under mandatory spending, the proposal included a $17 billion cut in SNAP funding for fiscal 2019, and $213.5 billion over ten years.

Trump proposed reducing federal subsidies for farm crop insurance premiums, but did not specify how much. The administration said the subsidy would decline from 62 percent to 48 percent. It also proposed a limit on eligibility for payments from commodity crop programs to producers with adjusted gross incomes of $500,000 or less; a limit on the eligibility for federal subsidized crop insurance programs to farmers with adjusted gross incomes of $500,000 or less; and it would reduce federal underwriting payments to private insurance companies that service crop policies.

The proposal would add $195 million to the Agricultural Research Service for buildings and facilities. Agriculture Secretary Sonny Perdue said the department needed to keep a tight budget in light of the $20.5 trillion federal debt.

Army Corps of Engineers. The administration requested $4.8 billion for the Corps, down from the $6 billion fiscal 2017 level. The administration also said it would lower by an unspecified amount the tax on import and export goods collected for harbor maintenance. The tax at the time was set at 0.125 percent of a cargo's value, and the proposal said a tax cut would add $265 million to the deficit in fiscal 2019, increasing each year to an estimated $345 million in fiscal 2027.

The White House also called for a new user fee on shippers along inland waterways to raise an estimated $1.78 billion over the next decade. The proposal did not specify an amount for the fee.

The plan also proposed selling the Washington Aqueduct to raise an estimated $120 million. The Corps had overseen the aqueduct since the conduit began operat-

ing during the Civil War and the administration wanted to privatize it, a proposal that caused some observers to fear it would lead to higher water bills for more than 1 million residents in the District of Columbia and Northern Virginia. Congress ultimately rejected the proposal.

Commerce. The budget request called for more than $9.8 billion for the Commerce Department, an increase of $546 million or 6 percent from fiscal 2017 levels. The administration proposed eliminating several programs that it said were duplicative or ineffective, including the Economic Development Administration, the Manufacturing Extension Partnership program, and several National Oceanic and Atmospheric Administration programs, such as coastal zone management grants and coastal research grants for universities.

The budget would boost the U.S. Census Bureau's funding ahead of the 2020 census—providing the bureau $3.8 billion, a $2.3 billion increase from fiscal 2017 enacted levels. Appropriators typically increased funding for the bureau at the end of each decade to prepare for the decennial survey, but census advocates said Trump's proposed boost was insufficient.

Trump's budget also would close outreach centers operated by the Minority Business Development Agency and reform the agency into a "policy office" that would advocate for minority businesses. In the previous fiscal year budget, Trump had proposed eliminating the agency.

Defense. The administration requested $716 billion for Department of Defense programs and activities, including $617 billion in base Pentagon spending and $69 billion for overseas contingency accounts, used for war operations, and $30 billion for Department of Energy nuclear programs and other smaller accounts. The request for a total of $686 billion for Defense was an $80 billion, or 13 percent increase, from the 2017 level, much of it to purchase more planes, ships, missiles, and high-tech equipment, including seventy-seven F-35 Joint Strike Fighters at a cost of $10.7 billion and twenty-four F/A-18E/F Super Hornets for the Navy at a cost of $2 billion. Also included in the request were funds for ten new ships. The request included $13.7 billion for such high-tech capabilities as hypersonic, autonomous, space, directed energy, electronic warfare, artificial intelligence, and cyber programs.

The budget also accounted for boosting troops levels by 25,900 above the current fiscal year, and spending $46.3 billion on the war in Afghanistan, $15.3 billion on ongoing conflicts in Iraq and Syria, and $6.5 billion for the European Defense Initiative—including $200 million to help Ukraine build up its defense operations as the government fought against Russian-backed separatists in eastern Ukraine.

Education. Trump asked for $63.2 billion in discretionary funding for the Department of Education, a $3.6 billion or 5 percent drop from fiscal 2017 levels. The bipartisan budget deal reached the week before precluded the president from seeking deeper cuts.

The White House sought authorization to create a $1 billion Opportunity Grants program that would provide scholarships for low-income children to attend private school, and called for increasing funding for programs that aimed to help students attend private and charter schools.

Energy. The president's request included $30.6 billion for the Department of Energy, up from $30.2 billion in fiscal 2017. The request included proposed cuts to research funding but increased spending on nuclear weapons maintenance and modernization. Before the bipartisan budget cap agreement, the administration's proposal was $29.2 billion for the department. Energy Secretary Rick Perry said the cuts reflected an effort to move DOE work to prioritize the acceleration of early research and development, rather than focusing on the late stages in moving technology to commercialization.

The budget request included $15.1 billion for nuclear weapons, a $2.3 billion increase from fiscal 2017, and $853 million for other Defense activities. Under the budget plan, the Office of Energy Efficiency and Renewable Energy would see the largest reduction. The bill would cut funding for the program from $2.1 billion in fiscal 2017 to $696 million. Funding for the Office of Nuclear Energy would be cut $259 million from fiscal 2017, to $757 million, but the Office of Fossil Energy would see an $81 million boost, to $502 million.

The administration proposed dividing the Office of Electricity Delivery and Energy Reliability into two accounts, one for reliability ($61 million) and one for cybersecurity ($96 million). Trump also sought $120 million to conduct a licensing review for the controversial Yucca Mountain nuclear waste site in Nevada and for an interim nuclear waste storage facility. The Yucca Mountain site, first designated in 1987, had encountered fierce political opposition for decades and Congress repeatedly had barred federal funding for the project.

The budget proposed eliminating the Advanced Research Project Agency–Energy, a politically popular program that funded high-potential energy projects that were too early in the experimental stage to draw private investment. The Government Accountability Office in December 2017 had found that the administration had withheld about $90 million in fiscal 2017 appropriated funds for the program.

The White House also sought to end the Title XVII Innovative Energy Loan Guarantee Program, which guaranteed loans to help accelerate deployment of innovative energy projects, and to close the Mixed Oxide Fuel Fabrication facility in South Carolina, which was planned to dispose of thirty-four tons of weapons-grade plutonium, turning it into fuel for commercial nuclear reactors. The National Nuclear Security Administration terminated the project, about 70 percent complete, the following October.

The administration also said it would generate $5.8 billion in deficit reductions by divesting of DOE-owned transmission line assets, including the Western Area Power Administration, the Southwestern Power Administration, and the Bonneville Power Administration.

Environmental Protection Agency. The White House proposed slashing the EPA's budget by more than 26 percent from fiscal 2017 levels, providing the agency $6.1 billion and cutting 21 percent of the workforce. The budget also would cut by 48 percent, from $475 million in 2017 to $246 million, funding for research and development.

Before the bipartisan budget deal, the president had planned a 34 percent cut to the agency's budget. Trump's budget also proposed $598.5 million in cuts to several environmental and climate programs that he said taxpayers should not fund, and reduced funding for grants for states to implement federal environmental laws and programs. The blueprint would eliminate funding for the Energy Star program that aimed to help companies develop energy-efficient consumer products, instead seeking to fund the program through user fees. Under the president's proposal, funding for the agency's Superfund program would be maintained at $1.089 billion, the same as enacted in fiscal 2017.

Federal Communications Commission. The president requested $333.1 million for FCC, a $21.2 million or 6 percent drop from fiscal 2018 continued funding levels but a boost from the fiscal 2017 level of $326.5 million. The request included about $322 million in base funding, $1.9 million to increase salaries and other office expenses, and 48.5 million in a one-time expenditure to upgrade information technology.

Federal Trade Commission (FTC). The budget request included $309.7 million, down from $313 million in fiscal 2017, for the FTC.

Health and Human Services. The request included $95.4 billion in discretionary spending, down from $86.7 billion in fiscal 2017, for HHS. Including mandatory spending for programs such as Medicare and Medicaid, the overall HHS budget would increase from $1.1 trillion in 2017 to $1.2 trillion in 2019.

Funding for such areas as HIV/AIDS, cancer research, and emergency preparedness would be cancelled under the administration's budget, while funding initiatives to fight opioid abuse would increase by $10 billion. Down the road, the White House planned for more than $1 trillion in cuts to such programs over ten years. However, the budget outlook assumed the unlikely scenario that Congress would dismantle the 2010 health care law (PL 111-148, PL 111-152) and replace it with a new plan that would reduce growth for Medicaid and exchange subsidies by about $675 billion. The administration plan assumed the existing law would be replaced with a plan such as that proposed in 2017 by Republican Sens. Lindsey Graham of South Carolina, Bill Cassidy of Louisiana, Ron Johnson of Wisconsin, and Dean Heller of Nevada. Their plan would have replaced expanded Medicaid funding and subsidies with block grants to states to finance health coverage in other ways. (Congress did not pass a health care overhaul.)

The White House plan also assumed Congress would approves changes to Medicare that would result in growth reductions of $554 billion over ten years.

Homeland Security. The budget outline called for $46 billion in discretionary funding for the Department of Homeland Security, an increase of $3.6 billion or 8.5 percent from fiscal 2017, mostly to crack down on illegal immigration. The request included $23 billion for immigration enforcement and border security.

Since Trump's presidential campaign, he had pushed for funding for a wall on the U.S.–Mexico border, and requested about $18 billion—divided between the fiscal 2018 and 2019 budgets—to build the wall. A $1.6 billion request in the 2019 budget was for sixty-five miles of wall in the Rio Grande Valley. In fiscal 2018 spending, the president sought $1.6 billion for the first seventy-four miles of wall, to be built between the San Diego area and Texas. The remainder of the $18 bill, according to OMB Director Mick Mulvaney, would be requested in ongoing negotiations with Congress to protect children of illegal immigrants enrolled in the expiring Deferred Action for Childhood Arrivals program. Trump was demanding funding for the border wall and other border security projects in exchange for protecting the so-called Dreamers, but Democrats were opposed.

The budget request also included

- $14.2 billion for Customs and Border Protection, an increase of more than 17 percent, in part to hire 750 more Border Patrol agents
- $8.3 billion for Immigration and Customs Enforcement, a nearly 30 percent increase from fiscal 2017, in part to hire 2,000 more agents
- $208 million for ICE to hire 300 new special agents focused on enforcement of immigration laws at worksites, human trafficking cases, and immigration fraud
- $2.5 billion to expand immigrant detention facility space

The administration's request included $6.7 billion in disaster relief funding, the same as approved for fiscal 2017, and $19 billion for FEMA, $1.9 billion for the Coast Guard, and $2.2 billion for the Secret Service (to hire another 450 agents, officers, and staff).

Housing and Urban Development. The president requested $41.2 billion in discretionary funding for HUD, down from $48 billion in fiscal 2017—a 14 percent cut. The administration proposed eliminating three grant programs:

- The Community Development Block Grant program (funded at $3 billion in fiscal 2017), which helped communities fund such projects as infrastructure improvement, economic development, community centers, housing rehabilitation, and public services
- The HOME Investment Partnerships Program (funded $950 million in fiscal 2017), which provided grants to states and localities to help build or rehabilitate affordable housing or provide rental assistance for low-income households
- The Choice Neighborhoods Program (funded $137 million in fiscal 2017), which helped struggling neighborhoods revitalize distressed public housing and address other necessary improvements in the area

The proposal also requested cancelling $137 million in unobligated fiscal 2018 funds for the Choice Neighborhoods program. Further, the proposal would reduce the Tenant-Based Rental Assistance program by $982 billion, dropping it to 1 percent below the fiscal 2017 enacted level.

The proposal included a $400 billion limit for loan guarantees by HUD's Federal Housing Administration, which typically provides mortgage insurance for first-time buyers. The amount was level with the fiscal 2017 funding. The White House also aimed to reduce funding for the Public Housing Operating Fund, the Native American Housing Block Grants program, and the Housing Opportunities for People with AIDS program.

Interior. The White House requested $11.5 billion in discretionary funding, a 15 percent reduction from fiscal 2017 enacted funding, for the Interior Department. The request included $792 million for all energy-related programs at the Department of the Interior—slightly more than the $791.2 million fiscal 2017 level—as it focused on the administration's desire to achieve energy dominance. The budget also would cancel contract authority for the Land and Water Conservation Fund ($28.1 million).

Of the request, $179 million would be budgeted for the Bureau of Ocean Energy Management, about $10.9 million above the 2017 level. That total would include $9.4 million for the bureau's continued rewrite of the five-year offshore oil and gas leasing program to allow offshore lease sales in areas that the Obama administration had closed off. Another $17.5 million was budgeted for a reorganization of the Interior Department into twelve unified regions, with boundaries defined by rivers and ecosystems rather than states. That plan would relocate many Washington officials to field offices.

The budget also estimated a cost of $6.8 billion over ten years to maintain a proposed "Public Lands Infrastructure Fund" of a maximum of $18 billion that would use some revenue from energy development on federal lands to pay for infrastructure projects on those lands.

Judiciary. The proposal included $7.2 billion, up from $6.8 billion in the fiscal 2017 enacted level, to fund the Supreme Court, federal district and circuit courts, and the U.S. Sentencing commission. It included $84 million for Supreme Court salaries and expenses, up from $76 million in fiscal 2017.

The administration sought a 27 percent boost, from $40 million in fiscal 2017, to $51 million, for fees paid to

jurors and commissioners. Federal courts at the time paid jurors $40 per day for serving on trial or grand juries.

Justice Department. The administration requested $28 billion for the Department of Justice, down slightly from $28.4 billion in fiscal 2017. The budget proposal included more than a 2 percent increase, to $14.2 billion, for federal law enforcement, including the FBI, as it sought to prioritizing fighting violent crime and the continuing opioid epidemic. The administration also said it would consolidate many offices and jobs to save taxpayers money. The DOJ planned to close two of six regional Bureau of Prisons offices and two of its seven minimum security prison camps, according to Assistant Attorney General Lee Lofthus.

The administration also planned to eliminate the State Criminal Alien Assistance Program, which was funded at $210 million in 2017. The program reimbursed state and local government for the costs of incarcerating undocumented immigrants charged with crimes. The budget also sought to reduce the COPS hiring program from 195 million to $99 million. The office of Special Counsel Robert S. Mueller III, who was looking into potential Russian interference in the 2016 elections, was budgeted at $10.4 million in the fiscal 2019 request.

Labor. Under the president's request, the Labor Department would be provided $10.9 billion in discretionary funding, $1.1 billion or 21.4 percent less than fiscal 2017 levels. The president requested a $105 million increase in apprenticeship training programs from the $95 million level in fiscal 2017, but a $407 million decrease for the Job Corps program, which would be achieved in part by closing certain low-performing Job Corps centers.

The White House sought $27 million for the Office of Disability Employment Policy, an $11 million reduction from fiscal 2017, and asked to eliminate a program aimed at helping low-income senior citizens find work. The administration called for a $2.1 million increase, to $375.9 million for the Mine Safety and Health Administration, and a $2.6 million boost for the Veterans' Employment and Training Service. The State Department sought $13 billion for diplomatic security programs, construction at embassies, and funding for international organizations—28 percent below the $18 billion level in fiscal 2017.

State Department. The administration asked for $39.3 billion for the State Department and the U.S. Agency for International Development (USAI). The fiscal 2017 spending level was 29 percent higher. The administration sought $6.4 billion for disaster aid and the Migration and Refugee Assistance account, an almost 18 percent decrease from the fiscal 2017 level of $7.8 billion total for the two accounts. Another $4.8 billion would be provided for the President's Emergency Plan for AIDS Relief, a 27 percent cut from the fiscal 2017 level of almost $6.6 billion, and $1.1 billion to support United Nations' activities, 20 percent below the fiscal 2017 level.

Funding for USAID, the Millennium Challenge Corporation, the Peace Corps, and bilateral economic assistance would drop by 31 percent from the 2017 level of $39.6 billion. USAID's budget would be cut 12.5 percent. The budget would cut by half the $170 million in fiscal 2017 funding for the National Endowment for Democracy, and would eliminate the emergency Food for Peace account.

According to the budget document, the State Department would create a U.S. Development Finance Institution to steer private investment funds toward certain developing countries, replacing the Overseas Private Investment Corporation. An unspecified amount would be provided to build a new embassy in Jerusalem, as President Trump in late 2017 recognized the city as Israel's capital. The budget request, however, did not include billions in aid cuts for countries that voted against the U.S. position on recognition of Jerusalem as the capital, which the president had threatened.

Transportation. The budget proposal would cut discretionary funding for the Department of Transportation programs and activities by 19.2 percent, or $19.3 billion, from the 2017 level to $115.6 billion. The president included in his budget a proposal to spend $200 billion over ten years to invest in infrastructure. Meanwhile, his request included cutting such popular transportation programs as the Transportation Investment Generating Economic Recovery discretionary grant program, and the Capital Investment Grant program at the Federal Transit Administration, and cutting grants in half for Amtrak.

The request included $60.9 billion in mandatory spending for highways, bridges, transit and other accounts, and projected the Highway Trust Fund—which finances most highway projects—would be depleted by the beginning of fiscal 2023. The president also included his request to privatize air traffic control, removing it from the Federal Aviation Authority, a proposal pushed by House Transportation and Infrastructure Chair Bill Shuster of Pennsylvania.

Veterans Affairs. The Department of Veterans Affairs was one of few accounts where Trump requested a funding increase: $85.5 billion in discretionary funding, an $11.1 billion or 15 percent increase from the 2017 enacted level. The plan included an extra $1.9 billion in discretionary funding for the Veterans Choice Program, which sought to help certain former service members access private care. The request also included $4.2 billion for information technology infrastructure to replace outdated data systems.

ECONOMIC OUTLOOK

The White House suggested that, if its proposed budget policies were approved, the nation would see a 3 percent economic growth over the coming decade. Yet the deficit was projected to continue to increase, to $873 billion in fiscal 2018, $984 billion in 2019 and $987 billion in 2020 before beginning to decline. The deficit was $665 billion in fiscal 2017.

The nonpartisan Congressional Budget Office in April 2018 had projected a continued rise in the federal budget deficit in the next few years before stabilizing between 2023 and 2028, increasing the federal debt to nearly 100 percent of GDP by 2028—the highest debt in any year since just after World War II. It predicted the result would be higher if a tax overhaul barred a significant increase in individual income taxes in 2026 and if funding for defense and nondefense discretionary programs was decreased.

The CBO said the deficit would rise from $665 billion in 2017 to $804 billion in 2018 and $981 billion in 2019, with deficits continuing to grow to $1.5 trillion by 2028. That projection was similar to the $1.1 trillion fiscal 2019 deficit predicted by the Committee for Responsible Federal Budget and Goldman Sachs. (In reality, the federal deficit in 2018 was $449 billion, equal to 3.9 percent of GDP, and $984 billion in 2019, equal to 4.6 percent of GDP.)

The CBO said its projected deficits in the next decade had increased since June 2017, when it had predicted a debt reaching 91 percent of GDP, or $25.5 trillion in 2027. The increase in its projected deficits, CBO said, was primarily due to the tax overhaul, called Tax Cuts and Jobs Act (PL 115-97), the Bipartisan Budget Act of 2018 (PL 115-123), and the Consolidated Appropriations Act of 2018 (PL 115-141). *(See above.)*

The CBO also said that real GDP (GDP adjusted for inflation) and real potential GDP would be greater in the next decade than previously expected due to the recent legislative changes. It also projected higher interest rates and a lower unemployment rate. CBO projected that real GDP would expand by 3.3 percent in 2018 and 2.4 percent in 2019, following a 2.6 percent growth in 2017, largely driven by consumer spending and business investment, as well as federal spending. Between 2020 and 2026, the real GDP growth would average 1.7 percent, and 1.8 percent in 2027 and 2028. (In reality, the real GDP increased 2. 9 percent in 2018, and 2.3 percent in 2019.)

But between 2020 and 2026, higher interest rates and prices, slower growth in federal outlays, and the expiration of reductions in personal income taxes would slow economic growth, CBO said. The CBO economic outlook was slightly stronger than the March 2018 Blue Chip Economic Indicators.

BUDGET RESOLUTION

The House and Senate did not devise a budget resolution for fiscal 2019. The two-year bipartisan deal (PL 115-123) reached in February had set discretionary spending targets for fiscal 2019, and Senate leaders were not interested in a reconciliation process to cut mandatory or entitlement program spending that would lead to partisan votes that could impact Republicans in the midterm elections.

Regardless of the Senate's plans, however, the House Budget Committee on June 21, 2018, approved a budget resolution in a party line, 21–13 vote. Rep. Tom McClintock, R-Calif., initially had criticized the plan for instructing the House authorizing committee to reduce the deficit by just $302 billion over ten years through the reconciliation process. He said the reconciliation instructions should be for $5.4 trillion in mandatory spending cuts over ten years, as reflected in the budget blueprint. However, McClintock voted for the measure in committee.

Before adopting the resolution, the committee rejected 28 Democratic amendments, including a proposal by Suzan Kay DelBene of Washington that would have increased budget authority to restore funding for the Supplemental Nutrition Assistance Program (SNAP) by reversing tax cuts in the 2017 tax overhaul (PL 115-97). The amendment was rejected 9–16.

Also by a 9–16 vote, the panel rejected an amendment by Democrat Michelle Lujan Grisham of New Mexico that would have added language stating that the Trump administration's policy of separating children from their family at the U.S.–Mexico border was "cruel and inhumane" and that taxpayer dollars should not be spent to implement the policy. The amendment also would have called on Congress to pass immigration reform legislation.

Several other Democratic amendments were rejected despite gaining some Republican support. Those proposals included

- An amendment by Rep. Barbara Lee of California to express opposition to the Overseas Contingency Operations account, which is exempt from discretionary budget limits. The amendment fell, 15–17. Republicans McClinton, Rob Woodall of Georgia, and Jason Lewis of Minnesota joined eleven Democrats to support the proposal
- An amendment by John Yarmuth of Kentucky that expressed support for the elimination of a so-called carried interest tax break, which permits asset managers to pay taxes on compensation at the lower capital gains rate. The amendment was rejected, 16–18. Republicans Glenn Grothman of Wisconsin, Matt Gaetz of Florida, and Lewis joined thirteen Democrats to support the proposal
- An amendment by Yarmuth to support a partial rollback of the previous year's tax cuts to finance full survivor annuities for about 64,000 military spouses. Republicans Bill Johnson of Ohio, Jack Bergman of Minnesota, and Gaetz supported the amendment, which ultimately was defeated 14–18
- An amendment by Rep. Hakeem Jeffries of New York to indicate support for erasing a $10,000 cap on itemized deductions for state and local property taxes, which was rejected 11–14. Republicans McClintock and John J. Faso of New York joined nine Democrats to support the amendment

The House Budget Committee's action was only symbolic, as the Senate had no intention to act. The Senate

Budget Committee held a hearing on February 13, 2018, but did not a draft a resolution for markup.

Fiscal Year 2019 Appropriations

With the fiscal 2019 appropriations process, Congress sought to get back on track and enact individual spending bills and send them to the president before the start of the new fiscal year. But with fiscal 2018 appropriations already delayed and time running out, lawmakers ultimately combined several bills into various minibus spending measures. Yet, again, disagreements over several issues—particularly the president's insistence on funding for his promised border wall—stalled progress on seven appropriations bills, forcing lawmakers to shut down part of the government and delay completion of the fiscal 2019 appropriations process until the next Congress.

Lawmakers began drafting the fiscal 2019 measures even before Congress had cleared the fiscal 2018 omnibus spending package. The first fiscal 2019 spending measure that Congress sent to the White House was a three-bill package (encompassing the Military Construction–Veterans Affairs, Legislative Branch, and Energy–Water spending measures), which President Trump signed in mid-September. It was the first time in a decade that Congress had delivered a spending bill to the White House on time.

The next minibus, a two-bill package (containing the Defense and Labor-HHS-Education bills), was cleared before the October 1 deadline, but Congress had to include a continuing resolution to keep open those remaining government agencies that had not had their fiscal 2019 funding approved. A four-bill omnibus tailed that measure. That package encompassed the Agriculture, Financial Services, Interior–Environment and Transportation–HUD measures. That left incomplete three more regular spending bills (Commerce–Justice–Science, Homeland Security, and State-Foreign Operations), which were continuing to move separately. Ultimately seven bills remained incomplete at the end of the Congress when negotiations stalled.

THREE-BILL MINIBUS

Both chambers jumped on the fiscal 2019 appropriations process quickly with the aim of breaking a trend in previous years of passing megaspending omnibus measures that comprised all the bills. After Congress cleared in two days the $1.3 trillion fiscal 2018 omnibus, called the Consolidated Appropriations Act of 2018 (PL 115-141), President Trump had signed the measure but said he would not sign another last-minute omnibus.

The House and Senate Appropriations committees moved their Military Construction–Veterans Affairs, Legislative Branch and Energy–Water appropriations bills rapidly to the floors, where they were wrapped into a single package for a final vote. However, with work delayed by fiscal 2018 spending negotiations and other priorities,

negotiations on the two versions were not finalized until September, and the president signed the minibus (HR 5895) shortly before the start of the new fiscal year.

House Action

House Republicans in late April discussed moving the least contentious of the appropriations bills to the floor and on to the Senate quickly, selecting the Military Construction–Veterans Affairs, Legislative Branch, and Energy–Water bills first.

Military Construction–Veterans Affairs. On April 26, 2018, the House Military Construction–VA Appropriations Subcommittee approved by voice vote a $96.9 billion fiscal 2019 spending bill, $4 billion or 5 percent above the fiscal 2018 level. Ranking Democrat Debbie Wasserman Schultz of Florida, however, criticized Republicans for including $69 million to fund a new military prison at Guantanamo Bay, Cuba.

On May 8, the House Appropriations Committee approved the $96.9 billion spending bill (HR 5786) by a vote of 47–0. Before approving the bill, the panel adopted a manager's amendment by subcommittee chairman Charlie Dent, R-Pa., that included, among other provisions, a provision stating that funding to build a $69 million new detention facility at Guantanamo Bay, Cuba, would be contingent on Congress passing authorizing legislation.

Legislative Branch. A House appropriations subcommittee on April 26 gave voice vote approval to a $3.8 billion spending for the legislative branch in fiscal 2019, $132 million more than the fiscal 2018 level. Funding for Senate operations would be approved by that chamber's appropriators. On May 8, the Appropriations Committee approved the Legislative Branch spending bill (HR 5894) on a 47–0 vote after adopting by voice vote a manager's amendment by subcommittee chairman Kevin Yoder, R-Kan., that would halt funding for former House speakers, who were entitled to keep an office on Capitol Hill for five years.

Energy–Water. On May 7, 2018, the House Energy–Water appropriations subcommittee approved, by voice vote, a $44.7 billion fiscal 2019 spending bill for water infrastructure and energy-related activities and projects. The bill would provide $1.5 billion more than the fiscal 2018 enacted level for such activities and $8.2 billion more than Trump requested. The measure would provide about $35.5 billion for the Department of Energy, up $1 billion from fiscal 2018; $7.3 billion for the Army Corps of Engineers, almost $500 million more than in fiscal 2018; and $1.6 billion for the Interior Department's Bureau of Reclamation, a $100 million boost from fiscal 2018.

On May 16, 2018, the House Appropriations Committee approved, by a 29–20 vote, the $44.7 billion spending for water infrastructure and energy-related projects (HR 5895). House Republicans then combined the Energy–Water bill with the Military Construction–Veterans Affairs and Legislative Branch spending bills to form a minibus spending measure (HR 5895).

On June 8, 2018, the House passed the $147 billion three-bill spending package in a mostly partisan vote of 235–179. In the final vote, sixteen Republicans voted with Democrats to oppose the package, while twenty-three Democrats voted for the measure.

The majority of Democrats objected to the GOP's environmental policy riders and funding priorities in the energy–water portion of the bill. Among the policy riders was one that would repeal the Waters of the United States rule, an Obama-era rule that expanded federal jurisdiction for enforcement of clean water regulations. The bill also included $268 million to restart the approval process for the Yucca Mountain nuclear waste site in Nevada.

Senate Action

Senate appropriators moved three individual spending bills to the floor, including the Energy–Water, Military Construction–Veterans Affairs, and Legislative Branch.

Energy–Water. On May 22, the Senate Energy and Water appropriations subcommittee gave voice vote approval to a $43.8 billion funding bill for energy and water-related programs and activities for fiscal 2019. The Senate Appropriations Committee on May 24, 2018, voted 30–1 to approve the bill (S 2975), which would provide $566 million more than the fiscal 2018 level and $7.2 billion more than Trump requested. The bill would provide $35 billion for the Department of Energy, $69 billion for the Army corps of Engineers, and $1.5 billion for the Interior Department's Bureau of Reclamation.

Sen. Lindsey Graham, R-S.C., voted against the bill because it included a provision to defund a mixed oxide fuel fabrication facility in his state, a facility that had suffered cost overruns and construction delays. Graham said he wanted the site to be finished so it could handle thirty-four metric tons of weapons-grade plutonium needed to be disposed of in accordance with a disarmament treaty with Russia. He opposed a plan to instead dispose of the plutonium at a defense facility in southeastern New Mexico, but Sen. Lamar Alexander, R-Tenn., chairman of the Energy–Water appropriations subcommittee, said the change would result in $30 billion in savings.

Military Construction–VA. The Military Construction-VA Appropriations Subcommittee approved, by unanimous consent, a fiscal 2019 (S 3024) bill that would provide nearly $98 billion in discretionary funding, a 5.7 percent increase from fiscal 2018. Two days later, the full Appropriations Committee approved the bill in a 31–0 vote. Before approving the measure, appropriators adopted by voice vote an amendment by Jeff Merkley, D-Ore., and Steve Daines, R-Mont., that would bar the Department of Veterans Affairs from using funds to implement agency policy that bars doctors from referring patients to medical marijuana clinics.

Legislative Branch. On June 14, the Appropriations Committee voted 31–0 to approve a fiscal 2019 legislative branch spending bill (S 3071) that would provide $4.79 billion in discretionary funding for the Senate, Library of Congress, Capitol police, and other legislative agencies—$90 million more than in fiscal 2018. The committee adopted, by unanimous consent, an amendment that would boost funding for Senate office accounts by $5 million in order to pay interns.

On June 18, senators voted 92–3 to invoke cloture (end debate) and proceed to the House's three-bill package (HR 5895). The Senate then agreed, via an amendment by Senate Appropriations Chairman Richard C. Shelby, R-Ala., to swap out the House bills for the bills approved by the Senate Appropriations Committee.

The Senate on June 25, 2018, passed its $146.6 billion version of HR 5895 by a vote of 86–5. Republicans Mike Lee of Utah and Rand Paul of Kentucky joined Democrats Kirsten Gillibrand of New York, as well as Edward J. Markey and Elizabeth Warren of Massachusetts in voting against the bill. Rather than fund the Yucca Mountain waste site, the Senate included a provision to fund a pilot interim storage program.

Final Action

Congress cleared HR 5895 in September after House and Senate negotiators met to resolve a number of differences between the House and Senate versions of the bill (HR 5895). For instance, the House version would allocate $44.7 billion for Energy–Water, and Senate's would provide $43.8 billion. Further, the House version carried several environmental policy riders not included in the Senate package. The measures had minor differences in the Military Construction–Veterans Affairs portions apart from a policy rider in the House bill instructing the Department of Veterans Affairs to use funds to prioritize research on the safety and medical effectiveness of cannabis, while the Senate bill aimed to lift agency policy that barred referrals to medical marijuana clinics.

At one point, conference negotiations were temporarily sidelined as talks continued about differing House and Senate funding levels for all twelve spending bills. If negotiators finalized spending levels on the three bills in the minibus package, that could impact the levels of the other nine spending bills that had not reached that point. After several weeks, conferees reached a deal on HR 5895. The measure would include $98.1 billion for military construction and veterans affairs projects and activities, a 5.8 percent increase; $44.6 billion for energy and water-related activities, a 3.2 percent increase; and $4.8 billion for the legislative branch, a 2.1 percent increase. Conferees agreed to drop all Republicans' partisan policy riders.

The Senate adopted, 92–5, the conference report on the three-bill package on September 12, 2018. Republicans Jeff Flake of Arizona and Rand Paul of Kentucky joined Democrats Kirsten Gillibrand, Ed Markey, and Elizabeth Warren in voting against the measure.

The House voted 377–20 to clear the minibus (HR 5895) on September 13, 2018. The measure was opposed by 18

Republicans and two Democrats (Reps. Ted Lieu of California and Jan Schakowsky of Illinois). The president signed the three-bill, $147.5 billion omnibus into law (PL 115-244) on September 21, 2018.

Highlights

The final three-bill package included $9 billion more for the agencies funded than Trump requested, and $6 billion more than in fiscal 2018. Lawmakers rejected almost $8.3 billion in cuts the president sought for Energy–Water accounts.

The president had sought cuts of more than 34 percent to many Energy Department programs, but lawmakers instead added $5.5 billion, above the president's request, to all DOE accounts, and provided another $2.2 billion for the Army Corps of Engineers, for a total that reached 46 percent above the request. Lawmakers also rejected Trump's requested 29 percent cut to the Bureau of Reclamation and added $501 million to his request.

TWO-BILL MINIBUS, STOP-GAP FUNDING

Beginning in June, the House and Senate Appropriations committees moved their versions of the Defense and Labor–HHS–Education spending bills to the floor. After the House had passed its Defense bill and before it passed the Labor–HHS–Education measure, the Senate moved its versions of the bills to the floor where leaders passed them as one package.

House and Senate negotiators then finalized a more than $850 million, two-bill package (HR 6157) shortly before the start of the fiscal 2019 year. The president had hinted he might veto the bill because it did not include his requested $5 billion for his border wall, so negotiators had included in the package a continuing resolution to keep the government funded through December 7. The president ultimately signed the measure into law (PL 115-245) on September 28, 2018.

House Committee Action

Defense. The House Appropriations Defense Subcommittee on June 7, 2018, approved a bill (HR 6157) to provide $674.6 billion in discretionary spending for defense and intelligence programs in fiscal 2019. The bill would provide $20 billion more than the fiscal 2018 funding level.

The measure included $9.4 billion to purchase ninety-three F-35 joint strike fighter jets, which were built at Lockheed Martin's facility in subcommittee Chair Kay Granger's Texas district. The Pentagon had requested funding for seventy-seven new strike fighter jets. On June 13, the full appropriations committee voted 48–4 to approve the $674.6 billion defense spending bill. The committee approved, by voice vote, an amendment by Mark Pocan that would require the Pentagon to report to Congress on U.S. support for Saudi Arabia in the Yemeni civil war.

Labor, Education, Health, and Human Services. Meanwhile, on June 15, a House appropriations subcommittee approved, by voice vote, a $177.1 billion fiscal 2019 spending measure for the departments of Labor, Education, and Health and Human Services. The bill would provide slight funding increases from fiscal 2018, including: $89.2 billion for HHS, $1.1 billion more than in fiscal 2018; $71 billion for the Education Department, a $43 million increase; and $12.1 billion for the Labor Department, an $89 million decrease.

The full Appropriations Committee on July 11, 2018, voted 30–22 to approve the $177.1 billion Labor–Education–HHS spending bill (HR 6470). The panel adopted, on a 31–21 vote, an amendment by Rep. Tom Cole, R-Okla., that would overturn a 1997 legal settlement, known as the Flores agreement, that barred undocumented children from being held in a detention facility with their parents for more than twenty days while immigration court proceedings were pending.

House Floor Action

The House passed, in a 359–49 vote, the $674.6 billion fiscal 2019 defense spending bill (HR 6157) on June 28. Before passing the bill, the House adopted, in a 252–157 vote, an amendment by Rep. Katherine M. Clark, D-Mass., that would add $14 million for the Defense Innovation Unit Experimental, a Pentagon office that sought to access the latest technology in the commercial sector.

Members rejected, 144–267, an amendment by Rep. Joe Courtney, D-Conn., that would have shifted $1 billion from several Defense Department programs to a Virginia-class submarine program. Courtney said the extra funding would enable the Navy to procure parts for two more submarines on top of the ten submarines that had been approved. The House also rejected, 160–251, a proposal by Rep. Bill Foster, D-Ill, that would have barred federal spending on space-based anti-missile interceptors. The full House did not consider the individual Labor–Education–HHS spending bill (HR 6470).

SENATE COMMITTEE ACTION

Labor, Education, and Health and Human Services. On June 26, a Senate appropriations subcommittee approved a $179.3 billion measure for Labor, HHS, and Education. The bill would provide $2.3 billion more for HHS and $541 million more for Education, as well as $92 million more for Labor, compared to fiscal 2018. On June 28, the Appropriations Committee approved, 30–1, the $179.3 billion spending bill (S 3158). Sen. James Lankford, R-Okla., voted against the measure.

Defense. Also on June 26, the Senate Defense Appropriations Subcommittee approved, by voice vote, the $675 billion draft spending bill for defense and intelligence programs, including funding for thirteen ships and righty-nine F-35 joint strike fighters for fiscal 2019. The Appropriations Committee approved the $675 billion spending bill (S 3159) on June 28.

In July, Senate Appropriations Chair Richard Shelby, R-Ala., and Senate Minority Whip Richard Durbin, D-Ill., advocated speeding up the appropriations process by combining the Defense measure (S 3159) with the Labor–HHS–Education bill (S 3158), the biggest nondefense spending bill. Combined, the bills would comprise about 63 percent of total discretionary spending for fiscal 2019. Leaders agreed to use the House-passed Defense bill (HR 6157) as the underlying vehicle for the passage.

On August 23, the Senate passed the $856.9 billion two-bill spending minibus (HR 6157) by a vote of 85–7. The measure was opposed by Republican Sens. Michael D. Crapo and Jim Risch of Idaho, Mike Lee of Utah, Jeff Flake of Arizona, Rand Paul of Kentucky, and Patrick J. Toomey of Pennsylvania, as well as independent Bernie Sanders of Vermont. Five Republicans and three Democrats did not vote: Sens. Bob Corker, R-Tenn.; John Cornyn and Ted Cruz, R-Texas; Deb Fischer, R-Neb.; John McCain, R-Ariz.; Mazie K. Hirono and Brian Schatz, D-Hawaii; and Patty Murray, D-Wash.

The package would provide $90.1 billion for HHS, up from $88.2 billion in fiscal 2018; $71.4 billion for the Education Department, up from $70.9 billion; and Labor would receive about $92 million less than the $12.2 billion it received in 2018. The bill would provide about $675 billion for defense and intelligence activities. The final vote on the package came after the committee approved a manager's amendment that included a provision to provide $1 million for HHS to develop regulations requiring drugmakers to include pricing information in their advertisements. That amendment also included a provision, offered by Kirsten Gillibrand, D-N.Y., that would provide $45 million to clean up perfluorooctane sulfonate and perfluorooctanoic acid contamination at military bases. The chemicals had been found to have contaminated drinking water and were suspected of causing a range of health problems for soldiers and veterans.

Final Action

On September 5, 2018, the House voted to go to conference with the Senate on a final two-bill spending package (HR 6157) to incorporate both the defense funding measure and the spending bill for Labor, Education, and HHS departments. House members agreed to the conference despite the fact that the full House had not considered the Labor–Education–HHS bill (HR 6470) approved by its Appropriations Committee, and appropriators agreed to the Senate's higher price tag for that portion of the bill.

On September 13, 2018, House and Senate negotiators agreed on a more than $850 billion package that would include

- $674.4 billion in discretionary spending for defense and intelligence activities, including $67.9 billion for overseas contingency operations (warfare)

- Nearly $178.1 billion for Labor, Education and HHS, about a $1 billion boost from fiscal 2018 funding and $10.7 billion more than President Trump requested. That included $90.3 billion for HHS, a $2.3 billion or 2.6-percent boost; $71.4 billion for Education, a $581 million or less than 1 percent boost; $12.1 billion for the Labor Department, a decrease of $128 million from fiscal 2018

GOP leaders also decided to tack onto the spending package a continuing resolution to keep the government funded through December 7, a move to avoid a shutdown of those agencies that did not have approved funding by October 1, the beginning of fiscal 2019.

On September 18, the Senate voted 93–7 to pass the conference report on the two-bill minibus. On Twitter on September 20, President Trump called the conferees' deal "ridiculous" because it did not include his $5 billion request to begin building a wall along the U.S.–Mexico border, and he threatened to veto the bill if it was cleared by Congress. The House on September 26, 2018, in a 361–61 vote, cleared the conference report for the president's signature, overcoming conservative Republicans' objections to the removal of policy riders from the Labor–Education–HHS portion of the bill. Trump, mostly via Twitter, continued to state his objections that the bill did not include funding for the border wall and continued to hint he might veto the measure. Suggesting Republicans might provide his requested funding after the midterms, the president signed the package into law (HR 6157; PL 115-245) on September 28, 2018.

FOUR-BILL MINIBUS

Lawmakers also took up a four-bill minibus that encompassed the Agriculture, Financial Services, Interior-Environment and Transportation–HUD spending measures. House and Senate appropriators got an early start with their drafts for the fiscal 2019 Agriculture, Financial Services, Interior–Environment and Transportation–HUD spending measures, moving them quickly to the floors of each chamber. The House passed a package that included Interior–Environment and the Financial Services bills in July. Before the House took up the other two bills, the Senate moved a package comprising all four measures (HR 6147).

House–Senate negotiations faltered amid disagreement on Republican's policy riders. After the president signed a stop-gap spending measure as part of the two-bill omnibus (PL 115-245), negotiations were postponed until after the 2018 midterm elections. Ultimately, a second stop-gap measure was signed into law to keep the government running through December 21 while lawmakers and the White House pursued negotiations. But the stalemate over the GOP policy riders as well as Trump's $5 billion request for a border wall led to a partial government shutdown when that stopgap expired. The shutdown continued into the next year.

House Committee Action

Agriculture. The Agriculture Appropriations Subcommittee on March 9, 2018, approved by voice vote a $145.1 billion fiscal 2019 spending bill, including $23.27 billion in discretionary funds, for the Department of Agriculture, Food and Drug Administration, and the Commodity Futures Trading Commission. The total was about $922 million less than the fiscal 2018 level.

On May 16, 2018, the House Appropriations Committee approved the $145.1 billion measure (HR 5961).

Before approving the bill, the committee adopted an amendment by Reps. Sanford D. Bishop Jr., D-Ga., and Tom Cole, R-Okla., that aimed to remove e-cigarettes from lengthy FDA market review and require the FDA to create a new regulatory process for e-cigarettes and nicotine vapor products. The bill also included a policy rider that would require the USDA to regulate products grown from cells for human consumption, a provision not included in the Senate counterpart (S 2976).

Financial Services. The House Financial Services Appropriations Subcommittee on May 24 approved by voice vote a draft $23.4 billion spending bill for financial services, providing about $100,000 more than the fiscal 2018 level. On June 13, the House Appropriations Committee voted 28–20 to approve the $23.4 billion spending bill (HR 6258). The bill would increase funding for the IRS, the White House, and federal courts. The bill would discontinue, for a second year, a $380 million grant program for election assistance and equipment for states while creating a new, $585 million account called the Fund for America's Kids and Grandkids. Republicans rejected, in a 21–30 vote, an amendment by Illinois Democrat Mike Quigley that would have shifted $380 million from the proposed fund to the Election Assistance Commission to finance state grants.

The bill included several policy riders, including language that would block some District of Columbia laws—such as the legalization of marijuana—from being enacted, place the Consumer Financial Protection Bureau under the appropriations process, and bar the Securities and Exchange Commission from implementing a rule that requires public companies to report their political contributions.

Interior-Environment. On May 15, the House Interior–Environment Subcommittee approved by voice vote a draft $35.3 billion spending bill for the Interior Department and the EPA. The bill would provide $8 billion for the EPA, a $100 million decrease from fiscal 2018, and $13.2 billion for the Interior Department, a $200 million cut. Democrats strongly objected to GOP policy riders, including provisions aimed at paving the way to repeal the Waters of the United States regulation and undercut other environmental protections laws such as the Endangered Species Act.

The Appropriations Committee voted 25–20 to approve the $35.3 billion spending bill (HR 6147) on June 6 after Republicans rejected a series of Democratic amendments targeting the Interior Department's reorganization plans, administration rollbacks of offshore oil leasing regulations, and fourteen environmental policy riders added by Republicans.

Transportation-HUD. The House Transportation–HUD Appropriations Subcommittee approved, by voice vote, a $71.8 billion fiscal 2019 spending bill, which would provide the departments of Transportation and Housing and Urban Development a 2 percent increase above the fiscal 2018 level. The measure was well above the White House request of $48 billion.

The full appropriations committee approved the bill (HR 6072) by a partisan vote of 34–17 on May 23. Democrats voted against the bill, saying they opposed the GOP policy riders and a proposed decrease in funding, from $1.36 billion in fiscal 2018 to $1.2 billion, for HUD's HOME Investment Partnerships Program that provided housing grants to states and localities. Five Democrats supported the bill: Sanford D. Bishop Jr. of Georgia, Henry Cuellar of Texas, C.A. Dutch Ruppersberger of Maryland, Peter J. Visclosky of Indiana, and Debbie Wasserman Schultz of Florida.

House Floor Action

On July 19, the House voted 217–199 to pass a spending package (HR 6147) that included the $58.7 billion Interior-Environment spending bill and the Financial Services appropriations measure. Senate leaders at the time already were talking about combining the two measures with the two bills funding the Transportation, HUD and Agriculture departments, and vowed to keep off policy riders such as those that weighed down the House's financial services portion of the package. The House had not considered Transportation–HUD or the Agriculture spending bills by the time the Senate approved a package comprising all four bills.

Senate Committee Action

Agriculture. On May 22, the Senate Agriculture Appropriations Subcommittee approved by voice vote a bill to provide $23.24 billion in discretionary funding and $121.8 billion in mandatory funding for the Agriculture Department in fiscal 2019. The full committee approved the bill (S 2976) by a 31–0 vote on May 24 after giving voice vote approval to a manager's amendment that would, among other things, maintain a ban on spending Agriculture funds to inspect horses slated for slaughter for human consumption.

Financial Services. The Senate Appropriations Financial Services Subcommittee gave unanimous consent to approve a draft $23.7 billion discretionary spending bill for financial services on June 19, 2018. The measure included $800 million for the purchase of the Transportation Department's headquarters in southeast Washington, which the department was renting. The Senate Appropriations Committee on June 21 approved, in a 31–0 vote, the $23.7 billion spend-

ing bill (S 3107). Before approving the bill, the panel adopted without objection a manager's amendment that, among other things, barred funds for the Office of Management and Budget to alter the annual work plan crafted by the Army Corps of Engineers and submitted to the appropriations committee. The House Financial Services Appropriations Subcommittee approved a similar provision in its bill.

Interior–Environment. A Senate appropriations subcommittee approved by voice vote $35.9 billion for the Department of the Interior and the EPA on June 12. The bill would provide a $600 increase from the fiscal 2018 funding level and $7.6 billion more than the White House requested. The bill would provide $8.1 billion for the EPA and $13.2 billion for the Department of the Interior. The Appropriations Committee unanimously approved the bill (S 3073) on June 14 after adopting a manager's amendment that included language by Sen. Tom Udall, D-N.M., ranking member of the appropriations subcommittee, that called on the EPA to comply with ethics standards. The amendment was in response to a series of reports about ethics and spending improprieties by the EPA under Administrator Scott Pruitt.

Transportation–HUD. The Transportation-HUD Appropriations Subcommittee approved by voice vote on June 5 a draft spending bill that would provide $71.4 billion in discretionary spending for the departments of Transportation and Housing and Urban Development—a $1.1 billion or 1.6 percent boost from fiscal 2018. The measure included $26.6 billion for DOT, a 3 percent drop, and $44.5 billion for HUD, a 4 percent increase.

The Senate Appropriations Committee on June 7 approved the $71.4 billion measure (S 3023) by a vote of 31–0. During the markup, appropriators approved several amendments, wrapped into two managers amendments. They included language by Republican Sens. John Hoeven of North Dakota and Daines to exempt truckers carrying livestock from a rule on the use of electronic logging devices. Another amendment by Democrat Joe Manchin III and Republican Shelley Moore Capito of West Virginia would require Amtrak to have at least one ticket agent in every state where it stopped.

Senate Floor Action

After the House passed a two-bill package (HR 6147) on July 19, the Senate replaced the package with its own bills funding the interior, environment (S 3037), and financial services (S 3107) departments, and attached the Agriculture (S 2976) and Transportation–HUD (S 3023) spending measures, boosting the package to $154.2 billion.

The Senate on August 1 passed, by a 92–6 vote, its four-bill spending package. Six Republicans opposed the package: Sens. Cruz, Ron Johnson of Wisconsin, Mike Lee of Utah, Paul, Ben Sasse of Nebraska, and Patrick J. Toomey of Pennsylvania. The Senate rejected several cuts proposed by the White House, including a proposal to cut $20 billion

from the Transportation–HUD spending bill, and instead increased funding.

Before passing the measure, senators adopted by voice vote a manager's package encompassing forty-six amendments that added noncontroversial provisions. The Senate rejected, 50–47, an amendment by Sen. Patrick J. Leahy, D-Vt., to include $250 million for grants to help states strengthen election system security. Senators also rejected, 14–84, an amendment by Lee to bar the FDA from using funds to determine whether only products made from cow's milk could be labeled as milk. An amendment by Tammy Baldwin, D-Wisc. to include $7 million for programs related to innovation, process improvement, and marketing of dairy products was adopted by a vote of 83–15.

Final Action

With hopes of finalizing nine of the twelve spending bills in time, House leaders in September appeared willing to consider a conference report on the Senate version of HR 6147, even though the House had not separately considered the Agriculture and Transportation–HUD measures. House and Senate conferees began discussing the four-bill package, but negotiations faltered amid disagreements, primarily on controversial policy provisions included by House Republicans. Congress already had included a stopgap spending measure in the two-bill minibus, which continued through December 7 funding for departments affected by the four bills, as well as the three outstanding measures (Homeland Security, State-Foreign Ops, and Commerce–Justice State bills), so House and Senate negotiators in late September delayed action until after the midterm elections.

OTHER APPROPRIATIONS BILLS

House and Senate appropriators also moved the three other fiscal 2019 spending bills (Commerce–Justice–State, Homeland Security, and State-Foreign Operations) through their committees by July. But progress halted when negotiations on the four-bill minibus faltered. Funding for the agencies affected by the three measures was continued through December 21 via two continuing resolutions before a partial government shutdown began and lawmakers returned to their districts.

House Action

Justice–Science. The House appropriations subcommittee on May 9 approved by voice vote a fiscal 2019 spending bill that would provide $62.5 billion in discretionary funding for Commerce, Justice, and Science programs—about 42.9 billion more than in fiscal 2018.

The House Appropriations Committee on May 17 approved the measure (HR 5952) on a 32–19 vote. Before approving the bill, the committee rejected by voice vote an amendment by Rep. Lucille Roybal-Allard, D-Calif., that would have barred the Justice Department from using funds

to prosecute undocumented immigrants who cross the border to seek asylum. The committee also rejected by voice vote a proposal by Rep. José E. Serrano, D-N.Y., that would have barred the Census Bureau from including a citizenship question on the 2020 census. Many observers said such a question could discourage immigrants from filling out the form.

Homeland Security. The House Appropriations subcommittee approved a draft spending bill (HR 6776) for the Department of Homeland Security by voice vote on July 19, 2018. The bill would provide $51.4 billion or 8 percent more in discretionary funds for DHS than in fiscal 2018. The measure included Trump's request for $5 billion to build a wall along the southern border with Mexico.

On July 25, the full Appropriations Committee approved the $51.4 billion in a party line vote of 29–22. Republicans rejected several Democratic amendments that would have shifted the $5 billion in funds for the border wall to other projects. The committee approved, by voice vote, an amendment by Homeland Security Appropriations Subcommittee Chair Kevin Yoder, R-Kans., that would require DHS to permit detained immigrants to make free phone calls, to perform more unannounced DHS inspections of detention facilities, and to allow members of Congress into those facilities.

Members also gave voice vote approval to an amendment by Yoder and the subcommittee's ranking member Roybal-Ballard stating that DHS "shall only separate a child from a parent if the parent has a criminal history, a communicable disease, or is determined to be unfit or a danger to the child." The department had separated more than 2,500 children from their parents between April and June 2018 before public outcry and congressional pressure forced the administration to halt the practice.

State-Foreign Operations. A House appropriations subcommittee approved by voice vote a fiscal 2019 draft spending bill that would provide $54 billion for the State Department, U.S. Agency for International Development, international organizations and banks, and other aid agencies. The measure, which included $8 billion in war spending, would match the fiscal 2018 level and provide $11.8 billion more than the administration requested.

On June 20, the House Appropriations Committee approved the bill (HR 6385) in a 30–21 vote. The panel adopted by voice vote an amendment by Debbie Wasserman Schultz, D-Fla., that would require the government to allow lawmakers to visit immigrant detention facilities. The committee also adopted by voice vote a manager's package of amendments that include, for example, a proposal that would grant USAID more flexibility in how to spend economic support funds to rebuild portions of Iraq destroyed by the terrorist group ISIS.

Senate Action

Commerce–Justice–Science. A Senate appropriations subcommittee by voice vote on June 12, 2018, approved a draft fiscal 2019 spending bill that would provide $63 billion

for Commerce, Justice, and Science programs—$3.4 billion above the fiscal 2018 level but $2.7 billion less than Trump requested. The full Appropriations Committee voted 30–1 to approve the bill on June 14. The bill would provide $11.57 billion for the Commerce Department, $30.7 billion for the Justice Department, $21.3 billion for NASA, and $8.1 billion for the National Science Foundation. Sen. James Lankford, R-Okla., voted against the measure, objecting that the discretionary funding level was above the subcommittee's official allocation and that the bill would bar Attorney General Jeff Sessions from interfering in states that legalize medical marijuana use. The bill would provide $11.57 billion for the Commerce Department, $30.7 billion for the Justice Department, $21.3 billion for NASA, and $8.1 billion for the National Science Foundation.

Homeland Security. A Senate appropriations subcommittee approved a $48.33 billion spending bill for DHS on June 19. The bill included $1.6 billion for sixty-five miles of fencing in the Rio Grande Valley on the U.S.–Mexico border. The Senate Appropriations Committee, in a 26–5 vote, approved the spending bill (S 3109) for DHS on June 21, 2018.

The bill would provide $55.15 in total funding, including $48.33 billion in discretionary funding. The no votes came from Democratic Sens. Tom Udall of New Mexico, Dianne Feinstein of California, Richard J. Durbin of Illinois, Jeff Merkley of Oregon, and Brian Schatz of Hawaii. Many Democrats objected that the bill would provide $1.6 billion for sixty-five miles of barriers in the Rio Grande Valley.

The committee adopted, by voice vote, a manager's amendment that included, for example, a proposal by Durbin that would require the DHS to continue to provide Congress data, twice a year, on parents of U.S. citizen children who are deported. The panel also adopted by voice vote an amendment by Merkley that would require the Immigration and Customs Enforcement office to explore alternatives to detention.

State-Foreign Operations. A Senate appropriations subcommittee on June 19 approved a $54.4 billion State-Foreign Operations spending bill, which would provide $400 million more than the fiscal 2018 level and $12.2 billion more than the president requested. The full committee approved the measure (S 3108) by a vote of 31–0 on June 21. Before approving the bill, the panel adopted by voice vote a manager's amendment that encompassed the language of a series of amendments, including a proposal by Durbin that would require the State Department and the U.S. Agency for International Development to report on allegations of sexual exploitation by partners of U.S. foreign assistance programs.

STOP-GAP FUNDING AND GOVERNMENT SHUTDOWN

With the last continuing resolution (PL 115-245) set to expire on December 7, 2018, and agreement not reached on spending measures for nine departments and dozens of

agencies, congressional leaders moved quickly to clear a stopgap spending measure to keep those portions of the government open through December 21. The stopgap measure (HJ Res 143) also would extend several expiring authorizations, such as those for Violence Against Women Act programs, Temporary Assistance for Needy Families, and the National Flood Insurance Program.

The Senate passed the resolution by voice vote on December 6 and the House cleared it the same day. The president signed the continuing resolution (HJ Res 143) into law (PL 115-298) on the morning of December 7. Negotiations on the seven remaining bills (the four-bill package and Commerce–Justice–Science, Homeland Security, and State-Foreign Operations) were on hold that same week as lawmakers mourned the death of former President George Bush.

Meanwhile, Senate Democrats hoped to convince Trump to accept a Homeland Security bill that would provide $1.6 billion for another sixty-five miles of fencing in the Rio Grande Valley, as included in the Senate bill (S 3109), rather than the $5 billion he had requested and that the House had included in its bill (HR 6776). The senators also hoped to wrap the other remaining six bills into one package that would include a stopgap funding bill to fund DHS through the end of fiscal 2019.

Trump would not budge on his $5 billion request, and negotiations halted on all remaining seven appropriations bills. The House in December passed a stopgap measure (HR 695) that would fund the nine cabinet departments and various agencies through February 8, and would include $5.7 billion for the border wall. Senate leaders, however, would not allow a vote on the measure until a deal had been reached on the remaining spending bills. Senate Republican negotiators wanted a full appropriations package that included the fiscal 2019 measures for the remaining agencies, along with wall funding that exceeded $1.6 billion and with $7.8 million in aid for victims of recent hurricanes, wildfires, typhoons, and other natural disasters.

The stalemate forced a partial government shutdown that began on midnight of December 22 and continued into the next Congress. The shutdown affected about 25 percent of federal agency operating budgets and led to the furlough of more than 380,000 federal workers. Another 420,000 workers would have to continue working without pay, according to estimates by the Democratic staff of the Senate Appropriations Committee.

The shutdown affected portions of the departments of Agriculture, Commerce, Health and Human Services, Treasury and State; the EPA, financial services such as the Securities and Exchange Commission and Commodity Futures Trading Commission; and some National Park services. Employees at the Department of Homeland Security and the Justice Department, as well as at the Federal Aviation Administration, were exempt from a lapse in government funding.

2019–2020

The 116th Congress opened with most of the government shut down as President Trump declined to sign further appropriations measures until Congress agreed to his request for $5 billion for construction of a border wall. Negotiations were further complicated as the 2018 midterm elections resulted in a divided Congress. Democrats retook control of the House, but Republicans increased their majority in the Senate by one seat, holding fifty-two seats to the Democrats' forty-six seats.

On January 25, 2019, the shutdown ended with agreement to a short-term funding package pending negotiations on a final appropriations package for fiscal 2019. Congress and the president in February agreed to a $333 billion fiscal 2019 spending package that included about $1.4 billion for new barriers along the U.S. border with Mexico.

A few months later, Congress followed with a $19.1 billion emergency supplemental measure to provide relief and recovery funds for communities damaged by natural disasters over the previous two years, and a $4.59 billion emergency funding measure intended to address a humanitarian crisis as a growing number of Central American migrants crossed the southern border into the United States.

Negotiations on fiscal 2020 spending were again bogged down by the president's request for sharp cuts to domestic programs and his calls for more money for a border wall. Congress set new discretionary spending caps for fiscal years 2020 and 2021, thereby avoiding a sharp reduction in spending that would have been required by a 2011 budget law and enabling appropriators to reject most of the president's requests for funding cuts. But Congress had to pass a series of stopgap funding measures to keep the government open while House and Senate leaders negotiated final spending measures, which included a package of four spending bills and a package of eight bills.

Democrats in 2019, however, failed in their effort to pass a two-year reprieve from a $10,000 cap on state and local tax deductions imposed by the 2017 tax code overhaul and in their effort to obtain more disaster relief for Puerto Rico, which continued to struggle in the aftermath of a series of hurricanes and earthquakes.

In 2020, the appropriations process was again delayed, but this time due to the economic and health emergencies created by the COVID-19 pandemic. Congress rushed to clear a series of aid packages to help stem the spread of the virus, fund research into potential vaccines, help small businesses stay afloat, and provide for low-income families and the growing number of unemployed workers. In December, Congress cleared a $1.4 trillion omnibus spending measure for fiscal 2021 that was packaged with more funding aid and tax breaks for Americans and businesses that continued to struggle during the pandemic.

Table 2.4 Taxes and Other Revenues as Percentage of Gross Domestic Product, 1935–2020

Fiscal Year	Individual Income	Corporate Income	Social Insurance	Excise	Other	Total
1935	0.7%	0.8%	—	2.0%	1.5%	5.1%
1940	0.9	1.2	1.8%	2.0	0.7	6.7
1945	8.1	7.1	1.5	2.8	0.5	19.9
1950	5.6	3.7	1.6	2.7	0.5	14.1
1955	7.1	4.4	1.9	2.2	0.5	16.1
1960	7.6	4.0	2.7	2.2	0.7	17.3
1965	6.9	3.6	3.1	2.1	0.8	16.4
1970	8.6	3.1	4.2	1.5	0.9	18.4
1975	7.6	2.5	5.2	1.0	0.9	17.3
1980	8.7	2.3	5.6	0.9	0.9	18.5
1985	7.8	1.4	6.2	0.8	0.9	17.2
1990	7.9	1.6	6.4	0.6	0.9	17.4
1991	7.7	1.6	6.5	0.7	0.8	17.3
1992	7.4	1.6	6.4	0.7	0.9	17.0
1993	7.5	1.7	6.3	0.7	0.7	17.0
1994	7.5	2.0	6.4	0.8	0.8	17.5
1995	7.8	2.1	6.4	0.8	0.8	17.8
1996	8.2	2.2	6.4	0.7	0.8	18.2
1997	8.7	2.1	6.4	0.7	0.7	18.6
1998	9.3	2.1	6.4	0.6	0.8	19.2
1999	9.2	1.9	6.4	0.7	0.9	19.2
2000	9.9	2.0	6.4	0.7	0.9	20.0
2001	9.4	1.4	6.6	0.6	0.8	18.8
2002	7.9	1.4	6.4	0.6	0.7	17.0
2003	7.0	1.2	6.3	0.6	0.7	15.7
2004	6.7	1.6	6.1	0.6	0.6	15.6
2005	7.2	2.2	6.2	0.6	0.6	16.7
2006	7.6	2.6	6.1	0.5	0.7	17.6
2007	8.1	2.6	6.1	0.5	0.7	17.9
2008	7.8	2.1	6.1	0.5	0.7	17.1
2009	6.3	1.0	6.2	0.4	0.7	14.6
2010	6.1	1.3	5.8	0.5	1.0	14.6
2011	7.1	1.2	5.3	0.5	0.9	15.0
2012	7.1	1.5	5.3	0.5	0.9	15.3
2013	8.0	1.7	5.7	0.5	0.9	16.8
2014	8.1	1.9	5.9	0.5	1.1	17.5
2015	8.6	1.9	5.9	0.5	1.1	18.2
2016	8.4	1.6	6.1	0.5	1.2	17.8
2017	8.2	1.5	6.0	0.4	1.0	17.2
2018	8.3	1.0	5.8	0.5	0.9	16.4
2019	8.1	1.1	5.9	0.5	0.8	16.3
2020*	8.2	1.2	5.9	0.4	1.0	16.7

SOURCE: Office of Management and Budget. *Budget of the United States Government, Fiscal Year 2021, Historical Tables* (Washington, DC: U.S. Government Printing Office, 2020), Table 2.3.

NOTE: The Social Insurance category includes Social Security, Medicare, railroad, and other retirement programs, and unemployment insurance. The Other category principally includes estate and gift taxes and customs duties. * indicates estimate

Fiscal Year 2019 Spending

Congress began in January with an immediate crisis as much of the government remained shuttered. Negotiations the previous year had stalled on seven remaining fiscal

2019 spending bills—affecting nine departments and scores of agencies—and on President Trump's request for $5 billion for construction of a wall along the U.S.–Mexico border.

The new Democratic majority in the House made eleven attempts to pass continuing resolutions to reopen those departments and agencies while talks continued, but the measures were blocked in the Senate. House Democrats also passed versions of the remaining spending bills, but Senate Majority Leader McConnell, R-Ky., declined to bring them to the Senate floor for a vote.

On January 25, 2019, Trump signed a measure (PL 116-5) that reopened the government for three weeks. The measure did not include the border wall funding he requested, but the House and Senate agreed to continue talks on that funding.

Ultimately, Congress cleared and the president signed into law (H J Res 31—PL 116-6) a measure that provided full-year funding for the seven remaining fiscal 2019 bills: Agriculture, Commerce–Justice–Science, Financial Services, Homeland Security, Interior–Environment, State–Foreign Operations, and Transportation–HUD.

The measure provided $333 billion in net discretionary funding, including $312.8 billion subject to the cap under the Budget Control Act, $12 billion in disaster relief, and $8.2 billion in Overseas Contingency Operation funding (war-related funding). The measure included $1.375 million for fifty-five miles of new fencing along the southern border, and a 1.98 percent pay raise for civilian federal workers.

BACKGROUND

In February 2018, Congress and the President had agreed to a two-year budget deal (PL 115-123) that raised discretionary spending caps for fiscal years 2018 and 2019. GOP leaders then packaged together several minibus spending measures, each of which encompassed several of the regular spending bills for fiscal 2019. Before the start of the fiscal year in October 2018, Congress cleared and the president signed a three-bill minibus (PL 115-244) that included the Energy–Water, Military Construction–VA and Legislative Branch spending bills, and a two-bill package (PL 115-245) that included the Defense and Labor–HHS–Education spending bills.

Talks continued during a lame-duck session of Congress on a third minibus, but negotiations were weighed down by President Trump's request for $5 billion to build a wall on the U.S. border with Mexico. Congress cleared and the president signed two stopgap spending measures to continue funding agencies affected by the remaining seven spending measures. The last stopgap funding, however, expired December 21.

The Senate had passed by voice vote another extension into February, but the president said he would not sign the bill. To appease the president, House GOP leaders then added another $5.7 billion for the border wall, along with disaster relief funding, before passing the measure. Without

a bipartisan agreement, however, the bill did not move, triggering a partial government shutdown affecting nine of the fifteen cabinet-level departments and several agencies, including the EPA, the Small Business Administration, and NASA.

GOVERNMENT SHUTDOWN AND STOPGAPS

The thirty-five-day government shutdown, which affected about 40 percent of the workforce, ended on January 25, 2019, when Trump signed into law a three-week continuing resolution (HJ Res 28— PL 116-5). In the weeks prior to passage of the measure, the House had continued to work on regular fiscal 2019 appropriations bills, most of which the president threatened to veto.

House Action

As soon as the new Congress was sworn in on January 3, 2019, the House voted 239–192 to pass a Democrat-crafted stopgap funding bill (HJ Res 1) to keep the Department of Homeland Security running at fiscal 2018 funding levels through February 9. The House also passed, in a 241–190 vote, a full-year, $272.4 billion funding measure (HR 21) for the other six fiscal 2019 funding bills. Those bills included the Agriculture, Financial Services, Interior–Environment, Transportation–Housing and Urban Development (HUD) spending measures—versions the Senate had passed as a package the previous August—and Commerce–Justice–Science and State-Foreign Operations measures, which the Senate Appropriations Committee had approved the previous June. Negotiators could not agree on several provisions in the final packages, including on the president's calls for border wall funds. Democrats were unwilling to give Trump more than $1.3 billion for the border wall.

Six Republicans supported the stopgap measure: Brian Fitzpatrick of Pennsylvania, Will Hurd of Texas, John Katko and Elise Stefanik of New York, and Christopher Smith and Jeff Van Drew of New Jersey. Seven Republicans supported the six-bill omnibus: Fitzpatrick, Hurd, Katko, Stefanik, Van Drew, Peter T. King of New York, Fred Upton of Michigan, and Greg Walden of Oregon.

The president issued veto threats on both House bills, contending they would underfund border security but exceed his budget request by nearly 20 percent for other programs, including for international affairs, the EPA and the Department of Housing and Urban Development. The House then proceeded to move spending bills individually. On January 10, the House voted 244–180 to pass the Transportation–HUD spending bill (HR 267) and voted 243–183 to pass the Agriculture spending bill (HR 265). On January 11, the chamber passed, by a vote of 240 to 179, a bill funding the Interior Department and the EPA (HR 266).

Also on January 11, the House voted 411–7 to clear a Senate-passed bill (S 24) that ensured federal employees back pay once the government shutdown was lifted. Seven

Republicans opposed the bill. Trump signed the back pay measure on January 16.

On January 15, a vote to pass another short-term funding measure (HJ Res 27) failed in the House on a vote of 237–187. The measure required a two-thirds majority to pass as it was considered under suspension of the rules. On January 23, the House voted 229–184 to pass another version of a stopgap measure (HJ Res 28) that would keep the government running through February 28. One Democrat, Alexandria Ocasio-Cortez of New York, opposed the bill, as did Michigan's independent Paul Mitchell and Libertarian Justin Amash. Six Republicans supported the bill: Brian Fitzpatrick of Pennsylvania, Jaime Herrera Beutler of Washington, Will Hurd of Texas, John Katko and Elise Stefanik of New York, and Christopher H. Smith and Jeff Van Drew of New Jersey.

Members on January 23 also voted 237–187 to pass a six-bill spending measure (HR 648) that had been negotiated by House and Senate conferees at the end of the previous Congress. Republicans mostly backed the president, with few exceptions. Before the House took up the bill (HR 648), the president had offered to pair his requested wall funding with protections from deportation for three years for those enrolled in DACA, and for those who came to United States seeking refuge from armed conflicts or natural disasters and had Temporary Protected Status. Democrats dismissed Trump's offer because it did not provide permanent DACA protections or a pathway to citizenship for them. On January 24, the House passed a stop-gap funding measure for the Department of Homeland Security (HJ Res 31) that would keep the agency funded through February 28.

Senate Action

On January 24, 2019, a Trump-backed spending plan—to combine the seven remaining fiscal 2019 spending bills with a $5.7 billion emergency border funding package, disaster aid, and immigration policy provisions—stalled in the Senate. Senators voted 50–47 against a motion for cloture to end debate, failing to reach the 60 votes necessary for the chamber to proceed to a vote on passage of the legislation. Also on January 24, senators, in a 52–44 vote, failed to invoke cloture on a proposal by Democratic Leader Charles E. Schumer of New York that would have reopened the government through February 8 at fiscal 2018 spending levels and provided more disaster relief. Both proposals had been offered as amendments to a House-passed spending bill (HR 268).

On January 25, federal workers missed a second paycheck, and the FAA halted flights in LaGuardia due to a shortage of air traffic controllers while delays occurred at other airports. Trump then announced he would sign a three-week continuing resolution to reopen the government. The Senate passed that resolution (replacing language in the House-passed minibus, HJ Res 28) by voice vote.

Final Action

The House cleared the three-week continuing resolution (HJ Res 28) by unanimous consent on January 25, 2019. Trump signed the measure into law (PL 116-5) on the same day, ending a thirty-five-day government shutdown, the longest in history. The measure did not include the $5.7 billion in border wall funding Trump wanted but allowed the government to open while negotiations continued on a border security package.

The shutdown had impacted 800,000 federal employees, about 40 percent of the federal workforce, who missed two paychecks. The shutdown also created turbulence in the stock market, affected federal contractors, and closed national parks.

Fiscal Year 2019 Appropriations

Seventeen House and Senate negotiators on February 11, 2019, announced a deal on a $333 billion spending package that would include the remaining seven fiscal 2019 spending bills and set aside $1.375 billion for new barriers along the U.S. border with Mexico—about the same as provided for fiscal 2018. Administration officials agreed to the deal, saying they might reprogram money from other programs to make up the rest of the $5.7 billion Trump requested for the border wall.

As part of the deal, House Democrats dropped a proposed 16,500 cap on the number of immigrant detainees that Immigration and Customs Enforcement could keep inside U.S. borders. Negotiators also agreed to fund beds for 40,520 detainees. That agreement was 5,000 more than House Democrats wanted, but below the 52,000 average daily population Trump requested, and a 17.4 percent cut from the September 30, 2019, level of 49,057. Six of the 2019 spending bills in the package entailed deals reached at the end of the previous Congress and reflected in the six-bill package (HR 648) House Democrats had approved in January.

Negotiators, meanwhile, dropped several policy riders, including a provision that would have ensured back pay for federal contractors for wages lost during the shutdown and another provision that would have extended authorization of the Violence Against Women Act, originally signed by President Clinton in 1994 (PL 103-322) and set to expire February 15, 2019.

House lawmakers filed a conference report on the measure on February 13, using as a vehicle the House-passed continuing funding resolution for the Department of Homeland Security (HJ Res 31). The Senate voted 83–16 to pass the conference report on February 14. Eleven Republicans and five Democrats (Cory Booker of New Jersey, Kirsten Gillibrand of New York, Kamala Harris of California, and Edward J. Markey and Elizabeth Warren of Massachusetts) voted against the measure.

Later on February 14, 2019, the House cleared HJ Res 31 by a vote of 300 to 128. Four freshmen—Alexandria Ocasio-Cortez of New York, Ilhan Omar of Minnesota,

Ayanna S. Pressley of Massachusetts, and Rashida Tlaib of Michigan—were among nineteen Democrats who voted against the measure. Republicans in the conservative Freedom Caucus, along with Rep. Tom Graves of Georgia, were among the 109 Republicans who opposed the bill.

President Trump signed the spending package into law (PL 116-6) on February 14. Trump also signed an emergency order to free up $6.7 billion more for the border wall, diverting $3.6 billion from military construction accounts, accessing $2.5 billion in reprogramming funds set aside for Pentagon counterdrug activities, and pulling $601 million from the Treasury's asset forfeiture fund. Democratic leaders and liberal groups quickly threatened court action.

HIGHLIGHTS

The $333 billion spending law (PL 116-6) increased funding for nine cabinet-level departments and several agencies by $7.4 billion, or 2.3 percent, over fiscal 2018 levels, and $54 billion or 24 percent more than Trump requested. The agreement extended several visa and immigration programs until September 30, 2019, including three pilot programs created under the Illegal Immigration Reform and Immigrant Responsibility Act of 1996 (PL 104-208): the E-Verify Program, the citizen attestation program, and the machine-readable document pilot program.

The measure allowed immigrants and their spouses and children to enter the United States to work for an organization in a religious vocation or to work for a tax-exempt religious organization. The bill also allowed aliens to enter the United States as students or teachers if they intended to return to their country of citizenship. Under the agreement, they could also bring a spouse or children. The measure maintained 3,000 work visas for qualified immigrants and increased the number of visas for temporary nonagricultural workers.

Table 2.5 Annual Caps on Spending

Fiscal Year	Caps in Trillions of Dollars	Year-to-Year Change
2011	$1.050	
2012	1.043	–0.7%
2013	1.047	0.4
2014	1.066	1.8
2015	1.086	1.9
2016	1.107	1.9
2017	1.131	2.2
2018	1.156	2.2
2019	1.182	2.2
2020	1.208	2.2
2021	1.234	2.2
2022*	1.522	8.6

NOTE: The table shows the annual caps for each fiscal year and the percentage change from the previous year. The caps essentially amounted to an actual freeze for fiscal 2012 and fiscal 2013 and a "real" or inflation-adjusted freeze for the remaining eight years. *2022 FY Budget is just the Biden Administration's request.

Discretionary Spending Caps

Fiscal Year	BCA (Billions)	Actual (Billions)
2012	$1.043	1.043
2013	1.047	1.043 (American Taxpayer Relief Act of 2012)
2014	973	1.012 (Bipartisan Budget Act of 2013)
2015	994	1.014 (Bipartisan Budget Act of 2013)
2016	1.016	1.067 (Bipartisan Budget Act of 2015)
2017	1.040	1.070 (Bipartisan Budget Act of 2015)
2018	1.066	1.208 (Bipartisan Budget Act of 2018)
2019	1.093	1.244 (Bipartisan Budget Act of 2018)
2020	1.120	1.118 (Bipartisan Budget Act of 2018)
2021	1.146	1.145 (Bipartisan Budget Act of 2018)

SOURCE: Congressional Budget Office. *Final Sequestration Report for Fiscal Year 2018* (April 2018), Table 2.

NOTE: Currently, there are no discretionary spending caps for FY 2022.

The following were among the provisions for each of seven regular fiscal 2019 appropriations measures:

Agriculture. Congress provided the Department of Agriculture $152.2 billion, slightly more than the $151.35 in fiscal 2018 and $13.23 billion more than the president requested. The funding included a slight reduction, from $71 billion to $70.48 billion, for food stamps, and dropped from $2 billion to $1.94 billion the funding for foreign assistance programs such as Food for Peace. President Trump wanted to reduce that funding to less than $205 million. The measure also boosted funding, from $6.97 billion to $7.4 billion, for agricultural programs.

The measure included $23 billion in net discretionary spending, $32 million more than in fiscal 2019. Congress cut funding for the Food Safety and Inspection Service by 1 percent, and for land conservation activities of the National Resources Conservation Service by 5 percent.

Commerce–Justice–Science. The measure provided $71.85 billion for the departments of Commerce and Justice and for NASA and other science programs, $390 million or 0.5 percent more than in fiscal 2018, and $5.75 billion or 8.7 percent more than the $66.1 billion Trump requested. The total includes $64.1 billion in discretionary funding, $4.5 billion more than in fiscal 2018 and $1.6 billion more than the White House requested. The funding included $30.93 billion for the Justice Department, $630 million more than the fiscal 2018 level and $2.1 billion or 7.3 percent more than Trump requested; $29.6 billion for science programs, $70 million or 0.2 percent more than in fiscal 2018 and $2.2 billion or 8 percent more than Trump requested; $11.4 billion for the Commerce Department, a $300 million or 2.7 percent boost from fiscal 2018, and $1.6 billion or 16 percent more than Trump requested. Funding for Commerce included a $1 billion increase, from $2.8 billion to $3.8 billion, for the Census Bureau.

Financial Services. The measure provided $45.9 billion for the Department of Treasury and related financial service agencies, down $1.8 billion or 3.8 percent from fiscal 2018 and $3.2 billion or 6.5 percent less than President Trump requested. The funding included $23.4 billion in discretionary funds, the same as in fiscal 2018 but $3.4 billion less than the president requested.

Funding for the IRS dropped $100 million from $11.4 billion in fiscal 2018 to $11.3 billion; Trump had requested a $100 million boost to $11.5 billion. The measure provided a 12 percent funding boost for the Department of Treasury's Office of Terrorism and Financial Intelligence, a 3 percent funding boost for the Financial Crimes Enforcement Network, and a 7 percent increase for the Alcohol and Tobacco Tax and Trade Bureau. Funding for independent agencies dropped more than $1 billion, including slight cuts for the Office of Personnel Management, the Federal Trade Commission, the Election Assistance Commission, and zeroing out of the budget for the Election Reform Program.

Homeland Security. The spending package included $63.3 billion for the Department of Homeland Security, nearly $53 billion or 45.4 percent less than in fiscal 2018 when appropriators included more than $59.3 billion in disaster relief funding and other aid. The fiscal 2019 funding included $49.4 billion in net discretionary spending, $1.7 billion or 3.5 percent more than in fiscal 2018 and $2 billion more than requested. In the final measure, funding for Customs and Border Protection was increased more than $1 billion, from the fiscal 2018 level of $16.4 billion to nearly $17.3 billion, or $580 million or 3.5 percent higher than Trump's request.

Lawmakers boosted funding for Immigration and Customs Enforcement by nearly $400 million, from $7.5 billion to $7.9 billion, about $900 million less than Trump requested. The bill also included a nearly $4.3 billion or 34 percent increase for the Federal Emergency Management Agency, from $12.3 billion to $16.6 billion, primarily to fund nondefense disaster relief. The president wanted to drop FEMA's budget by nearly $1.3 billion, or 10.6 percent, to $11.02 billion.

The measure included $1.375 billion for fifty-five miles of new fencing along the southern border, as well as $100 million for new border surveillance technology, $564 million for inspection equipment at land ports of entry to detect opioids and other contraband, and $415 million to address humanitarian needs of migrants crossing the border. The measure also provided for the hiring of 1,200 new Customs and Border Protection officers and an increase of nearly 5,000 immigrant detention beds over the fiscal 2018 level.

Interior and Environment. The measure provided $35.61 billion in discretionary spending for the Department of the Interior and the Environmental Protection Agency, nearly $1 billion less than the fiscal 2018 level but nearly $7.3 billion more than the president requested. Funding for the Department of the Interior programs and activities dropped about $100 million or 0.7 percent, to $13 billion. Funding for the EPA, meanwhile, stayed at nearly $8.1 billion, similar to the fiscal 2018 level, as Congress rejected the president's request to slash the agency's funding by about 23 percent to $6.2 billion. The Forest Service received a $400 million boost to $13.8 billion. The president had wanted to cut its budget by almost 14 percent to $11.56 billion.

State-Foreign Operations. The final measure included $54.2 billion for the State Department and foreign operations, a $200 million increase from fiscal 2018. The State Department received $12.09 billion, up $50 million from fiscal 2018 but nearly $1.5 billion less than the president's request of $13.57 billion. The measure decreased funding for Overseas Contingency Operations by one-third, from $12 billion to $8 billion, rejecting the president's request to cut the budget further, to $301.2 million, as he sought to wind down the U.S. involvement in wars overseas.

The total funding included $6.1 billion to combat HIV/AIDS, $3.4 billion for refugee assistance, and $528 million to help Central America respond to migrants trying to enter the United States. Congress also included $8.8 billion for global health programs, $3.3 billion for military assistance to Israel, $1.4 billion in security and economic assistance to Egypt, $1.5 billion for Jordan, $446 million for Ukraine, and $275 million for a Countering Russian Influence fund.

Transportation, Housing, and Urban Development. Congress provided $71.1 billion—$29 billion or 29 percent less than the fiscal 2018 level—for the Transportation Department and Housing and Urban Development. The president had sought less than $48 billion, combined, for the departments. (The fiscal 2018 level included nearly $30 billion in supplementary funding.)

The measure provided $86.5 billion for the Transportation Department, including $9 billion for new infrastructure. The final measure also provided for the release of $60 billion from highway and aviation trust funds. The total funding included $17.5 billion for the Federal Aviation Administration, $549 million less than in fiscal 2018; $49.3 billion for the Federal Highway Administration, $1.8 billion more than in fiscal 2018. Congress increased funding for the National Highway Traffic Safety Administration, the Pipeline and Hazardous Materials Safety Administration and the U.S. Maritime Administration, but cut funding for the Federal Motor Carrier Safety Administration, Federal Transit Administration, and Federal Railroad Administration.

The measure provided $44.2 billion for HUD, a $1.5 billion cut from fiscal 2018 but $12.5 billion more than the president's request of $31.69 billion. Congress rejected the

president's request to cut rental assistance, zero out the HOME Investment Partnership Program, and impose cuts in other areas.

Disaster Aid

Congress in mid-2019 cleared, and the president signed into law, a $19.1 billion emergency supplemental measure (HR 2157—PL 116-20) to provide relief and recovery funds for communities damaged by natural disasters over the previous two years.

BACKGROUND

Hurricanes, wildfires, typhoons, and volcanic eruptions damaged communities across the nation in 2018. In all, FEMA declared fifty-nine major disasters in 2018, and another twenty-seven by May 23, 2019.

Among the FEMA-declared disasters were rain and mudslides in wildfire-damaged areas of Montecito, California, in January; Hawaii's Kilauea volcanic eruption and area earthquakes from May to August; and flash flooding in Ellicott City, Maryland, in May.

Hurricane Florence hit the Carolinas in September, killing at least forty-three people, causing North Carolina's Cape Fear River to reach an all-time high of 8.27 feet in Wilmington and flooding communities. Then Hurricane Michael blew through Florida, Georgia, and the Carolinas in October, devastating Panama City, Florida, and nearly demolishing Mexico Beach.

Typhoon Yutu, a Category 5 hurricane, hit the Northern Mariana Islands in October, and record-breaking wildfires swept through Northern and Southern California in November. Meanwhile, Puerto Rico continued to struggle from the damage caused by Hurricane Maria in 2017.

INITIAL LEGISLATION

On January 16, 2019, the House voted 237–187 to pass a supplemental spending measure (HR 268) that packaged $14 billion in disaster aid with a three-week stopgap funding measure. Republicans opposed attaching the popular emergency spending to a stopgap measure, and then objected to Democrats' approval of an amendment by Jim McGovern, D-Mass., that would bar the disaster funds from being used for construction of a border wall on the U.S.–Mexico border. The House also adopted by voice vote an amendment by Pramila Jayapal, D-Wash., that would bar funds designated for Homeland Security from being used to construct or expand immigration detention facilities.

The Senate, however, was unable to get cloture, which would have ended debate and proceeded to a vote, on proposed amendments to the House bill (HR 268), and action on the bill stalled. Senate Appropriations Chair Richard Shelby introduced a $13.45 billion disaster funding measure as a substitute to the House bill (HR 268), but action again stalled on the Senate floor.

REVISED LEGISLATION

On April 9, House Appropriations Chair Nita Lowey introduced a $17.31 billion disaster aid measure (HR 2157). On May 10, the House voted 257–150 to pass the bill after approving a series of amendments that added about $1.8 billion in funding, raising the total price tag to $19.1 billion. Thirty-four Republicans supported the measure.

Among the amendments were

- A proposal by Neal Dunn, R-Fla., adopted by voice vote, that would add $685 million to repair military facilities affected by Hurricane Michael in October 2018
- An amendment by Joe Cunningham, D-S.C., that added another $270 million for Air Force facility repairs
- Two amendments by Cynthia Axne, D-Iowa, adopted by voice vote, to include $500 million for emergency highway repairs and $310 million to repair flood control projects
- An amendment by Ed Perlmutter, D-Colo., adopted 247–165, to add $50 million to improve the National Oceanic and Atmospheric Administration's weather forecasting capabilities

The measure included language that would require HUD to publish rules for how Community Development Block Grant (CDBG) funds appropriated in February 2018 (in PL 115-123) would be distributed for Puerto Rico and other affected areas. Many lawmakers had raised concerns that the money was not being distributed promptly.

Senate. Action

As the House moved on its disaster aid measure, the Senate held bipartisan negotiations on a separate aid package in which the White House and Republicans aimed to set more financial controls on Puerto Rico's management of funds from HUD. But negotiations stuck on several issues, including Trump's request for $4.5 billion for border funds and Appropriations Chair Richard C. Shelby's request for $2 billion a year in harbor maintenance funds.

In late May, Shelby, R-Ala., pulled his proposed change to the Harbor Maintenance Fund from the package while senators agreed to include a portion of the president's border funds but had not yet set an exact amount. Democrats also sought more CDBG funds for Puerto Rico.

The Senate on May 23 approved its version of the $19.1 billion disaster aid bill (HR 2157) by a vote of 85–8. The package would provide more than $4.6 billion to reimburse farmers for lost crops and livestock and to help rebuild communities affected by the disasters. It also would provide $3.25 billion for the Army Corps of Engineers' flood control and storm damage reduction projects, and nearly $3.2 billion to repair military bases. For Puerto Rico, the bill included $600 billion in nutrition assistance and $304 million in CDBG grants. The measure also

extended the National Flood Insurance Program through September 30, 2019. To break a logjam in negotiations, senators did not include humanitarian aid for migrants at the Mexican border, as the Trump administration requested, but agreed to revisit the issue after the weeklong Memorial Day recess.

Final Action

In the House, Republicans blocked three attempts to clear the Senate-passed disaster aid bill (HR 2157) by unanimous consent. When lawmakers returned from the Memorial Day recess on June 3, the House took up the bill under suspension of the rules, which required a two-thirds majority for passage, and cleared the measure by a vote of 354–58. The president signed the measure into law (PL 116-20) on June 6, 2019.

FUNDING HIGHLIGHTS

The following amounts were among the funding provided in the measure:

- $3 billion for agricultural programs
- $480 million for emergency forest restoration
- $435 million for watershed and flood prevention operations
- $558 million for the emergency conservation program
- $150 million for the rural community facilities program
- $600 million for nutrition assistance for Puerto Rico
- $25.2 million for nutrition assistance for the Commonwealth of the Northern Mariana Islands
- $18 million for nutrition assistance for American Samoa
- $5 million for the study of Puerto Rico disaster nutrition assistance

Emergency Border Funding

Congress in June 2019 cleared a $4.59 billion emergency funding measure (HR 3401) to help the administration address a growing surge of migrants from Central America crossing the border into the United States. The funding would help the Department of Homeland Security (DHS) detain illegal immigrants and process cases and would bolster the Department of Health and Human Services' Office of Refugee Resettlement, which cared for migrant children who were not accompanied by parents or caregivers.

BACKGROUND

Between fiscal 2000 and fiscal 2017, the number of migrants apprehended at the U.S.–Mexico border had been generally declining, from a peak of 1.64 million to a forty-five-year low of 303,916 in fiscal 2017. Apprehensions increased in fiscal 2018 to 404,142 and continued to increase into fiscal 2019.

In April 2019, U.S. Customs and Border Patrol (CBP) agents apprehended 109,144 migrants, which included those who had turned themselves in voluntarily and those caught entering illegally, according to the DHS. Of those, 8,897 were unaccompanied minors while 58,474 migrants were traveling in family units. In May 2019, CBP apprehended 132,856 migrants at the border, including 11,475 unaccompanied children.

The U.S. policy on the treatment of unaccompanied minor children migrating across the border was dictated by the Flores Settlement Agreement of 1997, the Homeland Security Act of 2002, and the Trafficking Victims Protection Reauthorization Act (TVPRA) of 2008. The TVPRA said Mexican children could be voluntarily returned to Mexico, while the United States would shelter children from other countries and then put them into formal removal proceedings in immigration court. Most of the children in recent years, however, were coming from El Salvador, Guatemala, and Honduras—known as the Northern Triangle Nations—thereby increasing the need for shelter and funding to handle cases.

CBP facilities quickly became overcrowded, leading border officials to drop migrants off at local communities that might be able to provide services. The Trump administration used temporary, unlicensed facilities to shelter unaccompanied minors while it sought to reduce the flow of migrants crossing illegally.

On May 1, 2019, President Trump requested about $4.51 billion in emergency supplemental funds to handle the increasing surge of migrants who were fleeing violence in Central America. His request included $1.1 billion for the DHS, divided between CBP and Immigration and Customs Enforcement (ICE).

Trump also continued to deploy military troops to the border, a practice he began in 2018. By June, 2,700 active-duty troops were spread across nine sectors and four border states, and 2,000 National Guard members were stationed in Texas, Arizona, California, and New Mexico to help border agents.

Some Republicans contended migrants were trying to take advantage of loopholes in the immigration system. Democrats urged the Trump administration to address why migrants were leaving their home countries. Many lawmakers were concerned about the care and treatment of migrant children, particularly those who crossed the border without family or caregivers.

Senate Action

Senate appropriators initially hoped to include border aid as part of the $19.1 billion disaster relief supplemental (HR 2157—PL 116-20). When that effort failed, they negotiated a bipartisan, $4.59 billion measure. The Senate Appropriations Committee on June 19 voted 30–1 to

approve the measure (S 1900). Jeff Merkley, D-Ore., provided the sole vote in opposition.

The bill would provide more than $1.3 billion for DHS, including $1.1 billion for CBP, $209 million for ICE, and $30 million for the Federal Emergency Management Agency (FEMA). The measure also would provide nearly $2.9 billion for the Department of Health and Human Services' Office of Refugee Resettlement, which cares for unaccompanied children. The Senate bill would require lawmakers to provide forty-eight-hour notice before visiting detention facilities where unaccompanied children were located.

House Action

On June 21, House Democratic appropriators unveiled a $4.54 billion supplemental funding measure (HR 3401) to address the crisis at the border. The bill would provide $1.49 billion for DHS, including $1.3 billion for CBP, $128 million for ICE, and $60 million for FEMA. The bill also would provide nearly $2.9 billion for the Department of Health and Human Services' Office of Refugee Resettlement, and would restrict HHS officials' ability to share information about potential sponsors with the DHS.

Following a proposal by the U.N. High Commissioner for Refugees, the bill would provide $200 million for a multiagency pilot program to process immigration requests. On June 25, the House, in a nearly party line vote of 230–195, passed its $4.54 billion measure (HR 3401). Four progressive Democrats voted against the bills: Alexandria Ocasio-Cortez of New York, Ilhan Omar of Minnesota, Ayanna S. Pressley of Massachusetts, and Rashida Tlaib of Michigan.

Before approving the bill, members adopted a manager's amendment by Appropriations Chair Nita M. Lowey, D-N.Y., that would limit to 90 days how long unaccompanied children could be held in facilities known as "influx shelters," which were not licensed. It also would require the CBP meet new standards to ensure the health and safety of migrants.

The measure also included provisions that would, for example, bar the president from blocking U.S. aid to the migrants' home countries. The White House immediately issued a veto threat, objecting to several provisions the president said were partisan.

Final Action

The Senate on June 26 voted 37–55 to reject the House bill (HR 3401) and instead insert the language of its own bill (S 1900). Three Democrats voted against the House bill: Edward J. Markey of Massachusetts, Joe Manchin III of West Virginia, and Jeff Merkley of Oregon.

The Senate then voted 84–8 to insert its own version. Subsequently, the Senate voted 84–8 to pass the $4.59 billion measure. Seven Democrats running for president did not vote. Six other Democrats voted against the bill: Mazie K. Hirono of Hawaii, Markey, Chris Van Hollen of Maryland, Merkley and Ron Wyden of Oregon, and Robert Menendez of New Jersey. Republican Sens. Mike Lee of Utah and Rand Paul of Kentucky also voted against the measure.

House Speaker Nancy Pelosi, D-Calif., then requested several changes to the Senate bill, focusing on higher standards for medical care and nutrition for migrant children, limiting the amount of time a child is kept in a detention facility, and boosting accountability and transparency. However, Pelosi later relented, saying she wanted to expedite assistance to the border.

On June 27, the House passed the Senate version of the bill (HR 3401) by a vote of 305–102. Six Republicans joined ninety-five Democrats and Michigan Libertarian Justin Amash to oppose the measure. The Republicans were Andy Biggs and Paul Gosar of Arizona, Mo Brooks of Alabama, Louie Gohmert and Chip Roy of Texas, and Thomas Massie of Kentucky.

Before clearing the measure, leaders withdrew an amendment that would have boosted money for humanitarian and processing needs while decreasing money from ICE, and would have strengthened safeguards for unaccompanied children, which would have increased the bill's total to $4.61 billion. The president signed the measure into law (PL 116-26) on July 1, 2019.

The measure allowed the DHS to continue to use temporary "influx shelters" to house unaccompanied minors in case of emergency, and required those facilities be sufficiently staffed. Children under thirteen, however, could not be held in those shelters. The measure did not provide funding for more detention beds or for the president's border wall.

Tax Extenders

The House Ways and Means Committee on June 20, 2019, approved four tax bills estimated to cost $174 billion. The measures would expand refundable tax credits for lower-income workers and families, renew thirty-two lapsed or soon-to-expire breaks for businesses and individuals, and expand retroactive benefits for married same-sex couples.

The measures did not advance further, however, as Republicans and some Democrats complained the measures were not fully offset and they opposed provisions to increase estate taxes.

The committee approved a measure (HR 3300) that would expand the Earned Income Tax Credit to more workers without children, and would make child tax credits fully refundable for certain households with children. The credits also would be offered for residents of U.S. territories.

The committee approved, in a 22–19 vote, an amendment that would increase the child tax credits from $2,000 to $3,000 for children under age four.

The measure was estimated to cost more than $130 billion over ten years, according to the Joint Committee on Taxation. The change would apply to anyone eligible for the credits under the 2017 tax overhaul law (PL 115-97), and would include married couples earning up to $400,000 a year. The measure also would increase the maximum refundable credit for children under age four by another $1,600, compared to $600 more for children ages four and older. The measure was not taken up on the House floor.

Also on June 20, the Ways and Means Committee approved, by voice vote, a measure (HR 3299) that would allow lawfully married same-sex couples to file claims for federal tax credits and refunds on returns back to the year of their marriage. The measure was estimated to cost $57 million.

The House passed the measure by voice vote under suspension of the rules on July 24. The Senate did not act on it. The Ways and Means Committee on June 20 approved, on a 25–17 vote, a $42.5 billion tax extenders bill (HR 3301) that would renew tax breaks that expired at the end of 2017 and 2018, and others scheduled to expire at the end of 2019. The measure proposed to pay for the lost revenue by ending the doubling of the estate tax exemptions, provided in the 2017 overhaul, three years earlier.

Before approving the measure, the committee rejected, in a 16–23 vote, a Republican amendment that would have made the tax extensions permanent. The bill was not taken up by the full House, but several provisions were included in COVID-relief measures in 2020.

The committee, by a 22–18 vote, approved another bill (HR 3298) that would boost childcare assistance grants to states under the Temporary Assistance for Needy Families program by $1 billion in each of the next two fiscal years. Three Democrats opposed the bill. The measure was not taken up on the House floor or by the Senate.

On July 2020, the House voted 250–161 to pass a bill (HR 7327) that would provide $179 billion in tax breaks, including $91 billion to expand and make fully refundable the child and dependent care tax credit. Twenty Republicans joined 230 Democrats to support it, while Michigan Libertarian Justin Amash joined 160 Republicans in opposition. The Senate did not take up the measure.

Fiscal Year 2020 Budget

President Trump on March 11, 2019, submitted a $4.75 billion blueprint for fiscal 2020 that would cut total discretionary funding by 1.8 percent in fiscal 2020. His budget proposed to boost military funding while cutting nondefense spending and included funds for his wall project along the U.S. border with Mexico. The White House proposed to stay within the caps that would be imposed by the 2011 debt ceiling and spending cuts law (PL 112-25). Republicans criticized Democrats for not acting on a budget resolution that would lay out a plan for spending, taxes, and the deficit over five or ten years, but divisions among Democrats made it too difficult to draft a budget resolution that would garner a majority vote.

On June 3, the Senate blocked consideration of a budget plan (S 1332), proposed by Sen. Rand Paul, R-Ky., that would have required trillions of dollars in spending cuts over ten years with the aim to balance to the budget. The Senate voted 22–69 against moving the plan for a vote by the full Senate as members of both parties opposed such severe spending cuts—Democrats to domestic spending and Republicans to military spending. In July, Congress cleared a two-year budget agreement that set new discretionary spending caps for fiscal years 2020 and 2021 and suspended the debt limit through July 2021.

PRESIDENT'S REQUEST

Trump's budget proposed to boost military funding, cut nondefense program spending and insert more funds for his promised wall along the Mexico border. The budget proposal said the administration would save $2.8 trillion over ten years by cutting nondefense discretionary programs, limiting health care costs, imposing tougher work requirements for welfare recipients, restructuring student loans, and more.

Under the president's budget, total discretionary spending—defense and nondefense—would be cut 1.8 percent in fiscal 2020 to $1.3 trillion. The budget suggested Congress did not need to raise the existing discretionary spending caps set in the 2018 budget deal.

The White House proposed a $33 billion boost for defense, 5 percent above the fiscal 2019 enacted level (PL 115-245) to $750 billion. Meanwhile, the proposed budget would cut nondefense spending by 5 percent to $567 billion. The administration also proposed to rescind $26 billion in unspent funds—including $20 billion from the Children's Health Insurance Program—to meet spending targets of the Budget Control Act of 2011 (PL 112-25). Trump's budget assumed $7.2 trillion in annual deficits for a decade and that it would take fifteen years to balance the budget.

ECONOMIC ASSUMPTIONS

The Trump administration's budget assumed the economy would grow at 3.2 percent in 2019 after subtracting effects of inflation. In January, the nonpartisan Congressional Budget Office had forecast a 2.3 percent real growth rate, the same that the Federal Reserve had forecast in December.

The White House also projected a 3.1 percent growth in 2020, and 3 percent each of the next four years. The CBO predicted 1.7 percent annual growth from 2020 through 2023, and the Federal Reserve predicted 2 percent growth in 2020, dropping to 1.8 percent in 2021 and 2022, and 2 percent thereafter. At the time, economists were concerned about signs of a recession for the coming year. Trump's growth forecast allowed the White House to plan for $2.8 trillion in revenue above the CBO's baseline over

the next decade, even with the assumption that 2017 tax cuts (PL 115-97) would be made permanent.

HIGHLIGHTS

The president's budget proposed severe cuts in funding for the EPA, including slashing its workforce and eliminating several programs addressing climate change; cutting mandatory funding for the nation's food stamps program; cuts to Medicare and Medicaid funding; the elimination of several HUD programs and reductions in rental assistance program funding; sharply reduced funding for K–12 education programs and federal student aid; reduced funding for several job training programs; and other major domestic programming cuts. The budget would increase funding for energy development and fossil fuel extraction.

The following were among the requests for each department:

Agriculture. The president proposed $22.8 billion in discretionary spending for the Department of Agriculture, a 6 percent decrease from fiscal 2019. The proposal included $2 billion above the budget caps for fiscal 2020 for wildfire fighting. The blueprint included a $17.4 billion cut in mandatory spending for the food stamp program, called the Supplemental Nutrition Assistance Program (SNAP), for fiscal 2020 and $219.8 billion in cuts over ten years. The administration also sought to limit farm, conservation, and crop insurance subsidies for farmers and ranchers with an adjusted gross income of no more than $500,000.

Defense. The White House requested $750 billion for defense programs and operations, a $34 billion or 4.7 percent increase from the fiscal 2019 level. That total included $718 billion for the Department of Defense and about $32 billion for Department of Energy nuclear weapons programs and other defense-related spending.

The total budget request included $3.6 billion for military construction projects (assumed to be for the border wall) and another $3.6 billion for other projects, which could be delayed if such funds were redirected to the border wall. The budget also included $165 billion for the Overseas Contingency Operations account, or war funding, and $9 billion for "emergency requirements." The OCO funding was a way to exceed the discretionary cap. Under the two-year budget deal (PL 115-13) reached in February 2019, total defense spending for fiscal years 2018 and 2019 was set at $700 billion and $716 billion, respectively. The OCO account in those years was $71 billion and $69 billion, while the Pentagon's base budget was $629 billion and $647 billion. The $165 billion OCO request for 2020 was $25 billion more than those two years combined.

The budget also assumed the creation of a new military branch called Space Force, though it did not specify a dollar amount to create the force.

Environmental Protection Agency. The White House requested $6.1 billion for the EPA in fiscal 2020, a 30 percent reduction from the fiscal 2019 level. The administration also called for the elimination of 2,000 full-time positions, 13 percent of the agency's workforce, resulting in 12,415 EPA employees, the lowest level since 2011, when the agency employed about 17,400 people. The budget would eliminate funding for several EPA programs focused on addressing climate change, such as Global Change Research, a federal program created by Congress to coordinate research on changes to the environment and climate, and fourteen voluntary climate-related global and multiagency partnerships.

The administration also proposed eliminating funding for some lead and radon monitoring programs, a program aimed at protecting the environment around the Gulf of Mexico, and the Safe Water for Small and Disadvantaged Communities Program, among other programs.

Health and Human Services. The president's budget request included $89.6 billion in discretionary funds for HHS in fiscal 2020, down from the $101.7 billion in fiscal 2019 enacted funding. The cuts primarily would affect the National Institutes of Health, which would receive $33 billion under the proposal, a $6 billion cut from fiscal 2019. The president, however, requested a $643 million increase for the Food and Drug Administration, to $6.1 billion. The funding increase would include revenue from a new fee on e-cigarette makers. The budget also would include $291 million for a new program aimed at ending HIV transmission in the United States, but would reduce global HIV/AIDS funding by 22 percent, to $3.85 billion. The administration called for $1.5 trillion in cuts to Medicaid and $818 billion in cuts to Medicare over ten years.

Housing and Urban Development. The administration proposed cutting discretionary spending for HUD by $8.6 billion or 16.4 percent, to $44.1 billion for fiscal 2020. The budget would eliminate the Community Development Block Grant program, which received $3.4 billion in fiscal 2019; the Public Housing Capital Fund, funded at $2.8 billion in 2019; and the HOME Investment Partnerships Program, which received $1.25 billion in fiscal 2019.

The administration aimed to reduce funding for HUD's rental assistance programs and the Public Housing Operating Fund. The budget would reduce funding for a housing assistance program for individuals with AIDS by $45 million, to $330 million. Meanwhile, the administration proposed increasing funding for project-based rental assistance by about $500 million, to $12 billion.

Education. The administration requested $62 billion for the Department of Education, an $8.5 billion or 12 percent decrease from fiscal 2019. The request

included the cancellation of unobligated Pell grant funds, and cuts to twenty-nine education programs, including after-school programs, 21st Century Learning Centers, and Title II-A grants that fund professional development for teachers and reduced class sizes, among other programs.

The White House proposed creating a single income-based student loan repayment plan, aiming to cut funding by $3.3 billion, and called on colleges to share responsibility for paying back federal student loans. The budget proposed $500 million to open or expand charter schools and $107 million to increase the number of magnet schools. The blueprint also proposed to make available $5 billion in tax credits annually for donations to private school scholarships, a proposal Education Secretary Betsy DeVos had presented in February.

Interior. The White House budget requested $12.8 billion for the Department of the Interior, a 5.2 percent or $700 million decrease from the fiscal 2019 level of $13.5 billion. The budget assumed the reopening of the Arctic National Wildlife Refuge for oil and gas drilling, as Congress permitted in the 2017 tax overhaul law (PL 115-97).

The administration's budget would reduce funding for wildfire management programs by 2 percent to $919.9 million. The White House requested a cut to the National Park Service budget to $2.7 billion from the $3.3 billion in fiscal 2019, but asked for $293 million to help address the agency's $12 billion deferred maintenance backlog. The White House also requested $28 million for reorganizing the Interior Department, including moving its headquarters from Washington, D.C., to a western state.

Labor. The administration proposed reducing discretionary spending for the Department of Labor by 10 percent or $1.2 billion, to $10.9 billion, by eliminating several programs, such as a community service employment program for older Americans and the Office of Disability Employment Policy. The White House also proposed to cut, by 41 percent, funding for the Job Corps program and to end the Agriculture Department's involvement in the program.

The White House proposed reorganizing and consolidating federal workforce programs, but to boost by 26 percent funding for the Transition Assistance Program that helps military veterans transition to civilian jobs. The administration proposed increasing fees employers pay for foreign worker visas and using the revenue to pay for some worker training programs. The budget request included funding for a new grant program to help states restrict improper payments in the federal-state unemployment program. The administration alleged that 13 percent of the program's payments, or $3.7 billion, are paid improperly. The administration proposed to create a new national paid family leave program for new parents, and proposed to move the Bureau of Labor Statistics from the Department of Labor to the Commerce Department.

NASA. The Trump administration requested $21 billion for NASA, $500 million less than in fiscal 2019 but including funds for space missions to carry cargo and astronauts to the moon, an unmanned research expedition to Jupiter's moon, Europa, and for commercial launch vehicles for both endeavors. The proposal also would fund the International Space Station and the James Webb Telescope, which NASA aimed to launch into space in 2021 to succeed the Hubble Telescope. The budget would not fund NASA's Office of Science, Technology, Engineering, and Mathematics Engagement.

State. The president's budget included $42.8 billion for the State Department, the U.S. Agency for International Development, overseas food assistance, and other international programs. The request represented a 23.5 percent cut to the $56 billion discretionary funding in fiscal 2019. The funding request included $29 billion for foreign operations and $13.7 billion for diplomatic activities and operations of the State Department. The request outlined a $1.4 billion cut to the embassy and diplomatic security account from the $6.1 billion level in fiscal 2019. The request included $500 million for the Countering Russian Influence Fund, about an 80 percent increase over fiscal 2019.

Transportation. The budget proposed $21.4 billion in discretionary funding for the Department of Transportation, a $5.1 billion or 19.2 percent reduction from the fiscal 2019 level of $26.5 billion. The budget also proposed a $3 billion cut in discretionary state highway aid, a $1 billion cut in discretionary mass transit capital investment grants, a $200 million reduction in transit infrastructure grants, a $500 drop in airport infrastructure grants, and a $1 billion cut in aid for Amtrak (the budget proposed recommended replacing several Amtrak routs with bus service). The budget would eliminate funding for a new port infrastructure grant program. The proposal included $1 billion for Trump's proposed competitive infrastructure grant program and a new $300 million competitive program for rural bridges.

The administration's budget also included $46.4 billion in nondiscretionary highway aid, up from $45.3 billion, and $10.2 billion in transit aid, an increase from $9.9 billion in fiscal 2019. The budget would not fund the Gateway rail tunnel and bridge project that would link New York and New Jersey. To finance an infrastructure program, the White House said the administration would fund $200 billion over 10 years, including $5 billion in fiscal 2020, with the aim to attract $1 trillion in private funding.

Treasury. The president's budget proposal included $13.1 billion for the Department of Treasury, a $400 million increase from fiscal 2019. That budget

included $11.5 billion for the IRS, boosting the agency's spending to the highest level since 2013. Trump said the increase was in part to enable the IRS to modernize its computer systems. The budget also would increase funding for the Office of Terrorism and Financial Intelligence by 5 percent, to $167 million, and would provide new funding of $13 million for Treasury's Office of Critical Infrastructure Protection and Compliance to provide cybersecurity for the U.S. financial services sector. The budget would eliminate funding for the Community Development Financial Institutions Fund, which seeks to help generate economic growth in distressed communities.

Justice. Under the administration's budget, the Justice Department would see a 5.5 percent or $1.7 billion decrease in funding, to $29.2 billion. The budget, however, included a $71.1 million increase for the Executive Office for Immigration Review to hire more immigration judges to handle a backlog of about 750,000 cases. The administration also sought funding for fifty more federal prosecutors to enforce immigration laws, and another $16.6 million for the FBI's role in vetting immigrants. The budget also included a $354 million increase for grants to help states and school districts increase school safety; $754 million for programs to help former prison inmates rejoin society; and $14 million for innovative programs to address the needs of individuals incarcerated in federal prison.

Veterans Affairs. The administration requested $93.1 billion in discretionary spending for the Department of Veterans Affairs (VA), a $6.5 billion or 7.5 percent increase from fiscal 2019. The request included $80.2 billion for veterans' health care programs, a $7 billion or 9.6 percent increase from fiscal 2019. The VA in July was scheduled to launch a new program aimed at expanding veterans' access to private medical care. The administration's budget also included $8.9 billion to implement the MISSION Act, which includes the private care program and expands benefits for caregivers; $9.4 billion for mental health services; and $4.3 billion for information technology projects.

TWO-YEAR BUDGET AGREEMENT

Congress in July 2019 cleared a two-year budget deal (HR 3877) that set discretionary spending caps for fiscal years 2020 and 2021, rejecting Trump's proposal not to increase the spending caps imposed by the 2011 debt ceiling and spending cuts law (PL 112-25). The measure also suspended the debt limit until July 31, 2021. The president signed the measure into law (PL 116-37) on August 2.

House Action

The House Budget Committee on April 3 voted 19–17 to approve a measure (HR 2021) that would raise the fiscal 2020 defense cap to $664 billion, $17 billion above the fiscal 2019 level, and the nondefense cap to $631 billion, $34 billion above fiscal 2019. The measure would raise the cap in fiscal 2021 to $680 billion and the nondefense cap to $646 billion in fiscal 2021. The measure would allow up to $69 billion in funding beyond the caps for defense spending and $8 billion for nondefense programs in fiscal 2020 and 2021.

Before approving the measure, the panel rejected six amendments, including

- An amendment by Chris Stewart, R-Utah, rejected by voice vote, that would have increased the cap on defense spending from $664 billion to $677 billion for fiscal 2020, and from $680 billion to $711 billion in fiscal 2021; increased funding for Overseas Contingency Operations from $69 billion to $73 billion in fiscal 2020, then reduced funding from $69 billion to $60 billion for fiscal 2021
- An amendment by Ro Khanna, D-Calif., that would have kept the defense cap for fiscal 2020 and 2021 at the fiscal 2019 level of $647 billion
- An amendment by Chip Roy, R-Texas, rejected by a 14–20 vote, that would have kept the nondefense caps at the levels set by the 2011 deficit reduction law
- A proposal by Bill Johnson, R-Ohio, rejected by a 14–20 vote, that would have barred the increased caps unless they were fully offset by cuts in mandatory spending
- A proposal by Kevin Hern, R-Okla., rejected 14–20, that would have eliminated adjustments that would permit spending beyond the caps for the 2020 census and IRS enforcement
- An amendment by William R. Timmons IV, R-S.C., rejected 14–20, that would have continued the discretionary spending caps beyond fiscal 2021

House progressives did not widely support the measure (HR 2021) and instead backed another deal reached with Senate Republicans and the White House. That deal, incorporated in HR 3877, would increase discretionary spending limits by nearly $324 billion over fiscal 2020 and 2021 when compared to the 2011 law, avoiding a $125 billion decrease set for 2020.

Under the measure, total defense discretionary spending would increase from $716 billion in fiscal 2019 to $738 billion during fiscal 2020 (a 3.1 percent increase) and to $740.5 billion in fiscal 2021. Nondefense spending would increase from $605 billion in fiscal 2019 to $632 billion in fiscal 2020 (a 4.5 percent increase) and $634 billion in fiscal 2021.

In total, discretionary budget would rise to $1.37 trillion in fiscal 2020, nearly 4 percent more than the fiscal 2019 levels. The measure would provide for $77.4 billion in offsets, and would suspend the debt limit until July 31, 2021. On July 25, 2019, the House voted 284–149 to pass the measure (HR 3877). The deal was supported by 132 Republicans and 16 Democrats.

Final Action

The Senate voted 67–28 to clear the two-year budget deal (HR 3877) on August 1. Five Democrats opposed the bill: Thomas R. Carper of Delaware, Joe Manchin III of West Virginia, Jon Tester of Montana, and 2020 presidential candidates Amy Klobuchar of Minnesota and Michael Bennet of Colorado. President Trump signed the measure into law (PL 116-37) on August 2.

The agreement paved the way for appropriators to begin working on fiscal 2020 spending measures, two months before the start of the fiscal year. The House Appropriations Committee had already marked up all twelve of its bills earlier in the year and passed 10 on the floor, but would need to trim them to meet the new caps. Senate appropriators had been awaiting a deal on discretionary spending before they started their work.

Fiscal Year 2020 Appropriations

The House and Senate reached agreement on fiscal 2020 appropriations in December 2020, more than two months after the start of the fiscal year. The delay again required lawmakers to pass short-term stopgap funding measures to keep the government open.

The House Appropriations Committee marked up all twelve of its fiscal 2020 appropriations bills in the first half of 2019 and passed 10 of the bills on the floor. The Budget Control Act of 2011 (PL 112-25) would have required a 10 percent cut in discretionary funding and Trump in his proposed budget proposed leaving that cap in place. Pending a new agreement on caps, House appropriators used their own set of caps, and the House on April 9 adopted a Democratic "deeming resolution" (H Res 293) that set a discretionary spending top line of $1.295 trillion for Fiscal Year 2020. However, after the House and Senate reached a two-year deal that raised defense and nondefense discretionary spending caps for fiscal 2020 and 2021, the House spending bills needed to be trimmed.

Senate appropriators, meanwhile, did not begin acting on their spending plans until the deal was reached on discretionary spending levels, but began with draft bills that included GOP spending priorities that sharply differed from House Democratic priorities and would increase funding Trump requested for the wall along the southern border. The Senate Appropriations Committee ultimately approved ten of its bills. Then, after the start of the fiscal year, the Senate passed its version of the House's four-bill package (HR 3055).

Lawmakers twice passed short-term stopgap measures (PL 116-59, PL 116-69) to keep the government open after the start of the fiscal year while it continued negotiations. House and Senate leaders in November agreed on discretionary allocations for the twelve spending bills, matching the caps in the two-year budget deal.

The agreement on spending allocations, the administration's agreement to drop its request for funding increases for the border wall, and the Democrats' decision to drop their mandate to zero out funding for the wall paved the way for Congress in mid-December to clear two minibus spending packages: a four-bill package (HR 1158) and an eight-bill package (HR 1865). The president then signed the measures, totaling $1.4 trillion, into law just before the last stopgap measure was to expire.

FOUR-BILL MINIBUS

On June 19, the House voted 226–203 to pass a minibus spending measure (HR 2740) that encompassed four regular spending bills. Seven Democrats voted against the measure, while no Republicans supported it. The Senate, however, did not pass it. The bill originally included five bills, but leaders dropped the legislative branch measure (HR 2779), approved by the committee May 9 in a 31–21 vote, because it did not include language to continue a freeze on members' pay.

The remaining four bills would provide $984.7 billion in discretionary spending for fiscal 2020, including $906.8 billion in spending subject to the Houses' discretionary cap of $1.295 trillion, $76.1 billion in uncapped OCO funding, and $1.8 billion in funding subject to a separate program integrity cap adjustment. Of the discretionary spending, $690.2 billion would be provided for the Department of Defense.

The four bills included

- Defense spending bill (HR 2968), which the Appropriations Committee approved May 21 in a 30–23 vote. The measure would provide $690.2 billion in discretionary funding for the Defense Department, $15.8 billion or 3 percent more than the fiscal 2019 level but $8 billion or 1 percent less than the president requested
- Energy–Water spending bill (HR 2960), approved in committee on May 21 by a 31–21 vote. The bill would provide $46.4 billion in energy and water projects, 41.8 billion or 4 percent more than in fiscal 2019 and $8.4 billion or 22 percent more than the president requested. The total included $37.1 billion for the Energy Department, a $1.4 billion boost from fiscal 2019, and $7.4 billion for the Army Corps of Engineers, a $357 million boost from fiscal 2019
- Labor–HHS–Education spending bill (HR 2740), approved May 8 by committee in a 30–23 vote. The measure would provide a total of $189.9 billion in discretionary spending, about 33 percent more than the president requested. The bill would provide discretionary funding of $13.3 billion for the Labor Department, $99.4 billion for HHS, and $75.9 billion for the Education Department
- State-Foreign Operations bill (HR 2839), approved in committee on May 16 in a 29–23 vote. The measure would provide $56.4 billion in discretionary funding, including 48 billion for OCO funding. The total was $2.2 billion more than the fiscal 2019 level and $13.7 billion more than the president requested

Before passing the bill, the House spent several days debating amendments, such as the following:

- An amendment by Rep. Jackie Speier, D-Calif., adopted 243–183, that would block the Pentagon from enforcing Trump's ban on transgender people from serving in the military
- An amendment by Steve Cohen, D-Tenn., adopted en bloc, that would block the State Department from spending funds at hotels or golf resorts owned or managed by the Trump organization
- An amendment by Gerald E. Connolly, D-Va., adopted en bloc, that would block Saudi Arabia from getting discounts on U.S. weapons systems purchases
- An amendment by Tim Walberg, R-Mich., adopted en bloc, that would bar funding for the Taliban insurgency in Afghanistan

As the four-bill package was considered on the House floor, the White House threatened to veto it if it was cleared. President Trump said he opposed the higher discretionary caps set by House Democrats, and he objected that Democrats demanded increases for defense be matched for nondefense spending.

Senate Action

On October 31, the Senate failed a motion on cloture, to end debate, on its version of the four-bill spending package (HR 2740) and its Defense spending measure (S 2474). Democrats objected to spending levels and funding of the border wall. The motion on cloture failed in a 51–41 vote, short of the sixty votes needed to proceed.

FIVE-BILL MINIBUS

On June 25, the House passed a $322 billion, five-bill minibus (HR 3055) by a 227–194 vote. No Republicans voted for the measure, and one Democrat, Ben McAdam of Utah, voted against it. The measure died after the Senate passed a different version.

The package, which House leaders put together using the Commerce–Justice–Science bill (HR 3055) as the vehicle, would provide a total of $383.3 billion in spending authority, including $321.9 billion in discretionary spending and $61.3 billion in spending from highway and aviation trust funds.

The package included the following appropriations measures:

Agriculture spending bill (HR 3164), approved June 4 by a vote of 29–21, which would provide $24.3 billion in discretionary funding, $1 billion or 4 percent more than in fiscal 2019 and $51.2 billion or 27 percent more than the administration requested. The total including mandatory spending would be $155.3 billion

Commerce–Justice–Science (HR 3055), approved May 22 by a vote of 31–20, which would provide $80.3 billion, $8.4 billion or 12 percent more than in fiscal 2019 and 11 percent more than the president requested. The measure would provide $16.4 billion for the Commerce Department, $5 billion or 44 percent more than in fiscal 2019 and 32 percent more than the administration requested. The bill also would increase funding for the Economic Development Administration by 78 percent, the International Trade Administration by 7 percent, National Institutes of Standards and Technology by 5.5 percent, the Patent and Trademark Office by 2 percent, and the National Oceanic and Atmospheric Administration by 11 percent. The Census Bureau would be funded at $8.4 billion, including $7.5 billion for the 2020 census. The bill would provide the Justice Department $31.9 billion, $1 billion or 3 percent more than in fiscal 2019 and $1.4 billion or 5 percent more than requested. The measure included the administration's request to increase funding for the Executive Office for Immigration Review by $109 million or 19 percent to hire up to 100 more immigration judges and support staff to handle a backlog of immigration cases

Interior–Environment (HR 3052), approved May 22 by committee, 30-21, would provide $35.9 billion in discretionary spending, $1.7 billion or 5 percent above 2019 level and $7.2 billion more than requested. The measure would provide $9.5 billion for EPA, rejecting president's proposed 23 percent funding cut and increasing funding by 8 percent. It also would provide $14.2 billion for Interior, 9 percent more than previous year and 20 percent more than president requested. The bill included $7.6 billion for US Forest Service, and $3.5 billion for Bureau of Indian Affairs programs

Military Construction–VA (HR 2745), approved May 9, 31–21, included $108.4 billion in discretionary funds, including $2.3 billion in emergency disaster funding and $921 million in OCO funding. The bill would provide $10.5 billion for base military construction activities, $207 million or 2 percent more than 2019 and $703 million or 6 percent less than requested. And it would provide $217.5 billion for Department of Veterans Affairs programs and services, including $94.3 billion in discretionary funding—$7.8 billion or 9 percent more than fiscal 2019 and $1.3 billion more than the administration requested

Transportation-HUD (HR 3163), approved June 4 by a vote of 29–21, included $75.8 billion in discretionary spending and $61.3 billion from highway and trust funds. The $137.1 billion would be $6 billion more than fiscal 2019 (when not including emergency supplemental appropriations) and $17.3 billion more than the administration requested. Under the bill, Transportation would receive $86.6 billion, including $25.3 billion in discretionary funds, while HUD would receive $53.1 billion

The measure also included about $1 billion to compensate lower-income federal contractors who did not receive paychecks during the thirty-five-day partial government shutdown that ended in January. The measure capped weekly compensation at the level of the worker's weekly compensation or $965, whichever was less. The measure would apply to an estimated 580,000 workers. The measure also included a provision to allow legislative branch agencies to hire individuals who were granted work authorizations under the Deferred Action for Childhood Arrivals (DACA) program.

Before the House voted to pass the measure, the White House threatened to veto it, saying the measure would cost 8.7 percent, or $25.7 billion, more than Trump requested. The administration also said it opposed several policy riders. Further, the bill was drafted before a deal was reached to raise discretionary spending caps.

The House considered 290 amendments, including

- An amendment, approved 238–104, that would bar the Justice Department from using funds to oppose the Obama-era health care law in court
- An amendment, adopted 267–165, that would block the federal government from enforcing marijuana laws in states that permit the sale and use of the drug
- Several amendments that would block the administration from conducting lease sales for oil and gas drilling in parts of the Atlantic and Pacific coasts
- An amendment, rejected 192–240, that would have barred the EPA from enforcing the Obama administration Clean Power Plan that was intended to reduce carbon emissions

Senate Action

The Senate passed its $214 billion, four-bill version of the House minibus (HR 3055) on October 31. That measure included

- Agriculture (S 2522), approved by committee September 19 in a 31–0 vote, which would provide $23.1 billion for the Agriculture Department and the FDA, $58 million more than the fiscal 2019 level
- Commerce–Justice–Science (S 2584), approved by the Appropriations Committee by a 31–0 vote on September 26. The bill would provide $78.9 billion, $7.5 billion or 11 percent more than in fiscal 2019. The measure would provide $70.8 billion in discretionary funding, and included a $3.7 billion increase, to $7.5 billion, for the Census Bureau
- Interior–Environment (S 2580), which the committee approved on a 31–0 vote on September 26. The bill would provide $35.8 billion for Department of the Interior and EPA programs, rejecting massive cuts requested. The bill would provide $9 billion for the EPA, $161 million above the 2019 level, and which the president wanted to cut by a third from the 2019 level; and $13.7 billion for the Department of the

Interior, which was funded at $13.5 billion in 2019 and which the president wanted to cut by 5.2 percent
- Transportation–HUD (S 2520), approved in committee on September 19 by a vote of 31–0. The measure would provide $74.3 billion for Transportation and HUD, $3.2 billion more than in 2019. The measure included $25.3 billion for the Department of Transportation and $48.6 billion for HUD

The measure did not include a Military–Construction VA measure, as the House bill did. Senate appropriators' drafting of that measure had been held up by continued partisan dispute over the president's border wall funding request.

The Senate approved the measure in an 84–9 vote. The Senate's measure came after the bipartisan cap deal (PL 116-37), so that the chamber's allocations were tighter than those in the House measures. Funding for the four regular spending measures was about $5 billion less than House funding for those measures.

Before passing the measure, senators voted 29–64 to reject an amendment by Sen. Mike Lee, R-Utah, that would have barred the federal government from using Land and Water Conservation Fund dollars to acquire public lands until after a $19.4 billion maintenance backlog was cleared.

Lawmakers voted 82–11 to adopt an amendment by Sens. Doug Jones, D-Ala., and Martha McSally, R-Ariz., that would suspend a law that required automatic spending cuts if the Highway Trust Fund's authorized spending for transit agencies exceeded estimated revenues. The move was to prevent public transit agencies from dealing with a 12 percent funding cut.

Senators also agreed to a manager's package, encompassing forty-five, mostly noncontroversial amendments. One of the amendments, however, would require the Commerce Secretary to publish in the Federal Register a report detailing the results of an investigation on whether imported cars and car parts constitute a threat to U.S. national security. Trump had used the report, which was kept secret, in May as reason to begin considering possible Section 232 national security tariffs or other actions on imported vehicles and parts from Japan and Europe. *(See Trade section.)*

STOPGAP MEASURES

As the start of the fiscal 2020 year approached and Congress had yet to clear any of the twelve regular appropriations measures, House Democrats on September 18, 2019, introduced a stopgap spending measure (HR 4378) that would keep the government running at fiscal 2019 levels through November 21. The measure also would reimburse the Commodity Credit Corporation for trade relief and other payments, providing the CCC with about $20.5 billion to prevent the fund from reaching its $30 billion borrowing limit. The House passed the bill in a 301–123 vote on September 19, with three Democrats voting against the measure and seventy-six Republicans supporting it.

The Senate cleared the measure (HR 4378) on September 26 by a vote of 81–16. All Democrats supported the measure, while sixteen Republicans voted against it. Before clearing the measure, the Senate voted 24–73 to reject an amendment by Sen. Rand Paul, R-Ky., that would have cut the bill's spending level by 2 percent. The president signed the measure into law (PL 116-59) on September 27.

On November 19, the House passed a continuing resolution spending bill to keep the government running through December 2020. The stopgap was attached as an amendment to the four-bill fiscal 2020 spending package (HR 3055) that the House and Senate had passed earlier. The Senate on November 21 voted 74–20 to clear the measure for the president's signature. Before clearing the measure, senators voted 73–20 to table an amendment by Sen. Paul that would have decreased spending by 1 percent.

The president signed the bill into law (PL 116-69) later on November 21, 2019. The bill continued funding for one month at fiscal 2019 levels, with a few exceptions. The Census Bureau, for example, was funded at a higher annualized rate of $7.3 billion due to the 2020 census.

The bill also

- Reauthorized until March three Foreign Intelligence Surveillance Act provisions that had been scheduled to expire December 15
- Continued several health programs for one month
- Extended authorization for the Export–Import Bank for another month
- Barred the cancellation of $7.6 billion in highway spending scheduled to occur on July 1, 2020, under the 2015 surface transportation law (PL 114-94)
- Codified a 3.1 percent pay raise for U.S. military troops, effective January 1, 2020

FINAL SPENDING PACKAGES

In mid-December 2019, Congress cleared two spending packages that combined the twelve fiscal 2020 appropriations measures and totaled $1.4 trillion in discretionary spending. The agreement came after congressional leaders, just before Thanksgiving 2019, reached agreement on discretionary allocations for each of the bills that were consistent with the caps set in the budget deal in July. Negotiators reached agreement after the administration dropped its demand for more money for the southern border wall and Democrats did not mandate zero funding for the wall.

Since Trump previously had vowed he would never sign an omnibus spending package again, House and Senate leaders on December sixteen unveiled two separate packages—a four-bill "security" spending package (HR 1158) and an eight-bill package (HR 1865).

FOUR-BILL PACKAGE

The House passed a $860.3 billion, four-bill spending package (HR 1158) by a vote of 280–138 on December 17.

The bill was opposed by seventy-five Democrats. The Senate cleared the bill by a vote of 81–11 on December 19. Four Republicans and seven Democrats opposed the bill: Republicans Mike Braun of Indiana, Ted Cruz of Texas, Josh Hawley of Missouri and Mike Lee of Utah; and Democrats Thomas R. Carper of Delaware, Kirsten Gillibrand and Charles E. Schumer of New York, Edward J. Markey of Massachusetts, Jeff Merkley and Ron Wyden of Oregon, and Chris Van Hollen of Maryland. The president signed the measure into law (PL 116-93) on December 20, 2019.

The measure included $767.6 billion subject to spending caps. The provisions for specific funding bills wrapped in the package included the following:

Commerce–Justice–State. Congress provided $70.7 billion in net discretionary spending for the Commerce, Justice and State Departments, $6.6 billion more than in fiscal 2019. The funding included $15.2 billion for the Commerce Department, including $7.6 billion for the Census Bureau; $32.6 billion for the Justice Department (including the FBI); and $22.6 billion for NASA and other federal agencies.

Defense. The bill provided $695.1 billion in discretionary funding for the Defense Department, $19.5 billion or 3 percent more than the fiscal 2019 level and $4.6 billion, or 0.5 percent less, than the president requested. The funding included $70.7 billion in OCO funding and $1.8 billion in emergency funding, as well as almost $10 billion for ninety-eight new F-35 planes, exceeding the funding request for twenty planes.

Financial Services (HR 1994). Lawmakers provided $23.8 billion in discretionary funding for financial services, a $669 million boost from fiscal 2019 levels but $370 million less than the president requested. The funding included a 3.1 percent pay raise for federal civilian employees, beginning in January 2020.

Homeland Security. The measure provided $50.5 billion in discretionary spending for the Department of Homeland Security, $1.1 billion more than in 2019 and $1.2 billion less than the president requested. The funding included $1.375 billion for continued construction of the U.S.–Mexico border wall, matching fiscal 2019 funding, although the president had requested $5 billion.

EIGHT-BILL PACKAGE

The House passed an eight-bill spending package (HR 1865) by a vote of 297–120 on December 17, with nearly all Democrats and less than half of Republicans voting for the measure. (The package was considered as a House amendment to a Senate amendment to an unrelated measure, HR 1865, that called for a commemorative coin in honor of the National Law Enforcement Museum.) The Senate voted 71–23 to clear the measure (HR 1865), which provided $540 billion in discretionary spending, on December 19. The president signed the bill into law (PL 116-94) on December 20 2019.

The measure included language from retirement savings legislation (HR 1994) that the House had passed earlier in the year. The measure also included provisions to

- Extend several health care programs through May 22, 2020
- Provide funding to restore the solvency of a coal miners pension fund and preserve health care benefits at risk due to bankruptcies of coal companies
- Provide a loan for capital improvements at the Presidio, a national park along San Francisco Bay
- Prohibit pay raises for members of Congress
- Increase to twenty-one the minimum age for purchasing tobacco products
- Repeal three taxes included in the 2010 health care law, which were expected to save 373 billion over ten years, according to the Joint Committee on Taxation
- Renew several tax provisions that had expired or were scheduled to expire January 1, 2020, including deductions for mortgage insurance premiums, college medical expenses; excise tax breaks for craft brewers and distillers; credits for employer-paid family and medical leave, investors in low-income communities, and faster depreciation for racehorse and motor sports complexes
- Extend through 2022 lapsed credits for biodiesel and short-line railroad maintenance
- Extend for seven years authorization for the U.S. Export–Import Bank (see page **151**)
- Extend for seven years, through December 31, 2027, the Terrorism Risk Insurance program (see page **60**)

The measure included $520.4 billion subject to discretionary caps. Funding for the eight spending bills included the following:

Agriculture. The bill provided $23.5 billion in discretionary funding for the Department of Agriculture, the FDA and related agencies, $183 million or 1 percent more than in fiscal 2019. Combined with mandatory spending on such programs as food stamps, the bill's funding totaled $154 billion. Funding included $98 billion for domestic food programs, $7.6 billion for agricultural programs; $39.1 billion for farm production and conservation programs, and $3.2 billion for rural development programs. The FDA received nearly $3.2 billion.

Energy–Water. The measure provided $48.3 billion in discretionary funding for energy and water programs, $3.7 billion or 8 percent more than the fiscal 2019 level and $10.3 billion or 27 percent more than the president requested. The funding included $24.3 billion for defense-related activities and $24.1 billion for nondefense activities.

The measure would provide $7.7 billion for the Army Corps of Engineers, $652 million or 9 percent more than in fiscal 2019 and $2.7 billion or 54 percent more than requested. The Energy Department received $38.6 billion, $2.9 billion or 8 percent more than in fiscal 2019 and $7.1 billion or 22 percent more than requested. Lawmakers rejected the president's request to eliminate the Advanced

Research Projects Agency–Energy research Program, instead boosting that program's funding from the fiscal 2019 level by $59 million, or 16 percent, to $425 million.

The bill did not include funding for the Yucca Mountain Waste Repository in Nevada or for an interim storage facility.

Interior–Environment. The measure provided $36 billion in discretionary spending for the Department of Environment and the EPA, $437 million more than fiscal 2019 funding and $5.8 million more than the administration requested. Lawmakers rejected the president's request to cut the EPA's funding by 23 percent and increased the agency's appropriations by $208 million to $9.1 billion. The bill provided $13.5 billion in discretionary funding for the Interior and related agencies—$545 million more than in 2019 and $2.1 billion, or 19 percent, more than the president requested.

Congress also rejected requested cuts to other agencies, instead increasing funding for the National Park Service, the Bureau of Land Management, the U.S. Geologic Survey, and the U.S. Fish and Wildlife Service. The measure provided $5.6 billion for Forest Service and Department of the Interior wildfire activities, a $1.6 billion increase from fiscal 2019 funding. The measure also increased funding for the Indian Health Service by 5 percent and provided slight spending boosts for the Smithsonian Institution and the National Endowments for the Arts and Humanities.

Labor–HHS–Education. Congress provided $184.9 billion in discretionary spending for the departments of Labor, Health and Human Services and Education, $4.9 billion or 3 percent more than in fiscal 2019 and $43 billion, or 30 percent, more than Trump requested. The departments and agencies also received $900 billion in mandatory funding (a 4 percent boost from fiscal 2019), including for Medicaid grants to states, payments to health care trust funds, and Social Security Supplemental Security Income benefits payments.

The measure provided $12.4 billion in discretionary spending for the Labor Department, $291 million more than in fiscal 2019 and $1.4 billion more than the president requested. Lawmakers rejected the president's proposal to eliminate funding for an employment program for older workers and for the Migrant and Seasonal Farmworkers program.

Under the measure, the Department of Health and Human Services received $94.9 billion, $4.4 billion more than in fiscal 2019 and $16.8 billion more than requested. The bill provided another $72.8 billion for the Education Department, $1.3 billion more than in fiscal 2019 and $8.7 billion more than requested.

Legislative Branch. The measure provided $5 billion in discretionary funds for the House, Senate, and legislative branch agencies such as the Library of Congress, the Government Publishing Office (GPO), and the Capitol Police. The total was $203 million or nearly 4 percent more than in fiscal 2019 and $239 million, or 4.5 percent, less than the legislative offices requested.

The measure included increased funding for the Capitol Police to boost security for lawmakers. The move was in response to a 2019 shooting at a practice for the annual congressional baseball game. The measure also maintained the freeze on members' salaries that had been in place since 2009.

Military Construction–Veterans Affairs. The measure provided $110.3 billion in discretionary funds for military construction and the Department of Veterans Affairs, $10.7 billion more than in fiscal 2019. The measure included $6.2 billion in disaster funding and $645 in Overseas Contingency Operations funding, or war-related funding.

Within the total funding, the measure provided $11.3 billion for base military construction, $983 million more than in fiscal 2019 and $73 million more than the president requested. It also provided $6.2 billion in emergency funds to repair damage to bases from hurricanes Florence and Michael, flooding in the Midwest, tornadoes in Louisiana, and earthquakes in California. The measure provided $216.5 billion for the Department of Veterans Affairs, including $91.9 billion in discretionary spending ($5.4 billion more than in fiscal 2019) and $124.9 billion in mandatory spending.

State-Foreign Operations. The measure provided $54.7 billion in discretionary funding, $467 million more than in fiscal 2019 and $11.3 billion more than the president requested. Congress rejected most of the spending cuts that Trump requested. The final measure included $9.1 billion for global health programs, $3.3 billion for military assistance to Israel, $1.4 billion for Egypt, $1.5 billion for Jordan, and $448 billion for Ukraine. The measure also included $520 million to respond to the flow of migrants across the border into the United States from Central America, and $6.3 billion to combat HIV/AIDS.

Transportation–HUD. Lawmakers provided $74.3 billion in discretionary funding for the Departments of Transportation and Housing and Urban Development, and $61.3 billion from highway and aviation trust funds. The total $135.6 billion in funding was $1.2 billion more than fiscal 2019 levels (not including emergency supplemental spending) and $15.8 billion more than requested.

The bill's total included $24.8 billion in discretionary funding for the Department of Transportation, $1.7 billion less than in fiscal 2019 but $3 billion more than Trump requested. HUD received $49.1 billion, $4.9 billion or 11 percent more than in fiscal 2019 and $12.9 billion, or 34 percent, more than requested. Lawmakers rejected the administration's request to end funding for the Community Development Block Grant program, community development loan guarantees, and HOME Investments Partnership programs.

SALT Repeal

The House on December 19, 2019, voted 218–206 to pass a bill (HR 5377) to provide a two-year reprieve from the $10,000 limit on state and local tax deductions, known as SALT, imposed by the 2017 tax code overhaul (PL 115-97). The Senate, however, did not take it up.

Under the measure, taxpayers could write off the cost of their state and local taxes when they file their returns for 2020 and 2021. The bill also would double the limit for married couples for 2019. The bill was a top priority among Democratic leaders as about a dozen Democrats had flipped Republican seats in the 2018 midterms in part with their pledges to undo the SALT cap, which they said disproportionately affected constituents in high-tax states such as New York, New Jersey, and California. Democrats proposed to cover the $184.5 billion loss in revenue resulting from the measure by permanently increasing the top marginal tax rate for individuals from 37 percent to 39.6 percent, returning it to the level before the tax overhaul.

The bill also included provisions to double the $250 deduction for teachers' out-of-pocket expenses and to create a new $500 deduction for paramedics, firefighters, and other first responders. While most Republicans opposed the bill, GOP Rep. Peter T. King of New York said it deserved support. Four other Republicans also backed the bill: Brian Fitzpatrick of Pennsylvania, John Katko and Tom Reed of New York, and Christopher H. Smith and Jeff Van Drew of New Jersey.

Sixteen Democrats opposed the bill: Alexandria Ocasio-Cortez of New York, Mark Pocan of Wisconsin, Cynthia Axne and Abby Finkenauer of Iowa, Kendra Horn of Oklahoma, Colin Allred of Texas, Joaquin Castro of Texas, Jared Golden of Maine, Ann McLane Kuster of New Hampshire, Susie Lee of Nevada, Ben McAdams of Utah, Stephanie Murphy of Florida, Chris Pappas of New Hampshire, Mark Pocan of Wisconsin, Abigail Spanberger of Virginia, and Greg Stanton of Arizona. Independent Paul Mitchell and Libertarian Justin Amash of Michigan also opposed the bill.

Before passing the measure, the House voted 388–36 to adopt a motion by Tom Rice, R-S.C., to include language that would bar householders with adjusted gross income above $100 million from benefitting from the measure, putting the $7 billion in savings from that change toward doubling the new deductions for teachers and first responders. Members then adopted by voice vote his proposal as an amendment to the measure.

The House Ways and Means Committee had approved the bill in a 24–17 vote on December 11. With the Senate refusing to act on the measure, House Speaker Nancy Pelosi, D-Calif., looked to add a SALT provision to a COVID-relief bill in 2020, but without success.

Disaster Relief for Puerto Rico

The House on February 7, 2020, passed a $4.9 billion emergency supplemental spending bill (HR 5687) that aimed to help Puerto Rico continue to recover from a series of natural disasters that wiped out homes, businesses, and infrastructure across the island and led to

thousands of deaths. The White House, however, insisted the president would veto a bill that provided more disaster aid for Puerto Rico. The Senate did not consider the bill.

BACKGROUND

Puerto Rico was still recovering from Hurricanes Irma and Maria. Irma was a Category 5 hurricane that passed north of the island on September 6, 2017, with tropical storm force winds and heavy rainfall cutting electricity and water, uprooting trees, and damaging homes and businesses. Maria was a Category 4 hurricane that hit September 20, further damaging buildings homes, boats, roads, and other infrastructure. Between September 2017 and February 2018, 2,975 people had died due to causes related to the hurricane damage, according to the Congressional Research Service.

A series of earthquakes followed in late 2019 and 2020, including a magnitude 5.8 quake that hit on January 6, 2020, destroying the natural rock arch at Punta Ventana, a popular tourist site. A magnitude 6.4 earthquake hit Puerto Rico on January 7, 2020, cutting off power on the island and leveling homes.

Action

House Democrats on January 16 released a $3.35 billion emergency funding package to help Puerto Rico with relief and recovery efforts. House Appropriations Chair Nita M. Lowey, D-N.Y. released an updated version of the package (HR 5687) on January 28, which boosted the package to $4.67 billion. The House Ways and Means Committee drafted the tax title of the bill, which was similar to a $6.8 billion provision in a bill (HR 3300) the committee had approved in June 2019.

The bill included about $21 billion in tax breaks and direct appropriations. Among the tax provisions were an expanded earned income tax credit and child tax credits for territorial residents. Also under the bill, the federal Treasury for five years would make matching payments to Puerto Rico for earned income tax credit expansions, while providing seventy-five cents on the dollar for U.S. Virgin Islands, American Samoa, Guam, and the Commonwealth of the Northern Mariana Islands. The bill also would make payments to territories for the cost of the child tax credits, with a maximum credit per child of $2,000, though $1,400 would be available as a refundable credit. Those provisions would be permanent and cost an estimated $13.5 billion, according to the Joint Committee on Taxation.

The bill also would dedicate $500 million of a $5 billion New Markets Tax Credit limit (set in December under PL 116-94) to Puerto Rico. The credits provided incentives for investors to support projects in low-income areas.

Lowey's bill also would call for the $13.50-per-proof gallon rum excise tax paid by U.S. producers and importers to be fully diverted to the governments of Puerto Rico and the U.S. Virgin Islands. The existing limit was $13.25 per gallon, which would drop to $10.50 in 2022. That provision was estimated to cost $1.7 billion. Lowey's bill would provide $3.26 billion in Community Development Block Grant funds and $1.25 billion for road repairs for Puerto Rico.

On February 7, 2020, the House voted 237–161 to pass the package, which totaled $21 billion in costs. Seventeen Republicans voted for the measure. The disaster aid portion totaled about $4.8 billion, including about $3.3 billion for CDBG funds, $1.25 billion for road repairs, and $210 million in food aid.

The House adopted by voice vote an amendment by Republican Jenniffer González-Colón, Puerto Rico's resident commissioner, that would add another $170 million for nutrition assistance for residents of Puerto Rico. The House also adopted an amendment by Republican Daniel Crenshaw and Democrat Lizzie Fletcher, freshman members from Texas, that would add $45 million to ensure victims of Hurricane Harvey who received Small Business Administration loans could access housing relief funds.

Members adopted by voice vote an amendment from Democrat Stacey Plaskett, a delegate for the Virgin Islands, to add $3 million to help repair the electrical grid in U.S. territories. President Trump, however, said he would veto the measure, in part because $44 billion already had been previously set aside for Puerto Rico disaster relief, and about half of that had been committed to specific uses but $8 billion remained unspent. The administration also said the measure's tax provisions, which composed about 75 percent of the ten-year cost, were unrelated to the disaster relief needs. Senate Republican leaders agreed, and the measure was not put on the Senate floor for a vote.

Fiscal Year 2021 Budget

PRESIDENT'S REQUEST

On February 10, 2020, the president submitted a $4.8 trillion fiscal 2021 budget request that again proposed deep cuts to domestic services and social safety-net programs, and would set the stage for sharply increasing debt and would not achieve a balanced budget for fifteen years. Although the bipartisan budget deal (PL 116-37) called for a $2.5 billion or 0.4 percent increase in nondefense discretionary spending, Trump proposed cutting that spending by $40 billion or 6 percent. His budget request included a total of $590 billion for nondefense discretionary spending, not including funds set aside for disaster relief and response.

Trump proposed a 0.3 percent increase, to $740.5 billion from $738 billion, for total defense discretionary spending, including the Overseas Contingency Operations account (war funding)—even though Democrats had said any increase for defense spending should be matched with an increase for nondefense spending. The budget did not include new major tax cut proposals, but did assume that tax cuts enacted in the 2017 law (PL 115-97) that were set to expire after 2025 would be extended, costing an estimated $1.4 trillion over the coming decade.

The administration's request included another $2 billion for a wall along the U.S.–Mexico border, more than the $8.6 billion he requested in the previous fiscal year. Congress had approved $1.375 billion for fiscal 2020.

ECONOMIC ASSUMPTIONS

The president assumed an economic growth rate of 3 percent per year over the next decade, which was more optimistic than the 1.7 percent growth the Congressional Budget Office predicted. With the onset of the COVID-19 pandemic, the economy instead contracted 3.5 percent — the worst decline since World War II.

Under the president's budget blueprint, the federal debt would grow to $23.9 trillion in 2030, up from $17.9 trillion in fiscal 2020. However, his budget predicted the debt would decline as a share of the economy, from 80.5 percent of gross domestic product to 66.1 percent of GDP in 2030.

HIGHLIGHTS

Agriculture. The president sought an 8.2 percent cut for the Department of Agriculture, to $21.8 billion from $23.8 billion in fiscal 2020. Among other changes, Trump sought to eliminate the $220 million McGovern-Dole Food for Education Program for low-income countries, reduce by 26 percent the budget for the Economic Research Service, and cut by $181.9 billion the food stamp program by, for example, providing some of recipients' monthly benefits in the form of a monthly box of food staples instead, and reducing the income eligibility level for farm subsidies.

Defense. The Pentagon's $740.5 billion request included a proposed shift of $3.8 billion from weapons programs to build more barriers on the U.S. border with Mexico. The proposal would take funds from such programs as the F-35 fighter jet, V-22 tiltrotor aircraft, and National Guard and Reserve Equipment.

In total, the Pentagon's budget plan would cut spending for weapons and equipment by $6.9 billion from the fiscal 2020 level, a nearly 5 percent reduction in the Department of Defense's procurement budget. The Army's procurement budget would drop by $453 million, to $24.9 billion. The Navy's budget would drop by $4.4 billion, to $61.6 billion, and the Air Force's procurement's budget would decrease $1 billion to $49 billion.

Education. The administration sought a 7.8 percent funding cut for Education programs, to $66.6 billion. The budget proposal would consolidate twenty-nine elementary and secondary school programs into one block grant program for states. The measure called for $5 billion annually for "education Freedom Scholarships" that could be used for technical education, special education, or private school education—a proposal Congress had previously rejected. The budget proposal also would have cut spending on federal student aid, and would eliminate certain loan programs, reducing funding for federal work--study programs, among other changes.

Energy. The budget proposal sought an 8.1 percent cut in funding for the Department of Energy, to $35.4 billion from $38.5 billion for fiscal 2020. The White House proposed a 19 percent funding increase for the National Nuclear Security Administration but a 28.7 percent funding cut for other Department of Energy programs. The president sought to cut by 75 percent the funding for the office of Energy Efficiency and Renewable Energy, and he proposed not funding the licensing process for the Yucca Mountain nuclear waste repository, contrary to early years when he sought such funding.

Environment. The Trump administration sought to cut funding for the EPA by nearly 27 percent, to $6.7 billion from $9.1 billion enacted for fiscal 2020. The president's budget called for eliminating fifty programs Trump deemed "wasteful," including various climate change and clean energy programs.

Health and Human Services. The budget blueprint proposed a $9.5 billion or 9 percent cut from the $106 billion in discretionary spending allocated for HHS in fiscal 2020, including decreases for the National Institutes of Health (NIH) and the Centers for Disease Control and Prevention (CDC). The White House also proposed $770 billion in mandatory funding cuts for HHS over ten years, affecting such programs as Medicare and Medicaid.

Homeland Security. The president sought a 3.4 percent or $1.6 billion boost, to $49.7 billion, in discretionary spending for the Department of Homeland Security. The request included $2 billion for a U.S.–Mexico border wall. The president also requested $182 million to hire 1,000 more border patrol agents and staff; $544 million for more than 4,600 additional Immigration and Customs Enforcement officers, prosecutors, and support personnel; and $317 million for non-wall border and trade security investments, and other requests.

Housing and Urban Development. Trump's budget request of $47.9 billion for HUD would have represented a 15.2 percent or $8.6 billion cut from the fiscal 2020 level. The White House sought to eliminate the Community Development Block Grant program, the Public Housing Capital Fund, and the HOME Investment Partnerships Program—which cost a combined $4.8 billion in fiscal 2020. The administration has proposed overhauling federal disaster relief programs.

Interior. The administration sought to cut funding for the Interior Department by 13 percent or $14.7 billion from fiscal 2020, to $12.7 billion. The budget blueprint indicated plans for opening the Arctic National Wildlife Refuge in Alaska for drilling, outlined in the 2017 tax overhaul law (PL 115-97), but did not specify the amount of funds that would be spent to open the refuge. The proposal also sought to set $796 million for energy development programs, including for oil, gas, coal and renewable energy, and $188.8 million for offshore energy and mineral development. The budget would cut by nearly 50 percent funding for the U.S. Geological Survey, and cut funding for federal land purchases.

Justice. The administration asked for a 2.3 percent or $730 million decrease in funding for the Justice Department, to $32.4 billion. The budget included $329 million for more federal law enforcement agents and personnel, $883 million for 100 immigration judges and support staff, $2.1 billion for U.S. Marshals Service prisoner detentions, $319 million to support a criminal justice overhaul law (PL 115-391) for programs that would help former prison inmates rejoin society, and $67 million for the Drug Enforcement Agency to target drug trafficking organizations.

Military Construction. The administration also requested $6.8 billion for military construction, a decrease of 31 percent or $9.9 billion from fiscal 2020. The request included $854 million for the Air Force, $2.1 billion for the Navy, and $1.1 billion for the Army.

NASA. The fiscal 2021 budget proposal included a 12 percent or $2.7 billion boost for NASA to $25.2 billion. Much of the funding increase would be targeted for a lunar landing mission. The White House sought to boost funding for deep space exploration from $6 billion to nearly $8.8 billion, for exploration technology from $1.1 billion to $1.6 billion, and for aeronautics from $783 million to $819 million. The budget plan would provide $3.3 billion for investment in a human landing system, which would take astronauts from a planned space station, called Deep Space Gateway, orbiting the moon to the lunar surface.

State and Foreign Operations. President Trump sought to reduce by about 21 percent, or $12 billion, funding for diplomatic operations and foreign aid. He requested about $43.9 billion for the State Department, U.S. Agency for International Development, and several small aid agencies—down from the $54.7 billion provided for fiscal 2020. The budget would eliminate funding for Food for Peace and McGovern-Dole child nutrition programs, the international disaster assistance fund, development assistance funding for foreign governments, and bilateral Economic Support Funds. The administration, meanwhile, sought sharp funding cuts for global health programs and other activities.

Transportation. The administration requested $21.billion in discretionary funding for the Department of Transportation, down 12.9 percent or $24.8 billion from fiscal 2020. The budget included $66.2 billion in mandatory spending, reflecting an 8 percent increase from 2020 levels.

The administration sought to reduce funding for the Federal Aviation Administration from $17.6 billion in fiscal 2020 to $17.5 billion in fiscal 2021 and boost FAA safety programs, including $36.7 million to improve FAA safety oversight following two Boeing 737 Max crashes that killed 346 people. The bill also would cut airport improvement program discretionary grants by $400 million to $3.4 billion, and cut by $225 million the port infrastructure development program. The president also sought cuts to Amtrak again and to the Essential Air Service program designed to provide air service to underserved, rural airports. The budget blueprint also proposed a 10-year reauthorization of surface transportation programs, and $190 billion in other infrastructure as part of the administration's 10-year plan for $1 trillion over a decade.

Treasury. The administration proposed a 2 percent increase to Treasury's budget to $13.35 billion, including a $528 million boost for the IRS, bringing that agency's budget to $12 billion. The budget also reflected a program to increase IRS collections. In addition, the blueprint proposed moving the Secret Service, and its $2.4 billion budget, from the Department of Homeland Security to the Treasury Department. Treasury oversaw the Secret Service prior to the September 11, 2001, terrorist attacks, and the administration hoped to direct the service's efforts to fighting complex criminal organizations responsible for financial crimes and cybersecurity threats.

Veterans Affairs. The White House requested a funding increase of $12.3 billion, or 13 percent more than fiscal 2020, to $105 billion for the Department of Veterans Affairs. The administration indicated about 80 percent of the funding increase would be budgeted for veterans' health care accounts. The VA expected to treat about 7.2 million veterans in fiscal 2021, a slight increase from fiscal 2020 as more Iraq and Afghanistan war veterans would enter the system.

BUDGET RESOLUTION

Democrats quickly rejected Trump's budget request, as did many Republicans. House Budget Chair John Yarmuth, D-Ky., indicated his committee did not intend to draft a budget resolution.

Congress did not need an annual budget resolution as the spending agreement reached in July 2020 (PL 116-37) set discretionary spending caps for defense and nondefense programs, totaling $1.375 trillion, for fiscal 2021. In February, Congress and the president also were looking toward the November elections, meaning bipartisan negotiations on any budget blueprint were unlikely to succeed.

COVID-19 Relief Funding

Congress in 2020 cleared five supplementary funding measures that provided about $3.5 trillion in relief to stem the spread of the COVID-19 virus, help businesses and unemployed workers during the worldwide pandemic, stimulate the economy, and support research into effective vaccines. The measures included

- Coronavirus Preparedness and Response Supplemental Appropriations Act of 2020 (HR 6074 — PL 116-123), providing $8.3 billion
- Families First Coronavirus Response Act (HR 6201— PL 116-127), providing an estimated $192 billion
- Coronavirus Aid, Relief, and Economic Security Act (CARES Act, HR 748 — PL 116-136), providing $2.1 trillion

- Paycheck Protection Program and Health Care Enhancement Act (HR 266 – PL 116-139), cleared April 23, providing $493.4 billion
- Consolidated Appropriations Act of 2021 (HR 113— PL 116-260), which provided $868 billion

The key COVID-19 relief measure was the $2.1 trillion CARES Act (HR 748) that included funds for direct payments to individuals, expanded unemployment benefits, and provided loans to small businesses that could be forgiven if they kept employees on the payroll, as well as aid to states and hospitals to respond to the pandemic.

BACKGROUND

On December 31, 2019, Chinese officials notified the World Health Organization (WHO) of several cases of pneumonia in Wuhan, China. On January 9, the WHO reported there were fifty-nine cases of the sickness in China that might be linked to a new coronavirus, which the WHO later called Coronavirus Disease 2019 or COVID-19.

The virus spread rapidly. On January 20, three more cases were reported in Thailand and Japan, and the U.S. Centers for Disease Control began screenings at JFK International, San Francisco International, and Los Angeles International airports. On January 21, the CDC confirmed the first COVID-19 case in the United States, while four individuals had died in China and another 200 people had been infected in that country. The WHO declared a global health emergency on January 31, 2020.

The Trump administration on February 2 barred foreign nationals who had been to China in the previous fourteen days from entering the United States, and mandated those who had already traveled back from China quarantine for fourteen days after arrival. On February 24, the White House asked Congress for $2.5 billion to respond to COVID-19, but most members of Congress said more would be needed.

On February 26, the CDC confirmed the first known instance of community transmission of COVID-19 in the United States. However, in April, health officials confirmed the first COVID-related death in the United States had occurred on February 6 in Santa Clara County. On March 11, the WHO declared the coronavirus outbreak to be a pandemic, and Trump announced a restriction on travel from Europe to the United States for thirty days.

Meanwhile, stocks plunged, with the Dow Jones Industrial Average falling 1,464 points to 20 percent below a record set the previous month. The Associated Press reported that the drop halted trading on Wall Street for the first time in more than twenty years, although it began to rebound with signs that the president would call on Congress to provide some relief.

On March 13, 2020, President Trump proclaimed the COVID-19 outbreak constituted a national emergency, pursuant to the Stafford Act Section 501(b), freeing up $50 billion in federal resources to combat the virus. It was the first time a president had unilaterally declared a nationwide emergency under the act, which authorizes FEMA assistance.

On March 15, Puerto Rico issued a mandatory state-at-home order, followed by California on March 19, with the aim to stem the spread of the virus. Over the next three months, forty-two states and territories issued mandatory state-at-home directives, which affected 73 percent of U.S. counties. The state-at-home orders resulted in several companies allowing employees to work remotely but many companies laid off or furloughed workers, with some businesses shutting down entirely.

On April 2, the Department of Labor reported that 6.6 million workers had filed for their first week of unemployment benefits in the week ending March 28—more than 3,000 percent above prepandemic levels. The previous week, 3.3 million initial claims had been filed, bringing the total unemployed to about 10 million. Meanwhile, businesses continued to lay off and furlough workers.

The unemployment rate reached 14.8 percent in April, then began to taper off, dropping to 6.7 percent by December 2020 as some states and localities began to relax some restrictions and companies adjusted to a remote workforce. But it remained above the prepandemic level of below 4 percent.

Many service industries were severely impacted, while states and localities needed support for COVID testing, hospitals and other medical centers needed protective gear and supplies, and companies needed financial aid to expedite research into COVID treatment and vaccines. The number of COVID-19 cases continued to surge, exceeding one million cases in the United States as of April 28.

OVERVIEW

As the economy took a nosedive and the number of COVID cases increased, lawmakers had set aside work on the regular fiscal 2021 spending measures and focused on clearing emergency aid.

In March, Congress cleared a coronavirus supplemental spending bill (HR 6074) that provided $8.3 billion in response to COVID-19, including $7.8 billion in emergency supplemental funding for the federal response to the outbreak, and $490 million for Medicare providers to provide telehealth medical services to patients.

Lawmakers quickly followed that with a measure (HR 6201) that provided $15.4 billion to help individuals and small business, mandating paid leave for individuals caring for a family member affected by the virus or for children whose school had closed. It also provided financial and nutrition assistance to low-income families, seniors and students, and mandated health plans cover COVID testing for free.

In April, Congress enacted the $2.1 billion Cares Act, after which Senate Majority Leader Mitch McConnell said lawmakers should pause and see the impact of the aid pro-

vided so far. Many Republicans also began raising concerns about the level of spending and its impact on federal deficits and the debt.

House Democrats in mid-May passed a $3.4 trillion aid package (HR 6800) that aimed to help those who were continuing to struggle or were unemployed because of the virus' impact on the economy. More than 22 million workers had lost their jobs in March and April. The bill would have extended and expanded many benefits previously enacted, such as unemployment, and provided more than $900 billion in aid for state and local governments. Republicans objected to providing another aid package so quickly and the Senate did not take up bill.

On May 15, Trump announced "Operation Warp Speed," an interagency partnership through the departments of HHS and Defense that would identify a set of vaccine candidates from private companies and dedicate essentially limitless funds for testing, human trials and manufacturing, including for increased manufacturing capacity.

The initiative, which aimed to acquire 300 million doses of an effective COVID-19 vaccine by January 2021 for Americans, was initially funded with $10 billion from the CARES Act. That year, the administration pledged $18 billion to the companies for vaccine development and doses. (The administration ultimately supported seven vaccine candidates through 2020, which were from Pfizer/BioNTech, Moderna, AstraZeneca/Oxford University, Johnson & Johnson's Janssen Pharmaceuticals, Novavax, Sanofi/GSK, and Merck/IAVI. Merck support was ultimately cancelled because its product was ineffective. On December 11, the FDA issued emergency use authorization for the Pfizer-BioNTech COVID-19 vaccine, and on December 18 the Moderna COVID-19 vaccine.)

Meanwhile, as the number of coronavirus cases continued to surge in the United States and unemployment and aid for small businesses were about to expire, negotiations began with the White House in late July on another aid package. Senate Republicans offered a series of virus response and relief bills estimated at $1 trillion, but the two parties disagreed on the level of unemployment aid and help for state and local governments.

After negotiations failed, President Trump in August signed four executive actions, which included $300 a week in extra federal unemployment aid, an extension on student loan payment suspensions, a moratorium on evictions of renters, and a suspension on the collection of federal payment taxes. In October, GOP senators offered a $519 billion aid bill (S 178). Democrats blocked it.

House and Senate lawmakers then negotiated another relief package. After several delays in negotiations, which required the passage of several continuing resolutions to keep the government funded, Congress cleared a $900 billion aid package as a part of the fiscal 2021 omnibus spending package (HR 113 —PL 116-260) at the end of December 2020.

CORONAVIRUS SUPPLEMENTAL

As of March 3, South Korea, Italy, and Iran had the largest outbreaks of COVID-19 outside China, according to the WHO. In the United States, the Centers for Disease Control reported 128 cases of COVID-19 had been confirmed in the United States and eleven deaths, including ten deaths in the Seattle area and one in California.

House Appropriations Chair Nita Lowey, D-N.Y., on March 4, 2020, introduced an $8.3 billion coronavirus aid package (HR 6074) to help federal agencies prevent, prepare for, and respond to the spread of the coronavirus, including testing on treatment. The House passed the measure in a 415–2 vote under a suspension of the rules on March 4, with Republicans Andy Biggs of Arizona and Ken Buck of Colorado voting no.

The measure included $7.8 billion in emergency supplemental funding to support the response to the outbreak and, at a cost of about $490 million, allowed Medicare providers to provide telehealth medical services to patients in their homes. Total funding included $6.5 billion for HHS (including $836 million for NIH; $3.1 billion for the Public Health and Social Services Emergency Fund; and $61 million for FDA), $1.3 billion for the State Department, $61 million for the FDA, and $20 million for the Small Business Administration (SBA).

The measure included $300 million for the government to buy drug treatments, test and eventually distribute vaccines when they were developed. USAID would receive $1.25 billion for global health programs, economic support funds, and diplomatic programs. About $136 million would reimburse federal programs tapped for initial response efforts, including a program to help low-income individuals and families.

The Senate cleared the bill on a 96–1 vote on March 5. Republican Rand Paul of Kentucky cast the lone vote against the bill, saying he wanted the bill's cost offset by cuts to foreign assistance programs. The president signed the measure into law (PL 116-123) on March 6, 2020.

FAMILIES FIRST ACT

On March 11, the number of COVID-19 cases in the United States exceeded 1,000 confirmed cases in twenty-eight states, and President Trump halted travel from Europe and appealed to Congress for more help in the form of an economic stimulus bill. The president, in a primetime address from the Oval Office, asked Congress to pass economic stimulus legislation that would designate another $50 billion for small business loans and give Americans a payroll tax cut. The president also said he would allow deferred tax payments for some individuals and businesses, which he said would inject $200 billion into the economy in the short term.

House Appropriations Chair Lowey, also on March 11, introduced the Families First Coronavirus Response Act (HR 6201), which aimed to provide an economic stimulus but did not include Trump's requested payroll tax cut. The

measure instead focused on provisions to help individuals and small businesses.

The bill would create a program to ensure sick and quarantined workers two weeks of emergency paid leave, require employers to provide more sick days for workers, and provide $1 billion in grant funding to help states manage and expand unemployment insurance programs. The measure would provide $1.2 billion for the Agriculture Department and HUD to boost nutrition assistance for low-income families, seniors, and students. The measure also called on private health plans to cover COVID testing for free, and for OSHA to create new workplace safety standards. The bill also would extend unemployment insurance and liability protections for manufacturers of face masks and other protective gear, and would suspend work requirements for food stamp recipients, among other provisions.

Republicans objected to the fact that the measure would require small businesses to provide paid leave. In bipartisan negotiations, Democrats agreed to add generous tax credits for those employers while narrowing the scope of paid sick leave and emergency leave. And instead of creating a new program, the measure would amend the Family and Medical Leave Act (PL 103-3) to provide up to twelve weeks of paid leave for employees who must quarantine or care for a family member in quarantine or a child whose school had closed.

On March 14, the House passed the estimated $192 billion (HR 6201) in a 363–40 vote, with forty Republicans opposing it. The Senate cleared the measure in a 90–8 vote on March 18. Eight Republicans opposed the bill: Marsha Blackburn of Tennessee, James M. Inhofe and James Lankford of Oklahoma, Ron Johnson of Wisconsin, Mike Lee of Utah, Rand Paul of Kentucky, Ben Sasse of Nebraska, and Tim Scott of North Carolina.

Before clearing the measure, senators rejected, 3–95, an amendment by Paul that would have required costs to be offset by ending U.S. involvement in the war in Afghanistan, transferring money from other accounts, and making permanent a law requiring individuals to have a Social Security number to receive the child tax credit. Senators also rejected, 50–48, an amendment by Sen. Ron Johnson, R-Wisc., that would have amended the bill to ensure workers would be eligible for up to fourteen weeks of unemployment insurance, paid at $1,000 a week or two-thirds of average weekly earnings, whichever was lower, retroactive to the beginning of March. Also, those receiving unemployment money would not have been counted in the unemployment rate. The president signed the measure into law (PL 116-127) on March 18, 2020.

CARES ACT

By the fourth week of March 2020, more than 86,000 cases of coronavirus had been reported in the United States, making it the nation with most confirmed cases in the world—and almost 1,300 people had died. There remained no known cure, effective therapeutic treatment, or vaccine to prevent COVID.

The economic impact of the spreading virus intensified as businesses and local governments took drastic actions. Many companies closed their doors, while state and local governments required the closure of schools, restaurants, bars, theaters, and other places. Many employers allowed workers to work remotely, but millions of service workers were laid off, heavily impacting travel, hospitality, restaurant, and retail industries. More than a dozen states called for residents to remain in their homes except for grocery shopping or other essential needs.

The stock market was plummeting; the Dow Jones Average had lost 37 percent of its value from its peak on February 12, though it began to rally when Congress indicated it was about to move another aid package. The unemployment rate was rising, and some economists predicted it could rise to 20 percent or more and the economy could contract up to 30 percent in the second quarter of 2020.

After clearing the first two aid packages, Senate Republicans developed another proposal (S 3548), estimated at costing almost $1 trillion, that would provide one-time cash payments to most Americans (up to $3,400 for married couples earning $150,000 and who had two children), low-cost loans for small businesses, and financial aid to such industries as airlines and health care. It also would defer payroll taxes paid by employers and provide some protections for student loan borrowers.

Democrats wanted to focus more on bolstering and extending unemployment benefits, and although Republicans included some of their proposals, Democrats twice blocked consideration of the GOP proposal on the floor. Democrats said the package, released by Senate Majority Leader Mitch McConnell, R-Ky., favored corporations rather than workers and did not provide sufficient support for hospitals and the broader medical system.

Late on March 24, the two parties reached a $2.1 trillion agreement and released the measure (HR 748) the next day. The Senate passed the measure late March 25 by a vote of 96–0. The House cleared the measure (HR 748) by voice vote on March 27, 2020. President Trump signed the bill into law (PL 116-136) the same day. The Coronavirus Aid, Relief and Economic Security Act, known as the CARES Act, provided about $300 billion in benefits for laid-off workers and low-income households through July 2020.

HIGHLIGHTS OF THE MEASURE

Among its provisions, the CARES Act

- Extended regular unemployment compensation by thirteen weeks after state benefits were exhausted, offering another $600 a week through July over state benefit levels
- Provided one-time payments to families of up to $1,200 per adult and $500 per child—for adults with adjusted gross incomes of up to $75,000 ($150,00 for married couples filing jointly)

- Offered employers a maximum tax credit of $5,000 per employee who was kept in their job
- Created a $349 billion loan program to help small businesses pay worker salaries and other expenses, with the loans forgiven if workers remained on the payroll (called the Paycheck Protection Program or PPP). The loans were made available to small businesses as well as small 501(c)(3) nonprofit organizations and small 501(c)(19) veterans' organizations
- Provided $454 billion to support credit facilities established by the Federal Reserve, funds that the Fed Reserve could leverage to provide $2 trillion to $4 trillion in loans to companies, industries, state and local communities
- Provided $78 billion to prop up the ailing domestic aviation industry
- Provided $150 billion to state and local government as reimbursement for efforts to respond to the coronavirus public health emergency
- Included $140.4 billion for health-related services financed through the Health and Human Services Department
- Provided $339.9 billion in emergency supplemental spending to help Americans during the crisis, with more than 80 percent directed to state and local governments
- Boosted food stamps and other assistance programs by $40 billion

PAYCHECK PROTECTION AND HEALTH CARE

The PPP loans authorized by the CARES Act were immediately popular. The loans were made on a first-come, first-served basis, and $349 billion in loan forgiveness had been committed in just two weeks. On April 7, the administration asked for a $251 billion increase in funding for the program to bring it to a total of $600 billion.

House and Senate Democrats also wanted more aid for state and local governments and hospitals. They proposed channeling half of the $251 billion request for PPP to smaller community-based financial institutions that could serve farmers, family, women, minority, and veteran-owned small businesses and nonprofits. They also wanted to direct another $65 billion of the request to the SBA Economic Injury Disaster Loan Program, and to provide another $150 billion for state and local governments and $100 billion for hospitals and medical providers.

The Republicans and White House said new state and local aid should be considered separately in May. The parties also disagreed on COVID-19 testing; Senate Democrats pushed for a national plan for testing, but the administration wanted to leave it to states to administer their own programs.

On April 21, the parties reached a bipartisan agreement on a $493.4 billion package aimed at helping small businesses and workers impacted by the pandemic. The package would offer $310 billion more in PPP loans, $50 billion for SBA Economic Injury Disaster Loans and $10 billion for other disaster grants. The agreement also would provide $75 billion to reimburse hospitals and other health care providers for costs associated with the pandemic, and $25 billion to help identify infections and mitigate the spread of the virus pending a vaccine.

On April 21, the Senate passed the measure by voice vote. The Senate used as a vehicle an unrelated House-passed fiscal 2020 interior appropriation bill (HR 266).

The House cleared the bill on April 23 by a vote of 388–5 after four hours of debate. The bill was opposed by Republicans Andy Biggs of Arizona, Ken Buck of Colorado, Jody B. Hice of Georgia, and Thomas Massie of Kentucky; and Democrat Alexandria Ocasio-Cortex of New York. Michigan independent Justin Amash voted present. The president signed into law the Paycheck Protection Program and Health Care Enhancement Act (HR 266 – PL 116-139) on April 24, 2020.

Executive Actions

As Congress failed to reach agreement on another economic recovery package, President Trump acted on his own. On August 8, 2020, President Trump signed a series of executive actions aimed at extending and expanding federal pandemic relief, including providing increased federal support for unemployment benefits.

The president signed a memorandum that directed funds to be diverted from FEMA's Disaster Relief Fund to provide another $300 per week in unemployment benefits, with aid capped at a total of $4 billion. States, however, were mandated to match 25 percent of the funding. Other measures included a federal eviction ban, a payroll tax suspension, and relief for student loan recipients.

FIFTH RELIEF PACKAGE

Senate Republican leaders in September proposed a $650 billion supplementary spending package to provide $300 a week in unemployment benefits through the end of the year and more money for the small business loan program, as well as $105 billion for schools, billions for virus testing and vaccines, and liability protections for businesses. Democrats opposed it and it fell short of the sixty votes needed for closure, to end debate and proceed.

Negotiations continued between House Democratic leaders, Senate Republicans, and the White House. The White House rejected a bill (HR 925) the House passed on October 1 that would have provided $2.4 trillion in aid. The president suggested instead a $1.6 trillion package. Democrats would not agree to a measure that went below $2 trillion, while Senate Republicans said they would not agree to more than $1 trillion in aid.

After the November elections, in which the Democrats won the presidency, negotiations began during a lame-duck session on a virus relief package that could be added

to an omnibus 2021 spending bill. With COVID infections and deaths still surging and many relief policies about to end, a deal was reached when Democratic leaders said they would support an estimated $900 billion package developed by a group of Republican and Democratic senators as well as some House members.

On December 21, negotiators released a final agreement that encompassed the omnibus fiscal 2021 spending bills and a $868 billion covid relief package. Hours later, the House passed the measure as an amendment to unrelated legislation (HR 133), amended by the Senate, that addressed U.S.–Mexico relations. Two votes were held on the measure: a vote on four of the spending bills, and a vote on the other eight spending bills, the COVID-relief package and other provisions. The House voted 359–53 to pass the package encompassing the COVID relief. The Senate cleared the full package by a 92–6 vote the night of December 21.

On December 22, Trump indicated he may not sign the measure into law. He said that the bill's provision for $600 stimulus checks for Americans was too low (he suggested $2,000 checks instead) and that much of the rest of the bill was "wasteful spending." On December 27, 2020, Trump signed the consolidated spending bill into law (PL 116-260). The House the next day took up legislation to increase the stimulus checks to $2,000, but the Senate did not take up the measure.

HIGHLIGHTS OF THE COVID-RELIEF PACKAGE

The bill provided specific aid for individuals and families affected by the pandemic by

- Providing for one-time direct payments to families of up to $600 for adults and children, with eligibility retroactive to CARES Act payments
- Extending into April 2021 federal unemployment benefits
- Providing through March 14 another $300 per week of unemployment benefits
- Providing $25 billion for financial aid to renters experiencing financial hardship due to the pandemic
- Extending through January 2021 an eviction moratorium
- Increasing monthly food stamp benefits by 15 percent through June 30, 2021
- Modifying SNAP eligibility to boost nutrition aid
- Providing about $600 million for other food aid programs

The bill provided aid for small businesses and nonprofits, aiming to help them keep afloat amid local government mandates for residents to stay at home. Among such provisions, the bill

- Extended Payment Protection Program, authorized in the CARES Act (PL 116-136), permitting new PPP loans to be guaranteed through March 31, 2021

- Expanded PPP loan eligibility for tourism boards, visitors' bureaus, certain nonprofits, local newspapers, and TV and radio stations
- Expanded business expenses that could be forgiven under PPP loans
- Allowed small businesses with 300 or fewer employees, and who had lost 25 percent in revenue, to apply for a second loan of up to $2 million
- Provided $284.5 billion for the PPP loan program and $50 million for the Small Business Administration to oversee and audit the loans
- Expanded and extended through June 2021 the temporary employee retention tax credit that allowed employers to claim tax credit on Social Security payroll taxes to offset costs of keeping employees on payroll
- Extended through December 31, 2021, the SBA Economic Injury Disaster Loan Advance Grant program, and provided $20 billion to create a special grant for businesses in low-income communities
- Provided $15 billion for grants to small live venue operators, theatrical producers, certain small independent movie theaters, and museums
- Provided $11.2 billion for support for farms and other agricultural producers, processors, and distributors affected by the pandemic
- Provided $400 million to help diary producers, $100 million for specialty crops, nearly $360 million for other farm and food activities, and $300 million for fisheries businesses
- Provided $9 billion for the treasury department to invest in community development financial institutions and minority-owned depository institutions that distribute loans and grants for small, minority-owned businesses; and $3 billion for grants and aid to Community Development Financial Institutions (CDFIs) to help economic recovery efforts in communities

The bill provided aid for local communities, schools, and transit services, including

- $82 billion to help schools, students, teachers and families with needs related to the pandemic, including returning to school
- $10 billion for grants to childcare providers
- $14 billion for public transit operators
- $1 billion for Amtrak
- $10 billion for state and local highway agencies
- $16 billion for aviation companies
- $2 billion for other transportation providers
- $7 billion for broadband internet activities

The bill also provided $63 billion for the Department of Health and Human Services to support pandemic-related activities such as research, development, manufacturing and distribution of vaccines, therapeutics, and diagnostic testing.

COVID-19 Loans

Congress in June 2020 cleared a measure (HR 7010) that aimed to make the federal loan program created in March under the CARES Act (PL 116-136) more flexible for small businesses struggling to reopen during the COVID-19 pandemic. The measure would amend the Small Business Administration's Paycheck Protection Program (created under the CARES Act, PL 116-136) that provided forgivable loans for companies affected by the pandemic.

The measure, introduced by Democrat Dean Phillips of Minnesota, aimed to make the program more flexible for small businesses. The measure would lower the amount of the loan companies would have to spend on payroll and increase, from eight weeks to twenty-four weeks, the time to spend the funds. The administration had required companies to use 75 percent of the loan amount on payrolls, while the measure would reduce that to 60 percent.

Under the law, companies had to repay PPP loan funds, at 1 percent annual interest, if they were not used for payroll and fixed costs within two years, a time frame set by the administration. The bill would set the time frame at five years. The measure also would extend the end date for applications to the PPP program from June 30 to the end of December 2020.

The House on May 28, 2020, voted 417–1 to pass the bill (HR 7010). Thomas Massie, R-Ky., cast the only vote against the bill. Also on May 28, the House rejected a measure (HR 6782), also introduced by Phillips, that would have required the SBA to disclose who received PPP and SBA Economic Injury Disaster Loan Program funds, how much they received, and some demographic information. The measure was rejected in a 269–147 vote, short of the two-thirds majority required for passage under suspension of the rules.

The Senate on May 21 had tried, but failed, to move its own measure (S 3833) that would have lengthened the period to use the loan funds from eight to sixteen weeks. The Senate measure would have allowed the funds to be spent on protective gear or other measures to prevent infection among employees or customers.

Sens. Angus King, I-Maine, and Steve Daines, R-Mont., introduced a companion to the House-passed bill, (S 3805) earlier in May. Senate Majority Leader Mitch McConnell, R-Ky., chose to take up the House measure. However, Republican Senators Ron Johnson of Wisconsin and Mike Lee of Utah held up consideration of the bill for several days as they insisted the PPP program expire in August rather than December.

On June 3, Johnson said he wanted House and Senate leaders to provide assurances that the bill would not extend the application deadline for businesses to apply for the loan. Senate Majority Leader Mitch McConnell agreed to print a letter providing such assurances. The Senate then cleared the measure (HR 7010) by unanimous consent. The president signed the measure into law (PL 116-142) on June 5.

Fiscal Year 2021 Appropriations

Congress in 2020 again failed to clear regular appropriations measures before the start of the fiscal year in October. This time the coronavirus pandemic disrupted House and Senate leaders and appropriators, forcing them to turn their focus to measures to help unemployed Americans, prop up the economy, and fund a series of health initiatives aimed at controlling the spread of the virus. Lawmakers also had to adjust as remote voting mechanisms were put in place so that they could vote on measures without entering the halls of Congress or the chamber floors.

The House in late June began working on its fiscal 2021 spending bills. In July, the House Appropriations Committee approved all twelve spending bills and the full House subsequently passed ten of the twelve bills, combining them into two packages (HR 7608 and HR 7617). The two packages encompassed all the regular spending bills except the Homeland Security (HR 7669) and Legislative Branch appropriations (HR 7611, approved by voice vote July 7) measures. The spending bills adhered to budget caps set for fiscal 2021 (PL 116-37) but House Democrats also included another $247 billion in emergency spending to address issues related to the pandemic or make repairs to infrastructure.

Meanwhile, Senate Republicans could not dissuade Democrats from attempting to add amendments to spending bills to address issues related to the pandemic, police reform, social justice, confederate statues, and military base names. The Senate Appropriations Committee did not take up any bill, nor did the full Senate, thereby forcing lawmakers to clear a series of five stopgap funding measures to keep the government running beyond the 2020 presidential and congressional elections.

After the November elections, Senate Republicans released drafts of all their spending bills. In late November, House and Senate appropriators agreed on funding allocations for the bills and began negotiations. Several provisions of spending measures were contentious, including those addressing veterans spending, Trump's border wall, and Immigration and Customs Enforcement detention beds.

Congress continued to keep the government open through stopgap measures until an agreement was reached on a $1.4 billion omnibus spending package (HR 133 — PL 115-260) that encompassed all twelve fiscal 2021 appropriations measures.

FOUR-BILL PACKAGE

The House on July 24 voted 224–189 to pass a $259.5 billion, four-bill package (HR 7608) for fiscal 2021. The bill would provide $259.4 billion in discretionary funding, including $211.2 billion subject to spending caps, $8.35 billion in war funding (OCO fund), $2.35 billion for wildfire suppression, and $37.5 billion in emergency funding. The White House, however, threatened to veto the bill if it was cleared, and the Senate did not take it up.

The four appropriations measures included in the package were the following:

- Agriculture spending bill (HR 7610), approved by the Appropriations Committee by voice vote on July 9, would provide $24 billion in discretionary funding for the Agriculture Department, FDA, and other agencies—$487 million or 2 percent more than in fiscal 2020 and $4.1 billion or 21 percent more than requested
- Interior-Environment measure (HR 7612), approved by the Appropriations Committee in a 30–19 vote on July 10, would provide $54.1 billion for the Interior Department, EPA and related agencies, including $36.8 billion subject to discretionary caps—$771 million or 2.5 percent more than in fiscal 2020 and $5.1 billion or 16 percent more than requested
- Military Construction–Veterans Affairs spending bill (HR 7609), approved by House appropriators in a 30–20 vote on July 9, which would provide $102.65 billion subject to caps—0.8 percent less than in fiscal 2020. The measure also would include $12.5 billion in emergency funding and $350 million for OCO funding
- State-Foreign Operations spending bill (HR 7608), approved by the House Appropriations Committee in a 29–21 vote on July 9, would provide $65.9 billion in discretionary funding, including $479 billion subject to discretionary caps (2.5 percent more than in fiscal 2020), $8 billion in OCO funding, and $10 billion in emergency funding related to the COVID-19 pandemic.

The bill's added $37.5 billion in emergency spending brought the total beyond the budget caps agreed to in a 2019 measure (PL 116-37). The package also included several policy riders opposed by the White House and Republicans. Such provisions would, among other things, overturn the administration's ban on federal funding for overseas groups that perform or promote abortions, bar the administration from shutting down Peace Corps activities in China, bar the administration from setting new restrictions on food stamps, require the National Park Service to remove statues and plaques commemorating the Confederacy, and bar the White House from using military construction funds for the border wall project.

SIX-BILL PACKAGE

On July 31, the House passed a $1.31 trillion, six-bill package (HR 7617) for fiscal 2021. No Republicans voted for the package, and twelve Democrats opposed it. As with the four-bill package, the Senate refused to take it up. The measure included $1.03 trillion in discretionary funding subject to caps, $68.4 billion in OCO funding, $1.9 billion for program integrity initiatives, and $210 billion in emergency funding during the COVID-19 pandemic.

The six appropriations measures included in the package included the following:

- Commerce–Justice–Science bill (HR 7667), approved by the Appropriations Committee on July 14 in a 30–22 vote, would provide $71.5 billion in discretionary funding subject to caps for the Commerce and Justice departments, NASA, and other science agencies—$1.7 billion or 3.5 percent less than fiscal 2020
- Defense spending bill (HR 7617), approved in committee by a 30–22 vote on July 14, would provide $694.6 billion in discretionary funding for the Department of Defense—$1.3 billion more than in fiscal 2020 and $3.7 billion or 0.5 percent less than the president's request
- Energy–Water bill (HR 7613), approved by appropriations in a 30–21 vote on July 13, would provide $49.6 billion for the Department of Energy and federal water projects—$1.3 billion or 3 percent more than in fiscal 2020 and $6.4 billion or 15 percent more than the president requested
- Financial Services measure (HR 7668), approved in a 30–22 vote on July 15, would provide $37.8 billion in discretionary spending for the Treasury Department, federal judiciary, and other executive agencies, including $24.6 billion subject to caps (3.4 percent more than in fiscal 2020), and $143 million for disaster relief for small businesses
- Labor–HHS–Education bill (HR 7614) approved by the House Appropriations Committee on July 13 in a 30–22 vote, would provide $198 billion in discretionary funds, including $182.9 subject to budget caps (a slight decrease from fiscal 2020), for the departments of Labor, Health and Human Services, and Education
- Transportation-HUD bill (HR 7616), approved by the Appropriations Committee in a 30–22 vote on July 14, would provide $75.9 billion in discretionary funds subject to caps for the Departments of Transportation and Housing and Urban Development—$1.7 billion or 2 percent more than in fiscal 2020 and $16.8 billion more than the president requested

Democratic leaders originally intended for the package to also include the Homeland Security funding bill (HR 7669), which had been approved in committee on a 30–22 vote on July 15, but opposition led by progressives led them to drop that measure from the package. Before passing the measure, the House voted 123 to 292 to reject an amendment by Rep. Rick W. Allen, R-Ga., that would have cut funding by 5 percent for the Labor–HHS–Education appropriations.

Members did adopt an amendment by Rep. Earl Blumenauer, D-Ore., to block the administration from interfering in state and tribal efforts to legalize cannabis, and an amendment by Lauren Underwood, D-Ill., to bar the White House from trying to dismantle the 2010 health care law in court.

STOP-GAP MEASURES

Following passage of the budget cap deal, House and Senate negotiators worked toward a deal on a fiscal 2021 spending package, but talks repeatedly were delayed over disagreements on funding for the president's border wall project, among other items. They were unable to close on an agreement before the start of the fiscal year on October 1, so they repeatedly passed stopgap funding measures to keep the government running while they finalized an agreement.

House Appropriations Chair Nita Lowey, D-N.Y., introduced a continuing appropriations measure (HR 8319) on September 21, 2020, to keep federal agencies funded through December 11. The measure also would have reauthorized for one year the surface transportation law, transferred $10.4 billion from the general revenue account to the highway account in the Highway Trust Fund, and transferred $3.2 billion to the mass transit account, as well as $14 billion to the Airport and airway Trust Fund. The measure, however, did not include Commodity Credit Corporation money for payments to farmers affected by the pandemic and the trade war with China, as requested by the White House and Republicans.

Democratic and Republican leaders then agreed to a revised continuing resolution (HR 8337) that extended government funding through December 11 and would provide more than $20 billion for payment to farmers, as well as nearly $8 billion for a pandemic-related program that funded subsidized meals for children who normally received them in school. The House passed the measure on September 22 in a 359–57 vote, with fifty-six Republicans and Libertarian Justin Amash of Michigan voting against the bill.

The measure also extended some provisions creating more flexible rules for eligibility for the food stamp program, and expanded the school meal program to include children who had been at childcare centers that had closed during pandemic. The measure also allowed the Navy to spend $1.6 billion in fiscal 2021 funds to start building a new Columbia-class nuclear-missile submarine, and $13.6 billion for highway and mass transit programs, and $14 billion for aviation programs.

The Senate cleared the measure on September 29 in a vote of 84–10. The president signed the bill into law (PL 116-159) on October 1, 2020.

On December 8, Lowey introduced another short-term funding bill (HR 8900) to keep the government open through December 18 as the House and Senate continued to negotiate fiscal 2021 appropriations. The resolution also would extend for one week several health care programs that were set to expire December 11.

The House on December 9 voted 343–67 to pass the one-week stop-gap measure. The Senate cleared the measure by voice vote on December 11, after leaders resisted efforts to attach measures addressing military policy, lawmakers' pay, and new tax rebate checks. The president signed the measure into law (PL 116-215) on December 11, 2020.

On December 18, the House passed another two-day continuing resolution (HJ Res 107) extending government funding through December 20. The measure was designed to give lawmakers another weekend to finalize negotiations on a fiscal 2021 omnibus spending bill.

The House passed the bill on December 18 by a vote of 320–60, surpassing the two-thirds majority required under suspension of the rules. The Senate cleared the bill by voice vote that afternoon.

On the evening of December 19, the president signed the measure into law (PL 116-225). At the end of the weekend, lawmakers needed more time to release the actual text.

The House on December 20 passed, in a 329–65 vote, a one-day continuing resolution (HJ Res 110). The Senate cleared the measure by voice vote immediately. The president signed the measure into law (PL 116-226) on the same day, giving congressional leaders until December 21 to clear an omnibus spending bill for fiscal 2021.

Lawmakers then hoped to avoid a government shutdown over Christmas while they processed the final 5,593-page omnibus spending deal. The House on December 21 voted 227–180 to approve a weeklong funding bill (HR 1520), keeping the government open through December 28, 2020. The House vote on the stopgap was part of a procedure rule (H Res 1271) on the omnibus measure. The Senate cleared the stop gap funding measure (HR 1520) by voice vote the same day, and the president signed immediately it into law (PL 116-246).

OMNIBUS SPENDING PACKAGE

Congress ultimately cleared a $1.4 trillion omnibus spending package (HR 133) for fiscal 2021, which President Trump signed into law (PL 115-260) on December 27. The package included $1.3 trillion in funding subject to discretionary budget caps, $77 billion in OCO funding, $17.3 billion for disaster relief cap adjustment, and $9.6 billion in emergency funding—$6.5 billion of which was related to the pandemic. It also included $900 billion in relief for individuals and businesses affected by the COVID pandemic, and funds for virus testing and distribution of vaccines.

In addition, the bill included provisions aimed at shielding patients from surprise medical billing. And the measure extended nearly forty temporary tax provisions, making some of them permanent. The measure also extended for about three years various federal health care programs, and included several authorization bills covering: aircraft certification reform; the Water Resources Development Act, and the Pipeline and Hazardous Materials Safety Administration. The measure also authorized classified amounts in fiscal 2021 funding for various U.S. intelligence agency activities. And the bill included provisions that would, among other things, promote the

development of clean and renewable energy over five years.

HIGHLIGHTS OF TAX PROVISIONS

The measure extended about forty temporary tax provisions, making some of them permanent. Those made permanent included a tax provision allowing all people, regardless of age, to deduct certain unreimbursed medical care expenses that exceed 7.5 percent of adjusted gross income. The bill also permanently reduced the federal excise tax rate and simplified recordkeeping requirements for small craft brewers, wineries and distilleries, enacted as part of 2017 tax law.

The measure also made permanent a commercial building energy efficiency tax deduction, the exclusion from income of tax stipends of up to $50 a month for volunteer firefighters and emergency medical responders, and the short line railroad tax credit for track maintenance.

The bill extended for five years tax provisions allowing individuals to exclude from gross income the debt forgiveness for the sale of a primary residence whose mortgage was "underwater," meaning more was owed for the property than it was worth. It also extended for five years the Work Opportunity Tax Credit—an elective credit for employers who hire individuals who are members of one or more of ten targeted groups—and the New Market Tax Credit, among other tax credits and incentives.

The measure extended for one year the production tax credits for onshore wind power and the energy efficient home construction credit; treatment of mortgage insurance premiums as qualified residence interest; health coverage credit on premiums for certain health insurance, among other tax incentives. It also extended through 2021 tax provisions that aimed to boost economic development for Native Americans. Further, the measure provided sixty days of tax relief for individuals and businesses in areas the president declared a disaster before January 1, 2020, which the Joint Committee on Taxation estimated would reduce revenues by $9.6 billion over ten years.

In addition, the measure

- Increased, to $3.50 per capita from $2.70, the 2021 federal allocation of Low-Income Housing Tax Credits for residents of disaster zones
- Suspended limitations on the deduction of charitable contributions associated with qualified disaster relief, and for uncompensated losses arising in disaster areas. The measure eliminated requirements that personal casualty losses must exceed 10 percent of adjusted gross income to qualify for deductions
- Exempted from early retirement plan withdrawal penalties any distributions for qualified disaster relief that do not exceed $100,000; provided flexibility for loans from retirement plans for disaster relief
- Provided employers affected by a declared disaster a tax credit for 40 percent of wages, up to $6,000 per employee

The following are highlights of each spending bill:

Agriculture. The measure provided $23.4 billion in net discretionary spending, $217 million more than in fiscal 2020. Including mandatory funding, the measure provided $208.9 billion—$52.1 billion or 33 percent more than in fiscal 2020, increasing funding for food stamps by $46.1 billion or 67 percent, commodity assistance programs by 24 percent, and child nutrition programs by 6 percent. It also slightly increased funding for most farm production programs while decreasing slightly the funding for rural development programs.

Commerce–Justice–Science. The bill provided $71.1 billion in discretionary spending subject to caps and $604 million in emergency spending for the departments of Commerce and Justice and for various federal science programs. The measure decreased funding for the Commerce Department by 41 percent, to $8.9 billion, in large part due to decreased funding for the Census Bureau with the completion of the 2020 census. The measure increased by 2 percent funding for the National Oceanic and Atmospheric Administration.

It increased funding for the Justice Department by 4 percent, including aid to state and local law enforcement and provided $25 million in funds to support investigation of police misconduct following a series of high-profile cases of alleged police brutality. Lawmakers provided another $5 million to create a database to track officer misconduct. The measure provided $31.9 billion for science-related agencies, 3 percent above the fiscal 2020 level, including a 4 percent boost for NASA, to $23.3 billion, and a 2.5 percent increase for the National Science Foundation, to $8.5 billion.

Defense. The bill provided $627.3 billion in net spending subject to caps and another $68.7 billion in OCO funding. The $696 billion total was $2.6 billion more than the fiscal 2020 level. The measure would fund a newly constituted Space Force and provide more than $10 billion for missile defense, $43.6 billion to procure more aircraft for the Navy and Air Force, and $23.3 billion for ten more Navy ships.

Energy–Water. The bill provided $49.5 billion in discretionary spending for energy and water programs and activities, subject to caps, $1.1 billion or 2 percent more than in fiscal 2020. The measure also included $2.3 billion in emergency spending for the Energy Department. The funding included a 23 percent increase for National Nuclear Security Administration weapon activities to fund nuclear warhead life extension programs and manage a backlog of deferred maintenance requests. The measure also increased by 4 percent funding for nuclear nonproliferation activities and increased by 2.5 percent funding for energy efficiency and renewable

MAJOR ACTIONS ON BUDGET AND TAX POLICY

Following is a chronology of the major actions on budget and tax policy taken during the 115th and 116th congresses.

2017

January 13: House and Senate adopt a fiscal 2017 budget resolution (S Con Res 3) that provides reconciliation instructions for a measure to repeal the Affordable Care Act of 2010.

April 28: Congress clears, and Trump signs into law (PL 115-30), a resolution to continue fiscal 2016 funding levels for most of the government through May 5, 2017.

May 3: The House passes an omnibus spending bill for fiscal 2017. The Senate clears the bill on May 4 and President Trump signs the bill into law (PL 115-31) on May 5.

May 4: The House passes legislation to reform the health care system as part of the budget reconciliation process. The Senate rejects its version of the measure on July 28. Reconciliation instructions expire September 30.

May 23: President Trump submits to Congress his fiscal 2018 budget request.

September 6: The House passes an emergency disaster relief bill to help communities with hurricane recovery, keep the government funded through December 8, and extend a suspension on the debt limit. On September 7, the Senate passes an amended version of bill. The House clears the measure and the president signs it into law (PL 115-56) on September 8.

October 12: The House passes an emergency spending bill providing aid for hurricane disaster relief in communities and food stamp funds for Puerto Rico. The Senate clears the bill on October 23 and the president signs it into law (PL 115-72) on October 26.

October 19: The Senate adopts a fiscal 2018 budget resolution (S Con Res 25) that includes reconciliation instructions for a tax overhaul measure and a measure to open the Arctic Wildlife Refuge in Alaska refuge to oil and gas drilling. The House adopts the Senate resolution on October 26.

December 8: President Trump signs into law (PL 115-90) a stopgap funding measure to keep the government open another two weeks.

December 19: The House adopts a tax reform overhaul measure. The Senate clears the measure on December 20, and the president signs it into law (PL 115-97) on December 22.

December 22: The president signs into law (PL 115-96) a continuing funding resolution to keep the government funded through January 19, 2018, and to provide funding for the Children's Health Insurance Program through March 2018.

2018

January 24: Congress clears and the president signs into law (PL 115-120) a three-week stopgap funding measure.

February 7: The Senate passes a bill to provide emergency disaster funding, fund the government through March 23, and set caps on defense and nondefense spending for fiscal years 2018 and 2019. The House clears the measure, and the president signs it into law (PL 115-123) on February 9.

February 12: President Trump submits his fiscal 2019 budget request.

March 22: The House approves a fiscal 2018 omnibus spending bill. The Senate clears the measure, and President Trump signs it into law (PL 115-141) on March 23.

September 12: The Senate passes the conference report on a minibus spending measure encompassing three appropriations bills. The House clears the measure on September 13, and the president signs it into law (PL 115-244) on September 21.

September 18: The Senate passes the conference report on a two-bill minibus spending measure. The House clears the measure on September 26, and the president signs it into law (PL 115-245) on September 28.

December 6: The Senate and House pass a stopgap funding measure to keep the government open through December 21. The president signs it into law (PL 115-298) on December 7.

December 22: Partial government shutdown begins.

2019

January 25: Congress clears and president signs into law (PL 116-5) a three-week stopgap funding bill, ending a thirty-five-day government shutdown.

energy programs, and included a 2 percent increase for the Army Corps of Engineers.

Financial Services. The measure provided $24.4 billion in discretionary spending for financial services, $281 million or 1 percent more than in fiscal 2020. The measure also provided $143 million in disaster funding and

$50 million in emergency funding, for a total of $37.5 billion in discretionary funding. The measure also included $22.9 billion in mandatory spending. Lawmakers boosted IRS funding by 3 percent, in part to modernize technology, and boosted funding for the Federal Communications Commission, the Federal Trade Commission, and the Securities and Exchange Commission. The measure pro-

February 14: Congress clears and the president signs into law (PL 116-6) a fiscal 2019 omnibus spending bill that includes funding for seven regular appropriations bills and provides funds for new barriers along the southern border.

March 11: President Trump submits his fiscal 2020 budget request.

May 23: The Senate passes a disaster aid bill. The House clears the bill on June 3, and the president signs the measure into law (PL 116-20) on June 6.

June 26: The Senate passes an emergency funding bill to address a surge of immigrants crossing the U.S.–Mexico border. The House clears the measure on June 27, and the president signs it into law (PL 116-26) on July 1.

July 25: The House passes a measure to set discretionary spending caps for fiscal years 2020 and 2021 and suspend the debt limit until July 31, 2021. The Senate clears the measure on August 1 and the president signs the bill into law (PL 116-37) on August 2.

September 19: House passes a stopgap spending measure to keep the government open through November 21. The Senate clears the measure on September 26, and the president signs it into law (PL 116-59) on September 27.

November 19: The House passes a stopgap spending bill to keep the government running through December 2020. The Senate clears the measure, and the president signs the bill into law (PL 116-69) on November 21.

December 17: The House passes a four-bill spending package and an eight-bill spending package. The Senate clears the minibus spending packages on December 19. The president signs the measures into law (PL 116-93, PL 116-94) on December 20.

2020

February 7: The Houses passes an emergency supplemental spending bill for Puerto Rico. The Senate does not consider the bill.

February 10: The president submits his fiscal 2021 budget request.

March 4: The House passes an emergency supplemental funding bill to provide health care research funding and support low-income individuals and families during the COVID-19 pandemic. The Senate clears the bill on March 5, and the president signs it into law (PL 116-123) on March 6.

March 14: The House passes an emergency funding measure to ensure employers give workers additional sick days, expand unemployment insurance programs, provide further assistance for low-income families, seniors and students, and call for health plans to cover COVID testing for free. The Senate clears the measure, and President Trump signs it into law (PL 116-127) on March 18.

March 25: The Senate passes a measure to provide one-time cash payments to most Americans, provide low-cost loans for small business and financial aid to certain industries, defer payroll taxes paid by employers, and provide protections for student loan borrowers. The House clears the measure, and the president signs it into law (PL 116-136) on the same day.

April 21: The Senate passes a measure providing additional aid for small businesses and workers impacted by the pandemic. The House clears the bill on April 23, and the president signs it into law (PL 116-139) on April 24.

August 8: President Trump signs executive orders aimed at extending and expanding federal aid during the pandemic.

September 22: The House passes a continuing resolution to fund the government through December 11. The Senate clears the measure on September 29, and the president signs it into law (PL 116-159) on October 1.

December 9: The House passes a one-week stopgap funding measure. The Senate clears the measure, and the president (PL 116-215) signs it into law on December 11.

December 18: Congress clears a two-day stopgap funding measure. The president signs the measure into law (PL 116-225) on December 19.

December 20: Congress clears and the president signs into law (PL 116-226) a one-day stopgap funding measure.

December 21: Congress clears an omnibus spending measure that is packaged with a COVID-19 relief package that extends unemployment benefits, expands the small business loan program, and provides funding for schools and billions in funding for testing and COVID-19 vaccines to halt the spread of the coronavirus. President Trump signs the measure into law (PL 116-260) on December 27.

vided a 1 percent pay raise for federal civilian employees and boosted by 4 percent the funding for federal courts.

Homeland Security. Congress provided $51.9 billion in discretionary spending subject to caps for homeland security activities and $17.1 billion in disaster funding, as well as $840 million in emergency funds. The measure included $1.375 billion to build fifty-six miles of wall along the U.S.–Mexico border, equal to funding in fiscal 2020, but reduced funding for ICE removal operations by 7 percent and did not provide funding for more ICE agents and officers.

Interior–Environment. The measure provided $38.5 billion in discretionary spending, including more

than $38 billion subject to caps—$118 million more than in fiscal 2020—as well as $64 million in mandatory funding. The measure increased funding for the EPA by 3 percent, to $9.2 billion, for the Interior Department by 1 percent, to $13.7 billion, and the U.S. Forest Service by 2 percent, to $7.4 billion. The measure provided $5.3 billion for wildfire fighting efforts of the Interior Department and the Forest Service.

Labor–HHS–Education. The measure provided $177.5 billion in discretionary spending for the departments of Labor, HHS, and Education. The measure also provided $971.4 billion in mandatory funding for Medicaid grants to states and other purposes.

The measure provided $12.5 billion in discretionary spending for the Labor Department, 1 percent more than the fiscal 2020 level. The measure boosted funding for apprenticeship programs by 6 percent, while increasing by 1 percent the funding for job training programs for youths and adults and for state unemployment insurance.

The measure provided $97 billion for HHS, 2 percent more than the fiscal 2020 level, including a 3 percent increase for NIH and 2 percent increases for Centers for Disease Control and Prevention, the Health Resources Services Administration, and the Substance Abuse and Mental Health Services Administration. The measure increased discretionary spending for the Education Department by 1 percent, to $73.5 billion.

Legislative Branch. The bill provided $5.3 billion in discretionary spending subject to caps—$251 million or 5 percent more than in fiscal 2020—and $10 million in emergency funding. The measure increased funding for the House by 8 percent, the Senate by 3 percent, the Library of Congress by 4 percent, the GAO by 6 percent, and the CBO by 4 percent. Funding for the architect of the Capitol was reduced by 2 percent, and a freeze on members' pay was continued.

Military Construction–Veterans Affairs. The bill included $112.8 billion in discretionary spending subject to caps and $350 million in OCO funding, as well as $138.7 billion in mandatory funding for veterans' pensions and benefits. Net capped funding was 9 percent above the fiscal 2020 level. The Department of Veterans Affairs received $234.2 billion, including $104.4 billion in discretionary funds—13 percent more than the fiscal 2020 level.

State-Foreign Operations. The bill provided $47.7 billion in discretionary funding subject to caps for the State Department and foreign operations, as well as $8 billion in OCO funding and $5.3 billion for COVID-related emergency funding. Of the emergency funding, $4 billion was for the GAVI Alliance, which provided vaccines to poor countries.

Transportation–HUD. The bill provided $75.4 billion in discretionary spending subject to caps for the Transportation Department and HUD, $1.1 billion more than in fiscal 2020. It also provided $718 million in emergency spending and authorized spending $61.4 billion from the highway and aviation trust fund. The measure included $86.7 billion for the Transportation Department, 0.6 percent more than in fiscal 2020, and $49.6 billion for HUD, 1 percent more than the fiscal 2020 level.

Chronology of Action on Trade Policy

President Trump launched a global trade war during his term in the White House, facing off with China, the European Union, and other countries. He said he sought to protect domestic manufacturing industries, boost the U.S. balance of trade, and protect national security interests.

While many members of Congress had long been concerned about alleged unfair trade practices—particularly China's monopoly of certain markets, subsidies for its state-owned enterprises, and alleged theft of U.S. intellectual property—lawmakers from both sides of the aisle became alarmed by Trumps' unilateral actions on tariffs. Congress, however, was limited in its ability to restrict the president's actions. The administration repeatedly claimed authority under Section 232 the Trade Expansion Act of 1962 (PL 87-794) and Section 301 of the Trade Act of 1974 (PL 93-618), which gave the president purview to act on trade policy without congressional approval in cases in which the Department of Commerce determined that domestic industry or national security was threatened.

Trump in 2018 imposed hefty tariffs on solar panels and washing machines to protect domestic industry. Then he imposed tariffs on steel and aluminum imports, which the administration said threatened national security because steel and aluminum are vital to the U.S. defense industrial base.

Subsequently, the administration

- Imposed tariffs on an increasingly broad array of Chinese goods to protest China's unfair trade practices for technology and intellectual property
- threatened tariffs on automobiles and autos, which the administration said threatened national security
- Threatened tariffs on Mexico to protest illegal immigration across the border
- Imposed tariffs on European Union and United Kingdom imports of aircraft parts, agricultural goods, and other products over a long-running dispute over subsidies for civilian aircraft
- Limited sales from U.S. companies to Semiconductor Manufacturing International Corporation, a major

Chinese semiconductor producer, and further restricted exports of semiconductor designs, software, and equipment to one of the industry's largest buyers

Lawmakers increasingly raised alarms about the heavy duties on imports from U.S. trading partners, saying they feared repercussions for domestic businesses and farmers.

U.S. Customs and Border Protection collected $74.4 billion in tariffs on imported goods during fiscal 2020, double what it collected on imports before Trump took office. But during Trump's term in office, China, the European Union, and other countries retaliated with their own tariffs, including on many agricultural goods.

China imposed four stages of tariffs from July 2018 to September 2019 in retaliation for four stages of U.S. tariffs on Chinese imports. The tariffs affected $68.4 billion of U.S. exports.

In mid-2018, the European Union, India, Turkey, and Russia imposed tariffs on $6.7 billion of U.S. exports in retaliation for U.S. tariffs on steel and aluminum. India's tariffs did not take effect until June 2019, after the Trump administration removed that country's eligibility to the Generalized System of Preferences, thereby cutting off that country's duty-free access to the U.S. market for a variety of products.

In November 2020, the European Union (EU) imposed more tariffs on $4 billion of U.S. exports in response to U.S. tariffs imposed a year earlier on EU aircraft and other goods. More retaliatory tariffs from China, Japan, and South Korea were expected in 2021.

Trump repeatedly said he sought to boost the U.S. balance of trade, but subsequent reports by the Department of Commerce showed that the U.S. trade deficit increased from $481 billion in 2016 to $679 billion in 2020. However, the Commerce figures also showed that the nation's trade deficit with China fell from $419 billion in 2018 to $311 billion in 2020. Still, several academic studies and accounts from industry observers indicated the tariffs increased uncertainty for businesses and put a damper on investment activity.

The tariff war particularly hurt U.S. agricultural trade with China. From 2010 through 2016, China had been the top destination for U.S. agricultural exports based on value. In 2017, Canada became the top destination for agricultural products, while China and Mexico tied for second. In 2018, agricultural exports to China declined further, dropping in value by 53 percent to $9 billion from $19 billion in 2017. By mid-2019, China was the fourth-largest destination for farm products from the United States—behind Canada, Mexico, and Japan.

In 2018 and 2019, Trump provided $23 billion in aid to farmers to make up for losses during the tariff war. The Trump administration ultimately negotiated a limited agreement with China that halted the escalating trade war but left most of the tariffs in place. The administration also renegotiated a 2012 trade pact with Korea and reached a limited trade deal with Japan. None of those deals required Congress's approval due to their limited scope.

Meanwhile, Trump also moved to—or threatened to—pull out of several global trade pacts. After he was sworn into office in 2017, he withdrew the United States from the Trans-Pacific Partnership Agreement, negotiated by President Obama with eleven other countries.

The president also said he wanted to pull out of the North American Free Trade Agreement that had been negotiated with Mexico and Canada in 1994. But in 2017, the administration agreed to renegotiate the pact. In 2018, Trump signed the rewritten deal that would continue many tariff-free lines of trade among the three countries but aimed to ensure more labor protections, improve access to the Canadian dairy market for U.S. industry, and set requirements for auto imports to be duty free. During the 116th Congress, lawmakers ratified the pact, called the United States–Mexico–Canada Agreement.

Trump also threatened to pull out of the World Trade Organization (WTO), and several Republicans said they would block such action. Ultimately, the president did not move to withdraw the nation from the WTO, which the United States had helped form in 1994 to set clearer global trade rules and settle disputes.

Table 2.6. Trade Balances (Millions of Dollars)

Year	Total	Goods	Services
2000	−3,69,685	−4,46,781	77,096
2001	−3,60,373	−4,22,370	61,997
2002	−4,20,665	−4,75,244	54,579
2003	−4,96,242	−5,41,643	45,401
2004	−6,10,837	−6,64,764	53,927
2005	−7,16,543	−7,82,805	66,262
2006	−7,63,532	−8,37,288	73,756
2007	−7,10,998	−8,21,198	1,10,199
2008	−7,12,351	−8,32,493	1,20,142
2009	−3,94,772	−5,09,695	1,14,923
2010	−5,03,090	−6,48,674	1,45,584
2011	−5,54,522	−7,40,999	1,86,477
2012	−5,25,906	−7,41,119	2,15,213
2013	−4,46,861	−7,00,539	2,53,678
2014	−4,83,952	−7,49,917	2,65,965
2015	−4,90,776	−7,61,868	2,71,092
2016	−4,79,458	−7,49,801	2,70,343
2017	−5,10,344	−7,99,343	2,88,999
2018	−5,78,594	−8,78,749	3,00,155
2019	−5,59,676	−8,57,260	2,97,584
2020	−6,53,989	−9,13,885	2,59,896

SOURCE: "U.S. International Trade In Goods and Services." Census.gov. United States Census Bureau. https://www.census.gov/foreign-trade/statistics/historical/index.html

NOTE: The information above reflects the trade balance in terms of annual goods (balance of payments basis), services, and total balance, exports and imports.

Initially, President Trump joined many conservative Republicans and business groups in calling to shutter the Export–Import Bank, a U.S. agency that helps support businesses seeking to export goods and services. But he changed course as the trade war with China continued. Congress ultimately cleared, and the president signed, a seven-year reauthorization of the bank. The Senate also confirmed several nominations to its board of directors, which had languished without a quorum since 2015.

U.S. TRADE REPRESENTATIVE

Robert Lighthizer, former deputy trade representative under President Ronald Reagan, served as President Trump's U.S. Trade Representative and helped lead the administration's tariff war as it sought to punish countries, particularly China, for alleged unfair trade practices that the administration said harmed domestic businesses and workers and threatened domestic security.

President-elect Trump nominated Lighthizer, a trade lawyer, on January 3, 2017. As deputy USTR, Lighthizer also had served as vice chair of the Overseas Private Investment Corporation. Lighthizer had repeatedly advocated protectionist policies during his career. As deputy trade representative for President Reagan, Lighthizer had threatened tariffs to persuade Japan and other countries to reduce their steel exports to the United States. In 2010, he told a congressional commission that the U.S. manufacturing crisis was due to America's trade relationship with China.

He backed a hard line on China, and shared Trump's view that the United States in previous decades had prioritized free trade with other countries to the detriment of domestic businesses, ignoring other countries' practices of subsidizing their industries. He viewed China as the greatest offender, using state subsidies to benefit its state-owned enterprises, stealing American trade secrets, and more.

During a March 14, 2017, hearing before the Senate Finance Committee, he promised strong enforcement of U.S. trade laws and said he would focus on increasing U.S. exports. He also pledged to address China's overproduction of steel and aluminum. Lighthizer had been a partner at Skadden, Arps, Slate, Meagher & Flom LLP, where he practiced as an international trade lawyer for thirty years. He represented many American steel producers who sought government protection from unfair trade practices abroad.

Senate Democrats said that in order for the nomination to move forward, Lighthizer needed a waiver or exemption from the Lobbying Disclosure Act of 1995 (PL 104-65) that barred individuals who had represented foreign entities in trade negotiations or disputes from serving as USTR. While at Skadden and Arps, Lighthizer had advised the Brazilian Ministry of Industry and Commerce in a trade dispute involving Brazilian and U.S. ethanol industries.

Democrats also wanted to package such a waiver with legislation extending health benefits for coal miners. Senate Finance Committee Chair Orrin Hatch, R-Utah, said Lighthizer's work with foreign entities predated the 1995 law so he did not need a waiver.

Ultimately, Hatch and Oregon Democrat Ron Wyden, the committee's ranking member, reached an agreement.

Hatch said he would back an extension of health benefits for retired coal miners and their spouses. In exchange, Wyden and the other Democrats agreed to drop their demands to combine the benefits with the waiver for Lighthizer's nomination.

On April 25, 2017, the Senate Finance Committee voted 26–0 to approve the waiver for Lighthizer. The waiver was included in the fiscal 2017 omnibus bill the president signed into law (PL 115-31) on May 5. On May 11, 2017, the Senate confirmed Lighthizer's nomination by a vote of 82–14.

Senate Democratic Leader Charles E. Schumer of Maryland said he agreed with Lighthizer on trade, but that he voted against the nomination because he was objecting to the White House firing of FBI Director James Comey in unrelated circumstances. Other Democrats who voted against the nomination included Sens. Richard Blumenthal of Connecticut, Kirsten Gillibrand of New York, Kamala Harris of California, Edward J. Markey and Elizabeth Warren of Massachusetts, Jeff Merkley of Oregon, Jack Reed and Sheldon Whitehouse of Rhode Island, and Brian Schatz of Hawaii.

Independent Sen. Bernie Sanders of Vermont also voted no, as did three Republicans. GOP Sens. John McCain of Arizona and Ben Sasse of Nebraska said they opposed the nomination because they were concerned Lighthizer did not appreciate the value of trade to their states and they were worried about the administration's plan to renegotiate the North American Free Trade Agreement. GOP Sen. Cory Gardner of Colorado also opposed the nominee, issuing a statement saying that he feared that Lighthizer's policies would hurt farmers and ranchers in his state.

2017–2018

Soon after taking office, President Trump took steps to follow through on his campaign pledge to pull away from free trade agreements that he said did not benefit U.S. businesses, punish other countries for unfair trade practices, and help boost U.S. manufacturing. Trump immediately withdrew the United States from the Trans-Pacific Partnership Agreement, a deal negotiated by former President Obama with another eleven countries but which had not been submitted yet to Congress. He also threatened to pull out of the North American Free Trade Agreement as well before agreeing to negotiate a rewrite of the 1994 pact with Mexico and Canada, which was completed by November 2018, although congressional review of the pact would have to wait until the next Congress.

In early 2017, Trump called on the Commerce Department to launch an investigation into the effects on national security of unfair prices for imported steel and aluminum. In 2018, he began imposing tariffs on imported washers and solar cells and modules, then imposed 25 percent tariffs on steel imports and 10 percent tariffs on aluminum, eventually expanding the tariffs to cover a wider range of products and igniting a global trade war with China, the European Union, and other countries. In fiscal 2019, the tariffs netted the Treasury about $71 billion, up about $36 billion since Obama's last year in office.

Members of Congress became increasingly concerned about the domestic effects of the tariff war, particularly on farmers whose agricultural products were among the goods that became targets of retaliatory tariffs. The USDA announced July 24, 2018, it would provide up to $12 billion in emergency relief to help farmers hurt by the trade war.

Trans-Pacific Partnership Exit

On January 23, 2017, President Trump signed an executive memorandum removing the United States from the Trans-Pacific Partnership (TPP) agreement, fulfilling one of his top campaign promises. Obama had signed the deal in 2016 with eleven other nations, but had not sent implementing legislation to Congress because he could not secure enough votes for approval.

White House Press Secretary Sean Spicer said the Trump administration would pursue direct trade deals with other countries rather than broad agreements such as TPP and the North American Trade Agreement (although the president did renegotiate the latter deal). Many farm groups had liked the TPP deal because it would have lowered tariffs and provided greater access to Asia Pacific markets.

Some Democrats in Congress applauded the Trump administration's withdrawal from TPP, but many Republicans criticized it. Republican Sen. John McCain of Arizona, chair of the Senate Armed Services Committee

and a former presidential candidate, said it was a "serious mistake" that would affect the domestic economy and the U.S. position in the Asia-Pacific region.

On April 12, 2018, as farm state lawmakers worried about damaging effects from a rising trade war with China, Trump said he asked National Economic Council Director Larry Kudlow and United States Trade Representative Robert Lighthizer to consider rejoining the TPP to help the farmers. The administration did not take such action.

NAFTA Rewrite

On November 30, 2018, President Trump, Mexican President Enrique Peña Nieto, and Canadian Prime Minister Justin Trudeau signed a rewrite of the North American Free Trade Agreement (PL 103-182). The 115th Congress, however, did not have time to review and approve the new agreement, dubbed the United States–Mexico–Canada-Agreement (USMCA), and action was postponed until the next Congress.

Democrats, set to take over the House following the November 2018 mid-term elections, said congressional approval was not guaranteed as they remained concerned about whether the agreement included sufficient provisions to ensure the protection of labor rights among workers that produced products or services imported to the United States. Democrats and Republicans also were concerned about continuing steel and aluminum tariffs on Canada and Mexico.

BACKGROUND

The North American Free Trade Agreement (NAFTA), which took effect on January 1, 1994, essentially eliminated most tariffs among Canada, Mexico, and the United States. The agreement was first drafted under President Reagan in 1987, negotiated by President George H. W. Bush, and took effect under President Clinton. During the 2016 presidential campaign, Trump said NAFTA was the "worst trade deal in history," because it led to a significant loss of U.S. manufacturing jobs. He said he wanted to toss out the deal but later was persuaded to renegotiate the agreement.

NEGOTIATIONS

On May 18, 2017, Trump sent Congress a ninety-day notice that he intended to renegotiate the NAFTA. The notice was required under the 2015 Trade Promotion Authority (PL 114-26), which allowed the president to negotiate international trade agreements with the promise Congress would not amend them before giving them an up or down vote.

Negotiations began on August 16, 2017, and continued for about a year. On September 29, 2018, the Office of the

United States Trade Representative (USTR) announced the three countries had reached an agreement on a rewrite of the NAFTA. Trump said he would sign the agreement and send it to Congress by end of November. After he signed it, the International Trade Commission had 105 days to consider the economic impact on U.S. industries, the agreement had to be made available to the public, and Trump had to send the agreement to both chambers of Congress for consideration.

Under the agreement, Canada's dairy supply management would give the U.S. dairy industry 3.6 percent of its market, up from 3.25 percent that the Obama administration had negotiated in the Trans-Pacific Partnership deal, from which Trump had removed the United States. Canada also would loosen export limits to allow more chicken, eggs, and turkey goods into its market, and stores in the Canadian province of British Columbia would have to carry American wines alongside local wines.

The agreement also would require that 75 percent of automobile content be made in North America. It retained the dispute settlement process of NAFTA under which countries could challenge each other's tariffs and other actions, and Trump dropped tariffs on Canadian and Mexican car imports.

However, the agreement did not lift steel and aluminum tariffs imposed on Mexico and Canada along with other allies. Those countries had pressed the administration to end the 25 percent steel tariffs and 10 percent aluminum tariffs on their exports in exchange for lifting retaliatory duties on farm goods. The USTR said talks about those tariffs were ongoing. Among other provisions, the agreement would require up to 45 percent of content in automobiles come from plants where workers earn at least $16 an hour.

Tariffs on Washers and Solar Panels

The Trump administration announced on January 22, 2018, it would raise tariffs on washing machines and solar panels to limit imports and protect the domestic industries, sparking concerns among members of Congress that the action would ultimately hurt domestic jobs and spark retaliatory tariffs on U.S. goods. The administration said the restrictions would last four years for solar panels and three for imported washing machines, but could be renewed. Tariffs on washing machines would be set at 20 percent the first year and drop to 16 percent by the third year, while tariffs on solar crystalline silicon photovoltaic cells and modules would start at 30 percent and decline to 15 percent the fourth year. The policy exempted 2.5 gigawatt solar panels.

Trump was the first president in sixteen years to impose penalties on foreign importers in order to protect the domestic industry. President George W. Bush had placed tariffs on foreign-made steel in 2002, but those tariffs had ended the next year after China, Europe, and other countries successfully challenged them before the World Trade Organization.

The decision came following rulings in several cases before the U.S. International Trade Commission (ITC), an independent agency. Suniva Inc., a Georgia-based solar manufacturer that filed bankruptcy in April 2017, and SolarWorld Americas Inc., an Oregon-based company that also was facing financial struggles, alleged cheap imports of solar cells and modules had hurt the U.S. domestic industry. ITC agreed with the companies' claims and recommended penalties to protect the domestic industry from cheaper imported products. China was the world's leader in solar panel manufacturing and, along with Malaysia, South Korea, Vietnam, and other Asian countries, was a top export of solar modules to the United States.

In an ITC case on washing machines, Michigan-based Whirlpool Corp. filed a petition on May 31, 2017, alleging that Samsung Electronics Co. Ltd. and LG Electronics Inc., both Korean companies, had moved their production from China to Vietnam and Thailand to dodge U.S. anti-dumping tariffs of up to 52.5 percent, thereby enabling the companies to import more washers to the United States and sell them at lower prices. The ITC supported Whirlpool's claim and recommended an annual cap of 1.2 million imported washer units.

In 2016, China exported an estimated $425 million worth of washers to the United States, Mexico exported $240 million, and South Korea exported $130 million. Samsung and LG were among the top exporters of washers to the United States.

Trump's actions sparked concerns on both sides of the aisle in Congress. Sen. Tim Scott, R-S.C., placed a hold on the Senate's consideration of nominees for the U.S. Trade Representative's office, saying he was dissatisfied with USTR Robert Lighthizer's response to his request to minimize the impact of the tariffs on imported washers, as well as his concerns that financial services were being addressed in renegotiations of the North American Free Trade Agreement. Scott lifted his hold in early February once Lighthizer assured him he was addressing the concerns.

On June 7, 2018, Sens. Martin Heinrich, D-N.M., and Dean Heller, R-Nev., introduced a measure that would roll back the administration's tariff on imported solar cells and panels. They said the tariff threatened jobs in their states. The Solar Energy Industry Association predicted the tariff would cost 23,000 jobs in 2018 and billions of dollars lost in investment. However, Senate Majority Leader Mitch McConnell, R-Ky., said he did not want the Senate to take up legislation that the president would not sign.

U.S.–China Trade War

The Trump administration in 2018 launched a trade war with China as it imposed a series of escalating and expanding tariffs on a range of Chinese imports. The war

MAJOR ACTIONS ON TRADE

The following is a chronology of major actions on trade policy between 2017 and 2020.

2017

April: Department of Commerce initiates investigations into U.S. steel and aluminum imports.

August: President Trump calls on U.S. Trade Representative (USTR) to investigate China's laws, practices, and actions affecting U.S. intellectual property and technology.

2018

January: Department of Commerce submits reports on steel and aluminum imports to president.

January 23: President announces actions on solar cells and modules and large residential washing machines, effective February 7.

March 22: USTR releases report finding China's polices burden or restrict U.S. commerce; President Trump signs memorandum proposing to implement tariffs on certain Chinese imports, initiate World Trade Organization case against China, and propose new investment restrictions on Chinese companies.

March 23: Trump administration imposes tariffs on steel and aluminum imports, with temporary exemptions for certain partners until May 1 (later extended to June 1).

April 30: President exempts South Korea from steel tariffs, imposes a quota arrangement.

May 23: Commerce Department initiates investigation into U.S. motor vehicle and parts imports.

May 31: Trump permanently exempts Argentina and Brazil from steel tariffs, and Argentina from aluminum tariffs, based on quota arrangements. Administration permanently exempts Australia from both duties without a quota.

July 6: U.S. imposes stage 1 tariffs on China.

July 18: Commerce Department initiates an investigation into imports of uranium and effects on national security based on industry petition.

August 23: Administration imposes stage 2 of tariffs on China.

September 24: Responding to China's retaliatory tariffs, U.S. imposes stage 3 of tariffs.

December 1: Trump announces talks with China to resolve U.S. concerns.

2019

February 17: Commerce Department sends report on motor vehicle imports to president (not released publicly).

March 4: Commerce initiates an investigation into imports of titanium sponge and effects on national security.

April 16: Commerce sends uranium report to president, but not released publicly.

May 5: Trump tweets that negotiations with China are moving too slowly and he will increase the stage 3 tariffs and impose stage 4 tariffs.

May 10: Administration increases stage 3 tariffs.

May 17: President announces that imports of automobiles and vehicle parts pose national security threat, tells USTR to negotiate a resolution with European Union, Japan, and others.

---

began when President Trump imposed tariffs on imported solar modules and washing machines, then levied heavy duties on steel and aluminum imports.

When imposing the penalties on steel and aluminum imports, Trump said he was protecting domestic industries for national security interests. Trump then extended and expanded the tariffs to billions of dollars' worth of hundreds of products in response to concerns about China's business partnering practices and trade rules that resulted in stolen U.S. intellectual property and technology, and unfairly benefited Chinese goods.

The increasing tariffs, imposed by the administration under authority of Section 232 of the Trade Expansion Act of 1962 (PL 87-794) and Section 301 of the Trade Act of 1974 (PL 93-618), provoked China to retaliate with tariffs on a range of U.S. products, particularly agricultural goods. Lawmakers of both parties complained the heightened

duties impacted industries and farmers in their districts. Several Republican senators pushed for legislation to impose congressional oversight over the president's actions, but Senate Majority Leader Mitch McConnell, R-Ky., and House Speaker Paul Ryan, R-Wisc., said they would not put to a vote legislation without the president's support.

STEEL AND ALUMINUM TARIFFS

On March 8, 2018, President Trump announced a 25 percent tariff on steel imports and 10 percent on aluminum imports, but exempted Mexico and Canada as they were in the process of renegotiating the North American Free Trade Agreement with the United States. Republican lawmakers tried to persuade the administration not to launch a tariff war, raising concerns that the tariffs could result in retaliatory actions against U.S. agricultural products and other goods. However, Congress could not over-

May 19: President exempts Canada and Mexico from steel and aluminum tariffs. The three countries announce process to reinstate tariffs if imports surge.

May 30: President Trump announces he will impose tariff on imports from Mexico beginning June 10 in response to concerns over illegal immigration into United States.

July 7: Trump tweets that administration reached agreement with Mexico suspending proposed tariffs.

July 12: President rejects Commerce Department findings that uranium imports threatened national security; president establishes U.S. Nuclear Fuel Working Group to develop ways to revive the domestic industry.

August: Trump tweets that China has not followed through with pledge to buy U.S. agricultural products; USTR releases two-part plan toward stage 4 tariffs beginning September 1.

August 23: Responding to Chinese retaliatory tariffs, Trump tells USTR to increase stage 1–4 tariffs.

September 1: United States imposes first part of stage 4 tariffs.

October 11: Trump suspends proposed October tariff increases, announces a forthcoming deal with China.

October 12: Trump announces plans to reinstate steel and aluminum tariffs on Argentina and Brazil due to currency issues.

October: Tariffs on certain U.S. imports from European Union go into effect.

December 2: USTR issues report on Frances Digital Services Tax that concludes the tax discriminates against major U.S. digital companies.

December 6: USTR requests comments on proposed tariffs on list of French products.

December 15: USTR suspends second part of stage 4 tariffs before they take effect.

2020

January 15: United States and China sign Phase One deal addressing some trade and investment issues, committing China to purchase $200 billion in additional U.S. exports, leaving most tariffs in place. USTR announces first part of stage 4 tariffs will be reduced on February 14.

January 21: France suspends its digital services tax for rest of 2020.

February 9: Trump imposes tariffs on derivative products of steel and aluminum.

February 21: USTR increases rate of additional duties on certain large civil aircraft and modifies a list of other products subject to additional tariffs.

June 6: Sen. Bob Corker, R-Tenn., introduces a measure to give Congress oversight of certain tariffs. The bill is not considered.

June 7: Sens. Martin Henrich, D-N.M., and Dean Heller, R-Nev., introduce bill to roll back the administration's tariff on imported solar cells and panels. The bill does not move.

July 16: USTR publishes list of imports from France to be subject to additional tariffs by January 6, 2021.

August 18: USTR modifies list of nonaircraft products subject to additional tariffs, effective September 1, 2020.

August 16: Trump reinstates tariffs on certain aluminum imports from China based on a surge in import volumes.

September 15: The administration announces it will revoke tariff on imported Canadian aluminum but would set a quota.

October 10: Trump announces solar tariff will be increased.

October 27: Trump withdraws reinstated tariffs on some aluminum imports from Canada.

rule the president's actions as he held executive authority for such actions under Section 232 of the Trade Expansion Act of 1962.

BACKGROUND

During the 2016 presidential campaign, Trump had pledged to boost domestic production and jobs in steel and to crack down on China's flooding of the steel market with cheap supplies that lowered global prices. China at the time was the world's largest producer of both products. On April 20, 2017, President Trump signed executive orders requiring the Commerce Department to launch investigations, under Section 232 of the Trade Expansion Act of 1962, to determine the potential national security effects of unfair prices for imported steel and aluminum. Section 232 permitted the president to adjust imports if the Commerce Department determined that certain products

were imported in such high levels, or under particular circumstances, that U.S. national security could be impaired. Trump was looking toward a military buildup and said the production of American steel was important to the country's defense industrial base.

Many lawmakers and American steel producers also said Chinese overproduction of steel and aluminum was undercutting U.S. products. The United States produced about 70 percent of the steel used domestically. In 2016, the United States imported 30 million metric tons of steel, including 789,153 metric tons from China and 5.1 million metric tons from Canada, according to the U.S. Census Bureau. The European Union was the second largest steel exporter to the United States.

In July, the Trump administration hinted it might impose tariffs on steel imports. That month, eighteen farm groups wrote a letter to Commerce Secretary Wilbur Ross

asking him to avoid a trade war and not use national security as a reason to limit steel and aluminum imports. They said many of U.S. agriculture's best markets were in countries that also supplied steel to America, and they feared retaliation.

On February 16, 2018, Ross publicly released the results of his investigation and called for a tariff of up to 24 percent on all aluminum and steel imports. Specifically, Ross recommended for steel: a global tariff of 24 percent on all imports, with a tariff of 53 percent on steel imports from Brazil, China, Costa Rica, Egypt, India, Malaysia, Republic of Korea, Russia, South Africa, Thailand, Turkey, and Vietnam. Imports from other countries would not be able to exceed their level of exports to the United States in 2017; and quotas on all countries would not be able to exceed 63 percent of their exports to the United States in 2017.

Ross's recommendations for aluminum included a global tariff of 7.7 percent on all imports, and a tariff of 23.5 percent or more on imports from China, Hong Kong, Russia, Venezuela, and Vietnam. Other countries' quotas could not exceed the level of their export to the United States in 2017. Ross recommended that aluminum imports from countries be barred from exceeding 86.7 percent of their 2017 exports to the United States.

Ross said the aim was to boost U.S. aluminum production from 48 percent of operating rate to 80 percent and U.S. steel production from 73 percent to 80 percent. Ross said imports of aluminum at the time accounted for 90 percent of primary aluminum use in the United States, and that between 2013 and 2016, employment in the aluminum industry had dropped 58 percent and six smelters had closed. Meanwhile, Ross said, U.S. steel imports were nearly quadruple its exports, while ten steel furnaces had closed since 2000 and jobs had declined by 3 percent.

GOP-leaning business lobbies immediately pressured the administration not to impose the tariffs. Many Senate Republicans said that the tariffs would negate the benefits of the 2017 tax overhaul (PL 115-97) and they feared a larger trade war could be ignited.

Two days before Trump announced his decision to impose the stiff tariffs, National Economic Council Director Gary Cohn, the White House's chief economic advisor, resigned over his disagreement with the president about the tariff issue. On April 30, the president said he would give an extended reprieve from the tariffs for Canada, Mexico, and the European Union as separate negotiations continued. The announcement came a few hours ahead of Trump's May 1 deadline to announce whether the United States would impose 25 percent import tariffs for steel or 10 percent for aluminum on Argentina, Australia, Brazil, Canada, Mexico, South Korea, and the European Union. EU leaders had pressed the administration to permanently exempt the twenty-eight-nation bloc. The White House subsequently set June 1 as the new deadline for the tariff announcement.

In May, the administration announced it had finalized a deal with South Korea on steel imports and had reached agreements in principle with Australia, Argentina, and Brazil. On May 31, the Trump administration said that on June 1 it would impose steel and aluminum tariffs on Mexico, Canada, and the European Union in order to pressure them to crack down on imports of the metals from China. The countries and the European Union would pay an additional 25 percent duty on steel and 10 percent on aluminum. Mexico, Canada, and the European Union threatened retaliation.

CONGRESSIONAL RESPONSE

Members of both parties in the House and Senate strongly criticized the administration's steel and aluminum tariff actions and feared retaliation could hurt their own districts and states.

In October 2017, Senate Minority Leader Charles E. Schumer, D-N.Y., said he would block action on two trade policy nominees because he said that President Trump had failed to act against countries such as China that subsidized their steel and aluminum products, undercutting prices for American goods. Schumer said he would place a hold on nominations of Gil Kaplan for undersecretary of Commerce for International Trade and Nazakhtar Nikakhtar for assistant secretary of Commerce, Industry, and Analysis until the administration took action.

However, a group of Republican lawmakers, including Sen. Roy Blunt of Missouri, Rep. Todd Young of Indiana, and Sen. Patrick J. Toomey of Pennsylvania, urged Trump not to launch a trade war. Sen. Jeff Flake, R-Ariz., said the steel and aluminum duties would lead to job loss and stymie economic growth. He introduced a measure to nullify the tariffs that the administration imposed, but the Senate did not consider the measure. Senate Finance Chairman Orrin G. Hatch also sharply criticized the administration's actions.

In March 2018, the House Ways and Means Committee grilled USTR Robert Lighthizer, seeking assurances that the tariffs on China imports would not affect the U.S. economy. Lighthizer said the U.S. economy would benefit. Lighthizer also said Trump would soon announce his decision on China's violation of intellectual property.

On June 6, 2018, Senate Foreign Relations Committee Chair Bob Corker, R-Tenn., introduced a measure that aimed to give Congress oversight of tariffs applied in the context of national security. Section 232 of the Trade Expansion Act granted the executive branch the authority to impose tariffs to protect the nation's interests, but many lawmakers said they believed Trump was abusing his power and using it against allies instead of adversaries.

Corker's measure, which had bipartisan support, would require a sixty-day window for Congress to review 232 actions of the administration. McConnell said he did not intend to take up Corker's bill as a standalone measure, but that someone might try to attach it to the fiscal 2019

defense authorization measure (S 2987). Corker's proposal never saw action, however. House Speaker Paul Ryan said the House would not take up such legislation without the president's support, although many business groups, including the Chamber of Commerce, wanted Congress to take such action.

The Senate Finance Committee on June 20 grilled Commerce Secretary Ross on the administration's tariff actions and potential economic repercussions, and Ross stood firmly in support of the heavy duties. During hearings, members of the House Financial Services and Senate Foreign Affairs committees on July 12 lambasted administration officials for the trade policy.

Google, Microsoft, the U.S. Chamber of Commerce, and other business interests spent millions lobbying Congress on the tariffs. On July 22, senators voted 88–11 to approve a motion by Corker and Pat Toomey to instruct conferees on an unrelated $147 billion spending bill (HR 5895) to include language giving Congress authority over presidential decisions to impose tariffs for national security reasons. The final spending bill did not include the language, however.

EXPANDED TARIFFS

Throughout 2018, President Trump repeatedly expanded tariffs to cover an increasingly broad array of Chinese products, and China imposed a series of retaliatory tariffs on U.S. products. Members of both parties in Congress raised alarms, particularly as the retaliatory tariffs affected farmers, the auto industry and other sectors, leading to billions of dollars in lost revenue. Senate Majority Leader Mitch McConnell, R-Ky., refused to allow the Senate to take up measures that aimed to impose congressional restrictions on the administration's actions. The tariff battle between the United States and China continued through 2019.

BACKGROUND

Since China began liberalizing its trade regime in the late 1970s, it had become America's largest trading partner and biggest source of imports, according to the nonpartisan Congressional Research Service. But U.S. policymakers and industry leaders had increasingly alleged that unfair trading and business practices by China adversely affected U.S. economic interests and contributed to job losses in certain domestic industries. Such alleged practices by China included cyber economic espionage on U.S. firms; ineffective enforcement of intellectual property rights; industrial policies, such as subsidies and trade barriers, that promoted and protected favored industries; and policies that influenced the value of China's currency.

In August 2017, the president asked the U.S. Trade Representative to investigate China's treatment of U.S. firms and industries seeking to enter, or already doing business in, Chinese markets. Trump called for the probe under Section 301 of the Trade Act of 1974 (PL 93-618),

which allowed the USTR to halt trade agreements or impose imports restrictions if it found that a trading partner was engaging in discriminatory or unreasonable practices that burdened U.S. industries.

The administration accused the Chinese government of requiring U.S. firms to enter joint ventures with Chinese firms and to share proprietary information, thereby facilitating intellectual property. China accounted for a major share of about $600 billion of U.S. intellectual property that was stolen annually, according to the administration.

The USTR on March 22, 2018, released a report that concluded China's trading policies and practices were unfairly burdening domestic industry. President Trump then signed a memorandum calling for the USTR to propose tariffs on Chinese imports, initiate a case against China before the World Trade Organization, and propose new investment restrictions on Chinese companies.

On April 3, 2018, the USTR released a preliminary list of 1,300 Chinese imports that would be hit with 25 percent tariffs as retaliation for China's treatment of U.S. businesses. The proposed tariffs covered a range of industries and consumer goods, such as the following:

- Machinery for meat preparation, box making, and printing, and textile equipment
- Magnetic disk drive storage units, parts of trash compactors, parts for aircraft electric generators, and television cameras
- Selected motorcycles and mopeds, parts of communications satellites
- Several types of microscopes, syringes, defibrillators, and military rifles and shotguns

Jay Timmons, chief executive officer of the National Association of Manufacturers, said the tariffs would boost costs for American manufacturers and consumers and might provoke China to retaliate.

On April 5, Trump said he was considering expanding tariffs on imports from China by $100 billion. He also told Agriculture Secretary Sonny Perdue to take steps to offset damages to farmers as result of an expected tariff war.

THREE STAGES OF U.S. TARIFFS

On June 15, the Trump administration said it would impose billions in tariffs on Chinese imported goods. The announcement was followed by three stages of tariffs.

On July 6, the administration imposed "stage one" tariffs of 25 percent on 818 product lines, affecting $34 billion in imports. In August, the administration imposed the second stage of tariffs, also of 25 percent, affecting another 285 product categories, totaling $16 billion of Chinese imports.

The tariffs primarily targeted aerospace and communications technology, robotics, industrial machinery, and new materials and automobiles. The lists did not include cell phones and televisions and other popular consumer goods.

After China imposed two rounds of retaliatory tariffs, the administration in September announced a third stage of additional Section 301 tariffs of 10 percent on $200 billion of imported goods from China.

CHINA'S RETALIATORY TARIFFS

Each stage of U.S. tariffs on imports prompted China to impose retaliatory tariffs affecting a range of American goods. On April 2, China responded to the U.S. steel and aluminum tariffs by imposing tariffs of 15 percent or 25 percent on 128 U.S. products, including ninety-four different food and agricultural items, particularly pork, fruit, and nuts.

In response to Trump's June 15 announcement that he would impose higher tariffs on more Chinese goods, China in July expanded the 25 percent retaliatory tariffs to cover a total of 697 tariff lines, including agricultural products such as soybeans. American agriculture exported about $22 billion of goods to China in 2017, with soybean exports accounting for about $14.2 billion, according to the Department of Agriculture.

In August, after the administration launched the second phase of Section 301 tariffs on Chinese imports, China imposed another 25 percent tariff increase on an expanded set of products, including agriculture-related products such as fishmeal, animal byproducts, wood products, and cotton waste. With the administration's expansion of import tariffs, China retaliated again by increasing tariffs on an expanded number of U.S. imports, including more agricultural products, by 5 percent or 10 percent.

Export–Import Bank Board

Through the 115th Congress, the Senate allowed the Export–Import Bank to languish without a quorum on its board of directors as conservatives balked at approving nominees for an agency they did not support. At the end of 2018, the board did not have any Senate-confirmed members and just an acting president. The bank's previous authorization was set to expire in September 2019, and President Trump had pledged to shutter the agency.

BACKGROUND

The Export–Import Bank of the United States, also called the Ex-Im Bank, was originally authorized in 1945 to provide financing and insurance to facilitate the export of U.S. goods and services. The Ex-Im Bank creation stemmed from two predecessor banks—which focused on U.S. trade with the Soviet Union and Cuba— that President Franklin D. Roosevelt created in 1934 as part of his New Deal program during the Great Depression.

For decades, the Export–Import Bank provided loan guarantees, credit insurance, and other support for U.S. businesses seeking to export goods and services. In recent

years, the bank's role had become increasingly controversial, pitting Democrats and moderate Republicans who supported the bank against conservatives who viewed it as corporate welfare. Much of the debate focused on the bank's role in private financial markets and whether government intervention was appropriate or beneficial.

Some lawmakers and business groups said the Ex-Im bank supported U.S. jobs by facilitating the export of goods and services that private financial institutions would not support due to market limitations or other reasons. However, conservative lawmakers and other opponents of the bank said the government should not assume such risks that the private sector would not take on, and they criticized the bank for selectively choosing what companies or products to support.

In 2015, Congress allowed the bank's authority to expire for five months before lawmakers cleared a reauthorization through September 30, 2019 (PL 114-94). That legislation also lowered the Bank's exposure cap—its total authorized outstanding and undisbursed financing and insurance—to $135 billion, among other changes.

When President Trump took office in 2017, he pledged to shut down the Export–Import Bank. The Export–Import Bank's charter called for a five-member board of directors, drawing from both political parties, to lead the bank. Members are presidentially appointed and Senate-confirmed. At least three members must be present to make up a quorum and conduct business. Beginning on July 30, 2015, the board lacked a quorum as members' terms expired and the Senate did not confirm any presidential nominations. That year, the board dwindled to two members. On March 20, 2016, Senate Banking Committee Chair Richard C. Shelby, R-Ala., who opposed the bank's renewal, said he would not approve nominees for the board.

LACK OF QUORUM

On January 8, 2017, the Homeland Security and Government Affairs committee approved the nomination of Mark L. Greenblatt as inspector general for the bank in voice vote. Greenblatt was serving as assistant inspector general for investigations at the Commerce Department.

On January 19, 2017, Fred Hochberg, who had served as president of the Export–Import Bank since 2009, resigned. At the time of his departure, Hochberg reported that the bank had about $30 billion worth of deals in its pipeline but could not approve them without a board quorum. He said the bank's business had dipped to a forty-year low.

After Hochberg left, President Obama, before his term ended, appointed Charles Hall to take over as acting chairman and president. Hall had served as the bank's executive vice president since November 2013. In April, newly inaugurated President Trump nominated former Rep. Scott Garrett, R-N.J., to head the bank. Garrett in previous years had been a fierce critic of the bank, and

had voted against its reauthorization in 2012 and 2015. His nomination was opposed by the U.S. Chamber of Commerce, the National Association of Manufacturers, and other business groups.

On December 19, 2017, the Senate Banking Committee voted 10–13 to reject Garrett's nomination. On the same day, the committee voted 20–3 to approve the nomination of Kimberly Reed to be vice president of the bank's board. The committee also approved three other nominees to the board: former Rep. Spencer Bachus III, the former Republican House Financial Services Chair, in 19–4 vote; and Judith DelZoppo Pryor and Claudia Slacik, each by 20–3 votes. The committee also approved, 23–0, the nomination of Mark Greenblatt to be inspector general of the bank. However, conservatives blocked the consideration of the nominees on the Senate floor.

Also in December, acting president Charles Hall left and acting first vice president Scott Schloegel, appointed in 2014, took over as acting head of the agency, but not as acting president. Schloegel departed in March 2018, and Ex-Im's executive vice president and chief executive officer Jeffrey Goettman took over as acting head of the agency. The departures left the agency without a single confirmed member on the board.

In April, Trump announced he was appointing Jeffrey Gerrish, a deputy United States Trade Representative, as acting president of the bank. The Senate on March 5, by voice vote, had confirmed Gerrish as deputy USTR for Asia, Europe, and the Middle East and Industrial Competitiveness.

On June 20, 2018, Trump withdrew Reed's nomination as vice president and nominated her as president. The Senate Banking Committee approved Reed's nomination as bank president in a 25–0 vote on August 23. By that point, the board was down to one member: Gerrish. The Senate did not act on any of the Banking Committee's approved nominees before the end of the 115th Congress.

U.S.–South Korea Pact

In 2018, South Korea and U.S. officials agreed to a revision of their 2012 trade pact that would limit steel exports to the United States and increase U.S. exports of vehicles to South Korea.

President Trump and South Korea President Moon Jae-in had first discussed negotiations during a June 2017 summit. U.S. Trade Representative Robert Lighthizer then convened special trade sessions to work out revisions of the earlier pact.

The two parties signed the deal on September 24, 2018. Korea's National Assembly ratified the agreement in a 180–5 vote on December 7, 2018. Trump did not need Congress to approve the deal because of its limited scope.

Under the pact, Korea agreed to limit its steel exports to the United States to 70 percent of the average of what it exported to the United States between 2015 and 2017, approximately 2.68 million tons. In exchange, the United States would exempt Korea from the 25 percent steel tariff the Trump administration had imposed on all steel imports.

In addition, South Korea would allow U.S. auto exports to double to 50,000 per year per manufacturer. The automobiles also would be exempt from Korea's stricter carbon dioxide emission requirements. The deal extended a 25 percent U.S. tariff on light-truck imports until 2041, rather than phasing those out in 2021, as per the 2012 agreement. Korea at the time was not exporting trucks to the United States, however. The agreement also called for reduced documentation required by Korean customs, which had been viewed as a nontariff barrier to trade.

WTO MEMBERSHIP

President Trump threatened to pull the country out of the World Trade Organization, an international group of 164 nations that the United States had cofounded in 1995 to oversee and administer global trade rules and settle disputes. As with other global organizations Trump criticized, he said the WTO threated U.S. sovereignty and hurt American businesses and workers.

Many previous administrations had said they were dissatisfied with the WTO and its slow consideration of trade cases, but Trump was the first president to threaten to pull the nation out of the Geneva-based organization. Among the complaints was that the WTO had not cracked down on China's failure to follow global trade rules. Other WTO members, as well as lawmakers, feared the entire organization would crumble if the United States did pull out.

On March 1, 2017, the administration submitted an annual trade report to Congress in which it indicated it would take "unilateral steps" if it believed the dispute settlement body of the World Trade Organization had exceeded its authorities. The report did not detail what actions the administration would take, but indicated the U.S. Trade Representative's Office had a number of remedies it could

(Continued)

WTO MEMBERSHIP (Continued)

use against other nations that take actions harmful to U.S. interests. In July 2018, Trump raised the idea of pulling the United States out of the WTO.

The WTO had succeeded the General Agreement on Tariffs and Trade, which the United States and twenty-two other countries had established in 1947. Both organizations were intended to create a more open, rules-based global trading system and to foster economic cooperation after World War II. However, many members and observers had complained in recent years that the WTO had become less effective and needed to modernize to address issues such as digital commerce.

The Doha Round of multilateral trade negotiations, which began in 2001, failed and members had since been unable to reach consensus on a new agreement. As a result, many countries had turned to negotiating bilateral and plurilateral agreements outside the WTO framework.

Kevin Brady, chairman of the House Ways and Means Committee, had complained that WTO was flawed but that he would take action to preserve the United States' membership if Trump moved to leave the WTO. Analysts said Congress could block Trump from pulling out of the WTO.

In hopes of spurring reform at the WTO, the Trump administration then blocked appointments of new jurists to the seven-member Appellate Body that reviewed appeals of disputes. The Obama administration also had blocked appointments. On December 11, 2019, the appellate Body lost its necessary quorum of three members and was unable to function.

During President Trump's term in office, he still turned to the WTO dispute settlement body to file charges of alleged trade abuses, including against China in regard to technology and intellectual property and the European Union for subsidies for its domestic manufacturer of civil aircraft.

2019-2020

The Trump administration continued to increase tariffs on an expanded line of Chinese imports, and China responded with several rounds of retaliatory tariffs, until negotiators reached a limited, short-term trade agreement. Domestic agricultural producers continued to suffer from the effects of the retaliatory tariffs, and the U.S. Department of Agriculture announced in July 2019 another $9 billion in aid for farmers.

In late 2019, Congress cleared a measure to reauthorize the Export–Import Bank for seven years. In 2020, lawmakers cleared legislation to implement the rewrite of the 1994 North American Free Trade Agreement, which largely continued tariff-free trade but added provisions to address digital trade, open access to the Canadian dairy market, and strengthen labor and environmental rules for the trading partners.

U.S.–China Trade Fight

In 2019, the Trump administration continued an escalating tariff war with China that the president had initiated the year before until the two countries reached agreement on some trading terms that would take effect in January 2020 and last two years. Most of the tariffs that had been imposed by either country, however, remained in effect. Several lawmakers raised concerns over the administration's actions but did not take formal action to end the dispute.

BACKGROUND

In early 2018, the Trump administration imposed heavy tariffs on steel and aluminum imports, which affected goods from China as well as other countries and the European Union. Subsequently, the administration sought to tamp down on alleged unfair business and trading practices of China by imposing three stages of higher and expanded tariffs:

- Stage 1: 25 percent tariff on 818 product lines, affecting about $34 billion in imports
- Stage 2: 25 percent tariff on 279 lines, affecting about $16 billion in imports
- Stage 3: 25 percent tariff on 5,733 import lines, affecting about $200 billion in commerce

China responded with retaliatory tariffs. In April 2018, China imposed tariffs of 15 percent or 25 percent on more than 100 tariff lines, and expanded the 25-percent tariff to 697 lines in July 2018. As a result, the tariffs affected most of the trade between the two countries and imposed increased prices on U.S. firms and consumers while posing disadvantages to U.S. exporters in the Chinese market.

China's tariffs primarily targeted agricultural products, along with a line of other products, but excluded turbojets and parts, semiconductors and related devices, certain plastics, and aircraft.

In 2018, U.S. agricultural exports to China had declined 53 percent, from $19 billion in 2017 to $9 billion. China from 2010 to 2016 was the top export destination for U.S. agricultural products, and dropped to second place with Mexico, behind Canada, in 2017. By mid-2019, China had become the fourth-largest market for U.S. agricultural exports behind Canada, Mexico, and Japan.

EXPANDED U.S., CHINA TARIFFS

On May 5, 2019, President Trump complained that talks with Chinese officials had yet to resolve U.S. concerns about China's business practices, particularly those affecting intellectual property rights, and threatened higher and expanded tariffs. On May 10, Trump increased the stage 3 Section 301 tariffs, which had been set on $200 billion of imports from China in September 2018, raising them from 10 percent to 25 percent. On May 17, the USTR published a proposed fourth stage tariff list that would impose up to a 25 percent tariff on $300 billion of U.S. imports.

China retaliated in June with increased and expanded tariffs from 5 percent to 10 percent on U.S. products and goods, most of them agricultural.

On August 1, Trump complained that China had not followed through on a pledge to buy U.S. agricultural products. He said he would impose the stage 4 tariffs of 10 percent, affecting almost all remaining Chinese products not yet covered by the previous stages of Section 301 tariffs. China retaliated by asking its state-owned corporations to halt all purchases of U.S. agricultural goods.

On August 14, the USTR proposed that stage 4 tariffs would be imposed in two phases affecting additional imports from China, the first taking effect on September 1 and the other on December 15. China retaliated by releasing two lists of U.S. products that would face another 5 percent or 10 percent increase in tariffs, effective September 1 and December 15.

President Trump on August 23 announced that on October 1, the first three stages of tariffs would be increased from 25 percent to 30 percent, and that the previously announced stage 4 tariffs would be higher—15 percent rather than 10 percent. The stage 4 tariffs, affecting $112 billion of Chinese imports, began in September.

China retaliated again, imposing another 5 percent or 10 percent tariffs on U.S. imports, including 695 different U.S. agricultural lines. The retaliatory tariffs by that point affected 1,053 U.S. agricultural tariff lines.

As talks between the countries resumed, China subsequently granted tariff exemptions on some U.S. imports, such as alfalfa. And the Trump administration postponed from October 1 to October 15 implementation of a 5 percent increase on the first three stages of tariffs. China

followed with an announcement that U.S. pork and soybeans would be exempted from additional tariffs.

U.S.-CHINA AGREEMENT

On January 15, 2020, China and the United States reached a "phase one agreement" that paused the escalating tariff war. The agreement called for China to make structural reforms and other changes to its trade practices in the areas of intellectual property, technology, agriculture, and currency and foreign exchange.

As part of the deal, China pledged to purchase an additional $200 billion U.S. agriculture, energy, and manufactured goods and services over the next two years. The additional purchases would include $40 to $50 billion a year in agricultural and seafood goods—or $12.5 billion more in 2020 compared to 2017 and $19.5 billion more in 2021 compared to 2017. Also in 2020, China pledged to buy $18.5 billion more in energy products than in 2017, and $33.9 billion more in 2021. For manufactured goods, China would buy $32.9 billion more in 2020 and $44.8 billion more in 2021. China promised to increase its purchases of U.S. services by at least $12.8 billion in 2020 and $25.1 billion in 2021.

The agreement also would require China to clear genetically modified agricultural products for sale more quickly by shortening the review and approval process. Also, holders of trade secrets would not have to prove actual losses before they could seek criminal investigations into misappropriation of a trade secret.

Senate Minority Leader Schumer and Richard E. Neal, chair of the House Ways and Means Committee, said the deal was weak and did not address China's use of industrial subsidies that provides its companies an edge in competing with companies from the United States. The agreement did not require congressional approval, however.

The agreement, to be implemented on February 14, established new U.S. tariffs on imports. Average tariffs remained elevated at 19.3 percent, more than six times higher than before the trade war began in 2018, according to the Peterson Institute for International Economics. And average Chinese tariffs on U.S. exports remained elevated at 21.2 percent, and covered 58.3 percent of U.S. exports, or about $90 billion of trade.

U.S.–MEXICO-CANADA AGREEMENT

Congress in early 2020 cleared legislation to implement the U.S.–Mexico–Canada Agreement to replace the 1994 North American Free Trade Agreement. The agreement continued largely tariff-free trade among the three countries, but added provisions to address digital trade, increase content requirements for automobile imports to qualify to be duty-free, provide greater access for the U.S. dairy industry to the Canadian market, and ensure Mexico complied with labor and environmental obligations.

The Congressional Budget Office estimated that implementation of the agreement would reduce federal deficits by $3 billion over a decade, mainly because of higher revenues from duties on vehicle parts that fail the higher content rules. The measure would provide $1 billion for the federal government to enforce the agreement.

BACKGROUND

The United States, Mexico, and Canada reached an agreement on the rewrite of NAFTA in September 2018, and signed the agreement in November 2018. In April 2019, the U.S. International Trade Commission issued a report concluding that the agreement would increase the gross domestic product by 0.35 percent after inflation, or $68.2 billion, and create 175,700 jobs. The ITC estimated U.S. trade with Canada and Mexico would increase about 5 percent.

However, the Peterson Institute for International Economics, a Washington, D.C. think tank, said that, apart from benefits for dairy producers, the agreement would be a drag on the economies of all three countries. The Institute said that, for example, provisions on auto content requirements would raise manufacturing costs, thereby hiking auto prices, which would reduce U.S. demand and lower auto exports, and would cost jobs as more machines were introduced to do the work.

Congress began reviewing the agreement in 2019. Under Trade Promotion Authority (PL 107-210), also known as fast-track trade authority, the president can negotiate an agreement that then must be ratified by Congress, but lawmakers cannot amend the treaty without sending it back to the signatories for consideration.

House Action

Before moving legislation to implement the agreement, House Speaker Nancy Pelosi, Ways and Means Committee Chair Richard E. Neal, D-Mass., and USTR Robert Lighthizer negotiated provisions for tougher enforcement of labor rights in Mexico, and agreed to drop language that would grant drug companies ten years of protection on biologics. The Mexican parliament ratified the modified agreement, and Canada said it also would approve the changes.

On December 17, 2019, the House Ways and Means Committee approved the bill in a voice vote. On December 19, the House approved the bill by a vote of 385–41.

Senate Action

On January 7, 2020, the Senate Finance Committee approved the measure (HR 5430) in a 25–3 vote. Patrick Toomey, R-Pa., Bill Cassidy, R-La., and Sheldon Whitehouse, D-R.I., voted against the bill.

The Senate Budget Committee approved the implementing legislation by voice vote on January 14. That same day, the Environment and Public Works voted 16–4 to approve the measure. Democrats Sheldon Whitehouse of Rhode Island, Kirsten Gillibrand of New York, Edward J. Markey of Massachusetts, and independent Bernie Sanders of Vermont opposed the bill.

The Senate Foreign Relations committee approved the bill by voice vote on January 15, 2020. On the same day, the measure was approved by

- The Senate Appropriations Committee in a 29–2 vote, with opposition from Democrats Jack Reed of Rhode Island and Brian Schatz of Hawaii
- The Senate Commerce, Science and Transportation Committee by voice vote
- The Health, Education, Labor, and Pensions Committee by a 22–1 vote, with Sanders casting the only no vote

On January 16, 2020, the Senate voted 89–10 to clear the bill (HR 5430) for the president's signature. The no votes came from Republican Patrick J. Toomey of Pennsylvania; Sanders; and Democrats Charles E. Schumer, the minority leader, and Kirsten Gillibrand, of New York; Kamala Harris of California; Whitehouse and Jack Reed of Rhode Island; Schatz; Cory Booker of New Jersey; and Markey.

Final Action

President Trump signed the implementing legislation into law (PL 116-113) on January 29, completing U.S. ratification of the three-nation agreement. The Canadian Parliament passed implementing legislation for the agreement in March. The Mexican parliament had ratified the agreement in December 2019.

HIGHLIGHTS

Automobiles

The following provisions were included in sections of the USMCA, which

- Increased, from 60 percent or 62.5 percent to 75 percent, North American content requirement for vehicles to qualify for duty-free status;
- Required that 70 percent of a vehicle's steel and aluminum originate in North America
- Required 40 percent to 45 percent of the automobile content be made by employees earning at least $16 an hour

Labor

With respect to labor, the USMCA

- Required each country to adopt and enforce labor rights recognized by the International Labor Organization
- Barred the import of goods produced by forced labor and aimed to ensure labor laws protected migrant workers
- Called for an independent, three-person panel that could request verification that workers at facilities in any of the three countries were not denied their rights under labor laws
- Established an interagency committee to monitor Mexico's implementation of labor reforms
- Required five U.S. government Department of Labor attachés to be posted in Mexico to monitor labor practices
- Created a framework to allow for an investigation of an independent panel of labor experts to investigate allegations of labor law violations and to impose penalties on exports from facilities found in violation

Environment

Concerning the environment, the USMCA

- Required each of the three countries to adopt and enforce various multilateral environmental agreements to which they had committed, such as the Montreal Protocol on Substances That Deplete the Ozone Layer.
- Created an interagency committee to monitor implementation of environmental obligations and recommend enforcement actions
- Called for attachés to be located in Mexico City to monitor compliance and enforcement with environmental laws

Agriculture

For agriculture, the agreement

- Required Canada to change its milk pricing system so that it considers the U.S. nonfat dry milk price and thereby eases market access for U.S. dairy exporters
- Required the United States to boost import quota levels for Canadian dairy
- The agreement addressed crops produced with all biotechnology methods and created a working group to facilitate the exchange of information on policies and trade matters related to those products

Alcohol

Regarding alcohol, the USMCA required the nations to be transparent on the sale, distribution, labelling, and certification of trade for wine and distilled spirits, treating each country's products the same as their own.

Digital Trade

In the area of digital trade, the agreement

- Barred customs duties on digital products distributed electronically, such as videos of software, and minimized limits on where data could be stored and processed
- Restricted governments' ability to require disclosure of property computer source code and algorithms
- Limited the civil liability of internet platforms for content from third parties

Copyrights and Trademarks

The USMCA required more consistent treatment of copyright, trademarks, and other rights so that outside

or foreign creators are granted the same protections as domestic creators.

Auto Tariffs

President Trump in 2019 threatened to impose hefty tariffs on imported automobiles and auto parts, saying the imports harmed domestic industry and posed dangers to national security. Congressional Republicans and Democrats, however, raised concerns that Trump was exceeding his authority and pledged to block tariff actions.

On May 23, 2018, Commerce Secretary Wilbur Ross had launched an investigation into automobile exports under Section 232 of the Trade Expansion Act of 1962, which allowed the administration to determine whether the imports were weakening the nation's economy and could impair national security. The investigation included the imports of cars, SUVs, vans and light trucks, and automotive parts.

The administration said that over twenty years, auto imports had grown from 32 percent to 48 percent of the U.S. vehicle market, while employment in car manufacturing had dropped 22 percent. The Commerce investigation was completed in February 2019, but its report was not publicly released. The president said the report concluded that U.S. auto imports posed a national security threat because they affected domestic producers and U.S. industry's research and development on which the U.S. military relied. Ross proposed the administration impose tariffs of up to 25 or 35 percent.

Trump threatened "high" tariffs on auto imports, saying they could amount to 25 percent, unless the U.S. concerns were addressed in new agreements with Japan, the European Union, and other trading partners. Several members of Congress raised concerns about the investigation and the threatened tariffs, including lack of transparency regarding the report; concerns that the president was abusing trade authority; and questions about the link between auto production and national security, the economic impact of auto tariffs, for example.

Sen. Bob Corker, R-Tenn. said he was concerned Trump was abusing authorities granted under the Trade Expansion Act, as did Sen. Lamar Alexander, R-Tenn. Alexander said the administration's actions could spark retaliation by Japan.

The Driving American Jobs Coalition, comprised of auto industry groups, formed to oppose potential tariffs. The European Union reportedly drafted a list of targets for retaliatory tariffs if the administration moved forward with auto tariffs. However, three groups supported measures to address auto imports: United Automobile Workers, the United Steelworkers, and the Forging Industry Association.

Sen. Jones, D-Ala., on January 15, 2019, introduced a measure (S 121) to halt the Commerce Department's investigation and launch a separate study of the domestic auto industry. Rep. Sewell, D-Ala., introduced a similar measure in the House on March 13, 2019. Lawmakers did not take up either bill. President Trump did not act on his threat of auto tariffs, and the administration did not release the Commerce Department report before the end of his term.

Aircraft Tariffs

A long running dispute between the United States and European Union over subsidies for large civil aircraft resulted in a tariff war between the two countries that expanded beyond aircraft to affect a number of other agricultural and industrial goods, eventually raising concerns among some in Congress. On October 18, 2019, the Trump administration, with approval from the World Trade Organization, imposed additional tariffs on $7.5 billion of U.S. imports from the European Union and the United Kingdom. The tariffs were in response to the WTO's conclusion that the European Union and the United Kingdom had not complied with a dispute settlement calling on them to withdraw subsidies on the manufacture of large civil aircraft.

The settlement had come after fifteen years of litigation at WTO involving U.S.-based Boeing and EU based Airbus. In that case, the United States had successfully argued that Airbus had received billions in illegal subsidies, which hurt Boeing's market share throughout the world. The tariffs were intended to pressure the European Union into ending the subsidies or negotiate an agreement with the United States. The October announcement indicated that the United States would impose tariffs of 10 percent on Airbus aircraft and 25 percent on a variety of agricultural and industrial goods.

In February 2020, the Office of the United States Trade Representative said it would raise tariffs on civil aircraft from the EU from 10 to 15 percent, and impose 25 percent tariffs on cheeses, meat products, liquor, and other goods. The tariffs affected French wine, Italian cheese, single-malt Scotch whisky, cookies and salami from France, and German coffee, among a variety of other products.

In August 2020, a bipartisan group of thirteen senators asked the USTR to remove the 25 percent tariffs on EU food, wine, and spirits. The senators said demand for the goods had declined, leaving imports and distributors with stockpiles of the products that may perish. The tariffs continued, however.

In November 2020, the European Union began imposing additional tariffs on about $4 billion worth of imports from the United States, including on aircraft, agricultural goods, and other products. The European Union charged that the United States had failed to abide by WTO subsidies rules by supporting Boeing, but the USTR said the alleged subsidy had been repealed seven months earlier. The dispute continued into the next administration and session of Congress.

Export–Import Bank Renewal

Congress in late 2019 passed legislation to renew the charter for the Export–Import Bank for another seven years, through December 31, 2026. The legislation included a provision to allow for the creation of a temporary board if the number of directors falls below a quorum, which would allow the bank to continue to approve transactions of more than $10 million. President Trump signed the measure into law (PL 116-59) even though in previous years he had pledged to shutter the U.S. agency, which helped provide credit and financing for American exports.

BACKGROUND

At the end of the 115th Congress, the Export–Import Bank's board of directors had only one member because conservative lawmakers had blocked consideration of nominees. Without a quorum, the bank could not approve transactions of more than $10 million and its business dropped to a 40 year low. In fiscal year 2014, the bank's last full year with a quorum, it authorized about $20.5 billion in deals. In fiscal 2018, it authorized about $3.3 billion.

Disagreements among lawmakers and business groups over the bank's role had caused a five-month lapse in its authorization in 2015 before Congress cleared a measure reauthorizing its charter through September 30, 2019 (PL 114-94). Still, the disagreements continued in subsequent years. Conservative business groups lobbied the administration and Congress to end the bank's authority, and many conservative Republicans considered the agency's trade credits and loan guarantees a form of corporate welfare.

President Trump initially intended to close the agency, but he changed his position and supported a renewal in order to compete with China. In May 2019, top economic aides Peter Navarro and Larry Kudlow said the bank would be critical to helping the United States compete with countries such as China that provide financing support for their own companies.

On May 2, 18 conservative groups, led by Americans for Prosperity, wrote to lawmakers urging them to oppose reauthorization of the bank, saying it distorted the free market. The National Association of Manufacturers, however, argued that many foreign competitors were backed by export credit agencies and that the Ex-Im helped levy the playing field.

INITIAL LEGISLATION

On March 27, 2019, Michigan Libertarian Justin Amash introduced a bill (HR 1910) that would terminate the Export–Import Bank, but it was not considered. When the Trump administration changed course and supported the agency's reauthorization, Rep. Patrick McHenry of North Carolina, the top Republican on the House Financial Services Committee, worked with Committee Chair Maxine Waters and the Trump administration to draft a reauthorization measure (HR 3407). The bill would renew the bank's authority for seven years, raise its exposure cap from $135 billion to $175 billion by fiscal 2026, and would create a temporary board that could approve large deals if the board of directors did not have a quorum.

However, negotiations with committee members fell apart before the panel took up a vote on the bill. Committee members disagreed on a provision that aimed to restrict trade deals with Chinese state-owned enterprises. Labor-backed Democrats said it would reduce the number of jobs. Denny Heck, D-Wash., said the provisions would unduly hurt Boeing Co., a major employer in his state.

Republicans had long complained, however, that Boeing had been a major benefiter of the Ex-Im Bank, which some conservatives dubbed the "Bank of Boeing." The next day, members of the Senate Banking Committee raised similar concerns about such a provision.

Sen. Kevin Cramer, R-N.D., on July 25 introduced a bill (S 2293) that would reauthorize the Export–Import Bank for ten years, raise the statutory cap to $175 billion, and allow for the creation of a temporary board. The Senate did not act on the measure.

SHORT-TERM EXTENSIONS

In September, Congress extended the bank's authority through November 21, 2019, in provisions that were included in a fiscal 2020 continuing appropriations measure (HR 4378). President Trump signed that measure into law (PL 116-59) on September 27. Another short-term reauthorization, to extend the bank's authority through December 20, was attached to another stopgap spending bill (HR 3055), which the president signed into law (PL 116-69) on November 21.

House Action

On October 28, Waters introduced another bill (HR 4863) that would reauthorize the bank for ten years, increase lending authority to $175 billion from $135 billion, and rename the bank the U.S. Export Finance Agency. The new measure would block the agency from financing projects directly involving Chinese military or intelligence services. McHenry, however, was dissatisfied, saying the bill did not go far enough to restrict trade with the Chinese.

On October 31, the House Financial Services Committee approved the bill in a 30–27 vote after considering fourteen amendments. The committee rejected eight Republican proposals that would have restricted the bank's ability to support trade deals with China state-owned enterprises. The committee also rejected amendments by Democrats Rashida Tlaib of Michigan and Ayanna S. Pressley of Massachusetts that would have placed environmental restrictions on the agency's activities.

On November 15, the House voted 235–185 to pass the bill. Thirteen Republicans voted for the measure, while four Democrats opposed it. Senate Republicans opposed the measure and did not want to take it up.

Final Action

On December 20, 2019, House and Senate conferees on a fiscal 2020 omnibus spending package (HR 1865) agreed to include provisions that would provide a seven-year reauthorization for the Export–Import Bank, including language from Water's second bill that aimed to encourage the bank to support small-business exports and renewable energy projects.

The House passed the measure (HR 1865) on December 17 in a 297–120 vote. The Senate cleared the bill by a vote of 71–23 on December 19. The president signed the measure into law (PL 116-94) on December 20.

BOARD OF DIRECTORS

The Senate in 2019 approved three nominations to the Ex-Im board of directors. The Banking Committee on February 26, 2019, gave voice vote approval to the three nominations:

- Kimberly A. Reed to a term that expires January 20, 2021, and to serve as the bank's president and chair. Reed previously headed the Community Development Institutions Fund in the Department of Treasury
- Judith DelZoppo Pryor for a term that would expire January 20, 2021. She had served as vice president of the Office of External Affairs for the Overseas Private Investment Corporation
- Former Republican Rep. Spencer Bachus III for a term that would expire January 20, 2023. Bachus served in the House from 1993 to 2015, including terms as chair and ranking member of the House Financial Services Committee

On May 8, the Senate voted 82–17 to confirm Reed's nomination, 77–19 to confirm Pryor's nomination, and 72–22 to confirm Bachus' nomination. The confirmations restored a quorum on the board.

Two other candidates were considered in committee but not by the full Senate. On March 12, the Senate Banking, Housing, and Urban Affairs committee approved the nomination of Claudia Slacik to the board for the term that would end January 2023. She had served on the bank board before from 2013 to 2016.

On June 18, the Banking committee approved the nomination of Paul Shmotolokha to be the bank's first vice president, serving until January 20, 2021. He had served as senior vice president of Alpha Technologies Inc. Those nominations were not confirmed on the Senate floor before the end of the Congress.

U.S.–Japan Agreement

President Trump and Japan Prime Minister Shinzo Abe in 2019 signed a small deal on agriculture and digital commerce that some observers hoped might lead to a broader trade deal affecting automobile and other industries. Congress did not have to approve the agreement because it was negotiated under Trade Promotion Authority (PL 114-26), which allows the president to finalize an agreement if it does not change U.S. law or reduce tariff rates by more than 5 percent.

Under the agreement, Japanese duties on $7.2 billion worth of U.S. agricultural goods would be gradually eliminated, and U.S. tariffs on some Japanese industrial and agricultural goods would be reduced. Separately, a digital commerce agreement established rules under which U.S. electronic commerce companies could compete in Japan.

Semiconductor Export Restrictions

On September 26, 2020, the Department of Commerce told American computer technology companies it was restricting sales to Semiconductor Manufacturing International Corporation, China's leading maker of computer chips, and its subsidiaries, due to concerns about national security. The letter said companies must obtain a license before making such sales. The Commerce department said it had determined that the Chinese company, an advanced maker of computer chips based in Shanghai, may divert materials for use by the Chinese military.

The action followed the administration's restrictions on exports to Huawei, a Chinese technology company, and restricted exports to dozens of other Chinese companies.

On May 15, 2020, the administration had issued a rule, effective in September, that would bar Huawei and its suppliers around the world from using American technology and software. The Semiconductor Industry Association raised concerns that the rule would create uncertainty in the global semiconductor supply chain.

A shortage of semiconductors already had been reported globally, affecting the technology and automobile industries. Semiconductors are small materials, usually made of silicon, that conduct electricity in products such as computers, smartphones, and cars. Many policymakers and members of Congress had expressed concerns about losing U.S. leadership in semiconductors, and they were concerned that China was moving to expand its industry.

On December 18, the Trump administration went a step further, adding Semiconductor Manufacturing International Corporation (SMIC), drone maker DJI, and dozens of other Chinese companies to the Commerce Department's Entity List, effectively cutting them off from U.S. suppliers. Meanwhile, two bills had been introduced during the 116th Congress that aimed to boost federal funding for semiconductor research and development: a bill (S.3933) introduced by Sen. John Cornyn, R-Texas, and a companion in the House (HR 7178) by Rep. Michael McCaul, R-Texas, and S 4130, introduced by Sen. Tom Cotton, R-Ark., though they did not see action.

CHAPTER 3

Homeland Security Policy

Homeland Security Policy

Homeland security issues often proved controversial during President Donald Trump's time in the White House. His nationalistic, isolationist views on immigration led to clashes with many members of Congress, particularly Democrats. Perhaps the most controversial flashpoint was Trump's campaign promise to build a wall along the U.S.–Mexico border. Although Trump had claimed Mexico would pay for the wall, hardly anyone believed that would happen. Instead, how or whether to pay for the wall caused many heated debates and was a contributor to a lengthy government shutdown in 2018–2019.

During Trump's presidency, the position of secretary of homeland security resembled a revolving door. There were two secretaries and four acting secretaries, leading to upheaval, chaos, and turmoil. The secretaries and acting secretaries often found themselves defending Trump's contentious policies, with most Republicans willing to listen to them and most Democrats in opposition. In 2017–2018, the Republicans held both houses of Congress along with the White House, but Democrats controlled the House in 2019–2020, with Republicans still in charge of the Senate.

In addition, during Trump's presidency, lawmakers investigated Russian interference with the 2016 presidential election. Trump, the suspected beneficiary of Russian actions, called such investigations "witch hunts," but, at least on the Senate Intelligence Committee, Republicans worked in a bipartisan way with Democrats to try to get to the bottom of what happened. The House Intelligence Committee's investigation, however, turned highly partisan and acrimonious.

Congress managed to pass various pieces of legislation relating to homeland security during Trump's presidency, although the vast majority of the homeland security bills introduced in this period did not become law. New homeland security laws included an extension to key provisions within the Foreign Intelligence Surveillance Act (FISA), a voluntary registry for firefighters affected by cancer, a fiscal 2021 intelligence authorization bill that was included in a larger piece of legislation, and a reauthorization of a September 11 victims' compensation fund. Legislation to block Trump from using military construction funds on his border wall was approved by the House and Senate, but after Trump vetoed it, Congress did not have enough votes to override.

Chronology of Action on Homeland Security Policy

2017–2018

Homeland security issues became a flashpoint in the 115th Congress, particularly matters relating to border security and President Donald Trump's goal of building a wall along the U.S.–Mexico border. Lawmakers, particularly Democrats but on occasion some Republicans, clashed with a series of homeland security secretaries and acting secretaries on various issues touching on the wall and the treatment of migrants attempting to enter the United States.

Congress did pass some legislation relating to homeland security priorities, but many pieces of legislation fell to the wayside, passed only by one house of Congress and not the other. In a two-year period where both the White House and both houses of Congress were in Republican hands, the process seemed to stall more often than not.

Legislation that was signed into law included an extension to key provisions within the Foreign Intelligence Surveillance Act (FISA) and a voluntary registry for firefighters affected by cancer.

In addition, the House and Senate intelligence committees were among the congressional panels holding hearings into Russian interference in the 2016 presidential election. While the Senate committee attempted to act in a bipartisan manner, the House committee devolved into partisan battles.

Reauthorizing Homeland Security Department

The House approved a bill (HR 2825) in 2017 to reauthorize the Department of Homeland Security. The Senate, however, did not take up the measure.

The Department of Homeland Security (DHS) was created in the wake of the September 11, 2001, terrorist attacks against the United States. The sprawling department included 22 agencies, including Immigration and Customs Enforcement (ICE), Customs and Border Protection (CBP), and the Transportation Security Administration (TSA). One priority for House Homeland Security Committee Chair Michael McCaul, R-Texas, in the 115th Congress was to reauthorize the department, and, he said, make it more efficient and more accountable. The 9/11 Commission, a bipartisan group formed to look into the attacks, had recommended creating a lone oversight mechanism for DHS, but congressional efforts to do so in the past had failed.

Eight separate House committees had jurisdiction over parts of DHS, making a single reauthorization bill difficult. But in January 2017, the committees agreed to work in a coordinated way on DHS oversight. In May 2017, the House Judiciary and Transportation and Infrastructure committees each marked up legislation focusing on authorizing the portions of DHS under their jurisdiction.

McCaul introduced the DHS Authorization Act, H.R. 2825, on June 8, 2017. The measure would create an outline for DHS organization, spell out posts that would be presidentially appointed, and reauthorize various grant programs, among other components.

The Homeland Security Committee approved the bill on June 14. In the course of debate, lawmakers considered a number of amendments. Among them, Rep. Filemon Vela, D-Texas, offered an amendment that would make it more difficult for DHS to invoke eminent domain when seizing land for President Donald Trump's wall along the U.S.–Mexico border. The amendment was defeated on a 12–14 vote. Another amendment, by Rep. Bonnie Watson Coleman, D-N.J., aimed at requiring DHS to turn down contracts with entities possibly connected to the Trump Organization. It was rejected on an 11–15 vote. The overall bill was approved by voice vote and sent to the House floor. On July 20, the House passed the bill on a vote of 386–41.

The Senate Committee on Homeland Security and Governmental Affairs, chaired by Sen. Ron Johnson, R-Wisc., approved its version of the bill on March 7, 2018, on a vote of 10–1. Sen. Rand Paul, R-Ky., was the only senator voting against it. During consideration of the measure, senators considered various amendments, including

26 amendments designed to bolster the country's cybersecurity defenses. The amendments were approved unanimously. The full Senate did not vote on the measure.

Border Security

Republican-backed measures to strengthen security at the U.S.–Mexico border, a priority of the Trump administration, were introduced in 2017 in the House and the Senate, but were not brought to either floor for a vote.

In the House, the Border Security for America Act of 2017, HR 3548, was introduced July 28, 2017, by House Homeland Security Committee Chair Michael McCaul, R-Texas. In the Senate, another Texas Republican, Senate Majority Whip John Cornyn, introduced the companion measure, the Building America's Trust Act, S 1757, on August 3, 2017. McCaul and Cornyn saw the four-year authorization measure as a way to ensure long-term focus on the issue.

The bills sought billions of dollars in construction for Trump's controversial border wall, as well as hiring thousands of additional Border Patrol and other enforcement agents. McCaul's bill would call for $10 billion toward the border wall; Cornyn's, $15 billion. The border wall was a key component of Trump's 2016 presidential campaign. Since the administration of George H. W. Bush, the United States had constructed areas of border wall, but Trump's approach was far more aggressive; the issue became one of the most hotly contested of his presidency.

On October 4, 2017, the Homeland Security Committee marked up HR 3548, passing the measure on a party line vote of 18–12. The bill would authorize $10 billion for the wall and $5 billion to hire 10,000 more agents and customs officers.

In the course of debate, Democrats offered various amendments, including one by ranking member Bennie Thompson of Mississippi that would have renamed the bill the "Taking Americans' Land to Build Trump's Wall Act"—an effort to focus on the privately owned lands that would likely be involved in wall construction. The amendment was defeated on a 10–17 party line vote.

In addition to the funding for the border wall and the additional agents, components of the bill included language ordering the secretary of Homeland Security secretary to make sure the U.S. Customs and Border Protection's (CBP) Air and Marine Operations underwent at least 95,000 annual flight hours; language requiring improvement in the department's physical infrastructure and construct, including the acquisition of additional U.S. Border Patrol stations and checkpoints; and language prohibiting the Interior or Agriculture departments from blocking CBP activities on federal land to prevent illegal entries into the United States or to undergo search-and-rescue operations.

The measure did not receive a vote on the House floor. The Senate measure did not progress to a committee markup.

FISA Reauthorization

Congress extended key provisions of the 1978 Foreign Intelligence Surveillance Act (FISA) in 2018, adding the legislation to an unrelated Senate bill (S 139). FISA was a 1978 law (PL 95-511) that had been updated over the years. It was initially drawn up following concerns over wiretapping conducted by the administration of President Richard Nixon as well as information from a congressional committee known as the Church Committee, chaired by Sen. Frank Church, D-Idaho, revealing that warrantless electronic surveillance had been around since President Franklin D. Roosevelt's administration. Under FISA, the government would need to obtain a warrant from a special FISA court to engage in foreign surveillance in instances where one person was a U.S. citizen. Short-term exceptions were made in cases of emergency or congressional declaration of war.

In the 115th Congress, lawmakers considered legislation focusing on the ability of U.S. intelligence agencies to gather electronic communication of foreigners possibly working against U.S. interests. Several bills were introduced, all designed to address expiring FISA provisions.

One such measure, introduced November 29, 2017, by House Intelligence Committee Chair Devin Nunes, R-Calif., was the FISA Amendments Reauthorization Act of 2017 (HR 4478). Under FISA, U.S. intelligence could collect information on non-Americans' electronic communications, but information would emerge on the activity of Americans during the course of that data collection. At issue was how to regulate the surveillance of those Americans. Nunes's bill, HR 4478, would permit the FBI and U.S. intelligence agencies to use a surveillance database to gather information on Americans without initially getting a warrant, and subsequently obtain the warrant if the information were to be part of a criminal case.

The Intelligence Committee approved the measure December 1, 2017, on a party line vote of 13–8. Democrats voted against the legislation because it included a provision cutting back on the use of "unmasking," or the idea of certain top officials seeking to reveal the identity of an American possibly in touch with a foreigner under surveillance. The Democrats did not think that provision belonged in the bill, saying it was too political an issue after President Donald Trump had made untrue allegations about the unmasking of Trump campaign officials by the Obama administration. An amendment by Rep. Adam Schiff, D-Calif., the ranking Democrat on the committee, to eliminate the unmasking language, was defeated on a party line vote of 8–13.

In addition to Nunes's bill, other FISA reauthorization measures included one backed by the Senate Intelligence Committee, which would offer greater flexibility to intelligence agencies; one introduced by Sens. Patrick J. Leahy, D-Vt., Mike Lee, R-Utah, and Ron Wyden, D-Ore., that would offer less flexibility; and one, HR 3989, approved by the House Judiciary Committee, that was in the middle.

On December 20, as the end-of-the-year reauthorization deadline approached, House leaders considered putting Nunes's bill on the floor for a vote, attaching it to a must-pass spending bill. But Nunes ended up pulling the measure after its language on warrantless searches sparked opposition from some other Republicans. And two senators, Wyden and Rand Paul, R-Ky., threatened to filibuster the measure once it reached the upper chamber. The next day, the House approved an extension to the FISA law through January 19, 2018, as part of its consideration of a stopgap spending bill. In January, the House Rules Committee put together a measure using an unrelated Senate bill, S 139, as the vehicle and HR 4478 as the underlying bill. During consideration of the issue, the committee approved an amendment supported by a bipartisan group including Reps. Justin Amash, R-Mich., and Zoe Lofgren, D-Calif., that would substitute the underlying bill with language from another bill called the USA Rights Act, HR 4124. That amendment, approved January 9 on a 6–3 vote, would require intelligence agencies to get a warrant before using the surveillance database. The full House considered S 139 on January 11. It voted down the Amash-Lofgren amendment, 183–233, before passing the overall measure on a vote of 256–164.

Next up was the Senate. Senate Majority Leader Mitch McConnell, R-Ky., moved quickly to block debate on the legislation. He filed for a cloture motion and filled the amendment "tree" with his own amendments. On January 16, the bill just managed to squeak past on a 60–38 cloture vote; 60 votes were necessary to move forward. Wyden and Paul were among those expressing their opposition to the measure.

The Senate approved the bill on January 18, on a vote of 65–34, thus extending the FISA authorizations for six years. The issues relating to warrantless surveillance continued to draw controversy, although the language involving the need to obtain a warrant later if the information would be used in a criminal case was a tightening of then-current procedures. Among those criticizing its passage were civil liberties groups and supporters of data privacy. Trump signed the measure (P.L. 115-118) into law January 19, 2018.

Fiscal Year 2018 Intelligence Authorization

An intelligence authorization bill for fiscal year 2018 was approved in the House but did not make it to the Senate floor. The legislation, HR 3180, would authorize spending amounts for seventeen intelligence agencies including the CIA, the FBI, and the National Security Agency; the topline amounts were classified. The measure was introduced by House Intelligence Committee chair Devin Nunes, R-Calif., on July 11, 2017.

The committee held a closed-door markup and approved the measure by voice vote July 13. Among its provisions, the bill would tell the director of national intelligence to publish an online report on cyber and foreign intelligence threats to national election campaigns. It also required a report on Russian efforts to influence foreign elections. Also in the bill was a clarification that intelligence contractors were permitted to meet freely with Congress as well as clarifications about issues including the requirements for investigative reports dealing with leaks of classified material.

The measure ran into procedural difficulties on the House floor July 24. It had been brought up under suspension calendar rules requiring a two-thirds vote to pass. Although the bill itself was not especially controversial, Minority Leader Nancy Pelosi, D-Calif., wanted Democrats to vote against it in an effort to get majority Republicans to bring the bill up under regular order, thus allowing debate and amendments to the measure. Pelosi's gambit was successful and Democrats blocked the bill, on a 241–163 vote.

A few days later, on July 28, the House passed the measure, on a vote of 380–35. There was still no debate on the measure, as the House Rules Committee had approved a closed rule July 27 permitting no amendments; the closed rule was approved by the House July 28 on a vote of 224–186. Democrats had filed amendments, including one by Rep. Adriano Espaillat, D-N.Y., that would forbid anyone who had pledged to destroy the government from appearing at National Security Council sessions—a swipe at controversial Trump advisor Steve Bannon. Rep. Jackie Speier, D-Calif., offered an amendment that would force the White House to turn in a report dealing with the unauthorized public disclosure of classified information—a move directed at Trump himself, who had been accused of disclosing such information on forums such as Twitter.

The Senate Intelligence Committee passed a 2018 intelligence authorization bill, S 1761, July 27 on a vote of 14–1, but it did not see a Senate floor vote. Among the legislation's priorities were ameliorating the intelligence community's prowess in detecting and understanding various forms of cyberattack, encouraging sharing of threat-related information between federal and state authorities, and bettering agencies' effectiveness using advancements in technology.

Fiscal Year 2019 Intelligence Reauthorization

In 2017, Congress failed to pass an intelligence authorization bill for fiscal year 2018. The House approved its measure, but the Senate did not vote on theirs. So in 2018, lawmakers tackled a measure dealing with intelligence reauthorization for both fiscal 2018 and 2019. The bill would authorize activities pertaining to intelligence in 16 agencies, including the CIA, FBI, and National Security Agency. Once again, however, the House passed its version and the Senate declined to vote on the measure.

The House measure, HR 6237, the Matthew Young Pollard Intelligence Authorization Act for Fiscal Years 2018 and 2019, was introduced June 27, 2018, by House

Intelligence Committee chair Devin Nunes, R-Calif. It was named for a Senate Intelligence Committee staffer who had recently passed away. The committee approved the measure by voice vote on June 28, 2018. Included in the bill was language telling the director of national intelligence (DNI) to report on foreign counterintelligence and cybersecurity threats to campaigns for federal office. The reports would be electronically published, thereby increasing transparency around the issue.

In addition, the measure would increase intelligence community funding by 1.9 percent over the Trump administration's budget. And the bill would order the FBI to regularly brief the intelligence committees about the work of its Foreign Influence Task Force, an entity created after charges of Russian interference in the 2016 election. The DNI would be required to provide information to Congress about Russian influence campaigns.

The House Rules Committee, in preparing the measure for the floor, voted 6–4 along party lines on July 11 for a structured rule that would allow twelve amendments but disallow others. One defeated amendment, by Rep. Alcee Hastings, D-Fla., would have required a White House cybersecurity coordinator; it was defeated on a party line vote of 4–6.

The following day, July 12, the House took up the measure. During debate, lawmakers approved various amendments, including ones requiring the DNI to inform Congress about terrorist groups' use of virtual currency and study how Russia is using that type of currency for money laundering and finance operations worldwide. The bill was passed on a vote of 363–54.

The Senate version of the bill, S 3153, also called the Matthew Young Pollard Intelligence Authorization Act for Fiscal Years 2018 and 2019, was introduced June 28, 2018, by Senate Intelligence Committee chair Richard Burr, R-N.C., and the committee approved the bill. The measure included language urging a faster process for federal workers to receive security clearances; the backlog had reached more than 700,000 cases. While Burr hoped the Senate would approve the measure by the end of September 2018, it did not receive a Senate vote.

Secure Elections

A bipartisan measure designed to make elections more secure was derailed in the Senate when some Republicans, including the Trump White House, expressed opposition. The bill, S 2593, the Secure Elections Act, was sponsored by Sens. James Lankford, R-Okla., and Amy Klobuchar, D-Minn. It never received a vote.

Although the bill had backing from a variety of senators, including Intelligence Committee chair Richard Burr, R-N.C., and vice chair Mark Warner, D-Va., the Senate Rules and Administrations Committee postponed a planned markup of the bill on Aug. 22, 2018, due to a lack of GOP support for the measure.

Among the issues under scrutiny was language in the bill requiring states and jurisdictions to hold postelection audits of federal elections, including primary contests, looking at a random sampling of ballots. The president of the National Association of Secretaries of State, Vermont Secretary of State Jim Condos, had expressed concern about the cost of including primary audits. Democrats had wanted to provide up to $250 million to cover the cost, but Republicans had opposed that idea.

One senator expressing opposition to the bill was Appropriations Committee chair Richard C. Shelby, R-Ala., a member of the Rules Committee who had chaired it in the past. He criticized the legislation as representing too much federal involvement in the election process.

In addition, the White House reportedly expressed opposition to the measure, saying the Department of Homeland Security could keep elections safe with the tools already at their disposal, and that the bill could force federal burdens onto state and local governments.

Debate over the legislation was occurring against a backdrop of concern among many in Congress about Russian interference in the 2016 election and the possibility that Russia could once again interfere in the upcoming November 2018 midterm elections.

The Secure Elections Act would have required states to use paper backup systems. It also would have given primary federal government responsibility to the Department of Homeland Security to disseminate information to federal entities and election agencies about election cybersecurity issues, including incidents, threats, and vulnerabilities. In addition, the bill called for the Election Assistance Commission (EAC), a bipartisan commission, to create a panel of independent experts who would create election cybersecurity guidelines, and to award grants to states and election agencies to implement those guidelines.

An earlier version of the bill, S 2261, had been introduced by Lankford in December 2017; the measure was revised in March 2018. Like S 2593, it did not advance.

Sanctions on Russia

Legislation to slap tough sanctions on Russian banks and energy companies if Russia interfered in U.S. elections was introduced January 16, 2018, by Sen. Chris Van Hollen, D-Md. The bipartisan bill (S 2313) was also sponsored by Sen. Marco Rubio, R-Fla., and backed by cosponsors from both parties. The measure was sent to the Senate Banking, Housing, and Urban Affairs Committee, which held hearings in August and September but did not vote on the bill.

The bill was introduced against a backdrop of concern over Russian interference in the 2016 election. Lawmakers hoped to clamp down on future Russian activities regarding upcoming elections. The measure would require that the director of national intelligence (DNI) decide, within 30 days of an election, if a foreign government interfered with the election, and report on that decision.

The president would impose specific sanctions on the foreign government if interference was found, and share information with Congress about the interference.

Among the types of interference are buying online ads to sway an election, using social media to disseminate large amounts of false information, and hacking election databases and websites as well as campaign email. If Russia were found to have interfered in an election, the actions would involve sanctions on various large Russian banks and energy companies. Some observers expressed concern that the bill would end up also penalizing U.S. allies in Europe, some of which could be affected due to their ties to Russian energy sources.

After President Trump seemed to agree with Russia's Vladimir Putin, at a meeting in Helsinki July 17 that Russia had not interfered with the 2016 election, the legislation gained eight additional cosponsors in the Senate.

The United States had sanctioned Russia on other occasions in recent years, including in 2017, when Congress passed legislation with sanctions affecting the country's energy, banking, and defense sectors. S 2313 was expected to take a harder line with greater economic impact on Russia. Ultimately, the bill did not advance to the Senate floor.

COMMITTEE INVESTIGATIONS INTO RUSSIAN ELECTION INTERFERENCE

Both the House and Senate intelligence committees held hearings beginning in 2017 focused on Russian interference with the 2016 presidential election. The U.S. intelligence community had concluded that Russia had interfered in the election in an effort to promote the candidacy of Republican Donald Trump over that of Democrat Hillary Clinton. But the two intelligence committees took different approaches to the matter. The Senate committee opted for bipartisanship, while the House committee deteriorated into partisan battles.

On March 20, 2017, in testimony before the House intelligence committee, FBI director James Comey revealed that the bureau, since July 2016, had been conducting a counterintelligence investigation into Russian interference in the 2016 election, including any possible links between Russia and the Trump campaign. The public hearing received a great deal of attention, and the committee planned a second set of hearings the following week.

Previously, House intelligence chair Rep. Devin Nunes, R-Calif., and ranking member Rep. Adam Schiff, D-Calif., had reportedly worked well together. But things started to break down, and just days after the public hearing, the committee was in the headlines for other reasons.

Nunes had learned information about potential surveillance of Trump transition officials during the period between the election and Trump's inauguration. The officials' communications, according to materials Nunes had been given, were intercepted incidentally by U.S. authorities conducting routine foreign surveillance. Instead of notifying his fellow committee members, he told the press and the White House, causing a furor of criticism and questions about whether he could lead an objective investigation. Nunes had served as an advisor to Trump's transition team, which had concerned Democrats before March 2017.

Reactions to Nunes's activities broke down largely along partisan lines, with Democrats blaming him for creating a politicized atmosphere and Republicans defending him and blaming Schiff for creating a partisan atmosphere. Nunes cancelled the second open hearing, which had been set for March 28. While Nunes reportedly apologized to committee Democrats in a closed-door meeting, the apology did not seem to ease the tension.

Problems continued into the following year. In early 2018, Nunes released a memo that cast aspersions on Justice and FBI officials, saying they had misled a Foreign Intelligence Surveillance court. The White House approved the release of Nunes's memo, but raised an issue when Schiff and other Democrats sought to release a response to Nunes's memo. The Democratic response was later released.

In March 2018, Nunes and committee Republicans released a report stating there was no collusion between the Trump campaign and Russia. Schiff and committee Democrats opposed the Republican statement. In the lead-up to the 2018 midterm election, Schiff said that if Democrats took over the House and he became chair, he would continue the Russia investigation.

On the Senate side, committee chair Sen. Richard Burr, R-N.C., and ranking member Sen. Mark Warner, D-Va., attempted to work in a bipartisan fashion. The committee announced January 13, 2017, that it would look into whether there were links between U.S. campaigns and Russia. The investigation also would include a review of U.S. intelligence assessments about Russian interference.

While Warner and Burr had clashed over issues, including the question of whether the committee would look into ties between U.S. campaigns and Russia, they tended to settle their disputes quietly. Among other differences, the Senate committee had managed to negotiate access to intelligence agency materials more smoothly; the House committee voiced complaints about the FBI and CIA in its pursuit of material. The House scheduled early public hearings with big-name officials, while the Senate chose to pursue less prominent officials at the start to gather information.

On June 8, the Senate committee heard from Comey, who had recently been fired by Trump. At the much-discussed public hearing, Comey accused Trump of lying and said he thought his firing was a way for Trump to interfere with the FBI's investigation into Russian election meddling. Days later, on June 13, Attorney General Jeff Sessions, who had recused himself from the Russia investigation, appeared before the committee, saying he did not participate in and was not aware of any collusion with Russia.

Burr and Warner, in October 2017, held a press conference, in which, among other things, they said they had found major efforts by Russia to disrupt the 2016 election, and that Russian interference was a threat for the upcoming 2018 elections. In June 2018, the committee released an update saying the panel did not dispute intelligence findings that Russia had interfered in the 2016 election. The committee planned to continue its work.

The intelligence committees were not the only panels looking into Russian interference. And in addition to the action on Capitol Hill, special counsel Robert Mueller, a former FBI director, was also probing the issue. Trump called the Russia investigations a hoax and tried to discredit them.

Counterterrorism Training Programs

In 2017, the House passed legislation that would update the Homeland Security Act of 2002 to add a Joint Counterterrorism Workshop Series. The bill, HR 3284, or the Joint Counterterrorism Awareness Workshop Series Act, was sponsored by Rep. Brian Fitzpatrick, R-Pa., and was introduced July 18, 2017. The measure was designed to help jurisdictions prepare for situations where multiple coordinated terrorist attacks would take place. Workshops had already been underway as of the time of the bill's introduction, held in more than thirty cities since 2011. The measure would authorize by statute the Joint Counterterrorism Awareness Workshop Series, which was coordinating the workshops. A Congressional Budget Office estimate said the measure would cost about $5 million over the 2018–2022 period.

The measure was referred to the House Committee on Homeland Security, which held a markup July 26. During committee consideration, Rep. Sheila Jackson Lee, D-Texas, withdrew an amendment that would have required yearly reporting on security benefits and costs of publishing images of structures around Joint Terrorism Task Force buildings in map phone apps and online. The committee favorably reported the measure, by voice vote, to the full House, and the House passed the bill on September 14, 2017, on a vote of 398–4.

On September 18, the Senate received the bill. It was referred to the Committee on Homeland Security and Governmental Affairs. There was no further action.

HOMELAND THREAT ASSESSMENT ACT

The House approved a bill, HR 2470, in 2017 that would amend the Homeland Security Act of 2002 to require the Office of Intelligence and Analysis within the Department of Homeland Security to assess the threat from terrorism against the homeland for the next five fiscal years. The first assessment would be made by 180 days after the bill was enacted, and annual assessments would be made for the next five years.

The bill, introduced by Rep. Mike Rogers, R-Ala., on May 16, 2017, was called the Homeland Threat Assessment Act. On May 18, the House Homeland Security subcommittee

on counterterrorism and intelligence marked up the bill and approved it by voice vote. The same day, the full committee, by voice vote, ordered the bill to be reported. The full House debated the bill on September 12, 2017, and approved it by voice vote.

The measure was received in the Senate September 13, 2017, and was referred to the Committee on Homeland Security and Governmental Affairs. There was no further action.

TERRORIST USE OF VIRTUAL CURRENCIES

In 2017, the House approved legislation that would require the Department of Homeland Security's Office of Intelligence and Analysis to come up with a threat assessment focusing on the use of virtual currency in terrorist activities and share that information with state, local, and tribal officials. The bill, HR 2433, the Homeland Security Assessment of Terrorists' Use of Virtual Currencies Act, was introduced by Rep. Kathleen Rice, D-N.Y., on May 16, 2017.

The House Homeland Security subcommittee on counterterrorism and intelligence approved the measure by voice vote on May 18, sending it on to the full committee, which approved it by voice vote the same day. The measure went to the full House, which considered it on September 12 and approved it by voice vote.

On September 13, the Senate received the bill. It was referred to the Committee on Homeland Security and Governmental Affairs. There was no further action.

DHS ROTATIONAL JOB PROGRAM

The House approved legislation in 2017 that would amend the Homeland Security Act of 2002 by requiring the Department of Homeland Security to create an Intelligence Rotational Assignment Program. The program would be available to analysts working in DHS's Intelligence Enterprise and other appropriate workers. The responsibilities pertaining to DHS's Homeland Security Rotation Program would apply here.

The bill, HR 2453, or the DHS Intelligence Rotational Assignment Program Act of 2017, was introduced May 16, 2017, by Rep. Mike Gallagher, R-Wisc. The House Homeland Security subcommittee on counterterrorism and intelligence approved the measure by voice vote on May 18. The same day, the full committee approved it by voice vote. The measure was considered on the House floor September 12, and approved by voice vote.

On September 13, the measure was received in the Senate and referred to the Committee on Homeland Security and Governmental Affairs. There was no further action.

Registry of Cancer Incidences

In 2018, Congress passed legislation focusing on studying the incidence of cancer among firefighters. The measure, HR 931, or the Firefighter Cancer Registry Act of

2018, was introduced February 7, 2017, by Rep. Chris Collins, R-N.Y., and referred to the House Committee on Energy and Commerce. The bill would create, via a grant or cooperative arrangement, a voluntary firefighter cancer registry that would gather relevant occupational and history information. The data could be linked to existing databases.

The Energy and Commerce Committee's subcommittee on health marked up the bill on June 29, 2017. It approved the measure, including an amendment to require information from state agencies for the registry, by voice vote. The full committee considered the measure on July 27, 2017, and approved it by voice vote. On September 12, 2017, the House approved the measure by voice vote.

On September 13, the Senate received the bill and referred it to the Committee on Health, Education, Labor, and Pensions. After a lengthy delay, the committee discharged the bill by unanimous consent on May 10, 2018. The Senate approved the measure with an amendment by unanimous consent the same day. The House, on June 22, approved the Senate bill, and on July 7, 2018, President Donald Trump signed it into law (PL 115-194).

Embassy Security

In 2018, both chambers of Congress passed different versions of legislation focusing on the security of U.S. embassies and diplomatic posts. However, they did not reconcile the differences.

The measure, HR 4969, or the Embassy Security Authorization Act, was introduced February 7, 2018, by Rep. Michael McCaul, R-Texas. The bill set out design and construction requirements that the State Department should follow when planning diplomatic buildings, in an effort to make the buildings safer.

On June 28, 2018, the House Foreign Affairs Committee marked up the bill. McCaul proposed a substitute amendment requiring a quarterly report about capital construction efforts overseas. Rep. Dina Titus, D-Nev., proposed an amendment stating that functionality and security should be balanced with accessibility when the State Department considered construction projects. Both these amendments were incorporated. The committee approved the bill by voice vote.

The House approved the bill by voice vote on September 5. The following day, the Senate received the bill and referred it to the Committee on Foreign Relations. On December 22, the committee discharged the bill by unanimous consent, and the same day, the full Senate approved an amended version of the bill by unanimous consent. It sent the amended measure back to the House, which did not take it up.

State-Sponsored Cyber Activity

In 2018, the House passed legislation that would impose sanctions on entities committing state-sponsored cyber-attacks on the United States. The measure, HR 5576, was introduced by Rep. Ted Yoho, R-Fla., on April 18, 2018.

Under the legislation, the president would designate individuals or entities involved in these attacks, and publish information in the *Federal Register* about these designees. The president could impose sanctions on these actors, including impacts on non-humanitarian U.S. development aid and U.S. security assistance.

The bill was referred to the House committees on Foreign Affairs, Financial Services, Oversight and Government Reform, and the Judiciary, and the Foreign Affairs Committee marked up the bill June 28. Yoho proposed a substitute amendment allowing the president to refrain from publishing the information in the Federal Register if the president believed that action was in the national interest or would help important law enforcement activities; the president would need to explain their actions to Congress. Rep. Gerry Connolly, D-Va., proposed an amendment adding language to the bill stating that five Russian entities and nineteen Russian individuals were cited March 15, 2018, for interfering with the 2016 election. Another amendment, by Foreign Affairs Committee chair Rep. Ed Royce, R-Calif., would direct U.S. officials to cooperate with international partners to deter cyberterrorism. Those amendments were included in the bill, which was approved by voice vote.

On September 5, the House approved the measure by voice vote. It was seen as making official what had been unofficial U.S. policy against those engaging in cyberterrorism. The following day, the bill was received in the Senate and referred to the Senate Foreign Relations Committee. There was no further action.

Global Election Practices

The House, in 2018, passed legislation authorizing the State Department to create a Global Electoral Exchange Program to promote best practices of election administration. The bill, HR 5274, was introduced by Rep. Joaquin Castro, D-Texas, on March 14, 2018.

It was referred to the House Foreign Affairs Committee, which marked the bill up and approved it by unanimous consent April 17. Castro introduced a substitute amendment revising public disclosure rules, and Rep. Dina Titus, D-Nev., introduced an amendment focused on equitable access to polling places and voting mechanisms by the disabled. Both were included in the bill.

On September 5, the House approved the measure by voice vote. The following day, the bill was received in the Senate and referred to the Senate Foreign Relations Committee. There was no further action.

Fiscal Year 2017 Homeland Security Appropriations

The process of finalizing funding for homeland security programs in fiscal year 2017 dragged into calendar year 2017, and into a new presidency, that of Donald Trump. President Barack Obama had signed two continuing

resolutions into law that continued the funding from the previous fiscal year, which had ended September 30, 2016.

The Trump administration asked for $3 billion in additional funding for the Department of Homeland Security, and this request was included in an overall appropriations bill known as the Consolidated Appropriations Act, which included funding for various agencies including DHS. The measure included $41.3 billion in discretionary homeland security funding, and also included $6.7 billion in major disaster funding and $163 million for overseas contingency operations. Trump signed the measure (PL 115–31) into law on May 5, 2017.

Fiscal Year 2018 Homeland Security Appropriations

Congress approved funding for homeland security programs for fiscal year 2018 in March 2018 as part of a massive spending measure, the Consolidated Appropriations Act (PL 115-123). The fiscal year had begun almost six months earlier, but Congress had passed various interim bills to keep funding going.

On May 23, 2017, the Trump administration requested $44.1 billion in discretionary funding for fiscal 2018 homeland security programs, along with an additional $6.79 billion for disaster aid funding for the Federal Emergency Management Agency (FEMA).

The House Appropriations Committee produced a bill, HR 3355, which included $44.3 billion in discretionary spending, slightly more than the administration's request. The subcommittee on homeland security approved the bill by voice vote on July 12, 2017. The measure included $13.8 billion for U.S. Customs and Border Protection (CBP), including $1.6 billion to begin work on Trump's border wall; $7 billion for U.S. Immigration and Customs Enforcement (ICE), and $10.5 billion for the U.S. Coast Guard.

On July 18, the full committee approved the measure on a party line vote, with only Republicans in support. Democrats protested the money for the border wall as well as other Republican-backed immigration priorities. Rep. Lucille Roybal-Allard, D-Calif., offered an amendment to cancel increases for CBP and ICE; the amendment was defeated on a party line vote of 22–30. Another of the amendments under consideration, from Rep. Mike Quigley, D-Ill., would use the money in question for emergency preparedness grants given to local first responders. His amendment was rejected by voice vote. Other Democratic amendments rejected by the committee included one from Roybal-Allard that sought to force DHS to continue the Obama administration's Deferred Action for Childhood Arrivals (DACA) program for undocumented immigrants brought to the country as children; the amendment was defeated on a party line vote of 22–30. Among the Republican-backed amendments that passed was one from Rep. Robert Aderholt, R-Ala., that would stop ICE from using appropriated funds to perform abortions; it was approved on a 29–21 party line vote.

On the Senate side, the Senate Appropriations Committee released a draft bill on November 21, 2017, that would provide $44.1 billion in discretionary spending, $6.8 billion in disaster relief, $559 million in emergency funding, and $163 million in overseas contingency operations. The full committee and the full Senate did not act on the measure.

Also in 2017 and 2018, Congress approved supplemental homeland security appropriations, mostly dealing with disaster relief: the first was signed into law October 26, 2017 (PL 115-72), the second on February 9, 2018 (PL 115-123).

Eventually, a consolidated appropriations bill was approved by both houses; the House passed it on a vote of 256–167 March 22, 2018, and the Senate approved it on a 65–32 vote March 23. It was signed into law by Trump on March 23. It provided $47.7 billion in discretionary spending for homeland security, and also included $7.4 billion for disaster relief and $163 million for overseas contingency operations.

Fiscal Year 2019 Homeland Security Appropriations

Congress approved funding for fiscal 2019 homeland security appropriations as part of a larger spending bill approved by Congress February 14, 2019, and signed into law (PL 116-6) by President Donald Trump February 15. The homeland security portion of the bill included $49.41 billion in discretionary funding, $12 billion for major disaster relief, and $165 million in Coast Guard Overseas Contingency Operations (OCO) funding. The administration had proposed $47.43 in discretionary homeland security spending for fiscal 2019.

On June 19, 2018, the Senate Appropriations subcommittee on homeland security approved a measure, S 3109, by voice vote including $48.33 billion in homeland security discretionary spending. The bill included $1.6 billion toward the controversial fence along the U.S.–Mexico border, one of Trump's priorities. Beyond the discretionary spending, the measure also included $6.65 billion toward disaster relief and $165 million for Coast Guard OCO funding.

Other specifics in the bill included $11.69 billion for FEMA, including $7.23 billion for the Disaster Relief Fund, $7.2 billion for Immigration and Customs and Enforcement, and $2.2 billion for the Secret Service.

On June 25, the full Appropriations Committee advanced the measure on a vote of 26–5. The nay votes were all from Democrats. During consideration of the bill, senators approved a manager's amendment from Sen. Shelley Moore Capito, R-W.Va., the subcommittee chair, that incorporated a variety of changes to the bill on issues including maritime ports of entry and public access to federal buildings. Also considered was an amendment from Sen. Jeff Merkley, D-Ore., that would require ICE to consider alternatives to detention; the provision was adopted by voice vote.

The House Appropriations Committee approved its bill, HR 6776, on a 29–22 party line vote, on July 25, 2018. The measure contained $54.1 billion in discretionary funding, more than the Senate version or the administration's request. A number of amendments were considered, including one from Rep. Kevin Yoder, R-Kan., chair of the Homeland Security Subcommittee, that would insert language stating that parents and children could only be separated at the border if the parent was deemed unfit, had a communicable disease, or had a criminal history. This amendment was approved by voice vote; it was a response to the Trump administration's controversial policy of separating migrant families at the border. Another amendment, from Rep. Pete Aguilar, D-Calif., would forbid money from the bill from being used to deport or detain Dreamers—undocumented immigrants who were brought to the country as children—who were serving in the military or were veterans. The amendment was approved by voice vote. Among other amendments considered was one from Rep. Lucille Roybal-Allard, D-Calif., that would move $750 million from border wall construction to a new Coast Guard icebreaker; the amendment was rejected along party lines, 21–29.

The process to fund the government did not go well in 2018 and led to a lengthy government shutdown from December 2018 to January 2019 that lasted thirty-five days. A key sticking point was the question of funding for Trump's border wall. Before and after the shutdown, the government was operating on continuing resolutions. In the end, Congress passed and Trump signed a spending bill that included homeland security funding in February 2019. Ultimately, just under $1.4 billion was provided for the wall, below Trump's request for $5.7 billion.

In addition, there were two supplemental spending measures that included DHS funding. The Coast Guard received $526 million in PL 116–20, and CBP, ICE, and FEMA received $1.34 billion in PL 116–26.

Homeland Security Leadership

Under President Donald Trump, the leadership of the Department of Homeland Security (DHS) often found itself mired in controversies. And during the four years of the Trump administration, there were multiple people at the head of the department.

The first secretary of homeland security under Trump was John F. Kelly, a retired Marine Corps general who had served as head of U.S. Southern Command. He became the first former military officer to head the department. Trump nominated Kelly on December 12, 2016, and the U.S. Senate confirmed him to the post on January 20, 2017, on a vote of 88–11.

Kelly was born in Boston, Massachusetts, in 1950, and graduated from the University of Massachusetts in 1976. He enlisted in the Marines in 1970, and was discharged as a sergeant in 1972. After his graduation, he was commissioned as a Marine officer, and retired from the service in 2016.

At his confirmation hearings January 10, 2017, before the Senate Committee on Homeland Security and Governmental Affairs, Kelly backed Trump's idea of building a physical barrier or wall between the United States and Mexico. He stated that his top priority was to stop undocumented immigrants and banned goods from crossing the border into the United States. However, he distanced himself from another controversial idea: creating a registry of Muslims or forbidding Muslims to enter the country.

But on January 31, Kelly met with lawmakers on Capitol Hill to discuss a Trump executive order banning nationals from seven mostly Muslim nations—Iran, Iraq, Libya, Somalia, Sudan, Syria, and Yemen—from coming to the United States. And on February 7, in his first testimony as secretary before the House Homeland Security Committee, Kelly defended the administration's policy but said it could have been delayed so he could have given Congress more preparation.

Kelly was also involved in the Trump administration's tough deportation policies against undocumented immigrants. Trump had promised to deport two to three million undocumented immigrants convicted of, or charged with, criminal offenses. The Obama administration had put a priority on deporting immigrants with records of violent crime.

Kelly met March 17, 2017, with a group of House Democrats to discuss the administration's immigration raids, the administration's idea of separating parents and children at the border as a deterrent, and the future of Dreamers, part of the Obama administration's Deferred Action for Childhood Arrivals (DACA) plan. After the meeting, many of the participants said Kelly was mostly dismissive of their concerns. His department disagreed with that characterization.

On April 5, Kelly appeared before the Senate Homeland Security and Governmental Affairs Committee to discuss border security issues, including the border wall and the arrest of families at the border. In his testimony, he ruled out the idea of a wall stretching along the entire border. Rather, he talked about barriers at strategic areas of the border. He credited the administration's tough immigration policies with contributing to a drop in the number of migrants arriving from Central America.

Kelly's frustration with opponents on Capitol Hill came through during a speech April 18, 2017, at George Washington University, where he said lawmakers who do not like the enforcement actions of the administration should "shut up" or change the law.

In the end, Kelly's tenure as homeland security chief was short. On July 28, Trump named him as his new White House chief of staff to replace Reince Priebus.

After Kelly left the department, his deputy, Elaine Duke, became acting secretary. Duke had been confirmed by the Senate April 4, 2017, on a vote of 85–14, as deputy secretary of homeland security. Before that, she served as

undersecretary of management. A 30-year federal government employee, Duke was not seen as especially controversial. She held management positions with the Navy and the Air Force, and was involved in the formation of the Transportation Security Administration (TSA), part of DHS.

Duke ran into a controversy on September 5, 2017, when she announced that the Trump administration would end the DACA program. The DACA recipients, undocumented immigrants who had been brought to the United States as children, had many supporters in Congress, and those lawmakers vowed to pass legislation to help the Dreamers stay in the United States. Finding consensus on this issue had proved challenging.

Meanwhile, the White House was searching for a permanent replacement for Kelly, and on October 11, 2017, Trump nominated Kirstjen Nielsen, a top aide to Kelly, as the new secretary of homeland security. Nielsen, born in 1972, graduated from Georgetown University and University of Virginia's School of Law. Her experience included working on Capitol Hill, in the White House, and as the founder and president of Sunesis Consulting LLC, a private consulting firm. She also had worked at TSA as the creator and manager of its legislative affairs office. At the time of her nomination, she was working as Kelly's top assistant at the White House.

At her hearing before the Senate Homeland Security and Governmental Affairs Committee November 8, 2017, Nielsen repeated what Kelly had told lawmakers earlier in the year: that she did not see the need for a wall along the entire U.S.–Mexico border. But she differed somewhat from Kelly's language on the subject of Dreamers, saying they deserved a permanent solution to their situation.

The following day, *The Washington Post* reported that Kelly, now Trump's chief of staff, was pressuring Duke, the acting secretary, to end the Temporary Protected Status of refugees from Honduras. Following that report, a group of Democratic senators, concerned about Nielsen's independence from Kelly, wrote to Committee Chair Ron Johnson, R-Wisc., asking for Nielsen to answer additional questions; the nomination vote was delayed for a few days while Nielsen responded. On November 14, the committee voted to advance Nielsen's nomination, on an 11–4 vote. Three Democrats joined the committee's Republicans in supporting her. On December 5, the full Senate approved Nielsen's nomination on a vote of 62–37. The no votes all came from Democrats and independent Sen. Bernie Sanders of Vermont.

In Nielsen's first months as secretary, she participated in various immigration initiatives, including tougher requirements for the Visa Waiver Program permitting foreigners from 38 countries to visit the United States without a visa, an end to Temporary Protected Status for refugees from El Salvador, additional vetting for refugees from 11 countries considered "high risk," and Trump's plan to ask border-state governors to deploy National Guard troops near the border to deter undocumented immigrants. Appearing before the Senate Judiciary Committee in January 2018, Nielsen was questioned about the White House's decision to turn down a bipartisan agreement in the Senate over the fate of DACA recipients; she told senators the administration did not think the plan would facilitate a decline in undocumented immigration. She also was asked about an Oval Office meeting January 11, 2018, in which Trump was said to have referred to Haiti and African countries as "shithole countries." She responded that she did not hear him say those words but that profanity and cursing had been uttered at the meeting.

The most controversial policy during Nielsen's tenure was the administration's decision to separate migrant parents from their children at the border. The policy was roundly denounced by many Democrats, some Republicans, civil rights groups, and civil liberties groups, among others.

At a hearing May 15, 2018, before the Senate Homeland Security and Governmental Affairs Committee, Nielsen categorized the policy as an effort to prosecute more adult migrants for crossing the border illegally rather than an effort to deter migrants from coming to the United States—although that rationale would also be used by the Trump administration. The adults would be referred to the Justice Department for prosecution, while the children would be under the auspices of the Department of Health and Human Services.

The policy was a fiasco; images of migrant children in cage-like structures spread across the world. Parents and children were separated for years in some cases; as of 2022, some families still had not been reunited. On June 18, 2018, Nielsen, while defending the policy at a White House briefing, said, "Congress and the courts created this problem, and Congress alone can fix it." House Minority Leader Nancy Pelosi, D-Calif., however, said Nielsen should resign, and even a number of prominent Republicans harshly criticized the policy.

In September 2018, after the Trump administration was forced to end the separation policy by bipartisan congressional opposition, Nielsen's department proposed a new rule that would permit lengthy detention of undocumented child migrants, a move that would end a longtime legal settlement that limited the amount of time a child migrant could be detained. The department also proposed a rule that would make it more difficult for immigrants on public assistance to get green cards.

Nielsen was among the government officials subpoenaed in February 2019 by the House Oversight and Reform Committee, which was looking into the child separation policy.

She continued defending Trump's policies as her time as secretary continued. In March 2019, she appeared before the House Homeland Security Committee, supporting Trump's decision to declare a national emergency at the border. At the contentious hearing, she clashed with

lawmakers about the family separation policy, among other issues.

Despite all her defenses of the president's policies, Trump grew dissatisfied with her performance, and he announced her resignation via Twitter on April 7, 2019. For the remainder of Trump's time in office, there was no confirmed secretary of homeland security. Instead, three men served as acting secretaries.

The first, Kevin McAleenan, was designated acting secretary by Trump on April 8, 2019. He had been confirmed as commissioner of U.S. Customs and Border Protection by the Senate in March 2018, and had been acting commissioner since January 2017. He had served in the federal government's senior executive service since 2006.

Among the DHS proposals during his time in the job was the "Remain in Mexico" plan under which many migrants would stay in Mexico while awaiting their hearing. McAleenan remained in the post for six months. On October 11, 2019, Trump—again via Twitter—announced that McAleenan would resign.

Next up was Chad Wolf, who had worked at DHS and also as a lobbyist. Wolf was sworn in November 13, 2019, after being confirmed by the Senate as undersecretary of the department's Office of Strategy, Policy, and Plans on a vote of 54–41. He had been serving in an acting capacity in that role, and now would become acting secretary of the entire department.

Shortly after Wolf's swearing-in, the heads of two House committees, Oversight and Homeland Security, questioned whether Wolf's appointment as well as those of McAleenan and Wolf's deputy Ken Cuccinelli were legal. Homeland Security Committee Chair Bennie Thompson, D-Miss., and Carolyn Maloney, D-N.Y., acting Oversight chair, requested that the U.S. Comptroller General examine whether the Trump administration acted legally to name these officials. The lawmakers cited documents indicating that succession rules may have been violated.

On August 14, 2020, the Government Accounting Office (GAO) said Wolf's and Cuccinelli's appointments were invalid because DHS had not followed proper succession protocols. Senate Democratic Leader Chuck Schumer of New York called on both men to resign. Later in the year, Wolf's appointment was ruled illegal by several federal judges during proceedings dealing with Wolf's role in trying to pause the DACA program.

Meanwhile, Wolf's first hearing before a congressional panel since assuming his post came on February 25, 2020, when he faced questions from the Senate Appropriations subcommittee on homeland security. Senators asked him about the Trump administration's request for $2 billion for the border wall, about whether DHS had enough respirators and masks to fight COVID, and about the policy forcing migrants to remain in Mexico.

Among the controversies during Wolf's tenure in the job were reports in July 2020 that tactical agents from DHS and the Justice Department, in fatigues with no identification on them, had rounded up protestors in Portland, Oregon, and placed them in unmarked cars. Wolf maintained that his department had the right to take those actions, but some lawmakers were outraged and planned to introduce legislation making these agents clearly show identification while on duty.

Wolf also faced two whistleblower complaints in September 2020. One involved a DHS whistleblower who accused Wolf of holding back an intelligence report dealing with the threat of Russian interference with the 2020 election, because it would have made Trump look bad. The other complaint detailed claims of medical neglect at an ICE facility in Georgia.

Wolf had been seen as an interim fix for the homeland security post, but he ended up staying in the position until almost the end of the Trump administration. On August 25, Trump said he would nominate Wolf to the permanent position of homeland security secretary. The Senate Committee on Homeland Security and Governmental Affairs held hearings on his nomination September 23, and approved his nomination September 30 along party lines, 6–3.

After Wolf condemned the January 6, 2021, insurrection by Trump supporters at the U.S. Capitol, Trump, by then a lame duck president, withdrew Wolf's nomination on January 7. Wolf resigned on January 11 but remained in the position to which the Senate had confirmed him in 2019. Trump's final acting secretary of DHS, for the remaining days of the administration, was Pete Gaynor, the administrator of the Federal Emergency Management Agency.

2019–2020

When dealing with homeland security issues, the 116th Congress, like its predecessor, featured furious debates over President Donald Trump's immigration policies, including his controversial wall along the U.S.–Mexico border. His various secretaries and acting secretaries of homeland security continued to clash with lawmakers, especially given that Democrats, after faring well in the 2018 House midterm elections, took control of the House in January 2019. The Senate remained under Republican control.

Once again, many homeland security-related pieces of legislation failed to become law, often seeing passage by only one house of Congress. But among the bills that did become law were a fiscal 2021 intelligence authorization bill, which was included in a larger piece of legislation, and a reauthorization of a September 11 victims' compensation fund. Legislation to block Trump from using military construction funds on his border wall was approved in both houses, but Trump vetoed it, and Congress did not have the votes to override the veto.

FISA Provisions

In 2020, the House and Senate each passed versions of legislation to reauthorize intelligence-gathering provisions under the Foreign Intelligence Surveillance Act (FISA) through December 1, 2023. But the chambers were unable to resolve their differences, and the legislation did not become law.

On March 10, 2020, Rep. Jerrold Nadler, D-N.Y., the chair of the House Judiciary Committee, introduced HR 6172, the USA FREEDOM Reauthorization Act of 2020. The bill was referred to the committees on Judiciary, Intelligence, Oversight and Reform, and Homeland Security. Three surveillance authorities were set to expire March 15, and the legislation would extend them. The authorities allowed the intelligence community to pursue lone wolf terrorists, use "roving wiretaps" not tied to a particular phone number, and collect business records. The legislation also made changes to FISA, including ending an already-suspended National Security Agency program that collected data on phone call records.

The House approved HR 6172 March 11, 2020, on a vote of 278–136. It was a bipartisan effort: 152 Democrats and 126 Republicans backed the measure while 75 Democrats, 60 Republicans, and one independent opposed it. Opponents' objections included a perceived lack of protection for civil liberties and of independent oversight of FISA orders.

The same day, March 11, the bill was received in the Senate. But the Senate did not vote on the measure until after the authorities had expired. Instead, the Senate voted March 16 by voice vote to pass a bill called S 3501, providing a seventy-seven-day extension to the lapsed authorities; the House did not take up this bill. Senate Majority Leader

Mitch McConnell, R-Ky., agreed to debate the House bill at a later point; Congress had become overwhelmed by matters relating to the COVID pandemic.

In May, the Senate returned to the FISA issue. On May 14, senators approved an amended version of the House bill, voting 80–16 in favor. The nay votes came from fourteen Democrats and two Republicans. Three amendments were considered, and one of them was approved; the amendments required sixty votes to pass.

One amendment, from Sens. Mike Lee, R-Utah, and Patrick Leahy, D-Vt., was approved on a vote of 77–19. The amendment would widen the mandate for naming of outside legal counsel in matters before the FISA court to add those featuring religious institutions, political figures, and other sensitive issues. Lee and Leahy saw it as a way to protect people who may not know they were targeted for surveillance. Another amendment, from Sens. Steve Daines, R-Mont., and Ron Wyden, D-Ore., that would stop warrantless surveillance of web browser search histories, fell short of passage by one vote, 59–37.

A third amendment, from Sen. Rand Paul, R-Ky., aimed to block the use of FISA court warrants against U.S. persons. It was easily defeated on a vote of 11–85. The amended measure returned to the House, where it ran into problems. Although Attorney General William Barr had worked with lawmakers to craft the original House measure, the Justice Department recommended President Donald Trump veto the Senate version, citing curbs on the ability to track terrorists and spies. Although the measure had been moving toward House floor consideration, it was pulled May 27. House Majority Leader Steny Hoyer, D-Md., cited Republican opposition to the bill for its removal from consideration. In addition, members had clashed over the inclusion of a proposed amendment similar to the failed Senate amendment on access to browsing history; the House Rules Committee had not permitted the amendment to be considered. And Trump had expressed opposition to the bill.

The House requested a conference with the Senate, voting May 28 to disagree with the Senate amendments and ask for a conference to resolve differences. The request was passed on a 284–122 tally; 211 Democrats and 73 Republicans voted yea and 21 Democrats, 100 Republicans, and one independent voted nay. On June 1, the Senate received the request. There was no further action.

Authorization of Intelligence Programs in Fiscal Year 2020

In 2019, the House passed legislation to authorize intelligence programs. The measure was not acted upon in the Senate. The bill, HR 3494, was introduced by Rep. Adam Schiff, D-Calif., the chair of the House Intelligence Committee, on June 26, 2019. The committee reported an amended bill

July 11. It was referred July 11 to the House Ways and Means Committee, which discharged it the same day.

The House debated the measure July 16, and considered a variety of amendments. Among them was an amendment proposed by Rep. Ted Yoho, R-Fla., requiring a report from the director of National Intelligence (DNI) on dangers posed by 5G technology and by telecom companies associated with a foreign adversary. The amendment, which passed by voice vote, was seen as a response to Chinese telecom firm Huawei, which created 5G wireless technology and had alleged connections to the Chinese government.

Rep. Tom Malinowski, D-N.J., proposed an amendment requiring a report to Congress dealing with financial or technological support for facial recognition programs that U.S. companies give China. The concern was that the government in China could be using these technologies on Uyghur and other ethnic minorities. The amendment passed by voice vote.

Rep. Adam Kinzinger, R-Ill., proposed an amendment requiring a report from the DNI about national security threats connected to international mobile subscriber identity-catchers, which track and intercept users of mobile phones, as used by foreign governments. The amendment passed by voice vote.

Rep. Stephanie Murphy, D-Fla., proposed an amendment requiring the DNI to report on the use of machine-manipulated video called "deepfakes" by countries including China and Russia. The DNI would need to let Congress know when a foreign entity has used this technology to interfere with U.S. political processes or elections. The amendment passed by voice vote.

Rep. Pramila Jayapal, D-Wash., proposed an amendment requiring a DNI report looking at the intelligence community's use of facial recognition technology, including risks to individuals' rights and privacy, and safeguards against those risks. The amendment passed by voice vote.

Rep. Kathleen Rice, D-N.Y., proposed an amendment requiring that an intelligence report required under the legislation be shared with local and state partners by the Homeland Security Department, dealing with terrorists' potential abuse of virtual currencies. The amendment passed by voice vote.

The House approved the overall bill on a vote of 386–31 on July 17, 2019. Voting yes were 226 Democrats and 171 Republicans. Voting no were 7 Democrats, 23 Republicans, and one independent.

The bill, officially named the Damon Paul Nelson and Matthew Young Pollard Intelligence Authorization Act for Fiscal Years 2018, 2019, and 2020, included reauthorization of various intelligence activities. The House had passed reauthorization bills for the past two years, but the Senate had not voted on them.

The bill's provisions would

- Set up a program of paid parental leave for employees of the intelligence community, twelve weeks of leave in the year following the birth or adoption of a child;
- Require the DNI's office to report on policies within the intelligence community for awarding contracts involving certain foreign countries, assessing the security and counterintelligence risks;
- Establish a Climate Science Advisory Council within the DNI's office to help assess climate security issues; and
- Move the National Intelligence University from the Defense Intelligence Agency to the office of the DNI.

The bill was received in the Senate July 18, and was referred to the Intelligence Committee. There was no further action.

Extending Surveillance Authorities

On March 16, 2020, Senate Majority Leader Mitch McConnell, R-Ky., introduced legislation, S 3501, designed to give lawmakers extra time to authorize various foreign intelligence programs. The Senate passed McConnell's amendment by voice vote that same day and sent it to the House, which did not vote on the bill.

The measure was necessitated because Congress had allowed certain provisions relating to surveillance powers to lapse. It would provide a seventy-seven-day extension, allowing members a chance to review issues relating to surveillance and privacy; lawmakers had been thrown off balance by the onset of the COVID pandemic. The provisions brought back under McConnell's measure included orders permitting the collection of people's business and other records through the Foreign Intelligence Surveillance Act (FISA) court, a roving wiretap provision allowing the government to target people who employ burner devices or often change phone lines to avoid being wiretapped traditionally, and "Lone Wolf" authorities permitting the FISA court to surveil possible terrorists operating outside formal networks. S 3501 retroactively approved the use of these provisions during the weekend the provisions were allowed to lapse.

Fiscal Year 2021 Intelligence Authorization Bill

In 2020, Congress passed language authorizing appropriations for intelligence programs for Fiscal Year 2021, which began October 1, 2020. The language, originally in a bill specifically focused on homeland security, HR 7856, was eventually incorporated into a massive appropriations bill, HR 133, which was signed into law (PL 116-260) on December 27, 2020, by President Donald Trump.

The original bill, HR 7856, was introduced July 30, 2020, by Intelligence Committee chair Rep. Adam Schiff, D-Calif. The measure included language authorizing a 1 percent increase in the U.S. intelligence community's fiscal 2021

budget over the administration's request. It asked the intelligence community to focus on Russia and China, in addition to climate change and pandemics. Agencies funded under the bill included the CIA, the National Security Agency, and the Military Intelligence Program. The overall funding level sought by the bill was classified.

The committee marked the bill up on July 31, in a closed session, and the measure was approved on a vote of 11–8, reportedly along party lines.

Among the provisions in the bill were some seemingly directed at the Trump administration and its actual or potential actions. One would make it illegal for federal officials to communicate details about a whistleblower at a spy agency to anyone involved in possible wrongdoing in the whistleblower's complaint. Another would make it illegal for a U.S. political campaign to take opposition research from a foreign national. The bill also would require the intelligence agencies to let Congress know if an administration asked for intelligence community support to combat domestic protests.

On the Senate side, the Senate Intelligence Committee marked up a bill introduced June 8, 2020, by interim committee chair Sen. Marco Rubio, R-Fla. The measure, S 3905, was considered that day by the committee in closed session and reported favorably on a vote of 14–1. The only senator voting against the measure was Sen. Ron Wyden, D-Ore. Ultimately, the authorization for intelligence programs' appropriations was included in HR 133, which was approved by both houses of Congress and signed into law in late December 2020.

Financial Crimes and Terrorism

In 2019, the House passed legislation, HR 56, that would look into new financial technologies and their use by terrorists. It would establish an Independent Financial Technology Task Force to Combat Terrorism and Illicit Financing, tell the Treasury Department to give a reward to someone who provides information leading to the conviction of a person involved with terrorist use of digital currencies, and set up the FinTech Leadership in Innovation and Financial Intelligence Program to help develop programs to find terrorist and illicit use of digital currencies. The measure, the Financial Technology Protection Act, was introduced January 3, 2019, by Rep. Ted Budd, R-N.C.

Budd had introduced similar legislation, HR 5036, in the 115th Congress. It was approved unanimously by the House Committee on Financial Services and passed by voice vote in the House. It stalled in the Senate.

This time around, the House again passed the bill by voice vote, on January 28, 2019. But once again, the measure did not progress in the Senate. It was received in the Senate January 29, 2019, and referred to the Committee on Banking, Housing, and Urban Affairs. There was no further progress.

Terrorist Use of Virtual Currencies

In 2019, the House passed legislation that required the Department of Homeland Security to make a threat assessment about terrorists' use of virtual currency. The bill was introduced January 10, 2019, by Rep. Kathleen Rice, D-N.Y. It called for the undersecretary for intelligence and analysis to prepare the assessment, along with other federal agencies, by 120 days from the bill's enactment. The information would be shown to state and local law enforcement.

On January 29, the House approved the bill by a vote of 422–3. The bill was received in the Senate that day and referred to the Senate Committee on Homeland Security and Governmental Affairs. There was no further action. In the previous Congress, the House passed an equivalent bill, but it failed to advance in the Senate.

Reauthorizing September 11 Victim Compensation Fund

In 2019, Congress passed legislation that in effect permanently reauthorized the September 11 Victim Compensation Fund of 2001. The measure, HR 1327, the Never Forget the Heroes bill, was introduced February 25, 2019, by Rep. Carolyn Maloney, D-N.Y. It would reauthorize the fund compensating victims of the terrorist attack of September 11, 2001, through Fiscal Year 2090. Claims could be filed through October 2089.

The fund was due to expire in December 2020, but claimants, including first responders with cancer diagnoses relating to their work in the wake of the attacks, continued to seek compensation. Originally intended to address those killed or injured in the attacks, a later version of the fund included help to people killed or affected by illnesses related to the attack. The current version called for a payment cap from the fund of $7.38 billion—an amount seen as inadequate to meet the victims' needs.

The House Judiciary Committee marked up the bill on June 12, 2019, and approved it by voice vote. On the House floor July 12, lawmakers approved the bill on an overwhelming vote of 402–12.

In the Senate, however, Sens. Mike Lee, R-Utah, and Rand Paul, R-Ky., raised obstacles. Lee placed a hold on the bill, and Paul objected when Sen. Kirsten Gillibrand, D-N.Y., called for unanimous consent to call up the bill for voting. Both senators tended to object to new spending unless paid for by cutting something else in the budget. Gillibrand sponsored the Senate version of the bill, S 546.

A Congressional Budget Office estimate predicted the bill would cost about $10.2 billion in its first decade with additional costs in subsequent years. The measure reached the Senate floor July 23, after Lee and Paul were given the right to offer amendments. Paul's amendment would seek cuts in various mandatory government programs to pay for the bill; it was defeated, 22–77. Lee's amendment would

cap the fund at $10.2 billion in the first decade and an additional $10 billion through 2092; it was defeated 32–66. Ultimately, the Senate voted 97–2 to approve the bill.

President Donald Trump signed it into law (PL 116-34) on July 29.

Acquisition Review Board in Homeland Security Department

In 2019, the House passed legislation, HR 2609, that would require the Department of Homeland Security (DHS) to create an Acquisition Review Board. The board would strengthen uniformity and accountability within the department's acquisition review process, review major acquisitions of at least $300 million, and review best practices. The bill was introduced May 15, 2019, by Rep. Dan Crenshaw, R-Texas.

On May 15, the House Homeland Security Committee approved the measure by voice vote. The bill was approved by the full House on June 11, on a vote of 419–0. It was received in the Senate the following day and referred to the Committee on Homeland Security and Governmental Affairs. There was no further action.

Border Security

In 2019, the House passed legislation that would create a new structure for dealing with migrants at the U.S.–Mexico border. The bill, HR 2203, was introduced April 10, 2019, by Rep. Veronica Escobar, D-Texas. The Trump administration's controversial policy of separating families at the border formed the political backdrop for this bill. As a result, the bill had strong support among Democrats and was opposed by Republicans. The Senate did not take it up.

The measure was referred to the committees on Homeland Security, Judiciary, and Ways and Means. On July 17, the Homeland Security Committee marked up the bill. At the markup, Rep. Mike Rogers, R-Ala., the ranking Republican on the committee, complained that Committee Chair Rep. Bennie Thompson, D-Miss., had introduced a substitute amendment without enough notification. Rogers attempted to strike consideration of the substitute amendment, but his move was rejected along party lines, 11–16. Thompson's substitute amendment, which would create a commission charged with investigating the treatment of migrants along the border by U.S. Customs and Border Protection (CPB), was adopted 16–12.

Among its other provisions, the bill would forbid a parent or legal guardian from being taken away from a child at, or near, a point of entry unless it was in the child's best interest; require the Department of Homeland Security to take people stopped by CBP to a long-term facility within seventy-two hours; and would not allow rules by the executive branch that turn away applications for asylum from migrants not applying in countries they travel through, force these applicants to wait outside the United States as their immigration proceedings continue, and limit the number of asylum applicants at a given port of entry.

The committee turned aside various Republican-sponsored amendments, including one by Rep. Debbie Lesko, R-Ariz., that would make changes in the bill's language, including adding a requirement that the comptroller general consider the effect of CBP rescue efforts on migrant deaths. The amendment was defeated along party lines, 11–16. Thompson and Lesko agreed to work on considering language for an amendment granting extra protections to minors trafficked across the border. Another amendment, by Rep. John Joyce, R-Pa., would eliminate language dealing with the establishment of a ten-member commission. It was rejected on a party line 11–16 vote. Among other amendments was one by Rep. Clay Higgins, R-La., that, among other changes, would eliminate language forbidding migrants from being kept in short-term detention more than seventy-two hours. This amendment also was rejected on an 11–16 party line vote.

The measure ran into difficulty after its passage, as there was debate among Democrats about various provisions in the bill. Three provisions were removed from the bill: one that blocked a Trump policy of having migrants wait in Mexico while their case was underway; one that would end a CPB practice of limiting the number of asylum applicants at a given entry point; and one that would repeal Trump's policy of forcing asylum seekers to try for asylum in other countries they passed through before reaching the United States.

On September 25, 2019, the House approved the bill on a vote of 230–194. The yea votes were all from Democrats. All Republicans voted against it, along with one Democrat and one independent. As passed, the bill's provisions included the establishment of a DHS ombudsman, the implementation of departmental accountability standards, and a border oversight panel. The ombudsman would make yearly evaluations of training programs for CPB and Immigration and Customs Enforcement (ICE) agents. During House consideration of the bill, members rejected an effort by Rep. Mark Green, R-Tenn., to recommit the bill back to the Homeland Security Committee to make changes. Green's effort failed on a 207–216 vote.

The bill was received in the Senate on September 26 and referred to the Committee on Homeland Security and Governmental Affairs. There was no further action.

Medical Screenings

In 2019, the House passed legislation that would establish uniform medical screenings for people stopped at the U.S.–Mexico border. The bill, HR 3525, the U.S. Border Patrol Medical Screening Standards Act, was introduced June 27, 2019, by Rep. Lauren Underwood, D-Ill.

The measure was referred to the Committee on Homeland Security, which marked up the bill July 17, 2019. Underwood added language requiring that migrants receive screening for vital signs; that a pediatric medical

expert be at every U.S. border patrol sector including processing centers and border facilities where 20 percent or more of the detainees are minors; and that the Department of Homeland Security (DHS) establish an electronic health records system and assess that system within 120 days. Underwood's amendment was passed by voice vote, as was the overall bill.

Among other components, the bill called for uniform medical processes to be established within thirty days of the bill's being signed into law and for DHS to screen the migrants they apprehended within twelve hours of stopping them. The House debated HR 3525 on September 26, 2019. Rep. Mark Green, R-Tenn., moved to recommit the bill back to the committee with instructions, seeking a change in the bill's language, but his motion was defeated on a vote of 202–213. The House then approved the bill on a vote of 230–184.

The measure was received in the Senate October 15, 2019. It was referred to the Committee on the Judiciary. There was no further action.

Border Wall

Congress voted in 2019 to block President Donald Trump from using military construction funds for his controversial wall along the U.S.–Mexico border, but Trump vetoed the measure, SJ Res 54, and Congress did not have the votes to override the veto.

Trump had declared a national emergency along the border in February 2019, a strategy that allowed him to move $3.6 billion in funds that had already been allocated to military construction projects, to help build his wall. The wall, part of his hardline approach to immigration, had been a key campaign pledge; at the time he had said Mexico would pay for it, which did not end up happening.

Sen. Tom Udall introduced SJ Res 54 on September 10, 2019. It called for an end to the national emergency, thus stopping Trump's ability to tap the military construction funds for the wall. The Senate Armed Services Committee discharged the measure September 25 by unanimous consent.

The measure reached the Senate floor the same day, and it passed the Senate on a vote of 54–41. Forty-three Democrats and eleven Republicans voted for the measure, while the no votes were all from Republicans. However, this margin was not enough to override an almost certain veto by Trump. The president already had vetoed a similar measure, HJ Res. 46, that had passed both houses of Congress earlier in the year but failed to reach the two-thirds threshold to override.

On September 27, the measure passed the House on a vote of 236–174. The yes votes came from 224 Democrats, 11 Republicans, and one independent; the no votes all came from Republicans. Again, this was not enough to override a veto—and Trump indeed opted to veto the bill October 15. The Senate took the measure up again October 17, but the vote, 53–36, failed to override Trump's veto.

Fiscal Year 2020 Homeland Security Appropriations

Congress approved spending for fiscal 2020 homeland security priorities as part of a larger appropriations bill in December 2019 and the bill was signed into law (PL 116-93). The bill included $50.47 billion in discretionary spending on homeland security.

The Trump administration, earlier that year, had requested $51.68 billion in discretionary spending. The House and Senate each produced their own bill, but differences—especially over whether to fund President Donald Trump's controversial wall between the U.S. and Mexico—led to delays in the process.

On June 11, 2019, the House Appropriations Committee marked up their version of the fiscal 2019 homeland security appropriations bill, HR 3931, and approved it along party lines, 29–20. The measure did not include any money for Trump's border wall. The bill would provide $63.8 billion in discretionary spending. It would offer a lower amount for both Immigration and Customs Enforcement (ICE) and Customs and Border Protection (CBP) than the previous year. ICE would get $7.67 billion and CBP, $13.8 billion.

In consideration of the bill, the committee adopted a manager's amendment by voice vote that included a requirement that ICE not make the deportation of people in danger in their home countries a priority. The manager's amendment also required, among other things, that money be used for social workers, medical professionals, and pediatricians to work with detained children.

The committee also adopted by voice vote an amendment by Rep. Debbie Wasserman Schultz, D-Fla., that would grant access to members of Congress, without notice, into immigrant detention facilities. Among other amendments approved was one by Rep. David Price, D-N.C., that would prevent federal dollars from being used to implement various Trump administration immigration policies; among them, it would essentially protect recipients of Deferred Action for Immigrant Children (DACA), undocumented immigrants brought to the United States as children. Price's amendment later came under scrutiny when a Congressional Budget Office estimate said it had brought the cost of the overall bill above the allotted limit.

Among the amendments rejected by the committee was an effort by Rep. Chuck Fleischmann, R-Tenn., to add $5 billion for the wall, the amount approved by the White House. It was turned down on a vote of 21–29; all Democrats and Rep. Will Hurd, R-Texas, voted against it, and all the yea votes were from Republicans.

The Senate, meanwhile, included $5 billion for the wall in its homeland security appropriations bill. On September 26, 2019, the Senate Appropriations Committee marked up its bill, S 2582, which included $53.2 billion in discretionary spending for homeland security. The bill offered $8.4 billion for ICE and $18.1 billion for CBP. Supporting the measure were sixteen Republicans and Sen. Joe Manchin, D-W.Va., and opposing it were fourteen Democrats.

CONGRESSIONAL RESPONSE TO DOMESTIC TERRORISM

In the years following the September 11, 2001, attacks on the United States, terrorism dominated many of the nation's headlines. The focus was on terrorism from abroad, as the 9/11 hijackers had come from Saudi Arabia and other Middle Eastern countries. And that focus continued, even though during the period of Donald Trump's presidency, domestic terrorism was a key issue facing the country. Domestic terrorism, according to the FBI, consists of "Violent, criminal acts committed by individuals and/or groups to further ideological goals stemming from domestic influences, such as those of a political, religious, social, racial, or environmental nature."

In August 2017, a "Unite the Right" rally in Charlottesville, Virginia, bringing together a variety of white supremacist groups, ended in bloodshed when a white supremacist rammed his car into a crowd of counterprotestors on August 12, 2017, leaving one woman dead. Trump declared at a news conference at Trump Tower in New York City on August 15, 2017, that there were "very fine people on both sides" of the issue. His comments would set the tone for much of his administration's response to domestic terrorism issues, especially issues involving right-wing domestic terrorism.

Much of the domestic terrorism taking place during the 2017–2020 period was caused by white supremacists. In 2020, white supremacists and their allies caused two-thirds of the incidents in the United States, according to data from the Center for Strategic & International Studies (CSIS). According to CSIS, there were 110 domestic terror attacks and plots that year, the most since data began to be collected in 1994; of those attacks, two-thirds were perpetrated by far-right actors and about 23 percent by those on the far left.

In Congress, little was accomplished on the issue of domestic terrorism. In 2020, the House passed the Domestic Terrorism Prevention Act of 2020, or HR 5602, introduced by Rep. Brad Schneider, D-Ill., on January 14, 2020. The bill sought to create new requirements to widen the availability of information on domestic terrorism and the links between it and hate crimes. Among other requirements, the bill would ask domestic terrorism workers in the Department of Homeland Security (DHS), the Department of Justice (DOJ), and the Federal Bureau of Investigation (FBI) to write joint reports on the issue and institute an interagency group to look into white supremacist and neo-Nazi involvement in the armed forces and federal law enforcement agencies.

The House Judiciary Committee marked up the bill March 11, 2020, on a vote of 24–2. During debate on the measure, some Republicans on the committee said they wanted the bill to include information on conservatives being threatened for their views. Rep. Greg Steube, R-Fla., introduced an amendment that would add the antifascist movement antifa and the Black Hebrew Israelite movement, as well as crimes against police. The amendment was adopted by voice vote. Other amendments under discussion included one from Rep. Ken Buck, R-Colo., seeking to add eighty-eight threats against conservatives to the bill. It was rejected on a party line vote of 9–19.

The House approved the bill by voice vote on September 21, 2020. It was referred to the Senate Judiciary Committee the following day but did not see Senate action.

Schneider had introduced similar legislation, HR 4918, on February 2, 2018. It was referred to the Judiciary and Homeland Security committees and later to various subcommittees but did not see further action.

Domestic terrorism legislation under consideration in Congress also included bills from Sen. Dick Durbin, D-Ill., who introduced S 894 on March 27, 2019, and S 3190 on January 14, 2020. Both bills would authorize dedicated offices in DHS, DOJ, and the FBI, to focus on domestic terrorism. They were referred to the Senate Judiciary Committee but did not see further action.

The events in Charlottesville were not the only high-profile incidences of domestic terrorism during the Trump administration. From 2017 to 2019, a series of mass shootings occurred in high schools, places of worship, and other locations.

In 2017, a gunman killed sixty people and wounded hundreds more at a country music festival in Las Vegas in the deadliest mass shooting in U.S. history. The same year, a gunman killed twenty-six people worshipping in a church in Sutherland Springs, Texas. Even Congress was not immune to the violence: a gunman shot at participants practicing for a congressional baseball game, seriously wounding Rep. Steve Scalise, R-La., a member of the House GOP leadership, and several other people.

In 2018, a gunman killed seventeen people at Marjory Stoneman Douglas High School in Florida. The same year, a gunman killed ten people at Santa Fe High School in Texas. A gunman killed twelve people at a country music bar in Thousand Oaks, California. And a gunman killed eleven people at the Tree of Life Synagogue in Pittsburgh as they were worshipping.

In 2019, a gunman, targeting Latinos, killed twenty-three people in a Walmart store in El Paso, Texas. Also in 2019, a gunman killed twelve people at a municipal building in Virginia Beach, Virginia.

Among the amendments under consideration was one from Sen. Jon Tester, D-Mont., that would take the $5 billion for the wall out of the bill and replace it with other priorities. It was rejected on a 14–17 vote, with Republicans and Manchin opposing it. Another Tester amendment taking funding out for the wall was rejected on a party line vote, 15–16. Among other amendments was one from Sen. Jeff Merkley, D-Ore., that would require timely medical

The COVID pandemic resulted in fewer people gathering in public, so 2020 did not see the same level of mass gun attacks. But 2020 did see other incidents, including an attempted kidnapping of Michigan Governor Gretchen Whitmer, a Democrat, by members of armed paramilitary groups opposed to her COVID-related restrictions.

In 2019 and 2020, Congress held a handful of hearings focused specifically on domestic terrorism. In 2019, after Democrats had taken control of the House, Homeland Security Committee Chair Rep. Bennie Thompson, D-Miss., opened a May 8 hearing on domestic terrorism with a statement criticizing the lack of attention paid to the issue under Republican leadership. He stated that "in recent years, we have seen a dramatic and disturbing rise in domestic terrorism—particularly far-right extremist violence tied to white supremacist extremism and white nationalism." Witnesses included officials from DHS, the DOJ, and the FBI.

Later that year, on September 6, 2019, the House Judiciary subcommittee on immigration and citizenship held a field hearing in El Paso, Texas, which is on the U.S.–Mexico border. The subject of the hearing was "Oversight of the Trump Administration's Border Policies and the Relationship Between Anti-Immigrant Rhetoric and Domestic Terrorism."

Rep. Jerrold Nadler, D-N.Y., the chair of the full Judiciary Committee, in his opening statement blamed the Trump administration for using "racist and inflammatory language against immigrants," adding, "Language such as this is dangerous and can have tragic consequences. The perpetrator of the horrific mass shooting here in El Paso last month used the term 'invasion' in his hate-filled manifesto and later told law enforcement officials that he was targeting 'Mexicans.'"

Meanwhile, on the Senate side, Sen. Ron Johnson, R-Wisc., chair of the Homeland Security Committee, held hearings on September 25, 2019, on the subject of "Countering Domestic Terrorism: Examining the Evolving Threat." Witnesses included scholars and an official from the Anti-Defamation League, George Selim, the group's senior vice president for national programs.

In his opening statement, Selim expressed outrage that more was not being done to combat domestic terrorism. He cited examples of domestic terrorism that included the El Paso shooting and the Tree of Life shooting, as well as a 2019 attack on a synagogue in Poway, California, that left one woman dead. "From my government experience, had these attacks been committed by ISIS, I can guarantee you the national security structure would be in crisis mode at this pernicious and severe threat to our communities. Where is that outrage and whole-of-government mobilization in the face of white supremacist terrorism?"

Selim also was called as a witness before a hearing January 15, 2020, of the House Financial Services Committee, which was looking into how domestic terrorism and extremism are funded. The same day, the House Homeland Security Committee's intelligence and counterterrorism subcommittee held the first of two hearings about antisemitic domestic terrorism.

At the hearing on antisemitism, subcommittee Chair Rep. Max Rose, D-N.Y., mentioned legislation he had introduced, the Raising the Bar Act, which aimed to set up a voluntary program to grade social media companies on their efforts to moderate terrorist content on their platforms. The bill, HR 5209, had been introduced on November 21, 2019, and referred to the Homeland Security Committee, but it did not see any action. Rose's subcommittee held a second hearing February 26, 2020, on antisemitic domestic terrorism.

FBI director Christopher Wray, appearing at a House Homeland Security Committee hearing September 17, 2020, on terrorist threats to the U.S. homeland, cited lone wolf actors as the biggest threat: "We see this lone actor threat manifested both within Domestic Violent Extremists ("DVEs") and Homegrown Violent Extremists ("HVEs"), two distinct sets of individuals that generally self-radicalize and mobilize to violence on their own." Within the group of domestic violent extremists, Wray said the top threat came from those identified as having racial or ethnic motivations.

Throughout the four years of Trump's presidency, his 2017 remarks about "very fine people" overshadowed any discussion of domestic extremism. Critics said he effectively winked and nodded at white supremacism; for example, at the first presidential debate between Trump and Biden on September 29, 2020, Trump referred to the Proud Boys, a white supremacist right-wing group, telling them to "stand back and stand by," which they—and many others—took as an endorsement of their activities. And he and his allies insisted that left-wing groups such as participants in the antifa movement were to blame for homegrown problems.

After Trump insisted that he had won the 2020 presidential election, a mob of his supporters attacked the U.S. Capitol on January 6, 2021, in an effort to stop lawmakers from certifying Biden's win. In the wake of the attack, the House impeached Trump for allegedly inciting an insurrection. The Senate acquitted him.

attention for children in DHS custody. It was rejected 14–17, with Republicans and Manchin in opposition.

Congress passed a continuing resolution September 27 that included homeland security funding; the fiscal year would end in a few days. On December 20, DHS appropriations were included in a larger bill that became PL 116–93. Ultimately, $1.375 billion in border wall funding was approved, the same amount as the previous year.

Among other provisions, the bill provided $14.9 billion for CBP and $8.1 billion for ICE.

Fiscal Year 2021 Homeland Security Appropriations

The fiscal year 2021 homeland security appropriations were approved in late 2020 as part of a larger spending bill (PL 116-260). The bill included the regular discretionary spending for Department of Homeland Security programs, as well as $2 billion in emergency supplemental appropriations for the Federal Emergency Management Agency (FEMA)'s Disaster Relief Fund to pay for COVID-related funeral expenses.

The House Appropriations Committee approved its fiscal 2021 homeland security appropriations bill, HR 7669, on July 15, 2020, on a 30–22 party line vote. It would provide $50.7 billion in homeland security spending. The bill would provide $14.6 billion for Customs and Border Protection (CBP) and $7.4 billion for Immigration and Customs Enforcement (ICE). It would stop ICE from using information gained from detained children in counseling sessions for enforcement purposes.

Among the amendments considered was one by Rep. Pete Aguilar, D-Calif., and Rep. Will Hurd, R-Texas, that would protect Dreamers—undocumented immigrants brought to the United States as children—from deportation; it was approved. Another amendment, by Rep.

Lucille Roybal-Allard, D-Calif., chair of the homeland security appropriations subcommittee, sought to allow international students to study in the United States even if their educational institutions offered only online courses during the pandemic. It was approved. The overall bill did not allow for additional spending on Trump's border wall, and Rep. Chuck Fleischmann, R-Tenn., proposed an amendment to allow border wall and additional immigration enforcement spending, but it failed, 22–30.

The House measure had been set for floor consideration as part of a massive appropriations package, but House Democratic leaders pulled it in July due to concerns including opposition from progressive Democrats opposed to the DHS agencies' role in enforcing immigration policies.

The Senate Appropriations Committee released a draft homeland security appropriations bill on November 10, 2020, that would provide $69.8 billion in spending. The Senate bill would give Trump almost $2 billion for his border wall, part of $15.5 billion that would go to CBP. ICE would get $8.8 billion.

Ultimately, interim spending bills were passed before the major consolidated bill was approved in late December. It allowed almost $1.4 billion for the border wall. Overall, it would provide about $69.9 billion in discretionary spending for homeland security, including almost $8 billion for ICE and $15 billion for CBP.

CHAPTER 4

Foreign Policy

Foreign Policy

During President Donald Trump's first and only term, protracted conflicts in the Middle East, including the ongoing wars in Syria and Yemen, as well as U.S. relations with allies in the region, were an important focus area for foreign policy legislation. Increased attention was also paid to U.S.–Russia relations, as Trump sought warmer relations with President Vladimir Putin amid mounting allegations and evidence that Russia had worked to influence the outcome of the 2016 election. Additionally, Trump's initiation of a so-called trade war with China prompted both members of Congress and administration officials to pursue a tougher stance against Beijing. China's neighbor, North Korea, also drew the administration's attention with its continued tests of ballistic missile and nuclear weapons technology, despite multiple rounds of sanctions meant to deter such activity.

At the start of his term, Republicans controlled both the House and Senate, but while Trump demanded and generally got their support, lawmakers did present some resistance to administration positions. Most notably, House and Senate appropriators repeatedly rejected Trump's proposed cuts to U.S. foreign assistance and contributions to the United Nations (UN). They also pushed for sanctions against Russia and Saudi Arabia—two countries with which Trump was keen to maintain alliances and build stronger relations. Democrats took control of the House midway through Trump's presidency, but outside of proposals for more extensive state-foreign operations spending, the change in leadership did not have a significant impact on foreign policy legislation considered during the 116th Congress, as many of the major bills were put forward by the Senate.

MIDDLE EASTERN CONFLICTS

When Trump took office, the Syrian civil war was entering its sixth year and showed no signs of abating despite repeated multiparty efforts to negotiate ceasefires and peace talks between the government of President Bashar al-Assad and rebel forces. The United States had reluctantly entered into the conflict in 2013, following United Nations confirmation that Assad's regime had attacked Syrian civilians with chemical weapons. Dozens of similar chemical attacks have since been conducted, and government airstrikes have repeatedly targeted civilian facilities and gathering places. Trump ordered targeted retaliatory strikes in response, and U.S. officials pushed for additional sanctions against the Syrian government and its supporters, as well as new UN Security Council resolutions condemning the Assad regime's actions. In 2018, Trump unexpectedly announced his intent to withdraw from the conflict, surprising lawmakers and high-ranking administration officials. His subsequent withdrawal of U.S. troops from northeastern Syria in October 2019 was met with considerable criticism in Congress, because it allowed the Turkish government to attack Syrian Kurds who were working with the rebel forces.

In Yemen, the ongoing conflict between the internationally recognized government of President Abdu Rabbu Mansour Hadi and the Houthi rebels who had pushed him out of office continued to exacerbate an unprecedented humanitarian crisis. The conflict, which had effectively become a proxy war between the Iranian-backed Houthis and a pro-Hadi coalition led by Saudi Arabia, resulted in the deaths of tens of thousands of Yemenis and pushed the country to the brink of famine. The contributing role that Saudi airstrikes played in this growing crisis raised questions about U.S. involvement in the conflict, which had to date centered on providing logistical and intelligence support for the Saudi-led coalition. According to the UN, roughly one-third of the airstrikes attributed to the coalition hit nonmilitary targets, killing civilians, destroying infrastructure, and hampering the delivery of humanitarian assistance. Concerns about the Saudi airstrikes prompted lawmakers to consider several resolutions reducing or withdrawing U.S. support for the conflict.

The Saudi government's actions, and the United States' alliance with it, were also called into question in the fall of 2018. Jamal Khashoggi, a Saudi journalist living in self-imposed exile in the United States, disappeared during an appointment at the Saudi consulate in Turkey. Khashoggi was a staunch critic of the Saudi royal family, including Crown Prince Mohammed bin Salman, who had been leading a push to quell dissent at home and abroad. Investigators later determined that Khashoggi had been assassinated by a team of Saudi agents. The U.S. intelligence community concluded those agents were acting on

orders from the crown prince, prompting outrage in Congress. Lawmakers demanded the Saudi government be held accountable for the incident, and pushed legislation condemning Khashoggi's murder, imposing new sanctions on Saudi officials, and restricting arms sales to the country. It also influenced lawmakers' stance on the conflict in Yemen, causing some Republicans who previously supported U.S. involvement in that war to call for withdrawal or a more limited scope of activity. Saudi officials denied the allegations, and Trump maintained that there was no conclusive evidence linking the crown prince with Khashoggi's death. He also emphasized that preserving the U.S.–Saudi partnership was critical, regardless of the tragedy, and exercised his veto power over congressional efforts to block a multibillion arms deal with the country.

With regard to Iran, Trump continued to criticize the Joint Comprehensive Plan of Action (JCPOA). The deal, under which Iran agreed to certain limitations on its nuclear activities, had taken effect in January 2016 and resulted in the lifting of select U.S. sanctions against the country. Trump was required by law to certify Iranian compliance with the deal every ninety days, which he did twice during his first year in office. In October 2017, however, Trump declined to certify the agreement, saying Iran had violated the deal's terms, despite the International Atomic Energy Agency's findings to the contrary. The United States remained a party to the JCPOA and Trump did not seek the renewal of related sanctions, but lawmakers in Congress—many of whom also criticized the deal and were skeptical Iran would abide by it long term—pursued other measures to tighten oversight of Iran's financial assets and business dealings.

RUSSIA

U.S.–Russia relations were often in the spotlight during Trump's presidency, due to the U.S. intelligence community's assessment that Russia tried to influence the 2016 presidential election through cyberattacks and disinformation campaigns, and that it did so with the goal of improving Trump's chances of winning. Reports of multiple contacts between Trump associates and Russian intelligence agents, including a purported discussion about potentially easing sanctions against Russian individuals and entities, added to

concerns about Russian meddling. In May 2017, Deputy Attorney General Rod Rosenstein appointed Robert S. Mueller III, a former director of the Federal Bureau of Investigation, as special counsel to lead an independent investigation into possible links or coordination between the Russian government and Trump campaign officials. Although Mueller confirmed that Russia attempted to influence the election, he also concluded that this effort was not coordinated with the Trump campaign. Trump claimed vindication and resumed his push for closer ties with Putin. He repeatedly denied the U.S. intelligence community's conclusions about malign Russian activities, for example, including his widely criticized statement during a joint press conference with Putin that while he had "great confidence" in his intelligence people, Putin was "extremely strong and powerful in his denial" that Russia meddled in the 2016 election. Trump also dismissed as "fake news" intelligence community reports that Russia offered to pay the Taliban bounties for U.S. soldiers killed in Afghanistan. Lawmakers remained concerned about Russian influence, however, and proposed various measures seeking either to prevent the easing of sanctions or impose new sanctions, as well as bolstering U.S. cybersecurity.

CHINA

A key element of Trump's campaign platform and his presidential agenda was combatting what he declared to be China's "unfair trade practices," including the provision of preferential treatment for state-owned businesses. At the beginning of 2018, his administration began implementing a series of tariffs on Chinese products and other trade barriers to try to pressure Beijing to change its practices, while providing a boost to U.S. manufacturing and reducing the U.S. trade deficit. Lawmakers in Congress appeared to take some cues from the administration's tougher stance on China: According to the Center for Strategic and International Studies, more than 360 China-related bills and another 75 nonbinding resolutions were introduced during the 116th Congress. While many of these focused on trade and commerce, several measures specifically targeted China's alleged human rights violations, including the unlawful detention and forced labor of ethnic and Muslim minorities.

Chronology of Action on Foreign Policy

2017–2018

The 115th Congress had limited success passing major foreign policy legislation during Trump's first two years in office, due in part to competing priorities. Fiscal 2018 and fiscal 2019 appropriations negotiations, for example, were not only delayed, they were also prolonged by partisan disagreements over immigration policy and border security. Additionally, a focus on passing significant tax reform legislation in 2017 prevented many measures that had been approved in one chamber from being considered by the other before year end.

Among the bills that did not pass due to a full legislative calendar were measures establishing new cybersecurity programs to protect internet-connected technologies at the U.S. State Department. Legislation imposing sanctions on Iranian financial assets and financial institutions that conduct transactions with North Korea also failed to pass both chambers. The latter was aimed at Chinese banks, whose services often help North Korea circumvent financial sanctions. Resolutions condemning Saudi Arabia's alleged role in Jamal Khashoggi's killing and withdrawing the United States from the Yemeni conflict gained approval in the Senate, but did not come up for consideration in the House before the end of the session. The incoming Democratic majority pledged to take up the measures in 2019.

Another failed effort in the Senate pushed for a new Authorization of the Use of Military Force (AUMF) specific to counterterrorism operations against the Taliban, al Qaeda, and affiliated extremist groups. The new AUMF would repeal or replace existing AUMFs that were approved following the September 11 terrorist attacks and had been used by several administrations to justify U.S. involvement in conflicts across the Middle East. The proposed bill did not proceed beyond the committee stage, however, because lawmakers could not agree on how much flexibility the AUMF should provide the president.

Congress did succeed in passing legislation requiring the president to impose new sanctions on certain individuals and entities in Russia, North Korea, and Iran. These measures were offered in response to concerns over Russian election meddling, North Korean weapons tests, and Iran's ballistic missile program, as well as its broader

influence in the Middle East. While the White House raised the possibility of a veto and Trump complained that the sanctions would harm U.S.–Russia relations and push American adversaries together, he ultimately signed the

Outlays for International Affairs

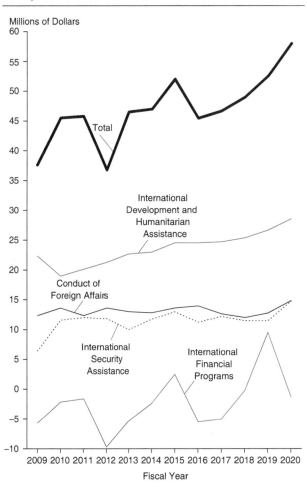

SOURCE: Office of Management and Budget, *Historical Tables, Budget of the United States Government: Fiscal Year 2021* (Washington D.C.: U.S. Government Printing Office, 2020), Table 3.2; * indicates estimate

NOTE: Total line includes some expenditures not shown separately. * indicates estimate

bill. Trump also signed a treaty document supporting the accession of Montenegro to the North Atlantic Treaty Organization (NATO) after the Senate consented to the treaty's ratification. Lawmakers characterized Montenegro's accession as important for countering Russian influence in the Balkans and bolstering the alliance's strength.

Fiscal Year 2018 State-Foreign Operations Funding

Negotiations over fiscal 2018 State-Foreign Operations appropriations were marked by several key challenges, including a major gap between the total spending levels proposed by the House and Senate. Fiscal 2018 was the first year for which newly inaugurated President Donald Trump could submit a budget, and his funding request for the U.S. State Department, United States Agency for International Development (USAID), and related agencies reflected both his dissatisfaction with the UN and his desire to significantly reduce U.S. foreign aid. The House's State-Foreign Operations appropriations package (HR 3362) more closely reflected the president's budget request, whereas the Senate rejected many of Trump's proposed cuts.

Overall, Trump proposed $54 billion in cuts to federal agencies, with the goal of reallocating those funds to defense spending. About $11 billion of that total was to come from the State Department's fiscal 2017 budget, making it the biggest target of Trump's spending cuts. Climate change prevention programs, such as USAID's Global Climate Change Initiative, would be eliminated under Trump's proposal, while funding for UN peacekeeping efforts, the World Bank and other development banks, and educational and cultural exchange programs would be reduced. Trump's budget also stipulated that economic and development aid be directed to countries of greatest strategic importance to the United States and that some military assistance be transformed from grants to loans.

Fiscal 2018 negotiations also began later in the year than usual, because Trump did not submit his budget request until March 15, 2017. (Such a delay is common for presidents in the first year of their first term.) Budget requests are typically submitted in February, with congressional subcommittees beginning their markup of appropriations language in March. In 2017, the House did not begin subcommittee markup until mid-June, leaving lawmakers in a crunch to get through as much of the appropriations process as possible before the August recess and beginning of the fiscal year on October 1.

The pressures of an already reduced timetable were exacerbated by a breakdown in deliberations over funding for the U.S. Department of Homeland Security—specifically, funds authorized for wall construction along the U.S.–Mexico border—and disagreements on immigration policy, which stalled progress on a consolidated appropriations package. Although Congress successfully passed several continuing resolutions to maintain funding while negotiations proceeded, the government shut down for three days in January while Trump and Senate Democrats discussed a possible solution to their divergence on immigration. The final fiscal 2018 omnibus was not approved until late March 2018—more than one year after Trump submitted his budget request.

House Action

The House Subcommittee on State, Foreign Operations, and Related Programs released its draft fiscal 2018 funding legislation on July 13. It proposed a smaller cut to state–foreign spending than Trump had, but still cut the topline budget by about $10 billion from fiscal 2017, for a total spend of $47.4 billion. That total included $12 billion for the war-related Overseas Contingency Operations (OCO) fund, which supports counterterrorism efforts in countries such as Pakistan, Iraq, and Afghanistan. It also included $1.5 billion for USAID operations, $6.1 billion for embassy security, $22.7 billion for bilateral economic assistance, and $8.8 billion for international security assistance to countries such as Israel ($3.1 billion), Egypt ($1.3 billion), and Jordan ($1.3 billion).

The bill supported many of the new administration's policy positions. One provision codified Trump's presidential memorandum expanding the application of the Mexico City Rule, which prohibits nongovernment organizations (NGOs) from receiving U.S. foreign aid if they perform or provide information about abortions. Under Trump's proposed expansion, the policy would be applied to *all* global public health programs, not just those that focus on family planning. Democrats staunchly oppose both the original rule and the proposed expansion, which lawmakers believe could adversely affect HIV/AIDS prevention and maternal and child health programs. The subcommittee's proposal also capped spending on family planning and reproductive health programs at $461 million and prohibited the provision of support to the UN Population Fund.

The UN Development Program and UN Women also saw funding cuts in the draft bill, with overall UN funding cut by about 18 percent. The bill also stipulated that the UN Human Rights Council would only receive funding if it enacted U.S.-sought changes to its transparency and Israel-related policies. Funding for the Intergovernmental Panel on Climate Change and Green Climate Fund—both UN-affiliated entities—was eliminated.

The full House Appropriations Committee conducted its markup of the bill on July 19. Democratic committee members pushed to amend the bill to remove the Mexico City Rule language and to restore support for UN initiatives and family planning programs, but these proposals were rejected. Perhaps the most notable change made to the bill was the addition of language prohibiting the secretary of state from executing organizational changes to the State Department or USAID without first obtaining congressional consent. This was a direct response to reports that the administration was considering an extensive

FOREIGN POLICY LEADERSHIP

The transition to a new presidential administration meant changes to every top foreign policy leadership position at the beginning of Trump's term in office. Many of these positions changed hands again midway through the Trump administration, due to several high-profile firings and resignations in 2018.

State Department

Speculation about who Trump would choose to be his secretary of state generated a list of potential candidates including former New York City mayor Rudolph Giuliani, former U.S. ambassador to the United Nations John Bolton, Senate Foreign Relations Committee Chair Bob Corker, R-Tenn., former speaker of the House Newt Gingrich, and South Carolina Gov. Nikki Haley. Giuliani was rumored to be the front runner until he withdrew his name from consideration, stating that he would focus on his private sector work instead.

Trump nominated Rex Tillerson, the CEO of ExxonMobil, on December 12, 2016. Tillerson's experience as head of a leading multinational oil and gas company gave some lawmakers cause for concern. Critics questioned the relationships Tillerson had developed with foreign leaders in his role as CEO, including Russian officials. During his tenure, for example, ExxonMobil signed a $500 billion deal with Russia for a joint drilling and shale development venture—a deal which prompted Putin to give Tillerson the Russian Order of Friendship Prize in 2013. The projects were ultimately delayed by the United States' imposition of sanctions against Russia for its aggressions toward Ukraine and Crimea.

Sen. Marco Rubio, R-Fla., was among the members of Senate Foreign Relations Committee who grilled Tillerson about his Russian connections during his confirmation hearing on January 11, 2017. Rubio asked Tillerson if he would consider Putin a war criminal because he authorized bombings of civilians in Syria and Chechnya, as well as if he would support additional sanctions against individuals involved in cyberattacks or seeking to undermine democratic institutions. Tillerson dodged many of these questions, but appeared to take a firmer stance than the president on some Russia-related issues, such as by stating that he would have recommended the United States provide arms and intelligence support to Ukraine in 2014 to help stop Russia's annexation of Crimea. Other senators probed Tillerson's stance on climate change, which he acknowledged the dangers of but said he did not consider it an imminent national security threat.

The committee ultimately approved Tillerson's nomination by a vote of 11–10 on January 23, 2017. He was confirmed by the full Senate on February 1 with a 56–43 vote.

Tillerson filled the top post at state for barely more than a year before Trump fired him on March 13, 2018. Tensions had reportedly been building between the two for months, as they repeatedly disagreed on various policy issues. Tillerson supported the nuclear deal with Iran, for example, and pushed Trump to recertify it, despite the president's disdain for the agreement. Tillerson also advocated a diplomatic approach to addressing the North Korean nuclear threat and supported talks with leadership versus Trump's threats of military action.

Central Intelligence Agency (CIA) Director Mike Pompeo was nominated as Tillerson's replacement. Democrats were strongly opposed to Pompeo's nomination because of his hawkish approach to foreign affairs. Sen. Rand Paul, R-Ky., also opposed Pompeo's nomination because of his support for the Iraq War and the use of harsh interrogation techniques. The Senate Foreign Relations Committee held Pompeo's confirmation hearing on April 12 and voted 11–9 to recommend his nomination on April 23. Pompeo was confirmed by the full Senate on April 26 by a vote of 57–42, with six Democrats voting in his favor.

John Sullivan was the deputy secretary of state under Tillerson and served as interim secretary between March 13 and April 26, 2018. Sullivan became the U.S. ambassador to Russia on December 20, 2019, at which point Stephen Biegun became deputy secretary.

United Nations

Trump nominated South Carolina Gov. Nikki Haley to serve as U.S. ambassador to the United Nations (UN) on November 23, 2016. Although Haley was widely viewed as a rising star in the Republican party, her selection was surprising. Haley frequently criticized Trump during the 2016 election cycle and had supported Rubio's primary campaign. She also lacked foreign policy experience.

Haley provided a clear contrast to Tillerson during her confirmation hearing on January 18, declaring Putin to be guilty of war crimes and advocating more sanctions against Russia. She was easily confirmed by the Senate on January 24, with a vote of 96–4, and became the first Indian American to serve on a presidential cabinet.

Like Tillerson, Haley did not remain in office for Trump's entire term. She announced her resignation on October 9, 2018, saying that she had accomplished her goals and wanted to return to the private sector. Trump nominated State Department spokesperson Heather Nauert to replace Haley, but Nauert withdrew from consideration in February 2019 after several reports surfaced that she hired a foreign nanny who was not authorized to work in the United States and that she had not paid the required nanny taxes in a timely manner.

(Continued)

FOREIGN POLICY LEADERSHIP (Continued)

After Nauert withdrew, Trump nominated Kelly Knight Craft, who had been serving as the U.S. ambassador to Canada since 2017. She had also served as an alternate delegate to the UN under former president George W. Bush. Craft's nomination was controversial, primarily because she is married to the CEO of one of the largest coal companies in the United States. During her confirmation hearing, Craft fielded questions about her knowledge of international issues, her position on climate change, and whether her family's business interests would interfere with her responsibilities as UN ambassador. Craft was confirmed by the Senate on July 31 in a mostly party-line vote and was sworn into office on September 12. Jonathan R. Cohen, the deputy representative to the UN under Haley, served as the interim ambassador until that time.

Central Intelligence Agency

Mike Pompeo was representing Kansas in the House when he was nominated to become Trump's first CIA director in November 2016. While Pompeo's fellow Republicans supported his nomination in the Senate, Democrats raised concerns that Pompeo supported expanded government surveillance of Americans' communications and the

increased collection of metadata by the National Security Agency. Democrats also expressed alarm at statements Pompeo made during his confirmation hearing on January 12, 2017, that indicated he was open to resuming the United States' use of waterboarding and other enhanced interrogation techniques. Although Democrats forced a three-day delay of Pompeo's confirmation vote, his nomination was ultimately approved by a full Senate vote of 66–32.

When Trump announced Pompeo's nomination to serve as secretary of state, he also nominated Pompeo's deputy, Gina Haspel, to become the new CIA director. Haspel's background as a former intelligence officer—and specifically her role in overseeing a CIA black site in Thailand where enhanced interrogation tactics were used—made her a controversial nominee. Several members of the Senate Select Committee on Intelligence had encouraged Trump to reconsider Haspel's nomination to the deputy position back in 2017 due to her alleged involvement in detainee torture and destruction of evidence of such treatment. However, Haspel had the support of several former CIA directors and directors of national intelligence. She also had enough support in the Senate to win confirmation on May 17, 2018, by a 54–45 vote, becoming the agency's first female director.

---

reorganization of both agencies, including the potential ending of certain core missions.

The bill was reported out of committee on July 24 by a unanimous vote. No further action was taken by the House.

Senate Action

The Senate was not expected to accept the size of the state-foreign operations cut proposed by the House. Indeed, the bill released by the Senate Appropriations Committee on September 7 (S 1780) provided $51.35 billion in funding—$4 billion more than the House proposal, and nearly $14 billion more than the president's request. Other key differences between the House and Senate bills include the Senate's proposed repeal of the Mexico City Rule, the provision of $585 million for bilateral family planning programs, and $37.5 million allocated to the UN Population Fund. The Senate bill provided more funding for UN peacekeeping efforts than that of the House, covering a minimum of 25 percent of the operations' estimated cost. Additionally, the Senate bill included the Taylor Force Act, which suspended roughly $328 million in economic assistance to the Palestinian Authority until it stopped making payments to the families of alleged terrorists who were killed or detained for attacking Israelis. No further action on this bill was taken by the Senate.

Consolidated Appropriations Negotiations

In early August, while both chambers were adjourned, the House Rules Committee announced that the House would take up consideration of eight appropriations bill when the summer recess concluded, including state-foreign operations, and called for the submission of amendments before the session resumed. (The House had approved a four-bill "minibus" in July.) Ultimately, these eight bills were combined with the minibus into one consolidated appropriations package (HR 3354).

Floor debate started on September 6 in the House and continued through September 14. A total of 342 amendments were considered during that time, but the Appropriations Committee's original state-foreign operations language was largely preserved. The bill was approved by a vote of 211–198 on September 14. Its total price tag of $1.23 trillion exceeded the spending caps set by the Budget Control Act (PL 112-25), meaning that lawmakers would either need to negotiate reduced appropriations or agree to new budget caps to avoid automatic spending cuts, also known as sequestration.

Once again, the House bill faced opposition in the Senate, where Democrats argued that topline spending levels were unrealistically low and objected to the inclusion of border wall funding in the homeland security portion of the omnibus. Lawmakers passed and Trump signed three

continuing resolutions to keep the government open while negotiations proceeded at a halting pace. The last of these measures extended government funding through January 19, 2018; a fourth measure failed to pass in the Senate before this deadline, prompting a three-day government shutdown from January 20 to January 22.

At issue was Trump's decision to rescind the Deferred Action for Childhood Arrivals (DACA) program in September 2017. Trump gave Congress until March 5, 2018, to come up with a replacement for the program, and Senate Democrats wanted to include language in the continuing resolution that would preserve protections for program participants, known as Dreamers. Senate Republicans were opposed to this approach, however. Senate Minority Leader Chuck Schumer, D-N.Y., met with Trump to negotiate a deal in which the Democrats agreed to provide more defense spending and border wall funding in exchange for Trump's support for legalizing Dreamers. But the White House later reversed course and sought further concessions from the Democrats, which they were unwilling to give. Only after Senate Majority Leader Mitch McConnell, R-Ky., promised to hold a vote on DACA and Dreamer status in February did Senate Democrats agree to approve a continuing resolution through February 9 that did not address either issue. A fifth continuing resolution was required to maintain government funding through March 23. Meanwhile, lawmakers negotiated a new two-year budget agreement (PL 115-123) to raise spending caps, providing relief from the threat of sequestration.

Final Omnibus

House and Senate foreign affairs committee leadership announced in early March that they had reached an agreement to resolve differences between their respective chambers' state–foreign operations spending proposals. The relevant text of the final omnibus bill (HR 1625) provided a total of $54 billion in funding for the State Department, USAID, and related agencies. The total included $11 billion in OCO funding for war-related activities, $9 billion for international security assistance, and $6 billion for embassy security. The bill maintained Trump's expanded Mexico City Policy, but it did not codify it. It increased funding for USAID family planning programs from $575 million to $608 million and provided $1.5 billion for UN contributions—a $108 million increase over fiscal 2017. The humanitarian relief budget also increased from the prior fiscal year, rising to a total of $7.6 billion. Of that amount, approximately $3.4 billion was provided for refugee assistance, while the remaining $4.3 billion was allocated for international disaster assistance. Another key provision increased funding for the Countering Russian Influence Fund from $150 million to $250 million.

The House approved the omnibus on March 22, and the Senate passed it the following day. Trump signed the bill into law on March 23 (PL 115-141).

Fiscal Year 2019 State-Foreign Operations Funding

No sooner had lawmakers approved fiscal 2018 funding than it was time to begin the fiscal 2019 appropriations process. Trump submitted his budget request to Congress on February 12, again proposing significant cuts to the State Department and other agencies to pay for increased defense spending, a border wall, and his administration's infrastructure plan. For fiscal 2019, Trump requested only $39.3 billion for state-foreign operations, with most spending reductions achieved through foreign aid cuts. However, Congress was not expected to follow the president's budget blueprint, since lawmakers had largely rejected similar cuts for fiscal 2018.

State-foreign operations funds were once again rolled into a consolidated appropriations package as Congress struggled to pass standalone bills for the different federal agencies. The extended fiscal 2018 appropriations process and the 2018 midterm elections tightened Congress' timeline for fiscal 2019 deliberations, but ongoing disagreements over border wall funding proved to be the biggest obstacle to spending negotiations. The longest government shutdown in U.S. history occurred from December 22, 2018, to January 25, 2019, as Democrats rejected Trump's request for $5.7 billion in border wall financing and the president refused to sign legislation that did not include the funding. The shutdown ended when lawmakers reached an agreement with Trump to pass a three-week continuing resolution (PL 116-5) and to establish a conference committee dedicated to negotiating appropriations for the U.S. Department of Homeland Security (DHS), including border wall construction. The final omnibus, including $54.2 billion for state-foreign operations, passed the House and Senate on February 14 and was signed by the president the next day (PL 116-6).

Senate Action

The Senate was first to release its draft appropriations bill (S 3107). As reported by the Appropriations Committee on June 21, the bill provided a total of $54.4 billion in state-foreign operations funding. Major provisions included

- $311 million in voluntary contributions to the UN and other international organizations
- $7.8 billion in humanitarian aid, including $4.4 billion for international disaster assistance
- $8.8 billion for global public health programs, and the same amount for international security assistance
- $1.35 billion for international financial institutions such as the World Bank
- About $5.7 billion for embassy security
- $515.5 million to implement the United States' strategy to address migration from Central America
- Increased funding for the Countering Russian Influence Fund

The bill also required the State Department and USAID to resume hiring staff at Obama administration levels and to consult with Congress before attempting to downsize or expand either agency. (Then-Secretary of State Rex Tillerson was seeking to reduce staffing by about 8 percent.)

The draft bill initially included the expanded Mexico City Policy and a prohibition on support to the UN Population Fund, but these provisions were removed during the committee's markup. Other notable amendments recommended the allocation of at least $632.5 million for family planning and reproductive health programs and provided $10 million in funding for the Intergovernmental Panel on Climate Change. No further action was taken by the Senate.

House Action

The House Appropriations Committee reported its version of the fiscal 2019 state-foreign operations spending bill (HR 6385) on July 16. Although the total funding level of $54 billion was similar to the Senate's bill, there were some notable differences. For example, the House bill did not provide any funding for the UN Population Fund, Human Rights Council, Green Climate Fund, or the Intergovernmental Panel on Climate Change. It also capped funding for family planning and reproductive health programs at $461 million—a cut of about $150 million from fiscal 2018 spending levels—and reduced voluntary and assessed payments to the UN and other international organizations by more than $220 million. The bill included the Mexico City Policy language, as well.

Notably, the committee's markup of the bill included adoption of an amendment by Sen. Debbie Wasserman-Schultz, D-Fla., which added language denying the use of government funding to block lawmakers from visiting U.S. facilities where "foreign national minors" are being detained or housed. The amendment was positioned as a direct response to the Trump administration's policy of separating undocumented migrant children from their parents at the U.S.–Mexico border, news of which had prompted domestic and global outrage. No further action on the bill was taken by the House.

Minibuses and Continuing Resolutions

With the start of the fiscal year approaching, Congress moved to pass two minibus spending deals in late September. Together, the legislation provided funding for agencies and programs typically covered by five standalone appropriations bills. This meant that lawmakers still had to negotiate the seven remaining bills, including one covering state-foreign operations spending. One of the minibuses, PL 115-245, also served as a continuing resolution, giving Congress until December 7 to finalize outstanding appropriations. A second continuing resolution was adopted on December 6, extending the deadline to December 21, following the death of former president George H. W. Bush.

Failure to agree on a third continuing resolution resulted in a government shutdown beginning on December 22. House appropriators worked to develop new language (HR 21) that would cover provisions typically included in five of the remaining standalone appropriations bills. It did not include border wall funding, but did provide continuing appropriations for DHS to allow time for further discussion on the issue. Draft text was released on December 31 and approved by the House on January 3, 2019. Senate Majority Leader Mitch McConnell, R-Ky., did not bring the bill up for consideration in the Senate because of the border wall omission.

The House tried again in late January with HR 648. This time the bill covered six of the outstanding seven appropriations bills; DHS was the only agency not included. House Appropriations Committee Chair Nita Lowey, D-N.Y., said the bill reflected formal conference agreements and informal talks that occurred between the House and the Senate in the fall. The state-foreign operations provisions included

- Total funding of $54.2 billion
- $5.1 billion for State Department operations
- $1.37 billion for USAID operations
- $8 billion in war-related funding via the OCO
- $9.15 billion for international security assistance
- $1.36 billion in contributions to the UN and other international organizations, reflecting a small cut of $100 million from fiscal 2018
- $7.8 billion for humanitarian assistance, including $3.4 billion to support refugees
- $3.1 billion for global public health, including $575 million for family planning programs

It did not include the Mexico City Rule or a prohibition on funding for the UN Population Fund. HR 648 was approved by the House on January 23, but the Senate did not consider the bill.

Meanwhile, Rep. Lowey had also proposed a new continuing resolution (HJ Res 28) that would provide appropriations though February 28, allowing the government to reopen for about three weeks. The measure did not include border wall funding, but lawmakers assured the president they would form a conference committee for the specific purpose of finalizing DHS' budget during the three-week stopgap period. The House approved the resolution on January 23, followed by the Senate on January 25. Trump signed the bill the same day (PL 116-5), and the shutdown officially ended.

Final Appropriations

The final consolidated spending package covering all outstanding appropriations (HJ Res 31) passed the House and Senate on February 14. The bill's state-foreign operations section preserved the key provisions of HR 648. Although the measure provided only $1.375 billion for

steel fencing along the U.S.–Mexico border, Trump signed the bill into law on February 15 (PL 116-6).

Countering America's Adversaries Through Sanctions

The U.S. intelligence community's conclusion that Russia interfered in the 2016 election, North Korea's continued testing of ballistic missiles, and ongoing concerns about Iranian influence in conflicts across the Middle East prompted Congress to consider various sanctions packages to respond to and deter future incidence of these activities. Early in 2017, the House and Senate deliberated over three separate sanctions bills—one for each of the three target countries—but ultimately combined them into the Countering America's Adversaries Through Sanctions Act to secure passage before the August recess. The bill cleared both chambers with little resistance at the end of July and it was signed by President Trump in August, despite the White House raising the possibility of a veto.

BACKGROUND

Congressional sanction measures initially focused on Russia, Iran, and North Korea due to major developments on the global stage in 2016. U.S.–Russia relations came under the microscope during the 2016 presidential election cycle, following accusations by U.S. intelligence officials that Russia conducted cyberattacks against the major political parties and other targets to undermine Americans' faith in democracy and the electoral system. An official, classified assessment by the Central Intelligence Agency confirmed these allegations in December 2016, as did an unclassified report released in January 2017, and further concluded that Russia intended to improve Trump's chances of winning the election through the attacks. President Barack Obama expelled Russian intelligence operatives from the United States, closed two compounds used by Russia for intelligence-related purposes, and imposed sanctions against Russian intelligence services and other entities in response to the intelligence community's findings. Meanwhile, multiple reports surfaced of repeated contacts between the Trump campaign and Russian intelligence agents, including news that Trump's first national security advisor, Michael Flynn, had discussed with the Russian ambassador the possibility of easing Obama-enacted sanctions on the country.

In Iran, the Joint Comprehensive Plan of Action (JCPOA) took effect. Signed by the United States, China, France, Germany, Russia, and the United Kingdom (U.K.) in July 2015, the JCPOA required Iran to significantly scale back its nuclear activities and capabilities in exchange for sanctions relief from the United States, United Kingdom, and United Nations. The International Atomic Energy Agency's verification in January 2016 that Iran was thus far in compliance with the agreement prompted U.S. officials to lift select sanctions, although the Obama administration said that some Iranian individuals and entities would remain sanctioned for their involvement in terrorism, human rights abuses, the Syrian and Yemeni civil wars, or Iran's ballistic missile program. Congressional Republicans remained skeptical that Iran would comply with the deal long-term, and sought additional opportunities to rein the country in without violating the JCPOA. Trump was also highly critical of the JCPOA, promising to "rip up" the agreement upon taking office.

Meanwhile, North Korea continued to test its ballistic missiles and nuclear technology in spite of a UN ban on such activities and several rounds of U.S. and UN sanctions. At least twelve such tests were conducted throughout 2016, including the purported underground detonation of a hydrogen bomb. Both the UN Security Council and the Obama administration approved new sanctions against North Korean individuals and entities, but its government remained unphased—ballistic missile tests resumed in July 2017. The effectiveness of sanctions against North Korea has repeatedly been questioned, due in part to its relationship with China, which remains a significant trading partner and has typically resisted efforts to implement and enforce harsh sanctions. The border between the two countries is also relatively porous, allowing smugglers to circumvent some sanctions as well. Also in 2016, North Korea detained American college student Otto Warmbier, charged him with subversion, and sentenced him to fifteen years of hard labor. After months of behind-the-scenes negotiations, Warmbier was released to the United States in June 2017, in a coma; he was taken off life support shortly after his return home.

Senate Action

Sen. Ben Cardin, D-Md., introduced the Countering Russian Hostilities Act of 2017 (S 94) on January 11, 2017. The bill required the president to block individuals who seek to undermine the cybersecurity of the United States or its allies on the Russian government's behalf, or who are responsible for serious human rights abuses in any territory occupied or controlled by Russia, from entering the United States or owning U.S. property. It also directed the president to impose financial and property sanctions against people who engage in transactions on behalf of Russian intelligence or defense; invest in Russian oil, natural gas, energy export pipelines, or civil nuclear projects; buy or facilitate purchases of Russian debt; or assist in privatizing state-owned assets. Sen. Cardin's bill was referred to the Senate Committee on Foreign Relations the same day, but it did not progress beyond the committee hearing stage. The chair of the committee, Sen. Bob Corker, R-Tenn., delayed consideration of the bill following a Trump administration request that the White House be given time to address concerns surrounding Russian relations—including the desire to reach an agreement ending the Syrian civil war—through diplomatic channels before sanctions were considered.

Months later, Sen. Corker introduced his own bill, the Countering Iran's Destabilizing Activities Act of 2017 (S 722). The bill's main provisions mandated sanctions against individuals directly and indirectly involved in Iran's ballistic missile program, required the president to sanction the Iranian Revolutionary Guard Corps (IRGC) branch of the military, and called for the assets of individuals and organizations engaged in certain arms deals with Iran to be frozen. The bill also authorized the president to impose sanctions on individuals responsible for extrajudicial killings, torture, or other gross violations of human rights in Iran. Sen. Corker and bill supporters claimed the legislation would not violate the terms of the JCPOA—a concern for some former Obama administration officials and those involved in the agreement's negotiation—because it targeted terrorism and Iran's ballistic missile program, not its nuclear activities. The bill stayed in the Committee on Foreign Relations for two months before markup was completed on the draft on May 25.

Also on May 25, the committee completed markup on S 1221, the Countering Russian Influence in Europe and Eurasia Act of 2017, which had been introduced on May 24. This was Sen. Cardin's second attempt to push through a Russia sanctions bill. Rather than the broader S 94, S 1221 focused on Russia's efforts to expand its influence in Central and Eastern European countries. Specifically, the bill characterized Russia's incursions into Abkhazia, South Ossetia, Crimea, Eastern Ukraine, and Transnistria as illegal. It authorized funds to push back against Russian influence in these areas, including by helping European Union and North Atlantic Treaty Organization (NATO) member countries enhance their energy security and better protect their infrastructure and elections from cyberattacks. The bill also authorized assistance to Ukraine to help reduce its dependence on Russian energy. The bill's narrower focus, and the Trump administration's lack of progress in its diplomatic engagement of Russia, prompted Corker to allow its consideration by the committee.

Both S 722 and S 1221 were approved by the committee and ordered to be reported favorably to the full Senate on May 25. Only S 722 was reported that day and placed on the Senate calendar, however. Sen. Cardin's bill was not reported out of committee until June 6.

Meanwhile, Senate Democrats began discussing the possibility of using the upcoming floor debate on Sen. Corker's Iran bill to force a vote on Sen. Cardin's proposed Russia sanctions, perhaps by offering S 1221 as an amendment to S 722. By this time, reports of additional contacts between Trump associates and Russian officials had surfaced, and Deputy Attorney General Rod Rosenstein had appointed Robert S. Mueller III as the independent counsel who would lead the investigation into Russia's alleged election meddling. Congressional Democrats were growing increasingly worried that Trump would try to ease or lift the sanctions Obama had imposed on Russia after the election. They were particularly driven to pass legislation

that would allow Congress to review and approve or prevent any attempts by the president to roll back sanctions.

On June 12, as the Senate deliberated S 722, Sen. Mike Crapo, R-Idaho, proposed an amendment adding sanctions against Russian mining, metal operations, shipping, and railways, as well as sanctions to combat corruption, sanctions evasion, human rights violations, malicious cyber activities, and supplying weapons to President Bashar al-Assad's regime in Syria. It also required the president to obtain congressional approval before lifting or easing existing sanctions against Russia.

The amendment was approved on June 14, 2017, by a vote of 97–2, and the revised bill passed the Senate on June 15 by a vote of 98–2. It was sent to the House for consideration the following day.

House Action

As the Senate deliberated Russia and Iran sanctions, the House considered the Korean Interdiction and Modernization of Sanctions Act (HR 1644). Introduced by Rep. Ed Royce, R-Calif., on March 21, 2017, the bill required the president to sanction individuals who buy North Korean coal or iron above UN Security Council–imposed limits, foreign persons who employ North Korean forced laborers, and individuals who sell fuel, aviation parts, and insurance to the government. It also made it illegal for foreign financial institutions to use correspondent accounts at U.S. banks to indirectly finance the North Korean government. Such accounts have been used by people and businesses to circumvent financial sanctions and trade prohibitions in the past. Royce's bill also increased limits on North Korean shipping and denied foreign aid to countries that engage in arms trade with North Korea, among other measures.

The bill was referred to the House committees on Foreign Affairs, Ways and Means, Financial Services, Transportation and Infrastructure, Oversight and Government Reform, and the Judiciary. The Committee on Foreign Affairs conducted bill markup on March 29. It was approved en bloc by voice vote along with several other measures, and reported out of committee on April 28. Debate on the House floor began on May 2. The bill passed with a vote of 419–1 on May 4, 2017, and was sent to the Senate that day.

House and Senate Negotiations

The Senate did not take up consideration of HR 1644, and the House did not move the Senate's combined Russia–Iran sanctions bill forward. However, in mid-July, House Majority Leader Kevin McCarthy, R-Calif., stated his intention to hold a vote on S 722 with HR 1644 added as an amendment, before the August recess. Democrats raised concerns that this would make the bill too unwieldy to pass the full Senate. Senate aides also suggested the amended bill would need to be marked up before floor consideration, with potential changes to include adding a ban on

American travel to North Korea to avoid future situations like that of Warmbier.

Sen. Corker proposed keeping the North Korea bill separate from the Russia–Iran sanctions package, and considering it along with another piece of North Korea-focused legislation (the Otto Warmbier Banking Restrictions Involving North Korea Act of 2017, or S 1591) later in the year. House Republicans rejected this proposal because they did not want to review North Korean sanctions again. There was also a mounting sense of urgency due to the recent completion of a Defense Intelligence Agency analysis concluding that North Korea could achieve a nuclear-capable intercontinental ballistic missile by 2018—a full three years sooner than previous estimates suggested.

After a full day of negotiations in July, Sens. Corker and McCarthy agreed to push forward with a compromise bill that combined provisions of all three pieces of legislation—S 722, S 1221, and HR 1644.

Final Action

The compromise bill, Countering America's Adversaries Through Sanctions Act (HR 3364), was introduced by Rep. Royce on July 24, 2017. Underscoring the bill's bipartisan nature, it was cosponsored by Reps. Steve Cohen, D-Tenn., Eliot Engel, D-N.Y., Steny Hoyer, D-Md., and Christopher Smith, R-N.J., as well as McCarthy.

As it related to Russia, the bill's major provisions required several Obama-ordered sanctions to remain in place and required the president to submit requests to Congress for approval before waiving or lifting certain sanctions. It authorized the president to impose sanctions on entities and individuals for malign activities involving cybersecurity, crude oil projects, financial institutions, corruption, human rights abuses, sanctions evasion, export pipelines, transactions with Russian defense or intelligence sectors, the privatization of state-owned assets by government officials, and arms transfers to Syria. It also required the State Department to work with the Ukrainian government to increase that country's energy security.

The bill's North Korea provisions increased the president's authority to sanction anyone who violated UN Security Council resolutions and required the U.S. State Department to submit a determination on whether North Korea should be designated a state sponsor of terrorism. (It had been removed from the list of designated countries in 2008 under then-president George W. Bush.) It prohibited U.S. financial institutions from maintaining accounts for foreign banks to provide indirect financial services to North Korea. The bill also prevented foreign governments that provide North Korea with defense services or technology, and those that receive defense-related products or services from North Korea, from obtaining U.S. foreign aid. Additionally, the bill called for sanctions against North Korean cargo and shipping, goods produced wholly or partly with forced labor, and foreigners who employ North Korean forced laborers.

Regarding Iran, the bill directed the president to sanction the country's ballistic missile and weapons of mass destruction programs, the IRGC and its affiliates, and sales or transfers of military equipment and the provision of related technical or financial assistance to Iran. Another key provision gave the president authority to sanction anyone responsible for human rights violations in Iran.

The bill was quickly referred to and reviewed by the House Committee on Foreign Affairs, in addition to the committees on Intelligence, the Judiciary, Oversight and Government Reform, Armed Services, Financial Services, Rules, Ways and Means, and Transportation and Infrastructure. Following a motion by Rep. Royce, the bill was brought to the House floor on July 25 for consideration under a suspension of the rules, meaning no amendments were allowed and a two-thirds vote was required to secure passage. After forty minutes of debate, the House voted 419–3 to approve the bill.

A full Senate vote was held on July 27. The bill was approved without amendment by a vote of 98–2, and sent to President Trump for his signature on July 28. Several White House officials raised the possibility that Trump would veto the bill because it would damage relations with Russia and make it more difficult to both end the Syrian war and partner to fight the Islamic State in the Levant. The president did sign the bill into law on August 2, albeit reluctantly. "The bill remains seriously flawed—particularly because it encroaches on the executive branch's authority to negotiate," he said in a statement. "This bill makes it harder for the United States to strike good deals for the American people, and will drive China, Russia and North Korea much closer together."

North Korea Banking Restrictions

Congress resumed consideration of additional sanctions legislation following their return from the August recess. Among the bills considered was the Otto Warmbier Banking Restrictions Involving North Korea Act of 2017 (S 1591), also known as the BRINK Act. Several committee hearings were held on the bill's proposed provisions and there was some discussion about combining it with another piece of North Korea-focused legislation, but the BRINK Act did not make it to the Senate floor, as Congress became consumed with passing tax reform legislation and appropriations bills at the end of the year.

BACKGROUND

The BRINK Act was an effort by Congress to push the Trump administration to take a tougher stance against major Chinese businesses and financial institutions that were still transacting with the North Korean government. China has traditionally resisted implementing or enforcing harsh sanctions against North Korea because the two countries have a significant trading relationship. This in turn has lessened the effectiveness of international eco-

nomic sanctions intended to deter North Korea from pursuing a nuclear weapons program.

Administration officials rejected calls by Congress to sanction Chinese entities, arguing that doing so would hinder diplomatic efforts to deal with perceived threats posed by China. However, an advisory issued by the U.S. Treasury Department in the fall of 2017 stated that "bank accounts used by sanctioned persons [in North Korea] are maintained predominantly at major Chinese financial institutions," providing fuel for Congress' push for more sanctions.

Senate Action

Sens. Chris Van Hollen, D-Md., and Patrick Toomey, R-Pa., introduced the bill on July 19, 2017. The draft bill's major provisions required the president to provide Congress with a list of financial institutions found to be providing financial or banking support to the North Korean government or previously sanctioned individuals. The president would then be required to sanction those institutions, either by freezing their assets or block their access to the U.S. financial system (e.g., opening or maintaining a U.S. bank account). Any U.S. institution involved in these transactions would face additional penalties if they did not take action to prevent such activities from occurring again. These provisions were modeled on similar sanctions the United States had imposed on Iran prior to JCPOA implementation—sanctions which were widely credited with enticing Iran to the negotiating table.

The draft bill also gave the president authority to suspend, renew, or terminate sanctions without prior congressional review or approval, but such actions would have to be reversed if Congress passed a joint resolution of disapproval. The president could also grant sanctions waivers to particular banks but had to provide Congress with fifteen days advance notice before doing so.

Other key provisions authorized the president to sanction anyone who provided financial messaging services to North Korean financial institutions or designated individuals. These messaging services are often used to conduct rapid transactions in circumvention of sanctions regimes. The president was also required to prohibit the manufacture, sale, purchase, transfer, import, or export of certain North Korean goods, services, and technology by a U.S. person or entity. Additionally, the bill allowed state and local governments to divest from or prevent investments in North Korea covered property worth more than $10,000, essentially permitting the divestiture of public employee benefit plan funds.

The bill was referred to the Senate Committee on Banking, Housing, and Urban Affairs, which conducted its first hearings on the legislation on September 7 and September 28, 2017. Testimony provided by Sigal Mandelker, undersecretary of the treasury for terrorism and financial intelligence, and Susan Thornton, the acting assistant secretary of state for the Bureau of East Asian and Pacific Affairs, echoed concerns voiced by other administration officials

that such sanctions would limit options for dealing with China. "It's also incredibly important that we have the ability to remain flexible," said Mandelker. "When our hands are tied in different ways, it keeps us from being agile in the way that you would want us to be agile in order to maximize that economic pressure."

In a unanimous vote, the committee approved a manager's package of amendments to the bill and ordered it reported to the full Senate on November 7. One of the agreed-upon amendments required the administration to report to Congress within three months on its strategy for dealing with North Korea, to include "the desired end state in North Korea and current United States objectives relative to security, economic, and illicit finance threats emanating from North Korea." Another amendment required the Treasury Department to brief Congress within one month on the resources it has allocated to administering various sanctions programs and its needs for additional resources, if any. This briefing was intended to help Congress understand if Treasury had enough staff and funding to effectively implement and enforce U.S. sanctions regimes.

The amended bill also codified four executive orders that imposed various sanctions on, or froze, the assets of designated individuals and entities in North Korea, as well as the shipping sector. It expanded the list of targets for mandatory sanctions to include individuals who

- Knowingly purchased significant amounts of North Korean coal, iron, iron ore, or seafood
- Deliberately imported North Korean textiles
- Facilitated a transaction of funds or property from the North Korean government in violation of UN Security Council resolutions
- Supported the exportation of North Korean workers
- Sold or transferred vessels to North Korea
- Misappropriated, stole, or embezzled public funds to benefit North Korea

Finally, the bill called for an analysis of the North Korean government's cyber capabilities and their potential to undermine U.S. national and economic security interests, including the U.S. financial system.

Sen. Van Hollen noted the important timing of the committee's bill approval following the November 7 markup, observing that it coincided with President Trump's visit to China. "I think it's important that when he arrives this committee has sent the signal to China and its government . . . that the United States means business and we intend to enforce these sanctions in order to bring North Korea to the negotiating table."

The bill was reported out of committee on November 16 and placed on the Senate calendar, but it did not reach the chamber floor. There was some discussion in December that the BRINK Act may be combined with the Leverage to Enhance Effective Diplomacy Act (S 1901). That bill made

it U.S. policy to achieve "complete, verifiable, and irreversible dismantlement" of North Korea's nuclear and ballistic missile programs, required the White House to determine if any of a specific list of Chinese businesses should be sanctioned for doing business with North Korea, and allowed the U.S. State Department to reduce its diplomatic presence in and terminate or reduce foreign assistance to countries not cooperating with U.S. efforts to isolate North Korea. The bills were not combined, however, and neither was considered by the full Senate.

Iranian Financial Oversight

Congress also resumed deliberations over additional sanctions against Iran after the August recess. Following passage of the Countering America's Adversaries Through Sanctions Act (HR 3364), the House started consideration of two smaller sanctions bills that sought to tighten restrictions on Iranian officials' financial assets and provide greater oversight for commercial aircraft sales to the country, respectively. While the House ultimately passed both bills in 2017, they did not progress through the Senate due to the prioritization of tax reform and appropriations legislation.

BACKGROUND

By the time House committee members began their consideration of the Iranian Leadership Asset Transparency Act (HR 1638) and the Strengthening Oversight of Iran's Access to Finance Act (HR 4324), President Trump had decertified the Iranian nuclear deal. The Iran Nuclear Agreement Review Act of 2015 (PL 114-17) required the president to verify to Congress every ninety days that Iran was complying with the terms of the JCPOA. Trump certified the agreement in April and July 2017; however, he announced its decertification in October, claiming that Iran had committed multiple violations. Notably, decertification did not withdraw the United States from the agreement, and Trump did not reimpose sanctions against Iran nor did he call on Congress to do so.

Germane to HR 4324 deliberations, one of the economic benefits Iran received through its compliance with the JCPOA was the ability to purchase commercial aircraft from the United States. Boeing and General Electric had since arranged to sell their planes to Iran Air, the state-owned airline. Some lawmakers and Trump administration officials claimed Iran was using planes purchased from these companies, as well as European manufacturer Airbus, for illicit activities and to advance its military objectives. "These planes were not solely used to transport passengers across Iran and the Middle East, but in many cases were used to transfer weapons and soldiers from Iran to Syria," said Rep. Roger Williams, R-Texas, in a statement following House passage of the bill on December 14. "While our brave men and women of the U.S. armed forces fight tirelessly across the Middle East, Iran uses American made aircraft to work against our own national security interests."

House Action

Rep. Bruce Poliquin, R-Maine, introduced HR 1638 on March 20, 2017. The bill's goal was to combat Iran's financing of terrorists and money laundering activities, as well as improve compliance with related financial sanctions. Its central focus was requiring the U.S. Treasury Department to submit a report to Congress within 270 days detailing

- Funds or assets directly or indirectly held by designated Iranian officials in U.S. and foreign financial institutions
- Whether those officials have an equity stake in a Treasury-sanctioned entity
- How the funds, assets, or equity interests were acquired and used
- Methods used by the named officials to evade money laundering and similar laws
- Recommendations for improving techniques to fight illicit uses of the U.S. financial system and for revising sanctions to prevent Iranian officials from using their assets to develop or buy ballistic missile technology
- How Treasury assesses the effectiveness of sanctions against Iran, as well as recommendations for improving its sanctions development and enforcement capabilities

The bill required the Treasury Department to submit a similar report each year for two years following the initial report.

Rep. Williams introduced HR 4324 on November 9, 2017. His bill required the Treasury Department to report to Congress within thirty days of authorizing a U.S. or foreign financial institution to export or reexport a commercial passenger plane to Iran. Those reports were to include a list of all financial institutions that had conducted such transactions since January 16, 2016, the JCPOA's effective date. They also needed to include either a certification that the transaction did not pose a money laundering or terrorism financing risk for the U.S. financial system and would not benefit an Iranian person who had knowingly transported weapons of mass destruction or provided support to terrorists, or a statement that Treasury could not make that certification. Additionally, the bill allowed the president to waive the reporting requirements for one year if he could certify to Congress that Iran had made substantial progress toward combating money laundering and terrorism financing risks, or it had significantly reduced its destabilizing activities in the region.

House Committee Action

The House Financial Services Committee completed markup on both HR 1638 and HR 4324 in mid-November. During deliberations, committee members adopted an amendment to HR 1638 that added nonbinding language advising the Treasury Department to "consider

acquiring information from sources that collect and, if needed, translate high-veracity officials records or provide search and analysis tools" to help it prepare the required reports to Congress and gain new insights on Iranian officials' commercial and financial relationships. As amended, the bill was approved by the committee in a vote of 43–16. HR 4324 was not significantly changed by the committee during markup. It was approved by a vote of 38–21. Both bills were reported out of committee on December 7.

House Floor Action

Floor debate on the two bills began on December 13, 2017. During consideration of HR 1638, the bill was renamed the Iranian Asset Reporting Requirement. Two amendments were adopted, as well. One, offered by Rep. Brad Schneider, D-Ill., added language stating that Iran could face economic sanctions for human rights abuses. An amendment from Rep. Grace Meng, D-N.Y., required the Treasury Department to include in its reports an assessment of the impact and effectiveness of U.S. economic sanctions against Iran. The final bill was approved the same day by a vote of 289–135.

Rep. Matt Gaetz, R-Fla., proposed the one amendment to HR 4324 that was adopted by the House. His amendment required the Treasury Department to certify that an aircraft sale would not benefit an Iranian individual who knowingly transported items used to establish the permanent presence of the Iranian military or an Iran-backed militia in Syria. This amendment was approved by voice vote. The other major action was Rep. Eric Swalwell's, D-Calif., motion to send the bill back to committee with instructions for it to be amended to require the Treasury secretary to certify that no financial institution involved in an aircraft sale to Iran had engaged in business with a foreign entity that had participated in, or authorized, cyberattacks against a U.S. election—namely, Russia. The motion was rejected 188–233. The final bill passed the House on December 14 with a vote of 252–167.

Senate Action

Both House bills were referred to the Senate Banking, Housing and Urban Affairs Committee, where a companion bill to HR 4324 was also awaiting consideration. None of these bills made further progress during the 115th Congress.

Montenegro's NATO Accession

In March 2017, the Senate passed by a nearly unanimous vote a resolution of ratification consenting to Montenegro's membership in the North Atlantic Treaty Organization (NATO). The vote helped pay the way for the Balkan state to become NATO's newest member, and was widely characterized by senators from both parties as an important step in the United States' efforts to limit Russian influence in the region.

BACKGROUND

Montenegro had been pursuing NATO membership since 2006, when it ended its union with Serbia. The newly independent Balkan state participated in various military cooperation agreements before receiving a formal invitation from NATO to join the alliance in December 2015. Accession negotiations over the terms of Montenegro's pending membership concluded in the spring of 2016, with NATO member representatives signing an official accession protocol document on May 19, 2016.

A country's addition, or accession, to the NATO membership must be ratified by all of the alliance's member states. (There were twenty-eight members at the time of Montenegro's accession.) In the United States, because NATO expansion involves a treaty, this required two-thirds of the Senate to approve a resolution of ratification. Such a resolution does not ratify treaties; it provides the Senate's advice and consent to the president to proceed with ratification.

The Senate Foreign Relations Committee previously considered and advanced a resolution of ratification in December 2016, but the measure was not taken up by the full Senate before the 114th session ended. Any treaties that are pending at the end of a Congress must be reintroduced and reapproved by the committee in the next session.

Montenegrin NATO membership was generally viewed as uncontroversial in Congress. Several senators, including Sens. John McCain, R-Ariz., and Ben Cardin, D-Md., advocated for the ratification resolution's swift passage, claiming it would help counter Russian influence. Russia strongly opposes NATO's expansion in the Balkans and Eastern Europe, believing it is an effort by the United States and Western nations to isolate the country, and had described Montenegrin accession as a "provocation." Preventing Montenegro from joining NATO was reportedly the main driver of an attempted coup in October 2016. Montenegrin officials have accused Russian intelligence operatives of plotting the coup and the prime minister's assassination.

Senate Action

The Senate Foreign Relations Committee re-endorsed Treaty Doc 114–12 by voice vote during a meeting on January 11, 2017. It did not progress to the Senate floor until March 27, following a motion by Senate Majority Leader Mitch McConnell, R-Ky., to invoke cloture and vote on the resolution of ratification. "With Russia's resurgence and quest for renewed great power status, NATO has given notice that it will stand up for Western democracies, too—and has continued to do so," he said. "[Putin] is intent on using all elements of national power to expand Russia's sphere of influence. He is also threatened by the examples of representative democracies anywhere near Russia's borders, and is accordingly trying to intimidate other nations from seeking entry into the alliance." The Senate voted 97–2 to approve Sen. McConnell's motion and begin debate.

One of the dissenters was Sen. Rand Paul, R-Ky. Paul's opposition was not specific to Montenegro's membership, but due to a concern that U.S. obligations to NATO cost too much and were overextending the military. "Currently, the United States has troops in dozens of countries and is actively fighting in Iraq, Syria, Libya, and Yemen (with the occasional drone strike in Pakistan)," said Sen. Paul in a written statement issued on March 15. "In addition, the United States is pledged to defend 28 countries in NATO. It is unwise to expand the monetary and military obligations of the United states given the burden of our $20 trillion debt."

Sen. Mike Lee, R-Utah, was the other no vote. He said he did not believe the benefits of Montenegro's addition to the alliance were sufficient to justify a collective defense commitment by other NATO members. Although Sens. Paul and Lee remained opposed to the resolution, it passed by another vote of 97-2 on March 28. President Donald Trump signed the United States' ratification document on April 11, 2017.

Withdrawal From Conflict in Yemen and Rebuke of Saudi Arabia

In 2018, as the Yemeni civil war entered its third year, the Senate began deliberating a series of bills and resolutions surrounding U.S. involvement in the conflict. Congressional Republicans initially resisted efforts to pass one such resolution, SJ Res 54, which sought to remove most U.S. forces from Yemen under the provisions of the War Powers Act. Yet Yemen's worsening humanitarian crisis and allegations that Saudi Arabia's royal family was involved in the murder of a dissident journalist who had been living in the United States prompted enough senators to change their position to allow the resolution to pass late in the year. However, senators approved the resolution knowing that it had no hope of progressing through the House, which had earlier adopted language preventing any such measure from coming up for consideration before year end.

BACKGROUND

Yemen's internal conflict started in 2015, when former president Ali Abdullah Saleh joined with a growing insurgency to push sitting president Abdu Rabbu Mansour Hadi out of office. The rebellion has been led by the Houthis, who have since taken control of Yemen's government, the capital city, and large swaths of the country. The conflict is also largely viewed as a proxy war due to Iran's backing of the Houthis and Saudi Arabia's leadership of a coalition supporting Hadi and his internationally recognized government.

The United States first became involved in the conflict in October 2016 when Houthi rebels attacked an American ship stationed off the coast of Yemen. A U.S. naval destroyer responded by firing upon three Houthi-controlled radar installations. Since then, the United States has provided logistical and intelligence for the Saudi coalition to help counter Iranian influence in the region.

The conflict has created an unprecedented humanitarian crisis. More than 100,000 Yemenis have been killed, and an estimated 18 million people had been classified as food insecure by 2018. Adding to these humanitarian concerns, Saudi-led airstrikes have killed thousands of civilians, with reports indicating that at least some of these attacks have purposely targeted civilians. This has prompted U.S. lawmakers and officials to not only criticize the Saudi government for sloppy operations but also question if the United States should continue to support the coalition. The Saudi government has responded in part by highlighting its provision of humanitarian aid, as well as efforts to improve the precision of its airstrikes.

Dissatisfied by progress toward a peaceful solution, the Senate considered and held floor votes on multiple pieces of legislation related to the conflict in 2017. None of these measures received sufficient votes to pass, but the number of senators supporting calls to reduce or withdraw U.S. assistance in Yemen grew over time.

Congressional reservations about the activities of the Saudi government sharpened into anger in October 2018, following the disappearance of Jamal Khashoggi, a Saudi journalist who was a staunch critic of the Saudi royal family, and specifically Crown Prince Mohammed bin Salman. Khashoggi relocated to the United States after facing government-sanctioned harassment in Saudi Arabia and became a writer for *The Washington Post*, where he kept up his criticisms and advocacy for democratic reforms. Khashoggi went missing after entering the Saudi consulate in Istanbul, Turkey, for an appointment. While Saudi officials initially claimed Khashoggi left the consulate unharmed, a team of Turkish investigators determined the journalist had been killed inside the building by a team of Saudi agents. The U.S. intelligence community subsequently concluded that the crown prince had ordered Khashoggi's murder as part of his ongoing crackdown on dissenters. Saudi officials denied the allegations. Despite congressional outrage, President Trump maintained that there was no conclusive evidence linking the prince to Khashoggi's death and that the U.S.–Saudi allyship—including a new, major arms deal—must be preserved.

Senate Action

Sen. Bernie Sanders, I-Vt., introduced SJ Res 54, a resolution directing the removal of U.S. armed forces from hostilities in Yemen, on February 28, 2018. It was cosponsored by Sens. Mike Lee, R-Utah, and Chris Murphy, D-Conn. As introduced, the resolution called for the removal of U.S. troops from Yemen, except for those who were specifically engaged in operations against al Qaeda or associated forces, within thirty days of the resolution's adoption and until Congress either declared war or granted a specific authorization for the use of force in the country. The resolution said Congress had the authority to direct the troops' removal under provisions of the War Powers Act (PL 93-148), which limits the president's ability to ini-

tiate or expand foreign military campaigns without congressional approval. U.S. involvement in the hostilities in Yemen had not been authorized by Congress, the resolution stated.

The resolution was referred to the Senate Foreign Relations Committee, where it stalled for nearly nine months. Sanders attempted to push the bill forward on March 20 by moving to discharge the committee, meaning the bill would move directly to the Senate floor, but his motion was tabled by a vote of 55–44. Sen. Bob Corker, R-Tenn., the committee chair, led the opposition to Sanders' motion, saying he opposed efforts to circumvent the committee's jurisdiction and promising that committee members would devote some time to discussing U.S. involvement in Yemen.

The result of these deliberations was SJ Res 58, proposed by Sen. Todd Young, R-Ind. Young's resolution was narrowly focused on cutting off Pentagon funding for the U.S provision of in-flight refueling for Saudi aircraft. The bill was reported out of committee on May 22, but it did not advance through the full chamber. (The U.S. Defense Department announced an end to such support in November.)

Debates over the Yemeni conflict and U.S.–Saudi relations resumed in the fall, after Khashoggi's death. Sen. Bob Menendez, D-N.J., introduced the Saudi Arabia Accountability and Yemen Act of 2018 (S 3652) on November 11, 2018. The bill's major provisions required the imposition of sanctions against Saudi individuals, including royal family members, who were responsible for, or aided in, Khashoggi's killing. It also required sanctions against individuals working to undermine Yemen's stability or block the flow of humanitarian goods and services, and prohibited the United States from providing in-flight refueling for Saudi aircraft engaged in the conflict. Another provision suspended the transfer of some weapons, including certain missiles, ammunition, ground vehicles, and aircraft, to Saudi Arabia. This bill also stalled in committee, however, because Sen. Corker wanted to revise the language to make the sanctions provisions discretionary, instead of mandatory; Sen. Menendez did not.

With reports emerging that Sanders and others might try to force a vote on SJ Res 54, the White House dispatched Secretary of State Mike Pompeo and Defense Secretary Jim Mattis to Capitol Hill on November 28, 2018, to provide a classified briefing on the Yemeni conflict. The White House also released a Statement of Administration Policy that expressed its strong opposition to the resolution's passage, which it said was based on "erroneous premise" because the United States was not engaged in hostilities. The United States "has provided limited support to member countries of the Emirati and Saudi-led coalition, including intelligence sharing, logistics, and, until recently, aerial refueling," and that level of support did not implicate the War Powers Act. The resolution would also "harm bilateral relationships in the region and negatively impact the ability of the United States to prevent the spread of violent extremist organizations such as al-Qaida in the Arabian Peninsula and ISIS in Yemen," the statement added, concluding that the president would veto the measure if it passed.

The same day, Sen. Sanders made another motion to discharge the Foreign Affairs Committee. This time, the Senate voted 63–37 to bring the resolution to the floor, underscoring the influence of Khashoggi's death and the worsening humanitarian crisis in Yemen on senators' positioning. Among those who remained opposed to the resolution, some cited concerns that a U.S. withdrawal would benefit Iran; others said they believed the War Powers Act was unconstitutional.

Senate Floor Action

The full Senate began consideration of SJ Res 54 on December 12, marking the first time since 1973 that the chamber had deliberated a resolution under the War Powers Act. Several amendments were adopted during the debate, including one bipartisan measure clarifying that "hostilities" included aerial refueling. Another amendment added language stating that nothing in the resolution was meant to influence or disrupt military operations or coordination with Israel. The Senate also agreed to add a requirement for the president, within ninety days of the resolution's enactment, to submit a report to Congress assessing the risks posed to U.S. citizens and Saudi civilians, as well as the possibility of regional humanitarian crises, if the United States ended its support for the Saudi coalition. A fourth amendment required the president to provide a separate report on the increased risk of terrorist attacks against the United States, its troops, and its allies if Saudi Arabia stopped sharing intelligence on the Yemeni conflict. The amended resolution passed by a vote of 56–41 on December 13, 2018.

As soon as passage was secured, Sen. Corker and twelve cosponsors introduced a separate joint resolution, SJ Res 69, supporting a diplomatic solution to the Yemeni conflict and condemning Khashoggi's murder. The resolution expressed the Senate's belief that Mohammed bin Salman was responsible for Khashoggi's death. It criticized Saudi Arabia for cooperating with and buying military equipment from Russia and China, stating that these activities posed challenges to U.S.–Saudi relations. It called for an immediate ceasefire in Yemen, the negotiation of a peace agreement, and it condemned the Houthis for human rights violations, as well as Iran for supplying the insurgency with weapons. Finally, the resolution declared that the United States had no statutory authority to be involved in the conflict, including the refueling of Saudi aircraft. The full Senate quickly approved SJ Res 69 by voice vote, without amendment, the same day it was introduced.

House Action

Even as the Senate pushed forward with these resolutions, there was a general understanding among senators that neither would make it through the House before the

end of the year. Indeed, House Republicans adopted language via a separate legislative vehicle stating that Yemen-related bills would not be considered during the remainder of the 115th session. However, House Democrats pledged to take up similar resolutions once they took control of the chamber in 2019.

Authorizing the Use of Force Against the Taliban

In the spring of 2018, a bipartisan group of senators led a fresh attempt to replace or repeal existing resolutions authorizing the president's use of force in the United States' ongoing war on terror. However, the Authorization for Use of Military Force of 2018 (SJ Res 59) never made it out of committee, as committee members could not agree on how much flexibility the measure should provide.

BACKGROUND

Per the War Powers Act of 1973 (PL 93-148), U.S. troops cannot be deployed for military engagements for more than sixty days without a formal declaration of war by Congress or a congressional authorization for the use of military force (AUMF). Congress passed one such AUMF (PL 107-40) in the days following the terrorist attacks of September 11, 2001, to allow then-president George W. Bush to "use all necessary and appropriate force" against those responsible and to prevent further attacks. This AUMF provided Bush with the legal authority to fight al Qaeda and the Taliban in Afghanistan. A second resolution, the Authorization of Military Force Against Iraq (PL 107-243), passed in October 2002, permitted Bush to wage war against Iraqi President Saddam Hussein's regime, which allegedly possessed weapons of mass destruction that were a threat to the United States.

Both AUMFs remained in place throughout Bush's two terms in office, as well as during President Barack Obama's administration. The 2001 AUMF's broad language was used by Obama to provide legal cover for his administration's counterterrorism efforts in Iraq and Afghanistan, but also in other countries and against emergent terrorist groups such as the Islamic State in the Levant (ISIL). This prompted criticism by some in Congress who argued the AUMF was intended only for fighting al Qaeda and the Taliban and thus did not give Obama the authority to conduct other operations—particularly against entities that did not yet exist in 2001. These lawmakers called for a new AUMF that would provide sufficient legal standing for the evolving war on terror. The Obama administration submitted a draft AUMF to Congress in 2015, but lawmakers disagreed on how broadly the new measure should be written, and it did not advance.

Sens. Tim Kaine, D-Va., and Jeff Flake, R-Ariz., tried in early 2017 to pass a resolution that would repeal the 2001 and 2002 AUMFs and replace them with a new authorization, but it did not gain traction in the Senate. However, calls for a new AUMF intensified that spring, after President Donald Trump ordered airstrikes against Syrian military facilities in response to the government's use of chemical weapons on its own people. Sen. Kaine was particularly vocal in claiming Trump had overstepped his authority and raising questions about the administration's rumored plan to maintain an "open-ended" military presence in Syria.

Senate Action

With Sen. Kaine as a cosponsor, Sen. Bob Corker, R-Tenn., introduced SJ Res 59 on April 16, 2018. The resolution had four other original cosponsors, as well: Sens. Flake, Chris Coons, D-Del., Todd Young, R-Ind., and Bill Nelson, R-Fla.

The resolution authorized the president to use "all necessary and appropriate force" against the Taliban, al Qaeda, ISIL, and other associated forces. The measure provided an initial list of these forces that included al Qaeda in the Arabian Peninsula, al Shabaab, al Qaeda in Syria (including the al Nusrah Front), the Haqqani Network, and al Qaeda in the Islamic Maghreb, but it also gave the president the power to designate additional organizations or individuals not listed. The resolution said it was necessary to provide such flexibility because the ongoing nature of the fight against al Qaeda and the Taliban had "evolved to include numerous non-state terrorist groups . . . that pose a grave threat to the United States." The resolution replaced the 2001 AUMF and repealed the 2002 AUMF. It also required the president to submit a report to Congress by January 20, 2022, and every four years thereafter about the use of military force under the resolution, including whether the AUMF should be repealed, modified, or preserved as written. Importantly, the AUMF could not be used to provide a legal foundation for military incursions against foreign governments.

Senate Committee Action

The resolution was referred to the Senate Committee on Foreign Relations, which held an initial hearing on May 16, 2018. As in past AUMF deliberations, committee members disagreed over how much flexibility to give the president in determining where and against whom to use military force to combat terrorism. Democrats and Sen. Rand Paul, R-Ky., wanted to include a "sunset" or specific date by which the AUMF would cease to be in effect. They also expressed concern that it gave the president and the U.S. Defense Department too much power to expand counterterrorism operations beyond the targets listed in the resolution language. Additionally, some committee members opposed language that only allowed Congress to limit the use of force in reaction to a presidential order, meaning that the president could conduct operations as he or she saw fit and lawmakers would have to pass a separate resolution to stop those operations. Doing so would require Congress to secure veto-proof majorities in both the House and Senate, which is difficult to achieve.

PROTECTING STATE DEPARTMENT COMPUTERS

Congress continued to confront an array of cybersecurity issues in 2018, ranging from election-related hacking concerns to the weaknesses of federal computer networks and other internet-connected information technology. Numerous data breaches had been reported by federal entities in recent years, such as two hacks of the Office of Personnel Management that resulted in the combined loss of more than 25 million personnel records. The State Department had been involved in several of these attacks, including an incident in April 2015 when hackers gained access to the White House's computer networks and sensitive information through the State Department's network.

In response to these challenges, several federal agencies had implemented "bug bounty" or crowd-sourced security programs to help identify and fix system gaps that could be exploited by hackers. These programs were modeled after similar initiatives in the private sector and essentially leveraged the time and skills of security researchers—sometimes referred to as "good hackers"—to identify weaknesses in agency IT in exchange for some form of compensation. In 2016, the U.S. Defense Department was among the first agencies to announce a bug bounty program, known as Hack the Pentagon, and has since expanded the initiative to include Hack the Army and

Hack the Air Force. The Internal Revenue Services and the General Services Administration have similar programs, as well. In 2018, members of Congress sought to further replicate this model and improve the U.S. State Department's cybersecurity with the Hack Your State Department Act (HR 5433).

House Action

Rep. Ted Lieu, D-Calif., introduced HR 5433 on April 5, 2018, with cosponsor Rep. Ted Yoho, R-Fla. The bill's major provisions required the secretary of state to design and implement a Vulnerability Disclosure Program (VDP) to improve the agency's cybersecurity. The VDP would provide security researchers with clear guidelines for testing the department's information technology for vulnerabilities and for reporting their findings. The program would also involve the creation of specific department procedures and infrastructure to fix the reported weaknesses. The secretary of state was also directed to submit a report to Congress within 180 days of VDP establishment, and every year for the next six years, on the number and severity of issues reported, which ones were fixed and which ones were outstanding, the resources used to implement the program, and estimated cost savings generated by the program, among other items.

Aside from Sens. Paul and Flake, Republican committee members countered that the AUMF should be broad because Congress would not be able to authorize the use of force against a new terrorist threat quickly enough to be effective and ensure national security. Democrats in turn highlighted that the 2001 AUMF was passed by Congress in only three days.

Sens. Flake and Kaine urged the committee to accept the resolution and consider it a compromise. "We have to judge this product against the reality and not what is optimal," Flake said during the May 16 hearing. "This is a bipartisan institution . . . You take what you can get sometimes." Committee members remained in a stalemate, however, and the resolution did not advance.

Additionally, the bill required the secretary of state to create a bug bounty pilot program to support the identification and reporting of vulnerabilities in the department's internet-facing technology. The program would provide compensation to participants who found previously unidentified weaknesses.

The House Foreign Affairs Committee conducted markup of the bill on May 9. The only changes considered and adopted were those put forward by Lieu as part of a substitute amendment. Lieu's amendment added language defining the term *bug bounty program* and limiting the pilot program's length to one year or less. The amendment further directed the secretary of state to consult with other government officials on the program's establishment, to ensure that it complimented existing scans of the agency's internet-accessible systems. Lieu's amendment also provided more time for the secretary of state to submit reports to Congress on the pilot program. The committee approved the amendment and revised bill by voice vote.

On September 25, Rep. Ileana Ros-Lehtinen, R-Fla., moved to suspend the rules and pass the bill on the House floor. Her motion and the actual legislation were both approved by voice vote.

Senate Action

The bill was referred to the House Committee on Foreign Affairs, which conducted its markup on May 9. Rep. Lieu offered his own amendment in the form of a substitute to the bill, making several relatively minor changes. These changes included adding a directive for the secretary of state to consult with other relevant government officials on its bug bounty program to ensure it complimented ongoing network and vulnerability scans of the department's internet-accessible systems. They also limited the duration of the bug bounty pilot to one year and extended the amount of time the secretary had to report on the pilot's outcomes, including the numbers of researchers who participated, vulnerabilities that had been identified and addressed, and issues that remained outstanding. The revised legislation was approved en bloc by voice vote with several other bills and amendments.

The Senate received the House-passed bill on September 26. It was referred to the Foreign Relations Committee, but consideration and markup were never scheduled due to the chamber's focus on negotiating annual appropriations measures.

2019–2020

Much of the major legislation pursued by the 116th Congress pertained to Middle Eastern conflicts, including a historic resolution directing the removal of U.S. troops from Yemen. Passage of this measure marked the first time in more than twenty years that Congress had called for the end of U.S. involvement in a conflict, but it lacked sufficient support to override Trump's subsequent veto. Lawmakers also failed to override Trump's veto of several measures seeking to block major arms deals with Saudi Arabia and the United Arab Emirates (UAE).

Other measures with a Middle East focus included a bill imposing new sanctions against the Syrian government. While the Senate approved this legislation, it did not gain passage in the House due to objections over the inclusion of anti-Boycott, Divestment, Sanctions (BDS) movement language. (This movement is a Palestinian-led effort to try to influence Israeli policies.) Resolutions disapproving of arms sales to Bahrain, Qatar, and the UAE failed to pass before the expiration of a statutorily required thirty-day congressional review period. Measures condemning the U.S. withdrawal from northern Syria and imposing sanctions against the Turkish government in response to its attacks on Kurdish groups did not pass, either.

Lawmakers pushed back against a Trump administration proposal to ease sanctions on select Russian companies, but they were unsuccessful in passing a resolution blocking this plan before a thirty-day review period expired. The Senate initiated consideration of a separate bill seeking to impose new sanctions against Russia, but while the measure had strong committee support, it did not receive a vote on the Senate floor due to fiscal 2020 appropriations negotiations.

Among the many China-related bills Congress considered during this two-year period was a measure supporting a strengthened U.S.–Taiwan alliance and advocating for increased international recognition and engagement of the Taiwanese government—a direct challenge to Beijing's efforts to erode the island's autonomy. This bill garnered nearly unanimous support in both chambers and was signed by the president. Another bill that gained passage sought to protect the human rights of China's Uyghurs and other ethnic minorities who had been detained under the pretense of an anti-extremist campaign. A separate measure that sought to provide special immigration and refugee statuses for Hong Kong residents—particularly those fearing persecution by the Chinese government—failed to pass, however, due to concerns that it could provide an opening for Chinese spies to infiltrate the United States.

Fiscal 2020
State-Foreign Operations Funding

Congress reached agreement on state-foreign operations appropriations for fiscal 2020 before the end of the calendar year, but two continuing resolutions were required to provide time for extended negotiations of two consolidated appropriations measures. One point of contention specific to state-foreign operations funding was a provision introduced by Sen. Jeanne Shaheen, D-N.H., which required USAID family planning and reproductive health contractors to abide by the government's anti-discrimination policies, meaning they could not deny individuals services based on marital status, sexual orientation, or other characteristics. While Shaheen and her Republican counterparts on the Senate Appropriations Committee had agreed to include this provision as an alternative to language blocking application of the Mexico City Rule, other conservatives—as well as faith-based groups and anti-abortion activists—expressed concern that it could effectively exclude faith-based groups from USAID contract opportunities. Additionally, Democrats in the House exercised their newly won majority to block or delay different iterations of combined fiscal 2020 spending measures as a way to fight certain Trump administration policies, including his diversion of military construction funds to build a wall along the U.S.–Mexico border.

The president's fiscal 2020 request, released on March 11, 2019, continued to push for spending cuts at the State Department and USAID, although his proposed reductions were not as steep as in previous years. This time Trump sought a total of $40 billion for state-foreign operations, representing a budget reduction of 23 percent. Both chambers rejected this total as insufficient, however, and the final appropriations bill (PL 116-94) provided $54.7 billion in total funding.

House Action

The House Appropriations Committee reported its proposed state-foreign operations bill (HR 2839) on May 20. It provided $56.4 billion in total funding, or $2.2 billion more than in fiscal 2019. Of that total, $17.2 billion was allocated for State Department operations and $1.7 billion was reserved for USAID operations. Other key provisions included

- $8 billion for war-related spending via the OCO
- $6.1 billion for embassy security
- $11.2 billion for international security assistance

- $1.5 billion for contributions to international organizations, with roughly $640 million for voluntary UN contributions
- $2.1 billion for UN peacekeeping operations, which was intended to fully pay the United States' current obligations (28 percent of costs) and pay off arrears from fiscal 2018 and fiscal 2019

The bill also included prohibitions on the use of approved funds to implement the Mexico City Rule or to withdraw from the Paris Agreement.

HR 2839 was ultimately rolled into a single package of four appropriations bills (HR 2740) that passed the House on July 19 by a party-line vote of 226–203. The Republican-controlled Senate was not expected to take up the bill due to concerns over its total price tag, as well as opposition to certain policy riders, such as those pertaining to the Mexico City Rule.

Senate Action

Senate appropriators did not release their own draft bill (S 2583) until September 18. Its proposed total, $55 billion, was less than that of the House bill. Some of the savings came from differences in proposed UN funding levels: The Senate bill provided only about $471 million for UN peacekeeping and limited contributions to 25 percent of operational costs. Other contributions to UN programs were limited to 22 percent of assessed costs. The bill also provided less funding for international security assistance, State Department operations, and USAID operations. It included $375 million for a new Countering Chinese Influence Fund, designed to combat malign Chinese activities and increase transparency surrounding the Belt and Road Initiative, a massive Chinese infrastructure project running between East Asia and Europe. It also provided $515 million in assistance to Central American countries to help address migration in the region.

The full Appropriations Committee completed its markup of the draft bill on September 26. It was during this markup that Shaheen's amendment was added. Her provision specifically required the Government Accountability Office (GAO) to evaluate the effectiveness of previously appropriated funds for family planning and reproductive health assistance, including an assessment of the process by which USAID selected contract awardees. USAID was also required to develop a mechanism through which complaints could be submitted about possible discrimination. Other related amendments increased funding for USAID family planning and reproductive health activities and allocated more than $32 million to the UN Population Fund.

Additionally, the committee adopted measures denying visas to officials from Turkey, Egypt, and Saudi Arabia who are responsible for the wrongful detention of U.S. citizens and nationals abroad. Another amendment forbade the U.S. Export–Import Bank from providing financial assistance for exports of nuclear technology and equipment to Saudi Arabia. Yet another provision required the State Department to report to Congress on Saudi diplomats suspected of aiding and abetting the disappearance out of the United States of Saudi citizens accused of serious crimes. The bill was reported out of committee on September 26, but no further action was taken by the Senate.

Final Consolidated Appropriations

The first of two continuing resolutions keeping the government open was passed and signed in late September (PL 116-59). This bill extended funding through November 21, but lawmakers still needed more time. The second continuing resolution (PL 116-69) was adopted and signed shortly before the November deadline, and provided funding through December 20. During this time, lawmakers successfully negotiated two consolidated spending packages.

The bill covering state-foreign operations provisions (HR 1865) passed the House on December 17 by a vote of 297–120. It passed the Senate on December 19 by a vote of 71–23. House and Senate negotiators had settled on $54.7 billion in total funding, which was less than either chamber had initially pursued but still a $500 million increase over fiscal 2019. Major provisions included

- $16.6 billion for State Department operations
- $1.7 billion for USAID operations
- $8 billion in OCO funding for war-related activities
- $9 billion for international security assistance, including $3.3 billion for Israel, $1.5 billion for Jordan, $115 million for Ukraine, and $1.3 billion for Egypt
- A $15 million increase for the Countering Russian Influence Fund, which raised the total allocation to $290 million
- Creation of a new Countering Chinese Influence Fund, with initial funding of $300 million
- $75 million for humanitarian and development projects in the West Bank and Gaza Strip
- $520 million for Central America to address root causes of the migration crisis, with half of that funding earmarked for the governments of Honduras, Guatemala, and El Salvador
- $1.5 billion for UN peacekeeping and another $1.5 billion for contributions to international organizations

The bill did not include Shaheen's USAID anti-discrimination language, nor did it include the House's prohibition of funding to implement the Mexico City Rule. Trump signed the bill into law on December 20, 2019 (PL 116-94).

Fiscal 2021
State-Foreign Operations Funding

The COVID-19 pandemic complicated the fiscal 2021 appropriations process both logistically and politically. Debates over relief packages intended to mitigate the pandemic's tremendous impact on the U.S. economy consumed much of Congress' time in the spring of 2020, pushing committee consideration and markup of appropriations packages later into the year. This contributed to the need for several stopgap funding measures, as did disagreements over whether to include additional COVID-19 relief in the final omnibus spending package.

While Trump proposed a record $4.8 trillion budget for fiscal 2021, his request included major cuts to areas such as foreign aid in favor of increased spending on defense and border security. The president sought $44.1 billion for the State Department, USAID, and related agencies, representing a roughly 21 percent reduction from fiscal 2020 spending levels. Trump proposed cutting funding for food aid programs, economic and development assistance accounts, refugee and humanitarian aid, peacekeeping operations, and other UN contributions. These cuts were not only rejected by both the House and Senate, but also the House proposed more than $65 billion in state-foreign operations spending, including emergency funds for global COVID-19 relief.

As deliberations stalled in late fall, Treasury Secretary Steven Mnuchin was dispatched by the administration to help negotiate the final omnibus bill and $900 billion in additional COVID-19 relief. Despite Mnuchin's involvement—and the administration's implied support for his work—Trump threatened to veto the measure, claiming the tax rebates it included were insufficient and the rest of the bill was full of unnecessary spending. Into the latter category, Trump placed state--foreign operations provisions such as foreign aid to Burma, Cambodia, Egypt, and Central America. With only a matter of days before the final continuing resolution expired, lawmakers scrambled to try to address Trump's concerns, but Republicans and Democrats failed to agree on corrective measures. At one point, Rep. Rob Wittman, R-Va., acting on behalf of Minority Leader Kevin McCarthy, R-Calif., proposed removing the state-foreign operations provisions from the omnibus and replacing them with a stopgap funding measure to allow more time for revisions, but this was rejected by his fellow lawmakers. Adding to congressional concerns was the possibility that the bill could be pocket-vetoed if the president failed to sign it before January 3, when the 116th session of Congress would be forced to adjourn.

Trump ultimately relented, signing the bill into law on December 27, 2020 (PL 116-260).

House Action

The House Appropriations Committee reported its proposed state-foreign operations spending bill on July 13. It provided $65.87 billion in total funding, including about $10 billion in emergency funding for global COVID-19 preparedness, response, and relief. The bill allocated $47.85 billion for the State Department, USAID, and related agencies, as well as $8 billion for war-related spending via the OCO.

Other major provisions authorized $3.55 billion in multilateral assistance, to be provided through international organizations and banks. This amount included full funding for the World Health Organization (WHO), which Trump had threatened to cut over its handling of the COVID-19 pandemic. Another $7.83 billion was appropriated for humanitarian assistance. The bill provided $750 million for family planning and reproductive health programs, as well as $55.5 million for the UN Population Fund. It prohibited the use of already-appropriated funds to implement the Mexico City Policy and included the Global HER Act, which permanently repealed the rule. Additionally, the bill approved $50 million in funding over five fiscal years to establish the People-to-People Partnership for Peace Fund under USAID and the Joint Investment for Peace Initiative under the U.S. International Development Finance Corporation, which would provide investments in people-to-people exchanges and economic cooperation, respectfully, between Israelis and Palestinians with the goal of supporting a negotiated and sustainable two-state solution.

House appropriators later combined these provisions with the interior–environment, agriculture, and military construction–veterans affairs appropriations bills to make a four-bill "minibus." Floor consideration of this combined appropriations package began on July 23 and continued through July 24, 2020. Lawmakers adopted 109 amendments, including those preventing the White House from using approved funds to withdraw from the WHO or NATO, denying the use of funds to enter into new contracts or grants with any Trump Organization–affiliated companies, and prohibiting the use of State Department funds to facilitate the export of air-to-ground munitions to Saudi Arabia or the UAE. The amended bill was approved 224–189, despite Republicans' opposition to including COVID-19 emergency funds in the fiscal 2021 appropriations bills. The White House also issued a policy statement threatening to veto the bill if approved, citing opposition to incorporation of the emergency funding, the bill's spending total, and several policy riders, such as a prohibition on the allocation of funds to military installations named for Confederate officers. The bill was sent to the Senate on July 30.

Senate Action

The Senate had planned to begin appropriations drafting and markups in late June, but this process was delayed due to disagreements about how to handle potential amendments related to pandemic relief. Senate appropriators finally released draft text for their state-foreign operations spending bill on November 10, but because it was so

late in the year, the text was not assigned a bill number and was essentially considered a marker of where the Senate was willing to begin omnibus negotiations.

Notably, the Senate language did not include any dedicated COVID-19 relief funds or related assistance, although it did approve $9.3 billion to bolster global health programs and prevent future pandemics. It provided $55.2 billion in total funding for the State Department and USAID and $8 billion for OCO war-related spending. Other key provisions included $6.1 billion for embassy security, $8.9 billion for international security assistance, and $3.4 billion for refugee assistance. The Countering Chinese Influence Fund was given $300 million, while the Countering Russian Influence Fund was to receive $290 million. The draft text maintained the Mexico City Policy and capped spending on family planning and reproductive health programs at $461 million.

Continuing Resolutions

Even before the Senate released its draft text, lawmakers negotiated the first of five continuing resolutions and stopgap spending bills needed to keep the government open until final funding was approved. The first continuing resolution passed the House on September 22 and the Senate on September 30, 2020, and extended fiscal 2020 funding through December 11. Another continuing resolution was adopted by the House on December 9 and the Senate on December 11, moving the funding deadline to December 18. That day, Congress passed a two-day stopgap bill to allow negotiations to continue over a weekend; this was followed by a one-day stopgap that kept the government open through December 21. At this point, lawmakers had reached an agreement and only needed to buy time for floor votes and enrolling the massive piece of legislation so it could be sent to Trump for signature. A final, week-long continuing resolution was approved on December 21, 2020, providing funding through December 28.

Final Omnibus

The state-foreign operations provisions of the Consolidated Appropriations Act of 2021 (HR 133) included $4 billion in emergency funding to help distribute COVID-19 treatments to developing countries. No additional funding was authorized for food assistance or broader health spending. The bill provided $55.5 billion in regular funding for the State Department, USAID, and related agencies, which was $10.8 billion more than the president requested and about $820 million more than fiscal 2020 appropriations.

The House passed the omnibus on December 21 using a procedural maneuver that allowed lawmakers to divide the bill for two votes, both of which received overwhelming approval. The Senate passed the omnibus the same day, by a vote of 92–6. The final bill was sent to the president on December 24; he signed it three days later (PL 116-260).

Sanctions Against Syria

Early in 2019, the Senate sought to pass the Strengthening America's Security in the Middle East Act (S 1), a package of several bills that were generally supported by the chamber but did not make it through Congress before the 115th session ended. The most notable of the bill's provisions proposed sanctions against the government of Syrian President Bashar al-Assad in response to its ongoing attacks on civilians in the country's long-running civil war. The bill's consideration was blocked by Senate Democrats until a spending bill covering the remainder of FY 2019 was approved, after which S 1 was passed by a comfortable margin. The House declined to take up the bill because Democrats objected to language opposing the Boycott, Divestment and Sanctions Movement (BDS) against Israel, however, the Syria sanctions were ultimately included in the National Defense Authorization Act for Fiscal Year 2020 (PL 116-92).

BACKGROUND

A defining characteristic of the Syrian civil war has been the government's deliberate targeting of civilian populations as it seeks to quell the internal rebellion and regain control of the country. Airstrikes have repeatedly targeted medical facilities, schools, markets, and residential areas. The government has also launched dozens of chemical weapons attacks against rebels and civilians alike since the war began in 2011. Syrian officials denied involvement in the attacks, or that they even took place, despite reports from the ground and considerable evidence collected by international observers. The United States led retaliatory strikes against select targets in Syria and, with Western allies, sought to apply political pressure on Assad's government, but neither effort—nor the United Nations' faltering attempts to broker peace—appeared to have much effect.

Senate Action

Sen. Marco Rubio, R-Fla., introduced S 1 on January 3, 2019, with cosponsors Cory Gardner, R-Colo., Mitch McConnell, R-Ky., and Roy Blunt, R-Mo. The bill's section on Syria—titled the Caesar Syria Civilian Protection Act of 2019—proposed measures "to halt the wholesale slaughter of the Syrian people," and included wide-ranging sanctions against Assad's government and its foreign associates. Major provisions required the president to impose sanctions on foreign persons who provide significant financial, material, or technological support to the government of Syria, a senior Syrian political figure, or an individual operating in a military capacity on behalf of the governments of Syria, Russia, or Iran. The president was also directed to sanction foreign individuals who did business with the Syrian oil or gas sector, sold aircraft or airplane parts to the Syrian government or associated foreign forces, or provided Syria with construction or engineering services. Another provision directed the U.S. Treasury

Department to determine if the Central Bank of Syria should be sanctioned for money laundering activities. The bill allowed the president to waive sanctions only if a specific set of criteria were met, including

- Syria and Russia were no longer conducting airstrikes that targeted civilians
- The Syrian government was no longer cutting off humanitarian aid to areas under siege
- All political prisoners were being released
- Syria, Russia, and Iran were no longer targeting community gathering places
- Syria was verifiably fulfilling its commitments under international agreements, including those limiting the use of chemical weapons
- Syria was holding people accountable for war crimes committed during the conflict

The bill also called for the president to submit to Congress a strategy for facilitating Syrians' access to humanitarian assistance.

Other portions of the bill pertained to U.S. relations with Israel and Jordan. Under the title Ileana Ros-Lehtinen United States–Israel Security Assistance Authorization Act of 2019, the bill reauthorized $3.3 billion in annual foreign military financing for Israel through FY 2028. It also extended loan guarantees to Israel through FY 2023 and authorized the president to provide Israel with precision-guided munitions that could be used to counter drones. The bill's second title, United States–Jordan Defense Cooperation Extension Act, extended the president's authority to expedite and waive surcharges on defense sales to Jordan through 2022, and directed him to submit a report to Congress on the costs and benefits of creating a fund to support private investment in the country. Finally, the bill's fourth title comprised the Combating BDS Act of 2019. This measure allowed state and local governments to divest from entities that attempt to use boycotts, divestment strategies, or sanctions to influence Israeli policies. (Supporters of the BDS Movement advocate for Israeli withdrawal from the Occupied Territories, removal of the West Bank separation barrier, and a right of return for Palestinians, among other policies.)

Senate Floor Action

The bill bypassed committee using an expedited parliamentary procedure, but its consideration by the full chamber was delayed despite five separate efforts to invoke cloture and begin deliberations. Democrats opposed each motion, arguing the Senate should not consider any other measures until it passed a spending bill covering the remainder of FY 2019. Majority Leader Mitch McConnell, R-Ky., countered that only appropriations measures likely to be signed by President Trump would be considered on the Senate floor. He also criticized Democrats for holding up bills that would be supported by a majority of the Senate.

With a short-term measure to reopen the government secured by January 25, and a consolidated appropriations bill (HJ Res 31) headed to conference, the Senate finally agreed to begin debate on S1 on January 29. Several amendments were approved during consideration, the most significant of which was a motion by McConnell to add nonbinding language expressing the sense of the Senate that there were ongoing national security concerns in Syria and Afghanistan and that withdrawals of U.S. troops from either country should be carefully considered. McConnell's language called on the administration to conduct a thorough review of military and diplomatic strategies in both countries, including an assessment of the risk that withdrawing could strengthen Russian and Iranian influence in the region and undermine efforts to negotiate peace in both countries. Additionally, the amendment called for the administration to define the conditions for the "long-term defeat of al Qaeda and ISIS" and to certify that those conditions had been met before initiating any significant withdrawal of U.S. forces from Syria or Afghanistan. The amended bill was approved by a vote of 77–23 on February 5, 2020.

House Action

House Democrats had signaled prior to the bill's passage in the Senate that they were unlikely to approve the measure due to the inclusion of anti-BDS language. The bill was held at the desk in the House following its receipt on February 6 and did not progress further.

Disapproving
Proposed Russia Sanctions Relief

Ongoing congressional concerns over malign activities linked to the Russian government prompted a Democrat-led effort to prevent the U.S. Treasury Department from easing sanctions against several companies owned by a designated Russian oligarch in 2019. While most Republicans joined with Democrats to easily pass a disapproving resolution in the House, there was insufficient Republican support for a similar measure in the Senate.

BACKGROUND

The Treasury Department's Office of Foreign Assets Control informed Congress on December 19, 2018, that the Trump administration intended to lift sanctions against several companies in which Oleg Deripaska, a sanctioned Russian oligarch, maintained a controlling interest. The companies—En+ Group, UC Rusal, and JSC EuroSibEnergo—were involved in aluminum mining, natural gas, energy production, and logistics. Deripaska had been sanctioned in April 2018, along with six other oligarchs who were close to Putin and twelve companies they controlled. Specifically, Deripaska was sanctioned for working in the Russian energy sector and having acted on

behalf of the Russian government. He also faced allegations of bribery, money laundering, extortion, racketeering, and connections to organized crime. The restrictions imposed against him and against the companies sought to make him a minority shareholder in those businesses.

Per the Countering America's Adversaries Through Sanctions Act of 2017 (PL 115-44), Congress had thirty days to pass a resolution in both chambers that disapproved of Treasury's plan in order to keep the sanctions in place. Democrats said the sanctions should be maintained, given Deripaska's close relationship with Russian President Vladimir Putin and his interactions with Paul Manafort, a former Trump campaign manager who was convicted of financial fraud as a result of the special counsel investigation into Russian election interference. Democrats generally argued that no sanctions relief should be provided to Russian oligarchs and entities until the investigation was complete.

Many Republicans also questioned the administration's position on sanctions easing, prompting Treasury Secretary Steven Mnuchin to visit Capitol Hill on January 15, 2019, and appeal to lawmakers for their support. "We have been tougher on Russia with more sanctions than any other administration," Mnuchin told reporters after the meeting. "We sanctioned Deripaska. He will continue to be sanctioned." Mnuchin also told lawmakers that Treasury had struck a deal with En+ Group, UC Rusal, and JSC EuroSibEnergo in which the companies agreed to reduce Deripaska's ownership stake and make him a minority shareholder.

Senate Action

Minority Leader Chuck Schumer, D-N.Y., introduced SJ Res 2, disapproving of the administration's plan to lift sanctions, on January 4, 2019. The resolution was referred to the Senate Banking, Housing and Urban Affairs Committee, but was discharged on January 15 without hearings or markup. Sen. Schumer quickly moved to bring the resolution to a vote on the Senate floor. Majority Leader Mitch McConnell, R-Ky., tried to table Schumer's motion, but his effort was rejected by a vote of 42 to 57, as eleven Republicans sided with Democrats to allow debate to begin.

The only significant effort to amend the resolution came from Sens. Tim Kaine, D-Va., and Chris Van Hollen, D-Md., who attempted to add language securing passage of a continuing resolution and consolidated fiscal 2019 appropriations bill that had passed the House on January 3. However, this amendment was rejected.

McConnell tried twice to invoke cloture, thereby ending debate and allowing for a vote, but neither motion garnered the sixty votes necessary to pass, meaning the resolution could not advance. Eleven Republicans continued to vote with the Democrats, including Sen. Marco Rubio, R-Fla., who argued that Treasury's agreement with the Russian companies was insufficient. Rubio noted that

although Deripaska himself owned only 35 percent of the companies' voting shares, he was able to influence another 17 percent of votes through his relationships with other companies and financial institutions, which effectively gave him a controlling interest.

House Action

In the House, Majority Leader Steny Hoyer, D-Md., introduced a companion measure, HJ Res 30, on January 15. Unlike the Senate resolution, the House measure was quickly and overwhelmingly approved by the full chamber on January 17. The vote of 362–53 in favor of the resolution included 136 Republicans who aligned with Democrats to oppose sanctions relief. The House resolution was sent to the Senate, where Sen. Schumer tried unsuccessfully to bring it to a vote. Since the Senate did not pass a disapproving resolution by the thirty-day deadline, the Treasury Department was able to lift the sanctions as planned.

Ending U.S. Involvement in Yemen

With their return to the majority in the House in 2019, Democrats sought to fulfill their promise to revive a resolution calling for the end of U.S. involvement in Yemen, which failed to pass the chamber in 2018. This time, both the House and Senate approved the measure, but it was vetoed by the president. Although the recent death of Saudi dissident journalist Jamal Khashoggi helped boost congressional support for cutting off U.S. military assistance in the Yemeni conflict, lawmakers were not able to muster enough votes for a veto override.

House Action

HJ Res 37 was introduced by Rep. Ro Khanna, D-Calif., on January 30, 2019. The resolution's language largely reflected the text of a resolution adopted by the Senate in the prior session (SJ Res 34). It directed the president to remove U.S. troops from "hostilities in or affecting Yemen" within thirty days, unless Congress authorized a later withdrawal date, declared war, or provided a Yemen-specific authorization of the use of military force. The resolution emphasized that withdrawal meant the United States could no longer provide in-flight fueling of Saudi aircraft. It also clarified that it did not apply to U.S. troops engaged in counterterrorism operations in Yemen. Additionally, the bill required the president to report to Congress on the risks of the United States ending its support for the Saudi-led coalition in Yemen, and of Saudi Arabia no longer sharing Yemen-related intelligence with the United States.

House Committee Action

The resolution was referred to the Foreign Affairs Committee, which conducted its markup on February 6. The measure was reported favorably, without amendment, by a vote of 25–17. This was a party-line vote, providing an

early indication that the measure may not have enough Republican support to override a Trump veto. Republican committee members expressed concerns about invoking the War Powers Act (PL 93-148) to remove troops from a situation in which they were only providing security cooperation, and were not involved in combat. If this resolution passed, they argued, similar measures could be used to restrict other types of U.S. security cooperation agreements, including those that provide training for foreign armies. Lawmakers were particularly concerned that such measures could be used to hamper the United States' support for and cooperation with Israel. Some lawmakers also worried that ending U.S. involvement in Yemen could drive Saudi Arabia to embrace closer relations with Russia.

House Floor Action

Floor debate began in the House on February 13, 2019. Two amendments were adopted, including one from Rep. Ken Buck, R-Colo., that added language clarifying that nothing in the resolution could be construed as influencing or disrupting U.S. intelligence, counterintelligence, and investigative activities in Yemen. The second amendment was offered by Rep. Elliot Engel, D-N.Y., and added language expressing the sense of Congress that it is in the United States' national security interest to combat anti-Semitism worldwide and to strongly support Israel.

As amended, the resolution passed by a vote of 248–177, marking the first time since 1993 that the House voted in favor of directing the U.S. military to withdraw from a foreign conflict.

Senate Action

The House-approved resolution was received in the Senate on February 14 and referred to the Committee on Foreign Relations, but the full chamber never considered the measure. Bills citing the War Powers Act typically enjoy privileged status in Congress, meaning their consideration cannot be blocked by leadership, but the new provision about supporting Israel and combating anti-Semitism effectively stripped the resolution of its privileged status. This meant that Senate Majority Leader Mitch McConnell, R-Ky., could prevent the measure from coming up for a floor vote. However, he was not able to prevent his Senate colleagues from forcing a vote on their own privileged resolution.

Sen. Bernie Sanders, I-Vt., had introduced SJ Res 7 on January 30, as a companion to the House bill. The Senate Committee on Foreign Relations discharged the resolution by unanimous consent on March 13, and floor consideration of the measure began the same day. The Senate adopted two amendments by voice vote before approving the resolution by a vote of 54–46. One amendment, offered by Sen. Rand Paul, R-Ky., added language clarifying that nothing in the resolution could be construed as authorizing the use of military force. The second amendment, from Sen. Marco Rubio, R-Fla., clarified that nothing in the

resolution could be construed as disrupting intelligence, counterintelligence, or investigative activities relating to threats in, or emanating from, Yemen that were conducted by or in coordination with the United States.

Resolving Differences

SJ Res 7 was received in the House on March 18 and considered by the full chamber on April 4. Rep. Michael McCaul, R-Texas, tried to amend the bill to include language stating it is in the United States' national security interest to oppose the Boycott, Divestment, Sanctions (BDS) movement, but his motion was rejected 194–228. The resolution was approved without amendment by a vote of 247–175. "We are reasserting our power and saying once and for all that the United States needs to end all support for Saudi Arabia's brutal war in Yemen," said Rep. Jim McGovern, D-Mass, during a press conference after the floor vote on April 4. "This is the first time in history that a Congress is sending a War Powers resolution to the president. We are . . . clawing back our constitutional responsibilities."

Final Action

The resolution was submitted to Trump on April 16; he vetoed it the same day. The Senate considered a veto override on May 2, but the effort failed by a vote of 53–45.

U.S. WAR CASUALTIES 2001–2020

War in Iraq

Year	Killed in Action	Noncombat Deaths	Wounded in Action
2001	0	0	0
2002	0	0	0
2003	315	173	2,427
2004	713	135	8,004
2005	673	171	5,948
2006	704	117	6,418
2007	764	137	6,130
2008	221	93	2,060
2009	74	75	688
2010	19	45	394
2011	34	25	223
2012	2	2	0
2013	0	0	0
2014	0	5	0
2015	1	7	5
2016	7	11	25
2017	5	20	26
2018	0	19	14
2019	3	9	12
2020	4	8	154
Total	**3,539**	**1,052**	**32,528**

NOTE: Figures include Operation Iraqi Freedom (2002–2021), Operation New Dawn (2006–2013), and Operation Inherent Resolve (2009–2022).

SOURCE: Defense Casualty Analysis System, U.S. Department of Defense (https://dcas.dmdc.osd.mil/dcas/app/conflictCasualties).

War in Afghanistan

Year	Killed in Action	Noncombat Deaths	Wounded in Action
2001	3	8	33
2002	18	31	75
2003	17	26	100
2004	25	27	218
2005	66	33	271
2006	65	33	403
2007	83	35	752
2008	132	24	804
2009	271	40	2,167
2010	437	61	5,267
2011	360	51	5,232
2012	237	77	2,963
2013	91	41	1369
2014	39	16	457
2015	10	11	77
2016	9	1	75
2017	12	3	111
2018	13	3	118
2019	17	6	196
2020	4	7	15
Total	**1,909**	**534**	**20,723**

NOTE: Figures include Operation Enduring Freedom (2001–2022) and Operation Freedom's Sentinel (2015–2022).

SOURCE: Defense Casualty Analysis System, U.S. Department of Defense (https://dcas.dmdc.osd.mil/dcas/app/conflictCasualties).

Sanctions Against Russia

Congress continued pushing President Trump to take a harder stance against Russia in 2019, proposing measures to bolster U.S. cybersecurity while imposing additional sanctions against individuals and entities supporting Russia's economy and malign activities. Although a draft Senate sanctions bill—the Defending American Security from Kremlin Aggression Act (S 482)—received strong committee support, it was sidelined by negotiations over fiscal 2020 appropriations and was not taken up by the full chamber.

BACKGROUND

At the beginning of 2019, members of Congress from both parties remained concerned about Russia's alleged election interference, mounting aggression toward Ukraine, and involvement in the protracted Syrian civil war. These concerns were further fueled by reports that President Trump was withholding details from his conversations with Russian President Vladimir Putin from other administration officials and lawmakers, as well as revelations that the Federal Bureau of Investigation (FBI) had opened an inquiry into whether Russia influenced Trump's 2017 firing of former FBI Director James Comey. Other reports indicated that Trump had privately discussed withdrawing the United States from the North Atlantic Treaty Organization (NATO), which would effectively cripple the alliance and allow Russia to expand its influence and potentially threaten European countries.

Senate Action

Sen. Lindsey Graham, R-S.C., introduced the Defending American Security from Kremlin Aggression Act on February 13, 2019. Key provisions of the draft bill included a prohibition on the use of funds to withdraw the United States from NATO, unless the Senate passed a resolution consenting to such action. It established an Office of Cyberspace and the Digital Economy within the U.S. State Department and made it a crime to manufacture, distribute, or possess communication-intercepting devices and "intentionally traffic in the means to access protected computers," including those used in an election system. The bill also required the president to impose sanctions on

- Russian individuals and entities that facilitate or benefit from Putin's corruption, including oligarchs and their family members
- Individuals and financial institutions that conduct financial transactions with an individual who "supports or facilitates malicious cyber activities"
- Individuals who sell, lease, or provide goods, services, or financing to develop or produce crude oil in Russia
- Individuals who made a significant investment in Russian liquified natural gas export facilities
- Individuals who support interference in democratic processes or elections

The bill also called on the administration to develop regulations banning U.S. persons from engaging in or facilitating the purchase of Russian sovereign debt, sales of which help generate revenue for the Russian government.

Committee Action

The Senate Committee on Foreign Relations did not mark the bill up until December 18. Committee Chair Jim Risch, R-Idaho, reportedly opposed the bill and sought to delay its consideration. However, he allowed the bill to come up for consideration after being pressured by members of both parties to let it proceed.

Several amendments were adopted during markup, including a manager's amendment from Sen. Bob Menendez, D-N.J., who added language requiring the State Department and the Office of the Director of National Intelligence (DNI) to submit a report to Congress on whether the Russian government is deliberately interfering with U.S. political processes, including elections. The amendment also clarified that some of the sanctions—specifically those targeting oligarchs, political figures, and sovereign debt transactions—would only be triggered if DNI confirmed Russian meddling. Additionally, the

amendment extended funding authorization for the Countering Russian Influence Fund through fiscal 2022, noting that funds would be used to counter disinformation campaigns and other efforts to influence U.S. democratic processes.

Other approved amendments included a measure from Sen. Ben Cardin, D-Md., which called for the U.S. attorney general to brief Congress on staffing levels needed to improve INTERPOL's technological operations. Sen. Jeff Merkley, D-Ore., offered an amendment stating that Russia uses its United Nations Security Council veto power to obstruct multilateral action aimed at addressing a number of global challenges, including in Syria, Ukraine, and Yemen, and called for the State Department to report on the pros and cons of expanding Security Council membership. Another adopted amendment offered by Merkley called for Russia to fully investigate human rights violations against the LGBTQ community in Chechnya.

Sen. Todd Young, R-Ind., proposed an amendment expressing support for the renewal of the New START nuclear arms reduction treaty between the United States and Russia. But Young withdrew the measure due to his committee colleagues' concerns that it could jeopardize the bill's chances of getting a floor vote. Young also received assurances from Risch that the treaty would come up for discussion in 2020.

The committee approved the revised bill by a vote of 17–5 and reported it out to the full Senate. The bill did not come up for debate on the Senate floor, however, as lawmakers prioritized fiscal 2020 appropriations.

Arms Sales to Bahrain and Qatar

Several arms deals between the United States and Middle Eastern countries came under congressional scrutiny in 2019, beginning with proposed sales to Bahrain and Qatar. Sen. Rand Paul, R-Ky., led an effort to disapprove of both deals in the Senate, but neither of his proposed resolutions passed before a statutory deadline for congressional review.

BACKGROUND

In May 2019, the Trump administration notified Congress of its intent to enter into two separate arms deals: Bahrain would pay $750 million for a munitions package supporting its fleet of F-16s, while Qatar would invest $3 billion to procure twenty-four Apache Attack helicopters and related equipment. Sen. Paul had been a staunch critic of recent U.S.–Middle East arms deals, arguing that the United States should not be sending more weapons to the region at a time of rising tensions between Iran and Saudi Arabia, and amid continued terrorist threats. "The Middle East is a hot cauldron continuing and continually threatening to boil over," he said during Senate floor debate on June 13. "I think it's a mistake to funnel arms into these century-old conflicts."

While some Republicans shared Sen. Paul's concerns, most supported the arms deals, characterizing them as a way of supporting American allies. "These sales, the two regarding Bahrain and Qatar, address the legitimate security interests of both countries and strengthen U.S. partnership with both countries," said Sen. Jim Risch, R-Idaho, from the Senate floor.

Senate Action

Sen. Paul introduced SJ Res 20, disapproving of the deal with Bahrain, on May 13, 2019. He introduced SJ Res 26, disapproving of the deal with Qatar, the following day. Both measures were referred to the Senate Committee on Foreign Relations, but neither was scheduled for markup.

On June 12, the White House issued a Statement of Administration Policy expressing strong opposition to SJ Res 20. The deal with Bahrain, it said, would improve the security of a major non-NATO ally and an "important security partner in the region." Bahrain "supports United States activities and priorities related to anti-piracy efforts in the Arabian and Red Seas, and is an important partner in countering Iran's nefarious activities and in countering al-Qaida and ISIS throughout the region," the statement explained, adding that the president would be advised to veto the resolution if it passed.

Sen. Paul moved to discharge both resolutions from committee consideration, thereby allowing them to come to a vote on the Senate floor, on June 13. His colleagues rejected the motions by votes of 43–56 and 42–57, respectively. The thirty-day deadline for congressional review passed before either resolution made it out of committee.

Supporting Taiwan Allies

Among the hundreds of China-related bills considered by the 116th Congress was the Taiwan Allies International Protection and Enhancement Initiative (TAIPEI) Act of 2019 (S 1678). The bill sought to help Taiwan strengthen its alliances around the world and was a direct response to mainland China's efforts to pressure countries to choose between maintaining diplomatic relations with Beijing and with Taiwan.

BACKGROUND

Although Taiwan has its own democratically elected government and has operated independently for decades, Beijing claims that there is only "one China" and that Taiwan is part of it. China also claims that Taiwan is bound to it and the pursuit of "national reunification" by the 1992 Consensus, and advocates a "one country, two systems" approach as has been applied in Hong Kong. In Taiwan, however, different officials and political parties hold varied views on the consensus' interpretation. Taiwan's current president, Tsai Ing-wen, has refused to explicitly accept the consensus while attempting to maintain cross-strait relations according to other policy documents and legislation.

Since Tsai took office in 2016, mainland China has discontinued official communications with Taiwan, blocked it from participating in a number of global meetings and events, and pressured countries to sever diplomatic ties with the island as a way to weaken international recognition of Taiwan's autonomy. China has also increased its air patrols and surveillance over Taiwan and has sent more warships and aircraft carriers through the Taiwan Strait—actions that observers say are meant to pressure the government and the Taiwanese people to accept unification. The Trump administration pursued stronger ties with Taiwan over China's objections, including through new arms deals and higher-level diplomatic contacts with Taiwanese officials.

Senate Action

Sen. Cory Gardner, R-Colo., introduced the TAIPEI Act on May 23, 2019. The bill stated that it should be the policy of the United States "to advocate, as appropriate, for Taiwan's membership in all international organizations in which statehood is not a requirement and in which the United States is also a participant, and for Taiwan to be granted observer status in other appropriate international organizations." It added that it should be policy for the president to advocate for Taiwan's membership or observer status in such international organizations as part of relevant U.S.–China bilateral engagements. Other key provisions authorized the secretary of state to consider modifying the United States' diplomatic presence in or provision of U.S. foreign aid to other countries to incentivize those countries in their relations with Taiwan. Additionally, the bill directed the secretary of state to submit a report to Congress within ninety days and every 180 days thereafter on actions taken by the United States to "reaffirm and strengthen Taiwan's international alliances around the world." These reports should also include a list of countries of concern that have acted to "alter the formal diplomatic ties with Taiwan or to otherwise downgrade official or unofficial relations," the bill said.

The TAIPEI Act was referred to the Committee on Foreign Relations. Full committee consideration and markup occurred on September 25, 2019. The committee adopted an amendment proposed by Sen. Gardner that made several changes to the bill, including the removal of language allowing the secretary of state to modify U.S. diplomatic presence in other countries and requiring the report on U.S. efforts to strengthen Taiwan's alliances. This language was replaced with new verbiage stating that the United States should support Taiwan's strengthening of official diplomatic relationships with Indo-Pacific countries and should consider increasing economic, security, and diplomatic engagement with nations that had demonstrably strengthened, engaged, or upgraded relations with Taiwan (or reduced such activities with nations that had downgraded their relations with Taiwan). Sen. Gardner's amendment also added language stating that the United

States should seek to enter into a free trade agreement with Taiwan.

The amended bill was approved by voice vote and was reported out of committee on September 26. The bill was considered on the Senate floor on October 29, 2019, and passed by unanimous consent the same day.

House Action

The Senate-approved bill was received in the House on October 31. After stalling in committee for roughly four months, the bill was brought to the House floor following a motion by Rep. David Cicilline, D-Rhode Island, to suspend the rules and pass the bill. Rep. Cicilline's motion was approved 415–0.

During debate, the House approved one amendment that added more language about U.S.–Taiwan trade relations, emphasizing Taiwan's significance as a U.S. trading partner and how continued economic relations between the two countries are mutually beneficial. It also called for the U.S. trade representative to consult with Congress on opportunities to strengthen bilateral trade and economic relations with Taiwan. As amended, the bill passed the House on March 4, 2020, by a vote of 415–0.

Resolving Differences

On March 11, Senate Majority Leader Mitch McConnell, R-Ky., made a motion to concur in the House's amendment to the TAIPEI Act. This motion was approved by unanimous consent, and the bill subsequently passed the Senate, also by unanimous consent. The final bill was submitted to President Trump on March 16. He signed it into law ten days later (PL 116-135).

Blocking Arms Sales to Saudi Arabia and UAE

Since President Donald Trump's announcement of a major arms deal with Saudi Arabia in 2017, Democrats in Congress had led a push to prevent or delay its enactment. Their objections centered around concerns that U.S. weapons may be used against civilians in the Yemeni civil war and could contribute to that country's urgent humanitarian crisis, but also Saudi Arabia's human rights abuses—including the government's alleged role in the 2018 killing of Jamal Khashoggi. While House and Senate Democrats succeeded in passing several resolutions disapproving of arms deal components in June and July 2019, they were unable to secure the two-thirds majority support needed to override Trump's veto of each measure.

BACKGROUND

In May 2017, President Donald Trump announced that he had reached a deal with the Saudi Arabian government to sell $110 billion worth of weapons and other defense equipment to that country. About $25 billion in sales were

reportedly in process, with additional sales to be agreed upon at a future date.

The announcement generated bipartisan criticism in Congress, where lawmakers raised concerns about providing the Saudis with weapons that could prolong the conflict in Yemen and contribute to its humanitarian crisis—particularly given accusations that Saudi airstrikes had deliberately targeted civilians. Major arms sales between the United States and foreign governments must undergo a formal thirty-day review in Congress, giving lawmakers several opportunities to approve or prohibit various components of the Saudi deal as they were submitted by the Trump administration. Purchases were initially approved in 2017 and 2018, despite Democrat-led efforts to block some sales. Then in the spring of 2018, Sen. Bob Menendez, D-N.J., placed an informal hold on consideration of any further arms sales to Saudi Arabia and the UAE until the administration addressed lawmakers' concerns that the weapons would be used to kill Yemeni civilians and provided more briefings on U.S. involvement in Yemen.

Menendez' hold effectively caused a nearly year-long delay in sales. Meanwhile, the murder of dissident journalist Jamal Khashoggi, allegedly orchestrated by the Saudi government, prompted greater congressional scrutiny and criticism of U.S.–Saudi relations—including the arms deal.

Then in May 2018, Secretary of State Mike Pompeo declared an emergency situation with respect to Iran and announced that the Trump administration would proceed to finalize an $8.1 billion arms package for the Saudis. Pompeo claimed that U.S. allies needed those weapons to deter Iran, and that if they did not procure them from the United States, they would buy them from Russia or China instead. The emergency declaration allowed the administration to circumvent the congressional approval process, which Pompeo pledged would be a one-time event. The move angered many in Congress, even some Republicans who generally supported the arms deals but did not believe congressional review should be bypassed, and set the stage for a Menendez-organized effort to pass multiple resolutions disapproving of the weapons sales.

Senate Action

On June 5, 2019, Sen. Menendez introduced twenty-two separate resolutions prohibiting a specific component of the $8.1 billion deal from going into effect. Three of the measures—SJ Res 36, SJ Res 37, and SJ Res 38—focused on weapons and technology that had already been manufactured and were ready to ship to Saudi Arabia and the UAE. SJ Res 36 disapproved of the sale of tens of thousands of precision-targeted munitions to Saudi Arabia; SJ Res 37 disapproved sales of about 60,000 smart bombs to the UAE; and SJ Res 38 sought to prohibit the sale of bomb fuse technology that supported precision-guided bombs to Saudi Arabia.

All twenty-two resolutions were referred to the Senate Committee on Foreign Relations, which discharged them by unanimous consent on June 19. Floor consideration by the full Senate began that day and continued on June 20, 2019. SJ Res 36 and SJ Res 38 were approved separately, each by a vote of 53–45. SJ Res 37 was adopted en bloc with the other nineteen resolutions, with a 51–45 vote.

"At the end of the day, these votes are not about any one president or any one arm sale," Sen. Menendez said during the Senate's floor deliberations. "There will be another president who will want to claim executive authority to run over Congress. We in this body must embrace our Article 1 responsibilities to ensure we serve as an effective check on whoever that president is."

The White House issued a Statement of Administration Policy strongly opposing the resolutions and warning of a presidential veto. The arms deal, it argued, "directly supports the foreign policy and national security objectives of the United States by improving the security of a friendly country that continues to be an important force for political and economic stability in the Middle East." Beyond negatively affecting the United States' bilateral relationships, it went on, the resolutions "would hamper our ability to sustain and shape critical security cooperation activities and would significantly hinder the interoperability between our nations," in addition to impacting Iranian deterrence capabilities.

House Action

The full package of Senate resolutions was received in the House on June 20. House leadership decided to bring only SJ Res 36, SJ Res 37, and SJ Res 38 up for a vote in July, since they were considered more time sensitive. All three were approved without amendment on July 17 by votes of 238–190, 238–190, and 237–190, respectively. Speaking on the floor, House Foreign Affairs Committee Chairman Eliot L. Engel, D-N.Y., characterized the resolutions as an effort by Congress to ensure it retained its constitutionally granted powers and hold other countries accountable for alleged human rights abuses.

White House Action

The three approved resolutions were sent to President Trump on July 24. He vetoed them the same day. The Senate considered motions to override the vetoes on July 29, 2019, but failed to reach the two-thirds majority necessary to overturn them.

Condemning U.S. Withdrawal From Northern Syria

HJ Res 77 was one of several pieces of Turkey-focused legislation brought forward in Congress in 2019 in response to a Turkish incursion against Kurds in northeastern Syria. Despite its quick passage in the House, the measure failed to advance in the Senate, where Majority Leader Mitch McConnell, R-Ky., warned of unintended consequences.

BACKGROUND

In December 2018, President Trump declared that ISIS had been defeated in Syria and made the surprise announcement that he planned to withdraw more than 2,000 U.S. troops from the country. Lawmakers from both parties were highly critical of the move—and the fact that Congress was not informed in advance—and Defense Secretary Jim Mattis was one of several administration officials who resigned in protest.

In Congress, lawmakers raised concerns that withdrawing from Syria would give Russia and Iran greater influence in the region, in addition to creating an opportunity for ISIS to reclaim territory. They were also concerned that Turkey, Syria's northern neighbor, would take advantage of the United States' absence to launch an attack against Syrian Kurds, who were critical partners in the fight against ISIS but are considered by Turkey to be a security threat.

Turkey invaded northeastern Syria on October 10, 2019. Trump and Turkish President Recep Tayyip Erdoğan had reportedly discussed the planned invasion during a phone call four days earlier. Soon after that conversation, the Trump administration announced it was withdrawing U.S. troops from the area and ceding responsibility for its protection to Turkey.

This decision also caught lawmakers by surprise and immediately generated bipartisan criticism. The backlash prompted the Trump administration to negotiate a five-day ceasefire with Erdoğan, during which the Kurds were supposed to withdraw further into Syria, away from the Turkish border. Neither side fully observed the ceasefire, however. The Turkish military continued firing on various border targets and some Kurdish groups remained in the territory.

House Action

Rep. Eliot Engel, D-N.Y., introduced HJ Res 77 on October 15, 2019, to declare the House's opposition to the U.S. withdrawal from northeastern Syria. "An abrupt withdrawal of United States military personnel from certain parts of Northeast Syria is beneficial to adversaries of the United States government, including Syria, Iran, and Russia," the resolution stated. Acknowledging the critical role played by the Kurdish-led Syrian Democratic Forces (SDF) in the fight against ISIS, the resolution noted the SDF had warned the United States that a Turkish invasion would "significantly decrease" its ability to continue that fight and to manage ISIS detainees held in the area. The resolution called on Erdoğan to "immediately cease" Turkey's unilateral action in the region. It further called for the United States to continue providing humanitarian support to Syrian Kurdish communities and to ensure that the Turkish military "acts with restraint." The resolution was quickly brought to a vote on the House floor under a suspension of the rules, and was easily passed by a vote of 354–60.

Senate Action

HJ Res 77 was received in the Senate on October 16. McConnell initially said the chamber would consider the measure, but cautioned that if it passed, it could have the effect of driving Turkey to establish closer ties with Russia than the United States. Roughly one week later, McConnell said he planned to introduce a new resolution explicitly stating the Senate's opinion that U.S. troops should remain on the ground in Syria—language that was not included in the House measure. However, such a resolution was not introduced, and the House measure did not advance. Neither did a Senate companion bill (SJ Res 57) that had been introduced by Sen. Robert Menendez, D-N.J., on October 15.

By early November, Democrats were accusing McDonnell of stalling HJ Res 77 and several other Turkey-related bills to provide the president with political protection. McConnell denied these claims, reiterating his concerns that passing such measures could have unintended impacts ranging from closer Turkish–Russian relations to greater anti-American sentiments in Turkey to economic consequences for the United States.

Sanctions Against Turkey

Congressional focus on Turkey's incursion into northeastern Syria included various proposals for imposing sanctions on Turkish officials and government entities. One such measure, the Protect Against Conflict by Turkey (PACT) Act (HR 4695), received overwhelming support in the House, but it was not raised for consideration in the Senate. Majority Leader Mitch McConnell, R-Ky., continued to caution against the bill's potential to create unintended consequences and deferred to committee leadership on how best to proceed.

BACKGROUND

Although prompted by the attacks against Syrian Kurds, the flurry of Turkey-related legislative activity was also motivated in part by lawmakers' growing frustration with the government of Turkish President Recep Tayyip Erdoğan. Recent provocations included Turkey's purchase of a Russian missile defense system that was seen as a threat to North Atlantic Treaty Organization (NATO) members' security, the arrest and detention of Americans and U.S. embassy employees in Turkey, and the use of force by Erdoğan's security guards to dispel protestors outside the Turkish ambassador's residence in Washington, D.C.

Additionally, Erdoğan was scheduled to visit the White House on November 13, as Congress was deliberating its options for sanctioning Turkey. Some lawmakers pushed for the passage of sanctions legislation before his arrival, in hopes of sending a message to Erdoğan that his actions would have consequences, even if President Trump was trying to move beyond the attacks in Syria.

House Action

Rep. Eliot Engel, D-N.Y., introduced the PACT Act on October 16, 2019. Rep. Michael McCaul, R-Texas, was the only original cosponsor of the bill, but more than 100 other members from both parties signed on as sponsors before the bill came to a vote.

The bill's major provisions directed the president to impose, within fifteen days, sanctions against Turkey's minister of national defense, minister of treasury and finance, the chief of the general staff of the Turkish Armed Forces, and the commander of the 2nd Army of the Turkish Armed Forces for their involvement in the Syrian invasion. It also directed the secretary of state to identify other Turkish officials and foreign persons who were involved in, or provided support to, the incursion. The president would be required to impose sanctions on those individuals as well. Additionally, the bill directed the president to sanction Halk Bankasi, a Turkish state-owned bank, as well as any foreign financial institution determined by the secretary of state to have knowingly facilitated significant transactions for Turkey's Armed Forces or defense industry related to invasion. Any of these sanctions measures could be temporarily waived by the president if it were "vital to the national security interests of the United States to do so" and Turkey had stopped its attacks in northern Syria.

Other provisions prohibited U.S. arms transfers to Turkey in situations where it was believed those weapons and other items could be used by the Turkish Armed Forces in its operations in northern Syria. The bill also called for the administration to submit a variety of reports to Congress, including an assessment of the national security threats posed by the Turkish invasion and the finances of Erdoğan and his family.

The bill was referred to the House Armed Services, Financial Services, Foreign Affairs, Judiciary, Oversight and Reform, and Ways and Means committees, but committee hearings and markups were not held. Instead, the bill was brought up to the floor for consideration by the full House on October 29, 2019, following an approved motion by Engel to suspend the rules and vote on the bill. The bill passed by a vote of 403–16 after limited debate.

Senate Action

The bill was received in the Senate on October 30 and held at the desk. McConnell declined to bring it before the full chamber, stating he would leave it to the relevant Senate committees to study the various sanctions measures that had been proposed against Turkey and their potential impact on U.S. national security and foreign relations. The bill faced resistance from some lawmakers who questioned what Congress could realistically expect to achieve by sanctioning Turkey and others who expressed concern about how sanctions may impact U.S.-Turkish relations in the long term. The PACT Act did not advance prior to the end of the session.

Addressing China's Human Rights Violations

Allegations of human rights abuses by the Chinese government were another focus of congressional action in 2020. Two bills introduced in March—the Uyghur Forced Labor Prevention Act (HR 6210) and the Uyghur Forced Labor Disclosure Act (HR 6270)—took specific aim at China's detention of Muslim minorities for purposes including forced labor. Both measures passed the House by comfortable margins but stalled in committee following their delivery to the Senate, as lawmakers disagreed about whether the bills' import disclosures and restrictions were the most effective tool for combatting forced labor. By contrast, a third bill proposed in the Senate—the Uyghur Human Rights Policy Act (S 3744)—focused on sanctions against those involved in human rights abuses in Xinjiang and earned quick approval in both chambers before becoming law in June.

BACKGROUND

In 2014, China launched the "Strike Hard Against Violent Extremism" campaign, which was widely criticized by international observers and officials as a pretext for the Chinese government to severely restrict the rights of ethnic minorities, including the mostly Muslim Uyghur minority, in the Xinjiang Uyghur Autonomous Region. China is believed to have established internment camps within and outside of Xinjiang, at which it has allegedly detained more than 1 million people. Detainees are reportedly subject to beatings and torture, deprived of food, and prevented from exercising religious and cultural freedoms. Those who have escaped or gained freedom have said the only way to do so was by demonstrating political loyalty to the Communist Party of China. Reports also indicate that many detainees are forced to labor at the internment camps or in factories. The bipartisan Congressional-Executive Commission on China's 2019 Annual Report, for example, found numerous reports of forced labor connected with the government's oppression of minorities in Xinjiang. Additionally, China has reportedly continued to harass Uyghurs and members of other ethnic groups who had legally immigrated to other countries—including those who moved to the United States to work or attend school.

In December 2018, President Trump signed the Asia Reassurance Initiative Act of 2018 (PL 115-409), which, among other measures, supported the promotion of human rights in the Indo-Pacific region, including by imposing sanctions against those entities or individuals who violated human rights or religious freedoms. In a few instances, human rights abuses were also cited as the rationale behind Trump's imposition of tariffs or other restrictions on trade with China—part of the so-called trade war intended to pressure China to abandon what Trump called unfair trade practices. While members of Congress generally agreed that the United States should do something to

address China's alleged human rights abuses and the plight of the Uyghurs, they struggled to reach consensus on the most effective means for doing so.

House Action

Rep. Jim McGovern, D-Mass., introduced the Uyghur Forced Labor Prevention Act (HR 6210) on March 11, 2020. The bill's major provisions prohibited the import of goods manufactured or produced in Xinjiang with convict labor, forced labor, or indentured labor. It also required the president to submit periodic reports to Congress on foreign entities and individuals that knowingly facilitated the forced labor of Uyghurs, Kazakhs, Kyrgyz, and other Muslim minority groups, or supported efforts to circumvent U.S. laws in this area. The president would then be required to impose visa and asset-blocking sanctions on the identified people and entities.

Additionally, the bill required securities issuers—which can include corporations and investment trusts—to file reports with the Securities and Exchange Commission (SEC) disclosing whether the issuer knowingly engaged in activities that helped create mass surveillance systems in Xinjiang, engaged with an entity that ran or built detention facilities for Muslim minority groups, or conducted a transaction with a sanctioned individual related to minority abuses. If a company reported any such activities, the president would then determine if it should be investigated or sanctioned, or face criminal charges.

The bill was referred to the Financial Services, Foreign Affairs, Judiciary, and Ways and Means committees, but was not marked up or advanced until September 22, when Rep. Joaquin Castro, D-Texas, moved to suspend the rules and pass the bill. The motion was approved by a vote of 406–3, and the bill passed the same day by the same margin.

Meanwhile, Rep. Jennifer Wexton, D-Va., introduced a separate but related measure, the Uyghur Forced Labor Disclosure Act (HR 6270), on March 12. The bill required securities issuers to publicly disclose—via the SEC—if they had imported goods or materials from Xinjiang, as well as the commercial activity, revenue, net profits, and future import plans related to those goods or materials. Issuers were also required to disclose if any of the goods or materials were connected to the region's forced labor camps. Wexton's bill effectively expanded upon one aspect of McGovern's proposal, in that it required disclosures not only for goods imported directly from Xinjiang, but also raw materials such as cotton that might be sourced from Xinjiang but used in manufacturing elsewhere.

Wexton's bill was brought up on the House floor on September 30 following adoption of a rule allowing consideration of it and several other pieces of legislation. During floor deliberations, Rep. Patrick McHenry, R-N.C., moved to send the bill back to the Financial Services Committee with instructions to amend it to delay the effective date until the SEC unanimously reported to Congress that the requirements would improve the lives of people in Xinjiang and target "bad actors" in the Communist Party of China more effectively than sanctions. McHenry's motion was rejected 184–229, and the bill ultimately passed the House by a vote of 253–163.

Senate Action

HR 6210 was received in the Senate on September 23 and referred to the Committee on Foreign Relations. HR 6270 arrived in the Senate on October 1, 2020, and was referred to the Banking, Housing, and Urban Affairs Committee. Neither bill progressed beyond the committee stage due to disagreements between senators about whether the disclosure requirements would be effective in combating China's forced labor practices and other human rights violations.

However, the Senate had passed its own bill, the Uyghur Human Rights Policy Act (S 3744), in the spring. Sen. Marco Rubio, R-Fla., introduced the measure on May 14, 2020, to "condemn gross human rights violations of ethnic Turkic Muslims in Xinjiang" and call for an end to "arbitrary detention, torture, and harassment of these communities inside and outside China." The bill's language described China's systemic discrimination against Muslim minority groups and declared that Beijing had violated international human rights laws and norms. Key provisions called for the president to condemn abuses committed against Muslim minority groups and other persons, and for Chinese officials to close internment camps and stop restricting minorities' human rights. The bill directed the president to submit a report to congressional committees of jurisdiction that identified any foreign person responsible for abuses against Muslim minorities in Xinjiang, such as torture, cruel and inhuman punishment, prolonged detention without charges or trial, and forced disappearances. Visa or asset-blocking sanctions must then be imposed against those individuals. Additionally, the bill required the submission of several reports to Congress, including a report on human rights abuses in Xinjiang and a separate report on efforts to protect ethnic Uyghurs and Chinese nationals living in the United States. Finally, the bill directed the Office of the Director of National Intelligence to report to Congress on Chinese policies in Xinjiang that constitute gross violations of human rights, as well as the extent of detentions and forced labor of Muslim minority groups in China.

This bill moved quickly through Congress, garnering unanimous consent on the Senate floor on May 14. The next day the bill was sent to the House, where it passed by a vote of 413–1 on May 27, 2020. The White House received the bill on June 8, and Trump signed it into law on June 17 (PL 116-145).

Protecting Hong Kong Residents

China's approval of a controversial national security law in Hong Kong prompted a series of reactions by U.S. officials, including a push in Congress to provide temporary

immigration protections for Hong Kong residents who were visiting or living in the United States, as well as a special refugee status for those fearing persecution by mainland China. While this proposal easily gained approval in the House, it was not taken up by the full Senate due to opposition by Sen. Ted Cruz, R-Texas, who blocked the measure from consideration.

BACKGROUND

Hong Kong is subject to the Chinese constitutional principle of "one country, two systems," which provides the city and surrounding administrative region with significant economic, legal, and administrative autonomy, as well as greater freedoms than Chinese mainland residents. Hong Kong has its own government, for example, and maintains a capitalist economic system. However, Beijing retains broader control of the territory, including its foreign affairs and defense policies.

In June 2020, the National People's Congress of the People's Republic of China passed a new national security law for Hong Kong that banned foreign collusion and subversive activities in the region. It also created a special police unit to conduct criminal investigations of alleged violations and place suspects under surveillance. The law was reportedly written without input from officials in Hong Kong and was immediately criticized by pro-democracy activists in the territory who expressed concerns that it could be used by mainland China to suppress opposition. Chinese officials countered that they passed the law because Hong Kong had failed to pass its own national security legislation.

Many foreign leaders also criticized China's actions, including President Donald Trump. On July 14, 2020, Trump revoked Hong Kong's special treatment status with the United States, which the territory has leveraged in its push to become a global financial hub. Trump's action effectively revoked license exceptions for U.S. exports and reexports to Hong Kong, as well as transfers within the region. It also ended U.S. exports of defense equipment and dual-use technologies to Hong Kong, suspended extradition agreements, terminated student exchange through the Fulbright program, and ended the provision of training for Hong Kong police and security services. Additionally, Trump signed the Hong Kong Autonomy Act (PL 116–149), which called for banks to cease transactions with individuals or entities working to undermine Hong Kong's autonomy. In a separate executive order, Trump granted U.S. officials the authority to sanction individuals involved in the development or implementation of the national security law, with a first round of sanctions announced in August 2020.

House Action

Rep. Tom Malinowski, D-N.J., introduced the Hong Kong People's Freedom and Choice Act (HR 8428) on September 29, 2020. The bill sought to provide temporary protected status (TPS) for qualified permanent Hong Kong residents who were living in or visiting the United States at the time. (TPS may be granted by the U.S. Department of Homeland Security if officials determine that a country's nationals may not be returned safely. It effectively provides a stay of deportation and a work permit for qualified individuals.) The bill also established a Priority Hong Kong Resident refugee status that allowed individuals to seek asylum in the United States if they had either played a significant role in supporting recent protests against the national security law or China's encroachment into Hong Kong's autonomy, or they had been arrested, charged, detained, or convicted for participating in the nonviolent exercise of certain rights. The bill further stated that Hong Kong would be treated as separate from mainland China for the purposes of calculating visa quotas.

The bill was referred to the Committee on Foreign Affairs, which conducted markup on October 1 and approved the bill the same day. It was brought up for consideration on the House floor on December 7, 2020, where it passed by voice vote.

Senate Action

HR 8428 was received in the Senate on December 8 and referred to the Judiciary Committee for consideration. On December 18, Sen. Richard Blumenthal, D-Conn., moved to discharge the bill from committee so it could be deliberated by the full Senate, but his motion was rejected. Sen. Ted Cruz, R-Texas, blocked further efforts to push the bill forward, claiming that Hong Kong refugees could be spies and that the law could create an opportunity for China to infiltrate the United States. Cruz also argued that the proposal was a ploy by Democrats to push for more open immigration policies across the board.

Blocking Arms Sales to UAE

Senate Democrats sought again in 2020 to block a proposed arms deal with the United Arab Emirates (UAE). Unlike in 2019, however, they lacked sufficient Republican support to advance resolutions disapproving of the deal before a thirty-day congressional review window expired.

BACKGROUND

On November 10, the Trump administration notified Congress of its intent to enter into an arms deal with the UAE worth roughly $23 billion. The sale would include up to fifty U.S. F-35 fighter jets, eighteen Reaper drones, and about 14,000 bombs and munitions. The deal was positioned as both a bolster of U.S. relationships in the Middle East and a reward for the UAE's decision to normalize relations with Israel.

The latter had occurred in August, when the UAE and Israel agreed to the Abraham Accord. The deal paved the way for future bilateral agreements on everything from

tourism and technology to health care and the environment, in exchange for Israel suspending its annexation of occupied West Bank territory. With the Abraham Accord, the UAE became the first Persian Gulf state and the third Arab nation to normalize relations with Israel.

The arms deal found plenty of advocates in Congress, with supportive lawmakers claiming it would improve Israel's regional security, now that it was engaging with the UAE, and was something the UAE deserved. But critics in the Senate questioned if the deal would adversely affect Israel's "qualitative military edge" over neighboring militaries—an advantage that U.S. arms deals are statutorily required to preserve. They also raised concerns the deal could lead to an arms race in the Persian Gulf or make Iran less likely to accept limits on its ballistic missile program in the future. Additionally, some expressed concern that the UAE would not be able to protect sensitive U.S. technology from Russia and China, both of which are major UAE trading partners.

Some lawmakers also objected to the manner in which the administration informed Congress of the deal. Typically, the leadership and staff of committees with jurisdiction over weapons sales are provided with various briefings on a proposed deal, giving them an informal opportunity to review an agreement's terms before Congress is officially notified and the thirty-day formal review process begins. In this case, however, the administration skipped the briefings, causing the formal review process to begin right away. This led some senators to complain that congressional review would be rushed. "We are being asked to support a significant transfer of advanced U.S. technology without clarity on a number of key details regarding the sale or sufficient answers to critical national security questions," said Sens. Bob Menendez, D-N.J., Jack Reed, D-Rhode Island, and Mark Warner, D-Va. in a joint written statement on December 9.

Senate Action

Menendez introduced two resolutions disapproving of the UAE arms deal on November 18, 2020. SJ Res 77 sought to prohibit the sale of the Reaper drones and associated munitions, technology, and equipment, while SJ Res 78 opposed the export of F-35 jets to the UAE.

Both measures were referred to the Senate Foreign Relations Committee following their introduction, but neither resolution was scheduled for deliberation. On December 9, with the thirty-day review period nearly expired, Menendez made separate motions to discharge both resolutions from the committee's consideration and bring them to a floor vote. The motion to discharge SJ Res 77 was rejected 46–50; the motion to discharge SJ Res 78 was denied 47–49.

Notably, several Republicans who voted to restrict arms sales to the UAE and Saudi Arabia in 2019 did not support these new resolutions. Congressional observers speculated that the UAE had bought some goodwill with these lawmakers by normalizing relations with Israel and by announcing its withdrawal from the war in Yemen in February 2020.

No further progress was made before the review window closed, meaning the Trump administration was allowed to proceed with the arms deal. However, the next Congress was expected to reconsider disapproval of the deal. There was also a possibility that incoming President Joe Biden would revisit the deal during his administration.

STATE DEPARTMENT REORGANIZATION

Secretary of State Rex Tillerson made reorganizing the State Department and the U.S. Agency for International Development (USAID) a top priority from the beginning of his tenure. This was partly a response to President Trump's signing of an executive memorandum in March 2017 that directed the heads of all federal agencies to submit proposals for improving the "efficiency, effectiveness, and accountability" of their agency. But Tillerson also made it clear that he believed the State Department was mismanaged, especially when compared to private companies, such as his previous employer ExxonMobil.

Reductions in Personnel

In terms of agency personnel, Tillerson stated that his goal was to reduce the agency's full-time staff by 8 percent and that this would be achieved through attrition and buyouts, not layoffs. This reduction was facilitated in part by Trump's announcement of a hiring freeze at all federal agencies, effective January 23, 2017. The Office of Management and Budget lifted the government-wide freeze in April, but Tillerson kept State's restrictions on new hires and promotions in place into 2018. The extended freeze had a particular impact on the agency's diplomatic corps because spouses of overseas employees could no longer be hired to fill positions at U.S. embassies, causing a shortage of personnel worldwide. A report issued by the State Department inspector general in August 2019 concluded that the hiring freeze had a major negative impact on employees' morale and undermined the agency's ability to execute key administration priorities.

Meanwhile, Tillerson was slow to fill top leadership positions and other key agency roles, leaving numerous bureaus and offices understaffed. This generated further

(Continued)

STATE DEPARTMENT REORGANIZATION (Continued)

resentment among agency personnel and contributed to dozens of senior staff members quitting or retiring early. An analysis of Office of Personnel Management data produced by *The Atlantic* found that the State Department's civilian workforce shrank by more than 6 percent overall during the first eight months of the Trump administration. Attrition in certain personnel categories was even higher: 12 percent of employees classified as belonging to the foreign affairs series left the agency during this time.

Reorganization Plan

To inform his broader reorganization plan, Tillerson polled state and USAID employees and conducted listening sessions with various staff members to collect their input on agency missions, effectiveness, and operations, as well as their suggestions for organizational reforms. Reports indicated that many employees stated the agency was poorly structured, lacked accountability, and did not treat its staff well. Significant reform recommendations included moving consular affairs responsibilities—such as the issuance of passports, visas, and other travel documents—to the Department of Homeland Security (DHS), as well as extending the length of foreign postings by one year to provide more consistency for overseas employees.

Following the survey and staff sessions, Tillerson produced a "Listening Report" with recommendations for organizational change that included modernizing the State Department's information technology and human resources systems. Notably, the report also called for USAID and the State Department to remain distinct, if coordinated, entities because development and diplomacy were two very different missions. This appeared to undercut speculation that Tillerson would seek to merge the two agencies.

In July 2017, Tillerson sent a cable to agency employees announcing that two consulting firms had been hired to further develop and implement a restructuring plan. Their work would be guided by five committees comprised of USAID and State Department staff, who would analyze and advise on different components of the agencies' operations. Tillerson said he intended to produce a final reorganization plan by the end of 2017, with implementation set to begin in 2018.

Although the reorganization effort appeared to be moving forward, details of Tillerson's plan were sparse. The lack of information—coupled with the president's proposal of deep cuts to the State Department and USAID budgets—caused rampant speculation and anxiety among agency staff that Tillerson would ultimately announce widespread closures or consolidation of State Department bureaus and offices, and that this would in turn cripple American diplomatic efforts and influence around the globe. Such closures did not occur, although Tillerson did eliminate dozens of special envoy offices with responsibilities that overlapped those of other agency bureaus.

Congressional Response

Lawmakers on both sides of the aisle pushed back on the administration's proposed budget cuts and Tillerson's reorganization efforts. Appropriators in both chambers dismissed the president's budget requests, stating that the allocations for foreign aid and operations were insufficient and ultimately approving significantly higher funding amounts. "I think this budget request is radical and reckless when it comes to soft power," said Sen. Lindsey Graham, R-S.C., during a hearing on state-foreign operations appropriations for fiscal 2018. The fiscal 2018 funding measure also provided an opportunity for lawmakers to limit Tillerson's reorganization plan: The final bill included language prohibiting Tillerson from executing organizational changes at USAID or the State Department without congressional consent.

Additionally, lawmakers repeatedly urged Tillerson to end the agency's hiring freeze. On December 5, 2017, a bipartisan group of senators wrote a letter to Tillerson saying the freeze was "adversely affecting America's Foreign Service and Civil Service professionals and putting our nation's ability to carry out diplomacy at risk." A separate letter penned by Democrats on the Senate Foreign Relations Committee called for Tillerson to provide more details on his reorganization plan, stating that Congress must be a "full partner in the development of the department's reorganization effort, budget and spending cuts, workforce changes and other significant plans." Lawmakers also added language to the fiscal 2019 state-foreign operations funding bill that required both agencies to resume hiring at Obama-administration levels and to consult with Congress before attempting to downsize or expand their staffs.

A Muted Plan

Tillerson sought to assuage the concerns of State Department personnel and lawmakers. He began discouraging the use of the term *reorganization*, saying it incorrectly implied major structural changes, and dismissed the possibility that consular affairs would shift to DHS. He and other agency officials also emphasized plans for smaller changes, such as upgrading State Department technology, improving agency training, and increasing the responsibilities of U.S.-based staff to alleviate the workload for overseas employees. Some observers interpreted this shift as Tillerson backing down from a more ambitious reorganization plan, whereas others said it showed he never intended to make sweeping reforms. Either way, Tillerson did not have an opportunity to see his plan to fruition after he was fired by Trump in March 2018. His successor, Mike Pompeo, largely abandoned Tillerson's efforts and ended the agency's hiring freeze.

CHAPTER 5

Defense Policy

Defense Policy

President Donald Trump came to office pledging to rebuild the U.S. military after years of spending cuts while subsequently bringing to a close what he called the endless wars the nation was fighting in the Middle East and Central Asia. During his four years in office, he oversaw a 20 percent increase in the Pentagon's budget, a tenuous peace agreement with the Taliban in Afghanistan, the creation of a new space-focused military branch, and multiple changes to programs benefitting veterans. However, his tenure was also marked by frequent rifts with U.S. allies, a growing threat posed by the Islamic State in Iraq and Syria (ISIS), the politicization of military leaders, and a heated conflict that nearly pushed the United States to the brink of war with Iran.

CONFLICTS IN THE MIDDLE EAST AND CENTRAL ASIA

When Trump took office in January 2017, he inherited the ongoing wind-down of the nearly two-decade $2 trillion U.S. military engagement in Afghanistan that had killed more than 3,500 U.S. and coalition troops and tens of thousands of Afghans. Although the combat mission ended in 2014, thousands of U.S. soldiers remained in the country training and equipping Afghan soldiers to prepare them to secure their own nation and fight terrorist networks, including ISIS. The president largely shared the public's sentiment that the United States was unlikely to achieve its objectives in Afghanistan with an ongoing military presence, and he was therefore willing to continue the effort of his predecessor to draw down troops.

To that end, the Trump administration set its policy goals on pressuring the Taliban to accept a peace agreement that would diminish its strength in the country and put the Afghan government on stable footing, in exchange for U.S. troop withdrawal. How the administration planned to go about that, however, was largely kept secret, though the president did at times share insight on Twitter, something that angered members of Congress, who at one point subpoenaed Department of State leaders in an attempt to learn more about negotiations with the Taliban. After nearly two years of on-again, off-again talks that began in early 2018, in February 2020 the United States signed a deal with the Taliban that could pave the way to an end of U.S. involvement in the country by the spring of 2021.

While Trump touted the agreement as fulfilling his campaign promise to bring the country's longest-running war to a conclusion, it was fragile at best and required the Taliban to meet several conditions, chief of which were severing its ties with al Qaeda and not attacking Afghan cities. There was also hope that the Taliban would enter into a separate peace deal with the U.S.-backed Afghan government, which was not included in the February 2020 agreement. In the end, while the president removed thousands of troops from Afghanistan, the Taliban failed to meet the conditions of the peace agreement.

In the Middle East, Trump oversaw U.S. forces engaged in a Saudi-led coalition to fight Houthi rebels in Yemen's civil war, airstrikes targeting terrorist networks in Syria, and troop withdrawals in Iraq and Somalia. Many of these

Figure 5.1 Outlays for National Defense

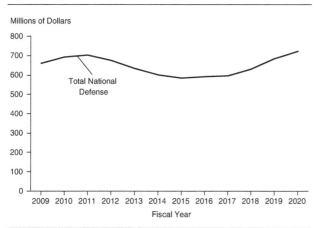

SOURCE: Office of Management and Budget, *Historical Tables, Budget of the United States Government: Fiscal Year 2021* (Washington DC: U.S. Government Printing Office, 2018), Table 3.2.

NOTE: Most of the expenditures, approximately 97 percent, were for military activities of the Department of Defense. Atomic energy defense activities accounted for most of the remainder. * indicates estimate

engagements renewed calls in Congress to either repeal or replace the 2001 and 2002 Authorization for Use of Military Force (AUMF). The AUMFs, passed in the wake of September 11, 2001, authorized military efforts in Iraq and Afghanistan to root out terrorist networks and those who had perpetrated the attacks. President Trump, like President Barack Obama before him, relied on these authorizations for other combat missions in the region. Independent bills and riders attached to larger pieces of legislation never passed, despite bipartisan support to sunset the previous AUMFs. Calls for their repeal reached a fever pitch in January 2020, when a U.S. airstrike in Iraq killed Iranian Maj. Gen. Qassem Soleimani, head of Iran's Islamic Revolutionary Guard Corps' Quds Force. In a classified briefing, the administration told Congress that they had intelligence indicating Iran was planning an attack against the United States. In turn, Iran struck two U.S. military installations in Iraq, though no U.S. casualties were recorded, and the rhetoric between the two countries quickly ratcheted up, raising questions about whether Trump's actions would push the country to war. Multiple pieces of legislation and amendments were proposed to overturn the AUMFs and prohibit the president from engaging U.S. forces in combat with Iran unless Congress authorized such activity or the United States was provoked. None of those bills or amendments succeeded, and the situation cooled, with Trump opting for sanctions instead of military force.

DEFENSE SPENDING

After years of cuts to defense spending under President Barack Obama—driven both by the economic toll of the Great Recession and the winddown of the wars in Iraq and Afghanistan—defense spending steadily increased under President Trump and in fact hit its highest levels ever. According to the president and some Pentagon leaders, the spending was crucial for maintaining military readiness in light of technological and warfighting advances being made by countries such as Russia and China.

Spending on defense activities remained subject to the Budget Control Act (BCA) of 2011 (PL 112-25), under which breached spending caps would result in across-the-board cuts known as sequestration. However, Congress passed two-year bipartisan budget agreements in both 2018 and 2019 to lift the BCA cap for fiscal years 2018, 2019, 2020, and 2021, and set higher spending levels that made it easier for legislators to reach a consensus on defense spending. These higher limits, however, did not stop members of Congress from looking for other ways to spend more than the set spending levels, such as through emergency spending proposals. Partisan disagreements over nondefense and tangentially related issues, however, kept Congress from passing stand-alone defense appropriations bills during the Trump administration, instead opting for bundled minibus and omnibus packages that gave members on both sides subtle victories.

Among these issues that slowed negotiations on defense spending was the construction of a proposed wall along the U.S.–Mexico border. As a candidate, President Trump promised to build a wall that would stop the flow of immigrants across the southern border, which he said Mexico would pay for. As president, Trump asked Congress for billions of dollars to fund the wall, but Democrats refused to provide anything. Instead, the president attempted to use the Pentagon's transfer authority to move funds between accounts in an effort to free up money for the wall. Democrats sought to limit his ability to do this, proposing policies within defense spending legislation and amendments that would drastically limit the Pentagon's transfer authority, which Republicans blocked. Funding for the wall arose in debates over nondefense appropriations bills as well, and was the impetus for a thirty-five day federal government shutdown from December 2018 to January 2019.

Figure 5.2 Outlays for Veterans

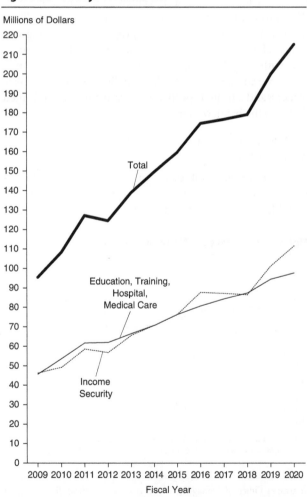

SOURCE: Office of Management and Budget, Historical Tables, *Budget of the United States Government: Fiscal Year 2021* (Washington DC: U.S. Government Printing Office, 2020), Table 3.2.

NOTE: Total line includes expenditures not shown separately. * indicates estimate

VETERANS CHOICE PROGRAM OVERHAUL

In 2014, the Department of Veterans Affairs (VA) faced a scandal surrounding its long-running service backlog problems. At some VA facilities, veterans were being forced to wait months for care, and some of them were dying in the interim, but the facilities were misreporting these instances or keeping appointments off the books to avoid the appearance of lengthy waits. Congress provided a temporary fix that year in the form of the Veterans Choice Program, which allowed veterans to seek care outside of the VA system if they met certain conditions, such as living more than forty miles from a VA facility or waiting more than thirty days for an appointment.

The program was widely popular, but also faced critical funding shortfalls, with the VA frequently reporting to Congress that they were spending money on private care as fast as Congress could appropriate it. In 2017, the year the Veterans Choice Program was due to sunset, Congress passed one bill eliminating its original expiration date and a second infusing billions more dollars into the program. They did so while also promising to find a longer-term fix for the situation.

The solution came in the form of the MISSION Act in 2018, which consolidated a variety of private care programs for veterans, including Veterans Choice, provided a $5.2 billion cash infusion, and removed the forty-mile/thirty-day restrictions on private care. Instead, veterans would now be able to seek covered care through a non-VA provider if they faced hardship in reaching a VA, the VA did not offer the services the veteran required, or a private care provider felt non-VA services were in the individual's best interest.

However, by making the switch, program funding moved from the mandatory to the discretionary side of the congressional ledger, meaning it would be subject to spending caps. Although the legislation passed by wide bipartisan margins in both chambers, this funding challenge—and the further privatization of VA care—worried Democrats. In subsequent years, Congress repeatedly found itself struggling to find ways to fund the new Veterans Community Care Program within statutory budget limitations.

Chronology of Action on Defense

2017–2018

With President Trump in the White House, Congress tried to move swiftly to utilize its majority in both chambers to pass legislation it had long sought during the Obama era. As is typical, the number of bills that passed the House far outpaced the Senate, where a slim 51–49 Republican majority prevented movement on most politically charged measures.

Nearly all the 115th Congress' defense-related work in 2017 and 2018 involved setting spending authorizations and providing appropriations for the Departments of Defense and Veterans Affairs. While largely considered "must-pass" legislation that draws broad bipartisan support, lawmakers struggled to reach consensus on stand-alone appropriation measures, instead opting to bundle the bills into minibus and omnibus appropriations packages. By doing so, Congress was able to move more appropriations measures to the president's desk before the start of the fiscal year. Perhaps more critically, however, bundling spending packages allowed members in each party to insert certain policy language that, if attached to a free-standing bill, could have threatened passage.

Both chambers were also largely able to avoid the significant topline spending disagreements that happened during the previous two Congresses by reaching budget agreements that raised spending caps above the 2011 BCA levels. Instead, where progress slowed, it was related primarily to leadership delaying decisions on how much of all government funds to allocate to each appropriations committee, disagreements about how much to provide to various defense and veterans programs, and partisan squabbles over the president's priorities, policy positions, and rhetoric. The intersection between policy and spending was most evident as Congress worked to pass fiscal year 2018 appropriations bills. After five continuing resolutions and a brief shutdown, it was not until six months into the fiscal year when the president finally signed a massive $1.3 trillion bill into law.

Lawmakers in the 115th Congress sought a number of changes to the popular Veterans Choice Program that allows veterans to seek care outside the VA under certain conditions. The House passed measures that would give veterans more options in which they could receive covered care when undergoing a bone marrow or organ transplant procedure. Both chambers passed—and the president signed—provisions that increased funding for the Veterans Choice Program and allowed it to continue past its original expiration date. The biggest change, however, came when the president signed legislation creating the Veterans Community Care Program that made permanent non-VA covered care for veterans who met certain conditions. While celebrated on both sides of the aisle, that 2018 legislation created new challenges for appropriators, who were now forced to fund the program within discretionary budget caps.

Fiscal Year 2018 Defense Authorization

The fiscal 2018 defense authorization bill was delayed slightly by a last-minute request from the Department of Defense to add a provision to the conference report that would allow the military to use drugs and medical devices not yet approved by the Food and Drug Administration (FDA) in emergency circumstances during a future conflict. Conferees initially included the provision, but drew backlash from the wider House and Senate membership, which threatened to derail passage of what was a broadly bipartisan bill. Ultimately, leadership decided to turn the Pentagon request into a separate bill, which passed both chambers by voice vote, allowing the defense authorization to move forward.

The final $692.1 billion authorization was $26.4 billion higher than the president's request, and included $626.4 billion for the Pentagon's base budget and another $65.7 billion for Overseas Contingency Operations (OCO), often referred to as war spending. The bill provided for $77.3 billion in spending above the amount allowable under the 2011 Budget Control Act. However, the legislation only authorizes the money. Appropriators would be unable to spend the full total unless Congress increased or eliminated the budget caps, neither of which happened in 2017.

In addition to setting the Defense Department's spending levels, the bill also set policy, authorized new weapons purchases, approved an increase in troop strength and pay, and called for multiple studies. Notably, the conference report and final measure did not include the authorization of a new arm of the military, a Space Corps that had been included in the House version.

The House passed the final authorization bill on November 14 and the Senate followed on November 16, 2017. President Trump signed the bill into law on December 12 (PL 115-91), and included a long signing statement, expressing his belief that many provisions interfered with his constitutional authority.

House Committee Action

On June 28, the House Armed Services Committee approved its fiscal 2018 defense authorization bill by a 60–1 vote. The bill would provide the Pentagon with $696.5 billion, $28.5 billion more than the Trump administration had requested, which itself was $54 billion more than total spending allowed by the Budget Control Act of 2011 (PL 112-25). The committee's version included $631.5 billion for the Pentagon's base budget, plus $65 billion for warfighting costs. The committee relied on $10 billion in OCO funding to augment the base budget, because these funds are not limited by the Budget Control Act. Committee leaders admitted that their proposal was unlikely to be enacted without significant changes to existing budget caps.

During the committee's markup session, members of both parties expressed their disagreement with President Trump on issues including defense spending priorities, climate change, and the proposed building of a wall along the U.S.–Mexico border. In the opening remarks of committee chair Mac Thornberry, R-Texas, he said the administration's budget proposal would "cut missile defense below current spending, cut shipbuilding accounts, add no additional soldiers to the Army, et cetera," all of which committee members rejected.

One notable area of bipartisan opposition to the president's proposal revolved around a wall at the U.S.–Mexico border. President Trump campaigned on the notion that once elected, he would build a wall along the full stretch of border to stop illegal immigration, and that he would force Mexico to pay for it. Although the committee had no jurisdiction over a wall on the border, it did adopt three amendments by voice vote that would block Pentagon funds from being used to build such barriers.

Committee members were less united on the idea of the creation of Space Corps, a new military unit that would be part of the Air Force and focus entirely on space. Rep. Michael R. Turner, R-Ohio, sought to block its immediate creation by proposing an amendment that would instead require a Pentagon study of the strategic need for the corps. The amendment was defeated by voice vote.

Debate in committee was also slowed over the Navy's Littoral Combat Ship. The shore-hugging vessels, built in two factories—one along the Great Lakes and another on the Gulf Coast—have a long history of maintenance problems. The Pentagon had requested authorization from Congress to fund one vessel, while the White House wanted two, and the committee bill provided for three. Democrats deemed the program wasteful, but an amendment to remove one ship from the bill was rejected 19–43.

House Floor Action

The House spent three days debating more than 200 amendments to the fiscal 2018 defense authorization bill before finally passing it by a widely bipartisan margin of 344–81 on July 14, 2017. The final House version would provide $688.5 billion in funds, well above existing budget caps, and contained provisions that would create a new space-focused military force, prioritize climate change, and call on the White House to develop a new AUMF. According to Thornberry, the bill would begin to undo what he called deep damage that the military had endured during years of spending caps. That argument and the bill's provisions even inspired Rep. Adam Smith, D-Wash., to vote for the legislation for the first time in three years. During floor debate, he noted that "U.S. national security is at risk," and espoused the likelihood that North Korea was aiming to develop a nuclear weapon that could strike the United States, which the Pentagon needed to be prepared to stop.

During debate, the House rejected an amendment, 208–217, proposed by Rep. Trent Franks, R-Ariz., that would require the Pentagon to study "violent" Islamic doctrine. The House also killed an amendment from Rep. Scott Perry, R-Pa., that would have eliminated language from the defense authorization bill that required the military to address and plan for the threat of global warming and rising sea levels.

Two of the most noteworthy provisions included in the House bill were an amendment from Rep. Tom Cole, R-Okla., calling on the president to provide Congress with a strategy, budgetary analysis, report, and legal justification for an AUMF. The provision did not go so far as to either outright eliminate or replace the existing AUMFs. The bill also authorized the creation of Space Corps, a new arm of the Air Force that would be dedicated entirely to space-focused missions. Notably, Secretary of the Air Force Heather Wilson objected to its inclusion, expressing concern that it only created new layers of bureaucracy.

Senate Committee Action

The Senate Armed Services Committee passed its fiscal 2018 defense authorization bill on June 28 after a closed-door markup session. It would provide $692 billion to the Pentagon, which included $60 billion for OCO funding. Like the House version, the Senate's draft also exceeded spending limits.

The bill provided billions of dollars for new fighters, ships, and advanced weaponry. This included $10.6 billion in authorization for ninety-four F-35 Joint Strike Fighters for the Air Force, Navy, and Marine Corps. In doing so, the panel demanded that the Department of Defense send to Congress a report on the affordability of operating these jets long term, expressing concern that the program lacks transparency and accountability. Another $739 million would go toward twenty-four new F/A-18E/F Super Hornet fighter jets, $2.9 billion for seventeen KC-46A aerial refueling tankers, and $1.6 billion for seventeen MC-130J aircraft.

Shipbuilding was another top spending item, with the committee authorizing $25 billion for thirteen new ships, including an extra DDG-51 Arleigh-Burke class destroyer and $1 billion in incremental funding for an amphibious assault ship. However, the bill did cut $300 million from aircraft carriers and set a $12 billion cap on any future carriers. It also reduced by $94 million the Littoral Combat Ship program, which has a history of cost overruns, schedule delays, and technical issues. The panel agreed with the Navy's goal of increasing its fleet to 355 ships, but noted that its budget might not cover new builds. Therefore, the committee asked the Navy to report on more cost-effective ways to build its fleet, including reactivating old ships or finding ways to extend the service life of existing ships.

Members of the military were set to receive a 2.1 percent pay raise in the committee's bill, but would also see higher TRICARE pharmacy co-pays, which would help the military offset the cost of special survivors benefits. The bill also boosted troop levels by 7,000, including 5,000 for active-duty Army, 1,000 for active-duty Marine Corps, 500 for the Army Reserve, and 500 for the Army National Guard. While increasing the number of troops, the bill targeted the Pentagon's bureaucracy, calling for a 20 percent reduction in deputy assistant secretaries of defense, a 10 percent reduction in senior executive service personnel, and the elimination of one assistant secretary from each military department.

Other key provisions in the bill focused on the Arctic and, among other things, called for a study of the Navy's Arctic capabilities, gaps that need to be addressed, and the authorization of six new icebreaker ships for the Coast Guard. It also called on the Defense Department to conduct an Artic wargame to assess its capabilities in the region, especially at a time of growing tension with Russia. The bill expanded the special immigrant visa program for Afghan interpreters and others who assisted the United States in combat missions in Afghanistan from 11,000 to 15,000, created a new $10 million fund for foreign forces and other groups or individuals who support Special Operations Forces, directed the departments of Defense and Homeland Security to develop recommendations on how the Army and Air National Guards could enhance border security while also gaining effective training, and required a plan from the Army on building a new ground combat vehicle prototype.

Senate Floor Action

On September 18, by a vote of 89–8, the Senate passed HR 2810, amended with S 1519, its own defense authorization language. As amended, the bill authorized $692 billion in discretionary funding for defense programs, including $60 billion in OCO funds.

Over the five days of debate on the bill, multiple senators expressed frustration at the speed at which the massive bill, and its many amendments, were being considered. The body adopted two packages of amendments, one with 104 amendments, and the second with forty-eight. The amendments included a $600 million authorization for the Navy's Littoral Combat Ship. The troubled program has two shipyards, one on Lake Michigan and the other on the Gulf Coast, and senators on both sides of the aisle from Alabama, Michigan, and Wisconsin were up for reelection in 2018. Another amendment would implement new measures at the U.S. Merchant Marine Academy in a bid to reduce instances of sexual assault, while another would, among other things, create an interagency management group to help curtail improper payments by federal agencies.

Other adopted amendments focused on U.S. foes Russia and North Korea. One, proposed by Sen. Joe Donnelly, D-Ind., was part of the 104-amendment package adopted by unanimous consent, and called for the creation of a strategy document on North Korea and the U.S. policy objective there. Another amendment, offered by Sen. Jeanne Shaheen, D-N.H., would ban the government from contracting with Kaspersky Lab, a Russian cybersecurity firm.

One of the most rancorous moments on the Senate floor during the five days of authorization debate related to Sen. Paul's proposed elimination of the 2001 and 2002 AUMFs. Senators speaking against the measure objected to the fact that the AUMFs would be eliminated without a dedicated replacement, which could cause chaos for U.S. troops overseas and confuse U.S. partners. In what would be its first AUMF vote in fifteen years, the Senate tabled Paul's amendment 61–36.

Conference and Final Action

While the House quickly moved to adopt the conference report by a vote of 356–70 on November 14, passage in the Senate was delayed after a last-minute Pentagon request to pass a separate bill that would grant expedited FDA approval of drugs and medical devices for battlefield emergencies. Initially, those working on the conference report included a provision that would give the Pentagon approval over certain drugs and devices, but that faced backlash from members outside the conference committee. In turn, the provision was removed and rewritten as a separate bill (HR 4374) that would expedite approval of unapproved medicines and medical products through the FDA in an effort to address military emergencies. The House and Senate cleared HR 4374 by voice vote on

November 15 and 16, respectively, and President Trump signed it into law on December 12, 2017 (PL 115-92).

After both chambers passed HR 4374, the Senate adopted the defense authorization conference report on November 16 by voice vote. The final bill authorized $692.1 billion for defense activities, including $626.4 billion for the Pentagon's base budget subject to spending caps, and $65.7 billion in uncapped OCO funds. The base funding was $77.3 billion higher than permitted under the Budget Control Act. The president signed HR 2810 on December 12, 2017 (PL 115-91).

The final bill included new funding for aircraft, missile defense, and shipbuilding, as well as provisions specifically targeting Russia, North Korea, and ISIS. Despite the overall winddown of efforts in Iraq and Afghanistan, Congress authorized $4.9 billion to train and equip Afghanistan's national army and other security forces and another $1.8 billion for a fund that aims to arm and train moderates in the fight against ISIS. Another $350 million was authorized for weapons for Ukraine in response to Russian aggression, and provided additional funding for the European Reassurance Initiative that sends equipment and U.S. forces to Eastern Europe. More than $15 billion went toward missile defense programs, including interceptors in Asia, cooperative programs with Israel, European missile defense, and assessments for more advanced systems in Hawaii and on the East Coast. The bill also called on the Missile Defense Agency to begin developing and testing a space-based antimissile system.

The military was authorized to receive $19.1 billion to procure Navy aircraft and another $19.2 billion for Air Force planes. This included ninety new F-35s, ten Poseidon surveillance aircraft, twenty-four F-18 Super Hornets, twelve V-22 tilt-rotor Marine aircrafts, seventeen new refueling aerial tankers, seventy-one AH-64E Apaches, ninety-two UH-60 Blackhawks, ten CH-47F Chinooks, four MH-47G Chinooks, thirteen Light Utility Helicopters, and new unmanned aerial vehicles and related missiles. Notably, most of the authorizations provided by Congress in the bill went beyond the White House request. Similarly, the $26.2 billion authorization for Navy shipbuilding was $6.3 billion more than requested and 50 percent higher than the previous funding authorization. That total included $5.9 billion for the construction and components of new attack submarines, $4.4 billion for aircraft carriers, $1.5 billion for three Littoral Combat Ships, and $5.3 billion for the next three DDG-51 destroyer vessels.

Spending on military equipment also included $2.2 billion for Army ground combat vehicles. The military housing and construction budget received $10.7 billion, cybersecurity initiatives received an $8 billion authorization, and the Energy Department was authorized $20.6 billion for defense-related activities, including nuclear weapons laboratories and environmental restoration and waste management.

The 2018 defense reauthorization provided for 20,300 additional soldiers and sailors, and an average 2.4 percent pay raise for military personnel, continued a special supplement to survivor benefits for those whose families are killed on duty, authorized $33.9 billion for defense health care programs, and banned the use of authorized funds for a new round of Base Realignment and Closure.

Fiscal Year 2018 Defense Appropriations

Like other annual appropriations work, negotiations on the fiscal 2018 defense appropriations bill were delayed by fiscal 2017 appropriations, a lack of set discretionary spending levels, and other competing congressional priorities. It was not until mid-June when the appropriations subcommittees began their markup process, but the halting progress left little hope that any appropriations measures would be enacted before the start of the fiscal year on October 1. In the end, Congress used five continuing resolutions (CR) to keep the government funded—with a brief, three-day shutdown between the third and fourth—and did not pass a final omnibus spending package until March 2018, with half the fiscal year already over.

The final $1.3 trillion measure signed by President Trump on March 23, 2018 (PL 115-141), allocated nearly $660 billion to defense programs, of which more than $589 billion was for the Pentagon's base budget and around $65 billion, for the warfighting Overseas Contingency Operations (OCO) account.

House Committee Action

The House Defense Appropriations Subcommittee approved a $658.1 billion appropriations bill on June 26 by voice vote, without amendment. The bill included $584.2 billion in discretionary base budget accounts as well as $73.9 billion in Overseas Contingency Operations (OCO) funding. These totals do not include military construction funds, which are included in the separate Military Construction–VA appropriations measure.

On June 29, the House Appropriations Committee took up the bill, approving it by voice vote with only one major amendment. The bill included identical topline numbers to that approved in the subcommittee, which was $68.1 billion above the fiscal 2017 enacted level and $18.4 billion more than the president had requested. The bill included a $28 billion fund to be spent at the discretion of the Secretary of Defense toward the implementation of a National Defense Strategy. That fund could go toward increased troop levels, research, operations, or other military procurement as the Pentagon saw fit to meet the security needs of the United States.

The amendment approved by the committee dealt with a new Authorization for Use of Military Force (AUMF). Specifically, it required that within eight months of the bill's enactment, a new AUMF must be passed to replace the 2001 and 2002 versions and must specifically address

present combat missions and threats. The committee version received no further action in 2017.

Senate Committee Action

The Senate Appropriations Committee released its version of a defense spending bill on November 21, well past the traditional October 1 deadline for setting fiscal year spending levels, but did not mark it up. Their bill would have allocated $650.7 billion to defense spending, to include $581.3 billion for core Pentagon and intelligence programs, $64.9 billion for overseas war spending, and $4.5 billion for missile defense programs.

The base total came in at more than $15 billion above President Trump's request, much of which would go toward buying additional warships and aircraft, upgrading facilities, and a larger pay raise for uniform members of the military, as well as weapons requested by military leaders.

The committee did not mark up its bill, and the draft measure received no further consideration in 2017.

Final Action

Congress passed, and the president signed, five continuing resolutions during the first six months of fiscal year 2018. The first three ran from October 1, 2017, until January 19, 2018, at which point federal funding lapsed for three days before a fourth CR passed, followed by the fifth and final CR, signed into law on February 9, 2018. The last stopgap measure gave Congress until March 23, 2018, to reach an agreement on spending measures or they would be forced to again provide a temporary solution.

On March 21, 2018, House and Senate appropriators announced that they had reached an agreement on draft language for the defense portion of the omnibus spending package congressional leaders were assembling. The language would give the Pentagon one of its largest budgets since World War II, totaling nearly $660 billion. Of that, $589.5 billion would go toward the Pentagon's base budget, while $65.2 billion went toward OCO funds (the Pentagon had already received another $4.7 billion for ship repairs and missile defense in one of the stopgap measures). These figures fell within the fiscal 2018 budget cap for discretionary defense spending, which was set at $629 billion through the February 2018 two-year budget agreement (PL 115-123). The final fiscal 2018 defense spending language included

- $11.5 billion for missile defense programs
- $23.8 billion for fourteen new ships
- $44 billion for certain aircraft, including ninety F-35 fighter jets
- $1.5 billion for defense medical research
- $1.3 billion for National Guard and Reserve equipment funding
- $800 million for Air Force space-focused programs
- A 2.4 percent pay raise for military personnel.

The measure also contained policy language prohibiting funds to acquire or transfer certain air defense systems to Ukraine, preventing the closure of the detention facility at Guantanamo Bay, Cuba, stopping funding from going toward a new round of base closures, and calling for an analysis from the White House on the cost and strategy to defeat various terrorist groups.

Once the full omnibus package was combined, leadership attached it as an amendment to HR 1625, an unrelated bill that had already passed both chambers. Doing so allowed them to expedite floor consideration. The House passed the $1.3 trillion omnibus measure 256–167 on March 22. In the Senate, where Majority Leader Mitch McConnell, R-Ky., was hoping for quick passage, it took hours of backroom negotiations to get certain members to drop their threats to block passage, with concerns ranging from the speed at which the bill had been put together to the renaming of a wilderness park in Idaho to excessive spending. The concerned senators relented, and the chamber passed the measure on March 23, 2018, 65–32. The president signed it into law the same day (PL 115-141).

Fiscal Year 2018 Military Construction–VA Appropriations

Although fiscal 2018 spending measures were supposed to be enacted by October 1, 2017, Congress was months behind schedule due to competing priorities, late enactment of fiscal 2017 appropriations, and also because the Appropriations subcommittees were hamstrung in beginning bill markup because the Budget committees had not yet set discretionary spending levels for the fiscal year. Without that number, subcommittees would not know how much they would be allowed to spend. Even so, some subcommittees began moving forward, with the Military Construction–VA bill being the first fiscal 2018 spending measure to be reported out of full committee in either the House or the Senate.

Despite that early progress, work on individual appropriations bills and smaller packages bogged down, and Congress had to pass five continuing resolutions (CRs) to keep the government funded. It was not until March 23, 2018, six months into the fiscal year, when the president signed an omnibus spending package for fiscal year 2018 (PL 115-141). Within that final measure was $92 billion for programs within the Military Construction–VA title, 12 percent more than fiscal year 2017 enacted levels.

House Committee Action

On June 12, 2017, the House Military Construction–VA Appropriations Subcommittee approved by voice vote an $88.8 billion spending measure for the programs that fall under its jurisdiction (HR 3354). This was $573 million below the White House's requested amount. Notably, the bill contained significant funding for a new VA electronic health record update, similar to the record system currently

used by the Department of Defense. However, because the VA had not yet provided a cost estimate or implementation plan, the subcommittee would hold back 75 percent of the funds dedicated to the project until it received additional information from the VA on how the project would proceed.

Three days later, on June 15, the House Appropriations Committee approved the Military Construction–VA appropriations bill by voice vote, marking the first spending measure reported out for fiscal 2018. Most of the $88.8 billion would go toward the VA, but the bill included a $2.1 billion, or 25 percent, boost from fiscal 2017 spending for military construction, raising the total funding level for construction projects to $10.2 billion.

There was little debate in the committee over the bill, though Democrats raised questions about what this $88.8 billion measure would mean for the other eleven appropriations bills that had yet to come out of committee, given that spending levels had not yet been set. They wondered about whether other committees would be forced to make cuts at the expense of the Military Construction–VA bill. Members also continued to call on Republicans and the White House to come to the negotiating table and find a way to raise discretionary spending limits set by the 2011 Budget Control Act (PL 111-25).

Senate Committee Action

On July 13, the Senate Military Construction–VA Appropriations Subcommittee approved a slightly larger $88.9 billion measure by voice vote (S 1557). That total included $78.4 billion in discretionary funds for the VA—$4 billion more than in fiscal year 2017—and $9.5 billion for 214 military construction projects, $1.8 billion more than the 2017 enacted level. Within the funding was $70.1 billion for veterans medical care, including $5.5 billion specifically for veterans of the wars in Iraq and Afghanistan and $316 million for treating traumatic brain injuries. Military construction funds included $1.4 billion for military family housing, $556 million for military medical facilities, $249 million for improvements to four overseas military schools, $575 million for National Guard and Reserve construction projects, $307 million for European Reassurance Initiative projects, and $331 million for the Overseas Contingency Operations funds for Middle Eastern projects. Arlington Cemetery was set to receive $81 million under the bill, while the American Battle Monuments Commission would receive $79 million.

In the Senate Appropriations Committee, members debated a handful of amendments. They adopted one that would give veterans easier access to medical marijuana in states where its use is allowed and also approved an amendment that would direct the VA to provide mental health care to veterans who received a less than honorable discharge from the military (though not those who were dishonorably discharged). Appropriators said that if a new

budget agreement was reached to raise spending levels, they would mark up the bill again to increase funding.

The bill did not receive a floor vote in 2017.

Final Action

With the prospects of a standalone bill dwindling, on July 27 the House voted 235–192 to approve a $790 minibus appropriations package that included the Military Construction–VA bill. The Senate, however, did not consider the legislation. On September 14, the House passed, 211–198, a $1.23 trillion omnibus package that encompassed all twelve regular appropriations bills. The bill surpassed the 2011 spending caps and had little chance of passing the Senate. However, it did mark the first time since 2009 when the House passed all twelve spending bills before the beginning of the fiscal year.

The two chambers in September agreed to a continuing resolution to keep the government funded until December 8, which was followed on December 7 by another CR to keep the government running until December 22, and a third through January 19, 2018. Disagreement over a variety of policy issues delayed passage of a fourth CR, resulting in a brief, three-day government shutdown. A fifth and final CR gave Congress until late March to reach an agreement on fiscal year 2018 appropriations.

The final fiscal 2018 $1.3 trillion omnibus spending package passed the House on March 22, 256–167, and the Senate on March 23, 65–32. President Trump signed the bill into law immediately after Senate passage (PL 115-141). The measure allocated $92 billion for programs within the Military Construction–VA title of the bill, which included $81.5 billion for the VA, up nearly 10 percent from the prior fiscal year; $68.8 billion for VA medical care accounts (notably, there was no specific boost for the Veterans Choice Program); and $10.9 billion for military construction, up 30 percent from fiscal 2017.

Fiscal Year 2019 Defense Authorization

Passage of the fiscal 2019 defense authorization bill, commonly referred to as the National Defense Authorization Act (NDAA) which authorizes funding and sets policy primarily at the Department of Defense and Department of Energy, marked the fifty-eighth year in a row that Congress had managed to move the legislation through both chambers and to the president's desk.

The NDAA is traditionally a bipartisan measure, though it spends months in markup and debate in subcommittees and committees where hundreds of amendments are proposed. Members in both the minority and majority often use the bill to set policies unpopular with the White House, because there is little threat of a veto. Work on the fiscal 2019 bill was no different, with controversial issues ranging from transgender troops serving openly to the development of new low-yield nuclear weapons to a military parade in the nation's capital.

Ultimately, the massive authorization passed both chambers and was signed by the president on August 13, 2018 (PL 115-232). In addition to setting various defense-related policies, the final measure authorized $708 billion in spending for defense and intelligence programs, which included $639.1 billion for the Pentagon's base budget and $69 billion for uncapped Overseas Contingency Operations (OCO) funds.

House Committee Action

Action in the House on the NDAA began in late April 2018, as the six Armed Services subcommittees filed their portions of the bill. The full Armed Services Committee met on May 7 for its annual markup, first reviewing each of the six subcommittee portions that addressed everything from whether to increase troop levels to whether the military should collect the email address of retiring service-members, then reviewing the full committee measure. Over the course of nearly fifteen hours into the early morning of May 8, the committee worked through hundreds of amendments.

Among one of the more contentious issues was a previously proposed bill from Armed Services Committee Chair Mac Thornberry, R-Texas, that he planned to fold into the NDAA. That bill would cut 25 percent from the $100 million budget for Pentagon support agencies by 2021 as well as eliminate a couple of small Pentagon organizations. These agencies handle various services, including logistics, contracting, and real estate. Democrats bristled at the idea, expressing concern that Thornberry's bill could make hasty spending reductions that without appropriate analysis could result in undue damage to basic Department of Defense functions. Rep. Anthony Brown, D-Md., proposed two amendments to limit Thornberry's proposal. The first, which was rejected by voice vote, would have called for an efficiency study of the Washington Headquarters Services, one of the support agencies Thornberry's package would close. His second amendment, which passed 33–28, required the Pentagon to undertake a feasibility study on whether it could transfer certain services currently offered by the Defense Information Systems Agency to other offices within the Pentagon.

The lengthy debate during the committee's markup also featured the question of whether the sage grouse and lesser prairie chicken should be kept off the endangered species list, an issue that has bogged down defense authorization legislation in the past. Supporters of the measure say that classifying the fowl as endangered limits usable training space on U.S. military bases. An amendment from Rep. Rob Bishop, R-Utah, proposed leaving the birds off the list for the next decade. The measure passed 33–28.

President Trump's border wall was the subject of multiple amendments, with committee members seeking alternately to ban its construction and admit that it could prove useful in stemming the flow of illegal immigrants. Rep. Ruben Gallego, D-Ariz., proposed an amendment that would prohibit the Pentagon from using any of its funds toward a border wall along the U.S.–Mexico border. Rep. Bradley Byrne, R-Ala., offered a substitute amendment noting that the Department of Homeland Security actually has jurisdiction in this area, and that the United States should be devoting all necessary resources toward border security. In response, Rep. Jim Langevin, D-R.I., proposed a perfecting amendment to override the Byrne amendment and stop defense funds from being used in wall construction. The perfecting amendment was rejected 33–28, while Byrne's amendment was approved.

A slew of amendments were proposed that would either limit or bolster U.S. engagement across the globe. Rep. Ro Khanna, D-Calif., offered an amendment to ban any funds in the bill from being used to refuel Saudi aircraft carrying out bombing runs against Houthi forces in Yemen. Democrats sought to reduce U.S. involvement in the region, where the long-running civil war and indiscriminate Saudi bombings had resulted in the destruction of infrastructure, hospitals, and schools, and the deaths of thousands of civilians. Republicans argued that if the United States drew back in its support, it could leave Iran in a place of strength and ultimately deepen the conflict. The amendment failed 19–42.

The final measure reported out of committee (HR 5515) by a vote of 60–1 authorized $708.1 billion in discretionary spending for the Pentagon, which included $69 billion in uncapped OCO funding. Other panels intended to authorize $7.9 billion to bring the total bill to the $716 billion cap established by the February 2018 bipartisan budget agreement (PL 115-123) that increased spending levels for fiscal years 2018 and 2019.

Senate Committee Action

On May 24, the Senate Armed Services Committee released the key provisions of their version of the NDAA, which had been marked up primarily behind closed doors. The panel's bill passed 25–2. It authorized $707.7 billion in funding, which included $617.7 billion in base Pentagon spending, $68.5 billion in OCO spending, and $21.6 billion for the Department of Energy. Another $8.2 billion in spending supported by the panel, but which was outside of their jurisdiction, could also be authorized and still fall within the $716 billion spending cap.

The committee also sought to add to the annual authorization the text of S 2098, a bill that would expand the Committee on Foreign Investment in the United States' (CFIUS) security reviews to include any deal that involves foreign control of specific U.S. assets situated near military installations, airports, and seaports. The bill also made some changes to the Department of Commerce export control program and would limit the ability of the president to lift sanctions imposed on certain Chinese companies.

For military equipment and capabilities, the Senate committee's bill provided $65 million for a somewhat

controversial low-yield submarine-launched ballistic missile, $7.6 billion for seventy-five F-35 fighter aircraft, and the procurement of ten new ships. Under the committee version, the military was also set to receive a boost in its ranks. The bill allowed for 485,741 active duty Army, 331,900 active duty Navy, 186,100 active duty Marine, and 325,720 active duty Air Force troops.

House Floor Action

The same week that the Senate Armed Services Committee began marking up its version of the NDAA, the House brought the measure to the floor for consideration. On May 23 and 24, the House waded through 168 amendments approved by the House Rules Committee for floor consideration. Many of those amendments were considered en bloc.

One contentious amendment offered by Rep. Jared Polis, D-Colo., would reduce by $198 million the funding authorization for the National Nuclear Security Administration's Weapons Account. That would bring total authorized funding for the program in line with the president's request. According to Polis and many other Democrats, the nation's existing nuclear arsenal should be enough to deter another nation considering a strike against the United States. Republicans countered that the United States was at risk of falling behind its adversaries who were quickly modernizing their nuclear capabilities. The amendment failed 174–239.

Republicans faced off against one another in a debate over where the Pentagon should buy its tableware. Two amendments, proposed by Reps. David McKinley, R-W.V., and Claudia Tenney, R-N.Y., would require the Pentagon to source its dinnerware and stainless steel flatware from U.S. manufacturers (McKinley and Tenney both represent districts with companies that manufacture these products). Thornberry's concern was that by approving the amendments, the Pentagon would be forced to spend more than necessary on plates and forks when that money could go toward other defense needs, and that there was no national security risk involved in allowing the Department of Defense to purchase these items from foreign manufacturers. Both amendments were defeated.

The House adopted seventy-four uncontroversial amendments by voice vote, many of which called for new studies and reports on specific operations abroad and how the Pentagon is spending its funds overseas. Rep. Mike Thompson, D-Calif., made a late-stage motion to recommit the NDAA to the House Judiciary Committee, asking them to report back with a gun control-related amendment that would expand background checks and authorize funding toward coordination and automation of the National Instant Criminal Background Check System. The measure was rejected 224–91. The House ultimately passed its fiscal 2019 defense authorization on May 24, 2018, 351–66.

Senate Floor Action

Senate debate on the NDAA stalled nearly as soon as it began on June 6, when Sen. Pat Toomey, R-Pa., objected to the motion to proceed because he first wanted a vote on an amendment he proposed that would require both chambers of Congress to approve, with a majority vote, any new CFIUS regulations with an economic impact estimated at $100 million or more per year. McConnell filed cloture on his original motion, and Toomey ultimately withdrew his objection. The Senate voted on cloture 94–2, but then Sen. Rand Paul, R-Ky., objected to allowing the NDAA to proceed unless the chamber first voted on his amendment that would help protect Americans from indefinite detention. On the evening of June 11, the Senate finally voted 91–4 to begin debating the NDAA the following day.

Before the chamber formally took up consideration of the measure on June 12, Sen. James Inhofe, R-Okla., who was managing the bill on the floor in place of Sen. John McCain, R-Ariz., who was battling brain cancer, announced that a number of amendments to the bill were being wrapped into a substitute amendment package which also included the Senate Armed Service Committee's version of the NDAA (S 2987). As is customary, the Senate was using the House-passed measure as its legislative vehicle. Within that package was a bipartisan amendment that would prohibit the U.S. government from subsidizing or buying anything from Chinese technology companies ZTE or Huawei and would also reinstitute export control violation penalties on those companies. While the president remained interested in allowing ZTE to continue to do business with the United States, members on both sides of the aisle and even the president's Secretary of Commerce wanted to punish the company for selling its products to Iran and North Korea, despite a U.S. sanction. Many also expressed concern that Huawei and ZTE, which is partially government owned, could pose a threat to national security if their products were used to spy on Americans. Two other amendments within the package would ban the Pentagon from selling F-35 fighter jets to Turkey, a rebuke to the nation that had been accused of giving North Atlantic Treaty Organization (NATO) allies' secrets to enemy countries.

During floor debate, senators reached an impasse over which amendments they wanted to include in the final bill. Sens. Bob Corker, R-Tenn., Rand Paul, R-Ky., and Mike Lee, R-Utah, submitted similar versions of amendments that would end the indefinite military detention of U.S. citizens. Both Paul and Lee requested unanimous consent to include their amendments, which Sens. Lindsey Graham, R-S.C., and Chuck Grassley, R-Iowa, objected to. In response, Paul and Lee asserted that, unless their amendments proceeded to a vote, they would object to all other amendments. Sen. Dick Durbin, D-Ill., objected to an amendment from Sen. Joni Ernst, R-Iowa, that would limit government funding for former presidents. The chamber declined to table two amendments, one from Sen.

Jack Reed, D-R.I., that would require that any new or modified nuclear weapons be authorized by Congress, and the Lee indefinite detention amendment.

Sen. James Inhofe, R-Okla., made multiple attempts to bring the situation under control, but eventually McConnell stepped in and filed three cloture motions: one on Toomey's CFIUS amendment, one on the substitute amendment to replace the House bill with the Senate version and a package of forty-five noncontroversial amendments, and one for the bill itself.

On June 14, the Senate rejected, 35–62 cloture on Toomey's amendment, voted 83–14 to invoke cloture on the substitute amendment, and finally voted 81–15 to invoke cloture on the defense authorization bill itself. The chamber agreed to the final bill on June 18, 2018, 85–10.

Conference and Final Action

On July 11, the conference committee convened to reconcile the differences between HR 5515 and S 2987. They released their conference report less than two weeks later on July 23, with both the House and Senate expressing a desire to approve the measure before their August recess.

The conference version authorized $708 billion in spending, among one of the largest defense spending measures since World War II, which included $639.1 billion for the base budget and $69 billion for uncapped OCO funds in support of operations in Afghanistan, the war on terror, and the fight against ISIS. The total was $16 billion more than the authorized fiscal year 2018 level, and $1.2 billion less than what the president initially requested.

The final measure included a 2.6 percent pay raise for uniformed military personnel and allowed for an additional 15,600 active-duty troops to be added to the military. The agreement also resulted in a significant boost for spending on equipment, authorized a submarine-launched low-yield nuclear warhead, and greatly increased funding for other new nuclear weapons. The fiscal year 2019 NDAA also included

- $10 billion to procure seventy-seven new F-35 aircraft
- $1.8 billion for ten Navy Poseidon aircraft
- $1.9 billion for twenty-four Navy F-18 Super Hornet aircraft
- $784 million for seven V-22 tilt-rotor aircraft for the Marines
- $2.4 billion for fifteen new refueling aerial tankers
- More than $3 billion for new drones and related missiles
- $1.2 billion for sixty-six new AH-64 Apache attack helicopters and upgrades and an equal amount for fifty-five new UH-60M multiuse Black Hawks
- $7.6 billion for new attack submarines
- $3.2 billion for another ballistic missile submarine
- $1.6 billion for three Littoral Combat Ships

Numerous other provisions were added to the measure specifically targeting U.S. foes Russia and China. This included $6.3 billion to provide equipment and U.S. troops to help nations in Eastern Europe protect themselves from possible Russian incursion. The bill also continued an existing ban on military cooperation with Russia and maintained the prohibition on U.S. government recognition of Russia's annexation of Crimea. However, struck from the final conference version was the provision included in the Senate version of the bill that would have banned U.S. exports to ZTE. President Trump overturned a previous ban against exports to ZTE.

Despite the push from House Armed Services Committee Chair Thornberry, the final agreement would neither eliminate the Washington Headquarters Service nor cut spending on certain Pentagon administrative functions by 25 percent. Instead, the Washington Headquarters Service would remain, and the Pentagon would be required to submit to Congress a report on the proposed budgetary cuts. The final measure also restricted the sale of F-35s to Turkey until Congress received and reviewed a report on strategic relations with and arms sales to the nation, and language pertaining to the sage grouse listing on the endangered species list was removed.

Notably, the final conference report thwarted Trump's attempt to hold a massive parade in the streets of Washington, D.C., to celebrate the nation's military strength. The bill banned the Pentagon from assigning any operational forces to the president's parade if it would impact the number of deployable troops. Defenders of the president's parade said it would help inspire a new generation of service members; opponents said the resources could be better used toward equipping troops, protecting the United States, and bolstering benefits for existing service members.

HR 5515 hit a technical snag before it could be approved by the full House. The House Ways and Means Committee objected to language in the bill related to sanctions under the 1987 Intermediate-Range Nuclear Forces Treaty that, according to the House parliamentarian, would affect revenue. The constitution requires that any revenue-related bills must start in the House, and this particular provision originated in the Senate. In turn, a sentence was added to the conference report reading "no provision affecting sanctions in this section or as an amendment made by this section shall apply to a sanction that affects the importation of goods." That technical change allowed the bill to move to the House Rules Committee, which swiftly approved its rules governing the eventual floor vote.

The House adopted the conference report on July 26, by a vote of 359–54. On August 1, the Senate voted 87–10 to approve the conference report and send the NDAA to President Trump for his signature. The president signed the NDAA on August 13, 2018 (PL 115-232).

Fiscal Year 2019 Defense Appropriations

In an effort to fully fund defense and intelligence budgets before the start of the fiscal year, Democrats and Republicans combined two of the largest appropriations packages, those for defense and Labor–Health and Human Services (HHS)–Education, into one bill. Passage, and the president's eventual signature on September 28, marked the first time since fiscal 2009 that the Department of Defense began its fiscal year funded.

The final $674.4 billion package, which included $606.5 billion for the Pentagon's base budget and $67.9 billion in warfighting funds, also increased troop levels, provided a pay raise for uniform military personnel, and authorized the purchase of dozens of new aircraft and ships (PL 115-245).

House Committee Action

The House Defense Appropriations Subcommittee released its draft language on June 6, 2018 (HR 6157). The bill would provide $674.6 billion in discretionary funds for defense and intelligence programs, which includes $68.1 billion for Overseas Contingency Operations (OCO). The total for core Pentagon programs was $17.1 billion higher than the fiscal 2018 enacted level, and much of that would go toward ninety-three F-35 fighter jets for the Air Force, Navy, and Marine Corps. The House fiscal 2019 defense authorization bill (HR 5515) only authorized seventy-seven of the aircraft, while the Senate's version authorized seventy-five. The panel's proposed legislation also provided more than $22 billion for warships, funding for medical research and preventing sexual assault, and gave all military personnel a 2.6 percent pay increase. The subcommittee marked up the bill in a closed-door session on June 7, before advancing it to the full House Appropriations Committee.

In early June, the House Appropriations Committee held its markup of the fiscal 2019 defense appropriations bill, voting on June 13, 2018, to send it to the House, 48–4. During consideration, the committee adopted four non-controversial amendments. One, from Rep. Mark Pocan, D-Wis., required the Pentagon to send a classified report to Congress on the ongoing support provided to Saudi Arabia as it relates to the civil war in Yemen. Another, from Rep. Chris Stewart, R-Utah, encouraged the continued development and deployment of cyber awareness tools; another, from Rep. Scott Taylor, R-Va., called for research and assessment of expanded military child care programs; and the fourth, from Rep. Mark Amodei, R-Nev., realigned $5 million in appropriations.

The committee also rejected, 22–30, an amendment from Rep. Barbara Lee, D-Calif., to repeal the 2001 Authorization for Use of Military Force (AUMF). Despite some Republican support on the committee for a repeal, those who voted against it did so because they felt the issue was outside of their purview. Similarly, the committee

rejected, 24–27, an amendment from Rep. Pete Aguilar, D-Calif., to ban the deportation of Deferred Action for Childhood Arrival recipients who had been honorably discharged from the military, with opponents saying it was outside the committee's jurisdiction.

House Floor Action

The full House began voting on the fiscal 2019 spending legislation the week of June 27, considering fifty-three amendments, including one from Representative Ruben Gallego, D-Ariz., that would ban certain government agencies from working with Chinese technology companies Huawei and ZTE. The companies are considered security risks and have been accused of violating U.S. sanctions, and though the Trump administration had eased restrictions on contracting with the groups, Congress sought to punish them further. It passed by voice vote. Other adopted amendments included those that would prohibit funds from being used to end reserve officers' training corps programs at certain higher education institutions, including any Historically Black College or University, one to provide $14 million for accessing commercial cutting-edge technology, and another to increase by $2 million funding for the Sexual Assault Special Victims' Counsel. A variety of other amendments within the bill shifted funding between programs.

Prior to passage, the House also rejected a number of amendments. One, defeated 114–267, was proposed by Rep. Joe Courtney, D-Conn., and would have removed $1 billion from certain Defense Department programs and shifted that money to the Virginia-class submarine program. Members from those states that would have been impacted by the $1 billion in cuts fiercely opposed the Courtney amendment. Three other rejected amendments dealt with money allocated to developing or purchasing weapons, including one from Rep. Bill Foster, D-Ill., that would bar appropriated funds from being used on space-based anti-missile interceptors. Foster's amendment was defeated 160–251.

Ultimately, the House approved the bill on June 28, 2018, 359–49, providing $674.6 billion for defense and intelligence programs, $20 billion more than the fiscal 2018 level. The final bill from the House preserved the funding for ninety-three fighter jets, $22.7 billion for new warships, and the 2.6 percent pay raise for all military personnel. It also provided for 15,600 new troops by the end of fiscal year 2019.

Senate Committee Action

On the same day that the House passed HR 6157, the Senate Appropriations Committee approved its version of the fiscal 2019 defense appropriations legislation (S 3159). The bill appropriated $675 billion in funds, the bulk of which went toward shipbuilding, the Defense Health Program, procuring military aircraft, and operation and maintenance accounts. During consideration, three

amendments were withdrawn, including one that would require regular monthly pay for National Guard troops who exceed their required training and duty days in a calendar year, another expressing the sense of the Senate that the president should use every tool at his disposal "to hold Russia and Putin accountable for attempts to undermine democracy in the U.S. and abroad," and a third that would provide $100 million for Israel's Iron Dome and short-range ballistic missile defense programs. The committee adopted by voice vote one amendment from Sen. Jeff Merkley, D-Ore., to require the Department of Defense to provide Congress with a report on low-yield nuclear weapons. They also adopted a managers amendment package by unanimous consent that would, among other things, block funds that would send F-35s to Turkey, require reports on reservist compensation and certain counterterrorism programs, and encourage the Navy to increase workforce development programs at its shipyards.

Senate Floor Action

In August, the Senate opted to bundle its defense spending measure with its Labor–HHS–Education appropriations bill in an attempt to speed up the appropriations process and move as many bills as possible to the president prior to the October 1 start of the fiscal year. Combined, the two bills account for nearly two-thirds of the total funding Congress appropriates each year. While historically the two bills are either passed separately or rolled into an omnibus funding package, pairing them meant that the chamber could find buy-in on both sides of the aisle: Democrats could leverage a funded start to the fiscal year for defense to get more money for health care programs, and vice versa. The Senate used the House-passed defense spending bill, HR 6157, as the legislative vehicle, despite the fact that the House had not yet voted on its Labor–HHS–Education measure.

The Senate spent the afternoon of August 23 arguing over an amendment from Sen. Rand Paul, R-Ky., that would ban federal funding for Planned Parenthood. Paul's amendment required only fifty votes to pass, and three Democrats were missing from the chamber that day. If Paul's amendment was attached to the spending legislation, it likely would have meant that the entire package would fail with Democrats voting as a bloc against it. Leaders in turn used a procedural tool to increase the vote threshold to sixty, after securing an agreement from Democrats that they would back down on attempting to force a vote on an amendment from Sen. Joe Manchin, D-W.V., to express the sense of the Senate that its legal counsel could defend provisions of the 2010 Patient Protection and Affordable Care Act in an ongoing lawsuit filed by the state of Texas. Paul's amendment received a vote but failed 45–48. The chamber went on to clear its Defense, Education–HHS–Labor spending bill 85–7, which would provide a total of $856.9 billion in funds for the titles within the bill.

Conference and Final Action

When conferees met to resolve differences between the House and Senate passed version of HR 6157, they were in relative agreement on the topline spending total for defense, which provided around $675 billion in both bills. They differed, however, in how those funds would be spent. For example, the House version authorized four more F-35 fighter jets and an extra Littoral Combat Ship, while the Senate wanted to provide $6 billion more for research and procurement programs focused mainly on space, artificial intelligence, and cyber.

On September 13, the conference committee announced that it had finished the compromise package, addressing differences primarily by choosing the higher of the two funding amounts in each bill. The final package provided $674.4 billion in discretionary funds, of which $606.5 billion was for the base budget and $67.9 billion, for OCO funding. The final bill also provided for

- 16,400 more troops
- A 2.6 percent pay increase for military personnel
- Ninety-three additional F-35 fighter jets
- Six V-22 Osprey tiltrotors
- Eight C-130J Super Hercules transport planes
- Three Littoral Combat Ships
- $10.3 billion for missile defense, including funds to help Israel develop new antimissile systems
- Millions of dollars in Senate-requested funds for new cutting-edge military research in systems in artificial intelligence, lasers, hypersonics, and machine learning.

On September 18, 2018, the Senate voted to approve the massive spending bill, 93–7. The House followed on September 26, voting 361–61 to send the measure to President Trump. The $855.1 billion combined Defense, Labor–HHS–Education bill also included a stopgap spending measure that would extend existing funding levels through December 7 for any agencies for which full-year appropriations had not yet been agreed to.

The president signed the final package on September 28 (PL 115-245) and subsequently issued a signing statement expressing his grievances with the measure. According to President Trump, the bill would "restrict the president's authority to control the personnel and materiel the president believes to be necessary or advisable for the successful conduct of military missions." Specifically, the White House took issue with prohibitions on moving the Navy's Pacific Command into Fleet Forces Command, a ban on transferring non-U.S. citizens held at Guantanamo Bay, Cuba, and a ban on developing nuclear armed interceptors of a missile defense system.

Fiscal Year 2019 Military Construction–VA Appropriations

The fiscal 2019 Military Construction–VA spending legislation was wrapped into a three-bill minibus package that was the first of the annual appropriations measures to clear both chambers and be signed by President Trump. The appropriation is often one of the easiest to pass, and generally does so with broad bipartisan support. The biggest sticking point during debate on the fiscal 2019 bill surrounded how to fund private medical care for veterans. Under a recently passed law that overhauled veterans' medical care (PL 115-182), funding for veterans who choose private or community care when they cannot readily access services at a VA facility moved from mandatory to discretionary, making it subject to funding levels set in February 2018 by the bipartisan budget agreement (PL 115-123). The final package allocated $98.1 billion to the Military–VA title. The president signed the legislation on September 21, 2018 (PL 115-244).

House Committee Action

On May 8, 2018, the House Appropriations Committee approved HR 5786, its $96.9 billion Military Construction–VA appropriations measure by a 47–0 vote. During debate, the panel rejected two amendments from Rep. Debbie Wasserman Schultz, D-Fla., one of which would have cut funds for a new "high value detention facility" at Guantanamo Bay, Cuba, and another that would ban the use of any Military Construction–VA funds appropriated for fiscal 2019 or earlier to be used toward construction of a wall along the U.S.–Mexico border. Both were rejected by voice vote. The committee did adopt one amendment, from Rep. Charlie Dent, R-Pa., to make the $69 million appropriation for the Guantanamo Bay detention facility contingent on separate authorization legislation. The measure was adopted by voice vote.

House Floor Action

In late May, the House bundled the Military Construction–VA appropriation bill with two other appropriations measures—Energy–Water and Legislative Branch—as a minibus, using HR 5895 (the Energy–Water bill) as the vehicle. Bundling some of the least controversial measures into a smaller package of legislation was widely viewed as an attempt by Republican leadership to move as many bills as possible to the president prior to the October 1 start of the fiscal year.

Debate slowed, however, as the chamber grappled with how to address a funding shortfall. In May 2018, when Congress restructured the Veterans Choice Program that allows veterans, under certain conditions, to seek care at private, non-VA facilities, it moved the program's funding from the mandatory side, where it was not subject to annual appropriations, to the discretionary side. Existing funding for the program was expected to quickly dry up,

meaning that legislators had to either make cuts elsewhere to get Veterans Choice to fit within budget caps or find a way to list it as emergency spending.

The House Rules Committee took up the issue during the first week of June. They blocked one proposal from Rep. Nina Lowey, D-N.Y., ranking member of the House Appropriations Committee, to ensure that the funds appropriated for so-called community care would not count toward discretionary spending caps. Instead, the committee adopted an amendment from Rep. John Carter, R-Texas, chair of the Military Construction–VA Appropriations Subcommittee to increase spending in the three-bill minibus by $1.138 billion without any cuts to other programs. By a 9–2 vote, the committee used a self-executing rule to add the amendment to the existing minibus. In doing so, when members voted for the rule, they were also approving the amendment.

On June 7, the House voted 225–187 to adopt the rules package, and followed with a 235–179 vote on June 8 to send the $147 billion three-bill minibus to the Senate. Sixteen Republicans voted against the bill, while twenty-three Democrats voted in favor.

Senate Committee Action

The Senate Military Construction–VA Appropriations Subcommittee approved its fiscal 2019 bill (S 3024) by unanimous consent on June 5, providing $98 billion in funding for the programs within its purview. This included a 6.1 percent boost to fiscal 2018 spending for the Department of Veterans Affairs. Notably, the panel punted to the full Appropriations Committee a decision about how to plug the Veterans Choice Program funding hole. The full Senate Appropriations Committee held its markup on June 7, reporting it favorably to the full Senate 31–0. One amendment adopted by the committee during debate, proposed by Sen. Steve Daines, R-Mont., would prohibit the VA from interfering with a veteran's ability to participate in a state-approved medical marijuana program or denying services to a veteran who participates in such a program.

Senate Floor Action

On June 14, Majority Leader Mitch McConnell, R-Ky., announced that he would soon bring for floor consideration the Military Construction–VA appropriations bill as part of the House-passed three-bill minibus. On June 18, the Senate voted 92–3 to invoke cloture on the motion to proceed on HR 5895, then adopted by voice vote an amendment swapping the House language for each underlying appropriations bill with the Senate language. Although there were plans to add an amendment to the bill during floor debate that would address the Veterans Choice Program funding gap, the final minibus, passed 86–5 on June 25, did not include any language or additional funding for the program, with senators instead deciding to let the situation resolve during conference with the House.

The final $98 billion package passed by the Senate included approximately $8 billion more in spending than the White House requested—something the president took issue with in a Statement of Administration Policy—but most of that money was connected to the Energy–Water appropriation.

Conference and Final Action

Many of the issues facing conferees related to Energy–Water policy riders in the bill, but under the Military Construction–VA title, members needed to work out how to address the expected Veterans Choice funding shortfall. On the Senate side, members wanted to exempt funding for the program from budgetary caps, while Republican members of the House, backed by President Trump, wanted to find cuts elsewhere. It became such a contentious issue that conferees called off their first public meeting that had been slated for early July. Negotiations also slowed over the summer because spending levels had not yet been set on the other nine appropriations bills, and any spending appropriated to the three titles in the minibus had the potential to impact the others.

Ultimately, conferees agreed to follow the House proposal for funding private medical care access for veterans, but increased their $1.1 billion set aside to $1.25 billion, remaining within the discretionary spending limit. House conferees said there was plenty of extra discretionary funding that could cover that total, but members from both chambers seemed to agree that a longer-term fix was needed to ensure ongoing funds for the program.

In total, the three-bill minibus provided $147.5 billion in spending, of which $98.1 billion went toward the Military Construction–VA title, a nearly 6 percent increase over fiscal 2018 funds. Negotiators signed off on the final bill on September 11, with Speaker of the House Paul Ryan, D-Wis., hailing the work as "the revitalization of our appropriations process," according to a statement from his office.

The Senate adopted the conference report on September 12, 2018, by a 92–5 vote, and the House followed the next day, sending the bill to President Trump on a 377–20 vote. The president signed the legislation at a southern Nevada VA hospital on September 21, 2018 (PL 115-244), marking the first time in a decade that three of the annual appropriations bills became law before the start of the fiscal year.

Other provisions included in the final package would

- Ban the use of appropriated funds from being used to close or realign Naval Station Guantanamo Bay or renovate, expand, or construct any facility in the continental United States for housing individuals detained at Guantanamo Bay
- Encourage the VA to address challenges facing homeless female veterans, undertake research into alternative pain care, and increase the number of rural health resource centers and home-based primary care programs
- Fund a pilot program to train veterans in agricultural vocations while simultaneously addressing their mental and behavioral health care needs
- Urge the VA to prioritize claims and appeals for elderly veterans and those in poor health and to investigate the potential use of medical marijuana for veterans
- Prohibit the VA from reprogramming certain funds between construction projects unless approved by Congress

Fiscal Year 2018–2019 Coast Guard Reauthorization

The traditionally uncontroversial, bipartisan reauthorization of the Coast Guard hit two major snags in 2017 and 2018. The first dealt with the regulation of ship ballast discharge, and the second speed bump came when a group of senators inserted a provision that would continue an exemption for a wooden paddle wheel boat to operate as a cruise ship on the Mississippi River, despite repeated safety concerns.

Senate Committee Action

On May 18, 2017, the Senate Commerce, Science, and Transportation Committee approved by voice vote S 1129, the annual Coast Guard reauthorization bill, overcoming last-minute opposition to a section of the legislation that would preempt certain federal and state regulations that control ballast water discharge—the water held in a ship that keeps it balanced—substituting instead less stringent Coast Guard standards. Concerns came from Democrats, including many along the Great Lakes, who were fearful that the dumping of ballast water under the revised standards would harm the fishing industry and drinking water, and introduce invasive species.

The bill would authorize $7.3 billion in funding for the Coast Guard for fiscal 2018 and another nearly $7.6 billion for fiscal 2019. The majority of the funding would go toward modernizing Coast Guard facilities and vessels, and also provided for the construction of a Coast Guard museum. Additionally, the bill called for survey and design work on a new icebreaker, created a short-term grant program for fishing safety, established a Center of Expertise for Great Lakes Oil Spill Preparedness and Response, and called for multiple other reports, studies, and audits.

House Committee Action

In June 2017, the House Transportation and Infrastructure Committee approved by voice vote HR 2518, which would reauthorize the Coast Guard for fiscal years 2018 and 2019. Only one amendment to the measure drew opposition during the committee markup. Rep. Rick Larsen, D-Wash., submitted an amendment that would give a shipbuilder in his district a Buy America waiver.

Shipbuilders in the United States are subject to the Jones Act (PL 66-261) which, among other things, requires that U.S. ships are built using domestic materials. The shipbuilder in question, Dakota Creek Industries Inc., exceeded the allowable foreign materials threshold under the Jones Act. Rep. John Garamendi, D-Calif., raised concern that by offering an exception to one company, other shipbuilders might see it as an opportunity to utilize more foreign-made products, which could ultimately weaken the Jones Act. However, the amendment moved forward. HR 2518 did not receive a floor vote in 2017.

Senate Floor Action

On April 18, Majority Leader Mitch McConnell, R-Ky., offered an amendment to S 140, a Native American water rights bill, that would remove the water rights language and replace it with the text of S 1129. The problem, however, remained ongoing Democratic opposition to the portion of the bill that allowed for the discharge of ballast water, with senators arguing that changing existing standards had the potential to irreversibly alter the ecosystem of the Great Lakes. Proponents of the provision said it would create more uniform, nationwide standards regulating ballast water and other ship discharges.

This bill also included a provision that would allow the Delta Queen, an old wooden paddle wheel boat, to operate on the Mississippi River as an overnight cruise ship, despite repeated warnings that the vessel was an unsafe fire hazard. The ship is the only one to have received several exemptions over the past several decades to continue operations without complying with flame-retardant material requirements. The last exemption ended in 2008 and had not yet been renewed by Congress, but Missouri Sens. Roy Blunt, a Republican, and Claire McCaskill, a Democrat, pushed a new exemption, determined to bring millions of tourist dollars and hundreds of jobs to areas along the river. (Previously, the Senate passed an exemption bill in 2017 that did not receive a vote in the House.) The Department of Homeland Security, which oversees the Coast Guard during peacetime, has repeatedly expressed its opposition to earlier attempts to exempt the Delta Queen. Those who support the ongoing exemption say it would result in improved safety, by requiring that 10 percent of the boat's structure be altered per year, with specific focus on combustible areas and new exits for evacuating the ship.

Ultimately, a procedural vote on S 140 failed. In the months that followed, Sens. John Thune, R-S.D., and Thomas Carper, D-Del., worked on compromise language to address the ballast concerns. In November, they announced final language for a reauthorization bill that would authorize $12.1 billion in spending for fiscal 2018 and $10.5 billion for fiscal 2019, and would also require the Coast Guard to apply Environmental Protection Agency (EPA) rules regulating invasive water species to ballast discharge. In a November 13, 2018, floor statement,

Carper said the bill would help prevent "polluted ballast water discharges from entering our waterways, minimize the risk of introduction of invasive species in the Great Lakes and other sensitive ecosystems, and maintain important environmental protections for our waters that are enshrined in the Clean Water Act."

On November 13, the Senate voted 93–5 to close debate on the measure, and on November 14, passed the reauthorization bill 94–6. The final bill sent to the House included both the ballast discharge language and the exemption from Coast Guard fireproofing regulations for the Delta Queen.

House Floor Action

On November 27, the House suspended the rules and agreed to S 140 by voice vote. The president signed the bill into law on December 4 (PL 115-282). As passed, the final measure authorized $12.1 billion in spending for fiscal year 2018, an increase of $1.7 billion from fiscal year 2017. Another $10.6 billion in discretionary funding was provided for fiscal 2019, which included $7.9 billion for operations and maintenance, $2.7 billion for infrastructure, and $29 million for research and development. The bill included both the exemption for the Delta Queen through December 1, 2028, and the EPA ballast regulations.

The bill created a national standard for ballast water and other ship discharges that pre-empt state law. The measures would help stop the spread of invasive species and would allow states to maintain regulation authority over specific vessel discharge, including sewage. Military and certain other vessels would be exempt from the new standards. The EPA would be required to develop vessel discharge pollution control standards in cooperation with the Coast Guard and governors within two years of the law's enactment.

The final measure called for various assessments of Coast Guard operations and strategic plans for meeting statutory requirements, established a Great Lakes Center of Expertise for oil spill response that would monitor and identify gaps in existing oil spill response capabilities, provide education and training to responders, and work to standardize oil spill response techniques. It also provided for the establishment of a National Coast Guard Museum in Connecticut. The measure reauthorized fishing safety and research grants, authorized the establishment of a canine currency detection team, and banned for eighteen months the closure or personnel reduction of any Coast Guard air facility that had been previously proposed for closure.

Authorization for Use of Military Force

After the September 11, 2001, terrorist attacks, Congress passed two Authorization for Use of Military Force (AUMF) bills in 2001 and 2002 that gave then-President George W. Bush authority to wage war in Iraq and

Afghanistan. The Obama administration used the legislation to continue military operations within Iraq and Afghanistan, carry out campaigns against the Islamic State of Iraq and Syria (ISIS), and target other terrorist groups both within and outside both nations. For years, lawmakers on both sides of the aisle argued that to continue the ongoing operations in the Middle East, a new AUMF was needed, one that could better support the evolving U.S. engagement in the region. Democrats and Republicans were unable to reach a consensus on new legislation during Obama's presidency, but again took up the issue during Trump's four years in office.

Senate Committee Action

After he took office, President Trump relied on the 2001 AUMF (PL 107-40) to target ISIS in Syria and other terrorist groups, including Al-Shabab in East Africa. In June 2017, a group of senators again set off to find a compromise on a new AUMF that would better define the current U.S. mission in the region. They placed their focus on a proposal sponsored by Sens. Jeff Flake, R-Ariz., and Tim Kaine, D-Va., who had tried unsuccessfully to pass similar legislation in the previous Congress.

Their new measure, SJ Res. 43, limited the scope of authority specifically to military action against al Qaeda, the Taliban, and ISIS. It also created a congressional oversight function that would give legislators the option to add other groups to the authorization as "associated forces." SJ Res. 43 would replace the 2001 and 2002 AUMFs and expire after five years unless Congress reauthorized it. The measure did not receive a committee or floor vote.

House Committee Action

In July 2017, the House Appropriations Committee also took up the issue, and approved an amendment to the defense appropriations bill (HR 3219) that would require a new AUMF within eight months of the bill's enactment. All but one Republican on the committee approved the measure, signaling that it had a greater chance at passage than previous AUMF overhaul attempts. Some Democrats and Republicans had publicly and privately expressed concern that by relying on the existing AUMF, Trump could land the United States in a new war in the Middle East.

However, Democrats wanted a more limited scope that prohibited significant ground invasions and that included a sunset provision requiring congressional reauthorization, while Republicans wanted to provide the president and Department of Defense greater leeway. The Rules Committee ultimately removed the amendment from the appropriations bill, and House Speaker Paul Ryan, R-Wis., expressed a desire for the administration to take the lead on a new AUMF. "I think it's in our interest to have a new one; I just want to make sure we have one that works for our warfighters," Ryan said at his weekly news conference. On September 7, the Trump administration said it would not propose a new AUMF, deciding instead that it already

had the legal authority it needed to target ISIS, al Qaeda, and other terrorist groups.

On October 12, 2017, Rep. Mike Coffman, R-Colo., introduced the Authorization for Use of Military Force Against al-Qaeda, the Taliban, and the Islamic State of Iraq and Syria (HJ Res. 118) that would repeal both the 2001 and 2002 AUMFs and replace them with a new measure specifically allowing for the use of "all necessary and appropriate force" to prevent terror attacks against the United States by al Qaeda, ISIS, or any person, but not a sovereign nation, that is part of a group or supports a group "engaged in hostilities against the United States" or U.S. armed forces and civilian personnel. The measure would expire after five years unless it was reauthorized. The bill was not marked up by the end of the year.

Senate Floor Action

The Senate again took up the issue of the AUMF while debating its defense authorization bill (S 1519). Sen. Rand Paul, R-Ky., proposed an amendment similar to that passed out of the House Appropriations Committee that would eliminate the 2001 AUMF within six months of the bill's passage. Some Republicans, including Senate Majority Leader Mitch McConnell, R-Ky., opposed any such provision, arguing that eliminating the AUMF without a replacement would create too much uncertainty for U.S. troops. Democrats were divided, with some, such as Sen. Kaine, supporting Paul's measure and others believing that the AUMF needed to be replaced rather than rescinded.

Paul's amendment was tabled on September 13 by a 61–36 vote and was not included in the final defense authorization bill. Senators again circulated a new AUMF draft in mid-December, however, it was not marked up by the end of the year.

Support for Disabled Veterans

In the spring of 2017, the House considered three pieces of legislation that specifically addressed the needs of disabled veterans. This included provisions increasing certain compensation, providing coverage for residential adaptations, and a new way to submit VA benefit appeals. All three made their way to the president's desk and were enacted.

House Committee Action

On April 5, 2017, the House Veterans Affairs Subcommittee on Disability Assistance and Memorial Affairs held a hearing on the first of these bills, HR 1329, the Veterans' Compensation Cost-of-Living Adjustment Act of 2017. The subcommittee reported it out favorably a few weeks later. Under the legislation, Congress directed the VA to increase the rates of veterans' disability compensation, the clothing allowance for certain disabled veterans, dependency and indemnity compensation for surviving spouses and children, and other allowable compensation. The increase, set to take effect on December 1, 2017, would

match the benefit increase provided under Old Age, Survivors, and Disability Insurance of the Social Security Act. On May 17, 2017, the full House Veterans' Affairs Committee held its markup, reporting the bill to the full House as part of an en bloc vote.

Another related bill was HR 3562, which would authorize the VA to provide residential adaptations for qualified veterans in vocational rehabilitation programs, at a cost of up to $77,307 per veteran with a service-connected disability. The full House Veterans' Affairs Committee held its markup on October 12, 2017, and reported the bill favorably to the full House by voice vote.

Perhaps the most consequential of the legislation impacting disabled veterans that was considered by the House Veterans' Affairs Committee was HR 2288, the Veterans Appeals Improvement and Modernization Act. The bill would create three "lanes" for a veteran to submit a benefits appeal, in an effort to reduce the amount of time former service members wait for decisions. The VA had long faced an appeals backlog; according to the panel, from fiscal 2015 to 2017 the appeals workload increased from an estimated 380,000 to 470,000, which the VA said would take five years to clear if no new appeals were filed. On May 17, 2017, the committee favorably reported the bill to the full House.

House and Senate Floor Action

There was little pushback on any of the veterans bills that came out of the House Veterans Affairs Committee. HR 1329 passed the full House by voice vote on May 23, was cleared by unanimous consent by the Senate on October 25, and was signed by the president on November 2, 2020 (PL 115-75). Similarly, HR 3562 sailed through both chambers, passing the House on November 6, 2017, 400–0, the Senate on May 16, 2018, by unanimous consent, and the president gave it his signature on June 1, 2018 (PL 115-177).

The House passed the original version of HR 2288 on May 23, 418–0. In the Senate, Sen. Rob Portman, R-Ohio, proposed a substitute amendment, which was adopted by unanimous consent on August 1, 2017, followed shortly by approval by unanimous consent of the underlying bill. During a pro forma session on August 11, the House agreed to the motion to concur on the Senate version of the bill by unanimous consent.

President Trump signed the legislation on August 23, 2017 (PL 115-55), saying at an address to the American Legion's national conference that the law would "get decisions much more quickly in a fraction of the time." Senate Veterans' Affairs Committee Chair Johnny Isakson, R-Ga., celebrated the enactment, issuing a statement after the president's signing that noted "for far too long, our veterans have faced unacceptable delays in their claims appeals. With this legislation, we're going to reduce the time it takes for our veterans to get a decision and increase the opportunity for them to receive their just benefits."

Protecting Veterans' Tax Credits

Under the 2010 Patient Protection and Affordable Care Act (ACA), often referred to as Obamacare, certain individuals can receive premium tax credits to help make the cost of purchasing insurance through the individual market more affordable. To qualify for the credit, a person cannot be otherwise eligible to receive another affordable health insurance option, such as one through an employer, Medicaid, or TRICARE, the military health benefits system.

However, there is an exception to the rule specifically for veterans, some of whom do not qualify for care through the VA while others simply choose to pursue private coverage. A 2012 IRS rule allows all veterans and their dependents to receive the premium tax credit if they purchase insurance on the exchange, even if they would otherwise qualify for VA health insurance. According to a report by the Urban Institute, a social policy think tank, between 2013 and 2015, that provision (which is not found in the law itself) resulted in a nearly 40 percent decrease in the number of uninsured veterans.

Since its inception, Republicans have attempted to dismantle the ACA through Congress and the courts. In 2017, with a majority in both the House and Senate and a Republican in the White House, the House passed, 217–213, an ACA replacement: the American Health Care Act (AHCA; HR 1628). Missing from the language of the bill, which never passed the Senate, was a carve out to allow veterans to receive the premium tax credit for purchasing insurance through the exchange.

An early version of the Republican bill did include the veterans' exemption. However, the language was removed in favor of using the budget reconciliation process. Budget reconciliation makes Senate passage easier by limiting amendments and debate and requiring only a simple majority to invoke cloture, rather than sixty votes. However, the process can only be used for bills related to spending and revenue, meaning nonbudgetary elements, such as the veteran tax credit exemption, had to be removed. The AHCA also did not include language that would direct the IRS to reissue the regulation, so it would be up to the Treasury Department and IRS to develop new regulations for veterans should the AHCA become law.

The omission riled Democrats. While Republicans held that veterans would not be impacted by the AHCA, Democrats disagreed. "Seven million veterans will lose their tax credit for their families in this bill," House Minority Leader Nancy Pelosi, D-Calif., said on May 16, 2017, at the Center for American Progress Ideas Conference. At a May 9, 2017, press conference, Sen. Richard Blumenthal, D-Conn., said the bill would "yank tax credits away from veterans unlike any other American." Sen. Tammy Duckworth, D-Ill., a combat veteran, said at a press conference that veterans would be forced "to pay thousands of dollars extra each year" under the AHCA,

and that as many as 8 million veterans could see their health care costs rise.

Notably, *The Washington Post* and *PolitiFact* took issue with the Democratic claims, pointing out that the overall impact was far more uncertain because the IRS had not weighed in on whether it would maintain the regulation. The Republican counterargument was that the 2012 IRS rule would continue to cover veterans; however, some legal experts disagreed, noting that there is no guarantee that the IRS would decide to apply its ACA rules to the AHCA.

In response to concerns about the tax credit, in 2017 Congress attempted to codify an Internal Revenue Service (IRS) regulation that gives a tax credit to veterans who choose to purchase health insurance through the exchange, but who are otherwise eligible for coverage under the Department of Veterans Affairs (VA). The debate over the bill language had more to do with Democrats' disinterest in entertaining additional Republican attempts to overturn the 2010 Patient Protection and Affordable Care Act (ACA) than the regulation itself.

House Committee Action

To address the controversy over veterans' tax credits, on May 4, 2017, Rep. Sam Johnson, R-Texas, introduced a bill (HR 2372) that would turn the IRS regulation into a law. The Veterans Equal Treatment Ensures Relief and Access Now (VETERAN) Act would modify the tax code so that an individual is not considered covered under VA health insurance unless that person is enrolled in the program's coverage. The language of the bill would codify the regulation as applicable under the ACA, or under the AHCA if it passed.

On May 24, the House Ways and Means Committee considered the legislation. Democrats offered ten amendments during debate, including those that would ban states from adding work requirements for veterans receiving Medicaid, restore a Medicare tax on high-income earners, further adjust tax credits for veterans to ensure they pay no more than 10 percent of the cost of premiums, and maintain the ban on health insurance companies discriminating against those with preexisting conditions. Nine of the amendments were ruled not germane. At one point, debate became heated, and Rep. David Schweikert, R-Ariz., accused Democrats of lying about the AHCA and its impact on veterans. "Never in 25 years on this committee have I heard anyone call another member a liar," said Rep. Richard E. Neal, D-Mass., the committee's ranking member.

Ultimately, the committee favorably reported HR 2372, by a 22–14 vote, with Rep. Ron Kind, D-Wis., joining Republicans in favor.

House Floor Action

On June 15, 2017, the House passed the VETERAN Act by voice vote; it was never considered in the Senate. After the vote, Rep. Phil Roe, R-Tenn., chair of the House Veterans' Affairs Committee, expressed confidence that the IRS would have maintained the exemption without HR 2372, but in a speech on the House floor said he was glad to "put an end to posturing over this issue and codify Congress' expectation." Because the AHCA also did not become law, the 2012 IRS regulation providing veterans an exemption to the premium tax credit remained in effect.

Veterans Choice Program Expansion

Throughout the 115th Congress, the House and Senate passed numerous pieces of legislation targeting different aspects of the Veterans Choice Program. Their early work included addressing funding shortfalls, changing the program's sunset date, and helping transplant patients. But in 2018, Congress voted to completely overhaul Veterans Choice, combining it with other similar VA offerings and establishing it as a permanent option for veterans.

Congress in 2017 sought to expand the Veterans Choice Program (PL 113-146), which allows veterans to use a private care provider if they would otherwise have to wait more than thirty days for an appointment or travel more than forty miles for care. What was initially in 2014 intended to be a temporary patch while seeking to improve VA services was a focus for President Trump, who promised on his campaign website to "ensure every veteran has the choice to seek care at the VA or at a private service provider of their own choice." The two bills that reached the president's desk in 2017 eliminated the program's expiration date and also provided additional funds to ensure the program would not run dry. In both instances, Democrats and Republicans expressed a desire to develop additional legislation that would continue to alleviate the burden veterans sometimes face when seeking care through a VA facility.

House and Senate Action

Sen. Jon Tester, D-Mont., sponsored S 544, the Veterans Choice Improvement Act. The bill would amend the Veterans Access, Choice, and Accountability Act of 2014 by eliminating the August 7, 2017, sunset date. In turn, the program could continue to operate until it ran out of funds. The Senate passed the measure by voice vote on April 3, 2017. The bill also made some changes related to record disclosure and payment processing, making the VA the primary payer for certain medical care where it was previously the secondary payer, and allowed for sharing of medical information with non-VA medical providers related to a veteran's care.

The legislation was approved in the House by voice vote on April 5, just days after the House Veterans' Affairs Committee had favorably reported a nearly identical bill, HR 369, which would also remove the sunset date and let the program continue to run until it had exhausted its funding. The Congressional Budget Office estimated that some $200 million would be left in the program after August 7. President Trump signed S 544 on April 19, 2017 (PL 115-26).

In the summer, Congress again returned to the issue of the Veterans Choice Program. This time, they cleared a $2.1 billion funding patch to keep the program running. S 114, the VA Choice and Quality Employment Act, passed the Senate on May 25 by unanimous consent. On July 24, the House took up the bill but failed on a motion to suspend the rules, 219–186, due to multiple objections raised by Democrats and some veterans groups. The chief concern was that the legislation as presented in the House included specific provisions to cover the $2 billion funding boost. These included extending both a reduction in pension payments provided by the VA for certain veterans in VA nursing care facilities and a fee collection requirement for certain VA-guaranteed housing loans.

In turn, House Veterans Affairs Chair Phil Roe, R-Tenn., proposed a revised package to the House Rules Committee that included appropriations for the Veterans Choice Program and medical facility lease renewals that lawmakers had been seeking for many years. The new package also included provisions to help with hiring and retention of VA employees. The House passed the revised measure on July 28, 414–0, and the Senate followed with a motion to concur on the House amendments on August 1. The president signed the bill into law on August 12, 2017 (PL 115-46).

Veterans Choice for Transplant Patients

Another Veterans Choice Program fix considered in the 115th Congress dealt specifically with care veterans are eligible for if they receive a transplant from a live donor who is not a veteran. Under existing law, a veteran was prohibited from using the Veterans Choice Program to receive coverage for a transplant from a live non-veteran donor. The program also placed restrictions on which treatment facilities a veteran could use when receiving a transplant, sometimes forcing veterans to travel long distances from their home. To address the situation, the House passed a bill in late 2017 that would allow veterans to access the Veterans Choice Program regardless of whether the live donor was a veteran.

House Action

On November 2, 2017, the House Veterans' Affairs Committee considered HR 1133, the Veterans Transplant Coverage Act of 2017, and HR 2601, the Veterans Increased Choice for Transplanted Organs and Recovery (VICTOR) Act of 2017, both of which addressed concerns about the existing service limitations for veterans who require a transplant. HR 1133, introduced by Rep. John Carter, R-Texas, would amend the Veterans Choice Program in two primary ways. First, it would allow the VA to cover a live donor transplant operation for an eligible veteran regardless of whether the donor is eligible for VA health care. Second, it would stipulate that the VA could provide for this operation at either a VA or non-VA care facility. These provisions extended to any necessary before- and

aftercare for the donor. Only one amendment was proposed to HR 1133, stipulating that care and services provided by the VA were subject to the availability of appropriations; that amendment was approved by voice vote, as was HR 1133.

The second, related piece of legislation considered by the committee on November 2 was HR 2601, introduced by Rep. Neal Dunn, R-Fla. The bill would amend the Veterans Choice Program to allow veterans who live more than 100 miles from a VA transplant center to instead seek organ or bone marrow transplant care and services at a federally certified non-VA facility that covers Medicare patients nearer to their home. According to the bill's supporters, research published in the *Journal of the American Medical Association* found that veterans who live long distances from VA transplant centers were less likely to receive a transplant, resulting in a greater likelihood of death for some patients. In turn, the bill sought to remove barriers to care by allowing veterans and their non-veteran live donors to receive a covered procedure whether at a VA facility or not.

One amendment was proposed during consideration, which eliminated the 100-mile requirement, and instead substituted language allowing veterans to seek transplant care at a non-VA facility if they faced unusual or excessive burdens related to geographical, environmental, or medical factors that made receiving care at a non-VA facility more appropriate. The amendment, along with the bill as amended, were approved by voice vote.

On November 7, 2017, under suspension of the rules, the full House passed both HR 1133 and HR 2601 by voice vote. Neither piece of legislation received a vote in the Senate. However, the provisions of HR 1133 were enacted as part of the VA MISSION Act of 2018 (PL 115-182).

Veterans Choice Program Overhaul

In the wake of a nationwide scandal over care delays at Department of Veterans Affairs (VA) facilities—that in some instances resulted in veteran deaths before appropriate care could be received—in 2014 Congress established the Veterans Choice Program (PL 113-146). The program allowed veterans to seek care at an eligible non-VA medical facility if that individual lived more than forty miles from a VA facility, had to wait more than thirty days for an appointment, lived within forty miles of a facility but faced certain transportation challenges, or lived more than twenty miles from a VA facility located in Alaska, Hawaii, New Mexico, or a U.S. territory (excluding Puerto Rico). The program was intended as a temporary fix while the VA worked on a longer-term solution to address care concerns, however, the program became hugely popular with veterans and when President Trump took office in 2017, he promised to continue, or even expand, the program. In 2017, Congress eliminated the program's original termination date (set for August of that year) and also provided additional funding to keep the program running while

DEFENSE LEADERSHIP

During President Trump's four years in office, he had multiple secretaries of defense. His first, James Mattis, brought extensive military experience to the White House. During his forty-three-year career, Mattis commanded the 1st Marine Division in Iraq and served as Commander of Marine Corps Combat Development at Quantico, Commander of U.S. Marine Forces Central Command in the Middle East, Commander of U.S. Joint Forces Command, NATO's Supreme Allied Commander Transformation, and Commander of U.S. Central Command. He directed forces during the Persian Gulf War, and the wars in Iraq and Afghanistan. Mattis retired from the armed forces in 2013 as a four-star Marine Corps General. Because the National Security Act prevents anyone from serving in the position of Secretary of Defense within seven years of their retirement as a commissioned military officer, Congress had to pass a bill providing Mattis an exemption to join the Trump administration, which the president signed on his first day in office, January 20, 2017 (PL 115-2). Mattis was subsequently confirmed by the Senate the same day, 98–1.

Mattis' tenure with the Trump administration was troubled, and the former Marine commander frequently disagreed with the commander in chief. Where Mattis favored close partnerships with U.S. allies and using the American military as a means to deter, rather than provoke, war, Trump was quick to dismiss global partnerships in favor of his "America first" agenda and often looked ready to use American military might at any moment. Some members of Congress came to rely on Mattis as a voice of reason and critical pushback against what they viewed as impetuous decisions by President Trump. Sen. Mark Warner, D-Va., referred to him in a Twitter post as "an island of stability amidst the chaos of the Trump administration." Mattis also argued against drawing down troops in Afghanistan, something Trump favored, instead advocating for additional forces to help end the war and stabilize the nation. Mattis also reportedly supported ongoing joint military exercises with South Korea, allowing transgender individuals to serve in the military, and the United States' involvement with NATO.

In December 2018, it was President Trump's announcement to remove all U.S. troops from Syria, where they were fighting the Islamic State of Iraq and Syria (ISIS), that resulted in Mattis' decision to leave the administration. Mattis, concerned that a withdrawal could threaten stability in the region as well as U.S. troops and allies, attempted to change Trump's mind, but ultimately resigned. In his resignation letter, Mattis wrote "because you have the right to have a Secretary of Defense whose views are better aligned with yours on these and other subjects, I believe it is right for me to step down from my position." Trump announced Mattis' resignation on Twitter, writing that "General Mattis

was a great help to me in getting allies and other countries to pay their share of military obligations. A new Secretary of Defense will be named shortly. I greatly thank Jim for his services!"

To succeed Mattis, Trump first nominated Patrick Shanahan, a former Boeing executive, but then withdrew the nomination after a background investigation revealed abuse allegations during Shanahan's divorce. Trump subsequently nominated Mark Esper on June 21, 2019, who had served for ten years on active duty in the U.S. Army and eleven years in the National Guard and Army Reserve before retiring in 2007. After leaving the armed forces, Esper served as chief of staff at the conservative Heritage Foundation, was former Sen. Chuck Hagel's legislative director, served as a staff member for various Senate and House committees, was the national security advisor for former Sen. Bill Frist, served the administration of President George W. Bush as Deputy Assistant Secretary of Defense for Negotiations Policy, and worked at Raytheon Company. Prior to his nomination as Secretary of Defense, Esper served in the Trump administration as the Secretary of the Army.

Esper differed from those who previously held the position in that he lacked deep military experience and high-level government knowledge. Even so, the Senate easily confirmed Esper, 90–8, on July 23, 2019, bringing to an end the longest period of time the nation had ever gone without a permanent Secretary of Defense. Unlike Mattis, during his time in the role Esper rarely appeared to be actively engaged in any of the administration's defense strategies, though his advisors said he preferred working behind the scenes. Esper kept a low profile, rarely commenting on administration policy or butting heads with the president in public, and the media widely speculated that he was infrequently involved in cabinet negotiations. One of Esper's most notable achievements was revising the National Defense Strategy to place a greater emphasis on threats coming from China and Russia, and their rapidly evolving armed forces and general disregard for international law.

Less than eighteen months into his tenure, on November 9, 2020, Trump ousted Esper, announcing in a tweet that the secretary was being terminated and replaced by Christopher Miller, the current director of the National Counterterrorism Center, a former Army Green Beret who served in Iraq and Afghanistan. Reportedly, the president had intended to fire Esper in the summer of 2020 for a number of reasons, including because Esper publicly disagreed with Trump's decision to use federal forces to quell racial justice protests in Washington, D.C. Miller did not receive Senate consideration.

During his tenure, Trump also appointed a new chair of the Joint Chiefs of Staff. On December 8, 2018, he announced via Twitter that Gen. Mark Milley, the Army's

chief of staff and a four-star general, would replace retiring Gen. Joe Dunford. Over his more than forty years in the armed forces, Milley held many staff and command positions, including commanding general of U.S. Army Forces Command, and had multiple operational deployments in countries such as Egypt, Iraq, Afghanistan, Haiti, and Somalia. Milley was confirmed by the Senate on July 25, 2019, by an 89–1 vote, and took the oath of office on September 30 of that year.

During his first year in the position, Milley attempted to distance himself from the politics of the White House, focusing instead on strengthening relationships with U.S. allies and keeping open lines of communication with nations such as Russia. In June 2020, however, the chair came under fire when he walked—in his combat uniform—with the president from the White House to Lafayette Square. Moments earlier, federal agents had forcibly removed racial justice protesters from the area. Milley had repeatedly discouraged the president from deploying federal troops during protests across the country following the killing of George Floyd by Minneapolis police, but Trump reportedly ignored him. According to those close to Milley, the general did not realize he was on his way to a photo op, but instead thought he would be reviewing National Guard and other troops deployed near the White House.

negotiations were ongoing about its future. After months of negotiations, in mid-2018, Congress created the Veterans Community Care Program, a permanent entity within the VA that consolidated various programs, including Veterans Choice, that gave veterans the option to seek care outside VA facilities.

House Committee Action

Since its inception, the Veterans Choice Program had burned through cash faster than Congress could provide it; according to an estimate from the VA, the program was set to run out of its annual funding by the middle of each year. In turn, Congress sought a solution to make permanent certain provisions of Veterans Choice while also fixing the perpetual funding shortfall. After extensive negotiations in the House and Senate, the resulting bill, HR 5674, would overhaul the Veterans Choice Program. It would be allowed to run for one year after the bill's enactment in its current form, after which time the program would be consolidated with seven others like it into a permanent Veterans Community Care Program. The draft legislation also provided $5.2 billion in funding, expanded a program that supports family caregivers, and added a provision for a review of the VA's assets. Starting in fiscal 2020, the funding for the Choice program would move from the mandatory to the discretionary side of the congressional ledger, meaning it would be subject to annual spending caps.

On May 8, 2018, when the bill came up for consideration by the House Veterans Affairs Committee, Chair Phil Roe, R-Tenn., encouraged panel members to support the bill as written, rather than trying to amend it, given the extensive work that had gone into balancing the desires of the VA, White House, and Congress. That did not stop Democrats from offering amendments, including one from Rep. Tim Walz, D-Minn., that would address the move of funds from mandatory to discretionary, which was rejected. The bill was favorably reported to the full House, 20–2.

The White House was a strong supporter of the measure, with press secretary Sarah Sanders saying on May 7, 2018, that it would transform the VA "into a modern, high-performing, and integrated healthcare system that will ensure our veterans receive the best healthcare possible from the VA, whether delivered in the VA's own facilities or in the community." Democrats, however, continued to have reservations, even those who supported the bill in committee. These worries rested on two primary points: that the program was not sustainably funded and that it amounted to the privatization of the VA's care system. Still, the bill had broad bipartisan support, and was also backed by multiple veterans advocacy groups.

House and Senate Floor Action

The House took up S 2372, the VA MISSION Act, the Senate's version of legislation to create the Veterans Community Care Program, easily passing it on May 16, 2018, 347–70 (the Senate Veterans Affairs Committee discharged the legislation on March 1 by unanimous consent and the full Senate agreed to the measure on the same day, also by unanimous consent). In addition to creating the newly combined Veterans Community Care Program and providing a $5.2 billion cash infusion, the legislation also eliminated the existing Veterans Choice Program rule that only covers veterans for non-VA facility services if they live more than forty miles away from a facility or are forced to wait more than thirty days for care. Instead, the legislation would let a veteran access outside care if the VA did not offer that specific service, or if a private provider deemed outside care to be in the best interest of the veteran. The bill also provided for a review of VA facilities and assets to determine which require modernization, realignment, or closure, and included provisions such as those that aimed to recruit and retain additional VA health care professionals and staff. To allay Democratic concerns about program funding, Senate leadership said they would take up the discretionary cap issue during consideration of the fiscal 2019 Military Construction–VA appropriation bill. The Senate agreed to the House changes on May 23, passing S 2372 by a vote of 92–5. The president signed it on June 6, 2018 (PL 115-182).

2019–2020

A highly charged political environment, largely driven by rhetoric at the White House, coupled with a Democratic-led House and Republican-controlled Senate, meant that passing any major defense-related legislation during the 116th Congress was unlikely. Or, as was the case of the annual National Defense Authorization Act (NDAA), required extensive conference negotiations to reach tenuous agreements that both parties could accept.

Progress during the second year of the 116th Congress was further hampered by the global COVID-19 pandemic, which forced the body to delay markups, meet virtually, and more narrowly focus their efforts on keeping defense programs funded and functioning, rather than drafting major overhauls to existing programs or implementing partisan wish lists. Ongoing partisanship came to a head in December 2020 when President Trump vetoed the hugely bipartisan NDAA, only the fourth such veto in the law's history. Both chambers of Congress easily passed veto overrides. While the president appeared to agree with the bulk of the package, he took issue with specific language, or lack thereof, addressing the renaming of military bases that currently bare the names of Confederate generals and stripping protections from social media platforms.

Continuing the theme of the previous years, Congress was again forced to fold defense, VA, and military construction appropriations into continuing resolutions and omnibus spending packages for fiscal years 2020 and 2021 rather than passing standalone spending bills. Because of split control, the spending measures required extensive negotiation related not to topline funding for defense programs, but rather over policies included in the measures. Some of the most contentious related to the ongoing fight over President Trump's desired wall along the U.S.–Mexico border, changes to the military court system to better protect individuals who file sexual assault allegations, limiting the president's war authority, and pulling troops out of Afghanistan.

Outside of keeping defense-related activities funded, Congress also took action on legislation to enhance care available to veterans, targeting mental and behavioral health with a series of bills. Among other things, these measures made grants to community organizations that work to prevent veteran suicide, covered the cost for veterans to seek emergency mental health treatment outside the VA system, expanded telehealth services, and ensured mental health providers would be available at each VA location.

Fiscal Year 2020 Defense Authorization

The National Defense Authorization Act (NDAA) traditionally enjoys broad bipartisan support. Debate on the massive fiscal year 2020 bill threatened to derail its streak of fifty-eight consecutive years of passage, however, as a Democratic-controlled House and Republican-controlled Senate struggled to reach a consensus on a number of hot-button issues. These included money for President Trump's border wall, low-yield nuclear weapons, the detention facility at Guantanamo Bay, and the topline number authorized for defense spending.

Full committee markup on companion pieces of legislation began in the House and Senate Armed Services Committees in June, and by late October, the conference committee was still far enough apart on a passable package that Sen. James Inhofe, R-Okla., filed a "skinny" NDAA, a barebones version of the annual legislation that simply met Congress' obligations. It was not until December 20, 2019, that the president signed the final fiscal year 2020 NDAA, which authorized $743.3 billion in spending that included $658.4 billion for the Pentagon's base budget and $71.5 billion for Overseas Contingency Operations (OCO) funds (PL 116-92).

Senate Committee Action

The Senate Armed Services Committee moved first on marking up its fiscal 2020 NDAA (S 1790), wrapping up its two days of closed-door meetings on May 22. The committee authorized $750 billion in spending for the Pentagon, in line with its budget request, divided as $642.5 billion for the base budget, $75.9 billion for war funding, and $23.2 billion for the Department of Energy's national security programs. Another $8.4 billion in spending outside of the committee's jurisdiction was also authorized.

Within its authorization, the committee gave the green light to $10 billion in funding for ninety-four new F-35 fighter jets, $948 million for eight F-15EXs, and $24.1 billion in new warships. The Senate did not authorize the president's requested $3.6 billion to fund a wall along the U.S.–Mexico border, dealing a significant blow to a key presidential priority, though it did authorize the creation of Space Force. The committee also blocked the delivery of and future sales of F-35s to Turkey unless that country could certify that it had not received a Russian-made air defense system.

House Committee Action

The House Armed Services Committee began its markup on June 12, considering the six panel bills and the chair's mark, a draft of the NDAA that reflected the priorities of committee Chair Adam Smith, D-Wash. Smith's version of the bill would authorize $733 billion in new defense spending, and this topline number quickly drew complaints from both sides of the aisle, as Democrats said it was too high, while Republicans felt it was too low to maintain a military postured to counter rising threats around the globe. Smith's bill also prohibited any Pentagon

funds from going toward the construction of a wall along the U.S.–Mexico border, stopped new detainees from being transferred to the military detention facility on Guantanamo Bay, banned the deployment of low-yield nuclear weapons, disallowed the sale of F-35 fighter jets to Turkey under certain conditions, and kept the Pentagon from reducing its active-duty troop levels in South Korea below 28,500. Smith's bill did provide $4.5 billion to support the ongoing U.S. engagement in Afghanistan, and included a provision that would make it easier for Afghans who supported the U.S. war effort to immigrate to the United States.

In the opening minutes of the full committee markup, Democrats and Republicans argued over the $733 billion authorization, with Republicans seeking $750 billion, in line with the bill drafted in the Senate. The higher total would be $34 billion above fiscal year 2019 defense funding, but, according to committee Republicans, was in line with what Pentagon officials thought was necessary.

The committee moved relatively quickly to approve the six subcommittee panel markups, with a few notable exceptions. The version from the Strategic Forces Subcommittee was among the most contentious, resulting in an hours-long debate on low-yield nuclear weapons. The subcommittee sought to stop the Trump administration from deploying these weapons, by blocking funding for the deployment of a submarine-mounted W76-2 warhead. Democrats argued that the limited damage caused by the weapon would make it more tempting to use, and therefore could push the United States closer to nuclear conflict. Republicans argued that not having the funding for deployment would leave the United States weaker and less prepared to compete with other nuclear armed foes. Rep. Liz Cheney, R-Wyo., proposed an amendment during subcommittee markup that would strike from the panel's portion of the bill the language blocking the weapon's deployment, but it was rejected in a party-line 8–10 vote. The full subcommittee went on to approve their mark 10–8, with all Republicans opposed. Cheney used the full committee markup to again propose amendments to remove the restriction on deployment of low-yield nuclear weapons; both of her amendments on the issue failed 26–30. Ultimately, the full committee approved the Strategic Forces Subcommittee markup with the deployment ban intact by a party-line 29–24 vote.

Another issue before the committee that sparked significant debate related to an amendment proposed by Rep. Jacky Speier, D-Calif., that would create a four-year pilot program in which a special prosecutor would handle sexual assault cases at U.S. military academies, removing them from the traditional chain of command. According to Speier, moving these cases outside the purview of the commandants of the service academies could have an impact on a decline in reporting rates, despite an increase in the number of sexual assaults. Rep. Mike Turner, R-Ohio, proposed a substitute amendment that mirrored one in the

Senate's version of the fiscal year 2020 NDAA that would instead require a review of the role the chain of command plays in these cases. Republicans expressed uncertainty about how Speier's proposal could upset the balance of power and undermine court martial authority. Turner's amendment was rejected 27–30, and Speier's was adopted by voice vote.

The House Armed Services Committee voted in favor of authorizing Space Force, with a perfecting amendment that would prohibit the new wing of the armed forces from using National Guard resources to establish its own force. The creation of this space-focused military service was a policy priority of President Trump's and one that Republicans had attempted to enact in the fiscal 2018 NDAA (PL 115-91) before it was removed by the Senate. Another issue stripped from the fiscal year 2019 NDAA that received support in the Democratic-controlled committee related to Iran. An amendment from Rep. Ro Khanna, D-Calif., which would bar the president from going to war with Iran unless either Congress declared war or the nation was attacked, resulted in a lengthy debate. Though some Republicans in both chambers had previously expressed support for limiting the president's powers as it relates to Iran, Republicans on the committee objected to the amendment's language, saying it was too limiting and would stop the United States from helping protect its allies in the region. Khanna ultimately withdrew his amendment, with Smith promising that it, or some variation of it, could have a vote on the House floor.

Republicans also scored mixed victories on removing language from the chair's mark related to Guantanamo Bay. They were able to strike the portion noting that the lack of transfers or repatriations of those prisoners who have been cleared for movement "poses serious policy and human rights concerns." They were not, however, successful in eliminating language that would ban new detainees at the facility (it was rejected on a party-line 26–31 vote). Another amendment to prohibit construction of a prison in the United States to replace Guantanamo Bay was also rejected 26–31, as was an amendment that would stop defense funds from going to transfer detainees from the prison. One Republican amendment related to the prison was passed, 29–28, specifically preventing detainees at the facility from being transferred to El Salvador, Guatemala, Honduras, Mexico, or Venezuela.

Rep. Mike Rogers, R-Ala., proposed three amendments to ensure President Trump would receive funding for his border wall, but all three were rejected 26–31. The first sought to strike language from the chair's mark that would prohibit the Pentagon from using its money to fund the wall, the second would have removed language targeting the president's ability to declare a national emergency over illegal immigration, and the third would have removed language limiting the president's ability to send troops to the border. A fourth border wall amendment, proposed by Rep. Vicky Hartzler, R-Mo., was also defeated along party

lines, and would have given the Pentagon the authority to spend its funds constructing a border barrier under the guise of counter-drug missions.

One of the final debates in the early morning hours of June 13 related to topline spending. Rep. Mac Thornberry, R-Texas, the committee's ranking member, introduced an amendment to authorize $750 billion in spending. Thornberry proposed to make up the difference between the chair's mark authorization and his proposal by giving the Pentagon funding for additional F-35 stealth fighters, hypersonic weapons development, construction of aircraft carriers, 5G infrastructure, and other weapons programs. The amendment was rejected 27–30, with one Democrat, Rep. Elaine Luria of Virginia, voting with Republicans.

In total, the committee spent twenty-one hours marking up its bill before sending it to the floor with a 33–24 vote. The final committee bill authorized $733 billion in spending for the Pentagon, made up of $622.1 billion for the base budget and $68.1 billion in uncapped Overseas Contingency Operations funds. The bill was deeply unpopular with many of the committee's Republicans.

Senate Floor Action

When the bill came to the floor, Senate Majority Leader Mitch McConnell, R-Ky., moved quickly to limit amendments and debate. In turn, Democrats threatened to filibuster over a variety of amendments, including one that would bar President Trump from going to war without the approval of Congress, and Sen. Rand Paul, R-Ky., indicated, as he had in years past, that he would block consideration of other amendments if his did not get a vote, including one that would allow the 2001 Authorization for Use of Military Force (AUMF) to expire.

Despite the rancor in the leadup to the vote, debate was relatively muted and the Senate passed its version of the NDAA on June 27 by a vote of 86–8, with three Republicans and five Democrats voting in opposition. The bill that passed the Senate largely tracked with the Pentagon's budget request, authorizing a total of $750 billion in spending.

To prevent any possible filibuster, McConnell scheduled an extended vote—one that ran past when the chamber had already approved the NDAA—to give senators the chance to vote on an amendment sponsored by Sen. Tom Udall, D-N.M., and co-sponsored by Sens. Mike Lee, R-Utah, and Paul that would block the Pentagon from using any funds for a conflict with Iran unless the use of force was authorized by Congress first. McConnell allowed the vote to run long so that those Democrats participating in a presidential debate had time to return to Washington. The motion failed 50–40; the unanimous consent agreement required sixty votes for adoption. Notably, the Senate had already approved, 90–4, an amendment sponsored by Sen. Mitt Romney, R-Utah, that expressed that the president has the authority to defend the United States and its people against military attacks launched by other nations. That amendment did not specifically mention Iran, but

was widely seen as a means to counter the language seeking to limit the president's authority with relation to the Middle Eastern country.

House Floor Action

After their July 4 recess, the House reconvened to consider the NDAA and it was already facing an uphill battle. Republicans looked likely to vote as a bloc against its passage, and coupled with the traditional group of Democrats who typically vote against the NDAA for any number of reasons including the total spending, it could have meant the bill's demise.

The Rules Committee gave the go-ahead to 439 amendments for floor consideration. This included the one Smith promised Khanna barring a war with Iran unless it was authorized by Congress or a means of self-defense, which was adopted 251–170. Another involving war powers was proposed by Rep. Barbara Lee, D-Calif., to repeal the 2002 AUMF. That was also adopted, 242–180. Other amendments approved by the House included those to limit arms transfers to Saudi Arabia and the United Arab Emirates, allow transgender individuals to join the military, ban the Pentagon from housing foreign nationals detained by immigration agents, and stop the Pentagon from spending money at the president's properties unless they could be reimbursed by Trump.

Amendments rejected by the House included those dealing with the immigration situation at the U.S.–Mexico border. One would block the president from sending U.S. troops to the border to enforce immigration laws, another sought to stop the Department of Defense from using their facilities to house unaccompanied migrant children, and a third would have banned the Pentagon from using its funds to detain undocumented immigrants at military facilities. The House also rejected, 115–307, an attempt to reduce the topline spending on the bill by $16.8 billion, along with a motion to recommit that would have put more money into military maintenance accounts and increased military pay. That motion was defeated 204–212. Notably, the House bill maintained language stopping the Pentagon from deploying low-yield nuclear weapons; an amendment from Turner to overturn that ban was rejected 201–221.

On July 12, the House approved its version of the fiscal 2020 NDAA (HR 2500), 220–197, authorizing $733 billion in Department of Defense spending. The bill did not receive any Republican votes, breaking with a longstanding tradition.

Conference and Final Action

As passed out of their respective chambers, the House and Senate fiscal 2020 NDAAs were vastly different on a number of critical issues, not least of which was the $17 billion gulf between the toplines on each bill. Other issues facing the conferees as they met in September included how to handle the Pentagon's low-yield nuclear weapons,

what prisoners could be sent to the detention facility at Guantanamo Bay, and whether the president needed congressional approval to take military action against Iran. For his part, President Trump had already announced that he would veto the House bill if it reached his desk.

Negotiators shied away from commenting on the bill's progress, though by late October there were indications it was not progressing well when Senate Armed Services Committee Chair Inhofe announced that he introduced a "skinny" NDAA that primarily included the critical authorizations but not the most contentious issues. Inhofe said he did not intend for his version of the legislation to act as a substitute for the full bill, but that if an agreement could not soon be reached, such a measure might be necessary.

The first week of December, Thornberry announced that the conference committee had reached an agreement on all of the critical issues facing them. On December 9, the committee filed its fiscal year 2020 defense authorization bill. It authorized $735 billion in national security spending, which included $658.4 billion for the Pentagon's base budget (with some of those funds going toward defense-related activities at the Department of Energy), $71.5 billion in Overseas Contingency Operations (OCO) funds, and $5.3 billion for disaster relief. The NDAA also authorized another $8.1 billion to fund defense programs that fall outside the House and Senate Armed Services Committees jurisdiction.

The bill authorized the creation of Space Force, to be housed as a branch within the Air Force (similar to the way the Marines fall under the Navy), gave military members a 3.1 percent pay increase, blocked Trump from withdrawing the United States from NATO, and stopped the Pentagon from reducing active-duty troops in South Korea below 28,500 without a specific certification from the Secretary of Defense. Stripped from the bill were the provisions that would block deployment of low-yield nuclear weapons, ban the Pentagon from using its funds for a border wall, and reverse the prohibition on transgender troops.

Despite progressives arguing that their party gave up too much during conference negotiations, the bill overwhelmingly passed the House on December 11, 377–48. A bipartisan majority of the Senate followed on December 17, 86–8. President Trump signed the NDAA into law on December 20, 2019 (PL 116-92).

Fiscal Year 2020 Defense Appropriations

Reaching an agreement on fiscal year 2020 defense appropriations was caught up in larger, related battles over President Trump's desire to build a wall along the U.S.–Mexico border and the ongoing impeachment inquiry into the president's decision to block, and later release, aid to Ukraine. Ultimately, the two chambers had to pass two continuing resolutions to prevent a government shutdown, and rolled all twelve annual appropriations measures into two larger bills, totaling a combined $1.4 trillion.

The final package containing defense spending allocated $695.1 billion for defense and intelligence programs, of which $622.6 billion was for the Pentagon's base budget, $70.6 billion for Overseas Contingency Operations (OCO) funds, and $1.8 billion for repairing military installations damaged by natural disasters. President Trump signed the measure into law on December 20 (PL 116-93).

House Committee Action

On May 14, 2019, the House Appropriations Defense Subcommittee unveiled its fiscal 2020 defense spending package (HR 2968), which would provide $690.2 billion to defense and intelligence activities, a 2 percent bump from the current fiscal year but $8 billion lower than President Trump's request. Of the total, $622.1 billion would go to the Pentagon's base budget, while $68.1 billion went toward the warfighting OCO account. The president had requested more toward OCO funds, which are not subject to discretionary budget caps, but Democratic leadership on the House Appropriations Committee rejected that as a budgetary gimmick.

The funding for the base budget was higher than the allocated spending cap for fiscal 2020, meaning either appropriators would need to reduce the topline or the chambers would need to agree to an increase in the year's defense spending cap to avoid across-the-board cuts. The bill proposed by the subcommittee was certain to draw the president's ire for limiting the Pentagon's ability to transfer funds from $9 billion to $1.5 billion, mainly as an effort to prevent the president from building a wall along the southern U.S. border. After a closed-door markup, the subcommittee advanced the bill to the full House Appropriations Committee on May 15 by voice vote. No amendments were included with the bill.

On May 21, the House Appropriations Committee voted 30–23 along party lines to advance the $690.2 billion fiscal 2020 defense appropriation bill to the full House, though appropriators readily admitted that the bill faced many hurdles, perhaps most pressing of which was a lack of topline spending agreement on which to base their decisions. The bill passed out of committee banned the sale of F-35 fighter jets to Turkey, funded ninety additional F-35s, and provided $15 million for Space Force operations and maintenance, well short of the president's $72.5 million request. The committee adopted five of the nine amendments it considered, including one to phase out the 2001 Authorization for Use of Military Force (AUMF), another prohibiting the Pentagon from using appropriated funds to pay for a war with Iran unless Congress authorized otherwise, and one requiring the withdrawal of any U.S. forces engaged in Yemen's civil war as part of the Saudi-led coalition. The committee rejected, 22–30, an amendment from Rep. Steve Womack, R-Ark., to increase OCO funds by $8 billion. It also rejected, 21–31, an amendment from Rep. Andy Harris, R-Md., that would have eliminated

language in the bill blocking the president from building a wall along the U.S.–Mexico border.

House Floor Action

The House wrapped the defense spending bill into a larger measure (HR 2740) that also included the annual appropriations language for Energy–Water, State–Foreign Operations, and Labor–Health and Human Services (HHS)–Education. At the time the $985 billion package passed the House 226–203 on June 19, the president had already threatened to veto it for a number of reasons, including the topline number (which was nearly $7 billion higher than the White House request) and a variety of Democratic policy riders. Seven Democrats joined all Republicans in voting against the bill.

Senate Committee Action

The Senate Defense Appropriations Subcommittee approved its fiscal 2020 defense spending bill (S 2474) on September 10 by voice vote, providing $694.9 billion toward defense and intelligence spending. Of that total, $622.5 was allocated to the Pentagon's base budget, another $70.6 billion went to the OCO, and a further $1.7 billion was provided in emergency disaster relief funding which would not be subject to the budget caps. The subcommittee did not include any amendments with the bill.

On September 12, 2019, the Senate Appropriations Committee favorably reported the bill to the full Senate, 16–15. The $694.9 billion represented a nearly 3 percent increase in funding for the Pentagon over fiscal 2019 levels, and provided for the purchase of ninety-six F-35 fighter jets, fourteen new warships, and a 3.1 percent pay increase for military personnel. The measure also fully funded M-1 tank upgrades, gave $10.6 billion to the Missile Defense Agency, and added $850 million to a National Guard equipment fund. After approving the bill, the panel tabled an amendment from Sen. Patrick Leahy, D-Vt., that would have blocked the president from using money appropriated in the measure to construct the southern border wall.

Conference and Final Action

In late September, with no additional movement in the Senate on either their defense language or that proposed in the House, the two chambers passed a continuing resolution (CR) to prevent a government shutdown and keep federal agencies funded through November 21. By October, the two parties again appeared at an impasse, with Democrats refusing to support any appropriations bills that came to the floor without some kind of agreement on funds for the border wall. Republicans balked, however, pointing to the August 2019 budget agreement (PL 116-37) that carried language barring any change in the funding transfer authority.

On October 31, Democrats in the Senate blocked an attempt by Senate Majority Leader Mitch McConnell, R-Ky., to bring HR 2740 for a procedural vote. At the time it hit the Senate floor, it was expected that the Senate would use the House package as its legislative vehicle for its Defense and Labor–HHS–Education bills, similar to what it had done the prior fiscal year. The cloture motion to advance the bill to the floor failed 51–41, with Democrats continuing to demand an agreement blocking the border wall. Without movement on the defense spending measure, or any appropriations bills, Congress was again forced to settle for a stopgap measure, funding the government at current levels through December 20.

One day before funding again ran out, House and Senate appropriators announced that they had reached an agreement on two large spending packages to cover all twelve annual appropriations measures (HR 1865 and HR 1158). Within HR 1158 was $695.1 billion in defense spending, a $19.5 billion increase over the previous year. Of that, $622.6 billion was directed to the Pentagon's base budget, while $70.6 billion went to OCO funds, and $1.8 billion was set aside for repairing military installations damaged by natural disasters. The defense portion of the bill also included

- $1.87 billion for ninety-eight F-35 fighter planes
- $985.5 million for eight F-15X fighter planes
- $23.9 billion for shipbuilding
- $1.7 billion for upgrading Army tanks
- $40 million for Space Force
- A 3.1 percent pay increase for military personnel
- $10.4 billion for the Missile Defense Agency
- $250 million for an initiative to counter Russian aggression

Notably, the bill left intact the Pentagon's nearly $10 billion threshold for reprogramming funds.

The House approved both packages, which totaled $1.4 trillion in spending, on December 17. HR 1158 was approved 280–138, while HR 1865 moved forward on a 297–120 vote. The Senate cleared both packages on December 19, voting 81–11 on the package containing the defense measure and 71–23 on the other. President Trump signed both bills into law on December 20 (PL 116-93, PL 116-94) with ninety minutes to spare before a government shutdown.

Fiscal Year 2020 Military Construction–VA Appropriations

After a thirty-five-day federal government shutdown from December 2018 to January 2019 predicated on President Trump's desire to fund the construction of a wall along the U.S.–Mexico border, House and Senate appropriators again found themselves hamstrung by partisan bickering over funds for the wall as they tried to work out the annual Military Construction–VA appropriations measure. Ultimately, two stopgap continuing resolutions (CR) were needed to stave off another shutdown before Congress

could deliver to the president two massive spending packages, which had all twelve annual appropriations measures divided between them. As signed into law on December 20, 2019, the package containing Military Construction-VA appropriations (PL 116-94), provided $110.4 billion to the programs within that budget.

House Committee Action

The House was the first to move on the fiscal year 2020 Military–Construction VA appropriations bill, with the Military Construction, Veterans Affairs, and Related Agencies Subcommittee beginning hearings on March 12, 2019. More than a month later, on April 30, the full House Appropriations Committee unveiled HR 2745, its draft $108.1 billion Military Construction-VA appropriations bill. That amounted to approximately $10 billion more than the enacted fiscal year 2019 level, much of which was going toward an 11 percent increase for veterans medical care to keep up with the growing costs of private health care services for veterans who cannot easily access treatment at a VA facility. Within the bill, the VA was set to receive $94.3 billion, or 9 percent more than the prior fiscal year.

The legislation, which provided $10.5 billion for military construction projects, also blocked any funds for military base projects from being used to build a wall on the U.S.–Mexico border. Specifically, the legislation stated that funds could not be "obligated, expended, or used to design, construct, or carry out a project to construct a wall, barrier, fence, or road along the Southern border of the United States or a road to provide access to a wall, barrier, or fence constructed along the Southern border of the United States." The provision spoke to an emergency declaration signed by the president that allowed him to divert as much as $3.6 billion in money previously appropriated for military construction projects to be used toward the wall. At the time the House committee released its draft bill, Trump had already vetoed a measure that would have rescinded the emergency declaration, and a court case was pending to block the declaration.

On May 1, the House Appropriations Military Construction and Veterans Affairs Subcommittee advanced the $108.1 billion appropriations measure to the full Appropriations Committee by voice vote without any amendments. The next week, on May 9, the full House Appropriations Committee advanced the bill to the floor on a largely party line 31–21 vote. The committee considered eight amendments during debate. Two amendments, one from Rep. Andy Harris, R-Md., that would remove language from the bill prohibiting funds from being used for a border wall and another from Rep. John Carter, R-Texas, that would transfer $7.2 billion in military construction funds to the Department of Homeland Security for border security, were both rejected. The committee also rejected an amendment that would have increased funding for the detention center at Guantanamo Bay, Cuba, from

$157 million to $245 million. The committee adopted five amendments, including one providing funding for military facility repairs in Nebraska that were damaged by flooding and another constructing child care development centers on military installations. The bill included no funding for the president's border wall, and an accompanying report said that the committee "must assert its role as a co-equal branch of the Federal government and insist upon the regular appropriation of funds" noting the "military construction dollars should be used only for the purpose they are provided, which is to support DOD's mission, service members, and their families."

House Floor Action

The full House took up the Military Construction-VA appropriations language as one title within a five-bill package (HR 3055), passing it mostly along party lines 227–194 on June 25, 2019. The full $322 billion package combined the annual appropriations measures for Commerce-Justice–Science, Military Construction-VA, Agriculture, Transportation–HUD, and Interior–Environment. The funding level appropriated in the bill was nearly 9 percent more than the White House requested, and was also above the discretionary spending limit allowed under the Budget Control Act of 2011 (PL 112-25). If there was no deal in place to raise those limits, the House-passed legislation would result in across-the-board spending cuts, otherwise known as sequestration. However, there was slim likelihood that the House measure would be signed into law, because the president had already indicated he would veto the measure not only over the topline number, but also because of the provision that blocked the transfer of funds to construct a wall on the southern border. Congress did eventually reach a two-year budget agreement raising spending caps in August 2019 (PL 116-37).

Senate Action

The Senate was slow to take up its version of the Military Construction-VA appropriation measure due to the disagreement between Democrats and Republicans over the president's border wall. Even on October 30, when the chamber voted to invoke cloture on a substitute amendment to HR 3055 to swap in their own appropriations language in place of the House-passed language for the underlying bills, they did so only for the four non-Military Construction-VA bills. On October 31, 2019, the Senate passed 84–9 its version of HR 3055, a four-bill spending package that did not include Military Construction-VA appropriations.

Conference and Final Action

With the new fiscal year already started, Congress was forced to abandon its plans to pass the twelve appropriations bills individually or as packages, and instead had to resort to two stopgap continuing resolutions to keep the government funded. Debate over that measure was nearly

delayed when Senate leadership and appropriators hit an impasse over which legislative vehicle to use to pass the stopgap language. While Senate appropriators wanted to preserve HR 3055 as the vehicle to help smooth later passage of a full fiscal year funding bill, McConnell and Senate Appropriations Chair Richard Shelby, R-Ala., wanted to swap for HR 265, a spending bill passed by the House in January 2019 during the shutdown. A similar argument cropped up in the House, but in the end both chambers passed the stopgap under HR 3055, with a 231–192 vote in the House on November 19 and a 74–20 vote in the Senate on November 20. President Trump signed the measure, which would fund the government through December 20, on November 21 (PL 116-69).

Two days later, on November 23, the chairs of the House and Senate Appropriations Committees reached an agreement on the funding level for each of the twelve annual appropriations bills, which would allow subcommittee appropriations work to move forward with a clear understanding of how funds could be allocated. In mid-December, appropriators unveiled a final, two-bill package that included all twelve appropriations bills. Appropriators opted not to send one omnibus piece of legislation to the floor, because the president had already said he would refuse to sign a one-bill package. Within the eight-bill package (HR 1865) was $110.4 billion for Military Construction–VA. The final deal allocated $1.375 billion for the wall along the U.S.–Mexico border, well short of the $8.6 billion the president requested, rejected the president's requested to backfill the $3.6 billion he was diverting from military construction to finance the wall, but preserved Trump's authority to redirect certain other funds for border barrier construction. At the time the bill was unveiled, the president had lost his case in district court to divert military construction funds under the emergency declaration, but the White House was likely to appeal.

Within the bill was $91.9 billion in discretionary funding for the Department of Veterans Affairs (VA), a $5.4 billion increase over the fiscal 2019 enacted level, of which $8.9 billion would go toward funding private care for veterans outside the VA system. Three months into the fiscal year, on December 17 the House voted to clear HR 1865 by a vote of 297–120, and the Senate followed on December 19, with a 71–23 vote. President Trump signed both appropriations packages on December 20, 2019 (PL 116-93, PL 116-94), with ninety minutes to spare before the stopgap funding ran out and the government shut down again.

Fiscal Year 2021 Defense Authorization

In 2020, the annual National Defense Authorization Act (NDAA) was almost derailed after Republicans refused to support the House-passed measure over a number of issues, including a Democratic provision that would stop the Pentagon from deploying low-yield nuclear weapons. Debate over the massive fiscal year 2021 NDAA was less partisan than usual, with members of Congress forced to grapple with the realities of the COVID-19 pandemic that meant their lengthy, in-person markups and floor debates were limited to fit within the confines of the federal government's social distancing guidelines. In turn, members focused more on crafting language that ensured the military had the resources it needed to continue its mission during a global pandemic, while setting aside some of the more hot-button issues that tend to slow debate. Despite quick passage through the bill's associated subcommittees, committees, and even both the House and Senate chambers, President Trump followed through on his veto threat, taking issue with the renaming of military installations and ships currently bearing Confederate names and the lack of a provision that removes certain protections from social media platforms. The House and Senate voted to overturn the veto, and the $731.6 billion NDAA was enrolled on January 1, 2021, marking the sixtieth consecutive time it became public law (PL 116-283).

House Committee Action

Committee work on the annual NDAA usually begins in late spring, but in March 2020, House Armed Services Committee Chair Adam Smith, D-Wash., indefinitely delayed the planned April 30 full committee markup amid the COVID-19 pandemic and the White House guidance on social distancing to slow the spread of the virus. Before either the subcommittees or full committee could meet, they had to make plans that would allow for appropriate distancing between members, which meant choosing larger meeting rooms, allowing some members to attend virtually, and limiting the number of staffers, reporters, and members of the general public who would be allowed to attend deliberations.

On June 21, the first subcommittee met and approved its portion of the fiscal 2021 bill. The Subcommittee on Intelligence and Emerging Threats and Capabilities held the committee's first ever fully remote meeting, and easily approved the language in the bill. The other five subcommittees that fall under the House Armed Services Committee quickly followed, with some meeting for less than thirty minutes to approve their panel's language.

Full committee markup took place on July 1. Smith opened the meeting, encouraging members to come together for swift passage, rather than continuing the trend of drawn-out all-night debates of years past. In his own opening remarks, Ranking Member Mac Thornberry, R-Texas, commented on the members who choose to participate remotely, saying it "degrades the legislative process, especially today where we sit for hours listening and learning from each other." The typically packed meeting room was sparse for deliberations, with members and staff scattered at least six feet apart from each other and many wearing masks.

Markup began with consideration of the six subcommittee portions of the bill, and there was little debate on

each. The committee quickly adopted the Tactical Air and Land Subcommittee mark, adding several amendments requesting briefings from the Army on various vehicle strategies, and the Seapower and Projection Forces subcommittee mark, which included a request for reports from the Navy on unmanned ships. The mark from the Intelligence, Emerging Threats, and Capabilities subcommittee was approved with provisions covering intellectual property theft and reporting and evaluation of COVID-19 capabilities and equipment.

The committee spent some time debating two amendments to the Readiness panel's language. The first would give the secretaries of the military branches the power to decide whether to remove or replace aging infrastructure on military bases (a power currently held by the House Armed Services Committee), and the second would let the Pentagon keep 50 percent of its unused budget from the previous year. Both amendments were withdrawn. The approved Readiness language did include a package of amendments that would, among other things, limit the use of Russian-sourced gas at U.S. military bases in Europe.

The Military Personnel subcommittee mark was approved with a large package of amendments, including those that would require the collection and analysis of the demographic data of military service academy applicants, give certain civilian employees access to commissaries and exchanges on military bases, and a variety of provisions seeking to combat sexual assault at military academies. The committee's final act was to approve the Strategic Forces Subcommittee language, which contained some minor amendments, before moving on to consideration of the full bill.

The committee considered a number of amendments to the full bill, including one that would block the Pentagon from using funds authorized in the bill to reduce the number of troops stationed in Germany, something the president had promised to do. Both Democrats and Republicans raised questions about the amendment, with some worried that it would tie the administration's hands and others questioning whether U.S. presence in the area would be better served by a diplomatic role. The committee ultimately adopted the amendment 49–7. In another troop drawdown amendment, the panel also approved, 45–11, language that would require certain conditions to be met before all U.S. forces could be withdrawn from Afghanistan.

As the committee's annual markup work continued, the members addressed an issue that had gained significant attention in recent months, as racial justice protests roiled the nation: military bases named after Confederate generals. President Trump had already refused to consider the renaming of bases, however, the committee approved an amendment, 33–23, from Rep. Anthony Brown, D-Md., that would require that any military installations named after a Confederate general be renamed within one year. Thornberry offered a watered-down version of the language as a perfecting amendment, but it was defeated.

The committee also weighed a deeply contentious amendment offered by Rep. Veronica Escobar, D-Texas, that would limit the president's use of the military under the Insurrection Act. Specifically, it would require the president to provide justification for deploying members of the military during times of domestic unrest. Republicans viewed the amendment as a knee-jerk response to the use of federal forces to quell unrest in cities around the country following the killing of George Floyd by police in Minneapolis in May. Democrats countered that the language did not stop the president from deploying forces domestically, but rather required that he have a compelling reason to do so. Bickering between members drew rebuke from the chair, who restored order before the committee rejected the amendment 25–31.

After thirteen hours of debate, the House Armed Services Committee sent the NDAA to the floor with a 56–0 vote. The final bill (HR 6395) authorized $731.6 billion for the Department of Defense and nuclear programs at the Department of Energy. The total would be divided between $662.6 billion for the Pentagon's base budget and $69 billion for uncapped Overseas Contingency Operations (OCO) funds.

Senate Committee Action

On May 26, the Senate Armed Services Committee announced that it would begin its NDAA markup the week of June 8. The Senate Armed Services Personnel Subcommittee, the only panel that holds a public markup, was the first to complete its work, which authorized a 3 percent military pay raise and 5,600 additional troops, meeting the Pentagon's request. Following long-standing tradition, the remaining subcommittees, as well as the full committee, conducted their work privately.

On June 10, the Senate Armed Services Committee marked up its fiscal 2021 NDAA (S 4049). It included two key provisions that were also circulating in the House at the time. The first, proposed by Sens. Joni Ernst, R-Iowa, and Kirsten Gillibrand, D-N.Y., would overhaul how the military's appellate judges review all courts-martial verdicts, making these military courts similar to civilian courts. In most civilian courts, appellate judges only review lower-court rulings for major evidentiary mistakes or procedural lapses, in essence giving greater power to the rulings of lower courts. In the military court system, an appellate court must reconsider all convictions by reading the lower-court proceeding's transcripts, then make a determination of whether the conviction is proven beyond a reasonable doubt and the witnesses are credible. The Ernst/Gillibrand provision was an attempt to improve the legal prospects of victims of sexual abuse, but the language was written so as to apply to all crimes that come before military courts.

The second key provision was proposed by Sen. Elizabeth Warren, D-Mass., and would create a commission to make recommendations on how to rename military

installations, ships, and other infrastructure that currently bear the name of a Confederate general. The language would give the Pentagon three years to make the recommended changes. The measure was approved by voice vote and had varying levels of support among Republicans in the Senate. Armed Services Committee Chair James Inhofe, R-Okla., voiced his opposition, but Senate Majority Leader Mitch McConnell, R-Ky., who would drive the NDAA's passage on the Senate floor, expressed a willingness to consider name changes. Sen. John Kennedy, R-La., took issue with the language, saying it unfairly targeted the South, and noting that he would consider proposing an amendment to instead rename all bases after medal of honor recipients.

House Floor Action

In mid-July, the House Rules Committee met to approve the rule that would govern floor debate on HR 6395. The rule allowed for one hour of general debate, equally divided between the chair and ranking member of the House Armed Services Committee, and also provided for consideration of 407 amendments.

The House moved quickly on July 20 through the amendments, passing most as massive en bloc packages with little debate. The first package, containing 155 amendments, was approved 336–71, and included provisions that would ban federal employees from installing TikTok on their work devices, create a national cyber director, and add new oversight to the annual nuclear weapon's budget. A second package of 239 amendments, approved by voice vote, included those that would require a report from the Federal Bureau of Investigation on domestic terror threats, require a review process for naming military installations after African American members of the armed services, and call for a study of the bio-weaponization of certain insects in the 1950s, 1960s, and 1970s. Other approved amendments designated new federal wilderness areas, prohibited new mining in portions of Colorado and Arizona, and banned additional nuclear testing. The House also adopted, 215–190, Escobar's amendment that would restrict the president's ability to invoke the Insurrection Act during periods of domestic unrest.

The House also rejected a slew of amendments. One, proposed by Rep. Ilhan Omar, D-Minn., sought to accelerate the withdrawal of U.S. troops from Afghanistan. It failed 129–284. Another, from Rep. Pramila Jayapal, D-Wash., would end the requirement that the military services send Congress a wish list of unfunded items. It failed 173–241, with Democrats and Republicans disagreeing over whether this amounts to an end run around congressional budgeting or provides a prudent way to understand the specific needs of the military. The House also overwhelmingly rejected an amendment from Rep. Mark Pocan, D-Wis., that would have cut 10 percent from the funds authorized in the bill, save for a few specific programs.

On July 21, the House voted 295–125 to pass the fiscal 2021 defense authorization bill, now named for Thornberry, who would retire at the end of the current Congress. The bill authorized $731.6 billion in national defense spending. Shortly before passage, the White House issued a Statement of Administration policy, taking issue with a number of provisions in the bill including renaming military bases and limiting emergency military construction projects. The statement threatened a presidential veto.

Senate Floor Action

On July 21, the Senate considered a number of amendments, each of which, per a previous agreement governing NDAA debate, needed to garner sixty votes for passage. Two dealt with the transfer of surplus military equipment to state and local law enforcement agencies through the Defense Logistics Agency. Over the past three decades, an estimated $6 billion in equipment has been transferred. The Obama administration placed some limitations on these transfers, which were rescinded by Trump, but the program has faced increasing scrutiny during the protests around the country throughout the summer of 2020. The first of these amendments was proposed by Sen. Brian Schatz, D-Hawaii. It would necessitate that state and local governments provide approval prior to any equipment transfer, require an accounting to Congress of all equipment, and bar jurisdictions from receiving any transfers for five years if they were found in violation of citizens' First Amendment rights. That measure failed 51–49. An alternate amendment, offered by Inhofe, would ban the transfer of certain equipment, including grenades and weaponized drones, and would require that any police force receiving surplus equipment train officers on deescalation and respect for citizens' rights. The Inhofe amendment passed 90–10.

The Senate also adopted amendments that would provide more money for a study of the effects of per- and polyfluoroalkyl substances (PFAS), so-called forever chemicals, in drinking water. That measure, proposed by Sen. Jeanne Shaheen, D-N.H., was adopted by voice vote. The Senate also approved, 96–4, an amendment from Sen. John Cornyn, R-Texas, to increase federal grants and incentives for semiconductor research and production, and another, proposed by Sen. Jon Tester, D-Mont., to add new diseases, including bladder cancer, to the list of those thought to be associated with exposure to certain chemicals during the Vietnam War. Tester's amendment was adopted 94–6.

The Senate tabled an amendment, 60–33, introduced by Sen. Paul to force the withdrawal of all U.S. troops from Afghanistan within a year. It also rejected, 23–77, an amendment from Sen. Bernie Sanders, I-Vt., to cut 14 percent from the Pentagon's budget, except for those funds set aside for personnel and certain health care programs.

Before its final vote on the fiscal 2021 NDAA, the Senate also blocked Democratic attempts to consider an

amendment that would require federal law enforcement officers deployed during domestic unrest to be identifiable, and would prohibit them from using unmarked cars to make arrests. That amendment came in response to video footage circulating on social media in cities such as Portland, Oregon, where eyewitnesses alleged that protesters were being arrested by individuals bearing no law enforcement identification. The Senate also rejected attempts to pass amendments that would set conditions for troop drawdown in Germany, protect service members from scams, and amend the language regarding changing military installation names. Ultimately, on July 23, the Senate approved its version of the NDAA, which would authorize $731.3 billion in defense spending, 86–14.

Conference and Final Action

With a looming presidential election and veto threats from the White House, leadership made clear in October that a final NDAA would not come before November 3. When the final conference report (HR 6395) was announced in early December, it included some of the more contentious language from the Senate—specifically that which would give the Nuclear Weapons Council the authority to certify whether the nuclear weapons budget for the Department of Energy is adequate—and maintained the Senate's language to strip some of the power from military appellate courts. It did not, however, include language that sexual assault victims have long advocated for that would move prosecution of these crimes outside the military chain of command. The final bill would authorize $731.6 billion for the Pentagon and certain Department of Energy programs for fiscal year 2021.

On December 8, the House voted 335–78 to pass the measure, but the Senate was temporarily delayed in its consideration when Sen. Rand Paul, R-Ky., raised a concern that language in the final bill would restrict the ability to withdraw all troops from Afghanistan; a provision in the legislation limited withdrawal only until certain conditions were certified in a report by the Secretary of Defense. On December 11, the Senate voted 84–13 to send the fiscal year 2021 NDAA to President Trump's desk.

Following passage, both the House and Senate began speaking with their members about an abbreviated holiday recess so that they could return to override a veto the president had for months been threatening. On December 23, Trump made good on his promise, relaying in his veto message that the bill "fails to include critical national security measures, includes provisions that fail to respect our veterans and our military's history, and contradicts efforts by my Administration to put America first in our national security and foreign policy actions. It is a gift to China and Russia." Not only did the president object to base renaming, but he was also frustrated that Congress failed to include a provision that would remove the liability shield social media companies have under Section 230 of the Communications Decency Act. The president had long been critical of platforms such as Twitter and Facebook using Section 230 to remove content, which the president viewed as a means to censor conservative voices.

The conference report had passed both chambers with overwhelming support, so there was little concern that Trump's veto would derail the NDAA's sixtieth consecutive year of becoming law. On December 28, House lawmakers voted 322–87 to override the veto, and the Senate followed, 81–13 on January 1, 2021 (PL 116-283).

Fiscal Year 2021 Defense Appropriations

As with the other bills that came before the House and Senate in 2020, their work on the fiscal 2021 defense appropriations legislation was delayed as lawmakers grappled to respond to the health and economic fallout from the global COVID-19 pandemic. In the end, Congress adopted a twelve-bill omnibus appropriations package to fund the government in fiscal year 2021, forgoing individual bills or smaller minibus packages. The final measure, signed by President Trump on December 27, provided $696 billion in funding for defense and intelligence activities (PL 116-260).

House Committee Action

On July 7, 2020, the House Appropriations Defense Subcommittee released its fiscal 2021 defense funding bill, which would give the Pentagon $626.2 billion for its base budget and $68.4 billion for the warfighting Overseas Contingency Operations (OCO) fund. The $694.6 billion bill also blocked the president from shifting Pentagon funds to cover construction of a wall along the U.S.–Mexico border and provided $1 million to help cover the cost of renaming military installations currently named after Confederate generals. Both proposals had previously been dismissed by the White House, and though the full House passed a similar border wall provision in its fiscal 2020 defense spending bill, it was removed during conference negotiations. The panel approved the bill by voice vote on July 8 after a brief, closed-door hearing, without any amendments.

The House Appropriations Committee took up the bill on July 14, voting along party lines 30–22 to send the measure to the House. The $694.6 billion in funds appropriated for defense and intelligence programs in fiscal 2021 represented a $1.3 billion increase above fiscal 2020 enacted levels, but $3.7 billion below what the White House requested. The House measure provided $22.3 billion for shipbuilding, $9.3 billion for ninety-one F-35 fighter jets, a 3 percent pay increase for military personnel, $801 million for a new Air Force One, and $2.8 billion toward the ongoing development of a new B-21 stealth bomber. The bill further prohibited the authorized funds from being used for nuclear testing and reduced from $9.5 billion to $1.9 billion the Pentagon's authority to transfer funds between accounts (essentially a maneuver to block the

border wall); Republicans continued to hold that changing transfer authorities was a violation of the most recent two-year budget agreement (PL 116-37). As it had in previous years, the bill also blocked the Pentagon from transferring any F-35s to Turkey.

During its consideration of the measure, the committee adopted three war-related amendments, all introduced by Rep. Barbara Lee, D-Calif. One blocked the military from using force against Iran unless authorized to do so by Congress or provoked, another would repeal within eight months of the bill's enactment the 2001 Authorization for Use of Military Force (AUMF), and the third would repeal the 2002 AUMF. Republicans accused Democrats of playing politics with critical defense funds, predicting that the bill would draw a presidential veto if it moved forward, especially with the base renaming and border wall provisions in place. As it did during its fiscal 2020 defense spending negotiations, the committee again rejected an amendment from Rep. Andy Harris, R-Md., to remove the provisions in the bill that would limit the president's ability to build a southern border wall.

House Floor Action

The House wrapped the defense spending measure into a six-bill appropriations package totaling more than $1.3 trillion (HR 7617), which also included the Commerce–Justice–Science, Energy–Water, Financial Services, Labor–Health and Human Services (HHS)–Education, and Transportation–Housing and Urban Development (HUD) appropriations measures. The Homeland Security spending bill was initially included in the measure, but the House struck it from the bill in a self-executing rule. During debate on HR 7617, the House adopted an en bloc package of amendments that included a provision blocking any appropriated funds from being used to carry out President Trump's April 2019 policy banning transgender individuals from joining the military. That amendment package was adopted by voice vote. Despite a veto threat, the House went on to approve the six-bill appropriations measure 217–197 on July 31, with twelve Democrats joining all Republicans in opposition.

Senate Action

The Senate Appropriations Committee did not unveil its $696 billion draft defense spending measure until early November. The topline number was similar to the enacted fiscal 2020 level, but more than $2 billion below President Trump's request. In the bill, Senate appropriators provided funding for ninety-six F-35 fighter jets—fifteen more than the Pentagon requested and five more than the House included in their bill—$10.2 billion for the Missile Defense Agency, $850 million for the National Guard's equipment account, and $21.4 billion for shipbuilding. The Senate version of the bill did not receive a floor vote.

Conference and Final Action

House and Senate negotiators again chose to forgo individual appropriations bills to fund the government in fiscal 2021, and instead used a $1.4 trillion omnibus package (HR 133) to cover all twelve regular appropriations measures. The defense portion of the bill provided $696 billion in funding for defense and intelligence activities, of which $68.7 billion was set aside for uncapped OCO funds. The final bill included

- $9.6 billion for ninety-six F-35 fighter jets
- $23.3 billion for ten warships
- $2.3 billion for a second Virginia-class submarine
- $500 million for an America-class amphibious ship
- $10.4 billion for the Missile Defense Agency
- $1.6 billion for nine Navy P-8 Poseidon patrol planes
- $344 million for sixteen MQ-9 Reaper drones
- $110 million for twelve MQ-1 Gray Eagle drones
- $950 million for the National Guard and Reserve Equipment Account
- A 3 percent pay raise for military personnel

Notably, the omnibus package did not include several House provisions that drew opposition from Republicans and the White House. The package dropped the repeal of the 2001 and 2002 AUMFs, the $1 million in funding for renaming bases, and the prohibition on using Pentagon funds for building a wall at the U.S.–Mexico border.

The House took up the funding package on December 21, using the process of dividing the question to first vote on one part of the bill and then another. The chamber passed the first portion, containing the defense bill, by a 327–85 vote and the second portion on a 359–53 vote. The Senate received the measures as one full package, which it cleared the same day 92–6. Both chambers had also sent the president that day a short stopgap continuing resolution (CR) to keep the government funded until the president could sign the omnibus measure; that CR was necessary because the first (H J Res 110) was set to expire.

On December 27, President Trump signed HR 133 into law (PL 116-260). He also sent to Congress a redlined version of the bill, asking the chambers to review those actions to which he objected. Congress did not act on the president's request.

Fiscal Year 2021 Military Construction–VA Appropriations

The COVID-19 pandemic hampered negotiations on the Military Construction–VA appropriations bill, as it did with most other congressional matters. A solution to pay for the health care for veterans who seek services outside a VA facility took top billing in negotiations, as it had in the two prior years. The final omnibus package signed by President Trump on December 27—which also included

COVID-19 relief elements—set aside $113.1 billion for military construction and VA projects (PL 116-260).

House Committee Action

The budget request from the Department of Veterans Affairs (VA) roiled Democrats on the House Appropriations committee in March 2020, after the department proposed a 13 percent increase in fiscal 2021 spending over the current year. Appropriators on both sides of the aisle noted that they were required to work within the agreement reached in 2019 (PL 116-37) that provided a modest increase in spending caps of $2.5 billion, or 0.5 percent, for all nondefense discretionary accounts. During an election year, the bipartisan pushback was unusual, because members tend to follow the VA's requests for whatever veterans need.

On July 5, the House Appropriations Committee released its draft fiscal 2021 Military Construction–VA appropriations bill, which would provide $115.5 billion, a $5.1 billion increase from fiscal 2020 enacted levels when $12.5 billion in emergency funds for the VA were figured in. In the bill, $10.1 billion would be directed toward military construction, $1.2 billion less than the current discretionary funding level, while the VA would receive $104.8 billion in discretionary funds, a $12.3 billion increase from the fiscal 2020 level. The $12.5 billion in emergency spending would mostly go toward covering the care for veterans who use non-VA services. Classifying the funding as "emergency" allowed Congress to avoid discretionary spending caps while still getting the VA more money for coverage. While House Republicans generally disagreed with classifying the funding this way, and the White House had opposed a similar measure in fiscal 2020 funding, Senate Republicans backed the provision during negotiations.

Notably, the committee also used the bill to weigh in on two hot-button issues in its draft bill. First, it blocked the president from diverting appropriated funds to construction of a wall on the U.S.–Mexico border. Second, it blocked funding for any projects on a military installation named after a Confederate officer, unless the location already had a plan in place to change its name.

On July 6, the House Subcommittee on Military Construction, Veterans Affairs, and Related Agencies approved the $115.5 billion bill by voice vote, reporting it to the full Appropriations Committee for consideration. Republicans voiced their concern about the provisions in the legislation that dealt with emergency spending for veterans health care, border wall funds, and Confederate base names during markup, but it did not stop the measure from moving forward.

The full House Appropriations Committee voted 30–20 on July 9 to advance the Military Construction–VA appropriations bill to the House on July 9. Only one Republican, Rep. Will Hurd, R-Texas, joined all Democrats in support of the measure. During debate, the committee rejected, 13–19, an amendment from Rep. Andy Harris, R-Md., that would remove language prohibiting the president from redirecting appropriated construction funds for the border wall. Harris said erecting a border barrier would help control the spread of COVID-19 while also slowing the flow of dangerous drugs into the United States; Democrats dismissed both arguments.

House Floor Action

The Military Construction–VA appropriations bill was rolled into a four-bill, $259.5 billion package also containing the Agriculture, Interior–Environment, and State-Foreign Operations measures (HR 7608). On July 23, a Statement of Administration Policy noted that "if H.R. 7608 were presented to the President in its current form, his advisors would recommend that he veto it." The statement listed a number of concerns of the administration, including the topline funding number, which the president wanted reduced, and provisions blocking him from using appropriated funds to construct the border wall. Regardless, on July 24, 2020, the House passed the bill 224–189. The full package provided $259.5 billion in discretionary funding, of which $115.5 was set aside for the VA, military construction, and related agencies. In total, the bill provided $37.5 billion in emergency funding not subject to discretionary spending caps, which would go toward veterans' health care, in addition to COVID-19 relief and infrastructure projects.

Senate Action

On November 10, Senate appropriators revealed their own $113.1 billion Military Construction–VA spending bill, of which $104.4 billion was discretionary spending for the VA, around $12 billion higher than the fiscal 2020 enacted level. Like the House-passed version, the Senate bill included $12.5 billion in emergency funds not subject to discretionary spending caps, much of which would go toward funding care outside the VA system for military veterans. The Senate bill also cut military construction funding, reducing it to $8.1 billion, or $3.3 billion below the fiscal 2020 enacted level.

Final Action

Getting the government funded required multiple continuing resolutions, including a one-week stopgap bill, which President Trump signed on December 11 (PL 116-215), to give Congress time to finish negotiations on the $1.4 trillion twelve-bill omnibus package (HR 133). Among the final details being hammered out by negotiators was how to classify VA spending for care outside a VA facility. House Republican leadership held firm that they would not support an emergency designation for the $12.5 billion in funds, which put them at odds with Senate Republicans. Ultimately, to push the full spending package through, Democrats and Senate Republicans allowed the emergency designation to be dropped, and appropriators

instead combined budgetary offsets and cuts from unspent appropriations to finance the program.

On December 21, negotiators announced that they had reached an agreement on the final text of HR 133, which included $113.1 billion in Military Construction–VA appropriations. That total provided $104.4 billion in discretionary funds, $12.5 billion more than fiscal 2020 levels, and $8.4 billion for military construction programs. In the bill was funding for four child development centers on military installations, money to encourage military officials to plan for the risks posed by extreme weather and climate change, and funds for modernizing the VA electronic health record system and improving VA-delivered health care.

The same day the final package was unveiled, the president signed a second seven-day stopgap to stave off a government shutdown (PL 116-246). The CR was not needed to provide more negotiation time, but rather to get the final legislation printed and signed before the prior stopgap ran out. Earlier in the day, the House passed the full omnibus measure using the dividing the question process, during which lawmakers first voted to pass the Commerce–Justice–Science, Defense, Financial Services, and Homeland Security pieces of the bill before voting on the remaining measures. The first vote was 327–85, while the second was 359–53. The Senate cleared the 5,593-page bill as one package, 92–6.

On December 22, the president posted a brief video on his Twitter feed, during which he called the omnibus package "a disgrace" and indicated he might not sign the legislation unless the $600 COVID-19 rebate checks designated for each American were increased to $2,000 and legislators removed what he called "wasteful and unnecessary items." However, on December 27, the president appeared to reverse course and signed the bill. He also sent a redlined version back to Congress, essentially a formal request for them to reconsider and remove certain items. Unsurprisingly, given that Trump was on his way out of office in January 2021, Congress did not consider his response.

VA Child Care Program

In 2011, Congress authorized a pilot program (PL 111-163) that would offer free childcare to veterans at participating VA health care facilities while the veteran received medical services, including mental health care. The program was popular with participants, who reported in a satisfaction survey that without the provision they would have either canceled their appointments or been forced to take their children with them. The program was reauthorized multiple times, but set to expire on October 1, 2019, without a new reauthorization. In February 2019, the House voted to make the popular program permanent. Although it passed overwhelmingly in the House, it did not receive a floor vote during the 116th Congress.

House Action

On January 29, 2019, Rep. Julia Brownley, D-Calif., the chair of the Veterans' Affairs Health Subcommittee, introduced HR 840, the Veterans' Access to Child Care Act, which would direct the VA to permanently provide childcare assistance at every VA facility in the country for eligible veterans receiving certain medical services at a VA facility. The bill previously passed the House in 2017, but was never taken up in the Senate. That version included spending offsets—such as extended caps on pension payments for certain Medicaid-covered nursing home–bound veterans along with higher home loan guarantee fees—to cover the anticipated cost of the childcare program. The lack of offsets in the 2019 version drew some mild concern from Republicans, worried about the five-year $120 million estimated cost in discretionary spending. Ultimately, however, those offsets did not stop fiscal conservatives from supporting the bill.

On February 8, 2019, the House passed the measure 400–9, sending the bill to the Senate, where it did not receive consideration. Sen. Patty Murray, D-Wash., introduced S 319, the Women Veterans and Families Health Services Act, on February 4, 2019, that included a similar provision regarding childcare services during VA appointments, but it, too, did not receive a vote in the Senate.

House Opposes Trump Transgender Troop Restrictions

The House in 2019 passed legislation opposing the president's decision to ban transgender troops from serving in the military. The Senate never took up the issue, though it frequently appeared as a policy rider in early versions of authorization and appropriations legislation.

In 2016, Obama-era Defense Secretary Ash Carter instituted a new policy allowing transgender individuals to openly serve in the military. It provided that anyone who had already transitioned could join the military, while anyone already in the military could transition during their time in the service.

After expressing opposition to the policy on Twitter, in August 2017 President Trump issued a memorandum that called on the Pentagon to begin discharging all transgender service members starting in March 2018. That order was temporarily blocked by a federal judge, and in turn Trump announced a second policy that would allow transgender individuals already serving in the military to remain but that would require them to serve under their gender assigned at birth. Again, the courts blocked the policy.

The Supreme Court stepped in, and in January 2018 ruled 5–4 to remove the preliminary injunctions and allow the White House policy to go into effect. On March 12, the Pentagon released the details of the new restrictions on transgender troops, which it said it would begin applying

on April 12. According to the memo, current military personnel would not be removed from the ranks so long as they had been stable in their gender for eighteen months and had completed all medical treatment required for gender reassignment. Any transgender individual who enlisted in the military would be permitted to do so only if they served at their birth-assigned gender, could show three years of stability in that gender, and had no recent problems with gender dysphoria. Anyone would be banned from enlisting if they ever had sex reassignment surgery, genital reconstruction surgery, cross-sex hormone therapy, or if they were currently living in a self-designated gender.

Democrats used their new position in the House majority in 2019 to take a stance on President Trump's policy that placed restrictions on transgender troops serving in the military. Although the measure, H Res 124, passed in the House on a largely party line 238–185 vote, the non-binding resolution had little impact on the revised policy.

House Action

On February 11, 2019, H Res 124 was referred to the House Armed Services Committee. The measure expresses opposition to the president's decision to ban transgender troops from serving in the military. It further encourages the Department of Defense not to follow through on the president's policies. Citing multiple studies and testimony delivered by military leaders, the resolution rejects the "flawed scientific and medical claims" on which the ban is based, and notes that transgender individuals had been openly serving since 2016, defending their nation, without disruption.

According to supporters of the resolution, the president's policies are much like the "don't ask, don't tell" policy, which kept gay and lesbian service members from serving openly until it was overturned by the Obama administration. They argued that the policies undermine military readiness and national security, and are nothing more than discrimination against transgender service members and enlistees. Supporters of the president's policy said that the military must be in a constant state of readiness, and openly transgender servicemembers may disrupt this focus. Further, they argued that all defense funding should go toward national security, not experimental health care needs.

When it reached the House floor on March 28, 2019, it was considered under a closed rule that would prohibit amendments. The bill passed on a largely party-line 238–185 vote, but was never considered in the Senate.

Apprenticeships for Veterans

In March 2020, the president signed into law a measure intended to make it easier for veterans to participate in apprenticeship programs and receive credit for their skills gained during their military service.

Senate Action

On March 12, 2019, Sen. Gary Peters, D-Mich., introduced the Support for Veterans in Effective Apprenticeships Act (S 760). According to lawmakers, apprenticeship programs can be especially helpful for veterans transitioning out of military service to boost their marketable skills. Veterans frequently struggle with unemployment, in part because the skills gained in the military do not easily transfer to many civilian jobs. S 760 sought to address this concern by requiring apprenticeship programs to account for a veteran's military skills, training, and experience when it comes to wages, standing, or credit. It would also require any new apprenticeship program to verify that they are aware of educational assistance available to veterans and their dependents through the GI Bill, and that they would make a good faith effort to obtain this assistance. The apprenticeship programs also had to affirm that they would not reject an otherwise valid application for their program simply because they did not want to go through the process of obtaining educational assistance. The Senate Committee on Health, Education, Labor, and Pensions discharged the bill to the Senate by unanimous consent on December 4, 2019, and the full Senate passed the measure by unanimous consent the same day.

House Action

The House took up S 760 on March 10, 2020. During forty minutes of debate, members expressed their support for programs that help connect veterans to well-paying jobs. One member, Rep. Susie Lee, D-Nev., noted that the Registered Apprenticeships covered under the measure have a 94 percent success rate at job placement after program completion and that those jobs have an average starting salary of $70,000 per year. On March 11, 2020, the House passed the measure 412–0. It was signed by the president on March 26, 2020 (PL 116-134).

Veterans Mental Health Care and Suicide Prevention

During the 116th Congress, the chambers passed multiple pieces of legislation addressing mental health care for veterans. Overcoming the shortfalls of existing laws had long been a priority for members on both sides of the aisle. According to the Department of Veterans Affairs (VA), an estimated twenty veterans commit suicide each day, a rate 50 percent higher than that of the general population. Fourteen of these deaths involve veterans outside of the VA system, and 70 percent involve a gun. President Trump signed all the measures into law.

Senate Committee Action

On May 22, 2019, the Senate Veterans' Affairs Committee began its consideration of S 785, the Commander John Scott Hannon Veterans Mental Health

Care Improvement Act of 2019, named after a former Navy SEAL who suffered from posttraumatic stress disorder (PTSD) and a traumatic brain injury before taking his own life. The bipartisan bill, sponsored by Sen. Jon Tester, D-Mont., would make a number of changes to existing VA programs, including by automatically enrolling veterans in VA health care for one year after leaving the armed services, unless they opt out. Primarily, however, the legislation sought to improve mental health care services for veterans by establishing grants for eligible organizations aimed at preventing veteran suicide, requiring access to alternative mental health therapies, assessing barriers to care, studying the effects of certain pharmaceuticals on veteran health, developing new clinical practice guidelines, expanding telehealth services, increasing the number of mental health providers, and establishing and tracking mental health care improvement goals. The VA took issue with some of the provisions that they considered duplicative as well as the one requiring certain alternative therapies, which Assistant Deputy Under Secretary for Health Teresa Boyd called scientifically unproven and not yet widely available.

The committee met again on January 29, 2020, for final consideration of the bill, during which a handful of amendments were proposed. One, from Sen. Sherrod Brown, D-Ohio, would have limited the VA's ability to collect overpayments, and a second, from Sen. Richard Blumenthal, D-Conn., would have added requirements that the VA's annual mental health care report include information on mental or behavioral health care services denied to veterans with a less-than-honorable discharge. Both amendments were withdrawn. Two amendments were adopted by voice vote. Sen. Kevin Cramer, R-N.D., proposed language allowing for the use of federal funds to establish partnerships for the purpose of researching hyperbaric oxygen therapy treatment for veterans. And Tester offered an amendment that would allow veterans to receive emergency mental health care in the community before being transferred to a VA facility or VA approved private doctor. As amended, S 785 was reported to the full Senate, 17–0.

House Committee Action

The House Veterans' Affairs Committee considered a litany of legislation targeting veteran mental health and suicide prevention. A number of bills received little pushback from either side of the aisle. One, HR 2333, the Support for Suicide Prevention Coordinators Act from Rep. Anthony Brindisi, D-N.Y., would require a report from the U.S. comptroller assessing the training, workload, responsibilities, and vacancy rate of VA suicide prevention coordinators. The committee approved that measure by voice vote on May 18, 2019 (it went on to be approved by both chambers and was eventually signed by the president on December 20, 2019 [PL 116-96]). On the same day, the committee advanced multiple other pieces of related legislation, including HR 2191 to protect veterans from benefit

denial or being labeled as having a substance abuse disorder for participating in a state medical marijuana program, one (HR 712) to require a study on the impact of medical marijuana on PTSD or chronic pain, and another (HR 2359) to assess a memorandum for increased access to alternative medicine. Other mental health measures approved by the committee at the time included HR 2340, requiring the VA to report to a member of Congress if a veteran commits suicide at a VA facility in their district, and HR 1812, which would allow National Guard troops activated under certain circumstances to receive mental health care at Vet Centers.

Perhaps the most contentious piece of legislation considered by the committee on the issue of mental health and suicide prevention was HR 3495, the Improve Well-Being for Veterans Act sponsored by Rep. Jack Bergman, R-Mich. The measure would, among other things, require the VA to award grants to organizations that provide or coordinate suicide prevention efforts for veterans and their families. The popular legislation, which garnered more than 220 cosponsors, was pulled from its scheduled markup on October 29, 2019, during a raucous committee hearing in which Republicans staged a walkout over an unrelated bill when Democrats blocked their attempts to introduce amendments. Committee Chair Mark Takano, D-Calif., who was trying to add oversight language to HR 3495, said he was still negotiating with Republicans and planned to bring the legislation for markup as soon as possible.

The key disagreement between Democrats and Republicans revolved around language that any organization receiving a grant must utilize a "collective impact model" requiring collaboration with at least six organizations, and provide a minimum of ten services while using grant funds. Republicans argued that the language would preclude many groups from participating in the program, especially those in rural areas that lack the ability to collaborate, which could leave pockets of veterans underserved. Takano countered that the model would ensure more comprehensive care and higher performance.

After the bill was pulled, Takano and Ranking Member Rep. Phil Roe, R-Tenn., introduced competing pieces of legislation. Takano's would give grant money to coordinating organizations only if they met certain standards, including those related to performance and location. Roe's language would prioritize local hubs providing mental health care, but would also allow grants to go to places providing direct clinical care, something Takano said he would oppose because he viewed it as a means to complicate the MISSION Act (PL 115-182). The competing pieces of legislation led to protracted negotiations between the committee's majority and minority staff. The November 20, 2019, hearing to review both bills turned sour when Takano and VA Secretary Robert Wilkie sparred over the accountability provisions in the bill and the work Wilkie had done behind the scenes in pressing for legislation. Wilkie had already sent a letter to Takano saying he could

not support HR 3495 as introduced because it would introduce too many barriers to care for veterans in need of mental health assistance.

On December 5, 2019, the committee met again to vote on the legislation. Takano introduced a substitute amendment, intended to address Republican concerns, though some members of the panel argued it did little to alleviate the fact that the bill was too limiting for many organizations to participate. Roe introduced four amendments to Takano's substitute amendment, each of which was defeated. One would require the VA to prioritize certain organizations for grant receipt and also implemented a number of reporting requirements, another would remove the "collective impact model" language, a third struck language requiring grant recipients to match VA funds up to a certain amount, and the final would add clinical treatment for emergent needs as a covered service. The committee adopted one amendment by voice vote, requiring that outreach about the grant program include U.S. territories, and another amendment, adopted 26–0, which allowed nontraditional or innovative treatment services to be covered under the program. Takano's substitute amendment was adopted 16–10, and HR 3495 was reported favorably to the full House by voice vote.

In mid-September 2020, the committee took up HR 8247, the Veterans COMPACT Act of 2020, which Takano introduced. The bill created multiple programs, policies, and reports related to VA suicide care, mental health treatment, and assistance for those transitioning out of the military. Specifically, it required the VA to provide or pay for emergency suicide care, regardless of discharge status or whether the care is received at a VA or non-VA facility. The committee conducted a brief markup with only one amendment proposed, by Takano, which would require a veteran receiving emergency suicide care outside the VA system to notify the VA within seven days of admission. The amendment, and the underlying bill, were approved by voice vote.

Final Action

After stalling for more than a year, on August 5, 2020, the Senate quickly passed by voice vote S 785 to expand mental health services for veterans. In introducing the bill, Sen. Jerry Moran, R-Kan., chair of the Senate Veterans Affairs' Committee, said the legislation would "make necessary investments in suicide prevention. It will improve and support innovative research. It will make improvements and increase the availability of mental health care."

After Senate passage, multiple House members, including Rep. Bergman who sponsored the IMPROVE Act, called on the chamber to take up HR 3495, which included many of the provisions in S 785. Takano and Moran, however, said they were looking for a path forward that would allow the House to pass S 785 without amendment if, in return, the Senate voted on separate pieces of legislation from the House under unanimous consent intended to

complement the bill and address the concerns of some representatives that S 785 did not go far enough toward preventing veteran suicide. Those bills included HR 1812 (the Vet Center Eligibility Expansion Act), HR 2359 (the Whole Veteran Act), and HR 8247 (the Veterans COMPACT Act).

On September 23, 2020, the House approved S 785 by voice vote. The $277 million bill would award grants to groups that coordinate or provide suicide prevention services, require a study on mental health biomarkers in veterans, expand telehealth services, require the placement of suicide prevention coordinators at each VA medical facility, and compel the VA and the Department of Defense to establish a plan to provide health care benefits to service members transitioning out of the military. On the same day the House passed S 785, it also cleared HR 8247 by voice vote.

On September 24, the Senate passed HR 1812 by unanimous consent. It followed with approval by voice vote of HR 2359 on October 1, and approval by unanimous consent of HR 8247 on November 10. In a press release, members of the House and Senate Veterans' Affairs Committees remarked on the importance of passing HR 8247 as a complementary piece of legislation. "This key legislation builds on the provisions in the Commander John Scott Hannon Veterans Mental Health Care Improvement Act to ensure veterans and their families receive the support, care, and services they need to live full, healthy lives following their brave service," said Roe. Tester said it would build on S 785 and ensure implementation of "the most effective tools to connect more veterans with life-saving care." The president signed S 785 on October 17, 2020 (PL 116-171), HR 1812 on October 20 (PL 116-176), HR 2359 on October 30 (PL 116-185), and HR 8247 on December 5, 2020 (PL 116-214).

Fiscal Year 2020–2021 Coast Guard Reauthorization

A House and Senate panel each passed a two-year Coast Guard reauthorization measure in 2019, however, the legislation never received a floor vote. Instead, the broadly bipartisan authorizing legislation was included with the fiscal year 2021 National Defense Authorization Act (NDAA).

House Action

On June 26, 2019, the House Transportation and Infrastructure Committee considered HR 3409, the Coast Guard Authorization Act of 2019. The bill would authorize the funding levels for fiscal 2020 and 2021 at $11.1 billion and $11.6 billion, respectively. The fiscal 2020 funding included an authorization of $8.1 billion for operations and maintenance, $2.7 billion for infrastructure, $13.8 million for research and development, and slightly more than $205 million for specific retiree health care fund

contributions. In fiscal 2021, the Coast Guard would be authorized $8.5 billion for operations and maintenance, $2.8 billion for infrastructure, $14.1 million for research and development, and $209.2 million for retiree health care fund contributions.

Additionally, the bill increased the Coast Guard's number of active duty personnel to no more than 44,500, while maintaining its allowable student loads. It further reauthorized $3 million each per fiscal year for fishing safety and research grants. During its consideration of the bill, the committee adopted an amendment by voice vote that included the text of HR 367 to provide the money necessary to pay both active duty and civilian Coast Guard employees and to provide death benefits and retirement pay if government funding lapsed during a shutdown. Committee Chair Peter DeFazio, D-Ore., said there was no reason for the Coast Guard to forgo pay when other members of the military had already been authorized the funds necessary to continue receiving a paycheck. The committee approved the reauthorization by voice vote on June 26, 2019, and the measure passed the full House by voice vote on July 24.

Senate Action

On July 31, the Senate Commerce, Science, and Transportation Committee considered its own Coast Guard reauthorization measure, S 2297.

During committee debate, the panel rejected two amendments, both offered by Sen. Mike Lee, R-Utah. The first would have created a program for companies to receive a waiver from requirements that transporting goods on ships between U.S. ports must be done on a U.S. flagged vessel, constructed in the country, and owned and run by U.S. citizens or permanent residents. The second amendment would have allowed for the building of Coast Guard vessels in countries outside the United States, assuming that second country was a North Atlantic Treaty Organization (NATO) ally and doing so would be cheaper. Both were rejected 4–22.

The Senate committee version of the bill did include an annual authorization for construction of new medium and heavy polar security cutters. Panel members agreed that having an icebreaking fleet was critical for national security and advancing U.S. interests in the Arctic. Like the House-passed measure, the Senate committee bill also authorized funds to pay Coast Guard members in case of a government shutdown, and authorized 44,500 active duty personnel.

The Senate committee measure differed slightly from that of the House in its funding. The Senate authorized research and development funding at $29.1 million for fiscal year 2020 and $29.9 million for fiscal year 2021, while the House reduced those levels to $13.8 million and $14.1 million, respectively. The Senate measure also authorized $8.8 billion for operation and maintenance activities in fiscal year 2020 and $8.4 billion for fiscal year 2021,

slightly higher than the House authorization the first year and lower, the second year.

The measure was reported to the Senate on September 26, without a written report from the committee. The standalone measure reauthorizing the Coast Guard never made it to the president's desk; instead, its provisions were wrapped into the 2021 defense authorization legislation that passed the House and Senate in December 2020. The president vetoed that legislation, but the veto was easily overridden in January 2021 (PL 116-283).

Restricting Military Action Against Iran

Under the War Powers Resolution (PL 93-148), or the War Powers Act as it is more commonly known, the president must give timely warning to Congress if U.S. troops will be sent overseas with the high probability of engaging in combat. The intent of the legislation was to ensure the executive and legislative branches shared in the decision making when it could take the country to war.

Since the September 11, 2001, terrorist attacks, the president's authority under the War Powers Act has routinely been called into question by members of both parties. Congress passed two Authorization for Use of Military Force (AUMF) bills in 2001 and 2002, permitting the use of force against nations, persons, or organizations suspected of being involved in planning, authorizing, committing, or aiding the September 11 attacks; the AUMFs also extended to preventing any future attacks. However, both Presidents Obama and Trump used those AUMFs to carry out strikes in Syria, East Africa, and other Middle Eastern nations. In turn, lawmakers argued about whether the AUMF should be revoked or replaced to allow for a more narrowly focused engagement against specific terrorists operating abroad.

On January 3, 2020, the United States launched a targeted drone strike in Iraq that killed Maj. Gen. Qassem Soleimani, head of Iran's Islamic Revolutionary Guard Corps' Quds Force. The president gave notice to Congress, as required under the War Powers Act, in a classified memo, noting that U.S. intelligence suggested that a strike by Iran against U.S. interests was imminent. Iran immediately threatened to retaliate, and the Pentagon announced that it would send 3,000 additional troops to the region. Iran did launch missile strikes against U.S. facilities in Iraq, however, there were no casualties or major damage. The White House subsequently appeared interested in deescalating the situation, by announcing sanctions and encouraging Iranian leaders to come to the negotiating table.

Some Democrats and Republicans expressed discontent with the way the situation was carried out. Democrats argued that the justification should not have been delivered in a classified manner, because something that could take the nation to war should be debated in an open forum. Some Republicans shared their opinion that the intelligence appeared weak and they felt bullied by the White

House to simply go along with whatever the president wanted. Others noted that the administration had compiled a list of fifty-two Iranian targets the United States would strike if Iran retaliated aggressively, some of which were cultural rather than military sites, which runs afoul of international law.

In another bid to express their displeasure with the president's policies, after the strike that killed the Iranian general Democrats in the House passed a nonbinding resolution calling on the president to end any U.S. military hostilities against Iran unless Congress expressly authorized such action. The Senate considered a similar measure, but it did not pass in 2020.

House Action

On January 8, 2020, Rep. Elissa Slotkin, D-Mich., introduced H Con Res 83, which directed the president to end the use of U.S. forces "in hostilities in or against Iran or any parts of its government or military" unless there's a congressional declaration of war or other specific authorization for such use of force. This direction would not apply if there was a need to defend the United States or U.S. interests and personnel against an imminent attack, nor would it apply to operations against al Qaeda or associated terrorist groups.

The concurrent resolution was referred to the House Foreign Affairs Committee on January 8, which took no action on the measure. On the same day, the House Rules Committee approved by a 9–4 vote the rules governing floor debate on the measure: two hours to be equally divided between each party, and waiving all points of order against provisions. The rules committee also struck Soleimani's name from the original language of the resolution. While committee chair Rep. Jim McGovern, D-Mass., did not find the deletion necessary, he believed it would make it more bipartisan. The House took up the measure on January 9, and it passed 224–194.

Notably, a concurrent resolution is not sent to the president to be signed into law or vetoed. Rather, it is a message from Congress that the president is free to ignore. The House opted to use the concurrent resolution so that it would receive privileged status in the Senate, and therefore expedited consideration. Using a different method would have given the minority the procedural motion to recommit and thus likely killed any chance of passage in the Senate.

Senate Action

On January 3, 2020, Sen. Tim Kaine, D-Va., introduced SJ Res 63, a legally binding resolution that used language similar to that proposed in the House. The joint resolution would "direct the removal of United States Armed Forces from hostilities against the Islamic Republic of Iran that have not been authorized by Congress." Immediately, some Republicans announced their support of the measure, noting that no president should have unlimited authority in the use of U.S. combat forces, especially at a time when it could mean deepening U.S. involvement in the region and perhaps sparking a war. Other Republicans said that it simply was not the right time for Congress to be debating the issue given the rising tension in the Middle East, and that any such issue should be dealt with either through a new AUMF or legislation that applied to all countries, not solely Iran.

On February 12, 2020, the Senate voted 51–45 to open debate on SJ Res 63. Eight Republicans crossed party lines, and because the resolution has privileged status under the War Powers Act, it did not need to reach the regular sixty-vote threshold to begin debate. However, no further action was taken on the measure in 2020. Even if it had passed the Senate and House, it would have likely received a presidential veto, which would have been difficult to override.

Repealing the 2002 Authorization for Use of Military Force

In the aftermath of the September 11, 2001, terrorist attacks, Congress passed two Authorization for Use of Military Force (AUMF) bills. The second, enacted in 2002, specifically authorized military action against Iraq, but has been used in the intervening years, along with the 2001 AUMF, as justification for military efforts in other African and Middle Eastern countries where the United States seeks to counter terrorist organizations including the Islamic State.

Since the early 2000s, support for U.S. military intervention in Iraq has waned. In a Gallup poll conducted from August 15 to 30, 2019, 50 percent of respondents agreed that it was a mistake to send troops to Iraq, while 45 percent said it was not a mistake. In 2003, only 23 percent thought it was a mistake to send in troops, compared to 75 percent in favor of the decision. In turn, over the years, legislators on both sides of the aisle have introduced bills that would either sunset the 2001 and 2002 AUMFs or replace them with something new. This extended into 2020 when Rep. Barbara Lee, D-Calif., tried unsuccessfully to repeal the 2002 AUMF.

House Action

Lee's bill, HR 2456, Repeal the Authorization for Use of Military Force Against Iraq of 2002, received more than 120 cosponsors, including one Republican, Rep. Thomas Massie, R-Ky., and one independent, Rep. Justin Amash, I-Mich. The House previously passed a similar amendment from Lee in 2019 when debating the fiscal 2020 defense authorization bill, but the language was stripped out during conference negotiations.

Lee's bill specifically targeted the 2002 AUMF, rather than the 2001 AUMF, because the Trump administration used it as justification for the drone attack that killed Iranian Maj. Gen. Qassem Soleimani in Iraq in January 2020. In floor remarks during debate on the measure, Lee compared the present situation to that before the war

ADDRESSING SEXUAL MISCONDUCT IN THE MILITARY

In 2020, the ongoing problem of sexual assault in the military made headlines when the body of twenty-year-old Army Spc. Vanessa Guillén was discovered in a shallow grave near Fort Hood in Texas. She had been missing for weeks, and prior to her disappearance twice reported being the victim of sexual harassment. An investigation revealed that her supervisors failed to report the incidents up through the chain of command, despite both Guillén and other soldiers coming forward to share their accounts. A further investigation found a "toxic culture" with ineffective leadership at Fort Hood, where women face a higher risk of sexual assault than any other females in the Army. More than a dozen officers were suspended, reprimanded, or relieved of their duties after the investigation into Guillén's death. Her suspected murderer, Army Specialist Aaron Robinson, was not one of the individuals thought to have sexually harassed Guillén, though he was accused of unrelated sexual misconduct. Robinson killed himself before murder charges were announced.

While Guillén's story tragically ended in her death, she was just one of the thousands of men and women in uniform who are sexually harassed or assaulted each year. A 2018 Department of Defense survey found that more than 20,000 service members had been subjected to some form of sexual assault, up 38 percent from 2016. Of those troops, only 38 percent reported the crime, a 41 percent decrease from 2016. According to the Pentagon, of the reported cases, 65 percent resulted in "disciplinary action," most of which was handled outside the court system. Research from RAND found that nearly half of these assaults targeted lesbian, gay, or bisexual service members. Further, their research estimated that 10,000 uniformed military personnel left the armed forces in a twenty-eight-month period after being sexually harassed or assaulted.

Over the years, the Pentagon has spent hundreds of millions of dollars on sexual assault prevention programs and trainings. However, according to RAND, these often amount to little more than PowerPoint presentations. Only the Air Force has full-time staff who oversee sexual misconduct prevention activities, while the other branches use short-term, rotating staff assignments.

To address the ongoing challenges facing the military, Congress has also stepped in and enacted various pieces of legislation. These measures include one that criminalized the nonconsensual sharing of intimate images and another that stripped provisions from the Uniform Code of Military Justice (UCMJ) that allowed verdicts to be overturned or sentences reduced for any reason (or even without a reason). Bills signed by the president have also removed "good military character" as a potential defense for those accused of sexual assault, and amended the UCMJ to give victims the option to appear at a preliminary hearing in their case rather than being forced to participate. Members in the House and Senate have also proposed, though the chambers have not enacted, legislation to provide more legal resources and support for victims of sexual assault and violence, establish a confidential reporting mechanism for assault claims, and create a system that lets victims report sexual assault without being punished for certain collateral misconduct, such as underage drinking.

During the 115th and 116th Congresses, one of the biggest pushes among some members was to reform how the military handles sexual assault cases, specifically by removing the statutory authority commanders have under the UCMJ to prosecute claims of sexual harassment and assault. Currently, after a sexual assault allegation is made, the military criminal investigative organization writes a report, which is provided to a Staff Judge Advocate (a military lawyer) who reviews it and recommends whether further action on the case should be taken. That recommendation goes to an officer in the accused's chain of command who will decide whether to convene a special courts martial or dismiss the issue. Typically, the commanders making these decisions have no legal background and are also often in a position of authority over the victim.

Advocates of removing a commander from sexual misconduct cases argue that one reason fewer than 40 percent of victims report their assault is because they fear retaliation. By eliminating commanders from their decision-making role in a case, victims may be more likely to come forward and more confident that the case will be handled impartially. Further, advocates say, career prosecutors are better qualified to make difficult legal decisions, especially in sensitive cases such as these.

Opponents, including some members of Congress and certain leaders at the Pentagon, argue that commanders are better positioned to understand the circumstances surrounding each case, and that removing their authority could weaken the overall command structure. They point to a report required under the fiscal year 2020 National Defense Authorization Act that found that an alternative system—in which judge advocates with significant experience in criminal litigation determine which cases go to trial—could create legal challenges, administrative burdens, and reduce a commander's overall disciplinary authority.

in Iraq began. "The 2003 invasion of Iraq was based on lies told by our own executive branch. In 2002, I stood here and urged us not to rush into war," Lee said. She encouraged her colleagues to pass the measure as a means of preventing the 2002 AUMF from becoming a justification for war with Iran. And, pushing back against Republicans and the White House who argued the amendment would tie the president's hands in defending U.S. interests, she noted, "repealing it would have absolutely no impact on the administration's ongoing military operations."

President Trump threatened to veto the measure, though in a tweet he also encouraged legislators to "vote their conscience." In a Statement of Administration Policy, the president said the legislation would limit the ability of forces in the region to protect U.S. interests "against ongoing threats from Iran and Iranian-sponsored proxies." According to the White House, through its Islamic Revolutionary Guard Corps-Quds Force, Iran directs terrorist organizations in Iraq, and "Iran and Iran-sponsored proxies continue to plan and execute attacks against United States forces in Iraq." The White House asserted that the 2002 AUMF provides critical authorities, used by two prior administrations, that allow U.S. forces to carry out their missions and defend themselves. Adopting the measure, the White House said, would "embolden our enemies" and "make the world less safe, less secure, and less free."

HR 2456 was offered as an amendment to HR 550, a noncontroversial Senate-passed measure that dealt with World War II medals, to avoid a motion to recommit. Republicans attempted to slow its consideration by offering unanimous consent requests to amend the rules governing floor debate and allow for a motion to recommit, but were blocked by Democrats.

On January 30, 2020, Lee's amendment passed 236–166, with eleven Republicans voting in favor and two Democrats opposed. The measure was not privileged in the Senate, and Senate Majority Leader Mitch McConnell, R-Ky., did not place it on the chamber's calendar.

CHAPTER 6

Transportation, Commerce, and Communications

Transportation, Commerce, and Communications

Major legislation to fix the nation's aging networks of highways, transit systems, power lines, public buildings, and other infrastructure was expected to be among the top priorities of lawmakers and the White House beginning in 2017. But such an initiative was sidelined pending a viable proposal to pay for such a package and while lawmakers worked to overcome partisan differences to clear annual transportation spending bills and a five-year reauthorization measure for the Federal Aviation Administration (FAA). The White House and Republicans also moved quickly to unravel several Obama-era rules governing internet service providers.

During the 2016 election campaign, President Donald Trump had pledged to push through Congress legislation intended to upgrade and modernize the nation's infrastructure, much of it built generations earlier. But his early proposal offered limited federal funding with the hopes of sparking major private investment. Meanwhile, Trump proposed significant cuts in federal transportation funding, cuts that were largely ignored by Congress—including his desire to privatize air traffic control.

After the start of the coronavirus pandemic in 2020, spending discussions focused on providing support for airlines and transit systems suffering a severe drop in ridership. Congress cleared several measures to provide payroll support for airlines and transit agencies.

Even before the pandemic, Transportation Security Administration was having a difficult time recruiting and retaining employees, including airport screeners, who complained of employer harassment and low salaries. Lawmakers considered, but did not clear a measure granting Transportation Security Administration employees the same collective bargaining rights enjoyed by other federal employees.

After two Boeing 737 Max airplanes crashed in 2018 and 2019, killing 246 people, Congress cleared legislation to reform the FAA's certification process for aircraft, engines and other components, minimizing the influence of aircraft manufacturers in the process and boosting FAA oversight of certification. Lawmakers also began discussing regulations for manufacturers of driverless vehicles, but,

amid low interest among Americans for such cars, they postponed any decisions.

Meanwhile, Congress reauthorized the Federal Communication Commission (FCC) for the first time in twenty-five years. The White House and congressional Republicans also moved to reverse a series of Obama-era rules. Among the rules that were reversed was a Federal Communications Commission's 2015 order that required internet providers to treat customers the same in terms of price and connection speeds, affecting websites such as Amazon that offer streaming services. The FCC voted to end the rule, and Democrats were unable to clear legislation to reverse the action.

Figure 6.1 Outlays for Transportation

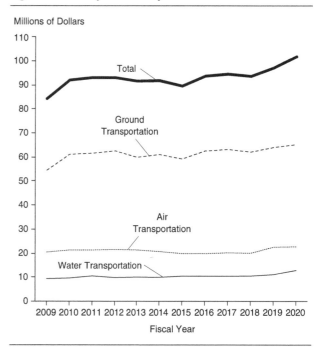

SOURCE: Office of Management and Budget. *Historical Tables, Budget of the United States Government: Fiscal Year 2021* (Washington DC: U.S. Government Printing Office, 2020), Table 3.2.

NOTE: Total line includes some expenditures not shown separately. * indicates estimate

262 CH. 6 TRANSPORTATION, COMMERCE, AND COMMUNICATIONS

Over Democrats' objections, Congress also blocked an Obama-era rule that would have required internet service providers to tell consumers what information they are collecting and how the information is being used or shared. Congress also repealed guidance for fining auto lenders that set higher rates for minorities.

Lawmakers, the Trump administration, social media companies, free speech advocates, and other public interest groups debated whether to amend federal law to end civil liability protections provided for social media companies that permit the distribution of disinformation, fake news, hate speech, or violence. Concerns were raised in the wake of the 2016 election and reports about the influence of Russian trolls that created fake Facebook accounts and provoked arguments among Americans about divisive issues. In the years leading to the 2020 election, more reports revealed the use of social media and artificial intelligence to disburse fake news and disinformation to influence political discussions. Congress failed to reach a resolution before the 2020 elections.

As in previous Congresses, lawmakers did not clear legislation to address whether states could collect taxes on online sales. The Supreme Court, meanwhile, in a June 2018 decision, opened the door to allow such tax collection.

Meanwhile, companies that stream music online were granted new protections from copyright infringement lawsuits under a measure signed into law by the president. Another measure the president signed into law aimed to make it easier for the blind and physically impaired to obtain access to foreign works of music and literature. Efforts to move the U.S. Copyright Office under Congress's control failed.

Chronology of Action on Transportation, Commerce, and Communications

2017–2018

Lawmakers during the 115th Congress cleared a five-year FAA reauthorization measure—the longest extension since 1982 and the first full reauthorization since 2012. The measure did not include Trump's plan to privatize air traffic control. Congress also cleared legislation to reauthorize the Coast Guard for one year.

President Trump in February 2018 unveiled a proposed infrastructure plan that called for spending $200 billion over ten years in order to spur up to $1.5 trillion in infrastructure spending from government and the private sector. His plan called for spending $20 billion per year for ten years to build and repair roads, ports, airports, energy infrastructure, rural broadband, and Veterans Affairs' hospitals.

Trump also proposed a twenty-five-cent increase in the federal gasoline tax to help pay for the plan, a proposal instantly rejected by both parties. Democrats also said the plan would impose heavy costs on state and local governments. Ultimately, lawmakers postponed consideration of a major infrastructure measure as they turned to other issues. Lawmakers did not include any of Trump's infrastructure proposals in fiscal 2018 or fiscal 2019 spending measures considered before the close of the 115th Congress.

Lawmakers passed several spending measures that boosted funding for Transportation programs above the president's requests, ultimately rejecting the administration's request to eliminate or reduce funding for several federal grant programs.

As in previous Congresses, lawmakers could not resolve how to maintain the dwindling Highway Trust Fund that had provided funding for most infrastructure projects since 1956. The fund was primarily financed by gas taxes, which had been set at 18.4 cents per gallon for gasoline and 24.2 cents per gallon for diesel in 1993 and remained unchanged. As lawmakers refused to hike the gas tax, neither they nor the administration proposed how to increase the fund.

Rep. Jeff Denham, R-Calif., led an unsuccessful effort to mandate uniform, nationwide meal-and-rest breaks for truck drivers. Provisions setting such a mandate were included in a series of funding bills as well as proposed FAA reauthorization measures, but they were ultimately dropped.

The GOP-controlled Congress also repealed a series of Obama-era rules, including a regulation that required metropolitan planning organizations in the same urban area to join together into a single organization or to issue unified plans. Congress also blocked an Obama-era rule that would have required internet service providers to tell consumers what information they are collecting and how the information is being used or shared.

Lawmakers cleared a measure aimed at ensuring online platforms comply with U.S. search warrants seeking emails stored on offshore networks without violating foreign data privacy laws. The new law led the Supreme Court to drop its consideration of a Justice Department lawsuit against Microsoft, which had refused to comply with a search warrant seeking emails in Ireland for a drug trafficking probe.

FAA Reauthorization

Congress during the 115th Congress cleared, and the president signed, a five-year reauthorization measure (PL 115-254) for the Federal Aviation Administration—the longest extension since 1982 and the first full reauthorization since 2012. Since October 2015, Congress had passed six short-term extensions of FAA authority while debate on a longer-term measure was delayed primarily by disagreement over whether to privatize management of the nation's air traffic control system.

BACKGROUND

Congress, under the 1958 Federal Aviation Act (PL 85-726), created the FAA to oversee the safe and

efficient use of national airspace and to regulate the aviation industry. The latest short-term authorization (PL 114-190) for the agency was set to expire on September 30, 2017. Efforts during the previous Congress to pass a six-year reauthorization had failed amid debate about a proposal by House Transportation and Commerce Chair Bill Shuster, R-Pa., that would have transferred management of the nation's air traffic control system from the FAA to a private, nonprofit corporation supported by airlines and other airport users.

In June 2017, Trump revived the idea, unveiling a plan that called for a new private nonprofit organization to manage air traffic control assets. The administration said the proposal would separate the operation from the congressional budget process, enabling the nonprofit to borrow money and thus modernize the air traffic control technology and more effectively implement, for example, new technology known as Next Generation Air Transportation System (NextGen), which in part would replace radar-based navigation with a satellite-based system.

Committee Democrats criticized the plan, calling it a giveaway of a public entity to private industry. They suspected the new entity would be controlled by the airlines. But Transportation Secretary Elaine Chao said the new entity would not raise a profit.

Democrats also estimated the air traffic control system's capital assets were worth billions and should not be given away for free, while Republicans argued the assets had depreciated in value over previous decades.

House Action

House Transportation Chair Shuster on June 22, 2017, introduced a six-year, $65.25 billion FAA reauthorization measure (HR 2997) that included a provision that would hand over air traffic control operations to a nongovernment entity in fiscal 2021. The provision was similar to the provision he had included in his 2016 reauthorization proposal, but with some changes. For example, while his latest proposal again would establish a board of directors with thirteen members, it would limit large passenger, regional, and cargo airlines to one vote each.

Shuster said the FAA had become inefficient, costly, and unable to keep up with developing technology. But Committee ranking member Peter A. DeFazio, D-Ore., said that privatizing the air traffic control system would jeopardize aviation safety and turn over taxpayer-owed assets to private interests.

Shuster's reauthorization bill would provide $51.1 billion in funding in each of the first three years, but would not reauthorize several major items (such as salaries, operations, and maintenance) after those three years as a result of spinning off air traffic control.

The bill also aimed to streamline the FAA's safety certification process for aircraft and aviation products. Shuster said the U.S. process had become too burdensome for

manufacturers competing in a global marketplace. He also said his bill would support innovation in unmanned aircraft systems and fund airport infrastructure.

Meanwhile, DeFazio and twenty-six other Democrats introduced their own reauthorization bill (HR 2800) that would not privatize air traffic control. Their bill also would address several controversies in the industries. For example, it would eliminate any cap on the compensation that airlines could provide passengers who are denied boarding. It also would bar airlines from refusing to board a passenger who had been approved by a gate attendant unless the passenger was considered a safety risk.

On June 27, The House Transportation and Infrastructure Committee approved Shuster's bill (HR 2997) by a vote of 32–25. During the more than nine-hour debate over eighty-six amendments, three amendments were adopted:

- a proposal by Del. Eleanor Holmes Norton, D-D.C., that would bar electronic cigarettes on passenger flights
- A proposal by Daniel Lipinski, D-Ill., that would require ticket agents with more than $100 million a year in revenue to adopt minimum customer service standards
- An amendment by Lou Barletta, R-Pa., that would have increased the funding authorization for the Airport improvement Program by about $1 billion more than the underlying bill, which set it at about $21.7 billion over six years. (Before the bill reached the House Rules committee, bill managers removed Barletta's provision to increase funding for airport construction projects.)

Republicans rejected, 24–34, an amendment by DeFazio that would have removed the provision to privatize air traffic control and would have substituted the Democrats' bill (HR 2800).

On July 12, 2017, the Congressional Budget Office said Shuster's proposal to hand over air traffic control to a nonprofit entity (which would be called American Air Navigation Service Corp.) would increase the federal deficit by $20.7 billion by fiscal 2027. The CBO estimated the nonprofit would spend about $3.5 billion more than the FAA through 2027 because it would need to finance capital spending.

In a July 18 preliminary legal analysis requested by committee ranking member DeFazio, the Congressional Research Service said the proposal to separate air traffic control from federal oversight could raise concerns about violations of the U.S. Constitution on three grounds: It would violate Congress's authority to levy taxes, violate the due process clause, and restrict the president's appointment power. However, the researchers cautioned that their analysis did not provide a "definitive conclusion" about the bill's constitutionality.

TRANSPORTATION, COMMERCE, AND COMMUNICATIONS LEADERSHIP

Transportation Secretary

Elaine Chao, a former secretary of Labor under President George W. Bush, served as President Trump's Transportation secretary for four years and loyally promoted his push for a major infrastructure package, to privatize air traffic control, and to block funding on a Northeast Corridor rail project before coming under scrutiny by the House ethics committee for her family's overseas financial dealings.

Trump nominated Chao, wife of Senate Republican leader Mitch McConnell, as Transportation secretary soon after winning the election in November 2020. The Senate swiftly confirmed her nomination, 93–6, on January 31, 2017, after telling senators that among her priorities would be advancing Trump's plan to invest up to $1 trillion in infrastructure over a decade. The Judiciary Committee had approved her nomination by voice vote a week earlier.

Chao had served as secretary of Labor under Bush for eight years—the only official to serve through both of the president's terms in the White House. Previously, she had worked in various federal departments, including as a White House fellow under President Ronald Reagan and director of the Peace Corps under Bush. She also had worked for Harvard's Kennedy School of Government and the Heritage Foundation, a conservative think tank.

In 2017, Chao immediately began urging Congress to support the president's forthcoming infrastructure plan, and promoted the White House's plan to remove air traffic control from the Federal Aviation Administration's responsibility and place it under a private, nonprofit entity that could better upgrade technology and improve aviation safety. She said the existing FAA air traffic control system was outdated and contributed to costly flight delays. House Transportation and Infrastructure Chair Bill Shuster, R-Pa., who in the earlier years had tried to advance legislation to privatize air traffic control, pushed legislation, but ultimately dropped the proposal amid Democratic opposition in order to clear an FAA reauthorization measure.

In 2018, Chao began pushing for a fix to the Highway Trust Fund, which relied on gas tax proceeds and whose balance was rapidly declining as funds were used for highway, road, and rail projects. The fund was projected to run out of money by the end of fiscal 2020, but the administration did not have proposals to fix the situation.

During debate on the president's infrastructure proposal and on the Highway Trust Fund, Chao also defended the president's opposition to the so-called Gateway Program, a $30 billion commuter rail, bridge, and tunnel project intended to connect New York and New Jersey under the Hudson River. She said the president just wanted New York and New Jersey to contribute more funds for the project rather than rely on hefty federal aid.

In 2019, Chao came under scrutiny by several media outlets for her financial holdings. Before joining the Trump administration, Chao held stock options in Vulcan Materials, an Alabama-based producer of crushed stone and asphalt. At the time of the hearing, Chao promised to sell her shares. But the Wall Street Journal reported in June 2019 that Chao had not sold her stock. Days after the report, the Department of Transportation announced Chao sold her stock shares, worth $250,000 to $500,000.

Chao also came under scrutiny for potential ethics violations for actions related to her family. Her father, until 2018, had run the family's shipping business, Foremost Group, and her sister Angela became chief executive of the company. Meantime, *The New York Times* reported a series of unusual requests Chao made on behalf of her family members, including a request to coordinate travel arrangements and include relatives in meetings with government officials. *The New York Times* also reported that Chao, who did not hold a position in Foremost, and her husband prospered as the company developed deeper ties to China.

In September, the House Committee on Oversight and Reform launched an investigation into whether Chao used her office to benefit her family's shipping company. After a preliminary review of the issues, House Transportation Chair Peter DeFazio, D-Ore., and House Oversight Chair Carolyn B. Maloney, D-N.Y., in December 2020 called on the Department of Transportation's inspector general to investigate.

Commerce Secretary

Billionaire Investor Wilbur L. Ross served as President Trump's Secretary of Commerce for four years. Vowing to boost U.S. exports and reform trade deals, Ross instead became the focus of probes into his financial holdings and potential ethics violations, and ultimately was held in contempt of Congress for not handing over certain documents related to the 2020 census.

During his confirmation hearing before the Senate Judiciary Committee, the seventy-nine-year-old vowed to make changes to the North American Free Trade Agreement, which Trump blamed for the loss of millions of industrial jobs. Ross also said he hoped to expand access for U.S. exports in other countries that play "fair" and "by the rules" and to strike back at those that limit or block American exports.

Ross had made his fortune by buying and selling struggling industrial companies. His financial disclosure filed with the Office of Government Ethics showed he had ties or investments with at least seventy corporations

(Continued)

in the United States, Bermuda, Brazil, Cayman Islands, China, Cyprus, France, Germany, Hong Kong, Ireland, Luxembourg, Japan, Mauritius, and the United Kingdom.

The Senate Commerce, Science, and Transportation Committee approved Ross's nomination by voice vote on January 24, 2017, and the full Senate confirmed the nomination in a 72–27 vote on February 27. The United Steelworkers union backed his confirmation. The union had supported Ross's revival of Bethlehem Steel, LTV Steel, and Weirton Steel by combining them into the International Steel Group, which became the largest steel operation in North America before he sold it to Mittal Steel in 2005.

Senate Democrats, however, raised concerns about Russian investors in the Bank of Cyprus, where Ross was a board member and vice president. Ross said he had only spoken to a major Russian investor once in 2014. Ross pledged to resign from those positions once he was confirmed.

Ross had vowed to divest his stock holdings in a number of corporations, but in June 2018, Citizens for Responsibility and Ethics in Washington called for a federal ethics probe into whether he lied about divesting his stock in Invesco, the firm he had managed before taking the position as Commerce secretary. The group also raised questions about his sale of shares in Navigator Holdings, a shipping firm that did business with a Russian energy firm. One of the directors of that firm was a Russian oligarch subject to U.S. sanctions and a son-in-law of Russian President Vladimir Putin.

On December 3, 2020, the Commerce Department's inspector general released a report detailing its investigation of Ross and complaints about lying about his financial holdings, making false ethics filings and suspiciously timed investments. The report concluded that Ross, in violation of federal regulations, had failed to avoid the appearance of ethical and legal breaches. The report said, for instance, that Ross had not listed all his assets on financial disclosure forms, and claimed to have divested holdings but did not. The report did not conclude that Ross knowingly lied, which would have been a crime.

In 2018, Ross also faced questions from Congress, as well as plaintiffs in a lawsuit, regarding his decision to add a citizenship question to the 2020 census. The question stated, "Is this person a citizen of the United States?"

The decennial count is used to determine electoral boundaries and funding disbursement for a variety of government programs and benefits. Census Bureau experts had advised Ross, who as Commerce secretary oversaw the Census Bureau, not to add the question. But Ross said the citizenship data was needed for enforcement of the Voting Rights Act. Immigrant and voting rights groups, however, asserted that the question was intended to discourage immigrants from filling out the census.

New York City, several states, local governments, and advocacy groups filed a lawsuit, contending the citizenship question would thereby undermine the accuracy of the population count. On June 27, 2019, the Supreme Court ruled that the Trump administration could not properly justify its decision to add a citizenship question to the census, effectively blocking the question. The Trump administration subsequently announced it would drop the question.

On July 17, 2019, the House voted, 230–198, to hold Ross, as well as Attorney General William P. Barr, in criminal contempt of Congress because they refused to turn over key documents related to the administration's attempt to add the citizenship question. The vote authorized the oversight panel to take Ross and Barr to federal court to enforce subpoenas for the material, and called for the Justice Department to criminally prosecute them (although Barr was head of the Justice Department). The Commerce and Justice departments and the White House issued statements condemning the vote as a political smear tactic against the administration.

In December 2020, the House Oversight and Reform Committee subpoenaed Ross for documents related to errors in finalizing 2020 census results. The committee released a series of leaked documents from the agency that indicated officials had found errors in more than 900,000 records, which could result in missing or double counting tens of thousands of people. The Commerce Department said it had turned over thousands of documents to the House.

Federal Communications Chair

Ajit Varadaraj Pai, a former lawyer for the Department of Justice and the U.S. Senate Judiciary Committee who advocated deregulation, became chair of the Federal Communications Commission in 2017 and immediately took steps to unravel the FCC's net neutrality rules. Pai, a Republican, had served as a member of the commission since 2011, nominated for the seat by President Obama based on the recommendation of Senate Republican Leader Mitch McConnell, R-Ky. As a minority member of the commission, Pai had voted against the 2015 rule that required internet service providers to treat online traffic equally in terms of price and connection speeds.

The Senate confirmed Pai's nomination as chair in a largely party line vote of 42–41 on October 2, 2017. Pai, a native of Kansas, became the first Indian American to chair the FCC. Pai had previously worked two years as an in-house lawyer for Verizon Communications, and joined FCC's general counsel office in 2007.

Pai had been serving as acting chair since January 2017, when he took over from former Chair Tom Wheeler. Maria Cantwell, D-Wash., and Ron Wyden, D-Ore., and other

Democrats vocally opposed Pai's confirmation, worried about his views on deregulation and his plans to unravel net neutrality rules.

Pai said he believed the FCC should help foster competition in the communications space. On March 1, 2017, the FCC voted, 2–1, to suspend implementation of a controversial broadband privacy rule that would have required internet service providers to tell consumers what data they were collecting and how the information was being used or shared.

Also under Pai's leadership, the FCC on December 14, 2017, voted along party lines, 3–2, to abolish the net neutrality rules. Democrats' subsequent efforts to overturn the FCC's decision failed.

In August, a Department of Transportation (DOT) inspector general report questioned the benefits the FAA cited in its multibillion-dollar NextGen program. The FAA had worked for several years on the program, but the project had suffered many delays and cost overruns. Shuster said the DOT report supported his proposal to privatize air traffic control.

Senate Action

On June 22, 2017, Sens. John Thune, R-S.D., and Bill Nelson, D-Fla., chair and ranking member of the Senate Commerce, Science and Transportation Committee, introduced a four-year, $68-billion reauthorization bill (S 1405) that did not include a provision to spin off air traffic control from the FAA. Several Republican senators, along with the majority of Democrats, had opposed privatizing air traffic control. The bill would provide $51 billion in funding for the first three years.

The Senate Commerce, Science and, Transportation Committee on June 29 approved the bill (S 1405) by voice vote after adopting several amendments that would, for example, loosen training requirements for commercial pilots and preempt state laws regarding rest breaks for truckers. The bill also would boost grant funding for the Airport Improvement Program through 2021. Under the bill, funding for the program would be boosted to $3.75 billion from $3.35 billion in the first year.

The committee also approved an amendment by Thune that would allow pilots in training to substitute certain training courses for flight hours. Thune said it could help airlines that were struggling to hire more pilots. Democratic leader Charles E. Schumer of New York opposed the added provisions and threatened to block the bill on the floor.

SIX-MONTH EXTENSION

Shortly before the existing FAA authorization was set to expire, the House took up a six-month extension of FAA programs. The bill (HR 3823) would authorize aviation trust fund spending at $1.67 billion over six months, consistent with half of the fiscal 2017 spending authorization level of $3.35 billion. The measure also would include provisions to help victims of hurricanes Harvey, Irma, and Maria.

The funding extension, through March 2018, was intended to allow lawmakers time to reach agreement on a longer-term bill. On September 25, the House rejected the six-month extension measure in a 245–171 vote, failing to reach the two-thirds majority required for the bill's passage under suspension of the rules. House Democrats had opposed the measure because Republicans had not included them in the drafting process; only a handful of Democrats voted with Republicans to support the bill.

After negotiations, the House on September 28 passed, in a 264–155 vote, the six-month extension. The same afternoon, the Senate, by voice vote, passed the measure after approving, by unanimous consent, an amendment by Bill Cassidy, R-La., to remove a provision that would have expanded private flood insurance under the National Flood Insurance program.

The same day, the House cleared the measure by unanimous consent. The president signed the measure into law (PL 115-63) on September 29, 2017.

SECOND EXTENSION

The House on March 22, 2018, approved, 256–167, a fiscal 2018 omnibus spending measure (HR 1625) that included another six-month reauthorization of FAA. The measure would provide $18 billion for FAA programs, $1.6 billion more than the fiscal 2017 level, through September 30, 2018. The measure also included $1.3 billion for NextGen air traffic control programs, $239 million more than the fiscal 2017 level.

The Senate cleared the measure (HR 1625) in a 65–32 vote on March 23. The president signed the legislation into law (PL 115-141) on the same day.

REVISED SIX-MONTH EXTENSION

On April 13, 2018, House Transportation Chair Shuster introduced a six-year, $103.2 billion FAA reauthorization measure (HR 4) that did not include his previous proposal to create a private nonprofit to oversee and operate air traffic control. The bill would authorize $83.1 billion for FAA operations, facilities, and equipment through fiscal 2023.

The House passed the bill on April 27, 2018, in a 393–13 vote. The measure would authorize $97 billion for aviation programs for fiscal 2019 through fiscal 2023. Republicans passed the bill over objections by the Trump administration, which opposed provisions affecting international aviation agreements. The administration opposed, for

example, a provision that would bar foreign air carriers from incorporating in a country outside the country where the majority of their owners reside. Labor groups said the provision would bar airlines from bypassing safety and labor regulations in more developed countries, but the administration said the provision would interfere with its authority to oversee such agreements.

The administration also opposed a provision, included from a House-passed measure (HR 4460), that would make changes to Federal Emergency Management Agency (FEMA) policy. DOT officials said changes to FEMA policy might result in higher spending on disaster relief efforts. But the administration supported a provision that would authorize $5.3 billion over five years for a new airport grant program that would prioritize spending on small, rural airports.

During floor debate, the House adopted, 212–190, an amendment by John J. Duncan Jr., R-Tenn., which would shield trucking companies from liability in certain cases if they followed training procedures. The House rejected, 113–293, an amendment by Tom McClintock, R-Calif., that would have abolished the Essential Air Service, which subsidized commercial flights to small, rural airports.

The House bill included a provision to direct the FAA to create policies and regulations on the certification and operation of supersonic aircraft, similar to a provision in the Senate bill (S 1405). Meanwhile, the Senate failed to act on its measure amid ongoing debate on Supreme Court nominee Brett Kavanaugh.

FIVE-YEAR EXTENSION

With time running out before the FAA authorization expired, House and Senate members of both parties negotiated a new, five-year reauthorization measure.

House Action

On September 26, 2018, the House passed the five-year measure (HR 302) in a 398–23 vote. The bill included provisions that would require flight attendants be permitted to rest after ten hours of work, establish a minimum for passenger legroom, and require revenue from a transportation security fee to be spent on transportation security costs. The final bill did not include a provision that would have preempted state laws on meal and rest breaks for truck drivers.

The aviation industry supported the bill, while the U.S. Chamber of Commerce complained it did not boost funding for the Airport Improvement Program or raise the maximum passenger facility charge airports were allowed to charge. Several non-FAA measures were added to the bill, including a measure to authorize the Transportation Security Administration and to reauthorize the National Transportation Safety Board. Just after passing the five-year reauthorization, the House passed a one-week extension (HR 6897) to give the Senate time to complete the Supreme Court confirmation process before turning to the long-term measure.

Senate Action

On September 28, 2018, the Senate cleared, by unanimous consent, the measure (HR 6897) providing a one-week extension—through October 7—of FAA authority. The president signed the measure into law (PL 115-250) on September 29. On October 3, the Senate cleared, 93–6, the bill (HR 302) that would reauthorize the FAA for five years.

Final Action

The president signed the five-year reauthorization measure into law (PL 115-254) on October 5, 2018. The final measure retained provisions calling on the FAA to set minimum requirements for passengers' legroom and to prohibit airlines from bumping passengers from a flight after they had boarded the plane.

While the last long-term reauthorization law (PL 112-95) restricted the FAA's ability to regulate drones, the new measure would allow the agency to regulate longer drone flights and drone operations at night or over people. Federal officials also would be allowed to disable drones that the Homeland Security and Justice departments viewed as security threats.

Coast Guard Reauthorization

Congress cleared a one-year reauthorization for the Coast Guard in late 2018 following a lengthy debate on provisions regarding potential new regulations on ballast water, which vessels used to maintain balance at sea but which could carry invasive species. The previous, two-year reauthorization was cleared in February 2016 (PL 114-120).

Senate Action

On May 18, 2017, the Senate Commerce, Science and Transportation Committee approved, by voice vote, a bill (S 1129) that would reauthorize Coast Guard operations through fiscal 2019, covering the agency's nearly 50,000 full-time, active-duty employees. The bill, introduced by Dan Sullivan, R-Alaska, would authorize $7.3 billion for fiscal 2018 and nearly $7.6 billion for fiscal 2019. Much of the funding would be authorized to modernize Coast Guard facilities, including building new vessels to replace outdated ships. The committee adopted an amendment by Richard Blumenthal, D-Conn., that would allow the Coast Guard to help fund the construction of a museum dedicated to the service.

But several Democratic senators from the Great Lakes region opposed a provision that would allow the Coast Guard to set regulations affecting ballast water, which vessels use to maintain balance at sea. The Democrats said it would preempt the Clean Water Act and federal and state regulations. Sen. Debbie Stabenow, D-Mich., said invasive species, such as Asian carp and foreign mollusks, which have been harming the Great Lakes,

were introduced in the region via ballast water. She said states should retain the authority to regulate ballast water. But Republicans said the measure would allow the creation of national standards. Committee Chair John Thune, R-S.D., said states could petition for stronger regulations if they could show that technology existed to support such standards.

In April 2018, when a Native American water rights bill (S 140) fell short of votes to advance, Majority Leader McConnell offered an amendment to replace its language with the text of the Coast Guard bill. But a vote to end debate on the bill fell short of the necessary sixty votes over the provision on ballast water.

Later, Chair Thune and Sen. Thomas R. Carper, D-Del., ranking member of the Environment and Public Works Committee, agreed on language that would require the enforcement of EPA's rules on ballast water, which are aimed at limiting the impact of invasive species. On November 13, 2018, the Senate voted, 93–5, to close debate on the measure and move to a vote.

The Senate passed the bill (S 140) in a 94–6 vote on November 14, 2018. The measure would authorize $12.1 billion for the Coast Guard, a $1.7 billion increase from fiscal 2017. The measure would authorize $7.9 billion for operating expenses and $2.6 billion for procurement, construction, renovation, and improvement in fiscal 2019.

The bill included a provision that would exempt the Delta Queen paddle wheel boat from federal law and Coast Guard regulations that require vessels with overnight accommodations for fifty or more passengers to be made of fireproof materials. Mississippi River state officials want the ninety-one-year-old wooden boat as a tourist attraction.

Final Action

On November 27, the House cleared the measure (S 140) for the president's signature by voice vote. The final bill included provisions that would require the Coast Guard to create a land-based backup to the Global Positioning System of satellites and to launch a land-based drone program. The president signed the measure into law (PL 115-282) on December 4, 2018.

Driverless Vehicles

The House in 2017 passed the first measure to address regulation and development of driverless vehicles, but a similar measure in the Senate failed to reach the floor. For several years, the federal government had been avoiding addressing its role in regulating autonomous vehicles, that is, reenvisioning existing vehicle standards and requirements that assumed a human driver. Both parties and the administration in the 115th Congress felt they should tread lightly into regulatory changes, while many technology representatives wanted Congress to first remove any barriers to testing.

House Action

The Digital Commerce and Consumer Protection Subcommittee of the House Energy and Commerce Committee on June 27, 2017, met to consider fourteen draft bills that sought to expedite deployment of driverless cars by lifting federal requirements for steering wheels, brake pedals, and other components not necessary for autonomous vehicles.

On June 19, the panel approved, by voice vote, a draft bill that aimed to expand testing and marketing of self-driving vehicles. The measure would expand the types of exemptions to federal safety standards that the National Highway Traffic Safety Administration could grant for driverless vehicles, such as not requiring brake pedals and steering wheels. The bill would require manufacturers of the cars to develop cybersecurity plans, and would bar states from drafting laws to regulate vehicle software.

As drafted, the bill included blank sections where bipartisan language could later be inserted before it moved to committee. Democrats said they wanted to revise language related to exemptions to Federal Motor Vehicle Safety Standards, for instance.

The full Energy and Commerce Committee on July 27 approved, 55–0, a measure (HR 3388) that would clarify the federal government's role in regulating autonomous vehicles. The bill would bar states and localities from regulating the design, construction, and performance of such vehicles. The bill also would encourage more testing and development of such cars by, for example, updating federal safety standards on who could develop and test the vehicles.

The bill also would authorize the secretary of Transportation to issue a rule requiring all new cars and trucks be equipped with alarm systems that alert the driver to check the rear seats, after the vehicle has been turned off, to ensure small children are not left inside. The House passed the measure (HR 3388) by voice vote on September 5, 2017. A coalition of groups representing state interests objected to the bill's provisions preempting state authority to regulate vehicles.

Senate Action

On September 28, 2017, Senate Commerce, Science and Transportation Chair John Thune, R-S.D., and committee member Gary Peters, D-Mich., introduced a bill (S 1885) on regulating autonomous vehicles. Like the House bill, the measure would aim to set national standards for self-driving vehicles by barring state and local governments from issuing their own regulations.

Thune's committee on October 4 approved the bill by voice vote after adopting an amendment by Sen. Bill Nelson, D-Fla., that would allow state and local governments to regulate the licensing, liability, and insurance for driverless vehicles.

Thune initially had considered including heavy trucks in the bill's provisions, but ultimately chose not to include them in order to retain bipartisan support. Thune had said

he believed regulations of self-driving vehicles should be addressed for various sizes of vehicles, but Peters had pushed for the exclusion of heavy trucks in the bill.

The committee approved an amendment by Richard Blumenthal, D-Conn., that would require, within two years of the bill's enactment, a rule requiring new vehicles of less than 10,000 pounds to be equipped with an alert system to remind the driver to check for a child in the backseat. Another Blumenthal amendment would reduce the number of annual federal exemptions that could be granted to makers of driverless vehicles, allowing 15,000 exemptions in the first year after the bill's enactment, 40,000 in the second year, and 80,000 each year thereafter.

Several Senate Democrats had safety concerns about the driverless technology and opposed moving the legislation. Several lawmakers and transportation experts also raised concerns about the need for modernized infrastructure on roads to accommodate driverless cars, and about consumer privacy. In December 2018, Senate Commerce Republicans made a last-minute push for the Senate to act on the legislation before the close of the 115th Congress, but to no avail.

Administrative Action

On September 12, 2017, Transportation Secretary Elaine Chao unveiled a federal policy on self-driving vehicles that stated automakers did not have to submit safety plans before testing technology. The policy updated 2016 guidance that recommended states require automakers to submit a safety assessment letter to the National Highway Traffic Safety Administration before allowing them to test their vehicles on state roads. The update clarified that such safety plans were not required. Chao released the updated policy the same day the National Transportation Safety Board issued a report that concluded the driver of a Tesla in a fatal 2016 crash relied too much on the autonomous function of the vehicle.

On October 4, 2018, Transportation officials issued another update to its policy, which continued to contain voluntary, rather than mandatory, guidance for makers of self-driving cars. The policy also encouraged a consistent, nationwide regulatory approach.

Truck Drivers' Breaks

Provisions to mandate uniform, nationwide meal-and-rest breaks for truck drivers were pushed in a series of funding bills and FAA reauthorization measures. The provisions were meant to clarify a 1994 law to block a 2011 California meal-and-rest-break requirement. California's law required employers to provide a thirty-minute meal break for employees who work more than five hours a day, and a second thirty-minute meal break for people who work more than ten hours a day. Other states require a different number of breaks per shift. The federal standard required drivers to take just one thirty-minute break during the first eight hours of driving.

The controversy stemmed from a July 2014 ruling by the Ninth Circuit Court of Appeals that Penske Logistics, a Reading, Pennsylvania-based trucking firm, must allow drivers paid meal and rest breaks as required by state law. California law required a thirty-minute meal break every five hours and a paid ten-minute rest break for every four hours of work. Penske had stood behind a 1994 federal law, known as the Federal Aviation Administration Authorization Act, that preempted state-level laws on drivers. The ruling spurred members of the House and Senate to reassert federal authority over truck drivers' time and pay.

An amendment by California Republican Rep. Jeff Denham was originally included in the House's five-year FAA reauthorization bill in April 2018, but it was dropped before a final bill was cleared in September. House Minority Leader Nancy Pelosi, D-Calif., had campaigned against the so-called "Denham amendment," saying it would erode safety standards set for drivers. Similar provisions were dropped from transportation spending measures.

Transit Planning

In a bipartisan move, lawmakers in 2017 repealed an Obama-era rule that required metropolitan planning organizations in the same urban area to join together into a single organization or to issue unified plans. The Federal Transit Administration and the Federal Highway Administration had finalized the rule in December 2016, one month before the end of President Obama's term.

Critics of the rule, which took effect January 19, 2017, said it could allow the creation of planning agencies covering large urban areas, including much of the Northeast, and those agencies would not have to take into consideration local concerns. Such an action, said Sen. Tammy Duckworth, D-Ill., would enable the governors of Indiana and Wisconsin, for example, to potentially block actions by the Chicago Metropolitan Agency for Planning.

By repealing the rule through legislation, Congress allowed the Department of Transportation an opportunity to revise it. If Congress had used the Congressional Review Act to nullify the rule, it would have prevented the agency from promulgating a similar rule.

Senate Action

Sen. Duckworth on March 2, 2017, introduced a bill (S 496) to repeal the rule on metropolitan planning organizations. On March 8, Majority Leader McConnell called on the Senate to discharge the bill from the Banking and Urban Affairs Committee and move it to the floor for consideration. The same day, the Senate passed the measure by unanimous consent.

House Action

On March 2, 2017, Rep. Daniel Lipinski, D-Ill., introduced a measure (HR 1346) to repeal the rule. Lipinski said the rule would force the consolidation of

some planning organizations that cross state lines, potentially stifling the concerns of local elected officials and creating obstacles to long-term planning. The House Transportation and Infrastructure Committee approved the measure by voice vote on March 29.

Final Action

On April 27, 2017, the House cleared the Senate bill (S 496) in a 417–3 vote. Reps. Earl Blumenauer, D-Ore., and Zoe Lofgren and Mark DeSaulnier, D-Calif., voted against the measure. The president signed the measure into law (PL 115-33) on May 12.

FCC Reauthorization

Congress in 2018 cleared legislation that reauthorized the Federal Communication Commission for the first time in twenty-five years. The last reauthorization had been enacted in 1990 (PL 101-396).

House Action

The Communications and Technology Subcommittee of the House Energy and Commerce Committee on October 11, 2017, approved, by voice vote, draft legislation that would reauthorize the FCC for two years. The bill would authorize $322 million for the FCC in each of fiscal years 2019 and 2020, with revenue raised through regulatory fees assessed by the commission. The draft bill included language that would require the FCC to provide more transparency in its rulemaking and to allow more public participation and comment. The language was identical to language in a measure (HR 290) that the House passed by voice vote on January 23. The provision was added in response to controversy surrounding the FCC's finalization of its broadband privacy rule in 2016. In petitions to reconsider the rule, opponents had cited a lack of transparency in the rule's development.

The Energy and Commerce Committee on February 14, 2018, approved the subcommittee-approved measure (HR 4986) to reauthorize the FCC for two years. The panel left undecided the amount of funding to help broadcasters cover relocation costs related to a forthcoming reshuffling of spectrum slots as a result of a 2017 auction that was completed to accommodate wireless providers. The FCC received $19.6 billion in bids in the incentive auction of eighty-four megahertz of spectrum that would be released by broadcasters and sold for wireless use. About $1.75 billion was set aside to compensate those broadcasters, but the broadcasters said the amount would not fully cover costs.

The committee's ranking member, Frank Pallone Jr., D-N.J., and Chair Greg Walden, R-Ore., said they would continue to work on that provision. Pallone had offered another measure (HR 3347) that would authorize $1 billion to help compensate broadcasters.

The House passed the two-year reauthorization measure (HR 4986) by voice vote, under suspension of the rules, on March 6, 2018. As passed by the House, the measure would provide $333 million for the FCC in fiscal 2019 and $339 million in fiscal 2020, an increase from the committee-approved bill. However, the bill still did not specify an amount to compensate broadcasters for moving television stations to new channels or FM radio equipment to accommodate wireless providers.

Final Action

House and Senate negotiators included provisions of the two-year FCC reauthorization bill (HR 4986) in the fiscal 2018 omnibus measure (HR 1625). The omnibus bill would authorize $333.1 million in fiscal 2019 and $339.6 million in fiscal 2020. The omnibus also included a provision authorizing $1 billion ($600 million in fiscal 2018 and $400 million in fiscal 2019) to help broadcasters cover the costs associated with accommodating wireless providers.

The House passed the bill by a 256–167 vote on March 22, 2018. The Senate, in a 65–32 vote, cleared the bill on March 23, and the president signed it into law (PL 115-141) on the same day.

Internet Sales Tax

During the 115th Congress, lawmakers failed to take action on legislation to address whether states could collect taxes on online sales from out-of-state vendors, while the Supreme Court took a step forward on the issue. On June 21, 2018, the Supreme Court, in a 5–4 decision, opened the door to allow states to collect sales taxes from out-of-state vendors. The ruling overturned the court's 1992 decision in *Quill Corp. v. North Dakota*, which had upheld a 1967 ruling that states could not require retailers to collect sales and use taxes from a company unless that company resided in the state. In that 1992 ruling, the court said Congress had the ultimate power to resolve the issue.

Forty-one states and the District of Columbia had asked the court to overturn its 1992 decision. Justice Kennedy said the 1992 ruling no longer made sense and had caused states to lose billions of dollars in sales tax revenue. He said a small warehouse in South Dakota, for instance, had to collect sales taxes for South Dakota. But if that same company had an online-only business across the border in Nebraska, it could sell the same items without collecting sales taxes for South Dakota.

Chief Justice John G. Robert, Jr., in a dissent, said it was up to Congress to consider any alteration to the rules that could disrupt the development of online commerce, which had become vital to the national economy. But in the years since the court's 1992 ruling, Congress had failed to take action, although a number of bills were considered. When the Supreme Court issued its ruling on the issue in 2018, several related measures (S 976, HR 2193, HR 2887) were pending before Congress, but the measures never saw action.

Data Privacy

Congress in 2018 cleared a measure aimed at ensuring Microsoft Corp. and other online platforms would comply with U.S. search warrants seeking emails stored on offshore networks without violating foreign data privacy laws. Supporters of such a law provision hoped it could resolve a pending Supreme Court decision on the Justice Department's lawsuit against Microsoft after the company refused to comply with a search warrant seeking emails in Ireland for a drug trafficking probe.

During oral arguments, several justices, including Justice Ruth Ginsburg and Sotomayor, had said that, in lieu of issuing a ruling on the case, Congress should enact a legislative solution.

In February 2018, Sen. Orrin G. Hatch, R-Utah, and Rep. Doug Collins, R-Ga., introduced companion bills (S 2383, HR 4943) called the Clarifying Lawful Overseas Use of Data (CLOUD) Act. Language from those bills was included in provisions of the final fiscal 2018 omnibus measure that the president signed into law (HR 1625, PL 115-141) on March 23, 2018. Those provisions expanded the reach of domestic search warrants authorized under the 1986 electronic communications law (PL 99-508) and encouraged reciprocal agreements between the United States and other countries to allow investigators to access emails stored on servers in the other country.

The case, *United States vs. Microsoft Corporation*, had been argued before the Supreme Court on February 27, 2018, but had not been decided before the president signed the omnibus measure into law. After the president signed the fiscal 2018 measure into law, Solicitor General Noel Francisco notified the Supreme Court of the passage of the so-called CLOUD Act provision included in the new law. That provision amended the Stored Communications Act of 1986 (18 U.S.C. §§ 2701-2712), requiring any U.S. company served with a court order to turn over data, regardless of where it was stored, provided it was within the U.S. company's possession.

Francisco also asked whether passage of the measure would affect the court's handling of the case. The government also obtained a new warrant for the information requested in regard to the case. The Supreme Court on April 17, 2018, declared the case moot.

Broadband Privacy Rule

Congress undid an Obama-era rule that would have required internet service providers to tell consumers what information they were collecting and how the information was being used or shared. In some cases, providers would have had to obtain consumers' explicit consent to sell their data for advertising purposes. Republicans said the rules put providers on unequal footing with other internet firms, such as Google and Facebook, which are subject to less restrictive standards set by the Federal Trade Commission.

BACKGROUND

The FCC had adopted, in a 3–2 vote, the privacy rule in October 2016 after its 2015 Open Internet Order reclassified internet service providers as common carriers and shifted privacy regulation of the providers from the Federal Trade Commission (FTC) to the FCC. Providers such as Comcast and Verizon said the change put them at a competitive disadvantage compared to other internet firms, which remained subject to the less restrictive standards of the FTC. So, under the rule, while the providers would have to wait for users to opt in and allow the use of their data, internet firms such as Google and Facebook could use such data until users opted out.

The internet service providers said the new rule would make it harder to attract advertising money based on consumers' usage data.

On March 1, 2017, the Federal Communications Commission voted, 2–1, to suspend the effective date of the broadband privacy rule, set for March 2. FCC Chair Ajit Pai and Michael O'Rielly, both Republican commissioners, had voted against the rule in 2016 and voted for the stay on the rule. Democrat Mignon Clyburn, who held the other commission seat, dissented. The stay would be effective until the commission reviewed petitions to revise or pull the regulation, which would impose new restrictions on internet service providers.

Senate Action

Sen. Jeff Flake, R-Ariz., on March 7, 2017, introduced a resolution (S J Res 34) to overturn the broadband privacy rule under the Congressional Review Act, under which Congress can repeal a regulation and bar the administration from subsequently promulgating a similar rule. Republicans on the Senate Commerce, Science, and Transportation Committee (of which Flake was not a member) supported the resolution. But Democrats criticized Flake for introducing the measure. Frank Pallone Jr., D-N.J., ranking member of the House Energy and Commerce Committee, said the resolution would impede the agency's ability to address the issue. On March 23, 2017, the Senate, in a party line vote of 50–48, approved the resolution to undo the privacy rule.

House Action

Rep. Marsha Blackburn, R-Tenn., introduced an identical resolution (H J Res 86) in the House on March 8, 2017. On March 28, the House passed the Senate resolution (S J Res 34) in a party line vote of 215–205, clearing it for the president's signature. President Trump signed the measure into law (PL 115-22) on April 3, 2017.

Privacy advocates and online consumers strongly opposed the legislation. After the measure was signed into law, at least thirteen states advanced their own internet privacy legislation.

Internet Access

The Federal Communication Commission voted to repeal so-called net-neutrality rules, issued under the Obama administration in 2015 to require internet service providers to treat consumers the same and not discriminate against any content providers, renewing a long-running debate between Republicans and Congress over the rules. Democratic efforts to block the FCC's latest ruling, however, failed in the GOP-controlled House and Senate.

BACKGROUND

In 2010, the FCC had issued an Open Internet Order that included three rules governing transparency, blocking, and unreasonable discrimination. The rules required "net neutrality"; that, is they required internet providers to treat customers the same in terms of price and connection speeds, affecting websites such as Amazon that offer streaming services. At the time, Republicans contended that former FCC Chair Julius Genachowski had overstepped his authority when he insisted on the rules.

In 2014, a federal court struck down most of the FCC's Open Internet rule that barred the throttling of speed and traffic. The court said the commission must allow broadband companies to offer content providers faster speed at a higher price, provided they did so within a "reasonable" standard. The FCC in 2015 issued a new rule that still required internet service providers to treat online traffic equally, but had moved its regulations to Title II of the 1934 Communications Act, which the agency used to regulate telephone companies and other carriers. The rules banned slowing down and blocking content as well as prioritizing service based on price.

AT&T and Verizon, through their trade group USTelecom, asked a three-judge panel of the U.S. Court of Appeals for the District of Columbia Circuit to overturn the rules. On June 14, 2016, the panel, in a 2–1 vote, upheld the rules. The U.S. Court of Appeals for the District of Columbia on May 1, 2017, declined to reconsider the June 2016 decision.

Under the Trump administration, the FCC sought to loosen the net neutrality rules. President Trump named Ajit Pai, an FCC commissioner since 2012 and an opponent of net neutrality, as the agency's new chair.

FCC PROPOSAL

FCC Chair Ajit Pai in April 2017, before the appeal court issued its statement, released a new net neutrality regulatory scheme. The plan would replace FCC's rules, passed by the Obama administration, with a set of voluntary guidelines that called on the technology industry for equal treatment in transmitting internet traffic. The scheme also would return oversight of online privacy to the Federal Trade Commission.

The FCC's proposal drew more than 1.6 million public comments, both pro and con, over the next month, with the number having reached 8 million by mid-July. Proponents of repealing net neutrality rules said a looser regulatory scheme could spur more investment to build out the Internet and reach into rural areas. The Internet Association, a trade group that represented such large firms as Facebook and Google, disagreed.

Democrats on the House Energy and Commerce Committee immediately said they would block such a plan to roll back net neutrality rules. On May 18, 2017, the FCC voted along party lines, 2–1, to begin taking steps to roll back the 2015 Open Internet Order that imposed net neutrality rules on internet providers.

Pai on November 21 circulated to the commission members a draft order to reverse the agency's 2015 Open Internet Order, which would allow internet service providers to treat internet users differently. The order would also change the transparency rule to require internet service providers to disclose practices such as blocking or throttling that affect users' internet access. The FCC and FTC would work together to enforce transparency, and states and localities would be barred from adopting rules that conflict with federal policies.

On December 14, 2017, the FCC voted, in a 3–2 party line vote to approve the order abolishing the 2015 net neutrality rules. The order eliminated bans on blocking, degrading, or charging fees for higher quality service or certain content. The order also treated internet service providers as informational services rather than common carriers, making them subject to a lighter regulatory approach consistent with the approach in place before 2015.

The Republican commissioners said the move would restore a competitive marketplace. Democrats said the order could be challenged in court because it went beyond reversing the 2015 order and conflicted with prior FCC rulings. On January 16, 2018, Democratic attorneys general from twenty-one states and the District of Columbia filed a federal lawsuit against the FCC to bar it from reversing the 2015 rules.

House Action

On December 19, 2017, Rep. Marsha Blackburn, chair of the Energy and commerce subcommittee on Communications and Technology, introduced a bill (HR 4682) that would create several internet fairness mandates. Her bill, for example, would bar internet service providers from blocking or degrading content on some websites. That measure did not see action.

Senate Action

The Senate on May 16, 2018, passed, in a 52–47 vote, a resolution that would nullify the FCC ruling on net neutrality, which was to take effect on June 11. The intent was to block the FCC's 3–2 decision in December 2017 to return net neutrality rules to where they were before 2015.

Critics said such a move would allow internet service providers to charge higher prices for faster speeds, thus handicapping small providers of web content.

Three Republicans—Susan Collins of Maine, Lisa Murkowski of Alaska, and John Kennedy of Louisiana—joined every Democrat to pass the resolution. Sen. Markey had introduced the resolution (S J Res 52) under the Congressional Review Act.

The House had a similar measure (H J Res 129), introduced by Rep. Mike Doyle, D-Pa., but it did not have enough support to reach the floor. The House also never acted on the Senate resolution before the end of the 115th Congress.

Copyright Protections

Congress during the 115th Congress cleared a measure to update U.S. copyright law in order to allow companies that stream music to avoid copyright infringement lawsuits. It also cleared a measure aimed at making it easier for the blind and physically impaired to access foreign works of music and literature. However, efforts to move a bill to place the U.S. Copyright Office under Congress's control stalled in the Senate.

MUSIC ROYALTIES

House Action

The House Judiciary Committee on April 11, 2018, approved a bill (HR 5447) that aimed to update music copyright law. The measure, introduced by committee Chair Robert W. Goodlatte, R-Va., included language from a bill (HR 4706) by Doug Collins, R-Ga., that would create a new system for digital music services such as Spotify and Pandora to license songs for streaming online.

The measure would create a collective of songwriters and publishers to oversee the creation of a publicly accessible database of song ownership information and manage royalty payments. In exchange for a fee, the streaming services could obtain a license to play any song in the database. The measure also would grant such companies retroactive protection from statutory damages for copyright infringement prior to January 1, 2018.

Collins' bill also included language from two other measures:

- A bill (HR 3301) by Rep. Darrell Issa, R-Calif., that would apply federal copyright law to sound recordings made prior to 1972
- A bill (HR 881) by Joseph Crowley, D-N.Y., that would create a process to distribute royalty payments to record producers

On April 25, 2018, the House passed Goodlatte's measure (HR 5447) by a vote of 415–0. Major songwriter groups, music publishers, and digital streaming companies supported the bill. Small independent groups, however, said the measure did not offer enough protection for the rights of individual songwriters.

Senate Action

The Senate Judiciary Committee approved, by voice vote, a companion bill (S 2823) to the House-passed measure (HR 5447) on June 28. Like the House bill, the Senate measure, introduced by Orrin G. Hatch, R-Utah, would grant digital streaming companies a license to provide customers digital copies or downloads of any song in an established database provided the companies follow certain requirements.

The measure also would provide federal copyright protections for recordings made between January 1, 1923, and February 15, 1972. Musicians such as Smokey Robinson, writer of classic '60s music, urged lawmakers to ensure compensation for musicians whose work was done before current copyright law became effective in early 1972.

Ron Wyden, D-Ore., introduced an alternative (S 2933) that would have provided copyright protection through 2025 for sound recordings made between 1922 and 1930 and ninety-five years of protection for recordings made between 1931 and 1972. Hatch's measure, as approved by the committee, also would standardize industry practices for royalty payments to sound producers, mixers, and engineers.

Final Action

On September 18, 2018, Hatch used a tax measure (HR 1551) as the vehicle for his music copyright measure, replacing the text with his revised language. The Senate passed the measure by voice vote the same day, after renaming it the Orrin G. Hatch Music Modernization Act, named for the senator who was a songwriter and violin and piano player. The measure would

- Provide a blanket statutory license for the distribution of music via digital download or streaming
- Create a collective that would collect and distribute royalties, as well as build a music database that would be publicly accessible
- Provide federal copyright protection for sound recordings made before 1972
- Create a process for music producers to be compensated from royalties collected from the use of sound recordings

The House on September 25 passed the bill by unanimous consent, clearing it for the president's signature. The president signed the bill into law (PL 115-264) on October 11, 2018.

AID FOR THE BLIND, PHYSICALLY IMPAIRED

Senate Action

The Senate Judiciary Committee on May 10, 2018, approved by a 20–0 vote a measure (S 2559) that would aim to make it easier for the blind and physically impaired to access foreign works of music and literature. Sen. Dianne Feinstein, D-Calif., ranking member of the committee, said the measure would help blind and disabled persons in developing countries gain access to books, for example.

The measure, introduced by Sen. Charles Grassley, R-Iowa, would expand a copyright exemption under a 1996 law (PL 104-197) to cover all literary and musical works that are reproduced in formats such as Braille, large print, and audio. Eligible persons and libraries could export or import works to or from more than thirty countries that are party to the Marrakesh Treaty, adopted by the World Intellectual Property Organization in 2013 to allow for the international exchange of books that serve people who are blind or visually impaired. The Senate passed the bill (S 2559) by unanimous consent on June 29.

House and Final Action

The House cleared the measure (S 2559) by unanimous consent on September 25. The president signed the measure into law (PL 115-261) on October 9, 2018.

U.S. COPYRIGHT OFFICE

The House Judiciary Committee on March 29, 2017, approved, by voice vote, a bill (HR 1695) that would move the U.S. Copyright Office under Congress's control and make the director of the office subject to a presidential nomination and Senate confirmation. The bill, drafted by Judiciary Committee Chair Robert W. Goodlatte, R-Va., would create a seven-member panel to approve a list of three candidates to the head of the Copyright Office and the president would make the final selection. The panel would include the following members: Speaker of the House, president pro-tempore of the Senate, majority and minority leaders of the House and Senate, and the librarian of Congress.

Traditionally, the librarian of Congress had chosen the register of copyrights, and the candidate did not require Senate approval. Many creative industry representatives wanted to bring in a candidate with more commercial experience—that is, who used copyrighted material. Goodlatte said his proposal would help reduce litigation.

The House passed the bill (HR 1695) by a 378–48 vote, on April 26, 2017. Before passage, the House adopted, 410–14, an amendment by Ted Deutch, D-Fla., that would allow the register of the Copyright Office to appoint a chief information officer to oversee information technology systems. The Senate did not act on the measure.

Auto Loans

Congress during the 115th Congress repealed 2013 Consumer Financial Protection Bureau (CFPB) guidance on fining auto lenders that discriminate against minorities by charging them higher rates. Lawmakers repealed the guidance by using the Congressional Review Act (CRA) (PL 104-121), a 1996 law that permits Congress to overturn agency rules within sixty legislative days of publication. In the case of the CFPB guidance, Republicans relied on a December 5, 2017, ruling from the Government Accountability Office (on treating the guidance as a rule under the CRA) and publication of the guidance the next day in the Congressional Record.

Senate Action

The Senate on April 18, 2018, passed a resolution (SJ Res 57) to repeal the 2013 CFPB guidance, which covered loans in which an auto dealer connects borrowers to a bank or finance company. The chosen lender and auto dealer can raise the loan's rate and split the extra income.

In some cases, the CFPB had found that minorities were charged higher rates. But Republicans questioned the bureau's research methodologies. Republicans also said that repealing the guidance would increase credit availability in auto lending markets.

House Action

The House passed the Senate's resolution (SJ Res 57) in a 234–175 vote on May 8, 2018, clearing it for the president's signature. Republicans said the Dodd-Frank Act (PL 111-203) barred the CFPB from regulating auto dealers, and that the former bureau director, Richard Cordray, issued the 2013 guidance without going through the full rulemaking process. The president signed the measure into law (PL 115-172) on May 21, 2018.

Transportation Appropriations

Throughout the 115th Congress, lawmakers and the administration passed a series of stop-gap governing funding measures as partisan wrangling hampered passage of regular appropriations bills, including the annual spending measures for the Department of Transportation. Ultimately, appropriators had to negotiate massive omnibus spending packages that could clear the final hurdles to the president's desk. Lawmakers ultimately granted about a $9 billion boost for Transportation programs between fiscal 2017 and fiscal 2018, rejecting President Trump's requests for deep funding cuts.

President Trump repeatedly urged Congress to slash funding for Transportation programs, in part by transferring air traffic control from the FAA to a nonprofit entity. He also requested Congress eliminate the Transportation

Investment Generating Economic Recovery (TIGER) grant program, which was intended to help states and localities fund highways, bridges, transit programs, and other surface transportation infrastructure; capital investment grants offered by the Federal Transit Administration (FTA); and Essential Air Service subsidies for air carriers that served small communities.

Democrats and Republicans disagreed on several policy provisions tucked into draft appropriations bills, including GOP provisions that aimed to block or limit funding for California's high-speed rail project and the Gateway rail project in Amtrak's Northeast corridor.

Rep. Jeff Denham, R-Calif., led opposition to federal funding for California's planned high-speed rail, which aimed to provide passengers between San Francisco and Los Angeles a two-hour-and-40-minute commute. The project repeatedly had been beset by construction challenges and political opposition. Voters had approved a 2008 referendum that allowed for the issuance of $9 billion in bonds for the project, and the Federal Railroad Administration, under the Obama administration, had granted a waiver that allowed construction to begin in San Joaquin Valley with $2.5 billion in funding from the 2010 American Recovery and Reinvestment Act (PL 11105). Denham and other critics objected that the money was promised before the state had matched funds, as typically required.

Over the next two years, the federal government awarded another $4 billion in funding. Then in June 2014 the state legislature and California Gov. Jerry Brown agreed to designate 25 percent of the state's annual cap and trade funds for the project. In early 2017, the state began considering contractors to help develop and manage the initial phase of construction. Two policy provisions that would have barred the Federal Railroad Administration from approving further federal grants for the rail project were not included in the final fiscal 2018 omnibus measure the president signed into law.

In March 2018, Trump threatened to shut down the government as he refused to sign a spending bill with funding for the Gateway project, a $30 billion commuter rail, bridge, and tunnel project intended to connect New York and New Jersey under the Hudson River. Trump reportedly tried to block funding for the project due to a political feud with New York Sen. Chuck Schumer, the Senate's Democratic leader.

The project was intended to expand and modernize Amtrak's Northeast Corridor line in New York City and New Jersey. The states had secured $1 billion in funding for the Gateway project, and under the Obama administration an agreement was made for another $900 million in federal funding.

New Jersey and New York officials said that, under the Obama administration, they and federal Transportation officials agreed that the states would cover half the costs and Amtrak and the federal government, the other half. The Trump administration refused to recognize the agreement, and complained that the states were not contributing enough, but Schumer said the Trump administration was unnecessarily stalling the project.

To gain support for a stopgap funding measure to keep the government running past March 23, 2018, congressional leaders had to leave out the $900 million in funding for the Gateway project. But they provided sufficient funding for Amtrak that could cover a portion of that promised support.

Fiscal Year 2017 Appropriations

When Congress opened in January 2017, the government was being funded under a continuing resolution (PL 114-254) developed by the Republican leadership of the previous Congress and cleared on December 5, 2016, after Trump's election as president. That measure, set to expire on April 28, 2017, was intended to provide time for the new president to set his mark on government spending. Congress cleared, and the president signed, another continuing resolution (PL 115-30) that extended funding through May 5.

On May 5, 2017, Trump signed into law a fiscal 2017 omnibus spending package (HR 244, PL 115-31) that included about $18.5 billion for Department of Transportation programs, slightly down from $18.6 billion in fiscal 2016. The decrease reflected an accounting move by Congress to take back spending power from states, thereby essentially rescinding $857 million of unused contract authority that had been distributed in previous years through the Highway Trust Fund to states.

The measure increased federal highway and transit formula grants to levels set in the December 2015 surface transportation reauthorization law (PL 114-94), and authorized spending $43.3 billion from the Highway Trust Fund for federal-aid highways and $9.7 billion for transit. The omnibus spending measure also provided $500 million for the TIGER program, the same level as for fiscal 2016. The federal grants were intended to help states and localities fund highways, bridges, transit programs, and other surface transportation infrastructure. The measure also included

- $12.4 billion in total budget resources for the Federal Transit Administration, including $9.7 billion for transit formula grants from the Highway Trust Fund. That amount would include $2.4 billion in capital investment grants offered by the Federal Transit Administration, and $150 million for Essential Air Service subsidies to air carriers that serve small communities
- $16.4 billion for the Federal Aviation Administration, $127 million more than provided in fiscal 2016 and $508 million above the administration's request
- $1.9 billion for the Federal Railroad Administration, an increase of $173 million above the fiscal 2016 level. The funding included $98 million for grants to

support rail infrastructure and passenger rail service improvements; $326 million for Amtrak's Northeast Corridor, which stretched from Washington, D.C. to Boston; and $1.17 billion to support Amtrak's National Network, its state-supported and long-distance service lines

- $3 million for the National Surface Transportation and Innovative Finance Bureau, which was created to consolidate several Department of Transportation programs
- $523 million for the U.S. Maritime Administration, a $123 million increase from fiscal 2016
- $644 million for the Federal Motor Carrier Safety Administration
- $911 million for the National Highway Traffic Safety Administration
- $264 million for the Pipeline and Hazardous Materials Safety Administration, including funding to ensure safe operations of underground natural gas storage facilities

The measure would provide $154.8 million to make the National Airspace System operate under a satellite navigation system, replacing radar.

In agreeing on the final omnibus measure, House and Senate negotiators had dropped a provision in the original House version of the bill that would have blocked the Federal Rail Administration from reimbursing California for costs related to its high-speed rail project. Negotiators also dropped a policy rider that would have preempted state laws regarding rest breaks for truck drivers.

The House passed the omnibus spending bill (HR 244) by a vote of 309–118 on May 3. The Senate cleared the bill on May 4 by a vote of 79–18.

Fiscal Year 2018 Funding

After passing a stopgap funding measure, Congress cleared an omnibus spending bill that included the $27.3 billion for Transportation programs for fiscal 2018. The Trump administration's budget request for fiscal 2018 had proposed a 12.7 percent funding reduction for the Department of Transportation, to $16.2 billion from the $18.6 billion in fiscal 2016. The White House proposed moving air traffic control from the FAA to a private non-profit entity, discontinuing a grant program for public rail transit and a grant program that aimed to finance transportation projects to spur economic growth. The president's budget also would cut the Essential Air Service program to save an estimated $175 million, as well as the TIGER program, to reduce federal funding for Amtrak.

House Action

On July 11, 2017, the House Transportation–HUD Subcommittee of the House Appropriations Committee approved a draft spending bill that would provide $17.8 billion in funding for the Department of Transportation. The bill would continue funding for the Capital Improvement Grant program, which Trump proposed to eliminate. But the measure would meet Trump's request to eliminate funding for the TIGER grant program.

The measure included a provision that would preempt states from making laws related to trucking rest breaks and bar federal funding for high-speed rail—provisions that Price said he opposed and would later seek to eliminate. The House Appropriations Committee approved, by a 31–20 vote, the transportation funding measure (HR 3353) on July 17. Committee Democrats criticized the bill for not providing more funding for a full infrastructure plan on par with Trump's request for a $1 trillion, ten-year package. But due to a lack of agreement on a budget blueprint, including a plan for how to pay for such a package, appropriators were limited to $56.5 billion to fund both the Transportation and the Housing and Urban Development departments.

Senate Action

On July 25, 2017, the Senate Transportation–HUD Appropriations Subcommittee approved, by voice vote, a draft fiscal 2018 spending bill that would provide $19.5 billion in discretionary spending for the Transportation department, a 6 percent increase above fiscal 2017. The bill would not include cuts Trump had requested to popular programs, such as the TIGER grant program and the Essential Air Service subsidy for commercial flights to small rural airports. The bill also did not include Trump's request to create a nonprofit entity to take over the FAA's air traffic control system.

The full appropriations committee approved the measure (S 1655) in a 31–0 vote on July 27. The measure also included a provision that would authorize airports to raise to $8.50 per ticket (a $4 increase) the Passenger Facility Charge that is passed on to passengers' ticket prices. Revenue from the fee was to be used to help fund construction and repair of airport infrastructure.

STOPGAP MEASURE

With fiscal 2017 funding set to expire on September 30, the House and Senate began considering a massive spending package that combined several spending bills. But before they completed that package, Congress cleared and the president signed on September 8, a stopgap spending measure (HR 601, PL 115-56) that continued government funding through December 8. Another stopgap spending measure (H J Res 123), which the president signed into law (PL 115-90) on December 8 continued government funding another two weeks. A third stopgap measure (HR 1370), which the president signed into law (PL 115-96) on December 22, continued government funding through January 19, 2018.

Disagreement over a fourth resolution to continue funding the government caused a partial government shutdown until Congress cleared, and the president signed, a

three-week stopgap measure (HR 195; PL 115-120) on January 24, 2018. A fifth stopgap measure (HR 1892; PL 115-123), signed on February 9, 2018, bought lawmakers another six weeks—through March 23—to agree on a full spending package.

Final Action

The House on September 14 passed, 211–198, a $1.23 trillion omnibus spending measure (HR 3354) that included the Transportation–HUD funding bill (HR 3353) and eleven other bills. During two weeks of floor debate before passage, the House considered 342 amendments that addressed issues ranging from immigration policy to environmental protection.

On March 21, 2018, House Republicans released a new omnibus spending bill that would increase Transportation spending to $27.3 billion, up from $18.6 billion in fiscal 2017 and the $16.2 billion requested by the administration. The measure would include $1.5 billion for TIGER grants, a program Trump sought to eliminate, as well as another $2.55 billion for federal-aid highway grants and $1 billion for the Airport Improvement Program.

The measure did not include Trump's request for an infusion of infrastructure spending, as he had outlined in a proposal in February. The measure also did not include a provision in the Senate funding bill (S 1655) that would have allowed airports to hike passenger facility fees.

The House approved the measure, 256–167, on March 22. The Senate voted 65–32 to clear the measure on March 23. On March 23, 2018, Trump signed into law the $1.3 trillion fiscal 2018 omnibus spending bill (HR 1625, PL 115-141), which included the $27.3 billion for Transportation programs.

The final measure provided

- $47.5 billion for the Federal-Aid Highways Program, of which $45 billion came from the Highway Trust Fund
- 18 billion for the Federal Aviation Administration
- $3.1 billion for the Federal Railroad Administration
- $13.5 billion for the Federal Transit Administration
- $3 billion for the National Surface Transportation and Innovative Finance Bureau
- $979.6 million for the U.S. Maritime Administration
- $844.8 million for the Federal Motor Carrier Safety Administration
- $947.2 million for the National Highway Traffic Safety Administration
- $272.3 million for the Pipeline and Hazardous Materials Safety Administration

Before debate on the final fiscal 2018 bill (PL 115-141) drew to a close in March 2018, Trump said he wanted to block funding for the Gateway project. That measure did not ultimately include provisions in the House spending bill (HR 3353) that would have assured $900 million for the Gateway Program, though funding for Amtrak's Northeast Corridor would provide an estimated $541 million for Gateway.

Fiscal Year 2019 Funding

With the fiscal 2019 budget process, Congress sought to get annual appropriations back on track and enact individual spending bills, although it ultimately combined several bills into omnibus spending measures. Action on a final measure to fund Transportation and HUD for fiscal 2019 was delayed until the next Congress.

Among the partisan disputes about fiscal 2019 funding was language regarding funds for the Gateway Program. Transportation secretary Elaine Chao said the administration was frustrated that New York and New Jersey relied on federal loans as their contributions to the project.

House Action

The House Appropriations Committee on May 23, 2018, approved, 34–17, a draft fiscal 2019 spending bill that would provide $71.8 billion in discretionary spending for the departments of Transportation and Housing and Urban Development, a 2 percent hike from fiscal 2018 funding.

Before approving the bill, the committee rejected, in a 21–29 vote, an amendment by David E. Price, D-N.C., the committee's ranking member, that would have stripped ten policy provisions from the bill. One of those provisions would bar states from enforcing laws requiring meal and rest breaks for truckers. Another provision would block funding for the high-speed rail project in California. Republicans backed the policy riders, pointing in particular to a provision that would bar U.S. transit systems from buying passenger cars and other transit assets from Chinese state-owned companies.

Senate Action

The Senate Transportation–HUD Appropriations Subcommittee on June 5, 2018, approved by voice vote a spending bill (S 3023) that would provide about $71.4 billion for the two departments in fiscal 2019. The measure would drop discretionary spending for the Department of Transportation by 3 percent, to $26.6 billion, while increasing HUD spending.

Lawmakers ultimately decided to move two omnibus spending packages. However, they could not agree on funding for a measure that combined funding for Transportation and HUD, Agriculture, Financial Services and Interior–Environment, forcing Congress to clear a stopgap funding measure (HR 6157, PL 115-245) for those departments in the meantime. Congress followed with a two-week stopgap funding measure (HJRes143, PL 115-298) that the president signed on December 7. Final action on the four fiscal 2019 spending measures was delayed until the 116th Congress.

2019–2020

The 116th Congress focused much of its attention on the coronavirus pandemic, including measures to help bolster ailing airlines and transit systems suffering from a decline of ridership and forced to furlough or lay off employees. Lawmakers ultimately cleared two measures to provide payroll support for the airline and transit industries, and cleared a measure to provide more than $25 billion in emergency funding for transportation services.

Meanwhile, Congress cleared a one-year surface transportation authorization bill as it again postponed debate on how to finance the repair or reconstruction of infrastructure across the nation. In the wake of two fatal crashes of Boeing's 737 Max airplane, Congress also cleared legislation intended to reform the FAA's certification process of aircraft and aircraft engines and components, in part to reduce the influence of manufacturers and to boost FAA training and oversight for certification.

Congress considered, but did not clear, legislation that would have granted Transportation Security Agents the same bargaining rights as other federal employees. Many lawmakers were concerned as the attrition rate of employees increased amid reports of employer harassment and low pay.

In 2019, lawmakers cleared a measure intended to allow the Army Corps of Engineers to spend money from the Harbor Maintenance Trust Fund on a backlog of harbor maintenance projects, including dredging. The action was in response to reports of problems at many of the nation's busiest ports.

Meanwhile, Democrats tried but failed to reverse the FCC's action that ended net neutrality rules governing internet service providers. Lawmakers did clear legislation aimed to push phone companies to identify robocalls and penalize businesses that use technology to make such calls.

Airline and Transit Relief

Congress during the 116th Congress cleared coronavirus response measures (HR 748, HR 133) that included provisions to provide payroll support for the airline and transit industries that were suffering from a severe decline in the number of passengers during the coronavirus pandemic, forcing airlines to ground planes and cancel aircraft orders. According to the Government Accountability Office, airline traffic in April 2020 was 96 percent lower than in April 2019 and remained 60 percent below 2019 levels throughout 2020. The decline affected airports, repair shops, and the supply chain.

Lawmakers in both parties generally agreed on the need to provide support for airlines, which the Federal Aviation Administration, in a January 2020 report, said accounted for about 5 percent of the U.S. economy. Efforts to pass a stand-alone measure to rescue the airlines, however, gave way to House Democrats' demands that any payroll support be part of a larger bill that rescued more industries as well as schools and households.

AIRLINE PAYROLL SUPPORT

Congress included funds to help finance airline employee and contractor paychecks in the $2 trillion coronavirus response law (HR 748, PL 116-136), known as the CARES Act, that Congress passed in March 2020. That law granted a total of $32 billion in payroll support for aviation workers. That funding, which would expire September 30, 2020, included $25 billion for passenger air carriers; $4 billion for cargo air carriers; and $3 billion for contractors. The measure also included $25 billion in support for transit.

The Senate passed the bill (HR 748) by a 96–0 vote on March 27, and the House passed the measure by voice vote on the same day. The president signed the measure into law (PL 116-136) on the same day.

PAYROLL SUPPORT EXTENSION

With payroll support included in the CARES Act set to expire September 30, 2020, Congress debated how much funding it should provide to extend the support as the pandemic continued and airline travel had not picked up. United Airlines, American Airlines, and other carriers said they would have to furlough employees if aid was not renewed.

Senate Action

Roger Wicker, R-Miss., chair of the Senate Committee on Commerce, Science and Transportation and Susan Collins, R-Maine, chair of the Senate Appropriations Transportation–HUD Subcommittee, on September 21 introduced a $28.5 billion measure (S 4634) to extend payroll support for airlines through March 2021. The bill would provide $25.5 billion for passenger air carriers, $300 million for cargo air carriers, and $3 billion for contractors. Treasury Secretary Steven Mnuchin endorsed the measure.

House Action

On September 22, 2020, Del. Stacey Plaskett, D-V.I., introduced a measure (HR 8345) that would provide nearly $29 billion to continue payroll support for airlines. On September 28, House Democrats tucked into a draft coronavirus-related spending bill another $25 billion to extend the payroll through March 2021. The bill would provide another $3 billion in payroll support for airline contractors and $300 million for cargo airlines, as well as $32 billion for transit companies, which also were suffering from a severe drop in ridership amid the pandemic. Other provisions included $13.5 billion in economic relief to airports

and $75 million for passenger air service for small communities. Another $2.4 billion would be provided for Amtrak.

The bill was not expected to go to the Senate for a vote, but was intended as a platform for further negotiations. The bill would provide $1 trillion less than would be provided by the bill (HR 6800) that the House passed in May. That House bill, however, did not include an extension for airline relief.

As Congress continued to debate whether and how to provide further relief for industries and Americans during the pandemic, the U.S. airlines on October 1 began furloughing tens of thousands of employees. House Speaker Nancy Pelosi, D-Calif., said she was willing to consider a stand-alone bill to extend payroll support for airlines in order to halt those layoffs, stepping back from her mandate that any measure be part of a broader COVID-relief package. On the same day, DeFazio introduced such a stand-alone measure (HR 8504). Pelosi, however, changed course a few days later, insisting on a measure that would provide support to more industries and to schools and households.

Final Action

As time ran out in the 116th Congress, lawmakers agreed to include in a COVID-relief bill (HR 133) another $15 billion to extend, through March 2021, payroll support for passenger airlines and $1 billion for payroll support for airline contractors. The bill also included a provision that would provide airline employees back pay from December 1, and would provide $14 billion in aid for transit; $10 billion for state highways; $2 billion for private motor coaches, buses, and ferries; $2 billion for airports and airport concessionaires; and $1 billion for Amtrak.

The House passed the measure by a vote of 359–53 on December 21, 2020. The Senate passed the measure in a 92–6 vote on the same day. On December 27, the president signed the measure into law (PL 116-260).

Surface Transportation Reauthorization

Failing to reach consensus on a long-term measure to help rebuild and modernize the nation's infrastructure, Congress cleared a one-year surface transportation authorization bill that would ensure continued financing, at existing levels, for states and localities already struggling during the coronavirus pandemic and economic downturn. Congress in 2015 had cleared a five-year, $281-billion highway authorization measure (PL 114-94) that was scheduled to expire September 30, 2020. House Democrats had hoped to pass a broader infrastructure package that aimed to modernize transportation systems and make infrastructure more resilient to natural disasters attributed to climate change, but the GOP-controlled Senate and the White House disagreed. Further, lawmakers could not agree on how to pay for a long-term measure without relying on a gas-tax hike.

Senate Action

On July 29, 2019, Sen. John Barrasso, R-Wyo., introduced a five-year surface transportation measure (S 2302) that would authorize $287 billion in spending from the Highway Trust Fund, about a 27 percent increase above the existing authorization level. Barrasso's measure aimed to fund repair and maintenance of roads, expedite permitting processes for major infrastructure projects, and make transportation systems resilient to natural disasters resulting from climate change. The measure included language from several bills aimed at reducing carbon emissions, including a bill (S 747) to reauthorize the Diesel Emissions Reduction Act, which helps reduce emissions from diesel-powered engines, and a committee-approved bill (S 383) that aimed to increase research into carbon capture, utilization, and sequestration.

The bill also would authorize $4.9 billion over five years for programs to improve protection of roads and bridges from natural disasters such as wildfires and mudslides. Another $1 billion would fund a competitive grant program to encourage states and localities to build hydrogen, natural gas, and electric vehicle fueling stations along highways.

The Senate Environment and Public Works Committee approved the measure (S 2302) in a 21–0 vote on July 30, 2019. The bill included a provision to restore nearly $7.6 billion in highway funding that was scheduled to be cut July 1, 2020. The 2015 highway measure (PL 114-94) had included the funding reduction in order to gain support for that bill's final cost. Barrasso also had introduced separate legislation (S 1992) to address the funding recission.

Barrasso's bill did not make it to the floor for a vote. In March 2020, Barrasso pushed for his highway reauthorization measure (S 2302) to be included in a stimulus package.

House Action

Highway and Transit Reauthorization. House Transportation Chair Defazio hoped to advance a broader measure than the Senate bill (S 2302) by focusing on building resilient infrastructure, reducing the U.S. reliance on fossil fuels, and improving the use of current infrastructure. The House Transportation and Infrastructure Committee Democrats on June 3, 2020, proposed a $494 billion, five-year highway reauthorization measure (HR 2) that targeted those priorities. The legislation would authorize $8.35 billion to help states meet greenhouse gas reduction goals and $6.25 billion for the construction of infrastructure that would be resilient to the effects of climate change-related events such as fires and floods. Another $60 billion would be authorized for rail infrastructure, including $29.3 billion for Amtrak (triple the existing level) and $350 million annually for grants to create electric vehicle charging and hydrogen fueling stations.

The legislation would immediately authorize $83.1 billion in fiscal 2021 to help state and local transportation agencies struggling during the coronavirus pandemic and related government and business shutdowns. For 2021,

the measure would eliminate a state-federal match requirement, thereby ensuring states would be eligible for the full federal funding. That language mirrored a provision in a measure (HR 6800) that the House passed May 15.

On June 18, 2020, the House Transportation and Infrastructure Committee approved by voice vote the $494 billion highway measure after considering nearly 300 amendments over two days and despite Republican objections that Democrats had not sought their input while drafting the bill.

The committee approved, 62–1, an amendment by Sean Patrick Maloney, D-N.Y., that would bar states and localities from using federal funds to purchase items from Chinese state-owned or subsidized companies. The amendment was in response to concerns that a growing number of Chinese companies were selling electric buses and trains in the United States.

Infrastructure Package. House Democrats on January 29, 2020, introduced a draft five-year $760 billion infrastructure package. The measure would authorize $329 billion for highways and bridges and would authorize funding to build electric-vehicle stations and alternative fueling options for other zero-emission vehicles. The measure also would include $105 billion for transit, $55 billion for rail investments, $30 billion for airport improvements, $50.5 billion for wastewater infrastructure, $86 billion to expand broadband, $12 billion for public safety communications, and $19.7 billion for harbor infrastructure.

On June 18, 2020, the same day the House Transportation committee approved the highway reauthorization bill (HR 2), House Democrats introduced a $1.5 trillion infrastructure package that included language from the highway bill, with funding to cover ten years. The measure included much of the same highway and climate-change-focused provisions as the Democrat's draft plan released in January, but it also included $100 billion for schools in high-poverty areas, $100 billion for affordable housing, and $25 billion for postal infrastructure.

Democrats remained undecided on how to pay for the measure. Highway programs typically are funded primarily by federal gas taxes. However, Congress had not raised the gas tax rate since 1993, when it was set at 18.3 cents per gallon, which had forced Congress to borrow from the federal government's general revenue fund since 2008 to pay for highway programs.

To cover the funding, the Democrats' latest plan would entail borrowing $145.3 billion—more than the cumulative $140 billion highway program had borrowed from general revenue since 2008. The package also included a proposal to resurrect and expand bond financing tools that could help states and localities raise money for projects.

On July 1, 2020, the House passed, 233–188, the $1.5 trillion infrastructure bill (HR 2), which included the five-year, $494-billion surface transportation reauthorization. The measure would require states to commit to reduce greenhouse gases and would include incentives for projects built with materials that would reduce greenhouse gas emissions.

Republicans in both chambers opposed the climate change provisions in the measure. Sen. Barrasso said the bill had no chance of passing the Senate, and the White House vowed to veto it if it was cleared. President Trump in his State of the Union address in February 2020 had endorsed the Senate's five-year, $287 billion bill that focused only on highway and transit; then he promoted a scheme for a $1 trillion, ten-year infrastructure plan.

Final Action

With both sides dug in on their respective measures, the House on September 22, 2020, passed, 359–57, a one-year extension of the 2015 highway law as part of a short-term government funding bill (HR 8337) that extended government funding through December 11, 2020. The Senate passed the measure (HR 8337) by an 84–10 vote on September 30. The president signed the measure into law (PL 116-159) on October 1. The measure authorized at least $12.6 billion for public transit investment, and dedicated $3.2 billion to the Mass Transit Account of the Highway Trust Fund.

Coast Guard Reauthorization

Congress in late 2020 cleared a measure to reauthorize the Coast Guard, as well as the Federal Maritime Commission, for two years. Congress had last reauthorized the Coast Guard and the commission in 2018 (P 115-282), and that law was set to expire at the end of fiscal 2019.

House Action

The House Transportation and Infrastructure Committee on June 26, 2019, approved by voice vote a two-year Coast Guard reauthorization bill (HR 3409). The measure would authorize $11.1 billion for the Coast Guard in fiscal 2020 and $11.6 billion in fiscal 2021. The measure included provisions that would authorize $29.1 million in fiscal 2020 and $29.6 million in fiscal 2021 for the Federal Maritime Commission. The House passed the measure (HR 3409) on July 24, 2019.

Senate Action

The Senate Commerce, Science, and Transportation Committee on July 31, 2019, approved, by voice vote, a two-year reauthorization measure (S 2297) for the Coast Guard. The measure would authorize $8.8 billion for fiscal 2020 and $8.4 billion for fiscal 2021. The measure also would authorize the construction of three heavy-duty ice breakers and three medium-duty icebreakers, granting $745 million for each cutter. Sen. Maria Cantwell, D-Wash., said the bill would strengthen U.S. presence in the Arctic, a growing shipping route. The measure also would call for the Government Accountability Office to study evacuation during tsunamis, orca protection programs, provisions to

increase recruitment and retention of women in the Coast Guard, and measures to prevent and handle oil spills.

Defense Authorization

House Action

As part of a $731.6 billion defense authorization bill (HR 6395), the House in July adopted an amendment by Peter A. DeFazio, D-Ore., that would reauthorize the Coast Guard and the Federal Maritime Commission for two years. The provisions would authorize $11.2 billion for the Coast Guard for fiscal 2020 and $11.9 billion for fiscal 2021—slightly more than the House panel-approved reauthorization bill.

DeFazio's provisions also would authorize $29 million in fiscal 2020 and $30 million in fiscal 2021 for the Federal Maritime Commission. Further, the amendment would authorize $650 million for a national security cutter, $645 million for a polar security cutter, $160 million for a Great Lakes icebreaker, and $265 million for four fast-response cutters. The House passed the bill in a 295–125 vote on July 21, 2020.

Senate Action

The Senate passed its defense authorization bill (S 4049) in an 86–14 vote on July 23, 2020. The measure included language, authored by Sen. Dan Sullivan, R-Alaska, to reauthorize the Coast Guard for fiscal years 2020 and 2021, to authorize the construction of three heavy polar security cutters, and to award contracts for three more.

The White House threatened to veto the defense authorization measure because it objected to several provisions, including language that would replace the names of military bases that honor Confederates and that would impose limits on how many U.S. troops could be withdrawn from Afghanistan and Germany. President Trump also objected that the measure did not remove legal liability shields for social media companies.

Final Action

House and Senate negotiators included in a final defense authorization bill (HR 6395) provisions to reauthorize the Coast Guard and Federal Maritime Commission for two years. The measure would authorize $11 billion and $11.7 billion, respectively, for fiscal years 2020 and 2021 for the Coast Guard; and $29 million and $30 million, respectively, for the maritime commission.

The House passed the conference report on the bill in a 335–78 vote on December 8, 2020. The Senate cleared, 84–13, the conference report on December 11, 2020.

The president vetoed the bill on December 23. The House overrode the veto in a 322–87 vote on December 28, 2020. The Senate overrode the veto and passed the bill (HR 6395) on December 31, 2020, by a vote of 81–13, thus enacting the measure into law (PL 116-283).

737 Max Air Safety

Congress during the 116th Congress cleared legislation to reform the FAA's certification process for airplanes and aircraft components. The measure was in response to two crashes involving the Boeing 737 Max. A 737 Max operated by Ethiopian Airlines crashed in March 2019, killing 157 people. The same model was involved in an October 29, 2018, crash of Lion Air flight 610 in Indonesia, which had killed 189 people. Three days after the second crash, the Trump administration grounded the planes.

Senate Action

In June 2020, Senate Commerce, Science, and Transportation Chair Roger Wicker, R-Miss., and ranking member Maria Cantwell, D-Wash., introduced a measure (S 3969) that aimed to reduce aircraft manufacturers' influence on the FAA's aircraft certification process, contending that Boeing's role in the certification of the 737 Max was not closely monitored. But the pair was forced to pull the bill from committee consideration in September when panel members could not agree on the bill's provisions nor on potential amendments.

House Action

On September 29, 2020, House Transportation and Infrastructure Committee Chair DeFazio and ranking member Sam Graves, R-Mo., introduced a similar measure (HR 8408) intended to increase oversight of the FAA aircraft certification process. The committee had just completed an eighteen-month investigation.

On September 30, the committee approved the measure by voice vote. The bill would require the FAA to reassert control over its Organization Designation Authorization (ODA) process, which enables the agency to outsource the certification process to employees of the airplane manufacturer. Critics of the process said it contributed to a lax regulatory compliance environment. Under the measure, the FAA also would have to review all its ODA holders every seven years and approve each individual selected to perform certification duties.

The measure would authorize $27 million annually from fiscal 2021 to fiscal 2023 for FAA to recruit and retain employees to help certify aircraft and components, and $3 million for each fiscal year to help fund resources to complete reviews of each person selected to perform certification duties.

The bill also would aim to eliminate conflicts of interest by setting "cooling off period" restrictions on Boeing employees who seek to work for the FAA or vice versa, and would bar FAA employees from a bonus or raise for meeting or exceeding a certification deadline. The bill also would call on FAA to research how pilots react to automated aircraft systems.

Rep. Paul Mitchell, R-Mich., refused to vote on the bill, saying the one day from the time of its introduction was

insufficient to allow for proper input from committee members. The House passed the bill (HR 8408) by voice vote on November 17, 2020.

FAA ORDER

On November 18, 2020, FAA Administrator Steve Dickson signed an order that allowed airlines to continue flying the Boeing 737 Max. The FAA also published a final directive on "airworthiness" for the aircraft, alerted the international community, and published 737 Max training requirements for pilots.

Senate Commerce Committee Chair Wicker said the FAA had taken sufficient steps before deciding to lift the ground order. House Transportation Chair DeFazio, however, harshly criticized the agency's oversight of the aircraft and the certification process.

Senate Action

On November 18, 2020, the Senate approved, en bloc with amendment, the measure (S 3969) to increase the FAA's oversight of the aircraft certification process and limit the influence of aerospace companies such as Boeing. The measure was similar to the House-passed measure (HR 8408), but bill managers had added provisions to increase whistleblower protections and ensure FAA worked with foreign civil aviation officials on safety management systems. The bill would grant the FAA authority to approve or remove Boeing employees conducting certification duties.

The panel approved a substitute amendment by Wicker that would, among other things, require the FAA to create a "National Air Grant Fellowship Program," authorizing $15 million annually between fiscal years 2021 and 2025 for one-year fellowships in the executive or legislative branch for individuals seeking to work on aerospace policy. Senate Commerce Committee Chair Wicker on December 18, 2020, released a report concluding that the two accidents of Boeing's 737 Max aircraft resulted in part from lapses in aviation safety oversight and failed FAA leadership. The report concluded that FAA managers had not been held accountable for failing to develop or deliver adequate training in flight standards and had retaliated against whistleblowers, permitted Southwest Airlines to continue to fly dozens of aircraft that were in unknown condition, and allowed Boeing to inappropriately influence the recertification testing of the aircraft.

Final Action

On December 21, 2020, congressional leaders released an omnibus spending bill (HR 133) that included language from the House and Senate bills (HR 8408 and S 3969) that aimed to reform the FAA's certification process for aircraft, engines, and other components. Provisions in the omnibus measure would authorize an independent panel to review Boeing's safety culture and its ability to perform certification functions delegated by the FAA, and the FAA would have to appoint aviation safety advisors to monitor airline employees or consultants involved in the certification process.

The bill would authorize $27 million for the FAA to hire engineers, safety inspectors and other employees to oversee safety, $7.5 million for a study on how people interact with technology on aircraft, and $2 million a year for an FAA Center of Excellence that would focus on automated systems.

The House passed the measure by a vote of 359–53 on December 21, 2020. The Senate passed the measure in a 92–6 vote on the same day. The President on December 27 signed the measure into law (PL 116-260).

TSA Workers

The House during the 116th Congress cleared a measure to grant Transportation Security Administration (TSA) employees the same collective bargaining rights enjoyed by other federal government employees. The Senate did not act on the measure.

BACKGROUND

When Congress authorized TSA's creation under a 2002 law (PL 107-296), in the wake of the September 11, 2001, terrorist attacks, lawmakers gave the TSA administrator the authority to set salaries and make personnel changes. In recent years, the TSA was reporting an increasing attrition rate among screeners at airports, which presented security risks at the nation's airports.

During a House Oversight and Reform Committee hearing on September 26, 2018, TSA Administrator David Pekoske said screener attrition was less than 20 percent, but the rate was still too high. He said the TSA was facing heavy costs for recruiting and training new screeners, and that attrition likely had an effect on security. In fiscal 2017, 64 percent of screeners who left TSA quit their jobs, according to Office of Personnel Management data, compared to about 35 percent of other federal employees who quit.

The committee also released a report that concluded that TSA officials had abused their power by, for example, transferring employees to jobs thousands of miles from their homes and retaliating against whistleblowers. In the fall of 2018, a jury trial uncovered on-the-job sexual harassment and an employee survey ranked TSA as the worst federal workplace. Experts blamed low morale in part on the low TSA salaries, which started at $32,617 a year for full-time screeners, with 15 to 39 percent eligible for "locality pay" for working in a costly area.

When Congress failed to reach agreement on a number of funding measures, a partial government shutdown began on December 22, 2018, causing many TSA screeners and other government workers to begin missing paychecks. Screeners began taking unscheduled leave and seeking

other jobs, increasing the security risk at many major airports, according to officials.

On January 23, 2019, Pekoske said that 7 to 10 percent of TSA's estimated 48,000 airport screeners had taken unscheduled leave in previous days, double the rate of a year earlier. Absences forced the closure of checkpoints at major airports such as Hartsfield-Jackson in Atlanta and Bush Intercontinental in Houston.

In May 2019, Democrats balked when the Trump administration announced it would send 400 TSA workers to the southwest border to help manage a surge in migrants. House Homeland Security Chair Bennie Thompson, D-Miss., said the move could worsen employee morale as well as heighten security risks at airports.

House Action

On January 29, 2020, the House Homeland Security Committee approved, in a party line 17–9 vote, a measure (HR 1140), introduced by Thompson, that would grant TSA employees the same collective bargaining rights enjoyed by other federal government employees. Thompson said the TSA personnel system needed to be remodeled to be more modern. The bill would permit the workers to take their grievances to a third party, would implement a pay structure, and grant workers protections under the Fair Labor Standards Act.

The committee's ranking Republican, Mike D. Rogers of Alabama, said the bill was too broad and would eliminate the agency's flexibility to make changes to respond to national threats. On March 5, 2020, the House passed the measure by a vote of 230–171, with fourteen Republicans joining Democrats in support. The House passed the bill after adopting by voice vote an amendment that would require Homeland Security to ensure that TSA does not hire individuals who had been convicted of a sex crime or an offense involving a minor (a crime or violence) or terrorism.

The House also adopted, 403–0, an amendment by Kim Schrier, D-Wash., that would require the TSA to provide employees with guidance and resources to protect against the coronavirus. Another amendment by voice vote, by Abigail Spanberger, D-Va., would bar TSA employees from using TikTok, a Chinese-owned social media video app, on U.S. government-issued mobile devices.

Sen. Brian Schatz had introduced a similar bill (S 944) on March 28, 2019. The Senate did not take up either measure.

Harbor Maintenance Trust Fund

Congress in 2019 cleared a measure to free up money in the Harbor Maintenance Trust Fund to be spent on harbor maintenance projects, particularly dredging projects. Lawmakers from coastal states had long been eager to free up more money to address a backlog of such projects. The House Committee on Transportation and Infrastructure

reported that channels at the nation's busiest fifty-nine ports were available less than 35 percent of the time because of maintenance work. Transportation Chair DeFazio said the Army Corps of Engineers had a $40 billion backlog in critical maintenance projects.

House Action

On May 8, 2019, the House Transportation and Infrastructure Committee approved, by voice vote, a measure (HR 2440) that would require all fees collected in the Harbor Maintenance Trust Fund to be used to maintain federally authorized harbors, as required by a 1986 law (PL 99-662).

The existing balance in the fund at that time was $9.3 billion, accrued from fees. Since 1986, the government had collected a fee from shippers. Under a 1990 budget bill, the fee started at .04 percent and increased to 0.125 percent of the value of the shippers' cargo. That law also implemented discretionary caps on spending for harbor maintenance, and the unspent fees accumulated. Chair Peter Defazio, D-Ore., said Congress had historically appropriated less than the amount of yearly revenue for harbor maintenance, and authorized the rest of the revenue to be spent on deficit reduction.

The committee-approved measure would lift the spending caps and allow lawmakers to appropriate the funds on harbor maintenance, such as dredging, and would grant authority to spend millions more in expected revenue over the next ten years. The Congress Budget Office estimated that $24.5 billion would be collected in the fund over the next decade.

Garret Graves, R-La., said shippers paid the tax with the understanding it would be spent on harbor maintenance. He said allocating the money for other expenses was embezzlement. But Mark Meadows, R-N.C., said the bill could pose budgetary problems for appropriators, particularly if harbor maintenance was considered a mandatory spending program. Congress typically declined to spend all trust fund revenue because of the discretionary spending caps.

The House on October 28, 2019, voted 296–109 to pass the bill. Senate Budget chair Michael B. Enzi, R-Wyo., and House Budget Committee ranking member Steve Womack, R-Ark., said they opposed the measure because it violated the Bipartisan Budget Act of 2019 (PL 116-37), which the president had signed in August, and would increase the deficit.

Senate Action

At the same time, Senate Appropriations Chair Richard Shelby, R-Ala., pushed to free up some money from the trust fund to help fund a disaster aid package for victims of hurricanes, wildfires, tornadoes, and other natural disasters. His provision was eventually dropped from a disaster aid package.

Shelby's provision was included in the stimulus bill (S 3548). But in contrast to the House bill (HR 2440) that

allowed the entire $9.3 billion balance in the fund to be spent, Shelby's measure would allow just the previous year's revenue to be spent. The $2 trillion coronavirus aid measure, the CARES Act, cleared in March 2020 (HR 758; PL 116-136) included a provision that allowed the previous two years of revenue in the Harbor Maintenance Trust Fund to be spent.

HOUSE AND FINAL ACTION

On July 15, 2020, the House Transportation committee approved, by voice vote, a Water Resources Development Act reauthorization measure (HR 7575) that would also release the nearly $10 billion in the Harbor Maintenance Trust Fund to be spent on dredging harbors. The House passed the bill by voice vote on July 29, 2020.

On December 8, 2020, the House passed, by voice vote, a measure to reauthorize the Water Resources Development Act (S 1811) that had been negotiated with the Senate and would free up $2 billion more from the Harbor Maintenance Trust Fund. The provision also mirrored the two-year spending authorization included in the coronavirus spending measure (PL 116-136).

The Water Resources bill, including provisions on spending from the Harbor Maintenance Trust Fund, was included in the large omnibus spending package (HR 133) that Congress cleared and the president signed into law (PL 116-260) before the end of the year. The final measure included a provision that authorized $500 million to be spent from the trust fund in 2021, and increasing amounts to be spent each year, eventually reaching $1.5 billion a year. That spending formula alleviated some senators' concerns about releasing the entire $10 billion at once.

Spectrum Auctions

The Federal Communication Commission (FCC) approved a plan to repurpose C-band spectrum that was being used by satellites to beam content to video and audio broadcasters. The plan aimed to further development of 5-G wireless. In addition, Congress cleared legislation to repeal a law that required the FCC to reallocate and auction off to commercial users spectrum in the T-band, a range of frequencies on the wireless spectrum that had been reserved for public safety agencies.

C-BAND AUCTION

The FCC on February 28, 2020, voted 32 to approve a plan to repurpose C-band, spectrum in the 3.7 GHz to 4.2 GHz frequencies, in order to further development of 5-G. Much of the C-band was being used by satellites to beam content to video and audio broadcasters and cable systems and was considered prime real estate. FCC proposed giving satellite companies "accelerated relocation payments" totaling $9.7 billion. The agency also proposed spending $3 billion to $5 billion to reimburse satellite companies for the cost of relocating their operations.

FCC planned to begin an auction of 280 megahertz of satellite C-band spectrum to 5G cellular networks December 8, 2020, and would allow satellite operators to collect up to $9.7 billion in incentive payments if they helped speed up the spectrum transfer, Chair Ajit Pai said February 6.

The FCC faced some criticism for moving without legislation. Measures in the House and Senate to address the allocation of C-band did not clear Congress.

House Action

The House Communications and Technology Subcommittee of the House Energy and Commerce Committee on March 10, 2020, approved by voice vote a measure (HR 4855) that would require the FCC to clear and reallocate via public auction between 200 and 300 MHz of what is known as C-band, in the 3.7 GHz to 4.2 GHz frequencies. The bill would require the frequencies to be used for the development of a fifth-generational wireless network, and to require that 20 MHz of that spectrum be reserved as "guard band."

Mike Doyle, D-Pa., chair of the subcommittee, said the auction could help address the need for rural broadband as well as rural telehealth, public safety communications, next generation 9-1-1, and other initiatives. The FCC estimated the auction could generate $77 billion in revenue. Lawmakers continued to negotiate how such revenue would be allocated.

Senate Action

Meanwhile, the Senate Commerce, Science and Transportation Committee approved, 14–12, a measure (S 2881) that would require the FCC by December 31, 2020, to launch a public auction to release at least 280 MHz of spectrum in the C-band available for 5G purposes. Before approving the measure, the panel approved a substitute amendment by Roger Wicker that would require the FCC to transfer to the general treasury at least 50 percent of the first $40 billion in gross proceeds from the auction, at least 75 percent of the next $10 billion, and at least 90 percent of any additional proceeds. It also would require that 10 percent of the gross proceeds be used to deploy broadband infrastructure in underserved or unserved areas as determined by the FCC. The Senate measure also would allow the FCC to transfer a portion of any remaining funds to licensees or grantees that relinquish their rights to use spectrum in the C-band.

T-BAND AUCTION

The Communications and Technology Subcommittee of the House Energy and Commerce Committee on March 10, 2020, approved a measure (HR 451), introduced by Rep. Eliot L. Engel, D-N.Y., that would repeal a 2012 law that required the FCC to reallocate and auction off to commercial users spectrum in the T-band, a range of frequencies on the wireless spectrum that had been reserved for

public safety agencies. Before approving the measure, the panel adopted an amendment by Walden, R-Ore., that would require the FCC to create rules that require that 9-1-1 phone service fees be dedicated to 9-1-1 services in the same jurisdiction.

The Energy and Commerce Committee approved, by voice vote, the measure on July 15, 2020. The House passed the measure, 410–5, on September 23, 2020. The measure was approved under suspension of the rules, which required a two-thirds majority vote for passage.

Sen. Edward Markey, D-Mass., introduced a similar bill (S 2748) in the Senate on October 30, 2019, but that chamber did not take up the measure. In December 2020, House and Senate negotiators included language from the House-passed measure (HR 451) in a fiscal 2021 omnibus spending measure (HR 133). That spending measure also included a provision that would require the FCC, before December 2021, to begin competitive bidding among nonfederal services for spectrum in the 3450 to 3550 megahertz bands in order to help develop the next generation 5G technologies.

The House passed the omnibus spending bill by a vote of 359–53 on December 21, 2020, and the Senate cleared the bill the same day by a vote of 92–6. Trump signed the measure into law (PL 116-260) on December 27, 2021.

SPECTRUM FOR EDUCATION

The FCC on July 11, 2019, approved, 3–2, a plan to action off a swath of spectrum that had been reserved for educational purposes since 1963. The plan would offer the 2.5 gigahertz band—the largest continuous swath of mid-band spectrum then available—to the highest bidders with hope of developing a fifth-generation wireless network.

Democratic commissioners Jessica Rosenworcel and Geoffrey Staks opposed the plan, saying it should remain for education, with the intent to close the gap between students who have Internet access and those who do not and, as a result, cannot complete homework. The two Democrats did approve a portion of the plan that would offer rural Indian tribes a chance to bid on the spectrum space. FCC Chair Ajit Pai, however, said the spectrum space was being underused.

Internet Access

Democrats during the 116th Congress tried again to restore the FCC's net neutrality rules, which the commission in 2017 had voted to repeal, but the Senate GOP leadership blocked their efforts.

The FCC, in a 3–2 party line vote in December 2017, had abolished Obama-era net neutrality rules that barred internet providers from throttling or blocking certain websites, or charging for certain content or faster service. Democratic initiatives to reverse FCC's 2017 order failed to gain traction during the 115th Congress.

The House Energy and Commerce Committee on April 3, 2019, approved, 30–22, a measure (HR 1644) that would restore the FCC's 2015 Open Internet Order that protected net neutrality. Republicans opposed the bill, saying it would pave the way for more government regulation.

The House passed the bill in a 232–190 vote on April 10, 2019. Before passing the measure, the House adopted, 423–0, an amendment by McAdams, D-Utah, that would clarify that the measure would not bar internet service providers from blocking unlawful content nor require

---

TRUCK DRIVERS' BREAKS

The Federal Motor Carrier Safety Administration (FMCSA) on May 14, 2020, finalized regulations that aimed to settle years of debate about how to give drivers flexibility on their driving hours yet prevent accidents caused by fatigue. The new rule would lengthen the maximum on-duty time for short-haul truckers, from twelve to fourteen hours, and extend the driving limit from 100 air miles to 150 air miles. Under certain poor driving conditions, drivers could extend their time by up to two hours.

The rule would change the previous requirement that said drivers had to take a thirty-minute rest period within the first eight hours of starting duty. Instead, they could take a break after working eight consecutive hours. Any on-duty time not spent driving could be counted as a break.

Regulations had been in the works since 2018 to give drivers more options on when they could take breaks.

FMCSA estimated the rules would save the trucking industry $274 million annually over ten years. Critics, including Advocates for Highway and Auto Safety, said the rule would extend drivers' workdays and reduce their opportunity to rest. Teamster General President James P. Hoffa said the same. However, the American Trucking Association and the Owner-Operator Independent Drivers Association said the rule would provide more flexibility for drivers.

The announcement of the new rules came when the trucking industry was suffering a myriad of challenges during the pandemic. Some trucking firms faced high demand, such as those delivering food to grocery stores or medical equipment to hospitals. But other firms, such as those servicing other retail industries, saw a drop in demand. Further, drivers said closure of highway rest areas were creating problems. Transportation Secretary Chao said the rules would help during the difficult time.

internet service providers to determine whether content is unlawful.

Markey, D-Mass., had introduced a similar bill (S 682) in the Senate on March 6, 2019. But the Commerce, Science, and Transportation Committee did not act on his measure, nor did the Senate take up the House-passed bill.

Robocalls

Congress in 2019 cleared legislation that aimed to require phone companies to identify robocalls and enforce penalties on businesses that use technology to initiate such calls. Robocalls targeting Americans had increased 64 percent between 2016 and 2018, reaching 47.8 billion in 2018, according to YouMail, an Irvine, California-based company that builds software to block such calls.

The Senate Commerce Committee on April 3, 2019, approved, by voice vote, a bill (S 151), that aimed to require phone companies to identify robocalls and would enforce penalties on companies or individuals that use automated telephone systems to make such calls. The measure would authorize civil penalties of $10,000 per call. The Senate on May 23 voted 97–1 to pass the measure, which was drafted by Sen. John Thune, R-S.D., and Edward J. Markey, D-Mass.

Thune said robocalls often involve scams intended to steal personally identifying information or money. Technological advances had enabled robocallers to easily target thousands of phones, making ineffective the Do Not Call Registry that was created in 2003.

The measure would call on the FCC, the Federal Trade Commission (FTC), the Consumer Financial Protection Bureau and the departments of Justice, Commerce, State, Homeland Security and other federal agencies, along with state attorneys general to report to Congress on ways to better deter such calls and criminally prosecute robocallers at the federal and state levels.

The House on July 24 passed, in a 429–3 vote, a similar measure (HR 3375) introduced by House Energy and Commerce Committee Chair Frank Pallone Jr. Negotiators agreed to include provisions of both bills in a final measure (S 151), which the House passed, 417–3, on December 4. The Senate cleared the measure by voice vote on December 19. The president signed the bill into law (PL 116-105) on December 30, 2019.

FCC RULING

Even before Congress cleared legislation to address robocalls, the Federal Communications Commission, on June 6, 2019, voted to give U.S. phone carriers authority to block robocalls based on the use of call analytics. Under the decision, customers would have to be informed of the practice and would have the ability to opt out.

Several trade groups, including the American Association of Health Care Administrative Management and the Consumer Banks Association, warned that many lawful calls could be erroneously blocked as a result. Democratic commissioners Jessica Rosenworcel and Republican commissioner Michael O'Rielly dissented in part to the ruling. Rosenworcel said the decision did not bar carriers from charging consumers for the block technology.

Transportation Appropriations

House and Senate appropriators in the 116th Congress again faced a series of partisan disputes, as well as disagreements between Democratic leaders and the White House, that necessitated the passage of several stopgap spending measures to keep the government running before they could finalize broad omnibus spending packages to fully fund the Department of Transportation and other agencies through fiscal 2021. A partial government shutdown that began on December 22, 2018, at the end of the previous Congress, continued into January 2019. The House moved several stand-alone spending bills while negotiations were attempted with the president, who was demanding funding for his border wall between the United States and Mexico.

After passing a stand-alone funding bill for the departments of Transportation and Housing and Urban Development, Congress and the president agreed to a stopgap measure that reopened the government. Congress then cleared an omnibus spending package in February 2019, weeks after ending a partial government shutdown and after resolving several disputes with Trump unrelated to transportation spending. House and Senate leaders resorted to passing similar omnibus spending packages for fiscal 2020 and fiscal 2021, tying the final omnibus spending package to a measure to provide relief for workers and businesses at the start of the coronavirus pandemic.

Fiscal Year 2019 Spending

When Democrats assumed the majority in the House in the 116th Congress, they sought to redraft lingering fiscal 2019 spending bills, including a measure for the Transportation Department and Housing and Urban Development. On January 10, 2019, the House passed, 244–180, a $71.4 billion spending bill (HR 267) for Transportation and HUD, $23.3 billion more than the president requested and $1.1 billion above the fiscal 2018 level. The measure would include $26.5 billion for Transportation programs.

Senate Majority Leader Mitch McConnell, R-Ky., refused to bring to the Senate floor any appropriations measure unless Trump said he would sign it, while a growing number of lawmakers supported efforts to pass a short-term spending bill. The House on January 23, 2019, passed, by 234–180, a six-bill spending package (HR 648) that would provide $26.5 billion for Transportation programs, a 3 percent decrease from the fiscal 2018 funding level of $27.3 billion. The reduction would result from a decrease, to $9 million from $1.5 billion, for Better Utilizing

Investments to Leverage Development (BUILD) grants, previously known as TIGER grants.

A standoff between congressional leaders and the president continued until January 25, when the Senate passed by voice vote a three-week stopgap (HJ Res 28) to end the partial government shutdown and allow lawmakers time to finish work on the remaining fiscal 2019 spending bills. The House cleared the measure by unanimous consent on January 25, and the president signed it into law (PL 116-5) on January 31.

Lawmakers then negotiated a $333 billion spending package (H J Res 31) that included $26.5 billion for Transportation programs and grants. The negotiated package dropped a provision in previous spending bills that had barred Houston from receiving funds for a light rail project unless the project was approved in a local referendum. Rep. John Culberson, R-Tex., who lost his seat in the 2018 election, had inserted the provision into spending bills since 2013 because many residents opposed one of the transit routes. Culberson also said he believed the local transit agency had not clearly stated the location of the route when it was approved in a 2003 referendum, according to the House Chronicle.

The Senate passed the measure by a vote of 83–16 on February 14. The House cleared the measure in a 300–128 vote on the same day, and the president signed it into law (PL 116-6) on February 15, 2019. The package included

- $3.25 billion for the Federal Highway Administration
- $204 million for the National Highway Traffic Safety Administration
- $2.87 billion for the Federal Railroad Administration
- $14.1 billion for the Federal Aviation Administration
- $3.47 billion for the Federal Transit Administration
- $1.12 billion for the Maritime Administration
- $246.7 million for the Pipeline and Hazardous Materials Safety Administration

Fiscal Year 2020 Spending

House Action

In May 2019, House appropriators unveiled a $137-billion Transportation–HUD spending bill, which would provide $25.3 billion in discretionary spending for Transportation programs. The House Transportation–HUD Subcommittee approved the measure by voice vote on May 23, 2019. House Appropriations approved the measure in a 29–21 vote on June 4. Before approving the measure, the committee rejected, by a 21–29 vote, an amendment by Rep. Mike Simpson, R-Idaho, that would have removed a provision that continued funding for California's high-speed rail project.

On June 25, 2019, the House passed, 277–194, a $322 billion five-bill spending package (HR 3055) that included the $25.3 billion for Transportation programs, slightly higher than the fiscal 2019 level. The bill included three policy riders that were not included in the Senate measure and that would preempt state standards on breaks for truck drivers, require the Transportation Department to post data on trucking companies' safety violations, and prevent the department from relaxing federal rules requiring truck drivers to take thirty-minute breaks every eight hours. The bill also would block the department from moving forward with a plan to cancel a grant for California's high-speed rail project or to require the state to refund money for the project.

Before passing its bill, the House adopted, 221–195, an amendment by House Transportation Chair DeFazio that would bar the Department of Transportation from using any funds to create a rule, or issue permits, that would authorize the transport of liquefied natural gas by rail tank cars. President Trump in April 2019 had signed an executive order calling on the Transportation department to create such a rule within thirteen months. Republicans, along with the natural gas industry said the order would make it possible for rural or underserved communities to obtain fuel. Democrats, backed by environmentalists, said transporting fuel by rail would create a risk for explosions and fires.

The House also approved, by voice vote, an amendment by Tom Malinowski, D-N.J., that would increase, by $6 million, funding for bus transit grants to help local governments buy low- or no-emission buses and develop related infrastructure, and to decrease by the same amount funding for grants to replace or acquire buses or bus facilities.

Senate Action

The Senate Appropriations Committee on September 19, 2019, approved a spending bill (S 2520) that would provide $25.3 billion in discretionary spending for the Department of Transportation. Both the Senate and House bills would provide $2 billion for Amtrak, $1.1 billion more than Trump requested. Both bills also would provide $17.7 billion for the Federal Aviation Administration, but would differ on how much to allocate for aviation safety—the Senate bill would spend $1.4 billion while the House version would spend $1.6 billion.

Final Action

As lawmakers continued to debate about funding levels, Congress cleared and the president signed two stopgap spending measures. On September 27, 2019, Trump signed into law a measure (HR 4378, PL 116-59) to continue funding the government at fiscal 2019 levels through November 21. A second measure, which the president signed into law (HR 3055, 116-69) on November 21, gave lawmakers until December 20 to reach an agreement.

Lawmakers ultimately negotiated a $555 billion omnibus spending package (HR 1865) that included eight spending bills to fund a range of government agencies, including the Department of Transportation. The $555 billion measure included $24.83 billion in discretionary

spending for the Department of Transportation, lower than the $26.5 billion approved for fiscal 2019 but above the president's $21.58 billion request.

The measure included

- $2.2 billion in discretionary funding for highway programs, including $781 million for the Surface Transportation Block Grant programs and alternative fuel infrastructure on highway corridors, and $1.15 billion for bridge repair and maintenance
- $17.6 billion in total budget resources for the Federal Aviation Administration, including a $67 million increase, above fiscal 2019 levels, for aviation safety
- $2.8 billion for the Federal Railroad Administration, including $2 billion for Amtrak's Northeast Corridor and National Network and $255 million for the Consolidated Rail Infrastructure and Safety Improvement grants
- $13 billion for the Federal Transit Administration, which would include $10.1 billion from the Mass Transit Account of the Highway Trust Fund
- $1 billion for the Maritime Administration
- $281 million for the Pipeline and Hazardous Materials Safety Administration to address safety concerns related to pipeline accidents and crude oil spills related to rail accidents

The House passed the measure by a vote of 297–120 on December 17, 2019. The Senate cleared the package on December 19 by a vote of 71–23. On December 20, 2019, Trump signed the fiscal 2020 omnibus appropriations package into law (PL 116-94).

Fiscal Year 2021 Spending

Hopes for a smooth fiscal 2021 appropriations process were quickly dashed as lawmakers turned their attention to the coronavirus pandemic and the need for emergency spending measures to provide aid for unemployed workers, help business stay afloat, and more.

House Action

In July 2020, House appropriators released a draft $75.9 billion fiscal 2021 spending bill for the departments of Transportation and Housing and Urban Development. The bill would include a total of $107.2 billion in spending (discretionary and mandatory) for the Department of Transportation, $21.1 billion more than in fiscal 2020 and $19.4 billion more than the president requested.

The measure would provide $18.1 billion for the Federal Aviation Administration, as well as $2.1 billion for Amtrak—$1.1 billion more than the president requested. The bill also would provide $3 billion for the Federal Railroad Administration, $18.9 billion for the Federal Transit Administration, $1.5 billion for aviation safety, and $15.9 billion for transit grants.

The measure also would include $61.9 billion for programs paid for by the Highway Trust Fund. In addition, the bill would provide $75 billion for pandemic recovery, including emergency funds for infrastructure: $8 billion in grants for Amtrak's Northeast Corridor and national network, $3 billion for National Infrastructure Investments, $5 billion for rail, $500 million for FAA facilities and equipment, and $2.5 billion for airport grants.

The $8 billion in emergency funds on top of the $2.1 billion in regular appropriations for Amtrak reflected an attempt by lawmakers to help boost the rail service, on which ridership had plummeted during the coronavirus pandemic. The House Transportation–HUD Appropriations Subcommittee approved the measure by voice vote on July 8, 2020.

Appropriators then packaged the measure with five other spending bills. The House on July 31, passed, by a 217–187 vote, the omnibus spending package (HR 7617). The measure would provide $107 billion for the Transportation Department (both discretionary and mandatory funds). In addition, it provided $25.7 billion in emergency funding for transportation services.

Before passing the measure, the House adopted, by voice vote, several blocks of noncontroversial amendments. Among those was an amendment by Reps. Tulsi Gabbard, D-Hawaii and Lloyd K. Smucker, R-Pa., that struck from the bill a provision that would have required certain communities to enter into a cost-sharing agreement with the Department of Transportation for a new Essential Air Service contract.

The House rejected, by voice vote, a package of GOP amendments that would have, among other things, eliminated the $25.7 billion emergency funding for transportation.

Senate Action

Meanwhile, neither the Senate Appropriations Committee nor the full Senate acted on spending measures as they failed to agree on what amendments could be considered. Congress in September cleared, and the president signed on October 1, a continuing resolution (HR 8337, PL 116-159) to keep the government running through December 11, past the November elections. President Trump on December 11 signed another, one-week stopgap funding measure (HR 8900, PL 116-215).

Final Action

After the November 2020 elections, Senate Republicans released all twelve of their draft fiscal 2021 spending bills. House and Senate appropriators then reached agreement on funding allocations for each bill and began negotiating details. Negotiators also agreed to attach a coronavirus relief bill to a year-end funding bill. The House on December 21 passed the massive $1.4 billion spending bill as an amendment to a Senate amendment on an unrelated measure (HR 133). The final vote entailed two votes: one on

four of the spending bills, and the second vote on the other eight spending bills (including the Transportation–HUD bill), the pandemic relief package, and some other legislative provisions. The House voted 359–53 to pass the aid package that included Transportation funding. The Senate that night cleared the measure by a vote of 92–6. The president signed it into law (PL 116-260) on December 27.

The measure included

- $2 billion for the Federal Highway Administration
- $211.2 million for the National Highway Traffic Safety Administration

- $2.8 billion for the Federal Railroad Administration
- $14.6 billion for the Federal Aviation Administration
- $2.8 billion for the Federal Transit Administration
- $1.2 billion for the Maritime Administration
- $260 million for the Pipeline and Hazardous Materials Safety Administration

The bill included $75.4 billion in net discretionary spending for Transportation and HUD programs. That total included $25.3 billion for Transportation programs, a slight increase from the $24.8 billion spent in fiscal 2020 and $21.7 billion requested by the president.

SOCIAL MEDIA'S IMMUNITY

Between 2017 and 2020, lawmakers from both parties, the White House, internet content providers, and free speech advocates engaged in extended debate about whether to limit liability protection for social media companies that permit the distribution of fake news, political disinformation, violent content, or hate speech. Congress failed to reach a resolution on legislation before the 2020 elections and the close of the 116th session.

At issue was Section 230 of the Communications Decency Act (PL 104-140), which former President Bill Clinton signed into law as part of the 1996 Telecommunications Act. Section 230 provided social media companies and websites broad legal immunity for content that users post. Under the law, social media companies and websites could restrict content that violated their terms of service, provided they acted in "good faith." That enabled them to choose what to leave online, what to remove, and what to label as false, without risk of being sued. In contrast, newspapers and other media formats did not enjoy the same immunity.

By passing the 1996 law, Congress had intended to protect new technology companies from costly legal challenges. In the years since, the number of people using social media platforms had grown rapidly. For example, the number of Facebook users had grown from 100 million in 2008 to more than 2 billion in 2019. And the Pew Research Center reported in 2018 that one in five Americans were regularly receiving news on social media.

Democrats and Republicans during the 115th and 116th Congress considered amending Section 230, but disagreed on what changes were needed. President Trump and some conservative Republicans contended that some social media companies were engaging in "selective censorship" of conservative views when they chose to remove certain content they considered "fake news" or hate speech. Democrats said social media platforms were not doing enough to prevent the spread of disinformation and hate speech and should be held responsible.

The debate about whether to amend Section 230 had begun well before the 115th Congress (2017–2018) as disinformation, violent videos, and fake social media accounts spread globally through the internet. In 2016, a Russian troll farm, called the Internet Research Agency and backed by the Kremlin, established fake Facebook accounts and provoked arguments among Americans about such divisive issues as race, immigration, police brutality and the 2016 presidential campaign, according to a Senate Intelligence Committee report released on October 8, 2019. Social media companies, meanwhile, did not tell users they had been exposed to disinformation, and they did not provide tools to bar the creation of such fake accounts.

In October 2017, executives from Facebook, Google, and Twitter told the Senate Judiciary committee that advertisements created by Russian-backed entities and automated non-advertising content created by Moscow-backed companies reached hundreds of millions of Americans during the 2016 elections. That month, Sen. John McCain, R-Ariz., Mark Warner, D-Va., and Amy Klobuchar, D-Minn., introduced a measure (S 1989) that would require social media companies to research and disclose information about sponsors of political advertising. The measure did not advance.

In early 2018, social media companies lobbied against potential new legislative mandates, saying they could root out fake news, terrorism-related material, and other content on their own. On April 6, 2018, Zuckerberg announced his company would require all advertisers to verify their identity and location. In May, his company announced it would begin labelling all political and issue ads on Facebook and Instagram, including who paid for them. But a year later, Zuckerberg told Congress he would welcome new regulations that would address how social media companies handle harmful content, election integrity, and privacy.

On June 13, 2019, several experts urged the House Intelligence Committee to amend the Communications Decency Act in order to address the increasing dangers

posed by artificial intelligence-enabled videos that provided fake depictions. At the time, many lawmakers and technology experts feared Russia, China, and other foreign powers would increasingly aggravate Americans' debate during the 2020 elections by distributing videos that voters could not discern were fake. At the time, artificial intelligence technology enabled a user to manipulate the video and audio of a person. The previous month, Facebook allowed on its platform a doctored video showing House Speaker Nancy Pelosi, D-Calif., slurring her words, appearing as if she was intoxicated. Facebook refused to take down the video.

Experts and some lawmakers also were increasingly concerned about a far-right conspiracy group known as QAnon, which spread messages around the internet stating that "deep state actors" were engaging in a global child sex-trafficking ring and distributed fake news during the 2020 election cycle. Social media companies did not block such fake news or disinformation campaigns and could not halt the creation of new accounts. In September 2019, Twitter banned thousands of accounts from the Middle East, including a previously banned account that had tweeted messages denouncing the investigation by Special Counsel Robert S. Mueller III into Russian involvement in the 2016 elections.

In 2019, Republicans increasingly complained about an anti-conservative bias as online publishers such as Twitter and Facebook allegedly censored only right-wing users and conservative viewpoints. In June 2019, Sen. Josh Hawley, R-Mo., introduced a measure that would remove the civil liability immunity for online publishers with more than 30 million active users in the United States or more than $500 million in global revenue. Companies would have to earn back their immunity by demonstrating to the Federal Trade Commission that they were politically neutral. A trade group representing Facebook, Twitter, Google, and other major internet platforms said such a measure would constrain the tech sector's growth and violate the Constitution because it would allow political appointees to oversee online censorship.

President Trump insisted platforms were not acting fairly when they chose to bar certain content or label it as fake news. On May 26, 2020, Twitter placed a fact-checking warning on two of Trump's tweets that claimed that mail-in ballots likely were fraudulent. Trump, via Twitter, accused the platform of stifling free speech. Two days later, the president signed an "Executive Order on Preventing Online Censorship" that called for limits on Section 230 protections. Trump accused social media platforms of engaging in "selective censorship," and called for the attorney general to propose federal legislation to restrict platforms' immunity from civil liability. The Justice Department on September 23 submitted a proposal to Congress.

As the November 2020 elections neared, cybersecurity experts warned Congress that a lack of federal support to battle disinformation about elections remained a concern, particularly as Trump's tweets about fraud continued to be spread by digital robots, or bots, many of them outside the United States. Many so-called "domestic terrorism" groups also were spreading fake news or disinformation through the internet. Joseph Biden, elected president in November 2020, said in January that he believed Section 230 should be revoked.

Violent Content

Lawmakers from both parties also called for greater scrutiny of such websites that shared violent content, but did not clear legislation to address the issue. Debate on the issue was heightened after an August shooting at a mall in El Paso by a suspect who appeared to have been following a white supremacist internet subculture. Virginia journalists Alison Parker and her cameraman had been shot on live television in 2015 by a former colleague. The shooter recorded and uploaded video to Facebook, and Google's legal team refused to remove the footage from YouTube.

Parker's father, Andy Parker, spoke at a National Press Club event on August 7, 2019, and urged Congress to revise the Communication Decency Act and bar "targeted harassment, incitement, and murder videos," and to remove liability protections to tech companies.

The liability issue had also been raised after a white supremacist, in March 2019, live-streamed an attack on two New Zealand mosques which left fifty-one people dead. Other mass shootings had been linked to such online communities as 4chan and 8chan. The website 8chan, a fringe message board, was considered by experts to be a haven for hate speech and violent content.

In the fall of 2019, Rep. Mike D. Rogers of Alabama, top Republican on the House Homeland Security Committee and his Chair Bennie Thompson, D-Miss., pushed for legislation to address the issue.

The House Homeland Security on October 23, 2019, approved by voice vote Thompson's measure (HR 4782) that would create a twelve-member bipartisan commission to study how online platforms had been used to perpetrate mass violence and exploited by foreign hackers, and how companies address misuse. The bill would require the Department of Homeland Security to evaluate connections between online platforms and incidents of violence and suggest how web platforms could bar the distribution of certain content without limiting free speech. The commission would not address amending Section 230 to limit social media companies' liability, however. The measure was not considered on the House floor.

(Continued)

SOCIAL MEDIA'S IMMUNITY (Continued)

Internet Predators

Senate Judiciary Chair Lindsey Graham, R-S.C., said he wanted to remove immunity for web platforms in order to also make them more accountable for the protection of minors online. In June 2019, *The New York Times* had published a story detailing how YouTube's algorithm increased traffic to family videos of children, luring views from people who watch sexually themed content. In the wake of the story, Graham's committee held a hearing into the dangers for children who use popular digital platforms such as YouTube and Snapchat.

After the hearing, Graham said he wanted to work with tech companies and experts to create a list of "best practices" to protect minors online and to determine whether technology companies were following them. He threatened that, if companies refused to follow such practices, they could lose their immunity protections under Section 230.

Meanwhile, YouTube said it continued to recommend videos featuring kids, but had changed its algorithm, had removed 800,000 videos in the first quarter of 2019 for violation of safety rules, and had disabled comments on videos featuring children. Sen. Hawley, R-Mo., in June 2019 introduced a measure (S 1916) that would bar video platforms from recommending videos featuring one or more minors. Platforms could face a penalty of up to $1,000 for each video or $10,000 per day. The 1998 Children's Online Privacy Protection Act (PL 105-277) aimed to protect children under the age of thirteen by requiring websites tailored to children to require parental consent to gather or use any data from the users.

Hawley, with Edward Markey, also introduced a measure (S 748) that would update the 1998 online privacy law to bar digital platforms from collecting personal data from anyone under age thirteen without parental consent, and anyone ages thirteen to fifteen without the user's consent. Neither bill saw action.

Pornography

Congress did limit immunity, however, for social media companies that knowingly promote or facilitate prostitution. On November 8, 2017, the Senate Judiciary Committee approved a measure (S 1693) by Rob Portman, R-Ohio, that would lift immunities for online platforms if they carry sex trafficking content. On December 12, 2017, the House Judiciary Committee approved by voice vote a similar measure (HR 1865), introduced by Ann Wagner, R-Mo.

The two bills approached the issue of liability differently, however. Wagner's bill, as amended by committee, would curb the immunity provided under Section 230 by allowing prosecution for intentionally promoting or facilitating prostitution, with penalties of up to ten years in prison. For cases involving prostitution of five or more persons, the penalty would rise to twenty-five years in prison. However, a prosecutor would have to prove that the company that provided the online platform specifically intended to promote or facilitate prostitution.

Portman's bill would make online companies accountable only if they knowingly facilitated a violation of federal sex trafficking laws. The House passed, 388–25, Wagner's bill (HR 1865) on February 27, 2018. The Senate cleared the measure, 97–2, on March 21, 2018. The president signed it into law (PL 115-164) on April 11, 2018.

In March 2020, Sen. Graham introduced a measure (S 3398) that would deny civil liability protections for technology companies that allow child pornography to be distributed on their platforms. The measure would force technology companies to prove they had taken steps to prevent the distribution of child pornography if they wanted protections under Section 230 of the Communications Decency Act. The measure would authorize the creation of a national commission to assess the companies' efforts. Members of the commission would include the attorney general, secretary of homeland security, the head of the Federal Trade Commission, and 16 other members appointed by lawmakers.

Democrats, however, wanted more oversight of internet content while Republicans wanted less. Critics of the measure also said it would inappropriately place political officials in charge of what was acceptable or not in online speech.

The Senate Judiciary approved the bill, 22–0, on July 2, 2020. The measure was not considered on the Senate floor.

Draft Trade Agreement

A trade agreement as finalized, and scheduled to be implemented July 1, 2020, would require U.S. trading partners to adopt laws modeled on Section 230.

A draft North American trade agreement, which would replace the 1994 pact with Canada and Mexico, in December 2019 included provisions granting tech companies immunity from lawsuits concerning third-party content in their platforms. Speaker Pelosi, as well as some Republicans such as Ted Cruz of Texas, had lobbied unsuccessfully for the U.S. trade representative to remove such language from the agreement. Congress can vote on legislation to implement an international trade agreement, but cannot change language in the agreement.

The House Ways and Means committee, by voice vote, approved a measure (HR 5430) to implement the agreement on December 17, 2019. On December 19, 2019, the House passed, 385–41, legislation implementing the U.S–Mexico–Canada Agreement (HR 5430). The Senate Foreign Relations committee approved, by voice vote, the measure on January 15, 2020. The Senate cleared the measure by a vote of 89–10 on January 16. The president signed the measure into law (PL 116-113) on January 29.

CHAPTER 7

Energy and Environment

Energy and Environment

President Donald Trump entered office seeking to promote domestic energy production and achieve independence from foreign imports. In two of his earliest executive actions, Trump approved the Keystone XL pipeline and the Dakota Access pipeline, which had been rejected and delayed, respectively, under the Obama administration. His support of opening coastal areas to oil and gas exploration provoked bipartisan opposition from local lawmakers. But mostly his proposals to open areas to oil and gas development such as the long-fought Arctic National Wildlife Refuge (PL 115-97) or national monuments in Utah met with lockstep Republican support and Democratic opposition.

During the 115th Congress, when Republicans controlled both chambers, GOP lawmakers joined Trump in overturning four Obama-era regulations under the 1996 Congressional Review Act, which had been wielded successfully only once before his administration. The act allowed lawmakers to nullify rules governing stream pollution from mining (H J Res 38), companies making foreign payments for resource extraction (H J Res 41), land-use planning (H J Res 44), and hunting in Alaska (H J Res 69). The Senate blocked a fifth attempt dealing with methane emissions (H J Res 36).

Democrats were unable to prevent Trump, who campaigned against business as usual in Washington, from upending previous energy and environmental policies. He withdrew from the Paris Accord, an international agreement negotiated during the Obama administration and aimed at reducing greenhouse gas emissions worldwide. He also scrapped Obama's Clean Power Plan to reduce emissions domestically from coal-fired power plants. Trump's Energy Department developed a plan to support coal-fired and nuclear power plants. And he scrapped regulations such as one governing the waters of the United States.

The debate became more antagonistic in the 116th Congress, when Democrats reclaimed control of the House. They proposed—unsuccessfully—a Green New Deal to curb climate change and opposed efforts to expand coastal drilling in the Atlantic and Gulf of Mexico. The administration reversed course from its goal of licensing the Yucca Mountain nuclear waste repository in the

political swing state of Nevada during the 2020 presidential election year, when GOP Sen. Dean Heller was seeking reelection.

Consensus was difficult to reach, but occasionally found on conservation measures. Lawmakers approved a permanent authorization for the contentious Land and Water Conservation Fund (S 47), which divided Republicans. They approved two water resource development laws (HR 3021, HR 7575) during the Trump administration, reviving a two-year authorization cycle for the first time in a decade. Lawmakers also approved major conservation bills for land (S 47) and animals (S 3051).

Appropriations battles played out consistently during the four years, with Trump proposing significant cuts and even the termination of programs while lawmakers

Figure 7.1 Outlays for Natural Resources and Environment

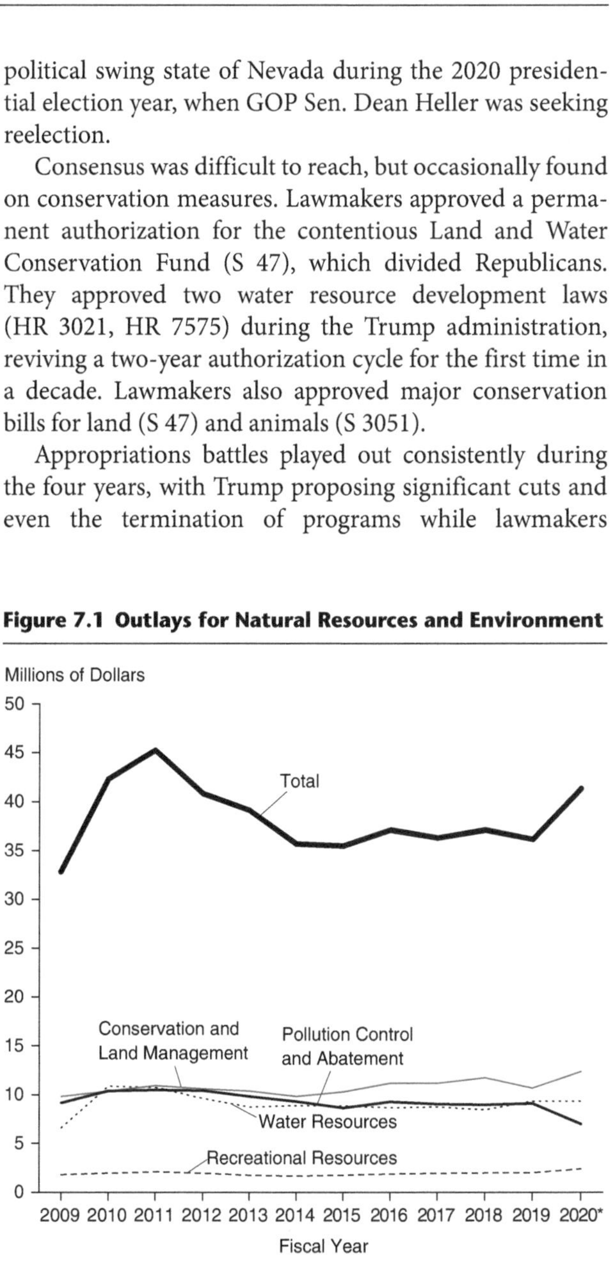

SOURCE: Office of Management and Budget, *Historical Tables, Budget of the United States Government: Fiscal Year 2021* (Washington DC: U.S. Government Printing Office, 2018), Table 3.2.; * indicates estimate

NOTE: Total line includes some expenditures that are not shown separately.

Figure 7.2 Outlays for Energy

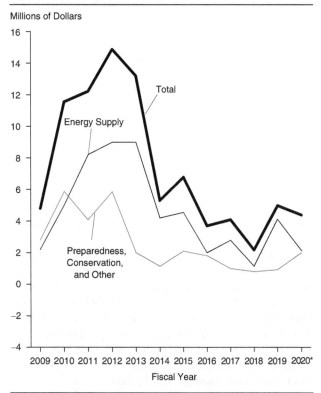

Millions of Dollars

SOURCE: Office of Management and Budget, *Historical Tables, Budget of the United States Government: Fiscal Year 2021* (Washington D.C.: U.S. Government Printing Office, 2020), Table 3.2.

NOTE: Total line includes some expenditures that are not shown separately. * indicates estimate

maintained the programs and usually provided significant funding increases. For example, the Trump administration proposed steep funding reductions of 43 percent in fiscal 2018 and 23 percent in fiscal 2019, but appropriators held funding steady. Trump proposed repeatedly to abolish or sharply reduce funding for the Advanced Research Project Agency–Energy, which conducts research deemed uneconomical by private industry. But appropriators boosted the program's funding from $380 million in fiscal 2018 to $427 million in fiscal 2021.

Chronology of Action on Energy and Environmental Policy

2017–2018

Republicans charged out of the gate in the 115th Congress on energy and environmental legislation by over-turning four Obama-era regulations and winning House approval of a fifth under the Congressional Review Act. President Donald Trump also wielded his executive power by approving the Keystone XL and Dakota Access pipe-lines. In addition, he withdrew from the Paris Accord on climate change and scrapped the Obama-era Clean Power plan to reduce emissions from coal-fired power plants. With Republicans in control of both chambers, Trump won approval of signature tax-cut legislation (PL 115-97) that also opened the Arctic National Wildlife Refuge in Alaska to drilling, a long-fought industry priority.

Bipartisanship was evident in several pieces of legisla-tion. Lawmakers agreed to a water resources development law (HR 3021), to revive a two-year cycle for the legislation for the first time in a decade. Congress cleared a trio of bills to spur nuclear research and better coordinate between federal facilities and private industry. But while Republicans and Democrats agreed on the need to update the Endangered Species Act, consensus proved elusive across several bills in both chambers.

Congressional Review Act

A 1996 law linked to former House Speaker Newt Gingrich's "Contract with America," which had only been used once successfully before the Trump administration, helped congressional Republicans overturn four Obama-era regulations dealing with natural resources and hunting. The Congressional Review Act (PL 104-121) allowed lawmakers to repeal certain rules under a fast-track pro-cess with a simple majority in the Senate. Senate Majority Leader Mitch McConnell, R-Ky., said Congress was directly attacking job-killing regulations he said the Obama admin-istration approved on its way out the door.

The House Rules Committee advanced by voice vote January 30, 2017, three resolutions to nullify Obama-era regulations under a closed rule, meaning no amendments could be made on the House floor. Two dealt with Interior and Energy issues:

- H J Res 38, from Rep. Bill Johnson, R-Ohio, proposed to strike an Interior Department Stream Protection Rule to limit runoff pollution from open pit coal mines
- H J Res 41, from Rep. Bill Huizenga, R-Mich., pro-posed to overturn a Securities and Exchange Commission (SEC) rule requiring companies to dis-close payments that oil, natural gas, and mining companies made to foreign governments

Rules Chairman Pete Sessions, R-Texas, said the Office of Surface Mining produced the Stream Protection Rule without input from states responsible for enforcing it. He said the resolution would protect hundreds of thousands of jobs nationwide by cutting red tape.

The controversial rule had been finalized in December 2016 after a seven-year rulemaking process. It was written to update a 1983 federal rule, but Republicans and some coal state Democrats quickly dismissed it as too economi-cally restrictive. The National Mining Association esti-mated the regulation would have rendered about 62 percent of coal reserves uneconomic. But the League of Conservation Voters criticized the resolution for threaten-ing the drinking water and public health of communities near coal mines.

The SEC rule was part of the 2010 Dodd-Frank finan-cial overhaul (PL 111-203), aimed at discouraging corrup-tion. But the regulation was fiercely opposed by oil companies, including Exxon Mobil, which was led by Secretary of State Rex Tillerson. Financial Services Chairman Jeb Hensarling, R-Texas, said the rule placed an unfair burden on companies that did not apply to foreign competitors, including providing proprietary information that could be obtained by foreign rivals such as state-owned companies in China and Russia. The SEC estimated

compliance would cost companies $591 million per year. But the ranking Democrat, Rep. Maxine Waters of California, said the rule helped fight corruption, provided investors with crucial information, and diminished political instability in resource-rich countries.

The House voted 235–187 on February 1, 2017, to repeal the SEC rule. The Senate voted 52–47 on February 3 to clear the measure without amendment. President Donald Trump signed the first repeal (PL 115-4) on Valentine's Day.

The House voted 228–194 on February 1 to repeal the stream rule. The Senate voted 54–45 on February 2 to clear the measure without amendment. Trump signed it (PL 115-5) on February 16, surrounded by miners. He was joined at the ceremony by McConnell and two Democrats, Sens. Heidi Heitkamp of North Dakota, and Joe Manchin III of West Virginia. "In other countries, they love their coal. Over here, we haven't treated it with the respect it deserves," Trump said February 16, 2017, at the White House. "This rule will eliminate a major threat to [coal] jobs, and we are going to get rid of that threat immediately."

The third nullification (H J Res 44—PL 115-12) eliminated a Bureau of Land Management (BLM) regulation for land-use planning. The rule finalized in December 2016 aimed to incorporate more public comment and transparency into the planning process that had not been updated in thirty years, according to BLM. But Republican lawmakers particularly in the West argued that the new system would centralize decisions in Washington and away from local stakeholders for development of energy extraction, logging, and grazing. Rep. Liz Cheney, R-Wyo., sponsored the resolution.

A White House Statement of Administration Policy on February 7, 2017, said "the rule does not adequately serve the state and local communities' interests and could potentially dilute their input in planning decisions." McConnell said March 7, 2017, on the Senate floor that the regulation had little to do with improving current policy and "really just represents another power grab pushed through by the Obama administration on its way out the door."

The House voted 234–186 to approve the bill on February 7 without amendments. The Senate voted 51–48 on March 7 to clear the bill without amendment. Trump signed it March 27, 2017.

The fourth measure (H J Res 69—PL 115-20) overturned an Interior Department rule governing hunting in Alaska. The Department of the Interior had finalized the rule August 5, 2016, to prevent "particularly effective" hunting methods on federal wildlife refuges in Alaska. The rule did not apply to subsistence hunting. Rep. Don Beyer, D-Va., said lawmakers who overturned the regulation tacitly supported the cruel and inhumane killing of wildlife on federal refuges. Beyer said the regulation would not have interfered with fair chase hunting, but with using planes and helicopters to shoot grizzly bears and wolves, or using steel-jawed leghold traps and wire snares. But Rep. Don Young, R-Alaska, called the rule illegal for violating Alaska's statehood act that granted it full authority to manage fish and game. Young said the rule took away that authority for sixteen wildlife refuges spanning more than seventy-six million acres, an area larger than many states.

The House voted 225–193 on February 16 to approve the resolution without amendment. The Senate voted 52–47 on March 21 to clear the resolution without amendment. Trump signed it April 3, 2017.

Methane Rule

Republican attempts to rescind one Obama administration methane rule were unsuccessful. One strategy was to approve legislation under the Congressional Review Act. Another was to use a rider on a fiscal 2018 appropriations bill.

Methane is a potent greenhouse gas. The Bureau of Land Management issued a so-called "venting and flaring" rule the previous November for oil and gas drillers to capture methane that would otherwise be released into the atmosphere. But that represented a problem in the Plains states, where there was a lack of infrastructure to ship captured methane to customers. President Donald Trump ordered the Interior Department to rework the rule even as lawmakers pursued a CRA resolution (H J Res 36) from Rep. Rob Bishop, R-Utah, to prevent the department from proposing a similar rule in the future.

The Rules Committee advanced the resolution by voice vote January 31, 2017, for a closed rule to prevent amendments during an hour of debate. The approval came after the committee rejected an amendment on a 4–9 vote from Rep. Jared Polis, D-Colo., that would have enabled reconsideration of the rulemaking due to the cost associated with striking methane regulation.

The House voted 221–191 on February 3, 2017, to approve the resolution, with four Democrats voting in favor and eleven Republicans against. But the Senate rejected it on a 49–51 vote, with GOP Sens. Susan Collins, Lindsey Graham, and John McCain opposing it. Collins and Graham had said they were concerned the resolution would prevent future steps to address methane.

Rep. Markwayne Mullin, R-Okla., also sought to prohibit the regulation of methane emissions through an amendment to an appropriations bill, but was ultimately unsuccessful. The House voted 218–195 on February 19, 2017, to adopt his amendment as part of the omnibus appropriations bill (HR 3394), but the provision was not included in the Senate version of the legislation or the final omnibus bill (PL 115-141).

EPA Science

The House passed two bills to make changes to regulations at the Environmental Protection Agency. The Senate, however, did not act on them.

A fight had raged for years at the Environmental Protection Agency over which science would justify regulations and policies the federal government adopted to deal with climate change and other thorny political issues. In May 2017, Pruitt touched off new controversy when he informed nine members approaching the end of their three-year term on the eighteen-member Board of Scientific Counselors, which helps determine the direction of scientific inquiry at the agency, that their appointments would not be renewed. By October 2017, Pruitt ordered that scientists and others who received agency grants should be barred from serving on its advisory committees. Pruitt said the directive would ensure that members of the panels are independent and free from potential interference.

But Sen. Thomas R. Carper, D-Del., said the move was part of Pruitt's battle against science. "Since he arrived at the agency, Mr. Pruitt has repeatedly worked to silence EPA scientists, deny the facts and discredit science inconvenient to his agenda; now he's trying to get rid of agency access to scientific advice altogether," Carper said in a statement October 31, 2017.

The House Committee on Science, Space, and Technology advanced two bills on March 9, 2017, to overhaul EPA regulations. One (HR 1430), which would have prohibited the EPA from proposing regulations by using science that is not open to the public or cannot be reproduced, was approved on a 17–12, party-line vote. Chairman Lamar Smith, R-Texas, said the days of "trust-me-science" were over. "The American people have a right to see the data that is used to justify EPA's costly regulations," Smith said in a statement March 29, 2017, when the House approved the measure.

But committee Democrats argued the public science requirement would require confirmation when catastrophic environmental events are impossible to recreate. Rep. Donald S. Beyer, D-Va., cited events such as the terrorist attacks September 11, 2001, and the volcanic eruption of Mt. St. Helens. Democrats also said the bill could allow private health information about cancer patients in drug trials to become public. Rep. Eddie Bernice Johnson, D-Texas, said the bill would cripple the EPA.

The committee advanced the other bill (HR 1431), which would have required business professionals on the Scientific Advisory Board to disclose conflicts of interest and disallow members who receive EPA grants, on a 19–14 vote along party lines. The bill's sponsor, Rep. Frank D. Lucas, R-Okla., said the measure addressed board shortcomings and deficiencies by guaranteeing a well-balanced, expert panel. But Democrats argued against disallowing scientists who receive EPA grants from serving. Johnson said that would eliminate top scientists in relevant fields from being considered.

The House voted 228–194 on March 29, 2017, to bar non-public science in developing EPA regulations. It then voted 229–193 on March 30, 2017, to restructure the EPA

board. Similar legislation had been approved in the previous two Congresses, but was ignored in the Senate.

The EPA under Administrator Scott Pruitt proposed a rule in April 2018 to do away with what the Trump administration called secret science. But after receiving more than 597,000 comments and holding a public hearing that drew about 100 speakers, the EPA released a regulatory agenda that said no rulemaking would be published until at least 2020.

Ozone

The House passed a bill (HR 806) to delay deadlines for states to comply with ground-level ozone standards set by the Obama administration. The measure, however, failed to advance in the Senate.

The EPA had issued new ozone standards under the Clean Air Act in 2008 to reduce the allowable pollutants harmful to people with asthma, children, and the elderly to 70 parts per billion from the previous 75. But the guidance for state compliance was not issued until 2015. The bill from Rep. Pete Olson, R-Texas, would have delayed implementation of the EPA's National Ambient Air Quality Standards from 2017 until 2025. The timeline for future reviews would have been once a decade rather than once every five years.

The House Energy and Commerce Environment Subcommittee voted 12–8 on June 15 to advance HR 806 after rejecting two Democratic amendments. The subcommittee voted 8–11 to reject an amendment from Rep. Raul Ruiz, D-Calif., that would have prevented enactment of the bill if the Clean Air Scientific Advisory Committee concluded it would have increased adverse health effects such as asthma or cardiovascular disease.

The subcommittee voted 6–11 to reject an amendment from Rep. Jerry McNerney, D-Calif., that would have struck a provision clarifying the bill would not authorize additional funds. The full committee voted 29–24 to advance the bill on June 28, 2017. The approval came after debate on several amendments.

The committee voted 22–29 to reject an amendment from Rep. Kathy Castor, D-Fla., that echoed Ruiz's proposal in the subcommittee. The committee voted 23–29 to reject McNerney's amendment again.

Rep. John Shimkus, R-Ill., proposed an amendment to grant more leniency to states failing to address ozone emissions beyond their control, which the committee rejected by voice vote. The House voted 299–199 to approve the bill July 18, 2017. The approval came after debate on a handful of amendments. The House rejected Castor's amendment again on a vote of 194–232.

Rep. Paul D. Tonko, D-N.Y., proposed an amendment that sought to strike a provision to allow EPA to consider technological feasibility when determining what level of pollution was safe. The House voted 182–241 to reject the proposal.

Rep. Donald S. Beyer Jr., D-Va., proposed an amendment to strike language that weakened the definition of exceptional events for monitoring air quality data. He said Americans value clean air, but that the country could not manage what it could not measure. But the House voted 191–235 to reject the proposal.

Rep. Jared Polis, D-Colo., proposed an amendment that aimed to close a loophole preventing aggregating emissions from any oil or gas exploration or production well, which was rejected on a 186–242 vote.

McNerney proposed an amendment to strike a section of the bill that said no additional funds would be authorized to carry out its requirements, which was rejected on a 190–236 vote. McNerney said the provision was a step by Republicans to add to EPA's workload without adding funding.

During the debate, Olson recalled how smog and ozone in 1972 prevented him from seeing Houston in the heart of the state's energy and chemical industries twenty-five miles from his home many days. But he said great progress had been made since then and he could usually see downtown Houston from forty miles away.

"Nothing in this bipartisan bill changes any air quality standard," Olson said on the House floor on July 18, 2017, when the bill was passed. "It is about making sure that our communities aren't penalized for pollution they can't control. It is about making sure that, when EPA sets a standard, they have to put out the rules to comply with that standard to our local communities at the exact same time."

But Democrats said the bill and its provisions to change the EPA's ozone review cycle would have rolled back the landmark Clean Air Act and its public health benefits.

"Plain and simple, the bill before us today would undermine the Clean Air Act as a safeguard of our public health law, and I encourage each and every Member of the House to oppose it," Tonko said on the House floor July 18, 2017.

Natural Gas Pipelines

The House in 2017 passed a bill (HR 2910) to streamline the Federal Energy Regulatory Commission's (FERC) review of natural gas pipelines under the 1969 National Environmental Policy Act. The controversial measure, however, was not taken up by the Senate.

The legislation, by Rep. Bill Flores, R-Texas, would have allowed the Federal Energy Regulatory Commission to invite federal or state agencies to consult on the authorization of pipeline projects. But the projects would still be subject to National Environmental Policy Act review. Flores said the bill aimed to modernize pipeline infrastructure and reduce energy bills. He cited dramatic benefits from greater access to energy, with Texas paying eleven cents per kilowatt-hour for electricity compared to twenty-one cents in Massachusetts. He said some areas lack pipeline infrastructure needed for natural gas and some state and federal agencies were failing to make timely decisions on pipeline permits. But Democrats argued that siting natural gas pipelines is often controversial and requires detailed regulatory scrutiny by FERC.

The House Energy and Commerce Subcommittee on Energy approved the measure by a vote of 17–14 on June 22, 2017, after rejecting a trio of Democratic amendments on 13–16 votes:

- The proposal from Rep. Bobby L. Rush, D-Ill., would have required FERC to consult with state governments before authorizing construction of natural gas pipelines
- The proposal from Rep. Frank Pallone Jr., D-N.J., would have struck a section of the bill to allow FERC to use data collected from aerial images
- The proposal from Rep. Kathy Castor, D-Fla., would have prevented the bill from taking effect until the Office of Management and Budget determined the bill would not duplicate other federal efforts and result in wasteful government spending

The full Energy and Commerce Committee voted 30–23 to advance the bill on June 28, 2017. As in the subcommittee, the approval came after the panel rejected a trio of Democratic amendments:

Castor revived her proposal and it was rejected on a 22–29 vote. Rush's proposed amendment would have prevented FERC from issuing an authorization permit unless the project was in the national interest, which was rejected on a 24–29 vote. Pallone's proposed amendment would have prevented the use of eminent domain to complete any project using a permit issued under the bill. The committee voted 24–29 to reject it.

The House voted 248–179 to approve the bill on July 19, 2017. The approval came after the defeat of a trio of Democratic amendments.

Rep. Bonnie Watson Coleman, D-N.J., proposed an amendment that would have made it harder for companies to use eminent domain to seize private land for pipelines. But the bill's supporters said it did not change eminent domain laws, and the proposal was rejected on a 189–239 vote.

Rep. Niki Tsongas, D-Mass., proposed an amendment that would have prohibited FERC from issuing a pipeline permit if the project was on lands managed by federal or local authorities for natural resource conservation or recreation. The proposal was rejected on a 180–249 vote.

Rep. Donald S. Beyer Jr., D-Va., proposed an amendment to improve FERC's public comment process, which was rejected on a vote of 192–236.

Wildfires

After wildfires scorched 9 million acres in 2017, Congress debated how to cover hundreds of millions of dollars in extra firefighting expenses. The House passed a

bill (HR 2936) that aimed to expedite the review process under the National Environmental Policy Act to remove trees after natural disasters or insect or disease outbreaks. But the Senate did not act on it.

Supporters said the measure responded to concerns about the increasing number of fires. But environmental groups called it a dangerous gift to the logging industry.

The House Natural Resources Committee voted 23–12 to advance the bill on June 27, 2017. The approval came after resolving a handful of amendments.

The committee adopted two amendments by voice vote. One, from Rep. Darren Soto, D-Fla., would require an arbitrator in forest management matters must be certified by the American Arbitration Association and not be a registered lobbyist. Rep. Scott Tipton, R-Colo., proposed to ensure categorical exclusion for insect and disease as part of the Healthy Forest Restoration Act would apply to forests with a relatively low interval of fire.

The committee rejected by voice vote another Soto proposal, which would have preserved the 2001 Roadless Rule limiting road construction and timber harvesting on roadless areas in national forests. Rep. A. Donald McEachin, D-Va., proposed to strike language streamlining Endangered Species Act assessments, which was rejected on an 11–22 vote. Rep. Raul M. Grijalva, D-Ariz., proposed to strike language directing the Bureau of Land Management to manage lands in Oregon and deposit timber revenue in the U.S. Treasury. The proposal was rejected on a 12–23 vote. Rep. Colleen Hanabusa, D-Hawaii, proposed to eliminate language aimed at expediting NEPA reviews of forest management projects, which was rejected on a 12–23 vote.

Despite the partisan votes, Democrats and Republicans agreed on the need to overhaul federal forest management amid drought and high temperatures. Lawmakers in both parties criticized President Donald Trump's proposed cuts to U.S. Forest Service and Interior Department budgets.

The House voted 232–188 to approve the bill Nov. 1, 2017. The approval came after debate on a number of amendments.

The House adopted a trio of amendments by voice vote. Rep. Kurt Schrader, D-Ore., proposed to strike "produce timber" as a forest management activity designated for categorial exclusion. Rep. Tony Cardenas, D-Calif., proposed to require the secretary of Agriculture to evaluate the feasibility, safety, and cost effectiveness of using unmanned aerial vehicles to support wildfire suppression, as well as forest restoration and management. And Rep. Peter A. DeFazio, D-Ore., proposed to add land exclusions including Yaquina Head Outstanding Natural Area, Wild and Scenic Rivers Acts, Wilderness Act, and lands managed under the National Trails System. The House voted 236–184 to adopt an amendment from Rep. Steve Pearce, R-N.M., to establish a pilot program to demonstrate tools and techniques for safeguarding natural resources.

Rep. Ro Khanna, D-Calif., proposed to strike a section on an arbitration pilot program for forest management from the bill. The amendment was rejected on a 189–232 vote.

Rep. Tom O'Halleran, D-Ariz., proposed to strike language revising regulations for extraordinary circumstances under NEPA. The House voted 194–226 to reject the amendment.

Tree Removal on Federal Land

The House passed legislation in 2017 that aimed to lessen one of the threats to wildfires on public lands. The Senate, however, did not take it up.

The growth of western wildfires spurred lawmakers to debate how to reduce the risk of power lines sparking the next conflagration. The House Natural Resources Committee voted 24–14 on April 27, 2017, to advance a bill (HR 1873) that aimed to require the secretaries of Interior and Agriculture to ensure rights-of-way for electrical distribution facilities on federal land have rules for trimming or removing trees that could catch fire.

The sponsors, Reps. Doug LaMalfa, R-Calif., and Kurt Schrader, D-Ore., sought to streamline the process for removing hazardous trees adjacent to electricity infrastructure such as power lines on Bureau of Land Management or Forest Service lands. LaMalfa said it was common sense to remove trees that are dangerously close to power lines, but that bureaucratic restrictions made the process too difficult. He said delayed removal of trees led to blackouts and forest fires.

The House voted 300–118 to approve bill June 21, 2017. The approval came after debate on several amendments.

Rep. Salud O. Carbajal, D-Ga., proposed an amendment to ensure owners of transmission and distribution facilities submit management plans, which was rejected on a 171–243 vote.

Rep. Kyrsten Sinema, D-Ariz., proposed an amendment that was adopted by voice vote to ensure Interior and Forest Service personnel involved in vegetation management decisions receive training on how unmanned technologies can be used to reduce the risk of wildfires. She said drones could help monitor transmission lines quickly and safely at a lower cost than helicopters, to reduce energy costs to consumers.

Rep. Donald S. Beyer, D-Va., proposed an amendment that was approved by voice vote to prohibit the loss of funds for wildfire suppression. The Senate Energy and Natural Resources Committee held a hearing on the bill September 19, 2017, but the panel held no votes on it.

Endangered Species Act

Democrats and Republicans agreed the 1973 Endangered Species Act (PL 93-205) needed an update. But they disagreed about which approach to take. Congress considered several bills but failed to clear any of them.

The law was credited by the Center for Biological Diversity with preserving 99 percent of the species under its protection from extinction, including the bald eagle and Yellowstone grizzly bear. Democrats sought to strengthen the protections because of concerns that climate change could eliminate half the world's plants and animals. Conservationists sought to increase funding for state grant programs, saying species should be protected before they become endangered.

But Republicans, especially from Western states, argued that the law had been abused in ways that hurt economic development, raised costs for businesses, and intruded on states managing wildlife. Conservatives sought to open public lands to fossil-fuel development. Agricultural communities feared their livelihoods would be sacrificed to protecting animals. And a coalition of Western governors asked Congress to give them more control over wildlife management.

Sen. Jim Risch, R-Idaho, proposed legislation (S 273) in February 2017 to limit protections for the sage grouse, but it languished in the Environment and Public Works Committee. The sage grouse became a lightning rod for complications in spending bills for years as the bird's habitat sprawled across 165 million acres across eleven states. A provision in the fiscal 2018 comprehensive spending bill (PL 115-141) prohibited the federal government from reviewing the status of the sage grouse as an endangered species.

A federal court vacated the Interior Department's Obama-era decision to partially end protections for gray wolves in the Great Lakes region on August 1, 2017. The Fish and Wildlife Service said the partial delisting was because wolves had recovered in the region including Minnesota, Michigan, Wisconsin, and parts of adjoining states. But the decision by the D.C. Circuit Court of Appeals in a case brought by the Humane Society said the department's 2011 order failed to reasonably analyze the impact of partial delisting.

The decision frustrated farmers and developers. The court decision came days after the Senate Environment and Public Works Committee advanced a bill (S 1514) from Sen. John Barrasso, R-Wyo., that aimed to end the protections for the wolves. The bill would have reauthorized through 2023 the North American Wetlands Conservation Act, the National Fish and Wildlife Foundation Act, the Chesapeake Bay Program, the Chesapeake Bay Gateways and Watertrails Network, and the Chesapeake Bay Gateways Grants Assistance Program. The panel advanced the bill on a bipartisan, 14–7 vote on October 5, 2017, but the bill featured a contentious provision to authorize the Interior secretary to remove gray wolves in Wyoming and the Great Lakes Region from protection under the Endangered Species Act. Sen. Thomas R. Carper of Delaware, the top Democrat on the panel, offered an amendment to strike the wolf language, but it was rejected on a 10–11 vote.

The committee adopted an amendment by voice vote from Sen. Dan Sullivan, R-Alaska, to allow the import of polar bear trophies from legal hunts in Canada before May 15, 2008. Democratic Sens. Jeff Merkley of Oregon and Benjamin L. Cardin of Maryland requested to be recorded as voting no. The Senate took no action on the bill.

In another piece of legislation, the fiscal 2018 budget resolution (H Con Res 71), Sen. Mike Lee, R-Utah, proposed amendment that would have prohibited an Endangered Species Act listing for just one state. But two fellow Republicans, Sens. Lamar Alexander of Tennessee and Susan Collins of Maine, joined Democrats in voting 49–51 to reject it on October 19, 2017.

In a series of actions on the House side, the Natural Resources Committee approved five bills October 4 to change the law, but the full House took no action on any of them. Four from Republicans were

- HR 717, from Rep. Pete Olson of Texas, would have allowed rejection of an endangered species listing based on economic impacts. The bill advanced on a vote of 22–13.
- HR 1274, from Rep. Dan Newhouse of Washington, would have mandated that federal agencies share supporting data with states and communities, and consider information from states, local and tribal governments. The bill advanced on a vote of 22–14.
- HR 3131, from Rep. Bill Huizenga of Michigan, would have limited fee recovery for bringing lawsuits under the Endangered Species Act against the government. The bill advanced on a vote of 22–16.
- HR 2603, from Rep. Louie Gohmert of Texas, would have prohibited the listing of non-native species. The committee advanced the bill on a vote of 23–16.

The one (HR 424) from a Democrat, Rep. Colin C. Peterson of Minnesota, would have directed the Interior Department to reissue rules delisting the gray wolf in the western Great Lakes region and Wyoming. The committee advanced the bill on a vote of 24–15.

NATIONAL MONUMENTS

Utah became ground zero in 2017 for fights over national monuments and the 1906 Antiquities Act that allowed presidents to designate land for federal protection. President Donald Trump shrank the boundaries of two national monuments: Bears Ears and Grand Staircase–Escalante. The move came amid an impasse over two bills from Utah lawmakers, who sought to change the way monuments are designated and to open areas around Escalante to mineral exploration.

Trump called former President Barack Obama's 2016 designation of Bears Ears an overreach of executive power. Trump vowed to tamp down abuses of the Antiquities Act, which presidents since Theodore Roosevelt have used to

protect environmentally and culturally significant areas. "These abuses of the Antiquities Act give enormous power to faraway bureaucrats at the expense of people who actually live here, work here and make this place their home," Trump said December 4, 2017, at the Utah State Capitol in Salt Lake City.

One of Trump's proclamations divided the 1.9 million-acre Grand Staircase–Escalante monument into three distinct monuments totaling 1 million acres. The other shrank Bears Ears from 1.35 million acres to 228,800 acres. The moves opened the areas to potential commercial and resource development. The executive action came amid a lack of legislative action on two bills.

Rep. Rob Bishop, R-Utah, proposed a bill (HR 3990) that aimed to prohibit monument designations less than fifty miles from another monument, require environmental reviews under the National Environmental Policy Act (NEPA) for monuments between 640 acres and 10,000 acres, and require more stringent reviews for monuments and approval from state legislatures for monuments from 10,000 to 85,000 acres. Bishop argued that Obama had made designations for political reasons rather than the scientific or architectural value, a problem he said his bill would fix. But conservation groups warned that the bill would damage the Antiquities Act and benefit industry. The House Natural Resources Committee voted 23–17 to advance the bill October 11, 2017, but it did not get a full House vote.

The other bill (HR 4558) from Rep. Chris Stewart, R-Utah, sought to establish an Escalante Canyons National Park of 243,241 acres within the national monument. The bill would have also codified the monument of 211,983 acres and the Kaiparowits National Monument of 551,117 acres. Stewart acknowledged that he wanted to open some of the land not in the protected areas to mineral exploration.

Democrats and conservationists opposed the move. Rep. Alan Lowenthal, D-Calif., said the bill would open the areas up potentially to development of oil, gas, tar sands, coal leasing, and hard-rock mining. The Natural Resources Committee held a hearing on the measure, but no vote.

ARCTIC NATIONAL WILDLIFE REFUGE

In a major setback for environmentalists, one element of the 2017 tax overhaul (PL 115-97) opened part of the long-debated Arctic National Wildlife Refuge (ANWR) to oil and gas exploration.

The 1.5 million-acre area, known as the coastal plain, had been set aside for potential development under the 1980 law that created the refuge (PL 96-487). Lawmakers debated whether to open the refuge amid high gasoline prices in 2005 and 2008, but Democrats and some Republicans blocked congressional approval in an effort to protect the pristine area from potential pollution from oil production.

The fiscal 2018 budget resolution (S Con Res 25) included reconciliation instructions to open the refuge to raise $1 billion in federal revenues over ten years. Sen. Lisa Murkowski, R-Alaska, had already proposed legislation (S 49) on January 5, 2017, to open a portion of ANWR to oil and gas development. The Energy and Natural Resources Committee voted 13–10 on legislative language to send to the Budget Committee as part of reconciliation to generate $1.1 billion in fees for oil and gas drilling rights over a decade. The ANWR provision was approved as part of the tax overhaul (HR 1). The Senate voted 48–52 on December 2, 2017, to reject an amendment from Sen. Maria Cantwell, D-Wash., that would have struck the title for ANWR.

Electric Grid Reliability

The U.S. electric grid was reliable, but regulatory and market challenges threatened coal-fired and nuclear power plants that can run without sunshine, wind, or occasionally dodgy natural gas supplies, according to an Energy Department report released a report August 23, 2017. The 187-page report echoed the Trump administration's focus on so-called baseload power, which can be provided without interruption, such as coal and nuclear power. But the report did not attack renewable technologies or the federal tax credits that support them, as advocates in those industries feared. The report called for federal energy market regulators to look for ways to assure investments in coal and nuclear power were rewarded, with a goal of ensuring grid resiliency during extreme weather events.

"Ultimately, the continued closure of traditional baseline power plants calls for a comprehensive strategy for long-term reliability and resilience," the report said. "States and regions are accepting increased risks that could affect the future affordability, reliability and resilience of electricity delivery for consumers in their region."

Storm damage raised concerns among lawmakers about how to make the grid more reliable. Hurricanes Harvey and Irma hit the mainland United States, causing power blackouts and leaving power lines down across streets. Puerto Rico and the U.S. Virgin Islands, territories in the Caribbean, were left in the dark for weeks.

While the Trump administration proposed to prop up coal-fired and nuclear power plants, a wide range of energy advocates said improving infrastructure could make the electric grid more reliable. Senate Environment and Public Works Chairman John Barrasso, R-Wyo., said lawmakers of both parties who visited Puerto Rico agreed on the need to build a stronger grid there. Homeland Security and Governmental Affairs Chairman Ron Johnson, R-Wis., said the grid was weak before the hurricane and offline afterward.

Advocates for an overhaul of hydropower licensing hoped the report would spur legislation as part of supporting power plants that operate around the clock. Hydropower produced about 10 percent of electricity

consumed nationwide, but Rep. Cathy McMorris Rodgers, R-Wash., and others sought to streamline licensing and the relicensing process for hydroelectric dams. The Energy and Commerce Committee advanced the bill (HR 3043) by voice vote June 28, 2017. The House voted 257–166 to approve the bill on November 8, 2017, but it languished in the Senate Energy and Natural Resources Committee.

MERCURY RULE

The Environmental Protection Agency embarked in August 2018 on a review of an Obama-era rule governing mercury pollution from coal- and oil-fired power plants. Mercury, a neurotoxin, has been found to endanger public health and is especially dangerous to children and pregnant women.

Thirty percent of the closures of coal-fired power plants in 2015 occurred in April, the month the rule called Mercury and Air Toxic Standard, went into effect, according to the Energy Information Administration. The standards imposed limits on pollutants including mercury, arsenic, chromium, and hydrochloric acid gas. The rule was one of the most expensive Obama environmental regulations, estimated to cost the industry $9.6 billion to comply, compared to $37 billion to $90 billion in public health benefits. The Supreme Court upheld the rule in June 2016.

Sens. Lamar Alexander, R-Tenn., and Thomas R. Carper, D-Del., jointly wrote the EPA to urge the agency to leave the rule intact—days before EPA announced its review. Sen. Susan Collins, R-Maine, joined Carper in introducing legislation (S 3394) to "establish a national mercury monitoring network to protect human health, safeguard fisheries," and track the environmental effects of reducing emissions. The Environment and Public Works Committee did not act on the bill.

The EPA finalized a rule April 16, 2020, that would eventually make it easier for oil and coal-fired power plants to release mercury and other toxic air pollutants, despite bipartisan opposition. The rule did not overturn the Obama standards outright, but altered their legal justification by recalculating the costs and benefits of the Mercury and Air Toxic Standard. The National Mining Association, which challenged the mercury rule in court, applauded the changes when they were proposed and said the Obama-era rule was a destructive and illegal assault on the coal industry.

King Cove Road

The House passed legislation to create a land swap in Alaska, but the Senate took no action on the measure. The bill (HR 218) from GOP Rep. Don Young offered for the state to give the Interior Department 43,093 acres of land in exchange for 206 acres of federal land within the Izembek National Wildlife Refuge and 131 acres in the Izembek Wilderness. The goal was to create a single-lane gravel road along an eleven-mile corridor connecting King Cove and an all-weather airport in Cold Bay. Young said the road was needed to provide access to lifesaving services and that nineteen people had died for lack of a road.

The House Natural Resources Committee approved the measure by voice vote on June 27, 2017. The ranking Democrat on the committee, Rep. Raul M. Grijalva of Arizona, said the bill was the latest move in a decades-long Republican attempt to build a road through the wildlife refuge. The panel rejected by voice vote an amendment from Grijalva that would have limited the time to build the road to seven years. The House voted 248–179 to approve the bill July 20, 2017. The approval came after the defeat of two amendments.

The House voted 190–234 to reject an amendment from Rep. Niki Tsongas, D-Mass., who proposed to require mitigation measures adopted in a previous law (PL 111-11) to ensure impacts on migratory birds, wildlife, and wetlands were minimized. Tsongas had argued that Congress approved similar land exchange legislation in 2009, but that after a four-year review with 70,000 public comments and 130 public meetings, former Interior Secretary Sally Jewell concluded the swap was not in the national interest. Young called the amendment mischievous and said it was trying to kill the project. He said the road would not hurt migratory birds or other wildlife, and he added that the 70,000 comments included only 100 from Alaskans.

The House voted 167–260 to reject a Grijalva amendment that sought to prohibit the land swap until $20 million in federal funds given to Alaska for King Cove transportation purposes were repaid. In June 2020, a federal judge ruled against Interior's proposed land exchange, a decision criticized by Alaska's congressional delegation. The lawmakers said from December 2013 to October 2019, residents of King Cove used 113 emergency medevacs including thirty-three by the Coast Guard.

Bureau of Reclamation

The House passed a bill in 2017 to make changes to the process for surface water storage projects, but the Senate did not take it up. The House Natural Resources Committee voted 24–16 on April 27, 2017, to advance legislation (HR 1654) that sought to allow the Interior secretary to coordinate federal and state water permits, with a goal of streamlining surface water storage projects. The committee also adopted an amendment by voice vote from the sponsor, Rep. Tom McClintock, R-Calif., that would have allowed water storage project groups to opt out of the streamlined process.

McClintock said water shortages resulted from stopping the building of reservoirs a generation early, because of laws that made the projects time consuming and cost prohibitive. He said water districts found it difficult to navigate the Byzantine maze of regulations with competing and overlapping requirements from federal agencies.

The House voted 233–180 to approve the bill June 22, 2017. The approval came after debate on two amendments. The House approved by voice vote an amendment from Rep. Doug LaMalfa, R-Calif., to enhance cooperation in the planning and construction of water storage projects. The House voted 179–232 to reject an amendment from Rep. Alan Lowenthal, D-Calif., that sought to exempt dam projects if they could harm commercial fisheries.

Sen. John Barrasso, R-Wyo., introduced a companion measure (S 677), and the Energy and Natural Resources Subcommittee on Water and Power held a hearing June 14, 2017. The committee did not vote on either bill.

Fiscal Year 2018 Interior and Environmental Appropriations

The fiscal 2018 spending bill for the Interior Department and environmental programs cleared Congress as part of a broader bill to fund the federal government through the remainder of the fiscal year. The House voted 256–167 to approve the omnibus March 22, 2018, and the Senate cleared it the next day on a vote of 65–32. President Donald Trump signed the legislation (HR 1625 PL 115-141) the same day.

The omnibus provided nearly $35.3 billion in discretionary spending for Interior and environmental programs, which was $3 billion or 9 percent more than the fiscal 2017 level and $8.1 billion or 30 percent more than the administration's request. The agreement rejected the administration's proposed 43 percent cut to EPA and kept the funding level for the agency at $8.1 billion, which included $149 million in rescissions.

The appropriations bill funded the Environmental Protection Agency and Interior Department, as well as its Bureau of Land Management, National Park Service, and Bureau of Indian Affairs. It also covered the Agriculture Department's Forest Service and the Department of Health and Human Service's Indian Health Service.

The appropriations process extended nearly halfway into the fiscal year. The House version of Interior–Environment spending legislation was approved by a vote of 211–198 on September 14, 2017, as part of a twelve-bill omnibus (HR 3354), but the Senate Appropriations Committee did not vote on its own bill before the eventual compromise legislation.

House Committee Action

The House Interior–Environment Appropriations Subcommittee approved by voice vote July 12, 2017, a draft bill that included $31.5 billion in discretionary spending, but Democrats indicated they would not support the measure. The bill would have cut spending at EPA, the Department of the Interior, and other agencies by 2.5 percent from the $32.3 billion enacted in the fiscal 2017 omnibus bill (PL 115-31).

Republicans ignored deep cuts the Trump administration proposed for EPA, but spending levels would still have been cut $528 million below the fiscal 2017 enacted level, or 7.4 percent, to $7.5 billion. The draft would have provided $3.4 billion to the Department of the Interior and Forest Service to prevent and combat wildfires. And it would have provided $1.2 billion for the Bureau of Land Management, or $46 million less than the previous year.

The draft bill included a rider to help the Trump administration bypass statutory and regulatory reviews to overturn the Obama administration's Waters of the United States rule. The measure would have also prohibited the Department of the Interior from proposing any rules listing the greater sage grouse as an endangered species. Another provision would have prevented the federal government from regulating lead in ammunition and fishing tackle under the Toxic Substances Control Act (PL 114-182) or any other law.

House Appropriations Chairman Rodney Frelinghuysen of New Jersey said Republicans identified ways to rein in federal bureaucracy. But Rep. Betty McCollum of Minnesota, the top Democrat on the subcommittee, said the provisions would have turned back protections for endangered species and undermined clear water and clear air protections while benefitting polluters.

The full Appropriations Committee approved the draft bill July 18, 2017, on a 30–21 vote. The bill would have provided $31.5 billion in discretionary spending for fiscal 2018, after defeating Democratic amendments to prevent the EPA and Interior Department from rolling back safeguards for endangered species, clean water and clean air, regulations Republicans argue are overly burdensome.

The White House had proposed to cut EPA spending by a third to $5.7 billion. But the bill spared EPA and other agencies from deep cuts the Trump administration proposed. It provided $7.5 billion to EPA, a 7.4 percent cut from the $8.1 billion enacted in fiscal 2017 (PL 115-31).

Rep. Mike Quigley, D-Ill., proposed an amendment that sought to prevent EPA Administrator Scott Pruitt from closing any of the agency's regional offices. But subcommittee Chairman Ken Calvert of California said the provision was unnecessary because the White House budget did not propose closing offices, and Republicans defeated the proposal on a 21–29 vote.

McCollum proposed to remove language in the bill allowing EPA to avoid statutory reviews when withdrawing from the Waters of the United States rule, which she said would give the agency unprecedented power. The panel rejected the proposal on a 19–31 vote.

Republicans also rejected by voice vote an amendment that would have required EPA, the Department of the Interior, the Forest Service and other agencies to consult with Congress before undertaking significant staffing changes. Interior Secretary Ryan Zinke had said he wanted to cut 4,000 jobs, partly through reassignments and buyouts. Rep. Chellie Pingree, D-Maine, said lawmakers hold

the purse strings for those changes, but the amendment was rejected by voice vote.

Rep. Andy Harris, R-Md., proposed one of the GOP amendments that were adopted. He proposed to preclude any federal funds from being used for assessments or construction of wind turbine projects within twenty-four miles of Maryland's shoreline. Rep. Chris Stewart, R-Utah, had another successful amendment to allow the "humane" euthanizing of wild horses on federal land, while prohibiting hunting them for processing or commercial benefits.

Senate Committee Action

The Senate Appropriations Committee released a draft in November 2017, one of its final four spending bills after the House approved its omnibus (HR 3354). But the committee did not act on its draft or the House omnibus before tackling the eventual compromise omnibus (HR 1625) while waiting on negotiations for higher spending caps.

The Senate version would have provided $32.6 billion in discretionary spending, including $507 million in emergency funding for fighting wildfires. The bill sought to allow the EPA to withdraw the Waters of the United States rule without statutory review. The bill would have provided $7.91 billion for EPA, $149.5 million less than enacted for fiscal 2017.

Final Action

Action on spending legislation was difficult because the two chambers began without agreement on discretionary spending and because the Trump administration did not submit a detailed budget proposal until late May 2017, a delay customary for new presidents. The 2011 Budget Control Act (PL 112-25) threatened to cut defense spending by $2 billion from the fiscal 2017 level and nondefense spending by $3 billion. A series of stopgap spending measures were required until the eventual omnibus compromise could be negotiated with new spending caps, with a three-day government shutdown in January 2018. Senate Majority Leader Mitch McConnell, R-Ky., and Minority Leader Chuck Schumer, D-N.Y., led negotiations after the shutdown that led to eliminating the sequester from the Budget Control Act and raising discretionary spending by $296 billion over fiscal 2018 and fiscal 2019. The deal (PL 115-123) also suspended the limit on public debt for nearly a year, to March 1, 2019. The deal gave appropriators the green light to develop full-year spending measures.

MAJOR PROVISIONS

Department of the Interior

The department received $13.1 billion, a 7 percent increase from the previous year despite the Trump administration requesting a cut in funding.

The funding included

- $3.2 billion for the National Park Service, an increase of $270 million or 9 percent. The funding included $45 million in construction funding for the Dwight

D. Eisenhower Memorial near the National Mall, after resolving years of disagreements between the Eisenhower family and architect Frank Gehry
- $3.1 billion for the Bureau of Indian Affairs and Indian Education, an increase of $204 million
- $1.6 billion for the U.S. Fish and Wildlife Service, an increase of $75 million or 5 percent
- $1.3 billion for the Bureau of Land Management, an increase of $79 million or 7 percent

Environmental Protection Agency

The EPA received nearly $8.1 billion, the same as the previous year. The House committee draft initially proposed $7.5 billion and the Senate draft, $7.9 billion. The bill maintained funding at $80 million for Brownfield projects, provided a slight increase of $3 million to the $1.1 billion Superfund remediation, and rejected the administration's proposal to end a number of state and tribal assistance grants, including the Great Lakes Restoration Initiative and the Chesapeake Bay Initiative. The measure prohibited EPA from issuing a rule requiring reporting of greenhouse gas emissions from manure management systems, from imposing reporting requirements about greenhouse gas emissions, and from regulating lead content in ammunition or fishing tackle under the Toxic Substances Control Act (94-469). The bill required EPA and the Energy and Agriculture departments to establish clear policies for the use of forest biomass to generate energy.

Forest Service

The agency within the Agriculture Department received $5.9 billion, an increase of $338 million or 6 percent. The agreement provided $3.1 billion, a $627 million or 26 percent increase, for core functions other than fighting wildfires such as maintenance of national forests.

Indian Health Service

This agency within the Department of Health and Human Services received $5.5 billion, an increase of $498 million or 10 percent. The funding includes $72 million for a new Indian Health Center Improvement Fund to help reduce disparities across the system.

Wildfires

The bill also appropriated $3.8 billion for fighting wildfires on public lands under the Forest Service and Department of the Interior. The funding equaled the ten-year average and managers said it would fully address operations for the two agencies.

Fiscal Year 2018 Energy and Water Appropriations

Congress appropriated $43.2 billion in fiscal 2018 for the Energy Department, Army Corps of Engineers, the Department of the Interior's Bureau of Reclamation and

other agencies, as part of the omnibus spending agreement (HR 1625 PL 115-141). The measure generally rejected significant cuts the administration had proposed by providing $4.8 billion, or 12 percent more than fiscal 2017, and $9 billion, or 26 percent more than the administration had requested.

House Committee Action

The House Appropriations Committee approved its draft bill (HR 3266) by voice vote June 28, 2017. The bill would have provided $37.6 billion in fiscal 2018 for energy programs and water projects, but would have ended the popular Advanced Research Project Agency–Energy (ARPA–E) program, which funds experimental energy research. That amount would have been $209 million than fiscal 2017 funding (PL 115-131), but still $3.65 billion more than the administration had proposed.

Subcommittee Chairman Mike Simpson, R-Idaho, said he followed the administration's request to zero-out ARPA–E as part of efforts to reduce federal spending. His draft also included policy language for the EPA and Army Corps of Engineers to more easily overturn the Obama administration's Waters of the United States regulation. The bill's language appeared to exempt repeal of the regulation from legal requirements of the Administrative Procedure Act (PL 79-404), which requires a justification for the withdrawal.

Rep. Marcy Kaptur of Ohio, the ranking Democrat on the subcommittee, said terminating ARPA–E would do real damage. Rep. Nita M. Lowey of New York, the ranking Democrat on the full committee, said Republicans knew the Waters of the United States rider and other controversial provisions would not be included in bipartisan legislation.

The measure sought to continue funding for the Mixed Oxide Fuel Fabrication Facility in South Carolina and to provide funding for the stalled approval process for the proposed Yucca Mountain nuclear waste repository in Nevada. The bill would also have allowed possession of firearms on Army Corps of Engineers' lands.

The full Appropriations Committee approved the draft by voice vote July 12, 2017. The measure would have provided $203 million less than 2017 funding (PL 115-31) and included a nearly $1 billion increase in Energy Department nuclear weapon activities, while slashing renewable and energy efficiency research funding by the same amount.

Rep. Matt Cartwright, D-Pa., proposed an amendment to reject most of the funding. But the committee rejected the amendment on a 22–30 vote.

Democrats also moved to strike all policy riders from the bill, including the one dealing with the waters of the United States. The amendment failed on a 20–32 vote.

The House voted 235–192 on July 27, 2017, to approve a four-bill minibus for spending bills for the military, energy programs and water projects, U.S. Capitol operations, veterans' benefits, and initial construction of the U.S.–Mexico border wall. But the defense spending breached budget limits, leaving the bill's fate unclear.

The House voted 211–198 on Sept. 14, 2017, to approve an omnibus of all twelve appropriations bills. But the bill violated spending caps from the 2011 budget law (PL 112-25), which would have triggered across-the-board spending cuts known as sequester, and it contained policy riders that were contentious in the Senate.

Senate Committee Action

The Senate Appropriations subcommittee approved its more generous version of the bill by voice vote July 18, 2017. The version would have provided $38.4 billion for energy- and water-related programs, which was $800 million more than the House version and $4.1 million more than the administration had requested. The bill provided more robust funding for energy research and development programs, including ARPA–E. The bill also directed the department to work on temporary storage options for nuclear waste other than Yucca Mountain in Nevada.

The bill would have granted the administration's request to halt construction of the Mixed Oxide Fuel Fabrication Facility in South Carolina. The project was intended to convert thirty-four tons of plutonium from nuclear weapons into fuel for civilian energy, under a 2000 disarmament treaty with Russia, but the project was over budget and behind schedule. Sen. Lindsey Graham, R-S.C., scrambled to salvage funding for the project by meeting with Energy Department officials and private contractors under a fixed-price contract, to relieve concerns about spiraling costs.

OMNIBUS HIGHLIGHTS

The bill provided $34.5 billion for the Energy Department, a $3.8 billion or 12 percent increase from the previous year and $6.6 billion or 24 percent more than requested. The bill increased funding for fossil energy research and development programs by 9 percent and provided a separate $50 million fund to support two coal technology programs.

The bill also provided Army Corps of Engineers with $6.8 billion for operations, investigations and construction, a $789 million or 13 percent increase from fiscal 2017 and $1.8 billion or 36 percent more than the administration had proposed.

The Advanced Research Projects Agency–Energy program, which develops energy technologies that are too risky to attract substantial private investment, received $380 million. The program received $306 million in fiscal 2017, but the administration had proposed just $26 million for fiscal 2018. The measure provided $252 million for the Strategic Petroleum Reserve in Texas and Louisiana, which was created after the oil embargo of 1973 and 1974, an increase of $29 million or 13 percent from the previous year.

The measure barred new nuclear nonproliferation projects in Russia and limited application of the Clean Water Act in agricultural areas such as farm ponds and irrigation

ditches. The bill provided $10.6 billion to maintain the nation's nuclear stockpile, a $1.4 billion or 15 percent increase from the previous year. The bill included $270 million to continue construction in South Carolina of a Mixed Oxide Fuel Fabrication Facility to convert weapons-grade plutonium into a safe fuel for civilian nuclear power generation.

The Bureau of Reclamation, which is responsible for 475 dams and 337 reservoirs that supply water to 31 million people and 10 million acres of farmland, received $1.5 billion. The amount was $163 million or 12 percent more than fiscal 2017 and $372 million, or 34 percent more than the administration had requested. The funding included $34 million to implement the San Joaquin River Restoration program, $41 million for the Central Valley Project Restoration Fund in California, $37 million for the California Bay–Delta Ecosystem Restoration account, and $11 million to complete the Central Utah Project.

ENERGY RESEARCH

Congress cleared a trio of bills to spur nuclear research and better coordinate between federal facilities and private industry. One bill (HR 6227 PL 115-368) from House Science, Space, and Technology Chairman Lamar Smith, R-Texas, directed the president to establish a ten-year National Quantum Initiative Program to coordinate research by industry, academia, and federal labs. The bill called for a five-year strategic plan followed by an additional five-year plan. The bill authorized $400 million over five years for the National Institute of Standards and Technology for the program. The bill also authorized $250 million over five years for the National Science Foundation to carry out research and educational programs on quantum information science and engineering. And the bill authorized $625 million over five years for the Energy Department's office of science to carry out the program.

Smith's committee advanced the bill by voice vote June 27, 2018. The approval came after adopting an amendment by voice vote from Rep. Randy Hultgren, R-Ill., that expanded the responsibilities of the National Quantum Coordination Office. The House approved the bill by voice vote September 13, 2018.

The Senate Committee on Commerce, Science, and Transportation advanced the bill by voice vote December 13, 2018. The full Senate approved the bill by unanimous consent after agreeing to a substitute amendment from Sen. John Thune, R-S.D., by unanimous consent.

The House voted 348–11 to approve the Senate amendment December 19, 2018. Smith said the bill leveraged the expertise on quantum physics for the storage, transmission, computing, and measurement of information. President Donald Trump signed the bill December 21, 2018.

Another bill from Smith (HR 589 PL 115-246) sought to promote international and domestic cooperation on the research and development of clean, affordable, and reliable energy. The House approved the bill by voice vote January 24, 2017, as one of the first actions of the new Congress. The Senate Energy and Natural Resources Committee advanced the bill without amendment March 8, 2018. The Senate approved the bill by voice vote after adopting an amendment by unanimous consent from Sen. Lisa Murkowski, R-Alaska, to strike provisions relating to nuclear energy innovation capabilities.

The House approved the Senate amendment by voice vote September 13, 2018. Smith said the bill would enable the Energy Department to partner with private industry and cut red tape in the transfer of technology. Trump signed the bill September 28, 2018.

Another research bill (S 97 PL 115-115) from Sen. Mike Crapo, R-Idaho, authorized creation of the National Reactor Innovation Center aimed at strengthening construction and testing of experimental reactors. Crapo said the bill brought together the technical expertise of national laboratories, the Energy Department, and the Nuclear Regulatory Commission to partner with private industry to prove the principles behind their research.

The Energy and Natural Resources Committee advanced the bill without amendment March 30, 2017. The Senate approved the bill by voice vote March 7, 2018, after adopting a Crapo amendment by unanimous consent to modify provisions for the advanced nuclear energy licensing cost-share grant program. The House approved the bill by voice vote September 13, 2018, and Trump signed it September 28, 2018.

LIQUEFIED NATURAL GAS

Congress considered a couple of bills aimed at streamlining the review process for so-called small-scale liquefied natural gas exports, but neither measure cleared the Senate. The House bill (HR 4606), from Rep. Bill Johnson, R-Ohio, would have required the Energy Department to approve applications to export up to 140 million cubic feet per day of natural gas to any country so long as the request qualified for an exclusion under National Environmental Policy Act regulations. The provision was likely to aid the shipment of natural gas to the Caribbean and Central American countries that are not interested in larger shipments.

Johnson said it was important for the country to take advantage of its abundant energy source with large reserves and technological advancements, but Democrats criticized the legislation as harmful to the environment. Rep. Frank Pallone Jr., D-N.J., said the bill sounded suspiciously like an earmark for Houston-based Eagle LNG Partners Jacksonville LLC because the Congressional Research Service said that was the only company to qualify.

The House Energy and Commerce Subcommittee on Energy voted 19–14 along party lines to advance the bill without amendments April 18, 2018. The full committee voted 35–15 to advance the bill May 9, 2018. The approval came after the adoption by voice vote of a Johnson amendment to clarify that the exports would be consistent with

the public interest and if the approval did not require an environmental impact statement or assessment under the National Environmental Policy Act.

The House voted 260–146 to approve the measure September 6, 2018. The approval came after the rejection of a couple Democratic amendments.

A Pallone amendment to insert the phrase "opportunity for hearing and public input" was rejected on a vote of 176–227. An amendment from Rep. Diana DeGette, D-Colo., to require that exports were produced using techniques to minimize methane emissions from leaks or venting was rejected on a 195–210 vote.

The Senate Energy and Natural Resources Committee took no action on the House bill. The panel advanced a companion measure (S 1981), from Sen. Bill Cassidy, R-La., without amendment on March 8, 2018, but neither bill got a Senate floor vote.

SEA LIONS

The House approved legislation (HR 2083) that aimed to protect endangered salmon and steelhead in the Pacific Northwest by selectively removing sea lions from the Columbia River. The Senate Commerce, Science, and Transportation Committee took no action on the bill.

The House Natural Resources Committee voted 21–14 on July 26, 2018, to advance the bill from Rep. Jaime Herrera Beutler, R-Wash. She said the bill would significantly improve the chances for survival of fish swimming upstream because the overcrowded sea lion population was decimating fish runs.

The bill sought to amend the 1972 Marine Mammal Protection Act by authorizing the National Oceanic and Atmospheric Administration to issue one-year permits allowing Washington state, Oregon, Idaho, the Nez Perce Tribe, the Confederated Tribes of the Umatilla Indian Reservation, the Confederated Tribes of the Warm Springs Reservation of Oregon, the Confederated Tribes and Bands of the Yakama Nation, the Columbia Inter-Tribal Fish Commission, and the Cowlitz Indian Tribe to kill a combined 100 sea lions pear year.

The House voted 288–116 to approve the bill on June 26, 2018. The approval came after the adoption of a couple of Democratic amendments by voice vote.

The amendment from Rep. Derek Kilmer, D-Wash., would have limited the bill to sea lions rather than all pinnipeds such as seals. The proposal from Rep. Juan Vargas, D-Calif., would have required the Interior secretary to report on the lethal taking of California sea lions on salmon stocks.

REV. MARTIN LUTHER KING JR. MEMORIAL

Congress designated the final resting place of civil rights leader the Rev. Martin Luther King Jr. in Atlanta as a national historic park. The bill (HR 267 PL 115-108) from another civil rights leader, Rep. John Lewis, R-Ga., changed the designation of what had been a national historic site.

The bill also adjusted the boundary of the site to include the Prince Hall Masonic Temple, the first headquarters of the Southern Christian Leadership Conference. Rep. Anthony Brown, D-Md., said the legislation would enhance the National Park Service's ability to tell and elevate King's story.

The House approved the measure by voice vote under a suspension of the rules March 15, 2017. The Senate Energy and Natural Resources Committee advanced it without amendment on March 30, 2017. The Senate cleared the measure by voice vote December 21, 2017. President Donald Trump signed the bill into law January 8, 2018.

ROUTE 66

The House approved legislation (HR 801) to designate Route 66 as a national historic trail. The Senate Energy and Natural Resources Subcommittee on National Parks held a hearing but took no vote on the legislation.

The sponsor, Rep. Darin LaHood, R-Ill., said Route 66 was known as the Main Street of America for spanning eight states from Illinois to California. Route 66 will celebrate its 100th anniversary in 2026, he said. Recognizing the highway as a historic trail would allow the National Park Service to support state and local governments in preserving, promoting, and developing the road, he said.

The House Natural Resources Committee advanced the bill by unanimous consent January 10, 2018, with an amendment from LaHood that would have barred the Interior secretary from using eminent domain or condemnation to carry out the bill. The amendment also clarified that the bill would not hinder development, production, or transmission of energy. The full House approved the bill by voice vote June 5, 2018.

STRATEGIC PETROLEUM RESERVE

The House approved legislation (HR 6511) to authorize the Energy Department to lease underutilized facilities of the Strategic Petroleum Reserve to private entities. The sponsor, Rep. Joe Barton, R-Texas, authorized the Energy Department to conduct a pilot program to lease underutilized facilities by making available the capacity to store 200 million barrels of petroleum products. Current law allowed the department to lease the facilities only to foreign governments.

The House Energy and Commerce Subcommittee on Energy advanced the bill by voice vote with no amendments September 6, 2018. The full committee advanced the bill by voice vote September 13, 2018, after adopting a Barton amendment by voice vote to authorize the department to use funds in the Energy Security and Infrastructure Modernization Fund to upgrade equipment and land improvements. The House approved the bill by voice vote September 25, 2018. The Senate Energy and Natural Resources Subcommittee on Energy held a hearing on the bill but no vote.

WATER RESOURCES DEVELOPMENT ACT

Congress cleared a water infrastructure bill with $6.1 billion in federal spending for twelve new Army Corps of Engineers projects and three previously authorized projects. The Water Resources Development Act (S 3021 PL 115-270) also included $4.4 billion for the state drinking water revolving loan fund program, which provides federal financing for states and utilities to provide drinking water infrastructure.

The bill was the third water development act to be enacted in six years, representing a return to the two-year cycle that industry members and supporters in Congress favored to keep projects on track. Congress had approved only two WRDA bills in the previous thirteen years.

The ultimate bill resulted from senators and representatives negotiating a compromise based on versions from the Senate Environment and Public Works, House Transportation and Infrastructure, and House Energy and Commerce committees. Staffers compiled the bill from a pair of other measures (HR 8, S 2800) that received unanimous committee support, along with an Energy and Commerce bill (HR 3387) to expand state drinking water revolving loan funds.

The Transportation and Infrastructure Committee advanced its initial bill (HR 8) by voice vote May 23, 2018, after adoption of twenty amendments. The measure would have authorized seven projects totaling $2.5 billion.

The authorized projects are the

- Houston–Galveston Navigation Channel Extension in Texas, with an estimated federal cost of $10.2 million and total cost of $15.6 million
- Ala Wai Canal flood risk management project in Hawaii, with an estimated federal cost of $199.2 million and a total cost of $306.5 million
- Mamaroneck–Sheldrake Rivers flood control project in New York, with an estimated federal cost of $51.9 million and total cost of $79.9 million
- St. Johns County, Florida, hurricane and storm damage risk reduction project, with an estimated initial federal cost of $5.7 million and initial total cost of $24.8 million. The project includes $9.8 million in federal funding for beach replenishment out of a total cost of $53.6 million
- St. Lucie County, Florida, hurricane and storm damage risk reduction project, with an estimated initial federal cost of $7.1 million and initial total cost of $20.3 million. The project includes $8.9 million in federal funding for beach replenishment out of a total cost of $33 million
- Sabine Pass to Galveston Bay hurricane and storm damage risk reduction project in Texas, with an estimated federal cost of $2.16 billion and total cost of $3.32 billion

- Espanola Valley, Rio Grande flood risk management and ecosystem restoration project in New Mexico. The project has an estimated federal cost of $40.1 million and a total cost of $61.7 million

The bill also would increase the authorization for the Savannah Harbor Expansion project and authorize modifications to the Norfolk Harbor and Channels navigation project in Virginia.

Shuster's manager's amendment, which was adopted by voice vote, authorized a flood risk management and restoration effort for Espanola Valley in New Mexico. The amendment called the Army Corps of Engineers to expedite completion of change report for a navigation project at Sault Saint Marie, Michigan. The amendment also required the Corps to submit a list within eighteen months of hydropower generating dams that had the greatest potential for development. And the amendment allowed a non-federal entity in Yuba River Basin in California to build a new levee.

The committee voted 22–34 to reject an amendment from Rep. Rick Nolan, D-Minn., that would have created an EPA grant program to help municipal water treatment facilities meet mercury limits for the Lake Superior basin.

Rep. Brian Mast, R-Fla., proposed an amendment approved by voice vote requiring the Corps to start a five-year demonstration project to develop technology to manage and reduce harmful algal blooms. Rep. Cheri Bustos, D-Ill., proposed an amendment adopted by voice vote to add language specifying the operation of navigation facilities at Crops water resources projects is an "inherently governmental" function.

The committee adopted the following amendments by voice vote en bloc from the following lawmakers:

- Elizabeth Esty, D-Conn., to require the Army secretary to study Corps development of innovative materials for water resources projects
- Esty, to require a study of regularly rotating Corps district commanders
- Sam Graves, R-Mo., to require the Corps of Engineers to study within eighteen months the impact of construction of an interception-rearing complex on the Missouri River
- Brenda Lawrence, D-Mich., to require a Government Accountability Office report on the Corps workforce, including diversity, recruitment, retention, retirements, credentialing, professional development, on-the-job training, and other readiness-related gaps
- Daniel Lipinski, D-Ill., to require an online list of real property the Corps holds an interest in
- Lipinski, to require the corps to enter into a memorandum of understanding with the Environmental Protection Agency to facilitate restoration activities at the South Fork of the South Branch of the Chicago River

- Mast, to allow nonfederal sponsors of authorized water resources projects to volunteer to have a project deauthorized
- Mast, to clarify the corps must provide technical assistance to nonfederal entities seeking it
- Mast, to expedite completion of the Lake Okeechobee regulation schedule review
- Rick Nolan, D-Minn., to require the Corps to research the management and eradication of aquatic invasive species, including Asian carp and zebra mussels
- Stacey Plaskett, D-V.I., to require Corps activity undertaken in response to a major disaster in U.S. territories to be paid entirely by the federal government, unless the president finds that the territory has the ability to pay the usual cost-share
- David Rouzer, R-N.C, to allow for the extension of a fifteen-year beach nourishment period
- Mark Sanford, R-S.C., to require a study of the consideration by the Corps of natural features and nature-based features in evaluating the feasibility of projects for flood risk management, hurricane and storm damage reduction, and ecosystem restoration
- Frederica Wilson, D-Fla., to allow the corps to provide credits for construction completed by a nonfederal entity, in lieu of reimbursement
- Don Young, R-Alaska, to increase from $50 million to $62.5 million the annual authorization for work on small river and harbor improvements and to increase from $10 million to $12.5 million the limit for a single project under the program
- Young, to require a study updating a 2009 study of relocation efforts for Alaska Native villages due to flooding and erosion threats
- Young, to require a Corps study on the best options to expedite waivers of nonfederal cost sharing for storm damage prevention and reduction, coastal erosion, and ice and glacial damage projects in Alaska

Rep. Dina Titus, D-Nev., proposed an amendment rejected by voice vote that would have increased the authorization for the Lake Tahoe Basin Restoration in Nevada from $25 million to $50 million.

The House voted 408–2 to approve the bill June 6, 2018, after dealing with dozens of amendments on the floor.

The Senate Environment and Public Works Committee voted 21–0 to advance its version of the bill (S 2800) on May 22, 2018. The bill authorized six Corps projects totaling $2.43 billion, without the Espanola Valley project in the House version. The bill echoed the authorizations for Savannah Harbor and Norfolk Harbor.

The committee adopted amendments en bloc by voice vote from

- Tammy Duckworth, D-Ill., to make technical corrections to existing law about transferring existing credits for flood control projects from one nonfederal sponsor to another, if approved by the assistant secretary of the Army for civil works
- Dan Sullivan, R-Alaska, to change the bill's definition of a Native American tribal organization for the purpose of being recognized as a nonfederal sponsor on projects
- Edward J. Markey, D-Mass., to require the Environmental Protection Agency to appoint at least one employee in each regional office to serve as liaison to minority, tribal and low-income communities
- Sheldon Whitehouse, D-R.I., to require the Corps to submit a report identifying ongoing and recently completed projects in coastal states, analyzing how these projects correspond to state-approved coastal plans and to recommend how state plans can be better incorporated into the Corps work

The House Energy and Commerce advanced its drinking water bill (HR 3387) by voice vote July 27, 2018. The bill authorized $8 billion for EPA's drinking water state revolving fund, which provides loans and grants to help communities improve their drinking water systems.

The bill directed states to spend at least 6 percent of the funding in disadvantaged communities and established a $5 million per year grant program to help schools remove drinking water fountains with lead pipes. The bill required all steel used in the projects to come from United States manufacturers.

The committee adopted a manager's amendment by voice vote. The amendment required the EPA within three years to monitor unregulated contaminants in water systems serving 3,000 to 10,000 people and authorized $15 million per year for required monitoring. The amendment also authorized $35 million per year for grants to assess the risks of water systems serving 3,000 to 10,000 people.

The final approval of the combined Water Resources Development Act—after bipartisan, bicameral negotiations—became a race against a hurricane. Sens. John Barrasso, R-Wyo., and Thomas R. Carper, D-Del., said Hurricane Florence heading for the southeastern coast in September 2018 illustrated the need for the legislation, which authorized projects for storm mitigation, flood control, and $100 million for drinking water systems inundated with storm water.

Sen. Richard M. Burr, R-N.C., temporarily blocked the legislation because the Senate version had not included language permanently authorizing the Land and Water Conservation Fund. The provision was not included the final version of the bill.

The House amended a Senate courthouse-naming bill (S 3021) with the compromise language on water projects and approved the bill by voice vote September 13, 2018. Rep. Peter A. DeFazio, D-Ore., voiced disappointment that the bill did not include a provision to automatically spend revenues from the Harbor Maintenance Trust Fund. Congress typically appropriates less than the taxes collected on imports shipped to U.S. ports.

The Senate voted 99–1 to approve the House-amended version of the bill October 10, 2018. President Donald Trump signed it October 23, 2018.

Fiscal Year 2019 Interior and Environmental Appropriations

The appropriations process for fiscal 2019 got off to a productive start. Congress approved five measures enacted in two bunches (PL 115-244, PL 115-245), including Energy–Water, that represented a combined 75 percent of discretionary spending before the start of the fiscal year October 1, 2018. But then the process broken down over the seven remaining bills, including Interior and environmental programs. Lawmakers opposed President Donald Trump's $5.7 billion proposal for border-wall funding, which sparked the longest partial government shutdown in history, for thirty-five days in December and January.

On January 3, 2019, the House approved the Interior spending bill as part of a six-bill minibus (HR 648), which contained the results of conferences of individual bills negotiated the previous year, as Democrats put pressure on Republicans to resolve the partial shutdown. The House then passed four individual spending bills, including Interior (HR 266). It eventually became part of a year-long omnibus (H J Res 31—PL 116-6). The omnibus raced through both chambers on February 14, 2019, with a House vote of 300–128 and a Senate vote of 83–16. Trump signed the bill the next day.

The omnibus provided $35.6 billion in discretionary spending subject to budget caps, which was $300 million or 1 percent more than fiscal 2018 and $7.3 billion more than the administration's request. The bill rejected the administration's proposed 23 percent cut to EPA and slightly increased funding for the agency. The bill also prevented proposed cuts to other agencies, increasing funding by 1 percent for the National Park Service, the Bureau of Land Management, the U.S. Geological Survey, and for core, nonwildfire functions of the U.S. Forest Service. The bill also provided $3.95 billion for wildfire activities of the Forest Service and Interior Department, which was $500 million more than the ten-year average for such spending.

House Committee Action

The House Appropriations Committee voted 25–20 on June 6, 2018, to advance the spending bill for Interior and environmental programs for fiscal 2019. The $35.3 billion bill would have provided about the same funding as fiscal 2018 and $7 billion more than the administration's proposal.

The committee considered twenty-six amendments as Democrats used the markup to criticize the Interior Department's reorganization plan, changes in offshore oil leasing regulations and fourteen policy riders they argued would have undercut laws such as the Endangered Species Act. EPA Administrator's Scott Pruitt's spending, security and personnel issues dominated the markup, with Republicans blocking most Democratic amendments on those matters.

One amendment, from Rep. Marcy Kaptur, D-Ohio, to limit the amount EPA can spend on fountain pens to $50, was approved by voice vote after reports Pruitt ordered a $1,560 set of twelve fountain pens. Rep. Betty McCollum of Minnesota, the top Democrat on the Interior–Environment subcommittee, said if the agency's leadership does not have a moral compass, Congress would step in to protect taxpayers.

Rep. Mike Quigley, D-Ill., offered an amendment to require the EPA to publicly disclose the travel costs within ten days of a trip by the administrator or deputy administrator. The amendment failed on a 21–26, party-line vote.

Rep. Mark Pocan, D-Wis., proposed $12 million more for the EPA's inspector general office, to keep up with numerous investigations of Pruitt. The amendment also failed on a 21–26, party-line vote.

Republicans argued that Democratic requirements appeared politically motivated. Subcommittee Chairman Ken Calvert, R-Calif., said other cabinet-level officials did not have to report travel within ten days.

Republicans added eleven amendments to the bill. One amendment sought to prevent the introduction of grizzly bears in Washington state's North Cascade ecosystem. Another change set buy-American standards for steel in EPA projects. Another one sought to limit judicial review of California water projects. And one change reallocated revenue sharing from oil activities in the Arctic National Wildlife Refuge in Alaska.

The bill would have provided $13.1 billion for the Interior Department, a $300 million decrease from fiscal 2018. EPA would have received $8 billion, a $100 million decrease from the previous year. The White House proposed to allocate $10.7 billion for Interior and $6.1 billion for EPA. Office of Management and Budget Director Mick Mulvaney sent a May 21 letter taking issue with the topline figures and threatened administration opposition to the bill. But Appropriations Chairman Rodney Frelinghuysen, R-N.J., said the bill would protect communities and support economic development.

The House voted 217–199 on July 19, 2018, to send a combined spending bill for Interior and environmental programs, and Financial Services, to the Senate. The approval came after the chamber spent two days debating

eighty-seven amendments, including several dealing with climate regulations and wildlife.

Rep. Markwayne Mullin, R-Okla., attached two amendments to thwart Obama-era regulations governing greenhouse gas emissions. The House voted 215–194 to prevent EPA from regulating methane emissions from oil and natural gas facilities. The House voted 215–199 to prevent rulemakings from calculating the social cost of carbon.

The House voted 213–202 to approve an amendment from Rep. Doug Lamborn, R-Colo., to block Preble's meadow jumping mouse from being added to the endangered species list. Rep. Steve Pearce, D-N.M., added two amendments to limit funding for listing the New Mexico meadow jumping mouse and the lesser prairie chicken.

Democrats complained that fourteen policy riders already on the bill dealing with implementation of the Endangered Species Act, Clean Air Act, and Clean Water Act should be left to authorizing committees. Rep. Betty McCollum, D-Minn., said provisions like Lamborn's did not belong on an appropriations bill.

Senate Committee Action

The Senate Appropriations Committee voted 31–0 on June 14, 2018, to approve its version of a spending bill (S 3073) for Interior and environmental programs. The unanimity came with a manager's amendment with language critical of EPA Administrator Scott Pruitt. The lack of controversy was notable after appropriators did not even mark up a bill for fiscal 2018 and the fiscal 2017 bill split along party lines.

The bill provided $35.9 billion, a $600 million increase from fiscal 2018, including $13.1 billion for the Interior Department and $8.1 billion for EPA. The House bill would have held funding steady. Part of the reason for the unanimity was because the Senate version contained none of the policy riders that House Democrats had opposed in their version of the bill.

Sen. Tom Udall of New Mexico, the ranking Democrat on the committee, provided the language in the manager's amendment that demanded agency officials comply with ethics standards. The provision came after Pruitt was under fire for ethics and spending scandals. The provision appeared toothless, but Udall said it sent a strong message.

The rest of the manager's package dealt with local issues such as language from Sen. Marco Rubio, R-Fla., voicing concern about unhealthy coral reefs and a provision from Sen. Joe Manchin III, D-W.Va., asking EPA to consult state representatives about dealing with toxic water contamination in Minden.

The bill was considered as part of a four-bill package (HR 6147) on the Senate floor. The manager's package of forty-six amendments included a provision from Sen. Lisa Murkowski, R-Alaska, to require by July 1, 2019, revised fish-eating advice from EPA and the Food and Drug Administration. The Senate voted 92–6 on August 6 to approve the four-bill package.

Final Action

Because the legislation was not approved until February 15, 2019, and due to the partial government shutdown, agencies received continuing appropriations before that date under continuing resolutions (PL 115-141 and PL 115-245) at the fiscal 2018 level. The Interior Department had 76 percent of its staff furloughed, which left national parks ungated and museums closed. The EPA had saved funds for carryover purposes, which funded normal operations during the first week of the shutdown, but then had 98 percent of its staff furloughed, including those involved in enforcement activities and making state grants. After the thirty-five-day shutdown and in a new Congress, the bill (HR 266) largely remained the same as what the Senate had passed the previous year and had included in the House's six-bill minibus (HR 21) that served as a vehicle to reopen the government.

The measure provided $35.9 billion in discretionary spending, which was $300 million more than fiscal 2018 and $6 billion or 20 percent more than the administration had requested. The bill rejected a 43 percent proposed cut to EPA and kept funding for the agency at the fiscal 2018 level, while increasing funding for the Forest Service's non-wildfire functions, the National Park Service, and the Bureau of Land Management.

MAJOR PROVISIONS

Interior Department

The department received $13.2 billion in discretionary funding, a $56 million increase over fiscal 2018 and $2.6 billion or 24 percent more than requested.

Departmental funding included

- $3.2 billion for the National Park Service, a $16 million or 0.5 percent increase from fiscal 2018 and $517 million or 19 percent more than requested
- $3.1 billion for the Bureau of Indian Affairs operations, which was $13 million more than fiscal 2018 and $663 million or 27 percent more than requested
- $1.6 billion for the Fish and Wildlife Service, a $20 million or 1 percent cut from fiscal 2018, but $349 million or 28 percent more than requested
- $1.3 billion for the Bureau of Land Management operations, an $11 million or 1 percent increase from fiscal 2018 and $320 million or 31 percent more than requested

Environmental Protection Agency

The bill provided $8.8 billion for the Environmental Protection Agency, which was about level with fiscal 2018 and $2.6 billion more than the administration requested after accounting for $182 million in recissions. The measure provided $26 million for Brownfield activities. The bill continued funding for geographic programs including the Great Lakes Restoration Initiative, in addition to

similar programs for Puget Sound and Chesapeake Bay. A program for the Long Island Sound and Gulf of Mexico would receive increases under the measure, and it would also fund a new unrequested Columbia River Basin program at $1 million. The bill provided $1.1 billion for Superfund activities, which equaled fiscal 2018 and was $3 million more than requested.

Forest Service

The agency within the Agriculture Department received $6.3 billion, which was $364 million or 6 percent more than fiscal 2018 and $1.6 billion or 35 percent more than requested. The figure included $3.1 billion for core functions other than fighting wildfires, a $14 million increase from fiscal 2018 and $851 million or 38 percent more than requested.

Indian Health Service

The agency within the Department of Health and Human Services received $5.8 billion, a $234 million or 4 percent increase from fiscal 2018 and $348 million or 6 percent more than requested. The bill rejected the administration's proposal for a new $150 million special diabetes program.

Wildfires

The measure provided $4.3 billion for fighting wildfires on public lands, including $3.2 billion in Forest Service funding for fires on national forest lands and $1.1 billion in Interior Department funding for fires on Bureau of Land Management, National Park Service, and Fish and Wildlife Service lands. The combined figure totaled $900 million more than the ten-year funding average.

Fiscal Year 2019 Energy and Water Appropriations

The final Energy–Water appropriations measure for fiscal 2019 was part of a $147.5 billion, three-bill package (HR 5895) that also covered Military Construction–VA and the Legislative Branch. The Senate voted 92–5 on September 12, 2018, to approve the measure. The House cleared it with a vote of 377–20 the next day. President Donald Trump signed the bill (PL 115-244) September 21, 2018.

The measure marked the first time since fiscal 2000 that the Energy–Water portion of federal spending was enacted before the September 30 fiscal deadline. The final Energy–Water bill boosted nuclear weapons programs while rejecting energy research cuts the Trump administration had proposed. The bill was closer to the Senate version than the House version heavy with policy riders. Senate Energy–Water Appropriations Chairman Lamar Alexander, R-Tenn., said lawmakers did not deserve an award for passing a bill, but that it was the first time in nearly a decade and it was within the budget.

House Committee Action

The House Energy–Water Appropriations Subcommittee advanced its bill May 7, 2018, by voice vote and without votes on amendments, with the expectation that Democrats would propose changes in the full committee. Rep. Marcy Kaptur of Ohio, the ranking Democrat on the panel, said proposals would deal with spending on clean energy and attempt to remove policy riders.

The $44.7 billion draft for fiscal 2019 would have provided $1.5 billion more than the previous year (PL 115-141) and $8.2 billion more than the Trump administration had requested. The bill would have provided $35.5 billion for the Energy Department, up $1 billion from the previous year; $7.3 billion for the Army Corps of Engineers, up $500 million; and $1.6 billion for the Interior Department's Bureau of Reclamation, up $100 million.

The bill included contentious policy riders, including $268 million for the proposed Yucca Mountain nuclear waste repository in Nevada and a provision to ease the repeal of the Obama-era Waters of the United States regulation. The bill would have provided $325 million for the Advanced Research Projects Agency–Energy, a $28 million cut from the previous year, rather than eliminate it entirely as the administration had proposed.

Energy–Water Chairman Mike Simpson, R-Idaho, said the committee long supported developing scientific research and development, with a goal of technological advancements to enable more abundant energy.

The House Appropriations Committee voted 29–20 to advance the bill on May 16, 2018.

The bill would have provided $2.1 billion for the department's Office of Energy Efficiency and Renewable Energy, a $200 million cut from fiscal 2018, and the $28 million cut for ARPA–E. Rep. Matt Cartwright, D-Pa., proposed an amendment to restore funding for those amendments to fiscal 2018 enacted levels. The committee rejected the proposal on a 21–28 vote.

Kaptur proposed an amendment to strike eight policy riders including making it easier to repeal the Waters of the United States regulation and prohibiting additional spills of dams on the Columbia and Snake rivers. The committee rejected the proposal on a 19–30 vote.

Simpson's manager's amendment was adopted by voice vote and was the only successful amendment. The measure included a provision directing the Energy secretary to report to Congress on the potential benefits of a nuclear waste repository in Nevada. The amendment also directed the Energy secretary to report on the cost and schedule to produce a new, low-yield nuclear weapon.

The full House voted 235–179 to approve the three-bill package June 8, 2018.

Senate Committee Action

The Senate Appropriations Committee voted 30–1 to advance its version of the Energy–Water bill on May 24, 2018. The draft bill would have provided $43.8 billion, a

$566 million increase from fiscal 2018 and $7.2 billion more than requested.

The committee considered four amendments to the bill and approved two. One was the manager's amendment. The other, from Sen. Joe Manchin, D-W.Va., sought to expand federal agency participation for moving the Appalachian Regional Commission's headquarters. The debate sparked a lengthy discussion of how to dispose of thirty-four metric tons of weapons-grade plutonium and develop new, low-yield nuclear weapons.

Sen. Lindsey Graham, R-S.C., proposed and withdrew an amendment to prevent the Energy Department from abandoning the MOX facility in South Carolina to convert weapons-grade plutonium into fuel for nuclear power plants. Graham complained that the country would drop the project that was 70 percent complete after signing a 2000 disarmament deal with the Russians.

Sen. Lamar Alexander, R-Tenn., said an Energy Department strategy to dilute and dispose of plutonium in a repository in southeastern New Mexico would have saved $30 billion. The approach was supported by both the Trump and Obama administrations. But Sen. Tom Udall, D-N.M., opposed the strategy because of safety concerns.

Democrats also voiced concerns about funding a low-yield weapon—the W76 warhead—as part of the recommendations from the Trump administration's Nuclear Posture Review. Sen. Dianne Feinstein, D-Calif., said the only purpose for the weapon would be to fight a nuclear war, which she said should frighten everyone. Sen. Jeff Merkley, D-Ore., proposed an amendment to redirect $65 million for the weapon to the department's nonproliferation account. The committee rejected the proposal on a 12–19 vote.

The full Senate voted 86–5 on June 25, 2018, to send the three-bill package to conference.

The approval came after a 62–34 vote to reject an amendment from Sen. Mike Lee, R-Utah, that sought to void the Waters of the United States rule. Twenty Republicans voted to kill Lee's amendment, despite some of them supporting it, to remove a contentious provision from appropriations so the bills could move more quickly.

On the contentious subject of Yucca Mountain, the Senate chose to fund a pilot interim storage program to consolidate waste from nuclear reactors in a temporary facility. The House voted 340–72 earlier in the year on a bill (HR 3053) that would have enabled both programs to go forward, a possible sign of compromise.

MINIBUS HIGHLIGHTS

The bill included $44.6 billion for the Energy–Water title, a $1.4 billion or 3.5 percent increase from the previous year (PL 115-141) and $8.1 billion or 22 percent more than the administration had requested. That figure provided $22.4 billion for defense-related activities, which was $600 million more than fiscal 2018, and $22.4 billion, an increase of $800 million, for nondefense activities.

The Energy Department received $35.7 billion, a $1.2 billion or 3 percent increase from fiscal 2018 and $5.5 billion or 18 percent more than requested. The $11.1 billion for nuclear weapons activities represented a 4 percent increase from the previous year and included $1.9 billion for nuclear nonproliferation programs, a 3 percent decline. The $6 billion for defense environmental cleanup activities was $36 million more than had been allocated the previous year. The allocation included $6.6 billion for science activities, which was 5 percent more than fiscal 2018 and 22 percent more than requested. It also included $1.3 billion for nuclear energy activities, a 10 percent increase from fiscal 2018 and 75 percent more than requested.

The Advanced Research Projects Agency–Energy, which the Trump administration proposed to eliminate, received $366 million, an increase from $353 million in fiscal 2018. The Army Corps of Engineers received $7 billion, a $172 million or 2.5 percent increase from fiscal 2018 and $2.2 billion or 46 percent more than requested. The Bureau of Reclamation within the Interior Department received $1.6 billion, a 6 percent increase from fiscal 2018 and 48 percent more than requested.

The measure removed any funding to revive the contentious nuclear waste site at Yucca Mountain in Nevada. The state's lawmakers, including GOP Sen. Dean Heller and Democratic Rep. Jacky Rosen, firmly opposed the waste site as they were locked in a tight race for Heller's seat. The House had included $268 million to restart a license application review for the project.

Policy riders included in the House version that were ultimately removed included

- Enabling firearms on Army Corps of Engineers lands
- Preventing the enactment of the Obama-era National Ocean Policy
- Preventing the Bureau of Reclamation to purchase water as outlined in the San Joaquin River Restoration settlement
- Exempting discharges of dredged or fill material from environmental review
- Preventing the use of the social cost of carbon in Energy Department considerations

2019–2020

Bipartisan agreements became more difficult to achieve in the 116th Congress, as Democrats regained control of the House. House Democrats pushed back against the Trump administration's proposals for more coastal drilling and argued for resolutions to curb climate change through the unsuccessful Green New Deal. Senate Majority Leader Mitch McConnell, R-Ky., called for a Senate vote to demonstrate its lack of majority support for the Green New Deal.

Talks also reached an impasse when lawmakers of both parties supported legislation, such as to reauthorize the National Flood Insurance Program.

Lawmakers found common ground on legislation for water projects and conservation for land and animals. They also found consensus on creating national museums for women and Latin Americans.

Land and Water Conservation Fund

Congress cleared a package early in 2019 to protect millions of acres of federal lands and to permanently reauthorize the Land and Water Conservation Fund, despite a last-minute hiccup the previous year.

The measure (S 47 PL 116-9), which resulted from months of negotiations and compromises, included sweeping protections for federal lands, the creation of four national monuments, and 1.3 million acres of federal wilderness designations. The monuments—three to be administered by the National Park Service and one by the Forest Service—totaled 1,750 acres, according to a congressional summary. The wilderness areas were in California, Utah, Oregon and New Mexico, resulting from locally driven proposals.

Sen. Lisa Murkowski, R-Alaska, said her legislation incorporated 100 bills dealing with pent-up demand from the lack of movement on public lands bills since 2014. "It is a substantive bill. There is no doubt about it," Murkowski said February 11, 2019, on the Senate floor. "It is substantive because of the many, many different, discrete, small provisions that have been incorporated into it."

The centerpiece of the legislation was the Land and Water Conservation Fund, which helps pay for federal land acquisition and lapsed in September 2018. Sen. Mike Lee, R-Utah, railed against the permanent authorization of the fund and fought unsuccessfully for an amendment to exempt Utah from federal land acquisitions and new national monument designations. "This bill perpetuates a terrible standard for federal land policy in the West, particularly for the state of Utah," Lee said February 11, 2019, on the Senate floor. "Utahns, and Americans, deserve better than the stranglehold that the Federal Government is exercising over so much of our country's lands."

The Senate tabled Lee's amendment on a 60–33 vote February 11, 2019. Sen. Joe Manchin III of West Virginia, the ranking Democrat on the Energy and Natural Resources Committee, called Lee's proposal a poison pill that could have blown up the legislation after months of negotiations. The Senate voted 92–8 to approve the bill on February 12, 2019.

The House voted 363–62 to approve the bill without amendment on February 26, 2019. Natural Resources Chairman Raul M. Grijalva, D-Ariz., had assured senators he would take up the bill if it were passed without significant changes. He called the bill one of the biggest bipartisan wins for the country during his time in Congress.

One of the bill's provisions dealt with the Arbuckle Project Maintenance Complex in Murray County, Oklahoma. The bill conveyed 2.83 acres, a small house, and the conservancy district's headquarters to the local office. Rep. Tom Cole, R-Okla., had tried since 2015 through bills that passed the House twice to convey the property that provided flood control, municipal water supply, and recreational water activities. President Donald Trump signed the bill March 12, 2019.

Paris Accord

As part of House Democrats' agenda to deal with climate change, they voted to oppose President Donald Trump's withdrawal from the Paris Climate Accord. The Senate, however, took no action.

Trump had announced June 1, 2017, that the United States would withdraw from the Paris Climate Accord, after foreign leaders failed to persuade him to stay in the agreement during a meeting of the world's seven largest economies, but he could not begin the withdrawal until November 2020. Republicans controlled both chambers of Congress, blunting meaningful opposition to the move.

The Obama administration had negotiated participation in the agreement in 2015 and it had gone into effect in November 2016, as countries agreed to cut their carbon emissions to slow the pace of global warming. The administration agreed to cut 26 percent to 28 percent of the country's emissions by 2025, compared to 2005 emissions.

Rep. Tim Ryan, D-Ohio, argued the United States should be more ambitious than the Paris goals because the threat from climate change was too great. Rep. Andy Barr, R-Ky., argued against the bill and said a thousand more pages in the Federal Register would not change the weather.

The House Energy and Commerce Committee voted 29–19 on April 4, 2019, to advance legislation (HR 9) to deny funding for Trump to withdraw. The Foreign Affairs Committee voted 24–16 on April 9, 2019, to follow suit.

The House voted 231–190 to approve the measure May 2, 2019. Democrats were joined by three Republicans in the 231–190 vote: Reps. Brian Fitzpatrick of Pennsylvania, Elise Stefanik of New York, and Vern Buchanan of Florida.

The House spent two days disposing of amendments to the bill. The chamber voted 189–234 to reject an amendment from Rep. Paul Gosar, R-Ariz., to remove the provision that would bar funding for the withdrawal. Rep. Adriano Espaillat, D-N.Y., proposed an amendment saying the Paris deal urges nations to agree to what he called climate justice, which was approved on a 237–185 vote. Rep. T.J. Cox, D-Calif., proposed an amendment to require the federal plan to cut emissions to consider employment, technology and energy costs, which was approved on a 259–166 vote.

Most Republicans opposed the measure and said it would put the United States at a disadvantage against large carbon emitters such as China and India. Rep. Andy Barr, R-Ky., said the United States should export so-called clean coal to address climate change.

The Senate did not vote on the measure. Senate Majority Leader Mitch McConnell, R-Ky., called the effort futile and argued it would handcuff the U.S. economy.

Drilling Bills

The House approved three bills in September 2019 to hinder President Donald Trump's drilling agenda, but the Senate Energy and Natural Resources Committee took action on none of them.

The legislation came with the memory of the 2010 BP oil spill in the Gulf of Mexico. The Deepwater Horizon explosion killed eleven people and spilled nearly 4 million barrels of oil into the Gulf.

Rep. Francis Rooney, R-Fla., proposed a bill (HR 205) to permanently ban oil and gas leasing in eastern areas of the Gulf off the Florida coast. The measure would have amended and made permanent a provision in a 2006 law (PL 109-432) that placed a moratorium on drilling in that area that was set to expire in June 2022.

The House Natural Resources Committee voted 24–12 to advance the bill June 19, 2019. Rep. Garret Graves, R-La., called the bill flawed and offered eight amendments. One, which would have specified the moratorium would not apply unless the secretary of the Department of the Interior confirmed it would not hurt national security through the reduction in federal revenues, was rejected on a 14–22 vote.

The House voted 248–180 to approve the bill September 11, 2019. The approval came after Rep. Paul Gosar, R-Ariz., proposed an amendment to prevent the bill from going into effect until the Interior and Labor departments certified the offshore energy moratorium would not eliminate a substantial number of jobs for minorities and women. The proposal was rejected on a 182–251 vote.

The second bill (HR 1941) was from Rep. Joe Cunningham, D-S.C., who proposed that would have permanently banned oil and gas leasing off the Pacific and Atlantic coasts. He said beaches, businesses, and a way of life should not be for sale.

Trump proposed adding those areas to its offshore leasing plan, as it seeks to expand the country's energy production. The plans met resistance from coastal lawmakers and governors from both parties, who feared damage from drilling to tourism and seafood industries.

The House Natural Resources Committee voted 22–12 to advance the bill June 19, 2019. Rep. Tom McClintock, R-Calif., proposed an amendment to strike the Pacific region from the bill, which failed on a 14–22 vote. Rep. Rob Bishop of Utah, the ranking Republican on the panel, proposed an amendment to make states adjacent to the planning areas ineligible for revenue from Outer Continental Shelf oil and gas leasing, including the Land and Water Conservation Fund. The committee rejected the proposal on a 14–22 vote.

The House voted 238–189 to approve the bill Sept. 11, 2019. Gosar proposed two amendments the House rejected. One would have changed the title to the "Russian Energy Reliance and U.S. Poverty Act," which was rejected on a 161–272 vote. The other repeated his jobs language, which was rejected on a 179–252 vote.

The third bill (HR 1146) was from Rep. Jared Huffman, D-Calif., who proposed to prevent the administration from opening the Arctic National Wildlife Refuge in Alaska to oil and gas drilling. The House Natural Resources Committee voted 22–14 to advance the bill May 1, 2019.

The House voted 225–193 to approve the bill Sept. 12, 2019, after rejecting three GOP amendments. Rep. Don Young, R-Alaska, proposed an amendment to stop blocking the oil and gas program until Alaska natives who live closest to the coastal plain were thoroughly consulted. The House rejected the amendment on a 193–230 vote. Gosar proposed his jobs amendment again, which was rejected on a vote of 184–237. Gosar's other amendment would have blocked the legislation until the Interior Department and U.S. Fish and Wildlife Service certified the bill would not harm caribou herds, which lost on a 187–237 vote.

Western Land Conservation

The House approved two bills to protect land in Arizona and New Mexico, but neither measure was acted upon in the Senate Energy and Natural Resources Committee. One bill (HR 1373) sought to prevent mining or mineral leasing on 1 million acres of federal land near the Grand Canyon, with a goal of preventing pollution of nearby land. Rep. Raul M. Grijalva, D-Ariz., said a uranium mine in the Kaibab National Forest a few miles from the south rim of the canyon opened in 1986 with assurances that its operations would not harm the groundwater. But he said 20 million gallons of groundwater polluted

with uranium and arsenic have come out after the mine pierced an aquifer in 2016.

"The situation is so dire that the mine operator regularly resorts to spraying this uranium-contaminated water into the air to speed evaporation," Grijalva said October 30, 2019, on the House floor. "On windy days, this spray has been known to travel off the site and into the surrounding areas and environment. Meanwhile, the mine shaft continues to fill with contaminated water."

The House Natural Resources Committee voted 21–14 to advance the bill July 17, 2019.

The approval came after a series of Gosar amendment proposals were defeated on 14–20 votes. Gosar proposed a substitute amendment to prohibit the bill from taking effect until the Interior secretary determined it would not hurt national security. He proposed to exclude Arizona's Fourth Congressional District from the bill. He also proposed to prohibit the bill from taking effect until the United States imported less than 30 percent of its uranium from hostile countries such as Russia. He proposed to change the title of the bill to the "Enhancing Soviet and Chinese Uranium Dominance Act." Further, he proposed to prohibit the bill from taking effect until the Interior secretary completed a mineral survey to determine there were no mineral resources in the area other than uranium.

Rep. Liz Cheney, R-Wyo., proposed an amendment to prohibit the bill from taking effect until the Interior secretary determined it would not hurt jobs available to Native Americans, other minorities, and women. The proposal was rejected on a 15–19 vote.

The House voted 236–185 to approve the bill October 30, 2019. The approval came after the rejection of three Gosar amendments. His jobs proposal that Cheney sponsored in committee was rejected again on a 185–240 vote. His proposal about the Fourth Congressional District was rejected on a 178–243 vote. And his proposal about the mineral survey was rejected on a 186–237 vote.

The other bill (HR 2181), from Rep. Ben Ray Lujan, D-N.M., sought to prevent mining on public lands within the Chaco Cultural Heritage Withdrawal Area. Rep. Deb Haaland, D-N.M., said the measure would protect the Chaco Culture National Historical Park from the impact of oil and gas extraction. The bill drew a ten-mile boundary around the park to protect its resources, she said. "As a 35th generation New Mexican and a descendant of the indigenous inhabitants of what is now the Southwest United States, I can say that there are few places more exceptional than the Chaco region," Haaland said October 30, 2019, on the House floor.

Republicans opposed the measure, noting its potential impact on revenue and jobs in the energy industry. Rep. Doug Lamborn, R-Colo., said the four counties surrounding the land produce $200 million in oil and gas revenues.

The House Natural Resources Committee voted 19–14 to advance the bill July 17, 2019. The approval came after the committee rejected a pair of Gosar amendments on 14–19 votes.

Gosar proposed an amendment that would delay the bill's effect until the Interior secretary determined it would not hurt development in the area or the economic value of mineral rights held by Native Americans in the area. He also proposed to limit the area covered by the bill to a six-mile radius around the existing Chaco Culture National Historic Park, which was rejected on a 14–19 vote.

The House voted 245–174 to approve the bill October 30, 2019. The approval came after the rejection of three GOP amendments. Gosar proposed to allow the exchange of federal land within the withdrawal area to a state trust or Indian tribe, which was rejected on a 191–233 vote. Gosar also proposed his economic value amendment again, which failed on a 181–243 vote. Rep. Jodey C. Arrington, R-Texas, proposed to allow oil and gas development if operators had previously worked in accordance with the Historic Preservation Act and regulations for archeological sites such as the Chaco Canyon Historical Park. The proposal was rejected on a 181–245 vote.

Clean Power Act

Senate Democrats in 2019 fell short in an effort to nullify an executive order by Donald Trump scrapping the Obama administration's Clean Power Plan. Trump, who had campaigned against climate change efforts such as the Paris Accord and in favor of coal-industry jobs, signed the executive order in March 2017. Former President Barack Obama's signature climate policy aimed to reduce greenhouse gas emissions from coal-fired power plants. Trump argued that federal regulations hurt the coal mining industry and his goal was to bring back those jobs. Trump's sweeping order rolled back a moratorium on new coal leases on public lands and a requirement that federal agencies consider climate change when adopting new rules. The order rescinded six Obama-era executive orders that instructed the government to prepare for the impact of climate change and outline the growing threat to national security that climate change posed.

Environmental groups criticized the move, saying it would surrender American leadership in dealing with climate change while leading to more emissions and deaths. Dan Lashof, United States director of the World Resources Institute, said in a statement August 21, 2018, that "Trump's dirty power plan" would represent "backward thinking that will lead to more pollution, more health problems, higher bills and less security."

The Clean Power Plan had placed the first caps on carbon emissions from power plants nationwide. Under the rule, states were to begin reducing greenhouse gas emissions from existing power plants by 2022 and cut emissions by 2030 by 32 percent from 2005 levels. But officials in twenty-seven states argued the plan usurped states' rights and would have killed jobs. A lawsuit from states blocked the regulation at the Supreme Court in February 2016.

Trump announced his executive order with Vice President Mike Pence, Interior Secretary Ryan Zinke, Energy Secretary Rick Perry, and EPA Administrator Scott Pruitt. "We have a very, very impressive group here to celebrate the start of a new era in American energy and production and job creation," Trump said at the Environmental Protection Agency on March 28, 2017. "The action I'm taking will eliminate federal overreach, restore economic freedom and allow our companies and our workers to thrive, compete and succeed on a level playing field for the first time in a long time."

The Senate voted October 17, 2019, on a resolution (S J Res 53) from Sen. Ben Cardin, D-Md., to nullify the EPA's rule, but it failed 41–53. The measure had been discharged from the Environment and Public Works Committee by unanimous consent.

Fiscal Year 2020 Interior and Environmental Appropriations

Congress and the White House agreed to a $1.4 trillion fiscal 2020 spending deal in December 2019 that continued to provide healthy increases for the Interior and Energy departments despite steep cuts proposed by Trump. Congress had approved funding for Interior and environmental programs as part of an eight-bill, $540 billion package (HR 1865 PL 116-94) of discretionary funding for fiscal 2020. A companion measure (HR 1158 PL 116-93) covered the other four appropriations bills in the closing days of the year. The approvals came after a bipartisan agreement (PL 116-37) in July to raise defense and nondefense discretionary spending caps for fiscal 2020 and 2021. Bipartisan cooperation on the spending measures contrasted sharply with the partisan divide over the House impeachment of President Donald Trump on charges he obstructed Congress and abused the power of his office in his dealings with Ukraine.

The House voted 297–120 to approve the eight-bill package on December 17, 2019. The Senate voted 71–23 to clear it on December 19, 2019. President Donald Trump signed it into law on December 20, 2019.

The bill provided $36 billion for Interior and environmental programs, $437 million more than fiscal 2019 and $5.8 billion more than the administration had requested. The agreement rejected the administration's proposed 23 percent cut to EPA and instead increased funding by $208 million to $9.1 billion. The bill also rejected proposed cuts to the National Park Service, Bureau of Land Management, U.S. Geological Survey, and U.S. Fish and Wildlife Service.

House Committee Action

The House Appropriations Interior–Environmental Subcommittee advanced its draft bill by voice vote May 15, 2019. The draft bill would have provided $39.5 billion, an increase of 10.9 percent from fiscal 2019.

The bill would have provided the Interior Department with $13.8 billion and the EPA with $9.5 billion. The draft bill's 8.1 percent hike for EPA in the Democratic-controlled House came in contrast to the Republican administration's proposal to cut agency funding by nearly a third, to $6.1 billion. The measure would have provided $5.2 billion for wildland fire management and $6.3 billion for the Indian Health Service. The draft bill also added $18 million for research and regulatory work on per- and polyfluoroalkyl substances, or PFAS, known as "forever chemicals." The measure included a provision that would have made it difficult for the White House to open up more of the nation's waters for oil and gas exploration. The provision prohibited the Department of the Interior from using funds for leading related activities until a five-year plan was finalized.

Subcommittee Chair Betty McCollum, D-Minn., said the legislation represented a shift in priorities to invest in public lands, the environment, and communities ignored in the past. Rep. Kay Granger of Texas, the ranking Republican on the full committee, said the exclusion of riders common to past bills dealing with hunting ammunition, wildlife conservation, and regulatory relief for farmers would make the legislation harder to approve.

The House Appropriations Committee voted 31–20 to advance the bill on May 22, 2019. The approval came despite complaints from Republicans that the bill would help balloon the federal debt and hurt fossil fuel developers and hunters.

The subcommittee's ranking Republican, Rep. David Joyce of Ohio, proposed an amendment to reduce funding for EPA's enforcement program. The committee rejected the proposal on a 22–30, party-line vote.

Senate Committee Action

The Senate Appropriations subcommittee advanced its version of the bill (S 2580) by voice vote September 24, 2019. The bill would have provided $35.8 billion, a $248 million increase from fiscal 2019. The National Park Service would have received $3.4 billion, an increase of $133 million, as it grappled with an $11 billion maintenance backlog. The bill would have provided $20 million for PFAS. The bill would have provided $13.7 billion for the Interior Department, $9 billion for EPA, $7.5 billion for the U.S. Forest Service, and $6 billion for the Indian Health Service.

Subcommittee Chairman Lisa Murkowski, R-Alaska, said the bill rejected unwarranted decreases in funding sought by the Trump administration. She and ranking Democratic Sen. Tom Udall of New Mexico said they did their best to limit contentious riders and to take into consideration priorities from members of both parties.

The Senate Appropriations Committee voted 31–0 to advance the bill without changes on September 26, 2019.

Final Action

As lawmakers sought to complete spending bills for the fiscal year, the Senate voted 84–9 on October 31, 2019, to approve a four-bill package of spending bills including Interior and environmental programs. Significant disputes remained between the chambers about top-line spending figures, despite the July budget agreement. The Senate's four-bill package allocated $5 billion less than the comparable House measures.

The Senate approval came after the chamber rejected a proposed amendment from Sen. Mike Lee, R-Utah, that would have prevented the federal government from acquiring new public lands with Land and Water Conservation Fund dollars until after a $19.4 billion maintenance backlog was cleared. The Senate rejected the proposal on a 29–64 vote. Lee had argued that the pattern of neglect would leave treasures for no one. But Udall, the subcommittee's ranking Democrat, said the amendment would have undermined the conservation fund.

The two massive appropriations packages were resolved in a rush as the clock ticked down toward the end of the year, as legislative leaders and White House officials negotiated spending disputes and tax extensions. The final bill provided $36 billion for Interior and environmental programs, a $437 million increase from fiscal 2019 and $5.83 billion more than requested from the Trump administration.

MAJOR PROVISIONS

Interior Department

The department received $13.5 billion in discretionary funding, which was $545 million more than fiscal 2019 and $2.1 billion or 19 percent more than the administration's request. The bill provided $62 million in mandatory funding and $300 million in adjustments to budget caps, leaving overall department funding at $13.9 billion.

The bill provided

- $3.4 billion for the National Park Service, a $155 million increase from fiscal 2019 and $636 million more than requested
- $3.2 billion for the Bureau of Indian Affairs and Bureau of Indian Education, a $149 million increase from fiscal 2019 and $449 million more than requested
- $1.6 billion for the U.S. Fish and Wildlife Service, which was $66 million more than the previous year
- $1.4 billion for the Bureau of Land Management, a $24 million increase from the previous year and $182 million more than requested

Environmental Protection Agency

The Environmental Protection Agency received $9.1 billion, a $208 million increase from fiscal 2019 and $2.8 billion or 46 percent more than requested. The funding included $2.7 billion for environmental programs and management accounts. The $4.3 billion in state and tribal assistance grants included $2.8 billion for Clean Water and Drinking Water State Revolving Funds and $89 million for Brownfield cleanups. The bill provided $1.8 billion for Superfund, a $25 million increase from fiscal 2019 and $139 more than requested.

The measure prohibited EPA from issuing a rule requiring the reporting of greenhouse gas emissions from manure management systems, blocked EPA from imposing reporting requirements regarding greenhouse gas emissions, and prohibited EPA from using funds to regulate lead content in ammunition or fishing tackle under the Toxic Substances Control Act (PL 94-469).

Indian Health Service

The service, which is part of the Department of Health and Human Services, received $6 billion, a $243 million increase from fiscal 2019. The total included $4.3 billion for health services, a $212 million increase from the previous year, and $912 million for health facilities, a $33 million increase.

Wildfires

The bill provided $5.6 billion for wildland firefighting under the Forest Service within the Department of Agriculture and the Interior Department. The total was $1.6 billion more than fiscal 2019. The total included $1.4 billion in base fire suppression funding and $2.3 billion in additional funding under the cap adjustment. Of the cap adjustment, $2 billion was from the Agriculture Department's Forest Service and $300 million from the Interior Department.

Despite Democratic opposition, the final bill included frequent GOP environmental riders. Appropriators in the Democratic-led House had not included the provisions, but they were included in the version from the Republican-led Senate. The policy provisions included

- Restrictions on listing the greater sage grouse as an endangered species
- Treating emissions from burning forest biomass as carbon neutral, to avoid limits on greenhouse gas emissions
- Prohibiting regulation of lead in certain types of ammunition and fishing tackle
- Restricting regulations from small incinerators in Alaska
- Prohibiting the government from regulating some greenhouse gases in the livestock industry, such as from manure management systems

The bill also set aside $43 million in new funding to address so-called forever chemicals, per- and polyfluoroalkyl substances or PFAS. Part of the provision aimed to establish drinking water and land cleanup standards.

Fiscal Year 2020 Energy and Water Appropriations

Congress approved funding for Energy–Water programs as part of an eight-bill, $540 billion package

(HR 1865 PL 116-94) of discretionary funding for fiscal 2020. A companion measure (HR 1158 PL 116-93) covered the other four appropriations bills in the closing days of the year. The agreements came after a bipartisan agreement (PL 116-37) in July to raise defense and nondefense discretionary spending caps for fiscal 2020 and 2021. Bipartisan cooperation on the spending measures contrasted sharply with the partisan divide over the House impeachment of President Donald Trump on charges he obstructed Congress and abused the power of his office in his dealings with Ukraine.

The House voted 297–120 to approve the eight-bill package on December 17, 2019. The Senate voted 71–23 to clear it on December 19, 2019. President Donald Trump signed it into law the December 20, 2019.

The Energy–Water title provided $48.3 billion in discretionary funding, which was $3.7 billion or 8 percent more than fiscal 2019 and $10.3 billion or 27 percent more than the Trump administration had requested. The funding included $24.3 billion for defense-related activities, $1 billion more than the previous year, and $24.1 billion for nondefense activities, an increase of $1.9 billion.

The Energy Department received $38.6 billion, which was $2.9 billion or 8 percent more than fiscal 2019 and $7.1 billion or 22 percent more than requested. Nearly half of the funding ($16.7 billion) was for nuclear weapons activities under the National Nuclear Security Administration, and another $6.3 billion was for continued environmental cleanup of defense facilities where nuclear weapons activities were conducted. The bill provided $7.5 billion for environmental cleanup for nondefense programs.

The bill rejected the administration's proposal to eliminate funding for the Advanced Research Projects Agency–Energy and provided $425 million, which was $59 million or 16 percent more than fiscal 2019.

The bill provided $2.8 billion for energy efficiency and renewable energy, which was $411 million or 17 percent more than fiscal 2019 and $2.4 billion more than requested. The bill provided $750 million for research and development of fossil fuels, $10 million more than the previous year and $188 million or 33 percent more than requested.

The Army Corps of Engineers received $7.7 billion, $652 million or 9 percent more than fiscal 2019 and $2.7 billion or 54 percent more than requested. The funding included $3.8 billion for operations and maintenance, $51 million more than the previous year, and $2.7 billion for construction projects, $500 million more than the previous year.

The Bureau of Reclamation, an Interior Department agency, received $1.7 billion, which was $110 million or 7 percent more than fiscal 2019 and $550 million or 50 percent more than requested. More than $1.5 billion of the funding was for the development, construction, management, and restoration of water resources. The bill included $55 million for the Central Valley Project Restoration

Fund, which was $7 million less than in fiscal 2019. The bill contained no funding for the proposed Yucca Mountain Waste Repository in Nevada nor any funding for interim storage of spent nuclear fuel.

House Committee Action

The House Appropriations Energy–Water Subcommittee advanced its draft bill by voice vote May 15, 2019. The bill would have provided $46.6 billion, a $1.8 billion or 4 percent increase from fiscal 2019. The Energy Department would have received $37.1 billion, or $1.4 billion more than the previous year under the bill rather than the $31.7 billion, or 12 percent cut, the Trump administration had proposed.

The Army Corps of Engineers could have received $7.36 billion, an increase of $357 million or 5 percent from fiscal 2019 and about $2.53 billion or 52 percent more than the administration had requested. The bill would have also provided $130 million for the Nuclear Regulatory Commission, $170 million for the Appalachian Regional Commission, and $22 million for the Northern Border Regional Commission. Subcommittee Chairman Marcy Kaptur, D-Ohio, said the bill would make critical investments to combat climate change and strengthen the country's energy and water infrastructure. Rep. Mike Simpson of Idaho, the ranking Republican on the panel, said there were many good things in the bill, but that he was disappointed it did not provide a path to licensing a nuclear waste repository at Yucca Mountain in Nevada.

The House Appropriations Committee voted 31–20 to advance the bill May 21, 2019. The approval, which made the bill one of the first appropriations measures to reach the House floor, came after the panel rejected Republican amendments to send money to a California dam project and to license Yucca Mountain as a nuclear waste repository.

The bill would have provided $46.4 billion for fiscal 2020, a $1.8 billion increase from fiscal 2019. The Energy Department would have received $37.1 billion, a $1.4 billion increase and 17 percent more than the administration had requested. The bill would have provided $7.36 billion for the Army Corps of Engineers, a 5 percent increase from fiscal 2019 and $2.53 billion or 52 percent more than the administration had requested. The Bureau of Reclamation would have received $1.65 billion, or $83 million more than the previous year.

Lawmakers offered five amendments, two of which were contentious. The ranking Republican on the subcommittee, Rep. Mike Simpson of Idaho, aimed to start the licensing process for Yucca Mountain. He said forty-eight of the committee's fifty-three members had nuclear waste in their states. But Subcommittee Chairman Marcy Kaptur, D-Ohio, said the change would divert funding from energy efficiency and renewable energy programs. The committee rejected the amendment on a 25–27 vote largely along party lines. Democratic Reps. Cheri Bustos of Illinois, Derek Kilmer of Washington, and Peter J. Visclosky of

Indiana voted for the provision. Rep. Mark Amodei, R-Nev., voted against it.

Rep. Ken Calvert, R-Calif., proposed an amendment to include federal funding for the Shasta Dam and Reservoir Enlargement Project in his state. The committee rejected the amendment on a 22–30 vote. Kaptur proposed an amendment to boost Everglades restoration funding from $63 million, the amount requested by the administration, to $200 million. The committee adopted the amendment by voice vote. Another amendment adopted by voice vote was from Rep. Dan Newhouse, R-Wash., to make small adjustments in funding for the Richland river corridor and the Richland community and regulatory support.

The full House agreed to consider the Energy–Water bill (HR 2960) as part of a four-bill package (HR 2740) totaling $985 billion. The House voted 226–203 on June 20, 2019, to approve the package, but the bill was considered doomed in the Republican-led Senate and White House for provisions overturning the administration's restrictions on access to abortions and blocking funds for a border wall.

Senate Committee Action

The Senate Appropriations Committee voted 31–0 on September 12, 2019, to advance its bill (S 2470). The bill would have provided $48.9 billion for Energy–Water spending, a $4.2 billion increase from fiscal 2019 and $10.8 billion more than the administration had requested. The unanimous vote was a rebuke to the White House, which sought to cut funding. Sen. Richard Shelby, R-Ala., said the legislation supports national priorities such as science and research, nuclear security, and critical infrastructure.

The Energy Department would have received $39 billion under the bill, $7.3 billion more than the administration had requested. The Army Corps of Engineers would have received $7.75 billion, or $2.9 billion more than requested. And the Bureau of Reclamation would have received $1.73 billion, or $63 million more than requested.

Despite the House omitting a provision for Yucca Mountain, the Senate bill sought to establish a pilot program for consolidated nuclear waste storage supported by Sens. Lamar Alexander, R-Tenn., and Dianne Feinstein, D-Calif. The program would have permitted the Energy Department to store nuclear waste at private facilities with approval from the Nuclear Regulatory Commission.

In another provision, the White House had moved to sell the Southeastern Power Administration, the Southwestern Power Administration, and the Western Area Power Administration, which function as federal utilities. The committee rejected the divestment and provided no funds to sell transmission assets. The bill would have provided $428 million to the Advanced Research Projects Agency–Energy, an increase of $62 million, despite the administration proposing to terminate it.

Final Action

As lawmakers struggled to complete spending bills for the fiscal year and extend tax legislation—and as the House moved to impeach President Donald Trump—the Energy–Water appropriations bill was folded into an eight-bill package that raced through both chambers in a few days. The House voted 297–120 to approve the eight-bill package on December 17, 2019. The Senate voted 71–23 to clear it on December 19, 2019. President Donald Trump signed it into law on December 20, 2019.

PFAS

A bipartisan bill won House approval early in 2020 to embark on a nationwide cleanup of widely used "forever" chemicals that persist in the environment and human body, but what was eventually included in legislation approved in the Senate left advocates disappointed.

Rep. Debbie Dingell, D-Mich., proposed legislation (HR 535) directing the Environmental Protection Agency within a year to designate per- and polyfluoroalkyl chemicals, or PFAS, as hazardous substances under the law (PL 96-510) that created federal Superfund sites. Rep. Larry Bucshon, R-Ind., warned that medical products such as catheter tubes use PFAS, so he urged caution in taking an all-or-nothing approach.

The chemicals are common in nonstick cookware, food packaging, furniture, carpeting, and military firefighting foam. The chemicals have been linked to numerous health problems, including cancers, thyroid disease, neurological development issues and reproductive problems.

The House Energy and Commerce Subcommittee on the Environment and Climate Change advanced the bill to the full committee by voice vote September 26, 2019.

The full committee voted 31–19 to advance the bill November 20, 2019. The panel voted 21–29 to reject an amendment from Rep. John Shimkus, R-Ill., that would have required the EPA administrator to come up with a drinking water standard for perfluorooctanoic acid (PFOA) and perfluorooctane sulfonic acid (PFOS). The proposal would have also directed EPA to require drinking water systems to monitor for unregulated PFAS, while preventing enforcement against the systems for five years.

The panel adopted an amendment by voice vote from Rep. Paul Tonko, D-N.Y., to require EPA to establish a maximum contaminant level for PFAS in drinking water, create a list of treatment technologies to remove detectable amounts of PFAS in drinking water, create a "safer choice" label for pots, pans and utensils that do not contain PFAS, and issue guidance for firefighters to minimize their exposure to PFAS.

The House voted 247–159 to approve the bill January 10, 2020, with twenty-four Republicans joining 223 Democrats. The approval came despite most Republicans arguing the bill was packed with bad policy and unworkable regulation. GOP lawmakers said it could stigmatize

communities designated as Superfund sites because of the chemicals.

An amendment adopted by voice vote from Rep. Antonio Delgado, D-N.Y., aimed to make it illegal for industrial operators to introduce PFAS into a sewage treatment system without first publicly disclosing information about the chemicals. Rep. Michael C. Burgess, R-Texas, proposed an amendment to delete a section from the bill that would require the EPA to clean up contaminated sites under the Superfund program. The proposal was rejected on a 161–247 vote.

Rep. Troy Balderson, R-Ohio, proposed an amendment that aimed to prevent the bill from taking effect until the EPA completed its own PFAS action plan. The proposal was rejected on a 170–239 vote.

The White House threatened to veto the bill if it passed the Republican-controlled Senate. The Senate Environment and Public Works Committee did not act on the House bill. A companion bill (S 638) from the panel's ranking Democrat, Sen. Thomas R. Carper of Delaware, was not marked up, but the conference report for the fiscal 2021 National Defense Authorization Act (HR 6395 PL 116-283) included some provisions to reduce forever chemicals. The defense legislation stopped short of wholesale cleanup efforts under the Superfund program; however, it ended Defense Department procurement of certain home goods, such as cookware and carpets. The legislation also speeded up plans to phase out a firefighting spray called aqueous film-forming foam, which features PFAS chemicals. The bill provided $15 million for the Centers for Disease Control and Prevention to study PFAS. More than 700 military bases were likely contaminated with PFAS, according to the Environmental Working Group.

PULSE NIGHTCLUB

The House approved legislation (HR 3094) to establish the National Pulse Memorial at the nightclub where forty-nine people were killed and fifty-three others injured in a 2016 shooting in Orlando, Florida.

Rep. Darren Soto, D-Fla., called the attack June 12, 2016, the single deadliest on the LGBTQ community at that time. He said the community came together after the attack with works of art, gifts and letters, and in candlelight vigils across the globe to grieve and remember. "The designation of the Pulse nightclub as a national memorial honors the lives taken, as well as the survivors, first responders, and an entire central Florida community," Soto said June 26, 2020, on the House floor. "Together, we will open minds and hearts and make the Pulse Memorial a national symbol of hope, love, and change."

The House Natural Resources Committee advanced the bill by voice vote March 11, 2020. The bill specified the memorial would not be part of the National Park Service and therefore would not be eligible for federal funds. The approval came after Chairman Raul M. Grijalva, D-Ariz., proposed an amendment adopted by voice vote that made

technical changes. The House approved the bill without amendment by voice vote June 26, 2020.

The Senate Energy and Natural Resources Committee took no action on the measure. Rep. Tom McClintock, R-Calif., said the House measure complemented a Senate resolution (S Res 246) from Sen. Rick Scott, R-Fla., that honored victims of the attack and the state of Florida's designation of June 12 as Pulse Remembrance Day. The Senate approved the resolution by voice vote June 12, 2020, the anniversary of the shooting. McClintock said a nonprofit called the onePULSE Foundation was created to memorialize those who had died. As a memorial, the designation would not require federal funds, he said.

LAND AND WATER CONSERVATION FUND

The Land and Water Conservation Fund received permanent funding, under a bill Congress cleared in July 2020. The bill (HR 1957 PL 116-152) permanently funded a federal pool of money raised largely from fees and royalties on offshore oil and gas drilling, with $900 million annually. It also allocated $9.5 billion over five years for the Interior Department to clear some of its backlog of maintenance, including at National Park Service sites. With rare bipartisan backing for environmental legislation, the bill directed money to five federal agencies: the Bureau of Land Management, the Bureau of Indian Education, the Forest Service, the National Park Service, and the U.S. Fish and Wildlife Service.

Within the backlog fund, the legislation allocated 70 percent to NPS projects and 15 percent to the Forest Service. States can apply for grants for outdoor recreation projects, such as parks, refuges, and other public lands. Interior Secretary David Bernhardt praised the legislation for funding maintenance at national parks and funding conservation projects.

Rep. Joe Cunningham, D-S.C., introduced the original bill (HR 7092), but House panels never voted on that measure. Instead, the Senate filled a House-passed tax bill (HR 1957) as a vehicle for land conservation legislation (S 3422) from Sen. Cory Gardner, R-Colo., which also was not marked up in committee.

Gulf Coast Republicans and opponents of federal land acquisition opposed the measure. The legislation was important for Gardner and Sen. Steve Daines, R-Mont., who faced competitive reelection campaigns and promoted the bill as a bipartisan benefit for their constituents. The Senate voted 73–25 to approve the compromise June 17, 2020, after two weeks of debate and no substantive amendments.

The House voted 310–107 to clear the bill July 22, 2020. More than eighty Republicans joined nearly every Democrat in supporting the bill. GOP Reps. Rob Bishop of Utah and Garret Graves of Louisiana led the opposition, noting that money flows into the fund from royalties on oil and gas drilling that were dropping during the COVID-19 pandemic because of a drop in oil prices. Rep. Raul

M. Grijalva, D-Ariz., said the bill enjoyed overwhelming bipartisan support. President Donald Trump signed the bill August 4, 2020.

CLIMATE CHANGE LEGISLATION

The House approved a climate-focused package of energy bills in September 2020 aimed at reauthorizing an Energy Department research program and allocating hundreds of millions of dollars for renewable energy programs, but the White House threatened to veto the bill and Republicans argued it would raise electricity costs and delay permitting for new energy projects. The Senate Energy and Natural Resources Committee took no action on it. The package (HR 4447) of thirty-eight bills included a long list of measures to combat climate change. The House Energy and Commerce Committee advanced by voice vote the initial bill from Rep. Tom O'Halleran, D-Ariz., on September 9, 2020. The bill aimed to establish an energy storage and technical assistance program. An O'Halleran amendment adopted by voice vote authorized $5 million per year for the Energy secretary to carry out the program.

The Rules Committee voted 7–3 on September 21, 2020, to modify the legislation into a thirty-eight-bill package for floor debate. The package would have authorized Energy Department programs including $1.6 billion for solar power, $815 million for hydropower, $671 million for advanced geothermal power, and $603 million for wind power.

The Advanced Research Projects Agency–Energy, a popular program the Trump administration sought to eliminate, would have been reauthorized through fiscal 2025 with a total of $3.3 billion. The package also would have authorized $250 million over a decade for energy-efficient building standards and $6 million for a new homeowner rebate program.

GOP Reps. John Shimkus of Illinois and Randy Weber of Texas estimated the nearly 900-page bill's price tag to be at least $135 billion. The White House issued a veto threat by opposing portions including a goal of cutting emissions of hydrofluorocarbons, or HFCs, which are potent greenhouse gases in refrigerants, aerosols, and heating-and-air-conditioning units.

The House voted 220–185 to approve the bill September 24, 2020. The approval came after adopting thirty-seven amendments in a series of votes. One from Rep. Josh Harder, D-Calif., directed the Energy Department to map wildfire risks for utilities. One from Rep. Alan Lowenthal, D-Calif., directed the Interior Department to create a public database of greenhouse emissions from federal lands. One from Rep. Deb Haaland, D-N.M., boosted funding for efficiency and renewable energy by 50 percent annually through fiscal 2025. The division received $2.8 billion, so Haaland's authorization could have pushed it above $5 billion. Democrats called it a down payment on a national agenda to address climate change, combined with a May

2019 vote (HR 9) to block President Donald Trump's withdrawal from the Paris Accord and the July 2020 passage of an infrastructure bill (HR 2).

NATIONAL FLOOD INSURANCE PROGRAM

The National Flood Insurance Program staggered through years of short-term extensions, as lawmakers were unable to agree on changes that would make it financially solvent and still affordable for homeowners.

The program (PL 90-448) was created in 1968 after private insurances increasingly left out flood insurance from homeowners' policies. The program run by the Federal Emergency Management Agency supports more than 5 million policies totaling $1.3 trillion in coverage, according to a 2020 report by the Congressional Research Service. A lapse in the program could disrupt the housing market because home buyers are required to buy flood insurance for mortgages in high-risk areas.

Lawmakers disagreed about how to overhaul the program, which has not kept pace with escalating costs, as more frequent and severe storms have hit the country. The program struggled to remain solvent since Hurricane Katrina hit New Orleans in 2005 and Superstorm Sandy, in 2012. With about $3.5 billion in annual premiums, FEMA paid more than $8 billion for claims from Hurricane Harvey and $1 billion for claims from Hurricane Irma.

The challenge for lawmakers is to keep the program affordable for homeowners while also balancing the books. As of August 2020, the program owed $20.5 billion even though Congress canceled $16 billion of debt in October 2017. Congress approved sixteen short-term extensions from 2017 through 2020 as lawmakers debated how to overhaul the program.

To shore up support, Republican leaders removed provisions opposed by lawmakers in flood-prone districts along the Gulf Coast, the Mississippi River, and the Eastern Seaboard who worried about the costs of higher premiums. Most Democrats also opposed the bill because of concerns over costs, which one lawmaker called draconian.

Insurance industry groups such as the American Insurance Association and the Property Casualty Insurers Association of America praised the short-term extensions of the program because of concerns about a lapse while lawmakers negotiated a long-term solution. The House approved a five-year bill (HR 2874) during the 115th Congress, but it went nowhere in the Senate. The Senate also did not act on any of its three reauthorization bills (S 1313, S 1368 or S 1571).

The House Financial Services Committee voted 30–26 to advance the bill (HR 2874) from Rep. Sean P. Duffy, R-Wis., on June 15, 2017. Every Democrat and Rep. Peter T. King, R-N.Y., voted against it. Duffy, the chairman of the Housing and Insurance Subcommittee, said the program's debt was evidence the status quo did not make sense. His legislation aimed to cap annual rate increases at 15 percent, down from 18 percent.

Duffy's manager's amendment, which was approved by voice vote, would have authorized the program for five years at $225 million per year for flood mitigation. The proposal would have required property sellers requiring flood insurance to notify any buyer about the hazard and any designation as a "repetitive loss" or "severe repetitive loss." The proposal would have allowed the federal program to provide coverage for a 10 percent surcharge if the buyer was unable to get private insurance and was otherwise prohibited from having a federal policy.

The committee adopted by voice vote an amendment from Rep. Gwen Moore, D-Wis., that would have allowed the Federal Emergency Management Agency administrator to create a community-based insurance pilot program. Rep. Claudia Tenney, R-N.Y., proposed an amendment to give the FEMA administrator 120 days to approve or deny a claim beginning when the claimant submits a signed proof of loss. The panel voted 31–25 to adopt the amendment.

The panel voted 26–29 to reject an amendment from Rep. Denny Heck, D-Wash., that would have struck language prohibiting the program from covering newly built structures in flood hazard zones.

The committee voted 26–30 to reject an amendment from Rep. Charlie Crist, D-Fla., that would have struck language to raise the minimum annual increase in premiums from 5 percent to 8 percent and struck a provision to increase the annual surcharge from $25 to $40.

Rep. Maxine Waters, D-Calif., proposed a substitute amendment with language from a Senate bill (S 1368) to reauthorize the program for six years, cap rate hikes at 10 percent, increase policy coverage from $250,000 to $500,000, authorize $800 million per year for advanced mapping methods, and freeze interest on the program's $24.6 billion in debt. The committee voted 25–31 to reject the amendment. The House voted 237–189 to approve the bill without amendment on November 14, 2017.

The Senate Banking, Housing, and Urban Affairs Committee took no action on it. The committee also took no action on the bill (S 1368) from Sen. Bob Menendez, D-N.J.; another bill (S 1313) from Sen. Bill Cassidy, R-La.; or another (S 1571) from Sen. Mike Crapo, R-Idaho.

WETLANDS CONSERVATION

Congress cleared legislation (S 3051 PL 116-188) in October 2020 to boost protection for wetlands, livestock, fish, waterfowl, and the Chesapeake Bay. Led by Sens. John Barrasso, R-Wyo., and Thomas R. Carper, D-Del., the bill authorized $60 million annually for fiscal years 2021 through 2025 for the 1989 North American Wetlands Conservation Act (PL 111-149) spanning the United States, Canada, and Mexico. In addition, it authorized $90 million for fiscal years 2020 through 2024 for the Chesapeake Bay Program. The bill also established a Chronic Wasting Disease Task Force at the U.S. Fish and Wildlife Service to deal with the illness in elk, deer, and

other animals. The bill also included provisions to help farmers protect livestock from predators and provide grants to states and Native American tribes to compensate livestock producers for losses due to federally protected species such as wolves and grizzly bears.

Barrasso called it the most significant wildlife conservation and sportsmen's legislation in decades.

The Senate Environment and Public Works Committee advanced the bill by voice vote December 17, 2019. The approval came after the committee adopted a series of amendments en bloc by voice vote.

An amendment from Barrasso and Carper clarified the funding for the chronic wasting disease study was subject to appropriations. The amendment from Sen. Jeff Merkley, D-Ore., added factors to successful conservation efforts under the Endangered Species Act to include determinations about putting animals on the list or changing their status from threatened to endangered. The amendment from Sen. Ben Cardin, D-Md., authorized the Chesapeake Bay Program at $90 million for fiscal 2020 and an additional $500,000 per year for five years.

The full Senate approved the bill by voice vote September 16, 2020. The House approved the bill by voice vote October 1, 2020. President Donald Trump signed it into law October 30, 2020.

ROBERT E. LEE STATUE

The House voted in December 2020 to remove a statue of Confederate Gen. Robert E. Lee from the Antietam battlefield in Maryland, but the Senate Energy and Natural Resources Committee took no action in the waning days of the session. The bill (HR 970) from Rep. Anthony G. Brown, D-Md., sought to remove the twenty-four-foot statue dedicated in 2003 on private ground that the National Park Service acquired two years later. He said the statue encouraged open rebellion against the United States and did nothing to teach about the dark lessons of history.

"As our nation continues to wrestle and reckon with racial inequality and injustice, it is past time that we take stock of these symbols that we display and the stories that we tell about our past, present, and future," Rep. Jared Huffman, D-Calif., said December 10, 2020, on the House floor.

The House Natural Resources Committee advanced the bill by voice vote September 30, 2020. The approval came after adopting by voice vote a Brown amendment to delay the deadline for the National Park Service to develop a plan for removing the statue from ninety days to 180 days. The House approved the bill by voice vote without amendment December 10, 2020.

WATER RESOURCES DEVELOPMENT ACT

Congress cleared another two-year bill for water projects in December 2020 that freed up $2 billion per year over five years for dredging harbors. The Water Resources Development Act included the dredging provision to

spend down roughly $10 billion in the Harbor Maintenance Trust Fund. The fund accumulated from fees from shipping cargo owners, which increased in 1990 from 0.04 percent to 0.125 percent of the value of cargo carried. The American Association of Port Authorities said the money would help address a significant backlog of maintenance needs.

This bill also authorized funding for Army Corps of Engineers projects for navigation, flood risk management, and ecosystem restoration. The bill established various pilot programs to address issues including flood risk management and hurricane and storm damage risk reduction in rural or economically disadvantaged communities.

After the House (HR 7575) and Senate (S 1811) each passed their own versions of the legislation, the eventual compromise hitched a ride on an omnibus spending bill (HR 133). President Donald Trump signed the measure December 27, 2020.

House action

The House Transportation and Infrastructure Committee advanced by voice vote its version (HR 7575) from Chairman Peter A. DeFazio, D-Ore. The bill would have authorized thirty-four Army Corps of Engineers projects, changed the federal cost share for inland waterway projects, and released $10 billion unspent in the Harbor Maintenance Trust Fund.

The committee voted 2–62 to reject an amendment from Rep. Scott Perry, R-Pa., that would have struck the harbor fund language and continued to hold the excess dollars. Perry argued the money should not be spent because of the country's dire fiscal situation, but DeFazio said not spending the money meant diverting it to other functions through appropriations.

DeFazio's manager's amendment, which was adopted by voice vote, added language dealing with flood risk management and storm damage risk reduction. The amendment directed the Army secretary to address harmful algae blooms in coastal and tidal waters of Louisiana and waterways of the Sacramento–San Joaquin Delta. The amendment amended the 1941 flood control law to allow the secretary to reimburse nonfederal sponsors for emergency response repair and restoration work.

Parochial issues in the amendment included a storm damage reduction project in Boston under a 2013 law (PL 113-2); a flood risk management project in Lower Cache Creek, California; a shoreline protection project in Oceanside, California; a coastal storm management project in Upper Barataria Basin, Louisianna; a replacement project for Bourne and Sagamore bridges in Cape Cod, Massachusetts; a flood risk management project in Rahway River Basin, New Jersey; a silting project in Port of Bandon in Oregon; and a storm damage risk reduction project in Bolongo Bay in the U.S. Virgin Islands.

Rep. John Garamendi, D-Calif., proposed an amendment that was adopted by voice vote to strike a provision from the 2014 water resources development law (PL 113-121) to terminate in-kind contributions from nonfederal project meeting the requirements of another project. Rep. Brian Mast, R-Fla., proposed an amendment that was rejected by voice vote to require the Army secretary to modify water infrastructure management in Central and Southern Florida. Rep. Stephen F. Lynch, D-Mass., proposed an amendment adopted by voice vote to amend the 1992 water resources development law (PL 102-580) to direct the Army secretary to expedite dredging of the Portsmouth navigation project in New Hampshire as a source of beach fill for Nantasket Beach in Hull, Massachusetts.

Rep. Abby Finkenauer, D-Iowa, proposed an amendment adopted by voice vote to direct the Army secretary to review policies for nonfederal entities developing contracts for local utilities.

The committee adopted an amendment from Perry by unanimous consent to require steel in Corps projects to be furnished and delivered in the United States. Rep. Brian Babin, R-Texas, proposed an amendment adopted by voice vote to modify a storm damage provision in the 1962 flood control law (PL 87-874) to reduce the risk of flooding in Port Arthur and Orange County, Texas. Rep. Garret Graves, R-La., proposed an amendment adopted by voice vote to direct the Army secretary to modify the 2010 Calcasieu River and Pass Dredged Material Management Plan. Rep. Gary Palmer, R-Ala., proposed an amendment adopted by voice vote to require the Army secretary to report on its outstanding studies with expected completion dates under the 2014 water resources development law (PL 113-121). The House approved the bill without amendment by voice vote July 29, 2020.

Final action

The Senate Environment and Public Works Committee advanced its version (S 1811) from Sen. John Barrasso, R-Wyo., by unanimous consent July 10, 2020. The full Senate approved the bill the same day by voice vote. The House passed a conferenced version of the bill (S 1811) by voice vote December 8, 2020. The compromise included a provision to free up $2 billion from the harbor maintenance fund for each of the five years of the bill, to spend down the roughly $10 billion.

URANIUM RESERVE

Appropriators set aside $75 million in the fiscal 2021 Energy–Water spending bill (HR 133 PL 116-260) to establish a national uranium reserve. President Donald Trump had proposed $150 million for the program and Senate appropriators unveiled a bill with $120 million, but the eventual compromise cut the administration request in half. Sen. John Barrasso, R-Wyo., had vocally supported creation of a bill (S 4897) to create the reserve. He said it would prevent the United States from being dependent on rival countries for nuclear fuel.

The Senate Environment and Public Works Committee voted 16–5 to advance his bill December 2, 2020. The bill would have required the Energy Department to report on the historical costs to store, manage, and dispose of spent nuclear fuel and high-level radioactive waste. The bill also would have authorized $100 million to clean up abandoned mine sites on tribal land and block uranium mined in the United States by companies that the Russian or Chinese governments control. The bill did not advance further, with the issue instead being taken up by appropriators.

WOMEN'S AND LATINO HISTORY

The Smithsonian Institution plans to establish a women's history museum and a Latino museum, as part of an omnibus spending package (HR 133 PL 116-260) Congress cleared in December 2020. Each bill—(HR 1980) from Rep. Carolyn B. Maloney, D-N.Y., and (HR 2420) from Rep. Jose E. Serrano, D-N.Y. —called for the Smithsonian Institution council to make recommendations to the Smithsonian's Board of Regents on the planning, design, and construction of each museum. Rep. Zoe Lofgren, D-Calif., said the women's museum could recount the contributions, accomplishments, and sacrifices of women including the Daughters of Liberty who helped spark the American Revolution, Harriet Tubman and the Underground Railroad before the Civil War, Susan B. Anthony and the fight for suffrage, and 6.5 million women who entered the labor force during World War II.

"However, these and countless other accomplishments by women notwithstanding, historical accounts, monuments, and museums disproportionately represent the achievements of men while neglecting those of women," Lofgren said February 11, 2020, on the House floor. "Furthermore, studies have shown that history textbooks discuss the accomplishments of men exponentially more often than those of women. This should change."

The House Administration Committee advanced by voice vote the Maloney bill November 12, 2019. The approval came after Rep. Mark Walker, R-N.C., proposed an amendment to direct the council to ensure diversity in political viewpoints when planning the content of the museum, which was adopted by voice vote. The House voted 347–37 to approve the bill without amendment February 11, 2020.

Rep. Tony Cardenas, D-Calif., said the country has more than 58 million reasons for a National Museum of the American Latino because they were largely excluded from history books. Cardenas said people deserve to learn the truth about Latinos. "We must teach our entire history, the beautiful, the glorious, and the horrors and the injustices," Cardenas said July 27, 2020, on the House floor. "Our story is the story of the United States of America. If we truly want to build a country that works for everyone, we must start by including everyone. We owe it to ourselves and our children to learn about Latino history in America."

The House approved the bill by voice vote July 27, 2020, although the House Administration, Natural Resources and Transportation and Infrastructure committees had not acted on it.

The Senate Rules and Administration Committee advanced the bill along with a companion measure for the women's history museum (S 959), from Sen. Susan Collins, R-Maine, by voice vote without amendment December 3, 2020.

CHEMICAL FACILITY SECURITY

Congress cleared a bill (HR 251 PL 116-2) in January 2019 that extended a chemical-security program for fifteen months so that a longer reauthorization could be negotiated. Under the Chemical Facility Anti-Terrorism Standards Program, security and industry stakeholders work together to identify high-risk facilities and ensure appropriate security measures.

Homeland Security Chairman Bennie Thompson, D-Miss., said a two-year extension would have been better, but that the program was set to expire the night of the final House vote January 17, 2019. He noted that the program aimed to stop catastrophes such as an explosion at a fertilizer plant in West, Texas, in April 2013 that killed a dozen first responders. "In short, allowing the program to sunset would make our communities less safe," Thompson said January 17, 2019, on the House floor. The House voted 414–3 to approve the bill January 8, 2019, with a two-year extension.

The Senate approved the bill by unanimous consent January 16, 2019, after adopting an amendment by unanimous consent from Sen. Ron Johnson, R-Wis., to have a fifteen-month extension. The House approved the change by voice vote January 17, 2019, and President Donald Trump signed the measure the next day.

Fiscal Year 2021 Interior and Environmental Appropriations

The House voted 327–85 to approve an omnibus spending bill (HR 133-PL 116-260) on December 21, 2020. The Senate cleared it 92–6 the same day. President Donald Trump signed the bill December 27, 2020.

The bill provided billions more than the administration requested, with $13.7 billion for the Interior Department and $9.2 billion for the Environmental Protection Agency. The bill added $2.35 billion for fighting wildfires after a year of large fires, bringing the total for Wildland Fire Management to $5.3 billion.

The bill blocked protecting the greater sage grouse under the Endangered Species Act. And the final bill dropped provisions to remove Confederate monuments from National Park Service sites, provisions that had been included in early House versions of the legislation. The bill also allocated $900 million to Land and Water Conservation Fund programs, which was required under a public lands bill (PL 116-152) approved earlier.

House Committee Action

The House Appropriations Subcommittee for Interior–Environment advanced its $36.8 billion draft bill (HR 7612) by voice vote July 7, 2020. The approval came despite Republican concerns about the level of discretionary spending and policy riders including a provision to remove Confederate symbols from National Park Service locations. For the first time in forty years, the bill treated funding for the Land and Water Conservation Fund as mandatory. The addition brought total funding in the bill to $54.1 billion.

The total included $5.73 billion to fight wildfires and $15 billion in emergency supplemental appropriations for critical infrastructure. The ranking Republican on the full committee, Rep. Kay Granger of Texas, criticized the spending as a departure from infrastructure priorities, but Subcommittee Chairman Betty McCollum, D-Minn., said the bill rejected dangerous policies and funding cuts proposed by the Trump administration.

The bill would have provided the Interior Department with $13.8 billion, an increase of $304 million from fiscal 2020 and $1.8 billion more than the administration requested. The total included $3.2 billion for the National Park Service; $1.6 billion for the Fish and Wildlife Service; and $1.3 billion for the Bureau of Land Management, including $72 million for sage grouse conservation.

EPA would have received $9.4 billion under the bill, a $318 million or 3.3 percent increase from fiscal 2020 and $2.67 billion more than the administration requested. The funding included $3.58 billion for core science and environmental programs, an increase of $210 million from fiscal 2020 and $822 million more than the administration requested. The total also included $555 million, an increase of $46 million from the previous year and $224 million more than requested, for geographic programs such as restoration of the Great Lakes, Chesapeake Bay, and Long Island Sound. The bill included $575 million for enforcement activities, an increase of $46 million from the previous year and $59 million more than requested. In addition, the bill included $12.9 million for work on per- and polyfluoroalkyl substances (PFAS) known as forever chemicals. Appropriations Chairman Nita M. Lowey, D-N.Y., said EPA's geographic programs protect the health of the American public.

The bill would have provided $3.5 billion for the Bureau of Indian Affairs, an increase of $188 million from the previous year and $562 million more than requested. And the bill would have provided $6.5 billion for the Indian Health Service in the Department of Health and Human Services, an increase of $445 million from fiscal 2020 and $199 million more than requested. McCollum said tribal communities were suffering disproportionately under the COVID-19 pandemic and that the funding would invest in the health, safety, and welfare of Indian Country.

The bill would have provided $4.36 billion for state and trial assistance grants, an increase of $119 million from fiscal 2020 and $1.52 billion more than requested.

Democrats included two provisions dealing with Confederate icons. One directed the National Park Service to remove all confederate commemorative works, and the other would have prohibited the service from displaying the Confederate flag except in special circumstances with historical context.

The bill also sought to prohibit authorizing oil and gas leasing on the Outer Continental Shelf that had not been scheduled before November 2016. Rep. David Joyce of Ohio, the ranking Republican on the subcommittee, criticized the bill for curbing energy development.

The bill also sought to deny funding for oil or gas leases within the Chaco Culture National Historic Park; for permits to import a sport-hunted trophy of an elephant or lion taken in Tanzania, Zimbabwe or Zambia; planning or constructing a forest development road in Tongass National Forest to harvest timber; and to approve a mine plan proposed within the Rainy River Watershed of Superior National Forest.

The full committee voted 30–19 to advance the $36.8 billion bill on July 10, 2020. The bill advanced with a party-line vote despite Republican criticism of policy riders. Rep. David Joyce of Ohio, the ranking Republican on the subcommittee, argued the partisan provisions aimed to stop the administration's efforts to cut red tape and took a step back on conventional energy development. Subcommittee Chairman Betty McCollum, D-Minn., said the bill rejected dangerous policies and funding cuts of the Trump administration while proposing new investments in environmental protection and land conservation.

Joyce proposed an amendment to increase to $6.7 billion from $1.2 billion the Bureau of Land Management's Energy and Minerals program for oil, gas, and coal management. The committee voted 19–30 to reject the proposal. Rep. Dan Newhouse, R-Wash., proposed an amendment to strike a prohibition against oil and gas leasing in Alaska's Coastal Plain, as authorized in the 2017 tax overhaul (PL 115-97). The proposal would have also struck a prohibition against harvesting timber in the Tongass National Forest in Alaska. The committee voted 19–30 to reject the amendment.

Rep. David Price, D-N.C., proposed an amendment to bar EPA from finalizing a proposed EPA rule issued in April 2018 to require all science used by the agency for regulatory action to be reproduced for review by the agency. The committee adopted the manager's amendment by voice vote. The amendment added language to require each agency to develop customer service standards. The amendment also directed the Forest Service to submit a report within ninety days outlining limits on ten-year firefighting contracts. Additionally, the amendment directed the National Park Service to convene the Cedar Creek and Belle Grove National Historic Park Advisory Commission to maximize the visitor experience at the battlefield. The House voted 224–189 on a four-bill package that included Interior and environmental programs on July 24, 2020.

Senate Committee Action

The Senate Appropriations Committee released its fiscal 2021 spending bills November 10, 2020. Senate Republicans would have funded agencies including Interior and EPA at lower levels than their counterparts, while providing higher levels of funding for Energy and the Army Corps of Engineers.

Despite the lack of committee votes, Sen. Patrick J. Leahy of Vermont, the ranking Democrat on the full committee, said the proposals resulted from bipartisan negotiations. He commended Chairman Richard C. Shelby, R-Ala., for releasing the draft bills so that senators could begin conference negotiations with their House counterparts. The draft bill would have provided $35.8 billion for Interior and environmental programs, compared to $36.8 billion in the House version and $36 billion enacted in fiscal 2020.

Final Action

The final omnibus spending bill (HR 133) provided $36.1 billion in discretionary spending for the Interior Department, Environmental Protection Agency and related agencies, a $118 million increase from fiscal 2020 and $4.5 billion more than the administration requested.

The bill increased funding for fighting wildfires and blocked attempts to the protect the greater sage grouse under the Endangered Species Act. The final version dropped provisions to remove Confederate monuments from National Park Service sites.

MAJOR PROVISIONS

Interior Department

The department received $13.7 billion, a $186 million increase from fiscal 2020 and $1.7 billion more than requested. The funding included

- $3.1 billion for the National Park Service, which was $44 million less than enacted in fiscal 2020 and $332 million more than requested
- $3.5 billion for the Bureau of Indian Affairs, which was $171 million more than fiscal 2020 and $544 million more than requested. The total rejected a new budget structure for the Bureau of Trust Funds Administration, but included the Office of Special Trustee, which received $108 million, the same as the previous year
- $1.6 billion for the U.S. Fish and Wildlife Service, which was $22 million more than fiscal 2020 and $205 million more than requested. The funding included $270 million for ecological services and $504 million for the National Wildlife Refuge System
- $1.3 billion for the Bureau of Land Management, which was $28 million less than enacted in fiscal 2020 and $90 million more than requested. Within that amount, the bill provided $74 million for sage grouse conservation, $31 million for renewable energy development and $116 million for the wild horse and burro program

Environmental Protection Agency

The agency received $9.2 billion, a $180 million increase from the previous year and $2.5 billion more than requested. The total included $3.5 billion for core science and environmental programs, which was $111 million more than the previous year and $724 million more than requested; $542 million for geographic programs, an increase of $32 million and $211 million more than requested, to help restore areas such as the Great Lakes, Chesapeake Bay and Long Island Sound; and $566 million for environmental compliance monitoring and enforcement activities, a $14 million increase and $41 million more than requested. The bill included $53 million for regulatory and cleanup work for per- and polyfluoroalkyl substances (PFAS) known as forever chemicals. The bill included $91 million for Brownfield cleanups, a $2 million increase from fiscal 2020, and $1.2 billion for Superfund, a $21 million increase and $127 million more than requested. The $12.5 million for environmental justice activities represented a $2.3 million increase from the previous year and a four-fold increase from the administration's request.

U.S. Forest Service

The bill provided $3.5 billion for non-fire-related activities at the service, which is part of the Agriculture Department, an increase of $324 million from fiscal 2020 and $527 million more than requested. After adjusting for the Land and Water Conservation Fund and restructuring of the Forest Service budget, the total represented a programmatic increase of $77.9 million.

Indian Health Service

The service received $6.2 billion, an increase of $189 million from fiscal 2020 and $57 million less than the administration requested. The bill rejected the administration's proposed program cuts and included $5 million for an HIV and hepatitis C initiative, $5 million for Alzheimer's and $5 million for a maternal health initiative. The total reflected the transfer of funds for tribal lease payments to a new indefinite appropriation account for these costs.

Wildfires

The bill provided $5.3 billion for Wildland Fire Management, including $2.35 billion to fight wildfires. The funding shifted $387 million to a non-fire portion of the Forest Service because of budget restructuring and the creation of a Forest Service Operations account. After the shift, the bill provided a $104 million programmatic increase for Wildland Fire Management.

The bill provided $900 million for Land and Water Conservation Fund programs, which was the mandatory level set in a public lands bill (PL 116-152). The allocation included $405 million for the federal program, $360 million for the state grants program, and $135 million for other nonfederal grant programs.

The bill prevented the department from applying the Endangered Species Act to the greater sage grouse, a flightless bird native to the western United States and Canada. The Trump administration did not support protection for the birds. The funding included $405 million for the federal program, $360 million for state grants, and $135 million for nonfederal grants.

Fiscal Year 2021 Energy and Water Appropriations

The House voted 327–85 to approve an omnibus spending bill (HR 133-PL 116-260) on Dec. 21, 2020. The Senate cleared it 92–6 the same day. President Donald Trump signed the bill Dec. 27, 2020.

The bill provided billions more than the administration had requested, with $39.6 billion for the Energy Department, $7.8 billion for the Army Corps of Engineers, and $1.7 billion for the Bureau of Reclamation. A boost for the department's division for Energy Efficiency and Renewable Energy—to $2.9 billion, a $2.1 billion increase from the administration's request— won bipartisan support.

The bill established a national uranium reserve, which Sen. John Barrasso, R-Wyo., had advocated to prevent the country from being dependent on rival countries for nuclear fuel. And the bill provided $27.5 million for interim storage of nuclear waste, after the Trump administration dropped its contentious support for a permanent repository at Yucca Mountain in Nevada.

House Committee Action

The House Appropriations Energy–Water Subcommittee advanced its draft bill (HR 7613) by voice vote July 7, 2020. The $49.6 billion bill provided a $1.3 billion or 3 percent increase from fiscal 2020 (PL 116-94) and $14.2 billion more than the administration requested. The legislation included funding for interim nuclear fuel storage and for restoration of parts of the Everglades in Florida. Subcommittee Chairman Marcy Kaptur, D-Ohio, said the bill provided historic funding for three Energy Department programs: $2.9 billion for Energy Efficiency and Renewable Energy, which was $2.1 billion more than requested; $435 million for the Advanced Research Projects Agency–Energy, which the White House had proposed to eliminate; and $7.1 billion for the Office of Science, which was $1.2 billion more than requested.

The bill would have provided $41 billion for the Energy Department, a $2.3 billion increase from fiscal 2020 and $5.1 billion more than the administration requested. The total included $18 billion for nuclear security programs, which was $1.3 billion more than requested; $7.5 billion for environmental management activities, which was $1.4 billion more than requested; and $1.4 billion for nuclear energy programs, which was $256 million more than requested.

The bill also would have provided $7.6 billion for the Army Corps of Engineers, which was $1.7 billion more than requested; and $1.7 billion for the Bureau of Reclamation, which was $518 million more than requested.

A previous sticking point in the annual funding process had been the proposed licensing for nuclear waste storage at Yucca Mountain in Nevada. The Trump administration did not demand the funding and the subcommittee's ranking Republican, Rep. Mike Simpson of Idaho, did not introduce an amendment to provide funding. The bill would have provided $27.5 million for interim storage of nuclear waste.

The bill also would have provided $175 million for the Appalachian Regional Commission, which was $10 million more than requested; $25 million for the Northern Border Regional Commission, which was $24.1 million more than requested; $15 million for the Delta Regional Authority, which was $12.5 million more than requested; $15 million for the Denali Commission, which was $7.7 million more than requested; and $1 million for the Southwest Border Regional Commission, which was $250,000 more than requested.

The bill also sought to bar funding for a wall along the border between the United States and Mexico and for the resumption of nuclear weapons testing. The country has not tested nuclear weapons since September 1992, but the Trump administration was reportedly considering resuming tests. The full Appropriations Committee voted 30–21 with few disputes to advance the bill on July 13, 2020.

Rep. Ken Calvert, R-Calif., proposed two amendments, but both were rejected by voice votes. The proposals would have directed funding to water storage projects and to the Shasta Dam and Reservoir Enlargement Project in northern California.

The committee adopted by voice vote an amendment from Kaptur to make technical changes to the bill. One change clarified that the bill barred funding for preparations for any explosive nuclear weapons test.

Rep. Dan Newhouse, R-Wash., argued the bill failed to do its job for lack of funding for Yucca Mountain licensing. Simpson said without a permanent repository, the interim storage sites envisioned in the bill would become permanent.

The House voted 217–197 on a six-bill package that included Energy–Water on July 31, 2020. The approval came after the House labored through 340 amendments to the package, with the most contentious focused on provisions outside the Energy–Water title. The legislation from the Democratic-led House challenged the Trump administration over policies including a ban on transgender individuals serving in the military, the exclusion of undocumented immigrants in the Census, and the zero-tolerance policy for prosecuting immigration offenses near the Mexico border. The House adopted 307 amendments and rejected 28 by voice vote, and a handful of proposals got stand-alone votes.

ENERGY AND ENVIRONMENT LEADERSHIP

EPA Administrator Scott Pruitt

Oklahoma Attorney General Scott Pruitt was confirmed February 17, 2017, as head of the Environmental Protection Agency, which he frequently tangled with in court. The 52–46 Senate vote came after Democrats debated into the night against him, saying he tried to dismantle the EPA and opposed Obama administration climate regulations. Two Democrats from mining states supported him: Joe Manchin III of West Virginia and Heidi Heitkamp of North Dakota.

The same dynamic—energy interests supporting him and environmentalists opposing him—trailed Pruitt after Trump named him December 7, 2016. Outside his confirmation hearing January 18, environmental advocates and Native American tribal demonstrators got into confrontations with Capitol Police. Coal miners from West Virginia supported him in the hope that he would revive their industry.

Pruitt resigned July 5, 2018, after "unrelenting attacks" on him and his family, as he put it in his resignation letter to Trump. News reports alleged he pressured aides to find a $200,000 job for his wife, installed a $43,238 soundproof privacy booth in his office for confidential conversations, and stayed in a $50-per-night condo rented from a lobbyist. The Government Accountability Office found the phone booth violated the law restricting improvements to secretarial furnishings costing more than $5,000 without congressional approval.

EPA Administrator Andrew Wheeler

The Senate voted 52–47 on February 28, 2019, to confirm former coal lobbyist Andrew Wheeler as head of the Environmental Protection Agency. The vote came despite Wheeler's work to weaken and delay national and global environmental protections. Sen. Susan Collins of Maine was the only Republican to oppose his nomination because of environmental concerns.

Wheeler, who served as deputy administrator before succeeding Scott Pruitt, had told senators the agency planned to finalize regulations for utility emissions and fuel-economy standards in 2019. The revisions aimed to slash less greenhouse gas emissions than the Obama-era regulations they replaced. Senators questioned the collapse of administration negotiations with California over a nationwide fuel-economy standard. Wheeler said nobody wanted a fifty-state deal more than him, but California sought tougher standards than the administration.

During his confirmation hearing at the Senate Environment and Public Works Committee, Wheeler would not commit to developing a new drinking-water standard for so-called forever chemicals during the final two years of Trump's term. But Sen. Shelley Moore Capito, R-W.Va., said he allayed her fears about EPA's plans for polyfluoroalkyl substances, or PFAS, which have been linked to health problems such as cancers and low birth weights in babies.

Interior Secretary Ryan Zinke

One-term Rep. Ryan Zinke, R-Mont., was confirmed March 1, 2017, as secretary of the Interior Department. The 68–31 Senate vote reflected one of the less contentious confirmations and showed bipartisan support for his pledge to keep public lands in federal hands.

President Donald Trump had named Zinke on December 15, 2016, with a goal of opening more public lands and coastal areas to oil, gas, and coal extraction. Zinke, a horse-riding acolyte of former President Theodore Roosevelt, told senators at his confirmation hearing that recreation and energy development did not have to be in conflict. Zinke studied geology at the University of Oregon and spent more than two decades as a Navy SEAL before entering politics.

Industry groups such as the Independent Petroleum Association of America and the National Rural Electric Cooperative Association welcomed his confirmation. Reaction from environmental groups was mixed. The National Wildlife Federation praised his support for keeping public lands under the federal government, but the Natural Resources Defense Council called Zinke part of Trump's polluter Cabinet.

Zinke announced his resignation with a tweet December 15, 2018. He said he was proud of his work for the administration but could not justify spending thousands of dollars defending himself against false allegations. The department's inspector general had investigated accusations about Zinke bringing his wife along on government travel and bringing his security detail on vacation to Turkey and Greece. Zinke reimbursed the government for his wife's travel and the inspector general found the department had no policy about the security travel accompanying him on vacation.

Interior Secretary David Bernhardt

The Senate voted 56–41 on April 11, 2019, to confirm David Bernhardt to lead the Interior Department after Ryan Zinke's departure. The vote brushed aside ethics issues for the former lobbyist for oil, gas and water industries, and a pending proposal to open the Atlantic Ocean to offshore drilling.

(Continued)

ENERGY AND ENVIRONMENT LEADERSHIP (Continued)

Bernhardt told the Senate Energy and Natural Resources Committee at his confirmation hearing that he would work to solve the maintenance backlogs at the National Park system, respect Native American tribes, crack down on sexual harassment in the department, and manage endangered species. He said he would tirelessly promote Trump's agenda for greater production of oil and gas on federal land. Coastal Republicans including Sens. Susan Collins of Maine and Marco Rubio and Rick Scott of Florida supported Bernhardt despite their concerns about the department's proposed five-year offshore oil and gas leasing plan.

The House Oversight and Reform Committee investigated whether Bernhardt, who served as Zinke's deputy, kept a private schedule on a Google document that was overwritten each day, a practice that could violate federal records laws. The department denied it happened.

The department's inspector general reported in August 2020 that political officials deliberately withheld sensitive records about Bernhardt during his confirmation process. In February 2019, his adviser Hubbel Relat directed staffers to temporarily withhold documents as part of a pending lawsuit, according to the inspector general. The department withheld 253 pages before releasing most of them in December, months after his confirmation.

Energy Secretary Rick Perry

Rick Perry's confirmation as Energy secretary on March 2 completed the triumvirate of President Donald Trump's energy and environment team. The 62–37 Senate vote also placed Perry atop a department he proposed to abolish during a 2011 Republican presidential debate, but he later said he regretted that position. "My past statements made over five years ago about abolishing the Department of Energy do not reflect my current thinking," Perry told the Senate Energy and Natural Resources Committee on January 19, 2017.

Perry enjoyed support from a number of Democrats, including Sen. Catherine Cortez Masto of Nevada. She said she expected him to prevent the designation of Yucca Mountain as a permanent repository for the country's nuclear waste. Perry told her at his confirmation hearing he could not give her a definitive answer, but that Republican Sen. Dean Heller and Gov. Brian Sandoval made their opposition loud and clear.

Perry advocated for an all-of-the-above research approach to energy, with support for fossil fuels and renewables. He also assured lawmakers that he would not purge administration officials who worked on climate programs.

Senate Committee Action

The Senate Appropriations Committee released its fiscal 2021 spending bills November 10, 2020. Senate Republicans would have funded agencies including Interior and EPA at lower levels than those of their counterparts, while providing higher levels of funding for Energy and the Army Corps of Engineers.

Despite the lack of committee votes, Sen. Patrick J. Leahy of Vermont, the ranking Democrat on the full committee, said the proposals resulted from bipartisan negotiations. He commended Chairman Richard C. Shelby, R-Ala., for releasing the draft bills so that senators could begin conference negotiations with their House counterparts. The draft bill would have provided $51.8 billion for Energy–Water, compared to $49.6 billion in the House version and $48.3 billion enacted in fiscal 2020.

Final Action

The final omnibus spending bill (HR 133) provided $49.5 billion for Energy–Water programs, a $1.1 billion increase from fiscal 2020 and $6.9 billion more than the administration requested. The total was closer to the House's $49.6 billion than the Senate's $51.8 billion.

The final compromise on the $1.4 trillion omnibus came after appropriators resolved a dispute over $12.5 billion for veterans' health care spending. Appropriators in both chambers initially agreed to designate the money as emergency spending, which would have allowed other programs under tight budget caps. But House Minority Leader Kevin McCarthy, R-Calif., opposed that strategy and the money was taken instead from unused funding in a children's health insurance program and by designating $2.3 billion in Energy Department science funds as emergency spending and rescinding two Obama-era loan programs that were also funded with emergency appropriations. The result was to lower the Energy–Water bill's regular allocation, which created room for spending under the nondefense cap.

The bill included $75 million to establish a national uranium reserve, a figure lower than the $120 million Senate appropriators proposed and half the White House request of $150 million. Sen. John Barrasso, R-Wyo., who was slated to take over as chairman of the Energy and Natural Resources Committee in the next Congress, had been a vocal advocate of the reserve. The bill also boosted funding for nuclear security and weapons, increased energy efficiency programs, and allocated money for temporary nuclear waste storage.

GREEN NEW DEAL

After Democrats regained control of the House in 2019, progressive lawmakers introduced nonbinding resolutions in the House and Senate in 2019 to combat climate change under what they called a Green New Deal. The proposals remained a lightning rod for criticism in both chambers and the only vote in the Senate favored opponents of the proposal.

Climate scientists have warned about an urgency to act fast to reduce climate-warming carbon emissions to stave off the worst effects of a hotter planet, including more frequent and damaging floods, hurricanes, wildfires, and droughts. The United Nations and U.S. agencies including the EPA, NASA, and Defense Department have warned that agricultural and economic disruptions could leave to international conflicts.

Polls found broad support for dealing with climate change, even if the details remained contentious. More than half of registered voters nationwide (56 percent) believed climate change to be an emergency, according to a Quinnipiac University poll in August 2020. Two-thirds of registered voters (67 percent) said more needs to be done—a high-water mark for the question first asked in December 2015, according to the poll. A U.S. Conference of Mayors survey of voters ages 18 to 29 in January 2020 found 80 percent considered climate change a major threat to human life on earth.

Amid growing public support to deal with the issue came broader institutional support. Thomas Smith, executive director of the American Society of Civil Engineers, said wildfires and devastating storms accelerated the urgency to invest in resilient infrastructure. The Business Roundtable, a lobbying group for some of the largest companies, supported efforts to reduce U.S. greenhouse gas emissions 80 percent from 2005 levels by 2050, and even contentious market-based carbon pricing to help get there. But the politics remained contentious.

Rep. Alexandria Ocasio-Cortez, D-N.Y., had 101 cosponsors for her resolution (H Res 109). The House did not hold a vote on her measure that sought to curb U.S. consumption of fossil fuels and reduce greenhouse gas emissions through more investment in clean infrastructure.

Contrary to GOP perspectives, the proposal did not call for an end to hamburgers or air travel. The resolution envisioned the U.S. embarking on a ten-year mobilization to boost the use of renewable energy, energy-efficient buildings, and low-carbon vehicles. Highlights included

- Shifting to carbon-free energy generation during a ten-year period
- Working with farmers and ranchers to reduce as much greenhouse gas "as is technologically feasible" because agriculture is the fourth-largest source of emissions, according to EPA data
- Providing affordable housing for all U.S. residents
- Reducing emissions from transportation as much as "technically possible," with access to public transit and high-speed rail

Republicans uniformly opposed the resolutions. Rep. Greg Walden of Oregon, the ranking Republican on the Energy and Commerce Committee, said the resolution threatened the entire U.S. economy and stretched into every corner of American life. The American Action Forum, a center-right think tank, estimated the proposal could cost between $53 trillion and $93 trillion. Rep. Paul Gosar, R-Ariz., said the plan would cost the average household an estimated $650,000 over ten years and cost an estimated 10.3 million jobs in the oil and gas industry.

Moderate Democrats were also wary. Rep. Paul Tonko, D-N.Y., chairman of the House Energy and Commerce Subcommittee on Environment and Climate Change said he embraced the goals of the resolution, but not the broader plan to remake the U.S. economy. While advocates educated Americans about the issue, Tonko said his goal as chairman was to develop tools to achieve goals through science- and evidence-based strategies.

In the Senate, Sen. Edward J. Markey, D-Mass., had fourteen cosponsors for his version (S Res 59) of the resolution. Senate Majority Leader Mitch McConnell, R-Ky., wanted a vote enthusiastically enough to introduce Markey's resolution as his own (S Res 8). The cloture vote March 26, 2019, was fifty-seven opposed, including four members of the Democratic Caucus, and forty-three present.

Democrats voted "present" because Republicans in both chambers could have bludgeoned Democrats who voted in favor of the resolution during the 2020 campaign, in states where climate risks carry less weight. The four members of the Democratic Caucus who voted no with Republicans were Sens. Doug Jones of Alabama, Angus King of Maine, Joe Manchin III of West Virginia, and Kyrsten Sinema of Arizona.

King, an independent who caucuses with Democrats, said the resolution had overly aggressive goals, but that he did not want his opposition to the political theater of the vote to be misconstrued as a lack of interest in dealing with climate change. Manchin, who represented the country's second-largest coal producer, said he opposed the resolution because it did not recognize the role fossil fuels play in the economy. The Senate vote put an end to efforts in the 116th Congress to pass Green New Deal legislation.

WHITE HOUSE EXECUTIVE ACTIONS

Some of the most important environmental policies during the 115th and 116th Congresses were made through executive orders by the Trump administration. These affected streams and wetlands, oil pipelines, the coal industry, and wildlife.

Waters of the United States

President Donald Trump campaigned to kill the Obama-era Waters of the United States rule and moved in his second month on the job to do just that. Trump signed an executive order February 28, 2017, directing the Army Corps of Engineers to review and reconsider the rule, which expanded federal authority over streams and wetlands under the Clean Water Act.

The Obama administration had said the rule was urgently needed to improve and simplify the process for identifying which waters needed protection. Environmentalists and Democrats feared that without such protections, pollutants such as pesticides could be dumped with impunity into the drinking water of millions of people and wildlife habitats. But the Sixth U.S. Circuit Court of Appeals placed the rule on hold in October 2015 after thirty-two states and agricultural groups sued. Landowners and farmers had fought the rule since its inception, arguing it represented a federal intrusion that criminalized activities on private property and hampered economic development.

The Army Corps of Engineers and the Environmental Protection Agency released a new rule February 14, 2018. The rule created six categories of regulated waters with eleven exemptions. The six categories were traditional navigable waters, tributaries, certain ditches, certain lakes and ponds, impoundments and adjacent wetlands. If the water did not meet one of the categories, it would not be considered among the Waters of the United States. The categories no longer covered included ditches, features that are wet only during rainfall, groundwater, stormwater control features, wastewater recycling, and converted cropland.

"The EPA so-called Waters of the United States rule is one of the worst examples of federal regulation and it has truly run amok, and is one of the rules most strongly opposed by farmers, ranchers and agricultural workers all across our land," Trump said February 28, 2017, at the White House while surrounded by farmers, housing developers, and county commissioners. "It's prohibiting them from being allowed to do what they're supposed to be doing. It has been a disaster."

Oil Pipelines

The Trump administration green-lighted two contentious pipeline projects—one from Canada and one in North Dakota—that the Obama administration had either rejected or delayed for environmental reasons. President Donald Trump got the ball rolling on the projects by signing executive memos January 24, 2017. In one, he invited TransCanada to resubmit its application and told the State Department to "take all actions necessary and appropriate to facilitate its expeditious review" of the Keystone XL pipeline. In the other, he told the Army Corps of Engineers to expedite the review of the Dakota Access pipeline of Energy Transfer Partners, which was already 90 percent complete.

The Obama administration had delayed for seven years and eventually rejected the Keystone XL pipeline from the oil sands of Alberta, Canada, to Nebraska before connecting to Gulf Coast refineries. But the State Department, which was led by former Exxon Mobil executive Rex Tillerson, issued a construction permit for the pipeline March 24, 2017. Calgary-based TransCanada Corp., which owned the project, called the permit a significant milestone for a project that was in the national interest for energy security and environmental issues.

U.S. District Judge Brian Morris in Montana halted the Keystone XL pipeline November 8, 2018, by ruling the Trump administration had not properly considered its impact on climate change or vulnerable animals. Trump blasted the decision. "It was a political decision made by a judge," Trump told reporters at the White House on November 9, 2018. "I think it's a disgrace."

Trump revoked the permit in March 2019, to let the company apply for another permit. Legal battles continued to rage over the pipeline, eventually reaching the Supreme Court. (President Joe Biden revoked the permit on his first day in office, January 20, 2021.)

For the other pipeline, Trump also reversed the Obama administration's decision to halt the contentious Dakota Access Pipeline by granting expedited environmental reviews. Construction resumed quickly and the pipeline started carrying oil in late March 2017, despite a pending court challenge from the Standing Rock Sioux tribe and environmental groups.

Environmentalists opposed the projects for helping unearth fossil fuels that would contribute to climate change. The Standing Rock Sioux had argued the pipeline risked contaminating their water source and that construction damaged sacred burial grounds.

Coal Jobs

Jobs in coal country were a top priority for President Donald Trump's administration, whether boosting the industry through subsidies or by reducing regulations. But the results were mixed amid market forces working against the industry in a bigger way than regulations.

The coal industry added 800 direct jobs in 2017, during Trump's first year in office, for a total of 50,500 jobs, according to the Bureau of Labor Statistics. But even with the increase, the number fell short of the 78,900 industry jobs five years earlier. The industry stood at 51,000 jobs in 2020, according to the bureau.

Energy experts pointed to industry trends for coal that had been declining for decades, as jobs became more automated and deposits were depleted. Hydraulic fracturing unleashed an abundance of cleaner, cheaper natural gas that electricity markets favor. Coal generated 30 percent of domestic energy in 2016 and 2017, down from nearly half a decade earlier, according to the Energy Information Administration. Natural gas rose to 32 percent of electricity generation in 2017, up from 22 percent in 2007.

To bolster jobs, the Energy Department proposed in September 2017 that coal and nuclear plants could run continuously during peak demand times and emergencies, in an effort to compete more favorably against natural gas and renewable sources. Under the proposal, power plants that could guarantee they had a three-month supply of fuel on-site would have received a financial reward for their crucial role in maintaining a reliable and resilient electric grid. The Federal Energy Regulatory Commission rejected the proposal January 8, 2018, saying the regulator would consult with grid operators for a different approach.

In June 2018, an Energy Department memo outlined potential proposals to rebuild coal jobs, including ordering grid operators to buy electricity from struggling coal and nuclear plants for two years, an emergency power typically employed for crises such as natural disasters. But other energy trade groups representing oil, gas, wind, and solar power criticized the plan and said it would lead to higher bills for consumers.

Sage Grouse Regulations

The Bureau of Land Management finalized a regulation in March 2019 changing protections for the greater sage grouse, a move praised by Western governors of both parties and criticized by conservationists. The regulation changed the management of the chicken-sized bird's habitat, to restore trust with state and local governments while easing regulatory burdens while ensuring responsible development of natural resources, according to acting Secretary David Bernhardt. The changes were negotiated with state officials from Wyoming, Nevada, California, Idaho, Oregon, Utah, and Colorado governing nearly 60 million acres.

Urbanization, wildfires, and invasive weeds decimated sage grouse populations in eleven Western states. Trump administration officials opposed 2015 Obama rules written with conservationists and recreation groups that some Western governors said ignored local voices. The Obama-era rule kept the bird off the endangered species list, but some Western lawmakers said there was a threat of more restrictive endangerment designation.

Gray Wolf Protections

The Interior Department dropped its protection of the gray wolf under the Endangered Species Act in November 2020, a long-held goal of Republican lawmakers, ranchers, and hunting groups. Critics of the protection have long cited the threats to livestock and ranching as reasons to remove the gray wolf from the endangered list, with state management instead. Interior Secretary David Bernhardt said gray wolf packs in the lower forty-eight states recovered sufficiently to justify the delisting. The Fish and Wildlife Service monitored the wolves for five years under the rule.

MAJOR PROVISIONS

The Energy Department received $39.6 billion, a $1 billion increase from fiscal 2020 and $4.5 billion more than requested. The Army Corps of Engineers received $7.8 billion, an increase of $145 million from the previous year and $1.8 billion more than requested. The Bureau of Reclamation, part of the Interior Department, received $1.7 billion, an $11 million increase from fiscal 2020 and $553 million more than requested.

The bill provided $2.9 billion for the Energy Department division for energy efficiency and renewable energy, a $2.1 billion increase from the administration request. Reps. Ralph Norman, R-S.C., and Raja Krishnamoorthi, D-Ill., said in a joint statement it was critical to pursue clean energy such as solar power. The funding included $20 million for cybersecurity, after Energy Secretary Dan Brouillette had warned in May 2020 that the department detected an increase in cyberattacks on national laboratories. Another division received $156 million, the same as in fiscal 2020, to focus on cybersecurity, energy security, and responding to emergencies.

The bill provided $6.4 billion for nuclear cleanup at military sites, an increase from $6.25 billion in fiscal 2020 and $4.95 billion requested by the administration.

The measure does not mention Yucca Mountain, the site of a proposed nuclear waste repository, but the bill provided $27.5 million for nuclear waste disposal, including $20 million for interim storage. The White House had announced abruptly that it did not support Yucca Mountain as a storage facility. Republicans criticized Brouillette for the change in a presidential election year and Rep. Dan Newhouse, R-Wash., said he was disappointed the administration was playing politics with nuclear waste.

Nuclear weapons fared well under the bill. The National Nuclear Security Administration received $19.7 billion, a $3 billion increase from fiscal 2020. The total included $15.4 billion for weapons activities, a $2.9 billion increase from the previous year.

CHAPTER 8

Agricultural Policy

Agricultural Policy

Agriculture was not a main focus of attention during the four years of the Trump administration, but Congress did succeed in passing a new multiyear, multibillion dollar farm bill, designed to replace the one that expired in the fall of 2018. The farm bill sparked debate between Democrats and Republicans over the Supplemental Nutrition Assistance (SNAP) program, previously known as food stamps, with Republicans seeking cuts and Democrats arguing in favor of the program.

The farm bill did not end up making controversial changes to the SNAP program, but other changes did emerge from the legislation. For example, domestic industrial hemp production was legalized, hemp was removed from the Controlled Substances Act, and hemp growers were permitted access to crop insurance. The hemp legislation was a particular priority for Senate Majority Leader Mitch McConnell, R-Ky., who saw hemp cultivation as a boon for his state.

Several more minor pieces of agriculture-related legislation made some progress during the 2017–2020 period, but none was signed into law. These included measures to ease pesticide regulations, encourage participation of women and underrepresented minorities from rural areas in science and technology, update rules pertaining to migrant farmworkers, and make it easier for farmers and forestry workers to participate in carbon credit markets.

Figure 8.1 Outlays for Agriculture

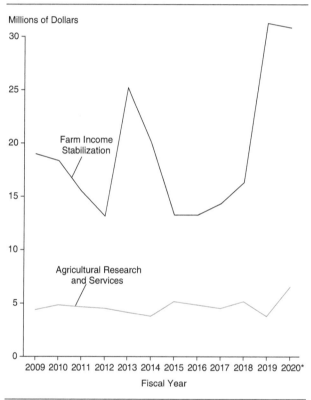

SOURCE: Office of Management and Budget, *Historical Tables, Budget of the United States Government: Fiscal Year 2021* (Washington DC: U.S. Government Printing Office, 2020), Table 3.2

NOTES: * indicates estimate

Chronology of Action on Agricultural Policy

2017–2018

Agriculture policy on Capitol Hill during the 115th Congress was dominated by the need to pass a massive new multiyear farm bill, as the previous one was set to expire in the fall of 2018. As had been the case in the development of the previous bill, much of the debate centered on the Supplemental Nutrition Assistance Program's funding, with many Republicans seeking to cut back on access to the program and many Democrats objecting. Also on the agenda was a bill aiming to make it more difficult for the Environmental Protection Agency and states to regulate pesticides. The legislation passed the House in 2017 but failed to advance to the Senate floor. The House also passed a measure attempting to increase the participation of women and underrepresented minorities from rural areas in science and technology. This measure also passed the House in 2017 but did not advance in the Senate.

Farm Bill

In the 115th Congress, the most important priority relating to agricultural programs was the passage of a multiyear, multibillion dollar farm bill, as the 2014 farm bill was set to expire in the fall of 2018. The massive bill focuses on laying out priorities for agriculture, conservation, crop insurance, nutrition, and rural development.

In years past, the farm bill had been seen as a bipartisan effort, with rural lawmakers backing the farm-related provisions and urban lawmakers coming on board in support of the food stamp components. But in more recent times, the farm bill had become yet another partisan battleground. The 2014 bill had taken almost three years to negotiate, resulting in the need to extend various farm programs past the expiration date, and the agriculture committee chairmen hoped to meet the September 30, 2018, deadline this time around.

Ultimately, it took a little longer, but, after some bumps in the road over issues including the Supplemental Nutrition Assistance Program, Congress approved the bill, known as H.R. 2 or the Agriculture Improvement Act of 2018, and it was signed into law (P.L. 115-334) by the end of 2018. The measure would expire at the end of fiscal year 2023, and the Congressional Budget Office estimated its cost at $428 billion over five years and $867 billion over ten years.

COMMITTEE ACTION

Both agriculture committee chairs, K. Michael Conaway, R-Texas, in the House and Pat Roberts, R-Kan., in the Senate, vowed to get moving early and avoid the problems faced with the previous farm bill. They were both aware of the need to pass a new five-year bill to reassure farmers anxious over the impact on the farm sector from the Trump administration's trade wars with various countries. But the two took very different approaches to creating their legislative product.

Adding to the mix, the Trump administration's fiscal 2019 budget sought less money for the Agriculture Department, major cuts to SNAP, and cuts to crop insurance and farm programs. The budget called for $213.5 billion in SNAP cuts over ten years; sought to make it more difficult for states to provide extensions beyond the typical three out of thirty-six months in SNAP benefits for single, able-bodied, childless adults; and wanted states to try to move more of these almost 3 million adults away from SNAP toward work. Regarding crop insurance premiums for farmers, the administration sought to cut from 62 percent to 48 percent the average federal share of the premiums, limit payment eligibility for commodity crop programs to those farmers having $500,000 or less in adjusted gross incomes, and give smaller government underwriting funding to private insurance companies servicing and writing the crop insurance policies.

In the House, Conaway, who took over the chairmanship in 2015, meaning this was his first time pushing through a farm bill, produced a partisan measure that sought to cut back on SNAP recipients' benefits. The measure called for stricter work requirements for SNAP recipients, requiring able-bodied workers ages eighteen to fifty-nine without children under six to participate at least twenty hours a week in job training or work to get their

benefits, a modification to the existing arrangement. The bill was approved April 18, 2018, on a strict party-line vote of 26–20. Ranking Democrat Collin Peterson of Minnesota had cut off negotiations on the measure, angered by the Republicans' approach. Among the amendments considered in committee was one by Rep. Steve King, R-Iowa, aimed at prohibiting states from imposing a condition or standard on the manufacturing or production of agricultural products involved in interstate commerce, and would permit those affected to seek damages in federal court. The measure was approved by voice vote. Another amendment, offered by Rep. Jeff Denham, R-Calif., would bar people from knowingly participating in efforts to procure dogs and cats for human consumption, and would make those actions a felony. It was approved by voice vote.

During the previous Congress, Conaway had held multiple hearings examining the SNAP program, which made up around 70 percent of spending in the farm bill and assisted more than 43 million people. SNAP had been the most contentious issue during the negotiation of the previous farm bill. Many Republicans tended to see the program as encouraging poor people to be dependent on the government, while many Democrats viewed it as a necessary stopgap for the poor to survive. In addition, the panel looked into other issues relating to the farm bill, in preparation for negotiating the massive measure.

Another component of the House farm bill was language to permit Environmental Protection Agency approval of pesticides without going through a review process designed to protect endangered species. Environmental organizations strongly opposed the language.

In the Senate, however, Chairman Roberts worked closely with Democrat Debbie Stabenow of Michigan, the ranking member, to create a bipartisan bill that avoided the controversy over SNAP. Stabenow had indicated that Senate Democrats would not back a bill with the House SNAP provisions included. The Senate measure won bipartisan support as the committee approved it on June 13 on a 20–1 vote, with only Sen. Charles Grassley, R-Iowa, in opposition.

One issue given prominence by Senate Majority Leader Mitch McConnell, R-Ky., was the legalization of domestic industrial hemp. Hemp, a less intoxicating relative of marijuana, had been under the regulation of the Controlled Substances Act, its domestic cultivation barred—although products using imported hemp were permitted. McConnell had backed a provision in the previous farm bill for a hemp pilot program, and touted its success in Kentucky. Now he sought to legalize domestic hemp. During the committee markup, Grassley, chairman of the Judiciary Committee, argued that McConnell's hemp legislation should have gone through his committee and that "any snake oil salesman" could market a hemp product without oversight.

Amendments considered during the committee markup included one by Sen. Amy Klobuchar, D-Minn., which would reauthorize energy programs under the farm bill at the current level, and would reimburse dairy farmers for participation in the Dairy Margin Protection Program. Klobuchar's amendment passed by voice vote. Another amendment, by Sen. John Thune, R-S.D., would raise the maximum acreage of environmentally sensitive land under the Conservation Reserve Program to 26.25 acres, let farmers graze livestock on one-third of the acres they enrolled in the program, and allow harvesting of hay on enrolled acres. The amendment was withdrawn after Roberts and Stabenow said the payments to participating farmers seemed low; the senators agreed to come up with a compromise in time for a Senate floor vote.

Meanwhile, interest groups had been making their voices heard throughout the process. Anti-hunger groups geared up to oppose cuts to the SNAP program. The Heritage Foundation, a conservative think tank, had urged the termination of government aid to farmers for crop insurance premiums and commodity crop support efforts, stating that instead of providing a benefit during periods of serious crop losses, the programs instead provided farmers with guaranteed income. And the dairy and cotton industries, concerned about ongoing low market prices for their products, sought increased aid from the new farm bill.

FLOOR ACTION

In a rebuke to the GOP leadership, the House rejected the committee's farm bill on a vote of 198–213 on May 18, 2018. Thirty Republicans voted with the Democrats to oppose the legislation. Some Republicans on the moderate side of the party voted against the bill because they didn't support the SNAP cutbacks. Other Republicans, from the conservative wing, voted against it to protest the floor schedule for unrelated immigration legislation. No Democrats supported the measure.

Conaway and Peterson joined forces during floor debate to oppose an amendment, sponsored by Rep. Virginia Foxx, R-N.C., seeking to change the sugar price support program. The amendment included language aimed at backing off on Agriculture Department efforts to limit domestic production. It failed on a 137–278 vote. Among other amendments considered on the floor was one proposed by Rep. Jim Banks, R-Ind., to repeal a joint EPA–Army Corps of Engineers rule, Waters of the United States, dealing with water pollution. The amendment was approved on a vote of 238–173.

The leadership brought the farm bill up again a month later when the unrelated immigration bills were no longer on the agenda. This time the farm bill passed, barely, on a 213–211 vote June 21. Again, the bill did not win any Democratic support. Twenty Republicans joined the Democrats in opposing the bill.

In the Senate, meanwhile, a bipartisan majority backed the bill the first time it came to the floor. The measure passed the chamber June 28 on a vote of 86–11. The opponents were all Republicans. The Senate bill did not include the controversial SNAP provisions found in the House bill, which made it a less partisan measure. It called for a

continuation of ongoing SNAP procedures, while asking the states for more accountability in the operation of their work-training programs and improved efforts to monitor the program for fraud.

During debate on the Senate floor, senators voted, 68–30, to table a SNAP-related amendment by Sens. John Kennedy, R-La., Ted Cruz, R-Texas, and Mike Lee, R-Utah, that would have cut food aid for able-bodied, single adults with no minor children. Other issues under discussion included a successful effort by Sen. Marco Rubio, R-Fla., to modify a provision relating to trade with Cuba. Sen. Heidi Heitkamp, D-N.D., had suggested language asking USDA, as it attempted to open new export markets, to include Cuba. Rubio's language would prevent USDA from using federal funds in agricultural export deals involving entities tied to the Cuban military.

CONFERENCE AND FINAL PASSAGE

Because the two chambers' versions were different, the House and Senate leadership appointed conferees—forty-seven from the House and nine from the Senate—to try to resolve the measure in a conference committee. The negotiations, at various points, seemed unlikely to succeed in a timely fashion, as the previous farm bill expired at the end of September. Some programs would continue to get their funding, including food stamps and crop insurance, but some others were at risk of lapsing.

Looming over the conference was the impact from the Trump administration's decision to impose tariffs on Canada, China, Mexico, and the European Union. Farmers were among those affected by retaliatory measures taken by those other countries, and were anxious for reassurance. At the same time as the cutbacks in export markets were underway, various crop prices were low, leading to additional concern.

Despite these pressures, conferees did not reach agreement before Congress broke for the November midterm elections. Democrats performed well in House elections, and prepared to take control of the chamber in January.

Ultimately, the conferees agreed on a bill resembling the Senate measure. Among the conferees was McConnell, and his hemp legislation made it into the final bill, legalizing domestic industrial hemp, removing it from the Controlled Substances Act, and permitting hemp growers access to crop insurance.

The Senate approved the farm bill December 11, 2018, on a vote of 87–13; the nays were all from Republicans. The House passed it the following day, 386–47. Forty-four Republicans and three Democrats opposed the bill. It was signed into law by Trump on December 20, 2018.

KEY PROVISIONS

Overall, the projected outlays under the 2018 farm bill included 78 percent for nutrition programs, 9 percent for crop insurance, 7 percent each for commodities and for conservation, and 1 percent for other programs.

Nutrition

The new law did not incorporate the changes sought by House Republicans to the SNAP program, which would have added work requirements and SNAP training and employment programs, although it did expand training and employment options a state could offer.

The law added changes intended to cut back on fraud and errors in the SNAP program. A National Accuracy Clearinghouse would make sure people were not getting SNAP benefits in multiple states. It also added funding for The Emergency Food Assistance Program, which assists low-income people in receiving food.

Crop Insurance

The farm law opted to include hemp as a crop eligible for federal crop insurance. Hemp was also added to the group of crops—potatoes, sweet potatoes, and tobacco—eligible for policies covering post-harvest losses. A new program for hemp was established under the oversight of USDA, in an effort to make commercial cultivation and marketing of the product easier.

Commodities

The new law allowed producers more leeway in moving between the Price Loss Coverage and Agricultural Risk Coverage revenue support programs. The law changed the definition of family farm to add cousins, nieces, and nephews to those eligible for farm program payments. The law increased loan rates under the sugar program.

The law made some changes to the dairy program, renaming the Margin Protection Program as Dairy Margin Coverage. It expanded the margin protection between milk prices and feed costs that producers can buy, and decreased coverage costs for the initial 5 million pounds of milk produced.

Conservation

The bill reauthorized the Environmental Quality Incentives Program and the Conservation Stewardship Program, the two biggest working lands programs, but cut their funding allocations.

The bill also reauthorized the Conservation Reserve Program, a key land retirement program. Under the new law, the program could grow from 24 million to 27 million acres. It also increased grazing and commercial efforts on the program's lands.

Pesticide Regulations

In 2017, the Republican-controlled House of Representatives passed a bill making it harder for the Environmental Protection Agency and states to regulate pesticides. The Senate did not vote on it.

The bill, HR 953, the Reducing Regulatory Burdens Act of 2017, was introduced by Rep. Bob Gibbs, R-Ohio, on February 7, 2017, and was referred to the House Transportation and Infrastructure Committee and the

House Agriculture Committee. It would amend the Federal Insecticide, Fungicide, and Rodenticide Act (FIFRA) and the Federal Water Pollution Control Act (also known as the Clean Water Act) to prohibit the EPA and states from requiring certain federal permits for the discharge of a federally approved pesticide from a point source—such as a pipe, channel, or tunnel—into navigable waters.

Gibbs described the existing process, under which farmers, ranchers, pesticide companies, and others needed to seek a permit under the National Pollution Discharge Elimination System to discharge a pesticide that was already federally approved as duplicative. But opponents expressed concern that the act would lead to additional water pollution. The House Agriculture Committee approved the bill by voice vote on February 16.

During floor debate on the measure on May 24, 2017, the House voted down an amendment, 191–229, offered by Rep. Elizabeth Esty, D-Conn., that aimed to ensure that existing clean water protections applied to the release of these chemicals into the environment. An amendment by Rep. Jared Huffman, D-Calif., calling for the protection of commercial, recreational, and subsistence fisheries from negative impacts of unregulated discharge also was voted down, 189–230.

The House approved the overall bill on a vote of 256–165. Voting in favor were 231 Republicans and twenty-five Democrats; 164 Democrats and one Republican opposed the bill. The House had previously passed similar legislation, but it failed to advance to the Senate floor, which was also the case in the 115th Congress. On May 25, 2017, the bill was sent to the Senate and referred to the Committee on Environment and Public Works.

Research Grants

A bill aimed at increasing the participation of women and underrepresented minorities from rural areas in STEM fields—science, technology, engineering, and mathematics—passed the House in 2017 but failed to advance in the Senate.

Rep. Grace Meng, D-N.Y., introduced HR 382, the 100 Years of Women in Congress Act, on January 9, 2017. It was referred to the House Committee on Agriculture. The measure sought to amend the Food, Agriculture, Conservation, and Trade Act of 1990 to designate the existing research and extension grants as Jeannette Rankin Women and Minorities in STEM Fields Program Grants.

Jeannette Rankin, a Republican from Montana, was the first woman elected to the House of Representatives, in November 1916. She served one term in the 65th Congress, from 1917 to 1919, and another term in the 77th Congress, from 1941 to 1943. She graduated from the University of Montana in 1902 with a degree in biology.

The House approved the measure on a voice vote March 20, 2017. It was sent to the Senate March 21 and referred to the Committee on Agriculture, Nutrition, and Forestry. The House also had approved the legislation in the previous 114th Congress, but it did not advance in the Senate.

Fiscal Year 2017
Agriculture Appropriations

Congress finally finished its fiscal year 2017 appropriations process in May 2017. The previous Congress had approved a continuing resolution that funded the government through April 28, 2017; the fiscal year ended September 30, 2017, just five months later.

The new legislation, HR 244, or the Consolidated Appropriations Act, included funding for agriculture programs. The bill called for more than $153 billion in agriculture-related spending, including mandatory spending of about $132.5 billion and discretionary spending of about $20.877 billion.

Mandatory spending tends to focus on items found in authorizing legislation—the multiyear farm bills passed by Congress, for example. The major items in the mandatory category include the Supplemental Nutrition Assistance Program (SNAP), child nutrition, and crop insurance. Discretionary spending often takes up the most attention during the writing of appropriations bills; the biggest items in this category in the agriculture appropriations bills include the Special Supplemental Nutrition Program for Women, Infants, and Children (WIC), agricultural research, and the Food and Drug Administration, which is part of the Department of Health and Human Services but falls under agriculture appropriations.

While the discretionary total for fiscal year 2017 was 2.9 percent lower than that of the previous year, various programs saw increases, including an additional $163 million for conservation programs and $119 million for rural development. The House and Senate approved the legislation on May 3 and 4, and it was signed into law (PL 115-31) May 5.

Fiscal Year 2018
Agriculture Appropriations

It took a while, but eventually Congress turned its attention to the fiscal 2018 appropriations, for the year beginning October 1, 2017. As had happened the previous year, agriculture appropriations ended up being funded in a larger appropriations bill. Lawmakers got off to a late start; they still needed to finish the fiscal 2017 appropriations, and the new Trump administration did not submit its full budget request until late May. To the dismay of many in the agriculture field, the Trump budget called for major cuts in such programs as SNAP and crop insurance.

The House Agriculture Appropriations subcommittee marked up its fiscal 2018 bill June 28, 2017, by voice vote, and the full committee passed an amended bill July 12, also by voice vote. Amendments to the measure included one introduced by Rep. Dan Newhouse, R-Wash., that would make legal foreign workers eligible for farm-worker housing; the amendment focused on temporary agricultural

workers. It passed by voice vote. Without action on many individual bills, the House approved a consolidated appropriations bill September 14 bringing together eight measures including agriculture. The measure included a discretionary total of nearly $20 billion. Cuts from the previous year's totals included rural development funding, down $262 million from the previous year; nutrition assistance, down $220 million; farm and conservation programs, down $199 million; department administration, down $123 million; and agricultural research, down $98 million.

On the Senate side, the agriculture appropriations subcommittee marked up its bill by voice vote July 18, 2017, and the full committee approved its amended version July 20 on a 31–0 vote. Amendments adopted in full committee included one by Sen. Tom Udall, D-N.M., that would ban USDA funding for inspections of horses designated for slaughter; and one from Sen. Lisa Murkowski, R-Alaska, that would ban commercial sale of salmon that was genetically engineered. Both amendments were approved by voice vote. The Senate version included a discretionary total of $20.53 billion. It called for reductions from the previous fiscal year of $119 million in rural development and $57 million in agricultural research. It also called for a $140 million increase in international food aid.

Because the fiscal year began on October 1, 2017, without a finished appropriations bill, Congress enacted a series of five continuing resolutions to keep the government funded. But in the course of these maneuvers, two brief government shutdowns occurred, from January 19–22, 2018, and again during the early part of February 9, 2018. The delays came about despite Republicans being in control of the White House, the Senate, and the House.

On February 9, Congress approved legislation known as the Bipartisan Budget Act of 2018 (PL 115-123), which provided appropriations for the remainder of the 2018 fiscal year. Among the changes in funding for agriculture-related programs were providing $2.36 billion to the Secretary of Agriculture to help alleviate losses from hurricanes and wildfires in 2017 that were not covered by other federal insurance programs; and making seed cotton a "covered commodity" for farm commodity programs.

Fiscal Year 2019
Agriculture Appropriations

Once again, agriculture appropriations passed Congress as part of a consolidated appropriations bill, well into the fiscal year—this time on February 15, 2019. The fiscal year had started more than four months earlier, on October 1, 2018. The measure included $23.03 billion in discretionary spending, $35 million more than the comparable figure from the previous year, and $129 billion in mandatory spending, an increase of $6 billion. The overall total was almost $152 billion.

The Trump administration had included $17 billion in agriculture spending in a budget proposal set forth on February 12, 2018.

The House subcommittee on agriculture appropriations marked up its bill by voice vote May 9, and the full committee approved an amended version of the measure on a 31–20 vote May 16. In the course of committee consideration of the measure, the panel approved an amendment relating to e-cigarettes on a 29–20 vote. The amendment, offered by Reps. Sanford Bishop, D-Ga., and Tom Cole, R-Okla., would ask the FDA to institute a new process to regulate e-cigarettes and nicotine vapor products, and would allow e-cigarettes not to be part of a group of products under stricter market review. Other amendments included one from Rep. Rosa DeLauro, D-Conn., that would eliminate language in the bill giving the USDA the power to regulate the new technology of creating products resembling meat from animal cells. DeLauro's amendment was rejected on a vote of 21–30. The House version included a discretionary spending total of $23.23 billion. Among the provisions were a $308 million increase in base FDA appropriations, a $79 million increase in agricultural research, and an additional $16 million for the Animal and Plant Health Inspection Service (APHIS). The House bill also included $121.82 billion in mandatory spending.

On the Senate side, the agriculture appropriations subcommittee marked up their bill by voice vote May 22, and the full committee approved an amended bill May 24 on a 31–0 vote. Added to the measure was language extending a ban on conducting inspections of horses set for slaughter for consumption by humans, using appropriated funds. The measure went to the Senate floor as part of a four-bill appropriations package, and passed on a 92–6 vote August 1. The bill's discretionary spending also totaled $23.23 billion. The provisions included a $159 million increase in base FDA appropriations and a $19 million increase for APHIS. Mandatory spending totaled $121.82 billion, resulting in an overall total of $145 billion.

Again, although Congress and the White House were under Republican control, the appropriations process foundered, leading to the longest federal government shutdown in history. The partial shutdown began December 22, 2018, and ran until January 25, 2019. Meanwhile, the November 2018 midterm elections led to a change in control of the House, with the Democrats taking over at the start of the new 116th Congress in January 2019.

Congress passed several continuing resolutions, and ultimately approved the FY 2019 Consolidated Appropriations Act (PL 116-6) on February 15, 2019. Among the provisions were an increase of $387 million in funding over the previous year for the four agricultural research agencies, an increase of $269 million in base FDA appropriations, and a $29 million increase for APHIS.

AGRICULTURE LEADERSHIP

Sonny Perdue was one of the few Cabinet officials in the Trump administration to remain in office for the entire four years of Republican president Donald Trump's term. Perdue was sworn in as Secretary of Agriculture on April 25, 2017, and left on January 20, 2021.

Perdue's background included eight years as governor of Georgia, service in the military and the Georgia state legislature, and experience as a veterinarian and a small businessman with a focus on agribusiness and transportation.

Perdue worked his way up in Georgia politics, beginning in the 1980s with service on the Houston County Planning and Zoning Board. He won a seat in the Georgia State Senate in 1990, where he remained through 2001, becoming majority leader and Senate president pro-tempore. He initially ran as a Democrat but switched to the Republican Party in 1998.

Perdue's victory as Georgia governor in 2002 marked the end of 131 years of Democratic control of the state's governorship. He won reelection to another four-year term in 2006.

A controversy over the state flag was seen as a major factor in the 2002 race. As governor, Barnes had backed changing the flag to eliminate the Confederate battle emblem, and a new state flag had gone into effect in 2001. Perdue, meanwhile, backed a referendum that would offer voters a choice, and yet another new flag, seen as a compromise between the old flag and the 2001 flag, was chosen under his governorship.

Trump announced Perdue as his choice to head the Agriculture Department on January 19, 2017, one day before Inauguration Day. This was the last of the traditional cabinet posts to be chosen. The incoming president had huge support from rural voters.

The Senate Agriculture, Nutrition, and Forestry committee held a hearing March 23, 2017, on Perdue's confirmation. The two-month delay reportedly resulted from issues over possible conflicts of interest with Perdue's financial assets. As governor, he had chosen not to put his assets in a blind trust, and had faced ethics complaints. After his nomination as secretary, Perdue opted to change his financial arrangements, putting his assets into a blind trust.

Perdue's hearing, unlike those for some other Trump nominees, was relatively amicable. A week later, the committee approved his nomination on a 19–1 vote. Democrat Kirsten Gillibrand of New York was the lone opposing vote.

After a short debate, the Senate voted 87–11 to confirm Perdue on April 24, 2017. Ten Democrats and one independent opposed his nomination. Farm groups tended to favor his confirmation, while some environmental groups opposed him, citing his connections to agribusiness and chemical companies.

Perdue took office at a time when farmers were not faring well economically. In addition, the Trump administration's focus on trade wars affected the agricultural community. The administration's budgets featured sharp cutbacks in agriculture-related programs, cutbacks that did not sit well with many on Capitol Hill. And Congress was gearing up to pass a new multiyear farm bill, which was eventually signed into law in December 2018.

One issue that arose during Perdue's tenure at USDA was the decision to move two department agencies, the National Institute of Food and Agriculture and the Economic Research Service, out of Washington, D.C., to Kansas City. As a result, many workers opted to quit to avoid moving, thus leading to a drain of knowledge at these research agencies.

The Trump administration had sought major cuts in the agencies' budgets, but Congress had balked. The agencies had conducted research on issues such as climate change and food stamps, and some observers believed the move was part of an effort to silence agency workers. Supporters of the move presented it as a way to get workers closer to the people they served.

Over the last few months of Perdue's tenure at USDA, a controversy emerged over Perdue's business practices. According to a report in *The Washington Post*, just around the time he was nominated to head the department, Perdue's company AGrowStar bought land in South Carolina from agriculture giant Archer-Daniels-Midland (ADM) for $250,000, far below market value. The property contained a grain storage site. After being confirmed as secretary, Perdue sold AGrowStar and its landholdings to an investor group. The ADM deal led to questions about whether Perdue may have faced a conflict of interest when considering questions affecting ADM.

2019–2020

The 116th Congress saw Democrats back in power in the House, providing a measure of divided government, given that the White House and Senate were controlled by Republicans. But the new Congress did not see much action on agricultural policy. The House approved a measure attempting to update rules pertaining to migrant farmworkers, but it died in the Senate. And a bill was introduced in the Senate to make it easier for farmers and forestry workers to participate in carbon credit markets, but it did not advance to the Senate floor.

Farm Workforce Bill

In 2019, the House passed legislation designed to update the rules governing migrant farmworkers working in the United States, making it easier for them to attain legal immigration status. Debate over the measure came against a backdrop of heated arguments concerning the overall issue of immigration amidst an increase of people seeking to enter the United States at the U.S.–Mexico border.

The bill, the Farm Workforce Modernization Act, or H.R. 5038, was introduced November 12, 2019, by Rep. Zoe Lofgren, D-Calif., It required applicants to have spent 180 days in U.S. agricultural work over the previous two years. If they qualified, they would get a five-year renewable agriculture visa. If they worked at least 100 days per year in agriculture, they could renew the visa. Applicants who wanted to progress toward legal permanent resident status would need to pay $1,000 and meet certain criteria based on the length of time they worked.

In addition, the bill sought to reform the process to make it easier for employers. They would be able to file their petitions for workers through one online portal rather than three (Department of Homeland Security, Department of Labor, and state workforce agencies). They also would be able to file one petition for different categories of workers rather than filing separately. Other provisions included a reduction in the cost of housing the workers.

The bill also would create a mandatory E-Verify system for agriculture workers while allowing due process for workers incorrectly singled out by the system. It was referred to the House Judiciary Committee, as well as Ways and Means, Education and Labor, and Financial Services. During consideration in the Judiciary Committee, the panel approved an amendment by Rep. Sheila Jackson Lee, D-Texas, permitting people with Temporary Protected Status or Deferred Enforced Departure residency programs to obtain permanent resident status through those programs. Among the amendments rejected was one by Rep. Steve Chabot, R-Ohio, that would not allow legal status for agricultural workers who had been convicted of driving under the influence in incidents where someone was killed or injured.

The House approved the measure December 11, 2019, on a vote of 260–165. In support of the bill were 226 Democrats and thirty-four Republicans, while 161 Republicans and three Democrats opposed it. One Democrat voted present.

While Lofgren and other backers of the measure presented it as a bipartisan compromise designed to help workers and employers, some Republicans cast it as an amnesty bill for undocumented workers. The bill was received in the Senate and sent to the Senate Judiciary Committee. There was no further action.

Carbon Credits

A proposal in the Senate aimed to make it easier for farmers and forestry workers to participate in carbon credit markets. The Growing Climate Solutions Act of 2020 was introduced by Sen. Mike Braun, R-Ind., on June 4, 2020. The legislation would have the U.S. Department of Agriculture create a voluntary certification program under which third-party verifiers and technical assistance providers could work with farmers, ranchers, and private forest landowners to help them cut back on greenhouse gas emissions, sequester carbon, or verify the processes involved in greenhouse gas credit markets. The bill, S 3894, was introduced against a backdrop of growing concern about climate change.

The bill was referred to the Senate Committee on Agriculture, Nutrition, and Forestry, which held hearings June 24. Testifying at the hearing were an Indiana farmer and representatives of the American Farm Bureau Federation, the National Farmers Union, and Land O'Lakes, who all spoke in favor of the legislation.

There was no further action on the measure in the 116th Congress.

Fiscal Year 2020 Agriculture Appropriations

It took until December 20, 2019, for Congress to pass a huge appropriations bill that included fiscal year 2020 funding for agriculture programs—more than two months after the October 1 start of the fiscal year. The measure, the Further Consolidated Appropriations Act (PL 116-94) included about $23 billion in discretionary spending for agriculture, as well as $129 billion in mandatory spending, reaching a total of $153 billion.

Compared to the previous year's bill, this new legislation saw a $235 million increase in foreign agricultural assistance, $229 million more in rural development, and a $175 million increase in rural broadband, among other changes.

In March 2019, the Trump administration had called for $19.2 billion in agriculture-related discretionary funds, which would have meant a $4.1 billion drop from the previous year.

The House Agriculture Appropriations subcommittee marked up a bill (HR 3164) by voice vote on May 23, and the full committee approved an amended version June 4 on a 29–21 vote. Among the amendments adopted was one introduced by Rep. Robert Aderholt, R-Ala., that would block the Food and Drug Administration from okaying research focusing on gene-editing of human embryos. It was adopted by voice vote. Among other actions, the committee rejected by voice vote an amendment by Rep. Andy Harris, R-Md., to make military personnel exempt from a proposal to increase the age to buy tobacco from eighteen to twenty-one. It rejected, on a vote of 23–27, another Aderhold amendment to move the minimum federal age for tobacco purchases from eighteen to twenty-one. The measure then went to the House floor, where, after debate over further amendments, it was approved as part of a five-bill "minibus" appropriation (HR 3055) June 25. The House bill called for $24.3 billion in discretionary spending.

On the Senate side, the Senate Agriculture Appropriations subcommittee marked up its version of the bill September 17, and the full committee approved an amended version (S 2522) September 19. As had happened on the House side, the Senate October 31 approved a minibus appropriation—four bills this time—including the agriculture funding. Among the amendments included was one by Sen. Martha McSally, R-Ariz., to give $3 million in grants to facilities offering shelter to domestic violence survivors and their animals. Another amendment included was by Sen. Sheldon Whitehouse, D-R.I.; it would provide $3 million to a working group examining the ocean farming of kelp and seagrass and how it affected oceans' acidity levels.

Among the differences in the two bills, the Senate bill called for $193 million more in agricultural research funding than the House bill, the House bill called for $407 million more in rural development than the Senate bill, and the House bill called for $159 million more in foreign agricultural assistance than the Senate bill.

Congress passed two continuing resolutions once the October 1 deadline came, avoiding a government shutdown. The consolidated bill was approved December 20.

Fiscal Year 2021 Agriculture Appropriations

Following the previous year's pattern, Congress approved a Consolidated Appropriations Act (PL 116-260) for fiscal year 2021 on December 27, 2020, almost three months after the start of the fiscal year. Agriculture programs were part of this larger package, with $23.4 billion in discretionary spending.

Also appropriated was $181 billion in mandatory spending, much of which came from supplemental spending on coronavirus assistance bills. The COVID-19 pandemic began in early 2020 and continued throughout the process of marking up the fiscal 2021 appropriations bills.

Among the changes from the previous year's bill were an increase of $231 million for the rural broadband program called ReConnect, and an extra $91 million in domestic nutrition programs. Back on February 12, 2020, the Trump administration released its budget plan, which called for $19.9 billion in agriculture-related spending, down $3.6 billion from fiscal 2020.

The House Agriculture Appropriations subcommittee marked up its bill July 6 by voice vote, and the full committee approved an amended measure July 9 (HR 7610). Among the approved amendments was one introduced by Rep. Sanford D. Bishop, D-Ga., that would allow the Food and Drug Administration to seek mandatory recalls of over-the-counter and prescription drugs. Another amendment approved by the committee, introduced by Rep. Chellie Pingree, D-Maine, would encourage swift action by the USDA to provide aid to the lobster industry and overall seafood industry. The measure, amended further, was included in a four-bill minibus that passed the full House July 24. The bill called for $23.97 billion in discretionary spending; it included more than $4 billion over the White House budget request.

On the Senate side, the agriculture appropriations subcommittee did not mark up a bill, and neither did the full appropriations committee. Late in the process, on November 10, 2020, the full committee's majority released draft appropriations bills in preparation for negotiations with the House. The Senate draft sought $23.3 billion in discretionary spending on agriculture programs.

Congress passed five continuing resolutions to keep the government running once the new fiscal year began. The consolidated bill was approved December 27.

MEATPACKING PLANTS AND COVID-19

The COVID-19 pandemic hit workers in meatpacking plants hard. Crowded conditions in these facilities led to the spread of COVID among these frontline workers. Outbreaks of the virus forced the closure of various facilities in the spring of 2020, as the disease was spreading across the country.

Some plants instituted new protocols, such as spreading workers out, placing dividers between them, and instituting more shifts so fewer workers would be at the plant at a time. But unions complained that not enough was being done to protect the workers. As plants began to close, the effect rippled through the economy. As of April 2020, the Commodity Futures Trading Commission stated that meat plants in the United States were operating at only about 60 percent capacity.

A *Washington Post* investigation published April 25, 2020, found that Tyson Foods, JBS USA, and Smithfield Foods, three major meat producers, did not offer protective equipment to all their workers. Some workers interviewed said they were asked to work even when sick. The three companies had closed fifteen plants due to COVID outbreaks, with meat production suffering a drop of at least 25 percent. The investigation showed that at least 3,300 meatpacking workers at plants run by these three companies and others had become infected with COVID, and at least seventeen workers had died.

Observing the tragedy, many people wondered if more could have been done. A ProPublica report from August 2020 indicated that in fact, the meatpacking and other related industries had been warned for years about the effects of a future pandemic. The George W. Bush administration had urged food and agriculture industry representatives, along with other industries, to prepare, arguing that in a pandemic, up to 40 percent of workers might not come to work because of fear, sickness, or quarantine. The ProPublica story said the food sector failed to heed these warnings, focusing instead on preventing illness among animals.

In recent years, government figures show almost 500,000 people worked in the field of animal slaughtering and processing: about 268,000 in red meat and about 230,000 in poultry. The top five meatpacking states were Nebraska, Iowa, Texas, Kansas, and Illinois. A report by the Economic Policy Institute think tank estimated that 37.5 percent of animal slaughtering and processing workers in the United States were foreign-born, with almost half of those workers coming from Mexico. Among the foreign-born workers, more than 70 percent were noncitizens.

The Trump administration opted to put out new guidance for meatpacking and processing workers on April 26, 2020. The Occupational Safety and Health Administration (OSHA) and the Centers for Disease Control and Prevention (CDC)'s interim guidance included new information on issues including cleaning of shared tools, screening employees for COVID, and practicing social distancing. However, critics charged that the guidelines were basically voluntary.

President Donald Trump issued an executive order April 28 that deemed meat processing part of the country's critical infrastructure. Some interpretations of the order indicated that he was ordering processing plants to stay open, while others saw it as more symbolic than anything else. Unions, meanwhile, argued that the order put workers' lives at risk.

In September 2020, six months into the pandemic, OSHA cited two plants—a Smithfield plant in South Dakota and a JBS plant in Colorado—levying fines totaling about $29,000 for failing to keep their workers safe during the pandemic. Critics said it was a small amount, given the toll COVID had taken on the industry.

Furthermore, a report by the U.S. Department of Agriculture's Economic Research Service, released in September 2021, found that the spread of COVID in meatpacking plants had led to higher rates of the virus in neighboring communities.

As of mid-April 2020, the rate of COVID in rural counties dependent on meatpacking was almost ten times as high as the rate in rural counties dependent on another industry. By mid-July, a reduction in the COVID rate in meatpacking plants led to the end of this difference. The study authors believed that efforts by the meatpacking industry to protect its workers contributed to this drop.

On July 28, 2020, Senator Cory Booker, D-N.J., introduced legislation called the Safe Line Speeds During COVID-19 Act of 2020 (S 4338). The bill would direct the Secretary of Agriculture to temporarily suspend faster line speeds at poultry and meat plants. The measure was referred to the Committee on Agriculture, Nutrition, and Forestry, but did not advance.

Although the 116th Congress did not pass legislation on the issue, a report issued October 27, 2021, by the House Select Committee on the Coronavirus Crisis found that the crisis in the meatpacking industry was more serious than previously reported. The committee, which began its investigation February 1, 2021, found that in the first year of the pandemic, at least 59,000 workers at five large meatpacking companies—JBS, Tyson Foods, Smithfield Foods, Cargill, and National Beef—had had COVID, and 269 workers had died. Earlier estimates had put the number of employees with COVID at 22,700.

The committee also reported that some companies failed to heed federal and state COVID warnings, did not move quickly enough to manage safety issues relating to the virus, and put company profits over safety for workers. In addition, the committee faulted the Trump administration

for not doing enough to protect the meatpacking workers, specifically mentioning the U.S. Department of Labor's decision not to issue an Emergency Temporary Standard that would have set out tougher, enforceable measures for employers to follow to protect workers from the pandemic.

The issue would continue to hold Congress's attention after the first year of the pandemic. Booker reintroduced his bill, along with Reps. Rosa DeLauro, D-Conn., and Bennie Thompson, D-Miss., in March 2021. The bill, now numbered S 713, was again referred to the Agriculture, Nutrition, and Forestry committee. In late 2021, Booker and Rep. Ro Khanna, D-Calif., introduced legislation, the Protecting America's Meatpacking Workers Act (S 3285), that aimed to strengthen protections for meatpacking workers. Among the bill's provisions were the establishment of a system to report publicly the number of workers who contracted COVID-19. The measure was referred to the Committee on Health, Education, Labor, and Pensions.

CHAPTER 9

Health and Human Services

Health and Human Services

President Donald Trump's tenure began with a push to fulfill a Republican campaign promise to repeal President Barack Obama's signature piece of legislation, the 2010 Patient Protection and Affordable Care Act (ACA). When that effort failed, the Republican-led House and Senate looked for other ways to chip away at ACA provisions, and successfully delayed or eliminated a number of the law's most unpopular pieces. After Democrats assumed control of the House during the 2018 midterms, they shifted the focus to strengthening the ACA and getting more funding to bolster other health programs in an effort to paint themselves as the party of health care ahead of the 2020 general election, especially given the COVID-19 pandemic. Despite the ratcheting up of partisan tensions, driven in part by a formal presidential impeachment inquiry, the 115th and 116th Congresses also made headway on bipartisan priorities, such as lowering prescription drug prices and passing measures to address the opioid crisis.

Figure 9.1 Outlays for Medicare and Medicaid

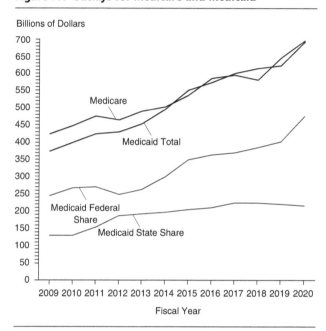

Billions of Dollars

SOURCE: Medicare: Office of Management and Budget, *Historical Tables, Budget of the United States Government: Fiscal Year 2021* (Washington DC: U.S. Government Printing Office, 2020), Table 3.2; Medicaid: Centers for Medicare and Medicaid Services, *2018 Actuarial Report on Financial Outlook for Medicaid* (Washington DC, Department of Health and Human Services, 2018); Congressional Research Services, *Medicaid Financing and Expenditures* (Washington DC, Congress, 2020); Centers for Medicare and Medicaid Services, *NHE Projections*, CMS.gov, 2021, Table 16.

NOTES: * indicates estimate. CMS has not released their latest actuarial reports so 2018–2020 are based on past projected estimates.

353

ACA Repeal Attempt

In 2010, Democrats leveraged their majority in the Senate to get a bill on President Obama's desk that would expand health care coverage for uninsured Americans while at the same time reining in the cost of health insurance. The final legislation, commonly referred to as Obamacare, included changes to employer-based health insurance, expanded the federally funded and state-administered Medicaid program, created state-based health insurance exchanges, and established federal subsidies to help offset the cost of health insurance purchased through the exchanges.

The law set minimum coverage requirements for health plans and barred insurance companies from refusing coverage to individuals with preexisting conditions. It also required any employer with more than fifty full-time equivalent workers to either provide health insurance or pay a penalty. And, any American who chose not to obtain health insurance would be penalized on their annual income tax filing. To help cover the cost of the legislation, a number of new taxes were included in the bill's language, such as a 2.3 percent tax on many medical devices, a tax on high-value employer-paid insurance plans (known as the Cadillac tax), a 3.8 percent net investment income tax, and a 0.9 percentage point increase in the Medicare payroll tax for individuals with income above a certain level.

While the idea behind the ACA was relatively popular with voters, many of its provisions—and the way it was pushed through Congress with only Democratic support—raised the ire of Republicans who promised to undo it either legislatively or through the courts. After Trump won the November 2016 election, Republicans began talking in earnest about how they could use their House and Senate majority to dismantle the ACA, though they needed to move cautiously because even some Republican voters feared losing the health insurance they gained under the law.

On January 10, 2017, incoming president Trump called on Republicans to repeal Obamacare the following week. Specifically, Trump wanted Republicans to eliminate the old law at the same time as they passed a replacement, instead of repealing the law and devising a replacement later. Taking the president's approach, some Republicans speculated, would help them hold their caucus together in the face of near unanimous Democratic opposition while also making sure they did not drastically increase the ranks of the uninsured.

In the spring, House Republicans introduced the American Health Care Act (AHCA), their repeal and replace attempt. The law would set the individual mandate penalty at $0, end Medicaid expansion, delay or repeal a number of the bill's taxes, and create funds to help states stabilize their health care markets. Dissension in the party's ranks resulted in additions to the bill, including those that set work requirements for Medicaid and eliminated the federal essential health benefits required for insurance plans. The House barely cleared the measure, but the Senate was never able to pass the AHCA or its own legislation because a handful of Republicans disagreed with either the provisions or the process. Instead, both chambers used other pieces of legislation—including annual spending bills and the Tax Cuts and Jobs Act of 2017—to effectively eliminate parts of the ACA, including the individual mandate.

Drug Pricing

Among President Trump's legislative priorities was finding a solution to rein in the rising cost of prescription medications. The price of many of the most commonly used prescription drugs had been rising faster than inflation, and was forcing some Americans to ration their care or make difficult choices about whether to spend their income on medication or other needs. In many wealthy nations, the government negotiates with pharmaceutical companies to set drug prices and keep their cost in check. In the United States, the federal government's focus has over time been toward helping generic and biosimilar products get to market faster and increasing pricing transparency as a means to lower prices.

During the 115th Congress, two bills made it to President Trump's desk intended to address transparency in drug costs. Specifically, the bills banned the use of the so-called gag clause, which prohibits pharmacists from alerting consumers when a certain medication would cost less if purchased out-of-pocket than with insurance. One measure dealt specifically with prescriptions covered under Medicare plans, while the other banned the use of gag clauses by health insurance companies that make their products available through group insurance and the health insurance exchanges. While the pharmaceutical sector did not push back on the legislation, they also indicated a belief that few companies use gag clauses anymore. Pharmacists, however, said they are frequently subjected to them.

In the final two years of President Trump's term, the House and Senate proposed a variety of bills intended to reduce the cost of prescription drugs. These included measures that would regulate certain agreements between brand name and generic drug makers, streamline the process for bringing over-the-counter medications to market, limit out-of-pocket prescription spending under Medicare, and require the Department of Health and Human Services to negotiate with drug makers on the prices of some of the most expensive prescriptions covered by Medicare. However, with divided control, the two chambers never reached a consensus on the best means for regulating drug costs. Many members of Congress expressed an ongoing desire to address the issue, though nothing made it to President Trump's desk.

Opioid Crisis

Historically, opioid-based medications, such as oxycodone, were prescribed only to treat extreme pain or for terminal illnesses. That changed in the 1990s, when pharmaceutical companies began pushing doctors to prescribe their use for a range of afflictions, and by 2017, according to the Centers for Disease Control and Prevention (CDC), more than 191 million opioid prescriptions were dispensed. Contrary to the information provided by the drugs' makers, opioids are highly addictive. In 2018, 10.3 million Americans misused opioids, according to the Substance Abuse and Mental Health Administration, and many of those individuals first came in contact with an opioid through a valid prescription. The proliferation of opioid addiction has had devastating consequences. In 2017, the CDC reported 47,600 opioid-linked overdose deaths. In addition to being a public health crisis, there is also a high economic cost associated with opioid addiction, estimated at tens of billions of dollars per year in lost productivity and state and local services.

In 2018, the president signed into law an omnibus package that included dozens of measures to help stem the opioid crisis. Provisions in the bill included additional funding for public health campaigns and outreach, new tools for community organizations to use in their fight against the epidemic, and changes to existing regulations that would help make it easier for some individuals to access and pay for the treatment they need. The law also encouraged multiple federal agencies, including HHS and the Food and Drug Administration, to study alternative treatments for pain management and identify other gaps that exist in treating drug addiction. To cover the cost of the legislation, estimated at $44 million over ten years, Congress included a variety of offsets.

During the 115th Congress, the two chambers also considered smaller pieces of legislation that focused on specific aspects of substance use disorders. One measure would have aligned the release of substance use treatment records more closely with the Health Insurance Portability and Accountability Act, allowing such records to be shared for certain uses without the express consent of the patient. Republicans said this would make accessing care easier, but Democrats objected, arguing that it could expose those seeking treatment to detrimental impacts, such as loss of a job or child custody. Another measure would provide Medicaid coverage for residential opioid abuse treatment at a facility with more than sixteen beds. The existing prohibition on such coverage dates back to an earlier Congress that sought to encourage more use of smaller community care facilities. While some legislators felt that the bill offering Medicaid coverage to patients at larger residential sites did not go far enough, it was wrapped into the omnibus bill signed by President Trump.

Chronology of Action on Health and Human Services

The first year of the 115th Congress was dominated by the Republican attempt to repeal and replace the 2010 Patient Protection and Affordable Care Act. That effort ulti-mately came up short, though Republicans were successful in further delaying the implementation of some of the law's taxes and zeroing out the individual mandate penalty.

2017–2018

Across the two years, the chambers also reauthorized the Food and Drug Administration's authority to collect drug and device maker user fees, extended funding for the Children's Health Insurance Program, and sought ways to address growing drug prices, the opioid crisis, and gaps in existing federal regulations.

Affordable Care Act Overhaul

An extensive amount of time during the first session of the 115th Congress was dedicated to the Republican campaign promise to repeal the 2010 Patient Protection and Affordable Care Act (ACA; PL 111-148, PL 111-152). After seven years of trying to dismantle the landmark achievement of the Barack Obama presidency through the courts and in Congress, the two chambers came up short of repealing the law in 2017. The House passed a repeal and replace measure (HR 1628) but the Senate was unable to do the same after Sen. John McCain cast a decisive "no" vote. Under separate pieces of legislation, the chambers did manage to amend or eliminate certain provisions from the bill, including the individual mandate that required all Americans to have a health insurance plan or face a penalty.

Budget Authority

The Senate set the stage for action to repeal the ACA during the first weeks of the 115th Congress when the chamber decided to use the budget reconciliation process to get legislation to President Trump's desk without a single Democratic

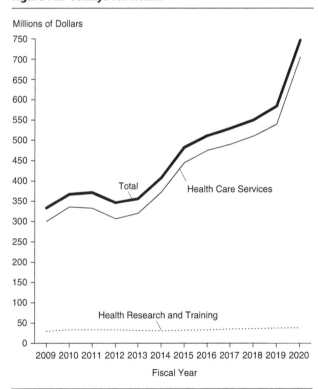

Figure 9.2 Outlays for Health

Millions of Dollars

Total

Health Care Services

Health Research and Training

2009 2010 2011 2012 2013 2014 2015 2016 2017 2018 2019 2020

Fiscal Year

SOURCE: Office of Management and Budget, *Historical Tables, Budget of the United States Government: Fiscal Year 2021* (Washington DC: U.S. Government Printing Office, 2020), Table 3.2.

NOTE: Total line includes expenditures not shown separately. * Indicates estimate

vote. While the procedural tool can only be used for legislation related to spending and taxation, it would allow Republicans in the Senate to overcome a filibuster with only their fifty-two seats. Democrats relied on budget reconciliation to enact the ACA over fierce Republican opposition, and Senate Republicans calculated that they could eliminate the spending portions of the ACA while leaving the rest of the law intact as they negotiated language with the House for a full replacement measure. The chamber had done the same during the previous Congress, sending HR 3762, which would strike spending-related portions of the ACA, to President Obama. The president vetoed the bill, and the House and Senate did not have enough votes for an override.

With this in mind, Republicans introduced S Con Res 3 to set budget authority and provide reconciliation instructions to the House Energy and Commerce and Ways and Means Committees, as well as the Senate Finance and Health, Education, Labor, and Pensions Committees, which would be tasked with drafting legislation to repeal the ACA. These committees were each asked to find at least $1 billion in deficit reduction over the next decade to offset the cost of a complete ACA repeal.

After invoking cloture on S Con Res 3, the Senate debated the resolution for fifty hours and considered dozens of amendments, none of which were adopted. In the early morning hours of January 12, 2017, the Senate voted 51–48 to approve S Con Res 3, with Sen. Rand Paul, R-Ky., the only Republican voting against the measure, expressing concern that use of budget reconciliation would leave too much of the ACA in place. Democrats staged a last-minute protest, using the roll call vote to stand and voice their opposition to the bill, over warnings of the chair that such remarks were not in order. Before the final vote, Sen. Bernie Sanders, I-Vt., said on the floor that 30 million Americans were set to lose their health care if Republicans repealed the ACA without a replacement, and that many could die without the care they need. "They have no alternative proposition," Sanders said of Republican efforts to repeal the ACA. "They want to kill [the Affordable Care Act], but they have no idea how they're going to bring forth a substitute proposal."

The House voted 227–198 in favor of S Con Res 3 on January 13, with nine Republicans in opposition. With that vote, the two chambers were able to begin working on legislation to implement an ACA repeal.

A few days later, at the request of Senate Democrats, the Congressional Budget Office (CBO) released a report estimating that had the 2016 attempt to dismantle Obamacare (HR 3762) been successful, the number of uninsured Americans would have grown by 32 million, while those with health care plans through the marketplace could have seen their premiums nearly double.

House Action

On March 7, Republicans introduced two bills containing implementing legislation and sent them to the House Energy and Commerce and House Ways and Means Committees, where they were approved the next day. On March 13, the

CBO issued its initial estimate that 52 million Americans would be uninsured under the measures and premiums would rise as compared to current law through 2020. Despite that prediction, and over Democratic opposition, the House Budget Committee combined the two bills into the American Health Care Act of 2017 (AHCA; HR 1628) and voted 19–17 on March 16 to send them to the floor.

The bill passed out of committee would effectively repeal one of the law's most unpopular provisions among Republicans—the individual mandate—by setting the penalty at $0. To encourage Americans to continue purchasing health insurance, the law required insurers to add a 30 percent surcharge on premiums for twelve months for any individual who went two months or more without health care coverage. The bill also zeroed out the penalty for the employer mandate. Additionally, the AHCA would

- Repeal the premium tax credit and cost-sharing reductions for individuals who purchase insurance through an exchange, replacing it with refundable tax credits
- Create a $100 billion Patient and State Stability Fund to help states stabilize their insurance markets through 2026
- End new federal funding for Medicaid expansion beginning in 2020
- Repeal or delay more than one dozen taxes, including the 3.8 percent tax on net investment income for certain taxpayers, the 2.3 percent medical device tax, the tax on high-value employer-paid insurance plans (Cadillac tax), annual fees on health insurers, the limitation on contributions to flexible spending accounts, and the 10 percent excise tax on indoor tanning services that involve ultraviolet radiation
- Ban, for one year, federal funding for Planned Parenthood
- Allow nongroup and small group insurers to charge up to five times more for premiums for older enrollees than younger ones
- Increase the cap on how much an individual can place in a health savings account to $6,550 each year per individual
- Require individuals to provide proof of citizenship or lawful presence in the United States before receiving Medicaid
- Amend how the federal government provides Medicaid support to states

House leadership quickly announced their intent to bring the bill to the floor the week of March 20, then almost immediately retracted their plans after members of the highly conservative House Freedom Caucus and some moderate Republicans revolted. In the weeks that followed, Republican leaders began modifying the existing bill. These changes included

- Preventing new states from opting into Medicaid expansion
- Allowing states to establish work requirements for certain Medicaid recipients

- Giving states the option to receive federal Medicaid funds as a block grant
- Granting states greater flexibility in use of their Medicaid funds
- Delaying the Cadillac tax until 2026 and repealing most other existing taxes effective for the 2017 tax year
- Eliminating in 2018 the requirement that qualified health plans provide ten essential health benefits, and shifting that power to the states to decide what must be included in a plan to be eligible for purchase using federal tax credits
- Removing small group market insurers from the 30 percent surcharge on individuals without continuous coverage
- Eliminating the requirement for an individual to provide documentation of U.S. citizenship or lawful presence in the country before receiving Medicaid coverage

Those changes gave Republican leadership assurance that they would have enough votes to secure the AHCA's passage. Before final passage, the House adopted two rules governing floor debate; one was a self-executing amendment that incorporated three changes into the bill. One restored the provision regarding minimum essential benefits, but gave states the option to seek a waiver. Another created an $8 billion fund to help individuals with preexisting conditions who see their premiums rise, and the third created a $15 billion federal risk sharing program.

As amended, on May 4, the House passed the AHCA 217–213. Twenty Republicans joined all Democrats in voting against it.

Senate Floor Action

In the Senate, Republicans announced that they would not take up the AHCA but rather planned to assemble their own bill and use the budget reconciliation process to pass it. Senate leadership said their bill would follow some of the House language but would also include additional funding for health insurance subsidies. As in the House, the Senate bill was drafted behind closed doors and the all-male group of thirteen Republican senators tasked with its creation were mum about the process, which drew criticism even from members of their own caucus. When asked for a timeline on the bill, Senate Majority Whip John Cornyn, R-Texas, would only say that once the chamber had fifty-one votes, they would bring it to the floor.

On June 19, Majority Leader Mitch McConnell, R-Ky., sent a draft of the Senate legislation to the CBO for review, which reported back a week later that the bill would increase the number of uninsured Americans to 49 million over the next decade. The Senate draft was also predicted to save $321 billion in the ten years after its enactment. Further, the average premium for a single individual would be 20 percent higher in 2018 than under the current law, and 10 percent higher in 2019. With that knowledge, some Republicans immediately came out against the bill, and movement on repealing the ACA was again thrown into question.

Republicans began floating the idea of passing a skinny repeal as a means to go to conference with the House, but many House conservatives did not support that approach. Regardless, on July 27, McConnell introduced a scaled-back repeal as an amendment to HR 1628. Rather than repealing the law in its entirety, the eight-page bill would

- Repeal the individual mandate
- Eliminate the employer mandate for eight years
- Eliminate the medical device tax for three years
- Raise the cap for three years on how much an individual can contribute to a health savings account
- Give additional funding to community health centers
- Defund Planned Parenthood for one year
- Give states the option to use waivers to roll back specific insurance regulations as long as they met certain requirements

A CBO projection released the same day said the skinny bill would see 15 million more people added to the uninsured rolls in 2018, and premiums would rise approximately 20 percent in all years between 2018 and 2026. The amendment, however, would save $135.6 billion over a decade.

After receiving assurances from weary Republicans that they would support the amendment, and indications from the House that they would go to conference, McConnell announced plans for a vote to take place the same evening the amendment was introduced. Vice President Mike Pence went to the Capitol, assuming that his vote would be needed as a tiebreaker. In the end, in the early hours of July 28, three Republican senators—Susan Collins of Maine, Lisa Murkowski of Alaska, and John McCain of Arizona—voted against the measure and it was defeated 49–51. The deciding vote was cast by McCain, who had only recently returned to Washington after a brain cancer diagnosis, in dramatic fashion: he walked into the chamber and flashed a thumbs down. According to Sen. McCain, he was driven to vote against the skinny repeal in part because of how the measure was drafted without any hearings or consultations with key stakeholders. At the White House, where the president had already been distancing himself from the effort, Trump tweeted "3 Republicans and 48 Democrats let the American people down. As I said from the beginning, let ObamaCare implode, then deal. Watch!"

Senate Republicans made one final effort to in 2017 to repeal the ACA. Republican senators, including Bill Cassidy, R-La., and Lindsay Graham, R-S.C., proposed a bill that would cap traditional Medicaid spending, repeal the individual and employer mandates, eliminate the tax on medical devices, allow insurers to charge people with preexisting conditions higher premiums, and replace federal funding for certain portions of the law with block grants to states that would expire in 2027. Several Republicans expressed their support, and leadership began

working to get the draft to the floor, mindful that their budget reconciliation process for fiscal 2017 was due to expire on September 30. However, on September 22, McCain announced that he would not support the legislation, noting that Democrats and Republicans needed to do a better job working together and that more information was needed on the bill's cost and impact. More senators announced their opposition in the days that followed, including Collins and Sen. Ted Cruz, R-Texas.

The Graham-Cassidy proposal never received a floor vote, and the ACA remained the law of the land with Republicans announcing that they wanted to move to their second-biggest priority: tax code reform. Within that bill was a provision eliminating the ACA's individual mandate starting in 2019.

ADDITIONAL AFFORDABLE CARE ACT LEGISLATION

Stymied in their efforts to overhaul the Affordable Care Act, Republicans instead targeted individual pieces of the far-ranging law. They succeeded in working with Democrats to repeal some controversial provisions. But several of their proposals failed to gain sufficient traction.

ELIMINATING THE INDEPENDENT PAYMENT ADVISORY BOARD

In an attempt to get control of Medicare spending, the 2010 Patient Protection and Affordable Care Act (ACA; PL 111-148, PL 111-152) established a fifteen-member commission made up of doctors and other health care experts, known as the Independent Payment Advisory Board (IPAB). That group, whose members would be appointed by the president and confirmed by the Senate, was charged with making recommendations on ways to cut Medicare costs if spending on the program was rising too fast. Republicans labeled it as one of the health care law's "death panels," with some of the party's supporters arguing that it was a means to ration care (the law includes a specific provision preventing the IPAB from rationing care, nor was it permitted to make decisions about an individual's health care). Given the slow growth of Medicare spending—and the political minefield the IPAB created—President Barack Obama never appointed anyone to sit on the committee, nor did President Donald Trump (the law's provision states that if the panel is never seated, it falls to the secretary of Health and Human Services to find cuts). However, that did not stop a bipartisan group of legislators from targeting the IPAB for elimination during the 115th Congress, which they successfully did through the Bipartisan Budget Act of 2018 (PL 115-123).

House Committee Action

On October 4, 2017, the House Ways and Means Committee considered HR 849, the Protecting Seniors Access to Medicare Act, introduced by Rep. Phil Roe, R-Tenn., which would terminate the IPAB. During markup, Republicans argued that the IPAB was not a cost-saving measure but rather a means to remove Congress and the American public from the health care decision-making process. "Putting Medicare on sustainable financial footing is a top priority for this Committee, but passing the buck to a handful of unaccountable bureaucrats is not the right approach," said Committee Chair Kevin Brady, R-Texas, in his opening remarks. Democrats, despite some of their members being counted among the bill's cosponsors, expressed concern about the cost of eliminating the panel. According to the nonpartisan Congressional Budget Office, repealing the IPAB would cost around $17.5 billion through 2027 in missed opportunities for spending reductions. They also criticized Republicans for focusing on the IPAB when there were more pressing challenges facing the country.

During markup, the committee approved by voice vote a substitute amendment from Brady that would revise the short title of the bill. They also rejected 15–22, a Democratic amendment that would prevent the IPAB from being repealed if the Centers for Medicare and Medicaid Services found that Medicare spending on prescription drugs was growing faster than the Consumer Price Index for All Urban Consumers. Another amendment was ruled not germane, and would have stopped HR 849 from taking effect until the House Ways and Means Committee chair sent to the secretary of the Treasury a request for President Trump's past ten years of federal tax returns and those of his businesses. Ultimately, the committee reported HR 849 favorably to the full House, 24–13.

House Floor Action

On November 1, the House Rules Committee voted 7–3 to advance to the floor its rule governing debate on HR 849. On the same day, the White House issued a Statement of Administration Policy expressing its support for the legislation. The statement noted that while Medicaid spending is on an unsustainable path, the IPAB amounted to little more than federal overreach that circumvented the power of Congress and the executive.

The following day, on November 2, the House voted 307–111 to pass HR 849, with seventy-six Democrats joining Republicans to pass the measure. The Senate never took up HR 849, however, its provisions were included in the Bipartisan Budget Act of 2018 (PL 115–123), which President Trump signed on February 9, 2018.

MEDICAL DEVICE TAX REPEAL

Within the 2010 Patient Protection and Affordable Care Act (ACA; PL 111-148; PL 111-152) was a provision placing a 2.3 percent excise tax on the sale of medical devices by a manufacturer, producer, or importer. That portion of the law had been a main component of Republican attempts to repeal or overhaul the ACA. Over the years, it has enjoyed some bipartisan support, especially from Democrats in districts with many medical device manufacturers. Like most provisions of the ACA, the tax went into effect in 2013. However, it was suspended from 2016 through 2018 and again delayed until 2020 as

part of a continuing resolution (PL 115–120). With control of both the House and Senate, and a Republican in the White House, eliminating the medical device tax was again on the Republican agenda during the 115th Congress. The House passed a repeal in July 2018, but the Senate never took up the bill. The tax was eventually eliminated under the Further Consolidated Appropriations Act, 2020 (PL 116–94), signed into law on December 20, 2019.

House Action

Among their many concerns with the ACA, Republicans have long argued—with some Democratic backing—that the medical device tax included in the health care law discourages innovation in the medical device sector, which could ultimately raise health care costs by inhibiting the development of new tools. Those Democrats who support the tax argue that repealing it would add to the federal deficit; in 2017, the Congressional Budget Office estimated that repealing the device tax could cost nearly $20 billion in the long term.

On July 23, 2018, the House Rules Committee took up HR 184, the Medical Device Tax Repeal (the measure bypassed committee markup). The closed rule, approved 8–4, allowed for one hour of debate and one motion to recommit (which offers a final chance to debate and amend a bill), and barred amendment debate. On the same day, the White House issued a Statement of Administration Policy, expressing its support for HR 184. According to the administration, repealing the tax would result in lower health care costs while at the same time protecting jobs. "This tax is an obstacle for patients seeking access to medical advances, and threatens to undermine the position of the United States as the global leader in healthcare investment and innovation," the statement read.

On July 24, the full House voted 283–132 in favor of a full repeal of the device tax. The vote marked the highest level of Democratic support of any attempt to repeal the device tax. The bill moved to the Senate where there was some hope among those in the medical device community that there would be enough Democratic support for a full repeal to pass. The Senate's companion legislation had multiple Democratic cosponsors, most of whom were from states with a high concentration of medical device manufacturers and who were also up for reelection in November 2018. However, neither the House nor the Senate version of the bill ever received committee or full floor consideration in 2018. The tax was eventually eliminated as part of the fiscal year 2020 omnibus appropriations bill signed into law on December 20, 2019 (PL 116-94). Because the tax was in a delayed status at the time it was repealed, it never actually went into effect.

SAVE AMERICAN WORKERS ACT

Under the 2010 Patient Protection and Affordable Care Act (ACA; PL 111–148, PL 111–152), employers with more than fifty full-time equivalent workers are required to furnish health insurance for any full-time employee.

The law defines "full-time" as anyone working thirty or more hours per week, and failure to provide coverage can result in a penalty. According to opponents of the provision, to avoid the significant fine, employers are forced to more carefully track worker hours to keep them under the cap, resulting in decreased flexibility and earning potential for employees, especially those who work in hourly, part-time, or seasonal positions. Supporters argued the opposite, saying that keeping the forty-hour workweek designation allows employers to hire more part-time employees to avoid the fine, thus decreasing the earning potential for millions of Americans who are forced to choose part-time instead of full-time employment, while also reducing health care coverage.

In 2018, the thirty-hour designation was another ACA target for Republicans. A measure revising the language of the law to stipulate that full-time means forty hours was slated for floor action, however, it was never debated during the final year of the 115th Congress in either the House or the Senate.

House Action

On September 14, 2017, Reps. Jackie Walorski, R-Ind., and Dan Lipinski, D-Ill., introduced the Save American Workers Act (HR 3798), which would amend the ACA to define full-time employment as forty hours per week. In a press release announcing the bill, Walorski said, "Obamacare's burdensome employer mandate and its redefinition of full-time workers are hurting middle class American families and crushing our job creators." Similar legislation passed the House in both 2014 and 2015, but never made it to then President Barack Obama's desk.

Like other ACA provision repeal or amend attempts, HR 3798 did not go through the markup process before moving to the House Rules Committee. On September 12, 2018, the Rules Committee held its proceedings on HR 3798, granting a closed rule that prohibited debate on any amendments. As approved by the rules committee, HR 3798 was packaged with four other measures seeking to change, delay, or suspend other portions of the ACA. The package included a measure (HR 1150) eliminating a 10 percent excise tax on indoor tanning, and another (HR 6718) to repeal a provision that requires health insurance companies to send covered individuals a statement certifying their coverage. Perhaps the most consequential piece of the package, other than the change to the full-time definition, was HR 4616, which would retroactively eliminate the employer mandate until 2019 and delay the 40 percent tax on certain high-cost health plans until 2023.

After the House approved the rule governing debate on September 13, 2018, it deferred any further action on the measure. Hurricane Florence delayed a House vote, and then the impending midterm election forced Republican leadership to again punt the measure. Traditionally, changes to the 2010 health care law have experienced greater success when they were rolled into year-end spending packages and

Republicans indicated some hope that might happen again in 2018. However, that goal never come to fruition.

SMALL BUSINESS HEALTH PLANS

While efforts in the House and Senate to repeal and replace the Patient Protection and Affordable Care Act (ACA; PL 111–148, PL 111–152) were ongoing, legislators were also working on multiple bills that would complement the larger measure. One of those would create rules allowing groups of small businesses to join together and offer their employees health insurance coverage. Over Democratic objections, the House passed a bill creating new pooled insurance plans, but the Senate never held hearings or a floor vote on the bill.

House Committee Action

On March 8, 2017, the House Education and the Workforce Committee held its markup of HR 1101, the Small Business Health Fairness Act. The measure would create a system in which small employers or professional associations could join together and create association health plans (AHPs). To ensure those plans were affordable, the association plans would be exempt from many of the state regulations that set minimum standards on what ACA-compliant health plans must include. However, the plans would still be subject to the same federal requirements applied to large employer plans.

Republicans argued that the legislation would ensure more workers have access to affordable health insurance coverage through their employers, ultimately giving consumers additional flexibility and choice in their health benefit decisions. Small businesses, they said, would have greater market power if they could work together to establish an insurance pool large enough to offer more cost-effective plans.

Democrats saw the opposite. In their mind, HR 1101 would weaken the protections offered to consumers under the ACA and push more insurance costs onto individuals. They also worried that this new category of plans would compete against existing individual and small group insurance offerings, which could disrupt the market and impact the state insurance exchanges to the detriment of individuals who choose to purchase insurance there. According to the bill's opponents, small businesses with younger, healthier employees would be incentivized to create insurance pools, while those businesses with older sicker employees would not be invited to join such plans.

Democrats also raised the fact that it seemed almost pointless to debate bills such as HR 1101 when other committees were working on dismantling the ACA. If successful, ACA repeal would pose a serious disruption to the health insurance landscape, and without knowing that bill's language or the impact it might have, spending time on complementary legislation was nonsensical, they said.

During committee markup, Democrats proposed and then withdrew six amendments. One amendment would have expressed the sense of the Congress that the body should not pursue health insurance reform until the Congressional Budget Office (CBO) issued its estimate of whether such action would lower insurance prices, provide better coverage, and not increase the number of uninsured Americans. Three other amendments would bar HR 1101 from going into effect if the CBO determined that it could increase premium costs in the small group market, for middle-class workers, or for older Americans. Another would stop the bill from taking effect if the CBO said that it would reduce coverage for substance abuse treatment. The sixth amendment, from Rep. Jared Polis, D-Colo., would allow for the importation of certain prescription medications from Canada and other countries so long as they met specific requirements. Polis also proposed an amendment that was ruled not germane and which would require health care service providers to make their prices publicly available; noncompliance would result in a penalty. The committee did adopt one substitute amendment that made technical changes to the language of the bill.

The committee voted 22–17 on March 8 to favorably report HR 1101 to the House, as amended.

House Floor Action

The House Rules Committee convened on March 20 to develop the rules governing floor action. The bill again sparked debate. Democrats asserted that allowing associations to create small insurance plans would drive up rates across insurance plans by diluting the pool of healthy individuals who participate in the exchanges or other small group markets. Republicans held firm that their bill was a net savings for those employed by small businesses who would now have greater access to low-cost plans. The committee recommended a rule providing one hour of debate and made one amendment. That amendment, from Rep. Jaime Herrera Beutler, R-Wash., would exempt existing association health plans from the bill's certification process and other requirements. Existing plans would still be required to follow other rules set in the bill, such as maintaining financial solvency.

Floor debate in the House took place on March 22, 2017. Rep. Beutler's amendment was adopted by voice vote. Before final passage, the chamber rejected, 179–233, a motion to recommit from Rep. Carol Shea-Porter, D-N.H., to send the bill back to the House Education and the Workforce Committee with instructions to add an amendment that would require the new pooled health insurance plans to cover treatment for substance abuse disorders.

The House passed HR 1101, as amended, largely along party lines, 236–175. The bill was never taken up by the Senate in 2017, and did not reach President Trump's desk.

SELF-INSURANCE PROTECTION

Another Republican measure targeting the Patient Protection and Affordable Care Act (ACA; PL 111–148, PL 111–152) was a bill that would remove stop-loss

insurance from existing regulations that govern health insurance plans. As with other similar measures, while the bill easily passed the House, the Senate did not have the votes to take it up.

House Committee Action

On March 2, 2017, Rep. Phil Roe, R-Tenn., introduced the Self-Insurance Protection Act (HR 1304). The bill dealt specifically with stop-loss insurance coverage, which self-insured health plans have the option to purchase to cover their insurance costs after claims reach a certain level. Stop-loss coverage is mainly used by employers that finance their own health insurance plans and provides them a safety net for the risk they assume. When an employer purchases stop-loss coverage, they are protected from unexpectedly large claims. Under existing law, these stop-loss options are regulated under the strict rules governing standard health insurance plans. HR 1304 would prohibit the government from regulating stop-loss coverage in the same way it regulates other insurance plans. Unlike most bills in the Republicans' health care overhaul plans, HR 1304 had bipartisan support, and both Democrats and Republicans saw it as a means to make health insurance more affordable for millions of Americans. (In 2016, 57 percent of workers were in plans that relied on stop-loss insurance.)

The House Education and the Workforce Committee marked up HR 1304 on March 8, 2017. Democrats proposed two amendments that were withdrawn. One would express the sense of Congress that health care reform efforts should not proceed until the Congressional Budget Office could verify whether such efforts would improve offerings and not negatively impact large numbers of Americans. The second withdrawn amendment sought to clarify that nothing in the bill would prevent states from regulating stop-loss insurance plans. One amendment, from Rep. Jared Polis, D-Colo., was ruled not germane. That amendment would have made available public health insurance options through the state exchanges. The committee ultimately reported the bill favorably to the House by voice vote. The bill was sent with a substitute amendment that made technical changes.

House Floor Action

On April 3, the House Rules Committee proposed a closed rule for debate of HR 1304. The rule provided for one hour of debate, waived all points of order against consideration of the bill, and provided for one motion to recommit. While Democrats did not outright endorse the bill during the Rules Committee meeting, they also indicated that they would not encourage their caucus to vote against it. On April 5, 2017, the House passed HR 1304, 400–16. It was never taken up in the Senate.

COMMON SENSE NUTRITION DISCLOSURE

Based on a provision in the 2010 Patient Protection and Affordable Care Act, by May 2017, restaurants with twenty or more locations were required to come into compliance with Food and Drug Administration (FDA) rules requiring them to publicly display calorie and nutrition information for their products. Although the deadline was extended by one year, Republicans introduced legislation in January 2017 that would give restaurants greater leeway in how they post calorie information and serving sizes, and would also protect them from certain civil litigation. While industry groups tended to disagree with the initial FDA rule, many in the restaurant sector also disagreed with the 2017 bill—though they also did not directly oppose it—fearing that it would create confusion. It was not until 2018 when the House passed a bill watering down the FDA regulations. The Senate never considered the House bill or their own companion piece of legislation during either session of the 115th Congress.

House Committee Action

In late January 2017, Rep. Cathy McMorris Rodgers, R-Wash., introduced HR 772, the Common Sense Nutrition Disclosure Act. The language was identical to a bill that passed the House during the previous Congress. The measure would provide flexibility to restaurants in how they display required nutritional information. For example, a nutrition disclosure statement on a menu board would be required to include the number of calories in the whole menu item, number of servings and calories per serving, or the number of calories per unit if the item has multiple servings. Businesses that take most of their orders over the phone would be permitted to provide their nutrition content online. The legislation also included carve outs for when a restaurant would be permitted to list nutritional values that differ from actual nutritional content, or when calorie ranges would be acceptable. Additionally, restaurants would not be held liable for civil action arising from a labeling violation, unless the suit was brought by a state or the federal government.

As they had in 2016, multiple associations representing the restaurant industry expressed concern about the bill, in part because restaurants and other food serving establishments had already spent time and money to come into compliance with the FDA regulations. Many public health groups were also against the new policies that would be created under the legislation, arguing that it allowed restaurants to hide the true nutritional information for high-calorie items. Supporters of the bill said it would give businesses more leeway and make it easier for them to comply. Additionally, supporters cited appreciation for the civil lawsuit protection, which they said would help avoid lawsuits that could arise when a menu item is changed to comply with a customer's dietary restrictions, thereby changing the calorie count.

When the House Energy and Commerce Committee marked up the bill in July, Democrats and Republicans were generally united in their support of the legislation,

though Democrats did express frustration that the bill further delayed implementation of the FDA's regulations and upended the effort that food service establishments had already done to comply. The committee considered two amendments during markup. One, from Rep. Kurt Schrader, D-Ore., was rejected 19–33, and would have struck from the bill language allowing certain establishments to post their calorie information online instead of on their premises. The second amendment, from Rodgers, would require the FDA to update its regulations in line with the bill's requirements within a year of the measure's enactment and would also give the administration the opportunity to choose a new deadline for compliance. The final vote in committee on July 27, 2017, to report the bill to the House was 39–14, with ten Democrats joining all Republicans in favor of the measure.

House Action

On February 5, 2018, the House Rules Committee approved a combined rule for consideration of three bills, including HR 772. The closed rule provided one hour of debate, waived all points of order against consideration of the bill or its provisions, and allowed for one motion to recommit. On the same day, the White House issued a Statement of Administration Policy, expressing the president's support of the bill. In it, the administration said HR 772 would better protect economic growth and job creation, while at the same time ensuring consumers have access to nutritional information.

The bill came to the floor on February 6, and it passed 266–157. Few saw any likelihood for the Senate to act on HR 772 or its companion legislation, S 261. While S 261 had Democratic cosponsors, some members of the party opposed the bill on the grounds that it continued to delay implementation of the labeling rules. On July 25, 2018, Sen. Roy Blunt, R-Mo., attempted to push the Senate to act on HR 772, but it failed to do so. Neither HR 772 nor S 261 passed the Senate in 2018.

HSA ELIGIBILITY AND PREMIUM TAX CREDITS

Among the bills considered in the House during the 115th Congress that would make changes to the provisions of the 2010 Patient Protection and Affordable Care Act (ACA; PL 111-148, PL 111-152) were two dealing specifically with health savings accounts (HSAs). Such accounts are available to those with qualified high-deductible health plans (HDHPs). The two measures would expand access to HSAs while also making more expenses allowable under HSA rules. These two tax-related bills passed the House but were never considered in the Senate.

House Action

The House Ways and Means Committee two-day markup of multiple bills addressing tax-related aspects of

the ACA was contentious, as each party lobbed criticisms at the other over the 2010 health care law and completely unrelated issues, such as child separation at the U.S.–Mexico border. During their July 11 and 12, 2018 debate, two bills under consideration, the Restoring Access to Medication and Modernizing Health Savings Accounts Act (HR 6199) and the Increasing Access to Lower Premium Plans and Expanding Health Savings Accounts Act (HR 6311), sought to amend the rules governing HSAs.

HR 6199 would make certain over-the-counter medical items, such as menstrual products, a qualified HSA or flexible spending account purchase, even without a prescription. It would also allow those accounts to be used for certain health and fitness expenses, including gym memberships. Further, the measure would let HDHPs pay for some medical services before the deductible kicks in, and let individuals with HDHPs plus another form of health care coverage contribute to an HSA. Individuals with an HDHP who are employed at a company that provides free or discounted onsite or retail clinic care would not be disqualified from setting up an HSA. The committee adopted one amendment to HR 6199 by voice vote, which set the bill's short title.

HR 6311 would expand HSA eligibility by allowing working seniors enrolled in Medicare Part A but who also have a qualified HDHP to set up an HSA account. It would also raise the cap on how much someone can contribute to their HSA account each year, and let those with bronze-level or catastrophic-level health plans qualify for an HSA. Further, the bill would let anyone buy a basic catastrophic health insurance plan (existing law restricted access to individuals under 30) and would also let those who qualify for premium tax credits purchase health insurance sold outside the exchanges. During consideration of HR 6311, the committee rejected two amendments. One, voted down 15–22, would strike language prohibiting funds from being used for any health care plan that funds abortion-related services. The other, rejected 16–23, would bar plans from charging higher premiums based on the insured's gender. The committee adopted by voice vote a substitute amendment that would, among other things, designate the bill's short title, and amend the definition of a grandmothered health plan.

During markup, Democrats argued that most of the HSA changes only benefited wealthy Americans because they are the most likely to have an account, and they also contended that the bill would do nothing to address the increasing costs of premiums and growing health care inequality in the United States. Republicans disagreed, saying their bills gave all Americans more control over their spending on health care.

HR 6199 passed out of committee 24–10. HR 6311 advanced to the full House 23–16.

On July 23, the House Rules Committee recommended closed rules for debate on both HR 6311 and HR 6199. And on July 25, both bills passed the House. HR 6199 was

approved 277–142, while HR 6311 passed 242–176. Neither bill received consideration in the Senate.

HEALTH INSURANCE ANTITRUST LOOPHOLE

A seventy-year-old antitrust exemption that gives health insurance companies the ability to share certain information related to analyzing risk and setting prices was the target of Congressional action in the early days of the 115th Congress. A bipartisan coalition of lawmakers who oppose the provision, found in the McCarron-Ferguson Act of 1945, argued that it encourages anticompetitive practice and market-distorting behavior among health insurers. In early 2017, the House sought to revive a 2010 attempt to eliminate that loophole. The earlier measure passed a Democratic-controlled House, 406–19, but never made it to the president's desk. The bill's popularity, however, left members hopeful that their 2017 attempt at striking the provision would be successful, but it suffered the same fate and never made it past a House vote.

House Committee Action

On February 28, the House Judiciary Committee held its markup of HR 372, the Competitive Health Insurance Reform Act, introduced by Rep. Paul Gosar, R-Ariz. The bill would amend the McCarran-Ferguson Act to strike the provision that grants health insurance companies certain antitrust protections. The committee favorably reported the measure by voice vote with a clarifying substitute amendment making clear that HR 372 would not eliminate the antitrust exemption available for certain industry practices, such as historical data sharing and common standardized insurance forms.

The House Rules Committee issued its recommendation for debate on HR 372 on March 20, calling for a closed rule providing one hour of debate. The rule prohibited amendments but did allow for one motion to recommit. The House approved the rule on March 21, 234–182; although many Democrats supported the underlying bill, they opposed the rule because it did not provide for amendments. The House went on to pass HR 372 on March 22, 416–7. One motion to recommit was rejected, 189–233, before final passage. That measure, from Rep. Jacky Rosen, D-Nev., would have sent the bill to the House Judiciary Committee asking for an amendment that would bar health insurers from varying their premiums by age in such a way that those over age fifty-five pay three times more than individuals under age twenty-one.

While the bill had wide bipartisan support in the House, its future was uncertain given pushback from the health insurance industry. Opponents of HR 372 said that the existing antitrust carve out for health insurers is incredibly narrow, and the allowable activities are already monitored by the states. Others argued that the loophole promotes competition and that its repeal could open the door for future Congresses to target other practices that may or may not be business friendly. HR 372 never received consideration in the Senate during the 115th Congress.

FDA Reauthorization

While the partisan wrangling continued over how to repeal and replace the 2010 Patient Protection and Affordable Care Act (ACA; PL 111–148, PL 111–152), Congress was also facing a September 2017 deadline for reauthorizing the Food and Drug Administration (FDA) authority to collect nearly $1.4 billion in annual fees for prescription medications, medical devices, generic medications, and biosimilar biological products. The money collected from drug and device makers primarily funds the salaries of the employees who review the applications drug and medical device companies submit for product approval. Leadership in both chambers sought to keep the process cordial, given that the reauthorization process tends to garner bipartisan support. However, in a highly charged political environment, the process slowed as members attempted to attach pet projects to the bill. In the end, the House and Senate got a bipartisan measure to the president's desk that reauthorized user fee collection through fiscal year 2022 and made a number of other small policy changes (PL 115–52).

Senate Action

The Senate moved first on an FDA reauthorization bill. The full Senate Health, Education, Labor, and Pensions Committee was scheduled to hold its consideration and markup of S 934 on May 10, 2017. However, that meeting was delayed by a day after President Donald Trump suddenly fired Federal Bureau of Investigation director James Comey and Democratic members took to the floor in protest. The committee convened on May 11, holding a ninety-minute markup. A significant portion of that time focused on an amendment proposed by Sen. Bernie Sanders, I-Vt., that would allow the United States to import certain medications from Canada, which are often lower cost, a savings that Sanders argued could be passed on to consumers. Republicans claimed that the FDA had in the past decided that it could not oversee the importation in a way that would ensure safety. Sanders countered that his amendment was focused on safety and would only allow for the importation of drugs that were already authorized by the FDA. The amendment never received a vote, however, because the committee's chair, Lamar Alexander, R-Tenn., first offered a motion to table it, which passed 13–10. While many committee members expressed a need to address the growing cost of prescription drugs, they wanted it to be taken up as a separate piece of legislation, not attached to a must-pass bill.

The committee did adopt three amendments before moving to a final vote. The first amendment required that, when reviewing applications, the FDA prioritize those for medications representing the first competition to another

drug already on the market that was at risk of a price spike. It also called on the agency to track drugs that might experience price hikes. The second amendment asked the FDA to work with the National Institutes of Health to review clinical trial accessibility and barriers and then issue guidance on how to broaden criteria to increase participation. They also adopted a substitute amendment that would allow regulations on some hearing aids and over-the-counter medications. Ultimately, the committee voted 21–2 to advance the underlying measure, as amended, with only Sanders and Sen. Rand Paul, R-Ky., voting against S 934. S 934 never received a floor vote.

House Action

On June 7, 2017, the House Energy and Commerce Committee took up consideration of HR 2430, its FDA user fee reauthorization bill. One contentious issue that threatened to derail the committee's action revolved around proposals from Reps. Brett Guthrie, R-Ky., and Morgan Griffith, R-Va., that would give drug manufacturers more leeway in communicating with providers about medications that have not yet gone through the FDA approval process. Democrats raised concerns that the language would make it easier for bad actors to give misleading information to providers. Griffith did not end up offering his amendment, while Guthrie withdrew his.

Before final passage, the committee adopted a variety of amendments, including a manager's package that made technical changes to the bill. Four adopted amendments dealt with medical devices. One addressed how medical devices are serviced by third parties, another would create a means for new uses of medical imaging devices, another would establish a pilot program to track the safety of certain medical devices once they come to market, and the final amendment would make it easier for the FDA to classify medical device accessories based on the risk of the accessory itself and not its parent device.

The committee's markup of the FDA bill centered largely on the cost of prescription drugs, and before voting unanimously to advance the measure to the floor, the committee adopted by voice vote an amendment from Rep. Jan Schakowsky, D-Ill., to express the sense of Congress that lawmakers would try to work with the White House to find ways to lower the cost of prescription medication. Another amendment dealing with prescription drug pricing, from Rep. Peter Welch, D-Vt., which would have allowed for the importation of certain medications from Canada, was rejected by voice vote. As approved by the committee, the bill struck a bipartisan tone and avoided controversial policy riders. In addition to the reauthorization language, the bill made some modest policy changes, such as those related to medical device regulation and generic drug approval timelines.

On July 10, the Energy and Commerce Committee released an updated version of HR 2430, to incorporate the amendments approved in committee and make a few other changes that addressed Senate priorities, to help smooth passage through both chambers. Changes in the draft would allow the FDA to require that adult cancer drugs also be tested in children, renew funding for the National Institutes of Health to test certain childhood cancer treatments, call on the FDA to review clinical trial participation, give the FDA the ability to regulate hearing aids as over-the-counter products, and make some changes to the process of approving generic drugs for market.

The amended version of HR 2430 reached the House floor on July 12, where it was approved by voice vote under suspension of the rules.

Senate Floor Action

While the House and Senate had to pass a bill reauthorizing the FDA's fee collecting authority by the time it expired at the end of September, they had set themselves a July deadline at which point they believed the FDA would begin issuing furlough notices to its workers, who are highly skilled and sought after by the private sector. On July 24, with no bill signed by the president but with general agreement between the two chambers on the bill's substance, the FDA announced that it would delay issuing those notices, giving Congress until the end of the fiscal year to get a bill done.

Senate consideration of the House bill was slowed over broader concerns about the chamber's action, or inaction, on an overhaul of the ACA. Additionally, one senator, Republican Ron Johnson of Wisconsin, had threatened to delay consideration of the FDA reauthorization if he did not receive a vote on a bill he introduced to increase access to experimental drugs (S 204). To stop Johnson from holding up the bill, Senate leadership allowed a vote to happen on Johnson's bill shortly before HR 2430 came up for a vote.

On August 3, the Senate passed HR 2430 94–1, with only Sen. Bernie Sanders, I-Vt., voting no. As passed, the bill renewed the FDA's user fee collection authority from fiscal year 2018 to fiscal year 2022, increased fee rates for the next five years, and made other minor policy changes. President Trump signed the measure on August 18, 2017 (PL 115–52).

Protecting Access to Care

In 2017, the House passed—but the Senate did not consider—a bill capping how much is paid out to victims of medical malpractice who receive their health insurance coverage through the federal government.

House Action

The House Judiciary Committee marked up HR 1215, the Protecting Access to Care Act, on February 28, 2017. The bill would create a standard for certain health liability claims, including medical malpractice suits, when the cost is covered by federal health insurance. The provisions of

the bill would limit to $250,000 noneconomic claims, such as those for pain and suffering, and set a three-year statute of limitations on lawsuits filed against medical practitioners. Additionally, health care providers would be shielded from liability if they prescribe an approved medical product that becomes part of a class action suit against the manufacturer or seller. Supporters said the bill was a means to slow rising health care costs, while Democrats argued that the measure infringed on states' rights to set medical malpractice law.

Democrats offered multiple amendments during debate, most of which were rejected. One would have exempted from the bill's provisions doctors who intentionally harm a patient, another would exempt certain medical errors, such as leaving a surgical instrument in a patient's body, and one would exempt nursing home negligence. Another amendment, from Rep. Hank Johnson, D-Ga., was initially adopted and then rejected on a motion to reconsider. That amendment would prohibit any provision in the bill from preempting a state constitution. The bill was narrowly advanced by the committee, 18–17.

On June 13, the House Rules Committee granted a structured rule for consideration of HR 1215, and the House took it up on June 28 (the bill was originally scheduled for an earlier floor vote, but was delayed after a shooting at a congressional baseball practice). During debate, House Democrats spoke out against the measure, accusing Republicans of limiting the relief offered to patients who are most severely harmed by negligence or malpractice, while shielding bad practitioners and medical device makers that sell dangerous items. To back their claims, they relied on 2016 data from Johns Hopkins University which found that medical errors are the third leading cause of death in the United States.

Prior to final passage, the House adopted three amendments, one letting a medical provider apologize to a patient without fear that the apology could be used as evidence against them. Another amendment would limit who could qualify as an expert witness, and the third set a statute of limitations for lawsuits.

The House passed the bill 218–210, with nineteen Republicans joining all Democrats in opposition. HR 1215 was never considered in the Senate.

Children's Health Insurance Program Funding

Since being signed into law in 1997 (PL 105-33), the Children's Health Insurance Program (CHIP) has enjoyed broad bipartisan support, and is regularly reauthorized either on or ahead of schedule. Beginning on October 1, 2017, however, the program lapsed for two months because Congress could not reach an agreement on its renewal. The disagreement rested not on policy but on offsets for the cost of the House version of the CHIP reauthorization. In

the end, the two chambers broke their stalemate in early 2018 after the Congressional Budget Office (CBO) released a new estimate of CHIP's long-term cost, and the program was reauthorized for four years as part of the Bipartisan Budget Act of 2018 (PL 115–123).

House Action

In 2017, reauthorizing CHIP was caught up in the larger battle between Republicans and Democrats as the former continued to try to overhaul the 2010 Patient Protection and Affordable Care Act (ACA; PL 111–148, PL 111–152). In the ACA repeal language floating in the House, Medicaid funding would be capped for the first time in the program's history. Democrats argued that doing so would ultimately impact CHIP, because the two programs work hand in hand. Under the ACA's Medicaid expansion provision, states received extra money from the federal government to enroll more families—and children—in Medicaid. If those federal funds went away, many children would be removed from the Medicaid rolls and would therefore shift to CHIP, which Democrats contended would significantly increase the program's cost.

At a June 23, 2017, hearing of the House Energy and Commerce Subcommittee on Health, committee Democrats held firm that maintaining the strength of CHIP depended on a fully funded Medicaid program. Republicans, while contending that Medicaid funding and CHIP reauthorization were separate issues, also noted that their health care overhaul bill would allow Medicaid to grow during the next decade; that growth, however, was predicted to be slower than under the ACA.

With the CHIP debate largely overshadowed by the ACA overhaul, members of Congress began to assert that they could delay CHIP's reauthorization to provide both parties and chambers time to come to a consensus on how to fund the program moving forward. They based this argument on information from the nonpartisan Medicaid and CHIP Payment and Access Commission's report indicating that most states had enough funds remaining to cover their programs through the end of 2017. According to their report, only three states and Washington, D.C., would exhaust their funding before then. Another report, by the Kaiser Family Foundation, said ten states would likely run out of money at some point in December.

In the intervening months, multiple states began raising the alarm that their funds were dangerously low. In a letter to the Minnesota congressional delegation, the state's Department of Health and Human Services commissioner wrote that the state would likely exhaust its funds in September. A letter from the Utah Department of Health to the Centers for Medicare and Medicaid Services warned that they had enough money to make it through December but after that point, without congressional intervention, they would need to suspend CHIP services and enrollment.

368 CH. 9 HEALTH AND HUMAN SERVICES

The House Energy and Commerce Committee began marking up its version of CHIP reauthorization (HR 3921), on October 4, 2017. Democrats were unhappy with the legislation, and the fact that it lacked bipartisan support. Specifically, they were frustrated about offsets in the House bill. These included higher premiums for Medicare recipients earning more than $500,000 per year, allowing states to disenroll lottery winners from their Medicaid rolls, and requiring that Medicaid recipients with another form of insurance have the secondary payer billed before Medicaid. Democrats questioned why House Republicans would want to pay for CHIP by reducing Medicaid services, given that individuals enrolled in Medicaid have lower incomes than those eligible for CHIP. Democrats offered an amendment during markup that contained various alternative offsets. For example, the amendment proposed changing when Medicare Advantage and Medicare Part D plans are paid, allowing the government to pay after the fact. The extra interest earned on the money while it was awaiting payment would go toward the cost of reauthorizing CHIP. The amendment was rejected.

The committee did adopt one amendment before passage, from Rep. Gus Bilirakis, R-Fla., to increase the cap on Medicaid payments for the U.S. Virgin Islands. The CHIP bill passed out of committee on a party line 28–23 vote.

House Action

Before HR 3921 hit the floor, the House Energy and Commerce Committee combined it with another piece of legislation, HR 3922, which extended for two years funding for community health centers and other safety-net programs. The combined bills, using HR 3922 as their vehicle, were submitted to the House Rules Committee as a substitute amendment. One other change was made ahead of the Rules Committee hearing, which struck the provision increasing Medicare premiums for seniors who earn more than $500,000 per year; the other offsets were maintained. However, by the time the rules package governing debate passed the House Rules Committee by a 7–3 vote, the Medicare premium adjustment had been readded to the bill.

During floor debate on November 3, Democrats and Republicans sparred over the offsets, with Democrats accusing Republicans of stealing money from the poor to give it to the less poor, while Republicans criticized Democrats for holding up the process of getting CHIP reauthorized. The Democratic concerns, however, were not enough to hold up passage. The House voted 242–174 to reauthorize CHIP for five years. Additionally, the bill would

- Require that Medicaid recipients have their supplemental insurance billed first, if applicable
- Cut $6.35 billion from the Prevention and Public Health Fund
- Allow states to remove lottery winners from Medicaid for a certain period of time

- Increase Medicare premiums for those earning more than $500,000
- Adjust the grace period for health exchange plans to thirty days or whatever a state opts to set it at
- Maintain the 23 percentage point enhanced CHIP federal funding match for the next two years, after which time the matching rate would decline to 11.5 percent in fiscal year 2020 and then return to its normal rate in fiscal year 2021
- Require states to maintain CHIP eligibility for programs run through Medicaid until 2019 (for children below 300 percent of the federal poverty line, the maintenance of effort requirements for enrollment would extend through fiscal year 2022)
- Extend funding for community health centers and certain other public health programs for two years

Within a week, with no movement on the bill in the Senate, states were continuing to remind their legislators about what would happen in the new year if Congress failed to reauthorize CHIP. In West Virginia, the state's CHIP board of directors voted to close enrollment at the end of February 2018 if Congress had not provided funds by then. According to the Centers for Medicare and Medicaid Services, it had redistributed leftover funding from prior fiscal years to fourteen states and territories in October and November to prevent them from exhausting their funding. Despite these warnings, HR 3922 never received a vote in the Senate.

Senate Action

The Senate was originally set to begin hearings and debate on CHIP reauthorization in May, however, their work was delayed after the House passed an ACA repeal bill and Republicans in the Senate introduced their own version of the legislation. It was not until mid-September, two weeks before CHIP funding was set to expire, when Senate Finance Chair Orrin Hatch, R-Utah, and the committee's ranking member Ron Wyden, D-Ore., introduced S 1827, a five-year CHIP funding renewal. Within their bill language, the federal government would continue its 23 percentage point enhanced CHIP federal funding match for the next two years, after which time the matching rate would decline to 11.5 percent in fiscal year 2020 and then return to its normal rate in fiscal year 2021. Their bill would also continue through fiscal year 2019 the ACA requirement that states must maintain CHIP eligibility; for children below 300 percent of the federal poverty line, the maintenance of effort requirements for enrollment would extend through fiscal year 2022. The bill would cost an estimated $8 billion, and did not come with any offsets.

On October 4, 2017, the Senate Finance Committee held its markup of S 1827. To help move the bill along, senators agreed not to introduce amendments in committee. Hatch said during markup that it was important for the committee and full Senate to move quickly on the

legislation, because funding for CHIP had already expired. The committee advanced the measure by voice vote. S 1827 never made it to a floor vote.

Final Action

With no final action on either the House or Senate version of CHIP reauthorization, and Democrats and Republicans still at loggerheads about whether offsets were necessary and, if so, where they should come from, the chambers instead turned to a funding patch. In the December 2017 continuing resolution to keep the government open (PL 115-96), Congress made a CHIP appropriation that they expected to keep the state programs functioning through March 31, 2018. State program officials and children's health advocates expressed concern that families were facing increasing uncertainty, and they encouraged the House and Senate to reach a long-term agreement for funding.

In January 2018, the Congressional Budget Office issued a report estimating that the provisions in S 1827 would increase outlays by $7.2 billion over ten years, but increase revenue by $8.2 billion. In part, the savings were driven by the elimination of the ACA individual mandate and other changes made by the Trump administration to health care regulations. The House and Senate ultimately attached a four-year CHIP renewal to the 2018 Bipartisan Budget Act (PL 115-123) enacted on February 9, 2018.

Right to Try

During the 115th Congress, the House and Senate worked on separate pieces of legislation that would offer protection to drug companies that provide experimental treatments to terminally ill patients. The Senate moved first on the legislation known as "right to try," passing a measure in 2017. The House attempted to pass its own version, but failed after Democratic leadership announced their opposition to the process used to rush the bill to a vote. In the end, the House took up and passed the Senate version, and President Donald Trump signed the bill on May 30, 2018 (PL 115–176).

Senate Action

Sen. Ron Johnson, R-Wis., introduced the Trickett Wendler, Frank Mongiello, Jordan McLinn, and Matthew Bellina Right to Try Act on January 24, 2017 (S 204). Under existing law, a terminally ill patient had to work with their doctor, a drug company, the Food and Drug Administration (FDA), and an institutional review board to get approval for an experimental drug's use. Johnson's bill would eliminate the federal government from the process, and give states the opportunity to define who qualifies as having a "terminal illness" and is therefore entitled to experimental treatments. The bill would also prevent the FDA from using experimental treatment outcomes when it reviewed a drug or device for authorization. Johnson's bill was intended to ease

the process of experimental treatment access for terminally ill individuals. Democrats, some Republicans, and even the pharmaceutical industry pushed back against specific bill provisions, arguing that allowing states to determine who qualifies as terminally ill would create a patchwork of regulations difficult for drug companies to follow. Many also wanted to see the FDA use the information gained from experimental use when assessing drug safety.

On August 2, Johnson released revised draft bill language that dropped the provision barring the FDA from using experimental outcomes and changed the eligibility provision to allow anyone with a "life-threatening disease or condition"—as defined by federal law—access to experimental treatment. His measure, which would protect drug companies that offer experimental treatments to terminally ill patients and reduce the paperwork required for individuals to seek these treatments, was fast-tracked in the Senate, after Johnson threatened to hold up a vote on a separate bill that would renew the fee collection authority of the FDA. On August 3, the Senate Health, Education, Labor, and Pensions Committee discharged the bill by unanimous consent, and it hit the floor the same day, where the Senate passed it by unanimous consent.

As passed in the Senate, the bill would protect drug manufacturers, distributors, prescribers, dispensers, and possessors from liability. The federal government would be required to allow for the manufacture, distribution, prescribing, and dispensing of prescription medications and medical devices that are authorized by state law and intended to treat someone who is terminally ill. Patients certified by a doctor as having exhausted all other treatment methods would be permitted access to these experimental methods. Any treatment allowable under the bill's provisions must meet certain requirements, including having successfully completed a Phase 1 clinical trial, still be under investigation, and not yet have been approved, licensed, or cleared for sale. At the time it passed in the Senate, more than two-thirds of states already had right-to-try measures in place.

House Action

While the Senate bypassed regular order and allowed its right-to-try bill to proceed without markup, the House opted for a full committee process. Before it could take up either the Senate's bill or its own version, however, patient advocacy groups began lobbying against the bill and even the FDA commissioner expressed concerns about the measures under consideration. According to those pushing back, the idea that the bill would increase access to experimental treatments was flawed, because the measure did not address the primary issues that stop patients from seeking and receiving experimental treatments: lack of supply, misunderstanding of the process, fear, and a risk of losing insurance coverage or hospice care. Additionally, according to the Government Accountability Office (GAO) the FDA is not the biggest barrier to access, and in fact approves about 99 percent of compassionate use requests for

experimental drugs. Rather, the GAO report found, drug companies do not pursue emergency use access because they are concerned about how the FDA will use outcome data from these cases, despite assurances that the agency reviewers are aware that terminally ill patients are likely to have adverse outcomes whether they use an experimental treatment or not. Patient advocates also said that taking the FDA out of the process could put more consumers at risk of exposure to dangerous medical devices or medications.

After President Trump called on Congress during his 2018 State of the Union Address to pass right-to-try legislation, the effort began anew in the House. Leadership on the Energy and Commerce Committee said they were talking with the FDA and White House to develop compromise legislation that addressed a number of concerns about the bill. Among these was the way the Senate bill classified who could qualify for experimental treatment. The FDA argued that under the Senate definition, someone with diabetes could technically qualify, because it is a long-term life-threatening condition. They wanted a more narrow definition that focused on those at more immediate risk of death. Republicans who backed the Senate bill worried that tightening the qualifications could prohibit some individuals from accessing experimental treatments, and both chambers raised concern that the Senate might not have the appetite—or the votes—to consider changes from the House. Patient advocacy groups, including the American Cancer Society Cancer Action Network, continued to oppose the Senate's right-to-try legislation, saying it could do more harm than good.

As a result of negotiations between the House, White House, and FDA, in mid-March 2018, the House was set to vote on a draft right-to-try measure under suspension of the rules. That version addressed the major concern of who has access to experimental treatments, defining an eligible illness as one where "there is a reasonable likelihood that death will occur within a matter of months" or a condition "that would result in significant irreversible morbidity that is likely to lead to severely premature death." Drug manufacturers would also be required to alert the FDA any time they make an experimental treatment available to a patient and would have to provide real-time updates on medical problems. While Republicans praised the changes, Rep. Frank Pallone Jr., D-N.J., ranking member on the House Energy and Commerce Committee, announced his opposition to the measure, saying it was unnecessary, rushed through negotiations, did not reflect a bipartisan consensus, and would give false hope to patients and their loved ones.

When the bill (HR 5247) came to the floor on March 13, it fell short of the two-thirds majority needed for passage under suspension of the rules, garnering only 259 votes in support. Republicans were undeterred, and began floating alternative methods for passage, such as bringing the bill to the floor under normal rules or considering the Senate-passed version.

On March 19, the House Rules Committee approved a closed rule for HR 5247. It came to the floor on March 21,

and passed 267–149. The House rejected one motion to recommit, from Rep. Pallone, that would send the bill back to the House Energy and Commerce Committee to add an amendment requiring the FDA to issue guidance on how to expand access to treatments under review, and provide a liability shield for manufacturers, certain medical personnel, and others involved in offering such treatments. Regardless of the House effort, there was no indication of a plan for reconciling the House-passed measure with the Senate's bill from the prior year, but House Republican leadership encouraged their counterparts in the Senate to quickly pass HR 5247. Sen. Johnson on March 23 attempted to ask unanimous consent for HR 5247's passage in the Senate. Minority Leader Chuck Schumer, D-N.Y., objected, but said that he was committed to working on a compromise to get something passed.

In mid-May, the House agreed to consider the Senate's version of right-to-try legislation, and S 204 hit the floor on May 22. By that time, its passage seemed guaranteed, despite some Republicans stating that they preferred the House version and criticizing the Senate for not taking it up, while most Democrats and patient groups continued to express their opposition. Republican leaders were inclined to vote for the Senate measure after assurances from the FDA that the agency could ensure safe implementation through its regulatory process. The White House also expressed support for the Senate bill, writing in a Statement of Administration Policy that "treatment decisions for those facing terminal illnesses are best made by the patients with the support and guidance of their treating physicians. This legislation will advance these principles."

The House passed S 204 on May 22, without amendment, 250–169, after rejecting a motion to recommit that would have added reporting requirements for the FDA and drug manufacturers on the use of experimental drugs. As passed, S 204 gave patients the ability to directly petition a drug manufacturer for access to experimental treatment that had already gone through a Phase 1 clinical trial, as long as they had exhausted other FDA-approved treatments and were not eligible to participate in a clinical trial. While manufacturers were under no obligation to provide the treatment, the bill sought to incentivize them to do so by adding a liability shield. President Trump signed the bill on May 30, 2018 (PL 115-176).

Abortion

With conservatives continuing to take aim at abortion, the House passed a trio of Republican-backed bills in 2017 and 2018 to impose restrictions on the procedure. None gained traction in the Senate, however.

FUNDING RESTRICTIONS

The first of the bills (HR 7) was a Republican priority, and it would permanently prevent federal tax dollars from being used to fund abortions. The House passed the measure on January 24, 2017, on a vote of 238–183.

The measure would not have necessarily altered actual funding. Since 1976, annual spending bills had included the so-called Hyde amendment, a provision that barred appropriated funds from being used for abortions or for health plans that provided coverage for abortions except in cases of rape or incest, or if the life of the mother was at risk. The provisions prevented Medicaid funds from paying for abortions.

But HR 7 went further in certain ways because it targeted insurance companies that covered abortions or individuals who used private money to pay for them. It would prohibit health insurers and small employers that provided abortion coverage from using refundable tax credits and cost-sharing reductions. Its restrictions extended to abortion coverage by plans sold on the insurance exchanges established by the 2010 Affordable Care Act (PL 111–148, PL 111–152).

The bill sponsor, Christopher H. Smith, R-N.J., said during the floor debate that the measure would ensure transparency about abortion coverage by health insurance plans. Democrats, however, said it would restrict the ability of women to obtain abortions. Democrat Jerrold Nadler of New York said it would effectively make abortions more expensive by preventing women from deducting local taxes for medical expenses that included abortion.

PROHIBITING ABORTIONS AFTER 20 WEEKS

The House next passed a bill that would prohibit abortions after twenty weeks with certain exceptions. The bill (HR 36), passed on October 3, 2017, by a vote of 237–189.

Sponsored by Republican Trent Franks of Arizona, the measure would impose fines or a prison sentence of up to five years on doctors who were in violation. It would allow abortions after twenty weeks in certain cases of rape or incest, or if the woman's life was in danger, although bill opponents said it would not create reasonable exceptions for rape or incest.

Abortions after twenty weeks were prohibited in seventeen states. Supporters of the bill said the United States was one of only seven countries that permitted such late-term abortions. They also said a fetus is able to feel pain after twenty weeks, and an abortion at that point could harm the health of the mother.

Opponents, however, dismissed such arguments as scientifically unfounded. They also argued there could be a pressing reason to have an abortion after twenty weeks, including a lethal medical problem in the fetus.

The White House issued a statement in support of the bill. But the Senate on January 29, 2018, defeated a companion measure (S 2311). The 51–46 vote fell well short of the sixty-vote requirement to limit debate on the bill.

LATE-TERM ABORTIONS

Almost exactly a year after passing the initial abortion measure, the House passed a bill on January 19, 2018, that would impose new restrictions on late-term abortions. The bill (HR 4712) would require a doctor to provide the same level of care for an infant who was born alive after an attempted abortion as for any other child born at the same stage.

Under the measure, by Rep. Marsha Blackburn, R-Tenn., health care professionals who violated the law could face up to five years in prison in addition to fines. Any provider who killed an infant who was born alive could face murder charges. If health care professionals witnessed violations, they would be required to report them to law enforcement officials. But the threat of prosecution did not extend to a woman who underwent an abortion in which the medical provider violated the law.

Congress in 2002 had passed bipartisan legislation, signed into law by President George W. Bush (PL 107–207) that extended legal protections to infants born alive after abortions. Colorado Democrat Diana DeGette, co-chair of the Pro-Choice Caucus, cited the 2002 law in arguing there was no need for HR 4712. She also said the government should not interfere with the medical judgment of health care professionals. Supporters of the bill, however, said it strengthened current law and provided essential protections for infants who survived a late-term abortion.

Health Emergency Preparedness Programs

In 2018, the House passed a bill to renew support for programs that help prepare the United States for infectious disease outbreaks and other health emergencies. The legislation was held up in the Senate due to a dispute over an unrelated bill, and the measure never made it to the president's desk.

House Action

On July 18, 2018, the House Energy and Commerce Committee held a markup of HR 6378, the Pandemic and All-Hazards Preparedness and Advancing Innovation Act. The bipartisan measure would renew and increase funding for federal programs intended to prepare the country for future public health emergencies and disease outbreaks. Money would be provided to programs including those that research possible vaccines and other treatments that would be critical during an emergency but which would not otherwise have a market. The measure would also provide additional funds for enhancing the nation's medical supply stockpile, and establish a committee to oversee what is purchased for the stockpile. Further, the bill would

- Require that emergency preparedness drills and response activities include pandemic influenza and other emerging diseases
- Call on the secretary of the Department of Health and Human Services (HHS) and director of the Centers for Disease Control and Prevention (CDC) to maintain a team specifically for addressing the needs of children during a health emergency

- Require multiple agencies to review the National Disaster Medical System to assess capacity, training effectiveness, surge capacity, and other issues
- Increase funding for the National Defense Medical System to $57.4 million per year through fiscal year 2023
- Expand a student loan repayment program for CDC employees who work on certain prevention activities
- Direct the HHS secretary to provide a report to Congress related to the national blood supply
- Increase to $670 million the annual funding authorization for grants to states aimed at health preparedness through fiscal year 2023
- Increase to $161.8 million through fiscal year 2023 the funding for CDC programs that train medical personnel
- Require the HHS secretary to enter into an agreement to evaluate hospital, long-term care, and other medical facility preparedness for emergencies
- Authorize $7.1 billion over ten years for the Project BioShield special reserve fund
- Compel the secretary of HHS to submit a report on support for vaccine development related to future epidemics
- Increase from $533 million to $610 million per year funding for the emergency medical supply stockpile

The committee adopted a manager's amendment during markup, by voice vote, that made various changes to the bill, such as adding new reporting requirements and establishing a new grant program to study infections acquired at certain health care facilities. The committee went on to approve the bill, as amended, by voice vote. On September 25, 2018, the House passed HR 6378 by voice vote.

Senate Action

In the Senate, the Health, Education, Labor, and Pensions Committee approved its version of pandemic preparedness legislation, S 2852, on May 23 by a vote of 22–1, with Sen. Rand Paul, R-Ky., the only dissenter. Floor action stalled, however, when the bill's sponsor, Sen. Richard Burr, N.C., refused to allow for a quick floor vote on S 2315, a measure from Sen. Johnny Isakson, R-Ga., that would make changes to how the FDA approves over-the-counter drugs, making their review more efficient in exchange for higher fees from drug manufacturers. Burr had previously voted against Isakson's measure when it was in committee, expressing skepticism that the FDA might not be a good steward of the money it collects from the pharmaceutical industry. In turn, Isakson also refused to allow a quick vote on S 2852.

In an effort to break the logjam, in December, House leadership combined HR 6378 with its own FDA over-the-counter regulation measure, HR 5333. Because both measures had already passed the House separately, HR 7328

sailed through passage, 367–9. The Senate, however, never took it up.

Prescription Drug Prices

As part of its plan to address the growing cost of prescription drugs, in 2018 the House and Senate passed two bills that would make drug prices more transparent for consumers. Both measures had broad bipartisan support, and faced little resistance from either side of the aisle or the pharmacy benefit managers who act as the intermediary between pharmacists and drug makers. President Donald Trump, who had been pressing Congress since his election to address drug prices, signed both pieces of legislation on October 10, 2018 (PL 115–262, PL 115–263).

Senate Action

On July 25, the Senate Health, Education, Labor, and Pensions Committee marked up the Patient Right to Know Drug Prices Act (S 2554), introduced by Sen. Susan Collins, R-Maine. The bipartisan measure sought to eliminate what are known as "gag clauses," provisions in health insurance plans that stop a pharmacist from telling a patient that a prescription would be cheaper if purchased out of pocket rather than through their insurance plan. Pharmacy benefit managers reported that most insurance plans already ban gag clauses, though pharmacists have routinely reported being subject to them. A 2016 survey by the National Community Pharmacists Association found

Figure 9.3 Outlays for Income Security

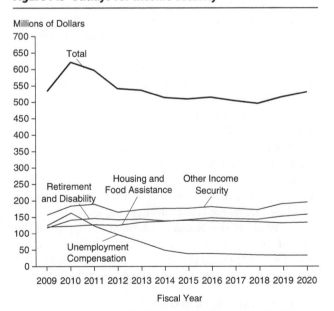

SOURCE: Office of Management and Budget, Historical Tables, *Budget of the United States Government: Fiscal Year 2021* (Washington DC: U.S. Government Printing Office, 2020), Table 3.2.

NOTES: * indicates estimate

that 59 percent of pharmacists surveyed had been restricted from sharing drug price information at least ten times in the prior month.

Collins's bill would specifically ban health insurance companies that offer their products on the exchanges created under the Patient Protection and Affordable Care Act (ACA; PL 111-148, PL 111-152) and group insurance plans from stopping pharmacists from offering pricing information.

Prior to passage, the committee adopted a manager's amendment that defined out-of-pocket costs to make it more difficult for insurers to craft language to get around the provisions on the Senate bill and established additional reporting and disclosure requirements for biosimilar biological products to help them get to market. The committee favorably reported S 2554 as amended by voice vote.

While S 2554 awaited further action, a similar bill, from Collins and Sen. Debbie Stabenow, D-Mich., reached the Senate floor. S 2553, the Know the Lowest Price Act, bypassed committee markup and instead was discharged by the Senate Finance Committee on the same day as it was considered on the floor. The measure would allow pharmacists to tell Medicare patients when it is cheaper to purchase a medication out of pocket. On September 4, 2018, the Senate passed S 2553 by unanimous consent.

The Senate returned to S 2554 in late September. While the bill was still nearly guaranteed to pass, it faced one hang up when it came to the floor. Sen. Mike Lee, R-Utah, sought to limit the scope of the legislation by applying the gag clause prohibition only to federally regulated self-insured plans. According to Lee, such a change was important because self-insured plans are mostly regulated at the federal level, while fully insured plans tend to be regulated by the states. Notably, Lee supported the ban on Medicare gag clauses, but said he did so because the federal government has a clear role in that program. Under Lee's amendment, many small group insurance plans and those sold on the exchange would be exempt from the bill's provisions. Multiple industry groups opposed Lee's amendment. On September 17, the Senate rejected Lee's amendment, 11–89. The Senate proceeded to pass S 2554, 98–2.

House Action

As S 2554 and S 2553 made their way through the Senate, a broader anti-gag clause bill was circulating in the House. On September 7, 2018, the House Health Subcommittee advanced HR 6733, a bill introduced by Rep. Earl Carter, R-Ga., a pharmacist and former pharmacy owner. That bill would disallow gag clauses in employer and individual health insurance plans, as well as the Medicare Advantage and Medicare Part D prescription drug plans. The House Energy and Commerce Committee favorably reported the bill by voice vote on September 13. As sent to the floor, the bill would bar pharmacy benefit managers, insurance companies, and other similar organizations from inserting gag clauses into their contracts with pharmacies that cover both private insurance and Medicare.

The House took no further action on HR 6733. Instead, on September 25, the chamber cleared both S 2553 and S 2554 under suspension of the rules by voice vote. The president signed both bills on October 10, 2018 (PL 115–262, PL 115–263).

Disapproving D.C.'s Death With Dignity Act

The House in 2017 attempted to disapprove of Washington, D.C.'s new law allowing physicians to prescribe life-ending medications to certain terminally ill patients. Ultimately, the thirty-day limit on congressional review ran out and neither the full House nor the Senate voted on the measure.

House Action

In December 2016, after two years of work on the measure, Washington, D.C., Mayor Muriel Bowser signed the Death with Dignity Act. The legislation, similar to that in place in five other states, was modeled after a 1997 law in Oregon that would allow a doctor to prescribe life-ending medication to a terminally ill patient who was sound of mind and met certain other requirements. As required, the law was transmitted to Congress in January 2017, starting the clock on the thirty-day period in which both chambers can pass a disapproval measure with a simple majority. Failure to do so allows the law to go into effect.

On January 12, 2017, Rep. Brad Wenstrup, R-Ohio, introduced a joint resolution to express Congress's disapproval of the Death with Dignity Act. The House Oversight and Government Reform Committee held its markup of HJ Res 27 on February 13, 2017, voting 22–14 to advance the measure to the full House. Democrats on the committee pushed their colleagues to vote against the measure, arguing in favor of the District's right to govern itself, while Republicans asserted their oversight authority for D.C. laws. The bill's supporters also suggested that, as written, the Death with Dignity law defined "terminal illness" too broadly and did not have adequate safeguards in place to protect patients. In a statement after the committee vote, Bowser said it showed residents of the city "that Congress has zero respect or concern for their will or the will of their elected officials."

Although committee passage cleared the way to a full House vote, the chambers had only thirty days to pass a disapproval resolution through both chambers from the time the District submitted the law. Because the Senate was unlikely to make the deadline to pass its own version of a resolution (SJ Res 4), the House never took up its version either.

While neither chamber formally disapproved of the Death with Dignity law by the deadline, Congress still had the power to limit its effect. In July, the House Appropriations Committee adopted an amendment from Rep. Andy Harris, R-Md., to add a rider to the Financial Services and General Government appropriations bill

(HR 3280) that would block funding for doctor-assisted suicides in the District, essentially preventing the city's law from taking effect. The House maintained that provision in its omnibus bill (HR 3354) that it passed in September. However, when the House and Senate went to conference committee to reach an agreement on full-year appropriations, the rider was dropped.

Emergency Use Authorization for Battlefield Medicine

In 2017, Congress passed a change to the Federal Food, Drug, and Cosmetic Act of 1938 that would give the Food and Drug Administration (FDA) the ability to expedite authorization for emergency use of certain unapproved medical products deemed necessary for members of the military if requested by the Department of Defense. The measure threatened to hold up passage of the bipartisan fiscal year 2018 National Defense Authorization Act (NDAA), but the two chambers reached a compromise and President Donald Trump signed the battlefield medicine measure on December 12, 2017 (PL 115-92).

House Action

Language in the fiscal year 2018 NDAA would have permitted the Department of Defense to authorize unapproved medical products for use on the battlefield, rather than first requiring that those products be approved by the FDA. Those who supported the provision argued that the FDA had not previously done a good enough job of expeditiously reviewing Pentagon requests to get critical drugs and devices to service members in harm's way. However, a group of lawmakers took issue with the idea of allowing the Pentagon to preempt the FDA's authority. In turn, Rep. Greg Walden, R-Ore., introduced a measure (HR 4374) on November 13, 2017, that would eliminate the language from the not-yet-passed NDAA and replace it with a provision amending the Food, Drug, and Cosmetic Act to allow the FDA to expedite consideration of certain medical products for battlefield use if the Department of Defense determines the product could be useful to prevent imminent risk to U.S. forces or prevent a life-threatening situation. The language in the bill was developed in cooperation with members from both parties in the House and Senate, along with the White House and FDA commissioner Scott Gottlieb.

On November 13, the House Rules Committee finalized their recommended rule for debate on the conference report to accompany the fiscal year 2018 NDAA (HR 2810). As part of that rule, they included a stipulation barring the House clerk from transmitting a message to the Senate stating that the House adopted the conference report, until the House received a message from the Senate that the chamber had passed HR 4374 without amendment. The House adopted the procedural rule and the conference report accompanying HR 2810 on November 14. The following day, the House passed HR 4374 by voice vote under suspension of the rules.

Senate Action

When HR 4374 moved to the Senate, the question was not whether the chamber would vote on the bill but when. Getting the NDAA passed is always a key priority for both Republicans and Democrats, and it had made it to the president's desk for fifty-five consecutive years. But there were some senators who objected to leaving the authority for emergency battlefield use approval to the FDA given what they saw as a poor track record of supporting the needs of the troops.

However, on November 16, Senate Majority Leader Mitch McConnell, R-Ky., received unanimous consent to send HR 4374 to President Trump for his signature, clearing the way for the Senate to finalize its work on the NDAA. President Trump signed the battlefield medicine bill on December 12, 2017 (PL 115-92).

Overdose Prevention and Patient Safety Act

In 2018, as part of a slate of action related to the opioid crisis, the House passed a bill that would align substance use disorder treatment records more closely with the privacy guidelines contained within the Health Insurance Portability and Accountability Act (HIPAA; PL 104-191). While Republicans said the bill would help those suffering from a substance use disorder more easily access care from different providers, Democrats argued that it opened those seeking treatment to the possibility of unintended consequences, such as job loss. The Senate never considered the bill.

House Action

Patient health records are protected by HIPAA, which sets guidelines for when records can be shared between providers, insurers, and others in the medical community. Substance abuse records are dealt with somewhat differently, and require that a provider keep those separate from other health information. Such records can only be shared with the express consent of the patient. On June 13, 2018, Rep. Markwayne Mullin, R-Okla., introduced HR 6082, the Overdose Prevention and Patient Safety Act, which would align the handling of substance use disorder treatment records with existing HIPAA guidelines for the purposes of payment, treatment, and other specified health care operations. The bill was nearly identical to one proposed by Rep. Earl Blumenauer, D-Ore., that advanced out of the House Energy and Commerce Committee on May 17, 2018, with some minor exceptions.

The House Rules Committee met on June 19 to recommend a closed rule for debate on HR 6082. During debate, Rep. Frank Pallone, D-N.J., worried that the underlying

bill would prevent people from seeking substance use treatment. "What happens is that people don't show up for treatment because they're afraid that they'll be stigmatized or lose their kid," he said, calling the bill "completely counterproductive" to the House's work to address the opioid crisis.

On the same day the Rules Committee advanced their recommendation, the White House released a Statement of Administration Policy, noting its belief that HR 6082 could improve care for those with substance use disorders. "Patients suffering or recovering from opioid addiction must access services from doctors, treatment facilities, and hospitals across an increasingly complex healthcare system," and HR 6082 "would enhance coordinated care while protecting patient privacy."

On June 20, the full House debated HR 6082. Some Democrats continued to express concern that the bill would prevent those with substance use disorders from seeking treatment out of fear that they could face a larger consequence. However, other members on both sides of the aisle agreed with the desire to prevent stigmatizing those with a substance use disorder but argued that creating a HIPAA carve out for them automatically implied a stigma. HR 6082, they contended, would ensure patients are receiving the highest quality care and avoid a situation where a provider might prescribe something to a patient that would unknowingly do them harm.

Before the final vote, Rep. Pallone made a motion to recommit the bill to the House Energy and Commerce Committee, requesting that it add an amendment striking language allowing for medical providers to see records related to substance abuse and instead calling on the secretary of the Department of Health and Human Services to find model programs to train providers on best practices for using and disclosing substance use records. The motion failed 175–240. The House went on to pass HR 6082, 357–57. The Senate never considered it.

Medicaid Coverage for Opioid Residential Treatment

With opioid addiction affecting Americans from coast to coast, Congress in 2018 considered a number of measures that would address the epidemic. One of these bills specifically sought to eliminate an existing Medicaid policy that restricts beneficiaries from using funds to cover residential treatment for a substance abuse or mental health disorder at a facility with more than sixteen beds. While the House passed its partial repeal measure, the Senate did not take it up.

House Committee Action

In May 2018, the House considered the Individuals in Medicaid Deserve Care that is Appropriate and Responsible in its Delivery (IMD CARE) Act (HR 5797), a bill introduced by Rep. Mimi Walters, R-Calif., that would partially suspend for five years the Medicaid Institutions for Mental Diseases (IMD) exclusion that bans the use of federal Medicaid dollars for residential treatment for mental health or substance use disorders if the facility has more than sixteen beds. Specifically, Walters's bill would allow beneficiaries between the ages of twenty-one and sixty-four years old to receive thirty days of inpatient treatment over the course of a year for an opioid use disorder. Under HR 5797, states would have the option to use the Medicaid state plan amendment process, instead of the 1115 Medicaid waiver, to bypass the existing prohibition on use of funds for opioid inpatient treatment. While approximately half the states have requested a 1115 Medicaid waiver to cover residential services for substance use and mental health care, supporters of Walters's bill said HR 5797 would speed up the process.

On May 17, 2018, the House Energy and Commerce Committee marked up thirty-four bills related to the opioid epidemic. One of the most contentious was HR 5797. Democrats agreed that the IMD policy should be eliminated, but expressed concern that the bill at hand was not the best way to do so, especially because it allowed a carve out only for opioid use disorders, no other types of substance use. Despite their opposition to the measure, Democrats did not request a roll call vote and the measure was advanced to the full House by voice vote.

More than one month later, on June 19, the House Rules Committee issued its rule governing debate on HR 5797. It provided for ten minutes of debate on three amendments. One, from Rep. Bobby Rush, D-Ill., would also allow use of Medicaid funds for eligible beneficiaries seeking treatment for a cocaine use disorder. Another, from Rep. Dan Kildee, D-Mich., would require states to provide additional information in their required reporting about access to community care for those with a nonsubstance use mental illness and the number of individuals with co-occurring disorders. The third amendment, proposed by Rep. Brian Fitzpatrick, R-Pa., would let states decide the level of care and length of stay for those covered under HR 5797's provisions. The rule included a self-executing amendment that, once adopted by the House, would modify the bill to include language giving states an incentive to voluntarily adopt a provision requiring Medicaid managed care organizations to spend 85 percent of their funds on medical care, rather than administrative costs, or face a payback requirement for fiscal years 2021 through 2024.

The White House released a Statement of Administration Policy on June 19, expressing its commitment "to leveraging every available tool in its arsenal to combat the scourge of opioid misuse and provide needed relief to American families and patients." According to the statement, HR 5797 would be consistent with the administration's current strategy to permit states to use their Medicaid resources to cover inpatient opioid abuse services.

HOUSE FLOOR ACTION

The full House took up HR 5797 on June 20, 2018. During debate, Democrats continued to assert that the existing waiver process was a better method for addressing the challenge of Medicaid coverage for mental health and substance use disorders. As written, they found the bill too narrow and limiting for states to fully address the challenges they face in providing appropriate coverage. Democrats also balked at the bill's price tag, estimated to be around $1 billion, and the fact that it did little to address resource availability.

The chamber passed the amendments from Reps. Rush and Kildee, while Rep. Fitzpatrick withdrew his amendment from consideration. The House rejected, 190–226 a motion to recommit from Rep. Betty Castor, D-Fla., that would send the bill back to the House Energy and Commerce Committee requesting an amendment that would replace the provisions in the bill with language giving states federal matching funds for those suffering from substance abuse disorders so long as the state extended Medicaid eligibility.

As amended, the House passed HR 5797 on June 20, 261–155. The bill never received Senate consideration. However, the provisions of HR 5797 were included in HR 6, an omnibus opioid abuse–related package signed by President Donald Trump on October 24, 2018 (PL 115-271).

Opioid Abuse

The House and Senate in 2018 passed an omnibus piece of legislation that packaged various measures intended to help address the opioid abuse crisis. The bill (PL 115-271), which President Trump signed on October 24, 2018, included enhancements for treatment and recovery programs, tools for community organizations, and more funding for prevention and public health outreach efforts.

House Action

In 2018 legislators in the House proposed dozens of bills aimed at addressing various aspects of the opioid crisis. Some dealt with how the Children's Health Insurance Program could cover substance use disorder treatment, others the privacy of treatment records, and still others called on various federal agencies to report on evidence-based health care practices that could help stem opioid use. To speed passage of these measures through both the House and Senate, on June 19, the House Rules Committee recommended a rule for general debate on HR 6, the SUPPORT for Patients and Communities Act, a bill to expand Medicare and Medicaid programs to cover opioid treatment. Their rules package included a self-executing rule that, upon adoption by the House, would add fifty-two opioid-related bills to the package—some of which had already passed and some that had not. In an effort to help smooth passage, the bills chosen for inclusion had bipartisan support.

The House approved the rule on June 20, and went on to debate HR 6 on June 22. The chamber considered seven amendments, adopting six by voice vote; the seventh was withdrawn. The adopted amendments included one to require the Food and Drug Administration to establish evidence-based forms of acute pain treatment. Three amendments called on the Department of Health and Human Services (HHS) to conduct surveys and issue reports and guidance on issues such as prescribing opioids during pregnancy, when to prescribe naloxone, and where service and funding gaps exist in treating drug addiction. A fifth amendment would require a report from the Government Accountability Office on existing policies that could have resulted in an increase in opioid-related deaths. A sixth amendment made technical changes to the measure.

As amended, the House passed HR 6, 396–14. While Democrats generally supported the bill, some also noted that there was still more work to be done given the magnitude of the crisis. As passed, HR 6 included a number of provisions, such as

- Adding requirements to state Medicaid programs to monitor those at risk for substance use disorder to limit their access to prescribers and dispensers
- Reinstating a reimbursement for postsurgical injections to encourage their use over opioids to treat pain
- Requiring the evaluation of whether telehealth services are effective in treating substance use disorder
- Authorizing certain nurses to prescribe buprenorphine to treat opioid use disorder
- Increasing the number of patients certain first-year providers can see

Also included were offsets intended to cover the bill's cost. These included one requiring Medicaid managed care organizations to spend at least 85 percent of their government funds on care instead of administrative costs or face a penalty. Another offset would increase from thirty months to thirty-three months how long a person's private insurance is billed before Medicare for end-stage renal disease. There was also an offset regarding reporting requirements for Medicare Part D prescription drug coverage intended to clarify when other insurance should be billed before Medicare.

Senate Action

On April 24, 2018, the Senate Health, Education, Labor, and Pensions Committee advanced its own opioid-related bill package by a 23–0 vote. S 2680 included more than forty measures that addressed aspects of the opioid crisis, such as medication disposal, patient information sharing, prescription monitoring, and greater coordination between various federal agencies to slow or prevent the importation of illegal drugs. During markup, the committee rejected three amendments, one of which was proposed by Sen. Bernie Sanders, I-Vt., that would hold drug companies

accountable for their role making and selling drugs that have contributed to the opioid epidemic. The committee adopted five amendments, including those to improve training for medical school students as it relates to medication-assisted treatment, expand alternative treatment options, and provide more resources to states. S 2680 never received a floor vote.

On September 17, the Senate passed HR 6, 99–1, after replacing the House text with its own substitute amendment. The Senate language encompassed seventy bills approved in the Finance; Health, Education, Labor, and Pensions; Commerce; Judiciary; and Banking Committees.

Final Action

After the Senate passed an amended version of HR 6 the two chambers went to conference to negotiate the differences between the bills. While they mostly mirrored each other, there were some key differences. For example, the Senate version did not include a House-passed measure that would partially eliminate the existing restriction on funding for Medicaid recipients seeking substance abuse treatment at a residential facility with more than sixteen beds. The House version would allow Medicaid reimbursement in these facilities for up to thirty days per year. The House bill also included language that would more closely align a patient's records related to substance use with the Health Insurance Portability and Accountability Act (HIPAA). Under existing law, patients had to give express consent to have records related to substance use shared with a medical provider. The House bill would eliminate that provision so that substance use records are shared in the way other patient information under HIPAA is shared.

On September 25, House and Senate negotiators released the language of their agreement on HR 6. While the HIPAA provision from the House-passed measure was dropped, the agreement would authorize Medicaid coverage for inpatient substance use treatment at a facility with more than sixteen beds for up to thirty days per year for individuals between the ages of twenty-one and sixty-five, so long as the person seeking treatment had a documented substance use disorder for at least one year. The final bill also overhauled drug monitoring programs, reauthorized the Office of National Drug Control Policy, renewed grant programs, supported early intervention, helped prevent drugs from being shipped through the mail, required disclosure of payments drug companies make to certain medical practitioners, limited the use of opioids in emergency departments, and encouraged the development of nonaddictive painkillers. The conference package maintained two of the House offsets: the one related to Medicaid managed care organizations and one requiring more reporting for Medicare Part D prescription drug coverage. After a Congressional Budget Office estimate indicated that the bill would cost $44 million over the next decade, conferees added two more offsets, one related to drug price

transparency and the other to the religious exemption offered under the 2010 Patient Protection and Affordable Care Act (ACA; PL 111-148, PL 111-152).

The House passed the compromise package on September 28, 393–8. The Senate followed on October 3, clearing the measure 98–1. President Trump signed the bill on October 24, 2018 (PL 115-271).

Home Visiting Program Reauthorization

In 2018, Congress reauthorized through fiscal year 2022 a federally funded program that sends certain professionals, including health care and social workers, into the homes of lower-income families in an effort to improve overall family and childhood outcomes.

House Action

The Maternal, Infant, and Early Childhood Home Visiting (MIECHV) program was created by the 2010 Patient Protection and Affordable Care Act (ACA; PL 111-148, PL 111-152) as a permanent follow-up to a fifteen-state pilot program started during the George W. Bush administration. MIECHV appropriates federal money to fund programs that send health care workers, social workers, and other professionals into the homes of families in communities with a history of poor child health outcomes or other risk indicators. The purpose of the program, which supports parents who opt in from pregnancy through their child's kindergarten enrollment, is to provide education and support that they might not otherwise receive in areas including healthy pregnancy, breastfeeding, nutrition, and positive parenting strategies. The overall goal is to break long-running cycles of poverty, abuse, and drug use. As with other federally funded health programs, MIECHV has to be reauthorized on a regular basis to ensure continued funding (the ACA provided a $1.5 billion appropriation for five years).

In June 2017, Rep. Adrian Smith, R-Neb., introduced the Increasing Opportunity and Success for Children and Parents through Evidence-Based Home Visiting Act (HR 2824) to reauthorize MIECHV through fiscal year 2022. While the legislation continued a condition that entities must prove their program's ability to meet certain benchmarks and other guidelines, Smith's bill added a new provision that would require grantees to provide matching funds under MIECHV beginning in fiscal year 2020. That quickly became a sticking point for Democrats, who worried that some programs could be forced to close if they could not meet the matching fund requirement.

When the House Ways and Means Committee took up the bill, Rep. Bill Pascrell, D-N.J., introduced an amendment that would strike language requiring state, local, and tribal grantees to provide a cost-sharing match. The amendment was rejected 13–21. An amendment from Rep. Suzan DelBene to eliminate cost sharing and provide additional funds to tribal organizations failed 15–22.

Democrats also attempted to include an amendment gradually phasing in a federal funding increase for the program from $400 million in fiscal year 2018 to $800 million by fiscal year 2022. That was ruled not germane, and their attempt to replace the bill's language in its entirety with a measure that would reauthorize the program and increase funding to $800 million with an offset, was rejected 15–21. Democrats also tried to strike some of the benchmarking language. For example, Rep. Pascrell introduced an amendment to remove the stipulation that a family's economic self-sufficiency be used to evaluate how effective an MIECHV program is. It was rejected 15–22.

The committee did adopt a substitute amendment by voice vote that changed the cost sharing requirements specifically for Native American tribes. In fiscal years 2020 and 2021, they would be eligible to receive grants without cost-sharing funds, but starting in fiscal year 2022 would need to meet a 30 percent cost sharing requirement. The full bill was reported favorably to the House, as amended, on a party line 22–15 vote on September 13. As sent to the House, the measure would

- Reauthorize MIECHV through fiscal year 2022
- Require grant recipients to track and report at specified intervals on their program's effectiveness and improvement in the economic conditions of participating families
- Give the secretary of Health and Human Services the authority to end funding for any program that does not meet designated benchmarks or reporting requirements
- Set state and local cost-sharing requirements at 30 percent in fiscal year 2020, 40 percent in fiscal year 2021, and 50 percent in fiscal year 2022
- Set cost sharing for tribal entities at 30 percent starting in fiscal year 2022.

The House Rules Committee on September 25 recommended a structured rule for debate on HR 2824 that made in order (or approved for debate) four amendments. One, from the bill's sponsor Rep. Smith, would allow states to account for staffing levels, community resources, and other requirements when determining how to run at least one of their MIECHV programs. Another, from Rep. Pascrell, again attempted to eliminate language requiring states to track increases in employment and earnings as part of a benchmark goal, and Rep. DelBene again made an attempt to strike language requiring Native American tribes to provide cost-sharing funds. The fourth amendment, from Rep. Stephanie Murphy, D-Fla., called on HHS to use the most accurate federal data available when determining how to allocate funding.

HR 2824 came to the floor on September 26, 2017. While Pascrell's amendment was rejected, 191–231, the other three were adopted by voice vote. Rep. DelBene made a motion to recommit the bill to the Ways and Means Committee, asking them to attach an amendment striking language to require grant recipients to demonstrate improvements in certain benchmarks and guidelines. It was rejected 191–232. As amended, the bill passed the House 214–209. It was never considered in the Senate.

Final Action

The Senate never took up HR 2824, nor did it consider its own bipartisan bill, S 1829, the Strong Families Act, which would reauthorize MIECHV funding without requiring state matching funds. Advocacy groups and many members of Congress raised concern that states would have to shut down their MIECHV programs if Congress failed to quickly reauthorize the program, which was due to expire on September 30, 2017.

It was not until February 9, 2018, when MIECHV was reauthorized, as part of the Bipartisan Budget Act of 2018 (PL 115-123). The program was reauthorized at $400 million per year through fiscal year 2022. Because the funding is on the mandatory side of the congressional ledger, it is not subject to annual appropriations.

Fiscal Year 2018 Health and Human Services Appropriations

The annual Labor, Health and Human Services (HHS), Education, and Related Agencies appropriations bill was added to a larger omnibus measure that did not reach President Donald Trump's desk until nearly six months after the start of fiscal year 2018. On March 23, 2018, Trump signed the $1.3 trillion measure into law (PL 115-141). Within the HHS portion of the bill, which funds agencies including the Centers for Disease Control and Prevention (CDC), National Institutes of Health (NIH), Centers for Medicare and Medicaid Services (CMS), Substance Abuse and Mental Health Services Administration (SAMHSA), and Administration for Children and Families (ACF), agencies were allocated $88.1 billion in discretionary funds, a more than 12 percent increase over the prior fiscal year.

House Committee Action

The House Appropriations Labor-HHS-Education Subcommittee voted 9–6 to advance the spending bill under its purview on July 13, 2017 (HR 3358). Of the total $156 billion measure, $78 billion was set aside for HHS, $542 million lower than the previous fiscal year. During markup, the committee rejected a Trump administration proposal to reduce the budget for the National Institutes of Health (NIH), instead increasing its budget by $1.1 billion. Democrats welcomed many of the provisions of the bill, though raised concerns that some of the decisions made by the Republican majority would be harmful to women's health. For example, the subcommittee planned to eliminate $286 million from family planning funds, which included a $25 million cut to Planned Parenthood. Policy riders in the bill also banned federal funding for Planned Parenthood and would stop researchers from using fetal tissue cells.

HEALTH AND HUMAN SERVICES LEADERSHIP

Prior to assuming office, President Donald Trump announced that he would nominate Rep. Tom Price, R-Ga., to head the Department of Health and Human Services (HHS). A sitting member of Congress, Price was also an orthopaedic surgeon and helped lead Republican opposition against the Patient Protection and Affordable Care Act (ACA). Democrats were critical of the nomination, pointing to Price's propensity toward restricting government funding especially when it came to health care programs, such as Medicaid and Medicare.

Republicans rallied behind him, with Speaker of the House Paul Ryan, R-Wis., tweeting that Price had "made health care his life's work. He is the absolute perfect choice for HHS Secretary." Price was confirmed on February 10, 2017, in a 52–47 vote, after a debate that focused significant attention on his investments in medical and drug companies at the same time as he was working on health policy in Congress. After his confirmation, Price's primary task was to help Republicans get the American Health Care Act (AHCA), their replacement for the ACA, passed through Congress. He failed to do so.

Price's short tenure as HHS secretary was clouded by questions about his spending habits, specifically those related to travel. After a *Politico* story revealed that the secretary was costing taxpayers hundreds of thousands of dollars in private jet usage, Price resigned on September 29, 2017. He was the shortest serving HHS secretary in U.S. history. An inspector general inquiry later found that Price had violated government travel rules on multiple occasions and wasted more than $300,000.

President Trump next nominated Alex Azar to fill the now vacant HHS secretary role. Azar previously served as deputy secretary at HHS during the George W. Bush administration, before going on to a leadership role at Eli Lilly and Co., a major pharmaceutical company. Trump claimed Azar's time with a drug maker would provide important insight into how to address runaway drug costs. During his confirmation hearings, Democrats argued the exact opposite, pointing to rising drug costs during Azar's time with Eli Lilly. Azar was ultimately confirmed by the Senate, 55–43, on January 24, 2018.

Where his predecessor focused on the legislative side of health-related issues, and shied away from excessive government intervention in medical practice, Azar's main priority was regulation. As such, he frequently looked for ways to limit the impact of the ACA, shift funding away from Planned Parenthood, and require more drug pricing transparency. Azar's role became more visible in early 2020 as the COVID-19 pandemic began sweeping across the country. On January 31, 2020, Azar declared a public health emergency as it related to the virus. Shortly thereafter, he was replaced as head of the White House Coronavirus Task Force, and stories began circulating in the media indicating that he had been sidelined by the Trump administration. Vice President Mike Pence soon became the task force lead, and it was not until late spring that Azar resurfaced, touting the administration's response to the crisis and blasting the World Health Organization for what he called its "failure" to warn countries about the COVID-19 pandemic.

In the last year of President Trump's tenure, perhaps the most recognizable member of his HHS team was Dr. Anthony Fauci, who had served since 1984 as director of the National Institute of Allergy and Infectious Diseases. Fauci was one of the lead members of the White House Coronavirus Task Force. In this role, Fauci was known for regularly contradicting Trump's statements. While the nation's top infectious disease expert walked a fine line to avoid openly criticizing the president, he frequently disagreed with Trump on the severity of the pandemic, possible treatments, its origins, and a timeline for safely reopening the country.

The subcommittee considered one amendment during debate. Language in the bill prevented HHS from using the funds appropriated to implement the 2010 Patient Protection and Affordable Care Act (ACA; PL 111-148, 111-152). At the time, Republicans had been working to dismantle the law, either through congressional action or via the courts. An amendment from Rep. Rosa DeLauro, D-Conn., would prevent HHS from implementing a Republican measure to overhaul or repeal the ACA if that bill either increased the number of uninsured Americans or increased premiums beyond a certain level. The committee rejected the amendment, 6–9.

On July 19, 2017, the House Appropriations Committee held an eleven-hour markup on HR 3358, ultimately voting 28–22 to advance the measure to the floor. The $156 billion bill was more than $21 billion higher than the president's budget request but $5 billion lower than current enacted levels. During debate, forty amendments were proposed, though few were adopted. One of the amendments agreed to, adopted at the start of the markup, was a manager's package that added certain directives to agencies and changed some funding in the HHS portion of the bill. This included an additional $10 million for the HHS Community Service Block Grant, and $6 million more for the CDC to spend on certain diseases that cause brain damage. Democrats introduced a variety of amendments— all of which were rejected—that would have increased

funding for other HHS areas, such as substance abuse treatment, family planning, public health emergencies, and vaccines. HR 3358 never received a floor vote.

Senate Committee Action

On September 6, 2017, the Senate Appropriations Labor–HHS–Education Subcommittee reported by voice vote S 1771, a $164.1 billion measure, which the full Senate Appropriations Committee passed the next day by a 29–2 vote. The bill included a major difference from the House bill, specifically related to family planning. While the House provided no money for family planning, the Senate's appropriations bill set aside $286 million for these programs and included a stipulation that the money could not go toward changing the rules of how that money is allocated. Essentially, this would block the White House from defunding Planned Parenthood. Although federal funds have been blocked from funding abortion for more than four decades, Republicans have regularly sought to deny funds to Planned Parenthood altogether, given that one of its many functions is providing abortion-related services.

House Floor Action

With the end of the fiscal year fast approaching, House Republican leaders in August proposed packaging a previously passed four-bill minibus (HR 3219) with the remaining eight regular appropriations bills, including Labor–HHS–Education. The House Rules Committee recommended two structured rules for debate on the combined package and made in order more than 340 amendments, most of which shifted funding around or made slight adjustments to program funding levels. The committee declined to include some of the most controversial amendments that had been proposed, including those dealing with family planning.

After the rule was approved, the Make America Secure and Prosperous Appropriations Act, 2018 (HR 3354), a twelve-bill $1.23 trillion omnibus, was debated on the House floor over two weeks in September. Ultimately, on September 14, 2017, the chamber voted 211–198 to send the bill to the Senate. Notably, the bill was in violation of the 2011 Budget Control Act (PL 112-25), and if enacted would have triggered across-the-board spending cuts known as the sequester. As passed, the bill had little chance of approval in the Senate, where Democrats objected not only to the funding levels but also to a variety of policy riders.

Final Action

In early September, Congress passed a stopgap funding bill that would give them until December 15, 2017, to reach an agreement on fiscal year 2018 appropriations. That was followed by four additional continuing resolutions (CRs) that each maintained funding at current fiscal 2017 levels. There was a brief three-day shutdown between the third and fourth CRs. The inability to reach a consensus on funding tended to have less to do with the topline numbers for each title covered in the omnibus package that passed the House and more to do with policy riders, especially those related to funding a wall along the U.S.–Mexico border. Democrats, along with some of their Republican colleagues, were hesitant to give President Trump the billions of dollars he had requested for one of his primary campaign promises.

As it related to the HHS portion of the bill, Planned Parenthood funding was a major sticking point for those responsible for reaching a compromise between the House and Senate spending bills. The House version barred funding from going to Planned Parenthood, while wording in the Senate bill would stop the White House from changing how grant allocations are made, meaning funding would continue for Planned Parenthood. Democrats wanted to ensure the organization could continue to receive federal dollars, arguing that it provides vital health care services, including cancer screenings, for men and women around the country. Republicans objected to setting restrictions on how funding is allocated.

On March 21, 2018, nearly six months into fiscal year 2018, the House Rules Committee met to set the rule governing floor debate on the massive, 2,232-page $1.3 trillion omnibus spending bill. To speed passage and avoid some procedural hurdles in the Senate, the bill was attached to an unrelated bill on human trafficking (HR 1625) that had already passed both chambers. The committee approved, 8–3, a rule for debate that did not allow for amendments. Members on both sides of the aisle complained about the rushed process for getting the bill to the floor, though leadership encouraged their members to vote for it given that there was little appetite in either Congress or the White House to pass another CR.

On March 22, the House voted 256–167 to pass HR 1625. The Senate followed later the same day, voting 65–32 to send the measure to President Trump's desk. With little time to spare before the existing CR expired, Trump signed the bill on March 23, 2018 (PL 115-141). At the time of signing, the president vowed to never again sign a bill that large that no one had time to read.

Labor–HHS–Education was the largest nondefense title in the omnibus package, receiving a $177.1 billion appropriation for the programs within its oversight, of which $88.1 billion went to HHS. This marked an increase of about $10 billion for HHS. Among other things, the bill

- Maintained the prohibition on federal funds from being used for abortion, except in instances of rape, incest, or when a mother's life is in danger
- Required the administration to disclose spending on the health insurance exchanges established under the ACA
- Increased by $3 billion money to address the opioid crisis

- Raised funding for the National Institutes of Health by $3 billion, which included more money specifically for Alzheimer's disease research
- Increased to $8.3 billion the appropriation for the CDC
- Left in place the funding for the Title X family planning grant program, which includes funds that go to Planned Parenthood
- Increased funding for the Child Care Development Block Grant and the program that provides heating assistance to low-income individuals
- Clarified that the CDC is not barred from awarding grants to study gun violence
- Banned the creation of embryos for research purposes and the use of federal funds for research programs in which embryos are destroyed
- Permitted state and local health departments to use federal funds in support of needle exchange programs, so long as those funds are not used to purchase syringes

Fiscal Year 2019 Health and Human Services Appropriations

The fiscal 2019 appropriations effort marked the first time since the fiscal 1997 cycle that full year appropriations were provided for Health and Human Services (HHS) before the start of the fiscal year. The Labor–HHS–Education measure was part of a two-bill package that also included the Defense bill. President Donald Trump signed the measure into law on September 28, 2018 (PL 115-245), providing $90.5 billion for HHS programs.

House Committee Action

After wrapping up the fiscal year 2018 appropriations process in March 2018, six months after the start of the fiscal year, House and Senate leadership expressed a desire to return to regular order, passing each of the twelve appropriations measures either individually or as smaller, minibus packages. To do this, some members indicated they would focus first on passing the least controversial spending bills, before moving on to the others to ensure that at least some could be enacted prior to the fiscal year.

On June 15, 2018, the House Education, Health and Human Services, and Education Appropriations Subcommittee approved its annual appropriations package (HR 6470) by voice vote, advancing it to the full Appropriations Committee. Despite using a voice vote to move the measure, Democrats were united in their opposition to the $177.1 billion bill, an amount unchanged from fiscal year 2018. Of that total, $89.2 billion would go to HHS, an increase of $1.1 billion over the current fiscal year. That boost went primarily to the National Institutes of Health (NIH) and the Centers for Disease Control and Prevention (CDC). The subcommittee did

not consider any amendments prior to their vote to approve the measure.

The total bill provided $89.2 billion in discretionary spending for HHS programs, including

- $6.7 billion for the CDC
- $38.3 billion for the NIH
- $5.5 billion for SAMHSA
- $4.3 billion for the Centers for Medicare and Medicaid Services
- $2.2 billion for the Administration for Community Living
- $6.5 billion for the Health Resources and Services Administration
- $334 million for the Agency for Healthcare Research and Quality

The measure provided no funding for the Title X family planning program, prohibited funds from being used to promote gun control, maintained the prohibition on federal funds being used for most abortions, banned the use of federal funds for syringe purchase by state and local needle exchange programs (except in certain circumstances), and blocked funds from going toward the ongoing implementation of the 2010 Patient Protection and Affordable Care Act (ACA; PL 111-148, PL 111-152).

It was almost a month before the House Appropriations Committee considered the Labor–HHS–Education bill. During a thirteen-hour markup, the committee debated more than fifty amendments, ranging from abstinence-only sex education to funding for Planned Parenthood to gun violence research. The committee did approve a manager's amendment that shifted money between programs in order to boost CDC and Substance Abuse and Mental Health Services Administration (SAMHSA) funding.

The committee thwarted Democratic attempts to add an amendment that would direct $10 million in CDC funds to be used specifically for research into gun violence. The committee also rejected an amendment that would restore $286 million to family planning funding and another to eliminate a restriction on federal funding going toward Planned Parenthood. Republicans also voted together to block an amendment that would strike language in the bill prohibiting funds from being used to continue implementation of the ACA. Adopted amendments included one directing HHS to report to Congress on the most frequently prescribed and highest-priced drugs for certain federal health insurance programs.

On July 11, the committee passed HR 6470, as amended, 30–22. The measure, which maintained the subcommittee's topline funding numbers, did not receive a floor vote.

Senate Committee Action

The Senate Appropriations Committee reported its Labor–HHS–Education bill (S 3158) on June 28, by a vote of 30–1. That $179.3 billion measure was the last of the

committee's twelve regular appropriations bills to move to the Senate for consideration. The bill provided $90.1 billion for HHS, up $2.3 billion over the current fiscal year. The funding increases included in the bill were part of an attempt to maintain a bipartisan spirit. For example, NIH would see record funding at $39.1 billion, the CDC and SAMHSA would receive an additional $0.6 billion each, and Alzheimer's research would receive $425 million more. Notably, the Senate version avoided the controversial provisions added in the House bill, and did not restrict ongoing implementation of the ACA or cut family planning funding.

Senate Floor Action

Instead of taking up S 3158 alone, the Senate decided to bundle much of the bill's language with HR 6157, the House Defense appropriations bill, which the House passed in late June. Because the Defense bill tends to receive broad bipartisan support, Senate leadership saw it as a means to also move the Labor-HHS-Education bill through both chambers, because the latter can attract controversial policy riders that bog down debate.

During floor debate, the Senate adopted thirty-one amendments to the two-bill $856.9 billion funding measure. These included a manager's amendment that contained, among other things, $1 million for HHS to create rules for drug makers to include pricing information in their advertisements. Other adopted amendments included those to provide more money for school mental health programs and neurological disease surveillance. Sen. Rand Paul, R-Ky., threatened to slow the bill's consideration over an amendment he proposed to bar federal funding for Planned Parenthood. On the Senate floor, Paul accused Republican leadership of trying to block consideration of his amendment through the so-called filling the amend-

ment tree procedural tool, in which the majority leader fills all opportunities to amend a bill. Worried that adoption of the Paul amendment could tank the entire package, Republican leaders reached an agreement with Democratic leadership, with the latter promising to back off a separate amendment related to ongoing legal proceedings over the ACA, if the vote threshold for Paul's amendment was raised from fifty to sixty. Paul's amendment ultimately failed, and the chamber went on to pass HR 6157 by a vote of 85–7 on August 23, 2018.

Final Action

Instead of voting on its own committee-passed Labor–HHS–Education bill, the House opted to go to conference with the Senate on HR 6157. In mid-September, negotiators announced that they had reached an agreement on the spending package, which would now also include a continuing resolution for any agencies that did not receive a full-year appropriation before the start of the fiscal year. To smooth passage, conferees removed controversial language, including the House-passed provisions blocking federal money for Planned Parenthood and eliminating the $286 million Title X family planning program.

The Senate passed the conference report on September 18, by a vote of 93–7. The next week, on September 26, the House passed the bill 361–61. Within the package, $178.1 billion in discretionary spending was allocated to the Labor–HHS–Education title, of which $90.5 billion would go toward HHS programs, a $2 billion increase over fiscal 2018. The bill provided $39.1 billion for NIH, $5.7 billion for SAMHSA, and $7.1 billion for the CDC. President Trump signed the bill into law on September 28, 2018 (PL 115-245), marking the first time in twenty-two years that the Labor–HHS–Education funding measure was enacted prior to the start of the fiscal year.

2019-2020

With Democrats in control of the House, the work during the first session of the 116th Congress moved from dismantling the 2010 Patient Protection and Affordable Care Act to bolstering the language within the bill and getting additional funding to the federal programs it established. Those efforts slowed in 2020, however, as the COVID-19 pandemic took hold and Congress shifted its focus to relief programs and supporting the development and availability of vaccines. Lawmakers also sparred over tobacco, raising the legal age to purchase tobacco from eighteen to twenty-one but falling short in efforts to ban flavored tobacco products.

Patient Protection and Affordable Care Enhancement

What was mostly a bipartisan desire to enhance health insurance purchased through the state and federal insurance marketplaces created under the 2010 Patient Protection and Affordable Care Act (ACA; PL 111-148, PL 111-152) was stymied by disagreement over how such a measure would address abortion. While the House passed a bill that would, among other things, give states funds to help their lowest-income citizens cover insurance costs, the Senate did not take it up.

House Committee Action

On March 6, 2019, the House Energy and Commerce Health Subcommittee began its consideration of a variety of measures aimed at strengthening the ACA, one of which was the Patient Protection and Affordable Care Enhancement Act (HR 1425). The bill would provide $10 billion per year for states to create reinsurance programs that help certain individuals afford plans on the exchanges. Under current law, those targeted by HR 1425 are not otherwise eligible for ACA subsidies, typically making plans on the exchange unaffordable.

During debate, Republicans raised concern that the bill did not include the Hyde Amendment, which is regularly attached to annual spending bills and which prohibits federal funds from being used to cover abortion except in certain instances. Democrats shot back that the provisions of the bill are modeled after those Republicans tried to pass in previous Congresses, and they criticized them for holding up passage of a bill that both sides of the aisle seemed to agree was necessary.

It was not until three weeks later, on March 27, when the subcommittee finally approved the bill. During a contentious markup, Republicans refused to support the bill because it did not expressly prohibit federal dollars from being used for abortions. Rep. Michael Burgess, R-Texas, introduced an amendment that would bar funding to state exchanges with plans that provide abortion-related care, but it failed 12–17. HR 1425 moved forward without any Republican support, 18–13.

When the bill moved to the full House Energy and Commerce Committee, Republicans again tried to attach an amendment blocking federal funds from being used for abortion coverage. The amendment offered by Rep. Cathy McMorris Rodgers, R-Wash., included a stipulation that such funds were barred except if the woman's life is in danger or in the case of rape or incest. That amendment was rejected by voice vote. Another Republican amendment was withdrawn before it could be considered. That substitute amendment, from Rep. Burgess, would authorize $2.5 billion for a fund to help states reduce the cost of health care and health insurance from plan years 2020 through 2022. There was also language in the amendment blocking states from using money in the stability fund to cover services related to abortion.

By voice vote, the committee adopted one amendment, from Chair Frank Pallone, D-N.J., that made technical changes to the bill and also added student health insurance coverage to plans that are excluded from the authorized reinsurance funding. On April 3, the legislation was favorably reported to the full House, as amended, 30–22.

House Floor Action

HR 1425 languished for the remainder of 2019, as Republicans remained staunchly opposed, making passage unlikely in the Senate. But the measure resurfaced in 2020 as Democrats hoped addressing the shortcomings in the ACA could help them in the coming November election. The Energy and Commerce Committee amended the bill's text, incorporating new provisions that they hoped would further expand the availability of insurance subsidies and make health insurance more affordable. To do this, the bill included language increasing insurance premium subsidies for individuals with a household income above 150 percent of the federal poverty line. Further, those earning more than 400 percent over the federal poverty line could receive tax credit subsidies. These Americans were not eligible for subsidies under the original language of the ACA, and have over time experienced large premium increases. The bill also required more outreach to consumers to help them understand the marketplaces and the benefits offered within them. It would provide enhanced federal benefits to states to encourage them to expand Medicaid eligibility, promote methods to lower drug costs, and provide permanent funding to expand the Children's Health Insurance Program (CHIP).

By the time it reached the Rules Committee on June 24, 2020, the bill incorporated pieces of multiple measures, including HR 6130 (Improving Awareness of Health Coverage Options Act), HR 6151 (Comprehensive Access to Robust Insurance Now Guaranteed for Kids Act), HR 6136 (Protecting Consumers from Unreasonable Rates Act), S 1400 (State Allowance for a Variety of Exchanges Act), S 1905 (Expand Navigator's Resources for Outreach, Learning, and Longevity Act), HR 3 (Elijah E. Cummings Lower Drug Costs Now Act), and HR 6149 (Medicaid

Report on Expansion of Access to Coverage for Health Act). The committee approved a closed rule for debate, which effectively barred the consideration of amendments not already reported by the House Energy and Commerce Committee, which would help smooth the bill's passage.

On June 29, the White House released a Statement of Administration Policy, noting that the president would veto HR 1425 if it reached his desk. In its statement, the administration accused Democrats of trying to pass a bill "that would send hundreds of billions of dollars to insurance companies in order to paper over serious flaws in Obamacare." Further, the administration alleged that the bill would use taxpayer money to eliminate competition from the insurance market and prevent more affordable options from being made available to consumers.

The same day the White House released its veto threat, the House passed HR 1425 largely along party lines, 234–179. Two Republicans voted in favor of the measure, while one Democrat opposed it. Before final passage, the chamber rejected, 187–223, one motion to recommit from Rep. Greg Walden, R-Ore., to send the bill back to the House Energy and Commerce Committee with instructions to add an amendment postponing the bill's implementation until the Department of Health and Human Services (HHS) could certify that the measure would not have a negative impact on the research, development, or approval of COVID-19 prevention and treatment medications.

As passed, HR 1425 would

- Give $10 billion to the states starting in fiscal 2022 to help lower the costs of plans offered on an insurance marketplace
- Make available $200 million in grants for states to establish state-based insurance marketplaces
- Provide $100 million to HHS to enhance its outreach activities about ACA offerings
- Expand eligibility for federal tax subsidies for insurance premiums
- Permanently authorize CHIP funding
- Permit states to expand CHIP and Medicaid eligibility
- Offer $200 million in grants each year through fiscal year 2024 to states to help them encourage more individuals to enroll in qualified insurance plans
- Give states financial incentives to expand Medicaid
- Require HHS to negotiate prices on certain prescription medications
- Allow Deferred Action for Childhood Arrivals program recipients to enroll in marketplace plans

As expected, the Senate did not consider HR 1425.

Insurance Outreach and Prescription Drugs

The House in 2019 passed a package of bills, half of which sought to strengthen the 2010 Patient Protection and Affordable Care Act (ACA; PL 111-148, PL 111-152) and the other half that made changes to drug pricing.

While Republicans supported the drug pricing measures, they objected to inclusion of the ACA provisions. The bill never received a Senate vote.

House Action

The House Energy and Commerce Subcommittee on Health marked up HR 987, a bill intended to increase the Department of Health and Human Services' (HHS) outreach about federal ACA exchanges, on March 27, 2019. It was approved by voice vote, and the full Energy and Commerce Committee took it up on April 3, sending it to the House with a 30–22 vote. As favorably reported by the committee, the bill would authorize $100 million per year beginning in fiscal year 2020 for HHS outreach and educational activities. HHS would be prohibited from using those funds to promote short-term health insurance plans that do not meet the ACA's minimum coverage requirements.

HR 987 went on to become the vehicle for a seven-bill package intended to improve access to high-quality affordable health care by strengthening the ACA and addressing drug pricing. In addition to the original text of HR 987, the six other bills included in the package were HR 1385, which would provide grants to states to establish ACA insurance exchanges; HR 1386, which would give $100 million for the Navigator program that conducts outreach to assist with exchange enrollment; and HR 1010, which restricted the ability of the Trump administration to expand the availability and duration of certain short-term insurance plans that do not meet the ACA's minimum standards. The package also included HR 965, which would give generic drug manufacturers greater power to sue drug makers who refuse to sell the generic company samples of their brand-name drugs. According to the Congressional Budget Office (CBO), the provision could save the federal government $3.5 billion over ten years. HR 938, which was also added to the package, would give the Food and Drug Administration (FDA) greater authority to start the 180-day clock on an exclusive sales period for the first generic drug to market if the FDA believes the generic company is unnecessarily delaying making its product available to consumers. The final bill in the package, HR 1499, would outlaw patent settlements when a manufacturer agrees to pay a generic drug company to settle a patent infringement claim out of court and the pair agree to a date after patent expiration for release of the generic to market. The CBO reported that HR 1499 and HR 938 could save a combined $894 million over a decade. Notably, drug makers lobbied against those two provisions, arguing that they would increase the cost of development and discourage generic drug makers.

Each of the seven bills added to HR 987 had passed out of the House Energy and Commerce Committee. The three drug pricing–related measures received bipartisan support, while the four ACA-related bills were reported to the full House on a party line vote. According to Democrats, it was important to combine the bills so that the savings from the drug pricing measures could be used

to offset the cost of the ACA programs. Republicans objected to combining the seven measures, because they supported congressional work on addressing the reason for high prescription drug costs but did not want to put federal funds toward ACA programs.

On May 14, 2019, the House Rules Committee recommended a rule providing ninety minutes of general debate. They also made in order twenty-seven amendments, each of which would receive ten minutes of debate. One of those amendments, from Rep. Larry Bucshon, R-Ind., would strike all of the bill's Title II, the portion that restored funding to promote exchange plans and gave money to states to set up marketplaces. Bucshon's amendment would also strike language restricting the availability of short-term insurance plans.

The House considered HR 987 on May 16, first adopting a variety amendments—primarily by voice vote—including those requiring new studies and reports, implementing certain training for insurance navigators, and calling for specific outreach about available insurance plans to certain groups including those with high health disparities. The House went on to pass the bill, as amended, 234–183, with five Republicans voting in favor. HR 987 never received a vote in the Senate.

Protecting Americans With Preexisting Conditions

In its bid to strengthen the 2010 Patient Protection and Affordable Care Act (ACA; PL 111-148, PL 111-152), in 2019 the Democratic-led House passed HR 986, a bill that would require the White House to rescind 2018 guidance that makes it easier for states to get approval for waivers that allow them to circumvent certain provisions of the ACA. The legislation was never considered in the Senate.

House Committee Action

In October 2018, the Trump administration issued guidance that would allow states to seek a waiver to offer cheaper, short-term health insurance offerings that do not meet some of the ACA's patient protection requirements. Opponents said the move was just another attempt by the White House to undermine the ACA, but in a way that was detrimental especially to individuals with preexisting conditions. Republicans countered that the president's guidance would encourage more innovation among the states to find ways to make health insurance more affordable. HR 986, the Protecting Americans with Preexisting Conditions, sought to stop the secretaries of Health and Human Services (HHS) and the Treasury from implementing or enforcing the administration's changes to so-called Section 1332 waivers. It would also bar those two departments from issuing substantially similar guidance.

The House Energy and Commerce Subcommittee on Health advanced the bill to the full committee on March 27, 2019, 19–13. The Energy and Commerce Committee favorably reported it to the full House a week later, on

April 3, by voice vote. The House Rules Committee met on May 7 to set the rules governing debate, voting 9–4 to approve a structured rule allowing for one hour of debate and making in order a dozen amendments, including three Republican amendments that would change the name of the bill to either "This Bill Actually Has Nothing to do with Protecting Americans with Preexisting Conditions Act," the "Nothing in This Bill Would Protect Individuals With Pre-Existing Conditions Act," or the "Insert Politically Punchy Title That Doesn't Reflect the Bill Substance Act."

House Floor Action

The House held its debate of HR 986 on May 9. In their floor statements, Democrats continued to criticize the White House for trying to dismantle portions of the ACA, while Republicans argued that the bill at hand had nothing to do with protecting people with preexisting conditions. They further asserted that the bill, if enacted, could do more damage by restricting states from trying out innovative methods to expand access to affordable insurance options. House Republicans were supported in that opinion by Centers for Medicare and Medicaid Services administrator Seema Verma who had recently said that the states did not have enough flexibility under Section 1332 guidance issued by the Obama administration. She also said, in a letter, that no waiver can undermine coverage for those with a preexisting condition.

During consideration, two amendments seeking to rename the bill were rejected while the third was withdrawn. The chamber adopted nine amendments. Most barred the HHS and Treasury departments from taking certain actions, including those that would increase insurance premiums, reduce affordability for those with preexisting conditions, cause individuals to lose coverage, decrease the number of enrollees, or reduce coverage availability for those with substance use disorders for plans that are at least as comprehensive as the essential health benefits required by the ACA. The chamber rejected, 182–231, a motion to recommit the bill to the Energy and Commerce Committee asking it to add an amendment noting that the October 2018 guidance does not amend Section 1332, nor does it allow HHS to waive protections for those with preexisting conditions.

The House ultimately voted to advance the measure 230–183, with four Republicans voting in favor. At the time of passage, no state had applied for a waiver under the October 2018 guidance. On October 24, 2020, Sen. Sherrod Brown, R-Ohio, sought unanimous consent to bring HR 986 for floor consideration, but it was not agreed to. The Senate also did not consider a similar bill from Sen. Mark Warner, D-Va. (S 466).

ACA Cadillac Tax Repeal

The 2010 Patient Protection and Affordable Care Act (ACA; PL 111-148, PL 111-152) contained an excise tax on high-premium insurance plans. Implementation of the

deeply unpopular so-called Cadillac tax was delayed twice by Congress, and in 2019 a large bipartisan group in the House voted to repeal it altogether.

House Action

The Cadillac tax places a 40 percent surcharge on certain high-cost employer-sponsored health insurance plans. It was one of a trio of taxes, including the medical device tax and health insurance tax, included to help cover the cost of the ACA. The Cadillac tax was also intended to slow the growth of health care spending. When employees have generous plans paid for by an employer, they often take advantage of health care they might not otherwise utilize if they had to pay out of pocket.

Since the ACA was implemented, various industry groups and labor unions have pushed Congress to repeal the tax, arguing that it could have the unintended consequence of making health care unaffordable for Americans who receive insurance through their employer. A bipartisan group of lawmakers also opposed the tax, and twice delayed its implementation, most recently to 2022. Economists were among those who supported implementation of the tax, fearing that its repeal would add to the federal deficit. In May 2019, the Congressional Budget Office projected that repealing the tax would cost $193 billion over the next decade.

That same month, Rep. Joe Courtney, D-Conn., asked Speaker Nancy Pelosi to place his bill (HR 748) that would repeal the tax altogether on the House "consensus calendar." Doing so would give the bill an easier route to a floor vote so long as it achieved at least 290 cosponsors. By the time it reached the House floor on July 17, HR 748 had more than 360 cosponsors. The bill was brought up under suspension of the rules, which limits debate but which requires a two-thirds majority for passage.

During floor debate, both Republicans and Democrats spoke on the floor in favor of repeal, arguing that it would help make health insurance more affordable, because many employers had moved toward offering high-deductible health insurance plans to avoid the tax, pushing more costs onto employees. "If we fail to repeal the Cadillac tax, we will leave working families with less health care coverage, higher out-of-pocket health care costs and little to no wage increases," said Rep. Richard Neal, D-Mass.

The bill easily passed, 419–6, on July 17. On December 19, Sen. Pat Toomey, R-Pa., made a unanimous consent request for the Senate to immediately consider HR 748. That move failed, and the Senate also did not take up its own version of a repeal, S 684, in 2019. However, the Cadillac tax repeal was included in the Further Consolidated Appropriations Act, 2020 (PL 116-94), signed by President Donald Trump on December 20, 2019. Notably, HR 748 went on to be used as the vehicle to pass the Coronavirus Aid, Relief, and Economic Security (CARES) Act in March 2020 (PL 116-136).

Tobacco Restrictions

Antismoking advocates won a partial victory in 2019 as Congress passed, and President Trump signed, legislation raising the minimum age for purchasing tobacco products from eighteen to twenty-one. However, lawmakers balked at passing legislation to prohibit flavored tobacco products despite rising concerns that they were enticing young people into becoming addicted to nicotine. The Trump administration, which initially moved toward banning the flavored products, ultimately backtracked on the issue.

Background

The debate over how strictly to crack down on e-cigarettes had its roots in a 2009 law, the Family Smoking Prevention and Tobacco Control Act, which passed Congress with bipartisan majorities and was signed by President Barack Obama. The law restricted marketing of tobacco products, required health warnings on labels, banned some flavored cigarettes and forced the manufacturers of new products, such as electronic cigarettes, to show that they did not undercut public health.

But the skyrocketing popularity of e-cigarettes among young people appeared to catch the Food and Drug Administration off guard, and it moved slowly to regulate them. Policy makers faced a difficult challenge in balancing the benefits of e-cigarettes, which appeared to be less harmful than the smoking of combustible cigarettes, with the risks of exposing young people to the allure of flavored varieties of liquid nicotine.

By 2018, e-cigarette use among high school students reached record levels, driven in large part by the popularity of a new device by Juul Labs Inc. that used liquid nicotine "pods" with flavors such as mango and cucumber. The popularity of e-cigarettes threatened to offset the overall decline in cigarette smoking in recent decades, with some advocates raising alarms about possible links to a national outbreak of lung illnesses.

President Trump announced on September 11, 2019, that his administration would halt the sales of flavored e-cigarettes. Health and Human Services Secretary Alex Azar said the FDA would issue a new policy within weeks that would require manufacturers to seek authorization from the FDA if they wanted to resume sales of flavored e-cigarettes, as opposed to e-cigarettes with the flavor of tobacco. But news broke on November 18, 2019, that the administration had decided to walk back that policy.

House committee action

One day after reports of the administration stepping back from a prohibition on flavored e-cigarettes, members of the House Energy and Commerce Committee on November 19 gave narrow approval, 27–24, to a bill that would impose such restrictions. One Republican, Fred Upton of Michigan, voted for it, while three Democrats broke party ranks and joined with most of the Republicans in opposition.

The bill (HR 2339) would increase the legal age to purchase tobacco products from eighteen to twenty-one. It would also ban tobacco products flavored with fruit and candy additives, as well as with mint and menthol except in cases in which the manufacturer provided sufficient evidence that the flavor was necessary to help adult smokers switch from traditional cigarettes and that it did not have an adverse health impact or cause nonsmokers to take up vaping. Expensive premium cigars would be largely exempted from the most stringent Food and Drug Administration regulation. The bill would also impose new taxes on vaping products and restrict how they could be advertised.

Supporters of the measure said the restrictions were needed to stem the epidemic of young people addicted to nicotine. Committee Chairman Frank Pallone Jr., D-N.J., the bill's sponsor, said the nation was facing the prospect of losing a generation to tobacco-related illnesses and premature death.

But Democrats found themselves divided over the issue. Some members of the Congressional Black Caucus debated whether menthol cigarettes and e-cigarettes should be exempted from any ban, reflecting differences over how best to respond to the popularity of menthols among African Americans.

Yvette D. Clarke of New York cited reports from the anti-tobacco nonprofit organization, the Truth Initiative, showing that nearly nine of every ten Black smokers used menthol cigarettes. She warned that implementing a ban on menthol tobacco products could contribute to the overpolicing of communities of color, although the House bill targeted manufacturers and shops, rather than consumers of menthol tobacco products. Others argued that the menthol flavor ban would deny Black people their cigarette of choice.

But other committee Democrats, including Congressional Black Caucus members, saw the issue through a much different lens. They contended that the very popularity of menthol tobacco products among communities of color made it especially urgent to ban menthol—especially considering the history of predatory marketing by Big Tobacco companies. They also said that menthol affected the way that users metabolize nicotine in a way that makes tobacco even more addictive.

The committee gave voice vote approval to an amendment by Clarke and Republican Michael C. Burgess of Texas that would provide educational materials to law enforcement and health care professionals about the FDA's regulatory authority. The language aimed to prevent profiling of African American smokers.

Concerns about the bill were also raised by Republicans on the committee, who warned that a flavor ban could spawn a black market of informal companies selling unregulated cartridges. They offered an amendment, which the committee rejected, that would have directed regulators, when considering whether to approve a flavored tobacco product, to also weigh whether rejecting it would "increase the likelihood that individuals will

purchase illegal or adulterated products on the illicit market." However, the committee gave voice vote approval to an amendment by Democrat Anna G. Eshoo of California that aimed to decrease black market sales by improving recordkeeping for tracking tobacco products from the point of manufacture.

The committee also gave voice vote approval to an amendment by Rep. Raul Ruiz, D-Calif., to increase civil penalties on vape shops that sell to minors, as well as require a Government Accountability Office report on e-cigarettes.

Burgess offered two amendments related to user fees, arguing that the FDA's Center for Tobacco Products had failed to be a good steward of fees levied on tobacco manufacturers to fund regulatory work. One amendment would have deleted a provision in the bill requiring the manufacturers of e-cigarettes and other vaping products to pay user fees. The committee rejected it, 22–31. Another amendment, which would have sunsetted all tobacco user fees, failed on a vote of 22–29.

TOBACCO 21

Congress passed the so-called tobacco 21 provision, raising the legal age for purchasing tobacco, on December 19, 2019, after adding it to an omnibus appropriations measure (HR 1865 — PL 116-94) to fund the government through the end of the 2020 fiscal year. It marked the first significant legislation since the 2009 law. The tobacco industry supported raising the legal age, which activists saw as a public relations maneuver meant to quell public concerns about increasing numbers of young people becoming addicted to tobacco. Nineteen states and hundreds of cities and towns had already raised the age to twenty-one. Two tobacco state senators—Majority Leader Mitch McConnell of Kentucky and Democrat Tim Kaine of Virginia—had introduced a bill (S 1541) earlier in the year to raise the legal purchasing age to twenty-one.

While anti-smoking advocates hailed the appropriations provision, they worried it would stall progress efforts to ban flavored nicotine products. Campaign for Tobacco Free Kids, a leading organization against flavored tobacco, said that raising the age to twenty-one was insufficient to stop the epidemic of young people using e-cigarettes. It continued to press lawmakers to ban flavored nicotine products.

House floor action

The House on February 28, 2020, passed HR 2339 by a vote of 213–195. Five moderate Republicans supported the bill. Of the seventeen Democrats who voted no, eight were members of the Congressional Black Caucus and the other nine represented conservative-leaning districts.

Supporters contended that the measure was essential to building on the recently enacted nationwide tobacco purchasing age of twenty-one, as well as filling in loopholes left by a decision by the administration to ban flavors in pod-based e-cigarettes such as Juul but keep them available in other vaping formats.

The floor debate highlighted concerns about the bill's disparate impacts. Some tobacco-state lawmakers and Congressional Black Caucus members argued that if Congress was going to target menthol, it should take the additional step of banning all tobacco products. Others warned that the measure could inadvertently affect communities of Middle Eastern descent by effectively doing away with hookah smoking, which almost always used flavored products.

Republicans criticized the bill for failing to tackle marijuana vaping. Some states permitted sales of flavored marijuana extracts for vaping, while other states that prohibited marijuana use were becoming home to black markets of marijuana vaping supplies. Such black market products were blamed for a high-profile outbreak of lung disease that had killed dozens of people and sickened thousands across the United States during the previous year.

Republicans also argued that the new taxes contained in the bill would damage public health by giving an incentive to former cigarette smokers to return to traditional smoking after having made the change to vaping. The White House threatened to veto the bill. With only a small number of Republicans supporting it, the Senate did not take it up.

Abortion

The Senate in 2019 and 2020 defeated three bills that would have imposed various restrictions on abortion. In each case, supporters fell well short of the sixty-vote supermajority needed to invoke cloture and advance debate. Even if the Senate passed the bills, there appeared to be scant opportunity for passage in the Democratic-controlled House.

TEXAS V. UNITED STATES

As enacted, the 2010 Patient Protection and Affordable Care Act (ACA) included what is known as the individual mandate, a provision that requires most individuals to purchase health insurance or face a penalty when they file their annual income return. In 2010, a group of twenty-six states, multiple individuals, and the National Federation of Independent Businesses challenged the mandate, arguing that it exceeded congressional authority to regulate interstate commerce. In a 5–4 decision on June 27, 2012, the Supreme Court held in *National Federation of Independent Business v. Sebelius* that the individual mandate was a constitutional use of Congress's authority to levy taxes.

Six years later, in February 2018, in *Texas v. United States*, eighteen Republican state attorneys general and two Republican governors filed a lawsuit in the Northern District of Texas arguing that the individual mandate is unconstitutional because Congress, as part of the Tax Cuts and Jobs Act of 2017, zeroed out the penalty for failure to purchase health insurance. Further, the plaintiffs argued, because the individual mandate is an integral part of the ACA, it cannot be separated from it, and the entire law must therefore be struck down. In April, two individuals joined the case, claiming that they were harmed by the ACA because they pay more for insurance and to comply with the law cannot buy a plan that matches their preferences. In June 2018, the Justice Department announced that it mostly agreed with Texas's position in the case, but still believed that some parts of the ACA were valid. In December 2018, a federal judge ruled that not only was the individual mandate unconstitutional, but it was also not severable from the ACA. Therefore, the entire law must be declared invalid. However, the judge declined to immediately overturn the law, instead granting a stay while the case was appealed.

When the Justice Department declined to appeal the district court ruling, in January 2019, the U.S. Court of Appeals for the Fifth Circuit allowed a group of seventeen states, led by California, to challenge the decision. Four additional states and the House of Representatives also joined the defendants, and two states—Maine and Wisconsin—withdrew as plaintiffs after Democrats won their states' gubernatorial elections. In December 2019, in a 2–1 decision on the newly titled *Texas v. California*, the appeals court partially upheld the lower court ruling, finding that the individual mandate was unconstitutional because it no longer provided revenue for the federal government. However, rather than ruling on whether the entire ACA should be struck down, it remanded the case to the district court to decide whether any portion of the ACA could be maintained without the individual mandate.

In turn, the plaintiffs appealed the case to the Supreme Court. The Court had to consider three specific questions when it heard arguments on November 10, 2020: Do the plaintiffs have standing to challenge the individual mandate? If they do, is the individual mandate unconstitutional? And, if it is, is it severable from the larger law? On June 17, 2021, in a 7–2 ruling, the Court held that the plaintiffs lacked standing to challenge the individual mandate because they could not prove personal injury traceable to the law. Because of this finding, the Court went no further in reviewing the individual mandate's unconstitutionality or its severability. As such, the ACA remained the law of the land. While Democrats in Congress celebrated the ruling, Republicans indicated a desire to move from a litigation phase to eliminate the ACA to a greater focus on legislative action to improve health care and health insurance for all Americans.

The votes occurred against the backdrop of states passing increasing restrictive abortion measures amid uncertainty over whether a more conservative Supreme Court would be less protective of the right to abortion. The first bill (S 109), rejected by the Senate on January 17, 2019, would permanently ban the use of tax dollars to fund abortions. The vote was 48–47. Two Democrats, Bob Casey of Pennsylvania and Joe Manchin III of West Virginia, crossed party lines to support it. Two Republicans, Susan Collins of Maine and Lisa Murkowski of Alaska, voted against it.

Sponsored by Roger Wicker, R-Miss., the bill was similar to the so-called Hyde amendment, a provision in annual appropriations bills that prohibited abortion funding. Like the Hyde bill, S 109 would make exceptions for rape, incest, and cases in which the life of the woman was in danger. But it would go further by banning subsidies for abortion and disallowing the use of tax credits to pay for plans that cover abortion in the 2010 health care law (PL 111-148, PL 111-152). It also would ban abortion in all federal health facilities.

The vote occurred during the partial government shutdown, which did not escape the notice of Democrats. Sen. Patty Murray, D-Wash., chided supporters for imposing restrictions on health insurance instead of voting to pay federal workers. Wicker, however, said it was important to welcome anti-abortion marchers who were coming to Washington to mark the anniversary of the 1973 *Roe v. Wade* decision that legalized abortion.

The following year, on February 25, 2020, the Senate failed to advance the other two bills. One of them (S 3275) would have banned abortions after twenty weeks with some exceptions for rape, incest, and protecting the life of the woman. The 53–44 vote fell short of the required supermajority threshold. A number of states had passed similar bans, although the courts had yet to sign off on them.

The other bill (S 311) would have imposed legal protections for infants born alive after an attempted abortion. It came somewhat closer to passage, 56–41, with all Republicans and three Democrats (Casey, Manchin, and Doug Jones of Alabama) supporting it.

Republican lawmakers framed it as an attempt to pass abortion restrictions on a bipartisan basis. Sen. Ben Sasse, R-Neb., said that even abortion supporters should agree to protect babies that have been born. Democrats, however, said an existing law (PL 107-207) already protected such infants.

Surprise Billing

The House and Senate considered related pieces of legislation that sought to end so-called surprise billing that occurs when an individual receives an unexpected bill from their health insurance company or medical provider after unknowingly receiving out-of-network care. While leadership in both chambers seemed intent on fast-tracking a surprise billing measure, or attaching it to a year-end spending bill, by the end of 2019 they were unable to reconcile their differences about whether to set a benchmark rate for providers and insurers to cover or develop an arbitration process. The issue remained a topic of debate in 2020, but no bill ever made it to a floor vote.

Senate Committee Action

On June 26, 2019, the Senate Health, Education, Labor, and Pensions Committee marked up S 1895, the Lower Health Care Costs Act, introduced by Sen. Lamar Alexander, R-Tenn. As introduced, the bill would make a variety of changes to health care coverage, costs, and services. It would, among other things, limit how much a health care provider or facility could bill a patient for certain emergency and nonemergency services provided out of network, make changes to existing regulations to speed up the approval process for generic and biosimilar drugs, create grant programs to support vaccinations, and require health insurers to make more pricing information easily accessible to consumers.

During debate, the panel considered a number of amendments. One, from Sen. Bill Cassidy, R-La., would require an insurance company to tell a patient if there are categories of providers for which the insurance plan does not have any in-network coverage for certain services, such as lab work. Cassidy's amendment was adopted by voice vote. Another approved amendment, from Sens. Tammy Baldwin, D-Wis., and Mike Braun, R-Ind., would require a pharmaceutical company with a drug that costs more than $100 and whose price rises 10 percent in one year or 25 percent in three years to make available information on the cost of its research, development, and advertising efforts. That amendment was adopted 16–7. By unanimous consent, the committee also adopted a manager's amendment raising the national age to purchase tobacco from eighteen to twenty-one. The amendment would also allow makers of generic drugs to bring civil suits against a brand-name pharmaceutical manufacturer if the latter failed to make available a sufficient quantity of samples of its brand-name drug upon request.

The committee rejected two amendments, both of which dealt with bill language requiring the Health and Human Services and Labor secretaries to partner with a nonprofit organization to create a health care claim database. Sen. Mike Braun, R-Ind., proposed replacing the language, while Sen. Rand Paul, R-Ky., wanted to eliminate the provisions.

Four amendments were withdrawn, including one that would allow the United States to import certain nonprescription sunscreens from specific countries, and another authorizing funding for the Teacher Health Centers Graduate Medical Education Program. An amendment from Sen. Chris Murphy, D-Conn., that would have required the Department of Health and Human Services

to produce a report explaining what would happen if Texas prevailed in its pending lawsuit challenging the constitutionality of the 2010 Patient Protection and Affordable Care Act's individual mandate, was ruled not germane.

Ultimately, the Senate panel went on to approve the measure, as amended, 20–3, on July 26. Less than two weeks later, the Congressional Budget Office released an estimate indicating that the bill could save $7.6 billion over a decade. The measure never received a floor vote, despite leadership indicating that they wanted to fast-track it. In part that was because of disagreement about whether a cap should be set on how much individuals can be charged for certain uses of out-of-network health care services or if payers and providers should instead use an arbitration process to reach an agreement on how much the company would pay. Those advocating for arbitration feared that a benchmark rate could hurt rural providers.

House Committee Action

A couple weeks after the Senate Health, Education, Labor, and Pensions Committee advanced their surprise billing legislation, Rep. Frank Pallone Jr., D-N.J., introduced a similar bill in the House. The No Surprises Act (HR 3630) would bar cost-sharing between the patient and insurance provider if an individual visits an emergency room that is out of network or has a procedure at an in-network hospital but one of the medical providers involved is out of network. When this happens, the provider would bill the insurer the median in-network rate for that area.

The House Energy and Commerce Committee Subcommittee on Health took up the bill on July 11 and advanced it by voice vote, despite some concern raised by both Democrats and Republicans that the legislation could force some providers to merge with larger hospital groups or close their business. Some lawmakers encouraged the subcommittee to adopt language from another bill, HR 3502, which would also prevent surprise billing, but which created an arbitration process for insurance companies to settle disputes with providers over service fees. Neither HR 3502 nor HR 3630 received a full committee markup or floor vote.

On July 17, 2019, the House Energy and Commerce Committee advanced HR 2328, the Community Health Investment, Modernization, and Excellence Act. During debate, the committee adopted a substitute amendment that added the text of HR 3630 to limit patient cost-sharing to in-network rates in certain situations when the patient cannot avoid using an out-of-network service. The committee also adopted an amendment from Reps. Raul Ruiz, D-Calif., and Larry Bucshon, R-Ind., to create an arbitration process between the provider and insurer in certain allowable instances when a provider says the in-network rate cannot cover its costs. HR 2328 did not receive a floor vote during the 116th Congress.

Further Action

In December 2019, House Energy and Commerce Committee and Senate Health, Education, Labor, and Pensions Committee leadership announced that they had reached a consensus on how to address surprise billing that maintained the arbitration process. Specifically, that process would be allowed in instances when the median in-network rate was higher than $750. Insurers would pay any bill under that amount at a benchmark rate, set at the median in-network rate for that specific geographic area. Also in December, the House Ways and Means Committee developed its own, competing proposal to address surprise billing, which included an arbitration provision. Leaders in both chambers thought they might be able to attach the language to an end-of-year spending bill, but facing intense lobbying from the medical industry and disagreement over exactly how to address billing issues, were ultimately unable to do so.

In February 2020, the House Education and Labor and Ways and Means Committees released draft proposals to address surprise billing, in hopes that they could attach some of the language to a bill extending funding for public health programs that was set to expire in May. Those two proposals included different ideas about how to address billing costs. The Ways and Means Committee measure would give providers and insurers thirty days to negotiate a payment, after which time either side could initiate the arbitration process for a bill of any cost. The Education and Labor proposal would require an insurer to pay an out-of-network provider the median in-network rate for the area for a cost up to $750. For costs above that amount, either side could rely on the arbitration process. Those proposals never received floor consideration in either the House or the Senate.

While Congress was unable to address the full scope of surprise billing issues during the 116th Congress, they did include a provision in the coronavirus relief law (PL 116-136) that banned any hospital receiving funds through that law to send a surprise bill for COVID-19 treatments.

Over-the-Counter Medication Approval Process

The Senate in December 2019 passed a long-stalled bill that would reduce the amount of time it takes to make changes to medications sold without a prescription. Despite having passed similar legislation three times prior, the House did not take up the Senate's 2019 measure.

Senate Action

On October 31, 2019, the Senate Health, Education, Labor, and Pensions Committee held its markup of S 2740, the Over-the-Counter Drug Safety, Innovation, and Reform Act. The bill would overhaul the regulation of over-the-counter (OTC) medications by streamlining

the process to approve new ingredients and update product labels. The bill would essentially eliminate the current regulation that requires an OTC drug to go through the formal rulemaking process to make changes, and instead allow the Food and Drug Administration (FDA) to issue an order that explains how an active ingredient can be used. The bill would also allow the FDA to collect new fees to help them hire more staff to facilitate faster approval of ingredient and labeling changes. Those fees were expected to generate $31 million through fiscal year 2025.

S 2740 was similar to a measure introduced in the Senate in 2018 that did not receive floor consideration. Sen. Richard Burr, R-N.C., blocked attempts in 2018 to advance the bill, arguing that the FDA was not a good steward of the other fees it collected, and should not be allowed to collect more. The House in the meantime passed three bills with language similar to S 2740, though none were considered in the Senate.

The Senate Committee advanced S 2740 by voice vote, and it came to the Senate floor on December 10. The chamber voted 91–2 to pass the bill. Sen. Burr was one of the two no votes. He said that he agreed with the purpose of the bill and the need to speed approval of new ingredients and labeling, but continued to disagree with the fees. The House never considered S 2740.

Medicare for All

In 2016, some candidates vying for the Democratic presidential nomination began touting proposals that would offer Medicare coverage to all Americans, regardless of their age, as a means to enact universal health care. The proposal resurfaced in 2019, with House and Senate Democrats attempting to enact legislation that would make those proposals a reality. Those efforts never received a committee vote, with Republicans standing united in their opposition and even some Democrats questioning whether the language floated made sense for the United States.

House Committee Action

House Democratic leadership bypassed a traditional committee markup in 2019 and sent their Medicare for All proposal straight to the Rules Committee. HR 1384, the bill under consideration, would move most Americans into government-sponsored health insurance plans. Proposed by Rep. Pramila Jayapal, D-Wash., it lacked the support of all the committee's Democrats, in part because the party was still divided on how to address health care in the lead up to the 2020 election. While they had staked out the position that health care is a human right and high costs are harming consumers, some of the party's members endorsed fixing that with a Medicare for All-esque plan, while others wanted to improve on the existing health care system and the 2010 Patient Protection and Affordable Care Act (ACA; PL 111-148, PL 111-152).

At the April 29, 2019, hearing, the committee heard testimony from individuals debilitated by various diseases who have struggled to afford coverage under their existing health insurance plans. The debate generally lacked partisan bickering and focused more on policy issues and the cost associated with implementing Medicare for All, as well as what it would mean for consumers and providers. While businesses and individuals would likely face higher taxes, Americans would not be spending on certain health care costs, such as premiums, deductibles, and copays. According to many estimates, shifting health care outlays to the government would cost upward of $30 trillion over a decade.

The Budget Committee was the next to take up Medicare for All, hearing testimony from the Congressional Budget Office. They were followed on June 12 by the Ways and Means Committee, where debate was a bit more heated than during the prior two hearings. Republicans criticized Democrats for trying to establish socialist control of the health care system, while Democrats alternately voiced support for either HR 1384 or building on the ACA. Republicans used the time to highlight the possible challenges of a single-payer system, such as high costs for the government, removing Americans from health insurance plans they like, lower reimbursement rates that could force some providers to close, and forcing consumers into a system with long wait times. Democrats relied on their witnesses to counter most of those arguments, though some panelists admitted that reimbursement rates were likely to fall, which could hit rural providers especially hard.

Over the year, multiple other measures were introduced in the House to establish some form of a single-payer public-run health system. These included HR 2452 (Medicare for America Act), HR 4527 (Expanding Health Care Options for Early Retirees Act), HR 2000 (a bill to establish a public health option), HR 1346 (Medicare Buy-In and Health Care Stabilization Act), HR 1277 (State Public Option Act), and HR 2463 (Choose Medicare Act). No bill made it past the committee stage, and Democratic leadership admitted that there was no easy path to passage of one measure, nor one definitive answer to addressing existing health care challenges. Even Speaker Nancy Pelosi, D-Calif., voiced support for strengthening the ACA over looking to a universal public option and raised concerns about the cost of the latter.

Senate Committee Action

Sen. Bernie Sanders, I-Vt., who was a leading advocate of a single-payer option on the campaign trail in 2016, introduced Medicare for All legislation in the Senate during the 116th Congress. S 1129 would set up a four-year transition to a single-payer system and would eliminate almost all individual copays, premiums, and deductibles; program participants would face a maximum $200 prescription drug copay each year. During the transition period, those already in most federal health care programs—such as the federal

exchange—would be shifted into Medicare, while other individuals would have the option to buy into the program. Once the program was fully phased in, it would enroll all U.S. residents and provide for automatic enrollment of those born in the United States or who gain residency status.

At an event unveiling his proposal, Sanders said the Medicare for All debate "really has nothing to do with health care. It has everything to do with greed and profiteering." Sanders's bill largely mirrored HR 1384, and both would cover a variety of services in addition to standard health care needs, including mental health treatment, dental and vision, emergency transportation, and treatment for substance abuse disorders. Unlike the House plan, Sanders's bill would rely on the existing Medicare fee schedule and alternative payments to reimburse providers; HR 1384 uses a combination of fee-for-service and a global budget to reimburse different providers.

Republicans quickly attacked the cost of the Sanders's bill, which did not include language on how it would be paid for (Sanders had previously floated various ideas for covering the bill's cost, including a new tax on the wealthiest Americans and income-based premiums imposed on either employees or employers). Opponents, including some Democrats, also questioned how an increase in taxes would impact American families.

Similar to those who backed the House measure, Sanders admitted that his bill had little chance of being enacted. S 1129 never received a committee or floor vote.

Prescription Drug Pricing

Under pressure from their caucus to do something to address the cost of prescription drugs prior to the November 2020 election, Democrats in late 2019 released drug pricing legislation that was marked up by three committees before full House passage. At the same time, the Senate was considering its own version, which was considered by many to be a more bipartisan approach to stopping drug price growth, but it never received a floor vote. By the conclusion of the 116th Congress, both Democrats and Republicans in the House and Senate appeared to agree that something needed to be done to address the high cost of prescription drugs, but they disagreed on the means to do so.

House Committee Action

In September 2019, Speaker of the House Nancy Pelosi, D-Calif., unveiled a large piece of legislation meant to tackle the rising costs of prescription medications. The bill would, among other things, require the Department of Health and Human Services (HHS) to negotiate with drug manufacturers to agree on lower prices for up to 250 of the most expensive drugs covered by Medicare. The drug makers would then be required to offer those same prices to commercial insurance plans. Any price increases in subsequent years could not exceed inflation. The bill also set a $2,000 limit for out-of-pocket spending for seniors covered by Medicare Part D, the program's prescription drug plan.

HR 3 was marked up on October 17 by both the House Energy and Commerce and Education and Labor Committees. During debate in the Education and Labor Committee, four Democratic amendments were proposed and adopted, while eight Republican amendments were proposed and rejected. Adopted amendments included those that called for new studies on the impact of the inflation cap and price negotiations, as well as one to ensure commercial plan copays did not exceed the HHS negotiated prices. As amended, the bill was approved by the committee 27–21. In the Energy and Commerce Committee, twenty-three amendments were up for debate. Those approved for inclusion included one to encourage the use of generic medications. As amended, the bill passed the committee 30–22. During both committee markups, a substitute amendment was adopted that increased from twenty-five to thirty-five the number of drugs that HHS would negotiate with manufacturers each year and required additional price transparency.

The House Ways and Means Committee marked up HR 3 on October 22. The panel debated thirty-two amendments and adopted only two. Those included one to rename the bill in honor of Rep. Elijah Cummings, D-Md., who died the week prior. They also adopted a substitute amendment that was similar to the language of that adopted in the Education and Labor and Energy and Commerce Committees. Of the thirty rejected, withdrawn, or not germane amendments, which included offerings from both Democrats and Republicans, were amendments allowing uninsured individuals access to negotiated prices, removing the language prioritizing the 250 most expensive drugs for negotiation, striking language to match drug costs to those paid by other wealthy nations, and requiring drug maker rebates to go straight to consumers at the point of sale. As amended, the bill was reported to the full House 24–17.

During the three committee markups, Republicans repeatedly accused Democrats of attempting to constrain innovation in the pharmaceutical sector, something that could limit important drugs from being developed and brought to market. Democrats, on the other hand, said the demands of Republicans were too closely aligned with drug manufacturers.

House Floor Action

In a Statement of Administration Policy released on December 10, 2019, the White House noted that while the president shared the belief that something needed to be done about prescription drug pricing, he would likely veto HR 3, because of "several provisions that would harm seniors and all who need lifesaving medicines." Specifically, the administration raised concern that the provision allowing for negotiation between HHS and drug manufacturers could result in price fixing, and questioned whether the bill would limit innovation in the market. In the statement,

the White House expressed the president's preference for drug pricing legislation under consideration in the Senate, and stated that "the Administration remains committed to working with both parties to pass legislation that will lower drug costs while encouraging innovation in the development of lifesaving medicines."

That same day, the Congressional Budget Office (CBO) issued its estimate of the cost of HR 3, noting that the bill would reduce spending by around $492 billion over a decade, while raising $45 billion in new revenue. Also on December 10, the House Rules Committee sent to the floor its recommended rule for debate on HR 3, which made in order twelve amendments. During committee debate, Republicans continued to question whether the bill, as written, would limit innovation. Republicans on the committee encouraged their colleagues worried about that issue to vote in favor of a substitute amendment that would eliminate price negotiation.

When the House convened on December 12, 2019, to consider HR 3, they first adopted the rules package which also adjusted some of the underlying bill's text. Changes included increasing the number of negotiated drugs from thirty-five to fifty and allowing employer-sponsored insurance plans to collect rebates from drug manufacturers if the cost of their products rose faster than inflation.

The Republican substitute amendment, which members of their caucus argued was more bipartisan than HR 3, was rejected 201–223, but did receive the support of eight Democrats. A number of noncontroversial amendments were adopted by voice vote, including those that would ensure HHS drug price negotiators do not have a conflict of interest, express the sense of Congress that the bill needs to positively impact minority and rural communities, authorize new grant programs, allow requirements to be implemented that require pricing information on drug advertisements, and increase funding for certain programs at the National Institutes of Health.

Prior to the final vote on the bill, Rep. Fred Upton, R-Mich., raised a motion to recommit that would require the addition of an amendment that would stop HR 3 from going into effect until the administration could verify that its provisions would not decrease the number of new drugs coming to market. The motion failed 196–226, and the House went on to pass HR 3 by a vote of 230–192, with only two Republicans voting in favor. As passed, HR 3 would

- Require HHS to negotiate the price for certain drugs that account for the highest volume of spending
- Require that negotiated prices be offered under Medicare, Medicare Advantage, and made available to private insurance plans
- Cap maximum negotiated prices at 120 percent of the average price paid by individuals in certain wealthy nations, including Canada, Japan, and the United Kingdom
- Require drug makers to issue rebates to the Centers for Medicare and Medicaid Services if a certain medication costs $100 or more and the price rises faster than inflation
- Reduce out-of-pocket Medicare prescription drug spending

The Senate never took up HR 3, where many members viewed it as a partisan exercise. Some Democrats and Republicans hoped that it could be a starting point for negotiations, but that never came to pass during the 116th Congress.

Senate Action

While the House debated HR 3, the Senate was working on its own drug pricing legislation. S 2543, the Prescription Drug Pricing Reduction Act, passed out of the Finance Committee in July 2019 and was reported to the Senate on September 25, 2019. Similar to the House measure, the Senate legislation would make multiple changes to the price of prescription medications covered by the Medicare and Medicaid programs. For example, the manufacturer of certain drugs whose price increases faster than inflation would be required to give a rebate to CMS, the Medicare Part D prescription drug out-of-pocket spending threshold would be reduced, and CMS would be required to publish certain information including drug discount and rebate availability.

The Senate bill never moved beyond committee, in part because leadership could not attract more Republican support. When the panel advanced the bill in July, all thirteen Democrats supported it, but only six of fifteen Republicans similarly voted in favor. Concerns raised by Republicans related to rebates for insulin and capping annual drug price growth under Medicare at inflation. The White House pushed the Senate to advance their bill, viewing it as a more bipartisan approach to lowering the cost of prescription drugs, and the Senate released an updated version of their legislation in December. Updates included a reduction in the out-of-pocket cost sharing paid by Medicare Part D beneficiaries, restricted drug plans from charging pharmacies retroactive fees, and made various other changes. However, it still did not address many of the concerns Republicans previously raised, and the new draft also did not receive a floor vote.

Classifying Fentanyl as a Schedule I Drug

In February 2020, the classification of fentanyl, a dangerously potent opioid, as a schedule I drug was due to expire. The House and Senate in response agreed to extend the classification, which is critical for law enforcement action, by fifteen months. The president signed the bill into law on February 6, 2020 (PL 116-114).

Senate Action

On January 16, 2020, the Senate passed by unanimous consent S 3201, the Temporary Reauthorization and Study of the Emergency Scheduling of Fentanyl Analogues Act.

The bill would extend the classification of fentanyl as a schedule I drug until May 6, 2021. It also directed the Government Accountability Office (GAO) to study such classification, and research fentanyl-related substances and their importation and report on best practices for controlling these drugs. Drugs listed under the Controlled Substances Act are considered to have the highest potential for abuse, and the classification allows law enforcement to prosecute individuals who make or distribute the drug. The Drug Enforcement Agency had been pushing for action in Congress in part because fentanyl and its analogues—those drugs designed to mimic the effect of fentanyl—are responsible for a significant portion of opioid deaths.

House Action

The House took up S 3201 on January 29, 2020, under suspension of the rules, which requires a two-thirds vote for passage. Prior to considering the bill, Democrats had been trying to work out an agreement that would amend the Senate language to address the concerns of some members of their party that the classification could have a disproportionate impact on minority communities and expose low-level offenders or those who do not know that a drug they possess contains a fentanyl analogue to severe penalties. However, they dropped those attempts in order to pass the Senate bill before the classification expired. The House vote was 320–88 in favor of S 3201.

President Donald Trump signed the bill on February 6, 2020 (PL 116-114). Members on both sides of the aisle indicated a desire to find a way to permanently classify fentanyl-related drugs as a schedule I substance after the GAO completes its study.

Child Care Funding and Tax Credits

During the COVID-19 pandemic, child care facilities across the United States shuttered, leaving parents scrambling to find care for children while also facing their own work challenges. In response, the House in July 2020 passed two measures, one that would provide funding for child care facilities to help them reopen and another to expand the child and dependent care tax credit to provide relief to families. Neither bill was considered in the Senate.

House Action

The House Rules Committee held a full proceeding for both HR 7027, the Child Care Is Essential Act, and HR 7327, the Child Care for Economic Recovery Act, on July 17, 2020. On July 20, the committee recommended a closed rule for debate. Less than two weeks later, on July 29, the pair of bills landed on the House floor.

The chamber first considered HR 7027. The bill would make available $50 billion in emergency funds for child care facility providers to help them reopen or stay open. The money could be used to cover staff salaries, regular

expenses, and fixed costs. The funding provided by the bill would be in addition to $3.5 billion in block grants provided to child care providers in the March COVID-19 relief package (PL 116-136).

Republicans objected to multiple components of the bill, including the ability of providers to use the funding for fixed costs, the total cost, and the fact that it would require providers to follow guidance from the Centers for Disease Control and Prevention regarding COVID-19 safety measures, even if those were at odds with state and local public health requirements. Rep. Cathy McMorris Rodgers, R-Wash., offered a motion to recommit the bill to the House Appropriations Committee to add an amendment removing a provision that required child care facilities to be in business as of March 1, 2020, in order to receive any funding. Republicans felt that the cutoff date could limit newer facilities from participating, especially home-based businesses. The motion was rejected 195–212, and the House went on to pass the underlying bill 249–163.

The House next moved to HR 7327, which would make available to states additional social services and infrastructure block grants for specific child care needs and also modify certain child and dependent care-related taxes. This included increasing the maximum child and dependent care tax credit, raising the income threshold at which point the credit begins declining, and making it fully refundable. According to Democrats, the overall purpose of the bill was to support low-income families who often spend the highest proportion of their income on child care expenses. The bill passed 250–161. The Senate did not consider either HR 7027 or HR 7327.

Fiscal Year 2020 Health and Human Services Appropriations

The annual Labor, Health and Human Services (HHS), Education, and Related Agencies appropriations bill was included as part of a larger spending package that Congress approved, and the president signed, in December 2019 (PL 116-94). The final law provided $94.4 billion in discretionary funds for HHS, but dropped a number of controversial policy riders related to health insurance and abortion that were included in the House-passed version of the bill.

House Committee Action

The House Labor, HHS, Education, and Related Agencies Appropriations Subcommittee advanced its appropriations bill on April 30, 2019, by voice vote. As sent to the full Appropriations Committee, the bill would provide $204 billion to the agencies within its purview, of which $99 billion would go to HHS. The HHS total was $8.5 billion higher than the total for the current fiscal year. The bill included new funding for a variety of programs supported by Democrats, as well as a restriction on White House efforts to prevent abortion. Although Republicans did not push for a roll call vote, they indicated that they did

not support the bill and noted that it was unlikely to pass in the Republican-controlled Senate.

The full House Appropriations Committee considered the Labor–HHS–Education bill (HR 2740) on May 8. At the beginning of the markup, the committee adopted by voice vote a manager's amendment that made some technical changes to the bill and also shifted around funding between programs. Most of the committee's action focused on two abortion-related amendments. One, proposed by Rep. Tom Cole, R-Okla., would bar federal funding from going toward abortion providers that do not provide critical medical care to a fetus born alive during an abortion procedure. The amendment failed, 23–29. A second amendment, from Rep. Martha Roby, R-Ala., would strike language in the bill that required the administration to distribute Title X funding to organizations regardless of whether they provide abortion services; at the time, the Trump administration was trying to block federal funds from flowing to Planned Parenthood. Roby's amendment was rejected by voice vote. The panel adopted two other amendments during markup, one making additional funding changes and another that would stop the Trump administration from enforcing a new rule that protected health care workers who refused to provide certain services or participate in procedures for religious reasons.

The committee favorably reported the bill to the House, 30–23. As amended, it would

- Allocate $99 billion for HHS, including $8.3 billion for the Centers for Disease Control and Prevention (CDC) and $41 billion for the National Institutes of Health (NIH)
- Require HHS to provide Congress monthly enrollment figures for insurance marketplaces
- Prohibit states from denying Title X funding to organizations that provide abortion-related services
- Require the Centers for Medicare and Medicaid Services (CMS) to use a set amount of funds to support ACA outreach and enrollment services

The full House never voted on an individual Labor–HHS–Education bill. Instead, HR 2740 was used as the vehicle for a four-bill fiscal year 2020 appropriations measure that also included Defense (HR 2968), State-Foreign Operations (HR 2839), and Energy–Water (HR 2960).

House Floor Action

During the week of June 10, the full House began consideration of HR 2740, its plan to move four annual appropriations measures to President Donald Trump's desk. The rule approved by the House Rules Committee made in order 106 amendments, of which seventy-seven were related to the Labor–HHS–Education title. Most of the seventy-seven amendments that the House would consider moved funding around between various HHS programs, though there were also amendments related to Democratic priorities that were sure to be nonstarters in the Senate. These included

measures that would block the Trump administration from stopping Title X family planning funding from flowing to organizations, such as Planned Parenthood, that provide abortion-related services, one requiring HHS to have higher standards for shelters used to house migrant children who come across the U.S.–Mexico border, and one limiting the administration's ability to implement a rule allowing the sale of short-term health insurance plans that do not meet the ACA's minimum coverage requirements.

The House approved dozens of amendments under the Labor–HHS–Education title, including those that blocked the administration from implementing a rule protecting health care workers who refuse to participate in, or offer, certain services because of their religious beliefs and one preventing the White House from blocking Title X funds from going to organizations that provide abortion-related services. The House also adopted the amendment stopping the White House from enforcing the rule allowing for the sale of short-term health insurance plans that do not meet ACA requirements, which Democrats referred to as "junk plans." The other adopted amendments primarily moved money between HHS programs. In total, the bill provided HHS $99 billion in discretionary funds, $9 billion more than in the current fiscal year.

On June 19, 2019, the House passed the spending bill 226–203, with Republicans united against the bill, while seven Democrats crossed party lines to vote against it. The bill, as passed, stood little chance of becoming law without major changes. The White House objected to the topline funding as well as the policy riders related to abortion and health insurance. And, without an agreement between the two chambers to raise spending limits, if enacted, HR 2740 would trigger the across-the-board spending cuts, known as sequestration.

Senate Action

The Senate did not hold a subcommittee or full committee markup of its version of a Labor–HHS–Education bill. A subcommittee markup was scheduled in September, but it was indefinitely delayed while the two parties argued over an amendment Democrats intended to propose that would stop the Trump administration from limiting the $286 million in federal Title X funds from going to organizations that offer, or refer patients to, abortion-related services.

On September 18, Republican leadership released their draft $178.3 billion Labor–HHS–Education appropriations bill. Of that topline, $93.4 billion would go toward HHS, or $2.9 million more than fiscal 2019. The language was released on the same day the Senate failed a procedural vote on HR 2740.

Final Action

Without agreement on any of the twelve regular appropriations bills, the House and Senate agreed to two continuing resolutions to maintain fiscal 2020 funding at 2019 levels and prevent a government shutdown while

negotiations continued. After months of work, negotiators unveiled two massive spending packages that covered all twelve bills. Labor–HHS–Education was included as Division A in HR 1865, an eight-bill spending package focused mostly on domestic programs. The House passed the bill 297–120 on December 17 and the Senate followed two days later, voting 71–23. President Trump signed HR 1865 into law on December 20, 2019 (PL 116-94), with ninety minutes to spare before a government shutdown.

As signed into law, the Labor–HHS–Education title received $184.9 billion in discretionary funding, $4.9 billion more than fiscal year 2019 and higher than the White House budget request. Of that total, $94.4 billion would go toward HHS. The bill included

- $41.68 billion for NIH
- $3.9 billion for mental health programs
- No new funding for the ACA
- $10.8 billion for public health prevention, surveillance, and preparedness programs
- $3.8 billion in funding to combat the opioid crisis
- $260 million for a White House HIV/AIDS elimination program
- $286 million for Title X family planning
- Language and funding for gun violence research

The final bill also eliminated three ACA taxes: the Cadillac tax on high-cost health insurance plans, a medical device tax, and a health insurer fee, and it raised the minimum age to purchase tobacco from eighteen to twenty-one. The final measure did not stop the president from implementing a rule that allowed the sale of certain short-term health insurance plans. It also did not include language blocking the White House from implementing a rule that prevented Title X funds from going to organizations that provide, or refer patients to, abortion-related services, nor did it include the House-passed language stopping a rule from going into effect that would strengthen protections for health care workers who refuse to provide certain services due to their religious beliefs.

Fiscal Year 2021 Health and Human Services Appropriations

Hampered by the COVID-19 pandemic, Congress failed to enact any of its twelve regular appropriations bills prior to the start of the 2021 fiscal year. Instead, all the measures were wrapped into one massive bill that President Donald Trump signed into law on December 27, 2020 (PL 116-260). As part of the combined spending and COVID-19 relief package, $97 billion was appropriated for the Department of Health and Human Services (HHS).

House Committee Action

On July 6, 2020, the House Appropriations Committee released its draft Labor–HHS–Education appropriations bill, and the Subcommittee on Labor, Health and Human Services, Education, and Related Agencies took it up the next day. The bill would provide $196.5 in regular discretionary funding for the agencies and programs within the bill, of which HHS would receive $96.4 billion, $1.5 billion higher than the fiscal year 2020 enacted level and more than $11 billion more than the president's budget request. Included in the language was a traditional rider known as the Hyde Amendment, which prevents federal funds from being used in most instances of abortion; however, the bill also included language that would block the Trump administration from restricting Title X family planning funds from going to organizations such as Planned Parenthood that either provide, or refer patients to, abortion-related services. The bill advanced 9–6 to the full Appropriations Committee.

On July 13, the Appropriations Committee held its markup of HR 7614. Although Democrats took issue with the inclusion of the Hyde Amendment, leadership said they would look for other ways to strike that federal policy outside of the appropriations process. Democrats blocked Republican attempts to strike language barring the president from changing how Title X funds are distributed. Republicans also failed to add language that would remove from the bill language prohibiting funds from being used to implement a rule that would provide religious employers an exemption from certain antidiscrimination labor protections.

The committee voted 30–22 to advance the bill to the House. As passed, it would provide $96.4 billion to HHS, of which $47 billion would go toward the National Institutes of Health (NIH) and $8 billion, to the Centers for Disease Control and Prevention (CDC). The bill also included $9 billion in emergency funding for the CDC, specifically related to public health emergency preparedness and response. The final bill also, among other things, restricted the Trump administration from changing how Title X grants are distributed, prohibited the implementation of a rule expanding religious protection for health care workers, and asked the Centers for Medicare and Medicaid Services (CMS) to use some of its funds to continue outreach and enrollment for the 2010 Patient Protection and Affordable Care Act (ACA; PL 111-148, PL 111-152). HR 7614 did not receive a floor vote on its own, however, it was included as part of a larger bill, HR 7617, considered by the House in late July.

House Floor Action

On July 28, the House Rules Committee finalized its recommended rule governing debate on HR 7617, a $1.31 trillion spending package that encompassed the Defense (HR 7617), Commerce-Justice-Science (HR 7667), Energy and Water Development (HR 7613), Financial Services and General Government (HR 7668), Transportation and Housing and Urban Development (HR 7616), and Labor-Education-HHS (HR 7614) spending bills. The rule made in order 340 amendments for the full package, of which ninety-two related specifically to the Labor–HHS–Education bill. During Rules Committee debate, Republicans repeatedly voiced concern

about policy riders, especially those in the Labor–HHS–Education portion related to family planning and religious liberty.

The full House voted 217–197 to send HR 7617 to the Senate. All Republicans voted against the bill, and twelve Democrats joined them. Prior to final passage, the House rejected, 123–292, an attempt to reduce by 5 percent the Labor–HHS–Education title discretionary funding.

Senate Action

The Senate did not hold a subcommittee or committee markup of its Labor–HHS–Education bill. However, on November 10, 2020, Appropriations Committee leadership released all twelve of their draft appropriations measures as a means to further discussions on fiscal 2021 funding.

Final Action

It was not until December 2020 when the two chambers agreed to final fiscal year 2021 funding. The combined twelve-bill appropriations measure (HR 133) provided $1.4 trillion in fiscal year funding plus nearly $900 billion for COVID-19 relief. The Labor–HHS–Education title was included in Division H of the bill. It would provide $97 billion for HHS, $2.1 billion more than the enacted 2020 level and $9.9 billion more than the president's budget request. Of that total, the funding was divided as follows:

- $42.9 billion for the National Institutes of Health
- $7.9 billion for the CDC
- $6 billion for the Substance Abuse and Mental Health Services Administration
- $7.5 billion for the Health Resources and Services Administration
- $338 million for the Agency for Healthcare Research and Quality
- $4 billion for the Centers for Medicare and Medicaid Services
- $24.7 billion for the Administration for Children and Families
- $2.3 billion for the Administration for Community Living
- $551 million for the Office of the Secretary
- $2.8 billion for the Public Health and Social Services Emergency Fund

In the House, leadership divided the bill into two portions before sending it to the Senate floor as one package. The portion of the bill containing the Labor–HHS–Education funding passed the House 359–53 on December 22. The Senate passed the combined bill 92–6 later that day. At the same time, the two chambers also passed a one-week stopgap funding measure to allow time to finalize the paperwork for the bill.

On December 22, President Trump released a video measure indicating that he might consider vetoing the spending bill if the $600 direct payments it provided under the COVID-19 relief provisions did not increase. Ultimately, Trump relented and signed the measure on December 27, 2020 (PL 116-260), but added a note to Congress requesting that they review and consider voting on changes to the provisions in the bill to which he objected. Congress opted not to do so.

CHAPTER 10

Education Policy

Education Policy

During Republican Donald Trump's presidential campaign, he offered only a handful of specific legislative proposals for improving education and gave the issue less attention than other recent GOP presidential candidates. George W. Bush, in contrast, had made K–12 education reform a keystone of his campaign, a focus that resulted in the No Child Left Behind (PL 107–110) law that set standards for school and student performance. And the previous GOP presidential candidate, Bob Dole, called for eliminating the Department of Education.

Among Trump's few specifics was a plan to limit the amount of income that people had to pay on college loans and a promise to push for funding for a school choice program to provide vouchers that low-income parents could use to send their children to any school they chose. In his inaugural address, he made one passing mention of education describing an "education system flush with cash, but which leaves our young and beautiful students deprived of all knowledge." In his first speech to a joint session of Congress, he described education as the "civil rights issue of our time" and again called for expanding school choice.

A version of the student loan relief proposal and a proposed $1.1 billion boost in federal support for school choice were included in the first Trump budget proposal sent to Congress. Versions of the student loan proposal and several bills to expand school choice were also introduced in the 115th and 116th Congresses, but none went anywhere. In fact, one of the biggest legislative accomplishments on education policy during the Trump presidency was not even in an education bill. Instead, it was in the president's keystone tax legislation, the Tax Cuts and Jobs Act of 2017 (TCJA)(PL 115–97). That law included a provision that allows people to use funds from 529 savings accounts, which were originally designed to be used only for college expenses, to pay for tuition for students attending private K–12 schools—up to $10,000 per year per student. The amendment adding that provision to the massive bill was approved by the Senate by one vote, 51–50.

Many of the other major policy initiatives on education during the Trump administration were done by executive action. This started with the executive order Trump signed on February 28, 2017, just weeks after being inaugurated, to implement a White House initiative to "promote excellence and innovation" at Historically Black Colleges and Universities (HBCU). The signing of the order came the day after an historic Oval Office gathering that included nearly 100 HBCU presidents. The presidential order moved the federal initiative on HBCUs to the White House from the Department of Education and created a President's Board of Advisors on HBCUs. The effort was widely lauded but some expressed skepticism about whether the Trump administration would follow through.

Two months before Trump took office, he laid down another major marker on education by announcing that he would nominate billionaire school choice advocate and philanthropist Betsy DeVos to run the Department of Education. The announcement set off a storm of protest by teacher unions and others in the education community. They said DeVos did not have the needed educational experience or credentials and was too closely linked to Republican politics. Her nomination and the Senate confirmation process became the first major confrontation between Trump and Democrats in Congress and ended with an historic first for a cabinet nominee: The vote by a vice president, in this case Mike Pence, was needed to break a tie and put DeVos in charge of the education department.

Several other education policy debates, even some that played out partly in Congress, were mostly in the world of regulations—the set of guidelines for implementing federal laws.

One of those key battles was over regulations passed late in the Obama administration to implement the Every Student Succeeds Act (PL 114–95), which was the successor to No Child Left Behind (PL 107–110). The regulation included standards on how states would rate schools and deal with parents who decide to remove their children from testing. The rules were finalized in November 2016 after the department received more than 21,000 comments on the draft proposal. Republicans said the rule gave too much federal control over schools. They employed the seldom used Congressional Review Act, targeting the regulation for removal in HJ Res 57. They also advanced another resolution, HJ Res 58, to ban the department's regulations on teacher preparation programs. Both were approved.

The Trump administration rolled back another Obama-era regulation when it revoked the so-called gainful employment regulation, which attempted to hold colleges and universities accountable if students who earned degrees failed to make enough money to repay their student loans. The administration argued the regulation unfairly targeted for-profit institutions.

When Democrats regained control of the House in the 116th Congress, they attempted to use the Congressional Review Act to roll back a Trump regulation that revised the process for a student borrower to obtain a discharge from a loan if a school committed fraud. HJ Res 76 passed both the House and Senate but was vetoed by Trump.

Even though the GOP held the "trifecta" for the first time since 2005 by controlling the White House as well as the U.S. House and Senate, only minor, noncontroversial education legislation passed in the 115th Congress. Those included HR 2353 (PL 115–24), which reauthorized legislation governing technical education programs; S 1866 (PL 115–64), which provided help to schools affected by hurricanes; and HR 3218 (PL 115–48), which expanded and restored GI education benefits for veterans.

The 116th Congress, with Democrats in control of the House, saw congressional consideration of legislation to reauthorize the Higher Education Act, HR 4674; to provide a way for college loan borrowers to remove a bad mark from their credit reports, HR3621; to direct the Department of Education to award grants to educational agencies to increase diversity in early childhood programs, and elementary and secondary public schools, HR 2639; and to provide college students with greater access to mental health resources, S1782. None won final approval.

Again, the most significant educational policy came in a spending bill, this time the fiscal 2021 omnibus spending bill and coronavirus relief package (PL 116–160). The bill reinstated Pell Grants for incarcerated students, restored Pell Grant eligibility for students defrauded by their institutions, and increased the maximum grant. It also simplified the Free Application for Federal Student Aid (FAFSA) application and forgave $1.3 billion in loans to Historically Black Colleges and Universities.

A handful of other minor education-related bills won approval during the 116th Congress and were signed into law. These included HR 943, the Never Again Education Act (PL 116–141), providing for expanded resources for teaching about what happened in the Holocaust; HR 276,

Figure 10.1 Outlays for Education

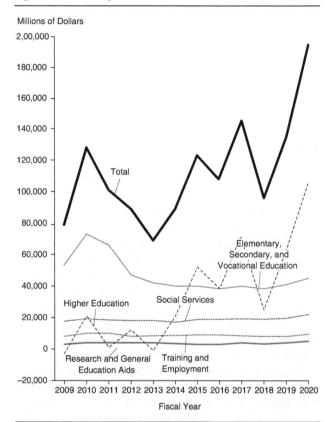

SOURCE: Office of Management and Budget, Historical Tables, Budget of the United States Government: Fiscal Year 2021 (Washington DC: U.S. Government Printing Office, 2020), Table 3.2.

NOTE: Total line includes expenditures not shown separately. * indicates estimate

Recognizing Inspiring School Employees, which added clerical, food, custodial, and other staff to a program honoring outstanding employees (PL 116–13); S1153, the Stop Student Debt Relief Scams Act (PL 116–251), which created criminal penalties for illegal access to student loan information and expanded the information made available to students about their loans when they leave school; and S461, the HBCU Partners Act (PL 116–270), which requires federal agencies to strengthen the ability of Historically Black Colleges and Universities to participate in federal programs including to compete for grants, contracts, and other agreements.

Chronology of Action on Education Policy

2017–2018

The major education accomplishments of the 115th Congress revolved around two goals of Republicans who controlled the White House and Congress: to reverse education regulations they believed gave federal officials too much power and to promote school choice. Congress passed two bills, HJ Res 57 and HJ Res 58, that rolled back Obama administration regulations that set standards for federal oversight of how states were implementing the Every Student Succeeds Act. And a provision in the Tax Cuts and Jobs Act of 2017 expanded school choice by allowing people to use up to $10,000 each year per student from savings accounts set up for college to pay tuition for students attending private elementary and secondary schools.

Regulation Rollback

Among the early targets of some Republicans in Congress at the start of the Trump presidency were regulations approved during the Obama administration that they believed exceeded the authority granted in the legislation they implemented. They used the Congressional Review Act, which gives Congress the ability within a specific timeframe to overturn an agency rule.

One of those regulations outlined what schools needed to do to implement the Every Student Succeeds Act. It included standards on how states rate schools and how to deal with parents who remove their children from testing. Rep. Todd Rokita, R-Ind., a witness at the hearing who introduced HJ Res 57, said the rule went too far in asserting federal power over decisions that should be left to states. "The result of the law is less flexibility for state leaders," he said.

Democrats objected that Republicans, by introducing the resolution, were reneging on a deal struck when the Every Student Succeeds Act (ESSA) was passed. Some feared the action would put school districts attempting to put together their plans for implementing ESSA in an awkward position. But Republican Sen. Lamar Alexander, R-Tenn., chair of the Senate Health, Education, Labor and Pensions Committee, downplayed the significance of the rule rollback, saying schools could still contact the Department of Education for advice without having it be in regulations. Plus, Alexander said the rule was illegal because it took action not outlined in the legislation.

The resolution moved quickly, introduced by Rokita on February 1, 2017, and passed the House Rules Committee five days later. The next day it passed the House 234–190. Only one Republican, Rep. Patrick Meehan of Penn., voted no, along with all the Democrats who voted that day. The Senate a month later approved the resolution, which could not be blocked with a filibuster, on a vote of 50–49 with Sen. Rob Portman of Ohio the only Republican senator to vote no.

The school assessment regulation was not the only one targeted by House Republicans. A second resolution, HJ Res 58, banned the department's Obama-era regulations on teacher preparation programs. The regulation, finalized in October 2016, required states to evaluate the effectiveness of teacher preparation programs at colleges and universities and report the results publicly.

The resolution removing the regulation passed the House 240–181 on February 7, 2017, on a mostly partisan vote. In the Senate, several moderate Democrats joined with Republicans to vote in favor of the resolution on March 8 and give it a slightly healthier margin of 59–40.

School Choice

Providing greater opportunities for school choice was another major educational policy theme of Trump and some congressional Republicans during his presidency. They scored a partial success, but Democrats succeeded in blunting their efforts. There appeared little chance of passing a standalone school choice bill, despite the GOP controlling the White House, and both Houses of Congress in the first two years of the Trump presidency. Instead Republicans found, and took, their opportunity using the age-old technique for passing difficult legislation: identifying a sure-to-pass or must-pass piece of legislation and riding on its back. In this case, the vehicle was the Trump tax cut bill, HR 1, the Tax Cut and Jobs Act of 2017 (PL 115–97).

The bill allowed up to $10,000 per year per student from 529 college savings plans to be used for elementary and high school as well. Conservative groups including the Heritage Foundation had championed expanding 529 programs. Americans held more than $253 billion in more than 12 million 529 accounts as of the end of 2015, according to the College Savings Plans Network.

Supporters of public schools, however, argued the provision would only benefit families who are able to afford the savings accounts. "Expanding education tax loopholes in order for wealthy families to stash away money for private school will hurt neighborhood public schools and students," said Lily Eskelsen García, president of the National Education Association, in a press release on November 2, 2017. School choice advocates admitted the provision would mostly benefit high-income families and looked for ways to give poor families greater choice of

BETSY DEVOS

Not since William Bennett called college students "beach bums" and the Chicago public schools a "blob" in the 1980s, had there been a secretary of education as controversial as Betsy DeVos. And unlike the nomination of Bennett, who won confirmation in the Senate on a 93–0 vote, it was DeVos' nomination itself and the unusually contentious confirmation process that set her apart.

Trump announced he would nominate DeVos on November 23, 2016, just days after his surprise victory in the presidential race. He called her a "brilliant and passionate education advocate." Sen. Lamar Alexander, the Tennessee Republican who was chair of the Health, Education, Labor, and Pensions (HELP) Committee, which would conduct the confirmation hearing on DeVos' nomination, immediately announced his support. Critics in the educational establishment and the Democratic party, however, called her unqualified, too political, and more interested in tearing down public schools than trying to improve them. House Democrats reacted to the nomination by forming the Public Education Caucus.

DeVos, from Michigan, was the former chair of the state's Republican Party. At the time of her nomination, she was the chair of the American Federation for Children. The group advocated for expanding choice in K–12 schools through charter schools and providing vouchers for parents to send their children to private schools. She and her husband, Dick, the son of a founder of Amway, donated $2.75 million to GOP candidates during the 2016 election cycle. Those donations along with her lack of experience in public schools or in secondary education set off an almost immediate backlash that continued to grow as her confirmation hearing date neared. Initial concerns focused on her campaign donations to GOP senators who would vote to decide her fate, including GOP Senate Majority Leader Mitch McConnell.

Another issue was the $5.3 million unpaid fine brought against a political action committee that DeVos was once involved with for violation of campaign finance laws. The fine by Ohio election officials was based on the illegal transfer of $870,000 from the All Children Matter PAC's Virginia office to an Ohio affiliate. Several senators sent a letter saying she should pay the fine, and Devos responded in a letter that she was "an unpaid volunteer director" at the organization and was not involved with the day-to-day management of it even though she remained listed as a director on the group's tax filings.

The HELP Committee on January 31, 2017, voted 12–11 along party lines to approve the nomination. At the committee's three and one-half-hour hearing for DeVos on January 17, Democratic members pressed her on her support for vouchers that would allow tax dollars to go to private and charter schools. Ranking Democrat Sen. Patty Murray of Washington accused DeVos of spending her career "fighting to privatize public education and gut investments in public schools." At one point, under questioning from Sen. Tim Kaine, D-Va., DeVos appeared not to understand the federal law mandating educational services for disabled students.

DeVos repeatedly said she supported public schools but said they were failing low-income students. Asked by Republican committee members about federal regulation of colleges and universities, she said she would review Obama administration rules, including gainful employment which put access to federal loan assistance at risk for schools whose graduates did not earn enough to repay their loans.

She promised to review sexual assault guidance issued in 2011 to ensure that the rights of victims and the accused would be protected. On other issues, such as how charter schools should be regulated and whether teachers should be able to bring guns in school as protection, DeVos deferred, saying those decisions should be left to state and local school officials. She also said she and her husband would stop making political donations if she were confirmed and she would only take a salary of one dollar.

But DeVos's confirmation by the full Senate was far from certain, especially because two of the committee Republicans, Sens. Lisa Murkowski of Alaska, and Susan Collins of Maine, who expressed reservations during the hearing, announced after it they would not vote for her before the full Senate. Democrats worked feverishly to peel off one other Republican vote, even holding the Senate floor overnight beginning the day before the vote. In the end, it took a historic first—the tie-breaking vote by Vice President Mike Pence—to confirm DeVos 51–50 as the 11th Secretary of Education on February 7, 2017.

Once installed as education secretary, DeVos's term took on a familiar pattern—reversing Obama-era policies on several fronts while going before Congress to defend Trump budgets that combined calls for increased funding for vouchers with overall deep cuts in education funding.

Among the policy changes were the following items:

- Withdrawing guidance that directed public schools to allow transgender students to use the bathroom that matches their gender identity. The Obama administration issued the guidance, but it never went into effect because of a legal challenge by several states
- Rolling back memoranda that directed the Federal Student Aid office to make sure that federal student loan servicers were helping students manage their debts and avoid going into default. In announcing the move, DeVos wrote that the department had a "duty to do right by both borrowers and taxpayers"

- Rewriting two rules that were intended to protect student loan borrowers and help them repay their debt. One of the Obama-era regulations, the borrower defense to repayment rule, was intended to allow borrowers who were defrauded by their for-profit college to have their federal student loans forgiven. That rule never went into effect. The second was the gainful employment rule, which was supposed to make sure college programs designed around a specific career did not leave graduates with more debt than they could repay. Republicans raised concerns that it unfairly targeted for-profit colleges (*See sidebar on gainful employment rule*)

DeVos's first budget proposal in June 2017 for fiscal 2018 called for a $9.2 billion cut, or 13.5 percent, for the education department. At the same time, she proposed increasing school choice programs by $1.4 billion. Some congressional Republicans joined with Democrats in rejecting the proposal. Two years later, Democrats were harsh as DeVos defended a proposed 12 percent decrease in discretionary spending in the Education Department. The department's final budget proposal under DeVos in 2020 proposed another 7.8 percent cut. It too was rejected by Congress.

DeVos's term as education secretary ended abruptly on January 7, 2021, when she resigned the day after protesters fueled by Trump's rhetoric invaded the U.S. Capitol. "There is no mistaking the impact your rhetoric had on the situation," she wrote to Trump in her resignation letter.

school, something Trump highlighted during his first speech to a joint session of Congress.

As it was, the 529 school choice provision made it through Congress by the barest of margins. The language was offered as an amendment by Sen. Ted Cruz, R-Texas, and was approved on December 1 when Vice President Mike Pence voted to break a 50–50 tie. Democrats succeeded in raising a parliamentary objection to language that would have allowed 529 funds to be used for home-schooling. The rest of the 529 provision remained, however, as the Senate gave the tax bill final approval just after midnight on the night of December 19 by a 51–48 margin.

Career Education

If expanding school choice was an example of partisan political warfare, reauthorization of the Carl D. Perkins Career and Technical Education Act (PL 115–224) was a study in bipartisan civility. The bill, HR 2353, enjoyed substantial bipartisan support at the outset, with twenty-nine Republicans and eleven Democrats signed on as cosponsors when it was introduced May 4, 2017.

The legislation reauthorized the career and technical education law through fiscal 2023 and increased funding levels. It modified the grant application process used by states and the method for evaluating the performance of the grants. At the same time, it blocked the Department of Education from withholding funds from states that did not meet certain performance measures.

Among other provisions was one requiring states to consult a variety of education and workforce stakeholders when creating their career and technical education plans. This meant employers and business leaders were involved for the first time in designing programs that helped prepare students for in-demand and emerging jobs. Local school districts were required to conduct an evaluation of their current programs and how those programs aligned with in-demand industry sectors or occupations.

This idea of a skills gap—that millions of jobs could not be filled because workers had not been trained in the proper skills—became one of the key arguments around which support gathered for the legislation. "Every one of us knows someone God has blessed with skills, talents, and ideas that do not fit the mold of traditional postsecondary education," said Rep. Virginia Foxx, R-N.C., on the House floor on July 25, 2018, during final debate on the legislation. "Because of that, they may not believe they have much to offer or much to gain by joining the workforce without the 'right' degree or diploma. But there really isn't a right degree or diploma."

The bill moved easily through the legislative process because it had already been vetted in the 113th and 114th sessions of Congress. The House Education and Workforce Committee held a brief markup on May 17, 2017, adopting one minor amendment on a voice vote. The Senate Health, Education, Labor, and Pensions Committee discharged the legislation to the Senate floor without a markup by unanimous consent.

The legislation received final approval in the Senate July 23, 2017, and in the House on July 25, both by voice vote.

Disaster Aid for Colleges and Students

Colleges and universities, and their students, were among the many victims of the three big hurricanes of 2017—Harvey, Irma, and Maria. And Congress moved swiftly to help them deal with the aftermath through the Hurricanes Harvey, Irma, and Maria Education Relief Act of 2017 (PL 115–64).

Hurricanes Harvey and Maria were the second and third most costly hurricanes in U.S. history and Irma comes in 6th, according to the National Oceanic and

Atmosphere Administration, costing an estimated total damage of close to $300 billion. The bill, S 1866, provided relief in areas the president had declared a major disaster or an emergency because of the three hurricanes. The legislation directed the Department of Education to waive matching fund requirements from schools located in the affected areas for two grant programs, one for the Federal Supplemental Educational Opportunity Grant Program (FSEOG) or the Federal Work–Study Program (FWS). In addition, it called for reallocating unspent funds in the two programs to help those students affected by the hurricanes. Also eligible for help were colleges and universities that were not located in an affected area but had enrolled students affected by the hurricanes and tropical storms.

The Department of Education later reported $10.4 million in unexpended funds from 2016 to 2017 from the Federal Work–Study program were initially reallocated to 904 schools. The department later reported an additional $16.3 million in unused work–study funds were sent to 1,173 schools and $4.4 million in FSEOG funds were sent to 272 schools.

The bill was introduced by Sen. Alexander on September 26, 2017, and passed the Senate by voice vote the same day. It passed the House by voice vote two dates later and was signed into law by President Trump on September 29.

Veterans GI Bill Benefits

Congress easily passed a measure (HR 3218 – PL 115–48) to expand the eligibility of veterans for assistance for college. The measure, called the Harry W. Colmery Veterans Educational Assistance Act, honored the Kansas man credited with writing the original GI bill (PL 115–48).

The measure provided veterans with lifetime access to education benefits instead of having them expire after fifteen years. Other changes included

- Providing additional funding for students studying science, technology, engineering, or math
- Restoring benefits to veterans who spent their gi bill aid on now-defunct for-profit schools

"The improvements and enhancements to the GI Bill . . . will empower service members, veterans, survivors and dependents for generations to come," said Rep. Phil Roe, R-Tenn., chair of the House Veterans Affairs Committee and the legislation's sponsor, during House floor debate on July 24, 2017.

The bill was marked up by the House Veterans Affairs Committee on July 19, 2017. Committee members gave voice vote approval to an amendment, sponsored by Rep. Kathleen Rice, D-N.Y., that required the Veterans Administration to make a new determination on disability claims that had been previously denied related to exposure to mustard gas during World War II. The committee reported the amended bill favorably to the House on a voice vote.

The bill passed the House 405–0 on July 24. The Senate, which did not hold a committee markup, passed the bill by voice vote on August 2.

Loan Counseling

The problem of students piling up huge amounts of college debt continued to capture the attention of policy makers. Americans owed more than $1.45 trillion in student loan debt. That made it a leading source of debt, behind housing debt, but still ahead of credit cards and auto loans. In the House, a bipartisan effort to address the problem by providing more rigorous counseling by colleges and universities for student borrowers once again made headway but did not receive final passage.

For the third consecutive Congress, Rep. Brett Guthrie, R-Ky, introduced the "Empowering Students Through Enhanced Financial Counseling Act." This bill (HR 1635) would have amended a portion of the Higher Education Act of 1965 to modify the loan counseling requirements that colleges and universities must meet for loans that come through federal student aid programs. Schools would have been required to provide annual counseling, not just when the student first becomes a borrower.

The bill also would have

- Expanded the pool of student borrowers covered by the requirement and added parents who borrow to pay for the child's education to the list of those subject to counseling
- Required each annual session to provide comprehensive information on the specifics of the loan

The session when the student was leaving school was to include details on the loan balance, monthly payments, and other information.

Republican Sens. Dean Heller of Nevada and Cory Gardner of Colorado along with Democratic Sens. Mark Warner of Virginia and Tim Kaine of Virginia introduced a companion bill, S 2081. "We should be empowering students to make smarter choices about their financial future," Warner said in a written news release dated November 7, 2017.

The House bill went to the floor without a committee markup. The rule governing debate made seven amendments in order, and all passed on voice votes. The amendments made additional requirements regarding the counseling process including informing students how to get additional aid if their financial circumstances changed and how much they would pay monthly if they qualified for income-based repayment options. Another amendment encouraged colleges to have students attend counseling sessions in person. The House bill passed that chamber 406–4 on September 5, 2017. It was the third year the bill passed the House, but never made it to the Senate floor.

HISTORICALLY BLACK SCHOOLS PUSHED INTO LIMELIGHT

During Republican Donald Trump's first presidential campaign, he targeted Black voters, arguing that he could do more for them than the Democratic Party had despite years of strong support by Black voters. To drive home that point, Trump made history in his first days in office by inviting the presidents of Historically Black Colleges and Universities to the White House to announce an initiative designed to give them a higher profile within the federal government and to offer other forms of assistance. The Oval Office photo op combined with the initiative thrust the more than 100 HBCUs into the forefront of the debate over higher education policy, where they stayed during the Trump presidency and his campaign for a second term.

The executive order itself simply transferred the director of the existing program from the Education Department to the White House. It also created a presidential advisory board on HBCUs and called for agencies to work with university officials to give them a better chance to earn grants and contracts from the federal government.

School leaders and others welcomed the attention drawn to the Black colleges and universities but said they also wanted to see whether the Trump administration would put money behind the rhetoric in its budget requests to Congress. Rep. Robert Scott, D-Va., ranking member on the House Education and Workforce Committee, said he feared that a Trump administration plan to spend more on defense would result in cutbacks for education, including HBCUs. Johnny Taylor, president of the Thurgood Marshall College Fund, said he planned to ask the administration to support a one-time payment of $25 billion to be directed at the schools.

For her part, Education Secretary Betsy DeVos got off to a rough start with leaders of these schools when she issued a statement after meeting with HBCU presidents equating her pet cause of school choice to the creation of Historically Black Colleges. "They started from the fact that there were too many students in America who did not have equal access to education," DeVos said in her statement. "HBCUs are real pioneers when it comes to school choice." Her comments prompted widespread criticism. Senate Democrat Sen. Patty Murray of Washington termed the comments tone-deaf given the legacy of racism the schools have faced.

The good feelings created by the February White House gathering were already beginning to wear off the next month when the White House budget proposal was released and it called for deep cuts in the Department of Education, with flat funding for HBCUs, and no increase in Pell Grant awards, which are particularly important to Black students. As the fall approached, frustration with the Trump administration had been growing among those in the HBCU community, including with the president's reaction to violence in Charlottesville, Va. After Heather Heyer was killed by a white supremacist who rammed his car into a crowd, Trump said there were "fine people on both sides." The next month only twenty-nine HBCU presidents showed up for an annual White House summit that was set up for them to lobby Congress and the administration.

But in February 2018, Trump earned praise from the HBCU community when he appointed Taylor, the former head of the Thurgood Marshall College Fund, as chair of the President's Board of Advisers on HBCUs. One month later, Education Secretary Betsy DeVos announced the cancellation of more than $300 million in federal relief loans that four Historically Black Colleges took out after Hurricanes Katrina and Rita hit in 2005.

On the legislative front, a House bill to reauthorize the Higher Education Act in the House, HR 4674, included provisions that would provide direct aid to HBCUs, and other minority-serving institutions. It also would expand the uses for grants to HBCUs and increase the availability of funds under the HBCU Capital Financing program. Most importantly, it would have permanently reauthorized the mandatory funds provided to HBCUs and increased the amount from $255 million per year to $300 million per year. That authorization had expired.

The bill passed out of the House Education and Labor Committee in 2019 on a party line vote with all Republicans opposed. It advanced no further. But congressional negotiations continued and, in the end, a bipartisan deal was reached which mandated permanent reauthorization of the mandatory funding for HBCU. Trump signed it into law (PL 116–91) on Dec. 19, 2019.

The president took credit for the legislation, first during a January speech when he said he had "saved" HBCUs and then during the third and final presidential debate with Joe Biden on October 22, 2020. However, PolitiFact, the fact-checking site, found that claim to be mostly false. It noted that while Trump signed the legislation reauthorizing HBCU funding, it was not clear how involved he was in the negotiations. Nor did funding for HBCUs appear to increase under Trump. Two university professors calculated at PolitiFact's request that HBCUs had received a total of $1.9 billion from the federal government in appropriations, grants, and contracts in the first half of Trump's first term in 2017–2018. That compared with $1.8 billion to $2.4 billion annually under President Barack Obama.

2019–2020

Heading into the 2018 midterm congressional elections, education was not among the key issues that Americans identified in polls. Two years of Donald Trump's no-holds-barred personal style had made Trump himself one of the focal points of the election. The economy, health care, and the Supreme Court were identified as key issues in a Pew Research poll, the latter because of the tense battle that fall over the nomination of Brett Kavanaugh to the high court.

Betsy DeVos's nomination and her administration of the Department of Education remained a source of frustration for opponents of Trump as well as the fact that GOP control of both the House and Senate provided critics with few opportunities to provide aggressive oversight of the administration's education policy. At the state level, education became a much bigger issue because of a rash of teacher strikes in 2018 combined with unhappiness with the level of funding for schools in some states.

When Democrats recaptured the majority in the House, they promised more oversight of DeVos and Trump educational policy, but it also added to congressional gridlock. The result was even less substantive legislative action in the final two years of the Trump presidency. Still, Sen. Lamar Alexander, a former Education Secretary and university president, who remained chair of the Senate Health, Education, Labor and Pensions committee, announced early in 2019 that he planned to focus on reauthorizing the Higher Education Act. Alexander said he had three goals: to make it easier for people to apply for federal student loans, to overhaul the loan process itself, and to ease the repayment system.

Alexander did not succeed. In fact, it was a House bill to reauthorize the Higher Education Act, HR4674 that advanced but only through the House Education and Labor Committee and no further.

Higher Education Overhaul

If there was one subject where it appeared that legislative action could be successful in the 116th Congress, it was an overhaul of the Higher Education Act. The House Education and Labor Committee passed an overhaul of the act in 2019, but Congress did not take further action on the measure.

The issue appeared ripe for action for several reasons. These included the skyrocketing cost of college tuition, the huge debt that saddled students when they left college, and the complexity of the process for applying for federal aid, all of which were among a long list of issues that had hit many households across the country. In addition, Sen. Alexander had made reauthorizing the Higher Education Act a goal before he retired from the Senate in 2020.

Originally passed in 1965, the law authorized a broad array of programs to assist students and their families in financing the cost of a postsecondary education. It also authorized programs that provide federal support to colleges and universities. The most prominent of these programs are those that provide financial assistance to students and their families. In fiscal 2017, about $122.5 billion was made available to about 13 million students under the programs. The law had been reauthorized several times including in 2008 when it was renamed the Higher Education Opportunity Act (PL 110–315).

As chair of the HELP committee, Sen. Alexander convened more than a dozen hearings on the subject. His resume as a former university president and education secretary gave him connections and credibility and he already had a reputation of being willing to work across the aisle. And at first, he seemed to have a willing negotiating partner in Sen. Patty Murray of Washington, ranking committee Democrat. In 2015, the two had worked together on the Every Student Succeeds Act (PL 114–95), which was the update to the No Child Left Behind law.

In the House, Rep. Scott, chairman of the Education and Labor Committee, and Rep. Foxx, the ranking Republican both had spoken about their desire to reauthorize the HEA. And Scott convened the first of five hearings on reauthorizing the HEA in March 2019.

Sen. Alexander introduced two bills that fall, the Student Aid Improvement Act, S 2557, and the FAFSA Simplification Act, S 2667. At about the same time, Scott introduced the first comprehensive overhaul, the College Affordability Act, HR 4674. The bill would expand the Pell Grant program and increase the maximum award by $500 and extend eligibility to fourteen semesters. It would replace the variety of student loan repayment plans with one fixed plan and one income-based plan. Those borrowers earning up to 250 percent of the poverty line would not have to repay their loans until their earnings improved.

Other provisions would have

- Expanded the Public Service Loan Forgiveness program to allow several additional groups to participate. The program allows loan forgiveness for people working for the government and nonprofits
- Reduced the number of questions on the FAFSA form
- Created a new grant program to invest in states that agree to waive community college tuition and fees
- Added several provisions to improve campus safety

Committee Democrats estimated the draft bill would cost about $400 billion over ten years.

But even before the markup of that bill began, Foxx and others were criticizing it. On October 29, 2019, in a joint statement with Rep. Lloyd Smucker, R-Pa., ranking member of the committee's higher education subcommittee, Foxx said the bill "does not address the underlying issue of

DEVOS REVERSES RULE ON COLLEGE LOAN ELIGIBILITY

Early in the second half of Trump's term, a major regulatory policy shift took place regarding "gainful employment." This phrase from the Higher Education Act referred to the idea that a college degree should allow someone to get a job that paid enough to repay the loans taken out to earn the degree. It had come to a head in 2010 and 2011 when then Sen. Tom Harkin, D-Iowa, was chairman of the Health, Education, Labor and Pensions committee, and orchestrated undercover investigations by the Government Accountability Office of for-profit colleges.

In many cases, undercover government investigators posing as prospective students were given false and misleading information about the programs at the schools; and some were subjected to dozens of phone calls urging them to sign up for classes. For-profit colleges challenged the validity of the investigations and successfully sued to block the initial regulation, but the revised one issued by the Obama administration in 2014 survived a legal challenge.

That regulation required schools to calculate how much students borrowed to complete various career programs, how much they earned in their jobs, and whether that income would allow them to repay their loans. If a program failed to provide graduates with an adequate income, students could lose access to federal loans. By 2017, the Department of Education had gathered data to determine which schools and programs were in violation, a necessary first step to triggering sanctions.

DeVos, however, delayed key parts of the rule in June 2017. The said she intended to revise it, but later she moved in late 2019 to rescind it entirely. She argued that the rule unfairly targeted for-profit colleges. The first gainful employment ratings released in 2017 found that most of the programs that failed the standards were operated by for-profit institutions. Repealing the rule would cost an estimated $6.2 billion over ten years in payments for grants and loans for programs that would have been removed from qualifying for federal aid.

Rep. Bobby Scott, D-Va., the chairman of the House Education and Labor Committee, said that repealing the regulation would "prop up low-quality for-profit colleges at the expense of students and taxpayers." The Education and Labor Committee subcommittee on higher education and workforce investment held a hearing on April 3, 2019, on how to hold colleges accountable, including gainful employment. The hearing was one of several the education committee convened as part of an effort to reauthorize the Higher Education Act.

It led to consideration of a comprehensive overhaul bill, HR 4674, the College Affordability Act, which included provisions reinstating the gainful employment requirement. That bill passed out of the Education and Labor Committee but went no further.

---

exploding college costs," and increased "burdensome requirements and bureaucratic red tape."

For her part, Murray objected to Alexander's piecemeal approach to legislation and said she favored a comprehensive bill such as what the House was considering. That bill totaled more than 1,000 pages. By this point most House Republicans were opposed and the legislative process, including a grueling three-day markup on October 29 through 31, 2019, in the education committee, was mostly partisan. The committee considered more than fifty amendments. Fifteen were approved, all but four offered by Democrats. Among those approved were these amendments:

- Adding a section that encourages institutions to implement comprehensive plans to address mental health and prevent suicide among students, offered by Rep. Susan Davis, D-Calif., and approved by voice vote
- Requiring institutions to disclose campus policies on background checks for employees and volunteers working with athletes and children, offered by Rep. James Comer, R-Ky., and approved by voice vote

Among those amendments defeated were these:

- Requiring institutions to disclose existing free speech policies to students, offered by Rep. Phil Roe, R-Tenn., and defeated 17–28

- Prohibiting schools from offering in-state tuition or reduced fees to people not lawfully in the United States, offered by Rep. Rick Allen, R-Ga., and defeated 19–26

The bill passed out of committee on December 30, 2019, on a partisan vote, with twenty-eight Democrats voting yes and twenty-two Republicans, no. And that marked the end of any chance for comprehensive reauthorization of the Higher Education Act. Congress and the country turned all of their attention to the coronavirus pandemic.

Omnibus Spending and Coronavirus Aid Bill

In the final days of the 116th Congress and the Trump presidency, significant education policy was made. As in the 115th Congress, the vehicle for these provisions was a must-pass omnibus spending and coronavirus aid bill, HR133, to fund the federal government in fiscal 2021.

The bill released by House and Senate leaders on December 21, 2020, included $73.5 billion for federal education programs, $785 million more than fiscal 2020 spending and $7 billion more than what the Trump White

House requested. The bill included education policies that had not been making progress on their own. They included

- Reinstating Pell Grants for incarcerated students and restoring Pell Grant eligibility for students defrauded by their schools. The maximum annual Pell Grant was also raised to $6,495, an increase of $150
- Adding $82 billion in emergency relief to the Education Department to help schools respond to the Covid pandemic, with $54.3 billion going to elementary and secondary schools and the rest to colleges and universities
- Providing across-the-board increases in federal funding for elementary and secondary education programs, including Title 1 grants serving low-income families
- Designating $2 billion for the career and technical education grants that had been a Trump administration priority

The retiring Sen. Alexander's goal of reducing the size and complexity of the federal student aid application, FASFA, also found a home in the legislation. The bill cut the form from 108 to thirty-six questions. And in a nod to a cause that Trump had embraced in his first days in office, the bill forgave $1.34 billion in loans made to Historically Black Colleges and Universities.

Democrat Rep. Scott, chair of the House Education and Labor Committee, praised it as marking a significant step toward improving the affordability of higher education. "Congress has a responsibility to expand access to quality higher education, which remains the surest path to the middle class," Scott said. Still, the legislation was not the comprehensive reauthorization of the Higher Education Act that many had hoped for.

The House approved the bill in two chunks, both with bipartisan votes, 327–85 and 359–53 on the evening of December 21, 2020. Later that night the Senate approved it, 92–6. Trump signed it into law, PL 116–260, six days later.

Student Loan Rule

Congress passed a resolution (HJ Res 76) in 2020 to try to overturn a Trump administration rule that scaled back protections for student loan borrowers. Lawmakers, however, failed to override a presidential veto. The measure marked the first time in the 116th Congress that Congress turned to the Congressional Review Act to block a regulation that had been promulgated by the Trump administration.

The rule by the Education Department made it harder for students to eliminate debt when arguing they were defrauded by a university. Borrowers who were defrauded had to demonstrate financial harm in order to have their debt partially or completely canceled. The rule also allowed for mandatory arbitration agreements and gave borrowers just three years after leaving an institution to file a claim. Republicans argued it was needed to counter a 2016 Obama administration rule that they said imposed protec-tions that were overreaching and costly to taxpayers. Democrats, however, said it placed an unreasonable burden on defrauded students.

The House on January 16 passed HJ Res 76 on a vote of 231–180 with six Republicans joining 225 Democrats in support. The Senate passed it 53–42 on March 11. Trump vetoed the resolution on May 29. The House, with a 238–173 vote on June 26, 2020, fell far short of the needed two-thirds margin for a veto override.

Bipartisan Education Bills

Several targeted education measures received bipartisan support and became law.

HOLOCAUST EDUCATION BILL

The Never Again Education Act, HR 943, was an attempt to improve access to educational materials about the Holocaust at a time of increased incidents of antisemitism and fading memories of the events surrounding the systematic killing of 6 million Jews and millions of others. The bill authorized $2 million for each of four years, which would be matched by donations and used by the director of the United States Holocaust Memorial Museum to develop and implement ways to teach about the Holocaust. These would include local and national workshops, teacher trainings, operation of a teacher fellowship program, and development of teaching materials. The director of the museum is also required to develop and maintain a special page on the museum's website that provides education resources.

The bill went directly to the House floor under suspension of the rules on January 27, 2020, and was approved 393–5. It was discharged by unanimous consent by the Senate Energy and Natural Resources Committee on May 13 and approved by the full Senate the same day by voice vote and became PL 116–141 on May 29.

RECOGNITION OF INSPIRING SCHOOL EMPLOYEES

The Recognizing Inspiring School Employees legislation, HR 276, is an attempt to bring attention to the many support staff who are key to successful schools. The legislation mandates that the Department of Education create an annual "Recognizing Inspiring School Employees Award Program." Eligible employees include clerical staff, food, custodial, transportation, health, and security staff. States are invited to nominate staff members and one would be chosen each year as the national award winner.

The bill went directly to the House floor under suspension of the rules on February 25, 2019, and was approved by a vote of 387–19. The Senate Committee on Health, Education, Labor, and Pensions discharged the bill by unanimous consent on March 28. The bill passed the Senate by unanimous consent the same day. It became PL 116–13 on April 12.

DEBT RELIEF SCAMS

The huge amount of student loan debt owed by Americans—estimated to be $1.6 trillion by 45 million Americans at the start of 2020—has spawned scammers who offer debt relief in exchange for exorbitant fees. It is illegal for a company to ask a consumer to pay a fee before they obtain debt relief, and many scammers also pretend to be from the government. There have been efforts to crack down on these scams, but the Department of Education's inspector general recommended that criminal penalties are needed.

The Stop Student Debt Relief Scams Act, S1153, does just that by making it a crime to knowingly use an account number issued to another person or that was fraudulently obtained to access DOE information technology systems for commercial gain. Violations are punishable by a fine or prison term of up to five years or both. The bill also requires institutions to caution borrowers about third-party student debt relief companies.

The Senate Committee on Health, Education, Labor, and Pensions discharged the bill by unanimous consent on December 1, 2020, and it passed the Senate by unanimous consent the same day. The House took up the bill under suspension of the rules on December 7 and it was passed that day by voice vote. It became PL 116–251 on December 22.

FEDERAL OPPORTUNITIES FOR BLACK COLLEGES AND UNIVERSITIES

The Historically Black Colleges and Universities Partners Act, S461, attempts to strengthen these institutions by better linking them to federal agencies. The bill requires every federal agency to submit a report each year describing efforts to strengthen the capacity of HBCUs to participate in agency programs. The plans are required to include ways to increase the ability of these institutions to compete for grants and contracts. The legislation also calls for creation of a President's Board of Advisors on HBCUs in the Department of Education or in the White House.

The bill was introduced in the Senate on February 12, 2019, and approved by voice vote the same day. The legislation was taken up in the House, without committee review, under suspension of the rules on December 7, 2020. The House approved the bill later that day 388–6. On December 31 it became PL 116–270.

Education Bills That Passed One Chamber

Several other education bills advanced in the 116th Congress but did not cross the finish line.

IMPROVING MENTAL HEALTH ACCESS FOR STUDENTS

The Improving Mental Health Access for Students Act, S1782, would have required institutions of higher education that participate in student-aid programs to share contact information for suicide prevention resources with students. The act also would have required student identification cards to include the National Suicide Prevention Lifeline, the Crisis Text Line, and contact information for campus mental health centers.

The bill was discharged by unanimous consent by the Senate Health, Education, Labor, and Pensions Committee without a markup on December 17, 2020. It was approved by voice vote in the Senate the same day. The House did not take it up.

REMOVING BAD CREDIT MARK FOR STUDENT BORROWERS

The Student Borrower Credit Improvement Act, HR 3621, was originally introduced on July 5, 2019, as a stand-alone bill that would allow students who missed a loan payment to get the bad credit report removed. It passed the House but was not taken up by the Senate.

The legislation required that the bad mark from a student borrower's credit report be removed if the person made nine on-time monthly payments during the following ten-month period. It passed out of the House Financial Services Committee on a 33–25 vote on July 16 after a substitute amendment was approved by the same vote.

On January 29, 2020, the bill came to the House floor as a vehicle for several other credit-related provisions that previously were separate bills. The legislation was renamed the Comprehensive Credit Reporting Enhancement, Disclosure, Innovation, and Transparency Act. During floor consideration, the House approved by voice vote an amendment offered by Rep. Donna Shalala, D-Fla., which called for the Government Accountability Office to study how credit scores harmed by loan defaults by student borrowers impacted applying for future loans. The legislation was approved later that day 221–189. The Senate did not take it up.

DIVERSITY IN EDUCATION

The Strength in Diversity Act, HR 2639, was an attempt to advance the cause of racial integration in public schools. The bill authorized funding for communities to develop and implement plans to address racial and socioeconomic segregation.

Planning grants would be used to study segregation in schools, evaluate current policies, and identify changes needed. Implementation grants would be used to recruit, hire, and train teachers to improve diversity; and to support activities in a district under a court-ordered desegregation plan.

The House Committee on Education and Workforce reported out the bill on May 16, 2020, by a 26–20 vote after approving a substitute amendment on a voice vote. The bill came to the House floor on September 15 and several amendments were approved by voice vote, including one that added new criteria for evaluating grant applications to ensure that the grant would lead to a meaningful reduction in racial isolation, and another that allowed use of grant funds to recruit and train school counselors. The legislation passed the House that day by 248–167. The Senate did not take it up.

Figure 10.2 Federal Spending on Education Rose Rapidly During Trump Presidency

While President Trump often submitted budget proposals that called for deep cuts, he signed spending bills from Congress that steadily increased the Department of Education budget.

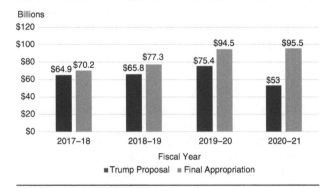

SOURCE: U.S. Department of Education, Budget History Tables.

Housing and Urban Aid

Housing and Urban Aid

By the time President Donald Trump took office in January 2017, the American housing market had largely recovered since the 2008–2009 housing crisis. New home sales for the year 2016 were at the strongest level since 2007. And in 2016, existing home sales were at the strongest level since 2006. However, affordable housing remained a vexing issue for federal policy makers, as did urban aid, an issue directly linked to the availability of affordable housing. From 2013 to 2015, "worst case needs for housing assistance persisted at high levels across demographic groups, household types, and regions," the Department of Housing and Urban Development said in its 2017 report to Congress, a document required annually.

Congressional lawmakers were divided over what to do about these problems. With Republicans holding House and Senate majorities during the first two years of GOP President Donald Trump's 2017–2021 White House term, policies focused on housing and urban aid took a mostly deregulatory bent. After Democrats won the House majority during the 2018 midterm elections, lawmakers in the chamber pushed for a more activist approach to expanding the nation's supply of affordable housing, and in providing federal aid to cities, among other policy goals.

These thorny policy issues already faced strong political headwinds. Affordable housing efforts by Democratic administrations had in the prior decades had mixed results and were often cited derisively by Republicans as examples of big government run amok. And, two years into the Trump administration, House Democrats had to push their housing and urban aid agenda through what was still a Republican Senate. They also faced a veto pen yielded by Trump—a reviled figure to many in the party whose own 1970s-era personal history tangling with the Justice Department over affordable housing discrimination spurred suspicion about him on the issue from many Democrats.

Complicating the challenge further, issues of race and class lurked just under the surface of policy debates on housing and urban aid policy. With Trump in the White House, these tensions bubbled up in public frequently, often in ugly, unseemly ways.

Then in March 2020 the COVID-19 pandemic struck the United States in full force, with about ten months left in Trump's term. Debate over long-term housing policy

Figure 11.1 Congressional Appropriations for Section 8 Tenant-Based Rental Assistance

HUD tenant-based assistance provides vouchers that very low-income families can apply toward rent. These serve the most economically vulnerable families in the country, HUD says, and represent the biggest share of HUD's budget.

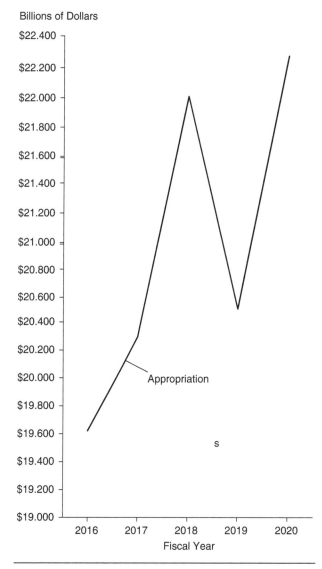

Billions of Dollars

source: U.S. Department of Housing and Urban Development, https://www.hud.gov/budget/additional

notes: * indicates congressional budget request

prescriptions turned to more immediate concerns about rent moratoriums and other efforts to help cash-strapped Americans keep their living quarters. During a period of months in mid-2020, the airborne pandemic—beyond the morbidity and cruelty of hundreds of thousands of American lives lost—left many U.S. workers unemployed. Shutdowns of dine-in service at restaurants and closures in a range of service industries led to the first bout of double-digit unemployment in more than three decades.

These strained economic circumstances complicated efforts to expand the affordable housing supply and to grow urban aid. Instead, immediate concerns focused on keeping Americans in the homes where they lived through such policies as a nationwide moratorium on evictions.

Chronology of Action
on Housing and Urban Aid

2017–2018

With Republicans holding majorities in the House and Senate during the first half of Trump's presidency, affordable housing-related legislation was rarely considered by either chamber. The individual bills were largely aimed at rolling back rules and regulations promulgated by the Consumer Financial Protection Bureau (CFPB). The CFPB had been founded in 2011 during the Obama Administration, as the brainchild of future Sen. Elizabeth Warren, D-Mass., with the goal of providing Americans consumer protection in the financial sector. CFPB's jurisdiction came to include banks, credit unions, foreclosure relief services, payday lenders, securities firms, and other types of financial companies. But the agency quickly became a bête noire of congressional Republicans, who considered it the epitome of government overreach, wielding too much unchecked power.

Some elements of the Trump administration's housing and urban aid agenda became law as pieces of larger, more prominent pieces of legislation. That included creation of investment "opportunity zones" aimed for low-income neighborhoods and easing lending requirements for some small banks.

Opportunity Zones

A bill by Sen. Tim Scott, R-S.C., S 293, to provide tax breaks for investments by businesses in low-income communities, got incorporated into the signature tax law enacted by President Donald Trump and congressional Republicans. The "opportunity zones" proposal was included in the Tax Cuts and Jobs Act of 2017 [PL 115-97], signed by Trump on December 22, 2017.

Scott had introduced the bill on February 2, 2017. It was referred to the Senate Committee on Small Business and Entrepreneurship. The bill saw no further action until Republicans put it into the tax package, a top GOP legislative priority. The tax package, among other provisions, lowered taxes for most Americans, as well as small busi-

ness owners, cut the corporate tax rate from 35 percent down to 21 percent, and limited mortgage interested deductions. The proposal drew fierce derision from Democrats, reflected in the 51–48 Senate vote on December 20, 2017, followed by a 224–201 vote in the House that same day.

Scott's proposal, in its original legislative form, had drawn bipartisan support. Of its fourteen cosponsors, half were Democrats, including Sen. Cory A. Booker of New Jersey, a former Newark mayor. Under this plan, investors would get tax breaks if they invested capital gains—profits earned from the sale of assets—in economically wanting areas of the country that were designated as Opportunity Zones. The idea was to flood underserved areas with an influx of money to jump-start their economies.

Supporters called Opportunity Zones a direct investment to parts of the country that did not particularly benefit from the post 2008–2009 economic crash recovery. When Scott introduced his Opportunity Zones bill, it drew little criticism. And because the proposal never went through the normal legislative process, with amendments offered and potential counterarguments considered, it largely flew under the radar screen until enacted as part of the Republican tax bill.

But since details of the proposal had not been thrashed about in the legislative process, lawmakers in subsequent years offered legislation to increase transparency and reporting requirements around the Opportunity Zones. Congress would not take action on any of those measures, however.

One Senate proposal came from Scott himself, S 2994, introduced on December 5, 2019. The bill was referred to the Committee on Finance but saw no further action. The measure would have included reporting requirements in the form of an annual report by the Treasury about the impact of Opportunity Zones.

Meanwhile Sen. Ron Wyden, D-Ore., introduced a bill, S 2787, which would have eliminated opportunity zones in

neighborhoods that were relatively wealthy or middle class. The bill also would have required the Government Accountability Office to issue a report every five years on the community impact of Opportunity Zones. Wyden expressed concern there were no safeguards in law to ensure taxpayers were not subsidizing politically connected businesspeople. If so, opportunity zones would offer little or no benefit to the low-income communities the program was supposed to help, Wyden said. Wyden's bill, introduced on November 6, 2019, was referred to the Committee on Finance and saw no further action.

House Majority Whip Jim Clyburn, D-S.C., introduced companion legislation in the House, HR 5042. Clyburn similarly raised concerns that the Opportunity Zone incentive would turn out to be a tax credit for rich investors, with limited benefits for low-income communities. Clyburn, like Wyden in the Senate, proposed changes that would have sought to nix zones he contended were not truly impoverished. Clyburn's bill also would have prohibited investments in certain developments such as casinos, stadiums, parking lots, or luxury apartments. The House proposal, introduced on November 12, 2019, was referred to the Committee on Ways and Means, and saw no further action.

Still, Scott throughout the Trump term touted the benefits of Opportunity Zones. In 2019, at a White House gathering, Scott said Opportunity Zones were working because property values in the designated areas had already increased by 20 percent. Scott added that the increased property value was a positive outcome since half of residents in the zones owned their properties.

Mortgages and Community Banks

The House passed a series of bills that made changes to mortgages as well as to regulations for community banks. Although the Senate did not act on those bills, key provisions were added to a banking deregulation bill that Trump signed into law in 2018 (S 2155 —PL 115-174).

HIGH-COST MORTGAGES FOR MANUFACTURED HOUSING

A bill (HR 1699) introduced by Rep. Andy Barr, R-Ky., aimed at streamlining regulations around the sale of manufactured houses, passed the House on December 1, 2017, on a 256–163 vote. Its main provisions were rolled into S 2155.

Manufactured houses are largely assembled in factories, and then transported to the plot of land where they will stand. That differs from the bulk of new homes, which are built on their permanent sites. Manufactured homes are significantly less expensive and are often first houses for young families.

Barr's bill would have established in law that a manufactured housing salesperson, who also assisted a customer during the mortgage loan process, could not then be labeled a mortgage "loan originator." That had become a real possibility—with the manufactured housing salesperson forced to choose one role over another and potentially give up business—due to a 2013 Consumer Financial Protection Bureau rule aimed at curbing predatory lending.

According to Barr, this CFPB rule often unintentionally snared and penalized people who sold manufactured housing. The CFPB rule, in this view, had harmed lower- and moderate-income families because manufactured home sellers were restricted in offering general financing information to potential buyers. HR 1699 specifically sought to clarify under federal law that a manufactured home salesperson would not be considered to have originated a loan when they helped a customer apply for a mortgage, or if the salesperson prepared loan information for the customer—that is, unless the salesperson were paid separately by a creditor, lender, or mortgage broker.

The measure was introduced on March 23, 2017. The House Committee on Financial Services, approved it, 42–18, on Oct. 12, 2017, with no amendments.

The bill sought to amend both the Truth in Lending Act of 1968, and the Secure and Fair Enforcement for Mortgage Licensing Act of 2008. The latter law established a series of mortgage lending requirements, to which manufactured home salespeople have been subject. After the bill passed the House, it was referred in the Senate to the Banking, Housing and Urban Affairs Committee, which did not take it up.

The policy goal of the bill, however, did end up getting enacted. The proposal's language was folded into a banking regulation bill (S 2155) signed by President Trump on March 24, 2018 (PL 115-174). S 2155 included a provision clarifying that a manufactured housing seller is not deemed a mortgage "loan originator" just because they provided a customer with some assistance in the mortgage loan process. The provision was one of several included by Senate Banking Committee Chair Michael D. Crapo, R-Idaho, which were aimed at reducing the regulatory burden regarding mortgage lending to help smaller institutions in the mortgage lending market. Sen. Joe Donnelly, D-Ind., had sponsored legislation (S 1751) such as—Barr's manufactured housing bill, which on August 3, 2017, had been referred to the Committee on Banking, Housing and Urban Affairs, without further legislative action.

The broader banking law, the "Economic Growth, Regulatory Relief, and Consumer Protection Act," eased banking regulations imposed by Dodd-Frank (PL 111-203) after the financial crisis of 2008–2009. The measure passed the Senate on March 14, 2018, on a 67–31 vote. It then cleared the House on May 22 on a 258–159 vote.

EXEMPTIONS FROM HOME MORTGAGE ESCROW REQUIREMENTS

The House, 294–129, passed a bill (HR 3971) on December 12, 2017, to ease mortgage rules for community banks. Key provisions of the bill became law after they were added to S 2155.

BEN CARSON CONFIRMED AS HUD SECRETARY

Ben Carson's nomination as Housing and Urban Development secretary was a controversial pick from the start. He was not a housing specialist by background. Carson came into public life after a renowned career in medicine and had a great story to tell about earned success and living out the American dream, all of which put Senate Democrats in the politically uncomfortable position of blocking a prominent African American nominee from joining Trump's Cabinet.

The soft-spoken Carson had grown up poor in Detroit. He went on to attend Yale University and the University of Michigan Medical School before becoming the first African American named as the head of pediatric neurosurgery at Johns Hopkins Children's Center in Baltimore. In 1987, Carson became famous for pioneering surgery to separate twins joined at the back of the head. In 2013, he entered the national political spotlight during the National Prayer Breakfast when he railed against the modern welfare state, with President Barack Obama sitting just feet away.

After losing out to Trump for the 2016 Republican nomination, the president-elect named Carson as his choice for HUD secretary. Senate Republicans praised the life story of a man who grew up in inner-city Detroit with a single mother who had a third-grade education.

Democrats in Congress took a mixed approach to Carson's nomination. Though she did not have a vote on Carson's confirmation, Rep. Maxine Waters of California, the top Democratic member on the House financial Services Committee, called it "appalling." "He is just another addition to the parade of unqualified individuals serving in the Trump Administration," Waters said in a March 2, 2017 statement, a sentiment echoed by many Democrats in no mood to compromise or cede any political ground to Trump.

Democrats on the Senate Banking Committee took a somewhat different approach. Many said during Carson's confirmation hearings that despite his lack of traditional background in housing policy or in managing a large bureaucracy, they would keep an open mind. And, after hearing Carson testify, several Democratic senators went on to praise his pledge to overcome that lack of experience by listening to experts about the needs of poor Americans with respect to temporary housing assistance. "A good CEO doesn't necessarily know everything about the business," Carson said. "But he knows how to pick those people and how to use them."

During the Senate confirmation hearing, on January 12, 2017, in the waning days of President Barack Obama's tenure, Carson said he would address the affordable housing crisis and the 11 million households that spend a high percentage of their income on rent. "There are a large number of people spending 30 to 50 percent of their income on housing," he said. "That's unacceptable." Carson further told lawmakers that he envisioned forging a more "holistic approach" to helping people and developing "the whole person." But he did not offer many details.

Under questioning from Democrats, Carson said HUD's rental assistance is "essential" to millions of Americans. HUD had a lot of worthy programs, Carson said, with a caveat. "We don't want it to be way of life," Carson said. "We want it to be a Band-Aid and a springboard to move forward." Carson also said he would like to see more partnerships with the private sector and religious groups.

Then, pressed by Senate Democrats, Carson also acknowledged that Trump had an ownership interest in a large Brooklyn development called Starrett City that received HUD funding. Carson said he had not discussed the housing project with Trump but pledged to work with the Senate Banking Committee should a conflict arise over the Starrett City project.

Carson's nomination cleared the Senate Banking, Housing and Urban Affairs Committee unanimously on January 24, four days after Trump's inauguration. While committee Democrats said Carson would not have been their choice for HUD secretary, they cited as reasons for their support his promises to address lead hazards in housing, homelessness, and other issues.

Carson's nomination then stalled for more than a month, with other Trump picks receiving more scrutiny and Democrats engaged in delaying tactics. In the interim, Trump lauded his HUD secretary-in-waiting, calling him a "totally brilliant neurosurgeon" who has saved many lives, during an appearance with Carson on a February 21, 2017 tour of the National Museum of African American History and Culture in Washington. "We're going to do great things in our African-American communities," Trump added later in the joint museum appearance. "And HUD has a meaning far beyond housing. If properly done, it's a meaning that's as big as anything there is, and Ben will be able to find that true meaning and the true meaning of HUD as its Secretary."

Carson was finally confirmed on March 2, on a 58–41 vote. The bulk of Senate Democrats were not as friendly to Carson's nomination as their brethren on the Banking Committee. Seven members of the Senate Democratic Caucus (including Independent Angus S. King Jr. of Maine) crossed over to back Carson's nomination. Five of the Democratic-aligned senators were Banking Committee members—Sherrod Brown, Ohio; Joe Donnelly, Ind., Heidi Heitkamp, N.D.; Jon Tester, Mont.; and Mark R. Warner, Va.—while two were not, King and Joe Manchin III, W.Va.

(Continued)

BEN CARSON CONFIRMED AS HUD SECRETARY (Continued)

All Senate Republicans voted in favor, except Sen. Johnny Isakson of Georgia, who was absent. Carson became the seventeenth member of President Donald Trump's Cabinet to be confirmed, leaving five nominations still awaiting a vote. (The final confirmation came on April 27, 2017, for Labor Secretary Alex Acosta.)

Change to Fair Housing Act

The Trump administration sought to cut HUD'S budget and several of its longstanding programs. Those efforts over four years met significant legislative pushback in Congress from both Democrats and Republicans. In some cases, though, the Trump administration was able to act unilaterally in tweaking and limiting affordable housing programs. For instance, HUD, under Carson's leadership, ended a rule meant to ensure the department's compliance with the Fair Housing Act of 1968.

The 2015 rule had been promulgated by HUD during President Barack Obama's administration. It sought to hold communities accountable for providing affordable housing by requiring that any jurisdiction that wanted to receive HUD funding had to document and publicly report patterns of racial bias.

In August 2018, HUD announced that it aimed to "streamline and enhance" the Obama-era rule on desegregation. Carson pitched as part of a broader effort to reverse zoning laws aimed at preventing housing growth, particularly in wealthy suburbs. Carson said HUD should be able to ease such exclusionary zoning, to build more housing and hopefully drive down costs by upping the supply. "After reviewing thousands of comments on the proposed changes to the [Affirmatively Furthering Fair Housing] regulation, we found it to be unworkable and ultimately a waste of time for localities to comply with, too often resulting in funds being steered away from communities that need them most," Carson said in a July 23, 2020 HUD statement.

Many housing advocates blasted the move, arguing the Obama-era rule, known as Affirmatively Furthering

Fair Housing (AFFH), should stay in place. The issue came to a head in July 2020, when HUD officially scrapped the Affirmatively Furthering Fair Housing rule. Instead, HUD put in a new policy, which effectively let municipalities just declare that they followed the 1968 Fair Housing Act. Localities did not have to provide documentation or other proof. They only had to pledge a "general commitment that grantees will use the funds to take active steps to promote fair housing," said the formal rule change.

The move drew swift pushback from congressional Democrats, in the run-up to its enactment and after. "Given what is at stake for families across the country, HUD should be taking steps to strengthen fair housing protections," a group of twenty-nine House Democrats, led by House Financial Services Committee Chairwoman Maxine Waters, Calif., wrote to Carson on March 20, 2020. "Yet with this proposed rule, the Trump Administration has chosen to upend the collaborative, participatory, data-driven framework under the 2015 rule that would have enhanced accountability under the AFFH mandate in favor of a framework that fails at the most basic level to focus on fair housing."

Congressional Democrats, though, were relatively powerless to reverse the decision. Since it had been issued as a federal rule change by HUD—an executive branch move—and because Democrats controlled only the House, with the presidency and Senate in Republican hands.

Still, at a June 9, 2020, oversight hearing by the Senate Banking, Housing and Urban Affairs Committee, Sen. Sherrod Brown of Ohio, the panel's ranking Democrat, blasted Carson, and the Trump administration over the pending rule change. The president and administration officials, including Carson, Brown said, were trying to "systematically dismantle basic civil rights protections that previous generations marched for and endured beatings for and laid down their lives for."

By that time the AFFH regulation had become fodder in the increasingly contentious 2020 presidential race tween Trump and Democratic nominee-in-waiting Joe Biden, the

---

HR 3971, the Community Institution Mortgage Relief Act, was approved by the House Committee on Financial Services on October 12, 2017, on a 41–29 vote. Sponsored by Rep. Claudia Tenney, R-N.Y., the bill aimed to roll back regulations enacted after the 2008–2009 financial crisis that required banks to set up escrow accounts for riskier borrowers. The regulations were put in place by the CFPB. The bureau intended the accounts to ensure that homeowners would have money set aside for expenses such as taxes and insurance. But Tenney said the CFPB rule had been too costly for small, community banks. These banks, Tenney noted, often have smaller staffs and

significantly less resources than larger institutions, forcing them to bear the brunt of costs to maintain escrow accounts for their customers.

In floor debate, the House adopted, by voice vote, the only amendment allowed under the rule. The amendment, by Rep. Brad Sherman, D-Calif., would have lowered the thresholds of assets a bank would need to be covered by the rule change, from $25 billion to $10 billion. The Sherman amendment also would have required loan servicing exemptions for banks with fewer than 20,000 mortgage loans, rather than 30,000, as originally proposed in Tenney's bill. This helped address the concerns of critics of

former vice president and thirty-six-year Democratic senator from Delaware. Trump used the pending AFFH regulation as a cudgel to win the support of suburbanites in swing states. "I am studying the AFFH housing regulation that is having a devastating impact on these once thriving Suburban areas," Trump tweeted on June 30, 2020. The president then cited his Democratic White House rival. "Corrupt Joe Biden wants to make them MUCH WORSE. Not fair to homeowners, I may END!" He went on to accuse Biden of pushing to "abolish our beautiful and successful suburbs."

A spokesman for Biden's presidential campaign, Andrew Bates, called the remarks an effort by Trump to deflect blame by his administration for its response to the COVID-19 pandemic.

Carson Ethics Questions and Scrapes with Lawmakers

Carson stayed in the cabinet through Trump's entire presidency, one of five Cabinet secretaries to do so (the other four were Treasury Secretary Steven Mnuchin, Agriculture Secretary Sonny Perdue, Commerce Secretary Wilbur Ross, and U.S. Trade Representative Robert Lighthizer). His relatively long tenure in office, however, was not without controversy. Most prominently, Carson came in for scrutiny over reports that HUD in late 2017 had spent $31,561 on a set of dining room furniture for the secretary's office. Carson defended the department's handling of the purchase of a dinette set. At a March 20, 2018, hearing before the House Appropriations Transportation–HUD Subcommittee, Carson said he was aware an old "dangerous" dining room table would be replaced and that he canceled the order once he learned of the high price.

Carson at the hearing touted his hiring of a new HUD chief financial officer, Irving Dennis, to ensure procurement rules were followed. Carson painted his response to the office furniture controversy as part of his commitment to HUD's fiscal frugality, which extended to proposed slashing of budgets for affordable programs. That response, though,

hardly mollified lawmakers. Several House members questioned Carson on the dinette set purchase, as well as the role his wife, Candy Carson, played in that purchase.

Carson said he was aware of $3,500 in decorating expenses that took place early in the administration, which he noted in a March 1, 2018 statement was "considerably less than the historical norm" since new department heads typically redecorate. Carson also said in March 20 testimony before the House Appropriations Subcommittee on Transportation, and Housing and Urban Development, and Related Agencies that he was aware of a fifty-year-old dining room table with exposed nails that was considered dangerous and needed to be replaced. "I left it to my wife," he said of the choice of dining room tables. But when he saw the bill, Carson said, he "immediately canceled" the order. "I'm not really big into decorating," Carson said at the March 20, 2018 hearing. "If it were up to me [the offices] would probably look like a hospital waiting room."

A year-and-a-half later, Carson was cleared of wrongdoing by HUD's inspector general. "We found no evidence indicating that either Secretary or Mrs. Carson exerted improper influence on any departmental employee in connection with the procurement," the inspector general said in its fourteen-page report released on September 12, 2019.

That hardly ended tensions with Congress, though, particularly after Democrats won the House majority in 2018 and party lawmakers were able to exercise oversight over HUD, along with other agencies in the Trump administration. Lawmakers at times clashed with Carson over basic knowledge about his agency and seeming competence for the job of secretary. At a May 21, 2009, House Financial Services Committee hearing, freshman Rep. Katie Porter, D-Calif., schooled Carson on the common abbreviation used to describe government-owned foreclosed properties. "An Oreo?" Carson replied, in response to a question from Porter about whether he knew the term REO (real estate owned). The clip quickly went viral and become fodder for late-night comics.

the bill, primarily Democrats, who said it would raise exemption thresholds too high and open the door for abusive practices. Through Sherman's amendment, they pushed successfully to scale back the deposits and accounts requirement to an increased level both parties earlier agreed upon. The amendment also required banks to hold the loan on their balance sheets for at least three years.

BANKS AND MORTGAGES

The House on February. 9, 2018, passed the Mortgage Choice Act (HR 1153) on a vote of 280–131. The Senate added key provisions to S 2155.

The bill, sponsored by Rep. Bill Huizenga, R-Mich., aimed to expand access to mortgages for lower- and middle-income home buyers. It would have changed the definition of what is known as a "qualified mortgage," which gives lenders legal protections. To be considered a "qualified mortgage," giving lenders legal protections, the points and fees on a home loan generally may not exceed 3 percent of the total loan amount, among other restrictions.

Huizenga's bill would have excluded from the points and fees calculation those fees paid to title insurance companies affiliated with the lender, and any escrow for future

payment of insurance. Those fees had been a source of irritation to lenders, who complained that including affiliated title fees in the 3 percent cap limited relatively safe loans from being included in the "qualified mortgage" category. Huizenga argued a home purchase is among the most important financial decisions made by families, who should be able to take advantage of what he deemed one-stop shopping when taking out a mortgage.

The House Committee on Financial Services approved HR 1153, without amendment, on November 14, 2017, by a 46–13 vote. During committee debate, some Democrats said the proposal would lead to the rollback of mortgage lending reforms instituted after the 2008–2009 financial crisis. Democrats said they were concerned that lenders would be allowed to increase the cost of loans while still being eligible for "qualified mortgage" protections.

COMMUNITY BANK REGULATIONS

The House on February 8, 2018, passed the Small Bank Holding Company Relief Act (HR 4771), on a vote of 280–139, without substantive amendment. Key provisions became law after the Senate added them to S 2155.

HR 4771, sponsored by Rep. Mia Love, R-Utah, aimed to make it easier for small banks to lend money in the communities where they operated. The bill would have directed the Federal Reserve to raise the threshold for its Small Bank Holding Company Policy Statement from $1 billion to $3 billion. Love and other supporters argued the move would have allowed smaller bank holding companies to hold higher levels of debt while also exempting them from certain Dodd-Frank Act minimum leverage and risk-based capital requirements.

The Committee on Financial Services had approved HR 4771, without amendment, on January 18, 2018, by a 41–14 vote. After the provisions were enacted as part of S 2155, the Federal Reserve Board on August 18, 2018, issued a rule to comply with the new law. It raised its Small Bank Holding Company Policy Statement total asset threshold from $1 billion to $3 billion.

TRID IMPROVEMENT ACT

The House on February 27, 2018, passed by voice vote the TRID (TILA-RESPA integrated disclosure) Improvement Act, HR 5078. But the Senate did not take up the bill. The House Committee on Small Business had approved the bill, by voice vote and without amendment, on November 20, 2019.

The legislation sought to override a series of mortgage-financing rules adopted by the CFPB, called Know Before You Owe. The bureau adopted the rule in October 2015 with the goal of assisting homebuyers in better understanding the home-closing process.

But Rep. French Hill, R-Ark., sponsor of HR 5078, said the CFPB rule had the opposite effect. In most states, the Know Before You Owe rule did not allow the calculation of a discounted rate known as "simultaneous issue." That is a rate title insurance companies provide to consumers when they simultaneously purchase a lenders policy and owners title insurance policy.

Hill argued a "simultaneous issue" rate would provide consumers with an effective discount on their owners' title insurance policy. The CFPB had been unwilling to fix the problem, leading to the need for congressional action.

Hill's bill to counteract the CFPB rule took on its TRID Improvement Act name in reference to the bureau's formal designation of the more popularly titled Know Before You Owe—TILA-RESPA integrated disclosure, or TRID. The acronym-filled title referred to the Truth in Lending Act of 1968 and The Real Estate Settlement Procedures Act of 1974, combined with the "integrated disclosure" component.

Hill said during floor debate on February, 27, 2018, that the discounted title insurance rate was important because it provided consumers with "an effective discount on their owners title insurance policy in order to protect their property rights as long as they own their home." The regulation, Hill added, had led consumers in more than half of the United States to receive confusing information about their title insurance costs.

HOUSING VOUCHERS FOR PEOPLE WITH SUBSTANCE ABUSE DISORDERS

The House on June 14, 2018, passed the HR 5735, the Transitional Housing for Recovery in Viable Environments Demonstration Program (THRIVE) Act, on a 230–173 vote after several amendments were adopted. The Senate did not take up the measure.

The THRIVE Act sponsored by Rep. Andy Barr, R-Ky., would have expanded housing options for individuals who were transitioning out of drug or alcohol addiction treatment. The measure was aimed at people completing an inpatient rehabilitation program or a prison sentence. These people, Barr said, often found themselves with limited long-term housing options. They frequently ended up in housing situations surrounded by people using the same drugs and other illegal substances whose habit they had broken while behind bars. The THRIVE Act, Barr said, rather than administering vouchers through public housing authorities, would have had the federal government give them directly to local nonprofit organizations in areas of the country with the highest rates of opioid-related deaths.

The THRIVE Act would have specifically moved 10,000 vouchers, or $83 million, away from the Housing Choice Voucher program to pay for transitional recovery housing for people with substance-use disorders. The Housing Choice Voucher system is the federal government's major program to help low-income families, the elderly, and the disabled afford private housing. Participants can use the vouchers to rent houses, townhouses, and apartments.

The proposal drew opposition from a group of national housing, homelessness, and recovery organizations, among

others. They contended the proposal would lengthen affordable housing waiting lists for low-income families, seniors, the homeless, and people leaving substance use treatment.

Rep. Maxine Waters, the ranking member of the House Financial Services Committee, praised Barr for trying to help people suffering from substance use. But, Waters added, doing so would take additional federal funds, not diversion of resources in an existing voucher program.

The House Committee on Financial Services approved the bill, on a 34–19 vote on May 22, 2018. The committee adopted by voice vote an amendment Barr offered, to expand criteria for entities eligible to participate in the rental voucher program to be required to demonstrate they had prior experience administering rental assistance vouchers and transition housing programs. Or they would have had to demonstrate a partnership with a public housing agency or a housing program of a state, local government unit, or Indian tribe.

The committee adopted by voice vote an amendment by Rep. Emanuel Cleaver, D-Mo., to replace the bill's provisions with language to authorize such sums as may be necessary to provide up to 10,000 rental assistance vouchers under the Housing Choice Program for families that have a member with a substance abuse disorder. That category would have included an opioid abuse disorder and those in recovery from an opioid abuse disorder. Cleaver's amendment also would have required the secretary of Housing and Urban Development to report to Congress, within five years of the bill's enactment of the program.

The committee rejected, on a 21–32 vote, an amendment by Rep. Charlie Crist, D-Fla., to require the HUD secretary, when selecting entities to receive rental assistance vouchers pursuant to the program, to ensure that those chosen would follow federal discrimination law. That definition would have included not discriminating against employees or covered individuals based on "sexual orientation, gender identity or expression."

The committee adopted by voice vote an amendment Rep. Maxine Waters, D-Calif., the panel's ranking member, to require a public housing agency or an owner to conduct an individualized review of the totality of circumstances—including a household's need for housing and the community's health and safety—when deciding whether to evict a household due to drug-related criminal activity of a household member or guest. The amendment would have further prohibited a public housing agency or owner from denying admission to federally assisted housing based on a conviction that was expunged, an arrest that did not result in a conviction or in noncriminal citations.

During House floor debate, lawmakers approved four amendments to the bill by voice vote. A manager's amendment was added by Barr that clarified selection requirements for nonprofit recipients of the federal housing vouchers. Rep. Dana Rohrabacher, R-Calif., offered an amendment that would have required local governments to

authorize which service providers could participate in the demonstration program. Rep. Gwen Moore, D-Wisc., proposed an amendment to ensure that tribal housing authorities would be eligible to participate. And Rep. Andy Biggs, R-Ariz., offered an amendment to remove the requirement to include recommendations for further continuation and expansion of the voucher program in a report to Congress.

The bill passed the House on a near party line vote. Republicans supported the measure 218–7, while Democrats opposed it 12–166.

MORTGAGE RECORDS

The House on April 27, 2017, passed HR 1694, the Fannie and Freddie Open Records Act of 2017, on a 425–0 vote after adopting several amendments as a substitute, which had been written into the text by the House Rules Committee. Despite the strong bipartisan vote, the Senate did not take it up after it was referred to the Senate Judiciary Committee.

The bill would have amended the Freedom of Information Act to require the Federal National Mortgage Association (Fannie Mae) and the Federal Home Loan Mortgage Corporation (Freddie Mac) to be subjected to the Freedom of Information Act (FOIA) public information disclosure requirements during any period in which they are under conservatorship or receivership. The measure would have been retroactive, applying to FOIA requests filed after enactment of the bill that related to any record created before it became law.

The bill was a throwback of sorts to the aftermath of the 2008–2009 financial collapse. It was sponsored by Rep. Jason Chaffetz, a Utah Republican who was chairman of the House Oversight Committee. Chaffetz resigned from the House on June 30, 2017, pursuing a career as a FOX News contributor, and author.

The bill aimed to treat the troubled housing entities like other federal agencies when it came to public access to documents. The Freedom of Information Act grants the public presumptive access—without explanation of justification—to certain executive branch records that have not been published. FOIA includes nine categories of exemptions from disclosure. That includes information touching on national security concerns or invasion of privacy, or that could hurt financial markets. Denial of requested documents through FOIA can be appealed administratively and ultimately settled in court.

Fannie Mae and Freddie Mac are congressional-chartered, stockholder-owned companies known as government-sponsored enterprises. Their goal is meeting affordable housing needs. But their public-private structure left Fannie Mae and Freddie Mac in a sort of legal netherworld when it came to the public's access to records about them—a topic of keen interest after the 2008–2009 financial crash.

In September 2008, due to steep losses and inadequate money in the bank, Fannie Mae and Freddie Mac agreed

Figure 11.2 Number of Households Getting Any Form of HUD Assistance and Number Specifically Getting Tenant-Based Assistance

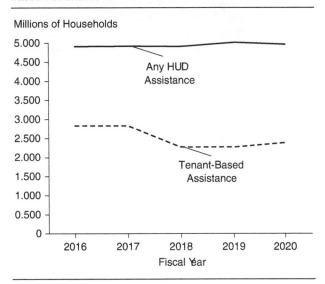

Millions of Households

SOURCE: U.S. Department of Housing and Urban Development, Assisted Housing annual datasets, https://www.huduser.gov/portal/datasets/assthsg.html

with the federal government to go into conservatorship. That meant the government took control, with the goal of returning the entities to financial health and shareholder control.

Both remained vital to the U.S. economy. Since the 2008–2009 financial crisis the two GSE's helped finance more than half of all new mortgages in the country. At the same time, with the housing pair under conservatorship, the government had purchased more than $150 billion in special stock issued by the organizations.

As stockholder-owned and -controlled companies, Fannie Mae and Freddie Mac would not normally be considered government agencies and subject to FOIA requests. That triggered waves of bipartisan outrage. In January 2011, with Republicans back in the House majority, Chaffetz introduced legislation to make Fannie Mae and Freddie Mac subject to FOIA, by requiring them to be considered federal "agencies."

The bill stalled amid protests from federal housing officials, who said making Fannie Mae and Freddie Mac subject to FOIA could generate substantial legal costs. The legislation was considered, but not taken up for a floor vote, repeatedly during subsequent sessions of Congress. So, House passage of the proposal in 2017 was a valedictory of sorts for Chaffetz, on his way out of Congress.

The House Committee on Oversight and Government Reform, the panel Chaffetz headed, approved the bill by voice vote on March 28, 2017. That came after the committee approved two amendments by voice vote. One, by Rep. Dennis Ross, R-Fla., made technical and conforming changes to the bill. The second, by Rep. William Lacy Clay, D-Mo., would have clarified that nothing in the bill would be construed to preclude or restrict disclosure of information regarding new products or significant new product terms prior to loan purchasing. As the bill was going to the floor a month later, the House Rules Committee by voice vote added an amendment by Chaffetz that would have created a fee structure intended to enable Fannie Mae and Freddie Mac to recover the entirety of their costs through fees to commercial requesters.

The House Rules Committee also by voice vote approved a substitute amendment by Chaffetz, which became part of the bill text, to stipulate that the existing exemption under FOIA for trade secrets and commercial or financial information also applied to the records of Fannie Mae and Freddie Mac. The amendment also would have provided that the provisions take effect six months after enactment.

Another tweak to the bill was part of the Chaffetz substitute amendment, by Rep. Hank Johnson, D-Ga., which would have stipulated that nothing in the bill be construed as precluding the traditional FOIA exemptions from applying to the records of Fannie Mae and Freddie Mac. An additional change to the bill covered by the Chaffetz amendment, by Del. Stacey Plaskett, D-V.I., and Rep. Michael E. Capuano, D-Mass., would have clarified that nothing in the bill could have been construed to preclude or restrict disclosure of information regarding new products or significant new product terms prior to loan purchasing.

2019–2020

House Democrats' sweeping wins in the 2018 midterm elections, which ushered the party into the majority for the first time in eight years, had dramatic effects on the push for housing and urban aid legislation. House Financial Services Chairman Jeb Hensarling, R-Tex., who touted himself as a free market purist, retired after the 2018 cycle. Hensarling was replaced as chair by Rep. Maxine Waters, D-Calif., a vocal advocate for expanding government programs in the housing and urban affairs realm.

Waters became the committee leader in 2019 after six years as ranking member. In addition to being the first woman and first African American to head the committee, Waters was the longest-serving Black woman in Congress. Waters had housing at the top of her priorities as chairwoman of the House Financial Services Committee, a position of power and prestige she gained through twenty-eight years in the House and the Democratic return to power. It was an unusual focus for a committee that traditionally had emphasized oversight of banks and financial markets. Nonetheless, her first committee hearing convened as chair, on February 13, 2019, examined an issue directly linked to affordable housing policy: "Homeless in America: Examining the Crisis and Solutions to End

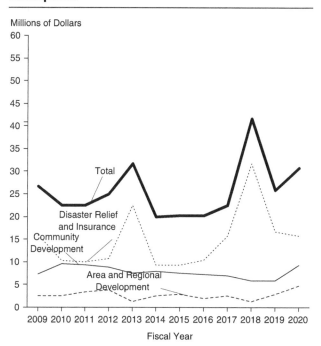

Figure 11.3 Outlays for Community and Regional Development

SOURCE: Office of Management and Budget, *Historical Tables, Budget of the United States Government: Fiscal Year 2021* (Washington DC: U.S. Government Printing Office, 2020), Table 3.2.

NOTES: * indicates estimate

Homelessness." Witnesses included representatives from the National Alliance to End Homelessness, the National Coalition for Homeless Veterans, and the National Coalition for the Homeless, among others.

Like so many congressional agendas, however, Waters's affordable housing push got upended when the COVID-19 pandemic struck the United States with full force in March 2020. Congress instead focused on shielding the housing sector from the worst impacts of the pandemic.

COVID-19 Assistance

The coronavirus pandemic, which would claim about 400,000 lives during the Trump presidency, also shut down large segments of the economy. Housing was one of the hardest-hit sectors. The impact of COVID-19 was immediate and severe on affordable housing for low-income residents and people of modest economic means. Many tenants faced job and income losses that prevented them from paying rent, buying food, and accessing health care.

When the pandemic struck, Congress in bipartisan fashion sought to extend rent relief and mortgage forbearance to millions of Americans forced out of work. During the pandemic's early months, Congress and President Donald Trump enacted several proposals related to housing. The provisions were not standalone legislation, but elements of broader, more sweeping bills.

Ultimately, two larger bills became law that directly affected housing—HR 748, the CARES Act [PL 116-136] and HR 133, the FY2021 Consolidated Appropriations Act [Public Law 116-260]. Another bill to put in place eviction moratoriums until the pandemic subsided, HR 7301, by Rep. Maxine Waters, died in the Senate.

THE CARES ACT

Congress passed the CARES Act, HR 748, on March 27, 2020, by voice vote. Amid a mounting national emergency, Trump signed it the same day (Public Law 116-136). The $2.2 trillion emergency spending bill aimed to deliver cash to individual Americans, businesses, and health care facilities, all reeling from the COVID-19 pandemic. The law, among other things, authorized the Internal Revenue Service to send $1,200 payments to millions of Americans. The law further created programs to disburse close to $1 trillion in business loans.

The CARES Act touched the housing realm directly, though none of its provisions were subject to debate or amendments, due to the harried and furious nature of the legislative process that pushed the proposal into law. The act, for instance, provided funding that some states and localities used to assist renters. And one of the law's most prominent provisions was its eviction moratorium, which drew bipartisan support. The eviction moratorium began

on March 27, 2020, and ended on July 24, 2020. (The Centers for Disease Control and Prevention subsequently imposed its own eviction moratorium.) Tenants covered by the law could not be forced to leave until a month after the law expired in late July, which came out to August 23. Similarly, landlords could not file notices forcing tenants to leave until August 23.

The CARES Act eviction moratorium, when it was in place under law for four months, applied to federally related properties. The law defined that as properties participating in federal assistance programs or with federally backed financing. That was thought to cover between 28 percent and 46 percent of occupied rental units in the United States.

The CARES Act's legislative history spanned more than a year, well before the COVID-19 pandemic emerged as a threat from China and spread worldwide in early 2020. HR 748 was originally introduced on January 24, 2019, by Rep. Joe Courtney, D-Conn. Introduced as the Middle Class Health Benefits Tax Repeal Act of 2019, the bill aimed to repeal a looming 40 percent excise tax on certain employer-sponsored health insurance plans known as the "Cadillac Tax," a provision of the 2010 Affordable Care Act (Public Law 111-148). The bill was referred to the House Ways and Means Committee. However, it saw no committee action, and on July 17, 2019, the House took it up under suspension of the rules, requiring a two-thirds majority for passage. The legislation passed the House 419–6.

The Senate received the bill on July 18 and placed it on the chamber's legislative calendar. But it saw no further legislative action for eight months. On March 20, to comply with the constitutional requirement that all bills for raising revenue must originate in the House, the Senate used HR 748 as a shell bill for the newly renamed CARES Act. The freshly inserted bill text, written by Senate Republicans and the Trump administration, aimed to provide direct cash payments to people making $75,000 or under annually, loan guarantees for impacted businesses and more resources for testing and development of vaccines, among other provisions.

House and Senate Democrats, however, were not enamored with many provisions in the Republican-written bill. On March 22, Senate Democrats blocked the bill in a key procedural vote, 47–47, when sixty votes were needed to cut off debate. The stock market plummeted the next day. A second procedural vote failed on March 23, on a 49–46 vote, with sixty votes still needed to move ahead.

House Speaker Nancy Pelosi, D-Calif., then indicated her chamber would prepare its own bill, with a $2.5 trillion price tag. But on March 25, senators reached a bipartisan agreement with the House on a $2.2 trillion bill. Spending provisions included $300 billion in one-time cash payments to people who submitted a tax return, $260 billion in increased unemployment benefits, creation of the Paycheck Protection Program, to help businesses continue paying their workers, and forgivable loans to small businesses.

On March 25, the Senate passed the $2 trillion bill on a 96–0 vote. In the House Democrats and Republicans were prepared to move the bill quickly to passage, clearing it for Trump's signature. When it came to the House floor on March 27, it passed by voice vote. The only note of dissent came from Thomas Massie, R-Ky., who tried unsuccessfully to force a roll call vote on the legislation, but was overruled by the House's presiding officer, Rep. Anthony Brown, D-Md. Trump signed the CARES Act into law hours later.

That ended Congress's role in enacting eviction moratoriums, although Waters attempted to pass a more sweeping moratorium (see HR 7301, below). But the issue would continue for another year. The Centers for Disease Control and Prevention put in place a separate eviction moratorium starting September 4, 2020, and ultimately extended it until 2021, when the Supreme Court struck it down. The CDC eviction moratorium was broader than the CARES Act, applying to all renters who attested to meeting income and other eligibility criteria as established in the law. This included attempting to obtain government assistance for rent and, if evicted, facing homelessness or overcrowded housing conditions. Renters had to assert their stay in their current housing by submitting a signed declaration of eligibility to their landlords.

COMBINED SPENDING AND COVID-19 RELIEF

The FY2021 Consolidated Appropriations Act (Public Law 160-260), HR 133, did not move nearly as quickly as the CARES Act in becoming law. After weeks of negotiations, Congress passed the combined fiscal 2021 spending and COVID-19 relief legislation on lopsided bipartisan votes on December 21, 2020, and Trump signed the measure into law on December 27.

On the housing front, the catch-all spending bill included $25 billion for states and localities to fund an Emergency Rental Assistance (ERA) program. The Emergency Rental Assistance program, administered by the Treasury Department, makes funding available to assist households that are unable to pay rent or utilities.

PL 116-260 established parameters for how the ERA funding could be used. Among other requirements, states and localities had to use the bulk of funds for financial assistance. The law defines that as assistance paying rent and utilities—including bills past due.

Renters are eligible for ERA funding if they are low-income, are experiencing financial hardship, or are at risk of homelessness or housing insecurity. The law directed those receiving grants to prioritize very low-income renters for assistance.

NO NEW CONGRESSIONAL EVICTION MORATORIUM FROM CONGRESS

Not all housing efforts tied to COVID-19 relief had such legislative success, though. The House, on a mostly party line vote of 232–180 and without amendment, on

June 29, 2020, passed HR 7301, the Emergency Housing Protections and Relief Act. The Senate did not take up the measure.

The bill included housing assistance programs and moratoriums on evictions, problems that had been exacerbated by the COVID-19 pandemic. Waters introduced the measure on June 24, 2020, during the pandemic's early months. The bill was referred to the Financial Services Committee, but Democratic leaders then routed it straight to the House floor. Democratic leaders saw it was an effective messaging tool against what they called the Trump administration's muddled response to the COVID-19 pandemic, as the infectious disease killed thousands of people a month, ravaged American households, and decimated the economy. As a result, many renters faced loss of income, and the inability to pay their rent.

The bill would have established a twelve-month moratorium on evictions covering all tenants, compared to a mortarium enacted earlier in the COVID-19 crisis that was part of the CARES Act (PL 116-136), which covered only properties with federally backed mortgages. HR 7301 also would have created an automatic suspension of mortgage payments for a single-family mortgage that became delinquent by sixty days during the public health emergency. Under current law, the borrower must request a forbearance. The automatic forbearance proposed by Waters's law also would have applied to certain reverse mortgages.

The proposal would have further extended the maximum period of forbearance for multifamily mortgages from ninety days to twelve months. Another provision of the bill would have increased the homestead exemption (generally, the equity in a residence that is protected from creditors in a bankruptcy proceeding) from $15,000 to $100,000.

Additionally, it would have extended eligibility for Chapter 13 bankruptcy, which enables individuals with regular income to develop a plan to repay all or part of their debts.

HOMELESSNESS

The Committee on Financial Services approved a bill (HR 1856) on March 28, 2019, that would have provided an additional $13.3 billion in mandatory funding over five years for Housing and Urban Development programs aimed at reducing homelessness. The programs would have been deemed permanent because, Waters said, they allowed individuals to stay until they could support themselves. The full House did not take up the measure.

House Financial Services Committee Republicans argued the bill had more to do with politics than policy, saying Waters refused to work with the GOP to address bureaucratic burdens in applying for HUD homelessness grants. All Republicans opposed the bill, but some indicated a willingness to work with Waters to tweak the text first.

The committee adopted by a voice vote an amendment introduced by Rep. Bill Posey, R-Fla., which would have prioritized awarding grants to applicants in communities that had adopted zoning policies and other housing regulations that encouraged private sector development of low-income housing. The committee also adopted, by voice vote, an amendment from Rep. Bill Huizenga, R-Mich., which would have clarified that faith-based organizations were eligible for the bill's grants.

Rep. Sean Duffy, R-Wisc., introduced an amendment that would have imposed some of the Green New Deal's goals as requirements for the grants. The committee voted unanimously against it.

FUNDING PROPOSALS FOR HUD

Trump signaled from the outset of his administration that housing and urban aid policies would be a lower priority. This was reflected in the administration's annual budget requests to Congress. Each budget proposal, to varying degrees, proposed large cuts to federal affordable housing programs. But Congress often refused to go along. For instance, Trump's fiscal year 2020 HUD budget proposal was $44.1 billion. That would have represented a cut of $9.6 billion, 18 percent below fiscal year 2019's congressionally enacted funding levels. In the end, Congress and Trump reached an agreement to go the other way on spending. The catch-all spending bill for fiscal year 2020, enacted in December 2019 with a government shutdown looming, boosted HUD's fiscal year 2020 budget.

In the Trump administration's four budget requests to Congress, HUD Secretary Ben Carson tried to eliminate or significantly scale back several longstanding programs his department operated. That included Community Development Block Grants, the Public Housing Capital Fund, HOME Grants, housing block grants for Native Americans, and the Choice Neighborhoods Initiative, among others. These efforts drew opposition even from Republican members of Congress. "Just like last year, we're unlikely to agree on a lot of the things you've put forward," Rep. Mario Diaz-Balart of Florida, the ranking Republican on the HUD appropriations subcommittee, told Carson during an April 3, 2019, hearing.

On the other side of the Capitol, later that same day at a Senate Appropriations subcommittee hearing, Sen. Susan Collins told Carson she was "deeply troubled" by many of the administration's proposals. "Low-income households face an affordable housing shortage across the country, and

(Continued)

in many locations that shortage is reaching crisis levels," Collins, a Maine Republican, told Carson.

Meanwhile, housing advocates over the course of four years argued slashing budgets for a range of programs would, among other consequences, exacerbate homelessness, and send prices for affordable housing skyrocketing—with a ripple effect of jacking up costs for buying homes throughout the economy.

Carson, for his part, insisted slashed housing programs were a painful but necessary element of broad cuts to many areas of the federal budget. At a March 20, 2018, hearing before the House Appropriations Transportation–HUD Subcommittee, Carson defended the Trump administration's proposed 14 percent slashing of his department's budget. That, and the elimination of three core programs, represented the "tough budget choices" needed to address the government's mounting debt, Carson said. "Our children's and grandchildren's futures depend on it," Carson said of the cuts. The requested level of funding "is sufficient to effectively administer our core programs, particularly as we are committed to running our programs more efficiently, spending every tax dollar with which we are entrusted wisely."

The gulf between the Trump administration's limited spending goals for HUD and congressional lawmakers' appetites for considerably larger budgets was on vivid display in the final round of negotiations between the opposing branches of government, in a catch-all spending bill, the Consolidated Appropriations Act, 2021 (HR 133, PL 116-260). Under the deal, HUD got $49.6 billion for fiscal 2021, which was a $561 million increase over the previous year. Notably, it was $12.3 billion more than Trump had requested in March.

Also under the spending law, the Office of Public and Indian Housing got $34.8 billion, a $2.3 billion boost over fiscal 2020's level. And the Office of Community Planning and Development received $8.3 billion for fiscal 2021. That was a $298 million increase over the fiscal 2020 enacted level, and $5.2 billion more than the Trump administration's request.

The Trump budget had proposed cutting the Choice Neighborhood's Initiative, a competitive grant for local leaders trying to help transform poor areas into mixed-income neighborhoods. The omnibus spending package instead spent $200 million on the Choice Neighborhood's Initiative, a $25 million increase from the prior fiscal year.

The fiscal 2021 spending package further allotted $40 million for the HUD–Veterans Affairs Supportive Housing for Homeless Veterans program, the same as the previous year's level. And the budget deal renewed a small voucher program for homeless individuals and families, giving it $43 million for fiscal 2021 after it went unfunded in 2020.

TRUMP'S TROUBLED AFFORDABLE HOUSING HISTORY

For news consumers of a certain generation, their first exposure to Donald Trump came not in his 2016 upset win for the presidency over Democratic rival Hillary Clinton, his 2004–2015 starring role in the television hit "The Apprentice," or his exploits as a swashbuckling New York real estate developer, chronicled at length in the 1980s by the New York tabloids. Rather they first learned of Trump from news reporters of a 1973 lawsuit brought against his family's New York City–area housing development company for alleged racial discrimination in apartment complexes it owned.

The Justice Department sued Donald Trump, his father, Fred Trump, and Trump Management to obtain a settlement in which the pair would promise not to discriminate. The case eventually was settled two years later after Trump tried to countersue the Justice Department for $100 million for making false statements. Those allegations were dismissed by the court.

Trump's friction-filled background with affordable housing may or may not help explain how as president decades later his administration took a lukewarm, at best, approach to programs run by the Department of Housing and Urban Development. Led by HUD Secretary Ben Carson, the Trump administration's proposed budgets repeatedly tried to slash the amount of money allotted to affordable housing programs. Congress rebuffed those efforts, usually with bipartisan support—frequently upping the amounts of money provided for housing and urban aid in appropriations bills that got enacted during Trump's term. Whatever the actual effect on public policy during Trump's White House term, congressional Democrats frequently cited the president and his family business's 1970s legal exposure as a reason his administration was so hostile to affordable housing programs.

The 1973 Justice Department lawsuit—which alleged Trump and his father were violating the Fair Housing Act of 1968 by refusing to rent units in their New York City buildings to African Americans—became a frequent rhetorical refrain for the president's Democratic opponents. Trump as presi-

dent frequently clashed with minority members of Congress, among others, who became proxies of sorts for his dim view of the nation's cities. This politically toxic mix exploded into public view in July 2019, through a series of the president's Twitter jabs at the city of Baltimore. Maryland's most populous city was a poster child of sorts for affordable housing programs funded by the federal government that had long been anathema to some conservatives. A forty-five-minute drive from Washington, D.C., congressional Republicans had long trekked north to Baltimore for photo ops of decayed housing projects, aimed at illustrating their warnings about the perils of big government programs run amok.

The bulk of the city—and more to the point its poorest areas—were represented by Democratic Rep. Elijah Cummings. With Democrats' capture of the House majority in 2018, Cummings became chair of the House Committee on Oversight and Government Reform. Cummings promised to aggressively investigate Trump's business dealings, and whether they presented conflicts of interest with his duties as president—along with more traditional topics such as the efficiency and performance of federal agencies.

Six months into Cummings's chairmanship he had become a frequent Twitter target of Trump's invective. The president on July 27, 2019, tweeted that Cummings's Baltimore district was a "disgusting, rat and rodent infested mess." "If he spent more time in Baltimore, maybe he could help clean up this very dangerous & filthy place," Trump wrote. The president argued that Cummings' "district is considered the Worst in the USA" and "no human being would want to live there."

Cummings quickly responded on Twitter. "Mr. President, I go home to my district daily," Cummings tweeted. "Each morning, I wake up, and I go and fight for my neighbors. It is my constitutional duty to conduct oversight of the Executive Branch. But it is my moral duty to fight for my constituents."

The social media dustup between Trump and Cummings would prove a high-profile drama at the end of the congressman's long career in public office. Cummings died on October 17, 2019, at age sixty-eight from "complications concerning longstanding health challenges," his spokesperson stated.

CHAPTER 12

Labor and Pensions

Labor and Pensions

President Trump took office in January 2017 amid a declining unemployment rate and sharp political divides in Washington which impeded Republican party leaders' efforts to address several priorities affecting labor, such as revamping job training programs and overhauling certain welfare programs to encourage more unemployed people to enter the workforce. Republicans also sought to reduce regulations on employers by overturning several Obama-era rules addressing overtime pay, sick days and employer liability, but several such rules quickly faced court challenges and Trump's labor secretary was slow to propose alternatives.

Between 2017 and 2019, the unemployment rate dropped from about 5 percent to below 4 percent. During the 115th Congress, lawmakers repeatedly sent to the White House stopgap funding bills and other measures that continued authorization for certain job training, welfare assistance, foreign worker visas, and other programs as Democrats and Republicans failed to reach agreements to overhaul or expand such programs.

The Trump administration pushed for increased and expanded job training programs to fill a so-called jobs gap as employers in certain industries said they could not find the skilled workers they needed to fill job openings. In January 2017, the Labor Department reported 5.6 million job openings, which increased to 6.3 million by January 2018 and to 7.6 million in January 2019, then dropped slightly to 6.4 million in December 2019.

Republicans controlled both the House and Senate in 2017 and 2018, but their margins were slim, with fifty-two seats in the Senate and 241 in the House. Disagreements among factions of their party also impeded negotiations on measures, and leaders were unable to get on track the annual appropriations process that in recent years repeatedly had stalled. At the start of the 115th Congress, the government was operating on a stopgap funding law (PL 114-254) that would expire on April 28, 2017.

Following the 2018 mid-term elections, Democrats took control of the House and reignited efforts to advance several labor priorities, such as measures to protect older workers and pregnant workers from employment discrimination, boost the minimum wage, expand worker rights, and bolster faltering union pension plans. But the GOP-controlled Senate did not take up such measures.

The parties found more common ground on a measure to encourage retirement savings.

After the start of the coronavirus pandemic in early March 2020, state and local governments mandated quarantines and barred large gatherings of people in restaurants, bars, and other businesses. Many companies temporarily laid off employees, and as the pandemic and related lockdowns continued, many small businesses began to shutter. The unemployment rate quickly shot up again, reaching 14.8 percent in April 2020 before slowly tapering off, to 6.7 percent by December 2020, when some states and localities began to relax some restrictions and companies adjusted to a remote workforce.

With the start of the pandemic, Congress expanded unemployment assistance and low-income benefits for workers who were laid off or working reduced hours. Trump signed several subsequent packages that extended and expanded such benefits.

Figure 12.1 Outlays for Social Security

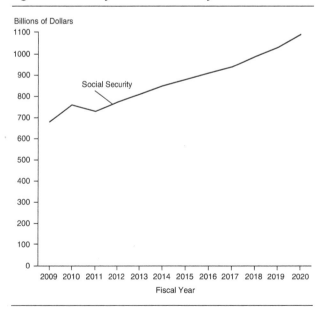

SOURCE: Office of Management and Budget, Historical Tables, *Budget of the United States Government: Fiscal Year 2021.*

NOTES: Total line includes expenditures not shown separately. * indicates estimate

Chronology of Action on Labor and Pensions

2017–2018

During President Trump's first year in office, the stock market climbed while unemployment fell, and certain industries reported a growing number of job openings. The unemployment rate hit a seventeen-year low, reaching 4.1 percent at the close of 2017 and dropping to 2.9 percent by the end of 2018.

The administration in 2017 immediately raised concerns about how to better match job training with the skills employers were seeking and thereby close a skills gap and fill a record 6 million job openings. Trump initially pushed to reduce funding for worker training and education programs overseen by the Labor Department while expanding industry apprenticeship programs. He backed off the funding cuts amid backlash from both Democrats and Republicans who wanted to protect programs in their districts, but he called on the Labor department to reduce red tape and allow industries to initiate and oversee new apprenticeship programs.

As in previous years, Republicans alleged that the existing welfare programs made it too easy for unemployed Americans to remain unemployed rather than seek work. The White House and GOP leadership wanted to increase work or job training requirements for welfare recipients in order to reduce spending on such entitlement programs that contributed to the federal deficit. Ultimately, such efforts failed, and Congress authorized several short-term authorizations to continue to provide for low-income and unemployed Americans.

Republican leaders on Capitol Hill also said they wanted to revamp Social Security Disability Insurance (SSDI), which was created in 1956 under an amendment to the Social Security Act and funded by payroll taxes. The Social Security Administration reported 8.9 million workers on disability in December 2015, more than double the number of two decades earlier. GOP proposals included barring people from receiving unemployment insurance and SSDI at the same time, changing qualification criteria and benefit payment formulas, redefining disability in the Social Security Act, and requiring those with lower back pain and arthritis to obtain physical therapy before applying for benefits.

The Trump administration in May 2017 proposed cutting benefits and requiring applicants to search for work while the Social Security Administration reviewed their applications for disability. The White House estimated such changes would save an estimated $48.8 billion over five years. Critics, though, quickly reminded Trump that he had pledged during the presidential campaign that he would not cut social security, Medicare, or Medicaid.

Discussions relaxed after Social Security trustees in July 2017 released a report stating that the program would be able to pay full benefits for recipients through 2028. A previous forecast estimated the program would be depleted by 2023. The trustees said there were fewer than expected applications. Meanwhile, debate continued about ensuring overtime pay for more workers, expanding foreign worker visas for seasonal industries, and ensuring workplace safety—particularly during the coronavirus pandemic.

Workforce Training

Republicans and Democrats agreed on the need to reform certain job training programs and find ways to fill the growing skills gap in the workforce, but many lawmakers resisted White House efforts to downsize programs favored by their constituents. Instead, Congress continued to authorize and slightly boost funding for many worker training programs. President Trump, meanwhile, issued an executive order calling on the Department of Labor to create a new system that would allow industry groups to develop and oversee their own apprenticeship programs.

FUNDING FOR JOB TRAINING

The fiscal 2017 omnibus spending package (HR 244, PL 115-31), which Trump signed into law on May 5, 2017, included $12.09 billion for the Labor Department, $83 million below the fiscal 2016 level. The measure included $90 million, a $5 million increase, for the Labor Department's apprenticeship programs, and maintained funding for most workforce and employment training programs.

But the administration's fiscal 2018 budget proposal called for a $2.4 billion (or 20 percent) funding reduction for the Labor Department to reduce the department's focus to "its highest priority functions" and to achieve savings to help boost military spending, the budget request said. The administration asked for funding reductions for job training programs and health and safety training grants. The following items were among the requests:

- Elimination of the Senior Community Service Employment Program, which helped low-income senior citizens find work, to save an estimated $433.5 million
- Closure of 125 underperforming Job Corps centers, which aimed to help disadvantaged youth, ages sixteen to twenty-four, find employment. The budget request estimated it would save about $237.5 million
- Reduction of technical assistance grants for employment programs for the disabled
- A $5 million reduction, to $90 million, for apprenticeship and vocational training programs
- Climination of the Occupational Safety and Health Administration's $11 million training grant program, which House appropriators said was ineffective

Rosa DeLauro of Connecticut, the top Democrat on the House Appropriations subcommittee, said in a March 16, 2017, statement that Trump's "proposal to cut job training by $2.5 billion at a time when he talks about getting Americans back to work is especially contradictory with his campaign promises." Labor Secretary Alexander Acosta, however, told the subcommittee in early June 2017 that the budget cuts were to better align "job training, job education and the skills the marketplace demands."

Nevertheless, in early 2018, Trump signed into law a $1.3 trillion fiscal 2018 omnibus spending bill (HR 1625, PL 115-141) that included $12.2 billion for Labor Department programs and activities, a boost of $192 million from fiscal 2017. The measure increased by $44 million funding for the Employment and Training Administration and increased by $15 million, to $1.7 billion, funding for Job Corps. However, congressional appropriators urged the Labor Department to take savings from closing selected Job Corps Centers to improve other centers. With the fiscal 2019 budget process, Congress then sought to get annual appropriations back on track and enact individual spending bills, although it ultimately combined several bills into large, omnibus spending measures.

On June 28, 2018, the House passed a measure (HR 6157), introduced by Rep. Kay Granger, R-Texas, which originally included only Defense Department appropriations for fiscal 2019. On September 18, 2019, the Senate approved, 93-7, a conference report on the bill that added to the underlying Defense Bill funding another $12.1 billion for the Labor Department, $94 million less than in fiscal 2018. It also included funding for the Health and Human Services, and Education departments, as well as a continuing resolution to keep other government agencies running through December 7, 2019.

The measure reduced overall funding for the Employment and Training Administration by $11 million (to $99 billion) due to reductions in unemployment compensations programs. The bill, however, increased, to $160 million, funding for apprenticeship programs and slightly boosted funding for Veteran Employment and Training programs.

On September 26, 2019, the House adopted, 361-61, the conference report on the measure. The president signed the bill into law (PL 115-245) on September 28, 2019, even though he had previously called the measure ridiculous because it did not include his request for a $5 billion down payment for his planned wall along the U.S.-Mexico border.

Career and Technical Training

On July 31, 2018, Trump signed into law (HR 2353, PL 115-224) a $1.2 billion measure that reauthorized career training and technical education programs. Members of both parties praised the measure for helping fund training programs that would help fill the skills gap.

The Carl D. Perkins Career and Technical Education Act was originally enacted as the Vocational Education Act in 1963 (PL 88-210) in response to growing technical change and a population explosion and to a need to move more Americans into jobs. The program aimed to develop and support academic and worker skills training for secondary and postsecondary students and facilitate connections between students and employers.

The law had last been reauthorized in 2006 (PL 109-270), when Congress expanded the programs to focus on skills beyond manufacturing and construction and include training in health care, information technology, and other industries. In the wake of the 2008 Great Recession, industry officials said they needed more skilled workers for certain technical positions, and experts called on Congress to better align training programs with employers' needs. The House in September 2016 had passed a bill that would have reauthorized the programs, but the measure stalled in the Senate amid disagreements about how much authority the Education secretary should have over the program and over the bill's proposed funding formula that would have reduced funding for programs in some states, particularly Wyoming.

BIPARTISAN MEASURE

On May 17, 2017, the House Education and the Workforce Committee approved, by voice vote, a bill (HR 2353) that would reauthorize the law through fiscal 2022 and aim to help workers gain new skills and help employers find workers to fill an estimated 6 million job openings. The bill, sponsored by Rep. Glenn Thompson, R-Pa., also would give states and local jurisdictions more control over the program, but would mandate states meet certain

performance goals, such as graduation and worker placement rates. During the markup, committee Chair Virginia Foxx, R-N.C., said, "Many employers can't find talent and high-tech skills they're looking for while many workers struggle to land good-paying jobs."

On June 22, 2017, the House passed the bill by voice vote. On June 26, 2018, the Senate Health, Education, Labor, and Pensions Committee approved, by voice vote, a similar measure (S 3217) during an executive session. On July 23, 2018, the Senate passed, by voice vote, the bill after amending it to extend the reauthorization through fiscal 2023 and increase its funding authorization, among other changes. On July 25, the House included the Senate's changes in its own measure (HR 2382) and cleared the bill for the president's signature.

The administration, in its fiscal 2018 budget proposal, had sought to cut the program by $148 million, or 13 percent below the fiscal 2017 level. Nevertheless, Trump signed the bill into law (PL 115-224) on July 31, 2018. The law, scheduled to be implemented July 2019, authorized $1.23 billion for the program in 2019, up from $1.19 billion in fiscal 2018. Funding would increase to $1.32 billion by fiscal 2024.

Energy Workforce

The House in 2017 passed legislation (HR 338) that aimed to boost training programs in the energy and manufacturing sectors, but the measure stalled in the Senate. As soon as the House opened the 115th session in January 2017, the GOP leadership pushed for action on the measure (HR 338), which would have required the Energy Department to prioritize its training programs for potential workers in the energy and manufacturing sectors. Under the bill, introduced by Rep. Bobby L. Rush, D-Ill., the Energy Department would have been required to work with colleges and outreach programs to help prepare women, minorities, and veterans for careers in the energy and manufacturing sectors. "This 21st Century workforce bill represents hope and opportunity for many of our citizens who feel they have been left out from the American dream," Rush said.

The House Energy and Commerce Committee approved the legislation by voice vote on June 12, and the House passed it by voice vote the same day. The Senate never took up the measure.

New Apprenticeships Program

While seeking to downsize certain job training programs, President Trump advocated an expansion of apprenticeships to help train workers in skills needed by industries that were struggling to fill the jobs gap.

On June 15, 2017, Trump signed an executive order calling on the Labor Department to expand apprenticeships and vocational training programs by making it easier for more industries to obtain certification of such programs. The order said development of such programs would be moved from the Labor Department to third-party entities such as trade groups, labor unions, and businesses, and would double, from $90 million to nearly $200 million a year, funding for apprenticeship grants. Administration aides said the order would reduce red tape.

Congress in 1937, with passage of the National Apprenticeship Act, also called the Fitzgerald Act, originally authorized the Labor secretary to set standards for apprenticeships. The order called for a review of such programs and said the Labor secretary could permit third-party entities to determine how programs meet certain quality standards.

The executive order defined an apprenticeship as an "arrangement that includes a paid-work component and an educational or instructional component, wherein an individual obtains workplace-relevant knowledge and skills." The existing definition prioritized on-the-job training and a schedule of wages.

Welfare Overhaul

The White House and Republican leaders in Congress sought to reduce the cost of some welfare programs that assisted unemployed and low-income people, but as negotiations on Capitol Hill stalled, lawmakers instead approved several short-term reauthorizations of key programs.

President Trump had said during the 2016 presidential campaign that he would not make cuts to the social safety net, but his early budgets proposed funding cuts for several entitlement programs. Retiring House Speaker Paul D. Ryan, R-Wisc., also pushed to reduce cash assistance and food stamp benefits for the poor with the aim to move more adults back into the workforce. Many Democrats, meanwhile, wanted to increase the basic cash assistance program for the poor, which had not been increased in more than twenty years. The Congressional Budget Office, in January 2017, said that without changes to the entitlement programs, federal annual deficits likely would more than double over the next ten years, rising from $559 billion in fiscal 2017 to $1.4 trillion in 2027. In early 2017, the Trump administration advocated cutting, by $800 billion over ten years, entitlement programs such as cash assistance for the poor and food stamps.

The administration said its fiscal 2018 budget blueprint aimed to save $21 billion in basic welfare benefits through the Temporary Assistance for Needy Families program, $193 billion through reductions in the food stamp program, $40 billion in Earned Income Tax Credit and Child Tax Credit programs, and $20 billion in other programs. President Trump and the GOP leadership also pushed to impose more work requirements for welfare recipients.

"We believe in the social safety net. We absolutely do," Office of Management and Budget Director Mick Mulvaney told reporters May 22, 2017, during a briefing

on the administration's proposed budget. "What we've done is not to try to remove the safety net for folks who need it, but try and figure out if there are folks who don't need it—that need to be back in the workforce."

In April 2018, Trump signed an executive order that called on federal departments and agencies to review welfare programs, enforce existing work requirements, and propose more stringent rules. Trump also sought to give states more flexibility in running their programs.

"Since its inception, the welfare system has grown into a large bureaucracy that might be susceptible to measuring success by how many people are enrolled in a program rather than by how many have moved from poverty into financial independence," the executive order said.

TEMPORARY ASSISTANCE FOR NEEDY FAMILIES (TANF)

Congress extended funding for the Temporary Assistance for Needy Families (TANF), a program offering cash benefits for certain low-income families, through several stopgap, or temporary, government spending measures in 2017 and 2018 (PL 115-30, PL 115-31, PL 115-245, PL 115-298). When the House and Senate failed to reach agreement on another short-term spending measure at the end of the 115th Congress, authorization for the program lapsed after December 21, 2018.

Congress created the TANF program in 1996 under the Personal Responsibility and Work Opportunity Act that overhauled the welfare system (PL 104-193). TANF replaced Aid to Families with Dependent Children, which had provided primarily cash assistance to low-income individuals. TANF imposed more work requirements and implemented a flexible grant funding program to help states prepare low-income families to care for children at home; promote job training, work, and marriage among low-income individuals; reduce unplanned pregnancies among single adults; and encourage the formation of two-parent families.

Federal grant funding for the program, totaling about $16 billion annually (with states putting in another more than $10 billion), had not changed since the program's creation. The Congressional Research Service estimated the grants' value, adjusted for inflation, had dropped by 36 percent in the intervening years.

Congress had last reauthorized TANF in the Deficit Reduction Act of 2005 (PL 109-171), and that authorization expired in 2010. Since then, Congress had renewed the program through more than two dozen short-term extensions, with the most recent extension (PL 114-254) scheduled to expire April 28, 2017.

On April 28, 2017, President Trump signed a measure into law (HJ Res 99, PL 115-30) that provided short-term government funding, including a provision to extend TANF funding through May 5, 2017. Then on May 5, 2017, the president signed into law a fiscal 2017 omnibus spending package (HR 244, PL 115-31) that extended the program's

authorizations and funding through September 30, 2018. That law also required the Department of Health and Human Services and the Department of Labor to develop a database of research projects analyzing services that aimed to move more TANF recipients into the workforce.

On May 24, 2018, the House Ways and Means Committee approved, in a 22–14 party-line vote, a measure (HR 5861) that would have reauthorized Temporary Assistance for Needy Families (TANF) through fiscal 2023 and changed how states managed the funds.

The bill, introduced by Adrian Smith, R-Neb., would have extended the authorization for family assistance grants and other grants related to responsible parenting, reentry services for incarcerated parents, and relationship skills training for married couples. The bill also would have limited eligibility to families with incomes below 200 percent of the federal poverty level. And rather than set work participation requirements on individuals, states would have had to meet certain employment outcome standards.

The bill would have continued the program's requirement that recipients work a minimum number of hours (usually twenty or thirty hours a week for single parents), and it would have allowed states more flexibility to spend funds on education and training. The measure also would have increased by 21 percent, to $3.5 billion annually from $2.9 billion in fiscal 2018, funding for states to provide childcare assistance. Democrats, however, said the bill did not specify that child-care assistance was a core tenet of the TANF program or an activity necessary to help recipients continue to work. Democrats also objected that the measure's funding authorization would not increase for TANF programs. When the bill languished after committee approval, House and Senate leaders extended the program's funding through December 7, 2018, in a continuing resolution (HR 6157), which the president signed into law on September 28, 2018 (PL 115-245).

Sen. Steve Daines, R-Mont., in November 2018 introduced a bill (S 3692) that was similar to the House reauthorization measure but also would have required states to penalize recipients who did not comply with work requirements. Daines said the country appeared to be suffering a worker shortage rather than a job shortage. "As my good friend, House Ways and Means Committee Chair Kevin Brady has said, 'We have gone from a country that asks where are the jobs to one that now asks where are the workers,'" Daines said on the Senate floor December 6, 2018.

On December 4, 2018, Senate Finance Chair Orrin G. Hatch, R-Utah, and ranking member Ron Wyden, D-Ore., introduced a narrower measure (S 3700) that would have authorized funding for up to ten demonstration projects that aimed to better collect information on welfare recipients and determine the best strategies to increase employment, earnings, and family stability.

The Senate measure also would have required states to have at least 20 percent of their recipients working or in job-training programs starting in fiscal 2021. Existing

rules allowed states, under certain conditions, to have no work requirements.

The Senate and House did not take up the reauthorization bills before the end of the session. Instead, negotiators agreed to extend authorization and funding for the program in a two-week government funding measure (HJ Res 143). On December 6, 2018, the House passed the measure by unanimous consent, and the Senate cleared the measure for the president's signature the same day. On December 7, 2018, the president signed the measure into law (PL 115-298).

The TANF program authorization and funding lapsed when the latest funding measure expired and triggered a partial government shutdown. The funding lapse, however, did not immediately impact welfare recipients because the latest quarterly grants had been distributed to states.

SUPPLEMENTAL ASSISTANCE NUTRITION PROGRAM (SNAP)

On December 20, 2018, President Trump signed into law (HR 2, PL 115-224) a measure that reauthorized the food stamp program through fiscal 2023. The measure, which renewed a series of federal agricultural programs, did not include expanded work requirements for food stamp recipients as the administration and congressional Republicans had desired. The Supplemental Nutrition Assistance Program (SNAP) provided food stamp benefits for more than 40 million individuals, most of them children, elderly, or disabled.

The House Agriculture Committee on April 18 approved, on a 26–20 party-line vote, a bill (HR 2) that would reauthorize SNAP for five years. The committee's bill, introduced by Rep. K. Michael Conaway, R-Texas, also would have imposed new eligibility criteria and work requirements on certain food stamp recipients. The current work requirements, contained in the welfare reform law passed in 1996 (PL 104-193), limited food stamp benefits to three months out of every thirty-six months for able-bodied individuals who did not work or attend work training a minimum of twenty hours a week. Under the same law, states or territories with high unemployment rates could request waivers from the requirements and thereby exempt able-bodied adults from the time limits on benefits.

On June 21, 2018, the House passed HR2, which included provisions to limit eligibility for food stamps. The Senate passed the bill June 28, 2018, but did not include the changes to eligibility requirements. The bill cleared for the president also did not include changes to eligibility or work requirements.

On December 20, 2018, hours before President Trump signed the so-called farm bill, Agriculture Secretary Sonny Perdue announced plans to propose a rule that would restrict states' abilities to exempt from work requirements any SNAP recipients, ages eighteen to forty-nine, who are "able-bodied adults" without dependents. The rule was formally proposed in February 2019, and finalized on December 5, 2019.

Overtime Pay

Congress and the administration failed to resolve long-term partisan disputes over how businesses should compensate employees who work more than forty hours in a week, while a federal district judge ruled against implementation of an Obama administration rule on overtime.

CONGRESSIONAL ACTION

On April 26, 2017, the House Education and the Workforce Committee approved, 22–16, a measure (HR 1180) that would have allowed private employers to offer workers compensatory time off rather than overtime pay for extra hours worked. Workers eligible for overtime could choose between more pay or compensatory time. Under the measure, workers who chose compensatory time but did not use it after a year could have received overtime pay for unused hours. During the markup, Republicans rejected several Democratic amendments, including a proposal by Blunt Rochester of Delaware that would have required employers to allow workers to earn seven paid days of sick leave. Another amendment, by Suzanne Bonamici of Oregon, would have enabled workers to earn interest on their pay if they did not take their compensatory time off and received pay instead. The committee rejected both amendments in party line, 16–22 votes.

The bill, sponsored by Rep. Martha Roby, R-Ala., would have amended the Fair Labor Standards Act of 1938 (PL 75-718). The House in previous years had passed similar versions of the bill.

On May 2, the House passed the bill in a largely party-line vote of 229–197. Republicans said the measure would allow workers to spend more time with their families, but Democrats argued that the measure still would not allow workers to decide when to use their compensatory time, leaving that to the discretion of employers.

Sen. Mike Lee, R-Utah, introduced a companion measure (S 801) in the Senate. Lamar Alexander, R-Tenn., chair of the Health, Education, Labor and Pensions Committee, said he supported the bill, but Sen. Patty Murray of Washington, the committee's ranking Democrat, said it would hurt workers.

"This is nothing but a recycled bad bill that would allow big corporations to make an end-run around giving workers the pay they've earned," Murray told *CQ Roll Call* after the House passed the measure. "That's wrong, and it's the opposite of what President Trump said he'd do on the campaign trail when he promised to put workers first."

She and other bill critics said that, instead, the GOP should back Democrat-sponsored bills that would hike the minimum wage, ensure workers sick leave (HR 1516), and create a national paid leave insurance program

(HR 947)—Democratic proposals that the House ultimately never acted on.

Several pro-labor groups strongly opposed Roby's measure, including The Leadership Conference on Civil and Human Rights, the AFL-CIO and Service Employees International Union, among others. But the Society of Human Resource Management and the pro-business Workforce Fairness Institute, among other groups, backed the measure.

The Senate bill did not see action.

LABOR DEPARTMENT RULE

During the previous session of Congress, the Obama administration had finalized a rule that aimed to increase the number of workers eligible for overtime pay. The rule essentially doubled, to $47,476, the annual salary level at which all workers would have to be issued overtime pay, equated to at least time-and-a-half for more than forty hours worked. Beginning in 2020, the salary cap would be adjusted for inflation.

House and Senate Republicans in the previous Congress had been moving to halt the rule's implementation, scheduled for December 1, 2016, when a federal district court judge in Texas imposed a temporary injunction that barred the rule from taking effect. A case filed by twenty-one states and a coalition of business groups then moved to the Fifth Circuit Court of Appeals.

In August 2017, U.S. District Judge Amos L. Mazzant halted the rule, saying the overtime regulation would override Congress' intent that eligibility for overtime pay should be dependent on a worker's job duties. Labor Secretary Alexander Acosta in 2017 said he was interested in increasing the ceiling of $23,660, set in 2004, but he said the Obama administration's rule went too high. The Justice Department in October said it planned to appeal the ruling in hopes of giving the Labor Department more flexibility in rewriting the regulation, but the Labor Department later said it would revise Obama's rule.

Foreign Worker Visas

In 2017 and 2018, Congress repeatedly gave the Homeland Security and Labor departments authority to increase H2-B visas for nonagricultural foreign workers to help seasonal industries such as seafood processing and landscaping, as negotiations to permanently expand the H-2B program failed. In the meantime, in April 2017, Trump signed an executive order he said would compel U.S. companies to hire more American workers and fewer immigrants.

BACKGROUND

The H-2 temporary worker program, designed for foreign workers filling temporary or seasonal jobs in the United States, was originally created by the Immigration and Nationality Act (INA) in 1952 (PL 82-414) and later amended by the Immigration Reform and Control Act of 1986 (PL 99-603). The INA limited the number of H-2B visas to 66,000 annually, exempting from the cap workers seeking a visa extension, change of employer, or change in employment terms.

In December 2016, Congress had reauthorized the program for four years and authorized another 1,500 visas for the next year. By May, more than 15,000 Afghans had applied. During Trump's presidential campaign, he had criticized the H-2B visa program, saying it encouraged companies to import cheap foreign labor rather than hire American workers.

FISCAL 2017 H-2B VISA INCREASE

In May 2017, negotiators in the House and Senate announced the fiscal 2017 omnibus spending bill (HR 244) would allow the Department of Homeland Security and the Department of Labor discretion to expand visa programs for seasonal industries, such as landscaping and seafood processing.

The bill also would provide another 2,500 visas under the Special Immigrant Visa program for Afghans who served as interpreters or provided other assistance to U.S. military after 9/11 attacks and who faced retribution from the Taliban. Due to a shortage of visas, the State Department had had to stop interviewing visa applicants in Kabul. The omnibus also would extend through the end of September the EB-5 visa program, which allowed foreign nationals to obtain a green card after investing at least $500,000 in a U.S. construction project that created jobs.

The House passed the measure on May 3. The Senate passed the measure on May 4, 2017. President Trump signed the bill into law (PL 115-31) on May 5, 2017.

The bill gave the Department of Homeland Security (DHS) limited discretion to issue visas beyond the annual cap. In June 2017, the Homeland Security Department said it would approve more work visas for seasonal employers in industries such as skiing, seafood, horse racing, landscaping, and hospitality. On July 17, 2017, Homeland Secretary John F. Kelley said the department would approve another 15,000 H-2B visas. (DHS had issued an additional 13,382 visas under leeway granted by the fiscal 2016 spending legislation.)

The H-2B Workforce Coalition, a group of hotels, restaurants and other seasonal businesses, said in July 2017 that the provision of another 15,000 visas was likely "too little too late" for businesses struggling to keep up with summer business. But program opponents, such as the Economic Policy Institute, said employers were not doing enough to attract American workers.

FISCAL 2018 INCREASE

The House on March 22, 2018, passed the fiscal 2018 omnibus (HR 1625), which would allow the Labor and Homeland Security departments to authorize more H-2B temporary work visas, above the cap of 66,000.

The language was similar to that included in the fiscal 2017 spending package.

The omnibus also would reauthorize for five months the EB-5 program, which had been plagued by allegations of waste, fraud, and abuse. Senate Judiciary Chair Charles E. Grassley, R-Iowa, said the program benefited wealthy cities such as New York City. In addition, the omnibus would reauthorize, for one year, two other immigration visa programs: the Conrad 30 program for foreign doctors working at rural hospitals and the Special Immigrant Religious Workers programs for ministers and other religious workers. It also would reauthorize, for three years, the E-Verify program, which allowed companies to verify their workers or potential hires were eligible to work in the United States.

The Senate passed the bill March 23, and the president signed it into law (PL 115-141) on the same day. The Department of Homeland Security announced on May 25, 2018, it would issue another 15,000 visas for remainder of fiscal 2018.

Meanwhile, members of both parties in the House remained frustrated that they could not pass a permanent boost in H-2B visas. In June 2018, William Keating, D-Mass., and Andy Harris, R-Md., said they would form a bipartisan coalition to boost visas permanently from 66,000 each fiscal year. "By not reforming this program, Congress is really turning their backs on local businesses," Keating said. But opponents to a permanent increase said the visas take away jobs from Americans, and Congress did not take up any legislation that would have provided a permanent boost.

EXECUTIVE ORDER

In April 2017, Trump signed an executive order, called "Buy America, Hire America," that ordered all government departments and agencies to enforce regulations on immigration fraud and proposed reforming the H-1B program to prioritize visas for the "most skilled or highest paid applicants." Under the existing system, applicants were selected in a lottery system, and Republicans had long sought to move away from such a system. Explaining the executive order, administration officials said program fees could be raised and priority could be given to applicants who hold master's degrees, for instance.

SECRETARIES OF LABOR

President Trump's two secretaries of Labor during his administration—R. Alexander Acosta (2017–2019) and Eugene Scalia (2019–2020)—shared Republicans' desire to reduce the regulatory burden on employers and worked to roll back or revise Obama-era rules on overtime pay, employer liability, and workplace safety while facing strong criticism from Democrats and labor groups for not prioritizing workers' rights and well-being. Acosta, a forty-eight-year-old former dean of Florida International University's law school and former assistant attorney general, was the first Hispanic to be confirmed to Trump's cabinet. "Alex is going to be a key part of achieving our goal of revitalizing the American economy, manufacturing and labor force," Trump said when he announced the nomination in February 2017.

Acosta had served as a National Labor Relations Board member from 2002 to 2003 under President George W. Bush. Later he served as assistant attorney general for the Justice Department's civil rights division during the Bush administration, then as U.S. attorney for the Southern District of Florida. While serving as U.S. attorney, Acosta's office had prosecuted lobbyist Jack Abramoff, terrorism suspect Jose Padilla, and founders of the Cali cartel. He was credited for the 2009 conviction of Charles Taylor Jr., son of Liberia's former leader, for torture.

But Acosta faced criticism for supporting a state-based plea deal offered to New York billionaire Jeffrey Epstein in 2008 to resolve a federal investigation into accusations that Epstein had paid underage girls for sexual acts. Acosta said the plea deal, which ensured Epstein would not face federal charges, was appropriate based on the evidence at the time. Acosta noted the deal required Epstein to register as a sex offender and serve thirteen months in jail.

During Acosta's confirmation hearing on March 22, Democrats raised concerns about Epstein's plea deal as well as about a 2008 Justice Department investigation that concluded, while Acosta was in charge of the Justice Department's civil rights division in southern Florida, he had ignored signs employees were being hired and assessed based on political affiliations. Many Democrats said they worried Acosta would allow conservative ideologues to shape the Labor department. Acosta replied, "As a former prosecutor, I will always be on the side of the law and not any particular constituency." The Senate on April 27, 2017, confirmed Acosta's nomination in a 60–38 vote, with eight Democrats and one independent voting in favor.

During Acosta's more than two years in office, he completed or nearly finished several top initiatives of the administration, including a new rule that raised the annual salary level at which all workers would have to be paid overtime for time worked beyond forty hours a week. The rule set a cap at $35,568, lower than the $47,476 cap set by an Obama rule that a federal judge had struck down in 2017.

Under Acosta, the Labor Department in April 2019 also proposed a rule to limit employers' liability for labor

law violations committed by contractors or franchisees. The rule would state, for example, when a locally owned McDonald's could challenge the McDonald's Corporation over compliance with minimum wage or overtime laws. The final rule went into effect on March 15, 2020, and immediately faced legal challenges.

The department also released a proposed rule to allow sixteen- and seventeen-year-old workers to operate devices to help lift hospital and nursing home patients, reversing a 2010 Obama-era rule that forbade teenagers from operating such devices. Labor groups and some Democrats warned the proposal could put teenagers at risk, but the administration and nursing home industry said it would create new job opportunities. The administration dropped the proposal in late 2019.

In June 2018, Acosta's Labor Department issued a rule that aimed to allow small businesses to band together and pool their employees under the same health insurance plan and thereby allow for lower premiums. Many Democrats, consumer advocates and the industry, however, criticized such plans because they would not be required to cover the ten categories of benefits required under the 2010 health care law (PL 111-148, PL 111-152). In April 2019, a federal judge struck down the rule.

Acosta also oversaw the development of a new Industry-Recognized Apprenticeship program, a Trump priority that aimed to allow more industries to develop and oversee on-the-job training programs with less government red tape. The program drew strong criticism from Democrats and labor groups who said the new system would not guarantee high-quality programs.

In July 2019, controversy over Acosta's handling of the 2008 sex crimes case involving Epstein resurfaced when federal prosecutors in Manhattan brought new child sex trafficking charges against Epstein. Controversy also swirled around Trump's past friendship with Epstein. On July 12, 2019, Acosta announced his resignation. "He felt the constant drumbeat of press about a prosecution which took place under his watch more than twelve years ago was bad for the Administration, which he so strongly believes in, and he graciously tendered his resignation," the president said on Twitter after appearing with Acosta at the White House. "This was him, not me," the president said of Acosta's decision to resign. He said Acosta had been a "great, great secretary."

Trump immediately named Acosta's deputy, Patrick Pizzella, to serve as acting secretary of Labor. Pizzella served as assistant secretary of labor under President George W. Bush and on the Federal Labor Relations Authority during Obama's term. He then nominated Eugene Scalia, fifty-six, son of late Supreme Court Justice Antonin Scalia, to serve as Labor secretary. Scalia was a partner in the corporate law firm Gibson, Dunn & Crutcher LLP. In the late 1990s and 2000s, he helped defend UPS against claims brought under the Americans with Disabilities Act in two cases.

He also helped represent SeaWorld after a killer whale attacked and killed a trainer in 2010 and the Occupational Safety and Health Administration (OSHA) determined that Sea World should have done more to protect workers. Bush had installed Scalia as Labor Department solicitor under a recess appointment in 2001. Scalia served in that role until 2003.

The Senate on September 26, 2019, confirmed Scalia's nomination in a 53–44 party-line vote. Before the vote, Republicans praised Scalia's work record. Lamar Alexander, R-Tenn., said "Eugene Scalia is well qualified to lead the Department of Labor with a steady hand at a time when workers' wages are up and unemployment is near record lows."

But Democrats criticized him for challenging administrative rules on behalf of businesses. Sen. Patty Murray, D-Wash., said Trump had "nominated a secretary of corporate interest," and criticized Scalia for his opposition to overtime rules, regulations on tipping practices and ergonomics (a Clinton-era rule designed to reduce repetitive stress injuries, which Congress later reversed), among other issues. During the confirmation hearing, Murray urged Scalia to put on hold the administration's proposed rules on overtime and joint employer liability, but Scalia refused.

Scalia soon was in the center of debate about extending unemployment benefits at the start of the coronavirus pandemic in 2020 and as the unemployment rate spiked. He repeatedly praised and defended the president's handling of the pandemic, and in June 2020 began to urge lawmakers to consider changing course on jobless benefits as the Labor Department had released a strong jobs report. He also defended OSHA's handling of workplace safety complaints amid the pandemic.

In December 2020, Scalia's department issued a final rule that allowed some contractors to discriminate against racial and religious minorities, women, and LGBTQ people in order to protect "religious liberty." The rule specifically said "religious organizations" that served as federal contractors would not have to comply with nondiscrimination and affirmative action requirements.

Before the White House changed hands in early January 2021, Scalia faced complaints from a Labor Department attorney who was leading a lawsuit against Oracle America Inc. Janet Herold, a regional attorney on the West Coast, complained Scalia meddled in the case to help Oracle, a Silicon Valley company closely aligned with Trump, and in December 2020 had tried to transfer her to a nonlegal post at a different Labor agency in Chicago. After Herold refused the transfer, Scalia fired her, nine days before the end of the Trump administration's term. The lawsuit against Oracle had been initiated in the final days of the Obama administration and sought $400 million for alleged systematic pay discrimination against female and minority employees.

2019–2020

Following the 2018 elections, Democrats took over the House and reignited efforts to increase worker protections, boost the minimum wage, expand overtime pay, and provide pay equity for female workers, for example. But such measures did not gain traction in the GOP-controlled Senate. The White House and Republicans also continued to push for restrictions on benefits for the unemployed and low-income workers while boosting job training.

But when the coronavirus pandemic began in early 2020, Congress and the White House turned their attention to providing expanded unemployment and welfare benefits to Americans as many businesses temporarily shuttered or laid off employees amid government-mandated quarantines. The unemployment rate, which had dropped to 3.6 percent by the end of 2019, began to rise again in March 2020, reaching a high of 13.3 percent in May before slowly dropping and reaching 6.7 percent by December 2020.

Welfare Benefits

During the 116th Congress, lawmakers continued to extend funding for the Temporary Assistance for Needy Families (TANF) program through short-term extensions to ensure continued cash-assistance benefits for low-income individuals and move them toward self-sufficiency. The previous extension (PL 115-298) expired December 21, 2018, after which TANF authorization expired briefly. The federal program provided quarterly payments to states, which were using reserves from previous payments or advancing their shares to the program so they could continue to support recipients. By the time the president signed another short-term reauthorization in late January, some observers said about half of states had run through their federal reserves or were close to running out.

House Ways and Means Committee Chair Richard E. Neal, D-Mass., and ranking member Kevin Brady, R-Texas, introduced a bill (HR 430) that would reauthorize the program for six months, through June 30, 2019. The House on January 14, 2019, passed the bill by voice vote. The Senate passed the measure by voice vote on January 22, 2019, and the president signed the measure into law (PL 116-4) on January 24, 2019.

On March 11, 2019, President Trump's fiscal 2020 budget proposal included provisions to scale back TANF, reducing block grants to states by 10 percent and eliminating the program's contingency fund that was created to help states provide residents emergency assistance during economic downturns. The White House's budget request said the proposed changes would ensure "states allocate sufficient funds to work, education and training activities," and that the changes would save $20.8 billion over ten years. Congress did not act on the proposed reductions as

it continued to provide short-term authorizations for TANF funding through the following measures:

- HR 2940, which extended program funding through September 30, 2019. The president signed the measure into law (PL 116-27) on July 5, 2019
- HR 4378, a short-term continuing resolution that included a provision to extend TANF funding through November 21, 2019. The president signed the bill into law (PL 116-59) on September 27, 2019
- HR 3055, a short-term continuing resolution, extended TANF funding through December 20, 2019. The president signed the measure into law (PL 116-69) on November 21, 2019
- HR 1865, a short-term continuing resolution to fund the government, which extended TANF funding through May 20, 2020. The president signed the measure into law (PL 116-94) on December 20, 2019
- HR 748, a measure that created the Coronavirus Relief Fund, extended TANF funding through November 30, 2020. The president signed the measure into law (PL 116-136) on March 27, 2020
- HR 8337, a short-term continuing resolution, extended TANF funding through December 11, 2020. The president signed the bill into law (PL 116-159) on October 1, 2020
- HR 8900, a short-term continuing resolution, extended TANF funding through December 18, 2020. The president signed it into law (PL 116-215) on December 11, 2020
- HJ Res 107, a short-term continuing resolution, extended TANF funding through December 20, 2020. The president signed it into law (PL 116-225) on December 18, 2020
- HJ Res 110, a short-term continuing resolution, extended TANF funding through December 21, 2020. The president signed it into law (PL 116-226) on December 20, 2020
- HR 1520, a short-term funding bill, extended TANF funding through December 28, 2020. The president signed it into law (PL 116-246) on December 22, 2020
- An omnibus spending package (HR 133) extended the programs through September 30, 2021. The president signed the measure into law (PL 116-260) on December 27, 2020

REAUTHORIZATION ATTEMPTS

Sen. Orrin Hatch, R-Utah, who had coauthored the Senate bill the previous session, had retired and his coauthor, Sen. Ron Wyden, D-Ore., did not resume the effort to complete a TANF reauthorization bill in the next Congress. Steve Daines, R-Mont., and Rep. Kevin Brady, R-Tex., introduced

companion measures in the House and Senate that were similar to a bill Brady had pushed through the House Ways and Means Committee in 2018.

Daines said on the Senate floor on March 13, 2019, that "a strong revitalized TANF program is urgently needed to close" the gap between the number of job openings and the skilled workers seeking those jobs. He also alleged the law had several loopholes that undercut its work requirements for recipients. The bills would have reauthorized the program until September 30, 2024, and would have increased childcare funding to $3.5 billion annually, up from $2.9 billion. It also would have required all able-bodied adults to participate in work-related activities for a minimum number of hours per month, and would have required individuals and case managers to develop employment goals and possible substance or mental health treatment programs for benefit recipients.

The measures also would have restricted TANF funds to help families earning below 200 percent of the federal poverty level, which was $42,660 for a family of three in 2019. Neither the House nor the Senate took up the measures.

Worker Training

APPRENTICESHIP PROGRAMS

The Trump administration issued a final rule to create a new apprenticeship program, parallel to an existing Labor Department program that Congress tried but failed to expand and reauthorize through fiscal 2025.

Labor Department Rule

Responding to a 2017 executive order, the Department of Labor in June 2019 proposed a rule to create Industry-Recognized Apprenticeship Programs, workforce training programs that included paid work and instruction to prepare individuals to work in a specific industry and occupation.

Finalized in March 2020, the rule set out criteria and steps for Labor to approve third-party entities—industry groups and unions, for instance—which would have authority to authorize and oversee apprentice programs. The system was designed as an alternative to the registered apprenticeship system. The rule took effect on May 11, 2020, and on September 23, 2020, the Labor Department announced it had approved eighteen "standards recognition entities" that would recognize apprenticeship programs in twenty industries and nearly 130 occupations. The first such apprenticeship program was announced October 1, 2020.

Controversy surrounded the creation of an industry-recognized apprenticeship program, with some critics saying the new system would allow creation of apprenticeship programs of varying quality. Many industry groups, however, applauded the system for reducing red tape. The rule initially excluded apprenticeship programs for the construction industry until a backlash from the industry forced Trump to back down.

House Bill

Meanwhile, on November 20, 2020, the House passed, 246–140, legislation (HR 8294) that would have reauthorized, and expanded, a Labor Department apprenticeship program through 2025. The program had changed little since it was first authorized in 1937.

The House Education and Labor Committee had approved the bill on September 24 in a 26–16 party-line vote. The measure would have expanded the program to cover preapprenticeships and youth apprenticeships and would outline workplace standards for such programs.

The measure would have authorized a $400 million grant program supporting apprenticeships for fiscal 2021. The amount would have increased to $800 million by fiscal 2025. Rep. Robert C. Scott, D-Va., the panel's chair, said during the September 24 markup, "There is no better time than now to invest in this proven program to help people get back to work as tens of millions of workers continue to receive unemployment benefits each week." Republicans wanted provisions that would support programs regardless of whether they were registered with the Labor Department, saying that would allow for more flexibility and innovation.

Before approving the measure, the committee adopted by voice vote two amendments with bipartisan support. The committee approved an amendment by Elise Stafanik, R-N.Y., that would ensure apprenticeship programs were included in lists of state eligible workforce training providers. The committee also approved an amendment by Rep. Dusty Johnson, R-S.D., which was further amended by Susan Wild, D-Pa., to direct the Labor secretary to create rules outlining a process for creating standards and requirements for various occupations eligible for the apprenticeship program.

House Rules Committee ranking member Tom Cole, R-Okla., said, "Democrats have . . . doubled down on the system as it is, not as it could be." Rep. Susan A. Davis, D-Calif., who introduced the bill, said she favors innovation, but believed funding should be directed toward programs that had been proven to work. The Senate did not act on the bill, and members vowed to reintroduce it in the 117th Congress.

Civilian Conservation Corp

In May 2019, the Trump administration said it would end the Job Corps Civilian Conservation Centers (CCC), laying off 1,100 employees, but the next month scrapped such plans amid bipartisan backlash. The CCC program, established in 1964, each year trained an estimated 4,000 individuals between the ages of sixteen and twenty-four to fight wildfires, help with disaster recovery, and handle other conservation jobs on public lands. At the same time,

the young workers earned GED diplomas and certifications in vocational trainings.

More than fifty lawmakers, including at least a dozen Republicans, wrote to Trump to urge him not to lay off workers in the civilian corps. The president immediately backed off the proposal.

Employee Discrimination

Democrats failed to push through Congress measures to protect pregnant workers and older workers from employment discrimination. Legislation to provide protection for female workers or job applicants facing discrimination due to pregnancy had been introduced in every session of Congress since 2012 but repeatedly failed due to a lack of bipartisan support. Such measures aimed to strengthen the Pregnancy Discrimination Act of 1978 (PL 95-555), passed as an amendment to the 1964 Civil Rights Act (PL 88-352).

On January 14, 2020, the House Education and Labor Committee approved, 29–17, a measure (HR 2694) that would have provided protections for pregnant workers. The bill would have required employers with at least fifteen employees to make accommodations for workers whose performance otherwise may be limited due to pregnancy, childbirth, or related medical conditions.

In 2015, the Supreme Court ruled in *Young v. UPS* (575 U.S. 206), that pregnant workers could bring claims against employers for not providing reasonable accommodations. However, under the ruling, workers had to prove they were denied accommodations provided to other workers with similar inabilities, said Rep. Robert C. Scott, D-Va. The bill would have provided pregnant workers the same protections provided other workers—based on race, color, religion, sex, or national origin—under the Civil Rights Act.

Two committee Republicans, Rep. Elise Stefanik of New York and James R. Comer of Kentucky, supported the bill. Other Republicans complained the bill did not provide any exemptions based on religious beliefs. Democrats said such exemptions would unfairly subject pregnant women to discrimination, including women whose employers did not support same-sex marriage, pregnancy out of wedlock, or abortion.

The committee rejected, 17–27, a substitute amendment by ranking member Virginia Foxx, R-N.C. that would have outlined religious exemptions. The House on September 21, 2020, approved the measure by a vote of 329–73, with 103 Republicans supporting it. The Senate did not take up the legislation.

The House also passed, 261–155, a measure (HR 1230) that would have protected older workers from discrimination. The measure, approved 27–18, by the Education and Workforce Committee on June 11, 2019, would have clarified federal employment laws to allow older workers to file claims against employers for discriminatory practice.

Republicans argued the bill would make it too easy for workers to allege discrimination. The Senate did not act on the bill.

Minimum Wage

Democrats also resumed their long-term campaign to boost the federal minimum wage, which had not been increased since 2009, when it was set at $7.25 per hour. Overcoming some sharp differences between progressive and moderate Democrats, the House on July 18, 2018, passed, 231–199, a measure (HR 582) that would have increased the minimum wage to $15 per hour over six years. The GOP-led Senate, however, did not act on an identical measure introduced by Sen. Bernie Sanders, I-Vt.

For years, Democrats had pushed to increase the minimum wage. More recently, fast-food workers and others were walking off their jobs in protest of wages, raising further awareness of the issue.

Several states also had increased their minimum wage. For example, New Jersey in January 2019 enacted a measure to boost its minimum wage to $10, and to $15 by 2024. California, Massachusetts, New York City, and the District of Columbia were scheduled for similar increases. Several other cities also were looking at boosts in their minimum hourly wages.

The Congressional Budget Office (CBO) reported in July 2018 that if the minimum wage was doubled to $15 per hour, fewer citizens would live in poverty but such a mandate on employers also could result in the loss of 1.3 million jobs by 2025. Democrats and Republicans used the CBO report to attack or support the legislation.

"That's literally the entire state of Oklahoma," Minority White Steve Scalise, R-La., said in a July 16, 2019, statement about the estimated job loss. But House Speaker Nancy Pelosi, D-Calif., said at a press briefing on July 18 that the measure would give "up to 33 million Americans a long overdue raise."

On March 6, 2019, the House Education and Labor Committee approved, 28–20, the measure (HR 582) to boost the minimum wage in a party-line vote. Before approving the measure, Democrats rejected, 20–28, an amendment by Rick W. Allen, R-Ga., that would have barred wage increases unless the unemployment rate for workers ages sixteen to twenty-four was below 8 percent during the previous year. Democrats similarly rejected six other Republican amendments that aimed, among other things, to create exemptions for small businesses and delay enactment of the measure until the effects of minimum wage increases were further studied.

The original measure, introduced by committee Chair Robert C. Scott, D-Va., would have gradually increased the wage to $15 per hour over five years. Some Democrats, however, said the five-year timeline could be too short for some states or regions where the cost of living, as well as income, was lower. Before the House approved the measure,

WORKPLACE SAFETY

The Trump administration and Republicans in Congress, in an effort to ease government regulation of businesses, moved to reduce workplace safety mandates on employers, raising concerns among labor unions and employees in a range of industries, particularly amid the spread of the coronavirus in 2020.

In early 2017, Republicans used the Congressional Review Act, a 1996 law that allows Congress to rescind agency rules without the possibility of a Senate filibuster, to roll back several Occupational Safety and Health Administration (OSHA) regulations created by the Obama administration, including

- A rule that expanded record-keeping requirements for workplace injuries and illnesses. On March 1, the House passed, 231–191, a resolution (HJ Res 83) that would end the rule under the Congressional Review Act. On March 22, 2017, the Senate passed the resolution in a 50–48 vote, and the president signed it into law (PL 115-21) on April 3, 2017
- A rule that required potential federal contractors to report violations of federal laws—a so-called blacklist rule. The House on February 2, 2017, passed, by 236–187, the resolution (HJ Res 37) to nullify the rule. The Senate passed the measure in a 49–48 vote on March 6, and the president signed it into law (PL 115-11) on March 27, 2017
- A rule limiting drug testing for unemployment compensation applicants. The House passed, 236–189, the resolution (HJ Res 42) to nullify the rule on February 15, 2017. The Senate cleared the resolution in a 51–48 vote on March 14, 2017. The president signed the measure into law (PL 115-17) on March 31, 2017

Meanwhile, OSHA focused on a less punitive approach to encourage businesses to comply with workplace safety requirements. Under President Obama, OSHA had favored an approach called "regulation by shaming" to crackdown on workplace safety violations. Under that approach, OSHA distributed messages to mainstream media and trade publications, as well as through its website, about a company's violations.

Under Trump, OSHA focused on helping businesses find best safety solutions, a method called "compliance assistance," rather than hand out enforcement regulations or shame businesses in the media. Trump made lists of workplace citations less prominent and removed names of injured workers from OSHA's website, while emphasizing tips for safer practices in the workplace and distributing information on voluntary compliance programs.

In 2017, the Trump administration delayed implementation of new beryllium and silica standards, but ultimately left both in place. The administration also halted work on rules to control combustible dust, protect workers from violence, limit the spread of infectious disease, and update exposure limits for a variety of chemicals. In addition, the administration revised other Obama-era regulations, such as rules on hard rock mining inspections, to reduce regulatory burdens on employers and reduce administrative costs. And Trump disbanded or sidelined five volunteer workplace safety panels that advised Labor on how to improve health and safety for workers.

After the start of the coronavirus pandemic, and as the virus quickly spread, thousands of workplace safety complaints were filed with OSHA. In May, Loren Sweatt, principal deputy assistant secretary for OSHA, said investigators had pursued almost 2,000 COVID-19 complaints, and issued one citation. But as with other workplace safety initiatives, the Trump administration said it was relying on guidance it provided to employers, rather than immediate fines or new rules specifically addressing the coronavirus.

Republicans supported such an approach, but Democrats argued employers had a responsibility to keep workers safe. Rep. Andy Levin, D-Mich., told the House Education and Labor Committee on May 18, 2020, that about 300 health care workers had died of coronavirus-related illnesses during the pandemic, and that three-quarters of OSHA inspections over the relevant period had been triggered by deaths. "To put it bluntly, OSHA is stepping in only once someone has died," Levin said. "Every day I get calls from workers who are terrified that they will become sick in their workplaces. Many worry not for their own lives, but for the lives of sick or elderly family members they reside with and support."

Levin criticized OSHA for not issuing an emergency temporary standard on infectious disease control. An Obama-era initiative, launched after the 2009 H1N1 pandemic, developed an infectious disease standard for work sites. Staff prepared a modified version when the coronavirus struck, but it was ignored, according to *The New Yorker*. And a National Employment Law Project report published in April 2020 concluded OSHA had fewer inspectors than it had had in forty-five years, and 42 percent of agency leadership positions were vacant.

On April 28, in a letter, AFL-CIO President Richard Trumka said the department's response to the pandemic

(Continued)

WORKPLACE SAFETY (Continued)

was "delinquent, delayed, disorganized, chaotic and totally inadequate." The next month, the labor union filed a lawsuit in the U.S. Court of Appeals for the District of Columbia, asking the court to order OSHA to issue an emergency temporary standard (ETC) to control workers' exposure to infectious disease in their workplaces.

Labor Secretary Eugene Scalia said new standards were unnecessary because OSHA already could penalize companies under the General Duty Clause, which requires employers to create a work environment "free from recognized hazards." On May 21, 2020, Sweatt told the House Education and Labor Committee in written testimony that the department had informal guidance for nursing homes, ride share services, meat packers, and other sectors to control the spread of the coronavirus.

Meanwhile, Rep. Robert C. Scott, D-Va., chair of House Education and Labor, introduced a measure (HR 6559)

that would have required the Labor Department to issue a standard for protecting employees from coronavirus in the workplace. His proposal was included in coronavirus relief legislation (HR 6800) the House passed May 15, but the Senate never took up that legislation.

OSHA did issue memorandums, on April 13 and May 19, 2020, announcing two revised enforcement policies, which increased the number of in-person inspections at workplaces and said employers must report a coronavirus case when it was confirmed as COVID-19, was work related, and met other criteria such as requiring first aid or sick days for the employee. The department also clarified that it would not enforce the reporting requirement on employers outside the health care, emergency response, or law enforcement sectors unless there was "objective evidence" the infection was work-related and such evidence was "reasonably available" to the employer.

---

it adopted a bill manager's amendment that extended the timeline to six years.

On the House floor, moderate Democrats considered helping Republicans modify the measure to exempt businesses with fewer than ten employees or an annual gross income of less than $1 million. Members of the Congressional Progressive Caucus threatened to vote against the bill if such language was added, and moderates backed off.

Overtime Pay

In September 2019, the Labor Department issued a rule that capped at $35,568 the annual salary level at which all workers would have to be paid overtime, equated to at least time-and-a half for more than forty hours worked. The rule ended a five-year fight to expand overtime pay to millions of workers.

The rule's salary cap was a boost from the $23,660 limit set in 2004, and was slightly higher than the $35,308 the administration had proposed March 7. But the cap was lower than the $47,476 annual salary limit set by an Obama rule, which a U.S. federal judge struck down in 2017. The Labor Department said Obama's rule would have made 4.2 million workers eligible for overtime pay, while the new rule would make 1.3 million workers eligible.

The Labor Department rule also did not require future changes to the cap to be tied to inflation.

Sen. Patty Murray, D-Wash., ranking member of the Senate Committee on Health, Education, Labor and Pensions, said in a September 24 statement, "This weak rule is a huge step back." Labor groups strongly criticized it, saying the salary threshold was too low. Committee

Chair Lamar Alexander, R-Tenn., issued a statement the same day, calling the rule a "reasonable update."

Pay Equity

The House on March 27, 2019, passed, 242–187, a measure (HR 7) that aimed to eliminate pay equity gaps in the workforce between male and female workers. The Senate did not act on the bill.

The measure would have tightened enforcement of gender discrimination laws, offering grants to train women in salary negotiation and awarding employers who offer equal pay, for example. Seven Republicans supported the bill. The bill would require employers to justify any pay disparity for women by explaining the business reasons for the pay difference. The Labor Department reported that women were making, on average, 80 percent of men's pay for the same job, with women of color making 53 percent and mothers averaging 71 percent of fathers' salaries.

Before passing the measure, lawmakers adopted by voice vote an amendment by Brenda Lawrence, D-Mich., that would require the Labor Department to report to Congress on the gender-based pay gap among teenagers in the labor force. The House passed similar bills in previous years, but no final legislation was enacted.

Foreign Worker Visas

A bipartisan group of House members and senators hoped to reform the visa program for temporary, non-agricultural workers and permanently increase the annual cap of 66,000, set in the Immigration and Nationality Act. Instead, authorization for the H-2B visa program was

extended through fiscal spending bills (HJ Res 31, PL 116-6; HR 1865, PL 116-94), all of which gave the administration some short-term flexibility in offering more visas.

The administration used that authority to issue another 30,000 such visas for fiscal 2019 and another 35,000 for fiscal 2020. Further provisions were made to increase other foreign worker visas during the coronavirus pandemic.

The president on February 15, 2019, signed into law a fiscal 2019 spending package (HJ Res 31, PL 116-6) that extended authorization for several visa programs through the end of the fiscal year, September 30, 2019. The measure also authorized the Homeland Security and Labor Departments to increase the number of H-2B visas, beyond the annual cap, for temporary nonagricultural work.

In March, Sens. Susan Collins, R-Maine, and Angus King, I-Maine, led a bipartisan group that sent a letter to Homeland Security Secretary Kirstjen Nielsen, urging her to increase the visa cap to 135,320, the number that had been available in fiscal 2008. The administration announced May 7 it would issue another 30,000 H-2B visas for fiscal 2019. The visas would only be available to returning workers who had been granted H-2B status during one of past three fiscal years.

Sen. Tom Cotton, R-Ark., criticized the administration's move to offer more visas, saying the U.S. immigration system "should prioritize the needs of U.S. citizens over cheap foreign labor," according to *CQ Roll Call*. But Sen. Chris Van Hollen, D-Md., said seasonal businesses, such as the seafood industry, had been "suffering from a total lack of labor so I support the administration using some authority to lift the cap level."

On May 8, 2019, the House Appropriations Committee approved a fiscal 2020 spending bill for the Labor Department that would have updated the way the federal government awarded H-2B visas to employers. Under the bill, the federal government would have allocated the visas on a quarterly system and would have avoided giving some employers multiple visas when other employers received none.

House leaders merged the labor funding measure into a four-bill omnibus spending package (HR 2740) that included language calling on the State Department to expedite Iraqi Special Immigrant Visa applications for those who had helped U.S. military forces. The measure also would have required the Statement Department inspector general report to evaluate the visa programs for Afghan and Iraqi workers.

That four-bill omnibus was merged into a larger, eight-measure omnibus spending bill (HR 1865) that the House approved on December 17, 2019. The Senate cleared the measure on December 20, 2019.

On December 20, 2019, the president signed the omnibus spending measure into law (PL 116-94). The law reauthorized the H-2B visa program, the EB-5 visa program for immigrant investors, as well as the Conrad 30 Program, which allowed certain foreign medical graduates an extension of the J-1 visa. Another provision reauthorized the E-Verify program that enables employers to confirm that potential foreign workers are eligible to work in the United States. The package also included a provision allowing the Department of Homeland Security to increase H-2B visas.

The next year, on February 26, 2020, a bipartisan group of senators urged Trump to raise the cap on seasonal worker visas again. Less than two weeks later, on March 5, the Homeland Security Department announced it would offer another 35,000 visas. Homeland Security officials would designate about 10,000 of the additional visas for nationals from Guatemala, El Salvador and Honduras, countries that had worked "to stem the flow of illegal migration in the region and encourage lawful migration to the United States," DHS said in a statement on the day of the announcement.

Immigration Restrictions

In April, amid efforts to control the spread of the coronavirus, the administration put in place immigration restrictions that suspended, for at least sixty days, the allocation of green cards to most immigrants seeking to live and work permanently in the United States. The restriction largely targeted families of immigrants not already in the United States.

In April, the Department of Homeland Security, responding to demands from farmers, allowed them to hire more workers who were holding H-2B visas and were already in the United States.

The president on April 28, 2020, signed an executive order invoking the Defense Production Act, declaring meat processing and packing plants part of the nation's critical infrastructure and therefore requiring them to continue operating during the pandemic. The Department of Homeland Security also said the H-2B temporary nonagricultural workers were essential to the food supply chain.

In May, the administration allowed meatpacking plants to rehire current workers who held H-2B visas but whose contracts or visas were expiring and would otherwise have to return home. The intent was to help plants coping with absenteeism and workers quarantined due to Covid-19 exposure. The administration gave employers until September 11, 2020, to enter new contracts.

On June 22, 2020, the White House extended the immigration restrictions it had implemented in April, expanding them to include workers on H-1B specialty visas (for workers in academia and the technology and health sectors). The federal government typically issued about 85,000 H-1B visas annually. The new order also barred people on H-4 visas who were spouses of foreign workers, most types of H-2B non-agricultural worker visas, most J-1 visas for exchange students and visitors, and L-1 visas that allowed companies to transfer foreign workers to U.S. outposts.

A senior administration official said the order would free up about 525,000 jobs. Sara Pierce, policy analyst at the nonpartisan Migration Policy Institute, said in a tweet

on June 22 that it "is beyond misleading to imply that blocking foreign nationals creates jobs 1:1."

On December 27, 2020, the president signed into law a $1.4 trillion fiscal 2021 spending package (HR 133, PL 116-260) that allowed Homeland Security again to increase the number of H-2B visas beyond the 66,000 annual cap. However, employers first would have to prove they tried to hire U.S. residents. The House had passed the bill December 21. The Senate cleared the measure the same day.

Union Rights

On February 6, 2020, the House passed, 224–194, a measure (HR 2474) that would have expanded worker rights under the 1935 National Labor Relations Act. The GOP-led Senate did not take up the measure.

Democrats said the bill would reverse the decline of union membership and boost the middle class, while Republicans said it would benefit labor bosses at the expense of workers. The measure would have extended collective bargaining rights to more workers and enabled the National Labor Relations Board to penalize employers who violate workers' rights.

Democrats noted the National Labor Relations Board did not have authority to levy fines against companies charged with violating workers' rights. The measure would have allowed the board to fine companies up to $50,000 per violation.

The measure also would have allowed more people classified as contractors to be granted employee status for the purposes of union organizing. Such a provision would have allowed workers for companies such as Uber and Lyft to organize among themselves or with other unions.

Rep. Robert C. Scott, D-Va., introduced the measure on May 2, 2019, amid a growing number of strikes among workers, and after California passed a law that granted more rights for contract workers and sparked a national debate about who should be classified as employees. The House measure would have changed who qualified as an employee, rather than as an independent contractor, but only for workers seeking to join a union.

Many business and industry groups lobbied against the bill, saying it would threaten small businesses and limit work opportunities for "gig workers" or independent contractors. The Coalition for a Democratic Workplace, a group of businesses, lobbied against a provision that would have required employers to provide to union leadership certain information on their workers, such as shift information, cellphone numbers, and addresses. Republicans said that requirement would violate privacy laws.

The House Education and Labor Committee passed the bill on September 25, 2019, in a 26–21 vote. Democrats turned back thirty-one GOP amendments that would have, among other things, mandated that union elections occur via secret ballot, required unions to be recertified at regular intervals, and required employees to prove they were legal citizens before joining a union. The committee approved, 27–21, an amendment by Lori Trahan, D-Mass., that would add language stating that suspending or withholding unemployment from an individual in an aim to influence their position in collective bargaining before a strike is an unfair labor practice. An amendment by Josh Harder, D-Calif., adopted 27–21, would impose a $100,000 civil penalty for unfair labor practices related to hiring or employment terms to influence a worker's decision whether to join a union.

"Strong union membership has not only been shown to increase productivity and reduce turnover, it also gives the middle class more purchasing power," Rep. Susan Wild, D-Penn., said during the markup. "Workers deserve a seat at the table because our economy does best when it grows from the middle out and not from the top down." Rep. Virginia Foxx, R-N. Car., ranking member of the Labor Committee, said the bill would impose "many indignities . . . upon American workers." Republican Sen. Lamar Alexander of Tennessee, chair of the Committee on Health, Education, Labor and Pensions, did not put the bill before his committee.

Pension Benefit Plans

Lawmakers failed to find a solution for struggling union pension plans and to lay out a plan to help shore up the Pension Benefit Guarantee Corporation (PBC). Congress did, however, take steps to help the ailing pension plans for miners and carpenters.

In August 2019, the Pension Benefit Guaranty Corporation (PBGC) said about 125 of 1,400 multiemployers plans were expected to become insolvent in 20 years. The plans, which covered 1.4 million people, had suffered from demographic shifts in industries such as in mining and trucking, with fewer workers paying into plans than the number of retirees receiving benefits. The PBGC also was expected to run dry by 2026.

On July 24, 2019, the House passed a $68 billion multiemployer pension bill (HR 397) by a vote of 264–169. The bill would have created a Pension Rehabilitation Administration within the Treasury Department, which would have made thirty-year loans at low interest rates to struggling plans.

The Ways and Means Committee had approved the measure in a 25–17 party-line vote on July 10, 2019. Before approving the measure, Democrats rejected eleven Republican amendments. Among the GOP proposals was an amendment by Jodey C. Arrington of Texas that would have required any pension plan that received a loan under the program to purchase insurance guaranteeing repayment. The committee rejected the amendment in a 17–24 vote.

The House Education and Labor Committee also had jurisdiction on the measure, which it approved in a party-line vote of 26–18 on June 11.

While most Republicans said Congress needed to do something to prevent pension fund failures, they criticized

the House bill as a "bailout." But Democrats said the bill would prevent more than 1 million recipients from losing most of their pension benefits, effects of which would ripple through the economy.

In November, Sens. Chuck Grassley, R-Iowa, and Lamar Alexander, R-Tenn., began drafting a proposal that would include a "front-end federal contribution" to the pension system, but that would provide less funding than the House bill. Still, the House and Senate failed to reach a deal before the end of 2020. Meanwhile, negotiators did include a $6 billion rescue of the failing United Mine Workers of America's pension plan in a consolidated spending bill (HR 1865) the president signed into law (PL 116-94) on December 20, 2020. Also, in a $1.4 trillion government funding and Covid-relief bill (HR 133, PL 116-260), Congress included provisions to help beneficiaries of a carpenters' pension plan that covered about 20,000 Missouri and Illinois employees. The measure reversed an earlier IRS decision that threatened the tax-exempt status of the plan.

The pension plan allowed members of the St. Louis Carpenters' Pension Plan to take early retirement, at age 55, even while continuing to work to train younger workers. The IRS, however, had ruled that benefit violated prior IRS rulings, thus threatening the promised benefits. The omnibus measure, signed by the president December 27, 2020, reversed that IRS ruling, allowing distributions to continue to such early retirees.

Retirement Savings

Congress approved a package of retirement savings incentives for American workers, rolling them into a year-end spending measure (HR 1865) that the president signed into law (PL 116-94) on December 20, 2019. The package, based on a bill (HR 1994) the House passed, 417–3, on May 23, 2019, would allow small companies to band together to form multiemployer retirement plans, such as 401(k) plans, even if the companies were not from the same industry. It also would increase the age requirement, from seventy-and-a-half to seventy-five years, for minimum distributions from such plans. The age limit had not been changed since 1986. The measure also would expand an existing tax credit as well as create a new credit to help small businesses cover the costs of launching plans for the first time.

The House Ways and Means Committee approved the measure (HR 1994) by voice vote on April 2, 2019. Rep. Richard Neal, D-Mass., chair of the committee, called it the largest retirement savings bill since the 2006 pension overhaul (PL 109-280). Neal said statistics indicated 10,000 baby boomers retire every day, the average Social Security benefit was under $18,000 a year, and 55 million Americans were not in a qualified pension plan.

The bill also would require inheritors of traditional Individual Retirement Accounts to withdraw all their funds within ten years, rather than over their projected lifetimes. Since the withdrawals were taxable as income, they would increase heirs' tax liability a total of $15.7 billion over ten years. That provision would not have applied to a spouse inheriting IRAs, and generally would affect the wealthy.

The measure also included a provision that would enable several community newspapers (those servicing cities with populations of 100,000 or fewer) to reduce their pension funding requirements. That provision was estimated to benefit about twenty news companies. The Senate was then poised take up the House bill, rather than a similar bill (S 972), sponsored by Sens. Ron Wyden, D-Ore., and Chuck Grassley, R-Iowa.

Efforts to pass the House bill stalled in the Senate, due to opposition from several lawmakers particularly Patty Murray, D-Wash., and Ted Cruz, R-Texas, who each blocked final action on the bill on the floor. Cruz held up the bill because he was displeased with revisions to a college savings provision in the House bill. Ultimately, congressional leaders rolled provisions of the House bill into the year-end spending bill (PL 116-94).

Unemployment Compensation

The long decline of the national unemployment rate continued through February 2020, then turned abruptly with the start of the coronavirus pandemic and accompanying government-mandated lockdowns. A sharp rise in unemployment claims spurred Congress and the administration to approve a series of measures that extended unemployment benefits, distributed tax rebates, and aimed to help stabilize small businesses and encourage companies to keep employees onboard.

BACKGROUND

The unemployment rate continued its gradual decline of previous years, dropping to 3.5 percent by February 2020, with 5.8 million unemployed—the lowest level since before the 2008–2010 recession. During the early months of the 2020 presidential campaign, Democratic candidates warned the numbers did not reflect the continuing hardship many Americans faced; they said young people were working for lower wages than their parents earned and were saddled with higher education debt, for instance.

Republicans, meanwhile, assailed the low unemployment rate as a victory for President Trump, who was running for reelection. A Wall Street Journal/NBC News poll in May 2019 also showed 51 percent of Americans approved of Trump's handling of the economy.

But as the country began to cope with the coronavirus pandemic, unemployment began to surge, reaching 13 percent in the second quarter of the year before dropping to 6.7 percent in the fourth quarter. Some people were able to work at home, but the numbers of workers facing temporary layoff or reduced hours increased. The pandemic and moves to contain it led businesses to suspend operations or shut down, resulting in high numbers of temporary layoffs.

The number of Americans unemployed increased dramatically over the year, according to the Bureau of Labor Statistics, from 6.2 million in February to 20.5 million in May 2020. Further, the unemployment rate for women in May 2020 (14.3 percent) was higher than that for men (11.9 percent), and the unemployment rate was lower for workers with higher education degrees.

The spread of the coronavirus also prevented many unemployed Americans from looking for jobs. The total number of civilian employed Americans decreased by 21 million between the fourth quarter of 2019 and the second quarter of 2020.

The Trump administration and Congress in early 2020 moved to provide emergency supplemental funding, primarily for the Department of Health and Human Services to handle public health emergency prevention and response activities related to COVID-19. The House on March 14 passed, 415–2, a measure (HR 6074) that would provide about $7.8 billion in discretionary supplemental funding. The Senate cleared the measure by a vote of 96–1 on March 5. The president signed it into law (PL 116-123) on March 6. The House and Senate then moved to pass relief measures for the growing number of unemployed and temporary laid-off workers as businesses suspended or downsized their operations.

Families First Act

On March 18, 2020, President Trump signed into law a measure (HR 6201, PL 116-227) that extended unemployment insurance and mandated companies provide free COVID testing and paid sick leave to those affected by COVID-19. The sick leave payouts would max out at $511 per day or $5,110 total for workers who were ill, quarantined, or seeking treatment. Lesser amounts would go to those caring for a dependent with the coronavirus.

The House passed, 363–40, its measure on March 14, 2020. In a pro forma session on March 16, the House passed, by unanimous consent, a slightly amended version to make some technical fixes. The measure would ensure fourteen days of paid six leave for workers and tax credits to help small- and medium-sized businesses comply with the mandate.

In the Senate, Majority Leader Mitch McConnell, R-Ky., on March 18 urged a vote for the bill, saying he was not going to let "perfection be the enemy of something that will help even a subset of workers." That day, the Senate cleared the bill by a vote of 90–8, with eight Republicans opposing it.

CARES Act

Congress in late March cleared and sent to the White House a $2.1 trillion package that extended unemployment compensation and expanded unemployment insurance to cover more workers.

The Coronavirus Aid, Relief and Economic Security Act, known as the CARES Act, included about $300 billion in benefits for laid-off workers and low-income households through July 2020. The measure also extended regular unemployment compensation by thirteen weeks after state benefits were exhausted, offering another $600 a week. And the measure offered employers a maximum tax credit of $5,000 per employee kept in their job, and boosted food stamps and other assistance programs by $40 billion.

On March 25, 2020, the Senate approved, 96–0, a House-passed bill (HR 748) after adding its own relief bill (S 3548). (The underlying House bill was a measure to repeal an excise tax on employer-sponsored health plans). The vote occurred after lengthy debate about the expansion of unemployment assistance, with some Republicans arguing that many laid-off workers would earn more on unemployment than they had been earning in their jobs. "I want to provide 100 percent of the salary while an American is laid off because of COVID-19, not a raise for not working. Not 200 percent of your income while on unemployment," Tim Scott, R-S.C., said during the Senate debate.

Minority Whip Richard J. Durbin, D-Ill, said lawmakers originally hoped states could ensure a full salary replacement for all jobless workers, based on their actual salaries. But the Labor Department said only a handful of states had computer systems that could provide such calculations. "They tell us it will take them months to reprogram their computers to make the simple calculation that says you never get paid more in unemployment than you were making on the job," Durbin said during the floor debate. The House cleared the measure (HR 748) by voice vote on March 27. President Trump signed the bill into law (PL 116-136) the same day.

House Relief Bill

The House on May 15, 2020, passed a $3.4 trillion relief bill (HR 6800) that would have extended the unemployment benefits that were provided under the CARES Act (PL 116-136) and scheduled to expire at the end of July. Democratic leaders hoped the measure would spark negotiations with Senate Republicans, but leaders of the two chambers could not agree on the size of the spending package.

The measure included nearly $1 trillion in aid to local and state governments, as well as $435 billion in direct payments to households. The House passed the measure by a vote of 208–199, with fourteen Democrats voting against it. Several moderate Democrats said the measure should have had more bipartisan support before the vote was held.

Senate Majority Leader Mitch McConnell refused to put the measure on the Senate floor, calling it a "liberal wish list." The White House threatened to veto the bill if it was cleared and urged a pause in negotiations until officials could review the effectiveness of the previous aid package passed in March.

In a June 4, 2020, report, the Congressional Budget Office said that if unemployment benefits were extended

through January 2021, unemployment would rise because five out of six eligible recipients would receive more money from the benefits than they would from their regular paycheck. But on June 16, 2020, Federal Reserve Chair Jerome Powell pushed Congress to increase spending to help the unemployed and limit economic damage from the pandemic. "There's a reasonable probability that more will be needed both from you and from the Fed," Powell told the Senate Banking Committee. He said low-income workers had been hit the hardest. Regional Fed presidents also called on Congress to do more.

As the end of July neared, nearly 18 million Americans remained unemployed, and millions of others were earning less than they had earned before the pandemic. Both Republicans and Democrats agreed further aid was needed but could not agree on how much. The GOP drafted a series of bills (S 4317, S 4318, S 4319, S 4320, S 4321, S 4322, S 4323, S 4324), all of which had much lower price tags than the House-passed measure.

On July 28, Republicans unveiled a $1 trillion aid package that would have provided a less generous extension of unemployment benefits but would have granted another round of tax rebate checks and expanded employment tax credits. Democrats immediately rejected the proposal as insufficient.

The parties continued to split on unemployment benefits. Republicans wanted a short-term extension of benefits, but Democrats wanted a longer guarantee of benefits. Democrats offered to decrease their original proposal in HR 6800 from $3.4 trillion to $2.2 trillion. The White House suggested it would be willing to accept a measure up to $1.5 trillion. The Senate briefly considered a $650 billion package (S 178). On September 10, 2020, a cloture vote failed, 52–47, not reaching the necessary sixty votes to end debate and move to a vote on the measure.

Executive Action

President Trump on August 8, 2020, signed a series of executive actions to extend and expand relief during the pandemic, including increased federal support for unemployment benefits. The president signed a memorandum that directed funds to be diverted from FEMA's Disaster Relief Fund to provide another $400 per week in unemployment benefits, with aid capped at a total of $4 billion. States, however, were mandated to match 25 percent of the funding.

House Relief Offer

On October 1, 2020, the House passed, 214–207, a $2.2 trillion aid package (HR 8406). All Republicans and eighteen Democrats voted against the measure, which would have offered another round of tax rebates of $1,200 per adult and expanded unemployment benefits among other things. It also included a $120 billion aid fund for the restaurant industry and $28 billion for the airline industry. Senate Republicans said the bill was too costly and did not take up the measure.

Unemployment Extension

On December 28, 2020, Trump signed into law a $900 billion stimulus package that provided continuing pandemic aid. By the time he had signed the measure, two unemployment programs had lapsed, causing a delay in benefits. Trump at the last minute had threatened a veto, saying the payments were too low; he had advocated $2,000 tax rebates per adult, but Republicans insisted on limiting the size of such payments to satisfy conservatives. House Democrats then vowed to bring up legislation to provide for $2,000 direct payments. Instead, the stimulus package, which was added to an omnibus funding bill, provided the following:

- Direct $600 payments to adult individuals with an adjusted gross income of not more than $75,000 a year, based on 2019 earnings. Heads of households with up to $112,500 or a couple making up to $150,000 would get twice that amount. Eligible families with dependent children would receive another $600 per child. Unlike the previous stimulus package, this one allowed spouses of undocumented immigrants to claim the benefit
- Extensions of several unemployment programs, reviving federal jobless benefits for eleven weeks. But the benefit, of $300 per week, was half the amount provided under the original stimulus package in the spring
- An extension of Pandemic Unemployment Assistance for freelancers and independent contractors, giving them another $100 per week
- $285 billion for loans to small businesses, under the paycheck protection program, to retain employees

Law and Justice

Law and Justice

Two issues dominated congressional consideration of law and justice issues during the Trump presidency: the impeachment of the president and the reshaping of the Supreme Court in a far more conservative direction. Congress also took up a number of other issues, successfully passing a major overhaul of the criminal justice system but falling short in efforts to make substantial changes to the immigration system or impose regulations on policing practices.

The specter of impeachment hung over Trump since Attorney General Jeff Sessions appointed a special counsel to look into allegations that his presidential campaign colluded with Russia to influence the 2016 election. Although the investigation by Special Counsel Robert S. Mueller III generated much speculation in Washington circles, Democrats were powerless to do much but cheer him on until they took control of the House after the midterm elections. Even then, despite months of investigations and much scrutiny of the Mueller report—finally issued in March 2019—they made little headway during much of their first year in power in determining whether Trump had committed impeachable offenses.

That changed in September 2019 with the revelations by a whistleblower that Trump appeared to use military aid to Ukraine as leverage to persuade that nation to announce an investigation into his presidential rival, former Vice President Joseph R. Biden. The House subsequently passed two articles of impeachment at the end of 2019 for abuse of power and obstruction of justice. But Democrats failed to win Republican support, and the Senate easily acquitted Trump in February 2020.

The episode made Trump the third president to be impeached in U.S. history, after Andrew Johnson and Bill Clinton. (He would subsequently be impeached again for encouraging the attack on the Capitol on January 6, 2021.) But he claimed vindication after his acquittal, and briefly rebounded in the polls. The debate over Trump's actions highlighted the seemingly intractable partisan divide on Capitol Hill. Whereas Democrats viewed Trump as willing to undercut U.S. security for his own political advantage, Republicans viewed him as exercising his legitimate authority over foreign policy.

Deepening partisan divisions were also evident when Republicans successfully confirmed all three of Trump's nominees to the Supreme Court. The new justices gave conservatives a 6–3 majority, with expectations that the court would roll back government regulations, bolster gun rights, and possibly overturn the 1973 *Roe v. Wade* decision that legalized abortion. But each nomination seemed to create even more partisan bitterness than the last.

Figure 13.1 Outlays for Law Enforcement

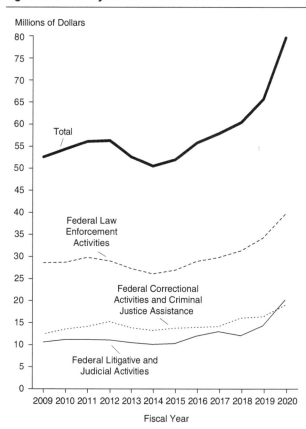

SOURCE: Office of Management and Budget, *Historical Tables, Budget of the United States Government: Fiscal Year 2021* (Washington DC: U.S. Government Printing Office, 2020) Table 3.2.

NOTES: * indicates estimate

Neil Gorsuch, a conservative appellate judge with impeccable credentials, was able to pick up the support of just three Democrats. That was partly due to Democratic outrage that Majority Leader Mitch McConnell, R-Ky., had held the seat open for a year, denying President Barack Obama the opportunity to fill it. But it also marked the increasing partisanship of battles over federal judgeships: the man Gorsuch replaced, Antonin Scalia, had been confirmed in 1986 by a vote of 98–0.

The Senate careened toward even more partisan rancor over the nomination of Brett Kavanaugh, another conservative appellate judge. His path to confirmation was disrupted by charges of sexual assault when he was a student. Republicans were infuriated by what they regarded as an underhanded attempt to destroy the reputation of an honorable judge, while Democrats fumed when the allegations were not investigated more thoroughly. In the end, Kavanaugh picked up just one Democratic vote.

Trump's third nominee, Amy Coney Barrett, could not even do that well with Democrats. She became the first Supreme Court nominee in 150 years to win confirmation without a single vote from the minority party. The issue had less to do with her credentials than with the timing: Republicans hustled to confirm her just days before the 2020 presidential election—a stark turnabout from their refusal to take a vote on Obama's Supreme Court pick for months leading up to the 2016 election.

Criminal Justice Overhaul

Lawmakers succeeded in making substantial changes to the criminal justice system when they cleared a sweeping measure at the end of 2018, known as the First Step Act. The legislation, supported by the White House advocacy groups across the political spectrum, inspired a rare alliance between conservative Republicans and liberal Democrats who worried that the existing criminal justice system was overly expensive and unfair.

The bill was the result of years of negotiations, and supporters managed to win enactment only by greatly narrowing its scope. Their goals were to lower the number of federal inmates by scaling back certain tough-on-crime policies and to provide more assistance to prisoners upon release to lower the rate of recidivism. To do so, the measure gave judges more discretion over some sentencing, scaled back requirements for some mandatory minimum sentences in certain cases, and expanded early release programs. It also created more job training and drug treatment programs for prison inmates.

Some conservatives warned that the measure could lead to higher crime rates, while some liberals worried that it fell short of a more expansive overhaul that had been pursued during the Obama administration. Supporters, however, noted that it was modeled after initiatives in several state prison systems that had successfully reduced costs and improved outcomes.

Immigration, Policing, and Guns

In several other areas, lawmakers failed to bridge their differences or made only modest progress. Perhaps most notably, Trump failed to win support for a comprehensive overhaul of the immigration system although he had pledged to crack down on illegal immigration during his 2016 presidential campaign. Congress, as had been the case for many years, could not find a balance between tightening security, cracking down on illegal immigration, and deciding whether to provide a path to citizenship for many of the estimated 10 to 11 million undocumented immigrants living in the United States.

Lawmakers also fell short in efforts to regulate police practices. They tried to tackle the issue after the highly publicized killing of George Floyd, a Black man who was killed by a Minneapolis police officer. The death, captured on video, galvanized coast-to-coast protests against police brutality and systemic racism. Both Republicans and Democrats agreed on the need to impose standards on police practices, but they pursued sharply different paths. House Democrats in 2020 passed a sweeping policing measure that would have greatly restricted chokeholds and

no-knock warrants among other provisions. Republicans wanted to take a more narrow approach, avoiding imposing federal mandates on local and state law enforcement agencies. In the end, efforts to pass legislation collapsed amid partisan finger-pointing in the run-up to the elections.

Finally, a spate of mass shootings spurred debate over measures to better regulate guns. Many Democrats wanted to expand background checks, ban bump stocks (which make semiautomatic rifles operate like a machine gun), and raise the legal age for purchasing semiautomatic guns to twenty-one. Although such proposals gained little traction, lawmakers turned to the appropriations process to provide funding to boost student safety in schools and strengthen the FBI background check system. They also ended the longstanding prohibition of federally funded research into gun violence. For their part, gun rights advocates won a victory in repealing an Obama-era rule prohibiting mentally impaired Social Security recipients from buying firearms. Republicans, however, scored an earlier victory in paring back a prohibition on mentally impaired people from buying firearms.

JUSTICE LEADERSHIP

With President Trump facing investigations for much of his tenure, his two nominees for attorney general came under intense scrutiny from Democrats who wanted reassurances that they would act independently of the president. In addition, Trump faced criticism in 2017 for forcing out FBI director James Comey, who was overseeing an investigation into his presidential campaign's ties to Russia.

Attorney General

Trump's announcement in November 2016 that he was nominating Sen. Jeff Sessions, R-Ala., for attorney general raised immediate concerns among Democrats. Sessions, who was Trump's earliest and most vocal supporter in the Senate, had consistently criticized many of President Barack Obama's policies on immigration and criminal justice issues. Civil rights advocates pointed to his failed 1986 nomination for federal judge, when witnesses testified that he used racially insensitive language and called major civil rights organizations "un-American." But the soft-spoken Sessions was popular with his Republican colleagues, who had the votes to confirm him, and his tough-on-crime policies appealed to many in the law enforcement community.

At his January 10, 2017, confirmation hearing, Sessions emphatically denied accusations of racism as "damnably false," and he reminded his Judiciary Committee colleagues of his twenty-year track record of working with them. "You know that I revere our Constitution and am committed to the rule of law," Sessions, seventy, told the senators. "And you know that I believe in fairness, impartiality and equal justice under the law." Despite facing intense opposition—

Sen. Cory Booker, D-N.J., took the extraordinary step of testifying against him—Sessions won confirmation on February 8 on a mostly party line Senate vote of 52–47.

Sessions had a tumultuous tenure of almost two years, ending with his forced resignation on November 7, 2018. Some of his troubles were outside his control: Trump's constant legal troubles kept the Justice Department in an uncomfortable spotlight. But Sessions managed the rare feat of angering both the president and congressional Democrats.

The problems began less than a month after he took office, when *The Washington Post* reported that he had spoken twice with the Russian ambassador while serving as a senior advisor to the Trump campaign. He had not disclosed those meetings at his confirmation hearing, despite being asked whether he had any contacts with Russian officials. In response, Sessions said he had decided to recuse himself from any Justice Department investigation into the 2016 campaign.

His announcement failed to mollify Democrats. It also angered Trump, especially when it opened the door in May for Deputy Attorney General Rod Rosenstein to appoint a special counsel, Robert S. Mueller III, to look into Russian interference in the 2016 election. Sessions became further embroiled in election controversy for playing a role in firing FBI Director James B. Comey, who had clashed with Trump over the FBI's Russia investigation. Testifying before the Senate Intelligence Committee in an often contentious hearing on June 13, 2017, Sessions adamantly rejected suggestions from Democrats that he had improper contacts with Russian officials during the elections and said he had "no recollection" of a reported third meeting with the Russian ambassador.

Even as he fended off congressional Democrats, Sessions had lost the confidence of Trump, who became publicly angry over federal investigations into his former campaign manager and former personal attorney. In a television interview in early 2018, Trump said he "put in an attorney general that never took control of the Justice Department."

Sessions's conservative policies at the Justice Department pleased fellow Republicans, while Democrats objected sharply to such decisions as reversing course on LGBT and civil rights policies that the Obama Justice Department had supported. Nevertheless, Democrats raised alarms when he was forced out just after the midterm elections, worrying that it could be Trump's first step toward shutting down the special counsel's investigation. Matthew Whitaker, who had served as Sessions' chief of staff and became acting attorney general, had publicly criticized aspects of Mueller's investigation.

Such concerns were somewhat tamped down by Trump's decision to tap William Barr as attorney general. A mainstay of the conservative establishment, Barr, sixty-eight, was a well-regarded corporate lawyer who had run the Justice Department from 1991 to 1993 under George H. W. Bush. But he had also praised Trump for firing Comey and questioned the political balance of Mueller's team, an issue that Trump had repeatedly tweeted about. With Democrats questioning Barr's willingness to stand up to Trump, the Senate confirmed him on a mostly party line vote of 54–45 on February 14, 2019.

Although Barr's tenure was less rocky in some respects than that of Sessions, it was not without controversy. Two days after Mueller delivered his final report to him, Barr summarized it in a four-page letter that appeared to largely exonerate the president. Democrats were furious, demanding that he share the entire report with him and later accusing him of misleading the American people. They also clashed with Barr over accessing administration documents, voting on July 17, 2019, to hold him in criminal contempt of Congress for refusing to comply with subpoenas seeking material about the administration's attempt to add a citizenship question to the census. After the Justice Department in September 2019 found that Trump had not crossed a legal line when asking the Ukrainian president to announce an investigation into former Vice President Joseph R. Biden, Democrats became more concerned than ever that Barr was acting as Trump's personal attorney rather than the independent head of the Justice Department.

The criticism escalated after the 2020 election, when Barr suggested there could be fraud involved with mail-in ballots. But he subsequently said the Justice Department had not found widespread fraud that would affect the results. Barr stepped down on December 23, just weeks before Trump left office. Despite his refusal to back Trump's claims about election fraud, the president warmly praised him, tweeting that he had done "an outstanding job."

FBI Director

Trump shocked Washington with his decision to fire FBI Director James B. Comey on May 9, 2017. There was an ongoing investigation into connections between Trump's 2016 campaign and Russian operatives, and speculation immediately swirled that the president was trying to protect himself. But Comey, appointed in 2013 by Obama to a ten-year term, had drawn sharp criticism from both parties for a series of questionable decisions. These included reopening an investigation, just before Election Day, into Democratic presidential nominee Hillary Clinton's use of a private email server and publicly acknowledging the FBI counterintelli-

(Continued)

JUSTICE LEADERSHIP (Continued)

gence investigation into potential ties between Trump associates and Russia.

Comey repeatedly clashed with Trump, refusing to pledge loyalty to him and then telling the Senate Judiciary Committee that it made him "mildly nauseous" to think that his investigation into Clinton may have affected the election. Although a White House spokesman initially said the firing was a Department of Justice decision, Trump himself, in an interview with NBC News on May 11, 2017, referenced the Russia investigation in his decision to fire Comey. "I said to myself . . . 'You know, this Russia thing with Trump and Russia is a made-up story.'" Comey would later say that Trump asked him to quash part of the probe.

A month later, Trump tapped Christopher Wray for FBI director. Wray, fifty, a litigation partner at King & Spalding law firm in Washington and Atlanta, had a traditional law enforcement background that included holding several prominent positions in the Justice Department under President George W. Bush. Most recently, he served as the assistant attorney general in charge of the DOJ's criminal division from 2003 to 2005—a position to which the Senate had confirmed him by unanimous consent.

This time, the Senate confirmed Wray on a strong bipartisan vote of 92–5 on August 1, 2017. Democrats were reassured by his strong statements about protecting the bureau's independence. Wray subsequently steered clear of controversy.

Chronology of Action on Law and Justice

2017–2018

Although much of the 115th Congress was marked by partisan fighting, Republicans and Democrats came together to pass a major overhaul of the criminal justice system. The new law, backed by the White House and advocacy organizations across the political spectrum, aimed to reduce the number of federal inmates and help former prisoners avoid committing new crimes.

Lawmakers also took modest steps to address gun violence, including using an appropriations measure to provide federal grant funding to boost student safety in schools and strengthen the FBI background check system. Gun rights advocates won a victory in repealing a rule prohibiting mentally impaired Social Security recipients from buying firearms.

But congressional efforts fell short in other areas. Repeated attempts to overhaul the immigration system collapsed because of differences over how much to focus on border security versus providing some immigrants with a path to citizenship. Even more targeted immigration proposals, such as stepping up certain types of enforcement, could not make it through Congress.

Republicans secured a major triumph for Trump by confirming his two picks for the Supreme Court. The nominations of Neil Gorsuch and Brett Kavanaugh overcame intense Democratic opposition and, in the case of Kavanaugh, allegations of sexual assault. As a result, conservatives strengthened their 5–4 Court majority.

Criminal Justice Overhaul

The House on December 20, 2018, cleared a sweeping, bipartisan criminal justice overhaul by a vote of 358–36, part of a year-end rush of legislation. The Senate had passed the measure, dubbed the First Step Act, 87–12, just two days earlier. The legislation (S 756—PL 115-391), a longtime priority for those who wanted to make substantial changes to the criminal justice system, came together because of the efforts of policymakers across the political spectrum, from conservative Republicans such as Senate Judiciary Chairman Charles E. Grassley of Iowa and House Judiciary Chairman Robert W. Goodlatte of Virginia to

liberal Democrats such as Sen. Cory Booker of New Jersey and Rep. Hakeem Jeffries of New York. It won support from the White House, thanks in part to the efforts of Trump's son-in-law, Jared Kushner.

The compromise bill was the product of years of negotiations, and it won resounding majorities in Congress only after supporters narrowed the scope of the legislation. A key goal was to lower the number of federal inmates, which had swelled because of tough-on-crime policies, and to provide more assistance to prisoners once they were released in order to keep them from committing new crimes and getting sent back to prison.

The bill made modest changes to sentencing, gave judges more freedom to hand down sentences below the mandatory minimum for nonviolent drug offenders, and reduced mandatory minimums associated with the three-strikes law for habitual offenders. The bill would create more job training and drug treatment for prison inmates, expand early release programs, prohibit the shackling of pregnant inmates, and largely bar the use of solitary confinement for juveniles.

Some conservatives, such as Sen. Tom Cotton, R-Ark., warned that the measure could lead to higher crime rates, while liberals fretted that it fell short of a more expansive overhaul that had been pursued during the administration of Barack Obama. But the majority of conservatives and liberals, prodded by a broad coalition of interest groups, viewed the existing criminal justice system as overly costly and unfair.

Many of the provisions in the First Step Act were modeled after initiatives in state prison systems that were successful in reducing costs and improving outcomes in the criminal justice system. The new law would not directly affect state prisons, where most of the country's inmates were locked up, but supporters said it could inspire more states to overhaul their approach to criminal justice.

BACKGROUND

With 2.1 million inmates in jails and prisons, the United States had more people behind bars than any other country. The nation's high incarceration rate sparked concerns

across the political spectrum, with policymakers across the political system raising alarms about the high cost to taxpayers and the human toll for those who were locked away for years.

In the 114th Congress, efforts to pass bipartisan criminal justice legislation (S 2123) failed, partly because of concerns by some Republicans that it would endanger public safety. The bill, known as the Sentencing Reform and Corrections Act of 2015, would have scaled back mandatory minimum sentences for many offenses, addressed sentencing disparities, and made other changes to the criminal justice system. Although the bill's supporters resumed their efforts in 2017, prospects for a compromise seemed uncertain at best, especially given that Trump had a tough-on-crime reputation.

But an unusual coalition of influential organizations, from the Koch brothers to the American Civil Liberties Union, continued to advocate for changes to the criminal justice system. Many on the left, including former President Barack Obama, had long decried perceived inequities in the treatment of offenders. They were joined by prominent conservatives, including anti-tax advocates such as Grover Norquist, as well as evangelicals, such as Chuck Colson, who founded the Christian nonprofit organization Prison Fellowship. They raised alarms about a prison system that they viewed as overly costly and fundamentally unfair. Advocates of prison reform had scored notable successes in several states by reducing incarceration rates for nonviolent criminals and investing in programs to reduce recidivism. Now they had their sights set on the federal level.

House committee action

The House Judiciary Committee on May 9, 2018, approved an early version of the legislation (HR 5682), which aimed to support federal prisoners' transition to society upon their release and reduce the chances that they return to crime. The measure won committee approval, 25–5, although Democrats wanted to add provisions that would have made changes to sentencing, especially mandatory minimum sentences.

Ranking Democrat Jerrold Nadler of New York voted against the bill, saying he was concerned that it could aggravate the inequitable treatment of offenders when they were investigated and sentenced. His motion to postpone consideration of the measure failed by voice vote.

Republicans said the bill would help ensure that prison funding was spent effectively while reducing the recidivism rate. They pointed to provisions on education and vocational training that would give offenders a greater chance of success upon their release.

HR 5682 would require the U.S. attorney general to create a risk assessment system for the Bureau of Prisons to determine the likelihood of recidivism for each prisoner. The assessment would evaluate the violent or serious misconduct of each prisoner and recommend recidivism

reduction programs, including when to provide incentives and rewards for those inmates who successfully participated. Prisoners could earn credits toward alternative custody options, such as a halfway house or home confinement, when they left prison. Offenders who were convicted of particularly egregious crimes, such as murders, would be excluded.

Addressing complaints about the treatment of pregnant prisoners, the measure would generally prohibit the use of restraints on pregnant women, as well as those giving birth and in postpartum recovery.

It would authorize $50 million per year from fiscal 2019 through 2023, with 80 percent of the funding used to implement the system and support associated programs and services.

The committee, on a party line 14–15 vote, rejected an amendment by Steve Cohen, D-Tenn., to make permanent a pilot program that would evaluate the effectiveness of moving certain nonviolent eligible elderly offenders from Bureau of Prisons facilities into home detention. The program would have added eligible terminally ill prisoners.

The committee gave voice vote approval to an amendment by Cedric Richmond, D-La., to increase the allowance for behavior credits for prisoner satisfactory behavior to up to fifty-four days for each year of the prisoner's sentence, as well as allowing credits for the last year of a prison term to be obtained on the first day of that last year. People currently in prison would be able to gain credit under the risk assessment system.

The committee also agreed by voice vote to an amendment by Matt Gaetz, R-Fla., that would require the Bureau of Prisons to create two pilot programs, one of which would focus on youth mentorship and another on prisoners and abandoned, rescued, or otherwise vulnerable animals. The programs would run for five years and be administered in at least twenty facilities.

In addition, the committee adopted by voice vote an amendment by Louis Gohmert, R-Texas, that would bar faith-based discrimination against any program, treatment, regimen, group, company, charity, person, or entity.

The committee rejected, on a party line vote of 15–14, an amendment by Steve Cohen, D-Tenn., to make permanent a pilot program that would determine the effectiveness of transferring certain nonviolent eligible elderly offenders from a Bureau of Prisons facility into home detention. The amendment also would have expanded the program to include eligible terminally ill prisoners.

By voice vote, the committee rejected an amendment by Sheila Jackson Lee, D-Texas, that would require the Bureau of Prisons director, within 270 days of the bill's enactment, to create a pilot program to allow women prisoners and the children born to them while in prison to live together. It would require that they be housed separately from the prison's general population. The amendment would allow a

child who was eligible to reside in a prison to stay until the age of thirty months.

House Floor Action

The House on May 22, 2018, easily passed HR 5682 even as doubts emerged that the bill would pass the Senate. The vote was 360–59.

Hours before the vote, Senate Judiciary Chairman Charles E. Grassley told an advocacy group that the bill was too narrow, and that he would press for a broader overhaul of the criminal justice system that would include changes to sentencing laws. That was the only way to win the support of Senate Democrats, he said.

House Judiciary Committee Chairman Robert W. Goodlatte, R-Va., acknowledged on the floor that some lawmakers would oppose the bill because it lacked sentencing measures. But he said the measure represented an important step toward reducing the recidivism rate.

Some prominent Democrats raised concerns about the House bill. Eric H. Holder Jr., who had been the first attorney general during the Obama administration, wrote an op-ed in *The Washington Post* that the measure "threatens to derail momentum for sentencing reform."

But some advocates of sentencing reforms rallied behind the bill. Families Against Mandatory Minimums, which wanted to do away with laws that required judges to impose harsh prison terms on even nonviolent drug offenders, praised provisions that could lead to a more just federal prison system. Shon Hopwood, a former federal inmate who had become a law professor and served on the organization's board, wrote in a blog post that he would not stop meaningful prison legislation when a sentencing bill faced dim prospects in Washington. "If the choice is prison reform or nothing, reform seems the obvious choice if you understand how meaningful the prison reforms have become," he wrote.

Senate Committee Action

The Senate Judiciary Committee on February 15, 2018, approved its version of the criminal justice bill. But the bill's sentencing provisions left Republicans divided, and the prospects for the full Senate taking up the measure appeared uncertain.

The legislation (S 1917), which passed 16–5, would reduce mandatory minimum sentences for nonviolent drug offenders and give judges more flexibility in sentencing even as it added some new mandatory minimums for certain crimes. It would also help released prisoners adjust to society.

Bill supporters, including Judiciary Committee Chairman Grassley, praised the measure for ending overly long prison sentences and saving taxpayer dollars. Grassley emphasized the bill's broad support across the political spectrum, with backing from groups that rarely found themselves working together, including FreedomWorks, the American Conservative Union, Prison Fellowship,

Families Against Mandatory Minimums, the NAACP, the American Civil Liberties Union, and the NFL.

But Attorney General Jeff Sessions announced one day before the vote that the administration opposed the bill. The sentencing provisions drew opposition from Republican senators and law enforcement groups.

The committee, 5–16, rejected an amendment by Ted Cruz, R-Texas, to exclude violent criminals from getting relief from their sentences. Cruz said the bill would fail without his language.

Joining Cruz in opposition to the overall measure were Republicans John Cornyn of Texas, Orrin G. Hatch of Utah, and Ben Sasse of Nebraska, as well as John Kennedy of Louisiana. Kennedy said a similar effort in his state had led to significant problems.

S 1917 would reduce the enhanced mandatory minimums for prior drug felons on three-strike penalty from life imprisonment to twenty-five years and from twenty years to fifteen years. It would focus the mandatory minimums on serious drug felonies and expand them to include serious violent felonies, while generally excluding nonviolent drug felonies. It would allow for sentence reductions for inmates who had been convicted of certain offenses prior to the bill's enactment, assuming certain conditions were met. It would allow judges more sentencing discretion in some cases and allow the retroactive application of a 2010 law (PL 111-220) that reduced the sentencing disparity between crack and powder cocaine.

Sentencing aside, it would require the Bureau of Prisons to make recidivism reduction programming available to all eligible prisoners within six years. Inmates would also receive time credit of up to five days for each period of thirty days of programming that they successfully completed, with low-risk inmates eligible for an additional five days of credit, while excluding certain inmates with previous convictions or violent crimes. As with the House bill, the attorney general would develop a risk and needs assessment system to determine the recidivism risk of all federal inmates.

Juveniles who were convicted as adults would be eligible to seek parole after twenty years. The bill would allow the compassionate release of offenders who had served a large portion of their sentences and were over the age of sixty with no record of violence, were terminally ill or in nursing homes. It also would create a National Criminal Justice Commission for a comprehensive review of the criminal justice system, and authorize $14 million over two years for the operation.

Final Action

The criminal justice overhaul effort stalled for much of 2018. Senators criticized the House approach as overly narrow, but a number of Republicans in both chambers, along with the White House, had objections to the sentencing provisions in the Senate bill. With little chance of finding consensus, Senate Majority Leader Mitch McConnell, R-Ky., did not plan on setting aside floor time for S 1917.

A broad and influential coalition of interest groups, however, continued to work toward a compromise solution. Lawmakers, hoping to make "smart-on-crime" changes to the criminal justice system, kept exploring ways to advance the measure with key administration figures, including White House adviser Jared Kushner. Trump continued to say that he wanted Congress to pass a bill.

Hopes for major criminal justice legislation dimmed at times, but they revived shortly after the midterm elections when Trump announced his backing of new compromise legislation. Although the legislation had yet to be finalized, Trump, flanked by lawmakers in the Roosevelt Room of the White House, urged passage of a bill that would reduce crime while giving Americans a chance at redemption. Trump said he would support a bill that provided low-risk inmates incentives to learn needed employment skills and obey the law upon their release, keep inmates closer to their families and communities and make "reasonable" criminal sentencing changes.

The new bill basically combined the provisions of the House-passed bill (HR 5682) with measures to change four areas of criminal sentencing. It would give judges more freedom to avoid large mandatory minimum sentences, take away some sentencing enhancements for defendants with prior state offenses, make retroactive the law that reduced the disparity of sentences for powdered versus crack cocaine, and limit how prosecutors could use firearm possession to boost mandatory minimum sentences. These sentencing provisions were more modest than those in S 1917, but they seemed more likely to garner critical Republican support. Grassley and fellow senators Richard J. Durbin, D-Ill., Mike Lee, R-Utah, and Lindsey Graham, R-S.C., worked on the bill with the White House.

Speaker Paul D Ryan, R-Wis., who had supported criminal justice efforts for years, indicated that the House could move forward if the bill had the necessary support in the Senate. Critically, the legislation received a key endorsement from the president of the Fraternal Order of Police.

With less than a month remaining in the 115th Congress, senators unveiled the compromise bill (S 3649) on December 12, 2018. Amid broad bipartisan support, McConnell announced a floor vote.

The bill included new measures to limit sentencing changes, thereby addressing concerns by law enforcement officials and a number of Republicans. It would prevent firearm offenders and fentanyl traffickers from early release from prison and specify conditions for supervised release from custody, according to a summary from the Senate Judiciary Committee. It also added eighteen offenses that would disqualify inmates from a program under which they could serve a latter part of their sentence in a halfway house or home confinement.

The compromise drew support from key House members, including Goodlatte and Doug Collins, R-Ga., who had cowritten the prison overhaul bill (HR 5682) that passed the House. But some Senate Republicans, including Tom Cotton of Arkansas and John Kennedy of Louisiana,

continued to oppose it out of concern that it would pose a threat to public safety, allowing the early release of many categories of violent criminals.

The bill was brought to the Senate floor as an amendment to an unrelated measure (S 756). Supporters, by votes of 32–67, 33–66, and 37–62, defeated three amendments by Cotton and Kennedy that would have further narrowed which prisoners would be eligible for early release. However, the Senate gave voice vote approval to an amendment by Cruz to keep violent offenders from being released early. The House passed the bill without amendments, and Trump signed it on December 21, 2018.

Provisions

The First Step Act (S 756—PL 115-39) has three main components: correctional reform through the establishment of a risk and needs assessment system at the Bureau of Prisons, sentencing reform consisting of changes in penalties for certain offenses, and the reauthorization of the Second Chance Act of 2007 (PL 110-199). The act also contains a number of other criminal justice–related provisions, including making certain changes in the way good time credits are calculated for federal prisoners, prohibiting the use of restraints on pregnant inmates, expanding the market for products made by the Federal Prison Industries, and requiring the Bureau of Prisons (BOP) to aid prisoners with obtaining identification before being released.

CORRECTIONAL REFORMS

Risk and needs assessment system

The correctional component of the First Step Act requires the development and implementation of a risk and needs assessment system at BOP. The Justice Department is required to develop the system within 210 days of enactment of the act.

The system must classify each prisoner as having a minimum, low, medium, or high risk of recidivism and assign prisoners to evidence-based recidivism reduction programs and productive activities to reduce this risk. The system periodically reassesses the recidivism risk of each prisoner and reassigns prisoners as appropriate to ensure that all prisoners have an opportunity to reduce their risk classification and are able to successfully participate in the programs. The system determines when to provide incentives and rewards for successful participation, as well as determining when a prisoner is ready to be transferred into prerelease custody or supervised release. Audio technology for program course materials will be provided to accommodate prisoners with dyslexia.

When developing the system, the Justice Department and the Independent Review Committee established by the First Step Act must review existing risk and needs assessment systems, develop recommendations regarding recidivism reduction programs and productive activities, and conduct ongoing research and data analysis. The system must be reviewed annually. The Justice Department will submit an annual report to Congress each year for five years starting in 2020.

Within 180 days of the development of the system, BOP is required to complete the initial risk and needs assessment for each prisoner, including those incarcerated before the act's implementation. BOP must begin assigning prisoners to appropriate recidivism reduction programs based on the assessment and begin to expand and add recidivism reduction programs and productive activities to effectively implement the system. All prisoners must have an opportunity to participate in risk reduction programs within two years of the initial assessments, with prisoners who are nearing their release data having priority for placement in the programs. High- and medium-risk prisoners must have priority for placement in the recidivism risk programs, with low-risk prisoners participating in productive activities. Prisoners must be reassessed at least annually, and reassigned if the reassessment shows changes in the risk of recidivism or specific needs.

The Justice Department must develop and administer a training program for BOP employees on how to use the system. The Justice Department must monitor and assess how the system is used at BOP, including an annual audit of the system's use.

Incentives and rewards

Incentives and rewards for prisoners in recidivism reduction programs may include additional phone privileges, and if available, video conferencing privileges, of up to thirty minutes a day and as much 510 minutes a month; additional visitation times; and transfer to a facility closer to the prisoner's release residence. Prisoners who successfully complete recidivism reduction programming may earn up to tendays of time credits for every thirty days of program participation, with additional time credits available to minimum- and low-risk prisoners who meet certain benchmarks. However, prisoners who were convicted of any one of multiple enumerated offenses (categorized as violent, terrorism, espionage, human trafficking, sex and sexual exploitation, repeat felon in possession of firearm, certain fraud, or high-level drug offenses) are ineligible to earn additional time credits regardless of risk level. Those subject to a final order of removal under immigration law are also ineligible for additional earned time credits. Earned time credits are reduced for prisoners who violate institutional rules or the rules of recidivism reduction programs and productive activities, although they can be earned back.

Prerelease custody

A prisoner is not eligible for prerelease custody until they

- Have earned an amount of time credits equal to the remainder of the imposed term of imprisonment
- Have shown a reduced risk of recidivism or maintained a minimum or low recidivism risk
- Have been determined to be a minimum or low risk to recidivate

A prisoner who is required to serve a period of supervised release after the term of incarceration and has earned time credits equivalent to the time remaining on the prison sentence can be transferred directly to supervised release, if the latest reassessment shows a minimum or low risk to recidivate. However, BOP cannot allow a period of supervised release to begin more than twelve months before the prisoner would otherwise be eligible to do so. A prisoner who has earned more than twelve months of additional time credits would need to serve the excess in prerelease custody.

Prisoners in prerelease custody are required to have twenty-four-hour electronic monitoring that enables the identification of their location and the time, and must remain in their residences, except to go to work or participate in other specific activities. Prisoners who demonstrate continued compliance with their conditions will have reduced restrictions to the extent practicable; those who violate conditions may face more restrictions or be returned to prison.

Reporting requirements

The act requires the submission of several reports. Two years after enactment and then annually for the next five years, the Justice Department must submit a report to Congress on the types of effectiveness of recidivism reduction programs and productive activities, the recidivism rates of prisoners who are released from federal prison, the status of prison work programs, and budgetary savings achieved by the act.

Within two years of enactment, the Independent Review Committee must submit a report to Congress that includes extensive information on prisoners who were ineligible for earned time credits, or who did not participate in recidivism reduction programming or productive activities, including their age, race, sex, and criminal history categories.

Within two years of BOP implementing the system and every two years thereafter, the Government Accountability Office is required to audit how the system is being used, including whether BOP is meeting requirements of the act and rates of recidivism to identify unwarranted disparities.

AUTHORIZATION OF APPROPRIATIONS

The First Step Act authorizes $75 million per fiscal year from Fiscal Year (FY) 2019 to FY 2023 for DOJ to establish and implement the system, with 80 percent directed to BOP for implementation.

Sentencing reforms

The First Step Act changed the mandatory minimum sentences for certain drug offenses, expanded the scope of the safety valve, eliminated the stacking provision, and made the provisions of the Fair Sentencing Act of 2010 (PL 111-220) retroactive.

Changes to mandatory minimums for certain drug offenders

The act reduces the twenty-year mandatory minimum (for an offender with one prior qualifying conviction) to a fifteen-year mandatory minimum and reduces the life sentence mandatory minimum (for offenders with two or more prior qualifying convictions) to a twenty-five-year mandatory minimum. It also changes the prior conviction criteria for mandatory minimum penalties, requiring that the offender's prior convictions meet the new criteria of a serious drug felony or serious violent felony, rather than any felony drug offense.

Expanding the safety valve

The act makes drug offenders with minor criminal records eligible for the safety valve provision, which allows judges to sentence low-level, nonviolent drug offenders to a term of imprisonment less than the mandatory minimum. It previously applied only to offenders with virtually spotless criminal records.

Eliminating the stacking provision

The act eliminates stacking by providing that the twenty-five-year mandatory minimum for a "second or subsequent" conviction for use of a firearm in furtherance of a drug trafficking crime or a violent crime applies only in cases in which the offender has a prior conviction for use of a firearm that is already final. Under prior law, two violations that were charged concurrently triggered the enhanced mandatory minimum.

Retroactivity of the fair sentencing act

The First Step Act authorizes courts to retroactively apply the Fair Sentencing Act of 2010, which increased the threshold quantities of crack cocaine sufficient to trigger mandatory minimum sentences. Qualified prisoners who petition the court can be resentenced as if the Fair Sentencing Act had been in effect at the time of their offenses.

Reauthorization of the second chance act

The First Step Act reauthorizes and makes certain changes to many of the grant programs that were initially authorized by the Second Chance Act of 2007 (PL 110-199). These include

- The Adult and Juvenile State and Local Offender Demonstration Program, authorized at $35 million annually from FY 2019 to FY 2023
- Grants for family-based substance abuse treatment, authorized at $10 million annually from FY 2019 to FY 2023.
- Grants to evaluate and improve educational methods at prisons, jails, and juvenile facilities, authorized at $5 million annually from FY 2019 to FY 2023.
- Careers demonstration training grants, authorized at $10 million annually from FY 2019 to FY 2023

- Offender Reentry Substance Abuse and Criminal Justice Collaboration Program, authorized at $10 million annually from FY 2019 to FY 2023
- Community-Based Mentoring and Transitional Service Grants to Nonprofit Organizations Program, authorized at $15 million annually from FY 2019 to FY 2023
- BOP Early Release Pilot Program expanded so that terminally ill offenders can be placed on home confinement
- A series of reentry research projects, authorized at $5 million annually from FY 2019 to FY 2023

Within five years of enactment, the National Institute of Justice is required to evaluate grants used by the Justice Department to support reentry and recidivism reduction programs at the state, local, tribal, and federal levels. The act also requires BOP to develop policies for wardens of prisons and community-based facilities to enter into recidivism-reducing partnerships with nonprofit and other private organizations, including faith-based and community-based organizations to deliver recidivism reduction programming. The act repeals certain Second Change Act programs: State, Tribal, and Local Reentry Courts program; Responsible Reintegration of Offenders program; and the Study on the Effectiveness of Depot Naltrexone for Heroin Addiction program.

Additional provisions

Modification of Good Time Credits. Federal prisoners can earn up to fifty-four days of good time credit for every year of their imposed sentence rather than for every year of their sentence served, as had previously been the case.

Secure Firearm Storage. The act requires BOP to provide a secure storage area outside of the secure perimeter of a correctional institution for qualified law enforcement officers employed by BOP to store firearms or allow this class of employees to store firearms in their personal vehicles in lockboxes approved by BOP. Those same employees are permitted to carry concealed firearms on prison grounds but outside of the secure perimeter of the correctional institution.

Prohibition on the Use of Restraints on Pregnant Prisoners. The act prohibits BOP or the U.S. Marshals Service from using restraints on pregnant inmates in their custody, with the prohibition on restraints remaining in effect until the inmate completes postpartum recovery. This prohibition does not apply if the inmate is determined to be an immediate and credible flight risk or poses an immediate and serious threat of harm to herself or others that cannot be reasonably prevented by other means, or if a health care professional determines that the use of restraints is appropriate for the medical safety of the inmate. In those cases, only the least restrictive restraints necessary to prevent escape or harm can be used. The BOP or U.S. Marshals Service cannot use restraints around the ankles, legs, or waist of an inmate;

restrain an inmate's hands behind her back; use four-point restraints; or attach an inmate to another inmate. If directed by a health care professional, correctional officials or deputy marshals shall refrain from using restraints on an inmate or shall remove restraints used on an inmate. If restraints are used on a pregnant inmate, the correctional official or deputy marshal who used the restraints must submit a report within thirty days describing how and why the restraints were used and any observable physical effects on the prisoner. BOP and the U.S. Marshals Service must develop training guidelines regarding the use of restraints on inmates during pregnancy, labor, and postpartum recovery.

Placement of Prisoners Closer to Families. The act generally requires BOP to house prisoners in facilities as close to their primary residence as possible, and to the extent practicable, within 500 driving miles. BOP must consider bedspace availability; the prisoner's security designation; programmatic needs, and mental and medical health needs; any request made by the prisoner related to faith-based needs; recommendations of the sentencing court; and other security concerns.

Home Confinement for Low-Risk Prisoners. BOP is required, to the extent practicable, to place prisoners with lower risk levels and lower needs on home confinement for the maximum amount of time permitted. BOP is authorized to place prisoners in prerelease custody on home confinement for 10 percent of the term of imprisonment or six months, whichever is shorter.

Increasing the Use and Transparency of Compassionate Release. A court, upon a petition from BOP, can reduce a prisoner's sentence and impose a term of probation or supervised release equal to the amount of time remaining on the prisoner's sentence if the court finds that "extraordinary and compelling reasons warrant such a reduction," or the prisoner is at least seventy years of age, has served at least thirty years, and is determined by BOP not to be a danger to any other person or the community. The act also requires BOP within seventy-two hours of a prisoner being diagnosed with a terminal illness to notify the prisoner's attorney, partner, and family about the diagnosis, inform them of their option to submit a petition for compassionate release on the prisoner's behalf, and provide the prisoner's partner and family with an opportunity to visit within seven days. BOP is also required to take certain steps to support the process of compassionate release. BOP must submit annual reports to the House and Senate Judiciary Committees that provides data on how BOP is processing applications for compassionate release.

Identification for Returning Citizens. BOP must assist prisoners and offenders who were sentenced to a period of community confinement with obtaining a social security card, driver's license or other official photo identification, and birth certificate prior to being released from custody. The bureau also has to establish prerelease planning procedures to help prisoners apply for federal and state benefits.

Expanding Prisoner Employment Through the Federal Prison Industries. The act authorizes the Federal Prison Industries (FPI, also known by its trade name, UNICOR) to sell products to public entities for use in correctional facilities, disaster relief, or emergency response; to the District of Columbia government; and to nonprofit organizations, although FPI is not allowed to sell office furniture to nonprofit organizations. BOP must set aside 15 percent of the wages paid to prisoners with FPI work assignments in a fund that will be payable to the prisoner upon release.

De-escalation Training. The act requires BOP to provide training to correctional officers and other BOP employees on how to deescalate encounters with a civilian or prisoner, and how to identify and appropriately respond to incidents that involve people with mental illness or other cognitive deficits.

Evidence-Based Treatment for Opioid and Heroin Abuse. Within ninety days of enactment of the act, BOP must submit a report to Congress that assesses the availability of, and the capacity of BOP to provide evidence-based treatment to prisoners with opioid and heroin abuse problems. The report must include a plan to expand access to evidence-based treatment for prisoners with heroin and opioid abuse problems, including medication-assisted treatment (MAT), where appropriate. After submitting the report, BOP is required to execute the plan. The act places a similar requirement on the Administrative Office of the United States Courts.

BOP Pilot Programs for Mentoring and Rescue Animals. The act requires BOP to establish two pilot programs, which will run for five years in at least twenty facilities. One will pair youth with volunteer mentors from faith-based or community organizations. The other uses prisoners to provide training and therapy to animals seized by federal law enforcement officers and to abandoned or rescued animals in the care of organizations that provide shelter and similar services.

National Prisoner Statistics Program. The act requires BJS to expand data collected under its National Prisoner Statistics program to include twenty-six new data elements related to federal prisoners. Among them are

- The number of prisoners who are veterans
- The number of prisoners who have been placed in solitary confinement in the past year
- The number of female prisoners who are known to be pregnant and the result of those pregnancies
- The number of prisoners who received medication-assisted treatment to treat a substance abuse problem
- The number of prisoners who are the parent or guardian of a minor child
- The number of assaults on bop staff by prisoners and the number of criminal prosecutions that resulted from those assaults

- The capacity of recidivism reduction programs and productive activities to accommodate eligible prisoners at each bop facility
- The number of prisoners enrolled in recidivism reduction programs and productive activities at each bop facility, broken down by risk level and by program, and the number of those enrolled prisoners who successfully completed each program

BJS is required to submit this data annually to Congress for seven years, starting one year after enactment of the act.

Federal Interagency Reentry Coordination. The act requires the attorney general to coordinate with the secretaries of Housing and Urban Development, Labor, Education, Health and Human Services, Veterans Affairs, and Agriculture, and the heads of other relevant federal agencies, as well as interested persons, service providers, nonprofit organizations, and state, tribal, and local governments, on federal reentry policies, programs, and activities, with an emphasis on evidence-based practices and the elimination of duplication of services. The attorney general must submit a report to Congress within two years of the enactment of the act that summarizes the achievements of the coordination, and includes recommendations on how to further reduce barriers to successful reentry.

Juvenile Solitary Confinement. The act prohibits juvenile facilities from using room confinement for discipline, punishment, retaliation, or any reason other than as a temporary response to a juvenile's behavior that poses a serious and immediate risk of physical harm to any individual. Juvenile facilities must try to use less restrictive techniques, such as allowing a mental health professional to talk with the juvenile, before placing the juvenile in room confinement. If the less restrictive techniques do not work and the juvenile is placed in room confinement, the staff of the juvenile facility is required to tell the juvenile the reason for room confinement and that he or she will be released upon regaining self-control and no longer posing a threat of physical harm. A juvenile who poses a continuing threat will be transferred to a facility or location where adequate services can be provided. The act prohibits juvenile facilities from using consecutive periods of room confinement.

Immigration

Despite repeated attempts to overhaul the immigration system, lawmakers in the 115th Congress failed to come to consensus over an issue that had defied resolution for years. President Trump had focused on illegal immigration during his 2016 campaign, decrying the government's failure to secure its southern border and warning that undocumented immigrants posed a major threat to the safety and prosperity of the nation. But he was unable to win passage of comprehensive immigration legislation. Congress, as in past years, could not find a balance between tightening

security, cracking down on illegal immigration, and determining whether many of the estimated 10 to 11 million undocumented immigrants living in the United States should be allowed to stay and have a path to citizenship.

BACKGROUND

Efforts to revamp immigration policy had simmered for years since a major initiative during the second administration of President George W. Bush collapsed in 2007. The number of illegal immigrants had more than tripled since 1990, even though illegal immigration had been expected to slow down after Congress last passed major immigration legislation: the Immigration Reform and Control Act (PL 99-604) in 1986. That law granted amnesty to 2.7 million people living in the country illegally while imposing tough sanctions on employers who hired undocumented workers. But the law had not been strictly enforced (1986 act, *Congress and the Nation, Vol. VII*, p. 717).

The unspoken fact was that there were many beneficiaries of the status quo, including businesses and families that employed illegal labor, as well as the immigrants themselves, who wanted any job they could get. Consumers also benefited from the lower-priced goods and services that resulted from immigrant labor. However, immigration became an increasingly deadly fact of life in isolated sections of Arizona, as smugglers sought to evade the stepped-up border enforcement and some immigrants could not survive the heat of the Sonoran Desert. The border enforcement also increased the number of undocumented immigrants who stayed in the United States instead of going back and forth to their home countries.

The larger impacts on the U.S. economy were mixed and uncertain. Although immigration advocates said the new arrivals filled the types of jobs that Americans did not want, some studies suggested that illegal immigration suppressed the wages of the least-skilled Americans. The effect on jobs became a larger concern after 2008 as displaced workers during the Great Recession, trying to support themselves and their families, faced an increasingly competitive job market. Another complicating factor was the effect of immigration on government spending. The federal government benefited by collecting income and payroll taxes from the 50 to 60 percent of illegal immigrants whose work was reported by businesses and individuals. But state and local governments struggled to foot the bill for health care, education, and other services.

During the Clinton administration, Congress in 1996 passed an enforcement-focused immigration law. A decade later, President George W. Bush made a concerted push for a new immigration policy, favoring an approach that would crack down on illegal immigrants while also allowing aliens to enter the country temporarily to work. But he could not overcome deep divisions among Republicans and Democrats, particularly on the treatment of illegal immigrants. With the Republicans in charge of both chambers in 2005–2006, the Senate followed Bush's

lead and passed a comprehensive immigration bill that aimed to both crack down on illegal immigration and create a guest worker program. But the House passed legislation focusing on border security and tough enforcement of immigration laws, especially in the workplace, and it would have punished those found aiding illegal immigrants. Many Republicans, along with a number of moderate and conservative Democrats, believed that granting illegal immigrants a path to citizenship sounded like amnesty. In the end, the only significant immigration bill to emerge during Bush's second term authorized 700 miles of fencing along the southwestern border with Mexico, as well as advanced surveillance technology along the entire U.S.–Mexico border.

By the latter part of Bush's administration, there was growing concern about the situation of Dreamers, young adult immigrants brought to the United States as children and educated in the United States, who were now seeking legal status to remain. Immigration advocates hoped for action after President Obama came into office, but neither he nor Democratic leaders during their control of Congress in 2009–2010 made major efforts on immigration, and focused instead on responding to the economic recession and financial crisis and on health care overhaul legislation. After Republican gains in the 2010 midterm elections, Obama turned to other tactics, using executive actions in 2012 to create the Deferred Action for Childhood Arrivals (DACA) program. This provided temporary, two-year protection from deportation to illegal immigrants who had been brought to the United States by their parents before June 15, 2007, who were under the age of sixteen at that time, and who had lived in the United States since then. DACA applicants also had to meet other standards, such as a clean criminal record and completion of high school or military service.

With the issue continuing to draw considerable attention, a bipartisan "gang of eight" senators in 2013 won Senate passage of a comprehensive immigration bill designed to beef up border security while setting in motion a process to grant citizenship to those in the United States illegally. But immigration efforts foundered in the House where a bipartisan group of lawmakers were divided over such issues as health insurance for illegal immigrants. Although Republicans won House Judiciary Committee approval of four smaller bills dealing with such issues as agricultural guest workers and employment verification, House GOP leaders declined to move any further, at least in part because of wariness among conservatives that passage of immigration legislation in the House might lead to conference negotiations that would favor the Senate approach.

With Congress deadlocked, Obama again flexed his presidential powers. After the 2014 midterm elections, he announced executive orders on November 20, 2014, that lifted the threat of deportation for an estimated 5 million illegal immigrants. He focused the government's immigration enforcement activities on national security threats, serious criminals, and recent border crossers. Republicans were infuriated, accusing the president of acting unilaterally instead of working with Congress to fix the immigration system. Senate Majority Leader Mitch McConnell, R-Ky., effectively killed chances for a comprehensive immigration bill in the 114th Congress when he declared during an August 6, 2015, news conference that Obama's executive actions the year before had "made it impossible for us to go forward."

Moreover, twenty-six states filed a lawsuit a month after Obama's order, setting up a showdown in the federal courts. In 2015, a three-judge panel of the U.S. Court of Appeals for the 5th Circuit ruled, 2–1, that Texas and the other states had a legal right to challenge the federal government because the states could face millions of dollars in costs if the immigrants got drivers' licenses and other benefits. As the case made its way to the Supreme Court, House and Senate Republicans filed separate briefs on behalf of the states challenging Obama's actions, arguing that the president had overstepped his authority. In June 2016, the shorthanded Supreme Court deadlocked 4–4 on the legal challenge to the Obama executive actions. This left in place the appeals court decision blocking the DACA program and leaving the administration powerless to do much more on immigration.

Donald Trump made immigration a centerpiece of his 2016 presidential campaign. He pledged to rescind DACA, build a wall along the U.S.–Mexico border, and suspend immigration from countries with histories of terrorism, sometimes using incendiary rhetoric to underscore his views of the issue. In a speech announcing his presidential bid on June 16, 2015, he said of immigrants from Mexico: "They're bringing drugs. They're bringing crime. They're rapists. And some, I assume, are good people." Such remarks, as well as later comments Trump made as president, led Democrats to accuse him of trying to exclude darker-skinned immigrants. They pointed to an Oval Office meeting in January 2018 when he complained that many immigrants came from "shithole countries" and that the United States should attract more immigrants from countries such as Norway.

As president, Trump repeatedly pressed for funds for a border wall and issued executive orders to restrict people from certain Muslim-majority countries from entering the United States. The Trump administration in September 2017 announced a plan to phase out DACA, but deferred the plan until March 5, 2018, to give Congress time to pass immigration legislation. Even though Congress ultimately would fail to meet the deadline, courts intervened to prevent the administration from ending the program.

Negotiations

Lawmakers in 2017 and early 2018 struggled to reach consensus on an immigration deal that would protect undocumented "Dreamers" and fulfill Trump's

enforcement priorities. A bipartisan group of six senators announced a deal early in January 2018, only to see it fall apart after Trump, who opposed it, set off a firestorm by using vulgar language to describe Haitian and African immigrants. As lawmakers tried to reach a compromise, they focused in particular on four issues:

- Border Security. Trump made clear that building a border wall was non-negotiable, and he asked Congress for tens of billions of dollars in funding. Leading Senate Republicans sided with him while sometimes suggesting a reduced funding level. Democrats opposed any funding for the wall, although they were amenable to enhanced border security measures such as border surveillance technology that was dubbed a "smart wall." The debate over the border wall would prove highly contentious throughout the Trump years, bringing the appropriations process to a halt at the end of 2018 and contributing to the nation's longest government shutdown.

- DACA. Both Democrats and Republicans said they wanted to provide Dreamers with a path to legal status, but they differed on what that would entail and the concessions that conservatives should receive in return. Whereas many Republicans coalesced behind a plan to provide Dreamers with three-year periods of temporary protected status, a bipartisan proposal (S 1615, HR 3440) known as the Dream Act would grant them a path to citizenship. Other plans floated by Republicans would have greatly limited the number of Dreamers who could obtain citizenship or temporarily limit Dreamers from bringing their extended family members to the United States.

- "Chain Migration." The White House and conservative lawmakers insisted on limiting the right of immigrants to bring their extended family members to the United States, a process known as family migration but derided by immigration hardliners as "chain migration." Family migration had contributed substantially to the number of immigrants in the United States. Some Democrats indicated a degree of flexibility on the issue, and bipartisan discussions looked into placing restrictions on the ability of Dreamers to bring in family members. But many conservatives wanted to go much further. One proposal (S 1720), by Sens. Tom Cotton, R-Ark., and David Perdue, R-Ga., would cut legal immigration by half and drastically limit an immigrant's ability to sponsor anyone but a spouse or a child under eighteen for a green card.

- Diversity Visas. The policy differences extended to a somewhat obscure Diversity Visa lottery that granted visas to 50,000 people annually from countries with historically low rates of U.S. immigration. Although largely overlooked, the program drew increased scru-

tiny after an Uzbek man who had come to the United States on a Diversity Visa veered his truck through a crowded New York City bike path in 2017, killing eight people and injuring eleven others in a highly publicized terrorist attack. Trump subsequently said that shutting down the program was a matter of national security.

While lawmakers tried to come up with a consensus on these and other issues, the White House announced an immigration plan in January 2018 that would offer a path to citizenship to an estimated 1.8 million Dreamers. It would also restrict family migration and appropriate $30 billion for a border wall and other security measures.

The package called for legalizing more than double the nearly 700,000 Dreamers enrolled in the Deferred Action for Childhood Arrivals program, providing them with a ten- to twelve-year pathway to citizenship, with requirements for work, education, and more. It also would direct $25 billion into a trust fund for Trump's proposed U.S.–Mexico border wall, as well as for ports of entry and exit, and improvements on the northern border. It would limit family-based immigration to spouses and minor children, disallowing parents, siblings, and others. The Diversity Visa Lottery program would be shut down, with those visas instead being redirected toward reducing backlogs in other visa programs, such as those for high-skilled workers and their families. In broad strokes, the plan would represent a move from family-based immigration, which gave preference to green card applicants who had family members in the United States, to a merit-based system that rewarded those with educational achievements and English fluency.

The plan won high marks from a number of Senate Republicans. McConnell praised the framework in a news release and said it pointed the way to "what's necessary for the president to sign a bill into law." But it drew fire from Democrats, who blasted it as xenophobic, and from conservative Republicans who strongly objected to providing Dreamers with a path to citizenship. In the House, conservatives rallied behind a bill (HR 4760) by Judiciary Chairman Robert W. Goodlatte, R-Va., that would offer Dreamers renewable periods of legal status but not a path to citizenship. The House bill would also cut legal immigration by about 25 percent, allow the Justice Department to withhold federal grant money from so-called sanctuary cities, and force employers to check the immigration status of their workers.

The political differences were clearly visible when Trump delivered his State of the Union address on January 30, 2018. More than two dozen Democrats invited Dreamers to attend the speech as their guests, while the president's guests, who sat with first lady Melania Trump, included an Immigration and Customs Enforcement agent and the parents of two teenage girls slain by undocumented gang members. The intensity of the issue was laid

bare when Rep. Paul Gosar, R-Ariz., said on Twitter that he asked Capitol police to "consider checking identification of all attending the State of the Union address and arresting any illegal aliens in attendance."

Trump used his speech to try to rally support for his plan, which he called "a down-the-middle compromise, and one that will create a safe, modern and lawful immigration system." But he continued to use contentious rhetoric, referring to Dreamers as "illegal immigrants" and criticizing undocumented immigrants who turned to gang violence. With House Republicans as well as Democrats opposed to key elements of the president's plan, it appeared to have faint prospects for congressional passage. Instead, Democrats and some Senate Republicans suggested narrowing the scope to DACA and border security, even though the White House and House Republicans insisted on addressing family migration and Diversity Visas as well.

Senate Action

The Senate on February 15, 2018, took up three major immigration proposals and rejected each one, delivering a major setback to efforts to overhaul the nation's immigration system. Each of the plans would have offered a path to citizenship for at least 1.8 million Dreamers in return for some degree of border security. None, however, could garner the requisite sixty votes to overcome a filibuster.

The proposals were attached to an unrelated tax bill, HR 2579, that McConnell tapped in an attempt to find a consensus on immigration. One proposal, which was supported by Trump and patterned after the hardline House plan, proved the least popular, failing on a vote of 39–60. Fourteen Republicans voted against it, while three moderate Democrats who faced difficult reelection battles in November—Joe Donnelly of Indiana, Heidi Heitkamp of North Dakota and Joe Manchin III of West Virginia—sided with the White House.

A bipartisan deal that was negotiated by Sens. Mike Rounds, R-S.C., and Angus King, I-Maine, fared somewhat better, winning fifty-four votes. Its key elements included providing a ten- to twelve-year path to citizenship for at least 1.8 million Dreamers and designating $25 billion for a border wall. Moderates in both parties supported it, but the White House undercut their efforts. Shortly before the vote, Trump tweeted that the proposal was a "total catastrophe," even though moderate Republican Susan Collins of Maine said it drew on key elements in the president's proposal.

Another bipartisan plan, by Sens. John McCain, R-Ariz., and Chris Coons, D-Del., won fifty-two votes. More narrowly tailored than the other plans, it would have offered the Dreamers a path to citizenship in return for some border security enhancements.

After failing to pass any of the three main proposals, senators also defeated a narrower plan, 54–45, by Republican Sen. Patrick J. Toomey of Pennsylvania. His proposal would have cut funding from so-called sanctuary cities that declined to cooperate with federal immigration officers.

House Action

The House voted down conservative and moderate immigration proposals, effectively delivering a death blow to a comprehensive overhaul of the immigration system in the 115th Congress. Despite months of negotiations, lawmakers could not bridge their differences over DACA, family migration, and other critical issues.

In an embarrassing setback for House leadership, the farm bill (HR 2) became a temporary casualty of the debate over immigration. In order to win the support of conservatives for funding levels in the farm bill, Republican leaders announced they had won support for HR 4760, the hardline immigration bill favored by the conservative House Freedom Caucus, and promised a vote in June. But the farm bill went down anyway on May 18, 198–213. Mark Meadows, the chairman of the Freedom Caucus and a no vote on the farm bill, said after the vote that leadership's plan for immigration "was not fully clear."

This set the stage for weeks of negotiations in which one seemingly promising agreement after another failed to gain traction. The discussions took place in the shadow of the Senate's failure to coalesce behind any plan, raising questions about whether a House bill, even if it mustered a majority on the floor, could ever be signed into law. Further roiling the waters, an insurgent group of moderate Republicans led by Rep. Jeff Denham, R-Calif., made steady progress on a plan to gather enough signatures on a discharge petition to force votes on the hardline immigration bill as well as other, more moderate immigration proposals. Although their efforts ultimately fell short, they came within a few signatures of achieving their goal. GOP leaders were left scrambling for a way to deter them, arguing that the discharge petition process would produce a bill that would be backed by more Democrats than Republicans and fail to pass muster with Senate Republicans or the White House.

Even as they excluded Democrats from negotiations, Republicans could not agree among themselves on a plan that would garner 218 votes. Although they generally rallied behind Trump's wall, they remained deeply divided over the issue of family migration as well as whether to provide Dreamers with a path to citizenship. They also lacked confidence that a House compromise could make its way through the Senate and win Trump's signature. The Goodlatte bill appeared to have little support in the Senate, given that a similar plan had won just thirty-nine votes. And even if a bipartisan bill (HR 4796) backed by moderate Democrats and most Republicans made its way through both chambers, it faced White House opposition.

As it turned out, the Senate would not be called upon to weigh in on a House-passed bill. The House on June 21 voted down the conservative bill, HR 4760, by a vote of 193–231. The measure would have granted legal status to Dreamers, authorized funds for the border wall, and cracked

down on asylum seekers. It also would have mandated the use of E-Verify, a system for business owners to ensure their employees may legally work in the United States. All 190 voting Democrats opposed it, along with forty-one Republicans. The Republican no votes included conservatives such as Louie Gohmert of Texas, who warned that it effectively provided amnesty to illegal immigrants, as well as moderates such as Mike Coffman of Colorado, who was trying to win a difficult reelection in a suburban district that had voted for Hillary Clinton in 2016. Underscoring the Republican disarray, the vote took place just minutes after GOP leaders delayed a vote on a second, more moderate proposal.

Six days later, the House scuttled what little chance remained of a comprehensive immigration measure when it rejected, 121–301, a bill (HR 6136) that would have created a path to citizenship for Dreamers. Taking place against the backdrop of an uproar over the administration's practice of separating undocumented children and their parents at the border, the bill included a provision in the compromise bill designed to keep families together while they remained in government custody. But Democrats and immigrant advocates dismissed it as ineffective, saying it contradicted current law and would lead to indefinite detention of asylum-seekers.

Other Immigration Measures

Conservative House members, with Trump's backing, coalesced behind several bills to crack down on undocumented immigrants. One of these (HR 3003), which passed on June 29, 2017, by a vote of 228–195, would have cut off federal funds to so-called sanctuary jurisdictions that did not allow their law enforcement agencies to cooperate with federal immigration enforcement. On the same day, the chamber passed a bill (HR 3004), known as Kate's Law, that would impose stiff penalties on convicted and deported criminals who reentered the country. The bill, passed 257–167, was named for a woman who was killed in San Francisco by a Mexican national who had committed multiple felonies and been repeatedly deported.

Lawmakers who wanted to impose tighter restrictions on immigrants viewed such narrowly focused enforcement bills as a fallback in case negotiations over more comprehensive immigration failed, while also keeping the contentious issue of illegal immigration in the spotlight. The Trump administration backed the limited bills, viewing them as important steps toward cracking down on undocumented immigrations, who the president viewed as a threat to public safety. Many Democrats, however, opposed the bills, portraying them as an effort by the White House to reduce the number of immigrants and close U.S. borders to refugees who were fleeing violence in their home countries.

Increased Immigration Enforcement

One of the more far-reaching Republican immigration bills, passed by the House Judiciary Committee in 2017, would have strengthened measures against undocumented immigrants. The House did not take up the legislation,

with Republican leaders instead focusing their attention on other immigration plans.

Under the bill (HR 2431), states and localities would gain specific authority to enact and enforce immigration laws that were consistent with federal statutes. Sponsored by Raul R. Labrador, R-Idaho, the measure extended the authority of federal deportation agents while taking steps against so-called sanctuary jurisdictions that refused to cooperate with federal immigration laws. It also would authorize the U.S. Immigration and Customs Enforcement to hire 12,500 additional officers and enable the agency to make arrests in cases where an individual was suspected to have committed a felony while unlawfully present in the United States. The bill also would establish new screening standards for the issuance of U.S. visas, including a requirement that certain applicants submit DNA tests and social media information.

The committee approved the measure on a party line, 19–13 vote on May 24, 2017, after a three-day mark-up in which Republicans turned back a series of Democratic amendments to scale back the bill. In a last-ditch effort to derail the measure, Democrats forced a vote to adjourn the committee. But the motion was rejected, 11–20.

Lawmakers sharply debated an amendment by Luis V. Guitierrez, D-Ill., that would have nullified an executive order by President Donald Trump, issued on January 25, 2017, instructing agencies on enforcing immigration law. With Democrats contending that the White House was criminalizing all undocumented immigrants, the amendment instead would have reinstated Obama administration policies that prioritized threats to national security, public safety, and border security. The committee rejected the amendment, 7–16, with the vote breaking down along party lines. The committee also rejected, 8–16, an amendment by Sheila Jackson Lee, D-Texas, that would have delayed, by seventy-two hours, the beginning of the removal period for undocumented immigrants who have been granted a provisional stay of deportation, are the subject of a pending challenge to a removal order, or are otherwise seeking to establish grounds to remain in the United States.

The committee rejected 11–18, an amendment by Brad Schneider, D-Ill., to exempt undocumented immigrants whose removal was deferred under the Obama administration's Deferred Action for Childhood Arrivals (DACA) program from the penalties in the bill. Although Democrats pointed out that DACA recipients came to the country as minors and had to meet such standards as a clean record and completion of high school or military service, Rep. Steve King, R-Iowa, said the program effectively rewarded them for breaking the law.

An amendment by David Cicilline, D-R.I., to strike language that would make changes to the process for extending temporary protected status, was rejected on a vote of 7–11. Temporary protected status was a special immigration status granted to immigrants who came from countries experiencing war, natural disasters, or other catastrophic events.

The committee adopted, 16–11, an amendment by Labrador that he said would help assuage Democratic concerns about penalties for illegal entry or presence in the country. The amendment would apply criminal penalties in the bill for such violations beginning ninety days after the bill's enactment.

Immigration and Criminal Gang Activity

Another Republican-backed bill, passed by the House on September 14, 2017, would make it easier to deport undocumented immigrants who are involved in criminal gang activity. The Senate, however, did not take it up.

The measure (HR 3697) passed on a 233–175 vote. Sponsored by Republican Reps. Barbara Comstock of Virginia and Peter T. King of New York, it was drawn from the more comprehensive measure (HR 2431) that the Judiciary Committee approved in May. Supporters said the legislation, backed by congressional Republicans and the White House, clearly showed that members of criminal gangs were not welcome in the United States. It gave expanded tools to law enforcement agencies to crack down on them.

The bill would give authority to the secretary of Homeland Security, in consultation with the attorney general, to designate a group, club, or organization of five or more people as a criminal gang if it was found to have committed certain offenses. Its foreign-born members would then be subject to swift deportation.

The criminal gang designation would apply to a group if any of its members had a felony drug offense, were suspected of bringing and harboring undocumented immigrants into the United States, obstructed justice, or were suspected of committing fraud in using identification documents. Comstock said the measure would help law enforcement combat the violent, transnational Mara Salvatrucha gang, known as MS-13, which had established a presence in Los Angeles, New York, and other U.S. cities.

The National Immigrant Justice Center said the bill would allow the Department of Homeland Security to designate churches and fraternities as criminal gangs if they sheltered immigrants. A fraternity whose members used expired identification documents to buy liquor could be similarly designated as a criminal gang, the group said.

Under the legislation, DHS could use classified details to designate a group as a criminal gang, putting the information beyond public reach. The bill would provide judicial review by the U.S. Court of Appeals for the District of Columbia of the government's designation, as well as the secret information used to come to such a conclusion. The National Immigrant Justice Center objected to the bill permitting a legal challenge only in one federal court.

Polygraph Waivers for Border Patrol Applicants

The House passed a bill (HR 2213) on June 7, 2017, that would waive polygraph testing requirements for certain Border Patrol applicants. The vote was 282–137, with fifty-one Democrats joining 231 Republicans in support. A similar measure won approval in the Senate Homeland Security and Governmental Affairs Committee but was not taken up on the Senate floor.

The House bill would forgo polygraph examinations for current law enforcement officers who had passed a polygraph, federal officials who cleared a background check, and veterans with three consecutive years of military service who passed background checks and held a security clearance. The goal was to accelerate the Customs and Border Protection (CBP)'s hiring process. The agency needed to add around 1,500 agents to meet its goal of 21,370 agents.

The Border Patrol had already sped up its hiring process while also improving retention of its current agents. In January 2016, it took the agency an average of 469 days to hire an agent compared with 165 days in March 2017. The CBP's attrition rate had fallen as well from 5.5 percent in fiscal 2015 to the current rate of 4.3 percent.

Supporters said the bill would advance Trump's goal of securing the nation's border with Mexico. Trump had called for 5,000 agents to be added to CBP without setting a specific time frame for reaching that goal. Debate over the bill came as the Border Patrol considered adopting a shorter version of the standard polygraph to speed up recruitment. The fiscal 2017 omnibus spending bill (HR 244) had included a directive to test alternative polygraph methods.

The House Homeland Security Committee approved HR 2213 by voice vote on May 3, 2017. The bill's sponsor, Rep. Martha McSally, R-Ariz., warned that CBP remained critically understaffed, and she said few applicants could wait 160 days or longer for a job. Opponents, however, worried that the measure would allow the agency to be infiltrated by the very threats it sought to prevent, with cartels recruiting people to apply for CBP positions. Rep. Zoe Lofgren, D-Calif., noted cases in which CBP officers had been found to have connections to drug cartels.

Rep. Bennie Thompson, D-Miss., the committee's ranking member, said the original congressional intent in requiring polygraphs was to prevent drug cartels from placing its members within the agency. Thompson, however, supported the bill. He said former CBP agents told him that a polygraph test could take as long as nine hours to complete.

The committee gave voice vote approval to an amendment by Thompson that would require CBP to provide the committee with information about how many polygraph waivers were requested, granted and denied, as well as reasons for denial. A comparable bill (S 595) won approval from the Senate Homeland Security and Governmental Affairs Committee on May 17, 2017. The vote was 9–2.

Supporters, such as Arizona Republican John McCain, said the legislation was needed to fill out the ranks of the Border Patrol more quickly. Sen. Kamala Harris, D-Calif., opposed the measure, saying she was concerned over misconduct issues involving some CBP agents. She contended

that it would be better to spend more time evaluating potential recruits.

Unaccompanied Alien Children

By a vote of 19–11, the House Judiciary Committee on July 26, 2017, approved a bill that would raise the "credible fear" threshold that the United States required of foreign nationals who were seeking asylum. The bill (HR 391) would also expedite the removal of children from Central America who traveled through Mexico to the southern U.S. border. The full House did not take up the measure.

Republicans, many of whom had worried that asylum-seekers were treated too leniently during the Obama administration, said the measure would reduce instances in which the system was abused while retaining protections for those with legitimate claims. Committee Chairman Robert W. Goodlatte, R-Va., said the current system enabled immigrants to merely get to the border and claim a fear of persecution back home in order to be admitted in the United States and enjoy years of freedom.

The policy, in Goodlatte's view, had spurred a massive migration surge of hundreds of thousands of unaccompanied children from Central America during Obama's second term. Under existing law, Mexican children could be quickly deported if they were found not to have credible fear claims, but Central American children, who comprised the majority of child border crossers, were handed over to the Health and Human Services Department and ordered to appear in immigration court.

The bill would alter this by giving authority to the Department of Homeland Security DHS to designate a country such as Mexico as a third-party nation to where children could be safely deported. It would also enhance the credible fear threshold by allowing Border Patrol agents to make the determination of whether claims made by a detained child migrant were "more probable than not," a responsibility currently delegated to immigration judges. Under the bill, federal funds could not be used to pay to help asylum seekers with legal representation when they appeared in immigration court.

The Trump administration supported the bill. With the nation already facing a massive backlog of immigration cases, Attorney General Jeff Sessions said the measure could help head off more attempts by child migrants to cross the border.

Humanitarian organizations, however, argued that the children—most of whom came from El Salvador, Guatemala and Honduras—were fleeing some of the world's worst gang violence and had no economic opportunity in their native countries. Democrats at the markup said the bill would prevent children with legitimate claims from gaining asylum in the United States. They also said it would do away with protections for undocumented relatives of U.S. veterans and service members.

Democrats proposed more than ten amendments to scale back the scope of the bill, but failed to win approval

of any. The committee rejected, 8–15, an amendment by Jerrold Nadler of New York that would have narrowed the bill's language pertaining to third-party countries. Nadler said at the markup that the provision as written could leave asylum seekers "stateless and in legal purgatory."

The committee also rejected, 8–14, an amendment by Pramila Jayapal of Washington that would refer Border Patrol agents to the Office of Professional Responsibility if they were accused of turning away asylum seekers. However, Republicans and Democrats joined together on an amendment by Goodlatte that would allow the Homeland Security Department to grant immigration parole to certain undocumented family members of active-duty service members. The amendment, passed 21–0, was a response to concerns by Democrats that a provision in the bill prohibiting DHS from offering parole to someone who would otherwise not be approved for refugee status would accidentally strip protections from family members of those currently serving in the armed services as well as relatives of Filipino nationals who fought for the United States in World War II.

Gun Violence

Despite a spate of mass shootings, Congress took limited action to address gun violence. Lawmakers used appropriations bills to provide federal grant funding to boost student safety in schools and strengthen the FBI background check system. They also ended the prohibition of federally funded research into gun violence. Gun rights advocates won a victory in repealing a rule prohibiting mentally impaired Social Security recipients from buying firearms. But lawmakers resisted more sweeping measures, including efforts by Democrats to regulate guns more strictly and by Republicans to loosen restrictions on concealed weapons.

The Trump administration took modest steps to curb gun violence. Following a mass shooting in Las Vegas in 2017 that left sixty people dead, it issued a rule prohibiting so-called bump stocks, which make semiautomatic rifles operate like a machine gun. After a mass shooting in 2018 at a high school in Parkland, Florida, that left seventeen people dead, Attorney General Jeff Sessions announced the Justice Department would funnel more grant money to local law enforcement agencies that wanted to hire officers for schools, and he ordered federal prosecutors to step up cases against people who lied in an attempt to get around the federal background check system to purchase a gun. Sessions also announced plans to get federal agencies that are required to report individuals to that system to certify that they are doing so, and help state and local agencies provide more records on mental health and domestic violence information.

Democrats wanted additional restrictions, and they wanted them imposed through congressional legislation, not administrative actions. But Republicans who controlled both chambers remained implacably opposed to

gun control. The country remained deeply divided along partisan lines when it came to gun control, which gave politicians little incentive to go against their base. In a Pew Research Center poll from June 2017, 79 percent of Republicans said it was more important to protect the right of Americans to own guns than to control gun ownership; 80 percent of Democrats answered the opposite. Three-quarters of gun owners say that gun ownership is essential to their personal freedom.

Democratic priorities included banning bump stocks, raising the legal age for purchasing semiautomatic guns to twenty-one, and—perhaps most controversial—banning assault rifles. None of these proposals, however, gained any traction in the 115th Congress, although Trump briefly expressed support for raising the legal age for certain gun purchases to twenty-one. Republicans, however, scored an earlier victory in paring back a prohibition on mentally impaired people from buying firearms.

CANCELING AN OBAMA-ERA GUN RULE

The Republican-led Congress on February 14, 2017, sent legislation to President Donald Trump that would stop a rule adding mentally impaired Social Security recipients to a list of those prohibited from buying firearms. The Senate voted 57–43 to approve a resolution (HJ Res 40) that would cancel the rule finalized in December, in the waning days of the Obama administration.

Under the rule, the Social Security Administration would send information to the nation's criminal background check system for gun purchases about people who receive disability insurance benefits based on a finding of mental impairment. The Obama administration estimated that 75,000 people a year would be added to the National Instant Criminal Background Check System under the rule, and law prohibited people from buying a gun if they had a mental health issue.

The issue of background checks for gun purchases, set against the backdrop of mass shootings in Orlando, Florida, and San Bernardino, California, had led to particularly heated debates in Congress in 2016, when Democrats staged a sit-in on the House floor and a talking filibuster in the Senate to demand votes on gun control legislation. Five senators who caucused with Democrats and who were up for reelection in 2018 joined Republicans to pass the measure: Democrats Joe Donnelly of Indiana, Heidi Heitkamp of North Dakota, Joe Manchin III of West Virginia, Jon Tester of Montana, and independent Angus King of Maine.

On February 2, 2017, the House voted 235–180, largely along party lines, to approve the resolution as part of the Congressional Review Act process. That process allows Congress to review regulations within sixty legislative days and overrule them with a simple majority vote in both chambers.

Democrats argued on the Senate floor Tuesday that the resolution would roll back an effort to keep guns out of the hands of mentally ill people. But they could not filibuster the resolution—and therefore could not stop it—unless they stuck together and also attracted votes from at least three Republicans.

Minority Whip Richard J. Durbin of Illinois argued that lawmakers had a responsibility to reduce gun violence. He warned that repealing the regulation would make it easier for severely mentally ill people to get guns. Democrat Dianne Feinstein of California took note of a 2011 case in Missouri in which a woman diagnosed with paranoid schizophrenia used her Social Security disability payments to legally buy a gun and later used it to kill her father.

But Republicans said the rule went too far and lacked constitutional protections. Senate Judiciary Chairman Charles E. Grassley of Iowa said it took away the Second Amendment right to buy or own a firearm from people who should not be in the background check system. He argued that many of the mental disorders that would trigger the rule were unrelated to gun safety, such as eating disorders, those that impact sleep, or disorders that could cause feelings of inadequacy, Grassley said. On February 28, 2017, Trump signed the resolution repealing the rule.

GUN PROVISIONS IN FISCAL 2018 OMNIBUS APPROPRIATIONS

Ultimately, lawmakers wound up rolling a pair of bills to reduce gun violence into the fiscal 2018 omnibus spending bill, which was signed into law on March 23, 2018 (HR 1625—PL 115-141). The measures provided grants to schools to bolster student safety and strengthened compliance with the background check system for firearm purchases. The bill also contained language permitting research into gun violence.

GRANTS FOR SCHOOLS

Lawmakers added a bipartisan measure to appropriations legislation to provide $1 billion over ten years in federal grant funding for school design and teacher training to bolster student safety. The measure was originally contained in a bill (HR 4909) that passed the House on March 14, 2018, by a vote of 407–10. The bill would reauthorize and modify the Secure Our Schools grant program to more explicitly focus on preventing student violence. It would authorize $75 million for fiscal 2018, and $100 million for fiscal years 2019 through 2028.

These provisions were rolled into the fiscal 2018 omnibus spending bill. They enjoyed support from both parties as well as White House backing.

BACKGROUND CHECKS

The background check measure proved more politically problematic. Sens. John Cornyn, R-Texas, and Christopher S. Murphy, D-Conn., introduced the bill to bolster enforcement of the National Instant Criminal Background Check System, known as NICS.

It would require federal agencies to certify twice per year that they are uploading relevant records to the NICS

and would establish implementation plans for submitting records. The bill was a response to a November 5 church shooting in Sutherland Springs, Texas, in which twenty-six people were killed. The gunman should not have been able to purchase a firearm, but the Air Force had failed to report his court martial conviction for domestic violence.

Although more than three-quarters of senators signed on as cosponsors, it failed to make its way to the floor. Republican senators Mike Lee of Utah and Rand Paul of Kentucky worried about the rights of individuals placed on a no-buy list. Sen. John Kennedy, R-La., said the database had flaws because a number of state and federal employees were not sending in data.

The House attached the original legislation to a controversial measure (HR 38) to allow those licensed to carry concealed weapons in one state to carry them in all states. It passed HR 38 on December 6, 2017, on a vote of 231–198. Supporters said the bill, a priority of the National Rifle Association, would help those who wanted to act in their own self-defense and also help them defend others. Opponents, however, said it would lead to more violence. At a December 4 markup of the bill, Republicans on the House Judiciary Committee rejected more than a dozen amendments by Democrats that would have excluded certain individuals from the concealed carry protections, including those convicted of misdemeanor domestic violence, assault on law enforcement, and drunk driving convictions. The committee then approved the bill on a party line vote of 19–11.

Although some Republicans threatened to oppose the omnibus spending bill unless it included the concealed carry language, lawmakers added the NICS measure without it.

Research Into Gun Violence

The omnibus spending law also opened the door to more government research into the causes of gun violence. That is because it clarified the Dickey Amendment, named after former Arkansas GOP Rep. Jay Dickey, which for more than two decades prohibited the Centers for Disease Control and Prevention from conducting research "used to advocate or promote gun control."

But the spending bill included report language approved by the secretary of the Health and Human Services Department, Alex Azar, who oversaw the CDC. It said the CDC could research gun violence, even though the Dickey Amendment barred it from funding research that promotes gun control. The provision in the May law split gun control advocates, with some viewing it as insufficient without a further congressional directive and specific research funding.

Protections for Special Counsel

With some in Congress worried that President Trump might fire Special Counsel Robert S. Mueller III, the Senate Judiciary Committee approved a bill (S 2644) by a vote of

14–7 to give protections to Mueller. Despite the bipartisan vote on April 26, 2018, the bill faced opposition by Senate Majority Leader Mitch McConnell, R-Ky., and never advanced to the floor.

The bill won committee approval over warnings by some Republicans that it would unconstitutionally infringe on a president's power. They also said the bill had no plausible path to becoming law, as neither the full Senate nor the House would pass it, and Trump would refuse to sign it even if it made it to his desk.

The markup took place hours after Trump responded to reports that he was considering firing Mueller or Rod Rosenstein, the Justice Department official who oversaw Mueller's probe, which focused on connections between Russian operatives and the 2016 Trump campaign. Speaking on *Fox and Friends*, he said he had no plans to do so but could change his mind.

"So, I'm very disappointed in my Justice Department. But because of the fact that it's going on, and I think you'll understand this, I have decided that I won't be involved," Trump said on April 26. "I may change my mind at some point because what's going on is a disgrace. It's an absolute disgrace."

The bill would give a special counsel ten days to ask a federal judge to determine whether a removal was for "good cause." If it was not, the special counsel would be allowed to stay in the position. The bill was written by Republicans Lindsey Graham of South Carolina and Thom Tillis of North Carolina and Democrats Cory Booker of New Jersey and Chris Coons of Connecticut. As amended by Chairman Charles E. Grassley of Iowa, it would require the executive branch to issue a report to Congress about when a special counsel is appointed or removed, or when the investigation of the special counsel concludes. It also would codify certain Justice Department regulations governing the special counsel.

The debate over whether the measure was constitutional focused on a 1988 Supreme Court decision, *Morrison v. Olson*, that a previous independent counsel law did not violate the separation of powers required by the Constitution. Justice Antonin Scalia, however, had written a much-discussed dissent arguing that Congress could not infringe on the prosecutorial powers of the executive branch.

Mike Lee of Utah offered an amendment that would have inserted language into the bill to state that Scalia's dissent was now "widely considered the law of the land across the political spectrum." The committee rejected it on a 6–15 vote.

In the end, four Judiciary Committee Republicans—Grassley, Graham, Tillis, and Jeff Flake of Arizona—joined the panel's ten Democrats to approve the bill. They said it would protect future special counsels as well as Mueller.

Later Action

In the House, Judiciary Committee ranking member Jerrold Nadler of New York tried to use a rule in September to force the committee to consider the House version of

the Senate legislation (HR 5476). Along with several other committee Democrats, Nadler said the unusual move was needed because of a number of Trump's comments, including criticism of Attorney General Jeff Sessions. But Nadler's gambit failed because he could not persuade committee Republicans to join Republicans in forcing a vote.

The issue returned to the forefront with the forced resignation of Sessions on the day after the midterm elections. Trump had repeatedly questioned the decision by Sessions to recuse himself from overseeing Mueller's probe, and his sudden departure stirred speculation that Trump may be moving to shut down the probe. Trump failed to assuage concerns when he announced that Matthew Whitaker, Sessions' chief of staff and a one-time critic of the probe, would become the acting attorney general.

In a press conference shortly before Sessions resigned on November 7, 2018, Trump said the Mueller probe should end. "This is a investigation where many, many millions of dollars has been spent, and there's no collusion," he said. "It was supposed to be on collusion. There's no collusion. And I think it's—I think it's very bad for our country, I will tell you. I think it's a shame," Trump said.

Democrats made a final attempt to protect Mueller, with Senate Minority Leader Charles E. Schumer, D-N.Y., and House Minority Leader Nancy Pelosi, D-Calif., proposing language to a year-end spending package that would prevent him from getting fired before he completed his work. But McConnell stood firmly against it. He contended that the legislation was unnecessary because Trump had never said he would shut down the investigation. He also said the proposal was probably unconstitutional. Senate Appropriations Chairman Richard Shelby of Alabama also opposed it, saying it would complicate efforts to reach an agreement on the spending package.

Mueller would continue the investigation, which wrapped up in 2019.

Presidential Pardon Power

With Democrats warning that President Trump could use his pardon powers to impede an investigation of him, the House Judiciary Committee, on June 26, 2018, rejected a resolution that would have directed the president and attorney general to share documents with the House on the president's use of pardon power within fourteen days after the legislation's adoption. The vote was 12–13.

The measure (H Res 928) would have required the president and attorney general to produce documents, records, audio recordings, memorandums, correspondence, or other communications that referred or related to a number of topics, including any presidential pardon issued on or after January 20, 2017. The measure would have encompassed pardons under consideration, including for Michael Cohen, President Trump's personal attorney, and Paul Manafort, the former chairman of the Trump presidential campaign. It also would have covered any consideration of the president's power to pardon himself,

which had become a topic of discussion among constitutional experts.

The committee rejected as out of order an amendment by Rep. Jamie Raskin, D-Md. It would have directed the president and attorney general to produce any departmental review of current laws to protect elections from foreign influence and any related communications with the executive office of the president. The amendment would also have included any communication or memorandum dealing with other topics, such as election infrastructure or foreign hacking attempts or operations.

Justice Department Documents

Amid sharp partisan differences, the House in 2018 adopted a resolution, 226–183, requiring the Justice Department to turn over documents pertaining to the FBI's investigation into allegations of Russian influence in the 2016 presidential campaign. The resolution (H Res 970) by Rep. Mark Meadows, R-N.C., passed on June 28 and gave Justice Department officials until July 6 to comply with requests and subpoenas issued by the House Intelligence and Judiciary committees.

The Republican interest in the documents stemmed from their concerns over potential violations by departmental personnel of the Foreign Intelligence Surveillance Act (FISA) during the 2016 campaign. These concerns centered on FBI surveillance of Carter Page and other aides on Trump's presidential campaign.

Top House and Senate Democrats assailed the resolution, urging Deputy Attorney General Rod J. Rosenstein and FBI Director Christopher Wray to resist Republican efforts to obtain thousands of pages of documents pertaining to the Russia investigation. In a letter to Rosenstein and Wray on June 27, 2018, Senate Minority Leader Charles E. Schumer of New York and House Minority Leader Nancy Pelosi, along with Senate Intelligence Committee ranking member Mark Warner of Virginia and House Intelligence Committee Adam B. Schiff of California, wrote, "With every disclosure, DOJ and FBI are reinforcing a precedent it will have to uphold, whether the Congress is in Republican or Democratic hands, of providing materials in pending or closed cases to the legislative branch upon request . . . It is imperative that you withstand pressure on DOJ and FBI to violate established procedures and norms."

The Justice Department and the FBI warned that turning over records requested by Republican lawmakers could jeopardize their investigation into the 2016 campaign, expose informants, and reveal vital national security information. But Republicans claimed that the FBI's investigation of the Trump campaign's ties to Russian entities and individuals was tainted and needed to be stopped. The partisan tangle extended to House Intelligence Chairman Devin Nunes, R-Calif., who faced sharp criticism after a secret trip to the White House in 2017 in which he looked at documents alleging that Page's identity had been revealed by former Obama administration officials. Nunes

subsequently recused himself from the committee's probe of the Russian interference. But he continued to seek additional documents from the Justice Department and the FBI.

Republicans on the House floor called for the removal of Rosenstein if the Justice Department failed to turn over the documents they were seeking. Rep. Paul Gosar, R-Ariz., said that if Rosenstein did not comply with the resolution, he should be held in contempt of Congress or face impeachment proceedings. Democrats, however, said the resolution was intended to protect Trump, not provide oversight.

Two days before House passage, the House Judiciary Committee had approved a similar resolution concerning Justice Department documents. The committee approved the resolution (H Res 938), 15–11, after adopting language added by Ohio Republican Jim Jordan to an underlying substitute amendment by Chairman Robert W. Goodlatte, R-Va. The Jordan amendment widened the scope of the resolution to compel the Justice Department to comply with subpoenas issued by the House judiciary and intelligence panels, provide all documents requested by Congress, and grant members of Congress and certain staff members with full access to unredacted documents.

A resolution of inquiry is an obscure legislative tool that Congress can use to obtain information from the executive branch. It must be marked up within fourteen legislative days of introduction. Alternatively, the resolution can be brought up for a floor vote under a privileged motion to discharge it from committee.

Rep. Jerry Nadler, D-N.Y., who said the language would interfere with the ongoing investigations of the Justice Department and FBI, raised a point of order at the markup that the Jordan amendment was not germane. Steve Chabot, R-Ohio, who was acting as the chairman at the time, supported the point of order. But the committee overruled Chabot, 16–13 with two members voting present.

The committee also rejected several Democratic amendments. One, by Steve Cohen of Tennessee, would have asked the Justice Department for all documents, communications, and meetings referring to or related to any investment by any foreign government or agent of a government in any entity fully or partly owned by Trump. The committee rejected it, 10–17. Another amendment, by Sheila Jackson Lee of Texas, would have asked for all documents, communications, and meetings concerning the separation of children from their families upon crossing the U.S. southern border and being placed in secure detention centers. It failed on a 11–16 vote. Although Democrats planned to offer additional amendments, the committee effectively cut off debate by agreeing, 16–11, to a motion by Rep. Matt Gaetz, R-Fla., to order the previous question.

The controversy over the investigation into the 2016 campaign would persist for the following two years. At the end of 2019, the Justice Department's inspector general released a scathing report that the FBI's justifications for surveilling Page contained "factual misstatements and omissions." The Justice Department acknowledged that it lacked probable cause to surveil Page in at least two of four warrant applications, each of which had been granted by the Foreign Intelligence Surveillance Court. The Republican-controlled Senate Intelligence Committee, however, concluded in 2020 that the FBI had been justified in its initial concerns about Page.

Child Protection

A trio of measures regarding the exploitation of children passed the House in 2017 but did not advance in the Senate amid partisan differences. Although Republicans said the bills would help close loopholes in child exploitation laws and ensure that those who sexually abuse a child are prosecuted to the fullest extent of the law, Democrats worried they would expand the use of mandatory minimum sentences and potentially lead to overly harsh sentences.

One bill (HR 1842), which the House Judiciary Committee approved by voice vote on April 5, 2017, would increase criminal penalties on those who were convicted of a violent crime and failed to register as a sex offender. Sponsored by Rep. John Ratcliffe, R-Texas, it would lock up the offender for a minimum of five years, and potentially up to thirty years.

Such penalties were required in federal, tribal, District of Columbia, and military law as well as the laws of U.S. territories and possessions. The bill would also require the penalties for state offenses.

New York Democrat Jerrold Nadler raised concerns at the committee markup that the bill would impose new mandatory minimum sentences on several additional classes of criminals. Ranking member John Conyers Jr. of Michigan offered an amendment that would have eliminated the mandatory minimum penalties in the bill while keeping the same maximum penalties. But the committee rejected it, 6–16, on a party line vote.

The House passed HR 1842 on May 22 by a vote of 371–30, with one member voting present.

The second bill (HR 1862), also passed by voice vote at the Judiciary Committee's April 5 markup, would change the definition of "illicit sexual conduct" to include all potential situations in which an adult defendant may abuse a child while traveling outside the United States.

Chairman Robert W. Goodlatte, R-Va., said this would help target offenders who had been able to avoid prosecution, and who even disseminate "how-to" guides to fellow sexual predators. But Democrats again objected to the bill's mandatory minimum sentences. The House passed HR 1862 on May 22, 2017, by a vote of 372–30.

A third bill (HR 1761) made it a crime to knowingly consent to the visual depiction or live transmission of a minor engaged in sexually explicit conduct. Sponsored by Rep. Mike Johnson, R-La., it was a response to a ruling by the 4th U.S. Circuit Court of Appeals in *U.S. v. Palomino-*

Coronado, in which the court sided with a defendant who had been convicted of producing child pornography. The court said that the facts in the case failed to prove intent to produce child pornography.

Republicans warned that the ruling created a loophole in the federal child pornography statute that would allow a defendant to deny a pre-formed specific intent to record a sexual offense of a minor. Democrats, however, opposed the measure, arguing that its mandatory minimum sentences could lead to unjust results.

The House Judiciary Committee approved HR 1761 on May 3, 2017, by voice vote. The House passed it 368–51 on May 25. Prior to passage, lawmakers rejected a floor amendment by Rep. Sheila Jackson Lee, D-Texas, that would have reduced the prison terms of those convicted of child pornography crimes in cases when they were no more than nineteen years old and no more than four years older than the minor involved, as long as the sexual conduct was consensual. The vote on the amendment was 180–238.

Civil Court Procedures

The House in 2017 passed two bills to make changes to civil court procedures. The Senate, however, did not take them up. Both measures had been considered in previous Congresses.

One bill (HR 720) would have reimposed penalties on federal lawsuits that were deemed to be frivolous. Courts had the option of sanctioning parties that file lawsuits for improper purposes or without evidentiary support. But they had not been required to since 1993.

The bill would have modified the Federal Rules of Procedure to require that plaintiffs pay the legal costs of parties harmed by a lawsuit, if the court determined the lawsuit to be baseless or frivolous. Such a requirement, Republicans said, would discourage people from filing baseless lawsuits.

The Judiciary Committee approved the bill along party lines, 17–6, on February 2, 2017. Ranking member John Conyers Jr., D-Mich., warned at the markup that the measure would reinstate the "deeply flawed version" of the rule that had been in effect before 1993 and lead to a steep increase in litigation costs. He and other Democrats also raised concerns that the measure would prevent judges from using their discretion in determining whether sanctions would be appropriate and discourage plaintiffs from filing civil rights lawsuits.

Lamar Smith, R-Texas, who sponsored the measure, countered that judges would still have discretion. He said that was because the bill would not change the criteria for determining whether a federal lawsuit was frivolous.

Democrats tried, but failed, to narrow the scope of the measure. On a party line vote, the committee, 10–19, rejected an amendment by Steve Cohen, D-Tenn., that would have exempted any claims that challenged the legality of a presidential executive order. Members also rejected, 11–18, an amendment by Conyers to exempt civil rights claims. The House passed the bill on March 10, 2017, 230–188.

The other bill (HR 725) would have established a uniform federal standard for federal courts to follow when remanding lawsuits back to state courts because of the fraudulent joinder of a local codefendant to the suit. The purpose, according to bill sponsor, Ken Buck, R-Colo., was to prevent lawyers from keeping a lawsuit in their preferred state court by fraudulently joining a local defendant to the suit. He said the measure would set clear guidelines for courts to determine when the joinder is fraudulent and, as a result, where the case would be heard. But Democrats opposed the bill, with Hank Johnson, D-Ga., saying it would make it easier for corporate lawyers to move cases to federal courts while making it harder for plaintiffs to add more defendants to their lawsuit.

The Judiciary Committee approved HR 725 without amendment on a party line vote of 17–4 on February 2. The House passed it on March 9, 2017, by a vote of 220–201, with one member voting present.

Disability Lawsuits

House Republicans won passage of a measure that they said would help prevent predatory lawsuits filed under federal disability rights legislation. Critics, however, assailed the legislation for potentially making it harder for the disabled to gain access to businesses such as restaurants, theaters, and other private establishments.

The House passed the bill (HR 620) on February 15, 2018, by a vote of 225–192. The Senate did not take it up.

The bill would require potential plaintiffs, prior to filing a lawsuit, to notify businesses that they believed were failing to comply with the 1990 Americans with Disabilities Act (PL 103-336). The original wording of the bill would have given the businesses six months to demonstrate their intent to comply, but an amendment adopted on the House floor shortened that timeline to four months.

The bill's supporters said it would improve business compliance with disability requirements because it would give them more time to comply and enable them to focus spending money on accommodating the disabled instead of paying attorneys' fees. Judiciary Chairman Robert W. Goodlatte, R-Va., said it would prevent unethical lawyers from abusing the law to pressure businesses into spending money to settle lawsuits instead of spending it on improving access for the disabled.

The bill, however, faced strong opposition from Democrats and disability rights groups. During the floor debate, the House gallery was filled with people who were blind or using wheelchairs. Protestors interrupted the final vote just before it began, and Capitol police removed more than a dozen people in wheelchairs from the gallery.

Rep. Jim Langevin, D-R.I., criticized the bill for ignoring the underlying problem of predatory lawsuits and predicted that it would lead to more businesses ignoring ADA

requirements. Langevin, who used a wheelchair after being paralyzed by an accidental shooting decades before, said during the floor debate that the measure would create an "obvious disincentive" for ADA compliance by giving businesses several months to properly implement a nearly three-decade-old law. Other opponents warned the bill, instead of reducing the number of frivolous suits, would merely delay them until after the compliance period.

Breaking party ranks were several House Democrats from California, where a law imposed higher penalties for violators and required them to pay the plaintiff's attorneys' fees.

In addition to shortening the compliance timeline, the House adopted three other floor amendments by voice vote. One would have made it easier for a non-lawyer to file a written notice of noncompliance with a business by eliminating a requirement that the notice cite the specific sections of the ADA that were allegedly being violated. Another required the Department of Justice to make educational publications available in languages other than English when developing a program that the bill required for promoting disability access. Another amendment clarified that business owners would be liable if they failed to make progress after the compliance period.

Lawmakers rejected, 188–266, an amendment by Langevin that would have removed all provisions from the bill except the requirement that the Justice Department create ADA educational programs. They also rejected, by voice vote, an amendment that would have allowed for additional punitive damages to be incurred for those businesses still in violation after the compliance period.

Juvenile Justice

The House passed a pair of bills by voice vote on May 23, 2017, to better support at-risk youth and juvenile offenders, as well as missing and exploited children. The Senate did not take them up.

One of the bills (HR 1808) would update and streamline the law that provides support for missing and exploited children and their families. It would require that grants through the National Center for Missing and Exploited Children be used to provide families with technical assistance and training to prevent, investigate, prosecute, and treat cases involving missing and exploited children. The grants would also support coordination with child welfare agencies and courts handling juvenile justice and dependency matters in addressing foster children missing from the state child welfare system; as well as in the identification, location, and recovery of victims of, and children at risk for, child sex trafficking.

The other bill (HR 1809) would reauthorize the Juvenile Justice and Delinquency Prevention Act through fiscal 2022. The act had not been reauthorized for fifteen years. The bill would require the Office of Juvenile Justice and Delinquency Prevention to prioritize the use of evidence-based strategies and current, reliable data to help reduce juvenile delinquency. It also mandated that the administrator of the office produce an annual plan for research and evaluation in areas critical to effectively serving youth.

The bill's sponsor, Jason Lewis, R-Minn., said the measure would help state and local leaders keep children out of the juvenile justice system. Supporters also said it would make important updates to protect youth who were brought into contact with the juvenile justice system. These included phasing out the detention of minors for acts that would not be considered adult crimes, such as truancy or underage drinking. Both bills received voice vote approval from the House Education and the Workforce Committee on April 4, 2017.

Medical Malpractice

House Republicans in 2017 narrowly passed a bill (HR 1215) to cap damages in medical malpractice suits. But the controversial measure failed to advance in the Senate, with Democrats, and some Republicans, opposing it.

The bill would have put a $250,000 cap on awards to victims of medical malpractice with some level of federal insurance, such as Medicare, Medicaid, or veterans' care. The limit would only apply to "noneconomic" damages—such as awards for pain and suffering—and not impose a cap on awards for monetary losses.

It also would impose a three-year statute of limitations on plaintiffs seeking to sue medical practitioners for damages. Another provision in the bill would prevent health care providers that prescribe an approved medical product from being liable as part of a class action against a manufacturer or seller of the product.

The health care industry, including the American Medical Association and the American Hospital Association, generally backed the legislation, saying malpractice suits increase the cost of health care by $50 billion to $100 billion per year. But plaintiffs' attorneys sharply objected. In a letter to House leaders in June, the American Bar Association argued that the caps would hurt patients who suffered the most harm. Military and veterans groups also opposed the bill, saying it could affect care for veterans and their families.

HOUSE COMMITTEE ACTION

The bill squeezed through the House Judiciary Committee by a single vote, 18–17, following a February 28, 2017 markup. All Democrats and one Republican, Ted Poe of Texas, voted against it.

Chairman Robert W. Goodlatte, R-Va., and other supporters said the bill would improve accessibility to health care and lower the cost of health care-related litigation. Iowa Republican Steve King, the bill's sponsor, said the specter of malpractice litigation is a factor in rising health care costs because of high malpractice insurance premiums as well as doctors ordering more tests to protect themselves from liability charges.

Democrats argued that medical malpractice laws should be left to the states. They said the bill would shield negligent doctors as well as drug and medical device companies selling dangerous products. They also pointed to data about the impacts of mistakes in the medical system, such as a 2016 study by researchers at Johns Hopkins University concluding that medical errors cause 250,000 deaths per year, making them the third-leading cause of death in the United States.

The committee rejected, 12–16, an amendment by John Conyers Jr., D-Mich., to create an exemption to the bill's limits in cases where a doctor intentionally harmed a patient, such as in the case of criminal actions. Republicans opposed the amendment, with King saying it would effectively negate the bill by enabling plaintiffs to make the case that any procedure performed by a doctor was with intent.

The committee, on party line votes, also rejected an amendment by Steve Cohen, D-Tenn., to create an exemption for medical errors, such as wrong-side surgery or a foreign object being left in a patient's body, and by Hank Johnson, D-Ga., that would have exempted cases involving nursing home negligence.

Johnson, in a bid to reframe the debate along the lines of states' rights, also offered an amendment that would prevent the bill from preempting any provision of a state constitution. His tactic seemed to have an impact, as several Republicans, including Ohio's Jim Jordan and Arizona's Trent Franks, initially supported the amendment. Even after the GOP leadership attempted to whip its members to change votes, the committee at first adopted the amendment, 16–15, with Raul R. Labrador of Idaho and Jim Sensenbrenner of Wisconsin joining the Democrats in voting yes.

But Sensenbrenner then offered a motion to reconsider the previous amendment. The committee, after some discussion and procedural motions, ultimately rejected the Johnson amendment although two Republicans crossed party lines to support it: Labrador and Texas Republican Ted Poe. The committee, by voice vote, did adopt an amendment by Goodlatte to strike a section of the bill that would allow parties to introduce evidence of a collateral source benefit, such as health insurance, into a health care lawsuit that involved injury or wrongful death.

HOUSE FLOOR ACTION

The House passed HR 1215 on June 28, 2017, on a vote of 218–210. Democrats who voted against it unanimously were joined by nineteen Republicans. Conservatives such as Poe and Louie Gohmert of Texas voted against the bill, arguing that it would preempt states trying to enact their own medical malpractice laws. Joining them were a group of lawmakers who were comfortable breaking party ranks, such as conservative Reps. Justin Amash of Michigan, Morgan Griffith of Virginia and Walter B. Jones of North Carolina, and moderates such as Ileana Ros-Lehtinen of Florida.

Conversely, several Republican members with medical training supported the bill. Rep. Phil Roe of Tennessee, an obstetrician and gynecologist, told his colleagues that "frivolous lawsuits" took some joy out of practicing medicine, and that more money went to attorneys than to victims of malpractice before a Tennessee enacted a law on medical malpractice lawsuits. The House adopted four floor amendments that were generally favorable to health industry defendants.

One of them, passed 222–197, would allow physicians to apologize to a patient without having the apology used as evidence against them in court. Three other amendments passed by voice vote. One would expand the bill's definition of medical services to include administrative services related to health care, another would place limits on who could qualify as an expert witness and how far the witness could travel to testify, and a third set the statute of limitations for the lawsuits.

The House rejected, 116–310, an amendment that would give defendants protection from liability if they proved they had complied with approved clinical guidelines.

Abuse of Young Athletes

Jolted by allegations of sexual assault against young athletes, Congress cleared bipartisan legislation to require reporting of alleged sexual abuse by adults authorized to interact with amateur athletes. President Trump signed the measure into law on February 14, 2018 (S 534 — PL 115-126).

Lawmakers acted after reports surfaced of sexual abuse of hundreds of young athletes and other victims over the previous two decades by coaches, doctors, and other adults affiliated with USA Gymnastics. Victims claimed that USA Gymnastics had failed to take action on the allegations, which included complaints against coaches who trained and abused young athletes in a number of states. A doctor on the U.S. women's national gymnastics team, Larry Nassar, was sentenced to up to 175 years in prison for sexually assaulting numerous amateur gymnasts.

S 534 mandated that national governing bodies, such as USA gymnastics and affiliated amateur sports organizations, immediately make reports of child abuse known to local or federal law enforcement authorities. It also allowed civil suits by minors to be filed against sex abuse perpetrators, clarifying that once a victim has established a harm occurred, the court will presume $150,000 in monetary damages. The civil statute of limitations for these cases was extended. In addition, the bill changed the charter of the U.S. Olympic Committee to include a new entity, the Center for SafeSport, which would be responsible for responding to reports of sexual misconduct within the U.S. Olympic and Paralympic Movements and for developing and implementing best policies and practices for preventing sexual and physical abuse of amateur athletes.

The Senate Judiciary Committee approved the bill by voice vote on May 11, 2017, and the full Senate passed an

amended version by unanimous consent on November 14. The House on January 29, 2018, passed an amended version by a vote of 406–3. The Senate then cleared it by voice vote on January 30.

SETTLEMENT FUNDS

The House passed Republican-backed legislation in 2017 that would have prohibited the Justice Department from requiring those who settle lawsuits with the federal government to give additional funds to third parties. Instead, the bill (HR 732) would allow settlement funds to go only to parties directly harmed by the settling party while barring government agencies from entering into settlement agreements that required the settling party to provide settlement funds to other groups. The Senate did not take up the measure.

House Judiciary Chairman Robert W. Goodlatte, R-Va., who sponsored the bill, said that the determination of how to use settlement funds should be made by congressional appropriators. He characterized the bill as an effort to prevent Justice Department from using settlements in a way that would circumvent congressional authority. For example, he cited a recent settlement by the Justice Department that required Volkswagen to spend $2 billion to fund an electric vehicle initiative that had not received any appropriated funding from Congress.

Goodlatte said HR 732 would not prevent the Justice Department from providing funds to parties that were harmed, but its main impact would be to channel remaining funds from the settlement to the Treasury rather than to a third party chosen by the administration. The Justice Department's authority in such cases, he said, should be limited to compensating the actual victims.

But John Conyers Jr. of Michigan, the ranking member of the House Judiciary Committee, said that secondary remediation is important for mitigating the general harm that can result from the behavior of the settling party. He also argued that existing laws already prohibited federal agencies from using settlements to supplement their budgets.

At the committee's February 7 markup, Democrats offered four amendments that would have carved exemptions to the measure. These included one by Conyers to exempt settlement agreements that directed funds to remediate indirect harms in cases of noncompliance with federal regulations related to lead in drinking water. The committee rejected the amendment, 10–14, with Michigan Republican Mike Bishop joining Democrats in support.

The committee rejected other Democratic amendments by party line votes. It then approved the bill on a party line vote of 17–8. The House passed the bill, 238–83, on October 24, 2017, after defeating Democratic amendments that would have carved out several exemptions.

Although the Senate did not take up the measure, House Republicans in 2018 amplified their criticism of settlements in their fiscal 2019 Interior–Environment spending report. They warned that a so-called sue-and-settle approach to regulations meant that outside parties such as environmental groups were filing lawsuits against agencies as a strategy to persuade courts to require regulatory spending and imposed rulemaking deadlines, even in areas that were not administration priorities. "The Committee is concerned that, as budgets shrink, agencies are forced to settle lawsuits quickly because they don't have funds available to complete court-imposed work," the report stated. "In addition, the courts are not concerned whether agencies have funding necessary to meet court mandates . . . As a result, the courts are playing an increasing role in determining how and where agencies use their funding."

The committee report directed the Department of the Interior, EPA, and the U.S. Forest Service to submit a report, within sixty days of enactment of the spending bill, about "detailed Equal Access to Justice Act (EAJA) fee information." That act required the federal government to pay the legal costs of plaintiffs who successfully sued the government. Similar language had appeared in spending bill reports for fiscal 2017 and 2018.

The issue also resonated with the Trump administration. In October 2017, EPA Administrator Scott Pruitt established new guidelines that were similar to those passed by the House. "We will no longer go behind closed doors and use consent decrees and settlement agreements to resolve lawsuits filed against the Agency by special interest groups where doing so would circumvent the regulatory process set forth by Congress," Pruitt said in a statement on October 16.

Targeting Law Enforcement Officers

The House passed two bills to stiffen penalties against those who target law enforcement officers. The Senate did not take up either.

One bill (HR 115) would have added the targeting, murder, or attempted murder of state or local law enforcement officers, as well as first responders, to the list of aggravating factors that courts and juries consider when determining whether to impose the death penalty. It was approved by the House Judiciary Committee on April 27, 2017, by a vote of 19–12.

Committee Chairman Robert W. Goodlatte, R-Va., said the bill would send the message that the targeting of law enforcement officers must not be tolerated. But Rep. John Conyers Jr. of Michigan, the committee's ranking member, said the legislation was not needed. While he said he supported laws to protect law enforcement officers, there was no evidence that law enforcement officers or first responders would be helped by the measure. He also raised concerns that it broadened the scope of the death penalty.

The committee adopted, 12–11, an amendment by Ken Buck, R-Colo., to add the targeting of first responders as an aggravating factor. The committee rejected, by voice vote, an amendment by Rep. Sheila Jackson Lee, D-Texas, that

would have required courts and juries to also consider life sentences without parole for those convicted of the murder, attempted murder, or targeting of a first responder. Two proposed amendments by Rep. David Cicilline, D-R.I., were ruled nongermane. One would have studied the appointment of defense counsel in capital cases, and the other would have authorized $5 million annually for defense lawyers assigned to capital cases. The House passed HR 115 on May 18, 2017, by a vote of 271–143.

The other bill (HR 5698) would have created a new federal crime for the targeting of law enforcement officers. Anyone who knowingly caused or attempted to cause serious bodily injury to an officer would face up to ten years in prison, a fine, or both. Increased penalties would be imposed if the crime resulted in death, or if it included kidnapping, attempted kidnapping, or attempt to kill. The House Judiciary Committee approved HR 5698 by voice vote on May 9, 2018. The House passed it, 382–35, on May 16.

Trump Tax Returns

The House Ways and Means Committee on March 28, 2017, thwarted an attempt by Democrats to compel the Treasury Department to release President Donald Trump's tax returns and other financial information regarding his debts and investments in foreign countries. Trump's taxes had been a matter of considerable speculation since he refused to release his returns during his 2016 campaign, breaking a forty-year tradition of every major party presidential candidate releasing their tax returns.

The committee voted along party lines, 24–16, to unfavorably report a Democratic resolution of inquiry (H Res 186) that would seek Trump's financial records. Such resolutions must be marked up within fourteen legislative days of introduction. The vote blocked the resolution from moving to the House floor, where Democrats could have offered a motion to discharge the resolution from the committee and force a vote on the measure.

House Ways and Means member Bill Pascrell Jr., who introduced the resolution, said the release of Trump's tax filings would reveal whether he had conflicts of interest or received emoluments in his unprecedented business arrangement. The Emoluments Clause of the Constitution bans government officials, including the president, from accepting gifts or compensation from foreign states or rulers. Given Trump's many business interests, critics warned that foreign governments could influence him by steering business to entities in which he had a stake.

Democrats also argued that Trump's tax returns could help inform an upcoming House debate over overhauling the tax code. They said the public should know if Trump would benefit from the proposed changes.

Republicans, however, said the Democratic resolution amounted to a political stunt because information regarding Trump's financial investments would not likely be found in his tax filings. Rep. James B. Renacci, R-Ohio, noted that Trump had submitted financial disclosure reports detailing more than 500 investment positions even though he had not released his tax returns. He said he had never seen a tax return that listed every investment.

The resolution of inquiry, within ten days of passage, would have directed the Treasury secretary to provide the House with Trump's tax returns for tax years 2006 through 2015. The Treasury also would have to provide any information on Trump's use of tax shelters, corporate structures, tax avoidance maneuvers, abatements, or other loopholes to reduce or eliminate tax liability.

Ways and Means Chairman Kevin Brady, R-Texas, had previously rebuffed a request by Pascrell for the committee to seek the Trump tax returns by using its authority under a 1924 law, telling reporters on February 13, 2017, that he would not be interested in allowing Congress to "rummage around in the president's tax returns for political purposes." Brady said the committee had never taken such a step to target a taxpayer.

Confirmation of Supreme Court Nominees

President Trump successfully placed two conservative justices on the Supreme Court, a major victory for Republicans. But the nominations sparked fierce clashes in the Senate as confirmation battles over judgeships continued to become increasingly partisan, with special-interest groups rallying to pressure senators in both parties. When Democrats in 2017 lined up to oppose the nomination of Neil Gorsuch, Republicans changed Senate rules to prevent filibusters against Supreme Court nominees. The following year, Democrats tried unsuccessfully to stop the nomination of Brett Kavanaugh over charges of sexual misconduct.

The confirmations left Republicans and Democrats alike embittered over the scorched earth tactics of the other party. With the Supreme Court serving as the final arbiter over some of the most polarizing issues of the time, including abortion, gun rights, same-sex marriage, and campaign finance, the make-up of the nine men and women on the nation's highest tribunal became increasingly consequential. The battles over Gorsuch and Kavanaugh, following the extraordinary decision by Senate Republicans in 2016 to deny a hearing for President Barack Obama's final Supreme Court nominee, Merrick Garland, raised concerns about how a president in the future could win confirmation of a Supreme Court nominee if the Senate was controlled by the opposition party.

Neil Gorsuch

The Senate confirmed U.S. Circuit Judge Neil Gorsuch to the Supreme Court on April 7, 2017, on a mostly party line vote of 54–45. Trump's successful nomination of the forty-nine-year-old Coloradoan capped a fourteen-month-long

battle over the seat of the late Antonin Scalia and restored the Court's 5–4 conservative leaning. But Democratic opposition resulted in Republicans doing away with the right of the minority party to filibuster future Supreme Court nominees, underscoring the increasingly high stakes over lifetime appointments to the nation's highest tribunal. The Senate had previously ended the filibuster against lower court nominees in 2013.

BACKGROUND

The Supreme Court had a vacancy when Trump came to office because the Senate had declined to replace Scalia, who died in his sleep unexpectedly in February 2016. Scalia was a longtime conservative icon, and Senate Majority Leader Mitch McConnell, R-Ky., made the strategic decision to refuse to hold hearings on Garland, arguing that the seat instead should be filled by the winner of the 2016 election. McConnell's intransigence stunned the Obama administration and infuriated Democrats. Garland was a veteran judge on the U.S. Court of Appeals for the District of Columbia Circuit with an impeccable resume and a reputation as a moderate liberal. Despite such credentials, his nomination galvanized conservatives in opposition because he would have shifted the ideological balance on the Court and given it a Democratic-appointed majority for the first time since 1968. By successfully blocking Garland, McConnell kept open the prospect that Republicans would be able to restore the Court's 5–4 conservative majority.

Although the Senate on occasion had rejected presidential nominees to the Supreme Court, it was exceedingly rare for the chamber to refuse to even take a vote. Republicans and legal conservatives defended McConnell's stand by claiming a historical tradition of declining to confirm a Supreme Court nominee in a president's final year in office. Democrats, however, pointed out that several Supreme Court nominees had been confirmed in the final year of a president's term—most recently, Anthony M. Kennedy in President Ronald Reagan's last year in office in 1988.

During the standoff over Scalia's seat, the short-handed Supreme Court was unable to decide controversial cases such as a review of the Obama administration's immigration executive actions because justices split 4–4. The court took fewer cases, largely avoiding the most decisive ones, while waiting for a ninth justice. Democratic anger over the treatment of Garland, and the high-profile role of the Court, made it almost inevitable that the confirmation of that ninth justice would be politically explosive.

Nomination and Initial Reactions

Less than two weeks after being sworn in, Trump on January 31, 2017, announced his nomination of Gorsuch. In a prime time event broadcast from the East Room of the White House, Trump touted Gorsuch as among the finest and most brilliant legal minds in the country, and a fulfill-

ment of his campaign promise to find the best judge in the country to replace Scalia. The president noted that Gorsuch clerked for two Supreme Court justices—Anthony M. Kennedy and Byron White—and gave up a lucrative career at a law firm for public service as a federal judge. "It is an extraordinary resume," Trump said. "The qualifications of Judge Gorsuch are beyond dispute."

Senate reaction largely followed partisan lines. Republicans on the Senate Judiciary Committee quickly announced their support of Gorsuch. Noting his substantial credentials, Chairman Charles E. Grassley of Iowa released a statement on January 31, 2017, in which he called Gorsuch "universally respected across the ideological spectrum as a mainstream judge who applies the law without regard to person or his own preferences." Grassley subsequently laid out an approximately six-week timeline for getting Gorsuch confirmed. He anticipated only one day of the senators publicly questioning the nominee, with three days of hearings overall.

Senate Democrats, however, wasted no time in assailing the nomination. In a statement issued just after the nomination, Minority Leader Charles E. Schumer of New York said he was concerned Gorsuch "hewed to an ideological approach," who sided with corporations over ordinary people and was hostile to women's rights. Ominously, Schumer announced that Gorsuch would be subject to the filibuster's sixty-vote threshold associated with a filibuster. With forty-eight senators who were Democrats or who caucused with them, that meant the minority could block the confirmation unless Senate Republicans took the fateful step of eliminating the filibuster for Supreme Court nominees.

In 2006, Gorsuch had won voice vote approval in the Senate after President George W. Bush nominated him to a seat on the U.S. Court of Appeals for the 10th Circuit, based in Denver. As a federal judge, Gorsuch had a solidly conservative career that has featured rulings on contraception and separation of powers cases. Like Scalia, he had a reputation for writing with unusual clarity as well as flair—a style that, coupled with his conservative jurisprudence, marked him to his supporters as a prime candidate to fill Scalia's seat. A fourth-generation Coloradoan, he would add geographic diversity to a Supreme Court dominated by justices from New York, New Jersey, and California. Indeed, Gorsuch noted when accepting the nomination that he had once clerked for Byron White, the last justice from Colorado "and the only justice to lead the NFL in rushing." The quip drew laughs, as White played pro football for three years and led the league in rushing in 1938.

Gorsuch, a one-time Senate page, graduated from Harvard Law School and then got a doctorate in legal philosophy from Oxford University. He worked at a Washington law firm and served in the Justice Department during the George W. Bush administration. His mother, Anne Gorsuch Burford, had served in the Colorado legislature before she became the first woman to lead the EPA in 1981 during the Reagan administration.

Gorsuch's experience on the bench meant he had a long record of rulings that could leave him open to attacks. In perhaps his most-discussed case, he wrote a concurring opinion in a 10th Circuit opinion that sided with the retail chain Hobby Lobby in its objection to a mandate in the 2010 Affordable Care Act (PL 111—148) to provide contraceptive coverage for employees. He wrote that company executives can seek guidance from religious faith on questions of moral culpability, such as the owners of Hobby Lobby, who said the mandate forced them to assist in ending life that begins at conception. The Supreme Court agreed with that 10th Circuit ruling in a 5–4 decision in 2014. In another decision addressing religious freedom, Gorsuch dissented from a 10th Circuit ruling that sided with an atheist group when it came to putting crosses on the side of Utah highways.

Such rulings heartened conservatives looking to bolster religious freedom and reign in federal regulatory power. But they raised concerns from progressives about abortion rights and other civil rights issues.

Those on the left also pointed to an opinion in which Gorsuch appeared to side with conservatives on an important aspect of regulatory law. In a 2016 case, *Gutierrez-Brizuela v. Lynch,* Gorsuch called for the Supreme Court to reconsider its 1984 ruling that created the Chevron doctrine, which required federal courts to side with a regulatory agency's interpretation of a statute unless it was unreasonable. Scalia had endorsed the Chevron doctrine in a speech early in his career on the Supreme Court but subsequently appeared to reconsider, writing in a 2014 dissent that too many important decisions were being made by government officials "rather than by the people's representatives in Congress."

The Chevron doctrine had become a major political divide. The House in 2016 passed Republican-backed legislation that would override the Chevron doctrine, with conservatives saying it would stop agencies from using regulations to push political priorities. Obama threatened to veto the bill and it died in the Senate.

For progressive groups, overturning the Chevron doctrine would mean courts would no longer defer to agency experts when it comes to enforcing regulations about the environment, labor and more. Deference to the Equal Employment Opportunity Commission and the Department of Education, for example, were central to the ongoing legal fight over transgender bathroom rights.

On other contentious areas of the law, such as the Second Amendment right to possess firearms and restrictions on money in politics, Gorsuch did not have much of a history.

While Gorsuch in the weeks after his nomination began making courtesy visits to senators, especially those on the Judiciary Committee, Democrats wrestled with how strongly to oppose him. In addition to their desire for revenge over the treatment of Garland, they faced pressure from liberal advocacy groups to do everything possible to block the nomination. Some moderate analysts, however,

urged Democrats to wait for another potential Supreme Court nominee to launch an all-out confirmation war. They noted that Gorsuch, by replacing Scalia, would not shift the ideological balance of the high court anyway.

Some Democratic senators, such as Kristen Gillibrand of New York, Jeff Merkley of Oregon, and Elizabeth Warren and Edward J. Markey of Massachusetts, promptly announced their opposition. Others, however, held their fire. Adopting a measured tone, Dianne Feinstein of California, the ranking Democrat on the Senate Judiciary Committee, said the committee needed to gather all the facts and then analyze them.

Sen. Claire McCaskill of Missouri, who faced a difficult reelection campaign in a state that Trump had won, said Gorsuch deserved a hearing despite what happened to Garland. Even though Republicans "should've given Merrick Garland a hearing," she told reporters shortly after the nomination. "I am not going to model my behavior after their terribly bad, historically precedent-setting behavior." Such comments gave hope to McConnell who wanted to find votes for Gorsuch among the group of ten Democrats who were up for reelection in 2018 in states that voted for Trump.

Some Democratic legal scholars also noted that Gorsuch had a reputation as an independent judge who would likely stand up to Trump if necessary. Neal Katyal, an acting solicitor general in the Obama administration who argued cases before the Supreme Court, wrote an op-ed column in *The New York Times* that argued Trump could have chosen a far more problematic nominee. He said he was confident that Gorsuch would uphold the law and, if necessary, say no to a president or Congress that failed to adhere to the Constitution.

This concern was underscored after Trump used the term "so-called judge" when referring to U.S. District Judge James Robart, who blocked the president's executive order temporarily banning all refugees as well as foreign travelers from seven Muslim-majority countries. Trump also tweeted that Robart's decision "is ridiculous and will be overturned!" Sen. Richard Blumenthal, D-Conn., told reporters on February 8, after a meeting with Gorsuch, that the nominee characterized Trump's tweet about Robart as "disheartening" and "demoralizing."

Senate Judiciary
Committee Hearing

Seeking to downplay the political nature of the judiciary, Gorsuch told the Senate Judiciary Committee on the opening day of his Supreme Court confirmation hearing on March 20 that judges are not "politicians in robes." He added, "If I thought that were true, I'd hang up the robe . . . Putting on a robe reminds us judges that it's time to lose our egos and open our minds." In defense of his judicial record, he noted that 97 percent of the decisions he participated in were unanimous, and that he had sided with the majority 99 percent of the time.

Grassley praised Gorsuch for having an unfailing commitment to constitutional order and the separation of powers. "His grasp on the separation of powers—including judicial independence —enlivens his body of work," Grassley said. For their part, Democrats reminded the nominee that he would have to stand up to the president if the administration encroached on protections of fundamental human rights.

The second day of the hearing lasted for eleven hours, featuring extensive exchanges between Gorsuch and the members of the committee. Gorsuch deftly avoided any type of major slip that could provide ammunition to liberal opponents. He sought to provide reassurances that he was not beholden to Trump, maintaining that he "would have no difficulty ruling for or against any party, other than what the law and the facts in a particular case require." Like previous Supreme Court nominees, he studiously avoided indicating how he would rule on issues such as abortion rights and campaign finance—sometimes to the frustration of Democrats. When he declined to even offer his personal views on past Supreme Court cases, arguing that judges should not hint how they would rule on those legal precedents, Democrats raised concerns that he was being too evasive. Mazie Hirono of Hawaii, the last Democrat to ask questions, told Gorsuch that he had "provided us less in the way of answers about the way you would approach cases than previous nominees to the Supreme Court."

Unperturbed, Gorsuch said repeatedly that he would not speak about legal issues that he might be called upon to rule on, telling the committee that he would keep an impartial reputation by judging cases only after they appeared before him. "The bottom line, I think, is that I'd like to convey to you from the bottom of my heart, is that I'm a fair judge," Gorsuch testified. "I can't guarantee you more than that, but I can promise you absolutely nothing less."

His unflappable performance and seemingly vague responses left Democrats frustrated. But it won praise from Republicans who appeared increasingly confident of his confirmation. "I respect your absolute resistance to being invited to put your personal opinions onto the issues that you will need to face as a Supreme Court justice if you are confirmed," said Sen. Michael D. Crapo, D-Idaho.

As the committee moved on to hear from outside witnesses, more Democrats began to announce their intent to vote no. They faced heavy pressure from organizations on the left to do everything possible to stop Gorsuch. More than twenty progressive groups, including NARAL Pro-Choice America and MoveOn.org, sent a letter to all Democrats on the last day of the confirmation hearing warning that Gorsuch as a justice would threaten "the rights of women, LGBTQ people, communities of color, and workers."

Sen. Bob Casey, D-Pa., said he would oppose Gorsuch because he worried that the judge's approach would not ensure fairness for workers and families in Pennsylvania. Sen. Bernie Sanders, I-Vt., told MSNBC that he would be voting against Gorsuch because the nominee "had nothing significant" to say about voter suppression or past Supreme Court decisions on campaign finance. Sen. Thomas R. Carper, D-Del., invoked the Republican response to the Garland nomination in his decision to oppose Gorsuch. Carper had voted for cloture on Justice Samuel Alito, a George W. Bush nominee, but he said this nomination was different due to the "shameful" treatment of Garland.

Schumer also announced his opposition, as well as announcing that he would support a filibuster. In a floor speech on March 23, 2017, Schumer said, "To my Republican friends who think that if Judge Gorsuch fails to reach 60 votes we ought to change the rules, I say: if this nominee cannot earn 60 votes, a bar met by each of President Obama's nominees, and President Bush's last two nominees, the answer isn't to change the rules—it's to change the nominee."

Republicans, however, stood firmly behind Gorsuch. They had previously shown little interest in doing away with the filibuster for Supreme Court nominations and had vehemently objected when Democrats in 2013 ended the filibuster against lower-court nominees as well as executive appointments. Now, however, they maintained that Gorsuch would be confirmed, one way or the other. McConnell laid out a timeline that called for the nomination to be on the floor of the Senate during the week of April 3 and then the confirmation on April 7.

Judiciary Committee Action

The Senate Judiciary Committee approved Gorsuch's nomination on a party line vote of 11–9 on April 3. Two senior committee Democrats, Feinstein and Patrick J. Leahy of Vermont, announced that they would oppose a floor vote, setting up a battle over the right to filibuster Supreme Court nominees. Leahy said that changing the filibuster rules would permanently damage the Senate. But, he added, "I cannot vote solely to protect an institution when the rights of hardworking Americans are at risk."

Republicans, united in support of Gorsuch, agreed that changing the filibuster rules would harm the Senate's judicial confirmation process. But they said the Democrats' intransigence left them no choice. Hatch said Democrats were politicizing the court and "we have no alternative" but to change Senate rules to put "a really fine judge" on the Supreme Court. For their part, three of the most endangered Democrats up for reelection—Donnelly, Heitkamp, and Manchin—said they would refuse to support a filibuster. They were joined by Sen. Michael Bennet, a Democrat from Gorsuch's home state of Colorado.

Final Action

The Senate narrowly confirmed Gorsuch on April 7 after Republicans ended the right of the minority to filibuster Supreme Court nominees. On April 4, McConnell announced on the floor that he would move to cut off debate on the nomination. This set up a vote on April 6 to

limit debate on the nomination, with a sixty-vote threshold. Assuming cloture was not invoked, McConnell would then launch the procedural maneuvering underlying the "nuclear option" to allow Gorsuch and future high court nominations to proceed via a simple majority.

Republicans blasted Democrats for trying to wage the first successful partisan filibuster of a Supreme Court nominee in the nation's history. For their part, Democrats fired back that the decision by the GOP majority to refuse to consider Garland's nomination was essentially a filibuster by another name.

On April 6, Senate Republicans invoked the so-called nuclear option to enable a simple majority of senators present to confirm Gorsuch and any future Supreme Court justice. Under this legislative maneuver, McConnell made a point of order that only a majority of senators—not sixty — were required to limit debate on Supreme Court nominations. The next step was for Nebraska GOP Sen. Deb Fischer, who was presiding in the Senate, to rule against McConnell, who then appealed the precedent of sixty votes.

All fifty-two Republicans responded by voting to overturn the presiding officer's ruling. This lowered the threshold to end debate on a Supreme Court nomination to a simple majority. Next, the Senate voted 55–45 to limit debate on the nomination. Donnelly, Heitkamp, and Manchin joined all fifty-two Republicans to advance the Gorsuch nomination, with the final confirmation vote scheduled for the next day. Other vulnerable Democrats such as McCaskill, however, continued to oppose the nomination.

Both sides traded blame during the floor debate. Republicans noted that Democrats began altering the confirmation process when they eliminated the filibuster for confirmations of district and appellate judges in 2013. "This is the latest escalation in the left's never-ending judicial war, the most audacious yet, and it cannot, and it will not stand," McConnell said. "There cannot be two sets of standards, one for the nominees of Democratic presidents and another for the nominees of Republican presidents."

Schumer, however, put the onus on the Republicans. He also warned that the filibuster for legislation may be eroded in time. "I hope that we can get together to do more in future months to ensure that the 60-vote threshold for legislation remains," he said. "But just as it seemed unthinkable decades ago that we would change the rules for nominees, today's vote is a cautionary tale about how unbridled partisan escalation will overwhelm our basic inclination to work together and frustrate our efforts to pull back." Democrats also warned that the end of filibusters for Supreme Court nominees would lead to more ideological nominees when the same party controlled the White House and the Senate because the minority party would not have any say.

The Senate on April 7 confirmed Gorsuch on a mostly party line vote of 54–45. Donnelly, Heitkamp, and Manchin joined fifty-one Republicans in support. GOP Sen. Johnny Isakson of Georgia was not present for the vote.

In the end, Gorsuch was supported by the fewest number of senators since Justice Clarence Thomas was confirmed in 1991 on a 52–48 vote. The confirmation battle marked a trend of increasingly partisan votes on Supreme Court nominees. Scalia, despite his staunch conservative reputation, had won confirmation in 1986 by a vote of 98-0. In the decades since, however, the opposition party turned sharply against more recent nominees regardless of their judicial experience. Samuel A. Alito, for example, a President George W. Bush nominee, picked up just four out of forty-five Democratic votes; while Elena Kagan, nominated by President Obama in 2010, was backed by just five out of forty-one Republicans.

Gorsuch was sworn in on April 10. He participated in his first oral arguments on April 17, 2017, providing the Supreme Court with a full complement of justices for the first time in fourteen months.

Brett Kavanaugh

The Senate strengthened the Supreme Court's conservative majority by confirming Judge Brett Kavanaugh on October 6, 2018. The 50–48 vote capped one of the most contentious confirmation battles in history, as Democrats first raised concerns about Kavanaugh's conservative judicial philosophy and then argued that he was not qualified because of allegations that he had committed sexual assault decades earlier. The remarkably bitter and partisan battle culminated in Kavanaugh and two accusers testifying before the Senate Judiciary Committee and a subsequent FBI investigation into the allegations.

Trump never wavered in his support of the nominee. In the end, Senate Republicans largely lined up behind Kavanaugh, while virtually all Democrats opposed him. A staunch conservative, Kavanaugh succeeded the retiring Anthony M. Kennedy, a swing vote who had been picked by President Reagan in 1988.

Nomination

Trump's nomination of Kavanaugh on July 9, 2018, set up a high-stakes confirmation battle months before the midterm election. In a prime time event broadcast from the East Room of the White House, Trump announced his decision to tap Kavanaugh to fill the vacancy left when Kennedy stepped down after thirty years on the high court. Trump had gradually narrowed down a list that originally included twenty-five potential nominees before finally picking one of Kennedy's former law clerks.

As a judge on the U.S. Court of Appeals for the District of Columbia Circuit since 2006, Kavanaugh, fifty-three, demonstrated a steadfast commitment to a conservative legal approach. He had ruled on some of the nation's most consequential and contentious legal fights over gun rights, health care, consumer protections, the environment and other federal laws and policies, and he had long been viewed as potential Supreme Court justice. Although no one could accuse Kavanaugh of inexperience, his lengthy

record in law and politics provided plenty of material for Democrats and their allies trying to stop his appointment. In addition to his time on the bench, he had served in the White House during the George W. Bush administration and worked on investigations into President Bill Clinton under independent counsel Kenneth W. Starr. He had also given numerous outside speeches.

The justice he would replace, Kennedy, had conservative leanings but was also a swing vote, sometimes siding with the Supreme Court's liberal wing on issues such as abortion rights, affirmative action, and LGBT rights. In one of his most notable decisions, *Obergefell v. Hodges,* Kennedy in 2015 ruled that same-sex couples have the constitutional right to marry. In contrast, Democrats worried, and Republicans hoped, that Kavanaugh would prove a more reliable conservative vote.

Trump called for a swift confirmation and robust bipartisan support for his nominee, citing Kavanaugh's "impeccable credentials, unsurpassed qualifications and a proven commitment to equal justice under the law." Senate Judiciary Chairman Charles E. Grassley, R-Iowa, quickly indicated his support, issuing a statement shortly after Trump's announcement that called Kavanaugh a "superb mainstream candidate worthy of the Senate's consideration." Democrats, however, quickly raised a number of concerns, including Kavanaugh's views on presidential power and whether a sitting president can be investigated. Sen. Dianne Feinstein of California, the Judiciary Committee's top Democrat, characterized Kavanaugh's views on health care, executive power, gun safety, worker protections, women's reproductive freedom, and environmental issues as "far outside the legal mainstream." Other members of the Senate Judiciary Committee also issued statements of opposition.

Democrats also criticized Republicans for pressing for the confirmation during an election year, as well as confirming a judge who might ultimately decide cases about Special Counsel Robert S. Mueller III's investigation into connections between the Trump campaign and Russian operatives during the 2016 election. In a much-discussed 2009 article, Kavanaugh wrote that Congress should consider passing a law to exempt a sitting president from criminal investigation, since the indictment and trial of a sitting president "would cripple the federal government." With the filibuster gone, however, the Democrats did not have the votes by themselves to stop a confirmation.

The July 9 White House announcement portended the fierce confirmation fight to come. Many Senate Republicans attended the announcement, but Sen. Susan Collins, R-Maine, declined her invitation. Democrats viewed Collins and Sen. Lisa Murkowski, R-Alaska, as two of the Republicans most likely to break party ranks because of their moderate positions on a number of issues and support of abortion rights. Collins, however, appeared reassured after meeting with Kavanaugh in August, telling reporters afterward that he had indicated that the decision

in *Roe v. Wade* was "settled law"—wording that was similar to that used by Chief Justice John G. Roberts Jr., during his confirmation process.

Three key Democrats facing difficult reelection battles—Joe Donnelly of Indiana, Heidi Heitkamp of North Dakota, and Joe Manchin III of West Virginia—also declined the invitation. All three had voted to confirm Gorsuch.

Kavanaugh had long been eyed by Republicans as a potential candidate for the Supreme Court because of his educational background and intellect, work with major Republican figures, and consistent commitment to a conservative legal approach, as embodied by such justices Clarence Thomas and Samuel A. Alito Jr. A native of Maryland whose mother served as a state judge, Kavanaugh went to Yale University for both his undergraduate and law degrees. His impressive—if sometimes partisan—resume included clerking for Kennedy as well as two appeals court judges, working on President George W. Bush's legal team during the highly contested 2000 presidential election recount in Florida, and serving in the Solicitor General's Office at the Justice Department and in the Office of the Independent Counsel under Starr, where he worked on investigations related to Bill Clinton in the 1990s. He also spent five years in the White House during the George W. Bush administration as associate counsel, a senior associate counsel, and as staff secretary.

Kavanaugh had already undergone a difficult confirmation fight. Bush first selected him for the D.C. Circuit court in 2003, but the Senate let the nomination die. Bush renominated Kavanaugh after winning reelection, and a divided Senate confirmed him in 2006 by a vote of 57–36 despite Democrats characterizing him as an inexperienced partisan ideologue.

Although his work on the D.C. Circuit drew praise from conservative legal experts, it provided Democrats with plenty of ammunition on conservative issues. Just months before his nomination, he dissented from a D.C. Circuit decision to allow a teenaged immigrant to get an abortion. He also frequently found himself on opposite sides of decisions with his colleague on the court, Merrick Garland, whose failed nomination to the Supreme Court still vexed Democrats. The two judges held conflicting views on such issues as police misconduct, criminal sentencing, and workers' rights.

Early sparring between Democrats and Republicans extended to the review of documents related to the nomination. Although Grassley aimed to begin confirmation hearings in early September, the National Archives and Records Administration said it would need until the end of October to fully review the voluminous documents related to Kavanaugh that the committee had requested. The alternative was for the committee to get most of the documents through a different process that allowed lawyers for Bush to review the paperwork and potentially withhold it on the grounds that it was privi-

leged. Democrats criticized that process as political. Grassley nevertheless insisted on the schedule, which would allow Kavanaugh to take his seat by the October 1 start of the Supreme Court's next term.

FIRST SENATE JUDICIARY COMMITTEE HEARING

From the opening minutes of the Senate Judiciary Committee hearing on September 4, 2018, the Kavanaugh confirmation was unusually contentious, with Democrats objecting to starting the hearing before all the Kavanaugh documents had been released, and Capitol Police removing about three dozen raucous protestors who shouted about the need for health care and access to abortion. Acknowledging the protesters, Feinstein said, "Behind the noise is really a very sincere belief it is so important to keep in this country—which is multi-ethnic, multi-religious, multi-economic—a court that really serves the people and serves this great democracy." She insisted the Democrats were not trying to disrupt the process but rather wanted time to vet the man who could be a key vote on such pressing issues as women's rights, civil rights, and environmental protection.

As the hearing room quieted down, Kavanaugh said in his opening statement that he would maintain his independence on the Court. The nominee, a sports fan and coach of each of his daughters' basketball teams, shared a number of sports metaphors. A good judge, he said, evoking a baseball metaphor that Roberts had used during his confirmation hearing in 2005, "must be an umpire—a neutral and impartial arbiter who favors no litigant or policy."

On the second day of the hearing, Kavanaugh underwent more than twelve hours of questioning and avoided making any major missteps that could have endangered his confirmation prospects. As each of the twenty-one committee members questioned Kavanaugh in turn, shouting protesters attempted to disrupt the hearing. Unruffled, Kavanaugh reassured the committee that he would not succumb to political pressure from the president or from Congress. When Grassley asked if he would have trouble ruling against the president who appointed him, Kavanaugh responded, "You're correct, no one is above the law in our constitutional system."

Democrats tried, without success, to pin Kavanaugh down on issues related to holding presidents accountable. Sen. Chris Coons, D-Del., repeatedly pressed the nominee on whether a president could fire at will a prosecutor who is criminally investigating that president. Kavanaugh said he could not weigh in on an issue that could come before the Court. "That's the kind of open question, gray-area question, that you would want to hear the briefs, get the oral arguments, keep an open mind on, what is the specific statute you have at issue," he said. He also told Sen. Jeff Flake, R-Ariz, that he would stay "three zip codes" away from commenting on a Trump tweet that criticized Attorney General Jeff Sessions for letting the Justice Department

bring criminal charges against two lawmakers who were early supporters of Trump's campaign.

As expected, Kavanaugh avoided questions from committee Democrats on such hot-button issues as health care, the constitutional right to abortion, presidential power, and campaign finance. When Feinstein pressed him about landmark cases establishing the right to abortion, Kavanaugh said access to abortion had been reaffirmed many times and was "precedent on precedent." He added, "I don't live in a bubble, I live in the real world. I understand the importance of the issue." He later said, however, that he would not answer whether he would overturn the 1973 abortion case, *Roe v. Wade*. Kavanaugh also fended off questions about racial discrimination, voting rights, and women's rights.

Friendlier questions from Republican senators gave Kavanaugh the opportunity to speak about tutoring students at a low-income school and volunteering at a homeless shelter. Taking a moment to address the protestors, he said, "I want to reassure everyone that I base my decisions on the law, but I do so with an awareness of the facts and an awareness of the real-world consequences." He added that he understood how passionately people feel about different issues, as well as the difficulties facing many Americans.

Judiciary Committee Democrats initiated an unusual showdown at the beginning of the third day of the hearing on September 6. Booker released documents about abortion and racial profiling that had been marked "committee confidential," saying his act was a form of civil disobedience. Other committee Democrats, frustrated by a process that had held back many documents related to Kavanaugh, backed Booker, who released more "committee confidential" documents later in the day via Twitter. Republicans dismissed the move as theatrics, pointing out that a number of the documents had already been cleared for release by the committee. Despite the drama, Kavanaugh continued to handle the hearing with aplomb, sidestepping Democratic queries about whether he respected Trump and his thoughts on the president's criticism of certain judges.

After the hearing, Democrats added a new line of attack, accusing Kavanaugh of being misleading or even lying under oath during his confirmation hearing. Schumer raised concerns about certain Kavanaugh responses about his work in the George W. Bush administration, while Leahy went as far as to write that Kavanaugh gave "untruthful testimony, under oath and on the record." Leahy had asked Kavanaugh at the hearing whether, during his work at the White House, he had received any Democratic committee documents obtained by a Republican staff member in 2002 and 2003. Kavanaugh testified that he never received any documents that appeared to be drafted or prepared by Democratic committee staff, but Leahy said "he got 8 pages of material taken VERBATIM from my files, obviously written by Dem staff, LABELED 'not [for] distribution.'"

Committee Republicans and the White House dismissed the allegations.

Determined to keep the nomination on track, Judiciary Committee Republicans on September 13 took the unusual step of setting a specific time for a committee vote. The committee, 11–10, agreed to vote on Kavanaugh's nomination at 1:45 p.m. on September 20. Democrats heatedly opposed the move, arguing it violated committee rules. They also tried, unsuccessfully, to have the committee subpoena documents from Kavanaugh's past jobs, including his advice as White House staff secretary in the George W. Bush administration, and they wanted to seek a reason why the Trump administration withheld more than 100,000 records as privileged.

Following up on the hearing, they also submitted more than 1,200 written queries to Kavanaugh. They received 263 pages of responses in which Kavanaugh added some additional thoughts but largely declined to give detailed answers on topic after topic, saying that the issue might come before the Supreme Court or that he could not recall certain aspects of his work during the Bush administration.

Sexual Assault Allegations

Kavanaugh's path toward confirmation, which appeared largely assured after the confirmation hearing, was nearly derailed when allegations surfaced of sexual assault when he was in high school and college. The allegations led to a high-stakes hearing before the Senate Judiciary Committee but ultimately failed to shake Republican support of his nomination. The situation was reminiscent of the contentious 1991 confirmation battle over Clarence Thomas, who was accused of sexual harassment by his coworker, Anita Hill. Thomas ultimately won confirmation to the Supreme Court.

The allegations began seeping out, somewhat mysteriously, when Feinstein's office issued a cryptic news release on September 13, 2018, about information that the senator had about Kavanaugh that was being kept confidential at the request of the individual who provided the information. One day later, *The New Yorker* published the contents of a letter that Feinstein sent to investigators from a woman who first approached Democratic lawmakers in July, alleging Kavanaugh had assaulted her in high school. The allegations were further detailed in media reports over the next few days: Christine Blasey Ford, a California college psychology professor, said she was fifteen, and Kavanaugh about seventeen, when he pinned her to a bed at a party, attempted to pull off her clothes, and covered her mouth when she tried to scream while a friend of Kavanaugh watched. She was able to free herself.

Kavanaugh categorically denied the allegation. The Judiciary Committee, on the same day that the article ran, received a letter from sixty-five women who knew Kavanaugh in high school to vouch for his reputation.

Coming at the height of the #MeToo movement, which revealed how allegations of sexual misconduct were routinely ignored or mishandled, the allegations put Republicans in a quandary. The fact that all eleven Republicans on the Judiciary Committee were men made the optics all that more difficult. Grassley initially indicated that the confirmation vote would proceed as planned on September 20, especially since the alleged assault occurred more than thirty years before and Feinstein had not reported the information in the weeks since first receiving the letter. But after at least two Republicans on the committee—Flake and Lindsay Graham of South Carolina—said the committee should hear from Ford, Grassley agreed to postpone the confirmation vote. Instead, he proposed a public hearing, originally scheduled for September 24, with both Ford and Kavanaugh. Trump also endorsed the idea of pausing the nomination. "If it takes a little delay, it'll take a little delay," he told reporters at the White House on September 17.

For several days, however, Grassley's approach seemed on the verge of falling apart. Committee Democrats wanted the FBI to reopen the background investigation into Kavanaugh and conduct a full probe before a public hearing. Ford expressed misgivings about testifying, and her lawyers, siding with Democrats, said an FBI investigation should be the first step in addressing the allegation, in line with calls from Senate Democrats. Senate Republicans, the Justice Department, and the White House all threw cold water on an FBI investigation, with Grassley arguing that such an investigation would not have any bearing on what Ford told the committee. Finally, Ford and the committee reached an agreement for her to testify on September 27.

Roiling the waters, new allegations emerged over sexual misdeeds. Deborah Ramirez, 53, who had attended Yale College with Kavanaugh, told *The New Yorker* that the federal appeals court judge sexually assaulted her at a college party in the 1980s. Separately, Michael Avenatti, a lawyer who had previously garnered attention by aggressively taking on Trump over alleged sexual conduct, said he had evidence of multiple house parties during the 1980s at which Kavanaugh and others plied women with alcohol and drugs to allow a "train" of men to subsequently gang rape them. His client, Julie Swetnick, subsequently said that Kavanaugh was present while she was gang raped at a high school party in 1982.

A beleaguered Kavanaugh vehemently denied the new allegations. As hundreds of protesters converged on Capitol Hill to oppose his confirmation, he sent a letter to the Senate Judiciary Committee that dismissed the allegations as "smears, pure and simple." He vowed not to withdraw his nomination. In response to Swetnick's allegations, he provided a response via a White House spokeswoman: "This is ridiculous and from the Twilight Zone. I don't know who this is and this never happened."

Trump and Senate Republicans continued to say they stood by Kavanaugh but also wanted to hear from his

accusers. They noted that the Ramirez claim lacked any independent confirmation and pointed to a *New York Times* story about its failure to find anyone to corroborate her account even after interviews with several dozen people.

Second Senate Judiciary Committee Hearing

The committee heard testimony from Ford and Kavanaugh on September 27, with Ford first detailing the alleged attack by Kavanaugh, and Kavanaugh then denying the allegations. Each of the two witnesses provided an opening statement and then took questions. Although the hearing appeared to do little to shake Republican support of the nominee, the committee agreed to postpone a confirmation vote for one week to enable the FBI to look into the matter.

The riveting hearing began with Ford, composed but tearful, providing stark details of the alleged assault in which a drunken Kavanaugh, she said, pinned her on a bed during a summer party in 1982 while he and his friend laughed. "I am here today not because I want to be," Ford said at the beginning of her testimony. "I am terrified. I am here because I believe it is my civic duty to tell you what happened to me while Brett Kavanaugh and I were in high school." Asked whether she was positive the person who assaulted her was Kavanaugh, she responded, "One hundred percent."

Kavanaugh heated and angrily denied the allegation, his voice sometimes roaring with indignation. He denounced the process as a "circus"—a description echoed by several Republicans—and told the panel, "you have replaced advise and consent with search and destroy." Unlike his previous appearance, he was openly hostile toward Democratic senators, sometimes insisting they answer the questions that they asked of him. He fought back tears as he spoke about the toll of the previous two weeks on his family and friends. "This whole two-week effort has been a calculated and orchestrated political hit, fueled with apparent pent-up anger about President Trump and the 2016 election," he said.

Republicans criticized Democrats for failing to take action for weeks on Ford's allegation, advising her on which law firm to hire, and leaking her allegations to the media. They said Democrats were more interested in blowing up the confirmation process until after the midterm elections than arriving at the truth. Democrats, for their part, continued throughout the hearing to press for an FBI investigation, saying the Republicans were trying to shortchange the allegations against Kavanaugh.

The format limited the opening statements to Grassley, who spoke of process and procedure, and Feinstein, who talked about Ford's strength and bravery in coming forward and referenced the "Me Too" movement. There was only a single round of questioning for senators, who had five minutes each. The Republicans deferred their questioning to a career sex crimes prosecutor from Arizona named Rachel Mitchell, who carefully and somewhat clinically took Ford through the details of her account.

The hearing was held in the relatively small space, Room 226 in the Dirksen Office Building, based on the Republican desire to minimize what Grassley and others termed a "circus" atmosphere and Ford's concerns about an overwhelming media presence. There were forty-eight press seats and seven video cameras, compared with 156 press seats and twenty-eight video cameras in the first Kavanaugh hearing. The area around the hearing room was restricted to prevent demonstrators from disrupting the proceedings.

Committee Vote and FBI Investigation

One day after the hearing, September 28, a sharply divided Senate Judiciary Committee advanced Kavanaugh's nomination to the Supreme Court on a party line vote of 11–10. But Flake said he wanted the FBI to conduct a weeklong investigation before the final confirmation vote on the Senate floor.

Flake, who was retiring, made his announcement after a thirty-minute delay in the committee vote during which he met with Democrats in an anteroom. He said the Democrats were "justifiably uncomfortable" in the Senate confirming Kavanaugh to a lifetime appointment without conducting due diligence on this nomination. The investigation, he insisted, would be brief and tightly focused on the current allegations. "This country's being ripped apart here," he said. Three key swing votes—Republicans Collins and Alaska's Lisa Murkowski and Democrat Manchin—also wanted an FBI investigation.

Bowing to the inevitable, Trump on September 28 ordered the FBI to reopen its background investigation into Kavanaugh. He made the decision after the Senate Judiciary Committee took the rare step of requesting the FBI look into the allegations at this late stage of the confirmation process. The committee asked the White House to limit the additional investigation to "current credible allegations" of sexual assault. Ford's attorney Debra Katz in a statement thanked the senators pushing for the FBI query, but said that the FBI should not be subject to "artificial limits as to time or scope."

For its investigation, the FBI tried to interview ten more people although one reportedly declined. One of the interviews was with Mark Judge, the friend of Kavanaugh who had been in the room when the alleged assault occurred.

Its forty-six-page secret report was placed in a secure room in the Capitol basement, where only senators and select staff could read it. Despite the considerable drama of senators going into and out of the room to read the single copy or get a briefing from staff, the report seemed to change few minds. Senators of both parties continued to stick to their positions while agreeing the report did not provide much new information.

Democrats said the report appeared to be very limited and lacked FBI interviews with Kavanaugh or Ford. Some said it failed to answer key questions. "We had many fears that this was a very limited process that would constrain the FBI from getting all the facts," Schumer said. "Those fears have been realized."

Ford's attorneys sent a letter to FBI Director Christopher Wray listing eight witnesses who they say should have been interviewed as part of the probe. "It took tremendous courage for Dr. Ford to come forward. As she testified before the Judiciary Committee, she was eager to talk to the FBI," they wrote. "The 'investigation' conducted over the past five days is a stain on the process, on the FBI and on our American ideal of justice."

Meanwhile, Kavanaugh's angry performance at the Judiciary Committee's second hearing stirred concerns in legal circles. Retired Supreme Court Justice John Paul Stevens, a lifelong Republican although a former leader of the court's liberals, said Kavanaugh's performance at the hearing should disqualify him. Several of Kavanaugh's former law clerks said they could not support him. More than 2,400 law professors signed a letter saying that Kavanaugh "displayed a lack of judicial temperament that would be disqualifying for any court, and certainly for elevation to the highest court of this land." Republicans, however, defended the nominee, saying he had been the target of a political hit job.

FINAL VOTE

A deeply divided Senate on October 6 confirmed Kavanaugh on a vote of 50–48. Manchin was the only Democrat to vote yes. Murkowski would have been the only Republican to vote no, but she voted present instead so that Sen. Steve Daines, R-Mont., would not have to travel back to Washington for the vote from his home state after his daughter's wedding. The final vote was conducted with senators sitting at their desks as their names were called.

The margin was the narrowest for any Supreme Court justice in modern history. The previous record had been set in 1991, when Clarence Thomas was approved 52–48 after weathering accusations of sexual harassment. But the Thomas confirmation did not divide senators as deeply along partisan lines, as the President George Bush nominee picked up eleven Democratic votes.

The battle over Kavanaugh resonated across the country like few other issues. Senators from both sides said they heard from constituents who were deeply moved by Ford's allegations and who sometimes shared their own stories of being sexually assaulted. Protesters on both sides of the issue confronted lawmakers in the Capitol amid an increasingly tense security atmosphere. Republicans and Democrats alike claimed the confirmation battle had energized their base just a month before the midterm elections. Within hours of Collins announcing her support for Kavanaugh, the president of NARAL Pro-Choice America

said that a website to fund an opponent to Collins crashed under the weight of increased traffic.

Kavanaugh was sworn in hours after the vote. Taking his seat with the eight other justices, he heard his first oral arguments three days later in a pair of criminal law cases.

Annual Appropriations Bills

The Department of Justice and other activities related to law enforcement were funded through the annual Commerce–Justice–Science appropriations bill. This measure, in addition to justice activities, funded the Department of Commerce and several science and other agencies, including NASA and the National Science Foundation. The 115th Congress consistently failed to pass the annual bill as a stand-alone measure. Instead, lawmakers repeatedly rolled into omnibus spending packages that included other appropriations bills.

FISCAL 2017 APPROPRIATIONS BILL

More than eight months behind schedule, Congress cleared the Commerce–Justice–State appropriations bill for the 2017 fiscal year, part of an omnibus appropriations bill (HR 244—PL 31) that included eleven annual spending bills for the remainder of the fiscal year that had begun on October 1, 2016. The House passed the massive, $1.163 trillion measure on May 3, 2017, by a 309–118 vote. The Senate cleared it the following day, 79–18, and President Trump signed it into law on May 5.

Provisions

The bill provided a total of $28.9 billion for the Justice Department, $142 million less than FY 2016 and $881 million less than requested. It appropriated $9.0 billion for the FBI, which was $208 million, or 2 percent, more than the FY 2016 level. The amount included $420 million for FBI construction, of which $323 million was to be used for the FBI's new headquarters, as well as $73 million for FBI instant background checks on gun sales. The bill required the agency to enhance its investigative and intelligence efforts related to terrorism, national security, and cyber threats, including strengthening its Cyber Division. For Justice Department legal activities, the measure provides $3.4 billion, a $39 million (1%) increase over FY 2016.

The measure provided $2.5 billion for activities of the Drug Enforcement Administration, a marginal increase over the FY 2016 level. Amid concerns about an increase in heroin availability and abuse, it included $12.5 million for four new heroin enforcement groups. The bill also contained $7.1 billion for the Federal Prison System and $1.3 billion for the Bureau of Alcohol, Tobacco, Firearms, and Explosives. It appropriated $2.7 billion for the U.S. Marshals Service.

The bill included a net $436 million for administrative review and appeals of immigration cases. Appropriators said the funding should be used to support at least an

additional ten immigration judge teams to oversee removal proceedings. The department was required to report to Congress on the backlog of immigration proceedings and the hiring of judges, as well as visa overstays.

The bill contained $2.1 billion for state and local law enforcement programs. This included $482 million for the Office on Violence Against Women and $222 million for Community Oriented Policing Services (COPS). It also included $103 million for the Justice Department's opioid initiative, which had been authorized by the Comprehensive Addiction and Recovery Act (CARE Act; PL 114–198).

The measure continued several provisions related to the military detention center at Guantanamo Bay, Cuba, including prohibiting the transfer or release of any detainee into the United States and prohibiting the acquisition or construction of any new prison to house detainees. It also barred the use of funds, other than those for the National Instant Criminal Background Check System, to facilitate the transfer of an operable firearm to a known or suspected member of a drug cartel unless enforcement personnel continuously monitored the firearm. It prohibited the implementation of firearms import or export criteria as well as the implementation of the Arms Trade Treaty until the Senate ratified the treaty. The bill prohibited any licensing requirement to export certain gun parts to Canada if they were valued at less than $500, while it permitted the importation of firearm and ammunition "curios and relics."

The measure prohibited the use of funds to pay for an abortion, except in the case of rape or to preserve the life of the mother, and it prohibited the use of funds to require any person to perform or facilitate an abortion. But it required the Bureau of Prisons to provide escort services to an inmate receiving an abortion outside of a federal facility. Appropriators also prohibited the Justice Department from enforcing federal marijuana laws in states that implemented their own laws to authorize the use, distribution, possession, or cultivation of medical marijuana.

FISCAL 2018 SPENDING BILL

Congress cleared the Commerce–Justice–Science annual spending bill on March 23, 2018, as part of an omnibus appropriations bill (HR 1625). Trump signed it the same day (PL 115-141).

House action

The Commerce–Justice–Science bill's journey began in the House Appropriations Committee, which approved it on July 13, 2017. The 31–21 vote followed unsuccessful Democratic attempts to add language on gun control and President Donald Trump's proposed border wall.

Chairman Rodney Frelinghuysen, R-N.J., said the bill would prioritize national security and law enforcement by targeting crime, illegal immigration, and terrorism. John Culberson, R-Texas, the chairman of the Commerce–Justice–Science Subcommittee, emphasized such priorities as an increase of $92 million for the FBI to fight terrorism

and cybercrime, $98 million more for the Drug Enforcement Agency, and funding for sixty-five new immigration judges.

But the subcommittee's top Democrat, Jose E. Serrano, said the bill's allocations needed to be increased. Democrats particularly objected to an $85 million cut to the Legal Services Corporation, which provided legal representation for the poor, and the elimination of Justice Department grant programs for hiring police and juvenile justice.

Serrano offered an amendment to add funding to many of the slashed programs, but Culberson said that would need to wait on a larger budget deal to allocate more money. The committee rejected the amendment, 22–30. The committee also voted down, 21–31, an amendment from Serrano to prohibit Justice Department funds from going toward litigation or an appraisal related to the acquisition of land or eminent domain for a wall or fence along the border with Mexico.

The committee also rejected, 20–32, an amendment from Nita M. Lowey, the ranking member on the full committee, that would have allowed the Justice Department to prevent firearm sales to those on terror watch lists, including the so-called No-Fly List. Republicans said it would infringe on the Second Amendment rights of Americans.

Debbie Wasserman Schultz offered two amendments, both rejected 22–30, that would have removed the security clearance of presidential adviser Jared Kushner, who was Trump's son-in-law. Kushner had reportedly attended a meeting with a Russian lawyer regarding damaging information about Hillary Clinton. The amendments would have blocked funding for security clearances for White House advisers who were either under a criminal investigation for aiding a foreign government or had deliberately omitted meetings with a hostile foreign government when filling out security clearance applications.

The bill was subsequently rolled into a $1.23 omnibus spending package (HR 3354) that the House passed on a mostly party line vote, 211–198, on September 14.

Senate action

The Senate Appropriations Committee approved its version of the Commerce–Justice–Science spending bill on July 27 on a lopsided, 30–1 bipartisan vote with James Lankford of Oklahoma voting no by proxy. But the full Senate did not take it up amid Democratic insistence on higher funding levels.

The bill provided $29.1 billion for the Justice Department. This represented an increase of $121 million over the previous year, including $213 million more for the FBI and $50 million more for the Drug Enforcement Agency. The bill increased funds for cybersecurity efforts, additional assistant U.S. attorneys to tackle violent crime, and sixty-five more immigration judges to work through a backlog of deportation and other immigration cases that can take years to resolve.

The committee, by voice vote, adopted a managers' amendment adding language to the bill report that directed

the leadership of the Justice Department "to adhere faithfully to all of its established processes and regulations regarding the operations of any Special Counsel."

The committee also agreed on an amendment to bar the Justice Department from spending funds to pursue medical marijuana cases against those who are following state laws, or to crack down on the cultivation of industrial hemp.

Final action

Following intensive negotiations over funding for a border wall and a record, thirty-five-day government shutdown, Congress cleared an omnibus appropriations package on March 23, 2019, that included the Commerce–Justice–Science spending bill.

Provisions

Appropriators agreed to provide $30.3 billion to the Justice Department, an increase of $1.35 billion over the fiscal 2017 level and almost $2 billion more than the administration request. This included $9.4 billion for the FBI, a 4.4 percent increase over FY 2017. No money was provided for the FBI headquarters consolidation plan that had been released the previous month because of questions over the revision of longstanding security requirements and changes to headquarters capacity in the national capital region, among other issues. Priorities for the FBI included an enhancement of its investigative and intelligence efforts related to terrorism, national security, and cyber threats, with a strengthening of its agency's cyber division. Appropriators directed the agency to improve the performance of the National Instant Criminal Background Check System operations and address background check demand. It also directed the FBI to make needed investments in counterintelligence and cyber-related investments to respond to foreign actors seeking to compromise democratic institutions and processes.

The measure provided $3.4 billion for Justice Department legal activities, including $2 billion for U.S. attorneys. It also contained $1.3 billion for the Bureau of Alcohol, Tobacco, Firearms, and Explosives and $2.6 billion for activities of the Drug Enforcement Administration. The U.S. Marshals Service received $2.9 billion. The bill provided $7.3 billion for the Federal Prison System and $543 million for Interagency Crime and Drug Enforcement activities.

Appropriators increased funding by $65 million for the Justice Department's Executive Office for Immigration Review, thereby paying for 100 new immigration judges and staff.

The measure contained $2.4 billion for state and local law enforcement programs, which was $375 million more than the Fiscal Year 2017 level and $965 million more than the administration requested. This included $492 million

for the Office on Violence Against Women and $276 million for Community Oriented Policing Services. The Office of Justice Programs received $1.7 billion for grants to state and local organizations for crime fighting, juvenile justice programs, and public safety officer benefits.

FISCAL 2019 APPROPRIATIONS

The 115th Congress failed to finalize a Commerce–Justice–Science bill for fiscal 2019. Instead, the 116th Congress cleared the spending measure as part of an omnibus appropriations package in February 2019.

House committee action

The House Appropriations Committee on May 17, 2018, approved a fiscal 2019 Commerce–Justice–Science spending bill on May 17, 2018, on a vote of 32–19. The bill (HR 5952) left Republicans and Democrats divided over provisions on gun control, among other issues.

The measure would provide $30.7 billion for the Justice Department. Key funding provisions included an additional $126 million to hire 100 immigration judges and staff at the department's Executive Office for Immigration Review to reduce a case backlog, an increase of $113 million for U.S. attorneys, and a $130 million spending boost for the Drug Enforcement Agency to step up efforts to combat opioids. The bill would seek to crack down on criminal activity involving guns, providing $75 million in grants for states to improve records for background checks on gun purchases and $100 million to buttress school safety.

The committee, by voice vote, rejected an amendment by Lucille Roybal-Allard, D-Calif., to prevent the Justice Department from spending funds to prosecute undocumented migrants who crossed the southern border to seek asylum. The committee also gave voice vote rejection to an amendment by Debbie Wasserman Schultz, D-Fla., that would have required sales of long guns to be reported if they occurred in states on the southwest border. Another amendment, by Barbara Lee, D-Calif., would have ended a requirement to delete background checks of gun purchasers. The committee rejected it, 20–31.

On another 20–31 vote, the committee also rejected an amendment by Nita R. Lowry, D-N.Y., to allow the Justice Department to block firearm sales to people on terror watch lists, including the so-called No-Fly List. Republicans raised concerns that it would infringe on the Second Amendment rights of Americans.

A closer vote occurred over another Lowry amendment, which would have prevented the Justice Department from spending any money to interfere in the special counsel's investigation. Culberson called it a "political stunt," arguing that existing law already barred federal money from interfering with such an investigation. The committee rejected the amendment, 23–27.

But the committee also adopted amendments to prevent the Justice Department from using funds to prevent states from implementing laws to legalize medical marijuana and to add report language encouraging the Drug Enforcement Agency to move quickly on applications to study marijuana effectiveness.

Senate committee action

In contrast with the partisan skirmishing over the House bill, the Senate Appropriations Committee on June 14 marked up its version of the fiscal Commerce–Justice–Science bill on a vote of 30–1. Committee members carefully avoided divisive issues such as immigration and gun control. The lone dissenting vote was cast by James Lankford, R-Okla. He opposed an accounting maneuver that freed up additional discretionary spending above the official allocation for the bill, as well as language preventing the attorney general from interfering with states that choose to legalize medical marijuana.

The bill would provide the Justice Department with $30.7 billion, matching the House number. Of this, $9.42 billion would go to the FBI. Funding for state and local law enforcement grants would total $3 billion.

An amendment by Lankford to prevent unobligated balances in the Crime Victims Fund from being used to offset other spending in the bill was rejected by voice vote. Senate appropriators had tapped $8.3 billion from the fund, which uses fines and penalties assessed on convicted federal criminals to compensate victims, to pay for other programs in the bill. This made it among the largest of "CHIMPs"—changes in mandatory spending—that appropriators used to meet funding priorities. Langford said the money should go to crime victims, but senators worried that the amendment would have a major impact on the funding priorities of both parties.

2019–2020

With the chambers controlled by different parties, the 116th Congress failed to clear legislation. House Democrats passed major progressive priorities focusing on police practices, immigration, voting rights and gun control, but the bills failed to gain traction in the Senate. Republicans, however, scored a major triumph when the Senate confirmed Amy Coney Barrett to the Supreme Court, overcoming unified Democratic opposition and cementing a 6–3 conservative majority on the nation's highest tribunal.

The impeachment of President Trump dominated the agenda for large parts of the 116th Congress. House Democrats, after launching multiple investigations into the administration throughout much of 2019, ultimately impeached Trump over allegations that he pressured Ukraine to investigate his political rival, former Vice President Joseph R. Biden. But they could not pick up Republican support for their efforts to remove the president. The Senate in early 2020 easily acquitted Trump on both counts of impeachment.

Policing

The highly publicized killing of George Floyd, a Black man who died after being handcuffed and pinned to the ground for more than nine minutes by a white police officer in Minneapolis on May 25, 2020, galvanized coast-to-coast protests against police brutality and systemic racism. Floyd's death had a particularly strong impact on the country because it was captured on video, but civil rights leaders emphasized that numerous other Black people had died at the hands of white police officers. With marches and protests sweeping across more than 150 cities in the months following Floyd's death and Black Lives Matter becoming an increasingly prominent movement, lawmakers moved quickly to introduce legislation to regulate police practices.

Republicans and Democrats, however, pursued significantly different approaches that could not be reconciled. Democrats passed a sweeping policing measure in the House while Republicans pursued a narrower bill in the Senate. Democrats generally favored decisive legislation to force state and local law enforcement departments to make changes, while Republicans wanted to avoid anything that would be viewed as a federal mandate. The two parties could not reach a middle ground over issues such as the extent to which the federal government should become involved in local policing, and efforts to pass legislation collapsed amid partisan finger-pointing. As Election Day loomed, some Democrats wanted to hammer their Republican opponents for failing to embrace far-reaching changes to policing that they thought were long overdue, while some Republicans positioned themselves as sensible reformers while criticizing progressives who wanted to defund, or even abolish, police departments.

The differences between the parties were reflected in the provisions of the Democratic-backed House bill (HR 7120) and the Senate GOP measure (S 3985). To House Speaker Nancy Pelosi, D-Calif., the Senate bill was "toothless." Senate Majority Leader Mitch McConnell, R-Ky., however, viewed the House bill as "typical Democratic overreach" and an effort to control as much as possible out of Washington. There were five particularly contentious areas where the House and Senate bills differed:

Chokeholds. Although neither bill would entirely ban chokeholds, the Democrats would make chokeholds a civil rights violation. It also defined *chokeholds* more broadly, including any pressure to the throat or windpipe or the restriction of blood or oxygen to the brain, whereas Republicans limited the definition to restricting an individual's ability to breathe. The GOP bill could also allow chokehold bans in cases in which deadly force was authorized. Both bills would withhold federal law enforcement grants from jurisdictions that did not ban chokeholds.

No-knock warrants. Concerned over the abuse of no-knock warrants, including a highly publicized case in which police in Louisville, Kentucky, who had a no-knock warrant killed a Black woman in her home, both Republicans and Democrats put some constraints on no-knock warrants. The Democratic bill went further, seeking to encourage states and localities to ban no-knock warrants in drug cases by disqualifying jurisdictions that do not from receiving federal law enforcement grants. The Republican bill would only require states and localities that receive such grant funding to annually report uses of no-knock warrants to the Justice Department, which would then compile and publish the information. The Republican measure would reduce grant funding to jurisdictions that do not comply with the reporting requirement.

Use-of-force data. Both bills sought to improve reporting on use-of-force incidents but used different approaches. The Democrats' bill would direct the Justice Department to set up a centralized database, and it mandated that any state and local law enforcement agencies receiving federal grant money report all data on use of force. Their bill called for DOJ tracking of other instances as well, including traffic and pedestrian stops and frisk and body searches. The bill would also establish and make public a national misconduct registry to track problem law enforcement officers, thereby preventing those officers from switching jurisdictions to avoid accountability. In contrast, the Republican bill

relied on an existing FBI database. It would require state and local law enforcement agencies that received federal grant money to report use of force incidents, to the FBI, which would be required to make the information public. The measure would reduce grant funding for states that do not comply with the reporting requirement.

Qualified immunity. One of the biggest divides between Democrats and Republicans had to do with the qualified immunity doctrine that shields police from lawsuits for actions performed on the job. The Democrats' bill would scale back qualified immunity by stating that arguments that "the defendant was acting in good faith, or that the defendant believed, reasonably or otherwise, that his or her conduct was lawful at the time when the conduct was committed" would not be a defense or warrant immunity in civil actions brought against law enforcement officers. Republicans, in contrast, did not include qualified immunity in the Senate bill.

Racial profiling. The Democrats would ban all law enforcement agencies from racial profiling. It would allow individuals to pursue "civil action for declaratory or injunctive relief" in cases of racial profiling. But the Republican measure did not include language on racial profiling.

Although the Democratic bill generally went much further, the Republicans included some accountability measures that the Democrats did not. The Senate bill, for example, would impose a twenty-year maximum sentence for officers who falsified police reports and a fifteen-year maximum sentence for federal law enforcement officers who engaged in a sexual act with individuals in their custody, regardless of consent. The measure also would authorize grants to state and local jurisdictions to adopt similar laws restricting police from engaging in sexual acts.

Trump, for his part, signed an executive order in June to address some policing issues. It encouraged state and local jurisdictions to adopt chokehold bans by directing the attorney general to refrain from certifying independent credentialing organizations unless those organizations required law enforcement agencies to ban chokeholds. The executive order used the same definition of chokeholds as the GOP bill and, like the Senate measure, provided an exception for "situations where the use of deadly force is allowed by law." It required the Justice Department to set up a database on excessive use of force. The executive order did not address no-knock warrants, racial profiling, or penalties for police misconduct.

House Committee Action

The House Judiciary Committee on June 17, 2020, approved HR 7120 on a party line vote of 24–14. The debate at times descended into deeply personal attacks between Republicans and Democrats, foreshadowing the partisan challenges to come.

Cedric L. Richmond, a Louisiana Democrat and former chairman of the Congressional Black Caucus, angrily accused Republicans of raising side issues such as abortion and the FBI investigation of Michael Flynn. "To my colleagues, especially to the ones that keep introducing amendments that are a tangent and a distraction from what we're talking about, you all are white males, you never lived in my shoes and you do not know what it's like to be an African American male," Richmond said. This touched off a heated back-and-forth, with Matt Gaetz, R-Fla., saying "Who the hell do you think you are?" as Chairman Jerrold Nadler, D-N.Y., banged the gavel for order.

The first three hours of the markup was consumed by just two Republican amendments. One focused on the FBI's investigation into Flynn, Trump's first national security adviser, and the other blamed Antifa for instigating violence, riots, and looting that happened during the protests about police misconduct. The pair of amendments clearly irritated the Democrats. California Democrat Ted Lieu, a native of Taiwan, cited his racial background as he said it was "offensive" at a debate over the killing of Black Americans to talk about "freaking Michael Flynn." The committee rejected both amendments on party line votes.

As the markup settled down, Republicans offered amendments that would have removed or scaled back language dealing with qualified immunity and no-knock warrants. An amendment by Andy Biggs, R-Ariz., would have replaced the bill's provisions with a requirement that federal law enforcement officers take a new training program on the use of deescalation tactics and techniques. Amendments by Gaetz and Greg Steube, R-Fla., would have removed language prohibiting or limiting the transfer of excess military equipment for counter-drug and border security activities. All the amendments were defeated by party line votes.

Senate Action

The Senate bill stalled when Democrats on June 24 blocked a Republican effort to bring it up on the floor. They argued that S 3985 was so inadequate that no amount of floor debate or amendments could repair its shortcomings, and they criticized Republican efforts to move it forward without going through committee or taking a bipartisan approach. The GOP bill also drew criticism from civil rights groups and the Congressional Black Caucus. Two Democratic senators—West Virginia's Joe Manchin III and Alabama's Doug Jones—and independent Angus King wanted to allow the bill to be taken up on the floor. Manchin said no bill was perfect, but it needed to be debated. The 55–45 vote left the chamber well short of the sixty votes required to move forward with the bill.

Tim Scott of South Carolina, the lone African American Republican senator and the sponsor of S 3985, said on the floor after the vote that he tried to work with Democratic senators, even offering as many as twenty amendments to repair the bill. But, he said, they walked out on him.

"This process is not broken because of the legislation," he said in a floor speech that included deeply personal stories from his sometimes troubled childhood. "This is a broken process beyond that one piece of legislation. It's one of the reasons why communities of color, young Americans of all colors are losing faith in the institutions of authority and power in this nation."

Richard J. Durbin of Illinois, the Democratic whip, said he was confident the Senate could pass a policing bill if it went through the Judiciary Committee in a bipartisan process. But lawmakers appeared far apart on several key issues, such as qualified immunity.

House Floor Action

Just one day after the Senate bill stalled, and eighteen days after the introduction of the House bill, the House passed HR 7120 on a mostly party line vote of 236–181 on June 25. The bill drew support from three Republicans: Will Hurd of Texas, Fred Upton of Michigan, and Brian Fitzpatrick of Pennsylvania.

The House rejected, 180–236, a motion to recommit the bill and replace its text with that of the Senate bill. Democrats otherwise did not allow any floor amendments.

During the floor debate, Democrats and Republicans blamed each other, even as they acknowledged that a massive public movement to address law enforcement misconduct and racial bias was unlikely to result in legislation making its way through a deeply polarized Congress. Republicans criticized Democrats for failing to take a bipartisan approach. Nadler, however, responded that Democrats had reached out to Republicans but that the Republicans would not share the text of amendments ahead of a markup or the floor action. Daniel Crenshaw, R-Texas, contended that the two sides could work together, noting the overwhelming bipartisan support for much of the bill.

But Republicans worried that some key provisions would undermine law enforcement, such as banning chokeholds or ending aspects of qualified immunity. Arizona Republican Debbie Lesko said certain provisions would effectively make criminals out of good police officers.

Both sides saw political advantages in the stalemate. Democrats pointed to polls showing overwhelming sympathy for the Black Lives Matter movement and concern about police practices at a time when Trump appeared to be sowing additional divisions by seemingly engaging in race-baiting. Republicans, for their part, highlighted the disorder and property destruction that marked some of the protests after Floyd's death, as well as the controversial demands of progressive activists to defund or abolish the police.

McConnell said the Senate would not take up the House bill. The White House issued a veto threat, saying it would "undermine law enforcement and make communities less safe." Pelosi, however, told reporters that the Senate bill would do "nothing" and be a nonstarter in the House.

Denouncing Senate provisions that would allow chokeholds in some circumstances, Pelosi said at a *Washington Post* event: "This is irreconcilable. Some things are just not reconcilable. That's it."

Border Wall

Congress in 2019 twice cleared legislation that would have terminated an emergency declaration by President Trump that he used to circumvent annual appropriations measures and redirect billions of dollars toward constructing his long-promised wall between the United States and Mexico. Trump vetoed the legislation both times, with lawmakers unable to muster the needed votes to override the vetoes.

The clash between the two branches of government began when Congress refused to provide Trump with his requested $5.7 billion of wall funding in the 2019 spending bill (PL 116-6). Instead, after a thirty-five-day partial government shutdown, Congress appropriated $1.375 billion for fifty-five miles of barriers along the U.S.–Mexico border.

Trump struck back on February 15, 2019, by declaring a national emergency along the southern border and asserting his authority under the National Emergencies Act of 1976 to move funding from other departments to construct the wall. The administration said it would tap $601 million from the Treasury Forfeiture Fund, $2.5 billion in drug interdiction funds, and $3.6 billion from military construction. These funds would be used for constructing steel primary pedestrian barriers ranging in height from eighteen to thirty feet, as well as secondary barriers that would provide a patrol zone. The White Housed stated that the military construction projects, which had broad support in Congress, would be delayed, not canceled.

Trump had made the border wall a centerpiece of his 2016 presidential campaign, saying it was needed to stop the influx of illegal immigrants. Since 2014, there had been a steady increase in the number of families and unaccompanied children arriving at the nation's southwest border, especially from the Central American countries of El Salvador, Guatemala and Honduras, where residents faced widespread poverty and violence. Although this tide of people raised alarms and became a prominent Republican campaign issue, the overall numbers of people intercepted at the border were much lower than in the early 2000s.

Trump's funding transfers to pay for the border wall gave the new Democratic majority an early opportunity to take on the administration's controversial immigration policies. Moving with unusual dispatch, the House passed legislation (H J Res 46) on February 26, 2019, that disapproved of Trump's emergency declaration.

Although Democrats picked up support from thirteen Republicans, the 245–182 vote was well short of the two-thirds margin needed to override a presidential veto. One

of the Republicans who broke party ranks, Kentucky Rep. Thomas Massie, distanced himself from the Democrats' immigration policies, instead emphasizing the importance of maintaining the separation of powers created in the Constitution. "I support President Trump and I support the wall," Massie tweeted before the vote, but "the appropriations process belongs within Congress."

Massie's comments foreshadowed the floor debate, which focused more on the extent of executive power and Congress's authority over spending than on border security. Rep. Joaquin Castro, D-Texas, who introduced H J Res 46, accused Trump of committing "constitutional cannibalism." Other Democrats argued that Trump's disregard for the appropriations process violated the adherence to the very constitutional principles that Republicans prided themselves on.

Republicans, however, accused Democrats of hypocrisy. Rep. Mark Meadows, R-N.C., the chairman of the conservative House Freedom Caucus, reminded Democrats that they did not object in 2012 when President Barack Obama bypassed Congress and claimed executive power in establishing the Deferred Action for Childhood Arrivals program, a maneuver that would subsequently divide federal judges. Republicans also emphasized the importance of securing the border, saying it was a necessary step to cracking down on illegal drugs and human trafficking.

Trump pledged to veto the resolution if it reached his desk. A White House statement, which blamed the continuing problem of illegal immigration on "antiquated laws and problematic court decisions," said the president had little choice but to declare a national emergency in order to confront the issue.

Although the resolution faced virtually impossible odds of becoming law, the Senate on March 14 passed it on a vote of 59–41. All forty-seven Democrats and twelve Republicans voted yes.

Each of the Republicans who broke party ranks said they agreed with Trump on the need for the wall. But they gave greater weight to the constitutional issues, saying the need to preserve Congress's power over government spending took precedence over the border wall. "The check on the executive is a crucial source of our freedom," said Sen. Lamar Alexander, R-Tenn., in a statement.

Supporters of the resolution said a president had never turned to the National Emergencies Act to spend money that he had previously requested and Congress refused to provide. Opponents responded that every previous president since Jimmy Carter had evoked the National Emergencies Act in one way or another. They said Trump needed to resort to executive authority because congressional Democrats were so intransigent over the wall.

Days before the Senate vote, Sen. Mike Lee, R-Utah, tried to head off the showdown between Congress and the White House by introducing a bill (S 764) that would have amended the National Emergencies Act of 1976 and made it more difficult for presidents to use it for longer-term policies. Under the bill, the emergency would end after thirty days unless both houses of Congress would vote to extend it. But the administration rejected this compromise. In the end, Lee voted for H J Res 46, saying it was imperative to prevent the president from acting like a king.

Just minutes after the Senate vote, Trump sent out a tweet with a single word: "Veto!" He followed through on this pledge the following day, issuing the first veto of his presidency. He called H J Res 46 "dangerous," "reckless," and "against reality."

The House on March 26, 2019, voted 248–181 in an unsuccessful effort to override the veto. An override would have required the support of two-thirds of those lawmakers present and voting, which in this case would have been 286 votes. The Democrats picked up one additional Republican vote, John Katko of New York, who had been absent previously.

The issue then temporarily moved to the courts. The House lost a lawsuit in June when a Trump appointee, Judge Trevor N. McFadden of the United States District Court for the District of Columbia, said the House did not have standing to stop the president from using his emergency powers for the border wall because it could not show that it had suffered appropriate injury.

In a separate case, a closely divided Supreme Court on July 26 ruled that the president could rely on its emergency powers to fund the wall while litigation proceeded over the issue. The 5–4, one-paragraph ruling in the case of *Trump v. Sierra Club* said the advocacy groups that filed suit did not appear to have legal standing. The Court's four liberals dissented.

Returning to the fray, lawmakers in September 2019 made another attempt to block the funding. Under the National Emergencies Act, Congress had the authority to vote again on Trump's declaration six months after he made it. House appropriators had already refused to provide funds for the wall in fiscal 2020 appropriations bills, while using a number of spending bill riders to restrict the administration authority to transfer funds.

This time the Senate struck first, voting 54–41 on September. 25 to pass the measure (S J Res 54) to disapprove of Trump's emergency declaration. Eleven Republicans joined a united Democratic bloc in support of the resolution. Speaking on the floor before the vote, Majority Leader Mitch McConnell, R-Ky., accused Democrats of framing the issue as a false choice between border security and the military construction projects that Trump was drawing from for wall funds. Congress, he said, could appropriate money for both. Democrats, however, continued to maintain that the issue had to do with Congress' constitutional authority.

The House passed S J Res 54 on September 27 by a vote of 236–174. Voting yes were all 224 Democrats, along with eleven Republicans and independent Rep. Justin Amash of Michigan. Supporters again framed the issue in terms of constitutional prerogatives.

Trump vetoed the measure on October 15. Two days later, an attempt by the Senate to override the veto failed by a vote of 53–36.

Immigration

Lawmakers did not attempt a comprehensive overhaul of immigration policies, as they had in 2017–2018. Instead, they tried to advance more targeted bills focusing on border security and conditions for migrants at the southwestern border, a path to citizenship for the children of undocumented immigrants, Trump's executive order to restrict travel from certain countries, and the per-country caps for employment-based green cards. As was frequently the case with the politicized issue of immigration, partisan differences sank their efforts.

Border Security

Amid outrage over the treatment of immigrants crossing the border with Mexico, Democrats and Republicans advanced competing bills to address the situation. The House in 2019 passed Democratic-backed legislation that would provide more oversight of the Department of Homeland Security, especially in its handling of migrants arriving at the southwestern border. House Democrats also weighed a number of other measures that would have required U.S. Customs and Border Protection to provide appropriate items to meet the shelter, hygiene, and nutrition needs of migrants; curb the expansion of detention facilities; improve the enforcement of detention standards; and even end the mandatory detention of migrants as well as reverse some of the 1990s laws that resulted in the current system. None made it into law. On the Senate side, the Judiciary Committee approved a Republican-backed bill (S 1494) that sought to reduce protections for migrant children in custody.

House Action

The House on September 25, 2019, passed legislation on a vote of 230–194 to create a DHS ombudsman and implement accountability standards for the department. The bill (HR 2203) would require the ombudsman to conduct annual evaluations of all training programs for agents under the department's Customs and Border Protection and Immigration and Customs Enforcement. It would also direct the ombudsman to submit a plan that would require Border Patrol agents and Immigration and Customs Enforcement officers to wear body cameras when engaged in border security activities and review policies and standards related to the treatment of migrants in custody.

The bill would establish a border oversight panel, which would evaluate enforcement policies and strategies along the southwestern border. The House acted amid revelations of inhumane conditions in both Customs and Border Protection facilities along the U.S.–Mexico border and Immigration and Customs Enforcement detention centers inside the United States. The Homeland Security Department's inspector general published reports of nooses dangling in detainees' cells, expired and spoiled food being served, and cells that were too crowded for migrants to sit. House hearings produced wrenching testimony, including a Honduran mother whose toddler daughter died in custody due to what she and her lawyers said was medical neglect. Lawyers in charge of detention oversight testified that Border Patrol was holding young children who had been separated from their families at the border, sometimes asking them to take care of even younger ones. All of the children appeared dirty, sick, and inconsolable, they said.

Democrats described these issues as gross institutional failures, reflecting a poorly run immigrant detention system that suffered from inadequate oversight. What was needed, they said, was legislation to create more safeguards for immigrants. Republicans, however, resisted efforts to make such changes, with some warning that creating more legal safeguards would backfire by encouraging more migration.

House Democratic leaders originally wanted to bring the bill to the floor before the August recess, but they faced disagreements within the party about some of the bill's original provisions. Lawmakers were particularly at odds over a proposal to end the Migrant Protection Protocols policy, also known as the Remain in Mexico program, which forces asylum seekers to wait in Mexico while their cases are being processed in the United States. Moderate Democrats shot down such a provision, warning that it would create more problems at the southern border if the policy was abruptly ended without offering anything to replace it with.

The White House strongly opposed both HR 2203 and another bill (HR 3525) that would seek to improve medical treatment for migrants by creating set standards and timelines for medical screening. It warned that the bills ignored efforts in the Department of Homeland Security (DHS) to achieve similar objectives and could divert resources needed elsewhere.

Senate Action

Taking a very different tact, the Senate Judiciary Committee on August 1, 2019, approved a bill that would reduce certain protections for migrant children. It did not advance further.

The bill (S 1494) by Chairman Lindsey Graham of South Carolina, approved on a vote of 12–10, aimed to stanch the flow of migrants to the southwest border. Graham said he wanted it to become part of larger negotiations between the House and Senate over immigration policy. Democrats sharply protested, saying the legislation was hastily pushed through and accusing Graham of breaking from longstanding committee procedures, both in his approach to scheduling and in not allowing any

Democratic amendments. They also opposed the bill's provisions.

The measure would strip several protections for migrant children and generally make it much more difficult to obtain asylum in the United States. It also would give more power to the Department of Homeland Security to make decisions on migrants without going through judicial review. In particular, it would modify the Flores agreement—a 1997 court settlement that required migrant children to be placed in the least restrictive setting and released from custody "expeditiously." A recent court ruling interpreted that to mean children needed to be released after twenty days.

S 1494 would have ended that limit as well as roll back standards of care for children in government custody. It would have made it more difficult for abused and neglected children to receive protection in the United States. As a result, Graham argued, migrants would be dissuaded from trying to make it to the border. Democrats, however, said it would increase problems at the border. Before the markup, about 150 immigrants' rights organization signed onto a letter opposing the legislation, arguing that it would "foreclose lifesaving protection and subject children as young as toddlers to prolonged and harmful incarceration."

Democrats also expressed anger over how the vote was scheduled. Sen. Patrick J. Leahy, D-Vt., who had served on the committee for decades, said the committee had changed and become "a conveyor belt of ultra partisan ideas." He angrily ripped up a copy of the committee rules, which he noted had been voted on by every committee member. In his defense, Graham said the markup on the bill had been scheduled for the previous week but it lacked a quorum because only one Democrat was present.

DREAMERS

The House delivered on a Democratic priority in 2019 when it passed a bill to grant permanent citizenship to up to 2.5 million undocumented immigrants. The Senate, however, did not take it up.

Known as the American Dream and Promise Act, the bill (HR 6) passed 237–187 on June 4. Seven Republicans crossed party lines to support it.

The legislation would provide legal status and a path to citizenship for adults, known as Dreamers, who had been brought to the United States as children by their undocumented parents. It also offered legal status to people living in the United States under the Temporary Protected Status and Deferred Enforced Departure programs. Immigrants who fell into one of those categories and who met certain education, employment, or military service requirements could become permanent legal residents and then proceed through the naturalization process to become U.S. citizens.

Democrats said it would allow immigrants to live without fear of deportation and continue contributing to the United States. The bill was backed by immigration rights groups and, as the vote was winding down, visitors in the gallery chanted, "*Si, se puede*" ("Yes, we can"). They cheered from the gallery when the vote was final, with some lawmakers applauding with them.

But Republicans assailed the bill, stating it would encourage even more migrants to come to the U.S.–Mexico border. Rep. Liz Cheney, R-Wyo., called it mass amnesty for millions.

The Center for American Progress, in partnership with the University of Southern California's Center for the Study of Immigrant Integration issued a report that estimated 2.1 million immigrants would be eligible under the measure for Dreamers and 460,000 immigrants would be eligible under the measures for TPS and DED recipients. The Congressional Budget Office estimated the bill would increase net deficits by more than $30 billion over ten years, as people in these programs applied for government benefits.

The Deferred Action for Childhood Arrivals (DACA) policy, which was the legal name for the Dreamers program, had been created during the administration of President Barack Obama. It quickly became embroiled in repeated legislative and judicial clashes. The 115th Congress had attempted to pass legislation that would have protected Dreamers from deportation, but lawmakers could not bridge differences over whether to grant citizenship to Dreamers and how to crack down on the continuing influx of illegal immigrants. When the Trump administration attempted to end the program, the courts blocked it.

Shortly before the House vote, the Trump administration threatened a veto if it advanced to the president's desk. "H.R. 6 would incentivize and reward illegal immigration while ignoring and undermining key administration immigration objectives and policy priorities, such as protecting our communities and defending our borders," the Office of Budget and Management said in a statement.

IMMIGRATION TRAVEL BAN

On a mostly party line vote, the House passed a measure on July 22, 2000, that would repeal the Trump administration's ban restricting travel from targeted nations and prohibit future presidents from implementing bans based on race or religion. The Senate did not take it up.

The measure passed 233–183 as part of a legislative vehicle (HR 2486). It would lift restrictions Trump had put on numerous countries since early in his presidency, including travel limits initially placed on a group of predominantly Muslim nations. It would also expand the Immigration and Nationality Act to prohibit discrimination based on religion.

Democrats said the Trump administration was motivated by prejudice when it banned visitors from seven Muslim countries, not by national security as the White House claimed. They argued that the ban violated fundamental U.S. values. Republicans, however, backed the White House, said its restrictions had been implemented

for the safety of the nation. They denounced Democratic lawmakers for calling Trump's travel restrictions a "Muslim ban."

Trump had imposed travel restrictions on a group of predominantly Muslim nations as one of his first presidential acts after he took office in 2017. His executive order prohibited visas for anyone traveling from Iran, Libya, Somalia, Sudan, Syria, and Yemen. The initial order also included Iraq, although that country was subsequently removed. Months later, the restrictions were extended to North Korea and to political officials from Venezuela.

The administration on February 22, 2020, extended the restrictions to include immigrant visas from Eritrea, Kyrgyzstan, Nigeria, and Myanmar. The order also barred Sudan and Tanzania from the diversity visa lottery program, which allocated 50,000 green cards at random every year to countries with low rates of immigration to the United States.

Trump said the travel ban was warranted because of national security. Immigration groups and civil rights organizations heatedly disagreed, saying it was implemented to keep out people from predominantly Muslim countries. Several federal courts initially blocked the ban. But the Supreme Court in 2018 sided with the administration, issuing a 5–4 ruling that Trump had sufficient national security justification to impose a policy that "says nothing about religion."

The House measure was approved by the Judiciary Committee on February 12, 2020, as a different bill (HR 2214). The vote was 22–10, with Republicans sharply opposing it.

IMMIGRATION CAPS

The Senate passed a bill in late 2020 that would eliminate the per-country caps for employment-based green cards, a system that critics viewed as discriminatory. The measure, which had been passed by the House in a different form, failed to make it into law because the House did not take up the final version.

The bill (HR 1044) would also increase the annual per-country cap on family-based immigrant visas from 7 percent to 15 percent, and it would impose measures to prevent abuse of the H-1B non-immigrant program. Only 70 percent of the total employment-based visas could go to H-1B workers after the bill's enactment. That portion would drop to 50 percent after nine years.

The legislation aimed to help reduce a backlog of more than 1.2 million green card applicants who wanted to work and obtain permanent residence in the United States. Sen. Mike Lee, R-Utah, who sponsored the bill, said it would end discrimination that was based on nationality in the employment-based green card system. Instead, it would enable applicants to be judged on their merits.

The Senate passed the bill (HR 1044) on a voice vote on December 3. The vote came after months of revisions by Democrats and Republicans. The House had passed the original bill, introduced by Rep. Zoe Lofgren, D-Calif., on a 365–65 vote in July 2019.

The Senate version included a provision by Lee that would deny entrance to, and adjust status for, immigrants determined by the Department of Homeland Security to be affiliated with the Chinese government military or the Chinese Communist Party. Lofgren warned the language could prevent final action in the House. Immigration experts raised concerns that it could effectively ban anyone who had a previous affiliation with the military forces in China, depending how the DHS interpreted it.

The United States allocated a total of about 1 million green cards annually to different categories of immigrants. Since 1965, it had placed a limit on how many visas can be given to applicants from any one country. In recent years, no single country could be allotted more than 7 percent of the total work visas.

Many advocacy groups argued that this was discriminatory, especially against citizens from India. Indian workers made up 75 percent of the employment-based backlog, and "recently backlogged Indian workers face an impossible wait of nine decades if they all could remain in the line," according to a 2020 report from the libertarian CATO Institute.

CAMPAIGNS AND VOTING RIGHTS

Democrats repeatedly fell short of one of their top goals in the 116th Congress: overhauling voting rights and other election-related issues such as campaign finance. Although the House passed several bills with the goal of making elections more secure, Senate Majority Leader Mitch McConnell, R-Ky., remained implacably opposed to advancing them in the Senate. As a result, even as the Mueller investigation uncovered evidence of foreign interference with elections, Congress did not pass major legislation in response.

HR 1

House Democrats first tried to tackle election procedures with a sweeping bill (HR 1) that would overhaul campaign finance, voting rights, ethics, and lobbying laws. Their aim was to reduce the influence of big money donations in politics, make it easier for Americans to vote, and set higher standards of ethics for politicians and government officials as part of an effort to clean up the political system. The measure passed the House but did not advance any further.

Supporters of the bill said it would improve the voting system, create more public transparency around the money aimed at influencing elections, reduce gerrymandering, and impose new conflict-of-interest rules on government officials. Republican opponents, however, worried that it would undermine local control of elections and potentially inhibit political free speech.

The ambitious measure, totaling about 700 pages, sought to expand ballot access by requiring states to offer

early voting and online and same-day voter registration. To tackle such issues as campaign financing and gerrymandering, it would create an optional 6-to-1 public matching system for political donations under $200 and mandate nonpartisan commissions to redraw the boundaries of congressional districts. Addressing concerns about conflicts of interest, the bill would establish new ethical standards for executive branch officials and Supreme Court justices, impose new restrictions on the work of federal officials when they leave the government, and tighten rules around registering as a federal lobbyist. In addition, it would revise the Foreign Agents Registration Act in order to strengthen federal oversight of foreign influence campaigns.

The Congressional Budget Office estimated the bill would cost close to $2.6 billion over six years.

The House Administration Committee approved the bill on a party line, 6–3 vote on February 26, 2019. Ranking member Rodney Davis of Illinois raised concerns that bill passage was being rushed so much that Democrats would take it to the floor before the Congressional Budget Office (CBO) could estimate its costs. Committee Chair Zoe Lofgren of California, however, said she expected a CBO score before a floor vote.

Each of the twenty-eight amendments that Republicans offered, which would have revised numerous parts of the bill, was rejected along party lines. One would have struck a provision requiring every state to implement online voter registration. Another would have deleted language requiring every state to adopt fifteen days of early voting. A provision of the bill allowing voters to make a sworn statement of their identity instead of other IDs required by some state laws was also targeted by an amendment.

In addition, committee Republicans tried unsuccessfully to delete the provision to create the 6-to-1 matching system on donations up to $200. That system, modeled after one in place in New York City elections, would offer candidates who opted in to receive public matching funds. The way it would work is if a voter, for example, were to donate $10 to a congressional candidate, the government would add in $60, for a total of $70. In order to qualify, candidates would have to forgo donations in excess of $1,000 per election, instead of the $2,800 per person limit that was in place for the 2019–2020 cycle.

With Republicans criticizing such a use of taxpayers' funds, Lofgren said her substitute amendment, unlike the original bill, would create a special fund in the Treasury Department to pay the matching funds. She said the system would be completely voluntary and not use any appropriated funds.

Democrats maintained their unity in support of the bill. But one Democrat, G.K. Butterfield of North Carolina, said he was concerned about bill language requiring polling places to be located within walking distance of a public transportation route. He represented a rural area where that would not be feasible. Lofgren assured him that the requirement was not absolute but merely called for polling places to be so situated to the greatest extent possible.

At a March 6 press conference, McConnell responded to the bill's progress in the House by insisting it would not be taken up on the Senate floor. He called it a "parade of horrible" and a "terrible proposal" and blasted specific elements of it. These included the 6-to-1 public matching system as well as a provision that would reduce the Federal Election Commission from six to five members with greater enforcement powers by the chair. The White House also opposed HR 1.

But McConnell indicated an openness to considering small and more targeted bills. In particular, he said he could support a prohibition on so-called ballot harvesting, which consisted of people collecting absentee ballots and passing them on to election officials. This practice was at the center of an election fraud controversy in the 2018 race for North Carolina's 9th Congressional District. Despite McConnell's opposition, the House passed HR 1 on a party line vote of 234–193 on March 8.

Democrats on the floor said the bill was needed to reassure voters that their voices mattered and to counter the political influence of well-monied special interests. They emphasized the importance of restoring ethics and accountability to government. Republicans, however, denounced it as federal overreach, and they also raised concerns about funneling taxpayer dollars into the campaigns of members of Congress through the matching system.

In response to such criticism, House Democrats had revised the bill to establish a "Freedom From Influence Fund" at the Treasury Department to pay for the optional public matching system. Instead of appropriated dollars, they said the money would come from corporate fines for tax fraud and other misdeeds. But Republicans said the system would officially embrace the use of corporate money in campaigns.

The partisan divide carried over to the Senate. Within weeks of the House vote, every Senate Democrat signed on to a bill (S 949) by Tom Udall of New Mexico that was their chamber's version of HR 1. True to his word, however, McConnell refused to bring it up.

SECURING FEDERAL ELECTIONS

With HR 1 stalled in the Senate, Democrats tried an alternative approach. The House passed a bill in June 2019 that supporters said would help secure federal elections. Once again, however, the Senate refused to take up the Democratic-backed measure.

The bill (HR 2722) would require voting systems to use backup paper ballots in federal contests. Additional provisions would require cybersecurity safeguards for hardware and software used in elections, bar the use of wireless communication devices in election systems, and require that electronic voting machines be manufactured in the United States. The measure would authorize $600 million

for states to bolster election security, as well as provide states with $175 million biannually to help sustain election infrastructure. Democrats said the bill would close dangerous gaps in the nation's election systems and provide needed security updates.

Republicans agreed that enhanced election security was necessary, but they contended that Democrats were going about it in a misguided way. They said the bill, like HR 1, would impose federal mandates on elections instead of allowing states to determine what would work best for them. They also pointed out that imposing additional regulations on which voting machines states could use would fail to address Russian interference, since Russians did not access voting machines.

At a June 21, 2019 markup by the House Administration Committee, Davis offered an amendment that would have replaced the legislation with a plan to simply offer states $380 million in grants, with a 25 percent match from states. The money would be used to secure elections and provide election officials with a top-secret security clearance in order to receive sensitive election security information. The committee rejected the amendment, 3–5.

Republican members also offered amendments that would strike sections in the measure to require states to use paper ballots and conduct risk-limiting audits. The amendments were also rejected.

Rep. Mark Walker, R-N.C., proposed an amendment to prohibit ballot harvesting. Butterfield said he could work with Walker on an amendment to address ballot harvesting, but the amendment as written was rejected 3–6.

The committee then approved HR 2722 on a party line vote of 6–3. With Democrats fast-tracking the bill, the House passed it on June 27 on a mostly party line vote of 225–184.

TARGETING FOREIGN INTERFERENCE

Undeterred, House Democrats sent a third election bill over to the Senate. McConnell, unmoved, refused to take it up.

Democrats characterized this third bill (HR 4617) as consisting of straightforward responses to what Congress was learning about Russian interference in the 2016 presidential election. The House on October 23, 2019, passed it on a nearly party line vote of 227–181, with a single Democrat voting no.

The legislation would require campaigns to report offers of foreign assistance to the FBI, restrict foreign nationals from the decision-making process of political action committees, and establish disclosure rules to keep foreign nationals from funding online advertisements about candidates, elections and national legislative issues, among other provisions. It also would make it a crime for candidates or their campaigns to give nonpublic information related to an American election to a foreign national. This was a response to the conclusion by Special Counsel

Robert Mueller that Trump's former campaign manager, Paul Manafort, gave polling data to a person associated with Russian intelligence.

House Republicans said the bill raised significant First Amendment concerns. They also said it failed to effectively address the problem of foreign interference in elections. For example, most of Russia's election interference was through unpaid posts on free social media sites, while the bill would address only paid ads for online platforms with more than 50 million unique monthly visitors. The result, according to Davis, would be to regulate $1.4 billion in political advertisements legally bought by Americans because of only $100,000 in ads purchased illegally by foreign nationals.

The House adopted thirteen amendments to the bill, including one from Rep. Eric Swalwell, D-Calif., that would require the immediate family members of a federal election candidate to disclose any foreign contacts to the candidate's campaign committee. Hours before the House vote, McConnell dismissed it as a piece of partisan messaging that, if enacted, would give the Federal Election Commission unprecedented power to regulate the online political speech of Americans. The White House issued a veto threat, stating that the measure would "produce harmful unintended consequences" without achieving the goal of reducing foreign interference in elections.

Gun Measures

The 116th Congress failed to pass major gun control legislation although it was a major Democratic priority. Amid concerns over continuing gun violence and mass shootings, House Democrats advanced proposals to broaden background checks, ban high-capacity magazines, establish a federal program for "red flag" laws allowing for temporary gun seizures from people suspected of being a danger to the public, expand bans on firearm ownership to people convicted of certain hate crime misdemeanors, and even enact a new assault weapons ban.

Most of these proposals were a nonstarter for Republicans, although red flag laws had some bipartisan support. Republicans focused more on strengthening enforcement of gun crimes, including a bill (HR 1339) by House Judiciary ranking member Doug Collins of Georgia that would codify a federal response center for mass violence, toughen penalties for stealing from gun stores, and authorize additional funds for federal gun prosecutions. For his part, Trump at times indicated support for modest gun control measures.

None of the Democratic proposals gained traction in the Senate. Instead Congress settled for appropriations language that would allow the Centers for Disease Control to spend $25 million on gun research.

Even if stronger laws passed, it appeared uncertain that they would survive Supreme Court review. In a landmark

2008 case, *District of Columbia v. Heller*, the court had affirmed Second Amendment protections for the right to keep and bear arms. Many legal experts believed the conservative wing of the court, bolstered by three Trump appointees, would broaden its interpretation of the Second Amendment.

BACKGROUND CHECKS

Democrats scored perhaps their most notable win on the issue of gun control when the House passed a measure to expand background checks for firearm sales. The 240–190 vote on February 27, 2019, fell mostly along party lines. Although it failed to become law, House passage marked a triumph for supporters in that it marked the first time in decades that the House had passed a stand-alone gun control bill that was not part of an appropriations measure.

The bill (HR 8), a priority for the new Democratic majority in the House, would mandate background checks for all firearm sales, including private and online transactions as well as those at gun shows. Under the existing law, background checks were required only for sales conducted by licensed firearms dealers. HR 8 exempted certain transactions, such as those involving hunting and law enforcement, and it did not impose requirements on gifts to family.

HR 8 set off a major partisan battle at a House Judiciary Committee markup on February 13. The committee approved the bill on a party line vote of 23–15 after Democrats defeated more than a dozen Republican amendments. Republican Jim Jordan of Ohio said Republicans had another ninety amendments, but Chairman Jerrold Nadler of New York forced a vote ten hours after the meeting had started.

Democrats repeatedly emphasized the strong public support for background checks. The Pew Research Center had found in October that 91 percent of Democrats and 79 percent of Republicans favored background checks for private gun sales and sales at gun shows.

Republicans, however, said the bill would fail to solve the problem of gun violence but instead only succeed in criminalizing gun transfers between law-abiding citizens and putting an unreasonable burden on them when buying or trading guns. They also said the only way to enforce the bill would be through a federal registry, which was a nonstarter among many conservatives. Collins argued that the bill would not deter criminals from acquiring firearms because they primarily obtained their firearms through means that were already illegal such as theft or straw purchases that were already illegal. What was needed, he said, was better enforcement.

When the full House took up HR 8 two weeks later, it narrowly rejected, 220–209, an amendment by Collins that would require the U.S. Immigration and Customs Enforcement to be notified if an undocumented immigrant failed a background check when attempting to purchase a firearm. The amendment was in the form of a motion to recommit. But the House passed an amendment by Madeleine Dean, D-Pa., clarifying that people who are at risk of suicide could give their gun to someone else without having to run a background check.

The Trump administration issued a veto warning because of concerns that that the bill's requirements ran counter to Second Amendment rights. The White House also criticized the bill for failing to include to exempt such transactions as giving a gun to a neighbor while on vacation or providing a gun to domestic violence victims who needed it for protection.

One day later, the House passed a companion measure (HR 1112) that would extend the time firearms dealers must wait for a response from the background check system before making a sale. The largely party line vote was 228–198.

ADDITIONAL GUN CONTROL MEASURES

Democrats on the House Judiciary Committee on September 10, 2019, advanced three more gun control bills during a lengthy, contentious, and sometimes emotional markup that underscored Republican opposition to restrictions on firearms. The bills did not advance further.

As the committee started to consider the legislation in the afternoon of the House's first full day after the summer recess, Nadler noted that fifty-three people had been killed in mass shootings during the month of August. The shootings had prompted a national address by Trump. Nadler said Democrats needed to act because of "the tragic gun violence that has engulfed this nation."

Democrats said there was broad public support for each of the three bills. The measures would allow judges to order guns taken from people thought to be a public danger (HR 1236), ban large-capacity magazines (HR 1186), and prohibit anyone convicted of a misdemeanor hate crime from owning a firearm (HR 2708).

As was the case with HR 8, Republicans contended the bills would infringe on Second Amendment rights while failing to make the country safer. McConnell said he would not bring them to the floor unless Trump said he would sign them into law—an unlikely scenario since the White House threatened to veto the bills should they make it through the Senate.

During the markup of more than four hours, Democrats determinedly rejected Republican amendments and approved the measures along party line votes. Lucy McBath, D-Ga., whose son was a victim of gun violence, choked back tears as she spoke about the pain of losing loved ones. "Inaction is unacceptable," she said.

Doug Collins, however, said the measures threatened basic rights without successfully targeting gun violence. For example, he said there were due process problems with HR 1236, which would establish a grant program to encourage states to adopt so-called red flag laws that allow

courts to take firearms away from people suspected of being a danger to the public. It would enable judges to take away firearms without notice or an opportunity to be heard in court, and on a low standard of evidence, Collins argued.

Equal Rights Amendment

Democrats rallied behind a resolution that would have removed the deadline for ratifying the Equal Rights Amendment (ERA) to the Constitution, barring discrimination on the basis of sex. Most Republicans, however, opposed it, and the Senate declined to act after the House passed it.

The resolution (HR Res 79) would remove the seven-year deadline that lawmakers had originally given the states to ratify the ERA after it passed Congress. The Constitution requires that three-fourths of state legislatures vote for a constitutional amendment for it to take effect, but it does not impose a timeline for them to do so. Congress had set the seven-year deadline for ERA ratification with a joint resolution in 1972. Under HR Res 79, the ERA would become valid whenever ratified by three-fourths of the state legislatures.

The nearly century-long history of the Equal Rights Amendment dated back to the first years after women gained the right to vote. The amendment, originally drafted by suffragist Alice Paul, was introduced in every Congress beginning in 1923. But it kept dying in committee until 1970, when Michigan Democrat Martha Griffiths forced a House floor vote with a discharge petition. After some alterations, the House passed her amendment in 1971 and the Senate followed suit in 1972, both with the two-thirds majority needed for a constitutional amendment. The proposed amendment simply stated, "Equality of rights under the law shall not be denied or abridged by the United States or by any state on account of sex."

The race was then on for three-fourths of the states to sign off on the amendment by 1979. More than half the states ratified it within the first year, and thirty-five states before 1977. Congress then extended the deadline for another three years to 1982 but no additional state legislatures voted to ratify, leaving the amendment three states short of the three-fourths requirement.

In recent years, the amendment garnered new attention in state governments. The Nevada legislature ratified it in 2017, and Illinois did so in 2018. Virginia then became the 38th state to ratify it on January 15, 2020, providing the needed three-fourths requirement—but decades after the deadline expired.

Muddying the waters, five states voted to rescind their ratification. But Article V of the Constitution did not grant states the ability to do so.

House Action

The House Judiciary Committee approved HJ Res 79 on November 13, 2019. The House passed it three months later.

The Judiciary Committee vote was 21–11, and it followed party lines. Chairman Jerrold Nadler, D-N.Y., noted that Virginia was preparing to ratify the Equal Rights Amendment. He called on members to pass the resolution so the Equal Rights Amendment could become the Twenty-Eighth Amendment to the Constitution. He and other Democratic members of the committee said the amendment was as relevant as when it was first proposed. Nadler recognized that legal precedent had prohibited most cases of discrimination on the basis of sex under the Fourteenth Amendment, but said the ERA was necessary to prevent these protections from being rolled back by future executive actions and court rulings.

But Republicans raised objections. Ranking member Doug Collins of Georgia questioned whether it would be possible to remove the seven-year deadline set in the 92nd Congress. He said lawmakers lacked the power to retroactively revive a constitutional amendment that had failed. Mike Johnson, R-La., said Congress would need to start over again with the amendment process in order to add the ERA to the Constitution.

Democrats responded that the Constitution does not contain any reference to a timeline. California Democrat Zoe Lofgren even questioned whether the original deadline for the ERA was valid, arguing that Virginia's ratification should be sufficient for the amendment to take effect even if Congress did not pass an extension.

Republicans also expressed concerns that the ERA would undermine efforts to restrict abortion. "Any limits on abortion, or denying tax-payer funds for abortion, could be seen as a form of sex discrimination and violation of this amendment," said Debbie Lasko, R-Ariz.

The House on February 13, 2020, passed HJ Res 79 on a vote of 232–183. Five Republicans crossed party lines to support the measure, while no Democrats voted against it.

Democrats argued that the amendment was about fairness and inclusion. They also contended that it would help boost the economy by giving women equal footing in the workplace. Republicans, however, maintained that the amendment was unconstitutional because the ERA had expired. They also continued to raise concerns about the amendment's potential impacts on abortion.

Senate, White House and Supreme Court Views

The Senate did not take up the resolution. Alaska Republican Lisa Murkowski and Maryland Democrat Benjamin L. Cardin led the effort to pass it. But Senate Majority Leader Mitch McConnell, R-Ky., declined to bring it to the floor, saying he was not a supporter. The Trump administration's Office of Legal Counsel stated that the ERA was "expired," although the administration did not have to sign off on the resolution if it passed.

Supreme Court Justice Ruth Bader Ginsburg, a feminist icon, also threw cold water on the idea. In a February 10 speech delivered as part of a celebration marking the 100th

anniversary of the Nineteenth Amendment, which gave women the right to vote, Ginsburg said she thought Congress should start over on the amendment. She expressed concern about changing the deadline and allowing additional states to ratify it, while disregarding those states that had rescinded their ratification. "I would like to see a new beginning," Ginsburg said.

LGBT Rights

The House in 2019 passed Democratic-backed legislation to extend legal protections to members of the LGBT community. The Senate, however, did not take it up.

The bill (HR 5) would prohibit discrimination based on sex, sexual orientation, and gender identity in public accommodations, education, federal funding, employment, and housing. It would amend the nation's landmark civil rights laws, including the Civil Rights Act of 1964 and the Fair Housing Act of 1968, to add sexual orientation and gender identity to the existing protected classes of race, color, religion, sex, and national origin.

The bill would allow individuals to access a shared facility, such as a bathroom or locker room, that corresponded with their gender identity. It also would enable the Justice Department to intervene in federal lawsuits regarding sexual orientation and gender identity.

Some states already prohibited discrimination against members of the LGBT community. But supporters, including sponsor David Cicilline, D-R.I., said it was important to establish protection on the federal level. They said it would help end the injustices faced by LGBT people, including families who were denied medical care and individuals who were fired for being transgender.

Republicans, however, raised concerns about the measure infringing on the rights of religious organizations by forcing them to take actions that violated their beliefs. They also said the bill's definition of gender identity was vague, creating uncertainty over how it would be applied. HR 5 defined gender identity as "gender-related identity, appearance, mannerisms or other gender-related characteristics of an individual, regardless of their sex at birth."

Similar legislation had failed to make it out of committee in the previous two sessions. This time, however, it won approval in the House Judiciary Committee on May 1 by a vote of 22–10 after a contentious markup. Action on the bill was briefly delayed when Republicans insisted on the clerk reading both the bill and a substitute amendment rather than dispensing with the reading, as was the customary practice.

On a party line vote, the committee rejected an amendment by Republican Louie Gohmert of Texas that would delete language stating that a law on religious freedom (PL 103-141) could not be used to defend discrimination on the basis of gender identity or sexual orientation in the areas covered in the bill. Cicilline defended the original bill language, saying it would not change the religious freedom law but would instead clarify that it could not be used to justify discrimination in certain cases.

The committee also rejected three Republican amendments related to gender identity. One, by Tom McClintock of California, stated that nothing in the bill would require a medical professional to affirm the "self-professed gender identity" of a minor. A second, by Mike Johnson of Louisiana, stated that nothing in the bill could deny a parent the right to be involved in their child's health care decisions, as had happened in British Columbia, Canada, when a father was prohibited from preventing a child's gender transition. A third amendment, by Greg Steube of Florida, clarified that nothing in the bill would require a "biological female to face competition from a biological male" in a sporting event. This addressed concerns about transgender women dominating women's sports events.

The House passed HR 5 on May 17 by a vote of 236–173. Eight Republicans voted in favor.

D.C. Statehood

The House passed a Democratic-backed measure in 2020 to admit the District of Columbia as the fifty-first state. Even though Republicans emphatically opposed the legislation and the Senate did not take it up, the House vote was hailed by advocates as the first time either chamber had passed a D.C. statehood bill.

The bill (HR 51) passed the House on June 26 on a vote of 232–180. It would establish virtually all of the current District of Columbia as the State of Washington, Douglass Commonwealth. But it would exempt the two square miles that included the Capitol, White House, National Mall, principal federal monuments and federal buildings adjacent to the National Mall, which would remain the District of Columbia and lack electoral rights. The bill would create an eighteen-member commission that would advise Congress on an orderly transition to statehood.

By giving the District a House member and two senators, the bill had substantial implications for the balance of power in Congress. Since the city was overwhelmingly Democratic, it was expected to provide Democrats with a notable boost on Capitol Hill.

Advocates noted that Washington's population of more than 700,000 was more than that of the states of Wyoming and Vermont. They said it was unfair for its residents to pay federal taxes (unlike residents in other U.S. territories) and not have congressional representation. In fact, they pointed out that the District paid more in federal taxes than twenty-two states, and more on a per capita basis than any of the fifty states.

Republicans raised constitutional concerns about the bill, saying it would violate the Twenty-Third Amendment, which grants D.C. residents the right to vote in presidential elections. Democrats downplayed that concern, although the bill called for the repeal of the Twenty-Third Amendment—a difficult task that would require the backing

of two-thirds of both chambers of Congress, as well as the approval of three-quarters of state legislatures.

The White House issued a veto threat, citing both the constitutional concerns as well as the potential for the new state to dominate the national government. Senate Republicans assailed the measure. One day before the House vote, Republican Tom Cotton of Arkansas took to the Senate floor to assail the bill, calling it "a naked power grab" because it would likely lead to two additional Democratic senators.

Those opposed to statehood also contended that, if the District wanted representation in Congress, it should be retroceded to Maryland. But Eleanor Holmes Norton, the sponsor of HR 51 and the District's nonvoting delegate, said Maryland had not given its consent for such a step. Under Article IV of the Constitution, "No new State shall be formed or erected within the Jurisdiction of any other State; nor any State be formed by the Junction of two or more States, or Parts of States, without the Consent of the Legislatures of the States concerned as well as of the Congress."

The House vote took place amid considerable tension between the White House and District leaders over how to handle protests against racism in the wake of the killing of a Black man, George Floyd, by Minneapolis police. D.C. Mayor Muriel Bowser and other local officials assailed the actions of federal law enforcement for clearing peaceful protesters from Lafayette Square with flash-bang grenades and pepper-spray projectiles during a Trump news conference.

Holmes said that only statehood could provide her constituents with true equality.

Statehood would confer other benefits as well. For example, if the District were a state instead of a territory, it would have been eligible for approximately twice the aid that it received in the $2 trillion coronavirus aid package that Congress passed in March.

HR 51 won approval from the House Committee on Oversight and Reform on February 11, 2020, on a party line vote of 21–16. Democrats batted away several Republican amendments. One, by Carol Miller of West Virginia, would set abortion regulations for the proposed state. Another, by Jody B. Hice of Georgia, called for a constitutional amendment on the creation of the state.

Marijuana Decriminalization

A Democratic bill to decriminalize marijuana passed the House in 2020 amid a raft of state measures to loosen marijuana laws. But the Senate did not take it up.

The bill (HR 3884) would remove marijuana from the schedule of illegal drugs established under the 1970 Controlled Substances Act. Marijuana had remained classified under the act as a highly dangerous drug with a high potential for abuse and no currently accepted medical use, despite ongoing research about its medicinal benefits.

Most people with federal marijuana convictions would have their records expunged, while those convicted of crimes in tandem with marijuana-related offenses could be resentenced. The bill would also prohibit the government from basing decisions about business loans, immigration status, or aid on marijuana use or a marijuana offense. Federal agencies that administered drug tests to job applicants could not deny anyone a security clearance based on marijuana use.

The bill would impose a 5 percent tax on marijuana sales that would fund job training, reentry services, health education programs, literacy programs, youth recreation or mentoring programs, legal aid, and addiction treatment. A new office in the Justice Department would oversee these grant programs.

The bill was meant to provide clarity and reduce the tension between increasingly liberal state policies and federal restrictions. By the time of the House vote after the 2020 elections, all but three states had loosened cannabis laws to some degree, according to the Congressional Research Service. Congress had turned to annual appropriations bills to prohibit funds from being used to pursue those people who acted within state medical marijuana laws, but it allowed exceptions. Furthermore, recreational users of marijuana remained vulnerable to the Department of Justice.

Marijuana was the most commonly used illicit substance in the United States. Americans appeared to be increasingly open to a less strict approach to the drug. The issue had appeared in five states in November 2020—Arizona, Mississippi, Montana, New Jersey, and South Dakota—with voters in each case approving measures to liberalize marijuana laws. The House vote also followed years of advocacy by the increasingly influential cannabis industry.

The House Judiciary Committee approved HR 3884 on November 20, 2019, by a vote of 24–10. Two Republicans, Matt Gaetz of Florida and Tom McClintock of California, joined Democrats in backing the measure.

Supporters pointed to the racially disparate nature of marijuana enforcement and the impacts on minority communities to argue why the bill was needed. Opponents did not directly criticize the idea of marijuana decriminalization, but they said the legislative process was rushed and the bill would not pass the Senate.

Although voting for the bill, Gaetz encouraged Nadler to have the committee mark up a measure (HR 2093) that would not impose federal marijuana law on individuals who were complying with state law. Nadler said that measure was inadequate because it would still limit the otherwise legal use of the banking system by cannabis businesses.

Ken Buck, R-Colo., proposed an amendment to insert the language of HR 2093 in place of the decriminalization language in HR 3884. But it was rejected by voice vote.

The committee gave voice vote approval to an amendment by Cedric L. Richmond, D-La., that would allow the

trust fund to be used for services addressing any collateral consequences from the "war on drugs" that had been waged during the presidency of Richard Nixon. Members also approved an amendment by Sheila Jackson Lee, D-Texas, modified by Gaetz, that would require the comptroller general to study the demographics of individuals who have been convicted of a federal marijuana offense. An amendment by Buck requiring the comptroller general to study the societal impacts of marijuana legalization won voice vote approval as well.

The House on December 4, 2020, passed HR 3884 by a vote of 228–164. Five Republicans supported the measure, while six Democrats voted against it.

The House floor debate took place against the backdrop of the COVID-19 pandemic and congressional efforts to provide relief for Americans facing health challenges, unemployment, and the threat of eviction. Republican opponents charged that the bill was frivolous but Democrats called it overdue.

Disparities in drug arrests were a focal point of the floor debate, spurred in part by months of racial justice protests after the police killing of Rodney King. Democrat Barbara Lee of California, co-chair of the Cannabis Caucus, cited statistics that Black and Latino people were more likely to be arrested and sentenced to long prison sentences. She said HR 3884 was a racial justice bill.

Republicans raised a number of concerns, such as why such a bill was even on the floor at a time when lawmakers were struggling to advance a major pandemic relief measure. Some also said the bill should have ensured that the Food and Drug Administration effectively regulated cannabis advertising and potency. Others worried that national decriminalization would lead to marijuana being federally regulated when it should be left to the states, although Democrats said the bill would prevent conflicts between state and federal laws.

Violence Against Women Act

Efforts to reauthorize the Violence Against Women Act collapsed amid disputes over a gun provision and conservative objections to other language. Democrats won passage in the House in 2019 with some Republican support. But the Senate, after months of fruitless bipartisan negotiations, did not take it up.

When the landmark law (PL 103-322) was first enacted in 1994 as a response to the prevalence of domestic and sexual violence, it marked a major effort on the federal level to reduce incidents of domestic violence and mitigate its impact on women's lives. The legislation created programs to enhance the investigation and prosecution of violent crimes against women and authorized grants to state and local law enforcement.

Over the years, Congress gradually expanded the law beyond its original focus on abuse between married partners. When last reauthorized in 2013, conservatives raised concerns over new provisions that extended protections to same-sex couples and allowed undocumented immigrants who were battered to obtain temporary visas. The act expired in late 2018 during the lengthy government shutdown. It was briefly reinstated in the January short-term fiscal 2019 spending deal (PL 116-5) before expiring again on February 15, as lawmakers did not include another extension in the agreement (PL 116-6) that provided for spending through the end of fiscal 2019. House Speaker Nancy Pelosi, D-Calif., believed that letting the law lapse would provide more incentive for the Senate to negotiate with the House on a multiyear reauthorization.

Lawmakers on both sides of the aisle said they wanted to take action to stop violence against women, which continued to be a national concern. A quarter of women reported experiencing severe intimate-partner physical violence, and one in seven had been stalked by an intimate partner to the point where she felt very fearful, or believed that she or someone close to her would be harmed or killed, according to the National Coalition Against Domestic Violence.

House Committee Action

The House Judiciary Committee on March 13, 2019, approved a bill (HR 1585) to reauthorize the Violence Against Women Act. As with previous reauthorizations of the law, the measure would expand programs and broaden the groups of people who are eligible for assistance. HR 1585 would require the Office of Violence Against Women to track cases across the country in which declinations to prosecute sexual assault cases occurred. The measure also would authorize grants for housing to victims of domestic violence so they could afford to stay in their homes. It would create a position at the Department of Housing and Urban Development to address domestic violence.

In response to the #MeToo movement, the measure would authorize grants for programs addressing sexual harassment and bullying. New provisions would support so-called red flag laws that aim to curtail the purchase and possession of firearms by individuals whom a court deemed to be a threat. The measure would also increase protections for gender and sexual minorities, which had been established in the 2013 authorization.

Republicans, however, said they could not support the bill because of some of the Democrats' provisions. John Ratcliffe, R-Texas, for example, objected to language in the bill that would allow victims to voluntarily enter into an "alternative justice response," a way to seek restitution outside of the court system. Ratcliffe warned that the provision would make it harder for prosecutors and judges to punish abusers.

Jim Sensenbrenner, R-Wis., raised concerns over bill language to allow Indian tribes to prosecute nontribal members for crimes committed on reservations, saying that it could infringe on the constitutional rights of nontribal members. He offered an amendment to delete the

language, but the committee rejected it on a party line vote of 9–16.

Democrats also defeated efforts by Republicans Louie Gohmert of Texas and Debbie Lesko of Arizona to delete language to extend protection to transgender individuals. Gohmert's amendment would have struck all references to gender identity and transgender people from the bill. Lesko's amendment included language to prohibit a victim service provider from placing a woman or child into a circumstance where they felt unsafe or their privacy may be violated. Although the amendment's vague wording temporarily caused confusion, Lesko, who was herself an abuse survivor, clarified that it was designed to stop women from being placed in shelters against their will with "biological males," her term for transgender women. Democrats objected to the claim that transgender women presented a danger to other women in shelters.

Both Gohmert's and Lesko's amendments were defeated on party lines.

Lesko introduced a second amendment with Rep. Steve Chabot, R-Ohio, that would have allowed faith-based organizations to establish their own standards when providing assistance. The committee rejected it on a party line vote. The committee also rejected, 14–19, an amendment by Ken Buck, R-Colo., to provide firearms training to combat future instances of sexual assault and dating violence. The committee gave voice vote approval to an amendment by Sheila Jackson Lee, D-Texas, requiring the Interior Department and the attorney general to submit a report with statistics on Indian women who were missing, murdered, or the victims of sexual assault.

House Floor Action

The House voted on April 4, 2019, to reauthorize the Violence Against Women Act. But differences over provisions that would restrict gun ownership and expand rights for transgender individuals foreshadowed problems to come.

The 263–158 vote split the Republican caucus. The bill, which had a Republican cosponsor—Brian Fitzpatrick of Pennsylvania—won support from thirty-three Republicans, with an additional Republican, Jeff Fortenberry of Nebraska, voting present. Even Republicans who supported the bill, however, warned that its restrictions on gun rights could undermine a politically popular bill, and they warned that Democrats erred by not agreeing to include the bill in the omnibus 2019 spending bill. "You're taking something that should be an easy bipartisan reauthorization of existing law and complicating it to make a political point," Tom Cole, R-Oklahoma, told Congressional Quarterly. "You're certainly free to do that, but in the meantime, you should have at least extended it through the fiscal year so that you can make whatever point and then sit down and negotiate." But Rep. Karen Bass, D-Calif., the bill's primary sponsor, said Congress needed to expand the 2013 reauthorization of the law in ways that would reflect the #MeToo Movement and respond to changes in society.

The most contentious provision would prohibit anyone convicted of a misdemeanor for domestic abuse or stalking from buying a gun. This would toughen the existing language, which applied only to felony convictions. The bill would also close the so-called boyfriend loophole by expanding gun prohibitions to include dating partners convicted of abuse or stalking.

Democrats said that a person who was convicted of domestic violence should not have access to a gun. Republicans, however, objected to introducing the contentious issue of gun control into a bill about the safety of women. The firearms provisions prompted the National Rifle Association (NRA) to weigh in against the measure and score lawmakers on how they voted on the bill, thereby affecting their much-watched NRA ratings.

Lawmakers also clashed over transgender rights. Lesko and other Republicans wanted to strip provisions in the measure that would allow transgender women to access women's shelters and serve in prisons that aligned with their gender identity. Instead, they wanted access and sentencing guidelines to continue to correspond with biological sex assigned at birth. Although Lasko voted against the bill, some Republicans did not oppose the transgender rights proposals included on the bill. Tom Reed of New York, for example, voted for the bill and said he was comfortable with its transgender language although he objected to gun provisions.

Prior to the final vote, lawmakers also debated provisions that affected Native American tribal justice jurisdiction. An estimated four out of five Native American women experience violence at some point in their lives, according to a report by the National Congress of American Indians. The House adopted two amendments by Democrat Deb Haaland of New Mexico related to Native American populations, including one to help federal, state, and tribal authorities share information in criminal databases. Haaland, one of the first Native American women elected to the House, reached across the aisle and teamed up with Republicans Paul Cook of California and Don Young of Alaska to propose the criminal database change.

HR 1585 also included a number of less controversial provisions. For example, it would make it a crime for a federal law enforcement officer to have sex while in the course of their official duties, regardless of whether it was consensual. Under an amendment passed on the floor, the bill would expand the National Domestic Violence Hotline to include texting features. The measure also expanded housing protections for victims, provided more assistance to Native American women, and authorized grants to enhance law enforcement tools.

Senate Negotiations

The Senate failed to vote on a reauthorization of the Violence Against Women Act despite months of negotiations by Sens. Joni Ernst, R-Iowa, and Dianne Feinstein,

D-Calif. Partisan differences centered on the gun control language, but the negotiators also struggled to reach agreement over issues involving LGBTQ protections and tribal jurisdiction. Feinstein wanted to use the House bill as a starting point, although Ernst and other Republicans criticized that bill as a nonstarter.

Senators on both sides of the aisle said that tackling violence against women remained a priority. Nevertheless, in a floor speech on November 7, 2019, Ernst said the negotiations had fallen apart and the bill had become swept up in election-year politics.

Senate Democrats the following week introduced the same reauthorization bill as the one passed by the House, even though Republicans opposed it. The entire Democratic caucus backed the bill, with several Democrats blaming the influence of the National Rifle Association for preventing passage.

Amy Coney Barrett Confirmation

President Trump established a conservative supermajority on the Supreme Court shortly before the 2020 election with his nomination of Amy Coney Barrett, forty-eight, a former law professor and reliably conservative federal appeals court judge. Trump and Senate Republicans moved quickly to fill the seat of Ruth Bader Ginsburg, a trailblazing women's rights advocate and liberal icon who died on September 18 at the age of eighty-seven after a long battle with cancer.

The replacement of a leading liberal with a staunch conservative marked a substantial triumph for Republicans who wanted to move the court decisively to the right. Trump's first two Supreme Court picks had replaced conservative justices. Democrats heatedly opposed the rapid confirmation process for Barrett, pointing out that Senate Majority Leader Mitch McConnell of Kentucky refused to hold hearings on President Barack Obama's Supreme Court nominee in a presidential election year. But they lacked the votes to block Barrett's path to the high court.

Nomination

Trump announced Barrett's nomination on September 26, 2020. The selection came as little surprise, since Barrett had long been viewed as a frontrunner for a Court opening. A New Orleans native, Barrett had graduated first in her class from Notre Dame Law School. She clerked for Supreme Court Justice Antonin Scalia, worked for the legal team representing George W. Bush in the legal battle over the 2000 presidential election and became a law professor at Notre Dame with a focus on statutory interpretation and judicial precedents.

Republicans lauded Barrett's conservative judicial philosophy as well as her personal story, including her family focus and the educational and geographic diversity her confirmation would bring to the court. If confirmed, Barrett would be the only justice with a degree from a law school other than Harvard or Yale, and she would bring a perspective of being raised in the South and living in the Midwest. She was a mother of seven children ranging in age from eight to nineteen, including one who had special needs and two adopted from Haiti. She would become the first mother of school-age children to serve as a justice. Republicans also noted her strong Catholic faith, while warning Democrats against questioning whether it would affect her ability to be fair.

When Barrett had been nominated by Trump in 2017 for a seat on the U.S. Court of Appeals for the Seventh Circuit, she encountered significant Democratic opposition. Sen. Dianne Feinstein, D-Calif., sharply questioned the nominee about an article she had cowritten calling for Catholic judges to recuse themselves in certain death penalty cases due to their moral objections to the death penalty, and she raised concerns about whether Barrett would uphold abortion rights, given her religious beliefs. Barrett said that she would follow the Constitution as a judge and not impose her personal convictions on the law. She won confirmation on a vote of 55–43, with just three Democrats supporting her.

When Trump introduced Barrett as his Supreme Court nominee, he praised her legal acumen. "She is a woman of unparalleled achievement, towering intellect, sterling credentials and unyielding loyalty to the Constitution," he said in the White House Rose Garden. Barrett, for her part, emphasized her conservative legal philosophy, linking her approach to that of Scalia, a leading proponent of originalism—a constitutional approach that seeks to interpret how laws were understood at the time they were written.

Both conservatives and liberals agreed that Barrett would firmly establish a 6–3 conservative majority that within months and over the years could push the Supreme Court rightward on contentious issues such as abortion rights, gun control, religious rights, immigration, and health care. Her supporters praised her intelligence, her relative youth, and her rock-solid conservative approach to the law. Democrats worried that she would vote to overturn the landmark 1973 decision establishing the right to abortion, *Roe v. Wade*, and side with court conservatives to strike down the Affordable Care Act (PL 111-148, PL 111-152), known as Obamacare, that had expanded health care to millions of people after narrowly surviving a judicial challenge.

Republicans announced an ambitious timeline to approve Barrett, with the confirmation hearing beginning on October 12 and a floor vote shortly thereafter. Their plans, however, were threatened not only by Democratic opposition, but also the COVID-19 pandemic, which temporarily halted proceedings. Trump fell ill with the novel coronavirus shortly after the Rose Garden ceremony announcing Barrett's nomination, and he had to spend several days at Walter Reed Army Medical Center. Republicans Mike Lee of Utah and Thom Tillis of North Carolina, who had been at the Rose Garden for the announcement, tested positive, prompting concerns that several other senators

may have been exposed. Two members of the Judiciary Committee, ranking member Feinstein and former committee chairman Charles E. Grassley, both eighty-seven, were at high risk for the virus because of their age.

Democrats invoked the pandemic as a reason to delay the hearing. Committee chairman Lindsay Graham, R-S.C., refusing to deviate from the schedule, said every senator had the option of attending the hearings virtually although votes would have to be cast in person. Democrats, however, argued that the significance of a Supreme Court confirmation demanded in-person attendance.

Confirmation Hearing

The Senate Judiciary Committee began its four-day confirmation hearing on October 12, with some members attending in person and others participating remotely. The health protocols limited the number of people in the room, preventing the type of protests that had occurred during the confirmation hearing of Brett Kavanaugh. Barrett declined to answer questions pertaining to specific issues and successfully avoided making the type of misstep that could derail her nomination. Each senator had ten minutes for an opening statement on the first day, and they firmly laid out their party's positions while taking shots at each other.

Democrats used their time to focus relentlessly on the potential for the Supreme Court to terminate the 2010 health care law, which was the target of a case backed by the Trump administration and set for argument November 10. The Democrats set up photos of people who would lose insurance coverage if the Supreme Court undid the health care law, and they spoke about their illnesses, lives, and hobbies. Sen. Mazie K. Hirono of Hawaii even talked about her own cancer diagnosis as she tried to persuade Republicans to slow the process.

Democrats also criticized Republicans for speeding a hearing just three weeks after Ginsburg's death and during a pandemic in which two committee members had recently tested positive for COVID-19 within the past two weeks. Democrat Chris Coons of Delaware scolded Republicans for behaving in a way that was "wrong" and "hypocritical" after blocking President Barack Obama's nominee to the high court just four years earlier because that vacancy arose in an election year.

Republicans shot back, criticizing Democrats for focusing on how Barrett might vote in particular cases instead of her qualifications. Ben Sasse, R-Neb., said it would politicize the courts to have judicial nominees precommit to certain outcomes in future court cases. Josh Hawley, R-Mo., accused Democrats of a "pattern and practice of religious bigotry" for targeting Barrett's religious faith as a reason to vote against her.

Despite the sometimes heated rhetoric, Graham conceded that the hearing was unlikely to change anyone's mind. "This is probably not about persuading each other," he said. "Unless something really dramatic happens, all Republicans will vote yes and all Democrats will vote no."

Barrett fielded questions on the second day of the confirmation hearing, saying little about contentious issues such as abortion, health care, and race relations. Asked by Feinstein if she agreed with Scalia that *Roe v. Wade* was wrongly decided, she said she would not grade precedents or weigh in on a particular legal issue. However, she said *Roe v. Wade* was not a "super precedent" considered beyond the possibility of being overturned. Barrett also said that her previous statements on abortion, including an advertisement she signed onto opposing it, were distinct from her role as a judge. "I do see as distinct my personal moral religious views and my task of applying laws as a judge," she said.

Barrett, however, did provide a few hints about how she might approach the court. She said she would only look at the legislative history of a statute if other options had been exhausted, regards herself as an originalist, and considers Scalia a model. She added, however, "I want to be careful to say that if I'm confirmed, you would not be getting Justice Scalia; you would be getting Justice Barrett."

Although she avoided weighing in on policies related to racism, Barrett gave a personal response to questions from Illinois Democrat Richard J. Durbin about the killing of George Floyd at the hands of police, which sparked nationwide protests and activism over racial justice. She described it as a serious and deeply personal issue for her multiracial family, which included two Black children adopted from Haiti. She said her seventeen-year-old daughter Vivian was particularly affected by Floyd's death. "We wept together in my room," Barrett said.

Durbin and other Democrats also pressed Barrett about her views on presidential power and the ability of Trump to pardon himself or delay November's election. Barrett said she did not believe anyone is above the law, but declined to weigh in on potential cases.

Barrett had just a pen and blank pad of paper on the otherwise bare witness table. She fielded questions without the help of reference material and took few notes. Early on the second day of the hearing, Texas Republican John Cornyn asked Barrett to hold up the materials she had been using to answer questions, and she displayed the blank pad of paper with the Senate letterhead at the top, smiling. "That's impressive," Cornyn said, pointing out the contrast with the binders and piles of materials that senators had in front of them.

Senate Judiciary Committee Action

The Judiciary Committee approved the confirmation on October 22. All twelve committee Republicans voted in favor. The panel's Democrats boycotted the meeting. Their chairs instead supported large photos of their constituents who they said would be harmed if Barrett was confirmed. They accused Republicans of violating panel rules in a rush to complete the process in time for Supreme Court oral arguments on November 10 in the case in which the Trump administration was asking the justices to wipe out the full 2010 health care law.

Graham refused to postpone the vote even though committee rules called for two members of the minority party to be present for a quorum. He blamed Democrats for the partisan divide over judicial nominees while praising Barrett's qualifications and legal expertise.

Final Action

The Senate on October 25 voted, 51–48, to cut off debate over the nomination. Two Republicans, Susan Collins of Maine and Lisa Murkowski of Alaska, joined Democrats in voting against the cloture motion, although Murkowski said she would vote to confirm Barrett.

One day later, on October 26, the Senate voted to confirm Barrett, 52–48. All Democrats as well as Collins voted no. It was the first time since 1870 that a Supreme Court nominee won confirmation without a single vote from the minority party. Collins said she crossed party lines because she did not believe in advancing a Supreme Court nomination right before a presidential election.

Democrats expressed outrage that the Senate took the vote just a week before Election Day after Republicans refused to consider Obama's nomination of Merrick Garland during a presidential election year. "There is no escaping this glaring hypocrisy," Schumer said. "No tit for tat, convoluted, distorted version of history will wipe away the stain that will exist forever with this Republican majority."

McConnell, however, blamed Democrats for the ever-escalating conflicts over judicial confirmations. He also noted that Barrett's legacy would far outlive the next election. "We've made an important contribution to the future in this country," he said on the Senate floor on October 25. "A lot of what we've done over the last four years will be undone, sooner or later, by the next election. Won't be able to do much about this, for a long time to come."

Appropriations Bills

As was the case in 2017–18, the 116th Congress could not pass the Commerce–Justice–Science bill as a standalone measure. Instead, lawmakers repeatedly rolled into omnibus spending packages that included other appropriations bills.

Fiscal 2019 Appropriations

The fiscal 2019 Commerce–Justice–Science spending bill was rolled into H J Res 31, an omnibus spending measure that the House and Senate passed on February 14, 2019, and Trump signed one day later. The measure provided $30.9 billion for the Justice Department, which was $638 million (2%) more than FY 2018 and $2.1 billion (7%) more than the amount requested by the administration. Compared with FY 2018, it increased funding for most federal law enforcement activities, including the FBI (2% more), the Drug Enforcement Agency (3.5% more), Alcohol, Tobacco and Firearms (2% more), and programs to support state and local law enforcement agencies (3% more).

For the FBI, Congress increased funding for counterterrorism, national security, and cybersecurity. The explanatory material accompanying the bill's report directed the FBI to report on increased instances of cyberstalking and threats, and it also called for FBI and U.S. attorneys to investigate and prosecute cyberstalking and other crimes involving internet threats to the fullest extent of the law. The measure included $75 million to improve the performance of the National Instant Criminal Background Check System. It also provided $385 million for the modernization of FBI facilities with an eye to enabling the agency to address high priorities outside the Washington, D.C., area.

The measure provided $3.3 billion for Justice Department legal activities, which was $57 million less than FY 2018 but $138 million, or 4 percent, more than requested. The agreement provided $1.3 billion for the Bureau of Alcohol, Tobacco, Firearms and Explosives (ATF)—$23 million (2%) more than FY 2018 and equal to the administration's request. It contained a number of restrictions on the activities of the ATF, which had drawn scrutiny from gun rights supporters because of its role in enforcing firearms laws. These included a prohibition on any functions, missions or activities of the ATF being transferred to other federal agencies or departments, and a prohibition on the use of funds to implement the Arms Trade Treaty (a multilateral pact that regulated the international trade in conventional weapons) without Senate ratification. The bill forbid the government from issuing regulations that would characterize certain shotguns as "non-sporting" due to military-style features. Federal agents could not facilitate the transfer of an operable firearm to any individual associated with a drug cartel.

The bill provided $2.3 billion in net funding for activities of the Drug Enforcement Administration. An additional $421 million was made available for DEA's Diversion Control Program with the goal of preventing controlled substances from being illegally diverted for illicit uses. This money, derived from the diversion control fund, resulted in a total of $2.7 billion that was available to the DEA for the fiscal year.

The measure also provided $7.5 billion for the Federal Prison System and $2.9 billion for the U.S. Marshals Service. An additional $560 million was appropriated for Interagency Crime and Drug Enforcement activities.

The legislation provided $563 million for 534 immigration judges and associated teams to conduct administrative reviews and hear appeals of immigration cases. This represented fifty-one more judges than authorized and funded for FY 2018. However only 395 immigration judges and teams were active as of the end of FY 2018, despite departmental efforts to accelerate the recruitment and hiring of immigration judges. Only 395 such teams were on board at the end of the fiscal year.

The measure included $2.5 billion for state and local law enforcement programs, which was some 62 percent more than the administration request. Most of this ($2.2 billion) funded grants to state and local organizations

for crime fighting, juvenile justice programs, and public safety officer benefits. Community Oriented Policing Services received $304 million to support local law enforcement agencies, while the Office on Violence Against Women received $498 million for prevention programs and prosecutions. Lawmakers, however, rejected the administration's $254 million request for the High Intensity Drug Trafficking Areas Program.

FISCAL 2020 APPROPRIATIONS

Lawmakers cleared the 2020 fiscal year Commerce–Justice–Science bill as part of a larger appropriations package in December 2019.

House committee action

Work on the funding measure began in the spring. The House Appropriations Committee on May 22, 2019, approved a fiscal 2020 Commerce–Justice–Science spending bill on a party line vote of 32–20. The bill would provide $32 billion for the Justice Department, an increase of $1.07 billion. The bill included an additional $110 million to hire immigration judge teams. It would increase funding for FBI personnel by $263.8 million for critical public safety missions such as counterintelligence and cybercrime enforcement.

Robert B. Aderholt of Alabama, the ranking member of the Commerce–Justice–Science subcommittee, said he and other Republicans supported much of the bill. But he criticized the overall spending levels, as well as a decision of Democrats to remove four firearm policy riders that have been in the bill for years.

Democrats rejected an amendment by Aderholt to cut a $10 million pilot grant program that would provide representation for detained immigrants entering the country illegally. Aderholt said that the program would encourage more illegal immigration as well as contradicting existing law that prohibited taxpayer funds from being spent on such a purpose. Democrats also voted down an amendment from Mario Diaz-Balart, R-Fla., to restore a provision from the previous year's spending bill that prohibited the use of funds for the transfer or release of detainees at the military's facility at Guantanamo Bay, Cuba, into the United States.

Much of the debate had to do with issues other than justice, such as preparations for the 2020 census. Democrats defeated an amendment from Florida Republican John Rutherford that would eliminate language in the bill designed to prevent inclusion of a question about citizenship on the 2020 census questionnaire—a major point of contention between the parties.

House floor action

The House on June 25 passed the Commerce–Justice–Science bill as part of an omnibus measure (HR 3055) that included five fiscal 2020 spending measures. The 227–194 vote largely followed party lines, and Republican opposi-

tion on the floor was aligned with a veto threat by the Trump administration, which raised concerns about spending levels and policy riders. On a vote of 267–165, the House adopted an amendment that would block the federal enforcement of marijuana laws in states that allowed the drug.

Senate committee action

The Senate Appropriations Committee on September 26, 2019, advanced its version of the Commerce–Justice–Science spending bill for fiscal 2020. The bill (S 2584) would provide $32.4 billion to the Justice Department, or $1.5 billion more than the current fiscal year, an increase of nearly 5 percent. Although the Trump administration had proposed eliminating the Legal Services Corporation, an independent nonprofit group that provided free legal aid to the poor, the bill would provide it with a 2.5 percent boost over the current year. The measure also would boost funding for programs to combat gun violence. Much of that money would go to the FBI for instant background checks on gun buyers and the Bureau of Alcohol, Tobacco and Firearms for enforcement, investigations and inspections.

The measure contained $75 million to implement the 2018 criminal justice overhaul law (PL 115-391). And it provided $500 million for grant programs under the Violence Against Women Act.

Senate floor action

The Senate passed the bill on October 31 as part of a $214 billion package that also included Agriculture, Interior–Environment, and Transportation–HUD spending bills. Less than two months later, senators on December 19 cleared the Commerce–Justice–Science bill as part of a larger, $860 billion spending package (HR 1158).

Provisions

The final bill contained $32.6 billion for the Justice Department, 5 percent more than in FY 2019. That amount included $3.4 billion for DOJ Legal Activities (3% more than in FY 2019), of which $2.25 billion was for U.S. Attorneys' offices.

It appropriated a total of $9.9 billion for the FBI (4% more than in FY 2019), $7.8 billion for the Federal Prison System (3.5% more), $3.3 billion for the U.S. Marshals Service (13% more), $2.7 billion for the Drug Enforcement Administration (a fractional decrease), and $1.4 billion for the Bureau of Alcohol, Tobacco, and Firearms (6% more). The measure also provided $2.8 billion for grants to state, local, and tribal law enforcement, which was 13 percent more than in FY 2019. And it called for an additional $502 million for grants through the Office on Violence Against Women (1% more than FY 2019), and another $343 million through the Community Oriented Policing Services program (13% more).

The bill appropriated $673 million for administrative reviews and appeals of immigration cases by the Executive

Office for Immigration Review, which was 19 percent more than in FY 2019. It also provided $440 million to the Legal Services Corporation, a modest boost over the fiscal 2019 amount. In a victory for Democrats, it included $25 million for the CDC to research firearms safety and gun violence.

FISCAL 2021

The Senate on December 21, 2020, cleared the fiscal 2021 Commerce–Justice–Science spending bill as part of a massive, $1.4 trillion omnibus spending package (HR 133) that included all twelve appropriations bills.

House committee action

The House Appropriations Committee approved the Commerce–Justice–Science bill on a party line vote of 30–22 on July 14, 2020. The measure, intended to spur changes in policing practices and protect civil rights, contained numerous, Democratic-backed provisions that would require local law enforcement agencies to make certain policy changes or lose federal grants. The committee action took place against the backdrop of nationwide protests over the killing of a Black man, George Floyd, by a Minneapolis police officer.

The chairman of the subcommittee, Rep. Jose E. Serrano of New York, said the goal was to put pressure on state and local governments to alter their laws on practices that had come under fire for being applied in racial ways, including the use of force and no-knock warrants. But Republicans raised concerns about taking decisions out of the hands of local leaders who knew their communities and nationalizing state and local law enforcement. They also argued that it would weaken efforts to reduce violent crime.

Somewhat similar to an authorizing bill about policing practices that stalled in the Senate, the appropriations measure sought to restrict controversial police practices. To receive Edward Byrne Memorial Justice Assistance and other Justice Department grants, law enforcement departments would have to meet certain requirements, including training in deescalation, elimination of racial profiling, use of force, and intervention if another officer used excessive force. In addition, departments would be required to prohibit chokeholds and no-knock warrants for drug cases.

The committee rejected several Republican amendments on party line votes that would have carved out certain exemptions from the requirements in the bill. One, by John Rutherford of Florida, would exempt Community Oriented Policing Services program grants. Another, by Mario Diaz-Balart, would exempt the Byrne grants or COPS grants used to better protect schools, such as installing metal detectors and locks. A third by Tom Cole of Oklahoma, would exempt federally recognized Native American tribes. Cole argued that many tribes could not afford such costly measures as obtaining accreditation for their agencies.

The bill included more than $400 million in grants for local police departments, both to provide an incentive for policy changes and to fund outside investigations of law enforcement.

Overall, the Justice Department would receive $33.2 billion under the spending bill, an increase of $973 million from the current fiscal year and a sizable boost over the administration request of $31.7 billion appropriation for the department.

Certain provisions seemed certain to draw opposition from the White House. These included $100 million for the Justice Department's so-called pattern and practice investigations meant to curtail unconstitutional policing. Attorney General William Barr criticized consent decrees with local police departments that were meant to prohibit civil rights violations, as did his predecessor, Jeff Sessions. Democrats also put an emphasis on civil rights investigations while boosting the FBI's budget by $235 million, to $9.7 billion. The bill also contained provisions to curb opioid abuse, hire immigration judges, further implement criminal justice overhauls, and reduce firearm-related crime.

House floor action

The Commerce–Justice–Science bill was rolled into a larger package (HR 7617) that contained five other appropriations bills. The House on July 31 passed it on a mostly party line vote, 217–197, defying a White House veto threat.

Final action

The Senate Appropriations Committee waited until after the elections to unveil its version of the fiscal 2021 spending bill on November 10. The committee did not mark up the bill.

The Senate measure did not include the controversial policing incentives that the House had passed. It would provide $33.7 billion for the Justice Department, including more than $10 billion for the FBI—a significant increase above both the House bill and the administration's budget request. The Senate version also gave significant funding increases to U.S. Attorneys offices, the Executive Office of Immigration Review, and the federal prison system.

The House and Senate on December 21 easily cleared the Commerce–Justice–Science spending bill as part of a massive package (HR 133) that included all twelve spending bills totaling $1.4 trillion. Trump signed it into law six days later (PL 116-260).

Provisions

The bill, which provided $33.7 billion for the Justice Department, greatly scaled back the House measures on policing. It bolstered programs and grants for police training, providing $153 million for local police department programs within the Justice Department, which was a $67 million increase over the previous fiscal year. The bill also would direct the Department of Justice (DOJ) to spend

$5 million on implementing an executive order that Trump had signed in June to create a national database of use-of-force incidents and alleged police misconduct. The Justice Department was required to develop national standards for police accreditation and provide evidence-based training for civil rights protection, use of force, and deescalation. It also had to review its own use-of-force policies. In addition, the bill appropriated $25 million for investigations into police misconduct, with an additional $5 million to create a database that would track misconduct.

The FBI received $10.3 billion, with funding provided for missions to counter terrorism, protect national security, and ward off cyber threats, as well as investigations of public corruption, organized crime, financial crimes, and human trafficking. The measure also provided $566 million for FBI construction to help the agency modernize its facilities and address its highest priorities outside the national capital area. It encouraged the FBI to work with the General Services Administration to submit a prospectus to Congress to construct a headquarters building in compliance with past Congressional directives. This was a response to a delay in the planned construction of a new FBI headquarters in the Washington D.C. region, influenced in part by the president's desire to keep the headquarters at its current site opposite the Trump Hotel on Pennsylvania Ave. in Washington, D.C.

The measure provided $3.6 billion for DOJ legal activities. It contained $2.3 billion for the Drug Enforcement Administration (DEA), in addition to a separate total of $460 million derived from the diversion control fund, which was available for DEA's Diversion Control Program to prevent controlled substances from being illegally diverted for illicit uses. A total of $1.5 billion was appropriated for the Bureau of Alcohol, Tobacco, Firearms and Explosives. The bill extended a prohibition on any functions, missions, or activities of the ATF being transferred to other federal agencies or departments. It also continued to prohibit federal agents from facilitating the transfer of an operable firearm to any individual associated with a drug cartel, which was known as the "Fast and Furious" provision.

The measure included $7.8 billion for the Bureau of Prisons, including $409 million for activities authorized by the 2019 First Step Act (PL 115-391) to provide programs for inmates intended to reduce recidivism. The U.S. Marshals Service received $3.6 billion. The measure also contained $550 million for Interagency Crime and Drug Enforcement activities and $14 million for the United States Parole Commission (2% more).

Appropriators provided $734 million for administrative reviews and appeals of immigration cases by the Executive Office for Immigration Review. This included $25 million for the Legal Orientation Program, which provided information about the immigration court process to individuals facing possible deportation proceedings.

Finally, it contained $3 billion for state and local law enforcement programs. This included $513 for the Office on Violence Against Women and $386 million for Community Oriented Policing Services, better known as COPS. It also included $394 million for anti-opioid abuse programs, $100 million for programs under the 2007 Second Chance Act (PL 110-199) to reduce recidivism and improve outcomes for people returning from prison, $90 million to improve police–community relations (including $35 million for body cameras), $85 million for states to upgrade criminal and mental health records for the FBI's National Instant Criminal Background Check System, and $79 million for school violence prevention.

Impeachment

The House delivered a historic rebuke of President Trump in December 2019, passing two articles of impeachment for abuse of power and obstruction of justice. The Senate acquitted him in February. The saga marked the third time in U.S. history that a president had been impeached, with each time culminating in a Senate acquittal. (A fourth impeachment occurred in 2021 when Trump faced allegations for inciting the January 6 insurrection that year, with the Senate again acquitting him, albeit by a narrower margin.)

Lawmakers in 2019 acted after allegations surfaced that Trump had solicited foreign interference in the 2020 presidential election. They also accused Trump of improperly obstructing their investigation by telling his administration officials to ignore subpoenas for documents and testimony. Their investigation found evidence that the president had withheld military aid and a White House invitation to Ukrainian president Volodymyr Zelensky unless Zelensky announced an investigation into Trump's political adversary, former Vice President Joseph R. Biden.

Some Democrats had raised the prospect of impeaching Trump from the time they won the House majority in the midterm elections. They launched a series of investigations into alleged administration misdeeds, including following up on the work of Special Counsel Robert S. Mueller III, who looked into charges of Russian meddling with the 2016 election. House Speaker Nancy Pelosi of California, however, resisted the desire of many in her caucus to impeach the president, fearing the political fallout of taking such an aggressive action without clear evidence of wrongdoing that met the constitutional standard of "high crimes and misdemeanors." But a whistleblower's revelation of Trump refusing to release congressionally appropriated money to Ukraine for political gain changed her calculus in September, and Democrats moved swiftly to investigate the charges and draw up articles of impeachment.

Although Trump's actions drew criticism from many across the political spectrum, Republicans argued they did not rise to the level of an impeachable offense. As a result, the House votes on impeachment largely followed party lines. In the Senate, Majority Leader Mitch McConnell of

Kentucky laid the groundwork for a brief trial and relatively quick vote for acquittal. Although all Democrats ultimately voted to convict the president, they were joined by just one Republican: Mitt Romney of Utah. After Trump's acquittal, he claimed vindication. He fired two witnesses who had provided damaging testimony to the House: Ambassador Gordon Sondland and Alexander Vindman, as well as Vindman's brother. Trump's poll numbers briefly surged, much as happened with President Bill Clinton after his own impeachment and acquittal. The entire episode left Democrats disheartened, and the partisan ill will on Capitol Hill seemed more bitter than ever.

INITIAL INVESTIGATIONS

By winning the House majority in the 2018 midterm elections, Democrats gained the means to investigate a president whom they viewed as irredeemably corrupt. The activities of Trump, his campaign, his administration, and his business were under scrutiny by Special Counsel Robert S. Mueller III and investigators with the state of New York, and a wave of lawsuits threatened to expose many of his once-private dealings. Several House committees launched investigations into Trump's business activities, including potential ties to Russia. Among their concerns were whether Trump was using the presidency to profit his own businesses and whether he was advancing his own interests, rather than those of the nation. The new chairman of the House Oversight and Reform Committee, Elijah E. Cummings, said one of his priorities was to show "there's a cop on the beat" (*Congressional Quarterly*, January 28, 2019).

Much of the conversation in Washington was dominated by Mueller's investigation into Russian interference in the 2016 election. By the beginning of 2019, seven people had pleaded guilty in the investigation, five of whom were former Trump aides, including former campaign manager Paul Manafort and former National Security Adviser Michael Flynn. Roger Stone, a highly visible adviser to Trump, was indicted on January 25. Democrats worried that the White House might try to shut down the investigation because, after the 2018 midterm elections, Trump had forced out Attorney Jeff Sessions, who had appointed Mueller, and replaced him with William Barr, a critic of the investigation. As it turned out, Mueller would be allowed to finish his report in March, although Democrats argued that Barr subsequently understated its findings.

Over the first eight months of 2019, Democrats focused primarily on four issues:

Financial improprieties. Three House committees made little progress into looking at potential conflicts of interest regarding Trump's business dealings and finances. The Financial Services Committee sought records from Trump's family businesses but faced court battles to obtain them. The Ways and Means Committee tried to get access to Trump's tax returns but was blocked by Treasury Secretary Steven Mnuchin. The Oversight and Reform Committee looked into whether Trump had violated the emoluments clause of the Constitution, but legal interpretations differed over the clause's prohibition on a president accepting gifts from foreign officials.

Obstruction of justice by the president. Evidence presented in Mueller's March 2019 report suggested that Trump made a number of attempts to thwart his office's nearly two-year investigation of Russian interference in the 2016 election. The Judiciary Committee subpoenaed testimony from former White House Counsel Don McGahn, who was allegedly asked by Trump to see that Mueller was fired, as well as from former Trump aides and advisers such as Corey Lewandowski, who was apparently told to order then-Attorney General Jeff Sessions to dismiss the special counsel. The White House challenged the subpoenas in federal court, delaying the investigation.

Hush money payments. Trump's former personal attorney, Michael Cohen, was sentenced to federal prison in 2018 after pleading guilty to two charges of violating campaign finance laws by arranging payments to a former Playboy model Karen McDougal and adult film star Stormy Daniels just before the 2016 election to keep them from going public about past affairs with Trump. Although U.S. attorneys in New York would end their investigation of the matter in the summer of 2019 without issuing additional indictments, House Democrats wanted to learn more about Trump's role in arranging the hush money.

Citizenship question on the 2020 census. The administration's attempt to add a question on citizenship to the 2020 Census, which was ultimately stopped by the Supreme Court, set off major partisan repercussions. The House voted in July to hold Attorney General William Barr and Commerce Secretary Wilbur Ross in contempt of Congress for refusing to turn over documents that might have shed light on Trump's role in trying to add the question to the census. The Oversight Committee wanted to learn whether the White House had attempted to manipulate the census for political gain.

Trump dismissed the investigations as politically motivated witch hunts and promised to adopt a "warlike posture." But his administration was swamped with records requests, such as a sweeping request by the House Judiciary Committee in March for documents from eighty-one agencies, entities, and individuals about alleged misdeeds that ranged from efforts to influence the Mueller investigation to hush money payments related to Stormy Daniels. At the same time, the chairmen of the House Intelligence Committee, the Foreign Affairs Committee, and the Committee on Oversight and Reform requested documents relating to communications between Trump and Russian

SPECIAL COUNSEL

The release of the report by the special counsel, Robert S. Mueller III, into ties between Donald Trump's 2016 presidential campaign and Russian officials was one of the more anticipated events during the Trump years. Mueller, a former FBI director, was appointed special counsel in May 2017, and it took almost two years for him and his team to wrap up their investigation and submit the resulting report on March 22, 2019, to Attorney General William Barr, who summarized it in a controversial, four-page letter that appeared to clear the president of wrongdoing. A redacted version of the report was publicly released the following month.

Supporters and opponents of President Trump alike wondered if it would serve as a catalyst for his impeachment. In the end, the 448-page report provided some ammunition to both sides, stating, "While this report does not conclude that the President committed a crime, it also does not exonerate him." The president aside, the special counsel's team indicted or got guilty pleas from thirty-four people, including a half-dozen former Trump advisors and a number of Russian nationals.

The report reached several conclusions that were damaging to Trump. It found that the Russian government illegally interfered with the 2016 presidential election and tried to help Trump win; that Trump's campaign advisers had a number of ties to Russia and wanted to benefit from Russian hackings that targeted Democrats; and that Trump tried repeatedly to impede the special counsel's Russia investigation.

The first volume of Mueller's report focused on the Russian effort to interfere with the 2016 presidential election, and whether any Trump associates were involved in that effort. It examined two major Russian government efforts to interfere with the election.

One was a social media propaganda operation, in which Russia's Internet Research Agency created fake online accounts to create positive views of Trump and negative views of his opponent, Democratic nominee Hillary Clinton. The investigation did not find evidence of any Trump campaign official becoming knowingly involved in these efforts.

Second, it looked into what the report called "Russian hacking and dumping operations." This began with Russian

President Vladimir Putin, including those relating to allegations that Trump had asked White House staff to destroy records of his conversations with Putin. "Impeachment is a long way down the road," Judiciary Chairman Jerry Nadler told reporters in early March, as he and other House leaders tried to downplay calls to begin formal impeachment proceedings. "We don't have the facts yet, but we're going to initiate proper investigations."

The conclusion of the Mueller investigation marked a major flash point between the administration and House Democrats. Mueller submitted his report to Barr on March 22, 2019. Two days later, Barr sent a four-page letter to Congress that characterized the report's conclusions. While the investigation found Russian interference in the 2016 election, Barr wrote, it "did not establish that members of the Trump Campaign conspired or coordinated with the Russian government in its election interference activities." He also said the special counsel "did not draw a conclusion" on allegations of obstruction of justice. "Deputy Attorney General Rod Rosenstein and I have concluded that the evidence developed during the Special Counsel's investigation is not sufficient to establish that the President committed an obstruction-of-justice offense," he wrote.

Barr's letter did little to end concerns about Trump's alleged misdeeds, especially because Democrats viewed him as acting more like Trump's personal defense lawyer than an independent attorney general. After weeks of Democratic demands to see the actual report, the Justice

Department released a redacted version on April 18. This failed to satisfy Democrats, who issued a subpoena for the full report and underlying investigative materials. When Barr refused, the House Judiciary Committee approved a resolution on May 8 to hold Barr in contempt of Congress over access to the full special counsel report. The resolution, approved 24–16, came after days of negotiations with the Justice Department over how many lawmakers and staffers could see and discuss the report and how much material they could view because of court orders protecting it. The administration exerted executive privilege over the materials that were subpoenaed, contending that they included sensitive national security information. But the Justice Department subsequently shared additional information with the committee, and the House held off on holding a floor vote on the contempt resolution.

By this time, a number of rank-and-file members wanted to begin impeachment proceedings, arguing that even the redacted version of Mueller's report outlined substantial evidence that Trump had engaged in obstruction of justice and other abuses. Pelosi continued to urge caution, saying that impeachment must be bipartisan and have public support. In the meantime, House Democrats began following leads laid out in the report. These included looking into Russian interference in the 2016 election and whether anyone on the Trump campaign colluded with the Kremlin, as well as whether Trump obstructed justice in attempting to stop the FBI and special counsel from investigating the alleged collusion. To do so, they sought testi-

intelligence officers hacking into the accounts of the Clinton campaign and Democratic Party organizations. Some of the hacked material was posted online by the Russians; other material was subsequently posted by WikiLeaks. The report did not suggest that Trump officials were involved in the hacking, but a section about the Trump campaign and the dissemination of hacked materials was heavily redacted.

The special counsel's office also investigated links and contacts between Trump associates and people with ties to Russia's government. It was trying to determine whether there was a conspiracy in which Russian assistance to the Trump campaign would be rewarded for favorable treatment in the future. After looking into a number of contacts, the office concluded that none of them constituted "an agreement to commit any substantive violation of federal criminal law."

The second volume of Mueller's report looked into events that could potentially implicate the president in obstruction of justice. Mueller wrote that he "determined not to make a traditional prosecutorial judgment" on whether Trump committed criminal obstruction of justice. This was based on a Justice Department decision that a sitting president could not be criminally prosecuted, as well as Mueller's belief that accusing a president of a crime would undermine his ability to govern and preempt impeachment. Mueller was therefore somewhat ambiguous on obstruction of justice, avoiding a judgment that the President committed crimes while adding that if Trump indeed "clearly did not commit obstruction of justice," he would say so.

The report detailed a number of instances in which the president attacked investigators and tried to control the investigation. It concluded that the president's "efforts to influence the investigation were mostly unsuccessful, but that is largely because the persons who surrounded the President declined to carry out orders or accede to his requests."

Although Mueller avoided coming to a conclusion on whether Trump's actions constituted a criminal obstruction of justice, he pointedly noted that Congress could have a role to play. The report stated, "We concluded that Congress has authority to prohibit a President's corrupt use of his authority in order to protect the integrity of the administration of justice."

mony from a number of officials including former White House counsel Don McGahn, who was mentioned in the Mueller report as a witness to several instances in which Trump may have obstructed justice.

Trump responded with increasing defiance toward the House investigation, which now encompassed six committees. Several administration officials, such as White House senior aide Stephen Miller, refused to testify, and Trump filed a lawsuit to stop congressional efforts to see some of his financial records. "We're fighting all the subpoenas," Trump told reporters outside the White House on April 24, 2019. Some Democrats saw this as further evidence of corruption, blasting the president for obstructing a congressional investigation. Lawmakers, however, faced the reality that they had limited options for moving forward. A vote to hold administration officials in contempt of Congress would not necessarily get lawmakers the information they sought, and filing lawsuits for certain documents could lead to yearslong legal battles. Democrats also had little support from congressional Republicans, who argued that the Mueller report vindicated the president. "Time to move on," Lindsay Graham, R-S.C., chair of the Senate Judiciary Committee, tweeted on April 23, 2019. A number of Republicans echoed Trump's contention that his political opponents may have tried to co-opt law enforcement agencies in an effort to undermine his campaign in 2016.

On June 11, House Democrats voted to bolster their oversight power by giving committees the authority to take Trump administration officials to court quickly. The reso-lution (H Res 430), which passed on a party line vote of 229–191, enabled the Democrats to skip the floor process and go directly to federal courts when enforcing subpoenas. It authorized lawsuits to enforce Judiciary Committee subpoenas seeking the full special counsel report from Barr and testimony from McGahn. It also allowed the committee to file a lawsuit seeking the release of grand jury information from the special counsel investigation, among other provisions.

By this time, more than 60 House members, or a quarter of the Democratic Caucus, had publicly expressed support for beginning impeachment proceedings. Pelosi, however, continued to hold her ground against taking such a momentous step. She called impeachment "divisive" and noted that fewer than half of House Democrats supported it.

The summer saw a continued escalation between House Democrats and the administration over several issues. On July 17, 2019, the House voted to hold Barr and Commerce Secretary Wilbur Ross in contempt of Congress over their refusal to cooperate with the chamber's probe into the administration's one-time attempt to add a citizenship question to the 2020 census. The 230–198 vote on the contempt resolution (H Res 497) came after weeks of administration resistance to subpoenas from the House Oversight and Reform Committee over the addition of the question. It also occurred a week after the White House dropped it from the census in the wake of a Supreme Court ruling that blocked the plan. Oversight and Reform Chairman Elijah E. Cummings, D-Md., assailed the administration in

a floor speech, saying it was "blatantly" obstructing the committee's probe. Republicans, however, continued to side with the president, with House Minority Leader Kevin McCarthy, R-Calif., criticizing the Democrats for pursuing political opportunities.

On July 24, Mueller appeared before the House Judiciary and Intelligence committees to provide much-anticipated testimony about the special counsel's 448-page report. But once again the Democrats were left frustrated as the televised hearings did little to change views of the president's behavior. A muted Mueller declined to go beyond the language of the report, telling members in his opening statement, "The report is my testimony. And I will stay within that text." Still, Democrats were able to score some points. When Nadler asked if he totally exonerated the president, Mueller replied "No." He also indicated that Trump may have been indicted if he was not a sitting president. Although the hearings failed to deliver a major blow to Trump, increasing numbers of Democrats supported impeachment, with more than half the 235 House Democrats calling for some formalized proceedings by early August.

But many Democrats wanted to move cautiously, with polls showing that only about a third of the public wanted the House to begin impeachment proceedings. Pelosi said the House should wait until the six ongoing committee investigations provided the "strongest possible case" for impeaching the president. Since the investigations continued to run into court delays, however, no one could say when the Democrats could put together a case—or even how formalized impeachment proceedings would differ from the committee investigations. Pelosi refused to provide a timeline for when she would move forward with impeachment. But, she said the process would not be endless.

The question of what constituted an impeachment proceeding continued to bedevil the House after the August recess. The House Judiciary Committee on September 12 approved a resolution for procedures related to an investigation into the possible impeachment of Trump on a party line vote of 24–17. But Democrats and Republicans argued over whether such a resolution actually meant anything. At the markup, Nadler declared that the resolution was "the necessary next step in our investigation of corruption, obstruction and abuse of power." This was important to Democrats in the context of the courts, where they could point to an impeachment investigation to strengthen their case to force witnesses to testify regardless of Trump's claim of executive privilege. But Doug Collins of Georgia, the ranking member, contended that the resolution did not give the committee any more authority than it already had. He also said the full House would have to take a vote before there were impeachment investigations.

Trying to move forward, the Judiciary Committee launched hearings into the possibility of impeachment on September 17. But two of the three witnesses did not show up on orders of the White House. The third, former Trump campaign manager Corey Lewandowski, answered questions only about the Mueller report, per instructions that he had received from the White House just the previous night. Although the hearing lasted more than five hours and generated some sparks, it clarified little beyond what was already known from the Mueller report. Only some new bombshell revelation, it seemed, could alter the fundamental dynamics around impeachment.

FORMAL IMPEACHMENT PROCEEDINGS

Revelations in late September that Trump had tried to pressure the president of Ukraine into investigating former Vice President Joseph R. Biden jolted the Democrats' views toward impeachment. Amid outrage that the president would potentially withhold congressionally appropriated military aid to an ally in his quest to dig up dirt on a political rival, Pelosi announced on September 24 that the House would move forward with a formal impeachment inquiry, although it was not initially clear what process that would take or where it would lead.

Lawmakers focused on a whistleblower's nine-page complaint, which made serious and detailed allegations in connection with Trump's July 25 telephone conversation with Ukrainian President Volodymyr Zelensky. "In the course of my official duties, I have received information from multiple U.S. government officials that the President of the United States is using the power of his office to solicit interference from a foreign country in the 2020 U.S. election," the whistleblower wrote in the official complaint, which was dated August 12, 2019. "This interference includes, among other things, pressuring a foreign country to investigate one of the President's main domestic political rivals. The President's personal lawyer, Mr. Rudolph W. Giuliani, is a central figure in this effort. Attorney General (William P.) Barr appears to be involved as well."

Trump's actions "pose risks to U.S. national security and undermine the U.S. Government's efforts to deter and counter foreign interference in U.S. elections," the whistleblower wrote. The letter described White House officials intervening to "lock down" all records of the call. In a sign of aides' potential concern, the records were moved to a system used for classified materials even though they "did not contain anything remotely sensitive."

The whistleblower wrote to a top government inspector general about being "deeply concerned" that the president's conversation with Zelensky amounted to "a serious or flagrant problem, abuse, or violation of law or Executive Order." This wording came directly from the U.S. criminal code and highlighted concerns about the commander in chief's conduct.

Soliciting such assistance for a personal political benefit would be a federal crime, House Democrats and some legal experts said. Republicans and White House officials, however, contended Trump did nothing wrong and was justified in asking the incoming Ukrainian leader to look into possible corruption by the former U.S. vice president and

his son. These different interpretations would be central to subsequent impeachment debate.

As details of the whistleblower's complain trickled out, with the White House on September 25 releasing a rough transcript of Trump's call with Zelensky and then the full complaint becoming public the next day, events took off at a dizzying pace. Trump's special envoy to Ukraine, Kurt Volker, resigned on September 27, 2019, which was the same day House Democrats issued a subpoena to Secretary of State Mike Pompeo. Three days later, House Democrats subpoenaed Trump's personal lawyer, Rudy Giuliani. Trump lashed out at Biden and his son at an October 2 press conference with the president of Finland, calling them "stone cold crooked," and a day later said both Ukraine and China should investigate the Bidens. Trump's legal woes deepened the next day when Volker provided the House with text messages showing that the administration asked Zelensky for a pledge to investigate the Bidens in exchange for a White House visit.

From the beginning, Trump insisted he did nothing wrong. "You take a look at that call, it was perfect," he told reporters on September 25, 2019, while denying that he sought help from another government to influence the 2020 U.S. election. "I didn't do it. There was no quid-pro-quo." He and his supporters also sought to undermine the whistleblower, saying the person had no firsthand knowledge of the alleged wrongdoing.

Undeterred, the House broadened its investigation and undertook a punishing schedule of depositions, which were taken outside public view. A roster of senior White House, Pentagon, and State Department officials defied Trump's orders and testified on the alleged scheme to hold up military aid to Ukraine until Kyiv agreed to investigate 2020 Democratic presidential candidate Joe Biden and his son Hunter.

Continuing its yearlong strategy, the administration sought to stymie the House investigations, arguing that the Democrats were pursuing an illegitimate effort to undo the 2016 election. Trump's attorneys argued that he could ignore all demands for testimony and documents in the absence of a floor vote in the House authorizing an impeachment inquiry. On October 8, the White House sent an eight-page letter to House Democrats stating that it intended to stop all cooperation with the "illegitimate" impeachment inquiry. The clash between Congress and the White House reached a crescendo in early October, when the State Department decided to block the U.S. Ambassador to the European Union Gordon Sondland from testifying before the Intelligence Committee, even though he was willing to appear. Committee Chairman Adam B. Schiff of California assailed the State Department decision as "obstruction of a co-equal branch of government." Some frustrated Democrats floated the option of using the House sergeant-at-arms to arrest officials who refused to appear before congressional committees, although leadership never appeared to take that seriously.

Meanwhile, Democrats were getting the message from the courts that they would have better success obtaining administration documents if they formalized their impeachment inquiry. In a hearing October 8 about whether the House Judiciary Committee should get grand jury materials from the special counsel report as part of an impeachment inquiry, Chief U.S. District Judge Beryl A. Howell questioned when she could know such an inquiry had begun if there was not a floor vote. It would be "easier for all of us" if the House simply took a vote, she said, although she subsequently granted the House Judiciary Committee's request for more documents.

With increased public support for an impeachment investigation and the Democrats readying public hearings into Trump's efforts to pressure Ukraine, Democrats at the end of October decided to take the step of formally launching impeachment proceedings. For the previous last month, they had conducted their impeachment inquiry largely behind closed doors. The impeachment resolution, which set guidelines for open hearings, laid the groundwork for the public phase of the impeachment probe.

FORMAL IMPEACHMENT INQUIRY

The House on October 31, over strong objections from Republicans, adopted a resolution that provided a roadmap for the Democrats to conduct the remainder of their impeachment inquiry into President Donald Trump. The 232–196 mostly party line vote on the resolution (H Res 660) put lawmakers formally on the record over the impeachment inquiry. Although it represented an important step in the impeachment process, the partisan nature of the vote foreshadowed the difficulties that Democrats would face in winning a Senate conviction. Furthermore, the Democrats lacked clear public support for the resolution. While polling showed support for impeachment grew in the initial couple of weeks after the disclosure of Trump's call with Zelensky, it had since plateaued.

The resolution directed five House committees to continue investigating whether Trump used his office to try to coerce the Ukrainian government to investigate Biden. It granted Schiff significant influence over the inquiry, allowing the Intelligence Committee chairman to question witnesses for lengthy periods without interruption in future public hearings. He also had the authority to release transcripts of private hearings and depositions and to block Republicans from calling witnesses. Overall, the resolution effectively gave Democrats control over nearly every aspect of the process, including which committees should hold public hearings and when to schedule them, which cooperative witnesses should testify and in what order, when to share incriminating information discovered in closed-door depositions, which articles of impeachment should be the focus, and when and whether to issue a report on their findings. The contents of such a report would be determined by Democrats.

House Republicans, not surprisingly, objected to the process. They argued during the floor debate that the

resolution gave too much power to the chairman. House Minority Whip Steve Scalise of Louisiana, who stood next to a sign that stated, "37 days of Soviet-Style impeachment proceedings," accused the Democrats of making all the rules to the extent of excluding the accused person from being in the room where testimony was being taken and questioning what was taking place. Some Republicans opposed even holding an investigation. Devin Nunes of California, the ranking member of the Intelligence Committee, accused Democrats of being obsessed with overturning the 2016 election.

Pelosi, taking to the floor just before the vote, said the resolution "ensures transparency." Countering Republican criticism, she said it enabled public hearings, set out procedures for the questioning of witnesses, and gave the minority the same rights in questioning witnesses as the majority.

In the end, 194 Republicans voted against the resolution and three did not vote. Two Democrats—Jeff Van Drew of New Jersey and Collin C. Peterson of Minnesota—voted with Republicans and another did not vote. Justin Amash of Michigan, an independent who had recently left the Republican party, supported the resolution.

One day before the House vote, the Rules Committee approved H Res 660 on a party line vote of 9–4. Republicans on the Rules Committee offered eighteen amendments, each of which was rejected by party line votes. One amendment, from Georgia Republican Rob Woodall, would have shifted responsibility for the impeachment probe from the Intelligence to the Judiciary Committee. Not only did Judiciary have jurisdiction over articles of impeachment, but it would permit Trump to have his counsel advocating for him. Democrats, however, said the Intelligence Committee would approach the investigation along the same lines as the Ken Starr independent counsel investigation during the Bill Clinton impeachment, which had not allowed input from Clinton.

Texas Republican Michael Burgess offered an amendment to remove the Financial Services and Ways and Means committees from the resolution. He claimed that the Democrats added those two committees to the resolution as a tactic to access Trump's tax returns and other information on his businesses. Burgess worried that the investigation would amount to a fishing expedition. Maryland Democrat Jamie Raskin retorted during the markup that they might "catch a whale."

HOUSE INTELLIGENCE COMMITTEE REPORT

The House Intelligence Committee on December 3, 2019, adopted a 150-page report that laid out the case for impeaching Trump for withholding military aid to Ukraine in exchange for Kyiv investigating his political rival, and for obstructing the House's probe. The report, written by the Democratic staff of the House Intelligence, Oversight, and Reform and Foreign Affairs Committees, detailed its findings after weeks of private and public testimony from

career bureaucrats and Trump appointees. The 13-9, party line vote released the impeachment report to the House Judiciary Committee for further action on the inquiry.

The preface of the report said Trump "subverted U.S. foreign policy toward Ukraine and undermined our national security in favor of two politically motivated investigations that would help his presidential reelection campaign." The committee found the evidence of Trump's misconduct to be "overwhelming, and so too is the evidence of his obstruction of Congress." Noting that Trump ordered many officials in his administration not to aid the committee in its probe, the report stated, "It would be hard to imagine a stronger or more complete case of obstruction than that demonstrated by the President since the inquiry began." At the same time, the report praised the "courageous individuals" who complied with subpoenas and provided evidence to the committee.

The report drew from two months of investigation, including public and private testimony from administration officials and diplomats who described Trump's efforts to pressure Ukraine into announcing investigations into Biden, while withholding military assistance and a coveted White House meeting for Zelensky, Ukraine's new president. The report concluded that Trump, acting both on his own in concert with his allies in the administration and outside of government, solicited Ukraine's interference in the 2020 presidential election.

In a sign of extraordinary partisan divisions, the report discussed phone records showing that the committee's ranking member, Devin Nunes of California, had been heavily involved in conversations with multiple Trump associates under scrutiny in the probe. Among these calls, Nunes spoke on several occasions to Rudy Giuliani, Trump's personal lawyer, at the same time that Giuliani was criticizing Marie Yovanovitch, the former U.S. ambassador to Ukraine, and planning to go to Ukraine in quest of negative material about Biden. Nunes had repeatedly criticized the way Schiff went about the investigation and called the inquiry a sham. Schiff had particularly left himself open to Republican attacks when he opened a hearing in September with what he would later refer to as a "parody" account of Trump's phone call in which he misquoted the conversation.

The president's Republican allies on Capitol Hill released their own report in advance of the committee report, condemning the impeachment effort as illegitimate. Written by the Republican staff of the Intelligence, Oversight and Foreign Affairs panels, the 123-page preemptive rebuttal argued that the evidence failed to prove the allegations against Trump and dismissed the impeachment inquiry as "an orchestrated campaign to upend our political system." It also argued that the evidence did not prove Democrats' allegations against Trump.

But the committee report outlined how Trump, by withholding $391 million in military assistance to Ukraine at a time that it was engaged in an active conflict with Russia,

could embolden Russian aggression in the region. The report also pointed out that Trump, when the whistleblower's allegations became public, requested that China also investigate Biden. "This continued solicitation of foreign interference in a U.S. election presents a clear and present danger that the President will continue to use the power of his office for his personal political gain," the report said.

The Intelligence Committee issued the report after taking private depositions followed by high-profile public hearings in November. The public witnesses, including largely unknown diplomats and bureaucrats, said that both the military aid and the promise of a White House invitation to Zelensky were contingent on Ukraine announcing investigations into Biden and his son. The president's defenders in Congress, however, argued that the witnesses in many cases lacked firsthand information of the president's intentions. They also pointed out that Ukraine eventually got the money without announcing an investigation, thereby throwing into question any allegations around a quid pro quo.

Under the rules of the impeachment hearings, Schiff or his staff could question the witnesses for forty-five-minute chunks, alternating with the minority for the same amount of time. Republicans could not call the witnesses they wanted to question, including Hunter Biden and the anonymous whistleblower. Frustrated by the rules and determined to throw up procedural objections, they temporarily added Rep. Jim Jordan, R-Ohio, to the Intelligence Committee. He was one of the most vocal and relentless of Trumps' defenders.

House Democrats, with an eye to winning over the public, used the hearings to build their case that Trump acted corruptly as well as undermine the various defenses that had been raised by Trump and congressional Republicans. To take aim at arguments that Trump's approach was common in foreign relations, Democrats raised questions during the first week of the hearings that led the acting U.S. Ambassador to Ukraine William Taylor, a Trump appointee, to say he had never seen another example of such an arrangement. Their questions also highlighted that the administration released the funds to Ukraine only after House Democrats launched a probe based on a whistleblower.

Jordan, however, emphasized that some of the witnesses were getting their information from other people. Republicans also pointed to statements by Zelensky, who had consistently said he was not aware of military aid being withheld during the call and that there was no pressure or threats.

But witnesses continued to provide evidence that was damaging to Trump. Gordon Sondland, U.S. ambassador to the European Union and a Trump donor and appointee, told the committee on November 20, 2019, that the holdup of military aid and a White House meeting for Ukraine in exchange for politically motivated investigations into the Bidens were indeed a quid pro quo. Sondland stressed that the president never directly told him U.S. military aid to Ukraine was contingent upon the politically motivated investigations, but he said he presumed "two plus two equals four." He also testified that he and other key players were acting at Trump's direction when they carried out the Ukraine pressure campaign.

One day later, Fiona Hill, a Russia expert who worked on Trump's National Security Council, delivered particularly forceful testimony. Using direct language, she offered firsthand knowledge of conversations and meetings with an array of key players and filled in the blanks left by conflicting and sometimes erratic testimony from previous witnesses. Hill rejected Republican claims that Ukraine intervened in the 2016 elections, and she reasserted that Russia had meddled—and was continuing to meddle—in U.S. politics. "Based on questions and statements I have heard, some of you on this committee appear to believe that Russia and its security services did not conduct a campaign against our country—and that perhaps, somehow, for some reason, Ukraine did," Hill said during the fifth day of public hearings. "This is a fictional narrative."

She warned that such fictions, deployed by Republicans for domestic political purposes, actually damaged the United States.

House Committee Action

The House Judiciary Committee on December 13, 2019, approved two articles of impeachment on separate 23–17 party line votes. The vote came on the third day of a contentious and starkly partisan markup in which Democrats rejected all five Republican amendments.

The committee's acrimonious debate ranged from constitutional law to crack cocaine. Even the timing of the vote provoked controversy. As the panel was preparing to vote on the articles shortly after 11:00 p.m. on December 12, 2019, Chairman Nadler gaveled out the markup. This enabled the committee to take its historic vote during normal business hours the next morning. But the maneuver infuriated Republicans. Doug Collins of Georgia, the top Republican on the panel, complained that Nadler did not consult him on the timing of the vote and that pushing it to Friday morning ruined many of the members' plans.

In one example of the committee's bitter divisions, Cedric L. Richmond, a Louisiana Democrat and a senior member of the committee, likened the enduring Republican support of Trump to Judas's betrayal of Jesus in the Bible. "Today I'm reminded of Judas—because Judas for 30 pieces of silver betrayed Jesus," Richmond said. "For 30 positive tweets for easy reelection, the other side is willing to betray the American people."

The marathon markup began with Collins raising a point of order to request that a heading be scheduled for Republicans to call witnesses to testify. Republicans had repeatedly sought testimony from Schiff, the White House whistleblower, and Joe Biden's son Hunter, but were blocked by Democrats. Nadler refused the request by Collins but

said he would be willing to work with Republicans on such a hearing after the markup.

Republicans then took aim at the first article of impeachment, which alleged that Trump abused his power by seeking help from Ukraine with his 2020 reelection bid. Ohio's Jordan offered an amendment to strike the first article, arguing that the Ukrainian government never announced an investigation into the Bidens in exchange for U.S. military aid. The committee defeated the amendment, 17–23, along party lines.

Republicans had made such an argument for months. In response at the markup, Rhode Island Democrat David Cicilline reminded members of testimony from senior State Department officials and other witnesses who appeared before the House Intelligence Committee and alleged wrongdoing by Trump, suggesting that the White House only provided the military aid after the whistleblower exposed their scheme.

The committee also voted along party lines, 17–23, to reject an amendment by Pennsylvania Republican Guy Reschenthaler to strike the second impeachment article, which alleged that Trump obstructed Congress. Reschenthaler argued that the Trump administration, far from obstructing the investigation, had provided the panel with thousands of documents and a number of witnesses. If Democrats wanted to settle a dispute between Congress and the administration over additional evidence, then the courts were the proper venue, Reschenthaler concluded.

Nadler defended the obstruction article, saying that Trump had barred witnesses from testifying and prevented Congress from obtaining documents without asserting executive privileges. The president's actions, Nadler said, amounted to an "usurpation of Congress' role."

Florida Republican Matt Gaetz offered an amendment to change the wording of the articles to state that Trump wanted to investigate "a well-known corrupt company, Burisma, and its corrupt hiring of Hunter Biden," instead of Joe Biden. Hunter Biden was a much-discussed Republican target, and Gaetz said he was unqualified to hold a lucrative spot on Ukrainian gas company Burisma's board while his father was vice president. He cited a recent profile of Hunter Biden in *The New Yorker* magazine that detailed Hunter Biden's crack cocaine usage, saying he was only added to the company's board because he was the vice president's son. The committee defeated that amendment as well along party lines, 17–23.

Arizona Republican Andy Biggs offered an amendment to add wording to the articles that Ukraine, after a delay caused by the Office of Management and Budget, ultimately received the military aid that Congress had appropriated. Like the other amendments, it was defeated along party lines.

The Biggs amendment reflected the Republican argument that the White House did not stall the aid to help Trump but to enable Washington to ensure that the government of Zelensky, who was newly elected, would use the aid to fight Russian soldiers and not to enrich oli-

garchs. "Democrats want to impeach the president for trying to ensure that taxpayer funds are spent efficiently and responsibly," Biggs said at the markup.

Democrats responded that the administration provided the aid to Ukraine only after the details of Trump's July 25 call with Zelensky became public. Expressing this viewpoint bluntly, California Democrat Karen Bass said, "The aid was released after the administration was busted."

House Floor Action

The House voted on December 18, 2019, to impeach Trump on charges of abuse of power and obstruction of Congress. The largely party line vote was 230–197 on the first article, which charged the president for abuse of power, and 229–198 on the second article, obstruction of Congress. Tulsi Gabbard, D-Hawaii, voted present on both articles. The floor debate featured fierce partisan clashes that reflected not only the seemingly unbridgeable polarization of the chamber but even a failure to agree on the basic facts regarding the president's actions.

For the Democrats, the case was relatively straightforward: Trump had withheld military aid and promised a White House meeting to Zelensky in exchange for a Ukrainian investigation of Joe and Hunter Biden. Intelligence Chairman Schiff warned that Trump posed a continuing threat to the nation. "The president and his men plot on," he said. "The danger persists. The risk is real. Our democracy is at peril."

Republicans countered that the Democrats were on a vendetta, using a "weaponized impeachment" to try to overthrow the president. In a particularly ferocious clash, Texas Republican Louie Gohmert cited a conspiracy theory, repeatedly debunked by U.S. intelligence agencies, that Ukraine had interfered in the 2016 election. When Nadler castigated this effort to "spew Russian propaganda on the floor of the House," Gohmert immediately began shouting, demanded that Nadler yield to him to respond and, after Nadler declined, marched over to him speaking intensely. Nadler did not appear to respond.

Andy Biggs of Arizona, the House Freedom Caucus Chairman, tried early during the proceedings to end them with a motion to adjourn. House Minority Leader Kevin McCarthy of California offered a privileged resolution (H Res 770) that would rebuke Democrats for their handling of the impeachment inquiry. Scalise later raised a point of order against the rule to adopt the articles of impeachment, arguing that the Democrats had disregarded the rights of the minority through the impeachment process. All these efforts were quickly brushed aside.

Underscoring the historic nature of impeachment, Pelosi remained in the chamber for most of the debate. She dressed in all black with a large brooch of the House mace, communicating her view of the "solemn and sad" need to exercise the House's constitutional power.

McCarthy, reflecting the widespread view of Washington, said Trump would survive the impeachment with a Senate

acquittal. "He is president today, he will be president tomorrow and he will be president when this impeachment is over," he said. Trump, at a campaign rally in Michigan during the House vote, shrugged off the impeachment. He said it was merely an attempt to "nullify" his 2016 election.

Senate Trial

The Senate began its impeachment trial on January 21, 2020, when it adopted trial rules proposed by Majority Leader Mitch McConnell, R-Ky. The trial wrapped up ten days later when the Senate narrowly rejected allowing subpoenas to call witnesses.

The timing of the trial was in doubt for several weeks while Pelosi held on to the articles of impeachment. She engaged in a waiting game with McConnell, who was openly supportive of Trump, she was willing to delay the trial, which Trump wanted to occur quickly. The Constitution does not specify how quickly the House must transmit impeachment articles to the Senate. Pelosi's goal was to win some concessions on the trial rules in the Senate, including the chamber agreeing to subpoena documents and witnesses, and she said she was not prepared to name impeachment managers until seeing what the trial process would look like. McConnell shrugged off Pelosi's tactic, saying he did not care if Pelosi did not send the articles to the Senate.

With McConnell refusing to budge, the House sent the articles of impeachment on January 15, 2020, after voting, 228–193, to adopt the resolution that officially appointed the seven House impeachment managers. The articles were physically walked to the Senate in a procession of the impeachment managers, much as occurred during the impeachment of President of President Bill Clinton in 1998. The Senate then formally notified Chief Justice John G. Roberts Jr., who would preside over the trial, and President Donald Trump, who was invited to attend and respond.

Pelosi chose a small and diverse group of seven managers, including three women and three minorities. Democrats noted the contrast with the thirteen white Republican men who managed the articles of impeachment for the House during the trial of Clinton. Schiff was the lead manager. The others consisted of Nadler; Hakeem Jeffries, chairman of the House Democratic Caucus; Val B. Demings of Florida, a Judiciary and Intelligence committee member and the former chief of the Orlando Police Department; Jason Crow of Colorado, an Armed Services Committee member and former Army Ranger; Sylvia R. Garcia of Texas, a Judiciary Committee member who had previously served as a city and county judge; and Zoe Lofgren of California, a senior member of the Judiciary Committee. Lofgren brought a lot of impeachment experience to the group; she was a Judiciary staffer during the Nixon impeachment inquiry and sat on the Judiciary panel during the Clinton impeachment.

The Senate on January 21, 2020, voted, 53–47, to approve the rules to govern the impeachment trial. The rules had been developed by McConnell, and they drew considerable criticism from Democrats even after Republicans agreed to give House impeachment managers and Trump's defense team twenty-four hours to make their arguments over three days, instead of the two days that McConnell initially proposed. Democrats had complained that the original two-day timeline would have deprived the public from viewing much of the proceedings, as they would start in the afternoon and stretch past midnight. In another concession, McConnell agreed to allow the automatic introduction of the impeachment House records into evidence. Under the original version of the rules, a vote would have needed to take place to admit the House records.

Nevertheless, Democrats said the majority leader was not following his pledge to follow the precedent set in the impeachment trial of Clinton. They worried that Republicans were rushing the trial in a way that would make it far more difficult to obtain documents and call witnesses.

The House managers began their three-day presentation on January 22 while senators sat quietly, forbidden from asking questions. On the first two days, they argued that Trump abused his office by withholding $391 million in military aid for Ukraine in exchange for that country announcing an investigation on Biden. The delay in providing the aid, they said, had impacts on the Ukrainian military. The reason the Ukrainian government never announced the investigation was because Trump got caught, they contended. They also cited historical citations and constitutional law in an attempt to rebut an expected argument by Trump's lawyers: that an impeachment is invalid without a crime.

On the third day, Schiff, a former federal prosecutor, laid out the House's case in his closing statement, arguing that Trump would "remain a threat to the Constitution" if he were allowed to remain in office. The California Democrat said the second article of impeachment, obstruction of Congress, was vital to preserving the power of Congress to investigate and impeach a president. He said no president had ever ordered the complete defiance of an impeachment inquiry.

For the Democrats, the immediate goal was to persuade four Republicans to break party ranks and agree to subpoena more witnesses and documents for the trial. But there were no signs that they were close to succeeding, let alone accomplishing the far more difficult goal of persuading twenty Republicans to create the needed two-thirds supermajority vote to convict Trump. Judiciary Chairman Graham, for example, said the Democrats needed to look to the upcoming election to remove Trump, not an impeachment trial. Republicans were particularly irked when Nadler said at the beginning of the trial that a vote to deny subpoenas for witnesses would be an "absolutely indefensible vote, obviously a treacherous vote." The comment drew a rebuke from Roberts and considerable criticism from the Republican senators he was trying to persuade.

The president's defense team, confident of victory, began to present their side on January 25, 2020. Using just two hours of their allotted time on the first day, White House counsel Pat Cipollone and his colleagues focused on what they called a lack of evidence and a flawed House investigation. They contended that, even though the president had done nothing wrong, the House was asking senators to subvert democracy by effectively tearing up ballots from the 2016 election.

On the second day of the Trump defense, the president's lawyers made their central argument: that the president could not be convicted without an actual criminal offense. Hammering home this argument was Alan Dershowitz, a former Harvard Law School professor and well-known defense attorney, who highlighted that he did not vote for Trump. Dershowitz's role was to put the charges against Trump in a constitutional context, working his way through history beginning with the Constitutional Convention in Philadelphia up to the present. The defense also argued that Trump worked to defend Ukraine, noting that he approved the delivery of lethal military weapons to that country after former President Barack Obama had blocked such weapons sales. They also contended that Trump's desired investigation into the Bidens was a legitimate endeavor to uncover corruption, and was not intended to give Trump an electoral edge.

On the final day of Trump's defense, they argued the Democrats' case amounted merely to politics. Cipollone closed the defense's case by urging senators to consider their role and the lasting impact that their decision could make on American history. He urged senators to put the Constitution above partisanship, a talking point that Democrats had also used in urging Republicans to step out from behind the GOP party line.

In all, the defense team used just ten of its allotted twenty-four hours. During the next two days of the trial, senators submitted written questions to Roberts, who then read them out loud, alternating between the majority and the minority. Many of the senators used the questions to advance their own points of view, with Republicans generally wanting to elicit a specific response from Trump's team and Democrats generally wanting a response from the House managers. Some senators used the rules to effectively put words in the mouth of the chief justice. In one question from Democrats Kamala Harris of California and Parry Murray of Washington, Roberts had to read Trump's comments on a recording about the former U.S. ambassador to Ukraine, Marie Yovanovitch. "Quote, 'Get rid of her, get her out tomorrow, I don't care, get her out tomorrow, take her out, okay,' end quote," Roberts read in a deadpan voice.

Utah Republican Mike Lee used a question to argue that the president was merely exercising his authority over the country's foreign policy. "Isn't it the president's place, certainly more than the place of career civil servants, to conduct foreign policy?" Roberts read Lee's question. In the

same way, Iowa Republican Charles E. Grassley's question to Trump's counsel made a key point for the defense: "Does the House's failure to enforce its subpoenas render its 'obstruction of Congress' theory unprecedented?"

Ohio Republican Rob Portman directed a question at Trump's counsel that reflected his ire at the House and concerns over prolonging the trial with additional witnesses. "Given that impeachment proceedings are privileged in the Senate and largely prevent other work from taking place while they are ongoing, please address the implications of allowing the House to present an incomplete case to the Senate and requesting the Senate to seek testimony from additional witnesses."

Two Republican swing votes on the issue of hearing from additional witnesses—Republicans Susan Collins of Maine and Lisa Murkowski of Alaska—submitted a question that asked, "Did President Trump ever mention Joe or Hunter Biden in connection with corruption in Ukraine to former Ukrainian President [Petro] Poroshenko or other Ukrainian officials, President Trump's Cabinet members, or top aides or others?" Patrick Philbin, the deputy White House counsel, said he was unable to answer because the House record did not contain the information.

One of the most pointed questions then came from Murkowski, who asked Trump's lawyers why the Senate should not call for the testimony of Trump's former national security advisor, John Bolton. In his upcoming memoir, Bolton reportedly claimed that Trump indeed was seeking to trade military aid for a political favor, just as Democrats alleged. In her query, Murkowski said the dispute about material facts "weighs in favor" of calling material witnesses.

The next—and highly anticipated—moment of the trial occurred on January 31, 2020, with the Senate voting, 49–51, to reject a motion to hear from additional witnesses or see new documents. This ended weeks of speculation over whether enough Republicans would break party ranks, and it sent the strongest signal yet that the Senate was solidly on track to acquit the president. Just two Republicans—Collins and Mitt Romney of Utah—joined all Democrats in supporting the motion. Minority Leader Charles E. Schumer of New York assailed the outcome, saying the Senate was holding a "sham trial."

The debate over additional witnesses focused in large part on whether Bolton should be asked to testify. Just hours before the Senate vote, *The New York Times* reported that Trump had told Bolton to pressure Ukrainian government officials to produce damning information on Democrats.

Schiff urged the Senate to make a complete and informed judgment, saying that more damaging information about Trump would continue to come out. Trump's lawyers argued that if the Democrats were to call witnesses, then they should also have the opportunity to call witnesses, including some who had testified before the House Intelligence

Committee without having to face cross-examination from Trump's defense team. They also reiterated that House investigators had failed to make their case.

The Senate then passed a resolution to bring the trial to an end and take a final vote on acquitting or convicting the president. Although the resolution (S Res 488) was drafted in agreement with Democrats, the 53–47 vote followed party lines. It came after Republicans blocked four Democratic amendments that served as a last-ditch effort to hear from witnesses.

The first of the amendments, offered by Schumer and defeated 53–47, would subpoena Bolton; acting White House Chief of Staff Mick Mulvaney; Robert Blair, a senior adviser to Mulvaney; and Michael Duffey, a senior Office of Management and Budget official. The amendment also would have subpoenaed documents from the administration related to Trump's decision to withhold military aid to Ukraine.

A second Schumer amendment to subpoena just Bolton failed more narrowly, 51–49. It picked up support from Collins and Romney, who said they wanted to hear from the former national security advisor.

A third Schumer amendment, also to subpoena Bolton, provided for a brief process with one day for a deposition and one day for public testimony before the Senate, with this occurring within five days of adopting the organizing resolution. That failed on an identical 51–49 vote.

The final amendment, by Democrat Chris Van Hollen of Maryland, would have required the Chief Justice Roberts to rule on motions to subpoena witnesses and documents, as well as any assertions of privilege in connection with those subpoenas. The Senate rejected it on a party line vote of 53–47.

Senate Acquittal

The Senate on February 5, 2020, acquitted Trump of both articles of impeachment, providing an anticlimactic ending to more than a year of investigations and high-profile debates that persuaded few in Congress to alter their views. Senators voted 48–52 to reject the House's abuse of power charge and 47–53 to reject the obstruction of Congress charge—far short of the two-thirds majority required for conviction. Romney was the sole senator to cross party lines, casting a vote to convict the president on the charge of abuse of power. In an emotional floor speech, the first-term senator and 2012 Republican presidential nominee said Trump made a "flagrant assault on our elec-

toral rights, our national security, and our fundamental values." He referred to his commitment to his faith and his oath "before God" to pursue justice impartially, and he called it the most difficult decision he had ever made.

Other previously undecided Republicans said they would acquit in the days leading up to the vote. Lamar Alexander of Tennessee said on the Senate floor that Trump engaged in "inappropriate" actions that were not impeachable. Alexander, along with Murkowski and Collins, criticized the House for rushing impeachment and said House Democrats should have summoned additional witnesses such as Bolton before impeaching Trump. Rejecting arguments from House Democrats that Trump had blocked witnesses from appearing, Senate Republicans said the House should have forced the issue in court.

Two Democratic swing votes from states that Trump had won in 2016—Joe Manchin III of West Virginia and Kyrsten Sinema of Arizona—voted for conviction on both charges.

In a statement, Manchin said, "I take no pleasure in these votes, and am saddened this is the legacy we leave our children and grandchildren. I have always wanted this President, and every President to succeed, but I deeply love our country and must do what I think is best for the nation." Sinema said just before the vote that Trump's actions were "dangerous to the fundamental principles of American democracy."

The acquittal came two days after the final arguments by the two legal teams. Schiff implored Senate Republicans to have the courage to remove Trump. He warned that the president otherwise would cheat in the upcoming election. But Trump's lawyers said it should be up to the voters to decide later in the year whether Trump should remain in office. Cipollone framed the impeachment as an effort to both overturn the 2016 election and interfere with the next one.

Trump was unrepentant, saying a day after the Senate vote: "We went through hell, unfairly. Did nothing wrong." Like Clinton, who saw his popularity rise after his acquittal in the Senate, he enjoyed a bump in the polls after the Senate verdict. His popularity waved, however, during the COVID-19 pandemic. Ultimately, he lost the 2020 election to Biden. His refusal to accept the outcome and his encouragement of the storming of the Capitol on January 6, when Congress was counting the electoral votes, would lead to his second impeachment and second acquittal in 2021, although this time more Republicans voted against him.

The Supreme Court, 2017–2020

The Supreme Court steered a generally conservative course during Donald Trump's single, four-year term as president from January 2017 through December 2020. The Court was poised to move further to the right after Trump's success in appointing three conservatives to the Court: Neil Gorsuch in 2017, Brett Kavanaugh in 2018, and Amy Coney Barrett in 2020. All three were confirmed by the Republican-majority Senate by historically narrow margins, in mostly party line votes.

With Justice Anthony M. Kennedy's retirement in 2018, the Court's four remaining liberal justices—Ginsburg, Breyer, Sotomayor, and Kagan—lost their most important occasional ally from among the Republican-appointed conservatives. Kennedy's retirement was critical, for example, in producing the decision by a 5–4 majority in 2019 to eliminate federal court jurisdiction over partisan gerrymandering cases.

Ginsburg's death in August 2020 weakened the liberal bloc further. Trump's appointment of the outspoken anti-abortion conservative, Barrett, created a lopsided 6–3 conservative majority and set the stage for a showdown in the Court's 2020 term on possibly overruling the landmark abortion rights ruling, *Roe v. Wade*.

The liberal bloc had few victories with Trump still in the White House, none of them equal in constitutional significance to Kennedy's 5–4 opinion in *Obergefell v. Hodges* (2015) that guaranteed marriage rights to same-sex couples nationwide. Even with Kennedy's retirement, however, the Court gave LGBT advocates a significant victory with a 6–3 ruling in two consolidated cases that extended the federal job discrimination law known as Title VII to prohibit discrimination in employment on the basis of sexual orientation, *Bostock v. Clayton County*, or on the basis of gender identity, *R.G. and G. R. Harris Funeral Homes, Inc. v. Equal Employment Opportunity Commission*.

Immigration and Citizenship

As presidential candidate in December 2015, Trump pledged before a political rally in South Carolina that as president he would impose a "total and complete shutdown of Muslims entering the United States until our country's representatives can figure out what is going on."

After taking office in January 2017, Trump acted on his campaign promise by issuing an executive order on January 27, one week after his inauguration, that banned foreign nationals from seven predominantly Muslim countries from visiting the country for ninety days, suspended entry of all Syrian refugees indefinitely, and prohibited any other refugees from coming into the country for 120 days.

Civil rights and immigrants' rights groups immediately filed multiple suits challenging the executive order in federal courts around the country. The cases eventually reached the Supreme Court under the name *Trump v. Hawaii* in time for oral arguments in April 2018. The 5–4 decision, issued on June 26 and divided along conservative-liberal lines, upheld Trump's actions based on what Chief Justice Roberts called "the broad discretion granted to [the president] . . . to suspend the entry of aliens into the United States." Roberts went on to reject the challengers' argument that the executive order violated the Establishment Clause by singling out Muslims because of what the plaintiffs called "religious animus." Roberts concluded that "national security justifications" were sufficient to uphold the order independent of any "unconstitutional grounds."

In one of two separate dissents, Breyer, joined by Kagan, argued that the order might be upheld if administered so as to allow waivers in some cases. Sotomayor, joined by Ginsburg, argued more forcefully that the order was "motivated by anti-Muslim animus" and "masquerades behind a façade of national-security concerns."

Buoyed by the victory at the Supreme Court, Trump continued to emphasize immigration and citizenship issues in policy pronouncements and in other cases that reached the justices. Trump failed in the most significant of the later cases, however, to rescind an Obama-era policy that granted a limited legal status to immigrants who arrived in the United States without papers as children. The Obama policy, adopted in 2012 and formally titled Deferred Action for Childhood Arrivals, was commonly known as DACA. With Obama in office, federal courts rejected efforts led by Republican states to invalidate the policy.

With Trump in office, the acting secretary of homeland security issued a terse memorandum rescinding the policy in June 2017. The administration's move drew several legal

challenges, including one brought by the University of California. That case reached the Court in its 2019 term under the name *Department of Homeland Security v. Regents of the University of California* (2020). Roberts led a five-justice majority in restoring DACA by finding the rescission to have been "arbitrary and capricious."

One year earlier, the Court had rebuffed Trump by ordering reconsideration of the administration's plan to include a citizenship question in the questionnaire being distributed for the 2020 Census. Various groups challenged the plan by Commerce Secretary Wilbur Ross on the ground that the citizenship question would deter some households from returning the questionnaire and thus result in an undercount. Roberts wrote a complex decision for overlapping majorities in *Department of Commerce v. New York* (2019) that found Ross's decision to be subject to judicial review and remanded the issue to the Census Bureau because of what Roberts called "a significant mismatch between the Secretary's decision and the rationale that he provided."

In other cases, the Court upheld tough enforcement policies that the government had adopted under previous administrations based on provisions in the Immigration and Nationality Act. The rulings in separate cases, *Jennings v. Rodriguez* (2018) and *Nielsen v. Preap* (2019), denied bail hearings to noncitizens during the often-protracted deportation proceedings. The 5–3 ruling in *Jennings* reversed a federal appeals court decision that would have required bond hearings after six months in detention. The 5–4 ruling in *Nielsen* held that noncitizens subject to mandatory detention because of criminal convictions were not entitled to bail hearings even if they had completed their criminal sentences. Alito led the conservative majority in both cases; liberal justices wrote strong dissents in both.

Criminal Law and Procedure

The Court's criminal law decisions over four terms included several that favored suspects or criminal defendants on Fourth Amendment issues but overall had no broad impact on police practices or policies, or on the conduct of criminal trials. The Warren Court's most important criminal law decisions survived intact with only minor modifications: the *Miranda* rules governing custodial interrogation of suspects, the exclusionary rule for suppressing evidence found after an unreasonable search or seizure, and the *Gideon* rule requiring appointment of defense counsel for indigent defendants.

The Court strengthened Fourth Amendment protections somewhat in two decisions that imposed limits on police surveillance of suspects. The 5–4 ruling in *Carpenter v. United States* (2018) required police to obtain a search warrant before obtaining a suspect's cell phone records to track the suspect's movements over time. Roberts wrote the opinion and gave the four liberal justices the needed

fifth vote to prevail. He reasoned that allowing the government access to a person's cell-site records violates the reasonable expectation of privacy in the person's physical movements.

In a more unified decision one month earlier, the Court ruled 7–1 that police engaged in hot pursuit of a motorist suspect must obtain a search warrant before following the suspect onto the suspect's property. Sotomayor based the decision in *Collins v. Virginia* (2018) on the historic practice of invoking the Fourth Amendment to protect both a home and the adjoining curtilage; Alito was the lone dissenter.

One term later, however, the Court held on a 5–4 vote that police need not obtain a search warrant before drawing blood from an unconscious motorist suspected of driving under the influence. Alito based his plurality opinion in *Mitchell v. Wisconsin* (2019) on the "compelling need" to obtain evidence of blood-alcohol content before it dissipates. Breyer, a Fourth Amendment pragmatist, provided the critical fifth vote for the decision; Sotomayor led three liberal justices in dissent and Gorsuch dissented separately.

The Court forced an important change in criminal trials in two states, Louisiana and Oregon, by holding on a 6–3 vote that the Sixth Amendment requires a unanimous jury verdict in criminal trials nationwide. Louisiana and Oregon were the only states that allowed non-unanimous verdicts under the Court's earlier precedent in *Apodaca v. Oregon* (1972). Gorsuch led the 6–3 majority in *Ramos v. Louisiana* (2020) in overruling the earlier decision; Alito, Roberts, and Kagan dissented.

Within the same term, however, the Court declined to adopt a nationwide rule defining the insanity defense in criminal trials. The 6–3 ruling in *Kahler v. Kansas* (2020) upheld the Kansas law that did not allow a defendant to claim insanity based on the inability to distinguish right from wrong. Writing for the majority, Kagan acknowledged that most states incorporated the "moral incapacity test," but she found no due process requirement for the test. Breyer led three liberal justices in dissent. The ruling upheld the murder conviction and death sentence imposed on a Kansas man, James Kahler, for killing four family members; he claimed that mental illness prevented him from recognizing his actions as morally wrong.

One year earlier, however, the Court established a constitutional limit on the common practice of state and local law enforcement agencies in forfeiting property that defendants used in committing crimes. The 9–0 decision in *Timbs v. Indiana* (2019) held that the Eighth Amendment's prohibition against "excessive fines" applies to civil forfeiture as practiced by state and local governments. Police in Indiana had seized Tyson Timbs's $42,000 SUV on the ground that he had used the vehicle to transport heroin. Timbs argued successfully in lower courts that the forfeiture was disproportionate to his offense, but the Indiana Supreme Court reversed by holding that the Excessive Fines Clause is not incorporated against the states.

Ginsburg wrote for seven justices in concluding that the prohibition against excessive fines is "fundamental to our scheme of ordered liberty." Thomas and Gorsuch concurred separately.

In a setback for defendants, however, the Court rejected an Alabama man's effort to invoke the Double Jeopardy Clause to prevent a federal prosecution for a firearm offense after he had already been convicted for a similar offense in state court. The 7–2 ruling in *Gamble v. United States* (2019) upheld the so-called dual sovereignty doctrine, which permits separate prosecutions by a state government and the federal government. Alito led the majority in concluding that separate prosecutions by the state and the federal government do not put a defendant twice in jeopardy for "the same offense," as the Fifth Amendment provides. Ginsburg and Gorsuch dissented separately.

The Court's ruling in various death penalty cases from state courts left existing capital punishment procedures largely unchanged. In a Mississippi case, however, the Court reversed a Mississippi man's murder conviction and death sentence because of the prosecutor's use of race in seating an all-white jury to try the Black defendant. Kavanaugh led the 7–2 majority in *Flowers v. Mississippi* (2019). The defendant, Curtis Flowers, was tried six times before he was convicted of killing four store employees. The Mississippi Supreme Court rejected Flowers's argument that the prosecutor violated Supreme Court precedent by using peremptory challenges to excuse Black prospective jurors. In reversing the conviction, Kavanaugh concluded that the trial judge was wrong in concluding that the prosecutor was not motivated by discriminatory intent. Thomas and Gorsuch dissented.

The Court's most significant capital punishment decision came in a method-of-execution dispute brought by a Missouri inmate, Raymond Bucklew, who claimed that because of a particular medical condition the state's lethal injection protocol posed the risk of excruciating pain for him during the execution in violation of the Eighth Amendment's prohibition against cruel and unusual punishments. Bucklew urged, in an as-applied challenge, that the state substitute use of nitrogen gas. In rejecting his claim in *Bucklew v. Precythe* (2019), the Court held on a 5–4 vote that Bucklew had failed to show that use of nitrogen gas was feasible, as required under previous method-of-execution decisions, or that it would substantially reduce the risk of pain during the execution. Gorsuch wrote the decision; the four liberal justices dissented.

The Court continued to adopt a skeptical approach toward expanding federal criminal jurisdiction. The unanimous decision in *Kelly v. United States* (2020) overturned the federal fraud convictions of two New Jersey officials, Anne Kelly and William Baroni, stemming from their use of a cover story to disguise the political motivation behind the rerouting of commuter traffic from New Jersey to New York. The rerouting caused massive traffic jams in the town of Fort Lee, New Jersey, as urged by New Jersey's

Governor Chris Christie to penalize the town's mayor for refusing to endorse his bid for reelection. Writing for the unanimous Court, Kagan concluded that the officials' scheme could not have violated federal fraud laws because it was not aimed at obtaining money or property.

The Court favored defendants in two other federal criminal cases. The Court's 7–2 decision in *Rehaif v. United States* (2019) held that the government must prove, in prosecuting an illegal alien for possession of a firearm, that the defendant knew that he belonged to the relevant category of persons barred from possessing a firearm. Breyer wrote the decision; Thomas and Alito dissented.

In a broader decision three days later, the Court in *United States v. Davis* (2019) struck down as unconstitutionally vague a sentence-enhancing provision that authorized longer sentences for anyone convicted of using, carrying, or possessing a firearm in connection with a "crime of violence." The provision, codified as 18 U.S.C. §924(c)(3)(A), included a definition of a crime of violence as a felony "that by its nature, involves a substantial risk that physical force against the person or property of another may be used in the course of committing the offense." Gorsuch wrote the majority decision, joined by the four liberal justices; Kavanaugh, Roberts, Thomas, and Alito dissented.

Also within the same week, the Court broadened the impact of the federal Sex Offender Registration and Notification Act (SORNA) by upholding, in *Gundy v. United States* (2019), the attorney general's decision to apply the act retroactively to sex offenses committed before enactment of the 2006 law. Conservative groups backed the petitioner's argument that the attorney general's decision violated the so-called "nondelegation doctrine," which limits the discretion for executive branch officials in exercising power delegated by Congress. In rejecting the argument, Kagan led a plurality of four justices in noting that the law specified that the attorney general should extend the act to all pre-SORNA offenses as quickly as possible. Alito provided the fifth vote for the decision; Roberts, Thomas, and Gorsuch dissented. Kavanaugh, appointed after the arguments, did not participate.

Individual Rights

Apart from First Amendment cases, the Court's decision to extend Title VII's prohibition against discrimination because of sex to discrimination based on sexual orientation or gender identity represented the Court's most important expansion of individual rights during the four-year period. The 6–3 ruling in *Bostock v. Clayton County* (2020) resolved three separate cases with lower federal appeals courts in conflict on the scope of Title VII's prohibition against sex discrimination.

The Eleventh Circuit Court of Appeals had rejected a Title VII complaint filed by a Georgia man, Gerald Bostock, after the county fired him from a position as child

welfare advocate after he was identified in a gay newspaper as participating in a gay softball league. In a separate case, the Second Circuit Court of Appeals upheld a gay man's Title VII complaint, after he was fired from a position as a skydiving instructor when a female client learned of his sexual orientation. Donald Zarda died in a skydiving accident during the litigation, but his sister continued the litigation against Altitude Express on behalf of his estate. In an en banc decision, the circuit court held that Title VII prohibits discrimination based on sexual orientation. Altitude Express asked the Supreme Court to review the decision.

In the third of the cases, the Sixth Circuit Court of Appeals upheld a complaint by the Equal Employment Opportunity Commission (EEOC) that a Detroit-area funeral home, R. G. and G. R. Harris Funeral Homes, violated Title VII by firing a longtime employee, Aimee Stephens, after she notified the funeral home's director that she was transitioning from male to female and would begin reporting to work as a transgender woman. The funeral home asked the Supreme Court to review the decision.

Gorsuch, a self-professed textualist, led a six-justice majority that included Roberts along with the four liberal justices in construing Title VII's provision to encompass sexual orientation and gender identity. "An employer who fires an individual merely for being gay or transgender violates Title VII," Gorsuch reasoned. Alito, Thomas, and Kavanaugh dissented in opinions that attacked Gorsuch's opinion for going beyond Congress's intent in enacting Title VII as part of the Civil Rights Act of 1965.

The Court had dealt a setback to LGBT advocates earlier with a ruling that set aside a penalty imposed on a Colorado baker for violating the state's antidiscrimination law by refusing to bake a cake for a gay couple's wedding. Kennedy based his majority opinion in the 7–2 decision in *Masterpiece Cakeshop Ltd. v. Colorado Civil Rights Commission* (2018) on comments made by some of the agency's members that indicated "hostility toward religion" in violation of the state's obligation of religious neutrality. The baker had claimed religious reasons for refusing the gay couple's order. Ginsburg and Sotomayor dissented.

The Court gave property rights advocates a significant procedural victory with a decision in 2019 that allowed property owners to file a takings claim in federal court without first having been denied compensation in state court proceedings. The ruling in *Knick v. Township of Scott* (2019) overruled a procedural requirement that the Court had imposed decades earlier in a case known as *Williamson County* (1985). Roberts led the 5–4 majority in concluding that the "state-litigation requirement imposes an unjustifiable burden on takings plaintiffs." Four liberal justices dissented.

The Court declined in a later case to extend the so-called *Bivens* remedy that the Court had created in 1971 for victims of constitutional violations by federal officers. The 5–4 ruling in *Hernandez v. Mesa* (2020) rejected a suit

by the parents of a Mexican teenager against the U.S. Border Patrol agent, Jesus Mesa Jr., who fatally wounded the youth while he was playing in a concrete culvert at the U.S.–Mexico border. Alito led four other conservatives in declining to extend the *Bivens* doctrine to a cross-border shooting by noting the Court's reluctance in prior cases to expand *Bivens* and the risk of interference with international relations. In a concurring opinion, Thomas, joined by Gorsuch, called for discarding the doctrine altogether. Ginsburg led the four liberal justices in a lengthy dissent.

First Amendment Cases

The Roberts Court continued to take an active role in protecting freedom of speech in a variety of contexts, with liberal justices in dissent. The Court also favored religious liberty claimants in a variety of contexts; two significant decisions required that parochial schools be included in general government programs offering assistance to schools.

FREEDOM OF SPEECH

The Court dealt public employee unions a significant financial setback by holding, on a 5–4 vote, that unions could not require nonmembers to pay a so-called agency fee to cover the unions' costs in administering collective bargaining agreements that cover union members and nonmembers alike. The ruling in *Janus v. AFSCME* (2018) upheld a complaint filed by a social worker in Illinois, who objected on First Amendment grounds to paying the mandatory $45 per month fee to the union, which he said helped finance lobbying positions that he opposed.

Alito led five conservatives in overruling an earlier decision, *Abood v. Detroit Board of Education* (1977), that had permitted a teachers' union to impose such fees on non-union members. Alito reasoned that the earlier decision had proved to be unworkable because of the difficulties that unions faced in calculating expenses to be covered by the agency shop fees. Kagan led four liberal justices in a strongly written dissent.

The Court divided along the same conservative-liberal lines in another decision in the same term, that struck down parts of a California law enacted in 2015 that required pro-life pregnancy centers to inform clients of the availability of abortion services from state-funded centers. The trade association representing the centers challenged the law as amounting to compelled speech in violation of their First Amendment rights. Thomas led the 5–4 decision in *National Institute of Family Life Advocates v. Becerra* (2018) in concluding that the law "unduly burdens protected speech." Breyer led the four liberal justices in dissent; he warned that the ruling could jeopardize other mandatory disclosure laws.

Within the same term, the Court also struck down a century-old Minnesota law that prohibited wearing campaign-related apparel at polling places. Roberts led the 7–2 decision in *Minnesota Voters Alliance v. Mansky* (2018) in

finding the law unconstitutionally overbroad. Sotomayor and Breyer dissented.

The Court also struck down, in two separate cases, portions of the federal trademark law, known as the Lanham Act, that prevented registration of trademarks with potentially offensive content. In the first of the rulings, *Matal v. Tam* (2017), the Court struck down a provision that prohibited registration of a trademark that might disparage individuals or groups. Simon Tam, founder of an all Asian American rock dance band, called the band "The Slants" in order to reclaim the ethnic slur as a badge of racial pride. Tam challenged the trademark office's refusal to register the mark. Leading the 8–0 decision, Alito concluded that the disparagement clause violated the First Amendment as improper viewpoint discrimination.

Two terms later, the Court followed by striking down a Lanham Act provision that prohibited registration of "immoral" or "scandalous" trademarks. The 6–3 decision in *Tancu v. Bruneti* (2019) favored a Los Angeles–based artist, Eric Brunetti, who created a line of streetwear that he branded as "FUCT"—for "Friends You Can't Trust." The trademark office refused to register the mark by regarding it as the past participle of a common vulgarity. Kagan cited the *Tam* decision as precedent in her opinion for the majority; Roberts, Breyer, and Sotomayor wrote separate opinions concurring in part and dissenting in part.

FREEDOM OF RELIGION

The Court discounted Establishment Clause concerns in two decisions that required government-funded assistance programs in Missouri and Montana to include parochial schools along with other schools. Roberts led the 7–2 majority in the first of the decisions, *Trinity Lutheran Church of Columbia v. Comer* (2017). The state had established a playground safety program to aid schools in resurfacing playgrounds with a rubber surface made from recycled tires. The state denied an application for assistance from a church-affiliated preschool and day care center in Columbia. In denying the application, the state cited a provision of the Missouri constitution that prohibited direct financial assistance to a church. The church filed suit against the state by arguing that the denial violated its right to free exercise of religion. In ruling for the church, Roberts agreed by concluding that the denial imposed a penalty on the free exercise of religion by denying an available benefit "solely on account of religious identity." Sotomayor and Ginsburg dissented.

Roberts again led a divided Court in extending the decision three terms later by requiring the state of Montana to include parochial school students in a program that allowed tax credits for families making donations to organizations that provided scholarships for students attending private schools. Parents who sought scholarships for students attending religious schools challenged the state's policy and brought the case to the Supreme Court after the Montana Supreme Court upheld the state's policy. Roberts led the 5–4 majority in *Espinoza v. Montana Department of Revenue* (2020) in concluding that Montana's constitutional provision prohibiting aid to any school controlled by a church amounted to improper discrimination against religious schools. The justices divided along conservative-liberal lines in ruling for the parents. The four liberal justices dissented in separate opinions written by Breyer, Ginsburg, and Sotomayor; Kagan joined the Ginsburg and Breyer opinions.

The Court extended another legal benefit to parochial schools in the same term by ruling in *Our Lady of Guadalupe School v. Morrissey-Berru* (2020) that church-affiliated schools are largely exempt from federal antidiscrimination laws in personnel decisions regarding teachers who teach religious subjects. The 7–2 ruling extended a previously recognized "ministerial exception" for parochial schools by rejecting suits filed by two teachers fired from Catholic schools in the Los Angeles area. One of the fired teachers filed suit under the federal Age Discrimination in Employment Act; the other teacher contended that she was fired in violation of the Americans With Disabilities Act after requesting leave for treatment of breast cancer. Alito led the majority in deferring to the schools' designation of the teachers as performing ministerial roles in their classroom instruction in secular as well as religious subjects. Sotomayor and Ginsburg dissented.

The Court had divided along the same lines one year earlier in dismissing an Establishment Clause challenge to the use of public funds in maintaining a large Christian cross as a memorial to World War I service members on public land at a major intersection in the Washington, D.C., suburb of Bladensburg, Maryland. Alito led the 7–2 ruling in *American Legion v. American Humanist Ass'n* (2019) with Ginsburg and Sotomayor again in dissent. Alito reasoned that the cross, funded by private donations ninety years earlier, had acquired "historical importance" despite its religious significance. In her dissenting opinion, Ginsburg found that the regional planning commission's role in maintaining the memorial violated the Establishment Clause. "By maintaining the Peace Cross on a public highway," Ginsburg wrote, "the Commission elevates Christianity over other faiths, and religion over nonreligion."

Election Law

The Court's decision in the partisan gerrymandering case, *Rucho v. Common Cause* (2019), marked an end to the justices' efforts over four decades to settle on a manageable standard to determine the limits of partisanship in redrawing legislative or congressional districts. The Court had entertained but rejected claims against partisan gerrymanders in a succession of four separate cases dating from 1986. After rejecting challenges to politically motivated redistricting plans in 1986 and 2004, the Court returned to the issue in the 2018 term by agreeing to hear a Democratic-backed challenge to Republican-drawn con-

gressional districts in North Carolina and a Republican challenge to Democratic-drawn congressional districts in Maryland. Ruling in the two consolidated cases at the end of the term, the Court issued a 5–4 decision definitively declaring political gerrymandering cases to be nonjusticiable in federal courts. With Kennedy's retirement, his successor, Brett Kavanaugh, provided the fifth vote needed for the decision. Writing for the conservative bloc, Roberts related the history of the prior cases and concluded that partisan gerrymandering claims had "proved far more difficult to adjudicate" than the one-person, one-vote claims raised in other districting cases. Kagan led the four liberal justices in a bitter dissent; she called the ruling an "abdication" *(See sidebar)*.

The Court had divided along the same lines one year earlier in a significant voting rights decision, *Husted v. A Philip Randolph Institute* (2018), that upheld voter deregistration procedures adopted by Ohio's Republican secretary of state for the 2018 election to remove voters who failed to provide change-of-residence notices. Democrats argued that the procedure violated a federal law, the National Voter Registration Act. Alito led the five Republican-appointed justices in upholding Ohio's procedures; Breyer led four liberal justices in dissent.

The Court issued two decisions in 2020 stemming from disputes relating to the 2016 and 2020 presidential elections. In the first of the rulings, *Chiafalo v. Washington* (July 6, 2020), the Court ruled unanimously that states can penalize so-called faithless presidential electors who fail to cast their votes as pledged. The issue arose after Washington's secretary of state imposed $1,000 fines on four electors who failed to vote for the popular-vote-winning Democratic nominee Hillary Clinton as pledged. Colorado's secretary of state dealt with a similar issue by discarding the vote cast by a faithless Democratic elector and replacing him with another elector. The nonconforming votes did not affect Donald Trump's 2016 electoral college majority over Clinton.

Ruling in the Washington case, Kagan concluded that states can "enforce a presidential elector's pledge to support the elector's party's nominee—and the state voters' choice—for president." The Court issued a one-sentence order in the Colorado case, *Colorado Dept. of State v. Baca*, on the same day, ruling for the state on the basis of the decision in the Washington case.

With Trump's apparent defeat in the 2020 election, Republican states led by Texas filed an original action in the Supreme Court on December 6, seeking to set aside Democrat Joe Biden's victories in four states that had changed election procedures during the campaign: Pennsylvania, Georgia, Michigan, and Wisconsin. Trump intervened three days later in support of Texas's petition. The Court dismissed the case on December 11 in an unsigned order, *Texas et al. v. Pennsylvania et al.* (2020). The order stated that Texas "has not demonstrated a judicially cognizable interest in the manner in which another State conducts its elections." Thomas and Alito dissented; they argued that the Court had no discretion to refuse to hear a state's original complaint against another state.

Business Law

Business interests generally fared well at the Supreme Court in cases that pitted companies against workers, consumers, and investors. As the 2019 term ended in mid-2020, the pro-consumer Constitutional Accountability Center reported that the Roberts Court's record since 2006 favored positions taken by the U.S. Chamber of Commerce in 70 percent of the cases in which the Chamber had filed amicus briefs.

Among major victories, the Chamber's position prevailed in a 5–4 decision, *Epic Systems v. Lewis* (2018), that rejected a union-backed effort to invoke the National Labor Relations Act (NLRA) to allow collective instead of individual arbitration of employee complaints. Gorsuch wrote for five conservatives in concluding in the majority opinion that the Federal Arbitration Act required enforcement of the arbitration clause at issue, which limited arbitration to individual complaints. Ginsburg led four liberal justices in a forceful dissent that labeled the decision as "egregiously wrong" in contradiction of the NLRA's "premise that employees must have the capacity to act collectively in order to match their employers' clout in setting terms and conditions of employment."

Within the same term, the Court dealt a potential setback to businesses engaged in e-commerce over the internet. The 5–4 decision in *South Dakota v. Wayfair, Inc.* (2018) allowed states to require retailers to collect and remit state sales taxes on purchases by the state's residents even if the company had no physical presence in the state. Kennedy led four conservative justices and Ginsburg in rejecting the physical presence rule established in two prior decisions, *Quill Corp. v. North Dakota* (1992) and *National Bellas Hess, Inc. v. Department of Revenue of Illinois* (1967). In litigating the case, South Dakota estimated that it lost $48 million to $58 million in sales taxes uncollected on ecommerce sales. A study by the General Accounting Office (GAO) estimated that states collectively lost between $8 billion and $33 billion annually in uncollected sales taxes under the prior rule.

Kennedy led the majority in concluding that the physical presence rule was "no longer clear or easily applicable." Roberts voiced concern in a dissenting opinion joined by three liberal justices that the decision could "disrupt the development of a significant and vibrant part of our national economy." The Chamber took no position in the case, but the trade association representing brick-and-mortar retailers supported South Dakota's position.

The Court issued several significant decisions favoring business interests in its 2019 term that protected companies to some extent from suits alleging violations of federal law. In one of those decisions, the Court voted 5–4 in *Thole*

v. U.S. Bank (2020) to make it harder for retirees in defined benefit pension plans to sue their employers for mismanaging the pension funds. Kavanaugh led the conservative justices in holding that retirees had no legal standing to sue the company unless the alleged mismanagement actually reduced their benefits. The four liberal justices dissented. The U.S. Chamber supported the bank's effort to dismiss the retirees' class action in a brief that warned the plaintiffs' position would invite "abusive and wasteful litigation." The dissenting justices argued instead that the bank's position would leave 35 million people with defined-benefit pension plans vulnerable to fiduciary misconduct by pension plan administrators.

Two months later, a unanimous Court held in *Comcast v. National Association of African-American Owned Media* (2020) that plaintiffs alleging racial discrimination in contracting under the federal civil rights law known as section 1981 must prove that race was the actual reason for failing to reach agreement on a contract. A trade association representing African American-owned media had sued the giant cable company, Comcast, for refusing to carry specialty channels they produced. Comcast rejected the programming by citing limited bandwidth and limited audience interest in the programming. The federal appeals court had rejected Comcast's effort to dismiss the suit and instead remanded the case to district court to allow the plaintiffs to try to prove that race played "some role" in Comcast's decision. Writing for eight justices, Gorsuch applied a traditional tort law requirement that plaintiffs in a section 1981 suit must "plead and prove that its injury would not have occurred but for the defendant's unlawful conduct." The U.S. Chamber supported Comcast's position by arguing that a "mixed motive" standard for section 1981 suits "would be difficult to administer."

The Court issued a major employment law decision as the 2019 term neared an end by ruling that the federal job discrimination law known as Title VII prohibits discrimination on the basis of sexual orientation or gender identity. Gorsuch led the 6–3 decision in *Bostock v. Clayton County* (June 15, 2020) in holding that Title VII's prohibition against discrimination because of sex encompasses discrimination on the basis of sexual orientation or gender identity. LGBT advocacy groups celebrated the ruling, while legal conservatives forcefully criticized it. The dissenting justices were Thomas, Alito, and Kavanaugh. A coalition of business organizations filed an amicus brief supporting the plaintiffs in the two companion cases decided together; they argued that federal protections for LGBT employees would benefit employers' ability to attract and retain employees and also would boost productivity.

The business community won its highest-profile victory for the term with an end-of-term decision that held the director of the newly established Consumer Financial Protection Bureau (CFPB) to be subject to removal by the president. In creating the new agency in 2010, the Democratic-majority Congress had provided that the agency would be headed by a single director with a fixed five-year term subject to removal by the president only for "inefficiency, neglect of duty, or malfeasance . . ." Business interests and political conservatives supported a legal challenge to the structure brought by a debt-servicing law firm on separation-of-powers grounds.

Roberts led the somewhat fractured 5–4 majority in *Seila Law v. Consumer Financial Protection Bureau* (June 29, 2020) in refusing to extend the tenure protections recognized for multimember federal agencies to the CFPB's single-director structure. Roberts reasoned that the broad authority granted to a tenure-protected agency head interfered with the president's authority over the executive branch. Kagan led four liberal justices in dissenting on the point. The business community's victory proved to be somewhat illusory, however, after a pro-consumer Democratic president, Joe Biden, took office in January 2021 and replaced the Trump-appointed CFPB director with a more consumer-friendly agency head.

One week before the CFPB decision, the Court dealt a setback to the financial sector by ruling that the Securities and Exchange Commission (SEC) can seek to force defendants in a securities fraud case to disgorge to victims the funds they received up to their net profits in the transactions. The 8–1 ruling in *Liu v. Securities and Exchange Commission* (June 22, 2020) held that disgorgement was appropriate "equitable relief" for the SEC to seek through a court suit. Sotomayor wrote the decision; Thomas was the lone dissenter.

The SEC had filed a federal court suit charging Charles Liu and his wife Lisa Wang with misappropriating most of the $27 million that they had raised from overseas investors for a planned cancer treatment center in the Los Angeles area. The district court granted summary judgment to the SEC requiring Liu and Wang to disgorge what the court called their "ill-gotten gains"—specifically, the full amount they had raised less their cash on hand.

The Supreme Court ruled instead that the defendants could be required to disgorge only their net profits, not the full amount they had raised. The decision remanded the case to the district court to reconsider the amount to be disgorged. Thomas dissented on the ground that disgorgement is not "a traditional equitable remedy."

COURT PULLS PLUG ON PARTISAN GERRYMANDERING CASES

The dishonorable and dishonored practice of drawing legislative and congressional district lines to advantage one political party over another dates as far back as the late 18th century when the practice acquired a derogatory name: gerrymandering. The term memorializes the 18th century governor of Massachusetts, Elbridge Gerry, who was blamed for drawing a legislative district that one opponent said looked like a "salamander." Gerry pronounced his surname with a hard *g*, but the term has come to be pronounced instead with a soft *g*.

The Court confronted the issue of partisan gerrymandering in a succession of cases that began in the 1980s, but justices failed to agree on a standard to determine when partisan considerations in drawing district lines went so far that they effectively limited equal political rights for voters. Struggling with the issues over three decades, the Court in 2019 finally gave up by holding, in a bitterly divided 5–4 decision, that federal courts have no jurisdiction to review challenges to partisan gerrymandering because those claims present political questions outside federal courts' authority.

The Court tentatively opened the door to partisan gerrymandering claims in a badly fractured decision in an Indiana case, *Davis v. Bandemer* (1986), brought by Democratic voters who were challenging Republican-drawn legislative districts. Justice Byron R. White led six justices in holding over the dissenting views of three justices that partisan gerrymandering claims are justiciable in federal courts. In his plurality opinion, White concluded that a districting plan could be invalidated only if it resulted in "effective denial to a minority of voters of a fair chance to influence the political process." Under that standard, the lower federal court rejected the Democrats' suit on remand. White's standard proved to be so demanding in future cases that no court struck down districting maps on partisan gerrymandering grounds over the next decade.

The Supreme Court set constitutional rules for the shape of legislative and congressional districts for the first time in a series of decisions in the 1990s dealing with what came to be called racial gerrymanders. The Court focused in the first of the decisions, *Shaw v. Reno* (1993), on the irregular shape of a congressional district in North Carolina drawn to connect predominantly African American neighborhoods in three cities. Over the next decade, the Court gave less emphasis to the shape of challenged districts but settled on a rule to require redrawing district lines if the predominant motive was to include or exclude minority voters.

The Court ruled inconclusively in two partisan gerrymandering cases early in the 21st century. The 5–4 ruling in *Vieth v. Jubilerer* (2004) dismissed a challenge by Democrats to Republican-drawn congressional districts in Pennsylvania. Writing for a plurality of four justices, Justice Antonin Scalia declared partisan gerrymandering claims nonjusticiable because there were no "judicially discernible and manageable standards" for judging such claims. Justice Anthony M. Kennedy left the door open to such claims in the future, however, in a separate, concurring opinion. Two years later, the Court considered partisan gerrymandering claims along with racial gerrymandering claims in a Texas case, *League of United Latin American Citizens v. Perry* (2006). Again, the Court failed to agree on a standard for judging partisan gerrymandering.

The Court tried again in two separate cases heard in the 2017 term. Plaintiffs in a Wisconsin case, *Gill v. Whitford* (2018), devised a mathematical standard that they called the efficiency gap to measure the degree of partisan imbalance in the legislative districting plan at issue. Roberts led a 5–4 majority in rejecting the suit on the ground that the plaintiffs lacked legal standing because they challenged the statewide map rather than their individual legislative districts. The Court also avoided a direct ruling in a second case, *Benisek v. Lamone* (2018), by holding in an unsigned, unanimous opinion that Republican voters challenging a Democratic gerrymander in Maryland had failed to show they were entitled to an injunction to redraw congressional districts within months of the next election.

The Court confronted partisan gerrymandering for the fifth time in the 2018 term in two separate cases that challenged congressional district maps in Maryland and North Carolina: a Democratic-drawn map in Maryland and a Republican-drawn map in the Tarheel State. The cases produced a single, bitterly divided 5–4 ruling, *Rucho v. Common Cause* (2019), that barred federal courts from considering partisan gerrymandering claims as political questions beyond the reach of the federal judiciary. The two cases that the justices agreed to hear illustrated that both major political parties engage in partisan gerrymandering when the opportunity to achieve political advantage with new district maps presents itself.

North Carolina case: The Republican-majority legislature and Republican governor of North Carolina produced a congressional districting plan in 2016 designed to preserve the Republican's 10–3 majority in the state's congressional delegation and aimed at resolving the still-pending racial gerrymandering case. The cochair of the committee that drew the maps explained the configuration by saying that it was impossible to draw a map to guarantee the GOP eleven seats.

(Continued)

COURT PULLS PLUG ON PARTISAN GERRYMANDERING CASES (Continued)

The state's Democratic party joined with the political reform group Common Cause and fourteen individual voters in challenging the plan on various grounds before a three-judge federal district court. They claimed that it violated the Equal Protection Clause by intentionally diluting Democratic votes and violated Democratic voters' First Amendment rights by retaliating against them based on their political beliefs. The three-judge court sustained all of the plaintiffs' claims in a ruling issued on January 9, 2018. The state appealed to the Supreme Court, which stayed the district court's order and remanded the case to the district court to reconsider in the light of the Court's new ruling in the Wisconsin case. The district court ruled again for the plaintiffs, with one judge dissenting, in a decision issued on August 27, 2018, that barred use of the district map in the 2018 elections.

The plaintiffs filed motions before the election asking the Supreme Court to affirm the decision; the state filed an opposition to the motions. The Supreme Court agreed to hear the appeal in an order issued on January 4, 2019, that postponed consideration of jurisdiction until oral arguments. The Court heard oral arguments in the two cases on March 26, 2019: the North Carolina case first, followed by the Maryland case.

Maryland case: The state's Democratic-controlled legislature and Democratic governor produced a congressional districting map plan in 2016 that disfavored the Republican incumbent in the state's easternmost congressional district and seemed likely to widen the Democrats' 6–2 majority in the state's congressional delegation. A three-judge court ruled for the Republican voters' challenge to the plan in a unanimous decision issued on November 7, 2018, and written by the lone Republican-appointed judge on the panel. Writing for the panel, Judge Paul Niemeyer found that the state had violated the plaintiffs' "representational rights and associational rights based on their party affiliation and voting history." The ruling ordered the state to draw new maps for the 2020 elections.

As in the North Carolina case, the plaintiffs asked the Supreme Court to affirm the decision, but the state opposed the request. The Court deferred a decision by agreeing on January 4, 2019, to hear a full round of arguments later. The Court later scheduled the case for arguments on March 26 along with arguments in the North Carolina case the same day, in time for a decision in both cases before the term's end in late June.

Ruling: The Court heard arguments in the two cases after Justice Kennedy, who had previously held out hope for finding a manageable standard for partisan gerrymandering claims, had retired in 2018, to be succeeded by his former law clerk, Brett Kavanaugh, then a judge on the D.C. Circuit Court. Kavanaugh, a former aide in the George W. Bush

White House, gave the other four Republican-appointed justices—Roberts, Thomas, Alito, and Gorsuch—the fifth vote they needed to pull the plug on partisan gerrymandering cases. Kagan led the four Democratic-appointed justices in a long and impassioned dissent that she summarized from the bench.

As senior justice in the majority, Roberts assigned the decision to himself and delivered the decision from the bench in an emphatic, ten-minute summary. Roberts began by acknowledging that the redistricting plans in both cases were "highly partisan, by any measure." He also stressed that the Framers were "familiar" with the practice that came to be known as gerrymandering but gave the states primary responsibility for congressional elections subject only to Congress's authority to "make or alter" any state regulations. In any event, Roberts concluded, "At no point was there a suggestion that the federal courts had a role to play."

Roberts noted the Court's failure to agree on a standard to apply in political gerrymandering cases, but he also acknowledged that lower courts had coalesced around a three-part test for such cases. In a final section, Roberts firmly closed federal courthouse doors to political gerrymandering cases. "We conclude," he wrote, "that partisan gerrymandering claims present political questions beyond the reach of the federal courts. Federal judges have no license to reallocate political power between the two major political parties, with no plausible grant of authority in the Constitution, and no legal standards to limit and direct their decisions."

The four Democratic-appointed justices—Ginsburg, Breyer, Sotomayor, and Kagan—dissented in an impassioned dissenting opinion that Kagan emphasized by summarizing from the bench. She opened by directly quoting her opening sentence: "For the first time ever, this Court refuses to remedy a constitutional violation because it thinks the task beyond judicial capabilities." Kagan continued with a sharp critique of the two instances of partisan gerrymandering before the Court. Those plans, she said, "deprived citizens of the most fundamental of their constitutional rights: the rights to participate equally in the political process, to join with others to advance their political beliefs, and to choose their political representatives."

Kagan closed with a bleak warning about what she called earlier in the opinion the Court's "nonchalance" in the face of increasingly sophisticated partisan gerrymandering. "Of all times to abandon the Court's duty to declare the law, this was not the one," she wrote. "The practices challenged in these cases imperil our system of government. Part of the Court's role in that system is to defend its foundations. Nothing is more important than free and fair elections. With respect but with deep sadness, I dissent."

CHAPTER 14

General Government

General Government

President Donald Trump's four years in office were marked by partisan disagreements over how the federal government spends its money and what it can and cannot regulate. Funding priority differences between Republicans and Democrats kept Congress from passing stand-alone appropriations bills and resulted in a thirty-five-day federal government shutdown that stretched from the end of the 115th Congress into the start of the 116th Congress. While that shutdown was predicated on the president's demand for money to build a wall along the U.S.–Mexico border, there were plenty of other disagreements between the two parties and chambers, including whether to provide pay raises to federal civilian employees,

how much to spend on grants to states for securing their election systems, how the District of Columbia is allowed to spend federal funds and local revenue, and whether to add money to the General Services Administration budget for addressing overdue building maintenance. When it came to regulations, Republicans generally sided with the president and his desire to repeal as many as possible, while Democrats attempted, often unsuccessfully, to keep existing rules from being overturned.

RESCINDING FEDERAL REGULATIONS

On the campaign trail, Trump promised to strike a more business-friendly approach than his predecessor and eliminate those federal regulations that he considered overly burdensome and a hindrance to economic development. During the 115th Congress, the House passed multiple bills that would not only eliminate certain existing regulations but also limit the ability of federal agencies to pass new ones in the future.

One measure approved in the House would create a commission charged with reviewing all existing regulations and making recommendations as to which could be rescinded, rolled back, or improved. Under the bill's provisions, an agency would not be permitted to replace a repealed regulation with something materially similar or that had the potential to create the same perceived problems as the initial regulation. Additionally, the bill would restrict agencies from enacting new regulations unless they could cut another one that was estimated to have the same cost. The House also passed a bill that would alter the rule-making process, requiring agencies to adhere to certain guidelines, such as forming evidence-based rulemaking determinations, looking for possible alternatives to the rule, weighing the costs and benefits of those alternatives, and following new reporting requirements for specific rules with a high economic impact.

Democrats were highly critical of each Republican attempt to amend the federal rulemaking process and eliminate existing regulations. They argued that the provisions in many of these bills would leave federal agencies without the ability to enact emergency regulations or those that were vital for public health and safety. During both committee markup and floor debate, Democrats attempted

Figure 14.1 Outlays for Science, Space, and General Government

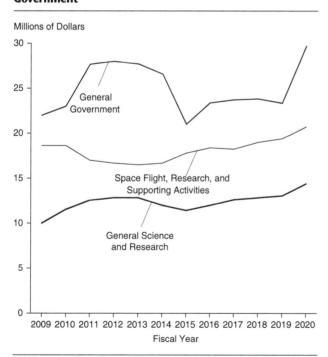

SOURCE: Office of Management and Budget, *Historical Tables, Budget of the United States Government: Fiscal Year 2021* (Washington DC: U.S. Government Printing Office, 2020), Table 3.2.

NOTE: Total line includes some expenditures not shown separately.
* indicates estimate

to exempt from the bills certain types of regulations, including those dealing with air protection, prescription drugs, and the incidence rate of specific diseases. Their efforts were largely unsuccessful.

While these rulemaking overhaul bills were never considered on the Senate floor, both chambers successfully advanced legislation repealing fourteen existing regulations, under authority provided to them by the Congressional Review Act.

FEDERAL WORKFORCE CHANGES

Democrats and Republicans at all levels of government have long argued over how much public sector employees should earn, especially when compared to workers in the private sector with similar responsibilities. In both the 115th and 116th Congress, the House and Senate considered multiple pieces of legislation that would adjust federal civilian employee wages.

Some of these measures were specific to a particular sector of the workforce. For example, one bill signed by President Trump changed the pay cap for Secret Service agents. Previously, many were not being compensated for overtime because the Treasury was restricted from paying these agents more than the GS-15 level, the highest available pay rate for civil servants on the General Schedule system, on a biweekly basis. This contributed to an ongoing attrition problem within the Secret Service, and pay issues were especially acute after Trump took office, because agents were racking up more overtime covering the president's trips to his homes in Florida and New Jersey, as well as the overseas business engagements and personal travel of the president's family. In 2016, Congress enacted legislation that increased the pay cap for those agents serving on a presidential candidate's detail, and in 2017 expanded that language to include other Secret Service agents as well.

The issue of raises for the federal civilian workforce was also addressed on multiple occasions. In years past, civilian employees received a wage hike equal to that offered to uniformed members of the armed services. President Trump, however, frequently sought to freeze civilian wages. Democrats argued that parity was critical, especially because in many instances both civilian and military workers perform the same duties. The call for a wage hike reached a fever pitch after the thirty-five-day federal government shutdown from December 2018 to January 2019 when many federal civilian employees went without a paycheck. After providing back wages to those workers, the House also took up a bill that would give them a 2.6 percent pay raise. While the legislation passed the House, it was not considered in the Senate. However in March 2019, the president lifted an earlier pay freeze and authorized a

congressionally approved 1.9 percent pay increase. Other wage increase language made its way into the fiscal year 2021 Financial Services and General Government appropriations measure that was wrapped into an omnibus bill, resulting in another pay increase for federal workers.

POSTAL SERVICE LEADERSHIP SCRUTINY

In May 2020, after vetting more than 200 candidates, the Postal Service Board of Governors selected Louis DeJoy to be the next postmaster general. DeJoy, who at the time of his selection was serving as the fundraising chair for the 2020 Republican National Convention, was a Trump megadonor and had no experience in United States Postal Service (USPS) operations. The selection of an outsider such as DeJoy came as little surprise, given that all the board's sitting members were Trump appointees and the president had long been critical of the USPS. Democrats were fiercely opposed to DeJoy's selection to lead the quasi-governmental body, who they saw as not only unqualified for the position but also too financially entrenched with Republicans, including the president, and businesses that compete with the Postal Service.

According to *CQ Roll Call*, Federal Election Commission records show that DeJoy had donated more than $214,000 to fifteen current House and Senate Republicans, including Senate Majority Leader Mitch McConnell, D-Ky., House Minority Leader Kevin McCarthy, R-Calif., Sen. Lindsey Graham, R-S.C., Rep. Martha McSally, R-Ariz., and Rep. Dan Bishop, R-N.C. Three additional members of Congress who received campaign contributions from DeJoy—Sens. Josh Hawley, R-Mo., and Mitt Romney, R-Utah, and Rep. Virginia Foxx, R-N.C.—were members of the Senate Homeland Security and Government Affairs Committee and House Oversight and Government Reform Committee, respectively, which has jurisdiction over the Postal Service and which, in 2020, held hearings about USPS finances, operations, and their role in facilitating the 2020 election. DeJoy also donated $1.24 million to campaign committees that supported Trump. DeJoy did make small donations in the past to Democrats, including Walter Mondale, Massachusetts governor Michael Dukakis, and Rep. Charles Rangel, D-N.Y.

While DeJoy was the first postmaster general since 1992 without experience in Postal Service operations, he touted his time utilizing USPS as a contractor during his reign at the helm of New Breed Logistics, which he took from a small transportation company to a large logistics firm that employs thousands. DeJoy also cited among his qualifications for the position his time in supply chain leadership with XPO Logistics, the firm that acquired New Breed Logistics.

Chronology of Action on General Government

2017–2018

Debate in the 115th Congress centered largely on two specific areas: regulatory reform and the federal workforce. While overhauling federal regulations was championed by President Trump, Congress often found itself at odds with the White House when it came to provisions dealing with the civilian workforce. Those differences became readily apparent in late 2018 when President Trump signed an executive order freezing worker pay at the same time as the two chambers were negotiating a fiscal year 2019 appropriations bill that included a 1.9 percent pay raise. Congress ultimately won out, but only after a thirty-five-day federal government shutdown—the longest in history—predicated on Trump's demand for billions of dollars to fund a wall along the U.S.–Mexico border. Two issues that previous Congresses sought to address—modernizing the Internal Revenue Service (IRS) and overhauling Postal Service operations to plug a massive funding shortfall—were considered in both chambers but fell short of the support necessary to make it to the president's desk.

Regulatory Accountability

When President Trump took office, he promised to eliminate Obama era regulations covering everything from drug testing unemployment insurance beneficiaries to dumping mining waste to oil and gas operations on federal lands to prepaid debit card fee disclosure. The business community, led by the U.S. Chamber of Commerce, rallied around the idea, noting that lifting regulations across multiple sectors would provide critical support for job creation and innovation, which they believed had been stifled by the Obama administration. After Trump took office, Republicans in Congress relied on the Congressional Review Act—a 1996 law that allows Congress to reverse a regulatory action with a simple majority so long as it does so within sixty days of when the regulation was submitted to Congress—to overturn fourteen regulations. And, in one of the first acts of the 115th Congress, the House considered legislation that would add new requirements for federal agency rulemaking; the Senate did not follow suit.

House Action

On January 3, 2017, Rep. Robert Goodlatte, R-Va., introduced the Regulatory Accountability Act (HR 5), which would amend the Administrative Procedure Act to require that agencies base their rulemaking determinations on evidence, consider the legal authority under which the rule can be proposed, look for possible alternatives and weigh their costs and benefits, and analyze the significance of the problem the rule seeks to address. The bill also implemented advance reporting procedures for major rules (those with an annual economic cost of $100 million or more) and high-impact rules (those with a cost to the economy of $1 billion or more), rules that involve certain legal or policy issues, and those that could have a negative impact on wages or jobs.

On January 9, the House Rules Committee reported out the rule under which debate on HR 5 would proceed, providing for consideration of sixteen amendments. The full House debated the amendments on January 11, easily rejecting nine proposed by Democrats, most of which sought to exempt certain regulations from the bill's provisions. These included one from Rep. Nydia Velazquez, D-N.Y., to remove provisions related to small businesses and require in-depth analyses of a rule's impact on small businesses. Another, from Rep. Debbie Castor, D-Fla., would have exempted certain rules intended to protect public health, such as those that reduce the incidence of cancer. Also rejected was an amendment from Rep. David Cicilline, D-R.I., to exempt rules related to the transmission of foodborne illness. An amendment from Rep. Hank Johnson, D-Ga., to exempt rules focused on improving employment, employee retention, and wages, especially for individuals with significant barriers to employment, was also rejected.

The House voted down an amendment from Rep. Raul Ruiz, D-Calif., to exempt rules pertaining to the safety of products and toys for children, and one from Rep. Robert Scott, D-Va., to exempt rules related to on-the-job health and safety. Another rejected amendment came from Rep. Paul Tonko, D-N.Y., and would exempt rules made under the 2016 Frank R. Lautenberg Chemical Safety for the 21st Century Act, while one from Rep. Raul Grijalva, D-Ariz., would eliminate the bill's provisions requiring that the Forest Service and Bureau of Land Management conduct analyses on the impact of small businesses before proposing rules dealing with land management plans. Shortly before the chamber voted on HR 5, the House rejected, 190–233, Democratic Florida Rep. Val Deming's motion to recommit—a procedural tool giving members a final opportunity to review and amend legislation—to the House Judiciary Committee requesting they report back with an amendment exempting rules that significantly lower the out-of-pocket cost to seniors for Medicare Part D prescription drugs.

The House adopted seven amendments during debate, all but one of which were proposed by Republicans. These included Rep. Goodlatte's amendment to prohibit a court from deferring to agency interpretation if, during review, it identifies a gap or ambiguity in a rule. It was adopted 237–185. Another amendment, from Rep. Steve Chabot, R-Ohio, was adopted by voice vote and required that agencies include economic assessments with their claims that a proposed rule would not significantly impact many small entities. Also adopted by voice vote was an amendment from Rep. Jason Chaffetz, R-Utah, requiring the issuance of guidelines necessitated by the rule within 270 days. The House passed, 260–161, an amendment from Rep. Collin Peterson, D-Minn., banning federal agencies from seeking public advocacy support for or opposition to a proposed rule. Another amendment, approved by voice vote, was proposed by Rep. Garret Graves, R-La., and would require agencies to compile reports every five years looking retrospectively at rules with an economic impact of more than $1 billion, their costs, and their benefits. An amendment from Rep. David Young, R-Iowa, passed by voice vote and would provide ninety days after a rule is issued for entities to comply. Florida Republican Bill Posey's amendment, which would require agencies to report on influential scientific information provided by the agency during the rulemaking process, also passed by voice vote.

As amended, the House passed HR 5 by a vote of 238–183. The Senate did not consider the measure during the 115th Congress.

Unfunded Mandates Information and Transparency

In another bid to address federal regulations, Republicans in Congress introduced a measure that would require certain agencies to report on any unfunded mandates imposed on the private sector or state and local government as a result of proposed regulations. According to Republicans, such a requirement gives the public and Congress more information on the impact of regulations. Democrats, on the other hand, argued that it would stall the regulatory process and could prevent important health and safety regulations from being enacted.

House Action

Rep. Virginia Foxx, R-N.C., introduced HR 50, the Unfunded Mandates Information and Transparency Act, on January 3, 2017. Among other things, HR 50 would require the Congressional Budget Office (CBO), if asked to do so by the leadership of a congressional committee, to assess the funding authorized for a certain piece of legislation against the costs of carrying out the required changes imposed on state, local, or tribal governments. It would also require agencies to analyze the prior impact of an existing regulation, when requested by the leadership of a congressional standing or select committee.

The House Oversight and Government Reform Committee held its markup of HR 50 on March 15, 2018. The committee adopted one amendment from Rep. Foxx, by voice vote, which authorized $1.5 billion annually from fiscal year 2018 through fiscal year 2024 for the CBO to cover the cost of carrying out the bill's provisions. The full bill was favorably reported to the House, as amended, 20–10.

On July 10, the House Rules Committee met to approve its rule governing floor debate of HR 50. The rule allowed for one hour of general debate on the measure and the consideration of four amendments. The full House took up the bill on July 13. During debate, the chamber rejected two amendments and adopted one, all by voice vote. The adopted amendment was proposed by Rep. Jamie Raskin, D-Md., and would require an agency to post online a record of any comments submitted by a nonfederal entity in response to a proposed regulation, or any record of a consultation with a nonfederal entity, within five days of the occurrence. One rejected amendment, from Rep. Watson Coleman, D-N.J., would strike language from the bill requiring independent agencies to comply with the bill's reporting requirements. Another rejected amendment, from Rep. Gerald Connolly, D-Va., would repeal all the bill's provisions if the U.S. gross domestic product did not increase at an average annual rate of 5 percent or more within one year of the bill's enactment. The House also rejected, 180–219, a motion to recommit from Rep. Joyce Beatty, D-Ohio, that would ask the House Oversight and Government Reform Committee to report back with an amendment exempting from the provisions any agencies responsible for protecting victims of domestic violence, assisting with background checks for school employees, protecting individuals against rape and sexual assault, and protect-

ing children from sex offenders. The full House passed HR 50, as amended, on July 13, 230–168.

Senate Action

On September 26, 2018, the Senate Homeland Security and Governmental Affairs Committee marked up HR 50. The committee considered one amendment, from Sen. Mike Enzi, R-Wyo., that would require the CBO, when possible, to study certain policies dealing with federal grant aid. It was adopted by voice vote. The committee voted 9–6 to send HR 50, as amended, to the floor, but the full Senate did not consider the bill during the 115th Congress.

Cutting Burdensome Regulations

Among Republicans' attempts to cut federal regulations was a bill that would create a commission to review existing regulations and determine which could be repealed or rolled back. This commission would be tasked with reducing the cost of federal regulation by 15 percent. The House passed a similar measure during the previous Congress, but it did not make it to the president's desk. The 2017 bill suffered a similar fate. While the House passed it along party lines, the Senate did not take it up.

House Action

On February 9, Rep. Jason Smith, R-Mo., introduced the Searching for and Cutting Regulations that are Unnecessarily Burdensome (SCRUB) Act (HR 998). The measure would establish a commission tasked with reviewing existing regulations to recommend which could be eliminated or reduced. One provision of the bill would give agencies the authority to determine how they want to cut regulations, but they would not be allowed to issue any new ones until they could eliminate those estimated to have the same cost as a proposed regulation. The bill also prohibited an agency from reissuing a rule if something similar had already been repealed or which would, after careful review, result in the same negative impact as something already rescinded. The nine-person commission charged with reviewing regulations, members of which would be appointed by the president and confirmed by the Senate, would end after five and a half years.

On February 14, the House Oversight and Government Reform Committee considered HR 998. According to committee Republicans, the purpose of the bill was to eliminate overly burdensome regulations, especially those that harm small businesses or prevent interested companies from entering the market. Democrats contended that the bill would leave agencies looking to implement emergency regulations hamstrung, while giving an unelected commission authority over an agency's areas of purview. Republicans countered that

while the commission could make recommendations on which regulations should be eliminated, Congress would have to pass a joint resolution before the agency would be formally required to strike it. Democratic attempts to exempt certain regulations from the commission's oversight—including those related to lead poisoning, whistleblowers, and the Clean Air Act—were rebuffed by Republicans, and ultimately the measure was advanced to the full House, 22–17.

On February 27, the House Rules Committee granted a structured rule for debate, providing for debate on twelve amendments, including those that would require the commission to consider a rule's impact to public health before recommending it for repeal, ban funding from being used to cover the cost of the bill, and exempt rules related to the relationship between federal and tribal governments as well as those that protect whistleblowers.

The House opened debate on February 28, adopting three amendments. These included one to bar anyone who was a registered lobbyist in the previous two years from serving on the committee. Another required the commission to consider the public health impact of regulation repeal, and one called on the commission to determine whether a regulation recommended for repeal had been submitted to Congress as required under the Congressional Review Act.

On the same day, the House rejected four amendments, including three that attempted to exempt certain types of rules from commission review, such as those governing airport noise restrictions, those related to national airspace system safety, and those that deal with the physical and cybersecurity of the bulk power system. The House also rejected an amendment that would remove a provision providing up to $30 million to carry out the bill and banning the use of other authorized or appropriated funds from being used to pay for the bill.

The House convened again on March 1 to continue its work on HR 998. The House rejected an additional five amendments that all sought to exempt certain rules from the commission's purview. This included those that protect whistleblowers from retaliation, those related to federal obligations to tribal governments and that support tribal sovereignty, those related to Clean Air Act enforcement, those providing financial assistance to education agencies that support children from low-income families, and those that provide consumer protections to student loan borrowers. The House also rejected, 190–235, a motion to recommit the bill to the House Oversight and Government Reform Committee asking it to report back with an amendment exempting laws governing bribery, and conflict of interest and financial disclosures for employees of the executive branch.

The full House passed the measure, as amended, on March 1, 2017, 240–185. The Senate did not consider it during the 115th Congress.

OVERTURNING OBAMA-ERA REGULATIONS

Perhaps one of the biggest achievements during Trump's early days in the White House was overturning more than one dozen regulations. Relying on the rarely used Congressional Review Act (PL 104-121), or CRA, Congress rescinded fourteen regulations, thirteen that were approved during the Obama administration and one enacted during Trump's first year in office. According to the White House, the termination of these regulations would save a combined $10 billion over the next two decades.

The CRA was enacted in 1996 and gives lawmakers the opportunity to overturn final rules issued by federal agencies with just a simple majority vote, so long as they do so within sixty legislative days of when the regulation was finalized (a provision within the law also gives an incoming Congress the chance to review the last sixty days of rules issued during the prior session). If Congress is successful in its attempt to block a regulation, not only is that regulation nullified, but an agency is also prevented from proposing a new regulation that is substantially similar unless Congress gives it the authority to do so. Prior to 2017, Congress only once successfully blocked a regulation, in 2001. They made five attempts to do so during Obama's two terms, but the president vetoed each one.

President Trump campaigned specifically on eliminating federal regulations that he saw as overly burdensome and a detriment to business innovation, economic growth, and job creation. During an October 2016 town hall event in New Hampshire, Trump told those gathered that he believed 70 percent of existing regulations could likely be repealed. According to his campaign staff, if elected Trump would specifically target regulations related to banking and finance, as well as those dealing with environmental protection.

During Trump's first year in office, Congress made fifteen attempts to repeal regulations through the CRA and was successful in fourteen of them. The one regulation they did not eliminate, which was enacted to make it more difficult and costly to develop oil and gas on federal lands, failed after Sens. John McCain, R-Ariz., Lindsey Graham, R-S.C., and Susan Collins, R-Maine, voted with Democrats against repeal.

In February, President Trump signed three CRA-driven regulatory repeals. One eliminated a Securities and Exchange Commission rule requiring that any company developing oil, natural gas, or minerals make public any payments of $100,000 or more per year per project to foreign governments or the federal government. Trump signed the repeal on February 14 (PL 115-4). Another did away with an Interior Department rule requiring coal companies to restore mined areas to their previous use and avoid any activity that would pollute streams or drinking water sources, or that increased the risk of floods or forest

damage. It was signed into law on February 16, 2017 (PL 115-5). Less than two weeks later, on February 28, the president also signed a repeal of a Social Security Administration rule that would add information on mentally impaired individuals who receive Social Security benefits to the list of those prohibited from buying guns (PL 115-8).

On March 27, Trump signed four regulatory repeals. One required any company bidding on a federal government contract valued at more than $500,000 to disclose allegations of labor law violations (PL 115-11), and another amended Bureau of Land Management procedures designed to increase transparency and solicit more public comment (PL 115-12). Two others were targeted at Education Department rules. One required states to evaluate and make public an annual report on the effectiveness of teacher training programs (PL 115-14), and another dealt with the accountability states use when measuring school performance (PL 115-13).

On April 3, President Trump rescinded an Interior Department prohibition on non-subsistence hunting and trapping that takes place on Alaska's national wildlife refuges (PL 115-20) and also eliminated a Federal Communications Commission rule that required internet service providers to get permission from customers before selling their personal information or internet browsing history to advertisers (PL 115-22). Ten days later, the president's signature negated a Health and Human Services Department rule banning states from denying federal family planning funds to Planned Parenthood and other health organizations that provide abortions (PL 115-23). On the latter, Vice President Mike Pence was called in to break a 50–50 tie in the Senate.

Four Labor Department rules were also rescinded in 2017. The first eliminated a Labor Department rule limiting when a state is permitted to test an unemployment benefit applicant for drug use (PL 115-17). Another repealed a rule exempting some local government-administered retirement savings plans from certain federal regulations (PL 115-24). A related rule that Congress opted to eliminate relaxed standards on states automatically enrolling private sector workers into state-administered retirement savings plans (PL 115-35). One additional Labor Department regulation eliminated under the CRA provided the Occupational Safety and Health Administration up to five and a half years to issue a citation to an employer that was not keeping records of serious injuries and illnesses for five years (PL 115-21).

Of the fourteen successful CRA repeals, one, the last passed in 2017, dealt with a regulation approved during Trump's tenure. It nullified the Consumer Financial Protection Bureau (CFPB) prohibition on mandatory arbitration clauses in consumer contracts. Often, companies

add such language to dissuade consumers from joining class-action lawsuits. The House voted largely along party lines to repeal the provision, but in the Senate Vice President Pence had to step in to break a 50–50 tie after Sens. Lindsey Graham, R-S.C., and John Kennedy, R-La., sided with Democrats. Trump signed the repeal into law on November 1, 2017 (PL 115-74).

The House made other separate attempts, outside of the CRA, to repeal regulations, though their success was more limited. One that made it to Trump's desk rescinded two Department of Transportation rules requiring that metropolitan planning organizations in one urban area either merge into a single organization or produce unified plans. Because Congress eliminated this regulation without using

the CRA, the department was left with the option of introducing a similar rule in the future. President Trump signed the recission on May 12 (PL 115-33). Other proposals did not clear both chambers. These included measures to eliminate specific National Labor Relations Board (NLRB) rules, such as one that lets workers file a petition to unionize and then hold their election in as few as eleven days later and another that would exempt Native American tribes and their businesses from NLRB jurisdiction.

The president also used his executive authority to block the enactment of regulations and review those already in effect. The result of these executive orders was mixed because undoing existing rules is a cumbersome and time-consuming process for federal agencies.

VA Accountability and Whistleblower Protection

In 2014, whistleblowers at the Department of Veterans Affairs (VA) exposed serious issues in the timely delivery of care to veterans. Some individuals were waiting months to see a doctor, at times dying before they could access life-saving testing or treatment. To avoid scrutiny, certain VA facilities were covering up these problems by keeping appointments off the books.

Since the scandal broke, Congress took multiple steps to improve the quality of care provided to veterans. In 2017, this work included passing new protections for whistleblowers and new authorities to demote or suspend VA employees for performance or misconduct issues. S 1094, the Department of Veterans Affairs Accountability and Whistleblower Protection Act, passed the House and Senate by overwhelming margins in early June and was signed by President Trump on June 23, 2017 (PL 115-41).

Senate Action

On May 24, 2017, the Senate Veterans Affairs Committee considered S 1094, introduced by Sen. Marco Rubio, R-Fla. The measure would establish an Office of Accountability and Whistleblower Protection within the VA, overseen by the assistant secretary for accountability and whistleblower protection. This office would be responsible for receiving information from whistleblowers; investigating misconduct, retaliation, and performance issues; and tracking any recommendations made in regard to whistleblower activities. These portions of the bill were intended to protect whistleblowers from retaliation while also providing training to supervisors on how to handle employees and their whistleblower filings.

As introduced, the bill also revised the VA's authority to suspend, remove, or demote employees or senior executives for performance or misconduct issues. Any individual removed from VA service who was later convicted of a felony related to their performance could have their annuity payment reduced. The measure would also give the VA the authority to recoup other monies from the former employee, such as bonuses, relocation expenses, or monetary awards. The VA was required to give any employee or executive advance notice of disciplinary action to provide them time to appeal the decision.

During markup, the committee considered five amendments, all of which were rejected by voice vote. One, proposed by Sen. Sherrod Brown, D-Ohio, would strike a provision in the bill allowing an administrative judge to uphold the secretary of the VA's decision about whether an employee should be demoted, suspended, or removed, if that decision was made due to evidentiary standards.

Sen. Richard Blumenthal, D-Conn., proposed two amendments. One dealt with annuity payments for VA employees removed from their jobs for performance or misconduct issues. Under Blumenthal's amendment, only those employees who were convicted of a felony related to their conduct would have their annuity payment reduced; individuals would be able to appeal any reduction to the Office of Personnel Management. Additionally, all VA employees would be subject to a thirty-day probationary period, the VA secretary would be required to create an annual performance plan for political appointees, and anyone whose employment was terminated by the VA would be barred from receiving payment from a federal contract for two years after their termination date. Blumenthal's other amendment would strip language from the bill related to annuity penalties.

Sen. Patty Murray, D-Wash., also proposed two amendments. One sought to give administrative judges the authority to uphold the VA secretary's decision to remove, demote, or suspend an employee if there was substantial evidence and the situation was considered a grievous

offense. Further, the measure called on the secretary of the VA to create a group that would recommend guidelines as to which types of misconduct qualify as egregious offenses. Murray also proposed a substitute amendment, replacing the existing bill language with that which would create an Office of Accountability and Whistleblower Protection within the VA to advise on accountability and whistle-blower disclosure. Among other things, this office would be led by an assistant secretary who would be appointed by the president. The new office would report to the House and Senate Veterans Affairs Committees on its activities throughout the year and would remain outside the report-ing chain of the VA's inspector general. The bill was reported favorably out of committee by voice vote on May 24, and the full Senate passed the measure by voice vote on June 6.

House Action

On June 12, the House Rules Committee passed its rules package for floor consideration of S 1094, and the full House took up the bill the next day. It easily passed the chamber 368–55. President Trump signed the bill on June 23, 2017 (PL 115-41).

Whistleblower Protection Act

The House and Senate in 2017 also passed stronger whistleblower protections for all federal agencies. S 585, the Dr. Chris Kirkpatrick Whistleblower Protection Act, would strengthen prohibitions that ban federal agencies from retaliating against whistleblowers. It passed both the House and Senate unanimously, and was signed by President Trump on October 26, 2017 (PL 115-73).

Senate Action

On March 8, 2017, Sen. Ron Johnson, R-Wisc., intro-duced S 585, named after Chris Kirkpatrick who in 2009 committed suicide after he was fired from his position as a psychologist at a VA facility in Tomah, Wisconsin. Before his death, Kirkpatrick reported the overmedication of patients at his facility. He was subsequently given a written reprimand and cautioned against criticizing other medical providers. Kirkpatrick was later fired from his position, which his union representative believed was related to his statements about overmedication and the facility's failure to properly discharge a potentially dangerous patient.

Johnson's bill sought to eliminate retaliation against people such as Kirkpatrick not only at the VA but across the federal government. His bill protected employees who disclose instances of fraud, waste, and abuse by requiring that federal agencies create penalties for super-visors who retaliate against their employees. Any super-visor found to have retaliated against a whistleblower would be suspended for at least three days on their first offense, and could be fired for their second offense. Supervisors would be provided fourteen days to appeal

the decision to their agency head, who could determine whether the punishment should stand. Johnson included in the bill language specifically calling on the VA to take steps to protect its employee's medical records and per-sonal safety.

On March 15, the Senate Homeland Security and Governmental Affairs Committee marked up the bill just off the Senate floor, rather than in its committee meeting room, due to an upcoming floor vote on an unrelated mea-sure. The bill was reported favorably to the Senate as part of an en bloc vote. The full Senate passed S 585 by unani-mous consent on May 25, 2017.

House Action

On October 10, the House Rules Committee consid-ered the package governing debate on S 585. The commit-tee declined to advance three amendments for floor debate. One would, among other things, provide supervi-sors thirty days advance written notice of any proposed disciplinary action, and prohibit an agency head from both proposing disciplinary action against a supervisor and deciding on the final action against that individual. Another amendment specifically addressed cases in which a whistleblower later committed suicide. The amendment would have required permission from the whistleblower's next of kin before any information related to the whistle-blower's allegation could be disclosed to the Office of the Special Counsel. The third amendment would have cre-ated a system to track how retaliation complaints are resolved. The final rule passed by the committee provided for one hour of general debate, split between the chair and ranking member of the House Oversight and Government Reform Committee, and prohibited consideration of any amendments.

During floor debate on October 12, Rep. Tom O'Halleran, D-Ariz., raised a motion to recommit the bill to the House Oversight and Government Reform Committee with a specific instruction that the committee report back on the bill with a new amendment that would add language extending the bill's provisions to any whistle-blower complaints about the violation of any law or regula-tion related to travel by an agency head or political appointee. The motion was rejected 190–232.

The full House went on to approve S 585, 420–0. President Trump signed the bill into law on October 26, 2017 (PL 115-73).

Federal Employee Antidiscrimination Act

Through various laws, regulations, and policies, the fed-eral government bans discrimination in its hiring and employment practices. In 2017, the House sought to expand on the existing prohibitions to require agencies to better track discrimination complaints and adjudication. The bill was never taken up by the Senate during the 115th Congress.

House Action

Rep. Elijah Cummings, D-Md., a stalwart supporter of antidiscrimination legislation, introduced the Federal Employee Antidiscrimination Act (HR 702) on January 27, 2017. The measure would require federal agencies to post on their websites any discrimination findings for at least one year. The notice must include certain details about the finding, such as the laws violated, and information for employees on their rights and protections available in cases of discrimination. Under the bill, federal agencies were provided sixty days from a final decision made on the discriminatory action or appellate decision issued by the Equal Employment Opportunity Commission (EEOC) to indicate whether disciplinary action had been initiated against the employee found in violation of antidiscrimination laws or policies.

Additionally, federal agencies were required to develop a system to track discrimination complaints and the conclusion of each case, and note on an employee's personnel record if an adverse action was taken and why. Federal agencies would also be called on to create Equal Employment Opportunity Programs to ensure complaints are fairly resolved, and the EEOC would be directed to refer discrimination findings to the Office of Special Counsel which could then pursue disciplinary action.

The measure was reported favorably by the House Oversight and Government Reform Committee, by voice vote, on February 2, 2017. The House passed it by voice vote on July 11, 2017. The Senate did not consider the bill.

Fairness for Breastfeeding Mothers

In 2017, the House passed—but the Senate did not consider—a bill to expand federal regulations ensuring that certain public buildings contain rooms for all nursing mothers, both employees and visitors.

House Action

Under existing law, federal buildings are required to have lactation rooms available for employees. On February 16, 2017, Rep. Eleanor Holmes Norton, D-D.C., introduced the Fairness for Breastfeeding Mothers Act (HR 1174) to expand existing provisions and ensure that all visitors to federal buildings have access to nursing rooms. According to the language of the bill, certain federal buildings that are open to the public and contain public restrooms must make available a space for mothers to nurse unless the building does not currently have a lactation room for employees, does not have available space that could be easily repurposed at a reasonable cost, or if a new space would need to be constructed and the cost of doing so would not be feasible. Federal buildings would not be permitted to use a restroom as a lactation room. Additionally, the room made available must be hygienic, shielded from public view, free from possible intrusion, and contain a chair, working surface, and electrical outlet (assuming the building has electricity).

The House Transportation and Infrastructure Committee agreed to the measure by voice vote on February 28, 2017, sending it to the full House for consideration. On March 7, 2017, the House approved the measure by voice vote. The Senate did not take up the bill during the 115th Congress.

Postal Service Reform

In an attempt to shore up United States Postal Service (USPS) finances, the House in 2017 passed legislation that would overhaul operations and employee benefits. Similar legislation was reported out of a House committee during the 114th Congress, but it never advanced beyond that. The measure considered in 2017, which according to the Congressional Budget Office (CBO) could reduce USPS costs by $6 billion over ten years, suffered a similar fate.

House Action

The USPS, a quasi-governmental entity, receives less than 1 percent of its annual funding from federal appropriations. Instead, it generates revenue from postage sales and the various services it offers. As technology has evolved and more communications move online, revenue from regular mail has steadily declined. Although package volume has increased, it hasn't done enough to keep USPS operating in the black. In 2006, Congress compounded the existing financial issues when it passed legislation requiring USPS to prefund anticipated retiree health care expenses by incrementally putting $56 billion into a prepaid account over the course of a decade. The intent was to protect taxpayers from shoring up any future unfunded liability. Yet the Postal Service quickly found itself unable to keep up with payments. These issues culminated in a massive budget shortfall, with fiscal year 2018 marking the Postal Service's twelfth consecutive year of net losses.

For its part, USPS has implemented changes to address its funding gap. For example, it slated for removal some sorting machines and large blue mailboxes with low usage. USPS has also recommended ending Saturday mail delivery, though Congress blocked the move, and it continues to increase the price of some mail pieces.

Over the years, Congress has also considered legislation to prevent ongoing financial strain on the Postal Service. Past bills have recommended five-day rather than six-day mail delivery, phasing out doorstep delivery, and allowing post offices to close based on low earnings. None, however, made it to the president's desk. When President Trump, a longtime critic of the Postal Service, took office, he pushed Congress to act, even going so far as recommending that USPS be privatized.

On January 31, 2017, Rep. Jason Chaffetz, R-Utah, made another attempt to address USPS shortcomings, introducing the Postal Service Reform Act (HR 756),

which was cosponsored by a bipartisan coalition of Democrats and Republicans. Under Chaffetz's bill, the Office of Personnel Management (OPM) would create Federal Employees Health Benefits plans specifically for USPS employees, annuitant retirees, and their families. Additionally, eligible retirees would be enrolled in Medicare and the portion USPS pays for their insurance premiums would decrease over time. The annual prefunding payments would also be recalculated each year.

Operationally, language was included in the bill that would allow USPS to raise first-class mail stamp prices by one cent, which the Postal Service said would have a significant impact on its finances. The bill would permit USPS to phase out doorstep delivery over time, instead pushing customers to centralized delivery addresses where mailboxes are grouped; however, for residential customers, that provision would require their consent. Before closing a post office, USPS would need to solicit feedback from customers and consider how easily customers can access other locations and the extent to which broadband and mobile service is available in the area.

The House Oversight and Government Reform Committee held its markup on March 16, 2017. Ranking member Rep. Elijah Cummings, D-Md., who also cosponsored the bill, encouraged committee members to refrain from offering too many amendments, fearing that attaching additional language to the bill, which had broad bipartisan support, could derail passage in the full House. Rep. Darrell Issa, R-Calif., ignored that recommendation and introduced four amendments. One, which was opposed by both Chaffetz, the committee's chair, and Cummings, would require the Postal Service to move to five-day delivery if it failed to reach a 2 percent net sales profit. Another would end doorstep delivery if 40 percent of a neighborhood's residents opted for centralized delivery; the remaining 60 percent of residents would have to request doorstep delivery each year. Another Issa amendment would move to centralized delivery if USPS failed to meet the 2 percent net sales profit threshold. All three amendments were withdrawn because Issa was unable to draw enough support. By voice vote, the committee rejected Issa's fourth amendment, which would push USPS to centralized delivery if it did not break even.

The committee did adopt two amendments, one, a substitute amendment that made technical changes to the bill, and another that required USPS to alert members of Congress if it planned to close a post office in the member's district. By voice vote, the committee advanced HR 756 to the full House. The same day, the committee also advanced HR 760, the Postal Service Financial Improvement Act. The bill, proposed by Rep. Stephen Lynch, D-Mass., would direct the Department of the Treasury to invest one-quarter of the Postal Service Retiree Health Benefits Fund into higher-yield securities. At the time, Treasury was only permitted to select low-yield Treasury-backed investments.

Despite strong committee support, both HR 756 and HR 760 were unable to generate enough backing in the full House for a floor vote in either 2017 or 2018. In the Senate, where Sen. Thomas Carper, D-Del., proposed a bill to make similar changes (S 2629), there was not enough agreement to even move the bill to a committee hearing.

Presidential Allowance Modernization

The House considered in late 2017 a measure that would change how much a former president earns annually after leaving the White House. The Senate never considered the bill during the 115th Congress.

House Action

Under the Former Presidents Act of 1958 (PL 85-745), after a president leaves office they are entitled to an annual pension that is equal to the base salary earned by a cabinet secretary that year ($226,300 in 2019 according to the Office of Personnel Management). They are also eligible for miscellaneous benefits, including office space and staff, travel expenses up to an annual cap, health benefits, and Secret Service protection.

On September 12, 2017, Rep. Jody Hice, R-Ga., introduced HR 3739, the Presidential Allowance Modernization Act, that sought to change how former presidents are compensated. Under the legislation, former presidents would receive an annual annuity of $200,000 per year, in addition to a monetary allowance set based on the number of years since the individual held office. For the five years beginning six months after the end of a president's term, they would receive $500,000 per year as an allowance, decreasing to $350,000 per year for the next five years, and $250,000 per year after that. Both the annuity and allowance would increase each year by the same percentage as Social Security benefits. Any former president whose earned income is more than $400,000 would have their allowance reduced dollar for dollar. In order to determine the allowance amount, former presidents would be required to provide to the Department of the Treasury a tax return or return information; the Treasury would not be permitted to use this information for any other means. If a former president holds a new elected or appointed office, benefit payments would temporarily stop, and all benefit payments would end thirty days after the former president's death.

Aside from the annuity, the bill limited a former president to monetary coverage for no more than thirteen office staff, and office space expenses would be reimbursable. The measure would also change existing coverage for the surviving spouse of a former president. Currently, spouses are eligible for a monetary allowance of $20,000 per year after the death of the former president; HR 3739 would increase this amount to $100,000 per year, with annual cost-of-living adjustments.

The House Oversight and Government Reform Committee reported the measure to the full House on September 13, 2017, and it passed by voice vote two months later, on November 13. The Senate never considered the bill.

Ensuring a Qualified Civil Service

Another piece of legislation concerning members of the federal workforce made changes to the probationary period for certain federal employees. Like many other measures considered during the 115th Congress, it passed the House but was never considered in the Senate.

House Action

In many cases, newly hired federal employees or supervisors complete a one-year probationary period during which their performance is assessed to determine whether they are the right person to fill the position. While in the probationary period, an employee or supervisor can be fired at any time, with few options for appeal.

Rep. James Comer, R-Ky., introduced a bill on October 31, 2017, that would extend the existing probationary periods for positions in the competitive service and Senior Executive Service from one year to two years. According to Comer, the Ensuring a Qualified Civil Service (EQUALS) Act (HR 4182) was intended to guarantee that those serving in certain positions were in fact the best people to fill the role. Democrats argued that the bill undermined the existing probationary regulations that protect employees from the politicization of their role or from being fired after becoming a whistleblower.

Under the bill's provisions, the two-year probationary period would apply to both those positions that require formal training or licensure as well as those that do not. Agencies would be required to make clear in a job posting the conditions of the probationary period, and those hired would be provided information on how to successfully complete their probationary period. Further, those overseeing someone on probation would be alerted no fewer than thirty days before the end of the probationary period, and certification would be made once an individual successfully completes the probationary period and is kept on as an employee.

On November 2, 2017, the House Oversight and Government Reform Committee held its markup of HR 4182. During debate, the committee considered one amendment, offered by Rep. Gerald Connolly, D-Va. Connolly's substitute amendment would require the Government Accountability Office (GAO) to conduct a study on agencies that have extended the probationary period from one to two years along with other probationary extensions for certain positions. The resulting report would be submitted to Congress within two years of the bill's enactment. The amendment was rejected by voice vote, and the committee went on to report the bill to the full house by a vote of 19–17.

The House took up the EQUALS Act on November 30 under a structured rule that allowed for consideration of a handful of amendments. One, from Rep. Alcee Hastings, D-Fla., would exempt from the lengthened probationary period anyone who had completed a term of service with organizations such as the Peace Corps or AmeriCorps. It was rejected 195–221. Connolly again tried to insert language requiring a GAO study, but it was turned down 193–223. Rep. Greg Gianforte, R-Mont., proposed an amendment that would require notification to those individuals in management and supervisory roles when the remaining time in the probationary period reaches one year, six months, three months, and thirty days. The amendment was adopted by voice vote.

The House passed HR 4182 on November 30, 2017, 213–204. The Senate took no action on the bill.

Secret Service Recruitment and Retention

When Trump assumed office, the Secret Service detail assigned to the president and his family frequently found themselves working overtime to cover trips to the family's residences in New Jersey and Florida along with overseas business and personal travel. At the time, the Secret Service was already facing a staffing crisis, due in part to compensation issues driven by overtime. The Treasury was prevented from paying Secret Service agents more, on a biweekly basis, than the GS-15 rate. This meant that agents working overtime were not compensated for those hours if it pushed them above the maximum allowable rate. In 2017, more than 1,000 agents were expected to exceed the cap. In turn, Congress passed legislation hoping to help entice more qualified individuals to join and remain with the Secret Service.

House Action

Seeking to address the attrition issue, on September 11, 2017, Rep. John Katko, R-N.Y., introduced the Secret Service Recruitment and Retention Act (HR 3731). The bill would extend through 2018 the Overtime Pay for Protective Services Act of 2016 (PL 114-311), which Congress passed to lift the pay cap for Secret Service agents assigned to presidential campaign detail, increasing the existing biweekly pay cap for agents.

The House Oversight and Government Reform Committee considered HR 3731 on September 13, 2017. Both Democrats and Republicans on the committee agreed that addressing the pay issue was critical for maintaining the Secret Service workforce. During markup, some members raised concerns that the Secret Service was incurring significant, unnecessary costs during the Trump presidency. But leadership on both sides of the aisle brushed those aside, noting that regardless of

who is in the White House, the Secret Service agents charged with protecting the president and their family should be fairly compensated for the hours they work. The committee favorably reported the bill to the full House by voice vote.

As passed out of committee, the bill would increase the maximum biweekly allowable pay for more than 1,000 Secret Service agents from the GS-15 level ($161,900 annually) to one step removed from the top of the Executive Schedule ($187,000 annually). Additionally, the bill required a report on multiple data points, including the impact of the increase, Secret Service recruiting and retention efforts, and details about Secret Service agents on detail to those other than the president. Under suspension of the rules, the full House passed HR 3731 by a vote of 407–4 on December 5, 2017.

Senate Action

On March 19, 2018, the Senate passed by unanimous consent a substitute amendment for HR 3731, then went on to pass the full bill, as amended, also by unanimous consent the same day. Because the language was amended in the Senate, the bill went back to the House, where it passed by unanimous consent on March 21, 2018. The president signed the overtime pay bill into law on April 3, 2018 (PL 115-160).

Social Security Fraud Prevention

In September 2017, President Trump signed into law legislation prohibiting federal departments and agencies from including an individual's Social Security number on any document sent by mail, unless it was determined that inclusion of the number was necessary.

House Action

At a time when an increasing number of Americans were facing data breaches, Congress acted to prevent Social Security numbers from accidentally falling into the wrong hands. On January 24, 2017, Rep. David Valadao, R-Calif., introduced HR 624, the Social Security Fraud Prevention Act. The bill would bar federal departments and agencies from including a person's Social Security number on any mailed documents. A provision allowed for departments and agencies to determine when inclusion of the number was important, and they were required to issue regulations indicating when this would be the case within one year of the bill's enactment.

The House Oversight and Government Reform Committee held its markup on February 14, 2017. It adopted by voice vote one substitute amendment, from Rep. Jason Chaffetz, R-Utah, extending from one year to five years the amount of time federal departments and agencies would have to comply with the new regulations. The committee favorably reported HR 624 to

the full House, as amended, by voice vote on February 14, 2017.

The measure passed the full House by voice vote on May 24, 2017. The Senate passed it by unanimous consent four months later, on September 6, 2017, and the president signed it into law on September 15, 2017 (PL 115-59).

Overhauling and Modernizing the IRS

The House in 2018 considered various pieces of legislation to modernize Internal Revenue Service (IRS) operations. While no single bill represented a full structural overhaul of the agency, members hoped that their work would begin laying the groundwork for future operational changes. These efforts in Congress came at a time when the taxation agency was already adjusting internal and public-facing procedures to implement the 2017 tax code overhaul (PL 115-97).

House Committee Action

On April 11, the House Ways and Means Committee held its consideration and markup of twelve IRS-related measures. One, HR 5444, the Taxpayer First Act, introduced by Rep. Lynn Jenkins, R-Kan., was a bipartisan package that would call on the IRS to create a portal for taxpayers to complete their 1099s online, allow the use of both credit and debit cards for tax payments, eliminate the IRS Oversight Board, and create new protections for certain low-income taxpayers that would prevent them from being referred to private debt collectors. The legislation also created a new Independent Office of Appeals within the IRS that would be tasked with reviewing administrative decisions and resolving tax controversies. It would also codify an existing program in which the IRS partners with private tax preparers to offer free services to certain low-income and elderly filers.

Another measure, HR 5445, the 21st Century IRS Act, introduced by Rep. Mike Bishop, R-Mich., included provisions to enhance IRS cybersecurity to better protect sensitive taxpayer information. The bill would require the IRS to establish public and private partnerships to help protect taxpayers from tax return fraud and would also call on the Electronic Tax Administration Advisory Committee to recommend ways to prevent fraud and identity theft. Language in the bill also directed the IRS to require more taxpayers to file their returns electronically, create an online platform for electronic 1099 filing, develop standards for accepting electronic signatures, and establish the IRS Chief Information Officer position, among other things.

There was broad bipartisan support for both HR 5444 and HR 5445—and the other ten measures considered by the committee on April 11, including those that would give Treasury Department employees the ability to advise

low-income filers of taxpayer clinics, require tax-exempt organizations to file electronic returns or statements, and direct the Treasury to create a program to provide personal identification numbers to any taxpayer who requests one when submitting their annual return. The friendly nature of the committee's work was a marked departure from the bitter battles that took place in 2017 when the committee was working on tax code overhaul legislation. The committee reported all the tax-related bills by voice vote.

House Floor Action

On April 18, the full House easily passed HR 5444, 414–0, and HR 5445, 414–3. As in committee, both Democrats and Republicans praised the legislation as a first step toward making the IRS more customer friendly and modernizing its systems. Democrats did express some concern that without additional funds, efforts to reshape the IRS could prove futile, but that would need to be dealt with through the appropriations process. The Senate never took up either HR 5444 or HR 5445.

In November, provisions from HR 5444 were added to a tax package (HR 88) that would extend certain tax cuts that had expired the year prior. That bill passed the House on December 20, 2018, 220–183. However, the Senate never took up the measure before the end of the 115th Congress.

Senate Action

On July 19, 2018, Sens. Orrin Hatch, R-Utah, and Ron Wyden, D-Ore., introduced their own tax modernization and taxpayer protection legislation. The bill reflected the House measures in many ways, but also included language that would allow IRS leadership to shift as much as $10 million in appropriated funds from one account to another specifically to prevent and address tax fraud. The Hatch-Wyden bill was never considered in a Senate committee.

Securing the International Mail Against Opioids Act

During the 115th Congress, the House considered dozens of bills to address various aspects of the opioid crisis, from treatment to housing to shipping drugs through the United States Postal Service (USPS). While many of these bills passed the House, few were considered in the Senate.

House Action

As part of its work on limiting the spread of dangerous opioid drugs such as fentanyl, on May 16, 2018, the House Ways and Means Committee advanced to the floor HR 5788, the Securing the International Mail Against Opioids Act. The bill, which was introduced by Rep. Mike Bishop, R-Mich., just one day earlier, would require that USPS provide to Customs and Border Protection (CBP) electronic data about the contents of packages sent from overseas and

a package's intended recipient. By December 31, 2018, USPS would need to provide this data for 70 percent of all international packages, increasing to 95 percent by December 31, 2022. Among other provisions, the bill would also call on CBP and USPS to work together to determine better ways to detect synthetic opioids and other harmful substances that are shipped through the mail. During markup, the committee approved one substitute amendment, which added a table of contents to the bill.

While seemingly benign, the bill faced opposition from a member of Bishop's own party. Sen. Rob Portman, R-Ohio, had introduced similar legislation in the Senate (S 372; a companion bill, HR 1057, was also introduced in the House), and argued that Bishop's bill did not do enough to allow law enforcement officials to intercept packages of synthetic drugs. Given the pushback, committee leaders met to reconcile the differences between Bishop's and Portman's bills to find something palatable to both chambers. The new language included stricter requirements for both USPS and CBP. Specifically, USPS would be required to refuse items for shipment that do not include the advance electronic data; civil penalties were established for acceptance of shipments without this information after 2020.

On June 12, the House Rules Committee granted a closed rule for debate on HR 5788. The rule included self-executing language changing the percentages of mail for which USPS must provide advance electronic data. By the end of 2018, USPS would still be required to submit the information for 70 percent of all packages coming from overseas, but 100 percent of shipments from China. And, by December 31, 2020, USPS must provide to CBP advance electronic data on 100 percent of all packages. There was an allowable carve out to the 100 percent provision, which would let CBP determine whether a country has the capacity to provide the required information, has a low volume of mail that could otherwise be screened in another way, and generally represents a low risk of violating U.S. laws. On June 14, 2018, the House voted 353–52 to pass the bill. It was sent to the Senate, where it did not receive a vote.

Fiscal Year 2018 Financial Services and General Government Appropriations

The fiscal year 2018 appropriations bill that funds multiple federal agencies, the White House, the Internal Revenue Service (IRS), the federal judiciary, and federal payments to the District of Columbia was wrapped into omnibus legislation that was not signed until halfway through the fiscal year. Negotiations were delayed for multiple reasons, including a lack of set discretionary spending levels, other congressional priorities, and late passage of fiscal 2017 appropriations. Congress passed a series of five

continuing resolutions (CR) to keep the government funded—and there was a brief three-day shutdown between the third and fourth CRs—before finally sending to President Trump a $1.3 trillion measure that he signed on March 23, 2018 (PL 115-141).

In the final bill, a $23.4 billion appropriation was slated for the Financial Services and General Government title for fiscal year 2018, up 9 percent from the prior fiscal year enacted level. Of that total, $11.4 billion would go toward the IRS, marking a rare budget increase for the agency, but one that legislators argued was necessary to help comply with the provisions of the 2017 tax overhaul (PL 115-97).

House Committee Action

On June 29, the House Financial Services Appropriations Subcommittee met to mark up its fiscal year 2018 appropriations bill (HR 3280) for the departments and agencies within its purview. Committee debate primarily centered on the 2010 Dodd-Frank financial regulatory law, election interference, and the General Services Administration (GSA) budget.

The $20.23 billion bill considered by the subcommittee included language from a House bill (HR 10) that would repeal Dodd-Frank, the legislation enacted after the 2008 financial crisis that overhauled financial regulation and established the Consumer Financial Protection Bureau (CFPB). Republicans have long seen the bill as an example of federal overreach and had been trying to undo its provisions since it became law. Subcommittee chair Rep. Tom Graves, R-Ga., noted during debate that he was "particularly excited about the financial reforms" that the fiscal 2018 appropriations bill included, which he said would help control what he viewed as the expensive and unaccountable CFPB.

Democrats raised concern about cuts to the Election Assistance Commission, which serves as the liaison between the Federal Bureau of Investigation and Department of Homeland Security, and which provides assistance to state and local governments to help them run accurate, secure elections. The appropriations measure would cut funding for fiscal 2018 from $9.6 million to $4 million. Democrats argued that the commission was even more important after Russian attempts to influence the outcome of the 2016 election. Republicans, however, noted that states are responsible for their own elections and the federal government does not need to spend money on something that is little more than a liaison. Rep. Mike Quigley, D-Ill., offered an amendment to restore the commission's funding to the $9.2 million included in the White House budget request, but it was defeated along party lines.

In total, the fiscal 2019 appropriations measure was $1.28 billion lower than the enacted fiscal 2017 level. The bulk of that cut was made to what GSA can spend on its Federal Buildings Fund, despite the agency asking for flat spending. According to Democrats, cuts to the GSA funds would put it even further behind on maintenance projects and new construction.

On July 13, the House Appropriations Committee held its markup of HR 3280, making multiple changes to the subcommittee's language. This included raising funding for the Election Assistance Commission to $7 million and inserting a manager's amendment to require the GSA to develop a plan within sixty days of the bill's enactment to consolidate the various FBI offices in the Washington, D.C., area into a single space. The committee maintained the large reduction in the GSA's Federal Buildings Fund and provided no funds for new construction.

During debate, Republicans rejected a number of amendments proposed by Democrats. This included one that would strike a provision preventing the IRS from enforcing the 2010 Patient Protection and Affordable Care Act (ACA) individual mandate that requires all Americans to have health insurance or face a penalty, and another that would have removed provisions in the bill that sought to roll back Dodd-Frank. Other Democratic amendments that did not pass included one to remove from the bill a provision denying funding to Washington, D.C., for abortion services unless the woman's life was in danger or in cases of rape or incest, another to restore funding to the Community Development Financial Institutions Program, and one eliminating language that would keep funds from the IRS in certain situations when determining the tax-exempt status of churches.

Ultimately, the committee approved the bill by a largely party line vote of 31–21, with only Rep. Henry Cuellar, D-Texas, joining all Republicans in support. The final bill passed out of committee provided $1.3 billion less than the fiscal 2017 omnibus legislation and was $2.5 billion below the president's budget request. The committee's bill would, among other things

- Maintain Treasury spending at the fiscal 2017 level
- Reduce by 8 percent federal payments to the District of Columbia
- Boost federal judiciary funds by 2 percent from fiscal 2017
- Cut funding to the Troubled Asset Relief Program inspector general by 10 percent and the IRS inspector general by 3 percent
- Cut Federal Communications Commission funding by 10 percent
- Stop the IRS from enforcing the individual mandate

House Floor Action

The full House did not take up the Financial Services and General Government appropriations measure as a stand-alone bill, opting instead to include it as part of a twelve-bill consolidated appropriations package. After two weeks of debate that included the consideration of 342 amendments, the $1.23 trillion omnibus legislation passed on September 14, 211–198. That total violated the 2011

Budget Control Act (PL 112-25) and, if enacted, would have triggered across-the-board spending cuts known as sequestration. While House Speaker Paul Ryan, R-Wisc., celebrated the bill's passage, noting that it was the first time since 2009 when the chamber had passed all its spending bills before the start of the fiscal year, it was unlikely to move in the Senate. There, Democrats objected to a number of the bill's policy riders and various funding levels.

Senate Action

The Senate Appropriations Committee did not release its draft Financial Services and General Government appropriations bill until November 20. Their bill would provide $20.8 billion to the agencies covered by the bill, $637 million less than the enacted fiscal 2017 level. Included in the draft bill was $11.1 billion for the IRS, $7.8 billion for the GSA, $7 billion for the federal judiciary, $1.8 billion for the Securities and Exchange Commission, $886.3 million for the Small Business Administration, $347 million for the Treasury Department, $322 million for the Federal Communications Commission, and $306 million for the Federal Trade Commission.

Democrats on the committee were opposed to language in the bill that would move CFPB's funding from the mandatory side of the ledger to the discretionary side and a provision to strike a portion of Dodd-Frank that prevents appropriators from intervening in CFPB's annual budget request. Democrats believed this would give Congress undue influence over the body and threaten its ongoing funding.

Notably not included in the Senate's draft legislation was a provision from the House bill that prohibited the IRS from enforcing the Patient Protection and Affordable Care Act (ACA) individual mandate. The committee did not hold a formal markup of the draft bill, nor was it considered by the full Senate.

Conference and Final Action

Between October 2017 and February 2018, Congress passed five CRs to keep the government funded. Between the third and fourth, funding lapsed for three days, prompting a brief federal government shutdown. The final stopgap measure, signed into law on February 9, 2018, gave Congress until March 23 to either reach an agreement on funding for the fiscal year or pass another CR.

Knowing that they would be unable to pass individual appropriations bills or smaller minibus packages, House and Senate appropriators combined all twelve regular appropriations bills into one omnibus package, which leadership attached as an amendment to HR 1625, an unrelated bill that had already passed both chambers, in order to expedite floor consideration. The $1.3 trillion omnibus measure passed the House on March 22, 256–167, and the Senate the following day, 65–32. President Trump signed it into law on March 23, 2018 (PL 115-141).

Within the massive, combined bill, the Financial Services and General Government title received $23.4 billion for fiscal year 2018. This marked a 9 percent increase over enacted fiscal 2017 levels, despite both the House and Senate proposing cuts to the spending bill's topline. In a rare move, Congress increased funding for the IRS, boosting it 2 percent above fiscal 2017 levels to $11.4 billion. The House and Senate agreed that this money was needed to help the IRS cover the cost of changing software and filing forms to comply with the 2017 tax code overhaul (PL 115-97). The final omnibus measure also gave $380 million to the Election Assistance Commission, specifically for grants to states to help them improve their election equipment and protect themselves from overseas interference, and maintained the large cuts to the GSA's Federal Buildings Fund. Additionally, the bill would provide

- $1.605 billion to the Securities and Exchange Commission
- $101 million for the Office of Management and Budget
- $7.1 billion to the federal courts
- $721 million for the District of Columbia

Fiscal Year 2019 Financial Services and General Government Appropriations

The fiscal year 2019 appropriations process began during the 115th Congress but stretched into the 116th Congress and resulted in a thirty-five-day federal government shutdown, the longest in history. It was not until February 15, 2019, that President Trump signed into law (PL 116-6) a seven-bill appropriation measure ·that included $23.42 billion in funding for the agencies covered by Financial Services and General Government appropriations.

House Committee Action

The House Financial Services Appropriations Subcommittee held its markup of the fiscal year 2019 spending bill on May 24, 2018 (HR 6258). The topline number in the bill—$23.4 billion—was nearly identical to that from fiscal 2018. Most agencies were set to receive the same funding from the year prior, while some funds were shifted around. Notable changes between fiscal 2018 and 2019 funding included the elimination of a $380 million fund that provides election assistance grants to states through the Election Assistance Commission and the creation of a new Fund for America's Kids and Grandkids. The latter became a lightning rod for Democrats in both the House and Senate. The program would set aside $585 million in funding that could only be used the year after the federal government has a surplus. While Republicans saw it as a means to encourage deficit neutrality, Democrats complained that it locked up money that could otherwise

go to critical needs. The subcommittee advanced the spending bill by voice vote.

The House Appropriations Committee took up HR 6258 on June 13. During markup, the committee considered twenty amendments. A number of those that were rejected dealt with policy riders popular with Republicans that have frequently found their way into the annual Financial Services appropriations measure. Democrats attempted to remove a provision barring the District of Columbia from using local revenue to cover the cost of abortion, which was rejected by voice vote. The committee also rejected amendments that would have restored the Federal Communication Commission's net neutrality rule, barred regulators from penalizing financial institutions that provide services to the marijuana industry, struck portions of the bill seeking to repeal Dodd-Frank, and allowed immigrants covered under the Deferred Action for Childhood Arrivals program to work for the federal government. Another rejected amendment would have added back the $380 million removed from the Election Assistance Commission to fund another year of grants for states. According to Republicans, ongoing grant funding in fiscal 2019 was unnecessary because more than one dozen states had yet to request funds from the fiscal 2018 set aside.

The final bill, which provided funding only $100,000 higher than the prior fiscal year, gave

- $11.62 billion to the IRS
- $735 million to the Executive Office of the President
- $7.27 billion to the federal judiciary
- $737 million to the District of Columbia
- $335 million to the Federal Communications Commission
- $737 million to the Small Business Administration
- $1.7 billion to the Securities and Exchange Commission

The House Appropriations Committee favorably reported the bill to the floor on June 13, 28–20.

House Floor Action

The House opted not to act on HR 6258 on its own, but rather bundled it with HR 6147, the fiscal year 2019 Interior–Environment appropriations bill. On July 16, the Rules Committee made in order eighty-seven amendments to the combined Interior–Environment and Financial Services spending bill, which was being brought to the floor as HR 6147. Among the seventeen amendments approved for floor debate related to the Financial Services title was one that would ban the United States Postal Service (USPS) from expanding its financial services offerings to more than money orders and international money transfers. Democrats were unhappy with the amendment, which was filed by Rep. Patrick McHenry, R-N.C., arguing that allowing USPS to provide additional banking services

would not only help shore up its long-running debt problem but also would make available services to low-income customers who otherwise turn to payday lenders.

The amendments debated on the $58.7 billion combined spending bill—of which $23.4 billion would go toward agencies covered by Financial Services and General Government appropriations—spanned two days. The McHenry USPS amendment was rejected 201–212. Adopted amendments included one that would bar the District of Columbia from enforcing parts of its Health Insurance Requirement Amendment Act and another stopping the district from using federal funds to seize property as it related to the district's health care insurance individual mandate.

The House passed the two-bill package 217–199 on July 19. The White House issued a Statement of Administration Policy on the measure, expressing concern that the House bill failed to adopt many spending cuts proposed by the administration. The House bill was $4 billion higher than the White House budget request for the agencies covered under the combined measure.

Senate Committee Action

On June 19, the Senate Financial Services and General Government Subcommittee held its hearing and markup of its version of the fiscal year 2019 Financial Services and General Government appropriations measure (S 3107). The committee's $23.7 billion discretionary spending plan was $3.2 billion less than the president requested and $16 million higher than the fiscal 2018 level. The slight difference in topline numbers between the House and Senate bills was primarily driven by the Commodity Futures Trading Commission, which the House funds through its Agriculture appropriations measure.

One of the biggest differences between the House and Senate spending bills was the amount spent on the IRS. The House bill sought to give the taxation agency $11.6 billion, or 2 percent more than was appropriated in fiscal year 2018, while the Senate wanted to provide $11.3 billion, a 1 percent decrease from the prior fiscal year. Much of the difference between the two bills came from higher spending in the House version on operations and business systems modernization. The Senate also proposed increasing funding by $1 billion for the General Service Administration (GSA) Federal Buildings Fund, much of which would go toward purchasing the Department of Transportation's headquarters in Washington, D.C. The department currently rents the space, and Sen. James Lankford, R-Okla., the subcommittee chair, said purchasing the campus could result in nearly $50 million in savings each year.

In addition to IRS and GSA spending, the Senate's Financial Services bill would provide

- $7.25 billion for the federal judiciary
- $728 million for the Executive Office of the President

- $310 million for the Federal Trade Commission
- $703 million for the District of Columbia
- $699 million for the Small Business Administration

Other language in the bill would

- Give the federal civilian workforce a 1.9 percent pay raise
- Prohibit any funds appropriated in the bill from giving a raise to the vice president or other senior political appointees
- Prohibit funds from going to paint portraits of federal employees
- Ban grants or contracts from going to those who have cheated on their taxes or those with felony criminal convictions

The committee reported the bill to the full Senate Appropriations Committee by voice vote. S 3107 never receive an Appropriations Committee vote and was never considered on the Senate floor.

Senate Floor Action

While S 3107 never received a vote, some of its provisions were included in a four-bill appropriations package, attached as a substitute amendment to HR 6147. In addition to the Financial Services title, the $154.2 billion bill included spending on the Transportation–HUD, Interior–Environment, and Agriculture bills. The topline was 29 percent more than the president requested for the agencies covered under the combined appropriation measure.

The Senate passed the spending package on August 1, 92–6. It marked the first time the full Senate had ever passed a Financial Services spending bill since the appropriations process was reorganized in 2007 and the Financial Services title was created. Its twelve failed attempts all resulted in the Financial Services appropriation being adopted as part of a year-end omnibus bill. Before final passage, the Senate adopted an uncontroversial en bloc amendment package, and also approved an amendment from Sen. Tammy Baldwin, D-Wisc., to provide $7 million for innovation and marketing programs related to dairy products. The Senate rejected an amendment that would have added $250 million in grants for states to help strengthen their election security systems. The chamber tabled an amendment to prohibit the District of Columbia from using funds appropriated in the bill to carry out its health insurance individual mandate. While the latter was scheduled for a vote, Senate Republican leadership sought to maintain a bipartisan spirit and keep riders likely to draw significant opposition out of the bill.

Conference and Final Action

When HR 6147 arrived in conference committee, negotiations stalled not on topline spending but on policy riders and the smaller pots of money that varied between the House and Senate bills. For example, while the House adopted the $585 million Fund for America's Kids and Grandkids, the Senate did not. Democrats in the Senate argued that it went against the fiscal 2019 budget agreement and prevented Congress from putting funds elsewhere, into programs that might save money in the long run. The House version of the bill would also allow President Trump to issue an executive order freezing civilian federal worker pay, while the Senate would provide a 1.9 percent pay raise.

Stalled negotiations forced Congress to pass two continuing resolutions to keep the government funded. The first provided appropriations until December 7, and the second until December 21. In that time, the House, Senate, and White House were unable to reach an agreement to either pass another CR or full fiscal year appropriations measures. The biggest challenge proved to be the wall along the U.S.–Mexico border that Trump promised to build once he assumed office. On the campaign trail, the president said that he would force Mexico to cover the cost, but when that money did not materialize, he instead looked to Congress to appropriate construction funds. For fiscal 2019, the president wanted $5.7 billion and announced that he would not sign any appropriations measure that did not include the money. In turn, funding for the federal government lapsed on December 22.

In January 2019, the 116th Congress began without funding for the federal government. While another stopgap ended the shutdown after thirty-five days, it was not until February 14 when both the House and Senate approved a seven-bill funding package that included the Financial Services and General Government title. The final bill appropriated $23.42 billion in discretionary funding to the agencies covered under this title. This included

- $12.7 billion for the Treasury Department, of which $11.3 billion was for the IRS
- $739 million for the Executive Office of the President
- $7.25 billion for the federal judiciary
- $726 million for the District of Columbia
- $339 million for the Federal Communications Commission
- $309.7 million for the Federal Trade Commission
- $1.67 billion for the Securities and Exchange Commission
- $715 billion for the Small Business Administration

The final bill also provided for a 1.9 percent pay raise for federal civilian employees and eliminated provisions that would have banned the District from using local revenue to implement certain local laws. The president signed the measure into law on February 15, 2019 (PL 116-6).

2019–2020

The 116th Congress was forced to make reopening the government and passing a fiscal year 2020 spending bill its first priority. Once they reached that milestone, the two chambers were able to move onto policy-related matters, though with Democrats controlling the House and Republicans holding the majority in the Senate, consensus was nearly impossible to reach and most legislation floated in 2019 never reached the president's desk.

The Postal Service took center stage during the second year of the 116th Congress. While in prior years the House and Senate searched for ways to address the long-running funding shortfall, in the wake of the COVID-19 pandemic and with the 2020 presidential election looming, focus shifted to maintaining operations at the level necessary to handle increasing mail volume. Again, however, the House and Senate found few areas in which they agreed, and no bills were signed into law.

Federal Civilian Workforce Pay Raise Fairness

During the thirty-five-day federal government shutdown that stretched from December 2018 into January 2019, tens of thousands of federal employees went without biweekly paychecks. Congress approved backpay for these workers, and as the checks began going out, the House was also looking for ways to give federal civilian workers a pay increase. During the 116th Congress, the House passed a 2.6 percent pay raise for most federal civilian employees, but the Senate never considered the bill.

House Action

On January 25, 2019, the same day the longest federal government shutdown in history came to an end, Rep. Gerald Connolly, D-Va., introduced a bill to increase by 2.6 percent the base pay for most federal civilian employees, matching a similar boost authorized for uniformed members of the military in 2018. As introduced, HR 790, the Federal Civilian Workforce Pay Raise Fairness Act, would also prohibit a pay increase for certain senior political appointees and the vice president. The bill would not limit other pay increases, such as bonuses, performance awards, or other similar monetary benefits offered to an employee.

Four days later, on January 29, the House Rules Committee approved, 8–4, a structured rule for debate of Connolly's measure. Democrats stated that the bill would help increase employee morale after the shutdown, while also bringing equality to civilian and military pay. Republicans on the Rules Committee raised two primary issues with the measure. First, that it should be more comprehensive and include provisions dealing with other aspects of federal employment, such as recruitment and retention. And, second, that it had not followed regular order by going through markup before being introduced to the full House.

The final rule approved by the committee included a self-executing amendment that would make the salary increase effective as of the date the bill was enacted, instead of retroactively. The amendment also struck from the bill language barring a pay increase for the vice president and certain senior political appointees. The final rule also made in order three amendments noting that employees of the Secret Service, Internal Revenue Service, and National Aeronautics and Space Administration would be eligible to receive the 2.6 percent pay increase. There was concern that the existing language of the bill did not cover those employees hired under special provisions at these three agencies.

The full House took up the bill on January 30. It adopted all three amendments approved for debate by the Rules Committee, and rejected 206–216 a motion to recommit from Rep. Susan Brooks, R-Ind., asking the House Committee on Oversight and Government Reform to report back with an amendment barring any government money from being used to fund a pay increase for someone disciplined for sexual misconduct on the job. As in the Rules Committee, while Republicans did not necessarily disagree with the idea of a pay raise, they did not like the speed with which it was rushed to the floor, and some of the chamber's most fiscally conservative questioned whether it made sense to allow government employees to earn more than those in the private sector performing similar jobs.

Ultimately, the House went on to pass the bill 259–161 on January 30, 2019. The Senate never considered the legislation.

In March, however, President Trump signed an executive order rescinding his earlier pay freeze and authorizing an across-the-board 1.4 percent pay increase for federal workers, with an additional 0.5 percent locality pay rate adjustment. The 1.9 percent raise was made retroactive to the first pay period of calendar year 2019. (Congress had already passed, and the president signed, the 1.9 percent pay increase as part of the fiscal year 2019 spending package; the executive order simply enacted it.)

Commission on the Social Status of Black Men and Boys

In May 2020, George Floyd died at the hands of Minneapolis, Minnesota, police as they attempted to arrest him for allegedly using a counterfeit $20 bill to buy cigarettes at a convenience store. Eyewitnesses shot a video of the confrontation between Floyd and police, which quickly

went viral, and which showed one officer, Derek Chauvin, kneeling on Floyd's neck for nearly nine minutes, during which time Floyd stopped breathing. Nationwide racial justice protests broke out, with participants demanding that police and government leaders do more to support communities of color and end racist police violence.

In Congress, both the House and Senate considered similar pieces of legislation that would establish a commission to study the issues that affect Black men and boys. The Senate version of the bill, S 2163, overwhelmingly passed both chambers and was signed by President Trump on August 14, 2020 (PL 116-156).

Senate Action

On June 25, 2020, the Senate Health, Education, Labor, and Pensions Committee discharged by unanimous consent S 2163, a bill introduced by Sen. Marco Rubio, R-Fla. The bill, which was modeled after a similar piece of legislation enacted in Florida, sought to create a body to study challenges facing Black men and boys in the United States. The Commission on the Social Status of Black Men and Boys would review the trends and consider issues including homicide rates, drug abuse, disparate income and wealth, school performance, poverty, violence, and incarceration rates. The nineteen-member commission would then create a publicly available report documenting their findings and the impact of government programs on these challenges.

The full Senate considered the measure the same day. It adopted one amendment, from Sen. Josh Hawley, R-Mo., that would ensure partisan parity on the commission by requiring the political party with fewer members on the commission to name additional participants. The Senate passed S 2163 as amended by unanimous consent on June 25, 2020.

House Action

After Floyd's death, Democrats in the House began talking about the possibility of bringing to the floor a bill initially proposed by Rep. Frederica Wilson, D-Fla., to create a similar nineteen-member commission under the purview of the U.S. Commission on Civil Rights to study the challenges facing Black males and release an annual report documenting their findings and making recommendations on how "to alleviate and remedy the underlying causes of the conditions." Wilson also modeled her legislation after the Florida commission, created during her time in the state legislature. According to Wilson, the purpose of the bill was to find a way to overcome the challenges facing Black men and boys before they come in contact with police and address community disparities to ensure they have the same opportunities as white males to become successful.

Ultimately, the House took up S 2163 on July 27, easily passing it 368–1. The president signed the bill three weeks later on August 14, 2020 (PL 116-156).

Delivering for America Act

Less than three months before the 2020 general election, Democrats in the House tried to pass legislation stopping the United States Postal Service (USPS) from continuing to implement changes that they feared could delay election mail at the same time as a record number of voters were expected to cast their ballots by mail. While the House was called back into session in the middle of its recess to vote on the measure, Senate Republican leadership refused to take action on the bill, noting that Postmaster General Louis DeJoy had already publicly stated that he was halting all ongoing changes—including taking sorting machines offline and prohibiting extra mail runs—until after election day.

House Action

On August 11, 2020, Rep. Carolyn Maloney, D-N.Y., introduced HR 8015, the Delivering for America Act, which would stop the USPS from making any changes to operations or the level of mail service. The bill would require operations to revert to those that were in place on January 1, 2020. That level must be maintained until 2021 or the end of the public health emergency related to the COVID-19 pandemic, whichever came later.

On August 16, House Speaker Nancy Pelosi, D-Calif., wrote in a Dear Colleague letter that she intended to call the chamber back into session before the end of its summer recess to vote on Maloney's bill. According to Pelosi's letter, changes implemented by DeJoy since he assumed his role in June—including eliminating overtime, closing processing centers, and holding mail at times when distribution centers were behind—had "devastating effects" on mail services. The speaker wrote that the changes were part of the president's "campaign to sabotage the election by manipulating the Postal Service to disenfranchise voters."

Before the House could consider Maloney's bill, DeJoy announced that he was postponing all Postal Service changes until after the November election. In an August 18 statement, the postmaster general said he wanted to "avoid even the appearance of any impact on election mail." His statement noted that the hours at post offices and processing facilities would remain the same, the large blue mail collection boxes would not be removed, and extra resources would be placed on standby to handle any influx of election mail. DeJoy's statement came as he was facing backlash from both Democrats and Republicans, who received a glut of complaints from constituents who encountered delays in receiving their mail and packages.

Despite the announcement, on August 19, House leadership released updated bill language that included a $25 billion supplemental funding boost for the USPS (the president was vehemently opposed to any additional funding, saying it could allow more people to vote by mail). A portion of these funds, $15 billion, would be set aside

specifically for the USPS inspector general. The House had previously passed in May a $25 billion boost for USPS operations in its COVID-19 relief package (HR 6800), but the bill never advanced in the Senate. The revised language would also require USPS to postmark all election mail the date it is received and treat all election mail as first class. Currently, while some states classify all election mail this way, other states treat it as bulk or marketing mail, which is a lower class of service that moves more slowly through the postal system. The revisions also included language allowing an individual harmed by a violation of the provisions of the bill to take civil action against the quasi-governmental body.

On August 21, the White House released a Statement of Administration Policy, threatening to veto HR 8015 if the bill made its way to the president's desk. According to the White House, the bill would not ensure the ongoing viability of the USPS, but would rather "arbitrarily give USPS $25 billion in 'emergency' taxpayer funding, without linking that funding to either the COVID-19 pandemic or the upcoming election." The administration said the bill would place burdensome restrictions on the Postal Service and failed to take the necessary steps to improve the long-term outlook of the system.

The House convened to consider HR 8015 on August 22. In its rule governing debate, the House Rules Committee struck the provision allowing individuals to take civil action against the Postal Service, one of many efforts Democratic leadership took to try and get more Republican support for the bill. Republican leaders encouraged their members to vote against the bill, arguing that the $25 billion funding infusion was unnecessary (despite being requested by the Postal Service Board of Governors) and that most operational changes had been ongoing for many years. During debate, the House rejected, 182–223, a motion to recommit that would have sent the bill to the House Appropriations Committee with instructions that it report back with an amendment that would bar the Postal Service from using funds provided under the bill to cover outstanding debt, and authorize disciplinary action against any USPS employee who knowingly obstructs election mail or attempts to interfere with the election in their official capacity, among other things.

The House ultimately passed HR 8015, 257–150, on August 22, 2020. Twenty-six Republicans voted in favor of the bill.

Senate Action

On August 13, 2020, Sens. Gary Peters, D-Mich., and Thomas Carper, D-Del., introduced the Senate's version of the Delivering for America Act (S 4527). Senate Majority Leader Mitch McConnell, R-Ky., made clear that the chamber would not consider the House bill, though he did express a willingness to tie additional funding for the Postal Service to a COVID-19 relief measure. S 4527, along with HR 8015, never received a vote in the Senate.

In December 2020, USPS did receive a $10 billion infusion of funds as part of a larger COVID-19 relief package. That money converted an additional borrowing authority loan into direct emergency relief that would not need to be paid back.

Nonpartisan Postmaster General Act

Democrats attempted to turn their frustration over President Trump's choice of DeJoy to lead the United States Postal Service (USPS) into legislation prohibiting individuals serving as postmaster general, deputy postmaster general, or on the Postal Service Board of Governors from undertaking certain political activities, fundraising or campaigning for candidates, or holding political office. However, no bill passed either the House or Senate in 2020.

House Action

On August 25, 2020, Rep. Carolyn Maloney, D-N.Y., introduced the Nonpartisan Postmaster General Act (HR 8109). The bill would restrict the postmaster general and deputy postmaster general, as well as members of the Postal Service Board of Governors, from holding a political position while in office or soliciting funds for either a candidate or political party while in their position. Additionally, the postmaster general and deputy postmaster general would be banned from actively participating in political management or campaigns. Anyone nominated to the position of postmaster general or deputy postmaster general must not have participated in political activities in the four years before their nomination.

On September 16, 2020, the House Oversight and Reform Committee marked up the bill, during which time they considered a handful of amendments. Maloney proposed a substitute amendment to her own bill, retitling it the Nonpartisan Postmaster General Act of 2020. The amendment was adopted by voice vote. Another adopted amendment, from Rep. Gerald Connolly, D-Va., added a provision to require nominees for the position of postmaster general or deputy postmaster general to submit certain financial disclosure forms before assuming office. Connolly said such language was critical because DeJoy held investments in companies that competed with the USPS. Rep. Jamie Raskin, D-Md., proposed an amendment to strike the portion of the bill prohibiting the appointment to the position of postmaster general or deputy postmaster general someone who had held political office in the prior four years. Raskin found possible constitutional issues with the ban. It, too, was adopted by voice vote. Republicans were critical of the amendments, and the underlying bill, viewing it as retaliation against DeJoy.

The committee also rejected five amendments. One, from Rep. Virginia Foxx, R-N.C., would strike the four-year prohibition language and would also eliminate language that bans Postal Service Board of Governor members from fundraising for a candidate or political party, holding elected office, filing paperwork to run for elected office, or

holding a position within a political party. Rep. Thomas Massie, R-Ky., proposed multiple amendments, including one to increase to ten years the maximum prison sentence for someone who forges or counterfeits a postmark stamp. Another would ban, from the time of the bill's enactment through January 6, 2021, any USPS employee from picketing or refusing to work if their actions slowed ballot delivery or impacted the federal election. His third rejected amendment would apply restrictions on taking part in political management or campaigns to all postmasters in the country. Another amendment that was not adopted, from Rep. Jody Hice, R-Ga., would ban—from the time of the bill's enactment through November 4, 2020—any USPS employee from representation or consultative functions during working hours, including those activities related to collective bargaining. The committee voted to report the bill, however, it was not considered by the full House during the 116th Congress.

Fiscal Year 2020 Financial Services and General Government Appropriations

As in years past, in 2019 Congress again failed to enact its Financial Services and General Government appropriations bill prior to the start of the fiscal year. Instead, two continuing resolutions were required to keep the government funded at fiscal year 2019 levels until the fiscal year 2020 levels were set. Ultimately, the Financial Services and General Government appropriations bill was included as part of the omnibus Consolidated Appropriations Act, 2020 (PL 116-93), signed by President Trump on December 20, 2019. It provided $23.8 billion to the Financial Services title.

House Committee Action

On June 2, 2019, House appropriators released their draft fiscal year 2020 Financial Services and General Government appropriations bill (HR 3351). It would provide $24.55 billion in discretionary funding for the White House, Treasury Department, Internal Revenue Service (IRS), District of Columbia, federal judiciary, and more than two dozen other agencies. The total was $1.4 billion more than the fiscal 2019 appropriated level, and $355 million more than the White House included in its budget request.

Within the bill were provisions that would provide federal civilian workers a 3.1 percent raise, eliminate earlier restrictions on Washington, D.C.'s spending on abortion, and language that would allow the IRS to issue guidance on the political activities of certain tax-exempt organizations. After a rare raise in the final fiscal 2018 spending bill—and subsequent cut in the fiscal 2019 legislation—the House draft measure boosted IRS funding to $12 billion, a $697.4 million increase over the prior fiscal year. Of this, more than half would be set aside for updating tax enforcement. The IRS was also slated to receive a nearly $300 million increase in its enforcement budget. Democratic leadership on the House Appropriations Committee also boosted funding for the Small Business Administration (up $280.4 million over the prior fiscal year) and federal judiciary (up $258.3 million). Additionally, the draft language

- provided $9.1 billion to the GSA, slightly lower than the prior fiscal year and less than the White House request
- increased to $741.3 million federal payments to the District of Columbia
- boosted by $7 million the Election Assistance Commission funding
- raised the Securities and Exchange Commission budget to $1.85 billion

One day later, on June 3, the House Financial Services Appropriations Subcommittee approved its version of the annual appropriations measure, allocating $24.9 billion to the programs funded by the bill. Republicans on the subcommittee encouraged Democrats to drop a number of the bill's provisions, arguing that it otherwise stood little chance of passage. Most of their concerns centered around blocking the president's ability to use money from the Treasury Forfeiture Fund to build a wall along the U.S.–Mexico border and providing more leeway to the District of Columbia in how it spends its money. When Republicans held the majority, they routinely added riders to appropriations legislation preventing the District of Columbia from enacting liberal social policies, including legalizing marijuana. Rep. Tom Graves, R-Ga., the subcommittee's ranking member, equated the D.C. language with handing the federal enclave a blank check with no oversight. Other policy riders contained in the bill addressed collective bargaining agreements and safe harbor for financial institutions providing services to marijuana businesses operating legally under state law.

The House Appropriations Committee voted 31–21 on June 11 to advance the $24.9 billion Financial Services and General Government appropriations bill to the House floor. The topline number was 8 percent higher than in fiscal 2019. The bill marked the end of the committee's work on its twelve annual appropriations measures, as it had already advanced the other eleven. Committee leadership admitted that their work was likely for naught, because there was no agreement with the Senate on topline spending and Republicans were strongly opposed to a number of provisions in the bill, including one that prohibited the president from using money from the Treasury Forfeiture Fund to build a wall along the southern U.S. border. The president had announced a plan to use more than $600 million from this fund to cover the cost of the wall. Appropriations Committee Republicans tried to push through an amendment that would strike that language, but it failed 21–31. Republicans in the House committee,

as in the subcommittee before them, also argued about policy riders related to the District of Columbia. While the bill language kept in place a restriction on using federal funds to pay for abortions, it did not stop the District from using local tax dollars for that purpose. An amendment from Rep. Martha Roby, R-Ala., to bar the District of Columbia from using local funds to cover the cost of abortions was defeated 21–27.

House Floor Action

The full House began debate on the Financial Services bill in late June, starting with consideration of forty-six amendments, ranging from increasing or decreasing funding to various programs to placing prohibitions on how agencies can use their money.

One of the most surprising debate moments came when Republicans proposed an amendment to HR 3351 that would increase by $10 million funding for the Treasury Department's Office of Terrorism and Financial Intelligence, specifically to support enforcing sanctions against Iran. Through the motion to recommit procedural tool, Republicans were able to successfully attach their amendment to the funding bill when thirty-seven Democrats voted for the measure. It marked the first time in four months that Democrats lost a procedural vote while in the House majority.

The final fiscal year 2020 Financial Services and General Government appropriations bill passed the House on June 26, 2019, 224–196. The $24.95 billion in discretionary funding included

- $12 billion for the IRS
- $7.9 billion for the federal judiciary
- $1.9 billion for the Securities and Exchange Commission
- $996 million for the Small Business Administration
- $741 million for the District of Columbia
- $178 million for the Executive Office of the President

It was unlikely that the House version would make it to the president's desk. Trump had already issued a veto threat, finding the topline number too high and disagreeing with the provision stopping him from using the Treasury Forfeiture Funds to build a wall along the U.S.–Mexico border. Of note, the House bill was only $355 million higher than the White House budget request. Republicans attempted to address the spending concern and proposed five amendments during debate that would have reduced the bill's topline by anywhere between 1 percent and 14 percent, but none was adopted.

Senate Committee Action

On September 19, 2019, the Senate Appropriations Committee took up its $24.2 billion fiscal year 2020 Financial Services and General Government measure, two days after the Financial Services Appropriations Subcommittee easily advanced the bill. S 2524 marked a $773 million increase over fiscal year 2019, but was around $800 million below the House-passed bill. During markup, the Senate Appropriations Committee adopted a handful of amendments, including one from ranking member Sen. Patrick Leahy, D-Vt., to provide $250 million in election security grants to the states through the Election Assistance Commission. That funding would be offset with an equal reduction in the amount provided to the GSA's Federal Buildings Fund. Although most of the committee members were cosponsors of the amendment, some Republicans raised concerns that more oversight was needed to determine how states were using the grant money. Getting the funding for election security was key for securing Democratic votes.

The final bill, approved by voice vote, provided

- $12.9 billion for the Treasury Department, of which $11.4 billion was for the IRS
- $717 million for the Executive Office of the President
- $7.4 billion for the federal judiciary
- $673 million for the District of Columbia
- $339 million for the Federal Communications Commission
- $312 million for the Federal Trade Commission
- $876 million for the Small Business Administration
- $1.8 billion for the Securities and Exchange Commission
- $9.6 billion for the GSA's Federal Buildings Fund

The full Senate never considered the committee's bill.

Conference and Final Action

By the start of the new fiscal year, no appropriations measure had cleared both chambers and made its way to the president's desk. Instead, Congress was forced to pass two continuing resolutions to keep the government funded at current levels until they could work out an agreement. When appropriations conferees met to package the individual appropriations measures, their work focused mainly on reaching agreements on the largest and most contentious funding bills. However, there were some differences for conferees to work out on the Financial Services title, including policy riders that were included in the House version but not in the Senate, and vice versa. For example, the Senate language approved in committee would prevent the District of Columbia from using local revenue to cover abortions or regulate marijuana. The House version blocked the president from using Treasury Forfeiture Funds to cover the cost of a wall along the U.S.–Mexico border and would stop certain federal facilities from relocating or closing.

In the final agreement reached by negotiators in mid-December, the Financial Services and General Government appropriations bill was bundled with three others—

Defense, Commerce–Justice–Science, and Homeland Security. Of that larger bill (HR 1158), $23.8 billion would go toward the Financial Services title. This funding included

- $13.1 billion for the Treasury Department, of which $11.5 billion was for the IRS
- $7.49 billion for the federal judiciary
- $339 million for the Federal Communications Commission
- $1.82 billion for the Securities and Exchange Commission
- $998 million for the Small Business Administration
- $331 million for the Federal Trade Commission
- $8.9 billion for the GSA's Federal Buildings Fund
- $714 million for the District of Columbia
- $15.2 million for the Election Assistance Commission
- a 3.1 percent pay increase for federal civilian workers

On the election security question, appropriators split the difference between the House and Senate and opted to provide $425 million for grants to help states secure their elections. Conferees also left in place policy riders that prevented the District of Columbia from using its funds toward covering the cost of abortion and regulating marijuana.

The House voted on December 17 to pass HR 1158 by a vote of 280–138. The Senate voted 81–11 on December 19, sending the measure to President Trump for his signature. The president signed the bill on December 20, 2019 (PL 116-93) with ninety minutes to spare before government funding ran out.

Fiscal Year 2021 Financial Services and General Government Appropriations

Congress delayed until summer their work on nonpandemic relief legislation, opting instead to focus on critical relief bills and putting in place safety protocol that would allow members to meet both in person and remotely to comply with federal social distancing requirements. As usual, the House was the first to produce its Financial Services and General Government appropriations language, voting it out of committee in July. It was not until December, however, that President Trump signed the final omnibus bill containing fiscal year 2021 appropriations. That legislation provided $24.4 billion to the agencies covered under the Financial Services and General Government title.

House Committee Action

On July 8, 2020, the House Financial Services Appropriations Subcommittee reported its Financial Services and General Government appropriations bill (HR 7668) to the House Appropriations Committee by

voice vote. Despite sending the $24.6 billion measure to the full committee, Republicans raised many objections about the bill, including its more than $67 billion in emergency infrastructure spending (the vast majority of which was set aside to bring broadband service to areas of the country with limited or no access), a provision that would block the president from using money from the Treasury Forfeiture Fund for constructing a wall along the U.S.–Mexico border, and the elimination of prohibitions included in past bills blocking the District of Columbia from using local revenue to pay for abortion services and barring the city from enforcing marijuana laws.

On July 15, the full House Appropriations Committee took up the bill. During markup, Republicans introduced multiple amendments to strike language from the bill, including the provisions banning President Trump from using Treasury Forfeiture Funds for the southern border wall and allowing the District of Columbia to use its local revenue to cover abortion services. All the Republican amendments were rejected. The committee did adopt, by voice vote, a manager's amendment that made a number of changes to the bill. The amendment added language specifying that $5 million provided to the Alcohol and Tobacco Tax Trade Bureau go toward enforcement and education about certain trade practices, struck language directing the Federal Communication Commission's broadband infrastructure grant rulemaking process, expressed the support of the committee for changing the metal content in coins if it would reduce costs, and expressed the committee's support for the development of 5G networks, among other things. The committee went on to favorably report the appropriations bill, as amended, 30–22.

The final $24.6 billion in discretionary funds approved by the committee was $808 million higher than the enacted fiscal 2020 level but $2.9 billion less than what the president requested. The bill provided

- $13.7 billion for the Treasury Department, including $12.1 billion for the IRS
- $741.2 million for the Executive Office of the President
- $7.8 billion for the federal judiciary
- $762.1 million for the District of Columbia; bill language also lifted the ban on the District's use of local revenue to fund abortion services, needle exchange programs, and legalize marijuana
- $19.1 million for the Election Assistance Commission
- $9.1 billion in spending authority for the General Services Administration's Federal Buildings Fund
- $939.4 million for the Small Business Administration
- $1.9 billion for the Securities and Exchange Commission
- $376.1 million for the Federal Communications Commission
- $341 million for the Federal Trade Commission

CHANGES AT THE POSTAL SERVICE

Perhaps more than Louis DeJoy's record of political contributions to Republicans, Democrats worried that his appointment would hamper Postal Service operations ahead of the 2020 presidential election. Due to the COVID-19 pandemic, many were opting to use a mail-in ballot to cast their vote to avoid crowded polling locations where the virus might spread more easily. Experts predicted that the November 2020 election was likely to see the largest portion of mail-in ballots in U.S. history.

After assuming his role on June 15, 2020, DeJoy began implementing multiple operational changes. These included eliminating hundreds of large blue public mailboxes, reducing overtime, shutting down some mail sorting machines and other agency infrastructure, and canceling additional deliveries. What Democrats saw an attempt to disenfranchise voters, DeJoy viewed as a means to help the agency dig out of its $160 billion budget shortfall. The new postmaster general also noted that many of the changes being made had been in the works before he took over, due to an ongoing decline in mail volume.

Almost immediately after the changes were implemented, stories began cropping up about Americans waiting weeks for critical letters and packages, including child support checks and medications. Farmers reported receiving dead animals, food shipments sat rotting in warehouses, and some people reported being charged late fees and penalties on bills that had not yet arrived. The changes came at the same time as USPS was facing an influx of mail due to ballot requests and more Americans opting to shop from home during the pandemic. USPS was also facing staffing issues across the country, with workers calling out sick after contracting COVID-19. The situation became so bad that in July, the Postal Service was forced to alert nearly every state that it might not meet its deadline for voters to receive and cast ballots.

Under pressure from Congress and facing a public backlash, on August 18 DeJoy announced that he was suspending any additional operational changes at the Postal Service until after the November election. He also agreed to reinstitute the use of overtime through the election. In announcing the decision, DeJoy said he wanted to avoid even the appearance of an impact on the November election and

said he would also ensure that resources were on standby in case mail volume reached unexpected levels. Speaker Nancy Pelosi, D-Calif., noted in her response to DeJoy's announcement that it could not undo any damage already done.

The USPS Inspector General released a report in November looking at the summer modifications and analyzing what impact they had, if any. According to the report, the changes—which also included reorganizing staff, changing working hours, eliminating early delivery starts, and ending some processing on Saturdays—individually did not have much of an impact, however, when taken together, significantly affected USPS operations. The report chided the Postal Service for failing to consider how its changes would impact mail service and poorly communicating the changes. The report did note that, as DeJoy argued, some alterations, such as removing blue mailboxes and certain sorting machines, were in the works prior to the start of his tenure. However, their investigation found that DeJoy accelerated these changes.

The Senate Homeland Security and Governmental Affairs and House Oversight and Reform Committees both called DeJoy to testify about slowed mail services and how the USPS was preparing for the November election. In each instance, the postmaster general testified that the changes he was implementing, while difficult, were critical for ensuring the long-term success of the Postal Service and stopping it from continuing to add to its deficit. DeJoy also reiterated that many of the changes were slated for implementation prior to his appointment, and that situations outside of his control, such as the COVID-19 pandemic and staffing challenges, were contributing to service instability. He also rejected the assertion that he cut overtime and repeated his commitment to getting election mail delivered on time.

DeJoy was not just facing backlash from the public and Democrats in Congress. Twenty Democratic state attorneys general also filed lawsuits against the postmaster general, accusing him of acting outside his authority to implement changes and not properly following federal procedure. These lawsuits sought to tie DeJoy's actions to statements made by President Trump, including those alleging that mail-in ballots are subject to high levels of fraud and claiming that additional USPS funding would only benefit Democrats.

House Floor Action

On the floor, the annual Financial Services appropriations bill was rolled into a larger, six-bill spending package (HR 7617) that also included Defense, Commerce–Justice–Science, Energy–Water, Labor–HHS–Education, and Transportation–HUD. Consideration of the $1.3 trillion package included debate on nearly 340 amendments, most

of which were bundled into larger en bloc packages to allow the House to move through them more efficiently. The House passed the package on July 31, 217–197, despite a veto threat from the White House. According to its July 30, 2020 Statement of Administration Policy, HR 7617 violated both the letter and spirit of the Bipartisan Budget Act of 2019 (PL 116-37). As it related to the Financial Services

title of the bill, the president took issue with a number of items, including the provision blocking him from using certain funds to build a wall along the U.S.–Mexico border, which according to the statement would "severely undermine" the president's ability to fully secure the border. HR 7617 never received a vote on the Senate floor.

Senate Action

The Senate released its draft Financial Services and General Government spending bill in November. Their topline appropriation was slightly more than $24 billion, 0.2 percent lower than the fiscal year 2020 level. Some areas covered by the legislation would receive small spending increases, including the federal courts (2%), Office of Management and Budget (5%), and Securities and Exchange Commission (4%), while cuts would be felt at the Small Business Administration (10%), Federal Trade Commission (6%), and District of Columbia (2%). The committee bill would also freeze federal civilian employee pay for 2021, differing from both the White House request and House bill that provided a 1 percent pay increase.

The Senate version included language prohibiting the District of Columbia from spending its local revenue on covering abortion services, enforcing laws that legalize marijuana use, and funding needle exchange programs. The committee did not take any further action on the bill.

Conference and Final Action

Between the COVID-19 pandemic, presidential election, and political disagreements over several government funding issues, it was not until late December that House and Senate negotiators unveiled an omnibus spending package that encompassed all twelve appropriations bills. To get to that point, however, Congress passed—and the president signed—five separate continuing resolutions to prevent a government shutdown.

The final $1.4 trillion package (HR 133) included $24.4 billion in discretionary funding for the agencies funded under the Financial Services and General Government title. That total was $281 million higher than the prior fiscal year. Among the biggest winners in the compromise bill was the IRS, which received a 4 percent spending boost to $11.9 billion over the fiscal 2020 level. That was lower than the 5 percent in the House version of the bill, but far larger than the Senate's version, which would have left the IRS budget flat. Other agencies that received spending increases included

- GSA (2%)
- Office of Personnel Management (9%)
- Federal Communications Commission (10%)
- Federal Trade Commission (6%)
- Securities and Exchange Commission (5%)
- Treasury Department (3%)
- Executive Office of the President (4%)
- Federal judiciary (4%)
- District of Columbia (2%)
- Election Assistance Commission (12%)

The bill maintained the House language providing a 1 percent pay raise for federal civilian employees, but followed the Senate's version on other language, such as maintaining the ban on the District of Columbia using federal money or its own local revenue to cover the cost of abortions. The District would also be restricted from implementing its marijuana law or enacting needle exchange programs.

The House passed HR 133 on December 21, 327–85 and 359–53 (the chamber used a procedural move to divide the bill into two portions for two separate votes), and the Senate followed on the same day, 92–6. President Trump signed the legislation on December 27 (PL 116-260). With his signature, he included a redlined version of the bill, asking the chambers to review provisions with which the president disagreed. Congress did not do so before the end of the session.

CHAPTER 15

Inside Congress

Inside Congress

Numerous forms of upheaval beset Capitol Hill during the 115th and 116th Congresses. The #MeToo movement targeting sexual harassment led to the political downfall of some lawmakers. A shooting at a congressional baseball practice seriously wounded House Majority Whip Steve Scalise of Louisiana and several others. The novel COVID-19 coronavirus overshadowed all other issues in 2020, forcing big changes such as remote hearings as well as proxy voting—the latter an especially controversial move.

But the primary source of upending how Congress functioned was President Donald Trump. The Tea Party movement—formed a decade earlier in opposition to what its adherents saw as President Barack Obama's excessive government overreach—morphed to conform to Trump's brand of "America First" populism. Few congressional Republicans were willing to defy Trump's demand for loyalty and publicly rebuke or oppose him. Several who did chose to retire rather than risk a tough primary-election challenge from a Trump-backed rival.

Trump showed a willingness to test political norms, including bypassing Congress. With Republicans' backing, he pushed for the diversion in 2019 of $3.6 billion in funds that lawmakers had slated for military construction to build a giant wall on the U.S.–Mexico border—a project that had been among the centerpieces of his 2016 campaign. House Democrats sued to block the move, calling it a violation of the constitutional separation of powers. But the U.S. Supreme Court sided with Trump in a 5–4 decision. Trump also regularly declined to swiftly fill Senate-confirmed positions in favor of installing "acting" leaders at agencies for months at a time. Just before leaving office, Trump pardoned multiple ex-House members who had been convicted of crimes.

His unabashedly partisan style delighted his Republican allies. Some left Congress to work for the president, with two House members—South Carolina's Mick Mulvaney and North Carolina's Mark Meadows—serving as White House chiefs of staff. But Trump greatly alienated Democrats, who regained a majority in the House in the 2018 midterm elections by emphasizing their differences with the president. Congress' attention shifted in 2019 and 2020 to Trump's initial impeachment over charges of abuse of power and obstruction of Congress stemming from allegedly soliciting foreign interference in his reelection bid. His role in instigating the January 6, 2021 insurrection at the Capitol that sought to overturn the Electoral College certification of Joe Biden as the next president prompted another impeachment and acquittal by sympathetic GOP senators.

One of the main ways in which Trump's presidency impacted Congress was through his relationships with both chambers' Republican leaders. In the House, Wisconsin's Paul Ryan resigned as Speaker in part over his frustration that Trump had made the normal process of legislating more difficult. His replacement was California's Kevin McCarthy, a vocal Trump booster. In the Senate, Kentucky Republican Mitch McConnell, as the majority leader, chose not to concentrate on passing bills—which Democrats could potentially block—in favor of working with the president to install Republican judicial nominees on the federal bench. Dozens of judges were confirmed, including three Supreme Court justices—a development that gave the high court a distinctly conservative cast.

A June 2021 survey by broadcast channel C-SPAN of 142 presidential historians found Trump ranked third from the bottom among all chief executives in terms of relations with Congress. He scored ahead only of Abraham Lincoln's predecessor and successor, James Buchanan, who failed to unite a fractured Democratic Party before the start of the Civil War, and Andrew Johnson, whose postwar attempt to remove a Cabinet official led to his impeachment. But in public opinion polls, the story was mixed. An average of 86 percent of Republicans approved of Trump's handling of his job during his tenure, compared with an average of 6 percent of Democrats—the widest partisan gap in approval for any president in the modern era of polling, according to the Pew Research Center.

INCREASED POLARIZATION

Congress displayed ample evidence of increased polarization during Trump's term. In CQ Roll Call's 2020 analyses of party unity voting, which split a majority of one party against a majority of the other, House Democrats got their way on 168 of 176 votes for a winning percentage of 95.5 percent. That figure was topped in the sixty-year history of CQ Roll Call's study only by 2019's 96.2 percent.

In the Senate, Republicans backed Trump 93 percent of the time over the entire course of his presidency. By comparison, Republican senators backed President George W. Bush 86 percent of the time during Bush's eight years as president. Democratic senators' votes demonstrated the exact opposite effect. They backed Trump 36 percent of the time during his term, well below their average support score of 51 percent for Bush's eight years.

Many lawmakers and congressional observers say a major contributor to Congress' polarization has been the inability of rank-and-file members to offer amendments to bills on the floor. In the House during the 115th Congress, the number of "closed rule" bills in which the majority permitted no amendments rose to 56 percent. That figure was higher than in any of the previous four sessions of Congress. Not a single bill was considered under an "open rule," in which members have the opportunity to offer unlimited amendments—the first time that had occurred since the 111th Congress in 2009 and 2010. In the Senate, just 466 amendments to bills were considered—more than the 384 amendments in the 113th Congress (2013–2014), but far fewer than the 891 in the 111th.

More than four in ten bills that became law during the 116th Congress ended up being passed during the final two months of its two-year term after the 2018 election—a period when partisanship traditionally wanes, according to the Pew Research Center. That figure represented the highest share of lame-duck legislation since at least the 93rd Congress of 1973–1974, the first years of the center's analysis.

The hardening of partisanship and increase in polarization mirrored shifts among Congress' constituents. The Pew Research Center has used an imaginary thermometer to measure partisan attitudes among the public. In 2019, the share of Republicans who gave Democrats a "cold" rating on a 0–100 thermometer rose 14 percentage points from 2016. Democrats' views of Republicans followed the same trajectory, with 57 percent giving Republicans a "very cold" rating, up from 41 percent three years earlier. After the January 6 insurrection, some Democrats said they had even less inclination to work with Republicans.

MAJOR LEGISLATION

Addressing the coronavirus as it spread across the United States consumed the bulk of Congress' attention in 2020. The Coronavirus Aid, Relief, and Economic Security Act (CARES Act, HR 748; PL 116-136) became law to provide relief for families, workers, and businesses. It included relief checks for individuals and forgivable loans for small businesses. Lawmakers also passed several bills that allocated billions of dollars for the Department of Health and Human Services and other federal agencies for coronavirus relief. Both chambers held numerous hearings on the Trump administration's response—with Dr. Anthony Fauci, director of the National Institute of Allergy and Infectious Diseases, becoming a frequent sparring partner and object of some Republicans' scorn.

Republicans' signature legislative achievement during Trump's presidency was the Tax Cuts and Jobs Act of 2017 (HR 1; PL 115-97), the largest tax overhaul in more than three decades. The law cut the corporate income tax rate from 35 percent to 21 percent. It repealed the corporate alternative minimum tax, which was aimed at ensuring a corporation pays at least some minimum amount of tax by limiting or eliminating certain deductions, credits, and other tax preferences. And it cancelled the penalty enforcing the individual mandate of the Patient Protection and Affordable Care Act, which had been President Barack Obama's signature achievement. The law also fulfilled a long-held goal of Alaska lawmakers to open the state's Arctic National Wildlife Refuge to oil and gas drilling, which environmentalists had staunchly opposed.

Republicans used the budget reconciliation process to enact the law to avoid the sixty-vote threshold needed to pass most Senate legislation. Under reconciliation, only a simple majority is required. Democrats complained the bill was crafted behind closed doors and amounted to a wish list for lobbyists. They also said the bill's tax cuts overwhelmingly gave an advantage to the country's wealthiest individuals.

As majority leader, McConnell guided three of Trump's nominees—Neil Gorsuch, Brett Kavanaugh, and Amy Coney Barrett—to confirmation. For Kavanaugh and Barrett, the circumstances were especially challenging. Kavanaugh overcame the testimony of a witness before the Senate Judiciary Committee, Christine Blasey Ford, that he had sexually assaulted her years earlier, a charge that he forcefully denied. Barrett was confirmed shortly before the 2020 election to fill the vacancy created by liberal icon Ruth Bader Ginsburg's death. Her confirmation came despite McConnell's earlier refusal to enable the confirmation of Obama's selection for the court in 2016, Merrick Garland, because the majority leader said that voters should decide which party should prevail in the election and thus get to pick the next justice.

Chronology of Action on Congress: Members and Procedures

2017–2018

The 115th Congress convened at noon on January 3, 2017. No major changes were made in the leadership of either chamber. There were seven new senators (5 Democrats and 2 Republicans) and fifty-two new representatives (25 Democrats, 27 Republicans) at the outset of its first session. At the start of the 115th Congress, congressional Republicans were eager to use their trifecta—a sweep of the White House, House and Senate—to bring major change to Washington. It was the first time that they had controlled all those governmental levers since 2007 during President George W. Bush's administration.

Numerous Republicans expressed confidence they could work successfully with Trump, but others said they were uncertain how things would unfold. As a candidate, Trump released few policy positions. He said he supported some of the House Republicans' ideas on addressing poverty and cutting taxes to stimulate economic growth, but he never formally endorsed their "Better Way" agenda or said whether he would make it a priority in his administration.

115th Congress: Organization and Leadership

In the House, Wisconsin's Paul Ryan had the strong support of his caucus in being elected as Speaker. Only one Republican—Kentucky's Thomas Massie—declined to back him. Massie instead voted for Florida Republican Daniel Webster, who had waged an unsuccessful challenge to Ryan in 2015 after the sudden resignation of Speaker John Boehner, R-Ohio.

The rest of the House Republican leadership team remained largely unchanged from the previous Congress. McCarthy carried over as majority leader, while Louisiana's Steve Scalise continued to serve as majority whip. Scalise was a gregarious lawmaker who counted numerous Democrats among his close friends despite having a strongly conservative voting record. Cathy McMorris

Rodgers of Washington state, a protégé of Boehner's who was briefly considered as Trump's secretary of Interior, continued to chair the House Republican Conference. One of her jobs was to recruit more women to the male-dominated GOP. The new chairman of the National Republican Congressional Committee was Steve Stivers, an up-and-comer who had been one of Scalise's top deputies. Indiana's Luke Messer, a former House aide and lobbyist, continued to lead the Republican Policy Committee, the caucus' in-house idea factory.

The House Democratic leadership also displayed few changes from the previous Congress. California's Nancy Pelosi, who had been the first female Speaker, continued as the minority leader. Pelosi beat back a challenge from Ohio's Tim Ryan, who argued that the party was too urban-centric and needed new leaders as well as a new economic agenda to win back voters from hard-hit rural districts. But he received just sixty-three votes to Pelosi's 134. Maryland's Steny Hoyer, an old-school politician with a much less partisan style than Pelosi, remained minority whip, while South Carolina's Jim Clyburn continued as assistant Democratic leader—a post Pelosi had created to ensure African Americans were represented at the party's top ranks. New Mexico's Ben Ray Lujan, a Pelosi loyalist, remained as Democratic Congressional Campaign Committee chair. The new caucus chairman was New York's Joseph Crowley, an energetic fundraiser and centrist.

In the Senate, the Republican leadership structure remained unchanged in the new Congress. McConnell remained his caucus' leader, a position he had held since 2007. John Cornyn of Texas, a close McConnell ally, remained at his post as the second-highest-ranking GOP senator and the caucus' chief vote-counter. John Thune of South Dakota continued as the conference chairman, reprising his role as the Republicans' chief public relations strategist. Wyoming's John Barrasso continued to lead the Republican Policy Committee. Utah's Orrin Hatch, as the

chamber's longest-serving member of the majority, remained president pro tempore. The only new arrival was Colorado's Cory Gardner—who had toppled incumbent Democrat Mark Udall in 2014—to chair the National Republican Senatorial Committee.

Bigger changes took place within the Senate Democratic leadership. New York's Charles E. Schumer formally became the minority leader after locking up the job a year and a half earlier, when Harry Reid of Nevada announced his retirement. The New York Democrat took the helm after serving a decade as caucus vice chairman, the No. 3 spot that Reid had created for him in 2006. Schumer also ran the Democratic Policy and Communications Center for five years, serving as the caucus' messaging guru. Schumer was known as a fierce advocate for Democratic priorities, a prolific fundraiser, and a loyal partisan.

Richard J. Durbin of Illinois maintained his No. 2 leadership position as whip, the top Democratic vote counter, which he had held since 2005. Durbin initially had been seen as a rival to Schumer for the majority leader post, but could not overcome his onetime Capitol Hill roommate's successful backroom politicking for the post. Durbin was a respected veteran who had long been among his party's leaders on providing Dreamers—the children of those who came to the United States illegally—with a path to citizenship.

Schumer, recognizing the immense popularity that Bernie Sanders had attracted among progressives during his presidential bid, expanded the leadership team to include the Vermont independent in the new role as Chair of Outreach. In that position, Sanders was tasked with trying to engage Americans who felt disconnected from the political process, many of them young people who were among Sanders' strongest supporters. The move came as Sanders also ascended to the ranking-member position on the Senate Budget Committee.

Another favorite of progressives, Massachusetts' Elizabeth Warren, became one of two Democratic conference vice chairs, joining the centrist Mark Warner of Virginia. Washington state's Patty Murray took the job of assistant leader, making her the third highest-ranking person within the Senate Democratic hierarchy. First-term Sen. Chris Van Hollen of Maryland became chairman of the Democratic Senatorial Campaign Committee. Van Hollen had chaired the House Democrats' counterpart committee from 2007 to 2011 when he served in the House. Michigan's Debbie Stabenow continued as chair of the Democratic Policy and Communications Committee, which sought to spread the party's message.

The party's largest and most influential internal caucuses saw varying degrees of transformation. The Congressional Progressive Caucus, which consisted of Vermont independent Sen. Bernie Sanders and seventy-eight House members, elected Democratic Reps. Raul Grijalva of Arizona and Mark Pocan of Wisconsin as its two co-chairs. Grijalva was one of the House's most liberal members and the ranking Democrat on the Natural Resources Committee, which he used as a platform to criticize fossil fuel development and advocate for renewable energy. Pocan, who was openly gay, also was a fierce progressive.

The Congressional Black Caucus—which in the 115th had its largest-ever membership with forty-nine members—chose Louisiana Democratic Rep. Cedric Richmond as its new chairman. Richmond had taken on voter-mobilization responsibilities for House Democrats in the 2016 campaign and was known as having forged close relationships with members in both parties. New Mexico Democratic Rep. Michelle Lujan Grisham became chairwoman of the Congressional Hispanic Caucus, which also boasted a record total of thirty-one members. Lujan Grisham was part of a Land of Enchantment political dynasty—Ben Ray Lujan was a distant cousin—who had served as the state's health secretary before coming to Congress.

The Blue Dog Coalition, a band of fiscally conservative Democrats that had seen its influence wane as House Democrats became more liberal, had eighteen members and five co-chairs in the 115th Congress: Jim Costa and Lou Correa of California, Anthony Brindisi of New York, Henry Cuellar of Texas, and Daniel Lipinski of Illinois. That membership figure represented a steep decline from the fifty-plus members who belonged to the group a decade earlier.

The Freedom Caucus, the group of the most conservative House Republicans, did not publicize its membership roster, but was believed to have about thirty-six members. Its chairman was North Carolina's Mark Meadows, a businessman and longtime GOP activist who was unafraid to tangle with his party's leadership. Another North Carolinian, Mark Walker, led the Republican Study Committee, a like-minded group in the House with 154 members. That figure represented almost two-thirds of the entire House Republican delegation. The Study Committee was the fastest growing of any of the caucuses, adding twenty-three Republicans to its ranks, according to a 2018 study by LegBranch.org.

A new congressional group made its debut in January 2017: the Problem Solvers Caucus, which sought to foster more bipartisan cooperation. It developed from meetings organized by the political reform group No Labels and heralded itself as having an equal number of Democrats and Republicans. Its first chairmen were Rep. Josh Gottheimer, D-N.J., a former speechwriter for President Bill Clinton, and Rep. Tom Reed, R-N.Y., who had forged a reputation over a decade as a moderate.

115th Congress: Committees

The 115th Congress had 214 committees and subcommittees—ninety-two in the Senate and 122 in the House. That figure was higher than in the previous two sessions

of Congress, but below the 223 in the 112th Congress (2011–2012).

In the House, committees began with relatively little top-level turnover, except for a few high-profile vacant slots at Appropriations, Energy and Commerce, and Education and the Workforce. Appropriations' new chairman was Rodney Frelinghuysen of New Jersey, a Republican who balanced a record as a foreign policy conservative and a fiscal and social moderate. At Energy and Commerce, Greg Walden of Oregon took over the gavel after compiling an impressive record recruiting candidates and raising money as the chairman of the National Republican Congressional Campaign Committee. And North Carolina's Virginia Foxx, an often-caustic critic of Democrats, ascended to chair Education and the Workforce.

The abrupt resignation in March 2017 of Utah's Jason Chaffetz as chairman of the Oversight and Government Reform Committee led to the elevation of South Carolina's Trey Gowdy to the post. A former federal prosecutor, Gowdy had led a special select committee from 2014 to 2016 looking at the Obama administration's actions before and during a terrorist attack in Benghazi, Libya. It specifically focused on former Secretary of State Hillary Clinton, who testified at length before the panel. Gowdy initially balked at chairing the Oversight panel, according to news media reports, but changed his mind after a number of colleagues lobbied him to do so.

Several lower-profile committees also had new leaders. Tennessee's Phil Roe took over at Veterans' Affairs, while Mississippi's Gregg Harper took the gavel at House Administration and Indiana's Susan Brooks ascended to chair the Ethics Committee.

On the House Democratic side, the 115th Congress opened with only one committee featuring a new ranking member—Budget, where Kentucky's John Yarmuth took over for Maryland's Chris Van Hollen after the latter's election to the Senate. The top spots on most other committees were helmed by veterans who had long been mainstays on those panels, such as Minnesota's Collin Peterson on Agriculture and Homeland Security's Bennie Thompson of Mississippi.

Michigan Rep. John Conyers Jr.'s resignation in December 2017 enabled New York's Jerrold Nadler to take the ranking-member post on Judiciary. In addition, the death of New York's Louise Slaughter in March 2018 meant that the Rules Committee's top Democratic slot passed to Jim McGovern of Massachusetts.

Senate committees also saw shifts in several top posts. On Banking, Housing and Urban Affairs, low-key and affable Idaho Sen. Mike Crapo took over for the term-limited Richard C. Shelby of Alabama. Barrasso took over Environment and Public Works from the term-limited James Inhofe of Oklahoma, bringing a less abrasive but no less conservative style than his predecessor. On the Democratic side, in addition to Sanders at Budget,

Vermont's Patrick J. Leahy assumed the new open ranking-member position on Appropriations, while Tom Carper of Delaware took that spot on Environment and Public Works.

In April 2018, the retirement of Mississippi Republican Sen. Thad Cochran handed the chairmanship of the Appropriations Committee to Shelby, another veteran Southerner with an avid interest in procuring federal money for his state. Shelby also assumed the chairmanship of the Appropriations panel overseeing spending for the Department of Defense, giving him an added way to help direct money to his state's military facilities. He relinquished the chairmanship of the Rules and Administration Committee, with the job going to Missouri's Roy Blunt.

The biggest structural change in any of the House or Senate committees was the creation of a new subcommittee on cybersecurity on the Senate Armed Services Committee. The move came in the wake of the intelligence community's detail linking of Russian officials to a comprehensive hacking campaign aimed at U.S. politicians and political organizations as well as think tanks and lobbying firms. The new subcommittee's chairman was South Dakota's Mike Rounds, who had earlier sponsored bills aimed at punishing Iran and North Korea for their hacking activities. Rounds aimed to help the new administration define when a cyberattack might require a military response.

115th Congress: Member Characteristics

The 115th Congress initially had 238 Republicans (including 1 nonvoting delegate and Puerto Rico's resident commissioner), 201 Democrats (including 4 delegates), and five vacant seats. The Senate had fifty-one Republicans, forty-seven Democrats, and two independents—Vermont's Bernie Sanders and Maine's Angus King—who caucused with Democrats. A record 115 women served: ninety-two in the House, including five delegates and the resident commissioner, and twenty-three in the Senate.

Almost one in five of the voting members of the House and Senate belonged to a racial or ethnic minority, making the 115th Congress the most diverse in history, according to the Pew Research Center.

African American representation included forty-nine House members and three senators. At the same time, there were a record forty-six Hispanics: forty-one in the House, including one delegate and the resident commissioner, and five in the Senate. Another record was set with eighteen members—thirteen representatives, two delegates, and three senators—being Asian Americans, Indian Americans, or Pacific Islander Americans. Two Native Americans served in the House.

Congress remained disproportionately white compared to the overall United States. But Pew Research found that the demographics of incoming freshman lawmakers in the 115th Congress more closely resembled the country's

increasingly racially and ethnically diverse population. Minorities accounted for twenty of the fifty-nine new members (34%) of the House and Senate. The 2020 U.S. census showed the non-white population was around 35 percent.

The overall average age of members was among the highest of any recent Congress, according to the Congressional Research Service. For House members, the average age was 57.8 years, up from 56.7 in the 112th Congress (2011–2012). For senators, the average age was 61.8, down slightly from the prior three sessions of Congresses. However, the average age of newly elected senators was 54.8, much older than the previous three sessions.

Public service/politics was members' dominant occupation, with 194 having that background in the House and forty-four in the Senate. That was followed by business, with 179 in the House and twenty-nine in the Senate, and law, with 168 in the House and fifty in the Senate. Half of the Senate's 100 members were House veterans.

The number of military veterans was on the decline, reflecting a trend of recent decades. At the outset of Congress, the Congressional Research Service found, 102 members—nearly 19 percent of the total membership—had served or were serving the military. By comparison, 64 percent of the members of the 97th Congress (1981–1982) were veterans, and in the 92nd Congress (1971–1972), 73 percent were veterans.

115th Congress: Rules

Of the rules changes adopted in both chambers early in the 115th Congress, the one that drew the most attention by far was Majority Leader Mitch McConnell's move in the Senate—dubbed "the nuclear option"—in April 2017 to eliminate the filibuster for Supreme Court nominees. His move expanded on a controversial action that Nevada's Harry Reid, as the Democratic leader, had taken four years earlier to lower the Senate vote threshold to fifty-one to confirm most presidential appointments. Reid, however, deliberately excluded nominees to the Supreme Court.

McConnell, R-Ky., was in the minority at the time of Reid's maneuver, and lamented it as a Democratic power grab. But one of his first big issues as majority leader in 2017 was to ensure the confirmation of Trump's choice of Neil Gorsuch to the high court. Democrats filibustered Gorsuch's nomination, prompting McConnell to engineer the nuclear-option response. His move—which in an earlier era of Congress would have been regarded as unthinkable—underscored the heavy partisan bitterness over major legislation in general and Supreme Court nominees in particular.

Democrats opposed Gorsuch for several reasons, including his conservative judicial philosophy and what they described as vague answers to questions during his confirmation hearings. But their main resentment stemmed from McConnell's decision to block any consideration of Obama's nominee Merrick Garland to the court a year earlier. All fifty-two Republicans voted for the change, and all forty-eight Democrats and those who caucused with the party opposed it.

In the House, Republicans at the start of the 115th Congress pushed through a rules package (H Res 5) on a strictly party-line vote of 234–193. Several of the package's provisions irked Democrats. One of them permitted the House sergeant at arms to levy a fine against a member who breached House decorum with use of an electronic device and added specific conduct that would be considered disorderly and subject to referral to the Ethics Committee. The change was widely seen as a response to Democratic members' 25-hour "sit-in" on the House floor in June 2016 to demand votes—using social media—on anti-gun violence legislation following the slaying of forty-nine people at a nightclub in Orlando, Florida.

Another contentious change was the reintroduction of the so-called "Holman Rule," which had been deleted from House rules in 1983. The rule allowed legislation on an appropriations bill when the effect of the amendment is to "retrench expenditures." Democrats argued that the rule allowed the majority party to circumvent the legislative process in order to fire or cut the pay of individual federal workers or groups of workers.

The resolution contained a variety of other, less controversial changes. The 104th Congress (1995–1996) added a provision requiring that each standing committee adopt, by February 15 of the first session of a Congress, its own oversight plan for the Congress. H Res 5 added a requirement that the committees include a statement concerning authorizations for programs or agencies within their jurisdiction. Those statements were required to identify programs or agencies with lapsed authorizations that received funding in the prior fiscal year, as well as programs or agencies with a permanent authorization that had not been subject to a comprehensive committee review.

Another change amended a provision on the number of subcommittees allowed for three committees. The change allowed the Armed Services Committee to have not more than seven subcommittees, the Foreign Affairs Committee to have not more than seven subcommittees, and the Transportation and Infrastructure Committee to have not more than six.

Depositions by committee members or their attorneys was the subject of a rules change. The authority for depositions was formally expanded to include all standing committees—plus the Select Committee on Intelligence—except for the House Administration and Rules committees. Another change was made requiring one committee member to be present at each deposition unless the witness agreed in writing to waive the requirement or the committee authorized the taking of the specified deposition without a committee member present, provided the House was not in session on the day of the deposition.

The rules resolution gave new authority to the Homeland Security Committee to close additional hearings. Before the 115th Congress, only the Appropriations, Armed Services, and Intelligence committees and their subcommittees were authorized to close five additional, consecutive days of hearings when voting to close a day of hearings. Other committees were limited to one day. The resolution also set a deadline of December 31, 2017, for the implementation of a searchable electronic version of legislation to be publicly available prior to the consideration of bills and joint resolutions.

A minor—but unusual—change to Senate rules that drew significant publicity was adopted in April 2018 after Sen. Tammy Duckworth, D-Ill., gave birth to a daughter. The change (S Res 463), approved unanimously, enabled senators to bring their newborn children onto the floor during votes. Duckworth had decided to take her maternity leave in Washington, D.C., instead of Illinois, to be able to be available to cast her vote if needed.

CRS Reports Made Public

In September 2018, the Library of Congress launched crsreports.congress.gov and started publishing nonconfidential Congressional Research Service reports there. CRS, an arm of the library that was informally known as Congress' think tank, conducts research on numerous issues and compiles historical and background information as well as statistics on Congress' behalf. It regularly updates its reports to reflect changes in events. For many years, the reports were not officially released to the public. Some organizations advocating for greater openness in government, such as the Federation of American Scientists, had made many of the reports available on their websites.

Presidential Nominations

For his initial Cabinet, Trump drew from an array of veteran Republicans in Congress as well as others who had previously held elected office. But he also picked conservatives without any prior political experience. They included longtime ExxonMobil leader Rex Tillerson as secretary of State; Wall Street executive Steven Mnuchin as secretary of the Treasury; retired Marine Gen. James Mattis as secretary of Defense; and onetime presidential rival Ben Carson as secretary of Housing and Urban Development.

The selections of Tillerson and Mattis, in particular, drew strong bipartisan praise. Tillerson was confirmed 56–43 in February 2017, though much of the opposition stemmed from Democrats' unease with Trump's early foreign policy pronouncements. Two Democrats—West Virginia's Joe Manchin and North Dakota's Heidi Heitkamp—joined Republicans in supporting his nomination, along with Maine's Angus King, an independent caucusing with Democrats. Mattis was confirmed 98–1 during Trump's first week in office after Trump signed a waiver exempting Mattis from a law that blocks senior officers from taking the defense secretary job within seven years of retirement. Mattis, at the time, had been out of uniform for three years.

Carson also picked up support from some Democrats, even though the renowned brain surgeon and author had no experience running a bureaucracy. He was confirmed 58–41 in March. Mnuchin was confirmed 53–47 in February amid several Democrats' arguments that his financial services experience served to highlight some of the problems that triggered the 2008 financial crisis.

Other Trump nominees, however, sailed to confirmation. They included Elaine Chao, a former secretary of Labor under President George W. Bush and the wife of McConnell, who was confirmed 93–6 as secretary of Transportation; former Texas Gov. Rick Perry, confirmed 62–37 to serve as secretary of Energy; and Alexander Acosta, a former prosecutor and investment banker, who was confirmed 60–38 as secretary of Labor. Acosta was nominated after Trump's original choice, fast-food executive Andrew Puzder, withdrew. Puzder had come under intense criticism from Democrats and liberal groups who accused him of mistreating workers and opposing an increase in the minimum wage. Conservatives also criticized Puzder's employment of an undocumented immigrant as a housekeeper and his failure to pay taxes for her services.

Puzder would not become the only nominee for a Cabinet post to withdraw amid controversy. In March 2018, Trump nominated Ronny Jackson, a Navy officer and the president's physician, to succeed David Shulkin, an Obama administration holdover whom Trump fired, as secretary of Veterans' Affairs. Senators of both parties expressed skepticism over Jackson's lack of management experience, and subsequent news reports detailed allegations by White House medical staff accusing him of creating a hostile work environment, excessive drinking on the job, and dispensing medication improperly. He withdrew from consideration after three days—only to be elected in 2020 as a Republican congressman from Texas.

Michigan GOP activist Betsy DeVos encountered an even more formidable wall of Democratic opposition in her path to becoming secretary of Education. A wealthy donor to many Republican causes, DeVos had almost no direct education experience. But she was an outspoken supporter of two areas of education with which many Democrats and teachers' unions sharply disagreed: charter schools and vouchers allowing students to use taxpayer dollars to pay tuition at private, religious, and for-profit schools. The Senate deadlocked 50–50 on her nomination in February after two Republican senators, Susan Collins of Maine and Lisa Murkowski of Alaska, called DeVos unqualified and voted against her. Vice President Mike Pence, serving as president of the Senate, broke the tie to confirm her 51–50, the first time in history that a vice president was required to do so.

Current lawmakers who were picked for Trump's Cabinet included Alabama Sen. Jeff Sessions, a prominent Trump

campaign supporter and leading advocate for sharply restricting immigration, as attorney general. Sessions came under fire from his onetime Senate colleagues for his views on race and civil rights. He had previously been nominated to be a federal district judge in 1986 by then-President Ronald Reagan, but allegations of racism torpedoed his nomination, which was voted down in committee.

Tensions over his nomination led to the rare use of a Senate procedure to silence Democrat Elizabeth Warren of Massachusetts for quoting a thirty-year-old letter written by Coretta Scott King, the late widow of the Rev. Martin Luther King Jr., that sharply criticized Sessions. He was confirmed on a 52–47 vote in February, with all but one Democrat—West Virginia's Joe Manchin—opposing his nomination.

Another member of Congress, Georgia Rep. Tom Price, also was confirmed on a party-line 52–47 vote in February to become secretary of Health and Human Services. His nomination spurred intense criticism from Democrats over his views on reining in the growth of Medicare and Medicaid as well as actively trading shares of medical and pharmaceutical companies while shaping health policy. Price denied any ethical lapses. But after confirmation, he became enmeshed in a controversy over his accumulating at least $400,000 in travel bills for chartered flights. Even prominent Trump allies condemned his actions, and Price resigned in September.

Price's resignation began a pattern of Trump starting to rely on acting agency heads without sending them to the Senate for confirmation. The president boasted that the situation gave him more control. Two HHS officials, Don Wright and Eric Hargan, filled Price's shoes as acting secretary, with Hargan serving until January 2018. The situation occurred again after retired Marine Gen. John Kelly stepped down as Homeland Security secretary to become Trump's chief of staff. Elaine Duke served as acting secretary from July until December 2017, when Kirstjen Nielsen was confirmed as secretary. At Veterans' Affairs, Robert Wilkie and Peter O'Rourke served as acting secretaries from March to July 2018, when Wilkie was confirmed as the secretary.

Yet another House member chosen for Trump's Cabinet was Montana Rep. Ryan Zinke as secretary of Interior. He won confirmation in March on a 68–31 vote, with seventeen Democrats supporting him. But Zinke, like Price, was dogged by ethics questions. The Justice Department began investigating whether a land deal Zinke had struck with the chairman of oil services giant Halliburton Inc. in his hometown of Whitefish, Montana, constituted a conflict of interest. He resigned in December 2018 after White House officials reportedly told him that he had until the end of the year either to resign or be fired.

Zinke's pro-fossil fuel stance often lumped him with Scott Pruitt, Trump's choice to head the Environmental Protection Agency. As Oklahoma's attorney general, Pruitt had led Republican states in challenging Obama's environ-

mental regulations and defending oil and gas interests. Environmentalists sharply objected to Pruitt's nomination, and he was confirmed on a 52–46 vote in February; Maine Republican Susan Collins joined all but two Democrats in voting "no." But like Price and Zinke before him, Pruitt became enmeshed in ethics scandals and investigations. News outlets reported that Pruitt spent about $43,000 on a soundproof phone booth for his office, along with thousands of dollars on first-class plane tickets and other luxury items. He resigned in July 2018, with his deputy, Andrew Wheeler, filling the job for several months in an acting capacity.

Kansas Republican Rep. Mike Pompeo, nominated as Central Intelligence Agency director, fared far better than Pruitt, Zinke, or Price. Although his views on electronic surveillance and torturing terrorism suspects drew the ire of some Democrats, Pompeo was confirmed four days into Trump's term on a 66–32 vote. His pugnacious style earned Trump's admiration. When Tillerson was fired in 2018 after having numerous reported behind-the-scenes conflicts with the president, Pompeo was confirmed as Tillerson's successor on a 57–42 vote. Among the ten Democrats running for re-election in states that Trump had won in 2016, five voted to confirm Pompeo and five voted against the nomination.

Another House member who was a prominent Trump booster, Pennsylvania Republican Tom Marino, served on the executive committee of Trump's 2016 presidential transition team. Marino was nominated in September 2017 as "drug czar," or director of the Office of National Drug Control Policy. But Marino withdrew a month later, following news reports that he had been the main architect behind a bill that protected pharmaceutical manufacturers and distributors and crippled the Drug Enforcement Administration's ability to address the opioid epidemic. Marino introduced the Ensuring Patient Access and Effective Drug Enforcement Act in 2014 and again in 2015, but it failed to advance both times.

Baseball Game Shooting

In June 2017, a gunman opened fire on House Republicans gathered and others at a baseball practice. The Capitol Police were present in Alexandria, Virginia, near Washington, at the morning practice for the annual charity game between Republicans and Democrats and killed the suspect in an exchange of gunfire.

The gunman was identified as James T. Hodgkinson of Belleville, Illinois. Hodgkinson was a left-wing political activist who had written numerous letters to a local newspaper on various topics, many of which bitterly condemned Republicans. A month before the shooting, Hodgkinson reposted an online petition in which he called for the destruction of Trump and other Republicans. He had also written a series of Twitter posts urging Democratic senators to filibuster the nomination of Neil Gorsuch to the U.S. Supreme Court.

The gunman traveled to the baseball field and opened fire, striking Scalise in the hip. A U.S. Park Police helicopter rushed him to MedStar Washington Hospital Medical Center. Doctors reported that after the bullet struck his hip, it fractured bones, damaged internal organs, and caused severe bleeding, causing his condition to initially be listed as "critical." He received multiple blood transfusions and underwent several surgeries to repair internal damage. Bullets also struck Matt Mika, an agricultural lobbyist attending the practice, multiple times in the chest and arm, injuring his lungs, sternum, and ribs. He was in critical condition immediately following surgery but was released from the hospital within a week.

Two of the Capitol Police officers assigned to protect Scalise also were injured. One of them, Crystal Griner, was shot in the ankle and briefly hospitalized. Another officer, David Bailey, was treated and released after sustaining a minor injury not caused by gunfire. Zack Barth, a legislative aide to Texas GOP Rep. Roger Williams, was shot in the calf. He was treated at the hospital and released. Williams sprained his ankle while jumping into a dugout during the attack.

After months of treatment, Scalise returned to the House chamber in September 2017 to a chorus of cheers and applause. He thanked Capitol Police and Rep. Brad Wenstrup, R-Ohio, a military veteran who had applied a tourniquet to Scalise's leg after the shooting—a move that doctors later said helped to save the congressman's life. The FBI in 2021 formally reclassified the shooting as an incident of domestic terrorism, following pressure from a number of lawmakers who were present on the field to reevaluate the conclusion that the shooter sought to die via "suicide by cop."

Stepped-Up Security for Members

The baseball shooting led to a reevaluation of congressional security practices. In a June 2017 letter to the Federal Election Commission, House Sergeant at Arms Paul D. Irving said the U.S. Capitol Police had investigated roughly 950 threatening communications against members since January, compared to 902 similar investigations during all of 2016.

Pointing to concerns about members' security in the House as well as in their district offices, the House in June 2017 adopted a resolution (H Res 411) that boosted the annual allowance for each members' office by $25,000. The Congressional Handbook also was updated to provide additional guidance for updating security equipment and measures at personal residences and other locations.

Some Republicans called for even stricter protection measures. Rep. Jody Hice, R-Ga., introduced a bill that would authorize a member of Congress carrying appropriate identification to carry a firearm for any lawful purpose in any state, or in any of the Capitol buildings other than the Capitol itself. The bill did not advance. Nor did a separate proposal from Rep. Mo Brooks, R-Ala., that would

have enabled members to carry guns in the Capitol itself and any other location except where the U.S. Secret Service was protecting the president or vice president and had banned any firearms.

Democrats spoke out against both measures. Eleanor Holmes Norton, the nonvoting delegate representing the District, said she feared such moves would only spawn more violence across the region.

A further debate over gun violence was touched off by the February 2018 shooting at a high school in Parkland, Florida, in which a former student killed seventeen people. Shortly after the Parkland shooting, the House Administration Committee approved a resolution that permitted House members to buy bulletproof vests and other security items. The resolution also allowed members to hire security personnel for events such as town halls, to guard their district offices during business hours, and to accompany them on official business.

Paul Ryan Steps Down

The highest-profile personnel move of the 115th Congress was the decision of Wisconsin's Paul Ryan in 2019 not to see another term and to step aside as speaker after just over three years in the job of being second in line to the presidency.

Ryan, Republicans' 2012 vice-presidential nominee, was a widely admired figure within his party's ranks who was often mentioned as a potential future presidential candidate. But he had to be talked into taking the job as speaker following the resignation of John Boehner in October 2015. Ryan was known as a policy wonk who vastly preferred the chairmanship of the tax-writing Ways and Means Committee to leading the fractious House Republicans. Trump, by contrast, showed little interest in legislative minutiae and put personality differences at the center of his frequent squabbles. Ryan grew openly tired of continually being asked to respond to Trump's remarks.

Trump and Ryan had a particularly uneasy relationship. Ryan had withheld his endorsement of Trump for a month after the real estate mogul clinched the 2020 nomination. The speaker denounced some of Trump's comments, such as when Trump said a judge presiding over a lawsuit against Trump University could not be impartial because his Mexican heritage was a sign of bias. Their relationship reached a low after the release, just weeks before the election, of a 2005 video showing Trump joking about sexually assaulting women. Days later, Ryan announced he would no longer defend Trump and that he would not campaign with the nominee. After that announcement, Trump criticized the speaker during campaign rallies and on Twitter.

As speaker, Ryan adopted a style similar to that of his predecessors in refusing to bring up any bills that lacked the support of the majority of his conference's members. That approach had worked well in the past, but the new

GOP arrivals were markedly more conservative than many veteran lawmakers. And his lieutenants, such as California's McCarthy, were more eager than Ryan to follow the president's path. Ryan had particular trouble with the Freedom Caucus, a group of the most strongly conservative House members who had stymied Boehner. The Freedom Caucus chairman was Mark Meadows, a North Carolina Republican who would later become Trump's chief of staff. The two men openly bickered on multiple occasions, such as in June 2018 when Republicans were seeking to bring up an immigration bill that Trump was eager to pass. Meadows erupted at Ryan on the House floor several times, then later told reporters the speaker had agreed to a deal on what would be contained in the compromise legislation, only to leave several provisions out of the final text. Republican aides sharply disagreed with Meadows' assertions.

Ryan had long made clear that his major priority in Congress was passing major tax legislation, and in 2017 he helped steer into law the Tax Cuts and Jobs Act. With that goal accomplished, and a number of veteran Republicans announcing in early 2018 that they would retire in anticipation of a strongly Democratic election that November, Ryan decided he would join them. In April 2018, he announced that after considerable deliberation, he would not seek another term but would continue serving as speaker until the following January when his term expired.

Ryan cited the personal toll the speaker's job had taken on him, particularly his time away from his family. Though he made no public mention of his feuds with Trump, in interviews for a subsequent book about Congress he made clear his deep frustration with the president's lack of understanding of government and penchant for attacking others. For the rest of his term as speaker, and for two years after leaving office, Ryan avoided directly criticizing Trump. But in May 2021, Ryan gave a widely publicized speech in which he warned about the dangers of conservatism resting on the appeal of a single person. He also condemned the January 6 rioting and the party's electoral losses of both the White House and the Senate. His remarks provoked a torrent of criticism from Trump and the ex-president's allies.

After he stepped down, Ryan tried to avoid a divisive contest between McCarthy and Scalise over the next Republican leader by endorsing McCarthy, who had lacked enough votes on the House floor to be elected speaker in 2015 following Boehner's departure. McCarthy's candidacy ran into trouble after he suggested that the House's select committee investigating 2012 terrorist attacks in Benghazi, Libya, was directly tied to an effort to politically damage presidential candidate Hillary Clinton. His withdrawal had initially prompted House Republicans to turn to Ryan. But McCarthy had resurrected himself politically among caucus members with his repeated willingness to help them—and with his firm embrace of Trump. Scalise eventually agreed not to challenge him.

Deaths

JOHN MCCAIN

McCain, R-Ariz., a senator since 1987 and his party's 2008 presidential nominee, revealed in July 2017 that he had been diagnosed with a brain tumor. At the time, McCain—a former Navy pilot who had endured more than five years of torture as a prisoner of war in Vietnam—chaired the Armed Services Committee.

McCain was one of his party's most prominent members for his hawkish national security views as well as his willingness to break from his party and the widespread media attention that those breaks commanded. He was an architect of a bipartisan 2002 law that sought to clamp down on campaign spending. He was also a fierce critic of "pork barreling"—member-added provisions to spending bills that he said were too often abused. And he worked with Democrats on pursuing an overhaul of immigration laws that went well beyond what many in his party were willing to accept. At the same time, he was one of the Senate's leading advocates of a strong military and the use of military power as key tools of foreign policy.

In his 2008 run for the White House against Barack Obama, McCain sought to portray himself as a greater agent of bringing about change in the country. He chose Alaska Gov. Sarah Palin as his running mate, which drew initial praise from Republicans. But Palin's rambling interviews and verbal miscues provided fodder for late-night comedians, and numerous analysts questioned whether she had enough experience to serve as vice president. He lost to Obama with 46 percent to Obama's 53 percent, the best percentage by a Democrat since 1964.

After announcing his cancer diagnosis, McCain underwent a procedure to remove a blood clot above his left eye. But he returned to the Senate less than two weeks later to cast a dramatic decisive vote against the Senate's repeal of the Patient Protection and Affordable Care Act—the health care overhaul championed by Obama. McCain also issued a statement blasting the Republican process of bypassing the regular procedure of letting committees work and called for greater bipartisanship.

Trump, with whom McCain had often feuded, was incensed by the move. But McCain backed Trump's subsequent push for a comprehensive tax overhaul. He cut back on his Senate duties in order to focus on his treatment, and did not cast any votes after December 2017. He died days before his eighty-second birthday in August 2018, and became the subject of worldwide tributes attesting to his courage and principle. McCain became only the thirty-first person in 166 years whose body lay in state in the Capitol rotunda.

Republican Jon Kyl, who had served alongside McCain representing Arizona in the Senate from 1995 to 2013, was appointed to serve the remainder of his former colleague's term. But Kyl resigned from the Senate in December 2018, saying he had no desire to finish the remainder of the unexpired term. He was succeeded by Arizona Republican Rep. Martha McSally, who had lost the election for

Arizona's other Senate seat to Rep. Kyrsten Sinema. McSally lost her bid for reelection in 2020.

Louise Slaughter

Rep. Louise Slaughter, D-N.Y., died in March 2018 after a career in Congress that covered sixteen years. Slaughter served as chair of the House Rules Committee from 2007 until 2011, and as ranking member from 2005 to 2007 and from 2011 until her death.

Slaughter was the lead House sponsor of the Genetic Information Nondiscrimination Act, a 2008 law that barred the use of genetic information in health insurance and employment. At the time of her death at age eighty-eight, Slaughter was the oldest sitting member of Congress and the last sitting member who had been born in the 1920s.

Ethics Investigations

ROBERT MENENDEZ

The Senate Ethics Committee, in a rare move, admonished Sen. Robert Menendez, D-N.J., in April 2018 over his relationship with a campaign donor and close friend. The ethics panel's bipartisan letter of admonition to Menendez was a warning and not considered an official disciplinary sanction.

The controversy involving physician and businessman Salomon Melgen had dogged Menendez for years, and had led the senator to temporarily step down in 2015 as ranking Democrat on the Foreign Relations Committee after becoming only the twelfth sitting senator in history to be indicted for a crime. The charges against Menendez were dropped after federal prosecutors failed to convict him following a nearly three-month trial.

Menendez had been accused of using the power of his Senate office to benefit Melgen's personal and financial interests. According to the indictment, Menendez intervened in a multimillion-dollar Medicare billing dispute on Melgen's behalf; helped obtain visas for several of Melgen's girlfriends; and lobbied State Department officials regarding a $500 million port security contract that a Melgen-owned company had with the Dominican Republic. The gifts that the senator allegedly received included travel and more than $750,000 in campaign contributions.

Melgen was convicted of bilking Medicare out of $73 million and sentenced to seventeen years in federal prison. (Trump commuted Melgen's sentence in one of his final acts in office.) But Menendez denied any wrongdoing, and a mistrial was declared in 2017 after a federal jury in Newark, New Jersey, said it was hopelessly deadlocked. Though he acknowledged during the trial that he had accepted gifts from Melgen, he said they were old friends and his not declaring the gifts on disclosure forms was an honest mistake. His admission opened the door for the Ethics Committee to take action over the gifts. Any gift from a friend worth more than $250 had to receive Ethics Committee approval and be declared in senators' annual financial disclosure reports.

The ethics panel said he used poor judgment and that his actions brought discredit to the chamber. It ordered Menendez to pay for any improper gifts that had not already been reimbursed, and officially closed its file on the case in 2019. Menendez ended up winning reelection in November with 54 percent of the vote, despite a campaign in which his GOP opponent, pharmaceutical executive Bob Hugin, repeatedly questioned Menendez's ethics and spent more than $36 million of his own money on attack ads and other expenses. Menendez and his allies, however, issued their own attacks accusing Hugin of raising drug prices.

REP. DUNCAN D. HUNTER

The Justice Department in 2017 began a criminal investigation into Hunter, R-Calif., and his wife Margaret Jankowski, who also served as his campaign manager, for alleged campaign finance violations. Both of them were indicted in 2018 on charges that included conspiracy, wire fraud, and violating campaign finance laws. Jankowski in 2019 pleaded guilty to corruption and named her husband as a co-conspirator in using campaign funds for personal expenses.

Federal prosecutors said Hunter had spent campaign funds on extramarital affairs with five women, including lobbyists and congressional staff. In December 2019, Hunter changed his plea to guilty on one count of misusing campaign funds, and the next month resigned his seat. In March 2020, Hunter was sentenced to eleven months in prison that were scheduled to begin in January 2021. But in December, just weeks before he left office, Trump pardoned both Hunter and his wife.

REP. CHRIS COLLINS

The FBI arrested Collins, R-N.Y., and his son in 2018, and both were charged with insider trading and making false statements. The congressman was accused of breaching the confidentiality of secret results of a drug trial for an Australian biotechnology company on which he served as a board member so that his son could trade the company's stock before the results were made public.

Three days later, Collins announced that he was suspending his bid for a fourth term in Congress, but later sought reelection. He predicted he would be exonerated of the charges against him. He won reelection, though his percentage dropped from 67 percent two years earlier to 49 percent. His opponent, Democrat Nate McMurray, initially conceded on election night, but reversed course the next morning, saying the race was too close to call. Collins eventually was declared the winner by about 2,500 votes.

Collins announced in September 2019 he would resign from the House and pleaded guilty the next day to the two charges. Trump pardoned Collins—who had been one of the president's earliest supporters in Congress—in December 2020, again just weeks before leaving office.

REP. JAMES RENACCI

The Office of Congressional Ethics began to investigate Renacci's, R-Ohio, social media accounts in 2018 after the Ohio Democratic Party filed an official complaint that claimed he improperly used official resources including his

congressional website and Twitter account to promote his campaigns for U.S. Senate and governor.

The office subsequently found in 2019 that staffers regularly took photos and videos of their boss performing official functions at the U.S. Capitol and transmitted them to his campaign for publicity purposes, and also occasionally performed campaign work in his official office. Renacci was not sanctioned for any violations because he had already left office.

Targeting Sexual Harassment

The #MeToo movement—named for the hashtag used on Twitter—against sexual harassment dominated the national conversation in 2017 following the multiple sex abuse allegations against film producer Harvey Weinstein, who eventually was sentenced to twenty-three years in prison for his offenses. Rep. Jackie Speier, D-Calif., was credited with spearheading the movement on Capitol Hill in October 2017 by sharing her story of sexual harassment from her time as a young congressional staffer and inviting others to do likewise. Using the hashtag #MeTooCongress, she posted a video on her YouTube page describing how a chief of staff had once forcibly kissed her. Four female Democratic senators—Elizabeth Warren of Massachusetts, Claire McCaskill of Missouri, Heidi Heitkamp of North Dakota, and Mazie Hirono of Hawaii—spoke of similar experiences on NBC-TV's Sunday *Meet the Press* show, drawing even more attention to the issue in Congress.

Speier and other harassment victims on Capitol Hill called the formal process of investigating allegations under the 1995 Congressional Accountability Act severely outdated and overly cumbersome. Under that process, they noted, the accuser had to first enter into thirty days of counseling with a legal counselor. After that time, the accuser would have fifteen days to agree to go into mediation with a representative within the office with whom they registered the complaint. That mediation would last at least thirty days. It was only after then that a formal complaint could be filed. Opponents of such a system of forced arbitration argued that it kept misconduct allegations—and resulting investigation findings—confidential and required employees to settle cases outside a court of law.

Speier—who had introduced an anti-sexual harassment bill in 2014 that never advanced—drew even more attention when she testified before the House Administration Committee that she knew of one sexual harasser in each party who was currently serving in Congress. Rep. Barbara Comstock, R-Va., also relayed a story of sexual harassment that forced a staffer to quit her job.

Speier and a bipartisan group of lawmakers introduced a bill seeking to hold Congress more accountable. The measure, which overhauled the Accountability Act, called for holding members of Congress personally liable for awards and settlements stemming from harassment and related retaliation they personally committed, including those who leave office. It also forbade them from paying out settlements with taxpayer funds and required them to foot the bill within ninety days or their wages could be garnished.

The bill kicked off a protracted debate. The House passed the bill in February 2018, with the Senate following suit three months later. But the two chambers had trouble reaching an immediate agreement. The Senate's bill called for a lawmaker to pay only in instances of sexual harassment and not for other forms of discrimination against a subordinate. It also narrowed the definition of harassment. Such language led critics to warn of loopholes that they said could make it more difficult to reach a sexual harassment claim because the wrongdoing can be categorized as discrimination.

The two sides finally reached a deal and both chambers passed the bill (S 3749—PL 115 397) into law in December 2018. Even some of the bill's supporters said it still did not go far enough. They noted that the new law applied only to sexual harassment charges and not to cases of alleged discrimination, such as denying a job to a woman because she may become pregnant.

*Resignations/Retirements Over Sexual
Misconduct Allegations*

By the end of 2018, allegations of sexual misconduct had ended the careers and campaigns of numerous members of Congress in that cycle.

Sen. Al Franken, D-Minn.: A radio broadcaster and model alleged in 2017 that Franken—a comedian and performer for *Saturday Night Live* before being elected—forcibly kissed her on a 2006 USO tour. He was also photographed placing his hands above the woman's breasts while she slept.

Seven additional women came forward with allegations of inappropriate behavior. Senate leaders, with Franken's encouragement, forwarded the allegations to the Ethics Committee for review. Two more accusations surfaced, one by an anonymous congressional aide about an attempted kiss and one by another congressional aide that Franken squeezed her waist before he took office.

More than two dozen Democratic senators called on Franken to resign before the ethics committee could review the allegations. In the face of growing pressure from the senators and women's organizations, he announced his intention to resign his seat in December. Minnesota Lt. Gov. Tina Smith was appointed to serve the remainder of his term.

A 2019 investigation in *The New Yorker* cast doubt on some of the original allegations against Franken. Several of his former colleagues said they regretted their earlier decision to call for his resignation without letting the ethics investigation proceed.

Rep. John Conyers Jr., D-Mich.: Conyers resigned in December 2017 after multiple allegations of sexual harassment during his forty-seven years in the House. Conyers was a revered figure among many African Americans nationally: He was a former chairman of the Judiciary Committee and a founder of the Congressional Black Caucus.

The allegations included charges from a former staffer that he inappropriately touched her during her thirteen years of working for him. She also said she witnessed Conyers touching other women in the office. According to the documents obtained by the news site BuzzFeed, one former staff member said she was fired because she would not have sex with Conyers. The publication also obtained affidavits from other staff members who said the congressman repeatedly harassed women working for him by requesting sexual acts.

Conyers initially denied all of the allegations against him. But amid an inquiry by the House Ethics Committee following revelations of a settlement two years prior for wrongful dismissal of a female employee, he announced his departure.

Rep. Trent Franks, R-Ariz.: Franks resigned in December 2017, after he was accused of offering $5 million to a female employee to be a surrogate mother of his children. She and another female employee worried that Franks wanted to have sex in order to impregnate them, according to an investigation by the House Ethics Committee.

Franks acknowledged that he had made staffers uncomfortable and that he had discussed fertility issues and surrogacy with two female staffers. But he denied the other claims. In resigning, Franks cited his wife's health, just as the Associated Press reported that Franks allegedly offered $5 million to a female employee to be a surrogate for him and his wife.

Rep. Patrick Meehan, R-Pa.: The New York Times reported in January 2018 that Meehan used thousands of taxpayer dollars to settle a sexual harassment claim brought by a female former staffer in 2017. She alleged that he grew hostile after she rejected his romantic advances. The staff member began to work from home to avoid Meehan's advances and ultimately left the job.

Meehan initially denied the allegations through a spokeswoman. But several months later, he abruptly resigned amid a House Ethics Committee investigation into his alleged conduct. He said that he would pay back the funds used for the settlement.

Rep. Tim Murphy, R-Pa.: Murphy resigned in October 2017, after revelations that he pressured a woman with whom he was having an affair to get an abortion. Murphy admitted to having an affair with the woman, whose relationship with him came to light through her divorce proceedings. The *Pittsburgh Post-Gazette* also published a memorandum from Murphy's chief of staff to Murphy complaining of the congressman's repeated harassment of staff and his abusive behavior, which the aide said had caused morale to deteriorate and made it extremely difficult to hire new employees.

Murphy was a fervent opponent of abortion during his nearly fifteen years in the House. A psychologist, Murphy was first elected to Congress in 2002, where he became an advocate for improving mental health care. Some of his mental health provisions were included in the 21st Century Cures Act, a broad health care bill signed into law at the end of 2016. After leaving office, he took a job with a government relations firm.

Rep. Joe L. Barton, R-Texas: Barton announced in November 2017 that he would not seek reelection to his 6th District seat in the House after reports of extramarital relationships with multiple women before his 2015 divorce. A lewd photo he had sent to one of the women circulated online the week before his announcement. A staunch advocate for the oil and gas industry, Barton was a former chairman of the Energy and Commerce Committee, and helped to steer a comprehensive 2005 energy bill into law. He briefly launched a run for minority leader that year, but dropped out when it became apparent he lacked enough support.

Rep. Ruben Kihuen, D-Nev.: Kihuen announced in December 2017 that he would not run for reelection in the wake of sexual misconduct allegations. The House Ethics Committee later concluded that Kihuen "made persistent and unwanted advances toward women who were required to work with him." BuzzFeed News reported that a former Kihuen campaign staffer had rebuffed multiple advances and that Kihuen had touched her without her consent. *The Nevada Independent* reported that a female lobbyist had received persistent and unwanted advances from Kihuen, through hundreds of text messages, and was also touched without her consent.

Rep. Blake Farenthold, R-Texas: Farenthold resigned from the House in April 2018, after a former aide charged him with sexual harassment. Tax dollars were used to pay an $84,000 settlement. The action came after Farenthold's former communications director in 2014 sued the congressman alleging gender discrimination, sexual harassment, and a hostile work environment. Both parties agreed to drop the case in 2015.

While Farenthold initially said he would reimburse the $84,000, he later declared that he had no intention of paying it back. The situation led Rep. Mark Walker, R-N.C., in 2019 to introduce the BLAKE Act (or Bad Lawmakers Accountability and Key Emends Act), which would block former members of Congress from lobbying their colleagues if they never repay taxpayer funds that they used to settle litigation.

Rep. Elizabeth Esty, D-Conn.: Esty announced in April 2018 that she would not seek reelection after reports that she had allowed a chief of staff in her House office to work for months after Esty had been told he had harassed, abused, and threatened a female staffer.

Other Resignations and Retirements

Mississippi Republican Sen. Thad Cochran resigned in April 2018, citing health concerns. Cochran had served in the chamber since 1978 and rose to chair the Appropriations Committee from 2005 to 2007 and again from 2015 to 2018. His resignation followed a series of news reports raising questions about whether he remained fit to serve because of his advancing age. He died in May 2019, a little more than a year after leaving office.

California Democrat Xavier Becerra resigned his seat in January 2017 to serve as the state's attorney general. Becerra had been one of the House's highest-profile Latinos over his two decades in office and had served as chairman of the House Democratic Caucus. He went on to become secretary of Health and Human Services under President Joe Biden in 2021.

South Carolina Rep. Mick Mulvaney resigned his seat in February 2017 after being nominated by President-elect Trump to head the White House Office of Management and Budget. Mulvaney would later serve as Trump's chief of staff.

Montana Rep. Ryan Zinke resigned his at-large seat in March 2017 after becoming Trump's secretary of Interior. He left the post in 2019 amid a cloud of ethics questions.

Georgia Rep. Tom Price resigned his seat in February 2017 after being named as Trump's secretary of Health and Human Services. Price, a physician, was a former chairman of the House Republican Policy Committee and was active on health care issues. He would resign after being dogged by controversies about his travel expenses.

Utah Republican Rep. Jason Chaffetz resigned in June 2017 after abruptly announcing his departure two months earlier. Chaffetz—who had been chairman of the powerful Oversight and Government Reform Committee—said he had a mid-life crisis and that he was disappointed in the Trump administration for not making enough immediate changes in the federal bureaucracy. Chaffetz became a Fox News contributor, commentator, and author.

West Virginia Republican Rep. Evan Jenkins announced his retirement from his 3rd District seat in May 2017 to run for the Senate. He lost the nomination and then resigned in September 2018 when he was appointed to the Supreme Court of Appeals of West Virginia. His seat was not filled until the regular election for the next Congress.

Oklahoma 1st District Republican Rep. Jim Bridenstine announced his retirement in November 2017 after Trump announced his intention to name him as NASA administrator. Bridenstine resigned in April 2018 after being confirmed.

Pennsylvania Democratic Rep. Robert A. Brady announced in January 2018 that he would not seek reelection to his 2nd District seat amid allegations that he conspired with former campaign strategists to pay a Democratic primary challenger in his district $90,000 to exit the race.

Pennsylvania Republican 15th District Rep. Charlie Dent, a well-regarded moderate and frequent Trump critic, retired in May 2018, amid threats from the president's allies to mount a primary challenge against him.

Ohio Republican Rep. Pat Tiberi resigned from his 12th District in January 2018, two months after he announced he would leave Congress to run the Ohio Business Roundtable. Tiberi had served in Congress since 1993 and was a close ally of John Boehner when Boehner was minority leader and speaker.

Virginia Republican Rep. Tom Garrett announced in May 2018 that he was an alcoholic and would not seek reelection to his 5th District seat. The admission came as the House Ethics Committee was investigating allegations that he used his congressional aides to run personal errands for him and his wife.

Arizona 9th District Democratic Rep. Kyrsten Sinema retired to run successfully for the Senate, replacing the retiring Republican Jeff Flake. Arizona 2nd District Rep. Martha McSally retired to run for U.S. Senator. She lost to Sinema, though she was appointed to fill the state's other Senate seat.

California 39th District Republican Rep. Ed Royce retired. He was a former chairman of the House Foreign Affairs Committee.

Colorado 2nd District Democratic Rep. Jared Polis retired to run successfully for governor of his state. Florida 6th District Republican Rep. Ron DeSantis resigned to run successfully for governor of his state. Hawaii 1st District Democratic Rep. Colleen Hanabusa retired to unsuccessfully run for governor of Hawaii. Idaho 1st District Republican Rep. Raúl Labrador retired to run for governor of his state; he lost in the primary to eventual winner Brad Little.

Indiana 4th District Republican Rep. Todd Rokita retired to unsuccessfully run for Senate. Despite losing, he won election in 2020 as the state's attorney general.

Indiana 6th District Republican Rep. Luke Messer retired to unsuccessfully run for Senate.

Maryland 6th District Democratic Rep. John Delaney retired to run for president. He failed to gain any traction in polls and dropped out in January 2020.

Minnesota 1st District Democratic Rep. Tim Walz retired to run successfully for governor of his state. Minnesota 5th District Democratic Rep. Keith Ellison retired to run successfully for state attorney general. Nevada 3rd District Rep. Jacky Rosen retired to run successfully for U.S. Senate, defeating incumbent Republican Dean Heller.

New Mexico 1st District Democratic Rep. Michelle Lujan Grisham retired to run successfully for governor of her state. New Mexico 2nd District Republican Rep. Steve Pearce retired to run for governor, only to lose to Lujan Grisham.

North Dakota at-large Republican Rep. Kevin Cramer retired to run successfully for the Senate, defeating incumbent Democrat Heidi Heitkamp. Pennsylvania 9th District Republican Rep. Lou Barletta retired to unsuccessfully run for the Senate.

South Dakota at-large Republican Rep. Kristi Noem retired to run successfully for governor. Tennessee 6th District Republican Rep. Diane Black retired to unsuccessfully run for governor.

Tennessee 7th District Republican Rep. Marsha Blackburn retired to run successfully for the Senate.

Texas 16th District Democratic Rep. Beto O'Rourke retired to run for the Senate, narrowly losing to incumbent Republican Ted Cruz.

Other House Retirements

California 49th District Republican Darrell Issa; Florida 15th District Republican Dennis Ross; Florida 17th District Republican Tom Rooney; Florida 27th District Republican Ileana Ros-Lehtinen; Illinois 4th District Democrat Luis Gutiérrez; Kansas 2nd District Republican Rep. Lynn Jenkins; Massachusetts 3rd District Democrat Niki Tsongas; Michigan 9th District Democrat Sander Levin; Michigan 11th District Republican Dave Trott; Minnesota 8th District Democrat Rick Nolan; Mississippi 3rd District Republican Gregg Harper; New Hampshire 1st District Democratic Rep. Carol Shea-Porter; New Jersey 2nd District Republican Frank LoBiondo; New Jersey 11th District Republican Rodney Frelinghuysen; Pennsylvania 6th District Republican Ryan Costello; Pennsylvania 13th District Republican Bill Shuster; South Carolina 4th District Republican Trey Gowdy; Tennessee 2nd District Republican Jimmy Duncan; Texas 2nd District Republican Ted Poe; Texas 3rd District Republican Sam Johnson; Texas 5th District Republican Rep. Jeb Hensarling; Texas 21st District Republican Lamar Smith; Texas 29th District Democrat Gene Green; Virginia 6th District Republican Bob Goodlatte; Washington 8th District Republican Dave Reichert

Senate Retirements

Thad Cochran of Mississippi; Republican Bob Corker of Tennessee; Republican Jeff Flake of Arizona; Republican Orrin Hatch of Utah

Special Elections

Alabama Senate

The 2017 election to fill the seat of Jeff Sessions after he was named Trump's attorney general was among the most unusual and tumultuous in recent congressional history. In one of the nation's most conservative states, Democrat Doug Jones overcame long initial odds to defeat Republican former state Supreme Court Justice Roy Moore. Jones' victory—the first by his party in a statewide race since 2008—came after *The Washington Post* published an article in which four women alleged that Moore inappropriately pursued them when they were teenagers and he was in his thirties. One of them alleged being sexually assaulted. Five more women also came forward, with two of them alleging assault.

Before he decided to run for the Senate, Moore was already unpopular among some Republicans in the state, who were dismayed by his controversial rhetoric and high-profile defiance of federal orders. Trump himself endorsed Luther Strange, who had been appointed to fill the seat after Sessions moved to the Justice Department. Strange lost to Moore in a Republican primary runoff even though he outspent his opponent by a ten-to-one margin, thanks

to a fundraising effort on his behalf led by Kentucky's Mitch McConnell.

Moore had twice been ousted from the state bench—first in 2003 for refusing to remove a Ten Commandments monument from the courthouse, and again in 2016 for ordering judges not to comply with the U.S. Supreme Court's same-sex marriage decision. But the allegations of the women became the tipping point for many national GOP leaders. The state's senior senator, Republican Richard C. Shelby, announced shortly before the December election that he could not vote for Moore, who had denied all the allegations as untrue and politically motivated. Moore did collect endorsements from a number of popular conservatives, including former Alaska Gov. Sarah Palin and ex-Trump adviser Steve Bannon.

Jones, a former U.S. attorney, won with 50 percent of the vote to Moore's 48.3 percent. Jones took office in January 2018, only to lose in November 2020 to another Republican, former football coach Tommy Tuberville.

Minnesota Senate

After Minnesota's Al Franken resigned in 2017, Democratic Gov. Mark Dayton appointed Tina Smith—his lieutenant governor and a former aide of his—to fill the seat. In the November 2018 special election, Smith defeated GOP state Sen. Karin Housley with ease, 53 percent to 42 percent.

Housley attacked Smith for being a hypocrite for opposing Supreme Court Justice Brett Kavanaugh's nomination by standing by Rep. Keith Ellison's campaign for attorney general, despite Ellison facing allegations of domestic abuse. (An attorney hired by the state Democratic Party could not substantiate the claims against him.) But Smith enjoyed a considerable advantage in fundraising. Two years later, in 2020, she won a general election to a full six-year term, defeating Republican Jason Lewis with 49 percent to Lewis' 44 percent.

Mississippi Senate

Following Thad Cochran's departure in April 2018, Mississippi Republican Gov. Phil Bryant named Cindy Hyde-Smith to fill the remainder of Cochran's term. Hyde-Smith previously was the state's agriculture commissioner and a state senator. She became the first woman to represent Mississippi in the Senate. Hyde-Smith went on to defeat Democrat Mike Espy, a former Agriculture secretary and congressman, in the special election runoff that November, 54 percent to 46 percent. Two years later, in a rematch, she easily defeated Espy again.

Shortly before the special election, Hyde-Smith was widely criticized for saying that if one of her supporters, Tupelo cattle rancher Colin Hutchinson, invited her to a public hanging, she would be in the front row. In a deep Southern state with a history of lynchings of African Americans, her remarks took on racial connotations. She at first refused to apologize, but later offered a conditional apology.

Pennsylvania's 7th District

Democrat Mary Gay Scanlon, an attorney, defeated Republican Pearl Kim and two other candidates in the special election for Pennsylvania's 7th District. The election coincided with the regular election on November 6, 2018.

The winner of the special election served in Congress until Republican Rep. Patrick Meehan's term expired in January 2019. Scanlon's special election also was held in conjunction with a regular election for a full two-year term in the new 5th District, which she also won.

Pennsylvania's 15th District

In November 2018, Democratic attorney Susan Wild defeated Republican ex-Olympic cyclist Marty Nothstein and Libertarian television reporter Tim Silfies in the special election for Pennsylvania's 7th District. The winner of the special election served in Congress until Republican Charlie Dent's term expired on January 1, 2019. Wild also defeated Nothstein and Silfies in the regular election for the newly drawn 7th District.

Pennsylvania's 18th District

Democrat Conor Lamb, a former Marine and prosecutor, won the special election for Pennsylvania's 18th District against Republican Rick Saccone in March 2018 by less than half a point. The race was too close to call immediately following the election, but Saccone conceded to Lamb a week later.

The special election was held to fill the vacancy created by the departure of incumbent Tim Murphy. It received attention from national figures on both sides of the aisle as an early sign of how Democrats could potentially retake the House that fall. Trump visited the state twice during the campaign, previewing his first trip with a tweet voicing support for Saccone and headlining a rally for the candidate during the second. Former Vice President Joe Biden campaigned for Lamb in March.

Kansas' 4th District

Republican Ron Estes won an April 2017 special election to represent the 4th District after Mike Pompeo was named to head the CIA. Estes received 52 percent of the vote to Democrat James Thompson's 46 percent. Before coming to Congress, Estes served as Kansas state treasurer and was a farmer and engineer.

In his 2018 bid to retain his seat, Estes faced a Republican primary challenger named Ron M. Estes, prompting legal action to differentiate the two candidates on the ballot. A state board allowed the congressman to be listed as "Rep. Ron Estes," and he won reelection. He won another term in 2020.

Montana's At-Large District

Businessman Greg Gianforte, a Republican, won a special election in May 2017 to fill the seat of Ryan Zinke for Montana's at-large district after Zinke was named Interior secretary. Gianforte won 50 percent of the vote against Democrat Rob Quist and Libertarian Mark Wicks.

The race attracted national attention after Gianforte angrily slammed to the ground a political reporter who sought to question him. Three Montana newspapers withdrew their earlier endorsements for him. Other Republicans condemned his actions, but said his future should be left to voters. After the election he was convicted of assault in state court, fined and sentenced to community service and anger-management therapy. Gianforte won a full term in 2018 but decided in 2020 not to run again.

California's 34th District

Democrat Jimmy Gomez won a June 2017 runoff special election in California's 34th District over fellow Democrat Robert Lee Ahn to fill the seat of Xavier Becerra, who had resigned to serve as the state's attorney general. The two candidates were the top vote getters in California's top-two primary system.

Gomez had served as the legislative and political director for the United Nurses Associations of California/Union of Health-Care Professionals and the political representative for the American Federation of State, County, and Municipal Employees. He easily won reelection in 2018 and 2020.

Georgia's 6th District

Republican Karen Handel won a June 2017 special election to fill the seat of Rep. Tom Price in the 6th District after Price was named secretary of Health and Human Services. Handel had a diverse portfolio of public- and private-sector jobs ranging from overseeing elections as Georgia's Secretary of State to heading the Fulton County Board of Commissioners to serving as vice president of the Susan G. Komen Foundation, which supports breast cancer research.

She defeated Democrat Jon Ossoff, who later went on to be elected to the U.S. Senate from Georgia in 2020. Handel lost to Democrat Lucy McBath in 2018 and again two years later in a rematch.

South Carolina's 5th District

Republican Ralph Norman, a wealthy developer, won his seat in a June 2017 special election to replace Mick Mulvaney, who resigned to become the director of the Office of Management and Budget in the Trump administration. Norman won the runoff over Democrat Archie Parnell by roughly 200 votes out of more than 35,000 cast. In the special general election that followed, Norman defeated Parnell by a slim 3 percent. The two had a rematch in 2018, with Norman winning easily.

Utah's 3rd District

Republican John Curtis, who had been mayor of Provo, won the November 2017 special election to replace Jason Chaffetz. Curtis easily beat Democrat Kathie Allen and

four other opponents with 58 percent of the vote. He easily won reelection in 2018 and 2020.

Arizona's 8th District

Republican Debbie Lesko, an Arizona state senator, won the April 2018 special election to replace departed Rep. Trent Franks, defeating Democrat Hiral Tipirneni with 53 percent of the vote. She beat Tipirneni by a wider margin that November and coasted to victory in 2020.

Texas' 27th District

Republican media consultant Michael Cloud won a June 2018 special election to fill the seat held by Blake Farenthold. The election came earlier than legally required because Texas officials wanted a member in Congress to represent the district as it recovered from Hurricane Harvey, which blasted the Houston area in August 2017.

Cloud easily beat Democrat Eric Holguin with 55 percent of the vote, increasing his share to 60 percent of the vote over Holguin in a November general-election rematch. He also won easily in 2020.

Ohio's 12th District

Republican businessman Troy Balderson won an August 2018 election triggered by the resignation of Pat Tiberi. Balderson edged out Democrat Danny O'Connor, 50.1 percent to 49.3 percent, then beat O'Connor again with 51 percent that November. He easily won reelection in 2020.

Michigan's 13th District

Democrat Brenda Jones, president of Detroit's City Council, won the November 2018 special election to fill John Conyers' seat. Jones defeated Constitution Party candidate Marc Sosnowski with 87 percent of the vote. Jones only served for two months. She ran for Congress again in 2020 but lost the Democratic primary to incumbent Democrat Rashida Tlaib.

New York's 25th District

Democrat Joseph Morelle, the New York State Assembly's majority leader, won the November 2018 special election to fill the remaining two months of the term of Louise Slaughter plus another two-year term. Morelle defeated Republican Jim Maxwell with 58 percent of the vote. He easily won reelection in 2020.

Notable Legislation

In the 115th Congress, 13,556 bills, resolutions and other legislation were introduced in both chambers—the most since the 111th Congress (2013–2014). Of that total, 1,085 measures were enacted or incorporated into law, according to GovTrack.us—a rate of 8 percent, the highest since the 101st Congress (1989–1990). No bills were vetoed, reflecting Republican control over both chambers and the White House.

Legislative Branch Appropriations

Funding for the 2018 fiscal year was provided in the Consolidated Appropriations Act of 2018 (PL 115-141), enacted in March 2018. The $4.7 billion provided by the act represented an increase of $260.0 million from the fiscal 2017 enacted level. The Government Accountability Office (GAO) received additional money through a supplemental spending bill (PL 115-123) that provided $14 million to GAO for audits and investigations relating to Hurricanes Harvey, Irma, and Maria and the 2017 wildfires that hit parts of the West.

Funding for fiscal year 2019 was provided in the Energy and Water, Legislative Branch, and Military Construction and Veterans Affairs Appropriations Act, 2019 (PL 115-244), which was enacted in September 2018. The $4.836 billion provided for the legislative branch represented an increase of $136.0 million, or 2.9 percent, from the fiscal 2018 enacted level.

Another $10 million in fiscal 2019 supplemental appropriations for GAO for audits and investigations related to hurricanes, 2018 wildfires, earthquakes, and volcano eruptions, and other disasters were included in HR 2157, which passed the House and Senate in May 2019. HR 2157 was enacted in June 2019 (PL 116-20). Neither spending bill for the legislative branch in the 115th Congress that became law raised the pay of lawmakers.

HR 72: GAO Access and Oversight Act of 2017

One of the most consequential bills in the 115th Congress addressing the institution's operations dealt with the Government Accountability Office, Capitol Hill's watchdog arm. The bill (HR 72; PL 115-3)—which passed easily—strengthened GAO's powers by authorizing it to obtain records it deemed necessary to carry its audit, evaluation, and investigative duties. It could obtain those records through bringing a civil action against a federal agency, if necessary, to compel it to produce a record.

The measure also clarified that privacy restrictions in the Social Security Act could not bar GAO's ability to obtain information or inspect records—including the National Directory of New Hires, or NDNH, a database that the office previously had been blocked from accessing. Bill sponsors said such a move would improve GAO oversight over a variety of federal programs, including unemployment insurance, student loans, and the Supplemental Nutrition Assistance Program food stamps program. Also under the bill, agency statements on actions taken or planned in response to GAO recommendations would have to be submitted to the congressional committees with jurisdiction over the pertinent agency program or activity, and the GAO.

The bill's passage followed the recent passage of a bill similarly boosting the powers of inspectors general, who serve as internal watchdogs at federal agencies. The House passed the bill by voice vote on January 4, 2017, with the Senate doing so 99–0 on January 17.

HR 469: Strengthening Congress' Ability to Intervene in Court Cases

The House on October 25 2017 passed a bill (HR 469) on a 234–187 vote that would expand Congress's ability to intervene in court cases involving constitutional challenges. But the measure never advanced in the Senate.

The bill, sponsored by Rep. Doug Collins, R-Ga., also sought to limit the process for using consent decrees or settlements to resolve litigation against the federal government. It would have required the use of alternative dispute resolution procedures that include industry and other stakeholders in negotiations. And it would have required the Treasury Department to publish information on its court-related payments.

The language concerning congressional intervention was drawn from a separate bill (HR 4070) sponsored by Rep. Robert Goodlatte, R-Va., chairman of the House Judiciary Committee. It would have required courts to allow the House or Senate to intervene in cases in which the Justice Department has decided to affirmatively challenge, or not to defend, the constitutionality of any provision of federal law or regulation or any federal policy. The House or Senate also could appeal any federal court decision that adversely affects the constitutionality of such a provision or policy.

The bill came about following the Justice Department's decision in 2011 to stop defending the Defense of Marriage Act (PL 104-199) after its lawyers determined that the law's definition of marriage as being between one man and one woman was unconstitutional. The same year, the department intervened in a case to argue that the court should strike down the definition. The House intervened to defend the law, participating in a series of cases culminating with the Supreme Court's decision in *U.S. v. Windsor*, finding Section 3 of the act to be unconstitutional.

Under the bill, the Justice Department would have to inform both chambers of its decision at least twenty-one days before a court deadline to intervene or appeal. Courts would have to accept as on time any congressional request to intervene filed within twenty-one days of a notification from the department. Current law called for the department to report to Congress within thirty days on any decision to challenge or not defend a provision or policy. The bill would require federal, state, and territorial courts to allow the House to intervene or participate in proceedings as a "friend of the court"—also known as *amicus curiae*—unless its request was late and would significantly delay the proceeding.

Democrats objected to the inclusion of the language. They noted that the measure had not been subject to a hearing or markup before the Judiciary Committee, depriving them of any ability to analyze it. Only two Democrats joined Republicans in supporting the bill.

Objections from the Sierra Club and other environmental groups proved to be an obstacle to the bill's progress. The groups argued that it prescribed burdensome, sometimes ambiguous steps that ended up favoring continued litigation over settlement. They also said it would delay and obstruct some environmental protection cases pending in federal courts. It became part of the League of Conservation Voters' 2017 legislative scorecard that was used in assessing the overall environmental credentials of lawmakers.

2019–2020

The 116th Congress convened at noon on January 3, 2019. There were nine new senators (2 Democrats, 7 Republicans) and eighty-nine new representatives (59 Democrats and 29 Republicans, with one open seat pending), as well as one new delegate (a Democrat) at the start of its first session.

The Democrats' recapturing of the House majority in the 2018 midterm elections dramatically altered Congress' course during the final two years of Trump's presidency. Democrats gained a net total of forty-one seats from the total number they had won in 2016—their largest gain of House seats since the 1974 elections following the Watergate revelations over GOP President Richard Nixon. The party's gains came as many Democrats ran for office out of frustration with gridlock or anger at Trump and his administration, as well as sometimes both.

But the Democratic Party did not get the blue tidal wave of support that some political analysts had projected. Nor did the GOP losses equal the "shellacking" that then-President Barack Obama famously described after his party's disastrous showing in his first midterm election in 2010, when control of both chambers switched over to the GOP. In the Senate in 2018, Republicans increased their majority by defeating Democratic incumbents in Florida, Indiana, Missouri, and North Dakota while holding open seats in Tennessee and Utah. In contrast, Democrats won two Republican-held Senate seats, defeating an incumbent in Nevada and winning an open seat in Arizona.

116th Congress: Organization and Leadership

Democrats' return to the majority meant the prospective return of California's Nancy Pelosi—who had been the first female Speaker—to the chair. She eventually did so, but not with ease. Much of the Democratic Caucus was hungry for change. Calls increased during the election cycle from Democratic incumbents and candidates asking for a new generation of leaders—with some of them explicitly stating they would not support the seventy-eight-year-old Pelosi, who had held her party's top leadership position for sixteen years.

In the months leading up to the election, however, the California Democrat repeatedly expressed confidence she would win the gavel. She did so again the day after the election when confronted with the question during a victory lap press conference at the Capitol. But she said she did not want to answer questions about the speaker's race, saying she preferred to keep the focus on Democrats' policy priorities. The "For the People" agenda that Pelosi and her leadership team crafted during the campaign had three main goals: lowering health care costs and prescription drug prices, increasing pay and driving economic growth by rebuilding the country's infrastructure, and cleaning up corruption in Washington.

The speaker sets the majority party's agenda and controls the floor schedule. They are also the lead negotiator for the House in matters involving the Senate and White House. Pelosi said she had more than proven herself in those areas, particularly holding her own in negotiations at a table where she had been surrounded by men. Among other things, she pointed to the Patient Protection and Affordable Care Act, the 2010 health care overhaul that was President Barack Obama's signature legislative achievement. Wanting a woman to be involved in those negotiations was one of the main reasons Pelosi remained in Congress. She said she had planned to retire if Hillary Clinton had won the 2016 presidential race.

At the Democrats' November postelection gathering, Pelosi got 203 votes on the caucus ballot. But her allies believed that was far lower than what she could earn on the floor during the formal vote. There were thirty-two "no" votes, three blanks, and one member was absent. The caucus temporarily changed its rules to allow for a "no" option on the speaker ballot to help Democrats who had promised during their campaigns to vote against Pelosi to fulfill that pledge. Typically, the only option for voting against a candidate in an uncontested race would be to leave the ballot blank or write in someone else's name. The thinking among Pelosi's supporters was that having an actual "no" vote on the ballot—which, while secret, members could take pictures of and share on social media—would be enough for most of them.

The California Democrat still ended up having to cut a handful of deals before the start of the 116th Congress with would-be opponents to shore up the support needed to win the floor vote, even though no one emerged to challenge her for the position. The one deal that vanquished the final opponents standing in her way came with a considerable price-tag: an agreement from Pelosi that she would not serve more than four additional years as speaker. Ultimately, of the 430 votes cast on the first day of the new Congress, Pelosi received 220—seventeen more than the number who backed her in November. She became the first speaker to reclaim the gavel after a hiatus in the minority since the legendary Sam Rayburn did so in 1955.

Fifteen Democrats did not cast ballots for her: Anthony Brindisi of New York backed former Vice President Joe Biden. Jason Crow of Colorado and Max Rose of New York supported Illinois Sen. Tammy Duckworth, while Joe Cunningham of South Carolina, Mikie Sherrill of New Jersey, Jared Golden of Maine, and Abigail Spanberger of Virginia supported their colleague Cheri Bustos of Illinois.

Other lawmakers voted for different colleagues. Ron Kind of Wisconsin supported civil rights icon

Rep. John Lewis of Georgia, while Ben McAdams of Utah supported Stephanie Murphy of Florida and Conor Lamb of Pennsylvania voted for Rep. Joe Kennedy III of Massachusetts. Kurt Schrader of Oregon backed Marcia Fudge of Ohio, who had publicly considered running for the position but endorsed Pelosi instead. Jim Cooper of Tennessee—a longtime Pelosi critic—voted "present," as did Elissa Slotkin of Michigan and Jeff Van Drew of New Jersey. In recognition of the provision in the Constitution enabling nonmembers of Congress to serve as Speaker, Kathleen Rice of New York backed Stacey Abrams, who had run against Republican Brian Kemp to become governor of Georgia and who had refused to concede losing to Kemp, declaring voter fraud.

Only one other House Democratic leadership contest was as contentious: The race for Democratic caucus chairman, which pitted New York's Hakeem Jeffries against California's Barbara Lee. Jeffries and Lee were both members of the Congressional Black Caucus, and their contest provided a tough choice for their colleagues within that group. The Black Caucus traditionally values seniority, and Lee had served seven terms more than Jeffries. But several members backing Jeffries said the opportunity for him to rise in leadership, potentially one day becoming the first Black Speaker, was among the reasons they voted for him. He won on a 123–113 vote.

Other leaders were elected by acclamation, including Maryland's Steny Hoyer as majority leader, the job he had held when Democrats had the House majority from 2007 to 2011. Hoyer had been a longtime political rival of Pelosi's, and his views were far closer to the center than hers, enabling him to maintain friendly relations with a greater number of Republicans. But Hoyer made it clear before the November election that he would not mount a challenge. Hoyer's ascension to majority leader enabled South Carolina's Jim Clyburn—the assistant Democratic leader, a job created earlier for him—to become majority whip, the job he also had held during Democrats' earlier tenure in the majority. His selection, with Jeffries, placed two African Americans in the top five House Democratic leadership posts.

To ensure that a Hispanic was also part of the top ranks, Pelosi named Ben Ray Lujan of New Mexico as assistant Democratic leader, the fourth-ranking leadership post. Lujan was a loyal Pelosi lieutenant who had chaired the Democratic Congressional Campaign Committee in the previous two election cycles. It helped pacify the caucus that Lujan's and Jeffries' relatively young ages—forty-six and forty-eight respectively—balanced out the much older Pelosi, Hoyer (who was also 79), and Clyburn (78).

Women attained positions in some of the rest of the leadership ranks. Massachusetts' Katherine M. Clark became Democratic caucus vice chair, while Illinois' Bustos took the reins of the Democratic Congressional Campaign Committee. Democrats added the position of Policy and Communications chair to serve as a landing spot for

Rhode Island's David Cicilline, who was openly gay. The absence of a woman of color on the new elected leadership team—and lingering frustrations over Lee's close loss to Jeffries in the caucus chair race—led Pelosi to appoint Lee as a cochair of the Democratic Steering and Policy Committee, which was in charge of making Democratic committee assignments. She joined current Steering cochairs Rosa DeLauro of Connecticut and Eric Swalwell of California atop the panel.

On the House Republican side, lawmakers kept California's Kevin McCarthy in the top slot as minority leader. He easily beat back a challenge from Jim Jordan of Ohio, a cofounder of the Freedom Caucus and one of the chamber's staunchest conservatives, winning a 159–43 vote. Jordan had made headlines in 2018 after former wrestling-team members he coached more than two decades earlier at Ohio State University accused him of failing to stop the team's doctor from sexually molesting them and other students. McCarthy's persistent efforts to endear himself to Trump—and his equally persistent fundraising on behalf of colleagues—helped him to prevail. Louisiana's Steve Scalise was unanimously elected as minority whip, keeping the same role he had held since 2014.

But the House Republican Conference had a new chairwoman: Wyoming's Liz Cheney. She won the job by voice vote after Washington state Rep. Cathy McMorris Rodgers decided not to seek another term in the party's leadership ranks. Cheney's father, former Vice President Dick Cheney, held the same job three decades earlier as Wyoming's congressman, and his hawkish views on national security helped pave the way for his daughter to elevate her profile—though Republicans would eventually learn that her willingness to speak her mind went sharply against the grain of the rest of the party.

Minnesota's Tom Emmer was elected the new National Republican Congressional Committee (NRCC) chairman. A former state legislator and the 2010 GOP nominee for his state's governorship, he was faced with the challenge of helping his party win back enough seats to regain control of the chamber in 2020. He took the position after serving as a deputy NRCC chair during the 2018 cycle. Also new to the leadership team were Republican Conference Secretary Jason Smith, R-Mo., an outspoken advocate for rural America's interests, and Republican Policy Committee Chairman Gary Palmer, R-Ala., who had founded a conservative think tank in his state.

The Senate, which remained under Republican control, nevertheless featured some leadership shifts on the GOP side as the Democrats continued with their same team from the previous Congress. Kentucky's Mitch McConnell became majority leader for the third consecutive Congress, and the second with Trump in office. But the new whip became South Dakota's John Thune, replacing the term-limited John Cornyn of Texas. Thune had previously been

the Republican conference chairman, and his ascension enabled other Republicans in the leadership ranks to move up one spot too. John Barrasso of Wyoming took over from Thune as chair of the Republican conference. Roy Blunt of Missouri took Barrasso's old job as Republican Policy Committee chair. Todd Young, an Indiana Republican, was elected chair of the Senate Republican campaign operation, the National Republican Senate Committee.

The change that drew the most public attention, however, was the election of Joni Ernst of Iowa to be the Republican Conference's vice chair. She was the first woman to be elected to the GOP leadership since 2009. Ernst's background was unique—she highlighted her family's roots in farming in a TV ad that mentioned her experience castrating hogs, and she also was deployed to Kuwait in the National Guard and rose to the rank of lieutenant colonel. She initially endeared herself to Republicans by winning an upset in 2014.

Several congressional caucuses featured new leadership. At the Progressive Caucus, Wisconsin's Pocan had a new co-chair for the 116th Congress—Pramila Jayapal, a progressive from Washington state who had taken office two years earlier. She had founded the organization OneAmerica to address the backlash, hate crimes, and discrimination against immigrant communities of color, primarily Muslims, Arab Americans, East Africans, and South Asians. The group's membership jumped to ninety-eight.

The new Congressional Black Caucus chair was California Democratic Rep. Karen Bass, a former California Assembly speaker who had drawn flattering comparisons to Pelosi for her leadership skills. Its membership ranks in the 116th Congress rose to fifty-five. At the Congressional Hispanic Caucus, an even-higher profile figure took over in Joaquin Castro, one of a pair of identical twins who were both seen as emerging figures within their party.

The fiscally conservative Blue Dog Coalition added to its leadership another lawmaker who was seen as an emerging star—Stephanie Murphy of Florida, who came with a compelling personal story of having escaped Vietnam as a baby and being rescued by the Navy at sea, then growing up to become a Pentagon analyst. She and Arizona Republican Tom O'Halleran joined New York's Anthony Brindisi and California's Lou Correa as cochairs. New Jersey's Josh Gottheimer and New York's Tom Reed continued as cochairs of the Problem Solvers Caucus.

For Republicans, both the Freedom Caucus and Republican Study Committee had new chairmen, each of whom had come to Congress just two years earlier. The Freedom Caucus' new leader was Andy Biggs, an Arizona Republican and ardent supporter of Trump's, especially on immigration issues. The Republican Study Committee's new chairman was Mike Johnson of Louisiana, a former talk radio host and another outspoken Trump ally.

116th Congress: Committees

The 116th Congress had 218 committees and subcommittees in the House and Senate—four more than in the previous Congress, but well short of the 295 two decades earlier in the 101st Congress (1989–1990). The return of the Democrats to the majority in the House meant seismic shifts in the operations of committees, particularly when it came to investigating Trump. In particular, the new leaders of three of the committees—Oversight and Government Reform, Judiciary, and Intelligence—commanded considerable attention, and eventually did much of the work that led to Trump's first impeachment.

During the first two years of the Trump administration, the Oversight and Government Reform panel faded from the spotlight as Republicans mostly shied away from the powers of probing the executive branch. New chairman Elijah E. Cummings, a Maryland Democrat with a forceful personality, made clear he would take the opposite approach in bird-dogging the administration on a number of fronts. His overarching goal, he said, was to gather the facts about perceived corruption in the Trump administration. He had spent the past two years calling on the panel to investigate reports of top administration officials' ethical blunders. As a sign of how seriously House Republicans took Cummings, they named as the panel's ranking member Jim Jordan of Ohio, a combative Trump defender.

New Judiciary Committee Chairman Jerrold E. Nadler of New York promised a similarly aggressive approach. Despite rampant speculation of impeaching Trump over Russian interference in the 2016 election, Nadler said he preferred to wait for Special Counsel Robert S. Mueller III's long-awaited report on the subject. But Nadler already had made advance preparations for action. Democratic committee staff issued a report in April 2018 that laid the predicate for action on election security, federal ethics rules, and obstruction of justice in the probe and whether Trump was financially benefiting from office. Committee Democrats sought documents on Trump's financial practices, communications between his campaign and Russian operatives, allegations that Trump Tower was wiretapped and the firing of FBI Director James Comey. They also sent sixty-four letters to the administration on issues from presidential advisor Jared Kushner's security clearance to Trump's allegations of voter fraud, and thirty-nine letters to Judiciary Committee or House leaders about issues including Trump's ban on travel from some Muslim-majority countries.

And on Intelligence, new Chairman Adam Schiff of California was constrained by the secret nature of much of his panel's work from publicly describing some of his aims. But Schiff's background as a former federal prosecutor and polished communicator would come to stand him in good stead with his chamber's leaders and eventually give him a national profile during the first impeachment—while earning him Trump's lasting enmity.

Other committees promised to join in on probing Trump and his administration. With Democrats taking control of the Homeland Security Committee under long-time Democratic leader Bennie Thompson of Mississippi, Trump's efforts were greatly complicated in his attempts to build a U.S.–Mexico border wall, and boost the Border Patrol ranks and hire thousands more deportation agents. An even bigger change loomed at Financial Services, where staunch liberal Maxine Waters of California took the gavel and promised a full-throated defense of the Consumer Financial Protection Bureau that Trump had opposed.

At Energy and Commerce, incoming Chairman Frank Pallone of New Jersey vowed to contest Trump's attempts to undo the Patient Protection and Affordable Care Act and to bolster his party's case for addressing climate change. Similarly, new Natural Resources Chairman Raul Grijalva of Arizona would prove to be a thorn in the administration's side over his repeated inveighing against Republican attempts to increase fossil fuel production on federal lands.

The change was not as immediate at the powerful tax-writing Ways and Means Committee. But new Chairman Richard Neal of Massachusetts held hearings on the impacts of the GOP-drafted tax overhaul, which had become law in late 2017 without getting a single Democratic vote. Neal also began a high-profile quest to seek Trump's personal income tax returns, which the president had steadfastly refused to release in the contradiction of years of prior presidential political practice.

Several other House committees were led by veterans who had long been eager to claim the gavel. On Appropriations, Nita M. Lowey of New York became the first female chair, promising to increase spending on domestic priorities. She worked with Texas Kay Granger, who became the first woman to serve as top Republican appropriator. On the Agriculture Committee, Collin C. Peterson, a conservative Democrat from Minnesota, ended up fulfilling early pledges to work closely with Republicans. So did New York's Eliot M. Engel, who assumed control of the Foreign Affairs panel, and Washington state's Adam Smith, who took over the Armed Services Committee.

Other new chairmen and chairwomen included John Yarmuth of Kentucky at Budget; Robert C. Scott of Virginia at Education and the Workforce; Ted Deutch of Florida at Ethics; Zoe Lofgren of California at House Administration; Jim McGovern of Massachusetts at Rules; Eddie Bernice Johnson of Texas at Science, Space, and Technology; Nydia M. Velazquez of New York at Small Business; Peter A. DeFazio at Transportation and Infrastructure; and Mark Takano of California at Veterans' Affairs. Other new Republican ranking members included Patrick McHenry of North Carolina, who gave up his spot as chief deputy whip to become the Financial Services Committee's ranking member; Texas's Michael McCaul, who moved to serve as the top Republican on Foreign Affairs after reaching his six-year term limit as chairman of the Homeland Security

Committee; Alabama's Mike Rogers, who replaced McCaul at Homeland Security; Georgia's Doug Collins, who left as House Republican Conference vice chair to claim the top GOP spot on Judiciary; Oklahoma's Frank Lucas, a former Agriculture Committee chairman who took the ranking post on Science, Space, and Technology; Missouri's Sam Graves, a pilot who moved in as top Republican on Transportation and Infrastructure; and Illinois's Rodney Davis, a former congressional aide who assumed the ranking spot on House Administration.

The biggest change at any of the committees was the creation of a new panel in 2019 to specifically address climate change. The Select Committee on the Climate Crisis was led by Florida's Kathy Castor, a close Pelosi ally who had compiled a strong pro-environment record since coming to Congress in 2007. It actually represented the revival of a similar panel that Pelosi had created during the party's early tenure in the majority. Republicans had abolished that committee after they assumed control in 2011.

To the dismay of some progressive Democrats clamoring for swift and sweeping legislative action, the new select committee was not granted the power to pass bills. Instead, its mission was largely to hold hearings to call more attention to the issue while coordinating with Energy and Commerce and other committees that did possess legislative jurisdiction on the subject. The panel's ranking Republican was Garret Graves of Louisiana, a former congressional aide. He had worked as then-Gov. Bobby Jindal's adviser on restoring the state's coast, which was being swallowed up as a result of effects blamed on a rapidly warming world. Unlike other Republicans, he saw a political need to act on the issue, particularly in protecting coastlines and developing bipartisan measures to mitigate and adapt to its most severe effects.

Democrats also set up another select committee, the Select Committee on the Modernization of Congress, to look at ways to make Congress more efficient, effective, and transparent. Its chairman was Washington state Democrat Derek Kilmer, a former business consultant who was known for his efforts at consensus building. Georgia's Tom Graves, a Republican who had chaired the Appropriations subcommittee on spending for the legislative branch, was vice chairman.

After Maryland Democrat Elijah Cummings' death in October 2019, New York Democrat Carolyn Maloney took over as acting chair of the Oversight and Reform Committee. Maloney had to fight to eventually defeat Virginia Rep. Gerald E. Connolly, first in the House Democratic steering committee (which voted 35–19 in her favor) and then in the House Democratic Caucus (which voted 133–86), to get the job permanently. She became the first woman to lead the panel. After taking the gavel, Maloney relinquished her position as chair of the Financial Services Committee's Investor Protection, Entrepreneurship, and Capital Markets Subcommittee. Known as a crusader for women's rights, Maloney fought

for access to women's health needs and reproductive rights in addition to combating sexual assault and human trafficking.

In the Senate, the continued Republican majority meant far fewer changes than in the House. But retirements and other moves created some shifts at the top spots on several committees.

One of the highest-profile moves was the decision of Iowa Republican Charles E. Grassley to take the chairmanship of the Finance Committee, a job he had held in early 2001 and again from 2003 to 2006. The Finance chairmanship opened up after the retirement of Utah Republican Sen. Orrin Hatch. Grassley had replaced Hatch as the Senate's president pro tempore, the majority party's longest-serving member, having been in the Senate since 1981 after six years in the House. He was a fiscal conservative who had made his reputation as a dogged overseer of numerous federal agencies he suspected of abusing their power and as Congress' leading champion of enabling government whistleblowing.

Grassley's move opened up the chairmanship of the Judiciary Committee, which went to South Carolina's Lindsey Graham. As Judiciary chairman in the 115th Congress, Grassley had overseen the controversial Supreme Court confirmations of justices Neil Gorsuch and Brett Kavanaugh. Grassley did occasionally accuse Trump's administration of ignoring his requests to conduct oversight. He also took the rare step in December 2017 of urging the president to rethink his nominations of two especially controversial judicial nominees; both were withdrawn from consideration. Graham, who ran a short-lived race for president in 2015, had transformed himself from a critic of Donald Trump as a candidate into one of the president's chief cheerleaders. He had worked in the past with Democrats, at great length, on the sharply divisive issue of overhauling immigration. But in taking over at Judiciary, Graham made clear that his foremost allegiance was now to a president with no interest in making the compromises necessary to craft a bipartisan deal.

The move upward of South Dakota's John Thune in the GOP leadership ranks opened up the chairmanship of the Commerce, Science and Transportation Committee, which went to Mississippi's Roger Wicker. An ardent conservative, Wicker had drawn attention for such moves as amending a transportation spending bill to allow Amtrak passengers to carry firearms and ammunition in checked baggage. As Commerce chairman, he worked on a comprehensive federal data privacy bill that would place enforcement authority in the hands of both the Federal Trade Commission and state attorneys general.

With the defeat of Florida Democratic Sen. Bill Nelson in 2018, the ranking member position on the Commerce panel went to Washington state's Maria Cantwell, a former technology executive. The only other Senate committee with a new ranking member at the start of the 116th was Homeland Security and Governmental Affairs, where

Michigan's Gary Peters took over for Missouri's Claire McCaskill after McCaskill lost her reelection bid. Tennessee Republican Bob Corker's retirement elevated Jim Risch of Idaho to the top spot on the Foreign Relations Committee. Risch, a former governor of his state, was more conservative than Corker and far more willing to hew to Trump's positions.

The retirement of Georgia Republican Sen. Johnny Isakson in December 2019 moved Republican James Lankford of Oklahoma into the chairmanship of the Ethics Committee. Lankford entered the Senate in 2015, winning a special election to replace Sen. Tom Coburn, R-Okla. He was a steadfast ally of Majority Leader Mitch McConnell.

116th Congress: Member Characteristics

The 116th Congress had 237 Democrats (including 4 nonvoting delegates), 197 Republicans (including 1 delegate and Puerto Rico's resident commissioner), two Independent/Libertarians, and five vacant seats. The Senate had fifty-two Republicans, forty-six Democrats, and two independents—Maine's Angus King and Bernie Sanders—who both caucused with the Democrats.

A record was set with the number of women—130—in Congress. Of that, 105 women, including three delegates as well as the Puerto Rico resident commissioner, served in the House and twenty-five served in the Senate. Of the 105 women in the House, ninety were Democrats, including two of the delegates, and fifteen were Republicans, including one delegate as well as the resident commissioner. Of the Senate's twenty-five women, seventeen were Democrats and eight were Republicans.

For the fifth Congress in a row, the 116th Congress was the most diverse in history, according to the Pew Research Center. More than one in five voting members (22%) were non-white. There was a record fifty-seven African American members (10.5% of the total membership) in the 116th Congress, five more than at the beginning of the 115th Congress, according to the Congressional Research Service (CRS). Fifty-four served in the House, including two delegates, and three served in the Senate. Fifty-three of the African American House members, including two delegates, were Democrats, with one Republican (Will Hurd of Texas). Two of the senators were Democrats and one was Republican (South Carolina's Tim Scott). Twenty-four African American women, including two delegates, served in the House, and one (California's Kamala Harris) served in the Senate.

Fifty-one members were Hispanic, 9.4 percent of the total membership—and another record number. Forty-six served in the House, including two delegates and the resident commissioner, and five in the Senate. Of the members of the House, thirty-seven were Democrats (including 2 delegates) and nine were Republicans (including the resident commissioner). Fourteen were women, including the resident commissioner. Of the five Hispanic senators

(3 Republicans, 2 Democrats), one (Nevada's Catherine Cortez-Masto) was a woman.

Yet another record was set with twenty members (3.8% of the total membership) being of Asian, South Asian, or Pacific Islander ancestry. Seventeen of them (16 Democrats, 1 Republican) served in the House, and three (all Democrats) were senators. Ten of the Asian, Pacific Islander, or South Asian American members were female: seven in the House and all three in the Senate. Harris was counted as being both African American and Asian, having had a Jamaican father and Indian mother.

The 116th Congress also saw the first Native American women ever to serve in the chamber: Democrats Sharice Davids of Kansas, a member of the Ho-Chunk people, and Deb Haaland of New Mexico, a member of Laguna Pueblo. In addition, the first two Muslim women in Congress were elected: Michigan's Rashida Tlaib and Minnesota's Ilhan Omar.

The average age at the beginning of the 116th Congress was 57.6 years for House members and 62.9 years for senators, CRS found. As in the previous Congress, the dominant occupation was public service/politics, with 184 House members and forty-seven senators having had that experience. That was followed by business (183 House members, 29 senators) and law (145 House members, 47 senators). Half of the senators were House veterans. The number of military veterans continued to decline, with ninety-six people—almost 18 percent of the total membership—either formerly or currently in one of the service branches.

116th Congress: Rules Changes

House Democrats used their new majority to push through dozens of rules changes. Many were intended to fulfill their campaign promises to make Congress more transparent and bipartisan. The final rules package was adopted 234–197, with only three Democrats voting against it. One of the three was freshman Rep. Alexandria Ocasio-Cortez, the youngest woman elected to Congress in history and an outspoken New Yorker who would become the leader of a group of progressive women known as "The Squad."

In an atypical move, three Republicans—Reps. Tom Reed and John Katko of New York and Brian Fitzpatrick of Pennsylvania—voted for the Democrats' rules package. They did so because of changes that the bipartisan Problem Solvers Caucus, to which they belonged, pushed to help bring about more two-party legislating. It marked the first time since 2001 in which members from the minority voted for the majority party's rules package.

One of the most prominent new rules was the reinstatement of "Pay-as-You-Go," commonly known as PAYGO. It required that revenue legislation and bills on entitlement or other mandatory programs should not add to the federal budget deficit or decrease a surplus. First implemented in the early 1990s, it was often waived by a vote of Congress. It was allowed to expire under Republican control of Congress in 1995. But Democrats first put it back in place when they regained the majority in 2007, changing the rules two years later to permit them to attach an "emergency" exemption. Two years later, Republicans took control again and modified the rule with a "cut-as-you-go" rule requiring new mandatory spending to be offset with cuts to existing programs. Many progressives—including Ocasio-Cortez—opposed PAYGO because they believed some policies that would have a larger economic benefit did not need to be paid for, such as expanding Medicare to cover all Americans.

In a nod to the divisions between the House and Senate, the rules package modified the so-called "Gephardt Rule" named for former House Majority Leader Richard Gephardt, D-Mo., to make it easier to suspend the federal debt ceiling. The Gephardt Rule required the House and Senate to jointly agree on the same budget resolution in order for the House to avoid what is typically a difficult vote on raising the ceiling. The new rule allowed the chamber to spin off a resolution "suspending" the debt ceiling to the Senate—without a House vote—once the House adopted its own version of a budget resolution.

Other changes also sought to make legislating on fiscal matters easier. One absolved the Congressional Budget Office and Joint Committee on Taxation from being required to produce a macroeconomic "dynamic" estimate of major legislation incorporating the effects of economic growth. Another removed a requirement for a three-fifths supermajority vote to raise revenue through federal income tax rate changes. And another change eliminated term limits for serving on the House Budget Committee. Previously, members could not serve for more than four Congresses out of a period of six successive Congresses, more than eight years out of a twelve-year period.

A further rules change enabled amendments to spending bills that raised federal spending. It removed "points of order" against amendments to appropriations bills that increased spending without offsetting spending cuts. Other points of order would still be able to be raised if an amendment did not comply with the overall limit on discretionary spending or the specific allocation assigned to each appropriations subcommittee. The House repealed the so-called "Holman rule" that Republicans had adopted in the previous Congress allowing floor amendments on appropriations bills to target individual salaries or workforce levels.

Multiple amendments sought to tighten ethics. The package required all House members—not just new members—to take ethics training. The rules also required members to reimburse taxpayers for settlements that that result from a member's discrimination of someone based on race, religion, sex, national origin, or disability, among other things. A separate change decreed that members who were indicted for certain felonies had to resign from lead-

ership and committee assignments until they were acquitted or the charges against them were dropped. Members and staff also were barred, as of January 2020, from serving on corporate boards, something that watchdog groups said raised too many potential conflicts of interest. And the existing prohibition on sexual relationships between members and their staff was extended to include members who serve on a committee on which a staffer works, even if that staffer was not their direct employee.

The rules package also included language to address whistleblowing—disclosures of information that a worker believes represents evidence of illegality, gross waste or fraud, mismanagement, abuse of power, general wrongdoing, or a danger to public health and safety. It created the Office of the Whistleblower Ombudsman, an independent and nonpartisan agency with the aim of developing best practices for House offices on how to safely and confidentially receive information from whistleblowers. Its first director was Shanna Devine, who had worked on the issue for years at the public watchdog groups Public Citizen and the Government Accountability Project.

Another new entity that the rules package created was an Office of Diversity and Inclusion charged with helping House members recruit, develop, and retain a diverse workforce. It was assigned to develop and conduct a survey to evaluate diversity in House employing offices. The director was Kemba Hendrix, who had been hired to lead a House Democratic diversity initiative in the 115th Congress.

Several rules changes sought to fix complaints from members in both parties about bills being rushed to the House floor. One required bills to be posted for a full seventy-two hours before a House vote. The change was an attempt to clarify the existing "three-day rule" that lawmakers said often was abused with bills being filed late at night on a first day and the House voting early on the third. In addition, the package required any bill being brought to the floor under a rule to have been reported out of committee and for there to have been at least one committee hearing relevant to the legislation.

Among other House rules changes were

- Overhauling the "motion to vacate," a legislative maneuver used to oust the speaker, so that it could only be brought up for a vote over the objection of leadership if offered at the direction of a party caucus or conference instead of just a single member
- Establishing some voting rights for delegates and the resident commissioner of Puerto Rico. The delegates and resident commissioner were permitted to vote on legislation, subject to immediate reconsideration in the House if their vote was collectively decisive. They also were granted the right to serve on joint committees
- Renaming the Oversight and Government Reform Committee as the Oversight and Reform Committee,

and the Education and the Workforce Committee as the Education and Labor Committee
- Maintaining an existing ban on wearing hats in the House while making clear that religious headwear was exempted. The exemption was to accommodate new Democratic Rep. Ilhan Omar of Minnesota, a Muslim American who wore a *hijab* or head scarf
- Enabling the use of a "Consensus Calendar." If a bill had 290 cosponsors and the relevant committee had not acted on the topic, a bill could be placed on the consensus calendar. The House was supposed to consider at least one bill a week from that calendar
- Removing the committee chair term limits that had been in effect under Republican-controlled sessions of Congress
- Changing procedures regarding committee oversight. The 115th Congress requirement that committees prepare and submit "authorization and oversight plans" was replaced with the requirement that chairs of committees develop oversight plans in consultation with the ranking member. A separate order also allowed committee counsel to take depositions without a committee member having to be present

Some rules changes were discussed but never pursued. Among those drawing the most attention was a reinstatement of earmarks, or member-added provisions to spending bills. Democrats had instituted a one-year moratorium on the practice in 2007, followed by a Republican-led ban in 2011. Trump encouraged the idea of their return, saying that they had helped warm relations between the parties. Proponents, including veterans in both parties, said they should be permitted to dictate where money should be directed in their states and districts. But Appropriations Chairwoman Nita Lowey, D-N.Y., announced in a letter in March 2019 that the idea lacked enough bipartisan agreement to move forward.

In the Senate, the most prominent rules change was aimed at enabling Trump to put more judges on the federal bench. By a 51–48 vote in April 2019, Senate Republicans adopted a change that reduced from thirty hours to two hours the maximum time allowed for debating most executive branch nominations after an initial vote to bring the matter to a close.

The action came after Majority Leader Mitch McConnell, R-Ky., complained that Democrats were abusing the thirty-hour allotment to draw out the confirmation time for judges and other nominees. Many political scholars noted, however, that McConnell had employed a similar tactic when Democrats were in the majority to slow down President Barack Obama's judicial nominees.

The rules change drew sharp protests from Democrats. They argued that they saw no need to limit debate on Trump's judicial nominees, whom they noted already were being confirmed at a record pace. They also noted that on average, the Senate had only used about three hours of

debate on average for each nominee. Finally, the Democrats said, the lifetime appointments granted to members of the judiciary required them to be permitted as much debate time as possible.

First Trump Impeachment

Trump's first impeachment thrust several House Democrats—and Republicans—into the spotlight. The trial in the Senate lasted two weeks and six days between January 16 and February 5. Legislative business did not stop outright during that period, but it did slow considerably.

Democrats accused Trump of abusing his office by pressuring Ukraine to investigate his political rivals ahead of the 2020 election while withholding a White House meeting and $400 million in security aid from that country's leaders. They also said Trump then obstructed the investigation into his misconduct by ignoring a host of subpoenas while refusing to allow key members of his administration to testify before Congress. It was the third time that a president had been impeached. Andrew Johnson and Bill Clinton were impeached, and both won Senate acquittal.

House Speaker Nancy Pelosi chose seven of her colleagues as impeachment managers to prosecute the abuse-of-power and obstruction-of-Congress articles resulting from Democrats' two-month investigation into the president's dealings with Ukraine. She sought a group that showed the party's ethnic, racial, and gender diversity and had experience in litigation as well as national security and law enforcement.

The impeachment manager with by far the highest profile was Intelligence Committee Chairman Adam Schiff, D-Calif., whom Pelosi chose as lead manager over Judiciary Chairman Jerrold Nadler, D-N.Y. Schiff was a Harvard Law-educated ally of Pelosi's and a former federal prosecutor, having spent six years in the U.S. Attorney's office in Los Angeles before coming to Congress. He already had greatly antagonized Trump with his frequent televised denunciations of what he called the president's grave misconduct. When the impeachment articles were unveiled, Schiff called the evidence against Trump both overwhelming and uncontested. He argued that the country could not wait for judicial rulings on the witnesses and documents that Trump had refused to provide because, he said, the president was certain to continue to abuse the process.

During the trial, Schiff earned praise from legal scholars for his efforts at articulating the case against Trump. Several of them, such as former acting solicitor general and Duke University law professor Walter Dellinger, said his opening trial statement was among the best legal performances they had ever seen. Even South Carolina Republican Sen. Lindsey Graham, who had been an impeachment manager during Clinton's trial, told CNN he had informed Trump himself what a good job Schiff had done, much to Trump's displeasure. Schiff chronicled his experiences in a 2021 book, *Midnight in Washington: How We Almost Lost Our Democracy and Still Could.* He said in the book and subsequent media interviews that he was shocked during the trial at how many Republican senators, to his mind, knew Trump was guilty after listening to evidence that they previously had not heard or seen, having gotten much of their prior information from Republican-leaning Fox News. But he said those senators were unwilling to sacrifice their jobs to vote to convict Trump.

Nadler had been a prominent defender of Clinton's during that impeachment trial, and his knowledge of the Constitution was put to use in drafting the articles of impeachment against Trump. His Judiciary panel also put out detailed reports about the constitutional underpinnings of the case against the president. But Nadler's temper flared during the trial. On the first day, White House counsel Pat Cipollone and Trump's personal lawyer Jay Sekulow described the congressman as a liar, prompting Nadler to respond in kind. Nadler also accused senators of treachery, with Sekulow responding that it was Nadler who was being treacherous. The rampant hostility led Supreme Court Chief Justice John Roberts, who was presiding over the trial, to admonish both sides and remind them of the historical gravity of the situation. After delivering the Democrats' closing statement in the proceedings, Nadler left the trial to be with his wife, who was battling pancreatic cancer.

Even with all of Nadler's experience in impeachment effort, the team of managers had someone with more—California Rep. Zoe Lofgren. She had been a staffer for the Judiciary Committee during the 1974 impeachment inquiry into Richard Nixon, and was a member of the panel during Clinton's impeachment. She had run for the chair of the Judiciary Committee, only to lose to Nadler. She later said in an interview with the *Stanford Daily* that unlike many of her colleagues, she did not openly seek to serve as a manager for Trump's trial, figuring her record made her a worthy candidate. She also said Trump's trial evoked some similarities to that of Nixon, who resigned in 1974 before facing impeachment. Both men allegedly abused their power, she noted, and it related to using that power to benefit in an election.

New York Rep. Hakeem Jeffries' choice as an impeachment manager was widely expected. Jeffries, a lawyer and frequent Trump critic, had risen quickly through his party's ranks since his election in 2012, and served as chairman of the House Democratic Caucus. Some political analysts speculated that he could one day succeed Pelosi. He was a close ally of hers, having taken her side in urging caution earlier when the Ukraine scandal came to light, and many progressives were clamoring for an immediate impeachment. Jeffries drew attention during the trial when he quoted a line from rapper Notorious B.I.G. to Trump lawyer Sekulow—a reference that drew laughter from several senators.

Another African American who was considered a rising political star, Florida's Val Demings, was also tapped for the impeachment team. She did not have a law degree, but had spent twenty-seven years with the Orlando Police Department, the last four as its chief. She also was one of just two Democrats serving on both the Intelligence and Judiciary committees. Lofgren said Demings was a logical choice, given her experience in courtrooms and familiarity with laying out evidence in helping to prosecute a case.

Lofgren also expressed admiration for another member of the impeachment team, Texas' Sylvia Garcia. A member of the Judiciary Committee, Garcia had spent five terms as presiding judge of the Houston Municipal System before becoming Houston city controller and a Harris County commissioner. In 2018, she and Veronica Escobar became the first female Hispanic members of Congress from Texas. During the trial, she was more measured in her rhetoric than other managers, making her less of a lightning rod for criticism.

Garcia said she never had been among those lobbying House leaders to serve as an impeachment manager. The final manager, Colorado freshman Jason Crow, also said he had never sought a spot—though Democrats said his surprise selection reflected their desire to bring direct national security experience to the effort. A former Army captain, Crow served in Iraq and Afghanistan before receiving his law degree. He was one of seven national security-oriented freshman lawmakers who had written an op-ed calling for an impeachment inquiry after the Ukraine scandal came to light. During the trial, Crow recounted his wartime experience in explaining why it was concerning that Trump held up aid to Ukraine in order to pressure its leader to damage his political rival. Schiff also said Crow was an asset to the House impeachment team in part because he represented a district far from the liberal coasts where 40 percent of voters did not belong to either party.

No Republican lawmakers served on Trump's trial defense team. The president had talked about such an idea before the trial, and some lawmakers publicly lobbied for the inclusion of Florida Rep. Matt Gaetz, a particularly outspoken and aggressive Trump backer. But *Politico* reported some of his advisers worried that putting such vociferous defenders in that position could distract from the solemn nature of the proceedings. The White House did name eight House Republicans to serve on his defense team, with the understanding that their job would be to work on public messaging in addition to behind-the-scenes strategy.

One of the leading team members was Georgia's Doug Collins, the Judiciary Committee's top Republican. He had accused Democrats of wanting to impeach Trump since the start of his presidency, even though Pelosi had held off immediate talk of impeachment after her party regained the majority. He compared the obstruction-of-justice charge against Trump to petulant children complaining they had not gotten their way. Collins ended up running in the 2020 primary for Georgia's Senate, but lost to incumbent Kelly Loeffler. Another hard-core partisan named to the team was Ohio's Jim Jordan, who was the top Republican on the Oversight and Reform Committee. Jordan regularly made the rounds of Fox News and other broadcast outlets to criticize Democrats' overreach and to argue that they never presented a coherent case. Just before leaving office, a grateful Trump awarded Jordan the Presidential Medal of Freedom, the nation's highest civilian honor.

Trump loyalist Mark Meadows of North Carolina, also part of the team, was rewarded one month after the Senate's not-guilty verdict with the job of White House chief of staff. And the president picked Texas' John Ratcliffe to serve as his national intelligence director. Two other members of the effort were Lee Zeldin of New York, who had emerged as a particularly vocal and caustic critic of Democrats' efforts, and Mike Johnson of Louisiana, a Judiciary Committee member and a former constitutional law attorney.

The final two GOP defense team members were women: Debbie Lesko of Arizona and Elise Stefanik of New York. Lesko had won a 2018 special election and was one of two women serving on the Judiciary Committee. She repeatedly contended in media appearances that the details of Trump's actions leading to impeachment had been blown far out of proportion by Democrats and the news media. Stefanik, who had an image as a moderate before becoming an ardent Trump defender, was frequently described as an ambitious young Republican star in the making. She depicted the impeachment effort as nothing less than an attack on American voters. Her high-profile defense during the trial and subsequent forums would catapult her into the House leadership in 2021 after Republicans voted to oust Wyoming Rep. Liz Cheney.

Coronavirus Impacts Congress

Just as it did across the globe, the COVID-19 coronavirus pandemic that became widespread in the United States during 2020 shook Congress. Like no event since the September 11, 2001, terrorist attacks in Washington, D.C., and New York City, the pandemic forced a significant overhaul in congressional operations.

It also hit Congress personally. Between February and June 2020, ten members of Congress tested positive for the virus, according to the legislative tracking website GovTrack.us. More than fifty others went into quarantine or self-imposed isolation after being exposed during that period. Dozens of lawmakers eventually were sickened, and one—GOP Rep. Ron Wright of Texas—died in February 2021. Another Republican House member who had been elected in 2020, Luke Letkow of Louisiana, died before the House reconvened in January of that year for the 117th Congress.

Congress closed the Capitol, along with House and Senate office buildings, to the public on March 12. Access was limited to members, staff, the news media, and visitors on official business. Those buildings would remain publicly closed for the remainder of the 116th Congress. The House began requiring lawmakers to wear protective masks during committee proceedings, though the Republican-controlled Senate implemented no such requirement and continued to conduct its business largely as usual.

A number of Republicans objected to wearing masks as an infringement on their freedom and refused to do so, even after being hit with fines of $500 per infraction. But after the non-mask-wearing Rep. Louie Gohmert, R-Texas, tested positive for the virus in July after interacting with numerous other lawmakers in the chamber, House Speaker Nancy Pelosi imposed a mask mandate on the floor for members and staffers. Lawmakers were permitted to temporarily take off their masks when speaking. The House sergeant-at-arms subsequently issued an additional set of rules upon Pelosi's direction requiring face coverings in all House office buildings.

Media outlets reported in March that several senators—including Republican Sens. Kelly Loeffler and David Perdue of Georgia, Richard Burr of North Carolina, James Inhofe of Oklahoma and Democrats Sen. Dianne Feinstein and Rep. Susan Davis of California—had sold various stocks in late January and early February as the Senate was beginning to hold briefings on the coronavirus. Lawmakers and aides were legally barred from trading stocks based on private information, but were permitted to buy shares based on public information they obtain on Capitol Hill so long as they disclose those trades within thirty days. The Justice Department found no evidence of wrongdoing in the cases, but government watchdog groups and some lawmakers said such an approach remained far too permissive and called for change.

The coronavirus did lead the chairman and ranking member of the Ethics Committee in April to issue a reminder of conflict-of-interest rules, laws, and regulations applying to members. In a memo to colleagues, Chairman Ted Deutch, D-Fla., and Vice Chairman Kenny Marchant, R-Texas, noted that the CARES Act contained a provision applicable to businesses in which senior government officials or their immediate family have an ownership interest. That provision barred companies in which members—or their spouse, children, daughter-in-law, or son-in-law— own 20 percent or more equity interest from receiving any loans, loan guarantees, or other investments.

The House changed its practices during votes to limit the number of members present on the floor at one time. This lengthened the time needed to complete a roll-call vote, and so it became common for the floor managers of bills to offer amendments "en bloc," or all together, to reduce the number of votes. But the virus' early spread spurred talk among Democrats of ending one of the House's long-standing, firmly-held traditions of lawmakers casting votes in person. In May, the House voted along party lines 217–189 to do so, with Pelosi citing the added the safety it would provide. The new rules immediately allowed for any member to vote remotely by giving precise, binding instructions to a proxy who was able to be on the House floor. They also provided, pending certification, for a process in which lawmakers eventually would be able to cast votes from home, either via a secure online portal or a videoconferencing system.

Republicans castigated the move as an unnecessary power grab. Many of those members represented states or districts in states that had led the push to reopen restaurants, schools and other shuttered places, and returning to Washington enabled them to show constituents they were practicing what they preached. The GOP-controlled Senate again refused to follow suit, though it did start to allow senators and witnesses to participate in committee hearings remotely by videoconference. In October 2020, the Senate had to delay its return from a recess by two weeks after three senators tested positive for the virus. When Senator Rand Paul, R-Ky., proposed a change to allow emergency voting, Majority Leader Mitch McConnell, his Kentucky counterpart, rebuffed the idea. In the months following the House's vote, only a lone Republican House member—Francis Rooney of Florida, who had announced plans to retire at the end of his term—broke ranks to cast a vote by proxy on the same day that Gohmert tested positive for the virus.

House Majority Leader Kevin McCarthy, R-Calif., along with twenty other Republicans and several of their constituents, filed a lawsuit in U.S. District Court for the District of Columbia in August that sought to overturn the move. Their central legal argument was that it violated the Constitution's requirement to assemble in person. District Court Judge Rudolph Contreras in August, however, ruled that the Constitution's Speech or Debate Clause prohibited lawsuits over Congress' legislative efforts. A three-judge panel from the U.S. Court of Appeals for the District of Columbia ruled, in a unanimous opinion, that the GOP's proxy voting lawsuit lacked jurisdiction because the court did not have the authority to intervene in decisions about House rules.

The virus did increase contact between members' offices and their constituents, according to an August 2020 survey by the Congressional Management Foundation. The survey found 82 percent of House and Senate senior staff said their offices were devoting more attention than before the COVID crisis to engaging constituents through online meetings, telephone town halls, and other methods. It showed 63 percent reported receiving more communications from constituents than before the crisis, while 59 percent reported having substantive interactions with more constituents.

The virus also transformed 2020's congressional political campaigns. Many Democrats eschewed in-person

politicking, relying mainly on telephone- and internet-based efforts. Some political analysts said the party's performance in House races in November—when it increased its party vote total by 5 million fewer votes than did the Republicans—resulted from such a sharp cutback in traditional campaigning.

By the end of the 116th Congress, the Clerk of the House recorded 709 separate instances in which lawmakers had used proxy voting. A handful of Republicans—mostly members who were retiring and had little to lose politically by reversing their position on proxy voting—joined Rooney in embracing it. After the violent January 6, 2021 insurrection at the Capitol, McCarthy told Republicans they could use proxy voting if they had concerns about their personal security.

Deaths

REP. JOHN LEWIS

The July 2020 death of Lewis, D-Ga., from pancreatic cancer at age eighty cast a deep pall over Congress. Lewis enjoyed near-universal respect on Capitol Hill as a hero of the civil rights movement, which gave him a national profile at a young age. As a lawmaker, he was willing to wield that clout and made his arguments in the stark moral tones of the civil rights era, championing federal programs that advanced his notions of economic and social justice.

The son of an Alabama sharecropper, Lewis burst into the national spotlight as a civil rights leader in the 1960s. He organized sit-ins, boycotts, and other nonviolent protests in the segregated South and was one of the thirteen original Freedom Riders seeking to integrate interstate bus travel. He helped form, and for several years led, the Student Nonviolent Coordinating Committee (SNCC), a youth-driven fulcrum of the civil rights movement that focused on civil disobedience. He was named chairman of SNCC in 1963, with twenty-four arrests under his belt and more than a dozen to come. At the time of his death, Lewis was the last surviving speaker from the 1963 March on Washington for Jobs and Freedom, the site of the Rev. Martin Luther King's iconic "I Have a Dream" speech.

Lewis was largely remembered for his actions during "Bloody Sunday," when state and local police attacked peaceful civil rights protesters seeking voting rights for Black people who were crossing the Edmund Pettus bridge in Selma, Alabama, on March 7, 1965, on their way to the state capitol at Montgomery. Lewis was badly injured, having had his skull bashed in, and the outrage sparked by images of the event inspired enactment of the landmark Voting Rights Act, signed into law by President Lyndon B. Johnson in August 1965.

Lewis was elected to the House representing an Atlanta-based district in 1986, compiling a staunchly liberal voting record. He initially challenged Nancy Pelosi for Democratic whip in 2002, eventually abandoning the race and switching his support to Maryland's Steny Hoyer. Lewis became a chief deputy whip in his party's leadership as well as a senior member of the powerful Ways and Means Committee. Lewis also achieved pop-culture icon status with the publication of a best-selling, three-part autobiographical graphic novel. For many years, he led members of Congress on pilgrimages to civil rights sites. He had pushed for fifteen years to create the National Museum of African American History and Culture, which opened on the National Mall in 2016. He also helped create the FBI's Cold Case Initiative, which reopens cases of racially motivated murders from past decades.

Lewis became the first African American lawmaker to lie in state at the Capitol. Democrats subsequently named legislation after him that was aimed at shoring up what they called deficiencies in the Voting Rights Act.

REP. ELIJAH CUMMINGS

Like Lewis' death, Maryland Democrat Elijah Cummings' death in October 2019 at sixty-eight after a long illness greatly saddened many in Congress. Cummings, elected in 1996, chaired the House Oversight and Reform Committee and drew attention for his principled stands on racially charged issues.

Cummings was a pioneer in American politics before his election to Maryland's 7th District in a 1996 special election, having served as the first African American speaker pro tempore in the Maryland General Assembly. He drew national attention as Secretary of State Hillary Clinton's leading defender during 2015 congressional hearings into her handling of the attack three years earlier on U.S. government facilities in Benghazi, Libya. The attack killed U.S. Ambassador J. Christopher Stevens and three other Americans.

On the Oversight panel, Cummings had led investigations into Donald Trump's business conflicts of interest, his possible violations of the Constitution's emoluments clause prohibiting the president from profiting from his office, and allegations of illegal hush payments to two former Trump paramours during the 2016 campaign. Despite the explosive nature of some of his committee's investigative work, Cummings remained popular on both sides of the aisle. He laid in state in National Statuary Hall outside the House chamber before his funeral.

REP. WALTER JONES

Jones, R-N.C., died in February 2019 at seventy-six after complications from a fall. He had represented North Carolina's 3rd District since 1995. Jones originally was an ardent proponent of the Iraq War, but changed his mind after attending the funeral of a Marine killed by a rocket-propelled grenade. He spent the rest of his days writing thousands of letters to the families of almost every fallen soldier in an attempt to atone for his 2002 vote as well as to comfort the families. He also was known for being one of the congressmen who pushed to rename the congressional

cafeteria's French fries "freedom fries" after France opposed the 2003 U.S. military action in Iraq.

JOHN D. DINGELL

Dingell, the longest-serving member of Congress in history, died in February 2019. Dingell represented a Michigan district in the House from 1955 to 2015. He chaired the Energy and Commerce Committee from 1981 to 1995 and from 2007 to 2009 and played a key role in passing numerous landmark bills, including the Clean Water Act, Endangered Species Act, and the Medicare Act. Dingell's father, John D. Dingell Sr., preceded him in the seat, and his wife, Debbie Dingell, assumed it after he left.

Early Resignations

Georgia Republican Sen. Johnny Isakson—who chaired the Senate Ethics Committee—resigned due to health reasons in December 2019, midway through his third term. Isakson died in December 2021.

Pennsylvania 12th District GOP Rep. Tom Marino resigned in January 2019, just two weeks after being sworn in for a fifth term. He cited health reasons and said he would take a job in the private sector. Marino's nomination to head the Office of National Drug Control Policy failed in 2017 over revelations that he had pushed legislation that would have hurt federal opioid investigations.

Wisconsin 7th District GOP Rep. Sean Duffy resigned from Congress in September 2019, citing a desire to spend more time with his family ahead of the upcoming birth of his ninth child. Duffy, a prominent Trump defender, became a lobbyist at BGR Group, a Republican-leaning firm. Democrat Katie Hill, elected in January 2019 to California's 25th District, resigned in November after acknowledging she had had an inappropriate relationship with a campaign staffer before being elected, but denied allegations of a relationship with a male staffer. Hill sued a British tabloid and two journalists for publishing nude photos of her without her permission. But a Los Angeles County Superior Court judge ruled that the tabloid was protected under the First Amendment and she was ordered to pay $220,000 in legal fees. North Carolina 11th District GOP Rep. Mark Meadows resigned in March 2020 after being named Trump's chief of staff.

Lawmakers Who Retired to Seek Other Office

New Mexico 3rd District Democrat Ben Ray Lujan, a member of his party's leadership, ran successfully for the Senate seat vacated by the retiring Democrat Tom Udall. Montana at-large Republican Greg Gianforte retired after two terms to successfully run for governor. Kansas 1st District Rep. Roger Marshall retired to successfully run for the Senate to replace Pat Roberts, who retired.

Other Retirements

Senate: Republican Lamar Alexander of Tennessee; Republican Mike Enzi of Wyoming; Republican Pat Roberts of Kansas; and Democrat Tom Udall of New Mexico.

House: Louisianna 5th District Republican Ralph Abraham; Utah 1st District Republican Rob Bishop; Indiana 5th District Republican Susan Brooks; Texas 11th District Republican Mike Conaway; California 8th District Republican Paul Cook; California 53rd District Democrat Susan Davis; Texas 17th District Republican Bill Flores; Georgia 10th District Republican Tom Graves; Washington 10th District Democrat Dennis Heck; North Carolina 2nd District Republican George Holding; Texas 23rd District Republican Will Hurd; New York 2nd District Republican Pete King; Iowa 2nd District Democrat David Loebsack; New York 17th District Democrat Nita M. Lowey; Texas 24th District Republican Kenny Marchant; Michigan 10th District Republican Paul Mitchell; Texas 22nd District Republican Pete Olson; Alabama 2nd District Republican Martha Roby; Tennessee 1st District Republican Phil Roe; Florida 19th District Republican Francis Rooney; Wisconsin 5th District Republican F. James Sensenbrenner; New York 15th District Democrat Jose E. Serrano; Illinois 15th District Republican John Shimkus; Texas 13th District Republican Mac Thornberry; Indiana 1st District Democrat Pete Visclosky; Oregon 2nd District Republican Greg Walden; North Carolina 6th District Republican Mark Walker; Georgia 7th District Republican Rob Woodall; and Florida 3rd District Republican Ted Yoho.

Special Elections

Arizona Senate

In one of the nation's most closely watched races, ex-astronaut and Democrat Mark Kelly beat Republican Martha McSally in the November 2020 special election to serve the remaining two years of the late Arizona Sen. John McCain's term. He won 51.2 percent to McSally's 48.8 percent on a night in which Democrat Joe Biden also won Arizona in the presidential race.

Arizona GOP Gov. Doug Ducey had appointed former Sen. Jon Kyl to fill the seat after McCain's death, but Kyl stepped down in December 2018, saying he had no desire to finish the term. That led Ducey to tap McSally, a House member who had lost the previous month's general-election race for the state's other Senate seat to Democrat Kyrsten Sinema. McSally's appointment proved highly controversial, with McCain's daughter Meghan, a prominent TV talk-show host, among those critical of the move.

Kelly had flown combat jets for the Navy during Operation Desert Storm before joining the space program. He made four trips in the space shuttle, two of them as commander. But his connection to politics had been limited to his role as the husband of Arizona Democratic

Rep. Gabrielle Giffords. She was seriously injured in a January 2011 assassination attempt and survived, but with a complex traumatic brain injury.

In December 2012, a shooting at Sandy Hook Elementary School in Connecticut killed twenty children and six teachers. A few weeks later, Kelly and Giffords—who had left the House earlier that year—launched a gun safety advocacy group, first named Americans for Responsible Solutions and later renamed Giffords: Courage to Fight Gun Violence.

Arizona was one of Democrats' top Senate targets in 2020 and regarded as a must-win if they were to gain the majority. State Democrats had been urging Kelly to run for years, and he proved himself to be a prolific fundraiser, bringing in $90 million through September to McSally's $57 million. McSally firmly aligned herself with Trump, but as the race tightened, she sought to distance herself. She declined at an October debate to say directly whether she was proud to support the president. Kelly, meanwhile, ran as someone who had never expected to be in politics but who had considerable experience solving difficult problems throughout his career.

Georgia Senate

The Rev. Raphael Warnock helped give Democrats a majority in the Senate with his win in Georgia's January 2021 special election runoff to fill the remainder of Republican Johnny Isakson's term after Isakson resigned due to health reasons. Warnock defeated Kelly Loeffler, whom Georgia Gov. Brian Kemp had appointed, 51 percent to 49 percent. The election came the same day as the general-election runoff in which Democrat Jon Ossoff beat GOP Sen. David Perdue—one day before the January 6 insurrection.

Warnock became the state's first Black senator and the first Black Democrat in a former Confederate state since Reconstruction. He grew up in Savannah public housing as one of eleven siblings and eventually became senior pastor at civil rights icon Martin Luther King Jr.'s former Baptist church in Atlanta, where he worked on social justice, health care, and other policies. Warnock had delivered the eulogy at the funeral for the late Rep. John Lewis of Georgia, another civil rights icon whose death was among several in 2020 from the 1960s-era fight for equality. Warnock spoke about civil unrest in the wake of police killings of Blacks that year.

The contest, along with the Ossoff–Perdue race, had become a final referendum on President Donald Trump as he begrudgingly left office. The runoffs took on added importance as Democrats failed to make inroads in several contested Senate races in November, leaving Georgia as the party's last potential pathway to the majority. Prior to the runoffs, Republicans had secured fifty seats and Democrats had captured forty-eight, including two seats held by independents who caucus with Democrats.

Loeffler was a wealthy businesswoman who was co-owner of the WNBA women's basketball team Atlanta Dream. She cast Warnock as a radical and charged that Warnock and other Democrats sought to raise taxes, open borders with Mexico, and socialize the health care system.

She emphasized her background of growing up on a farm and waitressing her way through college. She also said that she left behind a high-paying job as a senior executive at Intercontinental Exchange, the parent company of the New York Stock Exchange, in serving in the Senate. *The New York Times* reported, however, she received stock and other awards worth more than $9 million from the company. Although she had been poised to forfeit the compensation if she left the company, the terms were altered to give her the money. Adding to the controversy about whether she received a sweetheart deal was her marriage to Intercontinental Exchange's chief executive, Jeffrey C. Sprecher.

Warnock, like Ossoff, was the beneficiary of substantial organizing help from former Georgia gubernatorial hopeful Stacey Abrams. She and others orchestrated a Black turnout operation that nearly matched the turnout in the earlier general election. Black turnout was nearly 92 percent of that in November, while white turnout was lower, at 89.5 percent of the November total. Analysts also found that many of Trump's strongest backers, unhappy with Biden being declared the winner, stayed home and did not vote.

North Carolina's 9th District

Republican Dan Bishop won a September 2019 special election to succeed GOP Rep. Robert Pittenger. Bishop narrowly defeated Democrat Dan McCready, 51 percent to 49 percent. The 2018 midterm race for the seat was in question for months because of evidence of election fraud on the Republican side.

Pittenger earlier had lost in the May 2018 Republican primary and suspected that his challenger, Mark Harris, benefitted from ballot-stuffing in a county in which Harris received 437 absentee votes and the three-term incumbent won just 17. Harris went on to win the November general-election race over McCready. However, the state Board of Elections refused to certify the results of the race because of potential irregularities involving mail-in ballots. Some voters claimed that individuals came to their homes to collect their unsealed absentee ballots. Others alleged that they received never-requested absentee ballots. And multiple others came forward to claim that they were paid by a Republican political operative to collect absentee ballots. The state board eventually called a new election, but Pittenger declined to run. In the special election, Bishop—a lawyer who had served in the state House and Senate—also benefitted from Trump's backing. He defeated a different Democrat in November with 56 percent.

Pennsylvania's 12th District

Republican Fred Keller easily won a May 2019 special election to replace Tom Marino. Keller defeated Democrat Marc Friedenberg with 68 percent of the vote. A veteran state House member, Keller had the backing of Trump, who traveled to the district to hold a rally with the candidate. Keller beat a different Democrat with 71 percent in November.

North Carolina's 3rd District

Republican Greg Murphy easily won a September 2019 special election to fill the unexpired term of the late Rep. Walter Jones. Murphy was a physician and state representative who first prevailed over sixteen other candidates in a primary before beating Republican Joan Perry in a runoff. He then defeated Democrat Allen M. Thomas with 62 percent of the vote. In the general election, he won with 64 percent.

Maryland's 7th District

Democrat Kweisi Mfume, who had represented Maryland's 7th District from 1987 to 1996, won an April 2020 special election to return to the seat. Mfume left the House to become president of the National Association for the Advancement of Colored People (NAACP), only to step down in 2004 amid allegations that he had sexually harassed female employees.

After Rep. Elijah Cummings' death, Mfume announced he would seek his old seat. He first came out on top in a twenty-four-candidate Democratic primary, then defeated Republican Kim Klacik with 74 percent of the vote. The two faced off in a rematch in the November general election, with Mfume winning with 72 percent.

California's 25th District

Former Navy pilot Mike Garcia flipped the seat from Democrat to Republican in a May 2020 special election. Garcia beat Democrat Christy Smith with 55 percent of the vote to replace Democrat Katie Hill, who resigned after admitting to an affair with a campaign staffer.

His victory marked the first time the GOP flipped a Democratically held seat in California since 1998 and was widely viewed as a warning sign of the troubles facing House Democrats in the 2020 general election. In November, he barely edged out Smith in a rematch by 350 votes out of more than 338,000 cast.

Wisconsin's 7th District

Tom Tiffany, a Republican state senator, handily beat Tricia Zunker, a Democratic school board member, with 57 percent of the vote in the race to succeed GOP Rep. Sean Duffy. He beat Zunker in a November general-election rematch with 61 percent.

New York's 27th District

Republican Christopher Jacobs won a June 2020 special election with 52 percent over Democrat Nate McMurray to succeed Rep. Chris Collins, who had resigned following his guilty plea to insider-trading charges. Jacobs was a state senator and former Erie County clerk who also worked at the U.S. Department of Housing and Urban Development. He beat McMurray in a rematch in November with 60 percent.

Georgia's 5th District

Democrat Kwanza Hall defeated fellow Democrat Robert Franklin with 54 percent of the vote in a December 2020 election to fill the seat left vacant by Rep. John Lewis' death. The two had won the most votes in an earlier seven-candidate primary. Hall served only the final month of Lewis' term, with Democrat Nikema Williams having won the general election a month earlier.

116th Congress: Presidential Nominations

Few of Trump's choices for administration posts requiring Senate confirmation faced much difficulty with the process in the final two years of his administration. That included William Barr, whom Trump chose to replace Jeff Sessions as attorney general after Sessions fell out of favor with the president and resigned in November 2018.

Barr had served as attorney general under President George H.W. Bush from 1991 to 1993. In his testimony before the Senate Judiciary Committee to be confirmed a second time, Barr cited his experience as proof he could remain firmly independent. He would not commit to releasing Special Counsel Robert S. Mueller III's still-pending report on Russia's efforts to influence the 2016 presidential election. But he said he would protect the investigation and would release as much as possible. He was confirmed in February 2019 on a 54–45 vote, with three Democrats—West Virginia's Joe Manchin, Arizona's Kyrsten Sinema and Alabama's Doug Jones—bucking their party and joining Republicans.

Another veteran Republican lawyer, David Bernhardt, had an easier time in replacing Ryan Zinke as secretary of Interior. Bernhardt had served as acting secretary following Zinke's departure, serving in that capacity for more than a year before being nominated in February 2019. Environmental groups and liberal Democrats mounted strenuous objections to his nomination, citing his work as a lawyer for the fossil fuel industry. But Bernhardt was confirmed 56–41 in April, with New Mexico Democrat Martin Heinrich joining Manchin and Sinema in voting in favor.

Defense Secretary James Mattis' decision to step down—he announced in December 2018 he would do so in February 2019, but Trump essentially fired him and he left January 1—led to another long-term acting secretary in Patrick M. Shanahan. He came to the Pentagon in 2017

as a deputy secretary following a thirty-year career with defense contractor Boeing Co. Trump nominated Shanahan in May 2019, but he withdrew his nomination the following month after an FBI background investigation continued because of past incidents of family violence. That led Trump to turn to Mark Esper, the secretary of the Army and a former executive with Raytheon, another defense contractor. Esper was confirmed in July on a 90–8 vote.

The Labor Department also saw a personnel shuffle at the top. Alexander Acosta resigned as secretary in July 2019 over mounting criticism of his approval, as a former U.S. attorney, of a controversial plea deal that allowed child-trafficking ringleader Jeffrey Epstein to plead guilty to a single state charge of solicitation in exchange for a non-prosecution agreement. Trump nominated attorney Eugene Scalia, the son of the late Supreme Court justice Antonin Scalia, as Acosta's replacement. Scalia was confirmed in September on a 53–44 vote.

Another Cabinet official to be confirmed during Trump's administration was Dan R. Brouillette to replace Rick Perry as secretary of Energy. Brouillette, who had been Perry's deputy secretary, was confirmed in December 2019 on a 70–15 vote.

Trump continued to make frequent use of acting secretaries. One was Chad Wolf, who stepped in at the Homeland Security Department after Kirstjen Nielsen feuded repeatedly with Trump over whether she was aggressively pursuing his immigration policies and resigned in April 2019. Wolf, who had been Nielsen's chief of staff, was named acting secretary. But two House committee chairs—Mississippi's Bennie Thompson at Homeland Security and New York's Carolyn Maloney at Oversight and Reform—asked the U.S. comptroller general to review the legality of Wolf's appointment. They alleged that another former acting secretary, Kevin McAleenan, lacked authority to change the department's line of succession because Nielsen had not properly placed McAleenan first in the line of succession before resigning, and that McAleenan's change came after the 210-day limit to his authority had expired. Eventually, a federal judge ruled in November 2020 that Wolf was not lawfully serving as acting secretary. Wolf's nomination at Homeland Security was withdrawn a day after he had urged the president to strongly condemn the January 2021 riots over the Electoral College's certification of Biden as the new president. The White House denied that the withdrawal was related to his comments, and he continued to serve as the department's acting head until Trump's term ended two weeks later.

At the Environmental Protection Agency, Andrew Wheeler also was allowed to serve as acting secretary for more than six months after Scott Pruitt resigned in 2018. Wheeler eventually was nominated and confirmed 52–47 in February 2019.

One of the most unusual—and contentious—nominees during Trump's presidency involved an acting secretary.

Rep. John Ratcliffe, a conservative Republican from Texas, was nominated to serve as director of national intelligence in July 2019 after Dan Coats left the job. But senators in both parties questioned whether Ratcliffe's thin resume as a former prosecutor made him suited for such a high-profile national security post. Some spy agency officials expressed fears, publicized in the news media, that he would politicize intelligence. Ratcliffe withdrew his nomination.

That led to Trump's appointment of an acting national intelligence director—Richard Grenell, a former U.S. ambassador to Germany. During his three months in the position, Grenell embarked on a highly controversial effort to declassify sensitive records that were aimed at benefitting Trump politically. He also undertook steps to reorganize the intelligence director's office. Those moves alarmed lawmakers of both parties, leading Trump to decide to renominate Ratcliffe. He was confirmed on a 49–44 vote in May 2020.

Ethics Investigations

SEN. RICHARD BURR

Burr, R-N.C., came under scrutiny from federal investigators as well as Senate ethics panel members for his financial transactions as the coronavirus pandemic began to spread. The situation led Burr in May 2020 to temporarily step down as the Senate Intelligence Committee's chairman. But the Justice Department told Burr in January 2021 that it would not pursue any insider trading charges against him.

Records showed that in February 2020, Burr sold thirty-three stock holdings, worth collectively between $628,000 and $1.7 million, that had comprised a large share of his portfolio. The sales enabled him to avoid losses that other investors had incurred when the stock market later sharply headed downward as the virus engulfed the country. News reports said the FBI served him with a search warrant and seized his cell phone as part of its investigation—highly unusual moves requiring a signoff at the Justice Department's top levels.

Burr acknowledged that he sold much of his stock portfolio out of concern for the spreading pandemic. But he contended his trades were based entirely on information reported by financial news outlets in Asia, not any briefings he got as a senator.

Nevertheless, amid calls from interest groups for Burr's resignation, he said he would temporarily yield the Intelligence gavel to Florida's Marco Rubio, the next Republican in line on the committee. That move ended up leaving him on the sidelines when the committee this summer delivered the final report on its lengthy investigation into Russia's attempt to influence the 2016 election. Burr had won respect from colleagues in both parties by working closely with Virginia's Mark Warner, Intelligence's

ranking Democrat, to oversee the politically sensitive investigation in the face of continued criticism from Trump and his allies.

Burr also publicly encouraged the Ethics panel to examine his finances. The committee took no action by the end of the 116th Congress and did not publicly comment on the status of any investigation. Media outlets reported that he still faced a probe from the Securities and Exchange Commission over the issue. Burr said he would not seek another term when his expired at the end of 2022.

REP. DAVID SCHWEIKERT

The Ethics Committee said in July 2020 it had ordered Schweikert, an Arizona Republican, to pay a $50,000 fine and face a reprimand from the House after finding that he violated eleven House ethics rules. The committee said Schweikert had agreed to the penalty as part of an agreement to end a two-year investigation that found substantial reason to believe that he violated House rules, the Code of Ethics for Government Service, federal laws, and other standards.

The panel cited Schweikert for campaign finance violations and errors in reporting by his campaign committees, the misuse of his congressional allowance, pressuring official staff members to perform campaign work, and his lack of candor and due diligence during the investigation. Investigators concluded that over a seven-year period, Schweikert failed to disclose, or falsely disclosed, $305,000 in loans or loan repayments and failed to report more than $140,000 in campaign contributions. A report detailing the committee's investigation cited Schweikert's campaign as having accepted more than $270,000 from his then-chief of staff, Richard Schwab, which broke campaign finance laws.

The panel said it considered a House-level sanction of censure, one of the most severe kinds of reprimand against a member. But it said it ultimately sought a lesser sanction in large part because of the congressman's willingness to accept responsibility and agreement to pay the fine. Schweikert managed to win reelection that fall over Democrat Hiral Tipirneni with 52 percent of the vote in the solidly Republican suburban Phoenix district, one of the nation's wealthiest.

SEN. KELLY LOEFFLER

Loeffler, R-Ga., was among the senators who came under scrutiny over her stock dealings around the time of the coronavirus, though she denied any wrongdoing. In May 2020, Loeffler announced that she had turned over documents to the Justice Department, the Senate Ethics Committee, and the Securities and Exchange Commission. She also recused herself from a Senate agriculture subcommittee and vowed to divest from individual stocks.

The Ethics Committee, after examining stock transactions made by both Loeffler and her husband Jeffrey Sprecher, chairman of the New York Stock Exchange, said in June that it found no evidence of any violations of either federal law or Senate rules. Its decision came several weeks after Loeffler's office said the Justice Department had also dropped its investigation and that of several other senators.

SEN. CORY BOOKER

The Ethics Committee announced in December 2018 it would not act on a complaint against Booker, D-N.J., accusing him of releasing "committee confidential" documents during the Senate confirmation hearing for then-Supreme Court nominee Brett Kavanaugh. Judicial Watch, a right-leaning government watchdog group, filed the complaint. Booker had divulged about twelve pages of emails from Kavanaugh's time as a White House counsel related to an internal discussion on racial inequality and racial profiling. Republican staffers on the Senate Judiciary Committee, however, said that then-Chairman Charles E. Grassley, R-Iowa, had previously waived the confidential restriction on the documents.

A week later, Booker released an additional twenty-eight confidential documents from Kavanaugh's time with the White House counsel's office showing his work on a controversial Bush-era judicial nominee, Charles Pickering. The documents raised questions about whether Kavanaugh was honest when he testified during his 2006 appellate court confirmation hearing that he was not primarily involved in pushing Pickering's nomination. Booker criticized the classification process and said many documents did not deserve to be kept confidential.

REP. SANFORD D. BISHOP JR.

An Office of Congressional Ethics (OCE) report released in July 2020 found that Bishop, D-Ga., may have used thousands of dollars in campaign funds for personal expenses on gasoline charges for him and his family, greens fees at country clubs, luxurious trips, and school tuition. He also may have spent more than $16,000 in taxpayer money for joint Christmas parties, the report said.

The report was released because the House Ethics Committee decided to further extend an investigation into Bishop. The congressman's office released a statement at the time of the OCE report saying that he was aware of mistakes that his campaign had made. It said he had proactively reimbursed many of the charges that the office had identified and that he would continue to work with the ethics committee on the issue.

DEL. MICHAEL F.Q. SAN NICOLAS

The House Ethics Committee began an investigation in 2019 into whether Democrat San Nicolas misused campaign funds, accepted improper contributions, and engaged in an inappropriate sexual relationship with a member of his congressional staff. In May 2021 it announced it had extended an investigative panel's probe of the matter for the rest of the 117th Congress.

John Paul Manuel, the former campaign chairman for San Nicolas, told the Office of Congressional Ethics that

San Nicolas accepted $10,000 in unreported cash from a local businessman during his initial run for Congress in 2018. Campaigns are limited to accepting a maximum of $100 in cash from a particular source, according to the Federal Election Commission. San Nicolas' office told *The New York Times* that the delegate welcomed the opportunity for due process.

REP. LORI TRAHAN

The Ethics Committee in July 2020 cleared Trahan, D-Mass., over allegations that the freshman lawmaker failed to properly disclose the source of $300,000 in personal funds she loaned to her congressional campaign in 2018. Conservative groups filed complaints against Trahan following her initial victory, contending that she failed to properly disclose all her personal financial assets until after winning her House race.

Trahan later acknowledged mistakes with her initial disclosure filings as well as with campaign finance reports, filing amended versions of those documents. But the ethics panel said she had not violated any House rules.

REP. ROSS SPANO

The Office of Congressional Ethics in August 2019 transferred a report to the Ethics Committee saying there was a substantial reason to believe Spano, a Florida Republican, received loans that exceeded federal campaign contribution limits. The committee in November 2020 said it was deferring action on the matter, though Spano lost his primary election and the committee no longer had jurisdiction after he left office in January 2021.

Shortly after Spano was elected to Congress in 2018, the *Tampa Bay Times* reported that he borrowed $180,000 from two personal friends and subsequently lent his campaign $167,000, a potential violation of federal campaign finance law. Contributions from individuals for the 2018 election cycle were set at $2,700 per person. Spano's lawyer wrote to the Federal Election Commission saying that the candidate had made an honest mistake.

REP. BILL HUIZENGA

The Office of Congressional Ethics in November 2019 referred instances of campaign spending by Huizenga, R-Mich., to the Ethics Committee for further review. The office said his campaign funded trips by the congressman, his staffers and their families to Walt Disney World, making payments for meals, airfare and other items, and that there was a substantial reason to believe the spending was not legitimate. The Ethics Committee did not reach a decision by the end of the 116th Congress, though investigations can carry over into new sessions.

The Federal Elections Commission in June 2019 had a split 2–2 vote on whether Huizenga's campaign violated election law, leading them not to pursue the matter any further. Huizenga accused the ethics panel of conducting a politically motivated investigation initiated by the state Democratic Party. The panel is split evenly between Democrats and Republicans, although it is chaired by a Democrat.

REP. RASHIDA TLAIB

The Ethics Committee found in August 2020 that Tlaib, D-Mich., broke campaign finance rules by receiving a campaign salary when she was no longer a congressional candidate, but the panel determined she did not have any ill intent. Tlaib was a member of "The Squad," a high-profile group of progressive female Democrats.

The committee concluded that receiving a portion of her salary from campaign funds following the 2018 general election was contrary to federal election law, though it said she engaged in good faith efforts to comply with relevant requirements. It ordered her to pay back to her campaign the $10,800 that she improperly received when she was no longer a candidate.

January 6 Insurrection

The January 6, 2021 insurrection was the Capitol's most serious security breach since the War of 1812, when invading British troops burned the building. It represented Trump supporters' last-ditch attempt to swing the election in the president's favor. Trump had repeatedly declared for weeks that widespread election fraud had denied him a second term, though state officials and the Justice Department found no evidence of such fraud. Courts also threw out dozens of lawsuits that the Trump campaign filed contesting the results.

On the morning of January 6, Trump addressed a throng of supporters at a White House rally, vowing never to concede and urged his supporters to fight. Several members of Congress also spoke, including Alabama Republican Rep. Mo Brooks. He later said he was wearing body armor at the rally, leading Democrats to sharply question whether the intention to demonstrate was as peaceful as he and other Trump supporters contended. After the insurrection, California Democratic Rep. Eric Swalwell filed a novel lawsuit in U.S. District Court against Brooks and others for allegedly conspiring with Trump and fomenting the attacks. Brooks denied the allegations.

Afterward, the protestors moved down the street from the White House to the Capitol. As Vice President Mike Pence—who had spurned Trump's plea to reject the certification—and senators walked to the House chamber where the Electoral College certification was being held, some protestors stormed an outer barricade west of the Capitol. Eventually they overtook Capitol Police outside and made their way up the steps, breaking windows to gain entry. As that was occurring, suspicious packages that were later determined to be pipe bombs were found at the nearby headquarters of both the Democratic and Republican parties, forcing nearby buildings to be evacuated.

The rioters approached the House chamber where the certification was being held, forcing both houses of Congress to adjourn and evacuate. The building went into lockdown. One group of protestors came down a Senate hallway not far from several senators, but a Capitol Police officer diverted the mob in a different direction. That officer, Eugene Goodman, received the Congressional Gold Medal for his efforts. Another group of protestors breached a barricaded door leading to a lobby just outside the House chamber. As thirty-five-year-old Ashli Babbitt tried to climb through a broken section of the door, she was shot in the neck and killed by a different Capitol Police officer.

Gangs of protestors roamed the Capitol hallways, posing for photos, defacing relics, and defecating and urinating in spots. They entered several abandoned offices, including those of House Speaker Nancy Pelosi. Lawmakers huddled in other offices and tried not to be discovered, tweeting out their status. Some of them donned gas masks after being advised that tear gas was being used in the Rotunda. A number of Republican lawmakers directly implored Trump to call off the mob; the president did call for peace, but continued to tweet inaccurate claims of election fraud. More than two hours after protestors first breached the Capitol's grounds, the White House announced that Trump had summoned the National Guard. Biden appeared on TV to demand that Trump appear on television to end the rioting; Trump did not do so, but tweeted a video telling his supporters they were special and that they should go home.

After more than four hours, police and the National Guard started to clear the mob. One Capitol Police officer later compared the fighting with protestors to a medieval battle and said he was more fearful during that day's events than he was during his entire military deployment to Iraq. Outside the Capitol, protestors built a wooden gallows with a noose and chanted that they wanted to hang Pence. Washington, D.C. Mayor Muriel Bowser announced a 6 p.m.-to-6 a.m. curfew. Trump's Twitter and Facebook accounts were temporarily locked for policy violations, with companies announcing that they saw a risk in carrying content that could be interpreted as encouraging violence. The moves followed a barrage of criticism from Democrats that safety considerations outweighed those of free speech.

The Senate reconvened at 8 p.m. to certify the electoral vote total, with the House following suit about an hour later. Finally, at 3:42 a.m., Pence called a majority of the Electoral College votes for Biden. That came despite some Republicans' objections. Those objections were permitted under the Electoral Count Act, a 140-year-old law governing what Congress should do in the case of disputes about which candidate won in a state. Some of Trump's allies tried to twist the law to claim that the vice president, in presiding over the certification, could simply reject states' electors. The lawmakers specifically registered their refusal to certify the results in Arizona and Pennsylvania, two of the most hotly contested states between Biden and Trump. A total of eight Republican senators and 139 representatives voted to register those objections. Several other Republicans who said they had initially planned to do so reversed their positions, saying they could not proceed after such a direct and disturbing assault on the democratic process.

Immediately after the attacks, Capitol Police installed metal security fencing topped with razor wire around the Capitol perimeter. The fencing would remain in place for nearly four months, drawing complaints from residents of the nearby Capitol Hill neighborhood. Officials also called in National Guard troops to help police patrol the grounds, with almost 26,000 in place at the time of Biden's inauguration two weeks after the riots.

A bipartisan Senate investigation by the Homeland Security and Governmental Affairs and Rules and Administration committees found a series of breakdowns across multiple law enforcement agencies ahead of the attacks. It also said the Defense Department's hesitancy in responding was influenced by criticism of its aggressive response to protests around the country in 2020 after George Floyd, a Black man, was killed in Minneapolis while in police custody. But the report did not explore the root causes of the attack or Trump's role.

116th Congress: Legislation Introduced and Passed

In the 116th Congress, 16,601 bills, resolutions, and other measures were introduced—the most since the 95th Congress (1977–1978), according to GovTrack.us. Of that total, 1,229 were incorporated or enacted into law, a rate of 7 percent that was slightly below the 115th Congress figure of 8 percent.

Nine bills received a presidential veto without an override. One bill was overridden with ease—the $741 billion defense authorization bill for fiscal 2021 (HR 6395). Trump vetoed the bill because it lacked a repeal he had demanded of legal protections for social media companies, which he argued did not deserve such protection. Lawmakers, however, said the issue was not related to national security and was not worth holding up the bill. The House voted to override Trump 322–78 in December 2020, with the Senate following suit 81–13 a few days later.

Legislative Branch Appropriations

As in previous Congresses, spending on the legislative branch for fiscal years 2020 and 2021 was made part of a catch-all appropriations bills. And as in previous Congresses, the bills did not increase lawmakers' salaries.

House Democrats had included a pay raise of 2.6 percent, or $4,500, in their chamber's version (HR 2779) of the legislative branch spending bill. But Democratic leaders in June 2019 pulled that measure from a broader

appropriations package because of ardent Republican and Democratic opposition to the perennially sensitive proposal.

Senators and House members at the time earned $174,000 a year. Lawmaker pay had decreased by around 15 percent after taking account of inflation and other factors since 2009, according to the Congressional Research Service. But the Republican-controlled Senate had signaled earlier in the year that pay raises would be a tough sell.

Fiscal 2020 funding was provided in the Further Consolidated Appropriations Act (PL 116-94), which was enacted in December 2019. The $5 billion provided for the legislative branch represented an increase of $202.8 million, or 4 percent, from the fiscal 2019 level.

Fiscal 2021 funding came via the Consolidated Appropriations Act, 2021 (HR 133, PL 116-260), which was enacted in December 2020. The act provided $5.3 billion for legislative branch activities—an increase of $251.2 million or 5.1 percent, excluding emergency appropriations.

The Coronavirus Aid, Relief, and Economic Security Act (CARES Act, PL 116-136), enacted in March 2020, provided additional funding for the legislative branch. Some of that funding included $1 million for the Sergeant at Arms and Doorkeeper of the Senate and $9 million for "miscellaneous items." In the House, it covered $25 million for an account that funds various activities, but not lawmakers' salaries. The Capitol Police got an extra $12 million for salaries, while the Architect of the Capitol received $25 million for virus-related preparations and supplies around the Capitol complex.

H Res 430: Judiciary Authorized to Pursue Civil Lawsuits to Enforce Subpoenas

The House adopted a resolution (H Res 430) in June 2019 authorizing Judiciary Committee Chairman Jerrold Nadler, D-N.Y., to go to court to pursue civil enforcement of subpoenas issued to Attorney General William Barr and former White House Counsel Donald McGahn. The measure also made changes increasing power of House committees to pursue enforcement of additional subpoenas. It was adopted on a strict 229–191 party-line vote.

The vote came one day after Nadler announced a deal with the Trump Justice Department to give the committee access to documents in Special Counsel Robert S. Mueller III's investigation of Russia's efforts to influence the 2016 presidential election. Nadler and other committee Democrats sought notes from former White House officials as well as the FBI's interviews with witnesses. The investigation was among many that House committees had launched, including probes over obtaining Trump's tax records, spending for a U.S.–Mexico border wall, and efforts to add a citizenship question to the 2020 Census.

Barr had resisted providing the Judiciary Committee with the information, citing executive privilege. That resulted in the panel voting 24–16 along party lines in May

to hold Barr in contempt of Congress. The deal between Nadler and Justice officials put that means of seeking information on hold—though it did not apply to other ongoing House investigations. In July, the House voted 230–198 to hold both Barr and Commerce Secretary Wilbur Ross in contempt over their defiance of the Oversight and Reform Committee's subpoenas seeking information about the failed attempt to add a census citizenship question.

Questions about how much authority congressional committees should possess to issue and enforce subpoenas had stretched back for decades. Before 1975, only a few House committees had the power to issue subpoenas under House rules, with other panels being given authority as part of separate resolutions that had to be adopted by the House. As part of post-Watergate reforms to congressional oversight, some lawmakers called for changes. All committees and subcommittees subsequently were granted subpoena power, though a majority of committee members had to agree and the full House had to vote.

The June 2019 resolution altered that approach. It gave committee chairs the ability to go to court on behalf of their panels in an attempt to seek compliance with subpoenas without the full House first assenting. Instead, the chairs needed to obtain the so-called Bipartisan Legal Advisory Group made up of the speaker, majority leader, majority whip, minority leader, and minority whip. The group, which had been in existence since 1993, directed the activities of the House Office of General Counsel. The resolution made the vote of that group equal to a vote of the House.

Social Media and Congress

In a trend that mirrored the rest of the nation, the 116th Congress set records for social media use, with more than 2.2 million tweets on Twitter and Facebook posts in 2019 and 2020, according to a January 2021 Pew Research Center report. Those figures were well above those of the 114th and 115th Congresses and represented more than 3,000 posts and tweets for the median member during the two-year span.

Twitter was the most used platform, with more than 500 million shares and retweets, Pew found. It said the thirty members who had more than 1 million followers on Twitter—representing 6 percent of lawmakers who were active during the session—produced 10 percent of all congressional social media posts. Of those thirty, five were freshmen, including New York Democratic Rep. Alexandria Ocasio-Cortez, who had more than 12.7 million followers at the time of Pew's report.

As in the 115th Congress, the lawmaker with the most Twitter followers was Vermont independent and two-time presidential candidate Bernie Sanders, with more than 21 million followers at the time of the report. California Sen. Kamala Harris, who became vice president, was next with more than 16 million followers. After Ocasio-Cortez, the

most followed member was Utah Sen. Mitt Romney, the 2012 GOP presidential nominee, with more than 12 million.

Trump Pardons/Commutes Sentences of Ex-Members

Seven former members of Congress who had been convicted of crimes received clemency from Trump before he left the White House. Five received presidential pardons, while two had their prison sentences commuted. The actions dismayed many of Trump's critics, who called them a blatant abuse of power—especially since many of the lawmakers had personal or political connections to the White House and some were given in his final days in office.

The first ex-member to receive clemency was a Democrat—former Rep. Rod Blagojevich of Illinois. In February 2020, Trump commuted six years of Blagojevich's fourteen-year prison sentence. Blagojevich was sent to prison on corruption charges over his attempt—as the state's governor—in 2009 to sell the Senate seat that had been vacated by then-President Barack Obama. Blagojevich once appeared on the reality TV series "The Celebrity Apprentice" that Trump hosted before being elected. Trump had publicly been highly critical of his sentence, calling him a victim of the same forces that had investigated him for years.

The first two Republican lawmakers to receive Trump pardons—former Reps. Duncan D. Hunter of California and Chris Collins of New York—both were ardent supporters of the president. Their pardons came in December 2020. In March of that year, Hunter had been sentenced to an eleven-month prison term that was scheduled to begin in January 2021. Federal prosecutors said Hunter had spent campaign funds on extramarital affairs with five women, including lobbyists and congressional staff. In December 2019, Hunter pleaded guilty on one count of misusing campaign funds, and the next month resigned from his seat. A day after Trump pardoned Hunter, the president pardoned his wife Margaret, who pleaded guilty to the same crime.

Collins' pardon came the same day as Duncan D. Hunter's. The FBI arrested Collins and his son in 2018, and both were charged with insider trading and making false statements. The congressman was accused of breaching the confidentiality of secret results of a drug trial for an Australian biotechnology company on which he served as a board member so that his son could trade the company's stock before the results were made public. He pleaded guilty to the charges in September 2019, having narrowly won reelection the previous November.

Also in December, Trump commuted the remaining sentence of former Texas GOP Rep. Steve Stockman, who was sentenced in 2018 to ten years in prison after he was convicted of nearly two dozen felonies, including fraud. Authorities said Stockman misused $1.25 million in funds from political donors that were intended for charity to pay for expenses such as hot air balloon rides and a new dishwasher. He was also accused of planting an undercover intern in the state House office of a political rival.

One week before leaving office in January 2021, Trump pardoned former California GOP Rep. Randy "Duke" Cunningham, whose crimes became a central focus of Democrats in their successful campaign to reclaim control of the House in 2006. Cunningham a year earlier had admitted accepting at least $2.4 million in bribes. That included about $1 million in cash as well as rugs, antiques, furniture, yacht club fees, boat repairs, moving costs and vacation expenses, in exchange for using his seat on the Appropriations Committee to obtain earmarks on behalf of defense contractors. He was sentenced to eight years and four months in prison and was released in 2013. The pardon was conditioned on Cunningham paying millions in restitution and forfeiture claims.

That same day, Trump pardoned former Republican Rep. Robin Hayes of North Carolina. Federal authorities said Hayes participated in a scheme while GOP state chairman in which a wealthy insurance company magnate attempted to bribe the state insurance commissioner with $1.5 million in campaign funds in exchange for removing a top department regulator. He was then accused of lying to FBI agents in 2018. Hayes accepted a plea deal in 2019 on one count and was sentenced to one year of probation in addition to financial penalties.

On his next-to-last day in office, Trump pardoned former Rep. Rick Renzi, R-Ariz.,, who had been convicted in 2013 of racketeering, money laundering, and other federal charges related to a land swap scheme. Renzi served three years in prison and was released in 2017. Rep. Paul Gosar, another Arizona Republican and a staunch Trump supporter, were among those who lobbied the president to pardon Renzi.

Sidebar: The Squad

Few congressional freshmen commanded as much attention as "The Squad," four progressive female Democrats of varying ethnic and racial backgrounds elected in 2018. The lawmakers—Alexandria Ocasio-Cortez of New York, Ayanna Presley of Massachusetts, Ilhan Omar of Minnesota and Rashida Tlaib of Michigan—rankled President Donald Trump to the point that the House in July 2019 passed a resolution that condemned Trump's attacks on the women. At the same time, the group tangled with Speaker Nancy Pelosi and others in their party, accusing them of not moving far enough to the left.

Ocasio-Cortez gave the group its nickname on Instagram when the four lawmakers met after the November election. She already had been catapulted into the national political spotlight when she ousted Rep. Joseph Crowley, a member of the House Democrats' leadership, in a primary on her way to becoming—at twenty-nine—the youngest woman ever elected to Congress. She depicted Crowley as a member of the old party

SELECT COMMITTEE ON THE MODERNIZATION OF CONGRESS

Congress has made many attempts over the years to improve its functioning. In 2019, the House formed a bipartisan panel devoted to the task—the Select Committee on the Modernization of Congress. It compiled nearly 100 recommendations covering a range of areas such as technology and cybersecurity, procedures and scheduling, staff retention, and executive-branch oversight. Many were implemented, and the panel proved successful enough to be reauthorized for the 117th Congress (2021–2022) so it could continue its work.

The committee was a result of House members' frustrations with the legislative body's waning power and dwindling resources. It also stemmed from concerns on and off Capitol Hill about the revolving door between Congress and the lobbying world where—because of high turnover—lobbyists often wielded more institutional knowledge and policymaking ability than congressional aides. Six Democrats and six Republicans were chosen for the panel, with Washington Democrat Derek Kilmer named as the chairman. Kilmer was a former McKinsey & Co. management consultant and a leader of the centrist, business-friendly New Democrat Coalition. He served on the Appropriations Committee, which had a reputation as being one of Congress' chief sources of bipartisanship.

Another Appropriations member, Republican Tom Graves of Georgia, was named the select committee's vice chairman. A real estate developer before being elected, he developed an interest in modernizing Congress while chairing the Appropriations panel on the legislative branch in the 114th Congress (2016–2017). Other members brought a mix of relevant backgrounds: Democrat Emanuel Cleaver of Missouri was a former Kansas City mayor; Democrat Zoe Lofgren of California had led the Ethics and House Administration panels; Republican Rodney Davis of Illinois had spent sixteen years as a House member's projects director and was the top GOP member on House Administration; and Republican Bob Latta of Ohio had experience working on technology issues as a member of the Energy and Commerce Committee.

Congressional scholars and interest groups welcomed the committee's creation, even though as a select committee it lacked the power to write and pass legislation and could only offer suggestions to committees or the full House. They noted the explosive growth in lobbying over the previous two decades and the decline in congressional staff experience, with the median tenure among House aides dwindling to just four years. They also said many members of Congress lacked a crucial understanding of just how rapidly technology was transforming society.

The committee received an initial budget of just under $500,000 and a staff of three full-time employees plus three congressional fellows. It held a series of hearings at which it listened to lawmakers describe their desire to encourage more civility and transparency. Several of those who testified also lamented the annual congressional budget process as overly cumbersome and in need of an overhaul.

The panel released its first slate of recommendations in May 2019. It proposed a number of changes to the lobbying disclosure system, including new unique identification numbers for each lobbyist to clean up the current system's sometimes duplicative names. The committee also recommended that the legislative branch provide resources to finish an ongoing project of the House Clerk's office aimed at developing an automated system—using artificial intelligence—to analyze differences between proposed legislation and current law and to easily show what changes proposed amendments would make to bills. And it called on Congress to develop a central online hub that would list the expiration dates of all federal programs as well as when Congress needs to reauthorize various agencies, such as the Federal Aviation Administration.

The committee took smaller steps on its own to encourage greater bipartisanship. At its hearings, lawmakers switched up their seating order, with Democrats and Republicans interspersed instead of sitting together with their party colleagues. In adopting any recommendations, at least two-thirds of those voting had to be in favor.

Although the committee initially had been envisioned as a one-year effort, it received approval to carry over into 2020. At the end of 2019, it put forth another series of recommendations: Endorsing bipartisan retreats for lawmakers and their families; having lawmakers band together to purchase office technology in bulk to save taxpayer money; and updating House procedures to allow members to electronically add, or remove, their names as cosponsors of legislation.

By the end of 2020, the committee had issued ninety-seven recommendations. Of that total, the committee said more than 60 percent had been implemented or partially adopted, or were in progress. More than thirty of them were included in a measure (H Res 56), which the House adopted in March of that year on a 395–13 vote. It included such changes as making permanent the House Office of Diversity and Inclusion and allowing committees to submit electronic reports and members to add their names to bills digitally. Other recommendations were made part of the annual legislative branch appropriations bill, such as allowing newly elected members to hire and pay one transition staff member.

(Continued)

SELECT COMMITTEE ON THE MODERNIZATION OF CONGRESS (Continued)

One of the most prominent recommendations that the panel made was setting up a framework for the return of earmarks—member-added provisions to spending bills. Earmarks had come under intense criticism from congressional watchdog groups—as well as some lawmakers—as a waste of taxpayer dollars, and Republicans abolished the practice in 2011. The select committee called for their return via a competitive grant program aimed at supporting projects that originate at the local level and have support within the communities receiving a grant. A modified form of that proposal was put in place in 2021.

To address the budget process, the committee made a number of suggestions that were not fulfilled immediately. They included implementing a biennial rather than an annual congressional budget resolution to give Budget Committee members more time, while implementing a fixed deadline for Congress to complete action on that budget. Some members of Congress had advocated the concept of biennial budgeting for years. But critics of the approach argued that achieving any time savings depended on a willingness to make relatively few changes in the off year of the two-year cycle and—absent such restraint—there might be little or no time saved.

The select committee was given an authorization for the entirety of the 117th Congress. Panel members set about suggesting improvements that were made more urgent by the 2020 arrival of the coronavirus pandemic and the changes in operations that resulted.

---

establishment who was too close to business while refusing to accept any corporate contributions of her own. Before being elected, Ocasio-Cortez had been a community organizer who worked on Vermont Independent Sen. Bernie Sanders' 2016 presidential campaign. She amassed one of the largest Twitter followings of anyone on Capitol Hill—more than 4 million as of April 2019—with her frequent denunciations of Republicans.

Pressley also toppled an incumbent—ten-term Rep. Michael Capuano—on her way to becoming the first woman of color from Massachusetts to serve in Congress. She had been an aide to Rep. Joseph P. Kennedy II and Sen. John Kerry before being elected to Boston's City Council. Tlaib was another Democratic primary winner, beating first-term Rep. Brenda Jones. Tlaib had served six years in Michigan's House of Representatives and worked as an attorney at a national nonprofit public-interest law center. Omar, a Somali native who fled the war-torn country when she was eight years old, won the seat that had been held by Rep. Keith Ellison after he ran for Minnesota attorney general. She also was a former state representative.

Ocasio-Cortez used her position on the Oversight and Reform Committee to sharply question Trump administration officials. They included Commerce Secretary Wilbur Ross, whom she accused of lying about the administration's controversial decision to add a citizenship question to the U.S. Census. But she did not spare her Democratic colleagues. She warned a group of them that they could wind up on a list of primary election targets after several moderates defied the party to join Republicans in a vote on an immigration bill. Several weeks later, she urged her Twitter followers to halt donations to the Democrats' campaign arm because of its new policy to boycott consultants who worked for those challenging incumbents in primaries.

Tlaib and Omar also stirred controversy. Tlaib celebrated her swearing-in by using an expletive in calling for Trump's impeachment, and later publicly booed Hillary Clinton at a 2020 campaign event for Sanders. In one of Omar's tweets in February 2019, she implied that support for Israel was driven by campaign donations from pro-Israel groups. That led Pelosi and several other Democratic leaders to issue a statement calling her remarks deeply offensive, prompting Omar to apologize. Tlaib later criticized Democratic leaders for using non-white lawmakers as props to showcase the party's diversity and said the best way to honor diversity was not attempt to silence her and others.

The battling between Democrats and Republicans over immigration led Trump—who had made cracking down on those entering the United States illegally a centerpiece of his presidential bid—to take aim at the group. He tweeted in July that Democratic women who criticized his approach should "go back" to the broken, crime-infested places from which they came. Although the president did not mention the Squad's members by name, he was widely presumed to be targeting them. Democrats reacted with outrage. They introduced a resolution (H Res 489) contending Trump's comments legitimized and increased fear and hatred toward people of color and naturalized American citizens. It passed the House in July on a 240-187 vote, with only four Republicans joining all Democrats in favor. But it had little effect on Trump, who continued to mock the group.

The news media and political analysts focused on the relationship between Ocasio-Cortez and Pelosi, who at seventy-nine when Ocasio-Cortez entered Congress was a half-century older. Many said it symbolized a broader generational divide within the Democratic Party. Pelosi was a staunch liberal, but generally sought to build consensus

within her caucus. Ocasio-Cortez took a more activist approach, joining a group of 200 youth protestors in November 2018 in staging a demonstration outside Pelosi's office over taking more decisive steps on climate change.

The freshman subsequently joined Sen. Edward J. Markey, D-Mass., in introducing a nonbinding joint resolution (H Res 109, S Res 59) calling for a "Green New Deal." The plan called for reducing the greenhouse gas emissions blamed for a warming climate while addressing what the lawmakers said were related social justice and labor problems. Republicans widely denounced the proposal as socialism in disguise. They inaccurately depicted it as—among other things—an effort to stop Americans from eating beef because forests were emitting carbon dioxide as trees were chopped down to enable more cattle grazing.

The resolution attracted more than 100 cosponsors in the House, but Pelosi and other Democratic leaders refused to bring it up for a vote. Instead, they said the newly created Select Committee on the Climate Crisis would assemble legislation to address the issue, which would then be parceled out to various committees. Ocasio-Cortez and other backers of the Green New Deal said such a deliberative approach ignored the urgency that the issue demanded. That and similar remarks prompted Pelosi to respond that other House Democrats represented much more politically competitive districts and lacked the ability—or inclination—to take the Squad's far-left stands.

All of the Squad members won reelection in 2020. That included Tlaib, who faced the most serious primary challenge in a rematch with Jones. Tlaib pointed to her work on legislation, which included a 2020 bill aimed at protecting retirees' pension benefits (HR 5214, PL 116-126) that Trump signed into law.

The Trump Presidency

The Trump Presidency

President Donald Trump entered the White House with no experience in elective politics and upended Republicans and Democrats with unorthodox policies that did not always track with the long-standing priorities of either party. His major successes included a significant tax cut his first year in office, a rollback of regulations throughout his term, and the confirmation of three Supreme Court justices. But he did not fit neatly into standard partisan boxes. He disappointed fellow Republicans with trade tariffs, withdrawing troops from Syria and Afghanistan, and the occasional advocacy of spending beyond what they would support, such as for infrastructure or pandemic aid. At the same time, Trump battled Democrats through years of wide-ranging investigations of his finances for potential foreign influence on his administration, his dealings with foreign countries, and his namesake Trump Organization's dealings with the government for possible violations of the Constitution's emoluments clause. He turned management of the company over to his sons Donald Trump Jr. and Eric Trump after he was elected, but he continued to profit from it. His own Justice Department appointed Special Counsel Robert S. Mueller III, a former FBI director, to investigate Russian interference in the 2016 election, which led to convictions of short-lived National Security Adviser Michael Flynn and several political aides. Trump became the first president in history to be impeached twice. The first time, the House of Representatives charged him for dealings with Ukraine, and the second time it charged him with inciting an insurrection against the peaceful transfer of power to his successor. He was acquitted both times by the Senate.

The 2017 tax cut, which reduced individual and corporate tax rates, became Trump's signature legislative achievement. But he enjoyed several landmark victories. His overhaul of criminal sentencing laws became the biggest revamp of criminal justice in nearly three decades. He created a sixth branch of the military, the Space Force, as the first new branch since its parent Air Force was established in 1947. When he could not win approval of legislation, such as with his top priorities of border security and immigration, he resorted to executive actions. Almost immediately upon entering office, he blocked travel from six majority-Muslim countries. He reduced the cap on refugee admissions. And he consistently urged more construction of the wall along the southern border with Mexico, even when it meant shifting funds from the Pentagon in the face of congressional objections.

Trump's domestic policies were often unpredictable. He took credit for triggering the longest partial government shutdown in history, which stemmed from a dispute over funding for border security that lingered after workers returned to their offices with back pay. He named more acting Cabinet secretaries than his predecessors, arguing that their status gave him more flexibility in personnel matters while leaving departments with less certain leadership that could change on a whim. He drove out Attorney General Jeff Sessions, who had given him one of his earliest congressional endorsements for the presidency, for failing to curb the FBI probe and Mueller investigation of Russian interference that hung like a cloud for years over his administration. Trump also brought his daughter Ivanka Trump and son-in-law Jared Kushner into the White House as senior advisers.

Trump sometimes faced opposition from both sides of the aisle. Despite Republican misgivings over government spending, he discussed a $1 trillion infrastructure package with Democratic congressional leaders before abandoning the effort. Repetitious pronouncements about infrastructure week became a running gag. Trump's final year in office was dominated by the worst pandemic in a century, which killed nearly 400,000 Americans during that year. Near the end of his term, after Congress cut a deal for $600 payments to individuals to cope with COVID-19, Trump urged $2,000 payments in a proposal that went nowhere until his successor took office. The administration spent billions spurring the development of several vaccines completed for distribution in less than a year. But stay-at-home orders to curb the spread of the virus also devastated the economy. Trump's mixed messages on health recommendations for wearing masks and practicing social distancing resulted in confusion about how to combat the deadly virus, and he eventually got sick himself. His own

611

vaccination was not announced until after he left office. In contrast, Senate Majority Leader Mitch McConnell, R-Ky., who suffered from polio as a child, remained a staunch proponent of vaccinations.

In foreign policy, Trump often took positions considered unthinkable or at least unworkable. For example, he moved the U.S. embassy in Israel to Jerusalem despite the risk of inflaming tensions with Arab nations. Along the way, he often antagonized allies and embraced adversaries. Trump criticized Canada and Mexico over trade before renegotiating a North American trade agreement to replace the one under former President Bill Clinton. He threatened to leave the North Atlantic Treaty Organization, which was formed in the aftermath of World War II as a Cold War response to the Soviet Union, over the lack of defense spending by European allies. And he curbed the restoration of diplomatic relations with Cuba begun under former President Barack Obama. Trump also withdrew from three Obama-era pacts: the Trans-Pacific Partnership trade agreement, the Paris Accord on climate change, and an international deal to discourage Iran from developing nuclear weapons, each of which he called bad deals for the United States. Trump's first impeachment grew out of a call with the Ukrainian president that his own diplomats said amounted to a quid pro quo for that country to investigate former Vice President Joe Biden in exchange for military weapons in defense against the mutual adversary of Russia. Meanwhile, he sided with Russian President Vladimir Putin against his own intelligence community in the fight over whether Russia interfered in the 2016 election. Trump also became the first president to visit North Korea while in office, amid an ultimately unsuccessful effort to discourage leader Kim Jong-un from developing nuclear weapons.

Assembling the Administration

INITIAL APPOINTMENTS

Despite campaigning to drain the swamp of political insiders in Washington, Trump filled his Cabinet largely with white men who had been military generals, conservative House members, or political rivals for the Republican nomination for president. His initial nominees were all confirmed, despite controversies that led to the first tie vote in the history of cabinet nominees. A couple of the earliest members of the cabinet made relatively quick departures, one for another job in the White House and the other after a report critical of his private plane travel.

Betsy DeVos may have generated the most vocal opposition to becoming a cabinet member after Trump named her to become Education secretary November 23, 2016. DeVos was a prominent supporter of charter schools, school vouchers, and alternatives to public school. She was also a wealthy philanthropist, prominent Republican donor, and former chair of the Michigan Republican Party. Protesters attended her confirmation hearing January 31,

2017, at the Senate Health, Education, Labor, and Pensions Committee. Vice President Mike Pence broke the first tie vote in history for a Cabinet member, when the Senate voted 51–50 to confirm her February 7, 2017. GOP Sens. Susan Collins of Maine and Lisa Murkowski of Alaska joined Democrats in opposing DeVos.

Another controversial choice was GOP Rep. Tom Price of Georgia, an orthopedic surgeon, who was chosen November 29, 2016, to become secretary of the Department of Health and Human Services. Price had traded medical industry stocks and he quickly agreed to divest holdings in more than forty companies while denying he received or profited from nonpublic information about them. After some parliamentary scuffles, the Senate voted 52–47 along party lines to confirm him February 10, 2017. His tenure was relatively brief. The HHS inspector general announced September 22, 2017, that it would investigate his use of private planes for official business, and he resigned a week later. His successor was Alex Azar, a former drug company executive who previously served as general counsel and deputy secretary of HHS, and was a clerk for Supreme Court Justice Antonin Scalia.

Sen. Jeff Session, R-Ala., was rewarded for his early endorsement of Trump with a nomination to become attorney general November 18, 2016. Despite his twenty years in the Senate, Democratic colleagues lashed into Sessions in much the same way senators did in 1986, when charges of racism cost him a federal judgeship. Sessions at the time labeled the accusations "damnably false." At his January 10, 2017, confirmation hearing before the Judiciary Committee, protesters chanted, "No Trump, no KKK, no fascist USA." During floor debate February 7, 2017, Senate Majority Leader Mitch McConnell, R-Ky., and Sen. Elizabeth Warren, D-Mass., clashed when Warren tried to read into the record a 1986 letter by Coretta Scott King, widow of the Rev. Martin Luther King Jr., opposing Sessions' nomination to the federal bench. After some procedural maneuvering, the Senate voted 49–43 along party lines to uphold the ruling of the chair that Warren had violated Senate rules by impugning a fellow member. She was not allowed to speak for the remainder of the debate. The Senate voted 52–47 that evening to confirm Sessions.

One of Trump's more unexpected choices came when he picked Exxon Mobil CEO Rex Tillerson to lead the State Department. At his January 11 Senate Foreign Relations Committee confirmation hearing, Tillerson revealed policy differences with Trump, such as acknowledging that humans play a role in climate change. Democrats criticized Tillerson's ties to Russian President Vladimir Putin and autocrats in other oil-rich nations, as part of his work for energy giant Exxon. Several Republicans—including Sens. John McCain of Arizona, Lindsey Graham of South Carolina and Marco Rubio of Florida—expressed reservations about his stance on U.S.–Russia relations. But the Senate voted 56–43 on February 1 to confirm him.

Trump chose former Marine Corps Gen. James Mattis to become Defense secretary on December 1, 2016. But first Mattis needed Congress to pass a bill creating a special exemption to a law prohibiting former military officers from leading the department within seven years of active service. It was not a slam dunk. The Senate passed the waiver January 13, 2017, on an 81–17 vote, and the House cleared it hours later, 268–151. It was the first bill Trump signed into law. Mattis was confirmed Inauguration Day by a vote of 98–1, with Sen. Kirsten Gillibrand, D-N.Y., casting the lone "no" vote.

Trump chose another retired Marine Corps general, John Kelly, who oversaw combat in Iraq, to lead the Department of Homeland Security. Like Mattis, Kelly took issue with several of Trump's positions at his January 10, 2017, confirmation hearing. Kelly agreed with Trump's proposal to build a wall on the southern border, but he offered different perspectives on issues such as immigration from majority-Muslim countries, and the use of "enhanced interrogation techniques" that qualified as torture to extract information from terrorism suspects. The Senate voted 88–11 on Inauguration Day to confirm Kelly. He served only until July, when Trump named him to replace White House Chief of Staff Reince Priebus. Kelly's successor was Kirstjen Nielsen, a top aide to Kelly who had served as chief of staff at the Department of Homeland Security (DHS). The Senate voted 62–37 on December 5, 2017, to confirm her.

Trump picked former Texas Gov. Rick Perry, a former rival for the 2016 Republican presidential nomination, to lead the Energy Department on December 14, 2016. Perry had once suggested the department should be eliminated, but said he regretted espousing the idea at his confirmation hearing. "My past statements made over five years ago about abolishing the Department of Energy do not reflect my current thinking," Perry told the Senate Energy and Natural Resources Committee on January 19, 2017. He also endorsed the idea that human activity contributes to climate change. The Senate confirmed him March 2 with a vote of 62–37.

Dr. Ben Carson, another former rival to Trump in the GOP presidential contest, was nominated December 5, 2016, to become secretary of Housing and Urban Development. Carson was a renowned neurosurgeon who served as director of pediatric neurosurgery at Johns Hopkins University Hospital. But he had never held public office and lacked any obvious qualifications for the HUD job, a point Democrats hammered home at his Senate Banking, Housing, and Urban Affairs Committee confirmation hearing on January 11, 2017. The Senate voted 58–41 on March 2, 2017, to confirm him.

Carson weathered a storm over a $31,561 set of dining room furniture ordered for his secretarial suite. The department initiated procurement of the furniture in mid-2017 and obligated funds December 21, 2017, without getting congressional approval for the expenditure greater than $5,000 for redecorating. The department's inspector

general investigated and found no wrongdoing because HUD canceled the purchase March 1, 2018. (See the Ben Carson Confirmed as HUD Secretary box.)

Oklahoma Attorney General Scott Pruitt became a lightning rod for supporters and detractors when Trump nominated him December 7, 2016, to lead the Environmental Protection Agency (EPA). Pruitt had frequently tangled with the EPA in court. At his January 18 confirmation hearing before the Environment and Public Works Committee, Pruitt said he believed the climate is changing and human activity has some impact on it, but he questioned the extent of that impact. He said that while he would return most of the authority to regulate clean air and the environment to the states, it was the EPA's responsibility to regulate carbon emissions. And he told lawmakers he would keep the agency's endangerment finding that greenhouse gases pose risks to the environment and public health. Outside the hearing room, environmental advocates and Native American tribal demonstrators got into confrontations with Capitol Police trying to keep them from breaking into the room. Coal miners from West Virginia spent most of the day outside the hearing to show support for Pruitt, who they hoped would help revive their industry. The Senate voted 52–46 on February 17, 2017, to confirm him. Pruitt resigned July 5, 2018, after "unrelenting attacks" on him and his family, as he put it in his resignation letter to Trump. News reports alleged he pressured aides to find a $200,000 job for his wife, installed a $43,238 soundproof privacy booth in his office for confidential conversations, and stayed in a $50-per-night condo rented from a lobbyist. The Government Accountability Office found the phone booth violated the law restricting improvements to secretarial furnishings costing more than $5,000 without congressional approval.

Steve Mnuchin, an investment banker at Goldman Sachs, was named November 30, 2016, to become Treasury secretary. He had gained some notoriety as a Hollywood producer of such films as *Mad Max: Fury Road* and *Suicide Squad*. At his confirmation hearing January 19, 2017, before the Senate Finance Committee, Mnuchin faced tough questions about his tenure at OneWest, a bank that foreclosed on thousands of homes during the housing crisis. Mnuchin disputed that he had taken advantage of the hardships of others and said he worked diligently to help homeowners stay in their houses. "No one has credibly alleged that any laws, regulations or industry standards were violated by companies run by Mr. Mnuchin," Finance chair Orrin Hatch, R-Utah, said at the hearing. The Senate voted 53–47 on February 13 to confirm him.

Trump tapped Wilbur Ross, a billionaire financier, former steel industry executive, and frequent critic of the North American Free Trade Agreement, to become Commerce secretary on November 30, 2016. Ross ran the private equity firm W. L. Ross & Co. and previously worked with Trump to restructure debt for the Trump Taj Mahal casino and hotel in Atlantic City, New Jersey. Ross

PRESIDENT DONALD TRUMP'S CABINET

Following is a list of cabinet officers who served in the administration of President Donald Trump during his one term in office between January 20, 2017, and January 20, 2021. Dates given are for actual service in office, beginning with the cabinet officers' swearing-in date, which often varies from date of confirmation by the Senate. Only heads of the major departments are listed; offices that have been designated as cabinet level are not included.

Department Head	Dates of Service
Secretary of State	
Rex Tillerson	February 1, 2017—March 31, 2018
Mike Pompeo	April 26, 2018—January 20, 2021
Secretary of the Treasury	
Steve Mnuchin	February 13, 2017—January 20, 2021
Secretary of Defense	
James Mattis	January 20, 2017—January 1, 2019
Mark Esper	July 23, 2019—November 9, 2020
Christopher C. Miller (Acting)	November 9, 2020—January 20, 2021
Attorney General	
Jeff Sessions	February 8, 2017
William Barr	February 14, 2019—December 23, 2020
Jeffrey Rosen	December 23, 2020—January 20, 2021
Secretary of the Interior	
Ryan Zinke	March 1, 2017—January 2, 2019
David Bernhardt	April 11, 2019—January 20, 2021
Secretary of Agriculture	
Sonny Perdue	April 24, 2017—January 20, 2021
Secretary of Commerce	
Wilbur Ross	February 27, 2017—January 20, 2021
Secretary of Labor	
Edward Hugler (Acting)	January 20, 2016—April 27, 2017
R. Alexander Acosta	April 27, 2017—July 12, 2019
Eugene Scalia	September 26, 2019—January 20, 2021

Department Head	Dates of Service
Secretary of Health and Human Services	
Tom Price	February 10, 2017—September 29, 2017
Don J. Wright (Acting)	September 29, 2017—October 10, 2017
Eric Hargan (Acting)	October 10, 2017—January 24, 2018
Alex Azar	January 24, 2018—January 20, 2021
Secretary of Education	
Betsy DeVos	February 7, 2017—January 7, 2021
Secretary of Housing and Urban Development	
Ben Carson	March 2, 2017—January 20, 2021
Secretary of Transportation	
Elaine Chao	January 31, 2017—January 11, 2021
Steven Bradbury (Acting)	January 11, 2021—January 20, 2021
Secretary of Energy	
Rick Perry	March 2, 2017—December 2, 2019
Dan R. Brouillette	December 2, 2019—January 20, 2021
Secretary of Veterans Affairs	
David Shulkin	February 13, 2017—March 28, 2018
Robert Wilkie (Acting)	March 28, 2018—May 29, 2018
Peter O'Rourke (Acting)	May 29, 2018—July 23, 2018
Robert Wilkie	July 23, 2018—January 20, 2021
Secretary of Homeland Security	
John Kelly	January 20, 2017—July 28, 2017
Elaine Duke (Acting)	July 31, 2017—December 5, 2017
Kirstjen Nielsen	December 5, 2017—April 7, 2019
Kevin McAleenan (Acting)	April 11, 2019—November 13, 2019
Chad Wolf (Acting)	November 13, 2019—January 11, 2021
Pete Gaynor (Acting)	January 12, 2021—January 20, 2021

was backed by the United Steelworkers union after his revival of Bethlehem Steel, LTV Steel, and Weirton Steel into a combined company, International Steel Group. Ross was confirmed on February 27, 2017, by a vote of 72–27.

Trump chose Alexander Acosta, the dean of Florida International University's law program, on February 16, 2017, to become Labor secretary. Acosta was the first Hispanic nominated by Trump. The decision came less than a day after Trump's initial choice for the position, Andy Puzder, withdrew from consideration. The fast-food CEO had lost the support of GOP senators after a string of unfavorable news stories, including one that reported he

had employed a housekeeper not authorized to work in the country. Acosta had previously served as a National Labor Relations Board member and as assistant attorney general for civil rights in the Justice Department under President George W. Bush. Some Democrats voiced concerns that Acosta would not protect workers' rights and that he was too aligned with Trump's priorities. But the Senate voted 61–39 on April 25, 2017, to confirm him. His successor, corporate lawyer Eugene Scalia, was confirmed September 26, 2019, on a party line Senate vote of 53–44.

Rep. Mike Pompeo, R-Kans., was nominated November 18, 2016, to lead the CIA. Pompeo was a former Army tank

commander who graduated first in his class at West Point. At his Senate Intelligence Committee hearing January 12, Pompeo said he would refuse to restart the CIA's "enhanced interrogation" program, in which terrorism suspects had been tortured, if ordered to do so by the president. The Senate voted 66–32 on January 23, 2017, to confirm him.

Trump subsequently nominated Pompeo on March 13, 2018, to succeed Tillerson as secretary of State. Democrats criticized Pompeo, while head of the CIA, for saying Russian interference did not change the results of the 2020 election. But the CIA issued a statement reiterating its finding that the interference favored Trump. The Senate voted 57–42 to confirm Pompeo on April 26, 2018, a decline from his CIA confirmation. But Democrats could have dragged their heels longer, yet allowed the vote to proceed so Pompeo could attend a European meeting with NATO foreign ministers.

Trump chose one-term Rep. Ryan Zinke, R-Mont., on December 15, 2016, to become Interior secretary. Zinke studied geology at the University of Oregon and spent more than two decades as a Navy SEAL before entering politics as a self-described Theodore Roosevelt Republican. There was little resistance to Zinke at the Senate Energy and Natural Resources Committee, where he said his goal was to keep public lands in federal hands. The Senate voted 68–31 on March 1, 2017, to confirm him. Zinke announced his resignation with a tweet December 15, 2018, that said he was proud of his work for the administration, but could not justify spending thousands of dollars defending himself against false allegations. Among the reported scandals were allegations he named his wife Lolita as a department volunteer so she could travel with him at government expense, that he brought a security detail with him during an August 2017 vacation to Turkey and Greece, and that a staffer resigned after being required to walk Zinke's dog. The department's inspector general issued a report October 21, 2018, that found Zinke reimbursed the government for the cost of his wife's travel, that the department had no policy against the $25,000 security detail traveling with him on vacation, and that the dog-walking allegation was unfounded.

Rep. Mick Mulvaney, R-S.C., was named December 16, 2016, to lead the Office of Management and Budget. Mulvaney endured criticism from Democrats at two confirmation hearings in one day, when members of the Budget Committee and the Homeland Security and Governmental Affairs Committee challenged his views on Trump's tax proposals and cutting government aid programs. But Mulvaney's biggest challenge came from Sen. John McCain, R-Ariz., who told his House colleague he was "deeply concerned about . . . [his] lack of support for the military." Mulvaney reassured defense advocates on both sides that as OMB director he would support Trump's plans to boost Pentagon spending. The Senate voted 51–49 on February 16, 2017, to confirm him, as McCain sided with Democrats in opposition.

South Carolina Gov. Nikki Haley, who had little formal experience in foreign affairs, was nominated November 23, 2016, to become U.S. ambassador to the United Nations. Haley became the first Indian American chosen to represent the United States at the 193-member United Nations. Sen. Robert Menendez of New Jersey, the ranking Democrat on the Foreign Relations Committee, said at her January 18, 2017, confirmation hearing that she had moral fiber for calling to remove the Confederate flag from the state capitol in 2015, if not foreign policy experience. The Senate voted 96–4 on January 24, 2017, to confirm her.

Trump chose Elaine Chao on November 29, 2016, to become Transportation secretary. She had previously served as Labor secretary during the George W. Bush administration and as Peace Corps director, in addition to being the wife of Senate Majority Leader Mitch McConnell, R-Ky. The Senate voted 93–6 on January 31, 2017, to confirm her.

After a protracted search, Trump nominated David Shulkin to lead the Department of Veterans Affairs. Shulkin had been President Barack Obama's undersecretary in charge of the Veterans Health Administration. Shulkin was arguably the least contentious of Trump's cabinet nominees, as an internist with thirty years of experience in the hospital industry. The Senate voted 100–0 on February 13, 2017, to confirm him.

SUBSEQUENT CONTROVERSIAL APPOINTMENTS

Barr Succeeds Sessions at Department of Justice

Attorney General Sessions resigned under pressure November 7, 2018, the day after the midterm election. Trump forced his departure after months of dissatisfaction with Sessions for failing to prevent or curb the investigation of Russian interference in the 2016 election by Special Counsel Robert S. Mueller III.

Some senators were concerned that Barr would end Mueller's probe, but the nominee said he would only be removed for good cause. Barr, 68, pitched himself as an end-of-career professional who could return to the job he held from 1991–1993 under George H. W. Bush's administration.

Barr was later criticized for his handling of the release of Mueller's report, which the attorney general summarized in four pages before releasing a redacted version of the report weeks later. On other issues, Barr continued or expanded Trump's conservative policies and legal arguments governing immigration, civil rights enforcement, and LGBT employment discrimination.

Kirstjen Nielsen Takes Over at DHS

Trump nominated Kirstjen Nielsen on October 11, 2017, to succeed Kelly leading the Department of Homeland Security. Nielsen had been Kelly's deputy before he left to become chief of staff at the White House. Immigration issues dominated her confirmation hearing, where Nielsen

acknowledged a wall was not needed along the entire 2,000-mile border with Mexico and where Democratic senators pressed her to resolve uncertainties about the Deferred Action for Children Arrivals program. The Senate voted 62–37 to confirm her December 6, 2017. She faced scathing criticism over a Trump administration policy to separate parents and children accused of crossing illegally from Mexico into the United States, and eventually resigned in April 2019.

Ronny Jackson Withdraws Veterans Affairs Nomination

Trump nominated Rear Admiral Ronny Jackson, who served as one of his White House physicians, on March 28, 2018, to lead the Department of Veterans Affairs. But Jackson withdrew his nomination April 26, 2018, after Senate Democrats raised allegations against him including crashing a government vehicle while intoxicated, prescribing himself drugs, and asking a physician's assistant to supply the drugs when he got caught. Jackson denied the allegations, but withdrew to avoid being a distraction for the Trump administration. Trump then nominated Robert Wilkie, who easily won confirmation.

Louis DeJoy Becomes Postmaster General

Trump appointed Louis DeJoy, founder of a freight company and a Republican Party donor, to the U.S. Postal Service board of governors in May 2020 and he became postmaster general in June 2020. The founder and CEO of New Breed Logistics became a lightning rod for criticism from lawmakers of both parties after eliminating overtime, having distribution centers hold mail until the next day if operations were running late, and removing some mail collection boxes. The changes caused significant delays and touched off congressional investigations amid concerns that they could interfere in mail-in voting.

Acting Secretaries

Trump expanded the use of acting secretaries rather than worrying about winning Senate confirmation of his appointees. The number of acting Cabinet secretaries increased significantly under Trump, according to research by Stanford law professor Anne Joseph O'Connell. The research found Trump had thirty acting secretaries by the end of his third year, compared to twenty-three for former President Barack Obama or twenty-two for former President George W. Bush during eight years. Trump's acting secretaries spent 10 percent of their time in office during his first three years, compared to 3 percent for Obama and 2 percent for Bush.

Trump was unconcerned. "It's OK," Trump said February 3, 2019, on *Face the Nation* on CBS. "It's easier to make moves when they're acting."

The Pentagon had a series of short-term leaders after the departure of Secretary James Mattis. Patrick Shanahan served as acting secretary during the first half of 2019. He was succeeded for nearly a month by Mark Esper as acting secretary, who was succeeded by Mark Spencer for about a week in July 2019. Esper was then confirmed and served as secretary for more than a year before Trump tweeted November 9, 2020, that he was "terminated." Esper had split with Trump in June 2020 over whether active-duty military troops could be used to quell domestic disturbances after the death of George Floyd in police custody in Minneapolis. Christopher Miller, the former director of the National Counterterrorism Center, served as acting secretary of Defense during the final three months of the term.

Trump announced in a tweet December 14, 2020, that Attorney General William Barr stepped down effective December 23. Barr's departure left Deputy Attorney General Jeffrey Rosen, the former deputy secretary of Transportation, as acting attorney general for the final month of Trump's term. It was a tumultuous period that featured the attack on the Capitol on January 6, 2020.

Mick Mulvaney, a former Republican House member from South Carolina, served as acting White House chief of staff from January 2019 to March 2020, between the tenures of John Kelly and Mark Meadows. Mulvaney had previously served as director of the Office of Management and Budget, where he was confirmed by the Senate.

Ryan Zinke served as secretary of the Interior for the first two years of Trump's administration. His successor, David Bernhardt, served more than three months as acting secretary before he was confirmed.

On *Face the Nation*, Trump was asked whether it was a problem having acting officials as chief of staff, secretary of Interior, and secretary of Defense. "Some are doing a fantastic job," Trump said February 3, 2019. "I like acting because I can move so quickly. It gives me more flexibility."

Domestic Policy

Once in office, President Donald Trump pursued traditional Republican policies to lower taxes and reduce government regulations. He championed a reduction in personal and business income taxes that became a signature legislative achievement. He slashed regulations and worked with Congress to overturn a handful of Obama-era policies. Trump also took a hardline approach against illegal immigration, which included separating undocumented children from their parents when caught and advocating funding for a border wall forcefully enough to lead to a government shutdown.

But Trump's hands-off approach to the COVID-19 pandemic led to widespread criticism during his final year in office. He directed government funding toward development of several vaccines. But he also promoted untested treatments, ridiculed rivals for wearing masks, and disparaged testing as the virus killed hundreds of thousands of Americans.

CUTTING REGULATORY RED TAPE

From his first days in office, Trump sought to cut federal regulations. He abandoned proposals from his predecessors and eliminated hundreds of policies that had already been

adopted. After meeting with business leaders at the White House on January 30, 2017, Trump signed executive order 13771 to require that two regulations be eliminated in order to adopt any proposed regulation. The policy had the effect of shelving pending proposals and halting new ones from being considered.

"If you have a regulation you want, number one, we're not going to approve it because it's already been approved probably in 17 different forms," Trump said January 30, 2017, while signing the order surrounded by small business leaders. "But if we do, the only way you have a chance is we have to knock out two regulations for every new regulation."

The regulatory process is governed by a 1946 law that prescribes cumbersome procedures agencies must use to issue a new rule. Agencies must notify the public, take comment, review the input, and make revisions before issuing new directives, a process that can take years. Diane Katz, a senior research fellow in regulatory policies at the Heritage Foundation, a conservative think tank, found that Trump withdrew a higher proportion of new rules than either of the previous two administrations. She found he was the least active regulator since recordkeeping began in the 1990s, with just eight major rules finalized through June 30, 2017, only two of which increased regulatory burdens, she found.

In addition to Trump's executive action, Republicans used the Congressional Review Act to rescind fourteen of former President Barack Obama's regulations during the first months of 2017. The rules ranged from an Environmental Protection Agency effort to keep pollution out of streams to a Social Security Administration directive aimed at making it more difficult for the mentally impaired to buy guns. But Congress can only rescind rules that have been finalized. Trump was able to delay, rethink, or kill scores of other proposals.

Some of the rules that Trump abandoned were in the planning stages, such as a Transportation Department proposal to test truck drivers and train engineers for sleep apnea. But others had been finalized and were awaiting implementation. For example, the Labor Department proposed to increase the number of American workers eligible for overtime, but implementation of the rule was tied up in court when Trump took office, giving him an opportunity to negotiate with the corporations challenging it, to cover fewer workers. Still others were finalized and not yet in effect. The Agriculture Department had a rule governing organic livestock and poultry practices, which Trump delayed to potentially seek revisions.

The rollbacks affected rules of wildly varying significance. The EPA put the brakes on Obama's plan to regulate greenhouse gas emissions from power plants, a decision with global consequences. Trump sought to rewrite Occupational Safety and Health Administration regulations to limit exposure of workers in foundries to beryllium, a chemical that can cause lung disease.

Legal battles over the changes led to mixed results and uncertainty about the status of proposals. A federal appeals court in Washington blocked the EPA in July 2017 from suspending a regulation aimed at reducing methane emissions from new oil and gas wells, ruling that the agency had not justified its plan. But courts were also allies. A federal judge in Texas found Obama's overtime rule expanded eligibility beyond what the law allowed, which gave Trump's Labor Department time to rewrite the regulation.

By December 2017, Trump celebrated the rollbacks. He posed at the White House next to stacks of paper meant to represent regulations stifling American industry. He used golden scissors to literally cut red tape draped across the stacks of paper. Trump said there were about 20,000 pages in the code of federal regulations in 1960 and more than 180,000 pages at that point. He vowed to return to the 1960 level, saying he had withdrawn or delayed nearly 1,600 planned regulatory actions during his first year in office. He boasted of eliminating twenty-two regulations for every new one that was adopted, rather than just the two cited in his executive order. "The never-ending red tape in America has come to a sudden, screeching, and beautiful halt," Trump said at the White House on December 14, 2017. "Because of our regulatory and other reforms, the stock market is soaring to new levels."

The Trump administration reported in October 2018 that the administration saved $23 billion from 176 regulatory actions during fiscal year 2018. The administration issued 65 percent fewer "significant" rules, with costs that exceed $100 million per year, than the Obama administration and 51 percent fewer than the Bush administration during their first twenty-two months in office. In July 2020, Trump celebrated the reductions in "job-killing regulations" with an event at the White House on the South Lawn with Vice President Mike Pence, Cabinet members including Transportation Secretary Elaine Chao and Commerce Secretary Wilbur Ross and Environmental Protection Agency Administrator Andrew Wheeler. Trump said agencies exceeded the mandate in his executive order by eliminating seven rules for every one added, rather than just two, and by cutting $50 billion in costs. He said the return of incandescent light bulbs and appliances that worked were among the benefits of his slashing 25,000 of pages in federal regulations. Trump promoted his modified rules, such as one modernizing the National Environmental Policy Act to limit delays in infrastructure projects and another one replacing strict auto fuel standards with the Safer Affordable Fuel Efficiency Vehicles rule.

"We're here today to celebrate and expand our historic campaign to rescue American workers from job-killing regulations," Trump said at the White House on July 16, 2020. "Before I came into office, American workers were smothered by a merciless avalanche of wasteful and expensive and intrusive federal regulation."

One example of paring back regulations came when the Trump administration reduced safety regulations adopted in the wake of the Deepwater Horizon oil spill in the Gulf of Mexico, to reduce costly and cumbersome requirements

618 CH. 16 THE TRUMP PRESIDENCY

on industry. The Bureau of Safety and Environmental Enforcement finalized revisions to the Well Control Rule on May 2, 2019. The changes applied to regulations that had been established under the Obama administration after eleven workers were killed and the Gulf of Mexico was polluted with millions of gallons of oil when the well's containment device failed. The changes included reducing requirements for monitoring operations on offshore rigs and loosening standards for overseeing blowout preventer devices. The new rule allowed independent third-party contractors to conduct reviews of the preventers instead of mandatory government inspections. Interior Secretary David Bernhardt, a former oil and gas lobbyist, said in a statement May 2, 2019, from Port Fourchon, Louisianna, the rule "puts safety first, both public and environmental safety, in a common sense way."

OVERHAULING THE TAX CODE

Trump signed the most sweeping overhaul of the U.S. tax code since 1986 on December 22, 2017. The bill became his signature legislative achievement and gave Republicans a major victory heading into the midterm elections.

The Tax Cuts and Jobs Act (PL 115-97) significantly modified both the corporate and individual tax system. For corporations, the law cut the tax rate from 35 percent to 21 percent, bolstered expensing to encourage domestic business investment, and created a new territorial international tax system for U.S. companies with overseas operations. It also provided new breaks for the owners of "pass-through" businesses who pay taxes on their individual returns. For individuals, the law reduced existing tax rates and sought to simply tax filing so that far fewer people would file itemized returns by doubling the standard deduction and limiting itemized deductions. The law also doubled the child tax credit and increased the portion that is refundable, while eliminating numerous other deductions and credits. The law also served as a vehicle to repeal the mandate for individuals to secure health insurance, a key element to the 2010 Affordable Care Act, nicknamed Obamacare, and to open Alaska's Arctic National Wildlife Refuge to oil and gas drilling.

Trump celebrated the new tax law as one of the biggest tax cuts in history. Republicans said most taxpayers would enjoy a tax cut and simplification would allow taxpayers to file returns essentially on a post card. But Democrats derided it as a "tax scam," saying it represented a massive giveaway to corporations and the wealthy, including the president, while providing relatively little for middle-class families. Sen. Bernie Sanders, I-Vt., called it a moral and economic obscenity.

AFFORDABLE CARE ACT

Congressional Republicans failed repeatedly in efforts to repeal the Affordable Care Act, nicknamed Obamacare. The House voted at least seventeen times in 2017 to repeal all or parts of the 2010 law. The most dramatic failure came

July 28, 2017, when Sen. John McCain, R-Ariz., pointed his thumb downward to provide the decisive vote rejecting the so-called skinny repeal (HR 1628) on a 49–51 vote. His gesture provoked audible gasps in the Senate chamber, followed by applause.

Against that backdrop, Trump began on his first day in office signing executive orders and having executive agencies attack the law. His executive order January 20, 2017, sought to "minimize the unwarranted economic and regulatory burdens" of the health law. The order instructed agencies to "exercise all authority and discretion available to them to waive, defer, grant exemptions from, or delay the implementation of any provision or requirement of the Act that would impose a fiscal burden."

The Department of Health and Human Services began that day removing information about how to sign up for the coverage from the healthcare.gov website. The Internal Revenue Service said February 14, 2017, it would not reject tax returns that did not indicate whether a taxpayer had health insurance, a cornerstone of the law.

House Republicans introduced the American Health Care Act to repeal Obamacare on March 7, 2017. The Congressional Budget Office estimated the bill would result in 24 million people going without insurance by 2026. But after revisions in the Senate, McCain helped kill the effort. GOP Sens. Lindsey Graham of South Carolina and Bill Cassidy of Louisiana sought to replace Obamacare essentially by converting the federal program to block grants to states. But the effort ended in September with the opposition of GOP Sens. Susan Collins of Maine, Rand Paul of Kentucky, and McCain.

By January 2020, Kaiser Family Foundation polling found 53 percent had a favorable view of the law compared to 37 percent viewing it unfavorably. Guy Cecil, who ran the super PAC Priorities USA, said most Americans knew by then the benefits of Obamacare—such as protecting people with preexisting conditions from discrimination, preventing women from being charged more for health insurance and guaranteeing children can remain on their parents' health insurance until they are twenty-six years old—rather than just providing a government website that helps people shop for health insurance.

JUDICIAL APPOINTEES

Trump's judicial appointments represented one of the most outsized and long-lasting areas of influence from his administration. A simple majority was all he needed for confirmation of his nominees, after Senate Democrats changed the interpretation of the filibuster rule for district and circuit judges in 2013, and Republicans changed the rule for the Supreme Court in 2017.

The Senate confirmed 226 of Trump's judicial nominees—including three Supreme Court justices. For comparison, former President Barack Obama appointed 320 judges during an eight-year tenure and former President George W. Bush appointed 322 judges during the same

length of time, according to a Pew Research Center analysis of Federal Judicial Center data. The impact was more stark at the circuit level. Trump appointed fifty-four circuit judges in four years, compared to Obama's fifty-five and Bush's sixty-two during twice as long.

Trump's influence on the Supreme Court was embodied in Justices Neil Gorsuch, Brett Kavanaugh, and Amy Coney Barrett. Each was less than fifty-five years old when reaching the bench for a lifetime appointment, so they were expected to spend decades on the high court. Those confirmations to the high court were the most for a president since former President Ronald Reagan's four and the most for a one-term president since Herbert Hoover, according to the Pew Research Center.

Senate Majority Leader Mitch McConnell, R-Ky., changed the interpretation of the filibuster in order to confirm Gorsuch. McConnell had prevented Obama from filling the late Justice Antonin Scalia's seat for nearly a year before Gorsuch eventually occupied it. McConnell also stopped recognizing the opposition of home-state senators to appeals court judges—a process known as blue slips—to win more confirmations. "Working with the administration to appoint men and women to lifetime appointments who have this basic belief that the job of a judge is to follow the law I think is the most consequential thing I've been involved in during my career," McConnell said during a Louisville news conference September 11, 2018.

IMMIGRATION

One of Trump's top priorities from his first day in office was to curb illegal immigration. When he declared his candidacy at Trump Tower in 2015, Trump spoke of criminals and rapists crossing the border. He declared that he would build a wall along the southern border and have Mexico pay for it, when he announced his candidacy for president. He eventually siphoned money away from the Defense Department to contribute to that goal. He blocked travel from Muslim-majority countries. He even targeted visa travel and discouraged legal immigration. "I would build a great wall, and nobody builds walls better than me, believe me, and I'll build them very inexpensively, I will build a great, great wall on our southern border," Trump said in announcing his candidacy June 16, 2015, at Trump Tower in New York. "And I will have Mexico pay for that wall. Mark my words."

But his various efforts through executive orders, spending priorities, and wielding the bully pulpit had mixed results. The zero-tolerance policy for illegal immigrations arriving along the southern border sparked a firestorm of outrage that forced Trump to backtrack. Courts blocked him repeatedly. Congress fought his spending proposals.

Progress came slowly. Trump requested $1.7 billion for the border wall in fiscal 2017. Congress appropriated $341 million to replace or upgrade existing barriers at the border. Trump requested $1.57 billion for border security in fiscal 2018. The figure provided for forty-seven miles of new barriers and forty-eight miles of upgraded existing barriers, with $196 million for new border technologies. But the omnibus spending bill put restrictions that new or replacement barriers had to be built with existing technology rather than the concrete barriers Trump wanted. The thirty-five-day government shutdown from December 2018 to January 2019 resulted from an impasse over wall funding. At that point, Trump did not get the $5.7 billion he proposed for another 234 miles of barriers in fiscal 2019. After the partial shutdown, Congress appropriated $1.37 billion for fifty-five miles using existing technologies. After the shutdown, Trump declared a national emergency at the border, which allowed him to move $6 billion from the Pentagon and Treasury Department. The effort was challenged by several lawsuits. But neither the Senate nor House could muster the two-thirds majority needed to overturn Trump's veto of a resolution rejecting the national emergency. By May 2019, there were 654 miles of physical barriers along the 2,000-mile border and the administration replaced about seventy-five miles of barriers.

Zero-Tolerance to Illegal Immigration

Trump used his executive authority in April 2018 to launch his "zero-tolerance policy" aimed at prosecuting all adults attempting to enter illegally on the southwest border. Attorney General Jeff Sessions initiated the policy April 6. He directed U.S. attorneys to prosecute all adults caught entering the United States illegally, including those with children. The policy resulted in separating thousands of children from their parents and became a public relations disaster. Trump ended the policy by executive order June 20, less than seven weeks after it began.

The U.S. District Court for the Southern District of California issued a preliminary injunction June 26, 2018, saying children cannot be separated from their parents. The court set a July 10, 2018, deadline for the Trump administration to reunify children under the age of five who have already been separated. The Trump administration failed to meet the deadline. By July 26, 2018, the government had reunited 1,442 out of 2,551 children from ages five to seventeen. At that time, 711 children were not reunited and 431 had a parent who had been deported. The inspector general for the Department of Health and Human Services estimated in a report January 17, 2019, that thousands more children may have been separated under the zero-tolerance policy than previously reported.

Apprehensions at the Border

Trump's anti-immigrant rhetoric, zero-tolerance policy and increased border enforcement failed to discourage migrants from attempting to cross. A surge of families and unaccompanied minors from the "Northern Triangle" countries of Central America—El Salvador, Guatemala, and Honduras—continued during his administration as migrants fled violence and poverty in their home countries.

The Border Patrol had 16,605 agents along the southern border in fiscal 2017, compared to 8,580 in fiscal 2000, when apprehensions peaked at 1.6 million. With three shifts per day, the number of agents means about three agents per mile along the border. Apprehensions dropped steadily through 2017, when the number hit 310,000. Migrants continued to arrive in near record levels in 2019. In fiscal 2018, the Department of Homeland Security said 521,090 individuals were apprehended or deemed "inadmissible." By February 2019, the department said 76,103 people were apprehended, and in March the number was 103,492.

Deferred Action for Childhood Arrivals

Trump set a six-month deadline in September 2017 for Congress to pass a permanent legislative solution for undocumented immigrants who arrived as children, so-called Dreamers. The Obama administration created the Deferred Action for Childhood Arrivals program in 2012, to allow nearly 650,000 undocumented children to live and work without fear of deportation. But Democratic lawmakers sought legislation to make the status of Dreamers permanent, and proposals languished amid broader disputes about immigration. About 689,000 DACA recipients were in the country when Trump announced his plan, and by February 2019 there were still 673,340 active recipients.

The legislation that came closest to passing was from Sens. Mike Rounds, R-S.D., and Angus King, I-Maine. Under their amendment to an unrelated bill, 1.8 million young immigrants would have been granted legal status and $25 billon would have been allocated for the border security construction projects over ten years. Trump threatened to veto the legislation, saying it did not go far enough to accomplish goals such as ending family-based immigration and the diversity visa lottery program.

Reducing Refugee Admissions

Despite setbacks in other areas, Trump successfully used his executive authority to reduce refugee admissions to the lowest levels in history. Trump called tougher security screening "extreme vetting," according to the Pew Research Center.

Trump reduced the annual refugee cap from 70,000 under President Barack Obama to 45,000 initially and then 30,000 in 2019. Not even that many refugees arrived. In fiscal 2018, the United States admitted only 22,491 refugees, about half the cap for that year, according to the State Department. Secretary of State Mike Pompeo said the decision to lower the cap was driven by a backlog of asylum seekers, although the admissions and asylum processes are two separate systems. The number of Muslim refugees dropped precipitously, falling to 1,800 during the first half of fiscal 2018 from about 22,900 the year before, according to the Pew Research Center.

Before the cap reductions, the United States led the world in accepting refugees. The country resettled more than 3 million people since 1980, according to the Pew Research Center. The annual cap averaged 116,000 per year in the 1980s and 110,000 in the 1990s. Former Presidents Obama and George W. Bush generally set the cap at 70,000 or 80,000 per year.

Asylum Seekers

Asylum claims along the southern border skyrocketed during the last decade. In 2014, authorities interviewed 47,870 people reporting a "credible fear" of gang- or drug-related violence or civil strife if they returned home. In fiscal 2018, the number of claims reached 92,259 who either crossed the border illegally or went to ports of entry legally. More individuals from El Salvador, Guatemala, and Honduras sought asylum from 2013 to 2015 than in the previous fifteen years combined, according to Citizenship and Immigration Services data.

In June 2018, Attorney General Jeff Sessions announced limitations in which victims of domestic abuse and even gang violence would no longer qualify for asylum. "I understand that many victims of domestic violence may seek to flee from their home countries to extricate themselves from a dire situation or to give themselves the opportunity for a better life," Sessions said in a Justice Department ruling June 11, 2018. "But the asylum statute is not a general hardship statute."

Judge Jon S. Tigar of the U.S. District Court for the Northern District of California blocked the new rule, stating that it "irreconcilably conflicts" with immigration law. "Whatever the scope of the President's authority, he may not rewrite the immigration laws to impose a condition that Congress has expressly forbidden," Tigar wrote.

The administration has also tried to change asylum policies in 2019 by launching the "Migrant Protection Protocols," informally known as the Remain in Mexico policy. The policy forces migrants to wait in Mexico while their immigration cases are being processed. A U.S. District Court judge in California in April blocked the policy, but a panel of three appellate judges subsequently allowed it to go forward while they awaited arguments in the case.

On April 29, 2019, Trump signed a new order again designed to shift asylum policies more toward deterrence. The order charged fees to individuals who are applying for asylum and fees for asylum seekers to receive work authorizations. The memorandum also required immigration courts to adjudicate asylum claims within 180 days.

REVISING DODD-FRANK FINANCIAL REGULATIONS

Trump signed legislation (PL 115-174) on May 24, 2018, to reduce the regulatory impact of the 2010 Dodd-Frank law (PL 111-203), which was enacted after the Great

Recession fueled by the collapse of the housing market. For smaller banks, the bill reduced reporting requirements, simplified capitalization standards, lengthened the interval between examinations by regulators, and created new criteria to enable small banks to comply with qualified mortgage rules. The bill ended the requirement that banks with assets between $50 billion and $100 billion automatically be subjected to enhanced regulation by the Federal Reserve and provided discretion for the Fed to require enhanced regulation for banks with $100 billion to $250 billion in assets.

The bill also included consumer protection provisions such as allowing consumers to place security freezes on their credit reports at will without cost. The compromise was reached between Senate Republicans and moderate Democrats. But most Democrats opposed the measure, arguing that it could put taxpayers at risk of bank failures while allowing lenders to discriminate in mortgage lending.

A senior member of the House Financial Services Committee, Rep. Blaine Luetkemeyer, R-Mo., said the bill would provide relief from the regulatory behemoth of Dodd-Frank. He argued the law forced banks to devote too much effort to compliance and too little to making business loans. But the ranking Democrat on the committee, Rep. Maxine Waters of California, accused Republicans of trying to help banks that were already reporting record profits.

RIGHT TO TRY EXPERIMENTAL MEDICINES

Trump had campaigned on a proposal to make it easier for terminally ill patients to try experimental drugs. He spoke about it during his State of the Union speech. Vice President Mike Pence had been a champion of the so-called right to try bill. On May 30, 2018, Trump signed legislation (PL 115-176) into law. The legislation allowed patients to directly petition drug manufacturers for access to treatments that received initial approval from the Food and Drug Administration and were going through clinical trials. But drugmakers were not obligated to provide the treatments. Patients had to exhaust other FDA-approved treatments and not be eligible for clinical trials. Marc Short, White House director of legislative affairs, told reporters in a conference call May 25, 2018, that the bill would allow patients to have medicines that were not yet on pharmacy shelves.

The bill was contentious. More than 100 patient groups opposed the Senate version (S 204) in a letter the week of the House vote, saying it lacked safeguards for accessing investigational therapies outside clinical trials. House Energy and Commerce Chairman Greg Walden, R-Ore., sought to clearly define which patients would be eligible for experimental treatments. But House leaders approved the Senate version. House Majority Leader Kevin McCarthy, R-Calif., said the measure would give hope to

patients. The FDA had raised concerns about the Senate version applying to people with chronic life-threatening ailments such as diabetes. But FDA Commissioner Scott Gottlieb said he believed the regulatory process would ensure the bill was implemented safely.

CREATION OF THE SPACE FORCE

Trump proposed June 18, 2018, to create a sixth branch of the military called the Space Force within the Air Force. The distinction is similar to how the Marine Corps is part of the Navy. Generals had opposed such a plan for adding to the military bureaucracy when lawmakers proposed it in previous years. But Trump eventually won approval from Congress at the end of 2019.

A 2015 Pentagon report had outlined China's expanded emphasis on offensive space capabilities, such as deploying anti-satellite weapons capable of disabling U.S. satellites. Many of those potential targets are operated by the Air Force and provide the GPS capabilities used by air traffic controllers, power plants, and smart phones. A decade earlier, when one of its missiles blew up a decrepit Chinese weather satellite, China joined the ranks of Russia and the United States as the only countries to have destroyed space assets. Russia, always the United States' fiercest competitor in space, displayed its advancements in 2014 by launching two different satellites that tracked and intercepted the communications from European and U.S. military satellites. Experts said those Russian spy machines could also be used to crash into adversary satellites, which could take GPS offline—and, by extension, the terrestrial systems that depended on it.

Rep. Mike Rogers, R-Ala., had proposed a separate Space Corps so the new department could focus on threats to satellites and streamline purchasing. But Defense Secretary James Mattis sent a letter in July 2017 to Rep. Mike Turner, R-Ohio, who opposed the idea, saying he did not want to create a department with a narrower and more parochial approach.

Trump announced his goal of creating the Space Force as a defense priority during a meeting of the National Space Council. "When it comes to defending America, it is not enough to merely have an American presence in space. We must have American dominance in space," Trump said June 18, 2018, at the White House. "Very importantly, I'm hereby directing the Department of Defense and Pentagon to immediately begin the process necessary to establish a space force as the sixth branch of the armed forces. That's a big statement."

Opposition remained. Sen. Bill Nelson, D-Fla., said in a tweet June 18, 2018, that "generals tell me they don't want" to create a Space Force and "now is NOT the time to rip the Air Force apart." But Mattis told reporters after Trump's announcement that he was not opposed to creating a Space Force, just against rushing to solve a problem that had not been defined. Congress established the Space Force as part of

the 2019 National Defense Authorization Act (PL 116-48), which Trump signed December 20, 2019.

CRIMINAL JUSTICE OVERHAUL

Trump signed a major overhaul of the criminal justice system into law in December 2018. The First Step Act (PL 115-391) reduced mandatory minimum sentences for certain crimes and took steps to integrate former prisoners back into society. Two of the bill's most significant provisions reduced the "three strikes" penalty for drug felonies from life behind bars to twenty-five years and retroactively limited the disparity in sentencing between offenses involving crack and powder cocaine. The law directed the Justice Department to evaluate prisoners' recidivism risks so they could earn time in prerelease custody at the end of their term. The measure also generally prohibited restraining pregnant prisoners. The measure also expanded the information required to be collected by the National Prisoner Statistics Program. Trump supported the legislation in part because of the advocacy of his son-in-law, Jared Kushner, and Senate Majority Leader Mitch McConnell, R-Ky.

The law was a response to a significant increase in federal prisoners. The number of inmates under the Bureau of Prisons increased from about 25,000 in 1980 to more than 205,000 in 2015. The Government Accountability Office reported that the growing number of inmates resulted in double and triple bunking, with waiting lists for education and drug treatment, limited meaningful work opportunities, and increased inmate-to-staff ratios. Those factors could reduce safety in prisons and contribute to recidivism after prisoners leave, according to the report. Groups across the political spectrum called on Congress to help former inmates get a second chance.

FARM BILL

Trump signed a farm bill December 20, 2018, that Democrats described as largely keeping policies the same after the removal of House Republican provisions for stricter work requirements for the Supplemental Nutrition Assistance Program. The five-year bill (PL 115-334) set policies and reauthorized farm, conservation, nutrition, rural development, agricultural trade, and other programs. The Congressional Budget Office estimated it would cost $867 billion during the ten-year scoring window of fiscal 2019–2028.

Lawmakers who negotiated the compromise legislation—Reps. K. Michael Conaway, R-Tex., and Collin C. Peterson, D-Minn., and Sens. Pat Roberts, R-Kans., and Debbie Stabenow, D-Mich.—said it would provide stability for farmers, ranchers and others in agriculture dealing with several years of low market prices. The effects of recent U.S. tariffs and retaliatory duties by other countries have cut into sales to foreign markets. Among other things, a new farm bill would reauthorize farm programs that provide eligible farmers and ranchers payments when prices or revenues decline below preset levels. Peterson said the bill

was mostly status quo. The National Association of State Departments of Agriculture, National Association of Conservation Districts, the American Soybean Association, The Nature Conservancy, and other groups urged Congress to approve the compromise bill.

The Supplemental Nutrition Association Program, previously known as food stamps, was a major focus of the farm bill debate because it accounts for more than 70 percent of farm bill spending. House Republicans sought to remake the program by shifting money from food aid to labor programs. The House bill (HR 2) called for able-bodied adults ages 18 to 59 to meet more stringent work or training requirements in order to retain food aid. But the work requirements had been a sticking point. Democrats argued that the requirements would hurt the poor. No Democrats voted for the GOP bill in June, largely because of the SNAP provisions, and the bill passed the chamber on a 213–211 vote. The provisions were dropped in conference with the Senate.

The farm bill also removed hemp from the Controlled Substances Act, which legalized hemp production. The 2014 farm bill (PL 113-79), which had expired September 30, allowed limited hemp production for research projects approved and overseen by state and tribal governments.

Removing hemp's designation as a controlled substance akin to marijuana was a pet project of Senate Majority Leader Mitch McConnell, R-Ky. He said legalizing hemp could give farmers a new cash crop. The 2018 legislation also would make hemp farmers eligible for federally subsidized crop insurance.

MARIJUANA

Trump's Justice Department offered mixed signals about legalizing marijuana, as states increasingly regulated the industry. In January 2018, Attorney General Jeff Sessions rescinded a 2013 memo from Deputy Attorney General James Cole that sought to clarify when federal prosecutors should enforce federal law in states with legal cannabis. But a federal crackdown never materialized. Later, Attorney General William Barr chose not to contradict the Cole memo at his confirmation hearing, even as he called for uniformity between federal and state law.

"My approach to this would be not to upset settled expectations," Barr told the Senate Judiciary Committee at his confirmation hearing January 15, 2019. "However, I think the current situation is untenable and really has to be addressed. It's almost like a backdoor nullification of federal law."

In July 2019, attorneys general from thirty-three states filed comments with the Food and Drug Administration asking for help dealing with cannabis-related products such as hemp, but not marijuana. Cannabinoids are chemicals sold to people with a variety of ailments such as anxiety and stress. The attorneys general said the lack of oversight or testing requirements raised serious public health concerns.

The 2020 election saw five more states ease their marijuana laws. Arizona, Montana, New Jersey, and South Dakota each legalized marijuana use for adults at least twenty-one years old. Mississippi approved marijuana for patients with certain medical conditions. The additions left about one-third of the country living in states where recreational marijuana use is allowed.

LONGEST GOVERNMENT SHUTDOWN

The longest government shutdown in history straddled 2018 and 2019 before Congress resolved the thirty-five-day lapse in funding over a dispute with Trump over border-security funding. The ordeal forced 800,000 federal employees to miss two paychecks during the political impasse, although they were later reimbursed.

The fiscal year had begun auspiciously October 1, 2018, in one of the most successful appropriations seasons in decades, with funding enacted for five of the twelve annual spending bills (PL 115-244, PL 115-245). But Democrats regained control of the House in the November 6 election and Trump picked a fight over border security—even breaking with political precedent by taking responsibility for it. "I am proud to shut down the government for border security, Chuck, because the people of this country don't want criminals and people that have lots of problems and drugs pouring into our country," Trump told House Minority Leader Nancy Pelosi, D-Calif., and Senate Minority Leader Charles E. Schumer, D-N.Y., in an Oval Office meeting December 11, 2018. "So I will take the mantle. I will be the one to shut it down. I'm not going to blame you for it."

The Senate approved a stopgap spending measure December 19, 2018, that would have funded the remaining departments through February 8, 2019, with the understanding Trump supported it. But the next day, Speaker Paul D. Ryan, R-Wisc., and several other Republicans met with Trump and announced the House would add $5.7 billion for border security and $7.8 billion for disaster aid to the spending package. The move guaranteed conflict with the Senate.

The partial shutdown began December 22, 2018, a Saturday. No solution was found over the holidays and Democrats reclaimed control of the House on January 3, 2019. The House passed a full-year funding bill for six appropriations titles (HR 21) and a short-term bill for the Department of Homeland Security (HJ Res 1). But Senate Majority Leader Mitch McConnell, R-Ky., said he would only bring up a spending bill if it had enough support to pass Congress and be signed by Trump. A meeting January 9 between congressional leaders and Trump ended abruptly when Trump walked out, according to Schumer. Pelosi suggested January 16 that Trump postpone his State of the Union address from January 29 until after the shutdown ended.

As a sweetener, Trump proposed January 19 to extend the Deferred Action for Childhood Arrivals program for three years and provide Temporary Protected Status for immigrants who left countries because of natural disasters or unsafe conditions. In exchange, he sought $5.7 billion for physical barriers on the southwest border and restrictions on Central American children applying for asylum. But Schumer called it hostage taking.

The dispute wheezed to a halt with no clear resolution. On January 25, federal workers missed their second paycheck, and the Federal Aviation Administration briefly halted flights into New York's LaGuardia Airport due to a shortage of air traffic controllers. Trump delivered a Rose Garden speech announcing a three-week stopgap spending measure (HJ Res 28) and the continuation of negotiations over border security.

CHARTER SCHOOLS

Education Secretary Betsy DeVos focused on expanding privatization of public schools through charters, vouchers that help poor families pay private school tuition, and tax incentives. Funding for charter school grants grew from $333.2 million in fiscal 2016 to $440 million in fiscal 2019.

Charter schools grew out of the 1954 Supreme Court ruling in *Brown v. Board of Education*, which found segregated schools were unconstitutional. Southern states began putting public funds into vouchers so that students could attend all-white schools. But former Presidents Bill Clinton and George W. Bush each encouraged charter schools. Enrollment in charter schools tripled from 2005 to 2017, but then leveled off, according to the National Alliance of Public Charter Schools and the Education Department. In the 2017–2018 school year, 47.4 million students attended traditional public schools, 3.2 million attended public charter schools, and 5.8 million attended private schools from kindergarten through twelfth grade. By 2019, charter schools were authorized in forty-four states and the District of Columbia. Nearly half of D.C. students attend charter schools, despite hurdles the voucher program faces each year in Congress.

The 2017 tax overhaul included a provision to allow families to pay for public, private, and religious schools through savings accounts that previously only covered college. The provision from Sen. Ted Cruz, R-Tex., expanded so-called 529 college savings plans to include elementary and secondary tuition. Vice President Mike Pence broke a 50–50 tie vote to include the provision in the tax overhaul.

ANTITRUST

The Trump administration had a mixed reaction to antitrust issues, allowing some mergers to proceed while also filing a landmark antitrust case for the first time in a generation. AT&T completed its $85 billion acquisition of Time Warner in June 2018, after the Justice Department unsuccessfully sought to block the deal. Sprint merged with T-Mobile in April 2020 after the Justice Department and the Federal Trade Commission signed off on the deal. But the Justice Department and FTC began reviewing major social media companies in Silicon Valley and filed a landmark antitrust case against Google.

Four decades of deregulatory policies allowed tech titans such as Amazon, Apple, Facebook, and Google parent Alphabet to dominate their industries. Amazon and Apple each reached market cap valuations of $1 trillion. Google generated $136.8 billion in revenue in 2018. And Facebook boasted 2.3 billion monthly active users, or more than one-third of the world's population. With the growth came greater involvement in federal policy. Google spent about $21.7 million on lobbying in 2018, the eighth-highest amount of any single organization or company, according to data published by the nonpartisan Center for Responsive Politics. Amazon and Facebook also cracked the top twenty, spending $14.4 million and $12.6 million, respectively.

In September 2018, Attorney General Jeff Sessions held a meeting with attorneys general from eight states and the District of Columbia to discuss ways in which privacy issues from Facebook and other tech firms might be challenged as anticompetitive. Trump told Axios during an interview that aired November 4, 2018, that the administration was looking at potential antitrust violations on the part of Facebook, Amazon, and Google. The House Judiciary Committee announced its own investigation of tech companies and their potential monopoly power. On June 3, 2019, Chair Jerrold Nadler, D-N.Y., said the committee was investigating because "there is growing evidence that a handful of gatekeepers have come to capture control over key arteries of online commerce, content and communications." The panel's ranking Republican, Doug Collins of Georgia, also raised concerns.

The Justice Department filed a lawsuit October 20, 2020, against Google, accusing the company of anticompetitive business practices to maintain monopolies over its competitors in the online search and advertising industry. Google vowed to fight back, arguing that its success does not mean it did anything wrong. The case marked the first major antitrust enforcement case against a technology company since the case against Microsoft began in 1998 and ended in a settlement in 2002.

OVERTIME

The Trump administration expanded the number of people eligible for overtime with a final rule from the Labor Department on September 24, 2019. But the rule covered 3 million fewer people than had been proposed under the Obama administration.

The "standard salary level" to receive overtime pay for more than forty hours of work per week had last been updated in 2004, when it was set at $23,660 per year. Trump's Labor Department rule raised the level to $35,568, which made an estimated 1.3 million more workers eligible for overtime. But that rate fell far short of the Obama administration's $47,476 level, which would have made 4.2 million more workers eligible.

Business groups and conservative state attorneys general sued Obama's Labor Department to block the overtime expansion in U.S. District Court in Texas. The Trump administration declined to defend Obama's proposal when arguments were due in June 2017 and instead developed its own proposal.

PAID PARENTAL LEAVE

About 2 million federal employees won twelve weeks of paid parental leave under legislation that President Donald Trump's daughter, Ivanka, championed. The provision, folded into the Fiscal Year 2020 National Defense Authorization Act (PL 116-92), gave all federal civilian employees leave for the birth, adoption, or fostering of a child. Democrats had pushed for a broader set of benefits to cover family relations and illnesses, but still supported the compromise.

Rep. Carolyn B. Maloney, D-N.Y., called the provision long overdue. Ken Thomas, president of the National Active and Retired Federal Employees Association, said the change would provide employees with priceless time with their families.

The cost of the benefit limited its adoption in private industry. The Congressional Budget Office estimated the benefit would cost about $3.3 billion during the first five years. Marc Freedman, vice president for workplace policy at the U.S. Chamber of Commerce, said requiring full pay during parental leave would be an extraordinarily expensive benefit to provide. Trump signed the measure into law December 20, 2019.

STUDENT LOAN FORGIVENESS

Trump's Education Department rewrote the Obama administration's rules governing when federal student loan borrowers can have their debt wiped out because of a school's misconduct. The department announced the changes in December 2019 to take effect July 1, 2020. The new formula compares a student's earnings to the median earnings of a graduate who attended a comparable school. The wider the gap, the more qualified a student would be for loan forgiveness.

Congress moved to block the new rules, with ten GOP senators joining Democrats in the effort. Trump vetoed the legislation May 29, 2020, but the House upheld the veto and the rules took effect. Members of the House Education and Labor Committee had criticized the formula for providing students with only partial loan relief, even when defrauded by for-profit institutions. Education Secretary Betsy DeVos, however, said the department needed a proper methodology for forgiving loans. The department stopped processing claims for loan forgiveness in June 2018 and had 240,000 outstanding claims by the end of 2019.

ROBOCALLS

Frustration with robocalls was an issue that united Democrats and Republicans amid the divisive debate over Trump's first impeachment. The problem was that technological advances allowed robocallers to target thousands of phones with minimal effort, which some advocates said

rendered the 2003 Do Not Call registry obsolete. The Federal Communications Commission said U.S. consumers received nearly 4 billion robocalls per month in 2020, according to private analyses. FCC Chair Jessica Rosenworcel said she received the calls at home, at her office, on her landline, and on her mobile phone—and that she wanted to stop them, too.

Congress approved legislation (PL 116-105) requiring phone companies to verify that phone numbers are real and block robocalls without charging consumers extra money. The measure from House Energy and Commerce Chairman Frank Pallone Jr., D-N.J., and Senate Majority Whip John Thune, R-S.D., also increased enforcement against robocallers. The law pushed the Justice Department to bring more criminal prosecutions and gave the Federal Communications Commission more time and authority to investigate and punish illegal robocallers. Trump signed the bill into law December 30, 2019.

HOUSING POLICY

Trump's Department of Housing and Urban Development suspended indefinitely on July 23, 2020, an Obama-era regulation aimed at preventing racial discrimination in housing. Under the 1968 Fair Housing Act, the 2015 regulations required federal agencies as well as states, counties, and cities to "affirmatively further fair housing" (AFFH) in exchange for HUD funds. But Ben Carson, the HUD secretary, had criticized the regulation during his confirmation hearing January 12, 2017, at the Senate Banking, Housing, and Urban Affairs Committee. He said the regulation encouraged officials in Washington to dictate responses to alleged discrimination rather than having people report a problem and get a solution. Carson, who was Black, told the committee he did not have a problem with affirmative action, "but I do have a problem with people on high dictating it when they don't know anything about what's going on in the area."

Carson suspended the rule in 2018 and terminated it in 2020, replacing it with the Preserving Community and Neighborhood Choice regulation. The rule defined *fair housing* broadly to mean affordable, safe, decent, free of unlawful discrimination and accessible under civil rights laws. The rule also defined "affirmatively furthering fair housing" to mean any action rationally related to promoting any of the above attributes of fair housing. "After reviewing thousands of comments on the proposed changes to the Affirmatively Furthering Fair Housing (AFFH) regulation, we found it to be unworkable and ultimately a waste of time for localities to comply with, too often resulting in funds being steered away from communities that need them most," Carson said in a statement July 23, 2020, that accompanied the final rule.

The rule noted that "when the President reviewed the proposed rule, he expressed concern that the HUD approach did not go far enough." The rule came after Trump repeatedly tweeted criticism of the Obama-era rule and said it would destroy the suburbs. His criticism came during the presidential campaign, when racial justice protests roiled the country after the death of George Floyd in Minneapolis police custody and Trump was courting suburban voters.

Democrats blasted the approach. Senate Minority Leader Chuck Schumer, D-N.Y., said Trump was cutting fair housing laws and legalizing housing discrimination. Sen. Elizabeth Warren, D-Mass., accused the president of using racist fearmongering for political advantage.

SURPRISE MEDICAL BILLS

Congress cleared legislation in December 2020 aimed at shielding patients from surprise medical bills. Four committees—House Energy and Commerce, Ways and Means, and Education and Labor, and Senate Health, Education, Labor and Pensions—had worked for a year on legislation to protect patients from receiving unexpected bills from out-of-network doctors at an in-network facility or in emergency cases. The law established an arbitration process for resolving payment disputes between providers and health plans, and detailed factors the arbiter could consider when picking between the sides. Trump signed the measure December 27, 2020, as part of a year-end spending bill (PL 116-260).

Intense lobbying by industry groups had derailed the legislation earlier in the year. The legislation set up an independent dispute resolution process, without a minimum payment threshold for one side in a billing dispute to ask for arbitration. The agreement required the third-party arbitrator to consider several factors when choosing between the sides, including the median in-network rate, information about the provider's training and experience, the parties' market share, previous contracting experience between the parties, and the complexity of services provided. After a decision, the party that brought the dispute would not be able to take the same opponent to arbitration for ninety days. Patients were not required to pay more than their insurance plan's cost-sharing amounts, including deductibles, for both emergency and non-emergency situations when they cannot choose an in-network provider. Out-of-network providers were banned from balance billing patients if they did not inform the patients of their network status and the charges at least seventy-two hours before a procedure and the patient consented to that care.

The House Ways and Means Committee had pushed for the arbitration approach, which was favored by doctors and hospitals. But insurance plans and employers pushed for Congress to set a benchmark payment rate, which is what the other committees preferred.

HIGHWAY BILL

Trump, a real estate magnate, campaigned on his familiarity with construction as he proposed to spend $1 trillion on infrastructure over ten years. But funding an ambitious transportation program remained a tough sell for both

parties because of resistance to raising the gas tax, the primary source of revenue for the Highway Trust Fund, or to finding another stream of revenue. Congress has not raised the fuel tax since 1993, when it was set at 18.3 cents per gallon for gas or 24.3 cents per gallon for diesel.

Trump proposed to boost spending beyond highways and bridges to include projects for energy, water, wastewater, broadband, and even hospitals for veterans. For funding, the president cited public-private partnerships, asset sales, tax credits, and other tools. Each subject could be contentious on its own and the combination proved difficult to sell. House Transportation and Infrastructure Chair Bill Shuster, R-Pa., and Sen. John Thune, R-S.D., chair of the Commerce, Science and Transportation Committee, each said the key was figuring out how to pay for the package.

Trump's eagerness to cut federal spending also collided with his proposals for infrastructure. In March 2017, Trump proposed a so-called skinny budget that sought to eliminate a federal grant program for transit, cancel another grant program for surface transportation, and end the Essential Air Service that subsidizes flights to small airports. The proposals ran into fierce opposition. Another false start appeared in May 2017, when Trump's longer budget proposed to spin off air traffic control from the Federal Aviation Administration, sell electricity transmission assets, reduce restrictions on tolling interstate highways, allow the Department of Veterans Affairs to lease its unused facilities, and increase the commercial navigation fee on inland waterways.

Despite a summer lull, Trump drew the spotlight back to infrastructure on August 15, when he signed an executive order designed to speed construction of roads and bridges by putting a single federal authority in charge of approvals for environmental and other permitting requirements. Transportation Secretary Elaine Chao said the administration would release details of its funding proposals in the fall. But they never came. By March 2018, Shuster and Thune each voiced skepticism about Trump's plan to leverage federal dollars by forcing states to contribute more to projects. Lawmakers said after meeting with Trump that he would support raising the gas tax twenty-five cents per gallon, but that proposal never came to fruition. In 2019, the Senate and House committees each marked up rival versions of highway bills, but they did not advance.

By the end of Trump's term, the phrase "infrastructure week" had become the punchline of an administration that could not deliver. His initial announcement of infrastructure week in June 2017 featured a diatribe against former FBI Director James Comey for his investigation of Russian interference in the 2016 election. Democratic congressional leaders emerged from a White House meeting in April 2019 with an agreement to pursue a $2 trillion plan. But Trump derailed the plan weeks later, when he stormed out of another meeting with congressional leaders after three

minutes and gave a Rose Garden speech behind a lectern with a sign: "No Collusion, No Obstruction." Instead of talking about roads and bridges, he accused Special Counsel Robert S. Mueller III's investigation of Russian interference of being a hoax. "Instead of walking in happily into a meeting, I walk in to look at people that have just said that I was doing a cover-up," Mr. Trump said May 22, 2019, in the Rose Garden. "I don't do cover-ups."

CHINESE DRONES

One of Trump's last acts in office was to sign an executive order January 18, 2021, directing government agencies to assess security risks from Chinese-made drones and to prioritize removing them. Trump directed U.S. agencies to outline the security risks posed by drones built in adversarial countries including China, Russia, Iran, and North Korea. Trump also directed agencies to outline potential steps that could be taken to mitigate the risks, including discontinuing federal use of foreign-made drones and removal of foreign drones from federal service.

Drones "have tremendous potential to support public safety and national security missions and are increasingly being used by Federal, State, and local governments. Unmanned Aircraft Systems (UAS) are used, for example, to assist law enforcement and support natural disaster relief efforts," the executive order said. "Reliance on (drones) and components manufactured by our adversaries, however, threatens our national and economic security."

Chinese drones had prompted security warnings in the Trump administration about potential security risks when used by government agencies. The concern was that information collected by drones, such as video or geolocation data, could be transferred surreptitiously to the adversarial Chinese government. The Department of Homeland Security had warned U.S. businesses in May 2019 about "strong concerns about any technology product that takes American data into the territory of an authoritarian state that permits its intelligence services to have unfettered access to that data or otherwise abuses that data."

The Commerce Department had added SZ DJI Technology Co., the world's largest drone manufacturer, and dozens of other Chinese companies to a trade-restriction list called the Entity List. Commerce Secretary Wilbur Ross criticized China's ubiquitous surveillance in a statement December 18, 2020, and said DJI and other companies enabled wide-scale human rights abuses in that country.

PARDONS

Trump pardoned 143 people during his administration, with more than half during the final week, according to a Justice Department tabulation. The people receiving clemency included political figures, an in-law who ran afoul of the law, and at least one feminist. Some participants in the Capitol insurrection January 6, 2021, had expected blanket pardons to protect them from

prosecution, but Trump did not grant any. A sample of the pardons included

- Joseph Arpaio, the former sheriff of Maricopa County, Arizona, who was known for his tough enforcement against undocumented immigrants, on August 25, 2017, a month after his conviction of contempt of court
- Lewis "Scooter" Libby, former chief of staff to Vice President Dick Cheney, on April 13, 2018, for his conviction for obstruction of justice, false statements, and perjury. He was sentenced in 2007 to thirty months in prison and fined $250,000
- Dinesh D'Souza, a conservative commentator, on May 31, 2018, for his conviction for campaign contribution fraud. He was sentenced in 2014 to five years of probation and fined $30,000
- Bernard Kerik, the former New York City police chief, on February 18, 2020, for his conviction for obstructing the administration of the Internal Revenue Service, aiding in the preparation of false income tax returns, making false statements on a loan application, and making false statements. He was sentenced in 2010 to forty-eight months in prison and ordered to pay $187,931 in restitution
- Susan B. Anthony, the suffragette, on August 18, 2020, for illegal voting. She was fined $100 and the cost of prosecution in 1873
- Michael Flynn, the former national security adviser, on November 25, 2020, for making false statements to federal investigators about his interactions with Russians during the transition before Trump took office
- Duncan Hunter, a former House member from California, on December 22, 2020, for conspiracy to commit offenses. He was sentenced to eleven months in prison
- Roger Stone, the GOP political operative, on December 23, 2020, for obstruction of proceeding, false statements, and witness tampering. He was sentenced to forty months in prison and fined $20,000
- Paul Manafort, Trump's former campaign chair, on December 23, 2020, for subscribing to false income tax returns, failure to file reports of foreign bank and financial accounts, and bank fraud. He was sentenced in 2019 to forty-seven months in prison, fined $50,000, and ordered to pay $25,497,487 in restitution. He was also convicted of conspiracy against the United States and conspiracy to obstruct justice for witness tampering. He was sentenced to seventy-three months in prison and ordered to pay $6,164,032 in restitution
- Charles Kushner, the father of Trump's son-in-law and senior adviser Jared Kushner, on December 23, 2020, for sixteen counts of fraud and false statements, and retaliating against witness. He was sentenced in

2005 to twenty-four months in prison and fined $40,000
- Steve Bannon, Trump's political strategist, on January 19, 2021, for charges of conspiracy to commit wire fraud and conspiracy to commit money laundering
- Elliott Broidy, a venture capitalist and former finance chairman of the Republican National Committee, on January 19, 2021, on charges of conspiracy to serve as an unregistered agent of a foreign principal

COVID-19 PANDEMIC

Trump's final year in office faced the challenge of the worst pandemic in a century, with the spread of COVID-19. The number of U.S. deaths reached nearly 400,000 by the end of his term.

Trump declared the pandemic a national emergency on March 13, 2020, after the World Health Organization declared a pandemic two days earlier. The designation noted that 1,645 people had become infected nationwide, after the novel coronavirus was first detected in Wuhan, China, in December 2019. The statement said hospitals and medical facilities needed to assess their preparedness and prepare for a surge of new patients. The administration spurred the private development of several vaccines that proved overwhelmingly effective at preventing hospitalization or death from the respiratory virus. But Trump at times disparaged the advice of public health officials and often did not wear a mask to prevent the spread of the virus.

COVID-19 Relief

Congress approved several packages of economic relief in response to the pandemic. Lawmakers cleared a $2.3 trillion package in March 2020 called the Coronavirus Aid, Relief, and Economic Security Act (PL 116-136), which represented the largest financial rescue package in history and a tenth of the country's economy. The measure delivered nearly $910 billion in direct assistance to businesses through a mix of grants and loans. The legislation provided $454 billion through new Federal Reserve lending facilities for larger companies, with states and cities also eligible. The bill also provided $377 billion in loans to small businesses, much of which did not have to be paid back if used to maintain payroll. Airlines got $61 billion in aid, more than half in cash grants. And $17 billion in loans went to companies considered critical to national security. The measure also provided $590 billion in tax breaks, with a centerpiece of $292 billion in tax rebates for individuals and families.

About $480 billion was included to help contain and treat the disease through temporary increases in Medicare and Medicaid payments and funding for community health centers. Hospitals and other health care providers received $130 million, with another $17 billion for veterans' health care. Another $27 billion went toward stockpiling medical supplies, and research and development

on vaccines and drug treatments. States received $150 billion to refill depleted coffers, while states and localities got $31 billion for education, $25 billion for public transit systems, and $10 billion for airports. About $300 billion went to laid-off workers and low-income households, mostly through a $600-per-week increase in unemployment benefits. The package also contained $40 billion to boost food stamps, school meal programs, childcare funding and rental housing assistance. Trump signed the bill March 27, 2020.

Congress approved another package of COVID-19 relief (PL 116-260) totaling $900 billion. The package included $82 billion for schools struggling through the pandemic through the Education Department, $73 billion for the Department of Health and Human Services, $26 billion for farm programs, and a 15 percent increase in food stamp benefits for six months. But the provision for $600 payments to individuals based on income remained contentious. Trump initially balked after signing the measure. After signing it December 27, 2020, Trump called for increasing the payments to $2,000 checks for each adult, a move that Democrats embraced.

Senate Majority Leader Mitch McConnell, R-Ky., blocked repeated Democratic efforts to raise the $600 payments, which had income restrictions, to $2,000. "Socialism for rich people is a terrible way to help the American families who are actually struggling," McConnell said in a Senate floor speech December 31, 2020. The proposal became an issue in the Senate runoffs in Georgia, where Democratic challengers Jon Ossoff and Raphael Warnock supported $2,000 payments in their races against GOP Sens. David Perdue and Kelly Loeffler, who were noncommittal. Perdue and Loeffler each lost their races—and handed tie-breaking control of the Senate to Democrats in the next Congress.

Minimizing the Threat

But Trump minimized the threat from growing numbers of sick and dead. He drowned out health experts at White House briefings by suggesting unproven treatments for dealing with the virus. During the heat of the campaign, he ridiculed his Democratic opponent, former Vice President Joe Biden, for wearing a mask and for refusing to hold crowded rallies. And Trump hosted what his top expert in infectious diseases called a "super-spreader event" at the White House before he personally got sick and was hospitalized.

During daily White House briefings on the pandemic, Trump promoted untested and potentially dangerous treatments. At a task force briefing at the White House on March 20, 2020, Trump promoted hydroxychloroquine, a malaria drug with untested efficacy against the coronavirus, as a treatment and called himself "a big fan." But Anthony Fauci, the director of the National Institute of Allergy and Infectious Diseases, said "the answer is no" when asked at the briefing whether it was an effective treatment, calling the drug's promise "purely

anecdotal." On April 23, 2020, Trump said in the White House briefing room it would be "very interesting" to test whether shining an "ultraviolet or just very powerful light" on a person would eradicate the virus. He also said disinfectants knock out the virus, so he questioned whether there "is a way we can do something like that, by injection inside or almost a cleaning." Later during the same news conference, he clarified his comments to say the treatment "wouldn't be through injections," but rather "a cleaning and sterilization of an area." The suggestions set off a firestorm. The maker of Lysol said in a statement April 24, 2020, that "under no circumstances" should its products be used in the human body. The U.S. Surgeon General's office tweeted April 24, 2020: "PLEASE always talk to your health provider first before administering any treatment/medication to yourself or a loved one." The Maryland Emergency Management Agency tweeted April 24, 2020: "This is a reminder that under no circumstances should any disinfectant product be administered into the body through injection, ingestion or any other route."

Trump announced September 26, 2020, in the Rose Garden his choice of Amy Coney Barrett, a federal appeals judge, as his nominee to succeed Justice Ruth Bader Ginsburg at the Supreme Court. More than 150 people attended the outdoor ceremony and many did not wear masks or practice social distancing. In addition to the president and first lady testing later testing positive for the virus, others who were at the ceremony and later diagnosed with COVID-19 included former New Jersey Gov. Chris Christie, Trump aide Kellyanne Conway, Rep. Sens. Thom Tillis of North Carolina and Mike Lee of Utah, and University of Notre Dame President John Jenkins. Dr. Anthony Fauci, the head of the National Institute of Allergy and Infectious Diseases, told CBS News Radio's Steven Portnoy on October 9, 2020, that the announcement was a super-spreader event. "Well, I think the data speak for themselves," Fauci said. "We had a superspreader event in the White House and it was a situation where people were crowded together and not wearing masks."

Trump also seemed indifferent to the health risks the virus posed. On October 2, 2020, Trump announced that he and his wife Melania had each tested positive for coronavirus, which had killed more than 200,000 Americans by that point. His diagnosis came hours after aide Hope Hicks, who had traveled with him, tested positive. Trump was hospitalized that evening with symptoms of coughing and congestion. While hospitalized, Trump's daughter and senior adviser Ivanka Trump shared a picture October 3 on Twitter of him working at a conference table at Walter Reed National Military Medical Center that said: "Nothing can stop him from working for the American people." Trump briefly left the hospital October 4, wearing a mask for a short ride in a black SUV, to acknowledge supporters. He tweeted a video thanking

doctors taking care of him. "We're going to pay a little surprise to some of the great patriots that we have out on the street, and they've been out there for a long time and they've got Trump flags and they love our country," Trump said in the tweet.

Accelerating Vaccines

Despite disputes about treatments, the Trump administration accelerated the development of a COVID-19 vaccine through a partnership of the departments of Defense and Health and Human Services, called Operation Warp Speed. The departments obligated about $13 billion by December 31, 2020, to support the development, manufacture and distribution of vaccines, according to a Government Accountability Office report. The program adopted several strategies to accelerate vaccine development and mitigate risk. For example, different companies pursued different platforms to deliver the vaccine, including mRNA, a novel technology developed with the help of U.S. scientists that proved very effective. The companies also began large-scale manufacturing during clinical trials. By December 2020, two of the candidates—Moderna's and Pfizer/BioNTech's vaccines—received emergency use authorization from the Food and Drug Administration. Each vaccine was about 95 percent effective at preventing confirmed COVID-19 from occurring at least fourteen days after the second shot. Another three of the six candidates had entered the final stage of clinical trials by the end of January 2021. The companies released 63.7 million doses in that period, toward their contracted commitment to provide 200 million doses by March 31, 2021.

Even as vaccine development raced ahead, Operation Warp Speed left the decision-making for distribution largely up to the states and territories. The administration distributed vaccine doses to each jurisdiction based on population, but it was up to states to make key decisions about distribution and keeping the vaccines chilled, Gen. Gustave Perna, the chief operating officer for Operation Warp Speed, said during a November briefing. The cumulative number of deaths from COVID-19 reached 396,837 on January 20, 2021, according to *The Atlantic* magazine's analysis of data from the Centers for Disease Control.

Foreign Affairs

Trump pursued a nationalist and isolationist foreign policy he termed "America First." Whether through tougher border and immigration enforcement, or by restricting visas from countries he viewed as hostile, Trump argued that he was protecting the United States from foreign adversaries. He tapped a vein of frustration with long-running military conflicts overseas by withdrawing troops from Afghanistan and Syria, even when that meant overruling the concerns of Republican congressional leaders who warned against moving too hastily. Trump's America First policy marked a stark change in court from the internationalism that had dominated the U.S. approach to foreign policy since the end of World War II.

"We assembled here today are issuing a new decree to be heard in every city, and in every foreign capital and in every hall of power," Trump said during his inauguration speech at the Capitol on January 20, 2017. "From this day forward, a new vision will govern our land; from this day forward, it's going to be only America first. America first!"

Trump often seemed more comfortable with dictators than with democratically elected allies. He sided with Russian President Vladimir Putin against his own intelligence community dealing with Russian interference with the 2016 election. During a photo op with Putin at a meeting of the world's twenty largest economies June 28, 2019, in Osaka, Japan, Trump disparaged the assembled reporters. "Fake news," Trump said to Putin on June 28, 2018, in Osaka, Japan. "You don't have this problem in Russia. We have, but you don't have." Amid negotiations with North Korean leader Kim Jong un, Trump said that country had great economic potential. Kim "wrote me beautiful letters and they're great letters," Trump said Sept. 29, 2018, at a rally in Wheeling, West Virginia. "We fell in love."

In contrast, Trump blasted and badgered Australian Prime Minister Malcolm Turnbull during one of his first calls in office about refugees. Trump told Turnbull in the call January 28, 2017, from the White House "this is the most unpleasant call" before abruptly hanging up.

Trump foreign policies occasionally sparked friction with Republicans who favored free trade and opposed tariffs such as the ones he imposed on China. Trump negotiated a new trade deal with Canada and Mexico, to correct flaws in the previous, decades-old agreement for North America. But he chilled the diplomatic thaw with Cuba by restricting financial transactions. He also threatened to withdraw from the North Atlantic Treaty Organization in a dispute over the defense spending of European allies, but he never pulled the trigger.

Trump withdrew from several international pacts that had been negotiated by his predecessor that were never ratified by the Senate. He withdrew from a Pacific trade agreement of a dozen countries that aimed to curb China's influence in the region. He said he would negotiate trade deals with individual countries, but those never came to fruition. Trump withdrew from the Paris Accord on climate change, a pact of nearly 200 countries that agreed to limit greenhouse gas emissions. Despite the global consensus, Trump echoed Republicans complaining that the deal created an economic disadvantage for the U.S. economy compared to other industrial countries. And Trump withdrew from an international pact with Iran that aimed to curb its development of nuclear weapons in exchange for reduced sanctions. Trump argued the deal was ineffective at monitoring the country's secretive work.

Trump made groundbreaking strides with some countries, although sometimes without noticeable result. He moved the U.S. embassy in Israel to Jerusalem and helped

broker peace deals between Israel and two Arab countries. Trump held a summit with Russian President Vladimir Putin. Trump also made a landmark visit to North Korea as he sought to limit development of nuclear weapons. But talks petered out with no deal.

TARIFFS

Trump wielded tariffs on billions of dollars of goods from China, Mexico, and Canada as a key tool in his foreign policy agenda. He argued inaccurately that trade deficits meant American money lost. He also argued that balanced trade in goods would mean more manufacturing and more U.S. jobs. But the strategy raised domestic prices on goods and alienated him from fellow Republicans.

By some measures, he met his goals. Trump imposed 25 percent tariffs on imported steel in March 2018, with a goal of helping U.S. plants to work at 80 percent of capacity. U.S. plants had averaged working 74 percent of capacity from 2011 to 2016 and dropped to 72.3 percent in 2017. The American Iron and Steel Institute said capacity utilization after the tariffs reached 81.3 percent in May 2019. Trump's three rounds of tariffs on Chinese products—on $16 billion, $34 billion and $200 billion in imports—covered thousands of products. The Chinese retaliated with their own tariffs. The president received enormous criticism that the costs would simply be passed on to U.S. consumers, but administration officials said from the outset that consumer price increases would be too small to attract notice.

But the tariffs divided Trump from Republicans who supported free trade. Sen. Orrin G. Hatch, R-Utah, the chair of the Finance Committee said in a statement that tariffs would harm American and Chinese businesses and consumers, weakening the American economy, alienating allies, and undermining the competition with China.

In the broadest terms, Trump failed to meet his promises. The U.S. imported $911.1 billion in goods in 2020, more than it exported, according to the Census. The deficit widened from $850.9 billion in 2019, $870.4 billion in 2018 and $792.4 billion in 2017, according to the Census. The tariffs prompted retaliation against U.S. products. For example, soybean producers exported 30.3 metric tons from October 2018 through April 2019, which was down 25 percent from the same period a year earlier, according to the Agriculture Department's Economic Research Service. Pork producers faced a 62 percent duty in China, after that country boosted a 12 percent duty with a 50 percent retaliatory tariff. Counter tariffs also targeted motorcycles made in Wisconsin and bourbon produced in Kentucky, both states that Trump won.

TRANS-PACIFIC PARTNERSHIP

Trump issued an executive order on his first full day in office January 23, 2017, withdrawing the United States from the Trans-Pacific Partnership. The twelve-member group had agreed to a trade pact during the Obama administration, but Trump had made withdrawing from the agreement a campaign promise. Trump said leaving the pact would safeguard U.S. jobs and be a great thing for American workers.

The Obama administration negotiated the deal as part of an effort to bolster the American economic presence in Asia and counter China. But the pact negotiated in October 2015 was never ratified by the Senate, where Majority Leader Mitch McConnell, R-Ky., said the chamber would not vote on it. The order served notice of the U.S. departure to the other members: Australia, Brunei, Canada, Chile, Japan, Malaysia, Mexico, New Zealand, Peru, Singapore, and Vietnam.

Sean Spicer, the White House press secretary, said the administration would pursue trade agreements with individual countries, but not broad deals such as TPP and NAFTA. Trump campaigned against the deal as an example of a bad deal with foreign countries. Wilbur Ross, his Commerce nominee, said at his confirmation hearing that rules of origin on auto parts was a particularly bad provision in the deal because member countries could import up to 60 percent of auto components from a nonmember country that would be subject to lower tariffs.

Dan Ikenson, a trade expert at the Cato Institute, called the move unprecedented because the United States had never withdrawn from a trade agreement. The chair of the Armed Services Committee, Sen. John McCain, R-Ariz., criticized the withdrawal for representing a troubling disengagement from Asia. He said the departure would forfeit the opportunity to promote American exports, reduce trade barriers, open new markets, and protect American innovation. Sen. Ben Sasse, R-Neb., argued that the pact's stronger provisions should be retained.

TRAVEL BAN

During the presidential campaign in 2015, Trump called for a shutdown of Muslims entering the country after a shooting in San Bernardino, California. A couple of Pakistani descent shot and killed fourteen people and wounded twenty-two others.

One of Trump's first acts as president was to issue an executive order January 27, 2017, prohibiting visas for anyone traveling from Iran, Iraq, Somalia, Sudan, Syria and Yemen, which are all predominantly Muslim, for ninety days. The order also halted refugee resettlement for 120 days and indefinitely suspended the resettlement of Syrian refugees. Protests and chaos erupted at airports as even Muslims with legal permanent residency were prohibited from returning to the United States. Two days after the order, U.S. District Judge Ann M. Donnelly of New York issued a nationwide injunction.

A second version in March 6, 2017, removed Iraq from the list and removed the restriction on Syrian refugees. But U.S. District Judge Derrick Watson in Hawaii issued a nationwide order March 15, 2017, to block the Trump administration from implementing the revised ban. Eight

months later, on September 24, 2017, Trump issued a third order (Presidential Proclamation 9645) adding non-Muslim countries Venezuela and North Korea, as well as Chad, to the unwelcome list. The order also exempted permanent residents and visa holders. The Supreme Court upheld the third order June 26, 2018.

NATO FUNDING

As part of his America First agenda, Trump traveled to the North Atlantic Treaty Organization months into his term to demand that other countries in the alliance pay more to defend against threats from Russia, terrorism, and immigration. Trump complained that twenty-three of the twenty-eight member countries were not paying their share for a common defense. He urged each country to spend at least 2 percent of their gross domestic product (GDP) on the military. "This is not fair to the people and taxpayers of the United States," Trump said May 25, 2017, at NATO headquarters in Brussels, Belgium. "Over the last eight years, the United States spent more on defense than all other NATO countries combined."

NATO Secretary General Jens Stoltenberg had told an audience at George Washington University a month earlier that the alliance had turned a corner after years of decline. Military spending by European members and Canada increased by 3.8 percent or more than $10 billion in 2016, compared to a year earlier, he said.

SYRIA MISSILE ATTACKS

Trump ordered fifty-nine Tomahawk cruise missile strikes in April 2017 against Shayrat air base after Syria President Bashar al-Assad's chemical attack that killed at least eighty-six people. The U.S. military struck three Syrian targets in April 2018, days after another chemical attack on a Damascus suburb that killed nearly fifty people. The Syrian government denied involvement in the Douma attacks and called the missile strikes a violation of international law.

The second set of retaliatory strikes were delayed several days as U.S. officials deliberated with French and British leaders, whose forces participated in the strikes. "This massacre was a significant escalation in a pattern of chemical weapons use by that very terrible regime," Trump said April 13, 2018, in a nationally televised address. Experts concluded the attacks had little effect and did not alter Assad's behavior or decision-making. Lawmakers of both parties urged Trump and his team to fashion a long-term strategy for Syria. Sen. Jeanne Shaheen, D-N.H., supported the strikes, but said military efforts alone are not sufficient to deal with Syria's civil war. Sen. Roger Wicker, R-Miss., said the United States needed to make Bashar al-Assad pay a price.

The second set of missile strikes came at a time of heightened tensions with Russia in the Mediterranean Sea. Moscow sailed its Syria-based fleet of eleven warships. U.S. ships and combat aircraft moved around the region.

Experts warned that the situation could spiral out of control as tensions between the former Cold War rivals were at the worst since the 1980s. Sen. Tim Kaine, D-Va., said Assad should face consequences for war crimes, but that Trump should not initiate military action without a threat to American lives. Senate Foreign Relations Chair Bob Corker, R-Tenn., said a one-off strike was within any commander in chief's legal authorities.

PARIS ACCORD

Trump announced June 1, 2017, the United States would withdraw from the Paris Climate Accord, after foreign leaders failed to persuade him to stay during a meeting of the world's seven largest economies. The leaders of Germany, France, and Italy said in a joint statement issued by the office of German Chancellor Angela Merkel that they regretfully noted Trump's announcement and reaffirmed their commitment to speedily implement the 2015 pact of 195 countries negotiated during the Obama administration. Trump said the agreement carried draconian financial and economic burdens.

"So we're getting out," Trump said June 1, 2017, in the Rose Garden. "But we will start to negotiate, and we will see if we can make a deal that's fair. And if we can, that's great. And if we can't, that's fine."

The agreement had gone into effect the previous November after enough countries agreed to cut their carbon emissions as a way to slow the pace of global warming. The United States had agreed to reduce its carbon emissions by 26 percent to 28 percent from 2005 levels by 2025. Trump said compliance with the terms of the Paris Accord and onerous restrictions in energy would cost the country as much as 2.7 million jobs by 2025, according to the National Economic Research Associates. The same study found by 2040, compliance with the accord would cut production in paper 12 percent, cement 23 percent, iron and steel 38 percent and coal 86 percent, he said.

In addition to the withdrawal, Trump said the United States would also immediately stop contributing to the Green Climate Fund, a United Nations–affiliated organization that helps developing nations adapt to and mitigate the harmful effects of climate change. The remaining six members of the Group of 7 issued a statement noting the United States was not in a position to join the consensus, but that the governments of Canada, France, Germany, Italy, Japan, and the United Kingdom reaffirmed their commitment to the agreement.

Congressional Democrats called the decision to quit the Paris Accord disappointing after leaving the United States with Nicaragua and Syria as the only countries not participating in the global agreement. Sen. Thomas R. Carper of Delaware, the top Democrat on the Environment and Public Works Committee, called the decision baffling and profoundly disappointing. Republicans praised the move, including Senate Majority Mitch McConnell of Kentucky and House Speaker Paul Ryan of Wisconsin, who said the

accord would have driven up the cost of energy and hit middle-class and low-income Americans the hardest.

CUBA

The Obama administration had reestablished diplomatic ties with Cuba for the first time in fifty years, but the Trump administration rolled back several steps at allowing greater ties with the communist country ninety miles from Florida. Former President Barack Obama announced in 2014 that secret negotiations with then-President Fidel Castro and aided by Pope Francis would ease but not end all restrictions on travel, banking, and commerce under a long-standing embargo. Trump outlined the tougher stand with Havana in June 2017 with goals of denying U.S. dollars to the Cuban government, increasing pressure on President Raul Castro to end human rights abuses, allowing free elections, and returning U.S. fugitives. Trump issued a directive to the Commerce and Treasury departments to develop regulations aimed at ending individual person-to-person trips, to discourage tourist trips, and requiring travelers in other categories to keep detailed records subject to federal audits. U.S. travelers who stay at hotels or facilities operated by the Cuban government would be subject to scrutiny. Unless covered by exemptions, businesses would be in trouble for transactions with hotels or other entities operated by the military or intelligence services. "Effective immediately, I am canceling the last administration's completely one-sided deal with Cuba," Mr. Trump said June 16, 2017, in Miami.

Several Obama policies remained, including keeping an embassy open in Havana and allowing Cubans to maintain an embassy in Washington. Flights and cruise ship travel to the island continued. Business lobbyists who favored expanding ties with Cuba such as Airbnb initially said they would wait and see how the regulations played out.

The Trump administration announced in March 2018 that it would permanently slash its Havana embassy staff by about two-thirds because of mysterious ailments suffered by some on the diplomatic staff. The decision came six months after reducing the staff, as a deadline loomed for either returning them to Cuba or making the departure permanent. The State Department said the embassy would continue its core diplomatic mission.

More restrictions arrived in April 2019. John Bolton, Trump's national security adviser, announced a cap of $1,000 per quarter that families could send from the United States to relatives in Cuba, after the Obama administration lifted the limits. About $3 billion was sent to Cuba in 2016, according to the State Department. Bolton also announced sanctions against the Central Bank of Venezuela and against financial services company Bancorp in Nicaragua.

"The troika of tyranny—Cuba, Venezuela and Nicaragua—is beginning to crumble," Bolton said April 17, 2019, in Coral Gables, Florida. "The United States looks forward to watching each corner of this sordid triangle of terror fall: in Havana, in Caracas, and in Managua."

Trump announced in September 2020 that U.S. travelers would not be allowed to bring home Cuban cigars and rum, or stay in government-owned hotels, under regulations aimed at financially crippling the island's government. He made the announcement while honoring twenty veterans of the failed 1961 Bay of Pigs invasion of Cuba, which aimed to topple the government.

NORTH KOREA

Relations with North Korea veered from saber-rattling to landmark diplomacy during the Trump administration. The isolated country became a rising threat as it tested an intercontinental ballistic missile that analysts said had a range to reach the United States and accumulated as many as sixty nuclear weapons by August 2017. To combat the threat, the Obama and Trump administrations adopted six resolutions in 2016 and 2017 that banned more than 75 percent of North Korea's exports. Trump also raised the specter of launching a preventive military strike after one North Korea missile test. "North Korea best not make any more threats to the United States," Trump said August 8, 2017, at the White House. "They will be met with fire and fury like the world has never seen." The same day, Pyongyang declared it could conduct a nuclear strike on Guam, a U.S. territory in the western Pacific Ocean, if attacked.

Trump and Kim held the first summit between sitting presidents of the two countries on June 12, 2018, in Singapore. The leaders agreed to discuss normalizing relations between the countries, building a lasting peace, working to denuclearize North Korea, and returning the remains of U.S. troops missing since the Korean War in the 1950s. Trump became the first sitting president to set foot in North Korea, when he visited Kim Jong un, the country's leader, at the Demilitarized Zone. The two agreed to resume negotiations on an elusive agreement to limit nuclear weapons. Former Presidents Jimmy Carter and Bill Clinton had each visited Pyongyang, but only after leaving office.

A second summit between Trump and Kim was held February 27 and 28, 2019, in Hanoi, Vietnam. The summit ended without an agreement amid disputes over North Korea's denuclearization in exchange for relief from sanctions. North Korea's stance became tougher after the summit and the country began testing short-range ballistic missiles again in May 2019. Talks tapered off and North Korea later refused to engage with the United States or South Korea through 2020.

JERUSALEM

Trump formally recognized Jerusalem as the capital of Israel in December 2017. He moved the U.S. embassy in Israel from Tel Aviv to Jerusalem on May 14, 2018. Such a move had long been sought by bipartisan majorities in Congress, but had not been accomplished because of security concerns. "We cannot solve our problems by making the same failed assumptions and repeating the same failed

strategies of the past. Old challenges demand new approaches," Trump said December 6, 2017, at the White House. "My announcement today marks the beginning of a new approach to conflict between Israel and the Palestinians."

Most countries had embassies in Tel Aviv because Jerusalem remained a point of contention between Israelis and Palestinians. Israel occupied East Jerusalem in the Six-Day War in 1967, but Palestinians hoped to make it the capital of their independent state, if one is ever created. Nearly six in ten Republican respondents approved of moving the U.S. embassy, according to a poll by The Economist and YouGov. About half of Democrats said they strongly disagreed, according to the survey of 1,500 U.S. adults December 10 to 12, 2017.

The move had been debated for decades. In 1980, the United States abstained when the United Nations Security Council voted 14–0 to condemn Israel's declaration that Jerusalem was its capital. In 1995, Congress passed a law ordering the embassy's move. Then-President Bill Clinton allowed its enactment without his signature. Presidents George W. Bush and Barack Obama used a provision in the law allowing them to ignore it for national security reasons. Most other countries were firmly opposed to the move. The United Nations General Assembly voted 128–9 in December to condemn Trump's decision.

NATIONAL DEFENSE STRATEGY

Trump's first National Defense Strategy released January 19, 2019, shifted the focus from terrorism to rivalries with other superpowers of Russia and China. The eleven-page summary also warned of threats from rogue states such as North Korea and Iran, and of terrorism. The threats from those countries led to competition in air, land, sea, space, and cyberspace—all areas the United States once dominated, the report said. "Inter-state strategic competition, not terrorism, is now the primary concern in the U.S. national security," the unclassified portion of the report said. Instead, "the central challenge to U.S. prosperity and security is the reemergence of long-term strategic competition."

The strategy suggested to prevent or win a potential conflict would require a robust military buildup, strengthening alliances and making the Pentagon more efficient. The strategy called for deterring aggression in three regions: the Indo-Pacific, Europe, and the Middle East.

Defense Secretary James Mattis explained that the strategy was to expand the competitive space with adversaries and rebuild the U.S. military advantage. The first step was to rebuild the lethality of U.S. forces, making them more agile and innovative. The second step was to strengthen and expand the constellation of allies and partners. And the third was to ensure Congress and the American public that money was being spent wisely.

IRAN NUCLEAR DEAL

Trump announced May 8, 2018, that the U.S. was withdrawing from the Iran nuclear deal, called the Joint Comprehensive Plan of Action. The 2015 agreement negotiated by the Obama administration lifted sanctions on Iran in exchange for dismantling its nuclear program. But Trump's withdrawal had been widely telegraphed because he campaigned against it, saying Iran should do more to halt terrorism. "This was a horrible one-sided deal that should have never, ever been made," Trump said May 8, 2018, at the White House. "It didn't bring calm, it didn't bring peace and it never will." Iran said it would continue abiding by the terms of the deal and Britain, France, and Germany issued a joint statement saying the United Nations Security Council resolution endorsing the deal remained the binding international framework for resolving the dispute.

Secretary of State Mike Pompeo said the administration would drive for a new nuclear treaty that would compel Iran to make more nuclear concessions, accept limitations on its ballistic missile program, and cease its support of militant groups such as Hezbollah. He outlined demands such as Iran committing to never pursue plutonium reprocessing, stopping what uranium enrichment was allowed under the 2015 deal, and granting the United Nations nuclear watchdog unimpeded access to any site in the country. No new deal was negotiated.

TRUMP PUTIN SUMMIT IN HELSINKI

Trump met with Russian President Vladimir Putin in Helsinki, Finland, in July 2018 amid concerns about growing tensions between the countries thirty years after the end of the Cold War and threats from cybersecurity. "I have great confidence in my intelligence people, but I will tell you that President Putin was extremely strong and powerful in his denial today," Trump said at the summit news conference July 16, 2018, in Helsinki.

Trump met one-on-one with Putin for two hours with just interpreters. The Russian leader later said he told Trump his country had never interfered and would not interfere with U.S. elections. Putin also said he discussed extending a nuclear arms control agreement and ways to abide by the Intermediate Range Nuclear Forces Treaty, which Russia was suspected of having violated by testing and deploying ground-launched missiles. Three days after the summit, Director of National Intelligence Dan Coats said at the Aspen Security Forum that he was unaware of what was discussed.

Standing alongside Putin, Trump slammed Special Counsel Robert S. Mueller III's investigation as a disaster for the country and denied Kremlin involvement in the election, in contrast to the unanimous assessment of U.S. intelligence agencies. Mueller had already indicted more than two dozen Russian individuals including twelve intelligence officers for allegedly hacking and stealing Democratic Party emails. Mueller also charged and eventually convicted Trump's former campaign chairman Paul Manafort and former national security adviser Michael Flynn in the Russia probe—before Trump pardoned them.

Sen. John McCain, R-Ariz., the chair of the Armed Services Committee, called the summit a tragic mistake and said in a statement that no president had ever abased himself more abjectly before a tyrant. Sen. Richard M. Burr, R-N.C., the chair of the Intelligence Committee, did not target Trump in a statement, but said the committee found that Putin ordered the 2016 influence campaign and coordinated cyberattacks on state election systems to sow chaos and discord in the United States. Burr said any Putin lie about those activities should have been recognized by Trump.

RUSSIA SANCTIONS

The Treasury Department announced in December 2018 it would terminate sanctions against three of Russian oligarch Oleg Deripaska's companies, after intense lobbying from his allies. The department announced that Deripaska would take his ownership stake below 50 percent in all three entities while he himself would continue to face sanctions.

The move raised alarm among many Democrats and some Republicans because Deripaska would still control companies through relatives or other means. Deripaska had close ties to Russian President Vladimir Putin and was at one time connected to Trump's former campaign manager, Paul Manafort, who was convicted of financial fraud in 2018 as part of Special Counsel Robert S. Mueller III's investigation. But legislative efforts failed to block the Treasury Department's move. The House passed its bill with 136 Republicans joining all voting Democrats to uphold the sanctions one day after the Senate failed to do so (SJ Res 2).

SYRIA

Trump ordered the withdrawal of U.S. troops from Syria through a tweet December 19, 2018, that overruled his generals to halt fighting against the Islamic State. "We have won against ISIS," Trump said in a video in the tweet. The next day, Defense Secretary James Mattis resigned in protest with a letter citing differences over "treating allies with respect." Mattis agreed to remain through February 28, 2019, while Trump found a successor.

Trump's move took congressional Republicans by surprise. The Senate voted 70–26 on January 31, 2019, to adopt a nonbinding resolution that called al-Qaida and the Islamic State a continuing threat to U.S. security. The resolution condemned any "precipitous withdrawal" from Syria or Afghanistan. The move was one of the highest-profile disputes over foreign policy between Senate Majority Leader Mitch McConnell, R-Ky., and Trump.

In October 2019, Trump announced U.S. troops would step aside for a Turkish attack against Syrian Kurds, who had been key allies in the fight against the Islamic State. Turkey then invaded, killing dozens and displacing more than 180,000 people. The move provoked a critical resolution in the House, which voted 354–60 on October 16, 2019, on a resolution (HJ Res 77), to oppose the decision to end U.S. efforts to prevent Turkish military operations against Syrian Kurdish forces. On the day of the vote, Trump called the Kurds "no angels." Congressional Democratic leaders walked out of a White House briefing on Turkey's incursion with House Speaker Nancy Pelosi, D-Calif., saying she was praying for Trump's health. Trump called Pelosi a "third-rate politician" and tweeted out a picture of Pelosi standing and pointing at the president. McConnell called Trump's actions a grave mistake, but the resolution never came up for a vote in the Senate.

SAUDI ARABIA

The murder of journalist Jamal Khashoggi in October 2018 prompted Congress to reevaluate the U.S. relationship with Saudi Arabia. Trump prevailed in two key votes in 2019 over the war with Yemen and arms sales. The Yemen civil war resulted in as many as 60,000 deaths, according to some estimates, and the United Nations called the war the world's worst humanitarian crisis.

Senate Foreign Relations Chair Bob Corker, R-Tenn., said the death of the Saudi dissident and U.S. resident could tip the scales when it came to how the U.S. dealt with the kingdom in its war in Yemen. The House adopted a Yemen withdrawal resolution (HJ Res 7) in February. The Senate voted 54–46 on March 13, 2019, on a joint resolution (SJ Res 7) that aimed to direct the president to remove U.S. armed forces from hostilities in Yemen, including in-flight refueling of non-U.S. aircraft. The House rubber-stamped the Senate version in April.

In practical terms, however, the maneuvers had no effect. Trump vetoed the measure despite his long-standing opposition to having troops with foreign entanglements. Trump argued in a statement that the bill would "harm bilateral relationships in the region," while also objecting to language in the bill that defined "hostilities" to include mid-flight refueling. The Senate failed to override the veto.

In May 2019, the Trump administration announced it would sell $8.1 billion in arms to Saudi Arabia and the United Arab Emirates, after years of ratcheting up pressure on Iran. The announcement invoked a section of the Arms Export Control Act that allowed the administration to bypass congressional review. The Senate voted 53–45, with seven Republicans joining all voting Democrats on June 20, 2019, on a joint resolution (SJ Res 36) to disapprove of arms sales to Saudi Arabia, the United Kingdom, Spain, or Italy. The measure went to the House, which also adopted it easily. Trump vetoed the resolution as promised, and the Senate failed to override the move. It marked the second time in four months the administration prevailed on a matter dealing with the Saudis despite congressional opposition.

MIDEAST PEACE

Trump unveiled a Middle East peace plan that put Democrats in a political bind even though the Palestinians had already rejected the framework. Despite the lack of

consensus on the central conflict, Trump also brokered landmark peace deals between Israel and United Arab Emirates and Bahrain.

The administration released a 180-page proposal called "Peace to Prosperity" on January 28, 2020, that was the three-year brainchild of Jared Kushner, Trump's son-in-law and senior adviser. The plan aimed to give Israel nearly everything it had long sought, including control over an undivided Jerusalem and formal recognition of the settlements it had held since it seized the West Bank and Gaza Strip during the Six Day War in 1967. A White House outline of the proposal said it provided for a demilitarized Palestine living peacefully next to Israel, with Israel retaining security responsibility west of the Jordan River. Territory west of the river referred to Israel, the West Bank and Gaza Strip, which collectively had 4.4 million Palestinian Arabs. Palestinians and key Arab governments remained firmly opposed. Yousef Munayyer, a Palestinian American and executive director of the U.S. Campaign for Palestinian Rights, said the proposal was designed as a peace plan, but as a way to legitimize what amounted to apartheid.

Regardless of its unworkability, the plan divided Democrats. Sen. Patrick J. Leahy of Vermont, the top Democratic appropriator on the subcommittee that allocates billions in aid to Israel, said it is not a roadmap for peace, but for annexing settlements and territory. Sen. Christopher S. Murphy, D-Conn., who served on the Foreign Relations Committee and on Leahy's appropriations subcommittee, said the plan abandoned decades of work to create a two-state solution. But House Foreign Affairs Chairman Eliot L. Engel, D-N.Y., and Sen. Bob Menendez of New Jersey, the ranking Democrat on the Foreign Relations Committee, issued a joint statement that did not condemn the plan, but continued supporting a two-state solution.

Later that year, Trump hosted delegations in November at the White House from United Arab Emirates and Bahrain to normalize relations with Israel. The South Lawn ceremony featured Israel Prime Minister Benjamin Netanyahu, Bahrain Foreign Minister Abdul Latif al-Zayani and his Emirati counterpart, Abdullah bin Zayed al-Nahyan. The agreements called for the countries to open embassies and establish diplomatic and economic ties including tourism, technology, and energy. The deal was the first such agreement between Israel and an Arab state since a 1994 agreement with Jordan.

ABU BAKR AL-BAGHDADI

Trump announced October 27, 2019, that the leader of the Islamic State, Abu Bakr al-Baghdadi, had been killed the day before by U.S. forces in Syria. Trump said al-Baghdadi detonated a suicide vest after being cornered in a tunnel by U.S. forces. U.S. military forces had been planning an operation for a couple of weeks and several potential missions were canceled. Eight American

helicopters landed in northwest Syria and chased al-Baghdadi into the tunnel. "He died like a dog," Trump said October 27, 2019, at the White House. "He died like a coward. The world is now a safer place."

Trump thanked Russia, Turkey, Syria, Iraq, and the Syrian Kurds for supporting the mission. He also defended his decision to withdraw U.S. forces from Syria.

IRAN

Trump ordered a U.S. drone strike January 3, 2020, that assassinated Maj. Gen. Qassem Soleimani, who had led the Quds Force of the Iranian Revolutionary Guards Corps, while he was in Baghdad. A member of the Foreign Relations Committee, Sen. Christopher Dodd, D-Conn., said it could have been the most significant foreign leader the United States ever assassinated. Iran vowed harsh revenge for the attack. European leaders urged both sides to tamp down tensions.

The Iranian military launched missiles against U.S. military bases in Iraq on January 7, 2020. Nobody was killed, but 110 American troops were wounded.

The attack on Soleimani rekindled debate about authorization for the use of military force in the Middle East that Congress passed after the terror attacks September 11, 2001, which critics said was too legally flexible and outdated. But lawmakers were not able to broker a new deal.

Secretary of State Mike Pompeo said the strike was needed to stop an imminent attack on U.S. interests in the Middle East. But House Speaker Nancy Pelosi, D-Calif., said the assassination risked provoking a dangerous escalation of violence.

TALIBAN

The number of U.S. troops fluctuated over the years under Republican and Democratic administrations, as both sought to end the country's longest war. The Trump administration announced February 29, 2020, that it would completely withdraw U.S. forces from Afghanistan. Military leaders said they were reducing their footprint of 13,000 U.S. troops deployed to Afghanistan to 8,600 troops by mid-summer. But lawmakers of both parties were skeptical the Taliban would meet its obligations.

Gen. Kenneth McKenzie, commander of U.S. Central Command, said the United States would have sufficient time to monitor what the Taliban would do to make sure they were abiding by the agreement. "We don't need to trust them," McKenzie told the House Armed Services Committee on March 10, 2020. "We don't need to like them. We don't need to believe anything they say. We need to observe what they do, and we have the capability to do that."

Defense Secretary Mark T. Esper said at a Pentagon news conference in March 2020 that the path would be long, windy, and bumpy. The Trump administration ended without the withdrawal being completed. About 2,500 U.S. troops remained in Afghanistan on January 15, 2021, according to Acting Defense Secretary

Christopher Miller, which he said was the lowest level since 2001.

WORLD HEALTH ORGANIZATION

Trump froze funding for the World Health Organization (WHO) in April 2020 and announced in May that he was terminating the U.S. relationship with the World Health Organization over its response to Chinese officials blocking crucial data about the coronavirus outbreak in Wuhan. The administration made it official July 7, 2020, announcing it would withdraw effective a year later.

The move had little support in Congress. The House Appropriations Committee included $200 million explicitly for WHO in its fiscal 2021 State-Foreign Operations appropriations bill. Sen. Lamar Alexander, R-Tenn., the chair of the Health, Education, Labor and Pensions Committee, said he disagreed with the administration's decision. He said the WHO was valuable for international vaccine and prevention efforts.

OPEN SKIES

Trump announced in May 2020 he would withdraw from an arms control accord called the Open Skies Treaty, which was negotiated three decades earlier to allow countries to fly over each other's territory to assure that they were not preparing for military action. American officials had long complained that Moscow was violating arms treaties and in flagrant violation of the United Nations for the attempted annexation of Crimea and invasion of Ukraine. The problem with Open Skies was that Russia did not permit flights over a city where nuclear weapons were deployed that could reach Europe where nuclear weapons were deployed. Satellites were not covered by Open Skies.

"To this day, Russia is violating the Open Skies Treaty and completely defeating the purpose of that confidence and security-building measure," Ambassador Marshall Billingslea, Trump's special envoy for arms control, said May 21, 2020, at the Hudson Institute. "As we contemplate new negotiations as to whether Russia can become a reliable arms control partner, many have their doubts." Cale Brown, a State Department spokesman, announced months later that the U.S. had completed the withdrawal.

NAFTA USMCA

Trump negotiated a new trade agreement between the United States, Canada, and Mexico to replace the North American Free Trade Agreement (NAFTA). The pact had long been ridiculed by Democrats and labor unions for opening the door for U.S. manufacturers to shift production to Mexico's low-wage industrial sector. Trump had campaigned to either revamp the 1994 NAFTA or withdraw from it. Renegotiating the pact also benefitted Democrats for curbing the movement of manufacturing jobs to Mexico.

Under the U.S.–Mexico–Canada Agreement (USMCA), U.S. dairy, poultry, and egg products gained greater access to Canadian markets. Canada adopted a new quality-grading system for U.S. wheat. Canada also ended pricing schemes the U.S. dairy industry said kept Canadian skim milk powder prices at artificially lower levels, giving domestic producers an edge in sales to Canadian cheese makers over U.S. high-protein ultrafiltered milk.

Key changes that Democrats sought in implementing legislation included enforcement of labor provisions they believed would make it more difficult and expensive for U.S. manufacturers, particularly automakers, to shift production to Mexico. The changes won the endorsement of the American Federation of Labor and Congress of Industrial Organizations (AFL-CIO), but other unions such as the International Association of Machinists and Aerospace Workers opposed it. House Democrats' negotiations with the Trump administration in 2019 resulted in the removal of provisions that would have given pharmaceutical companies a ten-year pricing monopoly on biologic drugs in Mexico and Canada. The United States has twelve-year pricing exclusivity for biologics under the 2009 Biologics Price Competition and Innovation Act (PL 111-148), and Democrats worried that keeping the provisions in the agreement called USMCA would prevent future Congresses from reducing the U.S. timeframe to less than ten years.

The International Trade Commission, an independent agency, said real GDP would increase over several years by $68.2 billion, or 0.35 percent, and would add 176,000 jobs to the economy. The Congressional Budget Office estimated that the agreement would increase U.S. government revenue by $2.97 billion from fiscal 2020 to 2029, due to higher expected duty revenue on car and truck parts that do not meet stricter rules.

The Senate cleared the bill implementing the agreement by a vote of 89–10 on January 16, 2020, handing Trump a trade victory as senators prepared to serve as jurors in his first impeachment trial. Trump signed the bill (PL 116-113) on January 29, 2020.

Impeachments and Other Controversies

Trump took controversial stands throughout his administration, to promote his agenda and to keep rivals off balance. His unorthodox moves complicated his agenda and may have thwarted potential cooperation on bipartisan issues such as infrastructure as controversies dominated news coverage. Perhaps most significantly, his aggressive approach to the office culminated in two impeachments. Trump's personal negotiations with Ukraine's president—and his release in September 2019 of a summary of a call between them months earlier—sparked his first impeachment. His relentless skepticism about the results of the 2020 election and charges of fraud without evidence led to

THE TRUMP PRESIDENCY 637

his second impeachment, on a charge he incited an insurrection at the Capitol.

INVESTIGATIONS BY MUELLER, HOUSE COMMITTEES

Trump was the subject of numerous congressional investigations and a special counsel beginning in his first year in office. The investigations dogged him during his term, raising questions about whether he was profiting personally from serving in the White House or beholden to foreign powers because of his dealmaking before and during his administration. But Trump dismissed the investigations as partisan witch hunts. Most of the congressional probes ended inconclusively, the special counsel took no action on potential criminal charges, and two House impeachments each led to acquittals in the Senate.

Six House committees pursued inquiries, with demands meeting escalating stages of resistance. The Ways and Means Committee sought Trump's tax returns and Treasury Secretary Steven Mnuchin refused. The Oversight and Reform Committee subpoenaed Trump's financial documents from longtime accountant Mazars USA, which the president fought in court. The Intelligence and Financial Services committees jointly subpoenaed Deutsche Bank, a longtime lender to Trump, for financial records about his overseas debt, which the president is fighting in another lawsuit. By June 2019, the House Oversight and Reform Committee voted in June 2019 to hold Attorney General William Barr and Commerce Secretary Wilbur Ross in contempt for defying subpoenas about how a citizenship question was added to the census.

The Oversight panel also sought information about how security clearances were granted. And the committee investigated potential violations of the Constitution's emoluments clause, which prohibits the president from profiting personally from his office, over the Trump Organization's lease of the Old Post Office Building a few blocks from the White House for the Trump International Hotel. The General Services Administration (GSA) had selected Trump to operate a hotel in the building in 2012 and it officially opened October 26, 2016, days before the election. Because of his oversight of the General Services Administration, Trump essentially served as both landlord and tenant. A Government Accountability Office report found "serious shortcomings" in the lack of legal review about the emoluments clause. But Jack St. John, the GSA's general counsel, said investigators interviewed two dozen employees and reviewed 10,000 documents, and found no political influence exerted to obtain the lease.

The special counsel investigation raised the stakes with a criminal probe, rather than just civil disagreements about congressional investigations. Acting Attorney General Rod Rosenstein appointed Robert Mueller, the former FBI director, on May 17, 2017, as a special counsel to investigate Trump. U.S. intelligence agencies had concluded there was a wide-ranging Russian effort to influence the election, discredit Democrat Hillary Clinton, and help Trump. National Security Adviser Michael Flynn resigned over contacts with Russia's ambassador before the inauguration. Then-FBI Director James Comey testified to the House Select Intelligence Committee on March 20—just two months into the administration—and revealed a counterintelligence investigation into Russian interference in the 2016 election that began three months before votes were cast. Rosenstein's assignment to Mueller was to investigate any links or coordination between the Russian government and the Trump campaign, and any matters that arose directly from the inquiry.

After a twenty-two-month probe, the end of the investigation was as controversial as the beginning. Attorney General William Barr initially released a four-page summary of the 448-page report on March 24, 2019, saying it found no evidence that Trump's campaign conspired with Russia to sway the election. But Democratic critics argued he misstated the case when most of the two-volume report—other than redactions—was released April 18, 2019. The volume dealing with Russian interference concluded there was insufficient evidence to support a conspiracy, despite detailing a range of interactions between Trump associates and Russia.

"In sum, the investigation established multiple links between Trump campaign officials and individuals tied to the Russian government," the report said. "Those links included Russian offers of assistance to the campaign. In some instances, the campaign was receptive to the offer, while in other instances the campaign officials shied away. Ultimately, the investigation did not establish that the campaign coordinated or conspired with the Russian government in its election-interference activities."

The volume dealing with potential obstruction of justice found that Trump tried to thwart the investigation in several ways. He fired Comey, he ordered White House counsel Don McGahn to fire Mueller, which McGahn ignored, and Trump urged associates to pressure then–Attorney General Jeff Sessions to curb the inquiry. But Mueller made no decision on whether those actions justified criminal charges because Trump would have been unable to respond effectively. The Justice Department has a policy against charging sitting presidents criminally. "The president's efforts to influence the investigation were mostly unsuccessful, but that was largely because the persons who surrounded the president declined to carry out orders or accede to his requests," the report said. "Consistent with that pattern, the evidence we obtained would not support potential obstruction of justice charges against the president's aides and associates beyond those already filed."

Trump called the report a vindication in a tweet, saying, "No collusion. No Obstruction. For the haters and the

Radical Left Democrats—Game Over." Barr, who briefed reporters at the Justice Department before the report's release April 18, 2019, joined in a full-throated defense of the president, underscoring the report's conclusion that no one associated with the Trump campaign "conspired or coordinated with the Russian government to interfere in the 2016 election."

IMPEACHMENTS

The myriad investigations culminated in Trump becoming the only president in history who was impeached twice. Both ended with Senate acquittals. The first, for his dealings with Ukraine, ran along almost straight party lines in both chambers. The second, charging Trump with inciting the Capitol riot January 6, 2020, aimed to prevent him from holding federal office again. Seven Senate Republicans voted with Democrats to convict Trump, a stark change from the first trial, but still fell well shy of the two-thirds majority needed to convict the former president.

House Speaker Nancy Pelosi, D-Calif., had resisted declaring an impeachment investigation after Mueller's report about Russian interference in the 2016 and Trump's potential obstruction. But after that mammoth investigation, the House mounted the first impeachment within months. The case began with inspector general for the intelligence community, Michael Atkinson, alerting Congress that a whistleblower claimed Trump was pressuring Ukraine to investigate his Democratic political rival, Joe Biden, and his son.

Pelosi authorized an impeachment inquiry September 24, 2019. The next day, Trump released a summary of his July 25 call with Ukraine President Volodymyr Zelensky. The summary revealed Trump calling his U.S. ambassador "bad news" and asking to "do us a favor though" with an investigation of Biden, as Zelensky sought military assistance against Russia. Three House committees—Select Intelligence, Oversight and Reform, and Financial Services—took 100 hours of depositions from seventeen witnesses and held public hearings with a dozen witnesses, who described a private diplomatic effort in Ukraine directed by Trump's personal lawyer, Rudy Giuliani. Gordon Sondland, the U.S. ambassador to the European Union, testified November 20, 2019, at the Select Intelligence Committee hearing that he assured Ukraine officials at the White House on July 10 that a meeting would be arranged between Trump and Zelensky in exchange for investigations. "Mr. Giuliani's requests were a quid pro quo for arranging a White House visit for President Zelensky," Sondland said.

The House Judiciary Committee then drew up two articles of impeachment, charging Trump with abuse of power and obstruction of justice. The House voted 230–197 on December 18 to impeach Trump for abuse of power and 229–198 for obstruction of justice. All Republicans and two Democrats—Reps. Collin Peterson and Jeff Van Drew—opposed the article for abuse of power. Rep. Tulsi Gabbard, D-Hawaii, voted present. Rep. Justin Amash of Michigan, a Republican turned independent, supported both articles. Rep. Jared Golden, D-Maine, opposed the article for obstruction.

At the Senate trial, Trump's lawyers argued he had the authority to conduct foreign policy however he saw fit. On February 5, 2020, the Senate voted 48 to convict and 52 to acquit of abuse of power, and 47 to convict and 53 to acquit of obstruction. Sen. Mitt Romney, R-Utah, joined the Democratic Caucus in voting to convict Trump of abuse of power, but the votes were otherwise along party lines.

The second impeachment was even faster. Trump was charged with inciting the riot January 6 at the Capitol, which temporarily halted the counting of Electoral College votes confirming Biden's victory as president. A mob ransacked the building, breaking open doors and windows, chanting for Pelosi and Vice President Mike Pence, who was presiding over the count in his role as Senate president. Minutes after the Secret Service evacuated Pence from the Senate chamber, Trump tweeted, "Mike Pence didn't have the courage to do what should have been done to protect our Country and our Constitution." About 140 police officers were injured and police shot a woman to death at the Speaker's Lobby doors outside the House chamber. Attorney General Merrick Garland announced January 5, 2022—the day before the anniversary of the attack—that 500 people had been charged, including 100 people accused of attacking police officers.

A week after the attack—and a week before the end of Trump's term—the House voted 232–197 on January 13, 2021, to impeach him on a charge of inciting the insurrection. Ten Republicans, including Rep. Liz Cheney of Wyoming, the head of the House Republican Conference, joined Democrats in impeaching Trump.

At the Senate trial, Trump's lawyers and most Senate Republicans argued that he could not be held responsible for the actions of the mob. His defenders called the attack repugnant and said rioters must be brought to justice, but that Trump called for a "peaceful" protest while urging supporters to "fight" for the country.

On February 13, the Senate voted 57 to convict and 43 to acquit, which fell short of the 67 votes needed for conviction. Seven Republicans—Richard Burr of North Carolina, Bill Cassidy of Louisiana, Susan Collins of Maine, Lisa Murkowski of Alaska, Mitt Romney of Utah, Ben Sasse of Nebraska, and Pat Toomey of Pennsylvania—joined Democrats in voting for conviction. The Senate vote against Trump was the most bipartisan push for conviction of a president in history—Andrew Johnson and Bill Clinton were opposed only by members of the opposition party.

"The president promoted unfounded conspiracy theories to cast doubt on the integrity of a free and fair election because he did not like the results," Burr said in a statement after the vote. "When the crowd became violent, the

BATTLES WITH SOCIAL MEDIA

Trump revolutionized the use of social media for White House communications. He tweeted 25,000 times during his presidency, according to a count by CNN. He used the messages to reward his allies and bludgeon his adversaries at an average of eighteen times a day. But he eventually turned on the unfiltered messaging and was dumped from his favorite perches on Twitter and Facebook in the days after the January 6, 2021, Capitol insurrection.

In contrast to the melodious fireside chats of President Franklin Delano Roosevelt, Trump's tweets stampeded into the national conversation. He constantly assailed the news media. In a tweet July 2, 2017, he posted a video of himself at a professional wrestling match attacking a man whose head was represented by the CNN logo with the message #FraudNewsCNN. Trump often wielded tweets as insults to domestic or foreign rivals. In a tweet January 2, 2018, Trump taunted North Korean leader Kim Jong un for having a "depleted and food starved regime" and said Trump's "nuclear button" was "a much bigger & more powerful one than his." In a tweet July 14, 2019, Trump said progressive Democrats in the House came from "countries whose governments are a complete and total catastrophe, the worst, most corrupt and inept anywhere in the world." And Trump repeatedly fired aides on Twitter. In a tweet November 9, 2020, Trump said Defense Secretary "Mark Esper has been terminated." Trump named Mike Pompeo as Secretary of State in a tweet March 13, 2018, and thanked the incumbent Secretary of State Rex Tillerson for his service. Tillerson told reporters he had not spoken to the president and was not aware of why he was fired.

Trump often feuded with social media companies as they began to restrict his messages. Trump called for a repeal of Section 230 of the 1996 Communications Decency Act, which protects platforms such as Twitter and Facebook from being treated as publishers, and thus being held liable, for the messages that users post. After Twitter fact-checked several of his tweets about voting by mail, Trump signed an executive order May 28, 2020, aimed at overhauling Section 230.

Facebook suspended him January 7, 2021, after pulling individual messages that Trump posted at the height of the Capitol riot. In a video at 4:21 p.m. on January 6, 2021, he called the election "stolen from us" and said it was "fraudulent." Facebook said in a statement the video was removed at 5:41 p.m. for violating its Community Standard on Dangerous Individuals and Organizations. Trump posted a written statement at 6:07 p.m. that said the "sacred landslide election victory" was "unceremoniously viciously stripped away." Facebook removed that statement at 6:15 p.m. for violating the same policy and blocked him from posting for twenty-four hours. The temporary suspension eventually became a ban.

Twitter permanently suspended Trump on January 8, 2021, two days after the Capitol riot. The site said due to ongoing tensions in the United States and the global conversation about the violence at the Capitol, Trump's statements could be mobilized by different audiences to incite violence. Twitter said in a statement January 8, 2021, that Trump's tweets saying that the 75 million patriots who voted for him would "not be disrespected or treated unfairly in any way, shape or form!!!" and that he would not attend Joe Biden's inauguration January 20, 2021, were "in violation of the Glorification of Violence Policy and the user @realDonaldTrump should be immediately permanently suspended from the service."

president used his office to first inflame the situation instead of immediately calling for an end to the assault."

TAX RETURNS

Trump also faced legal battles over his tax returns. He repeatedly refused to release his tax returns publicly during the 2016 campaign, the first major-party nominee to refuse since 1976. He falsely said he could not release them while under audit by the Internal Revenue service. Two House committees subpoenaed his financial records, the Ways and Means Committee for six years of tax returns and the Oversight and Reform Committee for his accounting records from Mazars USA. Trump fought both cases to the Supreme Court, which refused to block their release. In addition, a New York grand jury subpoenaed eight years of personal and corporate tax returns from Mazars for a Manhattan district attorney investigation. Mazars provided the records to the prosecutor.

Trump also refused to release his returns during his 2020 campaign for reelection. *The New York Times* published a blockbuster article in September 2020 that found Trump paid no federal income taxes for eleven of eighteen years the paper examined.

Misrepresenting Facts

Fact checkers had a field day with Trump. *The Washington Post* reported that Trump made 30,573 untruths during his presidency, or an average of twenty-one per day. The tone was set on his first day in office, when Trump declared the inauguration crowd was so massive that it stretched to the Washington Monument and that it did not rain during his speech. Both statements were demonstrably false. Trump's untrue statements peaked on November 2, 2020—the day before his reelection defeat—when he barnstormed across the country making 503 false or misleading claims.

The subjects of the misstatements ran the gamut from accomplishments he sought to embellish, to failures that he chose to overlook. On December 22, 2017, when Trump signed the Tax Cuts and Jobs Act into law, he claimed it was the biggest tax cut in U.S. history, despite ranking eighth in the past 100 years, according to *The Washington Post*. When Special Counsel Robert S. Mueller III's report was released April 18, 2019, about Russian interference in the election and potential obstruction of the investigation, Trump claimed "total exoneration" despite the report saying it "does not exonerate" Trump. And when Trump was asked about the novel coronavirus January 21, 2020, he told CNBC at the World Economic Forum in Davos, Switzerland: "We have it totally under control. It's one person coming in from China, and we have it under control. It's going to be just fine." He declared a national emergency two months later, the country largely shut down, and nearly 400,000 Americans died from the virus during his final year in office.

Politifact.com awarded Trump its Lie of the Year for both 2017 and 2019, for statements that dealt with each of his impeachments. The 2017 statement was for saying Russian election interference is a "made-up story." The 2019 statement was for calling the whistleblower complaint about his Ukraine call "almost completely wrong."

ACCUSATIONS OF RACISM

Trump's incendiary rhetoric drew harsh criticism of racism. This came to the fore early in his presidency, when the Unite the Right rally in Charlottesville on August 11 and 12, 2017, attracted neo-Nazis and white supremacists who opposed the planned removal of a statue of Confederate Gen. Robert E. Lee. The mob carried tiki torches and chanted slogans such as "The Jews will not replace us." Violence the next day between protesters and counterprotesters led to the death of a woman, Heather Heyer, who was hit by a car, and injured dozens of others. At a Trump Tower news conference in New York on August 15, 2017, about infrastructure permitting, Trump said of the protests that "you also had people that were very fine people, on both sides." Trump said alt-left counterprotesters charged at their rivals with clubs in their hands. He called it a "horrible, horrible day," but said the left-leaning groups did not have a permit for their counterprotest, as did the white nationalists who were protesting "legally" and "innocently." "There are two sides to a story," Trump said.

Lawmakers from both parties quickly assailed Trump's comments. Rep. Ileana Ros-Lehtinen, R-Fla., said Trump moved to relativism when dealing with the KKK, Nazi sympathizers, and white supremacists. Sen. Brian Schatz, D-Hawaii, mentioned his Jewish heritage and said words could not express his disgust and disappointment. When Biden declared his presidential candidacy April 25, 2019, he released a video blasting Trump's language and saying the campaign would be a fight for the soul of the nation. "With those words, the president of the United States assigned a moral equivalence between those spreading hate and those with the courage to stand against it," Biden said in the video.

Even apart from Trump's rhetoric, civil rights groups complained that he rolled back measures that aimed to protect people from discrimination for race or sexual orientation. The Leadership Conference on Civil and Human Rights compiled a list of reductions in protections that occurred during the Trump administration, including the following:

- The first version of Trump's travel ban January 27, 2017, targeted majority-Muslim countries
- The Justice and Education departments rescinded Obama-era guidance February 22, 2017, that allowed transgender students to use bathrooms that match their gender identity
- Trump announced a prohibition July 26, 2017, against transgender people serving in the military
- The Justice Department sided September 7, 2017, with a Colorado baker, who refused to make a same-sex wedding cake by saying it went against his religious beliefs, in a Supreme Court case
- The Department of Housing and Urban Development indefinitely suspended May 18, 2018, implementation of a fair housing rule
- Nikki Haley, the U.S. ambassador to the United Nations, announced June 18, 2018, the U.S. withdrawal from the U.N. Human Rights Council
- The Justice Department issued new rules November 7, 2018, restricting the use of consent decrees for law enforcement agencies
- The departments of Homeland Security and Justice announced an interim rule November 8, 2018, blocking asylum claims from people who entered the United States outside legal ports of entry.

Trump denied any racist intent. When he was first running for election in 2016, he told *The Washington Post*, "Well, I am not a racist, in fact, I am the least racist person that you've ever encountered."

MOCKING RIVALS AND WORLD LEADERS

Trump prided himself on being unconventional during his campaign and his administration. He routinely mocked rivals, as he did when criticizing Sen. John McCain, R-Ariz., for his background as a prisoner of war in Vietnam. "I like people who weren't captured," Trump said at a campaign stop in Ames, Iowa, on July 18, 2015. He would also make up nicknames for adversaries, disparaging Sen. Elizabeth Warren, D-Mass., as "Pocahontas," for example, for falsely claiming Native American heritage.

Trump often resorted to name calling in disputes with other leaders. He called Paul Ryan, the former Republican House speaker, a "baby" after excerpts from Tim Alberta's book *American Carnage* quoted Ryan as saying Trump did not know anything about government and wanted to scold him all the time. "Paul Ryan was a terrible speaker," Trump told reporters July 12, 2019, at the White House. "Frankly, he was a baby. He didn't know what the hell he was doing."

After leaving a summit of the world's seven largest economies in Quebec, Canada, Trump called Canadian Prime Minister Justin Trudeau "very dishonest & weak" in a tweet June 9, 2018. Trudeau had said in a news conference at the end of the summit he would impose tariffs on the United States in response to Trump's steel and aluminum tariffs against Canada. Trump called Trudeau "meek and mild" in his tweet, in addition to dishonest.

Trump blasted Pope Francis after the pontiff questioned his Christianity in February 2016. The pontiff had told reporters aboard a papal flight that a person who thinks about building walls rather than bridges is not Christian. Trump made building a wall along the southern border with Mexico a keystone of his campaign. "For a religious leader to question a person's faith is disgraceful," Trump said in a statement February 18, 2016, as he campaigned against former Vice President Joe Biden, a Catholic. "No leader, especially a religious leader, should have the right to question another man's religion or faith."

DEFYING POLITICAL NORMS

Trump angered his political opponents by frequently defying political norms. On July 4, 2019, for example, he hosted a military parade on the National Mall called "Salute to America." He got the idea after attending a 2017 Bastille Day celebration in Paris. The display included a pair of M1 Abrams tanks before a military flyover featuring a B-2 bomber, F-35 Joint Strike Fighters, and V-22 Ospreys before a fireworks display. House Majority Leader Steny Hoyer of Maryland and other congressional Democrats complained the plans amounted to a campaign ad.

REPUBLICAN NATIONAL CONVENTION

Trump also used the White House as a stage for the Republican National Convention. Despite the Hatch Act prohibiting the use of public funds or personnel for electoral purposes, Trump accepted the nomination with a speech from the South Lawn. "Gathered here at our beautiful and majestic White House—known all over the world as the People's House—we cannot help but marvel at the miracle that is our great American story," Trump said August 27, 2020, at the White House.

One of his most controversial acts occurred after chain-link fences were erected around Lafayette Square, across the street from the White House, as a precaution during

the height of racial justice protests over the death of George Floyd in Minneapolis police custody. Federal authorities forcibly cleared a path through peaceful protesters June 1, 2020, so that Trump could walk across the park. He held a Bible aloft, in front of St. John's Church, in a widely criticized photo opportunity. He was joined by Attorney General William Barr, Defense Secretary Mark Esper, and chief of staff Mark Meadows. His daughter, Ivanka Trump, carried the Bible. Gen. Mark Milley, the chair of the Joint Chiefs of Staff, later said it was a mistake for him to attend. "I should not have been there," Milley said in a video June 11, 2020, for graduating officers at National Defense University. "My presence in that moment and in that environment created a perception of the military involved in domestic politics."

SHARPIE AND WEATHER MAP

Trump sparked a different kind of storm when talking about Hurricane Dorian in September 2019. He had been criticized for tweeting a warning that Alabama could be in the path of the storm, even though it was not. The National Weather Service in Birmingham corrected him with a tweet September 1, 2019, that said, "Alabama will NOT see any impacts from #Dorian" because it would be too far east.

When Trump held a map September 4, 2019, in the Oval Office that showed the potential paths Dorian might have taken, a Sharpie line was drawn on the map to include part of Alabama. "I know that Alabama was in the original forecast," Trump said at the White House on September 4, 2019, after a speech about opioids.

60 MINUTES

Trump attacked the news media throughout his administration, even while using it as a foil to amplify his messages. The most direct confrontation came October 22, 2020, when he stormed out of a White House interview with *60 Minutes* reporter Leslie Stahl and then posted the unedited interview on Twitter before the broadcast three days later.

When he boasted the greatest economy in history, Stahl told him it was not true. When she asked about spreading COVID-19 at a Rose Garden ceremony, Trump said he encouraged people to wear masks and she said he did not. When an off-screen voice gave a five-minute warning to end the interview, Trump walked out, saying, "I think we've had enough." Trump urged viewers in his tweet October 22, 2020, to compare Stahl's "constant interruptions and anger" with his "full, flowing and 'magnificently brilliant' answers."

REELECTION CAMPAIGN

Trump became the first president held to a single term since George H. W. Bush nearly three decades earlier, but it was not for lack of trying. He notified the Federal Election Commission the day he was inaugurated January 20, 2017,

that he qualified as a candidate in the 2020 race, even if his letter "does not constitute a formal announcement of my candidacy." As it turned out, his campaign was outspent by Democrat Joe Biden, with nearly $809 million compared to nearly $1.1 trillion, according to Federal Election Commission (FEC) documents. But money had not been decisive in 2016, when he raised $343 million to Democrat Hillary Clinton's nearly $586 million.

Trump faced headwinds during his final year when the novel coronavirus devastated the worldwide economy. During his stump speeches, Trump highlighted his signature tax cut, his slashing of federal regulations, growth in the economy and the appointment of hundreds of conservative judges, including three Supreme Court justices. His campaign slogans included "Keep America Great" and "Promises Made, Promises Kept."

Trump repeatedly promoted the low unemployment rate on the campaign trail. The unemployment rate declined from 4.7 percent when he took office in January 2017 to 3.5 percent in February 2020, according to the Bureau of Labor Statistics. But the economy shrank nearly 3.5 percent in 2020 during the pandemic, which prompted widespread economic shutdowns. The unemployment rate spiked to 14.2 percent in April 2020, according to the Bureau of Labor Statistics.

Investigations dogged Trump throughout his term. Successful prosecutions of his former National Security Adviser Michael Flynn and former campaign advisers such as Paul Manafort and Roger Stone kept the investigation of Russian interference in the 2016 election in the headlines for years. Trump appeared aware that former Vice President Joe Biden represented the biggest threat to his reelection, and his urging of Ukraine in mid-2019 to investigate Biden became the foundation for his first House impeachment, for which the Senate acquitted him.

Trump's approval rating averaged 41 percent during his term, according to Gallup's daily tracking poll. His rating peaked at 49 percent at five points early in 2020, but fell as low as 35 percent at a couple of points in 2017 and to 34 percent as he left office, according to Gallup. An average of national polls during Trump's administration found majority disapproval from almost immediately after he took office until he lost his campaign, according to FiveThirtyEight.com.

The coronavirus haunted Trump's campaign. He mocked Biden repeatedly for wearing a mask during the pandemic. One episode was at the first presidential debate September 29, 2020, at Case Western Reserve University in Cleveland. Trump said he wore masks, but not as much as Biden. "I don't wear masks like him," Trump said. "Every time you see him, he's got a mask." Trump denied Biden's claim that wearing masks and social distancing between then and January 2021 would save an estimated 100,000 lives. Trump quoted Fauci as saying "masks are not good" before changing his mind.

Trump had suspended in-person campaigning from March 2 through June 20, when he held a rally in Tulsa, Oklahoma. But he repeatedly criticized Biden for campaigning remotely from his home in Delaware. "I got a guy who stays in his damn basement all day long and I'm doing this," Trump said at a rally in Newport News, Virginia, on September 25, 2020. But Biden held fourteen public events during September 2020. He visited Kenosha, Wisconsin, on September 3 after Jacob Blake, an unarmed Black man, was shot by police. He met with union leaders in Lancaster, Pennsylvania, on September 7. And he spoke about manufacturing plans in Warren, Michigan, on September 9.

Biden eventually won with 306 Electoral College votes to Trump's 232 votes. The results, which Trump challenged after his defeat, nearly matched the 2016 results when he defeated Democrat Hillary Clinton with 304 Electoral College votes to her 227. Trump called his victory a landslide and his defeat a fraud.

Appendix

Glossary of Congressional Terms

AA—*(See Administrative Assistant.)*

Absence of a Quorum—Absence of the required number of members to conduct business in a house or a committee. When a quorum call or roll-call vote in a house establishes that a quorum is not present, no debate or other business is permitted except a motion to adjourn or motions to request or compel the attendance of absent members, if necessary by arresting them.

Absolute Majority—A vote requiring approval by a majority of all members of a chamber rather than a majority of members present and voting. Also referred to as constitutional majority.

Account—Organizational units used in the federal budget primarily for recording spending and revenue transactions.

Act—(1) A bill passed in identical form by the House and Senate and signed into law by the president or enacted over the president's veto. A bill also becomes an act without the president's signature if it is unsigned but not returned to Congress within ten days (Sundays excepted) and if Congress has not adjourned within that period. (2) Also, the technical term for a bill passed by at least one house and engrossed.

Ad Hoc Select Committee—A temporary committee formed for a special purpose or to deal with a specific subject. Conference committees are ad hoc joint committees. A House rule adopted in 1975 authorizes the Speaker to refer measures to special ad hoc committees, appointed by the Speaker with the approval of the House. *(See and compare Select or Special Committee.)*

Adjourn—A motion to adjourn is a formal motion to end a day's session or meeting of a house or a committee. A motion to adjourn usually has no conditions attached to it, but it sometimes may specify the day or time for reconvening or make reconvening subject to the call of the chamber's presiding officer or the committee's chair. In both houses, a motion to adjourn is of the highest privilege, takes precedence over all other motions, is not debatable, and must be put to an immediate vote. Adjournment of a chamber ends its legislative day. For this reason, the House or Senate sometimes adjourns for only a brief period of time, during the course of a day's session. The House does not permit a motion to adjourn after it has resolved into the Committee of the Whole or when the previous question has been ordered on a measure to final passage without an intervening motion.

Adjourn for More Than Three Days—Under Article I, Section 5, of the Constitution, neither house may adjourn for more than three days without the approval of the other. The necessary approval is given in a concurrent resolution to which both houses have agreed.

Adjournment *Sine Die*—Final adjournment of an annual or two-year session of Congress; literally, adjournment without a day. The two houses must agree to a privileged concurrent resolution for such an adjournment. A *sine die* adjournment precludes

Congress from meeting again until the next constitutionally fixed date of a session (January 3 of the following year) unless Congress determines otherwise by law or the president calls it into special session. Article II, Section 3, of the Constitution authorizes the president to adjourn both houses until such time as the president thinks proper when the two houses cannot agree to a time of adjournment. No president, however, has ever exercised this authority.

Adjournment to a Day (and Time) Certain—An adjournment that fixes the next date and time of meeting for one or both houses. It does not end an annual session of Congress.

Administration Bill—A bill drafted in the executive office of the president or in an executive department or agency to implement part of the president's program. An administration bill is introduced in Congress by a member who supports it or as a courtesy to the administration.

Administrative Assistant (AA)—The title formerly given to a member's chief aide, political advisor, and head of office staff. Today, the title most commonly used for such an individual is chief of staff. The administrative assistant often represents the member at meetings with visitors or officials when the member is unable (or unwilling) to attend.

Adoption—The usual parliamentary term for approval of a conference report. It is also commonly applied to amendments.

Advance Appropriation—In an appropriation act for a particular fiscal year, an appropriation that does not become available for spending or obligation until a subsequent fiscal year. The amount of the advance appropriation is counted as part of the budget for the fiscal year in which it becomes available for obligation.

Advance Funding—A mechanism whereby statutory language may allow budget authority for a fiscal year to be increased, and obligations to be incurred, with an offsetting decrease in the budget authority available in the succeeding fiscal year. If not used, the budget authority remains available for obligation in the succeeding fiscal year. Advance funding is sometimes used to provide contingency funding of a few benefit programs.

Adverse Report—A committee report recommending against approval of a measure or some other matter. Committees usually pigeonhole measures they oppose instead of reporting them adversely, but they may be required to report them by a statutory rule, chamber rule, or an instruction from their parent body.

Advice and Consent—The Senate's constitutional role in consenting to or rejecting the president's nominations to executive branch and judicial offices and treaties with other nations. Confirmation of nominees requires a simple majority vote of senators present and voting. Treaties must be approved by a two-thirds majority of those present and voting.

Aisle—The center aisle of each chamber. When facing the presiding officer, Republicans usually sit to the right of the aisle, Democrats to the left. When members speak of "my side of the aisle" or "this side," either literally or metaphorically, they are referring to their party.

Amendment—A formal proposal to alter the text of a bill, resolution, amendment, motion, treaty, or some other text. Technically, it is a motion. An amendment may strike out (eliminate) part of a text, insert new text, or strike out and insert—that is, replace all or part of the text with new text. The texts of amendments considered on the floor are printed in full in the *Congressional Record.*

Amendment in the Nature of a Substitute—Usually, an amendment to replace the entire text of a measure. It strikes out everything after the enacting clause of a bill or resolving clause of a resolution and inserts a version that may be somewhat, substantially, or entirely different. When a committee adopts extensive amendments to a measure, the panel often incorporates them into such an amendment. Occasionally, the term is applied to an amendment that replaces a major portion of a measure's text.

Amendment Tree—A diagram showing the number and types of amendments that the rules and practices of a house permit to be offered to a measure before any of the amendments is voted on. It shows the relationship of one amendment to the others, and it may also indicate the degree of each amendment, whether it is a perfecting or substitute amendment, the order in which amendments may be offered, and the order in which they are put to a vote. The same type of diagram can be used to display an actual amendment situation.

Amendments between the Houses—This is a method for reconciling differences between the House and Senate versions of a measure by passing the measure with successive amendments back and forth between the two chambers until both chambers have agreed to identical language.

Annual Authorization—Legislation that authorizes appropriations for a single fiscal year and usually for a specific amount. Under the rules of the authorization–appropriation process, an annually authorized agency or program must be reauthorized each year if it is to receive appropriations for that year. Sometimes Congress fails to enact the reauthorization (or authorization) but nevertheless provides appropriations to continue (or fund) the program, circumventing the rules by one means or another. *(See also Authorization.)*

Appeal—A member's formal challenge of a ruling or decision by the presiding officer or committee or subcommittee chair. On appeal, a house or a committee or subcommittee may overturn the ruling by majority vote. The right of appeal ensures the body against arbitrary control by the chair. Appeals are rarely made in the House and are even more rarely successful. Rulings are more frequently appealed in the Senate and occasionally overturned, in part because its presiding officer may not be of the same party or disposition as the Senate majority.

Apportionment—The action, after each decennial census, of allocating the number of seats in the House of Representatives to

each state. By law, the total number of House members (not counting delegates and a resident commissioner) is fixed at 435. The number allotted to each state is based approximately on its proportion of the nation's total population. Because the Constitution guarantees each state one representative no matter how small its population, exact proportional distribution is virtually impossible. The mathematical formula currently used to determine the apportionment is called the Method of Equal Proportions. *(See Method of Equal Proportions.)*

Appropriated Entitlement—An entitlement program, such as veterans' pensions, that is funded through annual appropriations rather than by a permanent appropriation. Because such an entitlement law requires the government to provide eligible recipients the benefits to which they are entitled, whatever the cost, Congress must appropriate the necessary funds.

Appropriation—(1) Legislative language that permits a federal agency to incur obligations and make payments from the Treasury for specified purposes, usually during a specified period of time. (2) The specific amount of money made available by such language. The Constitution prohibits payments from the Treasury except "in Consequence of Appropriations made by Law." With some exceptions, the rules of both houses forbid consideration of appropriations for purposes that are unauthorized in law or of appropriation amounts larger than those authorized in law. The House of Representatives claims the exclusive right to originate appropriation bills—a claim the Senate denies in theory but accepts in practice. *(See General Appropriation Bill.)*

At-Large—Elected by and representing an entire state instead of a district within a state. The term usually refers to a representative rather than to a senator. *(See Apportionment; Congressional District; Redistricting.)*

August Adjournment—A congressional adjournment during the month of August in odd-numbered years, required by the Legislative Reorganization Act of 1970. (In practice, Congress typically adjourns as well during August in even-numbered years.) The law instructs the two houses to adjourn for a period of at least thirty days before the second day after Labor Day, unless Congress provides otherwise or if, on July 31, a state of war exists by congressional declaration.

Authorization—(1) A statutory provision that establishes or continues a federal agency, activity, or program for a fixed or indefinite period of time. It may also establish policies and restrictions and deal with organizational and administrative matters. (2) A statutory provision, as described in (1), may also, explicitly or implicitly, authorize congressional action to provide appropriations for an agency, activity, or program. The appropriations may be authorized for one year, several years, or an indefinite period of time, and the authorization may be for a specific amount of money or an indefinite amount ("such sums as may be necessary"). Authorizations of specific amounts are construed as ceilings on the amounts that subsequently may be appropriated in an appropriation bill, but not as minimums; either house may appropriate lesser amounts or nothing at all.

Authorization-Appropriation Process—The two-stage procedural system that the rules of each house require for establishing

and funding federal agencies and programs: first, enactment of authorizing legislation that creates or continues an agency or program; second, enactment of appropriations legislation that provides funds for the authorized agency or program. *(See Appropriation; Authorization.)*

Automatic Roll Call—Under a House rule, the automatic ordering of the yeas and nays when a quorum is not present on a voice or division vote and a member objects to the vote on that ground. It is not permitted in the Committee of the Whole.

Backdoor Spending Authority—Authority to incur obligations that evades the normal congressional appropriations process because it is provided in legislation other than appropriation acts. The most common forms are borrowing authority, contract authority, and entitlement authority. *(See Borrowing Authority; Contract Authority; Entitlement Program; Spending Authority.)*

Baseline—A projection of the levels of federal spending, revenues, and the resulting budgetary surpluses or deficits for the upcoming and subsequent fiscal years, taking into account laws enacted to date and assuming no new policy decisions. It provides a benchmark for measuring the budgetary effects of proposed changes in federal revenues or spending, assuming certain economic conditions.

Bells—A system of electric signals and lights that informs members of activities in each chamber. The type of activity taking place is indicated by the number of signals and the interval between them. When the signals are sounded, a corresponding number of lights are lit around the perimeter of many clocks in House or Senate offices and corridors.

Bicameral—Consisting of two houses or chambers. Congress is a bicameral legislature whose two houses have an equal role in enacting legislation. In other national bicameral legislatures, one house may be significantly more powerful than the other. Most state legislatures are bicameral.

Bigger Bite Amendment—An amendment that substantively changes a portion of a text including language that had previously been amended. Normally, language that has been amended may not be amended again. However, a part of a sentence that has been changed by amendment, for example, may be changed again by an amendment that amends a "bigger bite" of the text—that is, by an amendment that also substantively changes the unamended parts of the sentence or the entire section or title in which the previously amended language appears. The biggest possible bite is an amendment in the nature of a substitute that amends the entire text of a measure. Once adopted, therefore, such an amendment ends the amending process. *(See Amendment in the Nature of a Substitute.)*

Bill—The term for the chief vehicle Congress uses for enacting laws. Bills that originate in the House of Representatives are designated as *H.R.* and are followed by a number assigned in the order in which the bills are introduced during a two-year Congress. Bills in the Senate are similarly designated except they begin with an *S.* Any bill that has not passed both houses of Congress in identical form at the end of a two-year Congress dies;

its proponents must introduce a bill again in the next Congress to seek its consideration. A bill becomes a law if passed in identical language by both houses and signed by the president, or passed over the president's veto, or if the president fails to sign it within ten days after receiving it while Congress is in session.

Bill of Attainder—An act of a legislature finding a person guilty of treason or a felony. The Constitution prohibits the passage of such a bill by the U.S. Congress or any state legislature.

Bills and Resolutions Introduced—Members formally present measures to their respective houses by delivering them to a clerk in the chamber when their house is in session. Both houses permit any number of members to join in introducing a bill or resolution. The first member listed on the measure is the sponsor; the other members listed are its cosponsors. *(See Hopper.)*

Bills and Resolutions Referred—After a bill or resolution is introduced, it is normally sent to one or more committees that have jurisdiction over its subject, as defined by House and Senate rules and precedents. A Senate measure is usually referred to the committee with jurisdiction over the predominant subject of its text, but it may be sent to two or more committees by unanimous consent or on a motion offered jointly by the majority and minority leaders. In the House, a rule requires the Speaker to refer a measure to the committee that has primary jurisdiction. The Speaker is also authorized to refer measures to additional committees with subject jurisdiction over one or more of a bill's provisions under House rules and to impose time limits on such referrals.

Bipartisan Committee—A committee with an equal number of members from each political party. The House Committee on Ethics and the Senate Select Committee on Ethics are the only bipartisan permanent full committees.

Borrowing Authority—Statutory authority permitting a federal agency, such as the Export-Import Bank, to borrow money from the public or the Treasury to finance its operations. It is a form of backdoor spending. To bring such spending under the control of the congressional appropriation process, the Congressional Budget Act requires that new borrowing authority is effective only to the extent and in such amounts as are provided in appropriations acts. *(See Backdoor Spending Authority.)*

Budget—A detailed statement of actual or anticipated revenues and expenditures during an accounting period. For the national government, the period is the federal fiscal year (October 1 to September 30). The budget usually refers to the president's budget submission to Congress early each calendar year. The president's budget estimates federal government income and spending for the upcoming fiscal year and contains detailed recommendations for appropriation, revenue, and other legislation. Congress is not required to accept or even vote directly on the president's proposals, and it often revises the president's budget extensively. *(See Fiscal Year.)*

Budget Act—Common name for the Congressional Budget and Impoundment Control Act of 1974, which established the basic procedures of the current congressional budget process; created the House and Senate Budget Committees; and enacted

procedures for reconciliation, deferrals, and rescissions. *(See Congressional Budget and Impoundment Control Act of 1974; Deferral; Impoundment; Reconciliation; Rescission. See also Gramm-Rudman-Hollings Act of 1985.)*

Budget and Accounting Act of 1921—The law that, for the first time, authorized the president to submit to Congress an annual budget for the entire federal government. Before passage of the act, most federal agencies sent their budget requests to the appropriate congressional committees without review by the president. Also established the Bureau of the Budget, forerunner of today's Office of Management and Budget. *(See also Budget; Office of Management and Budget.)*

Budget Authority—Generally, the amount of money that may be spent or obligated by a government agency or for a government program or activity. Technically, it is statutory authority to enter into obligations that normally result in outlays. The main forms of budget authority are appropriations, borrowing authority, and contract authority. It also includes authority to obligate and expend the proceeds of offsetting receipts and collections (that is, proceeds treated not as revenue but as negative budget authority). Congress may make budget authority available for only one year, several years, or an indefinite period, and it may specify definite or indefinite amounts. *(See Appropriation; Borrowing Authority; Contract Authority; Obligation; Outlays.)*

Budget Control Act—PL 112-25, legislation enacted in the 112th Congress, to provide for an increase in the statutory limit on the public debt in conjunction with other measures to reduce the budget deficit, including the creation of a Joint Select Committee on Deficit Reduction. The committee failed to report recommendations, thereby triggering automatic spending reductions.

Budget Enforcement Act of 1990—An act that revised the sequestration process established by the Gramm-Rudman-Hollings Act of 1985, replaced the earlier act's fixed deficit targets with adjustable ones, established discretionary spending limits for fiscal years 1991 through 1995, instituted pay-as-you-go rules to enforce deficit neutrality on revenue and mandatory spending legislation, and reformed the budget and accounting rules for federal credit activities. Unlike the Gramm-Rudman-Hollings Act, the 1990 act emphasized restraints on legislated changes in taxes and spending instead of fixed deficit limits. *(See Gramm-Rudman-Hollings Act of 1985.)*

Budget Enforcement Act of 1997—An act that revised and updated the provisions of the Budget Enforcement Act of 1990, including by extending the discretionary spending caps and pay-as-you-go rules through 2002. *(See Budget Enforcement Act of 1990.)*

Budget Process—(1) In Congress, the procedural system it uses to approve an annual concurrent resolution on the budget that sets goals for aggregate and functional categories of federal expenditures, revenues, and the surplus or deficit for an upcoming fiscal year; and to implement those goals in spending, revenue, and, if necessary, reconciliation and debt-limit legislation. (2) In the executive branch, the process of formulating the president's annual budget, submitting it to Congress, defending it before congressional committees, implementing subsequent budget-related legislation, impounding or sequestering expenditures as permitted by law, auditing and evaluating programs, and compiling final budget data. The Budget and Accounting Act of 1921 and the Congressional Budget and Impoundment Control Act of 1974 established the basic elements of the current budget process. Major revisions were enacted in the Gramm-Rudman-Hollings Act of 1985, the Budget Enforcement Act of 1990, and the Budget Enforcement Act of 1997. *(See individual entries for the laws named in this entry.)*

Budget Resolution—A concurrent resolution in which Congress establishes or revises its version of the federal budget's broad financial features for the upcoming fiscal year and several additional fiscal years. As with other concurrent resolutions, it does not have the force of law, but it provides the framework within which Congress subsequently considers revenue, spending, and other budget-implementing legislation. The framework consists of two basic elements: (1) aggregate budget amounts (total revenues, new budget authority, outlays, loan obligations and loan guarantee commitments, deficit or surplus, and debt limit); and (2) subdivisions of the relevant aggregate amounts among the functional categories of the budget. Although it does not allocate funds to specific programs or accounts, the Budget Committees' reports accompanying the resolution often discuss the major program assumptions underlying the functional amounts. These assumptions are not binding. *(See Budget Authority; Debt Limit; Federal Debt; Function or Functional Category; Outlays.)*

By Request—A designation indicating that a member has introduced a measure on behalf of the president, an executive agency, or a private individual or organization. Members introduce such measures as a courtesy because neither the president nor any person other than a member of Congress may introduce legislation. The term, which appears next to the sponsor's name, implies that the member who introduced the measure does not necessarily endorse it. A House rule dealing with by-request introductions dates from 1888, but the practice goes back to the earliest history of Congress.

Byrd Rule—The popular name of an amendment to the Congressional Budget Act that bars the inclusion of extraneous matter in any reconciliation legislation considered in the Senate. The ban is enforced by points of order sustained by the presiding officer. The provision defines different categories of extraneous matter, but it also permits certain exceptions. Its chief sponsor was Sen. Robert C. Byrd, D-W.Va.

Calendar—A list of measures or other matters (most of them favorably reported by committees) that are eligible for floor consideration. The House has four calendars; the Senate has two. A place on a calendar does not guarantee consideration. Each house decides which measures and matters it will take up, when, and in what order, in accordance with political considerations, rules, and practices.

Call Up—To bring a measure or report to the floor for immediate consideration.

Casework—Assistance to constituents who seek help in dealing with federal and local government agencies. Constituent service is a high priority in most members' offices.

Caucus—(1) A common term for the official organization of each party in each house. (2) The official title of the organization of House Democrats. House and Senate Republicans and Senate Democrats call their organizations "conferences." (3) A term for an informal group of members who share legislative interests, such as the Black Caucus, Hispanic Caucus, and Children's Caucus. These groups in the House are formally called Congressional Member Organizations and were formerly called Legislative Service Organizations. *(See Party Caucus.)*

Censure—The strongest formal condemnation of a member for misconduct short of expulsion. A house usually adopts a resolution of censure to express its condemnation, after which the presiding officer reads its rebuke aloud to the member in the presence of their colleagues.

Chairman—The presiding officer of a committee, a subcommittee, or a task force. Increasingly, the term *chairwoman* is used, reflecting the growing number of women in Congress who have gained seniority, or simply "chair." At meetings, the chair preserves order, enforces the rules, recognizes members to speak or offer motions, and puts questions to a vote. The chair of a committee or subcommittee usually appoints its staff and sets its agenda, subject to the panel's veto. The presiding officer in the House or Senate may be referred to as the chair.

Chamber—The Capitol room in which a house of Congress normally holds its sessions. The chamber of the House of Representatives, officially called the Hall of the House, is considerably larger than that of the Senate because it must accommodate 435 representatives, five delegates, and one resident commissioner. Unlike the Senate chamber, members have no desks or assigned seats. In both chambers, the floor slopes downward to the well in front of the presiding officer's raised desk. A chamber is often referred to as "the floor," as when members are said to be on or going to the floor. Those expressions usually imply that the member's house is in session. *(See Floor.)*

Christmas Tree Bill—Jargon for a bill adorned with amendments, many of them unrelated to the bill's subject, that provide benefits for interest groups, specific states, congressional districts, companies, and individuals.

Classes of Senators—A class under the Constitution consists of the thirty-three or thirty-four senators elected to a six-year term in the same general election. Because the terms of approximately one-third of the senators expire every two years, there are three classes.

Clean Bill—After a House committee extensively amends a bill, it often assembles its amendments and what is left of the bill into a new measure that one or more of its members introduce as a "clean bill." The revised measure is assigned a new number, reported to the House, and placed on the appropriate calendar.

Clerk of the House—An officer of the House of Representatives responsible principally for administrative support of the legislative process in the House. The clerk is invariably the choice of the majority party.

Cloakrooms—Two rooms with access to the rear of each chamber's floor, one for each party's members, where members may confer privately, sit quietly, or have a snack. The presiding officer sometimes urges members who are conversing too loudly on the floor to retire to their cloakrooms. *(See Chamber.)*

Closed Hearing—A hearing closed to the public and the media; a hearing conducted "in executive session" is a closed hearing. A House committee may close a hearing only if it determines that disclosure of the testimony to be taken would endanger national security; violate any law; or tend to defame, degrade, or incriminate any person. The Senate has a similar rule. Both houses require roll-call votes in open session to close a hearing.

Closed Rule—A special rule reported from the House Rules Committee that prohibits amendments to a measure or that only permits amendments offered by the reporting committee. *(See Rule.)*

Cloture—A Senate procedure that limits further consideration of a pending proposal to thirty hours to end a filibuster. Sixteen senators must first sign and submit a cloture petition to the presiding officer. One hour after the Senate meets on the second calendar day thereafter, the chair puts the motion to a yea-and-nay vote following a live quorum call. If three-fifths of all senators (sixty if there are no vacancies) vote for the motion to invoke cloture, the Senate must take final action on the cloture proposal by the end of the thirty hours of consideration and may consider no other business until it takes that action. Cloture on a proposal to amend the Senate's standing rules requires approval by two-thirds of the senators present and voting. *(See Nuclear Option.)*

Code of Official Conduct—A House rule that bans certain actions by House members, officers, and employees; requires them to conduct themselves in ways that "reflect creditably" on the House; and orders them to adhere to the spirit and the letter of House rules and those of its committees. The code's provisions govern the receipt of outside compensation, gifts, and honoraria, and the use of campaign funds; prohibit members from using their clerk-hire allowance to pay anyone who does not perform duties commensurate with that pay; forbid discrimination in members' hiring or treatment of employees on the grounds of race, color, religion, sex, disability, age, or national origin; restrict members convicted of a crime who might be punished by imprisonment of two or more years from participating in committee business or voting on the floor until exonerated or reelected; and restrict employees' contact with federal agencies on matters in which they have a significant financial interest. The Senate's rules contain some similar prohibitions.

College of Cardinals—A popular term for the subcommittee chairs of the appropriations committees, reflecting their influence over appropriation measures.

Colloquy—A discussion between members to put a mutual understanding about the intent of a measure or amendment on the record. The discussion may be scripted in advance.

Comity—The practice of maintaining mutual courtesy and civility between the two houses in their dealings with each other and in members' speeches on the floor. Although the practice is largely governed by long-established customs, a House rule explicitly cautions its members not to characterize any Senate action or inaction, refer to individual senators except under certain circumstances, or quote from Senate proceedings except to make legislative history on a measure. The Senate has no rule on the subject but references to the House have been held out of order on several occasions. Generally the houses do not interfere with each other's appropriations in the legislative branch appropriations bill, although minor conflicts sometimes occur. A refusal to receive a message from the other house has also been held to violate the practice of comity.

Committee—A panel of members elected or appointed to perform some service or function for its parent body. Congress has four types of committees: standing, special or select, joint, and, in the House, a Committee of the Whole. Committees conduct investigations, make studies, issue reports and recommendations, and, in the case of standing committees, review and prepare measures on their assigned subjects for action by their respective houses. Most committees divide their work among several subcommittees. With rare exceptions, the majority party in a house holds a majority of the seats on its committees, and their chairs are also from that party. *(See Committee of the Whole.)*

Committee Jurisdiction—The legislative subjects and other functions assigned to a committee by rule, precedent, resolution, or statute. A committee's title usually indicates the general scope of its jurisdiction but often fails to mention other significant subjects assigned to it.

Committee of the Whole—Common name of the Committee of the Whole House on the State of the Union, a committee consisting of all members of the House of Representatives. Measures from the Union Calendar must be considered in the Committee of the Whole before the House completes action on them; the committee often considers other major bills as well. A quorum of the committee is 100, and it meets in the House chamber under a chair appointed by the Speaker. Procedures in the Committee of the Whole expedite consideration of legislation because of its smaller quorum requirement, its ban on certain motions, and its five-minute rule for debate on amendments. The Senate does not use a Committee of the Whole.

Committee Ratios—The ratios of majority to minority party members on committees. By custom, the ratios of most committees reflect party strength in their respective houses.

Committee Report on a Measure—A document submitted by a committee to report a measure to its parent chamber. Customarily, the report explains the measure's purpose, describes provisions and any amendments recommended by the committee, and presents arguments for its approval. House and Senate rules prescribe the content of their committees' reports. The House requires its committees to write a report on legislation

reported to the House, the Senate does not. *(See Cordon Rule; Ramseyer Rule.)*

Committee Staff—Employees who assist the majority or minority party members of a committee. Most committees hire separate majority and minority party staffs, but they instead may hire nonpartisan staff, either professional and administrative staff or only administrative staff. Senate rules state that a committee's staff must reflect the relative number of its majority and minority party committee members, and the rules guarantee the minority at least one-third of the funds available for hiring partisan staff. In the House, each committee is authorized thirty professional staff, and the minority members of most committees may select up to ten of these staff (subject to full committee approval). Under House rules, the minority party is to be "treated fairly" in the apportionment of any additional staff resources. Each House committee determines the portion of its additional staff that it allocates to the minority; some committees allocate one-third, and others allot less. *(See Staff Director.)*

Committee Veto—A procedure that requires an executive department or agency to submit certain proposed policies, programs, or action to designated committees for review before implementing them. Before 1983, when the Supreme Court declared that a legislative veto was unconstitutional, these provisions permitted committees to veto the proposals. Language is still included in committee reports requiring agencies to seek committee approval before taking a specified action or type of action. Agencies usually take the pragmatic approach of trying to reach a consensus with a committee before carrying out an action, especially when an appropriations committee is involved. *(See Legislative Veto.)*

Concur—To agree to an amendment of the other house, either by adopting a motion to concur in that amendment or a motion to concur with an amendment to that amendment. After both houses have agreed to the same version of an amendment, neither house may amend it further, nor may any subsequent conference change it or delete it from the measure. Concurrence by one house in all amendments of the other house completes action on the measure; no vote is then necessary on the measure as a whole because both houses previously passed it.

Concurrent Resolution—A resolution that requires approval by both houses but does not need the president's signature and therefore cannot have the force of law. Concurrent resolutions deal with the prerogatives or internal affairs of Congress as a whole. Designated "H. Con. Res." in the House and "S. Con. Res." in the Senate, they are numbered consecutively in each house in their order of introduction during a two-year Congress. *(See, for example, Budget Resolution.)*

Conferees—A common title for managers, the members from each house appointed to a conference committee. The Senate usually authorizes its presiding officer to appoint its conferees. The Speaker appoints House conferees and under a rule adopted in 1993 can remove conferees "at any time after an original appointment" and also appoint additional conferees at any time. Conferees are expected to support the positions of their houses despite their personal views, but in practice this is not always the case. The party ratios of conferees generally reflect the ratios in

their houses. Each house may appoint as many conferees as it pleases. House conferees often outnumber their Senate colleagues; however, each house has only one vote in a conference, so the size of its delegation is immaterial. *(See Conference; Conference Committee; Conference Report.)*

Conference—(1) A formal meeting or series of meetings between members representing each house to reconcile House and Senate differences on a measure (occasionally several measures). Because one house cannot require the other to agree to its proposals, the conference usually reaches agreement by compromise. When a conference completes action on a measure, or as much action as appears possible, it sends its recommendations to both houses in the form of a conference report, accompanied by an explanatory statement. (2) The official title of the organization of all Democrats or Republicans in the Senate and of all Republicans in the House of Representatives. *(See Conferees; Conference Committee; Conference Report; Party Caucus.)*

Conference Committee—A temporary joint committee formed for the purpose of resolving differences between the houses on a measure. Major and controversial legislation may require conference committee action. Voting in a conference committee is not by individuals but within the House and Senate delegations. Consequently, a conference committee report requires the support of a majority of the conferees from each house. Both houses require that conference committees open their meetings to the public. The Senate's rule permits the committee to close its meetings if a majority of conferees in each delegation agree by a roll-call vote. The House rule permits closed meetings only if the House authorizes them to do so on a roll-call vote. Otherwise, there are no congressional rules governing the organization of, or procedure in, a conference committee. The committee chooses its chair, but on measures that go to conference regularly, such as general appropriation bills, the chairmanship traditionally rotates between the houses. *(See Conferees; Conference; Conference Report.)*

Conference Report—A document submitted to both houses that contains a conference committee's agreements for resolving their differences on a measure. It must be signed by a majority of the conferees from each house separately and must be accompanied by an explanatory statement. Both houses prohibit amendments to a conference report and require it to be accepted or rejected in its entirety, although specific disagreements may be presented to a chamber in a manner allowing the chamber to agree to its conferees recommendation. *(See Conferees; Conference; Conference Committee; Recommit a Conference Report.)*

Congress—(1) The national legislature of the United States, consisting of the House of Representatives and the Senate. (2) The national legislature in office during a two-year period. Congresses are numbered sequentially; thus, the 1st Congress of 1789–1791 and the 113th Congress of 2013–2015. Before implementation of the Twentieth Amendment in 1935, the two-year period began on the first Monday in December of odd-numbered years. Since then it has extended from January of an odd-numbered year through noon on January 3 of the next odd-numbered year. A Congress usually holds two annual sessions, but some have had three sessions and the pre-1935 67th Congress

had four. When a Congress expires, measures die if they have not yet been enacted.

Congressional Accountability Act of 1995 (CAA)—An act applying eleven labor, workplace, and civil rights laws to the legislative branch and establishing procedures and remedies for legislative branch employees with grievances in violation of these laws. The following laws are covered by the CAA: Fair Labor Standards Act of 1938; Title VII of the Civil Rights Act of 1964; Americans with Disabilities Act of 1990; Age Discrimination in Employment Act of 1967; Family and Medical Leave Act of 1993; Occupational Safety and Health Act of 1970; Chapter 71 of Title 5, *U.S. Code* (relating to federal service labor–management relations); Employee Polygraph Protection Act of 1988; Worker Adjustment and Retraining Notification Act; Rehabilitation Act of 1973; and Chapter 43 of Title 38, *U.S. Code* (relating to veterans' employment and reemployment).

Congressional Budget and Impoundment Control Act of 1974—The law that established the basic elements of the congressional budget process, the House and Senate Budget Committees, the Congressional Budget Office, and the procedures for congressional review of impoundments in the form of rescissions and deferrals proposed by the president. The budget process consists of procedures for coordinating congressional revenue and spending decisions made in separate tax, appropriations, and legislative measures. The impoundment provisions were intended to give Congress greater control over executive branch actions that delay or prevent the spending of funds provided by Congress. *(See Budget Process; Budget Resolution; Congressional Budget Office; Deferral; Impoundment; Rescission.)*

Congressional Budget Office (CBO)—A congressional support agency created by the Congressional Budget and Impoundment Control Act of 1974 to provide nonpartisan budgetary information and analysis to Congress and its committees. CBO acts as a scorekeeper when Congress is voting on the federal budget, tracking bills' compliance with overall budget goals. The agency also estimates what proposed legislation would cost over a five-year period. CBO works most closely with the House and Senate Budget Committees.

Congressional Directory—The official who's who of Congress, usually published during the first session of a two-year Congress. Contains statistical and other information on past Congresses and the current one as well as rosters of executive branch officials, foreign ambassadors, and other individuals.

Congressional District—The geographical area represented by a single member of the House of Representatives. For states with only one representative, the entire state is a congressional district. After the reapportionment from the 2010 census, seven states had only one representative each: Alaska, Delaware, Montana, North Dakota, South Dakota, Vermont, and Wyoming. *(See Apportionment; Gerrymandering; Redistricting.)*

Congressional Record—The daily, printed, and substantially verbatim account of proceedings in both the House and Senate chambers. Extraneous materials submitted by members appear in a section titled "Extensions of Remarks." A "Daily Digest" appendix contains highlights of the day's floor and committee action

plus a list of committee meetings and floor agendas for the next day's session.

Although the official reporters of each house take down every word spoken during the proceedings, members are permitted to edit and "revise and extend" their remarks before they are printed. In the Senate section, all speeches, articles, and other material submitted by senators but not actually spoken or read on the floor are set off by large black dots, called bullets. However, bullets do not appear when a senator reads part of a speech and inserts the rest. In the House section, undelivered speeches and materials are printed in a distinctive typeface. The term "permanent *Record*" refers to the bound volumes of the daily *Records* of an entire session of Congress, which are repaginated so that page numbers run consecutively through a whole session of Congress. *(See also* Journal.*)*

Congressional Research Service (CRS)—Established in 1914, a department of the Library of Congress whose staff provide nonpartisan, objective analysis and information on virtually any subject to committees, members, and staff of Congress. Originally the Legislative Reference Service, it is the oldest congressional support agency, except for the Library of Congress.

Congressional Support Agencies—A term often applied to three agencies in the legislative branch that provide nonpartisan information and analysis to committees and members of Congress: the Congressional Budget Office (CBO), the Congressional Research Service (CRS) of the Library of Congress, and the Government Accountability Office (GAO)—previously called the General Accounting Office. The Library of Congress also supports Congress in many ways, but provides numerous services to the public and to specialized users, including copyright and book cataloguing. *(See Congressional Budget Office; Congressional Research Service; Government Accountability Office.)*

Congressional Terms of Office—A term normally begins on January 3 of the year following a general election and runs two years for representatives and six years for senators. A representative chosen in a special election to fill a vacancy is sworn in for the remainder of the predecessor's term. An individual appointed or elected to fill a Senate vacancy usually serves until the next general election or until the end of the predecessor's term, whichever comes first.

Constitutional Option—*(See Nuclear Option.)*

Constitutional Rules—Constitutional provisions that prescribe procedures for Congress. In addition to certain types of votes required in particular situations, these provisions include the following: (1) the House chooses its Speaker, the Senate its president pro tempore, and both houses their officers; (2) each house requires a majority quorum to conduct business; (3) less than a majority may adjourn from day to day and compel the attendance of absent members; (4) neither house may adjourn for more than three days without the consent of the other; (5) each house must keep a journal; (6) the yeas and nays are ordered when supported by one-fifth of the members present; (7) all revenue-raising bills must originate in the House, but the Senate may propose amendments to them. The Constitution also sets out the

procedure in the House for electing a president, the procedure in the Senate for electing a vice president, the procedure for filling a vacancy in the office of vice president, and the procedure for overriding a presidential veto.

Constitutional Votes—Constitutional provisions that require certain votes or voting methods in specific situations. They include (1) the yeas and nays at the desire of one-fifth of the members present; (2) a two-thirds vote by the yeas and nays to override a veto; (3) a two-thirds vote by one house to expel one of its members and by both houses to propose a constitutional amendment; (4) a two-thirds vote of senators present to convict someone whom the House has impeached and to consent to ratification of treaties; (5) a two-thirds vote in each house to remove political disabilities from persons who have engaged in insurrection or rebellion or given aid or comfort to the enemies of the United States; (6) a majority vote in each house to fill a vacancy in the office of vice president; (7) a majority vote of all states to elect a president in the House of Representatives when no candidate receives a majority of the electoral votes; (8) a majority vote of all senators when the Senate elects a vice president under the same circumstances; and (9) the casting vote of the vice president in case of tie votes in the Senate.

Contempt of Congress—Willful obstruction of the proper functions of Congress. Most frequently, it is a refusal to obey a subpoena to appear and testify before a committee or to produce documents demanded by it. Such obstruction is a misdemeanor and persons cited for contempt are subject to prosecution in federal courts. A house cites an individual for contempt by agreeing to a privileged resolution to that effect reported by a committee. The presiding officer then refers the matter to a U.S. attorney for prosecution.

Continuing Body—A characterization of the Senate on the theory that it continues from Congress to Congress and has existed continuously since it first convened in 1789. The rationale for the theory is that under the system of staggered six-year terms for senators, the terms of only about one-third of them expire after each Congress and, therefore, a quorum of the Senate is always in office. Consequently, under this theory, the Senate, unlike the House, has not adopted its rules at the beginning of each Congress because those rules continue from one Congress to the next. Under Senate rules, a two-thirds vote of the senators present and voting is needed to invoke cloture against a filibuster of a proposed rules change.

Continuing Resolution (CR)—A joint resolution that provides funds to continue the operation of federal agencies and programs at the beginning of a new fiscal year if their annual appropriation bills have not yet been enacted; also called continuing appropriations. Continuing resolutions are enacted shortly before or after the new fiscal year begins and usually make funds available for a specified period. Additional resolutions may be needed after the first expires. Some continuing resolutions have provided appropriations for an entire fiscal year. Continuing resolutions for specific periods customarily fix a rate at which agencies may incur obligations based either on the previous year's appropriations, the president's budget request, or the amount as specified in the agency's regular annual appropriation bill if that bill has already been passed by one or both houses. In the House,

continuing resolutions are privileged after September 15. *(See Appropriation; Privilege.)*

Contract Authority—Statutory authority permitting an agency to enter into contracts or incur other obligations even though it has not received an appropriation to pay for them. Congress must eventually fund them because the government is legally liable for such payments. The Congressional Budget Act of 1974 requires, with a few exceptions, that new contract authority may not be used unless provided for in advance by an appropriation act. *(See Backdoor Spending Authority.)*

Cordon Rule—A Senate rule that requires a committee report to show changes the reported measure would make in current law. The rule was named after its sponsor, Sen. Guy Cordon, R-Ore. The House's analogous rule is called the Ramseyer rule. *(See Committee Report on a Measure; Ramseyer Rule.)*

Correcting Recorded Votes—The rules of both houses prohibit members from changing their votes after a vote result has been announced. Nevertheless, the Senate permits its members to withdraw or change their votes, by unanimous consent, immediately after the announcement. In rare instances, senators have been granted unanimous consent to change their votes several days or weeks after the announcement. Votes tallied by the electronic voting system in the House may not be changed. But when a vote actually given is not recorded during an oral call of the roll, a member may demand a correction as a matter of right. On all other alleged errors in a recorded vote, the Speaker determines whether the circumstances justify a change. Occasionally, members merely announce that they were incorrectly recorded; announcements can occur hours, days, or even months after the vote and appear in the *Congressional Record.*

Cosponsor—A member who has joined one or more other members to sponsor a measure. Joining on the day of introduction qualifies the member as an original sponsor.

Credit Authority—Authority granted to an agency to incur direct loan obligations or to make loan guarantee commitments. The Congressional Budget Act of 1974 bans congressional consideration of credit authority legislation unless the extent of that authority is made subject to provisions in appropriation acts.

C-SPAN—Cable-Satellite Public Affairs Network, which provides live, gavel-to-gavel coverage of Senate floor proceedings on one cable television channel and coverage of House floor proceedings on another channel. C-SPAN also televises selected committee hearings of both houses. Each house also transmits its televised proceedings directly to congressional offices.

Current Services Estimates—Executive branch estimates of the anticipated costs of federal programs and operations for the next and future fiscal years at existing levels of service and assuming no new initiatives or changes in existing law. The president submits these estimates to Congress with the annual budget and includes an explanation of the underlying economic and policy assumptions on which they are based, such as anticipated rates of inflation, real economic growth, and unemployment, plus program caseloads and pay increases.

Custody of the Papers—Possession of an engrossed measure and certain related basic documents that the two houses produce as they pass and then try to resolve their differences over the measure.

Dean—Within a state's delegation in the House of Representatives, the member with the longest continuous service; also the longest-serving member of the House.

Debate—In congressional parlance, speeches delivered during consideration of a measure, motion, or other matter, as distinguished from speeches in other parliamentary situations, such as one-minute and special order speeches when no business is pending. Virtually all debate in the House of Representatives is under some kind of time limitation. Most debate in the Senate is unlimited; that is, a senator, once recognized, may speak for as long as they choose, unless the Senate invokes cloture or agrees by unanimous consent to limit debate time.

Debt Limit—The maximum amount of outstanding federal public debt permitted by law. The limit (or ceiling) covers virtually all debt incurred by the government except agency debt. A congressional budget resolution sets forth the new debt limit that may be required under its provisions. *(See Budget Resolution; Federal Debt; Public Debt.)*

Deferral—An impoundment of funds for a specific period of time that may not extend beyond the fiscal year in which it is proposed. Under the Impoundment Control Act of 1974, the president must notify Congress that he is deferring the spending or obligation of funds provided by law for a project or activity. Congress can disapprove the deferral by legislation. *(See Congressional Budget and Impoundment Control Act of 1974.)*

Deficit—The amount by which the government's outlays exceed its budget receipts for a given fiscal year. Both the president's budget and congressional budget resolutions provide estimates of the deficit or surplus for the upcoming and several future fiscal years. *(See Budget Resolution.)*

Degrees of Amendment—Designations that indicate the relationships of amendments to the text of a measure and to each other. In general, an amendment offered directly to the text of a measure is an amendment in the first degree, and an amendment to that amendment is an amendment in the second degree. Both houses normally prohibit amendments in the third degree—that is, an amendment to an amendment to an amendment. *(See Amendment; Amendment Tree.)*

Delegate—A nonvoting member of the House of Representatives elected to a two-year term from the District of Columbia, the territory of Guam, the territory of the Virgin Islands, the territory of American Samoa, or the territory of the Northern Marianas. By law, delegates may not vote in the full House but they may participate in debate, offer motions (except to reconsider), and serve and vote on standing and select committees. On their committees, delegates possess the same powers and privileges as other members and the Speaker may appoint them to appropriate conference committees and select committees. Delegates are given an office budget according to the same formulas as representatives. *(See also Resident Commissioner from Puerto Rico.)*

Denounce—A formal action that condemns a member for misbehavior; considered by some experts to be equivalent to censure. *(See Censure.)*

Dilatory Tactics—Procedural actions intended to delay or prevent action by a house or a committee. They include, among others, offering numerous motions, demanding quorum calls and recorded votes at every opportunity, making numerous points of order and parliamentary inquiries, and speaking as long as the applicable rules permit. The Senate rules permit a battery of dilatory tactics, especially lengthy speeches, except under cloture or a unanimous consent agreement. In the House, possible dilatory tactics are more limited. Speeches are always subject to time limits and debate-ending motions. Moreover, a House rule instructs the Speaker not to entertain dilatory motions and lets the Speaker decide whether a motion is dilatory. However, the Speaker may not override the constitutional right of a member to demand the yeas and nays and in practice usually waits for a point of order before exercising that authority. *(See Cloture.)*

Discharge a Committee—Remove a measure from a committee to which it has been referred in order to make it available for floor consideration. Noncontroversial measures are often discharged by unanimous consent. However, because congressional committees have no obligation to report measures referred to them, each house has procedures to extract measures from committees.

District and State Offices—Representatives maintain one or more offices in their districts for the purpose of assisting and communicating with constituents. The costs of maintaining these offices are paid from members' official allowances. Senators can use the official expense allowance to rent offices in their home state, subject to a funding formula based on their state's population and other factors.

District Work Period—The House term for a congressional recess during which members may visit their districts and conduct constituency business.

Division Vote—A vote in which the chair first counts those in favor of a proposition and then those opposed to it, with no record made of how each member voted. In the Senate, the chair may count raised hands or ask senators to stand, whereas the House requires members to stand; hence, often called a standing vote. Committees in both houses ordinarily use a show of hands. A division usually occurs after a voice vote and may be demanded by any member or ordered by the chair if there is any doubt about the outcome of the voice vote. The demand for a division can also come before a voice vote. In the Senate, the demand must come before the result of a voice vote is announced. It may be made after a voice vote announcement in the House, but only if no intervening business has transpired and only if the member was standing and seeking recognition at the time of the announcement. A demand for the yeas and nays or, in the House, for a recorded vote takes precedence over a demand for a division vote.

Earmark—A set-aside within a measure, committee report, or conference report for a specific purpose. *(See Pork or Pork Barrel Legislation.)*

Effective Dates—Provisions of an act that specify when the entire act or individual provisions in it become effective as law. Most acts become effective on the date of enactment, but it is sometimes necessary or desirable to delay the effective dates of some provisions or to make them effective retroactively.

Electronic Voting—Since 1973 the House has used an electronic voting system to record the yeas and nays and to conduct recorded votes. Members vote by inserting their voting cards in one of the boxes at several locations in the chamber. They are given at least fifteen minutes to vote. However, when several votes occur immediately after each other, the Speaker or chair of the Committee of the Whole may reduce the voting time to five minutes (or less in some circumstances) on the second and subsequent votes. The Speaker or chair routinely allows additional time on each vote but may close a vote at any time after the minimum time has expired. Members can change their votes at any time before the Speaker announces the result. The House also uses the electronic system for quorum calls. While a vote is in progress, a large panel above the Speaker's desk displays how each member has voted. Smaller panels on either side of the chamber display running totals of the votes and the time remaining. The Senate does not have electronic voting.

Enacting Clause—The opening language of each bill, stating "Be it enacted by the Senate and House of Representatives of the United States of America in Congress assembled. . . . " This language gives legal force to measures approved by Congress and signed by the president or enacted over the president's veto. A successful motion to strike it from a bill kills the entire measure.

Engrossed Bill—The official copy of a bill or joint resolution as passed by one chamber, including the text as amended by floor action, and certified by the clerk of the House or the secretary of the Senate (as appropriate). Amendments by one house to a measure or amendments of the other also are engrossed. House engrossed documents are printed on blue paper; the Senate's are printed on white paper.

Enrolled Bill—The final official copy of a bill or joint resolution passed in identical form by both houses. An enrolled bill usually is printed on parchment. After it is certified by the chief officer of the house in which it originated and signed by the House Speaker and the Senate president pro tempore, the measure is sent to the White House for the president's signature.

Entitlement Program—A federal program under which individuals, businesses, or units of government that meet the requirements or qualifications established by law are entitled to receive certain payments if they seek such payments. Major examples include Social Security, Medicare, Medicaid, unemployment insurance, and military and federal civilian pensions. Congress cannot control their expenditures by refusing to appropriate the sums necessary to fund them because the government is legally obligated to pay eligible recipients the amounts to which the law entitles them. *(See Backdoor Spending Authority.)*

Equality of the Houses—A component of the Constitution's emphasis on checks and balances under which each house is given essentially equal status in the enactment of legislation and in the relations and negotiations between the two houses.

Although the House of Representatives initiates revenue and appropriation measures, the Senate has the right to amend them. Either house may initiate any other type of legislation, and neither can force the other to agree to, or even act on, its measures. Moreover, each house has a potential veto over the other because legislation requires agreement by both. Similarly, in a conference to resolve their differences on a measure, each house casts one vote, as determined by a majority of its conferees. In other national bicameral legislatures, the powers of one house may be markedly greater than those of the other.

Ethics Rules—Several rules or standing orders in each house that mandate certain standards of conduct for members and congressional employees in finance, employment, franking, and other areas. The Senate Select Committee on Ethics and the House Committee on Ethics investigate alleged violations of conduct and recommend appropriate actions to their respective houses.

Exclusive Committee—(1) Under the rules of the Republican Conference and House Democratic Caucus, a standing committee whose members usually cannot serve on any other standing committee. As of 2013 the Appropriations, Energy and Commerce (for Democrats beginning service in the 105th Congress), Financial Services (for Democrats beginning in the 109th Congress), Ways and Means, and Rules committees were designated as exclusive committees. The parties may choose to ignore or waive their rule for specific members. (2) Under the rules of the two-party conferences in the Senate, a standing committee whose members may not simultaneously serve on any other exclusive committee.

Executive Calendar—The Senate's calendar for executive business, that is, treaties and nominations. The calendar numbers indicate the order in which items were referred to the calendar but have no bearing on when or if the Senate will consider them. The Senate, by motion or unanimous consent, resolves itself into executive session to consider items on the executive calendar. The Senate's legislative calendar is the Calendar of General Orders, and is referred to colloquially as the Senate Calendar. *(See Executive Session; Nomination; Resolution of Ratification.)*

Executive Document—A document, usually a treaty, sent by the president to the Senate for approval. It is referred to a committee in the same manner as other measures. Resolutions to ratify treaties have their own "treaty document" numbers. For example, the first treaty submitted in the 113th Congress was "Treaty Document 113-1," a treaty on fishery resources in the South Pacific Ocean. *(See Ratification; Resolution of Ratification; Treaty.)*

Executive Order—A document signed by the president that has a policy-making or legislative impact on the management of the federal government's operations. Members of Congress have challenged some executive orders on the grounds that they usurped the authority of the legislative branch. Although the Supreme Court has ruled that a particular order exceeded the president's authority, it has upheld others as falling within the president's general constitutional powers. An executive order might also be explicitly or implicitly authorized by law.

Executive Privilege—The assertion that presidents have the right to withhold certain information from Congress. Presidents have based their claim on (1) the constitutional separation of powers, (2) the need for secrecy in military and diplomatic affairs, (3) the need to protect individuals from unfavorable publicity, (4) the need to safeguard the confidential exchange of ideas in the executive branch, and (5) the need to protect individuals who provide confidential advice to the president.

Executive Session—(1) A Senate meeting devoted to the consideration of treaties or nominations. Normally, the Senate meets in legislative session; it resolves itself into executive session, by motion or by unanimous consent, to deal with its executive business. It also keeps a separate *Journal* for executive sessions. Executive sessions are usually open to the public, but the Senate may choose to close them. (Closed committee meetings in the House and Senate are also referred to as executive sessions.) *(See Executive Calendar.)*

Expulsion—A member's removal from office by a two-thirds vote of their chamber; the supermajority is required by the Constitution. It is the most severe and most rarely used sanction a house can invoke against a member. Although the Constitution provides no explicit grounds for expulsion, the courts have ruled that it may be applied only for misconduct during a member's term of office, not for conduct before the member's election. Generally, neither house will consider expulsion of a member convicted of a crime until the judicial processes have been exhausted. At that stage, members sometimes resign rather than face expulsion. In 1977, the House adopted a rule urging members convicted of certain crimes to voluntarily abstain from voting or participating in other legislative business.

Extensions of Remarks—An appendix to the daily *Congressional Record* that consists primarily of miscellaneous material submitted by members. It often includes members' statements not delivered on the floor, newspaper articles and editorials, praise for a member's constituents, and noteworthy letters received by a member, among other material. Representatives supply the bulk of this material; senators submit little. "Extensions of Remarks" pages are separately numbered, and each number is preceded by the letter *E*. Materials may be placed in the Extensions of Remarks section only by unanimous consent. *(See Congressional Record.)*

Fast Track—Also called expedited procedures, this refers to any set of procedures applicable to a specific piece or specific subject of legislation. A fast track set of procedures circumvents or speeds up all or part of the legislative process to ensure or better ensure that a congressional decision is reached. Rulemaking statutes may prescribe expedited procedures for designated measures, such as statutes granting trade promotion authority to the president.

Federal Debt—The total amount of monies borrowed and not yet repaid by the federal government. Federal debt consists of public debt and agency debt. Public debt is the portion of the federal debt borrowed by the Treasury or the Federal Financing Bank directly from the public or from another federal fund or account. For example, the Treasury regularly borrows money from the Social Security trust fund. Public debt accounts for about 99 percent of the federal debt. Agency debt refers to the debt incurred by federal agencies such as the Export-Import

Bank but excluding the Treasury and the Federal Financing Bank, which are authorized by law to borrow funds from the public or from another government fund or account. *(See Debt Limit; Public Debt.)*

Filibuster—The use of time-consuming debate and parliamentary tactics by one member or a group of members to delay, modify, or defeat proposed legislation or rules changes. Filibusters are also sometimes used to delay urgently needed measures to force the body to consider other legislation. The Senate's rules permitting unlimited debate and the extraordinary majority it requires to invoke cloture make filibustering particularly effective in that chamber. Under the restrictive debate and other rules of the House, filibusters in that body are short-lived and infrequently attempted. *(See Cloture.)*

Fiscal Year—The federal government's annual accounting period. It begins October 1 and ends on the following September 30. A fiscal year is designated by the calendar year in which it ends and is often referred to as FY. Thus, fiscal year 2014 began October 1, 2013, ended September 30, 2014, and is called FY14. In theory, Congress is supposed to complete action on all budgetary measures applying to a fiscal year before that year begins. It rarely does so. *(See Budget.)*

Five-Minute Rule—A House rule that limits debate on an amendment offered in the Committee of the Whole to five minutes for its sponsor and five minutes for an opponent. In practice, the committee routinely permits longer debate by three devices: offering pro forma amendments, each debatable for five minutes; unanimous consent for a member to speak longer than five minutes; and special rule. Consequently, debate on an amendment could continue for hours or, more commonly today, be limited to ten or twenty minutes, with the amendment's proponent and an opponent each controlling half the time and yielding parcels of it to colleagues. In the absence of a special rule or unanimous consent, however, at any time after the first ten minutes, the committee may shut off debate immediately or by a specified time, either by unanimous consent or by majority vote on a nondebatable motion. *(See Committee of the Whole; Pro Forma Amendment; Rule.)*

Floor—The level of the House or Senate chamber where members sit and the houses conduct their business. When members are attending a meeting of their house they are said to be on the floor. Floor action refers to the procedural actions taken during floor consideration such as deciding on motions, taking up measures, amending them, and voting. *(See Chamber.)*

Floor Manager—A majority party member responsible for guiding a measure through its floor consideration in a house and for devising the political and procedural strategies that might be required to get it passed. The presiding officer gives the floor manager priority recognition to debate, offer amendments, oppose amendments, and make crucial procedural motions. The minority party member is referred to as the minority floor manager.

Frank—Informally, members' legal right to send official mail postage free under their signatures; often called the franking privilege. Technically, it is the autographic or facsimile signature used on envelopes instead of stamps that permits members and certain congressional officers to send their official mail free of charge. The franking privilege has been authorized by law since the first Congress, except for a few months in 1873. Congress reimburses the U.S. Postal Service for the franked mail it handles.

Function *or* Functional Category—A broad category of national need and spending of budgetary significance. A category provides an accounting method for allocating and keeping track of budgetary resources and expenditures for that function because it includes all budget accounts related to the function's subject or purpose such as agriculture, administration of justice, commerce and housing, and energy. Functions do not necessarily correspond with appropriations acts or with the budgets of individual agencies. As of 2013 there were twenty functional categories, each divided into a number of subfunctions. *(See Budget Resolution.)*

Gag Rule—A pejorative term for any type of special rule reported by the House Rules Committee that proposes to prohibit amendments to a measure or only permits amendments offered by the reporting committee.

Galleries—The balconies overlooking each chamber from which the public, news media, staff, and others may observe floor proceedings.

General Appropriation Bill—A term applied to each of the annual bills that provide funds for most federal agencies and programs and also to the supplemental appropriation bills that contain appropriations for more than one agency or program. *(See Appropriation.)*

Germaneness—The requirement that an amendment be closely related—in terms of subject or purpose, for example—to the text it proposes to amend. A House rule requires that all amendments be germane. In the Senate, only amendments offered to general appropriation bills and budget measures or proposed under cloture must be germane. Germaneness rules can be waived by suspension of the rules in both houses, by unanimous consent agreements in the Senate, and by special rules from the Rules Committee in the House. Moreover, presiding officers usually do not enforce germaneness rules on their own initiative; therefore, a nongermane amendment can be adopted if no member raises a point of order against it. Under cloture in the Senate, however, the chair may take the initiative to rule amendments out of order as not being germane, without a point of order being made. All House debate must be germane except during general debate in the Committee of the Whole, but special rules invariably require that such debate be "confined to the bill." The Senate requires germane debate only during the first three hours of each daily session. Under the precedents of both houses, an amendment can be relevant but not necessarily germane. A crucial factor in determining germaneness in the House is how the subject of a measure or matter is defined. For example, the subject of a measure authorizing construction of a naval vessel is defined as being the construction of a single vessel; therefore, an amendment to authorize an additional vessel is not germane.

Gerrymandering—The manipulation of legislative district boundaries to benefit a particular party, politician, or minority group. The term originated in 1812 when the Massachusetts leg-

islature redrew the lines of state legislative districts to favor the party of Gov. Elbridge Gerry, and some critics said one district resembled a salamander. *(See also Congressional District; Redistricting.)*

Government Accountability Office (GAO)—A congressional support agency, often referred to as the investigative arm of Congress. It evaluates and audits federal agencies and programs in the United States and abroad on its initiative or at the request of congressional committees or members. The office, created in 1921, was called the General Accounting Office until 2004.

Gramm-Rudman-Hollings Act of 1985—Common name for the Balanced Budget and Emergency Deficit Control Act of 1985, which established new budget procedures intended to balance the federal budget by fiscal year 1991. (The timetable subsequently was extended and then deleted.) The act's chief sponsors were senators Phil Gramm, R-Texas, Warren Rudman, R-N.H., and Ernest Hollings, D-S.C.

Grandfather Clause—A provision in a measure, law, or rule that exempts an individual, entity, or a defined category of individuals or entities from complying with a new policy or restriction. For example, a bill that would raise taxes on persons who reach the age of sixty-five after a certain date inherently grandfathers out those who are sixty-five before that date. Similarly, a Senate rule limiting senators to two major committee assignments also grandfathers some senators who were sitting on a third major committee before a specified date.

Grants-in-Aid—Payments by the federal government to state and local governments to help provide for assistance programs or public services.

Hearing—Committee or subcommittee meetings to receive testimony on proposed legislation or for oversight purposes. Relatively few bills are important enough to justify formal hearings. Witnesses often include experts, government officials, spokespersons for interested groups, officials of the Government Accountability Office, and members of Congress.

Hold-Harmless Clause—In legislation providing a new formula for allocating federal funds, a clause to ensure that recipients of those funds do not receive less in a future year than they did in the current year if the new formula would result in a reduction for them. Similar to a grandfather clause, it has been used most frequently to soften the impact of sudden reductions in federal grants. *(See Grandfather Clause.)*

Hold—A senator's request that their party leaders delay or halt floor consideration of certain legislation or presidential nominations. The majority leader usually honors a hold for a reasonable period of time, especially if its purpose is to assure the senator that the matter will not be called up during their absence or to give the senator time to gather necessary information.

Hold (or Have) the Floor—A member's right to speak without interruption, unless they violate a rule, after recognition by the presiding officer. At the member's discretion, they may yield to another member for a question in the Senate or for a question or statement in the House, but may reclaim the floor at any time.

Hopper—A box on the clerk's desk in the House chamber into which members deposit bills and resolutions to introduce them. In House jargon, to drop a bill in the hopper is to introduce it.

Hour Rule—A House rule that permits members, when recognized, to hold the floor in debate for no more than one hour each. A member recognized for one hour typically yields one-half of the time to an opposing member. In the instance of debate on a special rule, the majority party member customarily yields one-half the time to a minority member. Although the hour rule also applies to general debate in the Committee of the Whole, special rules routinely vary the length of time for such debate and its control to fit the circumstances of particular measures. *(See Rule, second definition.)*

House as in Committee of the Whole—A hybrid combination of procedures from the general rules of the House and from the rules of the Committee of the Whole, seen infrequently today and most often only when the House considers a private bill. *(See Private Bill.)*

House Calendar—The calendar reserved for all public bills and resolutions that do not raise revenue or directly or indirectly appropriate money or property when they are favorably reported by House committees.

House Manual—A commonly used title for the compilation of the rules of the House of Representatives, the Constitution, *Jefferson's Manual,* and rulemaking statutes, published in each Congress. Its official title is *Constitution, Jefferson's Manual, and Rules of the House of Representatives.*

House of Representatives—The house of Congress in which states are represented roughly in proportion to their populations, but every state is guaranteed at least one representative. By law, the number of voting representatives is fixed at 435. Five delegates and one resident commissioner also serve in the House; they may vote in their committees but not on the House floor. Although the House and Senate have equal legislative power, the Constitution gives the House sole authority to originate revenue measures. The House also claims the right to originate appropriation measures, a claim the Senate disputes in theory but concedes in practice. The House has the sole power to impeach (only the Senate convicts, however) and elects the president when no candidate has received a majority of the electoral votes. The House is sometimes referred to as the lower body. *(See Delegate; Lower Body; Representative; Resident Commissioner from Puerto Rico; Senate.)*

Immunity—(1) Members' constitutional protection from lawsuits and arrest in connection with their legislative duties. They may not be tried for libel or slander for anything they say on the floor of a house or in committee. Nor may they be arrested while attending sessions of their houses or when traveling to or from sessions of Congress, except when charged with treason, a felony, or a breach of the peace. (2) In the case of a witness before a committee, a grant of protection from prosecution based on that person's testimony to the committee. It is used to compel witnesses to testify who would otherwise refuse to do so on the constitutional ground of possible self-incrimination. Under such a grant, none of a witness's testimony may be used

against them in a court proceeding except in a prosecution for perjury or for giving a false statement to Congress. *(See also Contempt of Congress.)*

Impeachment—The first step to remove the president, the vice president, Supreme Court justices, or other federal civil officers from office and possibly to disqualify them from any future federal office "of honor, Trust or Profit." An impeachment is a formal charge of treason, bribery, or "other high Crimes and Misdemeanors." The House has the sole power of impeachment and the Senate the sole power of trying the charges and convicting. The House impeaches by a simple majority vote; conviction requires a two-thirds vote of all senators present.

Impeachment Trial, Removal, and Disqualification—The Senate conducts an impeachment trial under a separate set of twenty-six rules that appears in the *Senate Manual.* Under the Constitution, the chief justice of the Supreme Court presides over the impeachment trial of the president, but the vice president, the president pro tempore, or any other senator may preside over the impeachment trial of another official.

The Constitution requires senators to take an oath for an impeachment trial. During the trial, senators may not engage in colloquies or participate in arguments, but they may submit questions in writing to House managers or defense counsel. After the trial concludes, the Senate votes separately on each article of impeachment without debate unless the Senate orders the doors closed for private discussions. During deliberations senators may speak no more than once on a question, not for more than ten minutes on an interlocutory question and not more than fifteen minutes on the final question. These rules may be set aside by unanimous consent or suspended on motion by a two-thirds vote.

The Senate's impeachment trial of President Bill Clinton in 1999 was only the second such trial involving a president (the first being the impeachment trial of President Andrew Johnson in 1868). It continued for five weeks, with the Senate voting not to convict on the two impeachment articles.

Senate impeachment rules allow the Senate, at its discretion, to name a committee to hear evidence and conduct the trial, with all senators thereafter voting on the charges. The impeachment trials of three federal judges were conducted this way, and the Supreme Court upheld the validity of these rules in *Nixon v. United States* (506 U.S. 224, 1993).

An official convicted on impeachment charges is removed from office immediately. However, the convicted official is not barred from holding a federal office in the future unless the Senate, after its conviction vote, also approves a resolution disqualifying the convicted official from future office. For example, federal judge Alcee L. Hastings was impeached and convicted in 1989, but the Senate did not vote to bar him from office in the future. In 1992 Hastings was elected to the House of Representatives, and no challenge was raised against seating him when he took the oath of office in 1993.

Impoundment—An executive branch action or inaction that delays or withholds the expenditure or obligation of budget authority provided by law. The Impoundment Control Act of 1974 classifies impoundments as either deferrals or rescissions, requires the president to notify Congress about all such actions, and gives Congress authority to approve or reject them. *(See*

Congressional Budget and Impoundment Control Act of 1974; Deferral; Rescission.)

Inspector General in the House of Representatives—A position established with the passage of the House Administrative Reform Resolution of 1992. The duties of the office have been revised several times and are now contained in House Rule II. The inspector general (IG), who is subject to the policy direction and oversight of the Committee on House Administration, is appointed for a Congress jointly by the Speaker and the majority and minority leaders of the House. The IG communicates the results of audits to the House officers or officials who were the subjects of the audits and suggests appropriate corrective measures. The IG submits a report of each audit to the Speaker, the majority and minority leaders, and the chair and ranking minority member of the House Administration Committee; notifies these five members in the case of any financial irregularity discovered; and reports to the Committee on Ethics on possible violations of House rules or any applicable law by any House member, officer, or employee. The IG's office also has certain duties to audit various financial operations of the House that had previously been performed by the Government Accountability Office.

Instruct Conferees—A formal action by a house urging its conferees to uphold a particular position on a measure in conference. The instruction may be to insist on certain provisions in the measure as passed by that house or to accept a provision in the version passed by the other house. Instructions to conferees are not binding because the primary responsibility of conferees is to reach agreement on a measure and neither house can compel the other to accept particular provisions or positions.

Investigative Power—The authority of Congress and its committees to pursue investigations, upheld by the Supreme Court but limited to matters related to, and in furtherance of, a legitimate task of the Congress. Standing committees in both houses are permanently authorized to investigate matters within their jurisdictions. Major investigations are sometimes conducted by temporary select, special, or joint committees established by resolutions for that purpose.

Some rules of the House provide certain safeguards for witnesses and others during investigative hearings. These permit counsel to accompany witnesses, require that each witness receive a copy of the committee's rules, and order the committee to go into closed session if it believes the testimony to be heard might defame, degrade, or incriminate any person. The committee may subsequently decide to hear such testimony in open session. There are no Senate rules of this kind.

Item Veto—Item veto authority, which is available in some form to most state governors, allows governors to eliminate or reduce items in legislative measures presented for their signature without vetoing the entire measure, and sign the rest into law. A similar authority was briefly granted to the U.S. president under the Line Item Veto Act of 1996. According to the majority opinion of the Supreme Court in its 1998 decision *Clinton v. City of New York* (524 U.S. 417) overturning that law, a constitutional amendment would be necessary to give the president such veto authority. *(See Line Item; Line Item Veto Act of 1996.)*

Jefferson's Manual—Short title of *Jefferson's Manual of Parliamentary Practice,* prepared by Thomas Jefferson for his guidance when he was president of the Senate from 1797 to 1801. Although it reflects English parliamentary practice in his day, many procedures in both houses of Congress are still rooted in its precepts. Under a House rule adopted in 1837, the manual's provisions govern House procedures when applicable and when they are not inconsistent with its standing rules and orders. The Senate, however, has never officially acknowledged it as a direct authority for its legislative procedure.

Johnson Rule—A policy instituted in 1953 under which all Democratic senators are assigned to one major committee before any Democrat is assigned to two. The Johnson Rule is named after its author, Sen. Lyndon B. Johnson, D-Texas, then the Senate's Democratic leader. Senate Republicans adopted a similar policy soon thereafter.

Joint Committee—A committee composed of members selected from each house. The functions of contemporary joint committees involve investigation, research, or oversight of agencies or activities closely related to congressional work, although they might have regulatory authority over a legislative branch agency or function. Permanent joint committees, created by statute, are sometimes called standing joint committees. Only four joint committees existed as of 2013: Joint Economic, Joint Taxation, Joint Library, and Joint Printing. None has authority to report legislation.

Joint Explanatory Statement—This is a statement appended to a conference report that explains in plain English the conference agreement and the intent of the conferees.

Joint Resolution—A legislative measure that Congress uses for special purposes based on tradition. Similar to a bill, a joint resolution has the force of law when passed by both houses and either approved by the president or passed over the president's veto. Unlike a bill, a joint resolution enacted into law is not called an act; it retains its original title. Most often, joint resolutions deal with such relatively limited matters as the correction of errors in existing law, a single appropriation, or the establishment of permanent joint committees. They are also used for important matters such as declaring war or providing continuing appropriations and to carry out fast-track procedures included by Congress in some statutes. Joint resolutions, in addition, are used to propose constitutional amendments, which are submitted to the states for ratification when approved by a two-thirds vote in each house of Congress; these joint resolutions do not require the president's signature and become effective only when ratified by three-fourths of the states. The House designates joint resolutions as "H. J. Res." and the Senate as "S. J. Res." Each house numbers its joint resolutions consecutively in the order of introduction during a two-year Congress. Unless passed by both chambers in identical form before the end of a two-year Congress, joint resolutions die with the Congress's *sine die* adjournment. *(See Bill; Continuing Resolution; Fast Track.)*

Joint Session—Informally, any combined meeting of the Senate and the House. Technically, a joint session is a combined meeting to count the electoral votes for president and vice president or to hear a presidential address, such as the State of the Union message; any other formal combined gathering of both houses is a joint meeting. Joint sessions are authorized by concurrent resolutions and are held in the House chamber, because of its larger seating capacity. Although the president of the Senate and the Speaker sit side by side at the Speaker's desk during combined meetings, the former presides over the electoral count and the latter presides on all other occasions and introduces the president or other guest speaker. The president and other guests may address a joint session or meeting only by invitation.

Joint Sponsorship—Two or more members sponsoring the same measure.

Journal—The official record of House or Senate actions, including every motion offered, every vote cast, amendments agreed to, quorum calls, and so forth. Unlike the *Congressional Record,* it does not provide reports of speeches, debates, statements, and other items. The Constitution requires each house to maintain a *Journal* and to publish it periodically. *(See Congressional Record.)*

Junket—A derisive term for a member's trip at government expense, especially abroad, on official business but, it is often alleged, for pleasure.

Killer Amendment—An amendment that, if agreed to, might lead to the defeat of the measure it amends, either in the house in which the amendment is offered or at some later stage of the legislative process. Also called a poison-pill amendment. Members sometimes deliberately offer or vote for such an amendment in the expectation that it will undermine support for the measure in Congress or increase the likelihood that the president will veto it.

King of the Mountain (or Hill Rule)—*(See Queen of the Hill Rule.)*

LA—*(See Legislative Assistant.)*

Lame Duck—Jargon for a member who has not been reelected, or did not seek reelection, and is serving the balance of their term.

Lame Duck Session—A session of a Congress held after the election for the succeeding Congress, so-called after the lame duck members still serving.

Last Train Out—Colloquial name for last must-pass bill of a session of Congress.

Law—An act of Congress (in the form of a bill or joint resolution, the latter of which is not a constitutional amendment) that has been signed by the president, passed over the president's veto, or allowed by the president to become law without his signature.

Lay on the Table—A motion to dispose of a pending proposition immediately, finally, and adversely; that is, to kill it without a direct vote on its substance. Often simply called a motion to table,

it is not debatable and is adopted by majority vote or without objection. It is a highly privileged motion, taking precedence over all others except the motion to adjourn in the House and all but three additional motions in the Senate. It can kill a bill or resolution, an amendment, another motion, an appeal, or virtually any other matter.

Tabling an amendment also tables the measure to which the amendment is pending in the House, but not in the Senate. The House does not allow the motion against the motion to recommit, in the Committee of the Whole, and in some other situations. In the Senate it is the only permissible motion that immediately ends debate on a proposition, but only to kill it.

(The) Leadership—Usually, a reference to the majority and minority leaders of the Senate or to the Speaker and minority leader of the House. The term sometimes includes the majority leader in the House and the majority and minority whips in each house and, at other times, other party officials as well.

Legislation—(1) A synonym for legislative measures: bills and joint resolutions. (2) Provisions in such measures or in substantive amendments offered to them. (3) In some contexts, provisions that change existing substantive or authorizing law, rather than provisions that make appropriations.

Legislation on an Appropriation Bill—A common reference to provisions changing existing law that appear in, or are offered as amendments to, a general appropriation bill. A House rule prohibits the inclusion of such provisions in general appropriation bills unless they retrench expenditures. An analogous Senate rule permits points of order against amendments to a general appropriation bill that propose general legislation. In both chambers, such prohibitions may be waived by procedures such as special rules in the House, by failure of any member to make a point of order against such a provision, or by other means. *(See Authorization-Appropriation Process.)*

Legislative Assistant (LA)—A member's staff person responsible for monitoring and preparing legislation on particular subjects and for advising the member on them; commonly referred to as an LA. Today, members' offices typically employ a legislative director (LD) to oversee an office's LAs.

Legislative Day—The day that begins when a house meets after an adjournment and ends when it next adjourns. Because the House of Representatives normally adjourns at the end of a daily session, its legislative and calendar days usually coincide. The Senate, however, might recess at the end of a daily session, and its legislative day may extend over several calendar days or longer. Among other uses, this technicality permits the Senate to continue for procedural purposes on the same day or to save time by circumventing its morning hour, a procedure required at the beginning of every legislative day.

Legislative History—(1) A chronological list of actions taken on a measure during its progress through the legislative process. (2) The official documents relating to a measure, the entries in the *Journals* of the two houses on that measure, and the *Congressional Record* text of its consideration in both houses. The documents include all committee reports and the conference report and joint explanatory statement, if any. Courts and affected federal agencies might study a measure's legislative history for congressional intent about its purpose and interpretation.

Legislative Process—(1) Narrowly, the stages in the enactment of a law from introduction to final disposition. An introduced measure that becomes law typically travels through reference to committee; committee and subcommittee consideration; committee report to the chamber; floor consideration and amendment; passage; engrossment; messaging to the other house; similar steps in that house, including floor amendment of the measure; return of the measure to the first house; consideration of amendments between the houses or a conference to resolve their differences; approval of the conference report by both houses; enrollment; approval by the president or override of the president's veto; and deposit with the Archivist of the United States. (2) Broadly, the political, lobbying, and other factors that affect or influence the process of enacting laws.

Legislative Veto—A procedure, declared unconstitutional in 1983, that allowed Congress or one of its houses to nullify certain actions of the president, executive branch agencies, or independent agencies. Sometimes called congressional vetoes or congressional disapprovals. Following the Supreme Court's 1983 decision in *Immigration and Naturalization Service v. Chadha* (462 U.S. 919), Congress amended several legislative veto statutes to require enactment of joint resolutions, which are subject to presidential veto, for nullifying executive branch actions. Alternately, Congress may include in a statute a provision requiring congressional approval of a proposed executive action before its implementation. *(See Committee Veto.)*

Limitation on a General Appropriation Bill—Language that prohibits expenditures for part of an authorized purpose from funds provided in a general appropriation bill. Precedents require that the language be phrased in the negative: that none of the funds provided in a pending appropriation bill shall be used for a specified authorized activity. Limitations in general appropriation bills are permitted on the grounds that Congress can refuse to fund authorized programs and, therefore, can refuse to fund any part of them as long as the prohibition does not change existing law. House precedents have established that a limitation does not change existing law if it does not impose additional duties or burdens on executive branch officials, interfere with their discretionary authority, or require them to make judgments or determinations not required by existing law. The proliferation of limitation amendments in the 1970s and early 1980s prompted the House to adopt a rule in 1983 making it more difficult for members to offer them. The rule bans such amendments during the reading of an appropriation bill for amendment, unless they are specifically authorized in existing law. Other limitations may be offered after the reading, but the Committee of the Whole can foreclose them by adopting a motion to rise and report the bill back to the House. In 1995 the rule was amended to allow the motion to rise and report to be made only by the majority leader or their designee. The House Appropriations Committee, however, can include limitation provisions in the bills it reports.

Line Item—An amount in an appropriation measure. It can refer to a single appropriation account or to separate amounts within the account. In the congressional budget process, the term

usually refers to assumptions about the funding of particular programs or accounts that underlie the broad functional amounts in a budget resolution. These assumptions are discussed in the reports accompanying each resolution and are not binding.

Line Item Veto Act of 1996—A law, in effect only from January 1997 until June 1998, that granted the president authority intended to be functionally equivalent to an item veto, by amending the Impoundment Control Act to incorporate an approach known as enhanced rescission. Key provisions established a new procedure that permitted the president to cancel amounts of new discretionary appropriations (budget authority), new items of direct spending (entitlements), or certain limited tax benefits. It also required the president to notify Congress of the cancellation in a special message within five calendar days after signing the measure. The cancellation would become permanent unless legislation disapproving it was enacted within thirty days. On June 25, 1998, in *Clinton v. City of New York* (524 U.S. 417) the Supreme Court held the Line Item Veto Act unconstitutional, on the grounds that its cancellation provisions violated the presentment clause in Article I, clause 7, of the Constitution. *(See Item Veto; Line Item.)*

Line-Item Veto—*(See Item Veto; Line Item Veto Act of 1996.)*

Live Pair—A voluntary and informal agreement between two members on opposite sides of an issue, one of whom is absent for a recorded vote, under which the member who is present withholds or withdraws their vote to offset the failure to vote by the member who is absent. Usually the member in attendance announces that they have a live pair, states how each would have voted, and votes "present." In the House, under a rules change enacted in the 106th Congress, a live pair is only permitted on the rare occasions when electronic voting is not used.

Live Quorum—In the Senate, a quorum call to which senators are expected to respond. Senators usually suggest the absence of a quorum, not to force a quorum to appear, but to provide a pause in the proceedings during which senators can engage in private discussions or wait for a senator to come to the floor (a "dead quorum"). A senator desiring a live quorum usually announces their intention, giving fair warning that there will be an objection to any unanimous consent request that the quorum call be dispensed with before it is completed.

Loan Guarantee—A statutory commitment by the federal government to pay part or all of a loan's principal or interest or both to a lender or the holder of a security in case the borrower defaults.

Lobby—To try to persuade members of Congress to propose, pass, modify, or defeat proposed legislation or to change or repeal existing laws. Lobbyists attempt to promote their preferences or those of a group, organization, or industry. Originally the term referred to persons frequenting the lobbies or corridors of legislative chambers in order to speak to lawmakers. In a general sense, lobbying includes not only direct contact with members but also indirect attempts to influence them, such as writing to them or persuading others to write or visit them, attempting to mold public opinion toward a desired legislative goal by various means, and contributing or arranging for contributions to members' election campaigns. The right to lobby stems from the First Amendment to the Constitution, which bans laws that abridge the right of the people to petition the government for a redress of grievances.

Lobbying Disclosure Act of 1995—The principal statute requiring disclosure of—and also, to a degree, circumscribing—the activities of lobbyists. In general, it requires lobbyists who spend more than 20 percent of their time on lobbying activities to register and make semiannual reports of their activities to the clerk of the House and the secretary of the Senate, although the law provides for a number of exemptions. Among the statute's prohibitions, lobbyists are not allowed to make contributions to the legal defense fund of a member or high government official or to reimburse for official travel. Civil penalties for failure to comply may include fines. The act does not include grassroots lobbying in its definition of lobbying activities.

The act amended several other lobby laws, notably the Foreign Agents Registration Act (FARA), so that lobbyists can submit a single filing. The 1995 act repealed the 1946 Federal Regulation of Lobbying Act.

Logrolling—Jargon for a legislative tactic or bargaining strategy in which members try to build support for their legislation by promising to support legislation desired by other members or by accepting amendments they hope will induce their colleagues to vote for their bill.

Lower Body—A way to refer to the House of Representatives, which is sometimes considered pejorative by House members. One source of this designation is the design of the capitol in colonial Williamsburg. The House of Burgesses met in a chamber on the ground floor of the capitol; the Council met in a chamber on the second floor above the Burgesses's chamber.

Mace—The symbol of the authority of the House and entrusted to the office of the House sergeant at arms. Under the direction of the Speaker, the sergeant at arms is responsible for preserving order on the House floor by holding up the mace in front of an unruly member, or by carrying the mace up and down the aisles to quell boisterous behavior. When the House is in session, the mace sits on a pedestal at the Speaker's right; when the House is in Committee of the Whole, it is moved to a lower pedestal. The mace is forty-six inches high and consists of thirteen ebony rods bound in silver and topped by a silver globe with a silver eagle, wings outstretched, perched on it.

Majority Leader—The majority party's chief floor strategist, elected by that party's caucus, sometimes called floor leader. In the Senate, the majority leader develops the party's political and procedural strategy, usually in collaboration with other party officials and committee chairs, and serves as their party's principal spokesperson. The majority leader negotiates the Senate's agenda and committee ratios with the minority leader and usually calls up measures for floor action. The chamber traditionally concedes to the majority leader the right to determine the days on which it will meet and the hours at which it will convene and adjourn. In the House, the majority leader is the Speaker's deputy and possibly heir apparent, helps plan the floor agenda, leads the party's legislative strategy, and often speaks for the party leadership in debate. *(See (The) Leadership.)*

Majority Staff—*(See Committee Staff.)*

Managers—(1) The official title of members appointed to a conference committee, commonly called conferees. The ranking majority and minority managers for each house also manage floor consideration of the committee's conference report. (2) The members who manage the initial floor consideration of a measure. (3) The official title of House members appointed to present impeachment articles to the Senate and to act as prosecutors on behalf of the House during the Senate trial of the impeached person. *(See Conferees; Floor Manager; Impeachment Trial, Removal, and Disqualification.)*

Mandatory Appropriations—Amounts that Congress must appropriate annually because it has no discretion over them unless it first amends existing substantive law. Certain entitlement programs, for example, require annual appropriations. *(See Appropriated Entitlement.)*

Markup—A meeting or series of meetings by a committee or subcommittee during which members mark up a measure by offering, debating, and voting on amendments to it.

Means-Tested Programs—Programs that provide benefits or services to low-income individuals who meet a test of need. Most are entitlement programs, such as Medicaid, food stamps, and Supplementary Security Income. A few—for example, subsidized housing and various social services—are funded through discretionary appropriations.

Members' Allowances—Official expenses that are paid for or for which members are reimbursed by their houses. Among these are the costs of office space in their home states or districts; office equipment and supplies; postage-free mailings (the franking privilege); a set number of trips to and from home states or districts, as well as travel elsewhere on official business; telephone and other telecommunications services; and staff salaries. Other cost items are not allocated to individual members, such as the cost of offices in the congressional office buildings in Washington, D.C., or staff overhead such as health insurance, life insurance, and retirement.

Member's Staff—The personal staff to which a member is entitled. The House sets a maximum number of staff and a monetary allowance equal for each representative. The Senate does not set a maximum staff level, but it does set a monetary allowance for each senator based on the population of a senator's state. In each house, the staff allowance is included with office expense allowances and other allowances such as travel and mail in a consolidated allowance. Representatives and senators can generally spend as much money in their consolidated allowances for staff, office expenses, or other allowable expenses, as long as they do not exceed the monetary value of the consolidated allowance. This provides members with flexibility in operating their offices.

Method of Equal Proportions—The mathematical formula used since 1950 to determine how the 435 seats in the House of Representatives should be distributed among the fifty states in the apportionment following each decennial census. It minimizes as much as possible the proportional difference between the average district population in any two states. Because the Constitution guarantees each state at least one representative, fifty seats are automatically apportioned. The formula calculates priority numbers for each state, assigns the first of the 385 remaining seats to the state with the highest priority number, the second to the state with the next highest number, and so on until all seats are distributed. *(See Apportionment.)*

Midterm Elections—The general elections for members of Congress that occur in November of the second year in a presidential term.

Minority Leader—The minority party's leader and chief, strategist and spokesperson, elected by the party caucus; sometimes called minority floor leader. With the assistance of other party officials and the ranking minority members of committees, the minority leader devises the party's political and procedural strategy. *(See (The) Leadership.)*

Minority Staff—*(See Committee Staff.)*

Modified Rule—A special rule from the House Rules Committee that permits only certain amendments to be offered to a measure during its floor consideration or that bans certain specified amendments or amendments on certain subjects. Also referred to as a structured rule or a restrictive rule. *(See Rule, second definition.)*

Morning Business—In the Senate, routine business that is to be transacted at the beginning of the morning hour. The business consists, first, of laying before the Senate, and referring to committees, matters such as messages from the president and the House, federal agency reports, and unreferred petitions, memorials, bills, and joint resolutions. Next, senators may present additional petitions and memorials. Then committees may present their reports, after which senators may introduce bills and resolutions. Finally, resolutions coming over from a previous day are taken up for consideration. In practice, the Senate adopts standing orders that permit senators to introduce measures and file reports at any time, but only if there has been a morning business period on that day. Because the Senate often remains in the same legislative day for several days, it orders a morning business period almost every calendar day for the convenience of senators who wish to introduce measures or make reports. *(See Legislative Day; Morning Hour.)*

Morning Hour—A two-hour period at the beginning of a new legislative day during which the Senate is supposed to conduct routine business, call the calendar on Mondays, and deal with other matters described in a Senate rule. In practice, the morning hour rarely, if ever, occurs because the Senate today typically agrees to a period for morning business for its next meeting in a unanimous consent agreement at the end of a daily session. If the Senate recesses at the end of day rather than adjourns, the rule requiring morning hour does not apply when the Senate next meets. The Senate's rules reserve the first hour of the morning for morning business. After the completion of morning business, or at the end of the first hour, the rules permit a motion to proceed to the consideration of a measure on the calendar out of its regular order (except on Mondays). Because that normally debatable motion is not debatable if offered during the morning hour, the majority leader may, but rarely does, use

this procedure in anticipating a filibuster on the motion to proceed. If the Senate agrees to the motion, it can consider the measure until the end of the morning hour, and if there is no unfinished business from the previous day the Senate can continue considering it after the morning hour. But if there is unfinished business, a motion to continue consideration is necessary, and that motion is debatable. *(See Legislative Day; Morning Business.)*

Motion—A formal proposal for a procedural action, such as to consider, to amend, to lay on the table, to reconsider, to recess, or to adjourn. It has been estimated that at least eighty-five motions are possible under various circumstances in the House of Representatives, somewhat fewer in the Senate. Not all motions are created equal; some are privileged or preferential and enjoy priority over others. Some motions are debatable, amendable, or divisible, while others are not.

Multiple and Sequential Referrals—The practice of referring a measure to two or more committees for joint consideration (multiple referral) or successively to several committees in sequence (sequential referral). A measure may also be divided into several parts, with each referred to a different committee or to several committees sequentially (split referral). In theory this gives all committees that have jurisdiction over parts of a measure the opportunity to consider and report on them.

Before 1975, House precedents banned such referrals. A 1975 rule required the Speaker to make concurrent and sequential referrals "to the maximum extent feasible." On sequential referrals, the Speaker could set deadlines for reporting the measure. The Speaker ruled that this provision authorized him to discharge a committee from further consideration of a measure and place it on the appropriate calendar of the House if the committee failed to meet the Speaker's deadline. In 1995 joint referrals were prohibited. Measures are referred to a primary committee and also may be referred, either additionally or sequentially, to one or more other committees, but usually only for consideration of portions of the measure that fall within the jurisdiction of each of those other committees. In 2003, the Speaker was authorized to not designate a primary committee under "extraordinary circumstances."

In the Senate, before 1977 joint and sequential referrals were permitted only by unanimous consent. In that year, a rule authorized a privileged motion for such a referral if offered jointly by the majority and minority leaders. Debate on the motion and all amendments to it is limited to two hours. The motion may set deadlines for reporting and provide for discharging the committees involved if they fail to meet the deadlines. To date, this procedure has never been invoked; multiple referrals in the Senate, if made, continue to be made by unanimous consent.

Multiyear Appropriation—An appropriation that remains available for spending or obligation for more than one fiscal year; the exact period of time is specified in the act making the appropriation. *(See Appropriation.)*

Multiyear Authorization—(1) Legislation that authorizes the existence or continuation of an agency, program, or activity for more than one fiscal year. (2) Legislation that authorizes appropriations for an agency, program, or activity for more than one fiscal year. *(See Authorization.)*

Nomination—A proposed presidential appointment to a federal office submitted to the Senate for confirmation. Approval is by majority vote. The Constitution explicitly requires Senate confirmation for ambassadors, consuls, "public Ministers" (department heads), and Supreme Court justices. By law, other federal judges, all military promotions of officers, and many high-level civilian officials must be confirmed by the Senate. *(See Executive Calendar.)*

Nuclear Option—A popular name for a parliamentary maneuver to interpret Senate rules to allow the Senate to limit debate on most nominations by a simple majority rather than the sixty votes that had previously been required. The Senate invoked this option in 2013. Also referred to as the constitutional option.

Oath of Office—On taking office, members of Congress must swear or affirm that they will "support and defend the Constitution . . . against all enemies, foreign and domestic," that they will "bear true faith and allegiance" to the Constitution, that they take the obligation "freely, without any mental reservation or purpose of evasion," and that they will "well and faithfully discharge the duties" of their office. The oath is required by the Constitution, and the wording is prescribed by a statute. All House members must take the oath at the beginning of each new Congress. Usually, the member with the longest continuous service in the House swears in the Speaker, who then swears in the other members. The president of the Senate (the vice president of the United States) or a surrogate administers the oath to newly elected or reelected senators.

Obligation—A binding agreement by a government agency to pay for goods, products, services, studies, and so on, either immediately or in the future. When an agency enters into such an agreement, it incurs an obligation. As the agency makes the required payments, it liquidates the obligation. Appropriation laws usually make funds available for obligation for one or more fiscal years but do not require agencies to spend their funds during those specific years. The actual outlays can occur years after the appropriation is obligated, as with a contract for construction of a submarine may provide for payment to be made when it is delivered in the future. Such obligated funds are often said to be "in the pipeline." Under these circumstances, an agency's outlays in a particular year can come from appropriations obligated in previous years as well as from its current-year appropriation. Consequently, the money Congress appropriates for a fiscal year does not equal the total amount of appropriated money the government will actually spend in that year. *(See Budget Authority; Outlays.)*

Off-Budget Entities—Specific federal entities whose budget authority, outlays, and receipts are excluded by law from the calculation of budget totals, although they are part of government spending and income. As of 2005, these included the Social Security trust funds (Federal Old-Age and Survivors Insurance Fund and the Federal Disability Insurance Trust Fund) and the Postal Service. Government-sponsored enterprises are also excluded from the budget because they are considered private rather than public organizations.

Office of Management and Budget (OMB)—A unit in the Executive Office of the President, reconstituted in 1990 from the former Bureau of the Budget. The Office of Management and Budget (OMB) assists the president in preparing the budget and in formulating the government's fiscal program. The OMB also plays a central role in supervising and controlling implementation of the budget, pursuant to provisions in appropriations laws and other statutes. In addition to these budgetary functions, the OMB has various management duties, including those performed through its three statutory offices: Federal Financial Management, Federal Procurement Policy, and Information and Regulatory Affairs.

Officers of Congress—The Constitution refers to the Speaker of the House and the president of the Senate as officers and declares that each house "shall chuse" its "other Officers," but it does not name them or indicate how they should be selected. A House rule refers to its clerk, sergeant at arms, and chaplain as officers. Officers are not named in the Senate's rules, but *Riddick's Senate Procedure* lists the president pro tempore, secretary of the Senate, sergeant at arms, chaplain, and the secretaries for the majority and minority parties as officers. A few appointed officials are sometimes referred to as officers, including the parliamentarians and the legislative counsels. The House elects its officers by resolution at the beginning of each Congress. The Senate also elects its officers, but once elected, Senate officers serve from Congress to Congress until their successors are chosen, following a change in party control or an individual officer's death or retirement. *(See Clerk of the House; Parliamentarian; President Pro Tempore; Secretary of the Senate; Sergeant at Arms; Speaker.)*

Official Objectors—House members who screen measures on the Private Calendar and decide whether or not to object to the consideration of any one or more of them. *(See Private Bill.)*

Omnibus Bill—A measure that combines the provisions of several disparate subjects into a single and often lengthy bill. Omnibus appropriations bills have become commonplace in recent years.

One-Minute Speeches—Addresses by House members that can be on any subject but are limited to one minute. They are usually permitted at the beginning of a daily session after the chaplain's prayer, the pledge of allegiance, and approval of the *Journal,* although they may be permitted at other times, such as at the conclusion of legislative business. They are a customary practice, not a right granted by rule. Consequently, recognition for one-minute speeches requires unanimous consent and is entirely within the Speaker's discretion. The Speaker sometimes does not permit them when the House has a heavy legislative schedule, or limits or postpones them until a later time of the day.

Open Rule—A special rule from the House Rules Committee that permits members to offer as many floor amendments as they wish as long as the amendments are germane and do not violate other House rules. *(See Rule, second definition.)*

Order of Business (House)—The sequence of events prescribed by a House rule during the meeting of the House on a new legislative day, also called the general order of business. The sequence consists of (1) the chaplain's prayer, (2) reading and approval of the *Journal,* (3) the pledge of allegiance, (4) correction of the reference of public bills to committee, (5) disposal of business on the Speaker's table, (6) unfinished business, (7) the morning hour call of committees and consideration of their bills, (8) motions to go into Committee of the Whole, and (9) orders of the day. In practice, the House never fully complies with this rule. Instead, the items of business that follow the pledge of allegiance are supplanted by any special orders of business that are in order on that day (for example, conference reports; the discharge or private calendars; or motions to suspend the rules) and by other privileged business (for example, general appropriation bills and special rules) or measures made in order by special rules or unanimous consent. The regular order of business is also modified by unanimous consent practices and orders that govern recognition for one-minute speeches (which date from 1937) and for morning-hour debates, begun in 1994. By this combination of an order of business with privileged interruptions, the House gives precedence to certain categories of important legislation, brings to the floor other major legislation from its calendars in any order it chooses, and provides expeditious processing for minor and noncontroversial measures.

Order of Business (Senate)—The sequence of events at the beginning of a new legislative day, as prescribed by Senate rules and standing orders. The sequence consists of (1) the chaplain's prayer, (2) the pledge of allegiance, (3) the designation of a temporary presiding officer if any, (4) *Journal* reading and approval, (5) recognition of the majority and minority leaders or their designees under the standing order adopted by unanimous consent at the beginning of each Congress, (6) morning business in the morning hour, (7) call of the calendar during the morning hour (largely obsolete), and (8) unfinished business from the previous session day.

Organization of Congress—The actions each house takes at the beginning of a Congress that are necessary to its operations. These include swearing in newly elected members, notifying the president that a quorum of each house is present, making committee assignments, and fixing the hour for daily meetings. Because the House of Representatives is not a continuing body, it must also elect its Speaker and other officers and adopt its rules.

Original Bill—(1) A measure drafted by a committee and introduced by its chair or another designated member when the committee reports the measure to its house. Unlike a clean bill, it is not referred back to the committee after introduction. The Senate permits all its legislative committees to report original bills. In the House, this authority is referred to in the rules as the "right to report at any time," and five committees (Appropriations, Budget, House Administration, Rules, and Ethics) have such authority under circumstances specified in House Rule XIII, clause 5.

(2) In the House, special rules reported by the Rules Committee often propose that an amendment in the nature of a substitute be considered as an original bill for purposes of amendment, meaning that the substitute, as with a bill, may be amended in two degrees. Without that requirement, the substitute may only be amended in one further degree. In the Senate, an amendment in the nature of a substitute automatically is open to two degrees of amendment, as is the original text of the bill, if the substitute is offered when no other amendment is pending.

Original Jurisdiction—The authority of certain committees to originate a measure and report it to the chamber. For example, general appropriation bills reported by the House Appropriations Committee are original bills, and special rules reported by the House Rules Committee are original resolutions.

Other Body—A commonly used reference to a chamber by a member of the other chamber. Congressional comity discourages members from directly naming the other chamber during debate.

Outlays—Amounts of government spending. They consist of payments, usually by check or in cash, to liquidate obligations incurred in prior fiscal years as well as in the current year, including the net lending of funds under budget authority. In federal budget accounting, net outlays are calculated by subtracting the amounts of refunds and various kinds of reimbursements to the government from actual spending. *(See Budget Authority; Obligation.)*

Override a Veto—Congressional enactment of a measure over the president's veto. A veto override requires a recorded two-thirds vote of those voting in each house, a quorum being present. Because the president must return the vetoed measure to its house of origin, that house votes first, but neither house is required to attempt an override, whether immediately or at all. If an override attempt fails in the house of origin, the veto stands and the measure dies.

Oversight—Congressional review of the way in which federal agencies implement laws to ensure that they are carrying out the intent of Congress and to inquire into the efficiency of the implementation and the effectiveness of the law. The Legislative Reorganization Act of 1946 defined oversight as the function of exercising continuous watchfulness over the execution of the laws by the executive branch.

Parliamentarian—The official advisor to the presiding officer in each house on questions of procedure. The parliamentarian and their assistants also answer procedural questions from members and congressional staff, refer measures to committees on behalf of the presiding officer, and maintain compilations of the precedents. The House parliamentarian revises the House Manual at the beginning of every Congress and usually reviews special rules before the Rules Committee reports them to the House. Either a parliamentarian or an assistant is always present and near the podium during sessions of each house.

Party Caucus—Generic term for each party's official organization in each house. Only House Democrats officially call their organization a caucus. House and Senate Republicans and Senate Democrats call their organizations conferences. The party caucuses elect their leaders, approve committee assignments and chairmanships (or ranking minority members if the party is in the minority), establish party committees and study groups, and discuss party and legislative policies. On rare occasions, they have stripped members of committee seniority or expelled them from the caucus for party disloyalty. *(See Caucus.)*

Pay-as-You-Go (PAYGO)—A provision first instituted under the Budget Enforcement Act of 1990 that applies to legislation enacted before October 1, 2002. It requires that the cumulative effect of legislation concerning either revenues or direct spending should not result in a net negative impact on the budget. If legislation does provide for an increase in spending or decrease in revenues, that effect is supposed to be offset by legislated spending reductions or revenue increases. If Congress fails to enact the appropriate offsets, the act requires presidential sequestration of sufficient offsetting amounts in specific direct spending accounts. Congress and the president can circumvent this requirement if both agree that an emergency requires a particular action or if a law is enacted declaring that deteriorated economic circumstances make it necessary to suspend the requirement.

Permanent Appropriation—An appropriation that remains continuously available, without current action or renewal by Congress, under the terms of a previously enacted authorization or appropriation law. One such appropriation provides for payment of interest on the public debt and another the salaries of members of Congress. *(See Appropriation.)*

Permanent Authorization—An authorization without a time limit. It usually does not specify any limit on the funds that may be appropriated for the agency, program, or activity that it authorizes, leaving such amounts to the discretion of the appropriations committees and the two houses. *(See Authorization.)*

Personally Obnoxious (or Objectionable)—A characterization a senator sometimes applies to a president's nominee for a federal office in that senator's state to justify their opposition to the nomination.

Pocket Veto—The indirect veto of a bill as a result of the president withholding approval of it until after Congress has adjourned *sine die*. A bill the president does not sign but does not formally veto while Congress is in session automatically becomes a law ten days (excluding Sundays) after it is received. But if Congress adjourns its annual session during that ten-day period, the measure dies even if the president does not formally veto it.

Point of Order—A parliamentary term used in committee and on the floor to object to an alleged violation of a rule and to demand that the chair enforce the rule. The point of order immediately halts the proceedings until the chair decides whether the contention is valid. In some instances, a member may be able to reserve a point of order, hear the proponent's argument, and then insist on or withdraw the point of order. If the point of order is insisted on, the chair must rule.

Pork or Pork Barrel Legislation—Pejorative terms for federal appropriations, bills, or policies that provide funds to benefit a legislator's district or state, with the implication that the legislator presses for enactment of such benefits to ingratiate themself with constituents rather than on the basis of an impartial, objective assessment of need or merit. The terms are often applied to such benefits as new parks, federal office buildings, dams, canals, bridges, roads, water projects, sewage treatment plants, and public works of any kind, as well as demonstration projects, research grants, and relocation of government facilities. Funds released by the president for various kinds of benefits or government contracts approved by them allegedly for political purposes are also sometimes referred to as pork. *(See Earmark.)*

Postcloture Filibuster—A filibuster conducted after the Senate invokes cloture. It employs an array of procedural tactics rather than lengthy speeches to delay final action. The Senate curtailed the post-cloture filibuster's effectiveness by closing a variety of loopholes in the cloture rule in 1979 and 1986. *(See Cloture.)*

Power of the Purse—A reference to the constitutional power Congress has over legislation to raise revenue and appropriate monies from the Treasury. Article I, Section 8, states that Congress "shall have Power To lay and collect Taxes, Duties, Imposts and Excises, [and] to pay the Debts." Section 9 declares, "No Money shall be drawn from the Treasury, but in Consequence of Appropriations made by Law."

Preamble—Introductory language describing the reasons for and intent of a measure, sometimes called a whereas clause. It occasionally appears in joint, concurrent, and simple resolutions but rarely in bills.

Precedent—A previous ruling on a parliamentary matter or a long-standing practice or custom of a house. Precedents serve to control arbitrary rulings and serve as the common law of a house.

President of the Senate—One constitutional role of the vice president is serving as the president of the Senate, its presiding officer. The Constitution permits the vice president to cast a vote in the Senate only to break a tie, but the vice president is not required to do so.

President Pro Tempore—Under the Constitution, an officer elected by the Senate to preside over it during the absence of the vice president of the United States. Often referred to as the "pro tem," this senator is usually the member of the majority party with the longest continuous service in the chamber and may also be, by virtue of seniority, a committee chair. When attending to committee and other duties, the president pro tempore appoints other, usually junior, senators to preside.

Presiding Officer—In a formal meeting, the individual authorized to maintain order and decorum, recognize members to speak or offer motions, and apply and interpret the chamber's rules, precedents, and practices. The Speaker of the House and the president of the Senate are the chief presiding officers in their respective houses.

Previous Question—A nondebatable motion that, when agreed to by majority vote, cuts off further debate, prevents the offering of additional amendments, and brings the pending matter to an immediate vote. A decision to order the previous question is a decision saying that the debate and amending process are completed and the body is ready to move to a final vote on the main proposition. A special rule in the House may by its provisions allow some specified business despite a provision in the special rule ordering the previous question. It is a major debate-limiting device in the House; it is not permitted in the Committee of the Whole in the House or in the Senate.

Private Bill—A bill that applies to one or more specified persons, corporations, institutions, or other entities, usually to grant relief when no other legal remedy is available to them. Many private bills deal with claims against the federal government, immigration and naturalization cases, and land titles.

Private Calendar—The title for a calendar in the House reserved for private bills and resolutions favorably reported by committees.

Private Law—A private bill enacted into law. Private laws are numbered separately but in the same fashion as public laws. *(See Public Law.)*

Privilege—An attribute of a motion, measure, report, question, or proposition that gives it priority status for consideration. Privileged motions and motions to bring up privileged questions are not debatable.

Privilege of the Floor—In addition to the members of a house, certain individuals are admitted to its floor while it is in session. The rules of the two houses differ somewhat but both extend the privilege to the president and vice president, Supreme Court justices, cabinet members, state governors, former members of that house, members of the other house, certain officers and officials of Congress, certain staff of that house in the discharge of official duties, and the chamber's former parliamentarians. They also allow access to a limited number of committee and members' staff when their presence is necessary.

Pro Forma Amendment—In the House, an amendment that ostensibly proposes to change a measure or another amendment by moving "to strike the last word" or "to strike the requisite number of words." A member offers it not to make any actual change in the measure or amendment but only to obtain time for debate. *(See Five-Minute Rule.)*

Pro Tem—A common reference to the president pro tempore of the Senate or, occasionally, to a Speaker pro tempore. *(See President Pro Tempore; Speaker Pro Tempore.)*

Procedures—The methods of conducting business in a deliberative body. The procedures of each house are governed first by applicable provisions of the Constitution, and then by its standing rules and orders, precedents, traditional practices, and any statutory rules that apply to it. The authority of the houses to adopt rules in addition to those specified in the Constitution is derived from Article I, Section 5, clause 2 of the Constitution, which states, "Each House may determine the Rules of its Proceedings. . . . " By rule, the House of Representatives also follows the procedures in *Jefferson's Manual* that are not inconsistent with its standing rules and orders. Many Senate procedures also conform with Jefferson's provisions, but by practice rather than by rule. At the beginning of each Congress, the House uses procedures in general parliamentary law until it adopts its standing rules. *(See Rule, first definition.)*

Proxy Voting—The practice of permitting a member to cast the vote of an absent colleague in addition to their own vote. Proxy voting is prohibited on the floors of the House and Senate, but the Senate permits its committees to authorize proxy voting, and most do. In 1995, House rules were changed to prohibit proxy voting in committee.

Public Bill—A bill dealing with general legislative matters having national applicability or applying to the federal government or to a class of persons, groups, or organizations.

Public Debt—Federal government debt incurred by the Treasury or the Federal Financing Bank by the sale of securities to the public or borrowings from a federal fund or account. *(See Debt Limit; Federal Debt.)*

Public Law—A public bill or joint resolution enacted into law. It is cited by the letters "PL" followed by a hyphenated number. The digits before the hyphen indicate the number of the Congress in which it was enacted; the digits after the hyphen indicate its position in the numerical sequence of public measures that became law during that Congress. For example, the Budget Enforcement Act of 1990 became PL 101-508 because it was the 508th measure in that sequence for the 101st Congress. This system of numbering began in the late 1950s; before that, the number of the Congress in which a law was enacted was not part of the law's numerical designation. *(See also Private Law.)*

Qualification (of Members)—The Constitution requires members of the House of Representatives to be twenty-five years of age at the time their terms begin. They must have been citizens of the United States for seven years before that date and, when elected, must be "Inhabitant[s]" of the state from which they were elected. There is no constitutional requirement that they reside in the districts they represent. Senators are required to be thirty years of age at the time their terms begin. They must have been citizens of the United States for nine years before that date and, when elected, must be "Inhabitant[s]" of the states in which they were elected. The "Inhabitant" qualification is broadly interpreted, and in modern times a candidate's declaration of state residence has generally been accepted as meeting the constitutional requirement.

Queen of the Hill Rule—A special rule from the House Rules Committee that permits votes on a series of amendments, especially complete substitutes for a measure, in a specified order, but directs that the amendment receiving the greatest number of votes shall be the winning one. This kind of rule permits the House to vote directly on a variety of alternatives to a measure. In doing so, it sets aside the precedent that once an amendment has been adopted, no further amendments may be offered to the text it has amended. Under an earlier practice that took root in the 1970s, the Rules Committee reported "king of the hill" rules under which there also could be votes on a series of amendments, again in a specified order. If more than one of the amendments was adopted under this kind of rule, it was the last amendment to receive a majority vote that was considered as having been finally adopted, whether or not it had received the greatest number of votes. *(See Rule, second definition.)*

Quorum—The minimum number of members required to be present for the transaction of business. Under the Constitution, a quorum in each house is a majority of its members: 218 in the House and 51 in the Senate when there are no vacancies. By House rule, a quorum in the Committee of the Whole is 100. In practice, both houses usually assume a quorum is present even if it is not, unless a member makes a point of no quorum in the House or a live quorum or vote exposes the absence of a quorum

in the Senate. Consequently, each house transacts much of its business, and even passes bills, when only a few members are present. For House and Senate committees, chamber rules allow a minimum quorum of one-third of a committee's members to conduct many types of business. *(See Live Quorum.)*

Quorum Call—A procedure for determining whether a quorum is present in a chamber. In the Senate, a clerk calls the roll (roster) of senators. The House usually employs its electronic voting system. *(See Quorum.)*

Ramseyer Rule—A House rule that requires a committee's report on a bill or joint resolution to show the changes the measure, and any committee amendments to it, would make in existing law. The rule requires the report to present the text of any statutory provision that would be repealed and a comparative print showing, through typographical devices such as stricken-through type or italics, other changes that would be made in existing law. The rule, adopted in 1929, was named after its sponsor, Rep. Christian W. Ramseyer, R-Iowa. The Senate's analogous rule is called the Cordon Rule. *(See Committee Report on a Measure; Cordon Rule.)*

Rank or Ranking—A member's position on the list of their party's members on a committee or subcommittee. When first assigned to a committee, a member is usually placed at the bottom of the list, then moves up as those above leave the committee. On subcommittees, however, a member's rank may not have anything to do with the length of their service on it.

Ranking Member—(1) A reference to the minority member with the highest ranking on a committee or subcommittee. (2) A reference to the majority member next in rank to the chair or to the highest ranking majority member present at a committee or subcommittee meeting.

Ratification—(1) The president's formal act of promulgating a treaty after the Senate has approved it. The resolution of ratification agreed to by the Senate is the procedural vehicle by which the Senate gives its consent to ratification. (2) A state legislature's (or state convention's) act in approving a proposed constitutional amendment. Such an amendment becomes effective when ratified by three-fourths of the states. *(See Executive Document; Ratification; Resolution of Ratification; Treaty.)*

Reapportionment—*(See Apportionment.)*

Recess—(1) A temporary interruption or suspension of a meeting of a chamber or committee. Unlike an adjournment, a recess does not end a legislative day. Because the Senate might recess from one calendar day to another, its legislative day may extend over several calendar days or longer. (2) A period of adjournment for more than three days to a day certain.

Recess Appointment—A presidential appointment to a vacant federal position made after the Senate has adjourned *sine die*. Presidents have also argued that a recess appointment is possible when the Senate has adjourned or recessed for more than thirty days and for shorter periods, including times of recess when the Senate is conducting pro forma sessions. If the president submits the recess appointee's nomination during the next

session of the Senate, that individual can continue to serve until the end of the session even though the Senate might have rejected the nomination.

Recommit—To send a measure back to the committee that reported it; sometimes called a straight motion to recommit to distinguish it from a motion to recommit with instructions. A successful motion to recommit kills the measure. A motion to recommit with instructions is normally an attempt to amend a measure. In the House, the rules provide that minority will have a motion to commit or recommit a measure with or without instructions before a vote on final passage of the measure. The motion to recommit in the Senate may be offered during the amending process. *(See Recommit with Instructions.)*

Recommit a Conference Report—To return a conference report to the conference committee for renegotiation of some or all of its agreements. A motion to recommit may be offered with or without instructions. Once one chamber has approved a conference report, a motion to recommit is no longer possible since that vote dissolved the conference. *(See Conference Report.)*

Recommit with Instructions—To send a measure back to a committee with instructions to take some action on it, usually to amend it as provided in the instructions. In the House, the instructions must be written so that the measure remains on the House floor and does not literally return to committee. *(See Recommit.)*

Reconciliation—A procedure for changing existing revenue and spending laws to bring total federal revenues and spending within the limits established in a budget resolution. This procedure is triggered by the inclusion of reconciliation instructions directed at specific committees in a budget resolution. Congress has applied reconciliation chiefly to revenues and mandatory spending programs, especially entitlements. Discretionary spending is controlled through annual appropriation bills. *(See Budget Process; Budget Resolution.)*

Reconsider—A practice that gives a chamber an opportunity to review its action on any proposition. Any member who voted on the prevailing side can ask to reconsider the vote, creating, in effect, the opportunity for another vote on the same proposition. In practice, a proposition's proponents typically engage in a scripted dialogue where one member moves that the vote be reconsidered and a second member moves to lay that motion on the table, and the presiding officer then states that the motion to table has been agreed to. Invoking this procedure may create the anomalous situation of an opponent of a measure changing their "no" vote to a "yea" vote (or a proponent changing a "yea" vote to a "no" vote) to force a new vote. Not all votes on propositions may be reconsidered.

Recorded Vote—(1) Generally, any vote in which members are recorded by name for or against a measure; also called a record vote or roll-call vote. The only recorded vote in the Senate is a vote by the yeas and nays and is commonly called a roll-call vote. (2) Technically, a recorded vote is one demanded in the House of Representatives and supported by at least one-fifth of a quorum (forty-four members) in the House sitting as the House or at least twenty-five members in the Committee of the Whole.

Redistricting—The redrawing of congressional district boundaries within a state after a decennial census. Redistricting may be required to equalize district populations or to accommodate an increase or decrease in the number of a state's House seats that might have resulted from the decennial apportionment. While redistricting was traditionally a responsibility of state legislatures, and still is in most states, some states use commissions instead of or as a complement to the role of their state legislatures, and courts have become active players, sometimes imposing their own district maps on a state. *(See Apportionment; Congressional District; Gerrymandering.)*

Referral—The assignment of a measure to one or more committees for consideration; also called reference in the Senate. *(See Multiple and Sequential Referrals.)*

Report—(1) As a verb, a committee is said to report when it submits a measure or other document to its parent chamber. (2) A clerk is said to report when they read a measure's title, text, or the text of an amendment to the body at the direction of the chair. (3) As a noun, a committee document that accompanies a reported measure. It describes the measure, the committee's views on it, its costs, and the changes it proposes to make in existing law; it also includes certain impact statements. (4) A committee document submitted to its parent chamber that describes the results of an investigation or other study or provides information it is required to provide by rule or law. *(See Committee Report.)*

Representative—An elected and duly sworn member of the House of Representatives who is entitled to vote in the chamber. The Constitution requires that a representative be at least twenty-five years old, a citizen of the United States for at least seven years, and an inhabitant of the state from which they are elected. Customarily, members reside in the districts they represent. Representatives are elected in even-numbered years to two-year terms that begin the following January. Representatives may also be elected in special elections to fill a vacancy created by a death or resignation; they then serve until the next general election.

Reprimand—A formal condemnation of a member for misbehavior, considered a milder reproof than censure. The House of Representatives first used it in 1976. The Senate first used it in 1991. *(See also Censure.)*

Rescission—A provision of law that repeals previously enacted budget authority in whole or in part. Under the Impoundment Control Act of 1974, the president can impound such funds by sending a message to Congress requesting one or more rescissions and the reasons for doing so. If Congress does not pass a rescission bill for the programs requested by the president within forty-five days of continuous session after receiving the message, the president must make the funds available for obligation and expenditure. If the president does not, the comptroller general of the United States is authorized to bring suit to compel the release of those funds. A rescission bill may rescind all, part, or none of an amount proposed by the president, and may rescind funds the president has not impounded. *(See Congressional Budget and Impoundment Control Act of 1974; Deferral; Impoundment.)*

Reserve the Right to Object—A member's declaration that the member may object to a unanimous consent request. It provides an alternative to silence (acquiescence to the request) or to objecting, instead allowing the member making the reservation to clarify the requester's purpose, suggest an amendment to the request, express views, or undertake another purpose. The member reserving the right to object must ultimately withdraw the reservation, allowing the unanimous consent request to take effect, or object. *(See Unanimous Consent.)*

Resident Commissioner from Puerto Rico—A nonvoting member of the House of Representatives, elected to a four-year term. The resident commissioner has the same status and privileges as delegates. As with the delegates, the resident commissioner may not vote in the House but may do so in committee. *(See Delegate.)*

Resolution—(1) A simple resolution; that is, a nonlegislative measure effective only in the house in which it is proposed and not requiring concurrence by the other chamber or approval by the president. Simple resolutions are designated "H. Res." in the House and "S. Res." in the Senate. Simple resolutions express nonbinding opinions on policies or issues or deal with the internal affairs or prerogatives of a house. (2) Any type of resolution: simple, concurrent, or joint. *(See Concurrent Resolution; Joint Resolution.)*

Resolution of Inquiry—A resolution usually simple rather than concurrent calling on the president or the head of an executive agency to provide specific information or papers to one or both houses.

Resolution of Ratification—The Senate vehicle for consenting to ratification of a treaty. The constitutionally mandated vote of two-thirds of the senators present and voting applies to the adoption of this resolution. However, it may also contain amendments, reservations, declarations, or understandings that the Senate had previously added to it by majority vote. *(See Executive Document; Ratification; Treaty.)*

Revenue Legislation—Measures that levy new taxes or tariffs or change existing ones. Under Article I, Section 7, clause 1 of the Constitution, the House of Representatives originates federal revenue measures, but the Senate can propose amendments to them. The House Ways and Means Committee and the Senate Finance Committee have jurisdiction over such measures, with a few minor exceptions. *(See Budget Resolution.)*

Revise and Extend One's Remarks—A unanimous consent request to publish in the *Congressional Record* a statement a member did not deliver on the floor, a longer statement than the one made on the floor, or miscellaneous extraneous material. *(See Congressional Record.)*

Revolving Fund—A trust fund or account, the income of which remains available to finance its continuing operations without any fiscal year limitation.

Rider—Congressional slang for an amendment unrelated or extraneous to the subject matter of the measure to which it is attached. Riders may contain proposals that are less likely to become law on their own merits as separate bills, either because of opposition in the committee of jurisdiction, resistance in the other house, or the probability of a presidential veto.

Roll Call—A call of the roll to determine whether a quorum is present, to establish a quorum, or to vote on a question. Usually, the House uses its electronic voting system for a roll call. The Senate does not have an electronic voting system; its roll is always called by a clerk.

Rule—(1) A permanent regulation that a house adopts to govern its conduct of business, its procedures, its internal organization, behavior of its members, regulation of its facilities, duties of an officer, or some other subject it chooses to govern in that form. (2) In the House, a privileged simple resolution reported by the Rules Committee that provides methods and conditions for floor consideration of a measure or several measures.

Rule Twenty-Two—A common reference to the Senate's cloture rule, which is contained in Senate Rule Twenty-Two. *(See Cloture.)*

Second-Degree Amendment—An amendment to an amendment in the first degree. *(See Degrees of Amendment.)*

Secretary of the Senate—The chief financial, administrative, and legislative officer of the Senate. Elected by resolution or order of the Senate, the secretary is invariably the candidate of the majority party and usually chosen by the majority leader. In the absence of the vice president and pending the election of a president pro tempore, the secretary presides over the Senate. The secretary is subject to policy direction and oversight by the Senate Committee on Rules and Administration. The secretary manages a wide range of functions that support the administrative operations of the Senate as an organization as well as those functions necessary to its legislative process, including record keeping, document management, certifications, housekeeping services, administration of oaths, and lobbyist registrations. The secretary is responsible for accounting for all funds appropriated to the Senate and conducts audits of Senate financial activities.

Section—A subdivision of a bill or statute. By law, a section must be numbered and, as nearly as possible, contain "a single proposition of enactment."

Select or Special Committee—A committee established by a resolution in either house for a special purpose and, usually, for a limited time. Most select and special committees are assigned specific investigations or studies but are not authorized to report measures to their chambers. A select or special committee might, however, be given legislative authority in the resolution establishing it. Legislative authority allows legislation to be referred to the select or special committee, and provides the committee with authority to report measures to its parent chamber. *(See Ad Hoc Select Committee.)*

Senate—The house of Congress in which each state is represented by two senators; each senator has one vote. Article V of the Constitution declares that "No State, without its Consent, shall be deprived of its equal Suffrage in the Senate." The Constitution also

gives the Senate equal legislative power with the House of Representatives. Although the Senate is prohibited from originating revenue measures, and as a matter of practice it does not originate appropriation measures, it can amend both. Only the Senate can give or withhold consent to treaties and nominations from the president. It also acts as a court to try impeachments by the House and elects the vice president when no candidate receives a majority of the electoral votes. It is often referred to as "the upper body," but not by members of the House. *(See House of Representatives; Lower Body.)*

Senate Manual—The compilation of the Senate's standing rules and orders and the laws and other regulations that apply to the Senate.

Senator—A duly sworn elected or appointed member of the Senate. The Constitution requires that a senator be at least thirty years old, a citizen of the United States for at least nine years, and an inhabitant of the state from which they are elected. Senators are usually elected in even-numbered years to six-year terms that begin the following January; one-third of the Senate—known as a class—is subject to election every two years. When a vacancy occurs before the end of a term, the state governor follows state law on appointing a replacement or calling a special election to fill the position until a successor is chosen at the state's next general election to serve the remainder of the term. Until the Seventeenth Amendment was ratified in 1913, senators were chosen by their state legislatures.

Senatorial Courtesy—The Senate's practice of declining to confirm a presidential nominee for an office in the state of a senator of the president's party unless that senator approves.

Seniority—The priority, precedence, or status accorded members according to the length of their continuous service in a house or on a committee.

Seniority Loss—A type of punishment that reduces a member's seniority on their committees, including the loss of chairmanships. Party caucuses in both houses have occasionally imposed such punishment on their members, for example, for publicly supporting candidates of the other party.

Seniority Rule—The customary practice, rather than a rule, of assigning the chairmanship of a committee to the majority party member who has served on the committee for the longest continuous period of time.

Seniority System—A collection of long-standing customary practices under which members with longer continuous service than their colleagues in their house or on their committees receive various kinds of preferential treatment. Although some of the practices are no longer as rigidly observed as in the past, they still pervade the organization and procedures of Congress.

Sequestration—A procedure for canceling budgetary resources—that is, money available for obligation or spending—to enforce budget limitations established in law. Sequestered funds are no longer available for obligation or expenditure.

Sergeant at Arms—The officer in each house responsible for maintaining order, security, and decorum in its wing of the Capitol, including the chamber and its galleries. Although elected by their respective houses, both sergeants at arms are invariably the candidates of the majority party.

Session—(1) The annual series of meetings of a Congress. Under the Constitution, Congress must assemble at least once a year at noon on January 3 unless it appoints a different day by law. (2) The special meetings of Congress or of one house convened by the president, called a special session. (3) A house is said to be in session during the period of a day when it is meeting.

Severability (or Separability) Clause—Language stating that if any particular provisions of a measure are declared invalid by the courts the remaining provisions shall remain in effect.

Sine Die—Without fixing a day for a future meeting. An adjournment *sine die* signifies the end of an annual or special session of Congress.

Slip Law—The first official publication of a measure that has become law. It is published separately in unbound, single-sheet form or pamphlet form. A slip law usually is available two or three days after the date of the law's enactment. *(See Statutes at Large; U.S. Code.)*

Speaker—The presiding officer of the House of Representatives and the leader of its majority party. The Speaker is selected by the majority party and formally elected by the House at the beginning of each Congress. Although the Constitution does not require the Speaker to be a member of the House, in fact, all Speakers have been members.

Speaker Pro Tempore—A member of the House who is designated as the temporary presiding officer by the Speaker or elected by the House to that position during the Speaker's absence.

Speaker's Vote—The Speaker is not required to vote, and the Speaker's name is not called on a roll-call vote unless so requested. The Speaker might vote either to create a tie vote, and thereby defeat a proposal, or to break a tie in favor of a proposal. Occasionally, the Speaker votes to emphasize the importance of a matter.

Special Rule—*(See Rule, second definition.)*

Special Session—A session of Congress convened by the president, under their constitutional authority, after Congress has adjourned *sine die* at the end of a regular session. *(See Adjournment Sine Die; Session.)*

Spending Authority—The technical term for backdoor spending. The Congressional Budget Act of 1974 defines it as borrowing authority, contract authority, and entitlement authority for which appropriation acts do not provide budget authority in advance. Under the Budget Act, legislation that provides new spending authority may not be considered unless it provides that the authority shall be effective only to the extent or in such amounts as provided in an appropriation act. *(See Backdoor Spending Authority; Borrowing Authority; Contract Authority; Entitlement Program.)*

Spending Cap—The statutory limit for a fiscal year on the amount of new budget authority and outlays allowed for discretionary spending. The Budget Enforcement Act of 1997 required a sequester if the cap was exceeded. *(See Sequester.)*

Split Referral—A measure divided into two or more parts, with each part referred to a different committee. *(See Multiple and Sequential Referrals; Referral.)*

Sponsor—The principal proponent and introducer of a measure or an amendment.

Staff Director—The most frequently used title for the head of staff of a committee or subcommittee. On some committees, that person is called chief of staff, clerk, chief clerk, chief counsel, general counsel, or executive director. The head of a committee's minority staff is usually called minority staff director. *(See Committee Staff.)*

Standing Committee—A permanent committee established by a House or Senate standing rule or standing order. The rule also describes the subject areas on which the committee may report bills and resolutions and conduct oversight. Most introduced measures are referred to one or more standing committees according to their jurisdictions.

Standing Order—A continuing regulation or directive that has the force and effect of a rule but is not incorporated into the standing rules. The Senate's numerous standing orders, such as its standing rules, continue from Congress to Congress unless changed or the order states otherwise. The House uses relatively few standing orders, and those it adopts expire at the end of a session of Congress.

Standing Rules—The rules of the Senate that continue from one Congress to the next and the rules of the House of Representatives that it adopts at the beginning of each new Congress.

Standing Vote—An alternative and informal term for a division vote, during which members in favor of a proposal and then members opposed stand and are counted by the chair. *(See Division Vote.)*

Star Print—A reprint of a bill, resolution, amendment, or committee report correcting technical or substantive errors in a previous printing; so called because of the small black star that appears on the front page or cover.

State of the Union Message—A presidential message to Congress under the constitutional directive that the president shall "from time to time give to the Congress Information of the State of the Union, and recommend to their Consideration such Measures as he shall judge necessary and expedient." Customarily, the president sends an annual State of the Union message to Congress, usually late in January, presenting it in person in an address to a joint session.

Statutes at Large—A chronological arrangement of the laws enacted in each session of Congress. Though indexed, the laws are not arranged by subject matter, nor is there an indication of how they affect or change previously enacted laws. The volumes are numbered by Congress, and the laws are cited by their volume and page number. The Gramm-Rudman-Hollings Act, for example, appears as 99 Stat. 1037. *(See Slip Law; U.S. Code.)*

Straw Vote Prohibition—Under a House precedent, a member who has the floor during debate may not conduct a straw vote or otherwise ask for a show of support for a proposition. Only the chair may put a question to a vote.

Strike from the *Record*—Expunge objectionable remarks from the *Congressional Record*, after a member's words have been taken down on a point of order.

Strike the Last Word—*(See Pro Forma Amendment.)*

Subcommittee—A panel of committee members assigned a portion of the committee's jurisdiction or other functions. On legislative committees, subcommittees hold hearings, mark up legislation, and report measures to their full committee for further action; they cannot report directly to the chamber. A subcommittee's party composition usually reflects the ratio on its parent committee.

Subpoena Power—The authority granted to committees by the rules of their respective houses to issue legal orders requiring individuals to appear and testify, or to produce documents pertinent to the committee's functions, or both. Persons who do not comply with subpoenas can be cited for contempt of Congress and prosecuted.

Subsidy—Generally, a payment or benefit made by the federal government for which no current repayment is required. Subsidy payments may be designed to support the conduct of an economic enterprise or activity, such as ship operations, or to support certain market prices, as in the case of farm subsidies.

Sunset Legislation—A term sometimes applied to laws authorizing the existence of agencies or programs that expire annually or at the end of some other specified period of time. One of the purposes of setting specific expiration dates for agencies and programs is to encourage the committees with jurisdiction over them to determine whether they should be continued or terminated. *(See Authorization.)*

Sunshine Rules—Rules requiring open committee hearings and business meetings, including markup sessions, in both houses, and also open conference committee meetings. However, all may be closed under certain circumstances and using certain procedures required by the rules. *(See Closed Hearing.)*

Supermajority—A term sometimes used for a vote on a matter that requires approval by more than a simple majority of those members present and voting; also referred to as extraordinary majority. *(See Constitutional Votes; Suspension of the Rules (House).*

Supplemental Appropriation Bill—A measure providing appropriations for use in the current fiscal year, in addition to those already provided in annual general appropriation bills. Supplemental appropriations are often for unforeseen emergencies. *(See Appropriation.)*

Suspension of the Rules (House)—An expeditious procedure for passing relatively noncontroversial or emergency measures by a two-thirds vote of those members voting, a quorum being present.

Suspension of the Rules (Senate)—A procedure to set aside one or more of the Senate's rules; it is used infrequently.

Task Force—A title sometimes given to a panel of members assigned to a special project, study, or investigation. A task force might be convened by leadership, a party caucus or conference, or a committee. Ordinarily, these groups do not have authority to report measures to their respective houses.

Tax Expenditure—Loosely, a tax exemption or advantage, sometimes called an incentive or loophole; technically, a loss of governmental tax revenue attributable to some provision of federal tax laws that allows a special exclusion, exemption, or deduction from gross income or that provides a special credit, preferential tax rate, or deferral of tax liability.

Televised Proceedings—Television and radio coverage of the floor proceedings of the House of Representatives have been available since 1979 and of the Senate since 1986. They are broadcast over a coaxial cable system to all congressional offices and to some congressional agencies on channels reserved for that purpose. Coverage is also available free of charge to commercial and public television and radio broadcasters. C-SPAN carries gavel-to-gavel coverage of both houses. *(See C-SPAN.)*

Third Reading—A required reading to a chamber of a bill or joint resolution by title only before the vote on passage. In modern practice, it has merely become a pro forma step.

Third-Degree Amendment—An amendment to a second-degree amendment. Both houses prohibit such amendments. *(See Degrees of Amendment.)*

Three-Day Rule—(1) In the House, a measure cannot be considered until the third calendar day on which the committee report has been available. (2) In the House, a conference report cannot be considered until the third calendar day on which its text has been available in the *Congressional Record*. (3) In the House, a general appropriation bill cannot be considered until the third calendar day on which printed hearings on the bill have been available. (4) In the Senate, when a committee votes to report a measure, a committee member is entitled to three calendar days within which to submit separate views for inclusion in the committee report. (In House committees, a member is entitled to two calendar days for this purpose, after the day on which the committee votes to report.) (5) In both houses, a majority of a committee's members may call a special meeting of the committee if its chair fails to do so within three calendar days after three or more of the members, acting jointly, formally request such a meeting. In calculating such periods, the House omits holiday and weekend days on which it does not meet. The Senate makes no such exclusion.

Tie Vote—When the votes for and against a proposition are equal, it loses. The president of the Senate—the constitutional role of the vice president—may cast a vote only to break a tie.

Because the Speaker is invariably a member of the House, the Speaker is entitled to vote but usually does not. The Speaker may choose to do so to break, or create, a tie vote.

Title—(1) A major subdivision of a bill or act, designated by a roman numeral and usually containing legislative provisions on the same general subject. Titles are sometimes divided into subtitles as well as sections. (2) The official name of a bill or act, also called a caption or long title. (3) Some bills also have short titles that appear in the sentence immediately following the enacting clause. (4) Popular titles are the unofficial names given to some bills or acts by common usage. For example, the Balanced Budget and Emergency Deficit Control Act of 1985 (short title) is almost invariably referred to as Gramm-Rudman (popular title). In other cases, significant legislation is popularly referred to by its title number *(see definition (1) above)*. For example, the federal legislation that requires equality of funding for women's and men's sports in educational institutions that receive federal funds is popularly called Title IX.

Track System—An occasional Senate practice that expedites legislation by dividing a day's session into two or more specific time periods, commonly called tracks, each reserved for consideration of a different measure.

Transfer Payment—A federal government payment to which individuals or organizations are entitled under law and for which no goods or services are required in return. Payments include welfare and Social Security benefits, unemployment insurance, government pensions, and veterans benefits.

Treaty—A formal document containing an agreement between two or more sovereign nations. The Constitution authorizes the president to make treaties, but the president must submit them to the Senate for its approval by a two-thirds vote of the senators present. Under the Senate's rules, that vote actually occurs on a resolution of ratification. Although the Constitution does not give the House a direct role in approving treaties, that body has sometimes insisted that a revenue treaty is an invasion of its prerogatives. In any case, the House may significantly affect the application of a treaty by its equal role in enacting legislation to implement the treaty. *(See Executive Document; Ratification; Resolution of Ratification.)*

Trust Funds—Special accounts in the Treasury that receive earmarked taxes or other kinds of revenue collections, such as user fees, and from which payments are made for special purposes or to recipients who meet the requirements of the trust funds as established by law. Of the more than 150 federal government trust funds, several finance major entitlement programs, such as Social Security, Medicare, and retired federal employees' pensions. Others fund infrastructure construction and improvements, such as highways and airports.

Unanimous Consent—Without an objection by any member. A unanimous consent request asks permission, explicitly or implicitly, to set aside one or more rules. Both houses and their committees frequently use such requests to expedite their proceedings. If all members are silent, consent is given. If any member objects, unanimous consent is denied. *(See Reserve the Right to Object.)*

Uncontrollable Expenditures—A frequently used term for federal expenditures that are mandatory under existing law and therefore cannot be controlled by the president or Congress without a change in the existing law. Uncontrollable expenditures include spending required under entitlement programs and also fixed costs, such as interest on the public debt and outlays to pay for prior-year obligations. In recent years, uncontrollables have accounted for approximately three-quarters of federal spending in each fiscal year.

Unfunded Mandate—Generally, any provision in federal law or regulation that imposes a duty or obligation on a state or local government or private sector entity without providing the necessary funds to comply. The Unfunded Mandates Reform Act of 1995 amended the Congressional Budget Act of 1974 to provide a mechanism for the control of new unfunded mandates.

Union Calendar—A calendar of the House of Representatives for bills and resolutions favorably reported by committees that raise revenue or directly or indirectly appropriate money or property. In addition to appropriation bills, measures that authorize expenditures are also placed on this calendar. The calendar's full title is the Calendar of the Committee of the Whole House on the State of the Union.

Upper Body—A common reference to the Senate, but not used by members of the House. *(See Lower Body.)*

U.S. Code—Popular title for the *United States Code: Containing the General and Permanent Laws of the United States in Force on* . . . . It is a consolidation and partial codification of the general and permanent laws of the United States arranged by subject under fifty titles. The first six titles deal with general or political subjects, the other forty-four with subjects ranging from agriculture to war, alphabetically arranged. A supplement is published after each session of Congress, and the entire *Code* is revised every six years. *(See Slip Law; Statutes at Large.)*

User Fee—A fee charged to users of goods or services provided by the federal government. When Congress levies or authorizes such fees, it determines whether the revenues should go into the general collections of the Treasury or be available for expenditure by the agency that provides the goods or services.

Veto—The president's disapproval of a legislative measure passed by Congress. The president returns the measure to the house in which it originated without his signature but with a veto message stating his objections to it. When Congress is in session, the president must veto a bill within ten days, excluding Sundays, after the president has received it; otherwise it becomes law without his signature. The ten-day clock begins to run at midnight following his receipt of the bill. *(See Override a Veto; Pocket Veto.)*

Voice Vote—A method of voting in which members who favor a question answer "aye" in chorus, after which those opposed answer "no" in chorus, and the chair decides which position prevails.

Voting—Members vote in three ways on the floor: (1) by shouting "aye" or "no" on voice votes in the House; (2) by standing for or against on division votes; and (3) on recorded votes (including the yeas and nays), by answering "aye" or "no" when their names are called or, in the House, by recording their votes through the electronic voting system. In the Senate, members do not shout their position on voice votes; rather, the majority's position is presumed to prevail unless there is a request for a roll-call vote.

War Powers Resolution of 1973—An act that requires the president "in every possible instance" to consult Congress before committing U.S. forces to ongoing or imminent hostilities. If the president commits forces to a combat situation without congressional consultation, the president must notify Congress within forty-eight hours. Unless Congress declares war or otherwise authorizes the operation to continue, the forces must be withdrawn within sixty or ninety days, depending on certain conditions. No president has ever acknowledged the constitutionality of the resolution.

Well—The sunken, level, open space between members' seats and the podium at the front of each chamber. House members usually address their chamber from their party's lectern in the well on its side of the aisle or from their party's two tables among the House seats. Senators usually speak at their assigned desks.

Whip—The majority or minority party member in each house who acts as assistant leader, helps plan and marshal support for party strategies, encourages party discipline, and advises their leader on how colleagues intend to vote on the floor.

Yeas and Nays—A vote in which members usually respond "aye" or "no" (despite the official title of the vote) on a question when their names are called in alphabetical order. In the House, such votes are conducted by electronic device. The Constitution requires the yeas and nays when a demand for it is supported by one-fifth of the members present, and it also requires an automatic yea-and-nay vote on overriding a veto. Senate precedents assume the presence of a quorum and therefore require the support of at least one-fifth of a quorum, a minimum of eleven members with the present membership of 100. If a live quorum or vote has exposed the absence of a quorum, the yeas and nays will be ordered with the support of one-fifth of those present.

The Legislative Process in Brief

Note: *Parliamentary terms used below are defined in the glossary.*

INTRODUCTION OF BILLS

A House member (including the resident commissioner of Puerto Rico and nonvoting delegates of the District of Columbia, Guam, the Virgin Islands, and American Samoa) may introduce any one of several types of bills and resolutions at any time the House is in session by handing it to the clerk of the House or placing it in a box called the hopper. A senator usually introduces a measure by presenting it, along with a formal statement, to a clerk at the presiding officer's desk.

As the usual next step in either the House or the Senate, the bill is numbered, referred to the appropriate committee (or, in the House, committees), labeled with the sponsor's name and sent to the Government Printing Office so that copies can be made for subsequent study and action. House and Senate bills may be jointly sponsored and carry several lawmakers' names. Print and electronic versions of the bill are available to the public. A bill written in the executive branch and proposed as an administration measure usually is introduced by the chair of the congressional committee that has jurisdiction, as a courtesy to the White House.

Bills—Prefixed with "H.R." in the House, "S." in the Senate, followed by a number. Used as the form for most legislation, whether general or special, public or private.

Joint Resolutions—Designated "H. J. Res." or "S. J. Res." Subject to the same procedure as bills, with the exception of a joint resolution proposing an amendment to the Constitution. The latter must be approved by two-thirds of both houses and is thereupon sent directly to the archivist of the United States at the National Archives and Records Administration for submission to the states for ratification instead of being presented to the president for his approval.

Concurrent Resolutions—Designated "H. Con. Res." or "S. Con. Res." Used for matters affecting the operations of both houses. These resolutions do not become law.

Resolutions—Designated "H. Res." or "S. Res." Used for a matter concerning the operation of either house alone and adopted only by the chamber in which it originates.

COMMITTEE ACTION

With few exceptions, bills are referred to the appropriate standing committees. The job of referral formally is the responsibility of the Speaker of the House and the presiding officer of the Senate, but this task usually is carried out on their behalf by the parliamentarians of the House and Senate. Precedent, statute, and the jurisdictional mandates of the committees as set forth in the rules of the House and Senate determine which committees receive what kinds of bills. Bills are technically considered "read for the first time" when referred to House committees. Bills are read twice before being referred to Senate committees.

When a bill reaches a committee it is placed on the committee's calendar. Failure of a committee to act on a bill is equivalent to killing it and most fall by the legislative roadside. The measure can be withdrawn from the committee's purview by a discharge petition signed by a majority of the House membership on House bills. Both the House and Senate discharge bills from committees by unanimous consent, with the cooperation of committees. Other discharge options are available in both chambers.

The first committee action taken on a bill may be a request for comment on it by interested agencies of the government. The committee chair may assign the bill to a subcommittee for study and hearings, or it may be considered by the full committee. Hearings may be public, closed (executive session) or both. A subcommittee, after marking up a bill (considering amendments to it), reports to the full committee its recommendations for action and any proposed amendments.

The full committee then marks up and votes on its recommendation to the House or Senate. This procedure is called "ordering a bill reported." Occasionally a committee may order a bill reported unfavorably, especially if it must report a measure pursuant to a rule, rulemaking law, or chamber order. Most of the time a report, submitted by the chair of the committee to the House or Senate, calls for favorable action on the measure since the committee can effectively "kill" a bill by simply failing to take any action.

When the bill is reported, the committee chair instructs the staff to prepare a written report. The report describes the purposes and scope of the bill, explains the committee revisions, notes proposed changes in existing law and, usually, includes the views of the executive branch agencies consulted. Often committee members opposing a measure issue dissenting minority statements that are included in the report.

Usually, the committee "marks up" or proposes amendments to the bill. If they are substantial and the measure is complicated, the committee may order a "clean bill" introduced, which will embody the proposed amendments. The original bill then is put aside and the clean bill, with a new number, is reported to the floor.

The chamber must approve, alter, or reject the committee amendments before the bill itself can be put to a vote.

FLOOR ACTION

After a bill is reported back to the house where it originated, it is placed on the calendar.

There are four legislative calendars in the House, issued in one cumulative document titled *Calendars of the United States House of Representatives and History of Legislation.* The House calendars are

The Union Calendar to which are referred bills raising revenues, general appropriations bills, and any measures directly or indirectly appropriating money or property. It is the Calendar of the Committee of the Whole House on the state of the Union.

The House Calendar to which are referred bills of public character not raising revenue or appropriating money.

The Private Calendar to which are referred bills for relief in the nature of claims against the United States or private immigration bills that may be passed without debate when the Private Calendar is called the first and third Tuesdays of each month.

The Discharge Calendar to which are referred motions to discharge committees when the necessary signatures are signed to a discharge petition.

There is only one legislative calendar in the Senate and one "executive calendar" for treaties and nominations submitted to the Senate.

Debate

A bill is brought to debate by varying procedures. In the Senate the majority leader, often in consultation with the minority leader and others, schedules the bills that will be taken up for debate. If it is widely supported by senators it can be taken up in the Senate either by unanimous consent or by a motion agreed to by majority vote.

Senate debate is unlimited, unless it is limited by unanimous consent, rule, rulemaking law, or supermajority vote. Typically, the Senate attempts to invoke cloture to limit debate, which requires a three-fifths vote of all senators. If invoked, debate may continue for only another thirty hours. To invoke cloture on a proposed change to Senate rules, a two-thirds vote of all senators is required.

In the House, precedence is granted to a bill if a special rule is obtained from the Rules Committee. A request for a special rule usually is made by the chair of the committee that favorably reported the bill, after consultation with the majority party leadership. The request is considered by the Rules Committee in the same fashion that other committees consider legislative measures. The committee proposes a simple resolution (H. Res.) providing for the consideration of the bill. The Rules Committee reports the resolution to the House where it is debated and voted on in the same fashion as regular bills.

The resolutions providing special rules are important because they specify how long the bill may be debated and whether it may be amended from the floor. If floor amendments are banned, the bill is considered under a "closed rule."

When a bill is debated under an "open rule," germane amendments may be offered from the floor. A "structured rule" has become the most commonly used form of rule. In the resolution reported by the Rules Committee, those amendments that may be offered are listed and the duration of debate on each prescribed. Committee amendments always are taken up first but may be changed, as may all amendments up to the second degree, if permitted by the rule; that is, an amendment to an amendment to an amendment is not in order.

Duration of debate in the House depends on whether the bill is under discussion by the House proper or before the House when it is sitting as the Committee of the Whole House on the state of the Union. In the former, the amount of time for debate occurs under the one-hour rule, which allows members to hold the floor for one hour each. In practice, the member first recognized to speak moves the previous question after an hour, which

the House almost always approves and which ends further debate. In the Committee of the Whole the amount of time specified in the special rule for general debate is equally divided between proponents and opponents. At the end of general debate, the bill is often read section by section for amendment if it is considered under an open rule. Debate on an amendment is limited to five minutes for each side; this is called the "five-minute rule." In practice, amendments under an open rule are regularly debated more than ten minutes, with members gaining the floor by offering pro forma amendments or obtaining unanimous consent to speak longer than five minutes.

The House considers almost all important bills within a parliamentary framework known as the Committee of the Whole. It is not a committee as the word usually is understood; it is the full House meeting under another name for the purpose of speeding action on legislation. Technically, the House sits as the Committee of the Whole when it considers any tax measure or bill dealing with public appropriations or authorizations. Upon adoption of a special rule, the Speaker declares the House resolved into the Committee of the Whole and appoints a member of the majority party to serve as the chair. Instead of the required quorum of 218 for the House, the rules of that chamber permit the Committee of the Whole to meet when a quorum of 100 members is present on the floor and to amend and act on bills. When the Committee of the Whole has concluded consideration of a bill for amendment, it "rises," the Speaker returns as the presiding officer of the House, and the member appointed chair of the Committee of the Whole reports the action of the committee and its recommendations.

The Committee of the Whole cannot pass a bill; instead, it reports the measure to the full House with whatever amendments it has adopted. Before the vote on final passage, the minority under House rules is guaranteed one attempt to kill or change the bill. This attempt is called the motion to recommit. A motion to recommit with no additional language is an attempt to get a majority to vote to kill the bill. A motion to recommit with instructions is an attempt to get a majority to adopt the amendatory language that comprises the instructions. These motions rarely succeed. After this vote, the House votes to pass or reject the bill. Amendments adopted in the Committee of the Whole may be put to a second vote in the full House.

Votes

Voting on bills may occur repeatedly before they are finally approved or rejected. The House votes on the rule for the bill and on various amendments to the bill. Voting on amendments often is a more illuminating test of a bill's support than is the final tally. Sometimes members approve final passage of bills after vigorously supporting amendments that, if adopted, would have scuttled the legislation.

The Senate has three different methods of voting: an untabulated voice vote, a standing vote (called a division), and a recorded roll call to which members answer "yea" or "nay" when their names are called. The House also employs voice and standing votes, but since January 1973 yeas and nays have been recorded by an electronic voting device, eliminating the need for time-consuming roll calls.

After amendments to a bill have been voted upon and, in the House, the motion to recommit disposed of, it is "read for the third time." The final vote is taken and is followed by a pro forma motion to reconsider, which is laid on the table. With that, the bill has been formally passed by the chamber.

A-1 Image The Legislative Process in Brief

This graphic shows the most typical way in which proposed legislation is enacted into law. There are more complicated, as well as simpler, routes, and most bills never become law. The process is illustrated with two hypothetical bills, House bill No. 1 (H.R.1) and

Senate bill No. 2 (S.2). Bills must be passed by both houses in identical form before they can be sent to the president. The path of H.R.1 is traced by a black line, that of S.2 by a gray line. In practice, most bills begin as similar proposals in both houses.

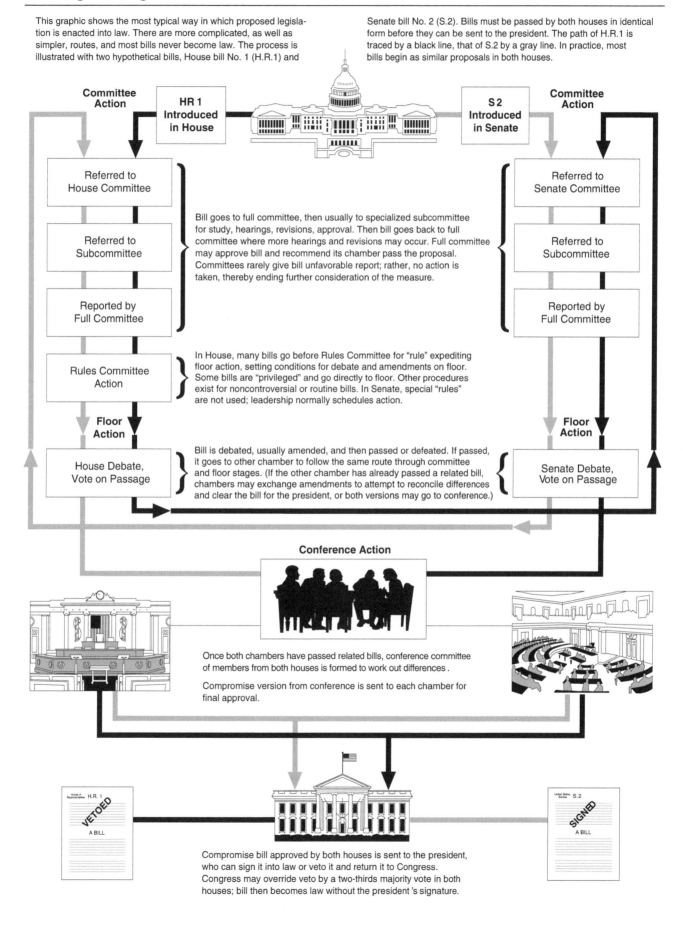

Committee Action

HR 1 Introduced in House

S 2 Introduced in Senate

Committee Action

Referred to House Committee

Referred to Senate Committee

Referred to Subcommittee

Referred to Subcommittee

Reported by Full Committee

Reported by Full Committee

Bill goes to full committee, then usually to specialized subcommittee for study, hearings, revisions, approval. Then bill goes back to full committee where more hearings and revisions may occur. Full committee may approve bill and recommend its chamber pass the proposal. Committees rarely give bill unfavorable report; rather, no action is taken, thereby ending further consideration of the measure.

Rules Committee Action

In House, many bills go before Rules Committee for "rule" expediting floor action, setting conditions for debate and amendments on floor. Some bills are "privileged" and go directly to floor. Other procedures exist for noncontroversial or routine bills. In Senate, special "rules" are not used; leadership normally schedules action.

Floor Action

Floor Action

House Debate, Vote on Passage

Bill is debated, usually amended, and then passed or defeated. If passed, it goes to other chamber to follow the same route through committee and floor stages. (If the other chamber has already passed a related bill, chambers may exchange amendments to attempt to reconcile differences and clear the bill for the president, or both versions may go to conference.)

Senate Debate, Vote on Passage

Conference Action

Once both chambers have passed related bills, conference committee of members from both houses is formed to work out differences .

Compromise version from conference is sent to each chamber for final approval.

H.R. 1 VETOED — A BILL

S.2 SIGNED — A BILL

Compromise bill approved by both houses is sent to the president, who can sign it into law or veto it and return it to Congress. Congress may override veto by a two-thirds majority vote in both houses; bill then becomes law without the president 's signature.

ACTION IN SECOND CHAMBER

After a bill is passed it is sent to the other chamber. This body may then take one of several steps. It may pass the bill as is—accepting the other chamber's language. It may send the bill to committee for scrutiny or alteration, or reject the entire bill, advising the other house of its actions. Or it simply may ignore the bill submitted while it continues work on its version of the proposed legislation. Frequently, one chamber may approve a version of a bill that is greatly at variance with the version already passed by the other house, and then substitute its contents for the language of the other, retaining only the latter's bill number.

Often the second chamber makes only minor changes. If these are readily agreed to by the other house, the bill then is routed to the president. Large or small differences between each chamber's version of a bill are commonly dealt with today by amendments between the houses, whereby the first chamber considers the changes of the second chamber, and may accept those changes, clearing the bill for the president, or respond with additional changes. The second chamber then considers the first chamber's additional changes and may accept them, clearing the bill for the president, or respond with additional changes. This exchange of amendments may continue until differences are resolved. If the opposite chamber significantly alters the bill submitted to it, or the houses are not able to reach agreement through an exchange of amendments, the measure may be "sent to conference." The chamber that has possession of the "papers" (engrossed bill, engrossed amendments, messages of transmittal) requests a conference and the other chamber may agree to it. If the second chamber does not agree, the bill dies unless subsequent parliamentary actions take place.

CONFERENCE ACTION

A conference works out conflicting House and Senate versions of a legislative bill. The conferees include senior members from the committees that managed the legislation who are appointed by the presiding officers of the two houses. Under this arrangement the conferees of one house have the duty of trying to maintain their chamber's position in the face of amending actions by the conferees (also referred to as "managers") of the other house.

The number of conferees from each chamber may vary from single to double or even triple digits depending on the length or complexity of the bill and the number of committees involved. But a majority vote controls the action of each group so that a large representation does not give one chamber a voting advantage over the other chamber's conferees.

Theoretically, conferees are not allowed to write new legislation in some parliamentary circumstances in reconciling the two versions before them, but this curb sometimes is bypassed. Many bills have been put into acceptable compromise form only after new language was provided by the conferees. Frequently the ironing out of difficulties takes days or even weeks. Conferences on complex and controversial bills sometimes are particularly drawn out.

As a conference proceeds, conferees reconcile differences between the versions, but generally they grant concessions only insofar as they remain sure that the chamber they represent will accept the compromises. Occasionally, uncertainty over how either house will react, or the positive refusal of a chamber to back down on a disputed amendment, results in an impasse, and the bill dies in conference even though each version was approved by its sponsoring chamber.

When the conferees have reached agreement, they prepare a conference report embodying their recommendations (compromises in the form of legislative text) and a joint explanatory statement. The report, in document form, must be submitted to each house. The conference report must be approved by each house. Consequently, approval of the report is approval of the compromise bill. In the order of voting on conference reports, the chamber that asked for a conference yields to the other chamber the opportunity to vote first.

FINAL ACTION

After a bill has been passed by both the House and Senate in identical form, all of the original papers are sent to the enrolling clerk of the chamber in which the bill originated. The clerk then prepares an enrolled bill, which is printed on parchment paper.

When this bill has been certified as correct by the secretary of the Senate or the clerk of the House, depending on which chamber originated the bill, it is signed first (no matter whether it originated in the Senate or House) by the Speaker of the House and then by the president of the Senate. It is next sent to the White House to await action.

If the president approves the bill, he signs it, dates it, and usually writes the word "approved" on the document. If he does not sign it within ten days (Sundays excepted) and Congress is in session, the bill becomes law without his signature, an extremely rare event.

If Congress adjourns *sine die* at the end of the second session the president can pocket veto a bill and it dies without Congress having the opportunity to override. While presidents have sought to pocket veto bills after the adjournment of the first session of a Congress, they and Congress have engaged in additional procedures surrounding these vetoes that have left it unclear whether or not constitutional authority for pocket vetoes exists in an intersession adjournment.

A president vetoes a bill by refusing to sign it and, before the ten-day period expires, returning it to Congress with a message stating his reasons. The message is sent to the chamber that originated the bill. If no action is taken on the message, the bill dies. Congress, however, can attempt to override the president's veto and enact the bill, "the objections of the president to the contrary notwithstanding." Overriding a veto requires a two-thirds vote of those present in each chamber, who must number a quorum and vote by roll call.

If the president's veto is overridden by a two-thirds vote in both houses, the bill becomes law. Otherwise it is dead.

When bills are passed finally and signed, or passed over a veto, they are given law numbers in numerical order as they become law. There are two series of numbers, one for public and one for private laws, starting at the number "1" for each two-year term of Congress. They are then identified by law number and by Congress—for example, Private Law 1, 112th Congress (or Private Law 112-1); Public Law 75, 113th Congress (or PL 113-75).

Congress and Its Members

Senate Membership in the 115th Congress

Membership at the beginning of Congress in 2017: Republicans 51; Democrats 47; Independents 2. Changes that occurred during the two year period are noted.

Alabama
Jeff Sessions (R)[1]
Richard Shelby (R)
Doug Jones (D) [3]
Luther Strange (R)[2]

Alaska
Dan Sullivan (R)
Lisa Murkowski (R)

Arizona
Jeff Flake (R)
John McCain (R)[4]
Jon Kyl (R)[5]

Arkansas
Tom Cotton (R)
John Boozman (R)

California
Dianne Feinstein (D)
Kamala Harris (D)

Colorado
Cory Gardner (R)
Michael Bennet (D)

Connecticut
Chris Murphy (D)
Richard Blumenthal (D)

Delaware
Tom Carper (D)
Chris Coons (D)

Florida
Bill Nelson (D)
Marco Rubio (R)

Georgia
David Perdue (R)
Johnny Isakson (R)

Hawaii
Mazie Hirono (D)
Brian Schatz (D)

Idaho
Jim Risch (R)
Mike Crapo (R)

Illinois
Dick Durbin (D)
Tammy Duckworth (D)

Indiana
Joe Donnelly (D)
Todd Young (R)

Iowa
Joni Ernst (R)
Chuck Grassley (R)

Kansas
Pat Roberts (R)
Jerry Moran (R)

Kentucky
Mitch McConnell (R)
Rand Paul (R)

Louisiana
Bill Cassidy (R)
John Kennedy (R)

Maine
Angus King (I)
Susan Collins (R)

Maryland
Ben Cardin (D)
Chris Van Hollen (D)

Massachusetts
Elizabeth Warren (D)
Ed Markey (D)

Michigan
Debbie Stabenow (D)
Gary Peters (D)

Minnesota
Amy Klobuchar (D)
Al Franken (D)[6]
Tina Smith (D)[7]

Mississippi
Roger Wicker (R)
Thad Cochran (R)[8]
Cindy Hyde-Smith (R)[9]

Missouri
Claire McCaskill (D)
Roy Blunt (R)

Montana
Jon Tester (D)
Steve Daines (R)

Nebraska
Deb Fischer (R)
Ben Sasse (R)

Nevada
Dean Heller (R)
Catherine Cortez Mastro (D)

New Hampshire
Jeanne Shaheen (D)
Margaret Hassan (D)

New Jersey
Bob Menendez (D)
Cory Booker (D)

New Mexico
Martin Heinrich (D)
Tom Udall (D)

New York
Kirsten Gillibrand (D)
Chuck Schumer (D)

North Carolina
Thom Tillis (R)
Richard Burr (R)

North Dakota
Heidi Heitkamp (D)
John Hoeven (R)

Ohio
Sherrod Brown (D)
Rob Portman (R)

Oklahoma
Jim Inhofe (R)
James Lankford (R)

Oregon
Jeff Merkley (D)
Ron Wyden (D)

Pennsylvania
Bob Casey Jr. (D)
Pat Toomey (R)

Rhode Island
Sheldon Whitehouse (D)
Jack Reed (D)

South Carolina
Lindsey Graham (R)
Tim Scott (R)

South Dakota
Mike Rounds (R)
John Thune (R)

Tennessee
Bob Corker (R)
Lamar Alexander (R)

Texas
Ted Cruz (R)
John Cornyn (R)

Utah
Orrin Hatch (R)
Mike Lee (R)

Vermont
Bernie Sanders (I)
Patrick Leahy (D)

Virginia
Tim Kaine (D)
Mark Warner (D)

Washington
Maria Cantwell (D)
Patty Murray (D)

West Virginia
Joe Manchin (D)
Shelley Moore Capito (R)

Wisconsin
Tammy Baldwin (D)
Ron Johnson (R)

Wyoming
John Barrasso (R)
Mike Enzi (R)

[1]Jeff Session was appointed Attorney General and resigned January 8, 2017.

[2]Strange filled in for Sessions on January 9, 2017 but was an unsuccessful candidate for Republican nomination to the unexpired portion of the term.

[3]Jones was elected in special election and served in Session's seat which was initially filled by Luther Strange.

[4]Senator John McCain passed away August 25, 2018.

[5]Kyl filled vacancy after McCain's death.

[6]Al Franked resigned January 2, 2018.

[7]Smith filled vacancy after Al Franken's resignation.

[8]Thad Cochran resigned April 1, 2018.

[9]Hyde-Smith filled vacancy caused by Thad Cochran's resignation.

House Membership in the 115th Congress

Membership at the beginning of Congress in January 2017: Republicans 238; Democrats 197. Changes during the 2017–2018 period are noted.

Alabama
1. Bradley Byrne (R)
2. Martha Roby (R)
3. Mike Rogers (R)
4. Robert Aderholt (R)
5. Mo Brooks (R)
6. Gary Palmer (R)
7. Terri Sewell (D)

Alaska
AL Don Young (R)

Arizona
1. Tom O'Halleran (D)
2. Martha McSally (R)
3. Raúl Grijalva (D)
4. Paul Gosar (R)
5. Andy Briggs (R)
6. David Schweikert (R)
7. Ruben Gallego (D)
8. Trent Franks (R)
   (resigned December 8, 2017)
   Debbie Lesko (R)
   (sworn in May 7, 2018)
9. Krysten Sinema (D)

Arkansas
1. Rick Crawford (R)
2. French Hill (R)
3. Steve Womack (R)
4. Bruce Westerman (R)

California
1. Doug LaMalfa (R)
2. Jared Huffman (D)
3. John Garamendi (D)
4. Tom McClintock (R)
5. Mike Thompson (D)
6. Doris Matsui (D)
7. Ami Bera (D)
8. Paul Cook (R)
9. Jerry McNerney (D)
10. Jeff Denham (R)
11. Mark DeSaulnier (D)
12. Nancy Pelosi (D)
13. Barbara Lee (D)
14. Jackie Speier (D)
15. Eric Swalwell (D)
16. Jim Costa (D)
17. Ro Khanna (D)
18. Anna Eshoo (D)
19. Zoe Lofgren (D)
20. Jimmy Panetta (D)
21. David Valadao (R)
22. Devin Nunes (R)
23. Kevin McCarthy (R)
24. Salud O. Carbajal (D)
25. Stephen Knight (R)
26. Julia Brownley (D)
27. Judy Chu (D)
28. Adam Schiff (D)
29. Tony Cardenas (D)
30. Brad Sherman (D)
31. Pete Aguilar (D)
32. Grace Napolitano (D)
33. Ted Lieu (D)
34. Xavier Becerra (D)
    (resigned January 24, 2017)
    Jimmy Gomez (D)
    (sworn in July 11, 2017)
35. Norma Torres (D)
36. Raul Ruiz (D)
37. Karen Bass (D)
38. Linda Sánchez (D)
39. Ed Royce (R)
40. Lucille Roybal-Allard (D)
41. Mark Takano (D)
42. Ken Calvert (R)
43. Maxine Waters (D)
44. Nanette Diaz Barragan (D)
45. Mimi Walters (R)
46. Luis Correa (D)
47. Alan Lowenthal (D)
48. Dana Rohrabacher (R)
49. Darrell E. Issa (R)
50. Duncan D. Hunter (R)
51. Juan Vargas (D)
52. Scott Peters (D)
53. Susan Davis (D)

Colorado
1. Diana DeGette (D)
2. Jared Polis (D)
3. Scott Tipton (R)
4. Ken Buck (R)
5. Doug Lamborn (R)
6. Mike Coffman (R)
7. Ed Perlmutter (D)

Connecticut
1. John Larson (D)
2. Joe Courtney (D)
3. Rosa DeLauro (D)
4. Jim Himes (D)
5. Elizabeth Esty (D)

Delaware
AL Lisa Blunt Rochester (D)

Florida
1. Matt Gaetz (R)
2. Neal P. Dunn (R)
3. Ted Yoho (R)
4. John Rutherford (R)
5. Al Lawson Jr. (D)
6. Ron DeSantis (R)
7. Stephanie Murphy (D)
8. Bill Posey (R)
9. Darren Soto (D)
10. Val Butler Demings (D)
11. Daniel Webster (R)
12. Gus Bilirakis (R)
13. Charlie Crist (D)
14. Kathy Castor (D)
15. Dennis Ross (R)
16. Vern Buchanan (R)
17. Tom Rooney (R)
18. Brian Mast (R)
19. Francis Rooney (R)
20. Alcee Hastings (D)
21. Lois Frankel (D)
22. Ted Deutch (D)
23. Debbie Wasserman Schultz (D)
24. Frederica Wilson (D)
25. Mario Diaz-Balart (R)
26. Carlos Curbelo (R)
27. Ileana Ros-Lehtinen (R)

Georgia
1. Buddy Carter (R)
2. Sanford Bishop (D)
3. Drew Ferguson (R)
4. Hank Johnson (D)
5. John Lewis (D)
6. Tom Price (R)
   (resigned February 10, 2017)
   Karen Handel (R)
   (sworn in June 26, 2017)
7. Rob Woodall (R)
8. Austin Scott (R)
9. Doug Collins (R)
10. Jody Hice (R)
11. Barry Loudermilk (R)
12. Rick Allen (R)
13. David Scott (D)
14. Tom Graves (R)

Hawaii
1. Colleen Hanabusa (D)
2. Tulsi Gabbard (D)

Idaho
1. Raul Labrador (R)
2. Mike Simpson (R)

Illinois
1. Bobby Rush (D)
2. Robin Kelly (D)
3. Dan Lipinski (D)
4. Luis Gutiérrez (D)
5. Mike Quigley (D)
6. Peter Roskam (R)
7. Danny Davis (D)
8. Raja Krishnamoorthi (D)
9. Jan Schakowsky (D)
10. Bradley Scott Schneider (D)
11. Bill Foster (D)
12. Mike Bost (R)
13. Rodney Davis (R)
14. Randy Hultgren (R)
15. John Shimkus (R)
16. Adam Kinzinger (R)
17. Cheri Bustos (D)
18. Darin LaHood (R)

Indiana
1. Pete Visclosky (D)
2. Jackie Walorski (R)
3. Jim Banks (R)
4. Todd Rokita (R)
5. Susan Brooks (R)
6. Luke Messer (R)
7. André Carson (D)

8. Larry Bucshon (R)
9. Trey Hollingsworth (R)

Iowa
1. Rod Blum (R)
2. David Loebsack (D)
3. David Young (R)
4. Steve King (R)

Kansas
1. Roger Marshall (R)
2. Lynn Jenkins (R)
3. Kevin Yoder (R)
4. Mike Pompeo (R)
   (resigned January 23, 2017)
   Ron Estes (R)
   (sworn in April 25, 2017)

Kentucky
1. James Comer (R)
2. Brett Guthrie (R)
3. John Yarmuth (D)
4. Thomas Massie (R)
5. Hal Rogers (R)
6. Andy Barr (R)

Louisiana
1. Steve Scalise (R)
2. Cedric Richmond (D)
3. Clay Higgins (R)
4. Mike Johnson (R)
5. Ralph Abraham (R)
6. Garret Graves (R)

Maine
1. Chellie Pingree (D)
2. Bruce Poliquin (R)

Maryland
1. Andy Harris (R)
2. Dutch Ruppersberger (D)
3. John Sarbanes (D)
4. Anthony Brown (D)
5. Steny Hoyer (D)
6. John Delaney (D)
7. Elijah Cummings (D)
8. Jamie Raskin (D)

Massachusetts
1. Richard Neal (D)
2. Jim McGovern (D)
3. Niki Tsongas (D)
4. Joe Kennedy (D)
5. Katherine Clark (D)
6. Seth Moulton (D)
7. Mike Capuano (D)
8. Stephen Lynch (D)
9. Bill Keating (D)

Michigan
1. Jack Bergman (R)
2. Bill Huizenga (R)
3. Justin Amash (R)
4. John Moolenaar (R)
5. Dan Kildee (D)
6. Fred Upton (R)

7. Tim Walberg (R)
8. Mike Bishop (R)
9. Sander Levin (D)
10. Paul Mitchell (R)
11. Dave Trott (R)
12. Debbie Dingell (D)
13. John Conyers Jr. (D)
    (resigned December 5, 2017)
    Brenda Jones (D)
    (sworn in November 29, 2018)
14. Brenda Lawrence (D)

Minnesota
1. Timothy Walz (D)
2. Jason Lewis (R)
3. Erik Paulsen (R)
4. Betty McCollum (D)
5. Keith Ellison (D)
6. Tom Emmer (R)
7. Collin Peterson (D)
8. Richard Nolan (D)

Mississippi
1. Trent Kelly (R)
2. Bennie Thompson (D)
3. Gregg Harper (R)
4. Steven Palazzo (R)

Missouri
1. Lacy Clay (D)
2. Ann Wagner (R)
3. Blaine Luetkemeyer (R)
4. Vicky Hartzler (R)
5. Emanuel Cleaver (D)
6. Sam Graves (R)
7. Billy Long (R)
8. Jason Smith (R)

Montana
AL Ryan Zinke (R)
    (resigned in March 1, 2017)
Greg Gianforte (R)
    (sworn in June 27, 2017)

Nebraska
1. Jeff Fortenberry (R)
2. Don Bacon (R)
3. Adrian Smith (R)

Nevada
1. Dina Titus (D)
2. Mark Amodei (R)
3. Jacky Rosen (D)
4. Ruben Kihuen (D)

New Hampshire
1. Carol Shea-Porter (D)
2. Ann M Kuster (D)

New Jersey
1. Donald Norcross (D)
2. Frank LoBiondo (R)
3. Tom MacArthur (R)
4. Chris Smith (R)
5. Josh Gottheimer (D)
6. Frank Pallone (D)
7. Leonard Lance (R)
8. Albio Sires (D)

9. Bill Pascrell (D)
10. Donald Payne Jr. (D)
11. Rodney Frelinghuysen (R)
12. Bonnie Watson Coleman (D)

New Mexico
1. Michelle Lujan Grisham (D)
2. Steve Pearce (R)
3. Ben Ray Luján (D)

New York
1. Lee Zeldin (R)
2. Peter King (R)
3. Thomas Suozzi (D)
4. Kathleen Rice (D)
5. Gregory Meeks (D)
6. Grace Meng (D)
7. Nydia Velázquez (D)
8. Hakeem Jeffries (D)
9. Yvette Clarke (D)
10. Jerrold Nadler (D)
11. Dan Donovan (R)
12. Carolyn Maloney (D)
13. Adriano Espaillat (D)
14. Joseph Crowley (D)
15. José E. Serrano (D)
16. Eliot Engel (D)
17. Nita Lowey (D)
18. Sean Patrick Maloney (D)
19. John Faso (R)
20. Paul Tonko (D)
21. Elise Stefanik (R)
22. Claudia Tenney (R)
23. Thomas Reed (R)
24. John Katko (R)
25. Louise Slaughter (D)
    (died March 16, 2018)
    Joseph Morelle (D)
    (sworn in November 13, 2018)
26. Brian Higgins (D)
27. Chris Collins (R)

North Carolina
1. G. K. Butterfield (D)
2. George Holding (R)
3. Walter B. Jones Jr. (R)
4. David Price (D)
5. Virginia Foxx (R)
6. Mark Walker (R)
7. David Rouzer (R)
8. Richard Hudson (R)
9. Robert Pittenger (R)
10. Patrick McHenry (R)
11. Mark Meadows (R)
12. Alma Adams (D)
13. Ted Budd (R)

North Dakota
AL Kevin Cramer (R)

Ohio
1. Steve Chabot (R)
2. Brad Wenstrup (R)
3. Joyce Beatty (D)
4. Jim Jordan (R)
5. Bob Latta (R)
6. Bill Johnson (R)
7. Bob Gibbs (R)
8. Warren Davidson (R)

9. Marcy Kaptur (D)
10. Mike Turner (R)
11. Marcia Fudge (D)
12. Pat Tiberi (R)
    (resigned January 15, 2018)
    Troy Balderson (R)
    (sworn in November 5, 2018)
13. Tim Ryan (D)
14. David Joyce (R)
15. Steve Stivers (R)
16. Jim Renacci (R)

Oklahoma
1. Jim Bridenstine (R)
    (resigned April 23, 2018)
    Kevin Hern (R)
    (sworn in November 13, 2018)
2. Markwayne Mullin (R)
3. Frank Lucas (R)
4. Tom Cole (R)
5. Steve Russell (R)

Oregon
1. Suzanne Bonamici (D)
2. Greg Walden (R)
3. Earl Blumenauer (D)
4. Peter DeFazio (D)
5. Kurt Schrader (D)

Pennsylvania
1. Bob Brady (D)
2. Dwight Evans (D)
3. Mike Kelly (R)
4. Scott Perry (R)
5. Glenn Thompson (R)
6. Ryan Costello (R)
7. Pat Meehan (R)
    (resigned April 27, 2018)
    May Gay Scanlon (D)
    (sworn in January 3, 2019)
8. Brian Fitzpatrick (R)
9. Bill Shuster (R)
10. Tom Mariano (R)
11. Lou Barletta (R)
12. Keith Rothfus (R)
13. Brendan Boyle (D)
14. Michael Doyle (D)
15. Charles Dent (R)
    (resigned May 12, 2018)
    Susan Wild (D)
    (sworn in January 3, 2019)
16. Lloyd Smucker (R)
17. Matt Cartwright (D)
18. Tim Murphy (R)
    (resigned October 21, 2017)
    Conor Lamb (D)
    (sworn in January 3, 2019)

Rhode Island
1. David Cicilline (D)
2. James Langevin (D)

South Carolina
1. Mark Sanford (R)
2. Joe Wilson (R)
3. Jeff Duncan (R)
4. Trey Gowdy (R)
5. Mick Mulvaney (R)
    (resigned February 16, 2017)

Ralph Norman (R)
    (sworn in June 26, 2017)
6. Jim Clyburn (D)
7. Tom Rice (R)

South Dakota
AL Kristi Noem (R)

Tennessee
1. Phil Roe (R)
2. Jimmy Duncan (R)
3. Chuck Fleischmann (R)
4. Scott DesJarlais (R)
5. Jim Cooper (D)
6. Diane Black (R)
7. Marsha Blackburn (R)
8. David Kustoff (R)
9. Steve Cohen (D)

Texas
1. Louie Gohmert (R)
2. Ted Poe (R)
3. Sam Johnson (R)
4. John Ratcliffe (R)
5. Jeb Hensarling (R)
6. Joe Barton (R)
7. John Culberson (R)
8. Kevin Brady (R)
9. Al Green (D)
10. Michael McCaul (R)
11. Mike Conaway (R)
12. Kay Granger (R)
13. Mac Thornberry (R)
14. Randy Weber (R)
15. Vicente Gonzalez (D)
16. Beto O'Rourke (D)
17. Bill Flores (R)
18. Sheila Jackson Lee (D)
19. Jodey Arrington (R)
20. Joaquin Castro (D)
21. Lamar Smith (R)
22. Pete Olson (R)
23. Will Hurd (R)
24. Kenny Marchant (R)
25. Roger Williams (R)
26. Michael Burgess (R)
27. Blake Farenthold (R)
    (resigned April 6, 2018)
    Michael Cloud (R)
    (sworn in July 10, 2018)
28. Henry Cuellar (D)
29. Gene Green (D)
30. Eddie Bernice Johnson (D)
31. John Carter (R)
32. Pete Sessions (R)
33. Marc Veasey (D)
34. Filemon Vela Jr. (D)
35. Lloyd Doggett (D)
36. Brian Babin (R)

Utah
1. Rob Bishop (R)
2. Chris Stewart (R)
3. Jason Chaffetz (R)
    (resigned June 30, 2017)
    John R Curtis (R)
    (sworn in November 13, 2017)
4. Mia Love (R)

Vermont

AL Peter Welch (D)

Virginia

1. Rob Wittman (R)
2. Scott Rigell (R)
3. Bobby Scott (D)
4. Donald McEachin (D)
5. Thomas Garrett Jr (R)
6. Bob Goodlatte (R)
7. Dave Brat (R)
8. Don Beyer (D)

9. Morgan Griffith (R)
10. Barbara Comstock (R)
11. Gerry Connolly (D)

Washington

1. Suzan DelBene (D)
2. Rick Larsen (D)
3. Jaime Herrera Beutler (R)
4. Dan Newhouse (R)
5. Cathy McMorris Rodgers (R)
6. Derek Kilmer (D)
7. Pramila Jayapal (D)

8. Dave Reichert (R)
9. Adam Smith (D)
10. Dennis Heck (D)

West Virginia

1. David McKinley (R)
2. Alex Mooney (R)
3. Evan Jenkins (R)

Wisconsin

1. Paul Ryan (R)
2. Mark Pocan (D)

3. Ron Kind (D)
4. Gwen Moore (D)
5. Jim Sensenbrenner (R)
6. Glenn Grothman (R)
7. Sean Duffy (R)
8. Mike Gallagher (R)

Wyoming

AL Liz Cheney (R)

NOTE: Changes that occurred during 2017 and 2018 are noted following the names of individuals who did not serve their full terms. Members of the 115th Congress also included delegates Aumua Amata Coleman Radewagen, R–American Samoa; Eleanor Holmes Norton, D–District of Columbia; Madeleine Z. Bordallo, D–Guam; Gregorio Kilili Camacho Sablan, D–Northern Mariana Islands; Stacey E. Plaskett, D–Virgin Islands; and resident commissioner Jenniffer González-Colón, R–Puerto Rico, AL–At Large.

Membership Changes, 115th and 116th Congresses

115th Congress

Member/Party	Died	Resigned	Successor	Appointed	Elected	Sworn In
Senate						
Jeff Sessions R-Ala.[1]		08/01/2017	Luther Strange, R	09/02/2017		09/02/2017
Luther Stranger, R-Ala.[2]		03/01/2018	Doug Jones, D		12/12/2017	03/01/2018
John McCain, R-Ariz.[3]	08/25/2018		Jon Kyl, R	09/04/2018		05/09/2018
Al Franken, D-Minn.[4]		02/01/2018	Tina Smith, D	12/13/2017		03/01/2018
Thad Cochran, R-Miss.[5]		01/04/2018	Cindy Hyde-Smith, R	03/21/2018		04/09/2018
House						
Trent Franks, R-Ariz.[6]		12/08/2017	Debbie Lesko, R		04/24/2018	05/07/2018
Xavier Becerra, D-Calif.[7]		12/01/2016	Jimmy Gomez, D		06/06/2017	11/07/2017
Tom Price, R-Ga.[8]		10/02/2017	Karen Handel, R		06/20/2017	06/26/2017
Mike Pompeo, R-Kan.[9]		01/23/2017	Ron Estes, R		04/11/2017	04/25/2017
John Conyers Jr., D-Mich.[10]		12/05/2017	Brenda Jones, D		11/06/2018	11/29/2018
Ryan Zinke, R-Mont.[11]		01/03/2017	Greg Gianforte, R		05/25/2017	06/27/2017
Louise Slaughter, D-Ny.[12]	03/16/2018		Joseph Morelle, D	06/11/2018		11/13/2018
Pat Tiberi, R-Ohio[13]		01/15/2018	Troy Balderson, R		07/08/2018	09/052018
Jim Bridenstine, R-Okla.[14]		04/23/2018	Kevin Hern, R		08/28/2018	11/13/2018
Pat Meehan, R-Pa.[15]		04/27/2018	Mary Gay Scanlon, D		06/11/2018	03/01/2019
Charles Dent, R-Pa.[16]		05/12/2018	Susan Wild, D		06/11/2018	01/03/2019
Tim Murphy, R-Pa.[17]		10/21/2017	Conor Lamb, D		03/13/2018	01/03/2019
Mick Mulvaney, R-S.C.[18]		02/16/2017	Ralph Norman, R		06/20/2017	06/26/2017
Blake Farenthold, R-Texas[19]		04/06/2018	Michael Cloud, R		06/30/2018	07/10/2018
Jason Chaffetz, R-Utah[20]		06/30/2017	John R Curtis, R		07/11/2017	11/13/2017

116th Congress

Member/Party	Died	Resigned	Successor	Appointed	Elected	Sworn In
Senate						
Martha McSally, R-Ariz[21]		12/02/2020	Mark Kelly, D		11/03/2020	12/02/2020
Johnny Isakson, R-Ga.[22]		12/31/2019	Kelly Loeffler	12/04/2019		01/06/2020
House						
Katie Hill, D-Calif.[23]		11/03/2019	Mike Garcia, R		05/12/2020	05/19/2020
John Lewis, D-Ga.[24]	07/17/2020		Kwanza Hall, D		12/01/2020	12/03/2020
Elijah Cummings, D-Md.[25]	10/17/2020		Kweisi Mfume, D		04/28/2020	05/05/2020
Chris Collins, R-N.Y.[26]		10/01/2019	Chris Jacobs, R		06/23/2020	07/21/2020
Walter B. Jones, R-N.C.[27]	02/10-/2019		Gregory Murphy, R		09/10/2019	09//2019
Tom Marino, R-Pa.[28]		01/23/2019	Fred Keller, R		05/21/2019	06/03/2019
Sean Duffy, R-Wisc.[29]		09/23/2019	Thomas Tiffany, R		05/12/2020	05/19/2020

[1]Resigned after being appointed as Attorney General by then President Donald Trump in 2018.

[2]Failed to be the Republican nominee and thus did not succeed in serving the rest of the unexpired term.

[3]John McCain died on August 25, 2018 after being diagnosed with a glioblastoma brain tumor in 2017.

[4]After being accused by multiple women of sexual impropriety (unwanted touches and kisses), Franken resigned on January 2, 2018.

[5] Resigned due to health concerns, and passed away May 30, 2019, about a year after his resignation.

[6]Forced to resign after allegations of sexual harassment made by female staffers. The House Ethics Committee conducted an investigation and found that Franks did not deny such claims and admitted that he engaged in conversations with female staffers about possible surrogacy arrangements. According to AP, he offered one woman $5 million if she was his surrogate.

[7]Resigned in 2017 to serve as California Attorney General after being appointed by then California governor Jerry Brown.

[8]Resigned after being appointed as 23rd Secretary of Health and Human Services by then President Donald Trump.

[9]Resigned after being appointed as the sixth director of the CIA from 2017 to 2018. Pompeo later served as the 70th U.S. Secretary of State on April 26, 2018.

[10]Conyer's resigned after being accused of sexual misconduct by three women, including former staffers. The House Ethics Committee conducted an investigation, and members of the House, including Rep. Nancy Pelosi and Rep. James Clyburn, called on Conyer's to resign.

[11]Resigned from Congress to serve as the 52nd Secretary of Interior after being appointed by then President Donald Trump.

[12]Louise Slaughter died on March 16, 2018 from complications after falling in her home.

[13]Resigned from Congress to serve as the president and CEO of the Ohio Business Roundtable, a nonprofit and nonpartisan organization.

[14]Resigned from Congress and served as NASA's 13th administrator.

[15]Resigned due to sexual misconduct allegations made by a woman who claimed that Meehan made unwanted advances and became hostile when feelings were not reciprocated. An investigation was conducted by the House Ethics Committee, a group from which he had his previous position as a member removed.

[16]Retired from office and announced that he would no longer seek reelection.

[17]Following extramarital affairs that lead to him asking a woman to have an abortion, Murphy resigned from office.

[18]Resigned from Congress after being selected as the director of the Office of Management and Budget by then President Donald Trump, serving from February 2017 to July 2020.

[19]Resigned following allegations of sexual misconduct made by Lauren Greene, a former staffer. The Office of Congressional Ethics rejected her claims and dismissed the case to the House Ethics Committee. Both Green and Farenthold reached an agreement and settled their lawsuit outside of court.

[20]Chaffetz did not seek reelection and made the decision to return to the private sector.

[21]After filling Sen. Jon Kyl's seat which was open after Sen. John McCain's death, McSally ran but failed to win a special election to secure her seat in Senate.

[22]Due to health concerns, Isakson retired from the House in 2019 and later died December 21, 2021.

[23]Resigned after an extramarital affair with a campaign staffer was revealed. The House Ethics Committee conducted an investigation, however, house rules do not forbid such relationships with campaign staffers.

[24]John Lewis died on July 17, 2020 due to pancreatic cancer.

[25]Cummings retired from Congress in 2017 after experiencing "longstanding health challenges."

[26]In 2018, Collins admitted to allegations made by the FBI of insider trading with Innate Immunotherapeutics stock. He suspended his reelection campaign but later chose to continue his efforts. However, in September 2019, court documents revealed his intention to plead guilty, which led him to submit his resignation later that day. He would eventually be pardoned by then President Donald Trump in December 2020.

[27]Walter B. Jones Jr died on February 10, 2019 due to related past health concerns.

[28]Resigned due to health concerns and a job opportunity in the private sector. The company focuses on the development of skill game devices.

[29]Resigned to tend to his wife and baby who was born with complications, including a heart condition.

Senate Membership in the 116th Congress

Membership at the beginning of Congress in 2019: Republicans 52; Democrats 46; Independents 2. Changes that occurred during the two year period are noted.

Alabama
Richard Shelby (R)
Doug Jones (D)

Alaska
Dan Sullivan (R)
Lisa Murkowski (R)

Arizona
Mark Kelly (D)
Martha McSally (R)[1]
Kyrsten Sinema (D)[2]

Arkansas
Tom Cotton (R)
John Boozman (R)

California
Dianne Feinstein (D)
Kamala Harris (D)

Colorado
Cory Gardner (R)
Michael Bennet (D)

Connecticut
Chris Murphy (D)
Richard Blumenthal (D)

Delaware
Tom Carper (D)
Chris Coons (D)

Florida
Marco Rubio (R)
Rick Scott (R)

Georgia
David Perdue (R)
Johnny Isakson (R)[3]
Kelly Loeffler (R)[4]

Hawaii
Mazie Hirono (D)
Brian Schatz (D)

Idaho
Jim Risch (R)
Mike Crapo (R)

Illinois
Dick Durbin (D)
Tammy Duckworth (D)

Indiana
Mike Braun (R)
Todd Young (R)

Iowa
Joni Ernst (R)
Chuck Grassley (R)

Kansas
Pat Roberts (R)
Jerry Moran (R)

Kentucky
Mitch McConnell (R)
Rand Paul (R)

Louisiana
Bill Cassidy (R)
John Kennedy (R)

Maine
Angus King (I)
Susan Collins (R)

Maryland
Ben Cardin (D)
Chris Van Hollen (D)

Massachusetts
Elizabeth Warren (D)
Ed Markey (D)

Michigan
Debbie Stabenow (D)
Gary Peters (D)

Minnesota
Amy Klobuchar (D)
Tina Smith (D)

Mississippi
Roger Wicker (R)
Cindy Hyde-Smith (R)

Missouri
Josh Hawley (R)
Roy Blunt (R)

Montana
Jon Tester (D)
Steve Daines (R)

Nebraska
Deb Fischer (R)
Ben Sasse (R)

Nevada
Jacky Rosen (D)
Catherine Cortez Mastro (D)

New Hampshire
Jeanne Shaheen (D)
Margaret Hassan (D)

New Jersey
Bob Menendez (D)
Cory Booker (D)

New Mexico
Martin Heinrich (D)
Tom Udall (D)

New York
Kirsten Gillibrand (D)
Chuck Schumer (D)

North Carolina
Thom Tillis (R)
Richard Burr (R)

North Dakota
Kevin Cramer (R)
John Hoeven (R)

Ohio
Sherrod Brown (D)
Rob Portman (R)

Oklahoma
Jim Inhofe (R)
James Lankford (R)

Oregon
Jeff Merkley (D)
Ron Wyden (D)

Pennsylvania
Bob Casey Jr. (D)
Pat Toomey (R)

Rhode Island
Sheldon Whitehouse (D)
Jack Reed (D)

South Carolina
Lindsey Graham (R)
Tim Scott (R)

South Dakota
Mike Rounds (R)
John Thune (R)

Tennessee
Marsha Blackburn (R)
Lamar Alexander (R)

Texas
Ted Cruz (R)
John Cornyn (R)

Utah
Mitt Romney (R)
Mike Lee (R)

Vermont
Bernie Sanders (I)
Patrick Leahy (D)

Virginia
Tim Kaine (D)
Mark Warner (D)

Washington
Maria Cantwell (D)
Patty Murray (D)

West Virginia
Joe Manchin (D)
Shelley Moore Capito (R)

Wisconsin
Tammy Baldwin (D)
Ron Johnson (R)

Wyoming
John Barrasso (R)
Mike Enzi (R)

Republicans	52
Democrats	46
Independents	2

[1]McSally filled vacancy caused by John McCain's death which was previously held by Jon Kyl. She was an unsuccessful candidate in the November 2020 special election.

[2]Sinema replaced Martha McSally.

[3]Resigned December 31, 2019

[4]Loeffler was appointed to fill John Isakson's seat but was an unsuccessful candidate for the remainder of the term.

House Membership in the 116th Congress

Membership at the beginning of Congress in January 2019: Republicans 200; Democrats 233; Independents/Libertarians 2. Changes during the 2019–2020 period are noted.

Alabama
1. Bradley Byrne (R)
2. Martha Roby (R)
3. Mike Rogers (R)
4. Robert Aderholt (R)
5. Mo Brooks (R)
6. Gary Palmer (R)
7. Terri Sewell (D)

Alaska
AL Don Young (R)

Arizona
1. Tom O'Halleran (D)
2. Ann Kirkpatrick (D)
3. Raúl Grijalva (D)
4. Paul Gosar (R)
5. Andy Briggs (R)
6. David Schweikert (R)
7. Ruben Gallego (D)
8. Debbie Lesko (R)
9. Greg Stanton (D)

Arkansas
1. Rick Crawford (R)
2. French Hill (R)
3. Steve Womack (R)
4. Bruce Westerman (R)

California
1. Doug LaMalfa (R)
2. Jared Huffman (D)
3. John Garamendi (D)
4. Tom McClintock (R)
5. Mike Thompson (D)
6. Doris Matsui (D)
7. Ami Bera (D)
8. Paul Cook (R)
9. Jerry McNerney (D)
10. Josh Harder (D)
11. Mark DeSaulnier (D)
12. Nancy Pelosi (D)
13. Barbara Lee (D)
14. Jackie Speier (D)
15. Eric Swalwell (D)
16. Jim Costa (D)
17. Ro Khanna (D)
18. Anna Eshoo (D)
19. Zoe Lofgren (D)
20. Jimmy Panetta (D)
21. TJ Cox (D)
22. Devin Nunes (R)
23. Kevin McCarthy (R)
24. Salud O. Carbajal (D)
25. Katie Hill (D)
    (resigned November 3, 2019)
    Mike Garcia (R)
    (sworn in May 19, 2020)
26. Julia Brownley (D)
27. Judy Chu (D)
28. Adam Schiff (D)
29. Tony Cardenas (D)
30. Brad Sherman (D)
31. Pete Aguilar (D)
32. Grace Napolitano (D)
33. Ted Lieu (D)
34. Jimmy Gomez (D)
35. Norma Torres (D)
36. Raul Ruiz (D)
37. Karen Bass (D)
38. Linda Sánchez (D)
39. Gilbert Ray Cisneros (D)
40. Lucille Roybal-Allard (D)
41. Mark Takano (D)
42. Ken Calvert (R)
43. Maxine Waters (D)
44. Nanette Diaz Barragan (D)
45. Katie Porter (D)
46. Luis Correa (D)
47. Alan Lowenthal (D)
48. Harley Rouda (D)
49. Mike Levin (D)
50. Duncan D. Hunter (R)
51. Juan Vargas (D)
52. Scott Peters (D)
53. Susan Davis (D)

Colorado
1. Diana DeGette (D)
2. Joe Neguse (D)
3. Scott Tipton (R)
4. Ken Buck (R)
5. Doug Lamborn (R)
6. Jason Crow (D)
7. Ed Perlmutter (D)

Connecticut
1. John Larson (D)
2. Joe Courtney (D)
3. Rosa DeLauro (D)
4. Jim Himes (D)
5. Jahana Hayes (D)

Delaware
AL Lisa Blunt Rochester (D)

Florida
1. Matt Gaetz (R)
2. Neal P. Dunn (R)
3. Ted Yoho (R)
4. John Rutherford (R)
5. Al Lawson Jr. (D)
6. Michael Waltz (R)
7. Stephanie Murphy (D)
8. Bill Posey (R)
9. Darren Soto (D)
10. Val Butler Demings (D)
11. Daniel Webster (R)
12. Gus Bilirakis (R)
13. Charlie Crist (D)
14. Kathy Castor (D)
15. Ross Spano (R)
16. Vern Buchanan (R)
17. Gregory Steube (R)
18. Brian Mast (R)
19. Francis Rooney (R)
20. Alcee Hastings (D)
21. Lois Frankel (D)
22. Ted Deutch (D)
23. Debbie Wasserman Schultz (D)
24. Frederica Wilson (D)
25. Mario Diaz-Balart (R)
26. Debbie Mucarsel-Powell (D)
27. Donna Shalala (D)

Georgia
1. Buddy Carter (R)
2. Sanford Bishop (D)
3. Drew Ferguson (R)
4. Hank Johnson (D)
5. John Lewis (D)
   (died July 17, 2020)
   Kwanza Hall (D)
   (sworn in December 3, 2020)
6. Lucy McBath (D)
7. Rob Woodall (R)
8. Austin Scott (R)
9. Doug Collins (R)
10. Jody Hice (R)
11. Barry Loudermilk (R)
12. Rick Allen (R)
13. David Scott (D)
14. Tom Graves (R)

Hawaii
1. Ed Case (D)
2. Tulsi Gabbard (D)

Idaho
1. Russ Fulcher (R)
2. Mike Simpson (R)

Illinois
1. Bobby Rush (D)
2. Robin Kelly (D)
3. Dan Lipinski (D)
4. Chuy Garcia (D)
5. Mike Quigley (D)
6. Sean Casten (D)
7. Danny Davis (D)
8. Raja Krishnamoorthi (D)
9. Jan Schakowsky (D)
10. Bradley Scott Schneider (D)
11. Bill Foster (D)
12. Mike Bost (R)
13. Rodney Davis (R)
14. Lauren Underwood (D)
15. John Shimkus (R)
16. Adam Kinzinger (R)
17. Cheri Bustos (D)
18. Darin LaHood (R)

Indiana
1. Pete Visclosky (D)
2. Jackie Walorski (R)
3. Jim Banks (R)
4. James Baird (R)
5. Susan Brooks (R)
6. Greg Pence (R)
7. André Carson (D)
8. Larry Bucshon (R)
9. Trey Hollingsworth (R)

Iowa
1. Abby Finkenauer (D)
2. David Loebsack (D)
3. Cynthia Axne (D)
4. Steve King (R)

Kansas
1. Roger Marshall (R)
2. Steve Watkins (R)
3. Sharice Davids (D)
4. Ron Estes (R)

Kentucky
1. James Comer (R)
2. Brett Guthrie (R)
3. John Yarmuth (D)
4. Thomas Massie (R)
5. Hal Rogers (R)
6. Andy Barr (R)

Louisiana
1. Steve Scalise (R)
2. Cedric Richmond (D)
3. Clay Higgins (R)
4. Mike Johnson (R)
5. Ralph Abraham (R)
6. Garret Graves (R)

Maine
1. Chellie Pingree (D)
2. Jared Golden (D)

Maryland
1. Andy Harris (R)
2. Dutch Ruppersberger (D)
3. John Sarbanes (D)
4. Anthony Brown (D)
5. Steny Hoyer (D)
6. David Trone (D)
7. Elijah Cummings (D)
   (died October 17, 2019)
   Kweisi Mfume (D)
   (sworn in May 5, 2020)
8. Jamie Raskin (D)

Massachusetts
1. Richard Neal (D)
2. Jim McGovern (D)
3. Lori Trahan (D)
4. Joe Kennedy (D)
5. Katherine Clark (D)
6. Seth Moulton (D)
7. Ayanna Pressley (D)
8. Stephen Lynch (D)
9. Bill Keating (D)

Michigan
1. Jack Bergman (R)
2. Bill Huizenga (R)
3. Justin Amash (L)

4. John Moolenaar (R)
5. Dan Kildee (D)
6. Fred Upton (R)
7. Tim Walberg (R)
8. Elissa Slotkin (D)
9. Andy Levin (D)
10. Paul Mitchell (I)
11. Hayley Stevens (D)
12. Debbie Dingell (D)
13. Rashida Tlaib (D)
14. Brenda Lawrence (D)

Minnesota
1. Jim Hagedorn (R)
2. Angie Craig (D)
3. Dean Phillips (D)
4. Betty McCollum (D)
5. Ilhan Omar (D)
6. Tom Emmer (R)
7. Collin Peterson (D)
8. Pete Stauber (R)

Mississippi
1. Trent Kelly (R)
2. Bennie Thompson (D)
3. Michael Guest (R)
4. Steven Palazzo (R)

Missouri
1. Lacy Clay (D)
2. Ann Wagner (R)
3. Blaine Luetkemeyer (R)
4. Vicky Hartzler (R)
5. Emanuel Cleaver (D)
6. Sam Graves (R)
7. Billy Long (R)
8. Jason Smith (R)

Montana
AL Greg Gianforte (R)

Nebraska
1. Jeff Fortenberry (R)
2. Don Bacon (R)
3. Adrian Smith (R)

Nevada
1. Dina Titus (D)
2. Mark Amodei (R)
3. Susie Lee (D)
4. Steven Horsford (D)

New Hampshire
1. Chris Pappas (D)
2. Ann M Kuster (D)

New Jersey
1. Donald Norcross (D)
2. Jefferson Van Drew (R)
3. Andy Kim (D)
4. Chris Smith (R)
5. Josh Gottheimer (D)
6. Frank Pallone (D)
7. Tom Malinowski (D)
8. Albio Sires (D)
9. Bill Pascrell (D)
10. Donald Payne Jr. (D)
11. Mikie Sherrill (D)
12. Bonnie Watson Coleman (D)

New Mexico
1. Debra A Haaland (D)
2. Xochitl Torres Small (D)
3. Ben Ray Luján (D)

New York
1. Lee Zeldin (R)
2. Peter King (R)
3. Thomas Suozzi (D)
4. Kathleen Rice (D)
5. Gregory Meeks (D)
6. Grace Meng (D)
7. Nydia Velázquez (D)
8. Hakeem Jeffries (D)
9. Yvette Clarke (D)
10. Jerrold Nadler (D)
11. Max Rose (D)
12. Carolyn Maloney (D)
13. Adriano Espaillat (D)
14. Alexandria Ocasio-Cortez (D)
15. José E. Serrano (D)
16. Eliot Engel (D)
17. Nita Lowey (D)
18. Sean Patrick Maloney (D)
19. Antonio Delgado (D)
20. Paul Tonko (D)
21. Elise Stefanik (R)
22. Anthony Brindisi (D)
23. Thomas Reed (R)
24. John Katko (R)
25. Joseph Morelle (D)
26. Brian Higgins (D)
27. Chris Collins (R)
    (resigned October 1, 2019)
    Chris Jacobs (R)
    (sworn in July 21, 2020)

North Carolina
1. G. K. Butterfield (D)
2. George Holding (R)
3. Walter B. Jones Jr. (R)
    (died February 10, 2019)
    Gregory Murphy (R)
    (sworn in September 17, 2019)
4. David Price (D)
5. Virginia Foxx (R)
6. Mark Walker (R)
7. David Rouzer (R)
8. Richard Hudson (R)
9. Dan Bishop (R)
10. Patrick McHenry (R)
11. Mark Meadows (R)
12. Alma Adams (D)
13. Ted Budd (R)

North Dakota
AL Kelly Armstrong (R)

Ohio
1. Steve Chabot (R)
2. Brad Wenstrup (R)
3. Joyce Beatty (D)
4. Jim Jordan (R)
5. Bob Latta (R)
6. Bill Johnson (R)
7. Bob Gibbs (R)
8. Warren Davidson (R)

9. Marcy Kaptur (D)
10. Mike Turner (R)
11. Marcia Fudge (D)
12. Troy Balderson (R)
13. Tim Ryan (D)
14. David Joyce (R)
15. Steve Stivers (R)
16. Anthony Gonzalez (R)

Oklahoma
1. Kevin Hern (R)
2. Markwayne Mullin (R)
3. Frank Lucas (R)
4. Tom Cole (R)
5. Kendra Horn (D)

Oregon
1. Suzanne Bonamici (D)
2. Greg Walden (R)
3. Earl Blumenauer (D)
4. Peter DeFazio (D)
5. Kurt Schrader (D)

Pennsylvania
1. Kirk Fitzpatrick (R)
2. Brendan Boyle (D)
3. Dwight Evans (D)
4. Madeline Dean (D)
5. Mary Gay Scanlon (D)
6. Chrissy Houlahan (D)
7. Susan Wild (D)
8. Matt Cartwright (D)
9. Daniel Meuser (R)
10. Scott Perry (R)
11. Lloyd Smucker (R)
12. Tom Marino (R)
    (resigned January 23, 2019)
    Fred Keller (R)
    (sworn in June 3, 2019)
13. John Joyce (R)
14. Guy Reschenthaler (R)
15. Glenn Thompson (R)
16. Mike Kelly (R)
17. Conor Lamb (D)
18. Michael Doyle (D)

Rhode Island
1. David Cicilline (D)
2. James Langevin (D)

South Carolina
1. Joe Cunningham (D)
2. Joe Wilson (R)
3. Jeff Duncan (R)
4. William Timmons (R)
5. Ralph Norman (R)
6. Jim Clyburn (D)
7. Tom Rice (R)

South Dakota
AL Dusty Johnson (R)

Tennessee
1. Phil Roe (R)
2. Tim Burchett (R)
3. Chuck Fleischmann (R)
4. Scott DesJarlais (R)
5. Jim Cooper (D)
6. John Rose (R)

7. Mark Green (R)
8. David Kustoff (R)
9. Steve Cohen (D)

Texas
1. Louie Gohmert (R)
2. Dan Crenshaw (R)
3. Van Taylor (R)
4. John Ratcliffe (R)
5. Lance Gooden (R)
6. Ron Wright (R)
7. Lizzie Fletcher (D)
8. Kevin Brady (R)
9. Al Green (D)
10. Michael McCaul (R)
11. Mike Conaway (R)
12. Kay Granger (R)
13. Mac Thornberry (R)
14. Randy Weber (R)
15. Vicente Gonzalez (D)
16. Veronica Escobar (D)
17. Bill Flores (R)
18. Sheila Jackson Lee (D)
19. Jodey Arrington (R)
20. Joaquin Castro (D)
21. Chip Roy (R)
22. Pete Olson (R)
23. Will Hurd (R)
24. Kenny Marchant (R)
25. Roger Williams (R)
26. Michael Burgess (R)
27. Michael Cloud (R)
28. Henry Cuellar (D)
29. Sylvia Garcia (D)
30. Eddie Bernice Johnson (D)
31. John Carter (R)
32. Colin Allred (D)
33. Marc Veasey (D)
34. Filemon Vela Jr. (D)
35. Lloyd Doggett (D)
36. Brian Babin (R)

Utah
1. Rob Bishop (R)
2. Chris Stewart (R)
3. John R Curtis (R)
4. Ben McAdams (D)

Vermont
AL Peter Welch (D)

Virginia
1. Rob Wittman (R)
2. Elaine Luria (D)
3. Bobby Scott (D)
4. Donald McEachin (D)
5. Denver Riggleman (R)
6. Ben Cline (R)
7. Abigail Davis Spanberger (D)
8. Don Beyer (D)
9. Morgan Griffith (R)
10. Jennifer Wexton (D)
11. Gerry Connolly (D)

Washington
1. Suzan DelBene (D)
2. Rick Larsen (D)

3. Jaime Herrera Beutler (R)
4. Dan Newhouse (R)
5. Cathy McMorris Rodgers (R)
6. Derek Kilmer (D)
7. Pramila Jayapal (D)
8. Kim Schrier (D)
9. Adam Smith (D)
10. Dennis Heck (D)

West Virginia
1. David McKinley (R)
2. Alex Mooney (R)
3. Carol Miller (R)

Wisconsin
1. Bryan Steil (R)
2. Mark Pocan (D)

3. Ron Kind (D)
4. Gwen Moore (D)
5. Jim Sensenbrenner (R)
6. Glenn Grothman (R)
7. Sean Duffy (R)
   (resigned September 23, 2019)

Thomas Tiffany (R)
   (sworn in May 19, 2020)
8. Mike Gallagher (R)

Wyoming
AL Liz Cheney (R)

204	Republicans
236	Democrats
1	Independent
1	Libertarian
7	Changes

NOTE: Changes that occurred during 2019 and 2020 are noted following the names of individuals who did not serve their full terms. Members of the 116th Congress also included delegates Aumua Amata Coleman Radewagen, R–American Samoa; Eleanor Holmes Norton, D–District of Columbia; Michael F.Q. San Nicolas, D–Guam; Gregorio Kilili Camacho Sablan, D–Northern Mariana Islands; Stacey E. Plaskett, D–Virgin Islands; and resident commissioner Jenniffer González-Colón, R–Puerto Rico, AL–At Large.

Congressional Leadership and Committees, 115th and 116th Congresses

Senate Leadership

President Pro Tempore, 115th Congress: Mike Pence, Ind.; Orrin Hatch, Utah.

President Pro Tempore, 116th Congress: Mike Pence, Ind.; Chuck Grassley, Iowa.

Republican Leaders, 115th Congress

Majority Floor Leader 115th Congress: Mitch McConnell, Ky.

Chief Deputy Whip 115th Congress: John Cornyn, Texas.

Democratic Leaders, 115th Congress

Minority Floor Leader 115th Congress: Chuck Schmer, N.Y.

Assistant Floor Leader 115th Congress: Patty Murray, Wash.

Minority Whip 115th Congress: Richard Durbin, Ill..

Republican Leaders, 116th Congress

Majority Floor Leader 116th Congress: Mitch McConnell, Ky.

Chief Deputy Whip 116th Congress: John Thune, S.D.

Democratic Leaders, 116th Congress

Minority Floor Leader 116th Congress: Chuck Schumer, N.Y.

Assistant Floor Leader 116th Congress: Patty Murray, Wash.

Minority Whip 116th Congress: Richard J. Durbin, Ill.

Senate Political Committees

Democratic Policy Committee—Debbie Stabenow, Mich., Chair (115th Congress and 116th Congress).

Democratic Senatorial Campaign Committee—Chris Van Hollen, Md., Chair (115th Congress); Catherine Cortez Masto, Mich., Chair (116th Congress).

Democratic Steering and Outreach Committee—Amy Klobuchar, Minn., Steering Chair; Bernie Sanders, Vt., Outreach Chair (115th Congress and 116th Congress).

Democratic Communications Center—Debbie Stabenow, Mich., Chair (115th Congress and 116th Congress).

National Republican Senatorial Committee—Cory Garden, Colo., Chair (115th Congress); Todd Young, Ind., Chair (116th Congress).

Republican Conference—John Thune, S.D., Chair (115th Congress); John Barrasso, Wyo., Chair (116th Congress).

Republican Policy Committee—John Barrasso, Wyo., Chair (115th Congress); Roy Blunt, Mo., (116th Congress).

House Leadership

Speaker of the House:

Paul Ryan, R, Wis., 115th Congress

Nancy Pelosi, D, Calif., 116th Congress

Republican Leaders 115th Congress

Kevin McCarthy, Calif., Majority Leader

Steve Scalise, La., Majority Whip

Patrick McHenry, N.C., Chief Deputy Majority Whip

Republican Leaders 116th Congress

Kevin McCarthy, Calif., Minority Leader

Steve Scalise, La., Minority Whip

Drew Ferguson, Ga., Minority Chief Deputy Whip

Democratic Leaders 115th Congress

Nancy Pelosi, Calif., Minority Leader

Steny H. Hoyer, Md., Minority Whip

James E. Clyburn, S.C., Assistant Leader

Democratic Leaders 116th Congress

Steny H. Hoyer, MD., Majority Leader

James E. Clyburn, S.C., Majority Whip

Ben Ray Lujan, N.M., Assistant Speaker

Political Committees

Democratic Congressional Campaign Committee— Ben Ray Luján, N.M., Chair (115th Congress); Cheri Bustos, Ill., Chair (116th Congress)

Democratic Steering and Policy Committees—Nancy Pelosi, Calif., Chair, (115th and 116th Congress); Rosa DeLauro, Conn., Co-Chair (Steering, 115th and 116th Congress); Eric Swalwell, Calif., Co-Chair (Policy, 115th and 116th Congress).

Democratic Caucus—Joseph Crowley, N.Y., Chair (115th Congress); Hakeen S. Jeffries, N.Y., Chair (116th Congress).

National Republican Congressional Committee—Steve Stivers, Ohio., Chair (115 Congress); Tom Emmer, Minn., Chair (116th Congress).

Republican Conference—Cathy McMorris Rodgers, Wash., Chair (115th Congress); Liz Cheney, Wyo., Chair (116th Congress).

Republican Policy Committee—Luke Messer, Ind., Chair (115th Congress); Gary J. Palmer, Ala., Chair (116th Congress).

Republican Steering Committee—Paul Ryan, Wis., Chair (115th Congress); Kevin McCarthy, Calif., Chair (116th Congress).

Congressional Committees

Following is a list of House and Senate leaders and congressional committees and subcommittees for the 115th and 116th Congresses. The committee listings are as of the beginning of both congresses. Some changes, usually because of resignations or death, occurred later.

Committee jurisdictions, party ratios, committee chairs and the dates of their service in that capacity, ranking minority members (in italics), and subcommittee chairs are included. Political and joint committees also are listed.

Senate Committees

AGRICULTURE, NUTRITION AND FORESTRY

Agriculture in general; animal industry and diseases; crop insurance and soil conservation; farm credit and farm security; food from fresh waters; food stamp programs; forestry in general; home economics; human nutrition; inspection of livestock, meat, and agricultural products; pests and pesticides; plant industry, soils, and agricultural engineering; rural development, rural electrification, and watersheds; school nutrition programs.

R 11–D 10 *(115th Congress)*

Debbie Stabenow, Mich.
Pat Roberts, Kan.

Commodities, Risk Management and Trade— John Boozman, Ark.
Rural Development and Energy—Joni Ernst, Iowa
Conservation, Forestry and Natural Resources—Steve Daines, Mont.
Nutrition, Specialty Crops and Agricultural Research—David Perdue, Ga.
Livestock, Marketing and Agriculture Security—Deb Fischer, Neb.

R 11–D 9 *(116th Congress)*

Pat Roberts, Kan.
Debbie Stabenow, Mich.

Commodities, Risk Management and Trade—John Boozman, Ark.
Rural Development and Energy—Joni Ernst, Iowa
Conservation, Forestry and Natural Resources—Mike Braun, Ind.
Nutrition, Specialty Crops and Agricultural Research—Deb Fischer, Neb.
Livestock, Marketing and Agriculture Security—Cindy Hyde-Smith, Miss.

APPROPRIATIONS

Appropriation of revenue; rescission of appropriations; new spending authority under the Congressional Budget Act.

R 11–D 10 *(115th Congress)*

Richard Shelby, Ala.
Patrick Leahy, Vt.

Agriculture, Rural Development, Food and Drug Administration—John Hoeven, N.D.
Commerce, Justice, Science—Jerry Moran, Kan.
Defense—Richard Shelby, Ala.
Energy and Water Development—Lamar Alexander, Tenn.
Financial Services and General Government—James Lankford, Okla.
Homeland Security—Shelley Moore Capito, W.Va.
Interior and Environment—Lisa Murkowski, Alaska
Labor, Health and Human Services, Education—Roy Blunt, Mo.
Legislative Branch—Steve Daines, Mont.
Military Construction, Veterans Affairs—John Boozman, Ark.
State, Foreign Operations, and Related Programs—Lindsey Graham, S.C.
Transportation, Housing, and Urban Development—Susan Collins, Maine

R 16–D 15 *(116th Congress)*

Richard Shelby, Ala.
Patrick Leahy, Vt.

Agriculture, Rural Development, Food and Drug Administration—John Hoeven, N.D.

Commerce, Justice, Science—Jerry Moran, Kan.
Defense—Richard Shelby, Ala.
Energy and Water Development—Lamar Alexander, Tenn.
Financial Services and General Government—John Kennedy, La.
Homeland Security—Shelley Moore Capito, W.Va.
Interior and Environment—Lisa Murkowski, Alaska
Labor, Health and Human Services, Education—Roy Blunt, Mo.
Legislative Branch—Cindy Hyde-Smith, Miss.
Military Construction, Veterans Affairs—John Boozman, Ark.
State, Foreign Operations, and Related Programs—Lindsey Graham, S.C.
Transportation, Housing, and Urban Development—Susan Collins, Maine

ARMED SERVICES

Defense and defense policy generally; aeronautical and space activities peculiar to or primarily associated with the development of weapons systems or military operations; policies related to cyber capabilities; maintenance and operation of the Panama Canal, including the Canal Zone; military research and development; national security aspects of nuclear energy; naval petroleum reserves (except Alaska); armed forces generally; Selective Service System; strategic and critical materials.

R 14–D 13 *(115th Congress)*

James Inhofe, Okla.
Jack Reed, R.I.

Airland Forces—Tom Cotton, Ark
Cybersecurity— Mike Rounds, S.D.
Emerging Threats and Capabilities—Joni Ernst, Iowa
Personnel—Thorn Tillis, N.C.
Readiness and Management Support—Dan Sullivan, Alaska
Seapower—Roger Wicker, Miss.
Strategic Forces—Deb Fischer, Neb.

R 14–D 13 *(116th Congress)*

James Inhofe, Okla.
Jack Reed, R.I.

Airland Forces—Tom Cotton, Ariz.
Cybersecurity—Mike Rounds, S.D.
Emerging Threats and Capabilities—Joni Ernst, Iowa
Personnel—Thorn Tillis, N.C.
Readiness and Management Support—Dan Sullivan, Alaska
Seapower—Daivd Perdue, Ga.
Strategic Forces—Deb Fischer, Neb.

BANKING, HOUSING, AND URBAN AFFAIRS

Banks, banking, and financial institutions; price controls; deposit insurance; economic stabilization and growth; defense production; export and foreign trade promotion; export controls; federal monetary policy, including Federal Reserve System; financial aid to commerce and industry; issuance and redemption of notes; money and credit, including currency and coinage; nursing home construction; public and private housing, including veterans' housing; renegotiation of government contracts; urban development and mass transit; international economic policy.

R 13–D 12 *(115th Congress)*

Mike Crapo, Idaho
Sherrod Brown, Ohio

Economic Policy—Tom Cotton, Ark.
Financial Institutions—Patrick Toomey, Pa.
Housing, Transportation, and Community Development—Tim Scott, S.C.
Security and International Trade and Finance—Ben Sasse, Neb.
Securities, Insurance, and Investment—Dean Heller, Nev.

R 13–D 12 *(116th Congress)*

Mike Crapo, Idaho
Sherrod Brown, Ohio

Economic Policy—Tom Cotton, Ark.
Financial Institutions and Consumer Protection—Tim Scott, S.C.
Housing, Transportation, and Community Development—David Perdue, Ga.
Security and International Trade and Finance—Ben Sasse, Neb.
Securities, Insurance, and Investment—Patrick Toomey, Pa.

BUDGET

Federal budget generally; concurrent budget resolutions; Congressional Budget Office.

D 12–R 11 *(115th Congress)*

Mike Enzi, Wyo.
Bernie Sanders, Vt.

R 11–10 *(116th Congress)*

Michael Enzi, Wyo.
Bernie Sanders, Vt.

No standing subcommittees.

COMMERCE, SCIENCE, AND TRANSPORTATION

Interstate commerce and transportation generally; Coast Guard; coastal zone management; communications; highway safety; inland waterways, except construction; marine fisheries; Merchant Marine and navigation; nonmilitary aeronautical and space sciences; oceans, weather, and atmospheric activities; interoceanic canals generally; regulation of consumer products and services; science, engineering, and technology research, development and policy; sports; standards and measurement; transportation and commerce aspects of outer continental shelf lands.

R 14–D 13 *(115th Congress)*

John Thune, S.D.
Bill Nelson, Fla.

Aviation Operations, Safety, and Security—Roy Blunt, Mo.
Communications Technology, and the Internet—Roger Wicker, Miss.
Consumer Protection, Product Safety and Insurance—Jerry Moran, Kan.

Oceans, Atmosphere, Fisheries, and Coast Guard—Dan Sullivan, Alaska
Science and Space—Ted Cruz, Texas
Surface Transportation and Merchant Marine—Deb Fischer, Neb.

R 14–D 12 *(116th Congress)*

Roger Wicker, Miss.
Maria Cantwell, Wash.

Aviation Operations, Safety, and Security—Ted Cruz, Texas
Communications Technology, and the Internet—John Thune, S.D.
Consumer Protection, Product Safety and Insurance—Jerry Moran, Kan.
Oceans, Atmosphere, Fisheries, and Coast Guard—Cory Gardner, Colo.
Surface Transportation and Merchant Marine—Deb Fischer, Neb.

ENERGY AND NATURAL RESOURCES

Energy policy, regulation, conservation, research, and development; coal; energy-related aspects of deep-water ports; hydroelectric power, irrigation, and reclamation; mines, mining, and minerals generally; national parks, recreation areas, wilderness areas, wild and scenic rivers, historic sites, military parks, and battlefields; naval petroleum reserves in Alaska; nonmilitary development of nuclear energy; oil and gas production and distribution; public lands and forests; solar energy systems; territorial possessions of the United States.

R 12–D 11 *(115th Congress)*

Lisa Murkowski, Alaska
Maria Cantwell, Wash.

Energy—Cory Gardner, Colo.
Public Lands and Forests—Mike Lee, Utah
National Parks—Steve Daines, Mont.
Water and Power—Jeff Flake, Ariz.

R 11–D 9 *(116th Congress)*

Lisa Murkowski, Alaska
Joe Manchin, W.Va.

Energy—Bill Cassidy, La.
Public Lands and Forests—Mike Lee, Utah
National Parks—Steve Daines, Mont.
Water and Power—Martha McSally, Ariz.

ENVIRONMENT AND PUBLIC WORKS

Environmental policy, research, and development; air, water, and noise pollution; construction and maintenance of highways; environmental aspects of outer continental shelf lands; environmental effects of toxic substances other than pesticides; fisheries and wildlife; flood control and improvements of rivers and harbors; nonmilitary environmental regulation and control of nuclear energy; ocean dumping; public buildings and grounds; public works, bridges, and dams; regional economic development; solid waste disposal and recycling; water resources.

R 11–R 10 *(115th Congress)*

John Barrasso, Wyo.
Tom Carper, Del.

Clean Air and Nuclear Safety—Shelley Moore Capito, W.Va.
Fisheries, Water, and Wildlife—John Boozman, Ark.
Superfund, Waste Management, and Regulatory Oversight—
  Mike Rounds, S.D.
Transportation and Infrastructure—James Inhofe, Okla.

R 11–D 10 *(116th Congress)*

John Barrasso, Wyo.
Tom Carper, Del.

Clean Air and Nuclear Safety—Mike Braun, Ind.
Fisheries, Water, and Wildlife—Kevin Cramer, N.D.
Superfund, Waste Management, and Regulatory Oversight—
  Mike Rounds, S.D.
Transportation and Infrastructure—Shelley Moore Capito, W.Va.

FINANCE

Revenue measures generally; taxes; tariffs and import quotas; reciprocal trade agreements; customs; revenue sharing; federal debt limit; Social Security; health programs financed by taxes or trust funds.

R 14–D 12 *(115th Congress)*

Orrin G. Hatch, Utah
Ron Wyden, Ore.

Energy, Natural Resources, and Infrastructure—Dean Heller, Nev.
Health Care—Patrick Toomey, Pa.
International Trade, Customs, and Global Competitiveness—
  John Cornyn, Texas
Social Security, Pensions, and Family Policy—Bill Cassidy, La.
Taxation and IRS Oversight—Robert Portman, Ohio
Fiscal Responsibility and Economic Growth—Tim Scott, S.C.

R 15–D 13 *(116th Congress)*

Chuck Grassley, Iowa
Ron Wyden, Ore.

Energy, Natural Resources, and Infrastructure—Tim Scott, S.C.
Health Care—Patrick Toomey, Pa.
International Trade, Customs, and Global Competitiveness—
  John Cornyn, Texas.
Social Security, Pensions, and Family Policy—Rob Portman, Ohio
Taxation and IRS Oversight—John Thune, S.D.
Fiscal Responsibility and Economic Growth—Bill Cassidy, La.

FOREIGN RELATIONS

Relations of the United States with foreign nations generally; treaties; foreign economic, military, technical, and humanitarian assistance; foreign loans; diplomatic service; International Red Cross; international aspects of nuclear energy; International Monetary Fund; intervention abroad and declarations of war; foreign trade; national security; oceans and international environmental and scientific affairs; protection of U.S. citizens abroad; United Nations; World Bank and other development assistance organizations.

R 11–D 10 *(115th Congress)*

Bob Corker, Tenn.
Ben Cardin, Mass.

Africa and Global Health Policy—Jeff Flake, Ariz.
East Asia, The Pacific, and International Cybersecurity Policy—
  Cory Gardner, Colo.
Europe and Regional Security Cooperation—Ron Johnson, Wis.
Multilateral International Development, Multilateral Institutions, and International Economic, Energy, and Environmental Policy—Todd Young, Ind.
State Department and USAID Management, International Operations, and Bilateral International Development—
  Johnny Isakson, Ga.
Near East, South Asia, Central Asia, and Counterterrorism—
  James Risch, Idaho
Western Hemisphere, Transnational Crime, Civilian Security, Democracy, Human Rights and Global Women's Issues—
  Marco Rubio, Fla.

R 12–D 10 *(116th Congress)*

Jim Risch, Idaho
Bob Menendez, N.J.

Africa and Global Health Policy—Lindsey Graham, S.C.
East Asia, The Pacific, and International Cybersecurity Policy—Cory Gardner, Colo.
Europe and Regional Security Cooperation—Ron Johnson, Wis.
Multilateral International Development, Multilateral Institutions, and International Economic, Energy, and Environmental Policy—Todd Young, Ind.
State Department and USAID Management, International Operations, and Bilateral International Development—
  Johnny Isakson, Ga.
Near East, South Asia, Central Asia, and Counterterrorism—
  Mitt Romney, Utah
Western Hemisphere, Transnational Crime, Civilian Security, Democracy, Human Rights and Global Women's Issues—
  Marco Rubio, Fla.

HEALTH, EDUCATION, LABOR, AND PENSIONS

Education, labor, health, and public welfare in general; aging; arts and humanities; biomedical research and development; child labor; convict labor; domestic activities of the Red Cross; equal employment opportunity; handicapped people; labor standards and statistics; mediation and arbitration of labor disputes; occupational safety and health; private pensions; public health; railway labor and retirement; regulation of foreign laborers; student loans; wages and hours; agricultural colleges; Gallaudet University; Howard University; St. Elizabeth's Hospital in Washington, D.C.

R 12–D 11 *(115th Congress)*

Lamar Alexander, Tenn.
Patty Murray, Wash.

Children and Families—Rand Paul, Ky.
Employment and Workplace Safety—Johnny Isakson, Ga
Primary Health and Retirement Security—Mike Enzi, Wyo.

R 12–D 11 *(116th Congress)*

Lamar Alexander, Tenn.
Patty Murray, Wash.

Children and Families—Rand Paul, Ky.
Employment and Workplace Safety—Johnny Isakson, Ga.
Primary Health and Retirement Security—Mike Enzi, Wyo.

HOMELAND SECURITY AND GOVERNMENTAL AFFAIRS

Homeland Security Department except the Coast Guard, Transportation Security Administration, Federal Law Enforcement Training Center, Secret Service, Citizenship and Immigration Service, immigration and commercial functions of Customs and Border Protection and Immigration and Customs Enforcement, and customs revenue functions; Archives of the United States; budget and accounting measures; census and statistics; federal civil service; congressional organization; intergovernmental relations; government information; District of Columbia; organization and management of nuclear export policy; executive branch organization and reorganization; Postal Service; efficiency, economy, and effectiveness of government.

R 8–D 7 *(115th Congress)*

Ron Johnson, Wis.
Claire McCaskill, Mo.

Permanent Subcommittee on Investigations—Rob Portman, Ohio
Federal Spending Oversight and Emergency Management—Rand Paul, Ky.
Regulatory Affairs and Federal Management—James Lankford, Ohio

R 8–D 6 *(116th Congress)*

Ron Johnson, Wis.
Gary Peters, Mich.

Permanent Subcommittee on Investigations—Rob Portman, Ohio
Federal Spending Oversight and Emergency Management—Rand Paul, Ky.
Regulatory Affairs and Federal Management—James Lankford, Ohio

INDIAN AFFAIRS

Problems and opportunities of Native Americans, including Native American land management and trust responsibilities, education, health, special services, loan programs, and claims against the United States.

R 8–D 7 *(115th Congress)*

John Hoeven, N.D.
Tom Udall, N.M.

R 7–D 6 *(116th Congress)*

John Hoeven, N.D.
Tom Udall, N.M.

No standing subcommittees.

JUDICIARY

Civil and criminal judicial proceedings in general; national penitentiaries; bankruptcy, mutiny, espionage, and counterfeiting; civil liberties; constitutional amendments; apportionment of representatives; government information; immigration and naturalization; interstate compacts in general; claims against the United States; patents, copyrights, and trademarks; monopolies and unlawful restraints of trade; holidays and celebrations; revision and codification of the statutes of the United States; state and territorial boundary lines.

R 11–D 10 *(115th Congress)*

Charles Grassley, Iowa
Dianne Feinstein, Calif.

Antitrust, Competition Policy, Consumer Rights—Mike Lee, Utah
Crime and Terrorism—Lindsey Graham, S.C.
The Constitution—Ted Cruz, Texas
Immigration and The National Interest—John Cornyn, Texas
Oversight, Federal Rights and Agency Action—Ben Sasse, Neb.
Privacy, Technology and the Law—Jeff Flake, Ariz.

R 12–D 10 *(116th Congress)*

Charles Grassley, Iowa
Dianne Feinstein, Calif.

Antitrust, Competition Policy, Consumer Rights—Mike Lee, Utah
Crime and Terrorism—Josh Hawley, Mo.
The Constitution—Ted Cruz, Texas
Immigration and The National Interest—John Cornyn, Texas
Oversight, Federal Rights and Agency Action—Ben Sasse, Neb.
Privacy, Technology and the Law—N/A

RULES AND ADMINISTRATION

Senate rules and regulations; Senate administration in general; corrupt practices; qualifications of senators; contested elections; federal elections in general; Government Printing Office; *Congressional Record*; meetings of Congress and attendance of members; presidential succession; the Capitol, congressional office buildings, the Library of Congress, the Smithsonian Institution, and the Botanic Garden; purchase of books and manuscripts and erection of monuments to the memory of individuals.

R 10–D 9 *(115th Congress)*

Roy Blunt, Mo.
Chuck Schumer, N.Y.

R 10–D 9 *(116th Congress)*

Roy Blunt, Mo.
Amy Klobuchar, Minn.

No standing subcommittees.

SELECT ETHICS

Studies and investigates standards and conduct of Senate members and employees and may recommend remedial action.

D 3–R 3 *(115th Congress)*

Johnny Isakson, Ga.
Christopher A. Coons, Del.

D 3–R 3 *(116th Congress)*

Johnny Isakson, Ga.
Christopher A. Coons, Del.

No standing subcommittees.

SELECT INTELLIGENCE

Legislative and budgetary authority over the Central Intelligence Agency, the Defense Intelligence Agency, the National Security Agency, and intelligence activities of the Federal Bureau of Investigation, and other components of the federal intelligence community.

R 10–D 9 *(115th Congress)*

Richard Burr, N.C.
Mark Warner, Va.

R 10–D 9 *(116th Congress)*

Marco Rubio, Fla.
Mark Warner, Va.

No standing subcommittees.

SMALL BUSINESS AND ENTREPRENEURSHIP

Problems of small business; Small Business Administration.

R 10–D 9 *(115th Congress)*

Jim Risch, Idaho
Jeanne Shaheen, N.H.

R 10–D 9 *(116th Congress)*

Marco Rubio, Fla.
Ben Cardin, Md.

No standing subcommittees.

SPECIAL AGING

Problems and opportunities of older people including health, income, employment, housing, and care and assistance. Reports

findings and makes recommendations to the Senate but cannot report legislation.

R 9–D 8 *(115th Congress)*

Susan Collins, Maine
Bob Casey, Pa.

R 8–D 7 *(116th Congress)*

Susan Collins, Maine
Bob Casey, Pa.

No standing subcommittees.

VETERANS' AFFAIRS

Veterans' measures in general; compensation; life insurance issued by the government on account of service in the armed forces; national cemeteries; pensions; readjustment benefits; veterans' hospitals, medical care and treatment; vocational rehabilitation and education; soldiers' and sailors' civil relief.

R 8–D 7 *(115th Congress)*

Johnny Isakson, Ga.
Jon Tester, Mont.

R 9–D 8 *(116th Congress)*

Johnny Isakson, Ga.
Jon Tester, Mont.

No standing subcommittees.

House Committees

AGRICULTURE

Agriculture generally; forestry in general, and forest reserves other than those created from the public domain; adulteration of seeds, insect pests, and protection of birds and animals in forest reserves; agricultural and industrial chemistry; agricultural colleges and experiment stations; agricultural economics and research; agricultural education extension services; agricultural production and marketing and stabilization of prices of agricultural products, and commodities (not including distribution outside the United States); animal industry and diseases of animals; commodities exchanges; crop insurance and soil conservation; dairy industry; entomology and plant quarantine; extension of farm credit and farm security; inspection of livestock, poultry, meat products, seafood and seafood products; human nutrition and home economics; plant industry, soils, and agricultural engineering; rural electrification; rural development; water conservation related to activities of the Department of Agriculture.

R 26–D 20 *(115th Congress)*

Michael Conaway, Texas
Collin C. Peterson, Minn.

Commodity Exchanges, Energy, and Credit—Austin Scott, Ga.
Conservation and Forestry—Marcia Fudge, Ohio

Nutrition—Glenn Thompson, Pa.
General Farm Commodities and Risk Management—Rick Crawford, Arkansas
Biotechnology, Horticulture, and Research—Rodney Davis, Ill.
Livestock and Foreign Agriculture—David Rouzer, N.C.

D 25–R 22 *(116th Congress)*

Collin C. Peterson, Minn.
Michael Conaway, Texas

Commodity Exchanges, Energy, and Credit—David Scott, Ga.
Conservation and Forestry—Abigail Spanberger, Va.
Nutrition—Marcia Fudge, Ohio
General Farm Commodities and Risk Management—Filemon Vela, Texas
Biotechnology, Horticulture, and Research—Stacey Plaskett, V.I.
Livestock and Foreign Agriculture—Jim Costa, Calif.

APPROPRIATIONS

Appropriation of the revenue for the support of the government; rescissions of appropriations contained in appropriation acts; transfers of unexpended balances; new spending authority under the Congressional Budget Act.

R 30–D 22 *(115th Congress)*

Rodney Frelinghuysen, N.J.
Nita Lowey, N.Y.

Agriculture, Rural Development, Food and Drug Administration and Related Agencies—Robert Aderholt, Ala.
Commerce, Justice, Science and Related Agencies—John Culberson, Texas
Defense—Kay Granger, Texas
Energy and Water Development, and Related Agencies—Michael Simpson, Id.
Financial Services and General Government—Tom Graves, Ga.
Homeland Security—John Carter, Texas
Interior, Environment, and Related Agencies—Ken Calvert, Calif.
Labor, Health and Human Services, Education and Related Agencies—Tom Cole, Okla.
Legislative Branch—Kevin Yoder, Kan.
Military Construction, Veterans Affairs, and Related Agencies—Charlie Dent, Pa.
State, Foreign Operations, and Related Agencies—Hal Rogers, Ky.
Transportation, Housing and Urban Development, and Related Agencies—Mario Diaz-Balart, Fla.

D 30–R 23 *(116th Congress)*

Nita Lowey, N.Y.
Tom Cole, Okla.

Agriculture, Rural Development, Food and Drug Administration and Related Agencies—Sanford Bishop Jr., Ga.
Commerce, Justice, Science and Related Agencies—Jose Serrano, N.Y.
Defense—Pete Visclosky, Ind.

Energy and Water Development and Related Agencies—Marcy Kaptur, Ohio
Financial Services and General Government—Mike Quigley, Ill.
Homeland Security—Lucille Roybal-Allard, Calif.
Interior, Environment, and Related Agencies—Betty McCollum, Minn.
Labor, Health and Human Services, Education, and Related Agencies—Rosa DeLauro, Conn.
Legislative Branch—Tim Ryan, Ohio
Military Construction, Veterans Affairs, and Related Agencies—Debbie Wasserman Schultz, Fla.
State, Foreign Operations, and Related Agencies—Nita Lowey, N.Y.
Transportation, Housing and Urban Development, and Related Agencies—David Price, N.C.

ARMED SERVICES

Ammunition depots; forts; arsenals; Army, Navy, and Air Force reservations and establishments; common defense generally; conservation, development, and use of naval petroleum and oil shale reserves; Department of Defense generally, including the Departments of the Army, Navy, and Air Force generally; interoceanic canals generally; including measures relating to the maintenance, operation, and administration of interoceanic canals; Merchant Marine Academy, and state maritime academies; military applications of nuclear energy; tactical intelligence and intelligence related activities of the Department of Defense; national security aspects of merchant marine, including financial assistance for the construction and operation of vessels, the maintenance of the U.S. shipbuilding and ship repair industrial base, cabotage, cargo preference, and merchant marine officers and seamen as these matters relate to the national security; pay, promotion, retirement, and other benefits and privileges of members of the armed forces; scientific research and development in support of the armed services; selective service; size and composition of the Army, Navy, Marine Corps, and Air Force; soldiers' and sailors' homes; strategic and critical materials necessary for the common defense.

R 34–D 28 *(115th Congress)*

Mac Thornberry, Texas
Adam Smith, Wash.

Tactical Air and Land Forces—Michael Turner, Ohio
Military Personnel—Mike Coffman, Colo.
Readiness—Joe Wilson, S.C.
Seapower and Projection Forces—Rob Wittman, Va.
Strategic Forces—Mike Rogers, Ala.
Emerging Threats and Capabilities—Elise Stefanik, N.Y.
Oversight and Investigations—Vicky Hartzler, Mo.

D 32–R 25 *(116th Congress)*

Adam Smith, Wash.
Mac Thornberry, Texas

Tactical Air and Land Forces—Donald Norcross, Ohio
Military Personnel—Jackie Speier, Calif.
Readiness—John Garamendi, Calif.
Seapower and Projection Forces—Joe Courtney, Conn.
Strategic Forces—Jim Cooper, Tenn.
Emerging Threats and Capabilities—Jim Langevin, R.I.

BUDGET

Congressional budget process generally; concurrent budget resolutions; measures relating to special controls over the federal budget; Congressional Budget Office.

R 21-D 14 *(115th Congress)*

Steve Womack, Ark.
John A. Yarmuth, Ky.

D 19-R 13 *(116th Congress)*

John A. Yarmuth, Ky.
Steve Womack, Ark.

No standing subcommittees.

EDUCATION AND THE WORKFORCE

Measures relating to education or labor generally; child labor; Columbia Institution for the Deaf, Dumb, and Blind; Howard University; Freedmen's Hospital; convict labor and the entry of goods made by convicts into interstate commerce; food programs for children in schools; labor standards and statistics; mediation and arbitration of labor disputes; regulation or prevention of importation of foreign laborers under contract; U.S. Employees' Compensation Commission; vocational rehabilitation; wages and hours of labor; welfare of miners; work incentive programs.

R 22–D 18 *(115th Congress)*

Virginia Foxx, N.C.
Bobby Scott, Calif.

Early Childhood, Elementary and Secondary Education— Todd Rokita, Ind.
Workforce Protections—Bradley Byrne, Ala.
Higher Education and Workforce Training—Brett Guthrie, Ky.
Health, Employment, Labor and Pensions—Tim Walberg, Mich.

D 28–R 21 *(116th Congress)*

Viriginia Foxx, N.C.
Bobby Scott, Calif.

Early Childhood, Elementary and Secondary Education— Gregorio Sablan, M.P.
Workforce Protections—Alma Adams, N.C.
Higher Education and Workforce Training—Susan Davis, Calif.
Health, Employment, Labor and Pensions—Frederica Wilson, Fla.

ENERGY AND COMMERCE

Interstate and foreign commerce generally; biomedical research and development; consumer affairs and consumer protection; health and health facilities, except health care supported by payroll deductions; interstate energy compacts; measures relating to the exploration, production, storage, supply, marketing, pricing, and regulation of energy resources, including all fossil fuels, solar energy, and other unconventional or renewable energy resources; measures relating to the conservation of energy resources; measures relating to energy information generally; measures relating to (1) the generation and marketing of power (except by federally chartered or federal regional power marketing authorities), (2) the reliability and interstate transmission of, and ratemaking for, all power, and (3) the siting of generation facilities, except the installation of interconnections between government water power projects; measures relating to general management of the Department of Energy, and the management and all functions of the Federal Energy Regulatory Commission; national energy policy generally; public health and quarantine; regulation of the domestic nuclear energy industry, including regulation of research and development reactors and nuclear regulatory research; regulation of interstate and foreign communications; travel and tourism; nuclear and other energy.

R 31–D 24 *(115th Congress)*

Greg Walden, Ore.
Frank Pallone, Jr., N.J.

Commerce, Consumer Protection, and Competitiveness—Bob Latta, Ohio
Communications and Technology—Marsha Blackburn, Tenn.
Energy and Power—Fred Upton, Mich.
Environment—John Shimkus, Ill.
Health—Michael Burgess, Texas
Oversight and Investigations—Tim Murphy, Pa.

D 31-R 24 *(116th Congress)*

Frank Pallone, Jr., N.J.
Greg Pallone, Jr., Ore.

Consumer Protection and Commerce—Jan Schakowsky, Ill.
Communications and Technology—Mike Doyle, Pa.
Energy—Bobby Rush, Ill.
Environment and Climate Change—Paul Tonko, N.Y.
Health—Anna Eshoo, Calif.
Oversight and Investigations—Diana DeGette, Colo.

ETHICS

D 5-R 4 *(115th Congress)*

Susan Brooks, Ind.
Theodore E. Deutch, Fla.

D 5-R 5 *(116th Congress)*

Theodore E. Deutch, Fla.
Kenny Marchant, Texas

No standing subcommittees.

FINANCIAL SERVICES

Banks and banking, including deposit insurance and federal monetary policy; economic stabilization, defense production, renegotiation, and control of the price of commodities, rents, and services; financial aid to commerce and industry (other than transportation); insurance generally; international finance; international financial and monetary organizations; money and credit, including currency and the issuance of notes and redemption thereof; gold and silver, including the coinage thereof; valuation and revaluation of the dollar; public

and private housing; securities and exchanges; and urban development.

R 34–D 26 *(115th Congress)*

Jeb Hensarling, Texas
Maxine Waters, Calif.

Consumer Protection and Financial Institutions—Blaine Luetkemeyer, Mo.
Housing, Community Development, and Insurance—Sean Duffy, Wis.
Investor Protection, Entrepreneurship, and Capital Markets—Bill Huizenga, Mich.
National Security, International Development, and Monetary Policy—Andy Barr, Ky.
Oversight and Investigations—Ann Wagner, Mo.
Terrorism and Illicit Finance—Stevan Pearce, N.M.

D 34–R 27 *(116th Congress)*

Maxine Waters, Calif.
Patrick T. McHenry, N.C.

Consumer Protection and Financial Institutions—Gregory Meeks, N.Y.
Diversity and Inclusion—Joyce Beatty, Ohio
Housing, Community Development, and Insurance—William Lacy Clay, Mo.
Investor Protection, Entrepreneurship, and Capital Markets—Brad Sherman, Calif.
National Security, International Development, and Monetary Policy—Emanuel Cleaver, Mo.
Oversight and Investigations—Al Green, Texas

FOREIGN AFFAIRS

Relations of the United States with foreign nations generally; acquisition of land and buildings for embassies and legations in foreign countries; establishment of boundary lines between the United States and foreign nations; export controls, including non-proliferation of nuclear technology and nuclear hardware; foreign loans; international commodity agreements (other than those involving sugar), including all agreements for cooperation in the export of nuclear technology and nuclear hardware; international conferences and congresses; international education; intervention abroad and declarations of war; measures relating to the diplomatic service; measures to foster commercial intercourse with foreign nations and to safeguard American business interests abroad; measures relating to international economic policy; neutrality; protection of American citizens abroad and expatriation; American National Red Cross; trading with the enemy; U.N. organizations.

R 26–D 21 *(115th Congress)*

Edward R. Royce, Calif.
Eliot L. Engel, N.Y.

Africa, Global Health, Global Human Rights, and International Organizations—Chris Smith, N.J.
Asia and the Pacific—Ted Yoho, Fla.
Europe, Eurasia, and Emerging Threats—Dana Rohrabacher, Calif.

The Middle East and North Africa—Ileana Ros-Lehtinen, Fla.
Terrorism, Nonproliferation, and Trade—Ted Poe, Texas
Western Hemisphere, Civilian Security, Migration and International Economic Policy—Jeff Duncan, S.C.

D 26–R 21 *(116th Congress)*

Eliot L. Engel, N.Y.
Michael McCaul, Texas

Africa, Global Health, Global Human Rights, and International Organizations—Karen Bass, Calif.
Asia, the Pacific, and Nonproliferation—Brad Sherman, Calif.
Europe, Eurasia, Energy, and the Environment—Bill Keating, Mass.
International Development, International Organizations and Global Corporate Social Impact—Joaquin Castro, Texas
The Middle East, North Africa and Global Counterterrorism—Ted Deutch, Fla.
Western Hemisphere, Civilian Security, Migration and International Economic Policy—Albio Sires, NJ

HOMELAND SECURITY

Overall homeland security policy; organization and administration of the Department of Homeland Security; functions of the Department of Homeland Security; border and port security (except immigration policy and non-border enforcement); customs (except customs revenue); integration, analysis, and dissemination of homeland security information; domestic preparedness for and collective response to terrorism; research and development; transportation security.

R 19–D 12 *(115th Congress)*

Michael McCaul, Texas
Bennie G. Thompson, Miss.

Border and Maritime Security—Martha McSally, Ariz.
Counterterrorism and Intelligence—Pete King, N.Y.
Cybersecurity and Infrastructure Protection—John Ratcliffe, Texas
Emergency Preparedness, Response, and Communications—Dan Donovan, N.Y.
Oversight and Management Efficiency—Scott Perry, Pa.
Transportation Security—John Katko, N.Y.

D 18–R 13 *(116th Congress)*

Bennie G. Thompson, Miss.
Mike Rogers, Ala.

Border Security, Facilitation, and Operations—Kathleen Rice, N.Y.
Cybersecurity, Infrastructure Protection, and Innovation—Cedric Richmond, La.
Emergency Preparedness, Response, and Recovery—Donald Payne Jr., N.J.
Intelligence and Counterterrorism—Max Rose, N.Y.
Oversight, Management, and Accountability—Xochitl Torres Small, N.M.
Transportation and Maritime Security—Lou Correa, Calif.

HOUSE ADMINISTRATION

Accounts of the House generally; assignment of office space for members and committees; disposition of useless executive papers; matters relating to the election of the president, vice president, or members of Congress; corrupt practices; contested elections; credentials and qualifications; federal elections generally; appropriations from accounts for committee salaries and expenses (except for the Committee on Appropriations), House Information Systems, and allowances and expenses of members, House officers, and administrative offices of the House; auditing and settling of all such accounts; expenditure of such accounts; employment of persons by the House, including clerks for members and committees, and reporters of debates; Library of Congress and the House Library; statuary and pictures; acceptance or purchase of works of art for the Capitol; the Botanic Garden; management of the Library of Congress; purchase of books and manuscripts; Smithsonian Institution and the incorporation of similar institutions; Franking Commission; printing and correction of the *Congressional Record*; services to the House, including the House restaurant, parking facilities, and administration of the House office buildings and of the House wing of the Capitol; travel of members of the House; raising, reporting, and use of campaign contributions for candidates for office of representative in the House of Representatives, of delegate, and of resident commissioner to the United States from Puerto Rico; compensation, retirement and other benefits of the members, officers, and employees of the Congress.

R 6–D 3 *(115th Congress)*

Gregg Harper, Miss.
Robert A. Brady, Pa.

D 6–R 3 *(116th Congress)*

Zoe Lofgren, Calif.
Rodney Davis, Ill.

Elections—Marcia Fudge, Ohio

JUDICIARY

The judiciary and judicial proceedings, civil and criminal; administrative practice and procedure; apportionment of representatives; bankruptcy, mutiny, espionage, and counterfeiting; civil liberties; constitutional amendments; federal courts and judges, and local courts in the territories and possessions; immigration and naturalization; interstate compacts, generally; measures relating to claims against the United States; meetings of Congress, attendance of members and their acceptance of incompatible offices; national penitentiaries; patents, the Patent Office, copyrights, and trademarks; presidential succession; protection of trade and commerce against unlawful restraints and monopolies; revision and codification of the Statutes of the United States; state and territorial boundaries; subversive activities affecting the internal security of the United States.

R 24–D 17 *(115th Congress)*

Bob Goodlatte, Va.
Jerrod Nadler, N.Y.

Regulatory Reform, Commercial, and Antitrust Law—Tom Marino, Pa.
Constitution and Civil Justice—Steve King, Iowa

Courts, Intellectual Property, and the Internet—Darrell Issa, Calif.
Crime, Terrorism, Homeland Security, and Investigations—Trey Gowdy, S.C.
Immigration and Border Security—Jim Sensenbrenner, Wis.

D 24–R 17 *(116th Congress)*

Jerrod Nadler, N.Y.
Doug Collins, Ga.

Antitrust, Commercial, and Administrative Law—David N. Cicilline, R.I.
Constitution, Civil Rights, and Civil Liberties—Steve Cohen, Tenn.
Courts, Intellectual Property, and the Internet—Hank Johnson, Ga.
Crime, Terrorism, and Homeland Security—Karen Bass, Calif.
Immigration and Citizenship—Zoe Lofgren, Calif.

NATURAL RESOURCES

Public lands generally, including entry, easements, and grazing; mining interests generally; fisheries and wildlife, including research, restoration, refuges, and conservation; forest reserves and national parks created from the public domain; forfeiture of land grants and alien ownership, including alien ownership of mineral lands; Geological Survey; international fishing agreements; interstate compacts relating to apportionment of waters for irrigation purposes; irrigation and reclamation, including water supply for reclamation projects, and easements of public lands for irrigation projects, and acquisition of private lands when necessary to complete irrigation projects; measures relating to the care and management of Indians, including the care and allotment of Native American lands and general and special measures relating to claims that are paid out of Native American funds; measures relating generally to the insular possessions of the United States, except those affecting the revenue and appropriations; military parks and battlefields, national cemeteries administered by the secretary of the interior, parks within the District of Columbia, and the erection of monuments to the memory of individuals; mineral land laws and claims and entries thereunder; mineral resources of the public lands; mining schools and experimental stations; marine affairs (including coastal zone management), except for measures relating to oil and other pollution of navigable waters; oceanography; petroleum conservation on the public lands and conservation of the radium supply in the United States; preservation of prehistoric ruins and objects of interest on the public domain; relations of the United States with the Native Americans and the Native American tribes; disposition of oil transported by the Trans-Alaska Oil Pipeline.

R 23–D 17 *(115th Congress)*

Rob Bishop, Utah
Raúl M. Grijalva, Ariz.

Energy and Mineral Resources—Paul Gosar, Ariz.
Federal Lands—Tom McClintock, Calif.
Indian, Insular, and Alaska Native Affairs—Doug LaMalfa, Calif.
Oversight and Investigations—Raul Labrador, Idaho
Water, Power, and Oceans—Doug Lamborn, Colo.

D 22—R 19 *(116th Congress)*

Raúl M. Grijalva, Ariz.
Rob Bishop, Utah

Energy and Mineral Resources—Alan Lowenthal, Calif.
Natural Parks, Forests, and Public Lands—Debra Haaland, N.M.
Indigenous Peoples of the United States—Ruben Gallego, Ariz.
Oversight and Investigations—TJ Cox, Calif.
Water, Oceans, and Wildlife—Jared Huffman, Calif.

OVERSIGHT AND GOVERNMENT REFORM

Civil service, including intergovernmental personnel; the status of officers and employees of the United States, including their compensation, classification, and retirement; measures relating to the municipal affairs of the District of Columbia in general, other than appropriations; federal paperwork reduction; budget and accounting measures, generally; holidays and celebrations; overall economy, efficiency, and management of government operations and activities, including federal procurement; National Archives; population and demography generally, including the census; Postal Service generally, including the transportation of mail; public information and records; relationship of the federal government to the states and municipalities generally; reorganizations in the executive branch of the government.

R 21–D 15 *(115th Congress)*

Jason Chaffetz, Utah
Elijah Cummings, Md.

Environment—Blake Farenthold, Texas
Government Operations—Mark Meadows, N.C.
National Security—Ron DeSantis, Fla.
Health Care, Benefits, and Administrative Rules—Jim Jordan, Ohio
Information Technology—Will Hurd, Texas

D 24–R 17 *(116th Congress)*

Ayanna Pressley, Mass.
Jim Jordan, Ohio

Civil Liberties—Jamie Raskin, Md.
Economic and Consumer Policy—Raja Krishnamoorthi, Ill.
Environment—Harley Rouda, Calif.
Government Operations—Gerald Connolly, Va.
National Security—Stephen Lynch, Mass.

RULES

Rules and joint rules (other than rules or joint rules relating to the Code of Official Conduct), and order of business of the House; recesses and final adjournments of Congress.

R 9–D 4 *(115th Congress)*

Pete Sessions, Texas
Louise M. Slaughter, N.Y.

Legislative and Budget Process—Rob Woodall, Ga.
Rules and Organization of the House—Doug Collins, Ga.

D 9-R 4 *(116th Congress)*

Jim McGovern, Mass.
Tom Cole, Okla.

Expedited Procedures—Jamie Raskin, Mass.
Legislative and Budget Process—Alcee Hastings, Fla.
Rules and Organization of the House—Norma Torres, Calif.

SCIENCE, SPACE, AND TECHNOLOGY

All energy research, development, and demonstration, and projects thereof, and all federally owned or operated nonmilitary energy laboratories; astronautical research and development, including resources, personnel, equipment, and facilities; civil aviation research and development; environmental research and development; marine research; measures relating to the commercial application of energy technology; National Institute of Standards and Technology, standardization of weights and measures and the metric system; National Aeronautics and Space Administration; National Space Council; National Science Foundation; National Weather Service; outer space, including exploration and control thereof; science scholarships; scientific research, development, and demonstration, and projects thereof.

R 21-D 16 *(115th Congress)*

Lamar Smith, Texas
Eddie Bernice Johnson, Texas

Space—Brain Babin, Va.
Environment—Andy Briggs, Ariz.
Energy—Randy Weber, Texas
Research and Technology—Barbara Comstock, Va.
Oversight—Darin LaHood, Ill.

D 22-R 16 *(116th Congress)*

Eddie Bernice Johnson, Texas
Frank Lucas, Okla.

Space and Aeronautics—Kendra Horn, Okla.
Environment—Mikie Sherrill, N.J.
Energy—Lizzie Pannill Fletcher, Texas
Research and Technology—Haley Stevens, Mich.
Investigations and Oversight—Bill Foster, Ill.

PERMANENT SELECT INTELLIGENCE

Legislative and budgetary authority over the National Security Agency and the director of central intelligence, the Defense Intelligence Agency, the National Security Agency, intelligence activities of the Federal Bureau of Investigation, and other components of the federal intelligence community.

R 12-D 9 *(115th Congress)*

Mike Conaway, Texas
Adam Schiff, Calif.

CIA—Frank LoBiondo, N.J.
Department of Defense Intelligence and Overhead Architecture—Chris Stewart, Utah

Emerging Threats—Tom Rooney, Fla.
NSA and Cybersecurity—Tom Rooney, Fla.

D 13-R 9 *(116th Congress)*

Adam Schiff, CA
Devin Nunes, CA

Counterterrorism, Counterintelligence, and Counterproliferation—Andre Carson, Ind.
Defense Intelligence and Warfighter Support (DIWS)—Terri Sewell, Ala.
Intelligence Modernization and Readiness (INMAR)—Eric Swalwell, Calif.
Strategic Technologies and Advanced Research (STAR)—Jim Himes, Conn.

SMALL BUSINESS

Assistance to and protection of small business, including financial aid, regulatory flexibility, and paperwork reduction; participation of small business enterprises in federal procurement and government contracts.

R 12-D 9 *(115th Congress)*

Steve Chabot, Ohio
Nydia M. Velazquez, N.Y.

Agriculture, Energy and Trade—Rod Blum, Iowa
Health and Technology— Aumua Amata Coleman Radewagen, Am. Samoa
Economic Growth, Tax and Capital Access—Dave Brat, Va.
Investigations, Oversight and Regulations—Trent Kelly, Miss.
Contracting and Workforce—Steve Knight, Calif.

D 14-R 10 *(116th Congress)*

Nydia M. Velazquez, N.Y.
Steve Chabot, Ohio

Underserved, Agriculture, and Rural Business Development—Abby Finkenauer, Iowa
Innovation, Entrepreneurship, and Workforce Development—Jason Crow, Colo.
Economic Growth, Tax and Capital Access—Andrew Kim, N.J.
Oversight, Investigations, and Regulations—Judy Chu, Calif.
Contracting and Infrastructure—Jared Golden, Maine

TRANSPORTATION AND INFRASTRUCTURE

Transportation, including civil aviation, railroads, water transportation, transportation safety (except automobile safety), transportation infrastructure, transportation labor, and railroad retirement and unemployment (except revenue measures); water power; the Coast Guard; federal management of emergencies and natural disasters; flood control and improvement of waterways; inspection of merchant marine vessels; navigation and related laws; rules and international arrangements to prevent collisions at sea; measures, other than appropriations, that relate to construction, maintenance and safety of roads; buildings and grounds of the Botanic Gardens, the Library of Congress, and the Smithsonian Institution and other government buildings within the District of Columbia; post offices, customhouses, federal courthouses, and merchant marine, except for national security aspects; pollution of navigable waters; and bridges and dams and related transportation regulatory agencies.

R 32-D 28 *(115th Congress)*

Bill Shuster, Pa.
Peter A. DeFazio, Ore.

Aviation—Frank LoBiondo, N.J.
Coast Guard and Maritime Transportation—Brian Mast, Fla.
Economic Development, Public Buildings, and Emergency Management—Lou Barletta, Pa.
Highways and Transit—Sam Graves, Mo.
Railroads, Pipelines, and Hazardous Materials—Jeff Denham, Calif.
Water Resources and Environment—Garret Graves, La.

D 37-R 29 *(116th Congress)*

Peter A. DeFazio, Ore.
Sam Graves, Mo.

Aviation—Rick Larsen, Wash.
Coast Guard and Maritime Transportation—Sean Maloney, N.Y.
Economic Development, Public Buildings, and Emergency Management—Dina Titus, Nev.
Highways and Transit—Eleanor Holmes Norton, D.C.
Railroads, Pipelines, and Hazardous Materials—Daniel Lipinski, Ill.
Water Resources and Environment—Grace Napolitano, Calif.

VETERANS' AFFAIRS

Veterans' measures generally; cemeteries of the United States in which veterans of any war or conflict are or may be buried, whether in the United States or abroad, except cemeteries administered by the secretary of the Interior; compensation, vocational rehabilitation, and education of veterans; life insurance issued by the government on account of service in the armed forces; pensions of all the wars of the United States, readjustment of service personnel to civil life; soldiers' and sailors' civil relief; veterans' hospitals, medical care, and treatment of veterans.

R 13-D 7 *(115th Congress)*

Phil Roe, Tenn.
Tim Walz, Minn.

Disability Benefits and Memorial Affairs—Mike Bost, Ill.
Economic Opportunity—Jodey Arrington, Texas
Health—Brad Wenstrup, Ohio
Oversight and Investigations—Jack Bergman, Mich.
Technology Modernization—Frank Mrvan, Ind.

D 16-D 12 *(116th Congress)*

Mark Takano, Calif.
Phil Roe, Tenn.

Disability Benefits and Memorial Affairs—Elaine Luria, Va.
Economic Opportunity—Mike Levin, Calif.
Health—Julia Brownley, Calif.
Oversight and Investigations—Chris Pappas, N.H.
Technology Modernization—Frank Mrvan, Ind.

WAYS AND MEANS

Revenue measures generally; reciprocal trade agreements; customs, collection districts, and ports of entry and delivery; revenue measures relating to the insular possessions; bonded debt of the United States; deposit of public moneys; transportation of dutiable goods; tax-exempt foundations and charitable trusts; national Social Security, except (1) health care and facilities programs that are supported from general revenues as opposed to payroll deductions and (2) work incentive programs.

R 24–D 16 *(115th Congress)*

Kevin Brady, Texas
Richard Neal, Mass.

Health—Pat Tiberi, Ohio
Oversight—Vern Buchanan, Fla.
Trade—Dave Reichert, Wash.
Human Resources—Adrian Smith, Neb.
Tax Policy—Peter Roskam, Ill.
Social Security—Sam Johnson, Texas

D 25–R 17 *(116th Congress)*

Richard Neal, Mass.
Kevin Brady, Texas

Health—Lloyd Doggett, Texas
Oversight—John Lewis, Ga.
Trade—Earl Blumenauer, Ore.
Social Security—John Larson, Conn.

Joint Committees

Joint committees are set up to examine specific questions and are established by public law. Membership is drawn from both chambers and both parties. When a senator serves as chairman, the vice chairman usually is a representative, and vice versa. The chairmanship traditionally rotates from one chamber to the other at the beginning of each Congress. However, the Committee on Taxation chairmanship rotates at the start of each session with the House having the chair in the first session and the Senate in the second session. In the alternate sessions the House and Senate members have the vice chair.

ECONOMIC

Studies and investigates all recommendations in the president's annual Economic Report to Congress. Reports findings and recommendations to the House and Senate.

Rep. Patrick Tiberi, R-Ohio, Chairman, (115th Congress)

Sen. Mike Lee, R-Utah, Vice Chair (115th Congress)

Sen. Mike Lee, R-Utah, Chair (116th Congress)

Rep. Carolyn Maloney, D-N.Y., Vice Chair (116th Congress)

LIBRARY

Management and expansion of the Library of Congress; receipt of gifts for the benefit of the library; development and maintenance of the Botanic Garden; placement of statues and other works of art in the Capitol.

Rep. Gregg Harper R-Miss., Chair (115th Congress)

Sen. Richard Shelby, R-Ala., Vice Chair (115th Congress)

Sen. Roy Blunt, R-Mo., Chair (116th Congress)

Rep. Zoe Lofgren, D-Calif., Vice Chair (116th Congress)

PRINTING

Probes inefficiency and waste in the printing, binding, and distribution of federal government publications. Oversees arrangement and style of the *Congressional Record*.

Sen. Richard Shelby, R-Ala., Chair (115th Congress)

Rep. Rodney Davis, R-Ill., Vice Chair (115th Congress)

Rep. Zoe Lofgren, D-Calif., Chair (116th Congress)

Sen. Roy Blunt, R-Mo., Vice Chair (116th Congress)

TAXATION

Operation, effects, and administration of the federal system of internal revenue taxes; measures and methods for simplification of taxation.

Rep. Kevin Brady, R-Texas, Chair (115th Congress)

Sen. Orrin Hatch, R-Utah, Vice Chair (115th Congress)

Rep. Richard Neal, D-Mass., Chair (116th Congress)

Sen. Chuck Grassley, R-Iowa, Vice Chair (116th Congress)

Postelection Sessions

A postelection session of Congress often is labeled a lame duck session. It takes place after an election for the next Congress but before the official end of the current Congress. As a result members who participate in the lame duck session are from the existing, or current, Congress, not from the Congress that will convene as a result of the just-held elections.

Lame duck sessions in the modern sense began in 1935 after the Twentieth Amendment to the Constitution was ratified in 1933. This amendment specified that regular congressional sessions would begin on January 3 of each year unless Congress passed a law designating a different date. Also, terms of members of Congress begin and end on January 3 of odd-numbered years, regardless of the date that a Congress officially ends its session. Originally the Constitution specified much later starting dates in recognition of the difficulty of travel in the early years of the nation, but those dates meant that lame duck sessions occurred in the second session of every Congress. In the modern sense, post–1935, a lame duck session is any meeting of Congress after election day in even-numbered years but before the following January 3.

Between 1935 and 2017, Congress held twenty-one lame-duck sessions.

1941. The 76th Congress actually had adjourned in 1939 but President Franklin D. Roosevelt called the legislators into special session—technically, the third session of that Congress–to deal with the threat of war in Europe. However, little of substance was accomplished during the lame duck session.

1942. By this year the United States was at war with Germany, Japan, and Italy but little was done during the period as legislators decided to leave many major decisions to the next Congress. Congress did approve bills on overtime pay for government workers and to provide for the military draft of eighteen and nineteen-year-old men.

1944. World War II was well along by this time, which meant Congress faced a host of exceptionally important issues including postwar universal military training, continuing the war effort, Social Security taxes, a rivers and harbors bill, and various postwar reconstruction matters. But, like the previous several lame duck sessions, legislators decided to postpone most actions until the new Congress convened in 1945.

1948. The 1948 postelection session of the 80th Congress lasted only two hours. Both chambers swore in new members, approved several minor resolutions, and received last-minute reports from committees. In addition to final floor action, several committees resumed work. The most active was the House Un-American Activities Committee, which continued its investigation of alleged communist espionage in the federal government.

1950. After the 1950 elections, President Harry S. Truman sent a "must" agenda to the lame duck session of the 81st Congress. The president's list included supplemental defense appropriations, an excess profits tax, aid to Yugoslavia, a three-month extension of federal rent controls, and statehood for Hawaii and Alaska. During a marathon session that lasted until only a few hours before its successor took over, the 81st Congress acted on all of the president's legislative items except the statehood bills, which were blocked by a Senate filibuster.

1954. Only one chamber of the 83rd Congress convened after the 1954 elections. The Senate returned November 8 to hold what

Congressional Lame Duck Sessions

Year	Congress	Dates
1941	76th	Adjourned January 3, 1941*
1942	77th	Adjourned December 16, 1942*
1944	78th	November 14, 1944–December 19, 1944
1948	80th	December 31, 1948 (two-hour session)
1950	81st	November 27, 1950–January 2, 1951
1954	83rd	November 8, 1954–December 2, 1954
1970	91st	November 16, 1970–January 2, 1971 (Senate)
1974	93rd	November 18, 1974–December 20, 1974
1980	96th	November 12, 1980–December 16, 1980
1982	97th	November 29, 1982–December 23, 1982 (Senate)
		November 29, 1982–December 21, 1982 (House)
1994	103rd	November 29, 1994 (House)
		November 30, 1994–December 1, 1994 (Senate)
1998	105th	December 17, 1998–December, 19, 1998 (House)
2000	106th	November 13, 2000–December 15, 2000 (House)
		November 14, 2000–December 15, 2000
2002	107th	Adjourned November 20, 2002 (Senate)*
		Adjourned November 22, 2002 (House)*
2004	108th	November 16, 2004–December 7, 2004 (House)
		November 16, 2004–December 8, 2004 (Senate)
2006	109th	November 13, 2006–December 8, 2006 (House)
		November 13, 2006–December 8, 2006 (Senate)
2008	110th	November 19, 2008–December 10, 2008 (House)
		November 17, 2008–December 11, 2008 (Senate)
2010	111th	November 15, 2010–December 22, 2010 (House)
		November 15, 2010–December 22, 2010 (Senate)
2012	112th	November 13, 2012–January 3, 2013 (House)
		November 13, 2012–January 2, 2013 (Senate)**
2014	113th	November 12, 2014–January 3, 2015 (House)
		November 12, 2014–December 16, 2014 (Senate)
2016	114th	November 14, 2016–January 3, 2017 (House)
		November 14, 2016–January 3, 2017 (Senate)
2018	115th	November 13, 2018–January 3, 2019 (House)
		November 13, 2018–January 3, 2019 (Senate)
2020	116th	November 9, 2020–January 3, 2021 (Senate)
		November 9, 2020–January 3, 2021 (House)

* Congress stayed in session.

** The Senate did not adjourn *sine die*.

has been called a "censure session," a continuing investigation into the conduct of Sen. Joseph R. McCarthy, R-Wis. (1947–1957). By a 67–22 roll call, the Senate on December 2 voted to "condemn" McCarthy for his behavior. In other postelection floor action, the Senate passed a series of miscellaneous and administrative resolutions and swore in new members.

1970. President Richard Nixon criticized the lame duck Congress as one that had "seemingly lost the capacity to decide and the will to act." Filibusters and intense controversy contributed to inaction on the president's request for trade legislation and welfare reform. Congress nevertheless claimed some substantive results during the session, which ended January 2, 1971. Several major appropriations bills were cleared for presidential signature. Congress also approved foreign aid to Cambodia, provided interim funding for the supersonic transport (SST) plane, and repealed the Tonkin Gulf Resolution that had been used as a basis for American military involvement in Vietnam.

1974. In a session that ran from November 18 to December 20, 1974, the 93rd Congress cleared several important bills for presidential signature, including a mass transit bill, a Labor–Health, Education and Welfare appropriations bill, and a foreign

assistance package. A House–Senate conference committee reached agreement on a major strip-mining bill but President Gerald R. Ford vetoed it. Congress approved the nomination of Nelson A. Rockefeller as vice president. It also overrode presidential vetoes of two bills: one broadening the Freedom of Information Act, a second authorizing educational benefits for Korean War and Vietnam-era veterans.

1980. The lame duck session of the 96th Congress was productive, at least until December 5, the original adjournment date set by congressional leaders. By that date a budget had been approved, along with a budget reconciliation measure. Ten regular appropriations bills had cleared, though one subsequently was vetoed. Congress had approved two major environmental measures—an Alaskan lands bill and toxic waste "superfund" legislation—as well as a three-year extension of general revenue sharing.

After December 5, however, the legislative pace slowed noticeably. Action on a continuing appropriations resolution for those departments and agencies whose regular funding had not been cleared was delayed, first by a filibuster on a fair housing bill and later by more than 100 "Christmas tree" amendments, including a $10,000-a-year pay raise for members. After the conference report failed in the Senate and twice was rewritten, the bill was shorn of virtually all its "ornaments" and finally cleared by both chambers on December 16.

1982. Despite the reluctance of congressional leaders, President Ronald Reagan urged the convening of a postelection session at the end of the 97th Congress, principally to pass remaining appropriations bills. Rising unemployment—and Democratic election gains in the House—made job creation efforts the focus of the lame duck Congress, however. Overriding the objections of Republican conservatives, Congress passed Reagan-backed legislation raising the federal gasoline tax from four cents to nine cents a gallon to pay for highway repairs and mass transit. Supporters said the legislation would help alleviate unemployment by creating 300,000 jobs.

Congress eventually cleared four additional appropriations bills, packaging the remaining six in a continuing appropriations resolution that also included a pay raise for House members. Conferees dropped funding for emergency jobs programs to avert a threatened veto of the resolution. The lame duck session also was highlighted by Congress's refusal to fund production and procurement of the first five MX intercontinental missiles. This was the first time in recent history that either house of Congress had denied a president's request to fund production of a strategic weapon.

1994. Congress reconvened to reconsider, and ultimately approve, the Uruguay Round pact strengthening the General Agreement on Tariffs and Trade (GATT). The bill had been submitted September 27, 1994, by President Bill Clinton under fast-track rules for trade legislation, which allowed each chamber only an up-or-down vote on the bill without amendments. But the rules also allowed every chairman with jurisdiction to take up to forty-five days to review the bill. Sen. Ernest F. Hollings, D-S.C., demanded his forty-five days, forcing the Senate leadership to schedule a two-day lame duck session. Clinton asked the House to approve the bill before the October adjournment but the Democratic leadership delayed consideration. The House reconvened for a one-day session November 29 and passed the GATT bill by a wide margin. Following a twenty-hour debate November 30 and December 1, the Senate gave overwhelming approval to the bill.

1998. The House reconvened in December for a remarkable and historic event: to vote on the impeachment of a president. After a tumultuous political year, House Republicans pushed through articles of impeachment for what they believed was President Clinton's lying under oath. The event was characterized by a year-long political chasm between House Republicans, who led the effort for impeachment, and Democrats in both chambers. It also was characterized by charges of sexual misconduct involving Clinton and release of a controversial and in places graphic report about sexual conduct of the president that Republicans defended as necessary to prove their case. The report was prepared by an independent prosecutor. In the short time the House was in session it voted—largely along party lines in favor of impeachment charges, which would be tried, and rejected, by the Senate early in the following year.

2000. Congress returned after the 2000 elections largely to complete action on appropriations measures that had remained unfinished as President Clinton continued to wrestle with his Republican adversaries in Congress over spending priorities. Partisan fighting over spending and taxes had been one of the principal matters that divided the White House and Capitol Hill during the latter years of Clinton's presidency. The year 2000 was no exception as Congress was unable to avert its annual pileup of appropriations bills at the end of the session. The pileup was exacerbated in 2000 because of the controversial presidential elections that were not decided until a Supreme Court decision in December awarding contested Florida electoral votes to Republican George W. Bush. With the GOP about to reclaim the White House, party members in Congress suddenly had new leverage in the final bargaining over appropriations. The lame duck session lumbered into mid-December when an omnibus package was used to close the books on four spending bills and move other unrelated legislation.

2004. Congress came back after Republicans scored impressive gains in the fall elections that returned Bush to the White House and increased GOP control of both chambers of Congress. The additional votes meant the GOP was strongly positioned to push Bush's legislative program in the 109th Congress. But before they could get there important legislative matters remained for the 108th Congress. The most important was a sweeping overhaul of the U.S. intelligence community, Congress's last major act of the year. It came only at the prodding of the independent, bipartisan National Commission on Terrorist Attacks Upon the United States—better known as the 9/11 commission—and the powerful lobbying of some of the victims' families of those attacks. In addition, all but four of the appropriations bills had been left hanging when Congress went out of the elections break. Congress bundled the other nine into an omnibus bill during the lame duck session and cleared it on November 20.

2006. Legislators returned after the 2006 midterm elections to a wholly new playing field because Democrats had recaptured control of both chambers, although the Senate by a one-vote margin. The principal agenda for the postelection session was completion of appropriations bills, only two of which (defense and homeland security) had been completed. A continuing resolution keeping the government operating was set to expire November 17. Dealing with several expiring tax benefits also was on the list of actions needed. But much of the plan never got going as Democrats decided to fund the government until February 15, 2007, through additional continuing resolutions, thereby leaving all the other regular appropriation bills to die. But some work was

done. A package of tax benefits was completed in connection with a trade package. Perhaps most significantly, Congress approved a bill allowing President Bush to negotiate a nuclear power agreement with India, one of the president's most significant foreign policy accomplishments. The Senate also confirmed Robert M. Gates as defense secretary to replace Donald Rumsfeld.

2008. The main focus of attention in the postelection session was the continuing financial crisis in the United States and worldwide, but the elections, like those two years earlier, had put a new cast on events. In the elections, Democrats had improved their margin in the House and significantly increased it in the Senate and had won the presidential contest when Barack Obama defeated John McCain by a comfortable 53–47 percentage margin. This meant that governmental activity to stave off an economic collapse that many economists thought would rival the Great Depression of the 1930s was left to coordination of action between the outgoing Bush administration and the new Obama administration. Congress, which had passed a $700 billion package of aid for the financial services industry before the election, was left with little to do. One major effort failed: With the nation's three principal auto manufacturers facing bankruptcy, Congress considered providing $14 billion in loans to the companies from an existing program. The House passed the bill but the Senate did not go along. As a result, Bush later provided $13.4 billion in loans to the automakers from the funds previously approved to save the financial services industry.

2010. The 111th Congress turned out to be one of the odder two-year periods because of the amount of significant, and highly controversial, legislation that became law. Earlier in the year, Democrats forced through a far-reaching health care reform bill; later in the summer, they passed a financial regulation overhaul that grew from the vast economic collapse that started in 2008. These actions alone would have made the 111th Congress exceptionally notable, and hardly required a lame duck session.

But one was to occur anyway and it too turned out to be significant. The postelection session was unusual because it came after an election in which Democrats, previously riding high with their successes, took a beating when Republicans surged back to recapture the House majority. Even President Obama acknowledged his party had taken a "shellacking" in the election. Although little was expected in the session after the voting, Congress extended income and estate taxes, approved a conditional repeal of the ban on gays in the military, and approved ratification of a nuclear arms treaty with Russia. The tax legislation also included a year-long extension of extra benefits for long-term unemployed persons. Congress also approved a food safety bill and worked out funding to keep the government operating into 2012.

2012. For the eighth time in a row, going back to the 105th Congress in 1998, legislators in 2012 returned after the national elections—in which the political divisions in Washington were largely repeated—to deal with tangled issues that the divisions had blocked from resolution before the voting took place. But unlike the lame duck session two years earlier, only the most pressing issues were addressed, and then only—as many observers noted—by kicking cans down the road.

The issues, mainly taxes and spending, were so intractable that the 112th Congress went past New Year's Eve right up to the January 3 deadline when the Constitution decreed it had to end. It was the first time in forty-two years that Congress slid past the turn of the calendar and evening celebrations.

In fact, there was little to celebrate in legislative terms. The legislators struck a deal on the looming deadline that had come to be called the fiscal cliff, which at the end of 2012 would have sent tax rates for all Americans back to levels last seen more than a decade earlier. The "cliff" described not only the expiration of an array of earlier tax cuts that were put in place as temporary but also an existing law that would force across-the-board spending cuts of some $109 billion, starting January 2, 2013.

The deal that emerged permanently extended the existing reduced tax rates for most taxpayers, while allowing rates on higher earners (above $400,000 for individuals and $450,000 for couples) to rise. A long-standing fight over federal estate taxes was settled, and a permanent "patch" was included for the alternative minimum tax to limit that levy from reaching into middle class incomes. The bill also extended long-term unemployment benefits for another year.

On the other hand, the across-the-board cuts, known as a sequester, were only delayed until March 1, 2013. Backers of the extension said it would give Congress time to work out a compromise. But Congress did not, and the forced cuts began then.

The 112th Congress did end, with the House adjourning a few minutes before the required session's end and the Senate merely allowing the clock to run out. Traditionally, at the end of a Congress, leaders make a ceremonial telephone call to the president and then hold news conferences about their accomplishments. None of that occurred for the 112th.

2014. The 113th Congress returned after the midterm elections to finalize an omnibus spending bill, which combined omnibus appropriations for most agencies with a short-term continuing resolution for the Department of Homeland Security. The legislation, which passed the House narrowly before being cleared by the Senate, included a number of controversial measures such as a ban on funding to implement a referendum decriminalizing marijuana in the District of Columbia. It also extended the moratorium on state and local internet access taxes until October 1, 2015.

In addition, lawmakers also scaled back some financial regulations in the Dodd-Frank Act, and they agreed to a one-year extension of popular tax credits. They also gave overwhelming bipartisan approval to a fiscal 2015 defense authorization bill.

Lawmakers debates but failed to pass several politically contentious proposals. These included bills that would have granted the president fast-track trade authority and that would have approved the Keystone XL pipeline.

2016. With Republicans poised for control of both the White House and Congress after the 2016 elections, lawmakers returned to town to warp up business on several significant pieces of legislation. They agreed to a continuing resolution to extend fiscal 2017 funding through April 28, 2017. The legislation included provisions to address the drinking water in Flint, Michigan, which contained high amounts of lead.

Lawmakers passed the 21st Century Cures Act, authorizing funding for medical research and an accelerated review process for new drugs and medical devices. They also overwhelmingly passed a fiscal 2017 defense authorization bill, and they voted for legislation, which Obama allowed to become law without his signature, that extended sanctions on Iran.

2018. Amid Democratic preparations to take control of the House after the midterm elections, Congress cleared a major bipartisan bill overhauling the criminal justice system. The bill aimed to lower the number of federal inmates by scaling back certain tough-on-crime policies and providing more assistance

to prisoners upon release to lower the rate of recidivism. Lawmakers also passed a farm bill that reauthorized agriculture and nutrition programs for five years and reauthorized the Coast Guard.

Congress failed to clear an omnibus appropriations bill, however. President Trump insisted on $5.7 billion for construction of a wall on the U.S.–Mexico border, but congressional Democrats adamantly opposed such funding. As a result, a record thirty-five-day government shutdown began on December 22.

2020. Against the tense backdrop of President Trump refusing to concede the election to Democrat Joseph R. Biden Jr., Congress overrode Trump's veto of the $731.6 billion fiscal 2021 defense authorization bill. The largely bipartisan measure ensured the military had the resources it needed to continue its mission during the COVID-19 global pandemic, but Trump took issue with removing Confederate names from military installations and ships as well as the lack of a provision that would have removed certain protections from social media platforms.

The president, however, signed a $1.4 trillion omnibus spending measure for fiscal 2021 that was packaged that contained funding aid and tax breaks for Americans and businesses who were struggling during the COVID-19 pandemic, as well as funds for virus testing and distribution of vaccines. The massive measure also contained provisions to protect patients from surprise medical billing and to extend nearly forty temporary tax provisions, making some of them permanent.

Senate Cloture Votes, 1917–2020

The filibuster, identified by the public primarily as nonstop speech, has been an enshrined Senate tradition throughout the chamber's history but became a focus of increasing criticism in the twentieth century as a device to thwart majority decisions. It was not until 1917 that the Senate adopted a rule, known as cloture, that allowed a majority—albeit a supermajority—to end a filibuster and bring a measure to a vote. The number of votes required to invoke cloture has varied over the years, standing at sixty in 2012 if there are no Senate vacancies. (The actual rules required a three-fifths majority of members to invoke cloture; the Senate has 100 members.)

Even with the rule in place, however, the number of filibusters and attempts to invoke cloture was limited until the 92nd Congress in 1971–1973. From that time on, and especially after 2000, cloture attempts expanded greatly as the character of the Senate changed from what one scholar called "communitarian" and deliberative to individualistic, increasingly partisan, and media driven. This pattern was seen during the 1990s also. In both decades, deep-seated partisan divisions in Congress led both parties to try whatever tools worked to block the initiatives or judicial or executive appointments of the other.

In the ten Congresses during the twenty years from 1971 to 1991, cloture was attempted no less than thirteen times in each two-year period, and on the average, twenty-five times each Congress. As dramatic as that growth was, it paled against the expansion in the following eleven Congresses from 1991 through 2012. During those eleven Congresses from the 102nd through the 112th, cloture votes were taken an average of nearly sixty-three times for each two-year period.

During this two decade period, cloture was typically used more for political and legislative maneuvering than to consider far-reaching national issues. For example, senators might start or threaten a filibuster to gain leverage for a matter completely unrelated to the legislation before the Senate. In one instance during President Barack Obama's first term, his nomination to head a new consumer protection bureau was blocked by a filibuster even through most senators agreed the nominee was qualified. The opposition to him centered, rather, on Republican demands that the bureau as enacted in a previous Congress be restricted in ways that reflected their unhappiness with the agency's powers.

The filibuster also was used increasingly in this period to thwart the choices of both Republican and Democratic presidents for positions in the federal judiciary, as each party saw control of the courts as core, nonnegotiable interests of their political bases.

CHANGES IN THE RULE

The Senate's ultimate check on the filibuster is the provision for cloture, or limitation of debate, contained in Rule 22 of its Standing Rules. The original Rule 22 was adopted in 1917 following a furor over the "talking to death" of a proposal by President Woodrow Wilson for arming American merchant ships before the United States entered World War I. The new cloture rule required the votes of two-thirds of all the senators present and voting to invoke cloture. In 1949, during a parliamentary skirmish preceding scheduled consideration of a Fair Employment Practices Commission bill, the requirement was raised to two-thirds of the entire Senate membership.

A revision of the rule in 1959 provided for limitation of debate by a vote of two-thirds of the senators present and voting, two days after a cloture petition was submitted by sixteen senators. If cloture was adopted by the Senate, further debate was limited to one hour for each senator on the bill itself and on all amendments affecting it. No new amendments could be offered except by unanimous consent. Amendments that were not germane to the pending business and dilatory motions were out of order. The rule applied both to regular legislation and to motions to change the Standing Rules.

Rule 22 was revised significantly in 1975 by lowering the vote needed for cloture to three-fifths of the Senate membership (sixty if there were no vacancies). That revision applied to any matter except proposed rules changes, for which the old requirement of a two-thirds majority of senators present and voting still applied.

In a further revision of the rule, the Senate in 1979 limited post-cloture delaying tactics by providing that once cloture was invoked, a final vote had to be taken after no more than 100 hours of debate. All time spent on quorum calls, roll-call votes and other parliamentary procedures was to be included in the 100-hour limit.

When the Senate decided to televise its floor proceedings in 1986, it further tightened up the time on postcloture debate. Rule 22 was revised to reduce to thirty hours, from 100, the time allowed for debate, procedural moves and roll-call votes after the Senate had invoked cloture to end a filibuster.

Following is a list of the 1,386 cloture votes taken between 1917, when Senate Rule 22 was adopted, and the end of 2016. Those in **bold type**, 676, were successful; 710 votes, 51.2 percent, were not.

Senate Cloture Votes

Issue	Date	Vote	Yeas needed
Versailles Treaty	November 15, 1919	78–16	63
Emergency tariff	February 2, 1921	36–35	48
Tariff bill	July 7, 1922	45–35	54
World Court	January 25, 1926	68–26	63
Migratory birds	June 1, 1926	46–33	53
Branch banking	February 15, 1927	65–18	56
Colorado River	February 26, 1927	32–59	61
Disabled officers	February 26, 1927	51–36	58
D.C. buildings	February 28, 1927	52–31	56
Prohibition Bureau	February 28, 1927	55–27	55
Banking Act	January 19, 1933	58–30	59
Anti-lynching	January 27, 1938	37–51	59
Anti-lynching	February 16, 1938	42–46	59
Anti-poll tax	November 23, 1942	37–41	52
Anti-poll tax	May 15, 1944	36–44	54
Fair Employment Practices Commission	February 9, 1946	48–36	56
British loan	May 7, 1946	41–41	55
Labor disputes	May 25, 1946	63–77	54
Anti-poll tax	July 31, 1946	39–33	48
Fair Employment	May 19, 1950	52–32	64
Fair Employment	July 12, 1950	55–33	64
Atomic energy Act	July 26, 1954	44–42	64
Civil Rights Act	March 10, 1960	42–53	64
Amend Rule 22	September 19, 1961	37–43	54

Issue	Date	Vote	Yeas needed		Issue	Date	Vote	Yeas needed
Literacy tests	May 9, 1962	43–53	64		Consumer Agency	July 30, 1974	56–42	66
Literacy tests	May 14, 1962	42–52	63		Consumer Agency	August 1, 1974	59–39	66
Comsat Act	August 14, 1962	63–27	60		Consumer Agency	August 20, 1974	59–35	63
Amend Rule 22	February 7, 1963	54–42	64		Consumer Agency	September 19, 1974	64–34	66
Civil Rights Act	June 10, 1964	71–29	67		Export-Import Bank	December 3, 1974	51–39	60
Legislative reapportionment	September 10, 1964	30–63	62		Export-Import Bank	December 4, 1974	48–44	62
Voting Rights Act	May 25, 1965	70–30	67		**Trade reform**	December 13, 1974	71–19	60
Right-to-work repeal	October 11, 1965	45–47	62		Export-Import Bank	December 14, 1974	49–35	56
Right-to-work repeal	February 8, 1966	51–48	66		**Fiscal 1975 supplemental funds**	December 14, 1974	56–27	56
Right-to-work repeal	February 10, 1966	50–49	66		Export-Import Bank	December 16, 1974	54–34	59
Civil Rights Act	September 14, 1966	54–42	64		**Tax law changes**	December 17, 1974	67–25	62
Civil Rights Act	September 19, 1966	52–41	62		**Social services programs**	December 17, 1974	70–23	62
D.C. Home Rule	October 10, 1966	41–37	52		**Rail Reorganization Act**	February 26, 1975	86–8	63
Amend Rule 22	January 24, 1967	53–46	66		**Amend Rule 22**	March 5, 1975	73–21	63
Open Housing	February 20, 1968	55–37	62		**Amend Rule 22**	March 7, 1975	73–21	63
Open Housing	February 26, 1968	56–36	62		Tax reduction	March 20, 1975	59–38	60
Open Housing	March 1, 1968	59–35	63		**Tax reduction**	March 21, 1975	83–13	60
Open Housing	March 4, 1968	65–32	65		**Consumer Advocacy Agency**	May 13, 1975	71–27	60
Fortas nomination	October 1, 1968	45–43	59		**Senate staffing**	June 11, 1975	77–19	64
Amend Rule 22	January 16, 1969	51–47	66		New Hampshire Senate seat	June 24, 1975	57–39	60
Amend Rule 22	January 28, 1969	50–42	62		New Hampshire Senate seat	June 25, 1975	56–41	60
Electoral College	September 17, 1970	54–36	60		New Hampshire Senate seat	June 26, 1975	54–40	60
Electoral College	September 29, 1970	53–34	58		New Hampshire Senate seat	July 8, 1975	57–38	60
Supersonic transport	December 19, 1970	43–48	61		New Hampshire Senate seat	July 9, 1975	57–38	60
Supersonic transport	December 22, 1970	42–44	58		New Hampshire Senate seat	July 10, 1975	54–38	60
Amend Rule 22	February 18, 1971	48–37	57		**Voting Rights Act**	July 21, 1975	72–19	60
Amend Rule 22	February 23, 1971	50–36	58		**Voting Rights Act**	July 23, 1975	76–20	60
Amend Rule 22	March 2, 1971	48–36	56		Oil price decontrol	July 30, 1975	54–38	60
Amend Rule 22	March 9, 1971	55–39	63		Anti-school busing amendments	September 23, 1975	46–48	60
Military Draft	June 23, 1971	65–27	62		**Anti-school busing amendments**	September 24, 1975	64–33	60
Lockheed loan	July 26, 1971	42–47	60					
Lockheed loan	July 28, 1971	59–39	66		**Common-site picketing**	November 11, 1975	66–30	60
Lockheed loan	July 30, 1971	53–37	60		Common-site picketing	November 14, 1975	58–31	60
Military Draft	September 21, 1971	61–30	61		**Common-site picketing**	November 18, 1975	62–37	60
Rehnquist nomination	December 10, 1971	52–42	63		**Rail reorganization**	December 4, 1975	61–27	60
Equal job opportunity	February 1, 1972	48–37	57		**New York City aid**	December 5, 1975	70–27	60
Equal job opportunity	February 3, 1972	53–35	59		**Rice Production Act**	February 3, 1976	70–19	60
Equal job opportunity	February 22, 1972	71–23	63		**Antitrust amendments**	June 3, 1976	67–22	60
U.S.–Soviet arms pact	September 14, 1972	76–15	61		**Antitrust amendments**	August 31, 1976	63–27	60
Consumer Agency	September 29, 1972	47–29	51		**Civil rights attorneys' fees**	September 23, 1976	63–26	60
Consumer Agency	October 3, 1972	55–32	58		Draft resisters pardons	January 24, 1977	53–43	60
Consumer Agency	October 5, 1972	52–30	55		Campaign financing	July 29, 1977	49–45	60
School busing	October 10, 1972	45–37	55		Campaign financing	August 1, 1977	47–46	60
School busing	October 11, 1972	49–39	59		Campaign financing	August 2, 1977	52–46	60
School busing	October 12, 1972	49–38	58		**Natural gas pricing**	September 26, 1977	77–17	60
Voter registration	April 30, 1973	56–31	58		Labor Law revision	June 7, 1978	42–47	60
Voter registration	May 3, 1973	60–34	63		Labor Law revision	June 8, 1978	49–41	60
Voter registration	May 9, 1973	67–32	66		Labor Law revision	June 13, 1978	54–43	60
Public campaign financing	December 2, 1973	47–33	54		Labor Law revision	June 14, 1978	58–41	60
Public campaign financing	December 3, 1973	49–39	59		Labor Law revision	June 15, 1978	58–39	60
Rhodesian chrome ore	December 11, 1973	59–35	63		Labor Law revision	June 22, 1978	53–45	60
Legal services program	December 13, 1973	60–36	64		**Revenue Act of 1978**	October 9, 1978	62–28	60
Rhodesian chrome ore	December 13, 1973	62–33	64		**Energy taxes**	October 14, 1978	71–13	60
Legal services program	December 14, 1973	56–29	57		Windfall profits tax	December 12, 1979	53–46	60
Rhodesian chrome ore	December 18, 1973	63–26	60		Windfall profits tax	December 13, 1979	56–40	60
Legal services program	January 30, 1974	68–29	65		Windfall profits tax	December 14, 1979	56–39	60
Genocide Treaty	February 5, 1974	55–36	61		**Windfall profits tax**	December 17, 1979	84–14	60
Genocide Treaty	February 6, 1974	55–38	62		Lubbers nomination	April 21, 1980	46–60	60
Government pay raise	March 6, 1974	67–31	66		**Lubbers nomination**	April 22, 1980	62–34	60
Public campaign financing	April 4, 1974	60–36	64		Rights of institutionalized	April 28, 1980	44–39	60
Public campaign financing	April 9, 1974	64–30	63		Rights of institutionalized	April 29, 1980	56–34	60
Public debt ceiling	June 19, 1974	45–48	62					
Public debt ceiling	June 19, 1974	50–43	62					
Public debt ceiling	June 26, 1974	48–50	66					

Issue	Date	Vote	Yeas needed	Issue	Date	Vote	Yeas needed
Rights of institutionalized	April 30, 1980	53–35	60	**National Gas Policy Act**	November 3, 1983	86–7	60
Rights of institutionalized	May 1, 1980	60–34	60	**Capital punishment**	February 9, 1984	65–26	60
Bottlers' antitrust immunity	May 15, 1980	86–6	60	**Hydroelectric power plants**	July 30, 1984	60–28	60
Draft registration funding	June 10, 1980	62–32	60	Wilkinson nomination	July 31, 1984	57–39	60
Zimmerman nomination	August 1, 1980	51–35	60	Agriculture funds, fiscal 1985	August 6, 1984	54–31	60
Zimmerman nomination	August 4, 1980	45–31	60	**Agriculture funds, fiscal 1985**	August 8, 1984	68–30	60
Zimmerman nomination	August 5, 1980	63–31	60	**Wilkinson nomination**	August 9, 1984	65–32	60
Alaska lands	August 18, 1980	63–25	60	**Financial Services Act**	September 10, 1984	89–3	60
Vessel tonnage/strip mining	August 21, 1980	61–32	60	**Financial Services Act**	September 13, 1984	92–6	60
Fair Housing amendments	December 3, 1980	51–39	60	**Broadcasting of Senate proceedings**	September 18, 1984	73–26	60
Fair Housing amendments	December 4, 1980	62–32	60	Broadcasting of Senate proceedings	September 21, 1984	37–44	60
Fair Housing amendments	December 9, 1980	54–43	60	**Surface Transportation Act**	September 24, 1984	70–12	60
Breyer nomination	December 9, 1980	68–28	60	**Continuing funds**	September 29, 1984	92–4	60
Justice Department authorization	July 10, 1981	38–48	60	**Anti-apartheid**	July 10, 1985	88–8	60
Justice Department authorization	July 13, 1981	54–32	60	Line-item veto	July 18, 1985	57–42	60
Justice Department authorization	July 29, 1981	59–37	60	Line-item veto	July 23, 1985	57–41	60
Justice Department authorization	September 10, 1981	57–33	60	Line-item veto	July 24, 1985	58–40	60
Justice Department authorization	September 16, 1981	61–36	60	Anti-apartheid	September 9, 1985	53–34	60
Justice Department authorization	December 10, 1981	64–35	60	Anti-apartheid	September 11, 1985	57–41	60
State, Justice, Commerce, Judiciary funds	December 11, 1981	59–35	60	Anti-apartheid	September 12, 1985	11–88	60
Justice Department authorization	February 9, 1982	63–33	60	Debt limit/balanced budget	October 6, 1985	57–38	64
Broadcast Senate proceedings	April 20, 1982	47–51	60	Debt limit/balanced budget	October 9, 1985 [1]	53–39	62
Criminal Code Reform Act	April 27, 1982	45–46	60	**Conrail sale**	January 23, 1986	90–7	60
1982 supplemental funds	May 27, 1982	95–2	60	**Conrail sale**	January 30, 1986	70–27	60
Voting Rights Act	June 15, 1982	86–8	60	**Fitzwater nomination**	March 18, 1986	64–33	60
Debt limit increase	September 9, 1982	41–47	60	Washington airports transfer	March 21, 1986	50–39	60
Debt limit increase	September 13, 1982	45–35	60	**Washington airports transfer**	March 25, 1986	66–32	60
Debt limit increase	September 15, 1982	50–44	60	Hobbs Act amendments	April 16, 1986	44–54	60
Debt limit increase	September 20, 1982	50–39	60	Defense authorization, fiscal 1987	August 6, 1986	53–46	60
Debt limit increase	September 21, 1982	53–47	60	Aid to Nicaraguan contras	August 13, 1986	59–40	60
Debt limit increase	September 22, 1982	54–46	60	**Aid to Nicaraguan contras**	August 13, 1986	62–37	60
Debt limit increase	September 23, 1982	53–45	60	**South Africa sanctions**	August 13, 1986	89–11	60
Antitrust Equal Enforcement Act	December 2, 1982	38–58	60	**Rehnquist nomination**	September 17, 1986	68–31	60
Antitrust Equal Enforcement Act	December 2, 1982	44–51	60	**Product liability reform**	September 25, 1986	97–1	60
Transportation Assistance Act	December 13, 1982	75–13	60	Omnibus drug bill	October 15, 1986	58–38	60
Transportation Assistance Act	December 16, 1982	48–50	60	**Immigration reform**	October 17, 1986	69–21	60
Transportation Assistance Act	December 16, 1982	5–93	60	Contra aid moratorium	March 23, 1987	46–45	60
Transportation Assistance Act	December 19, 1982	89–5	60	Contra aid moratorium	March 24, 1987	50–50	60
Transportation Assistance Act	December 20, 1982	87–8	60	Contra aid moratorium	March 25, 1987	54–46	60
Transportation Assistance Act	December 23, 1982	81–5	60	**Relief for the homeless**	April 9, 1987	68–29	60
Jobs funding/interest withholding	March 16, 1983	50–48	60	Defense authorization, fiscal 1988	May 15, 1987	52–36	60
Jobs funding/interest withholding	March 16, 1983	59–39	60	Defense authorization, fiscal 1988	May 19, 1987	58–41	60
International trade/interest withholding	April 19, 1983	34–53	60	Defense authorization, fiscal 1988	May 20, 1987	59–39	60
International trade /interest withholding	April 19, 1983	39–59	60	Campaign finance	June 9, 1987	52–47	60
Defense authorizations, 1984	July 21, 1983	55–41	60	Campaign finance	June 16, 1987	49–46	60
Radio broadcasting to Cuba	August 3, 1983	62–33	60	Campaign finance	June 17, 1987	51–47	60
				Campaign finance	June 18, 1987	50–47	60
				Campaign finance	June 19, 1987	45–43	60
				Kuwaiti tanker reflagging	July 9, 1987	57–42	60
				Kuwaiti tanker reflagging	July 14, 1987	53–40	60
				Kuwaiti tanker reflagging	July 15, 1987	54–44	60
				Wells nomination	September 9, 1987	65–24	60
				Campaign finance	September 10, 1987	53–42	60
				Campaign finance	September 15, 1987	51–44	60
				Defense authorization, fiscal 1988	October 1, 1987	41–58	60
				Kuwaiti tanker escort	October 1, 1987	54–45	60
				Verity nomination	October 13, 1987	85–8	60

Issue	Date	Vote	Yeas needed
War powers compliance	October 20, 1987	67–28	60
Nuclear waste depository	November 10, 1987	87–0	60
Campaign finance	February 26, 1988	53–41	60
Polygraph protection	March 3, 1988	77–19	60
Intelligence oversight	March 15, 1988	73–18	60
Risk notification	March 23, 1988	33–59	60
Risk notification	March 24, 1988	2–93	60
Risk notification	March 28, 1988	41–44	60
Risk notification	March 29, 1988	42–52	60
Campaign spending limitations	April 21, 1988	52–42	60
Campaign spending limitations	April 22, 1988	53–37	60
Immigration legalization program extension	April 28, 1988	40–56	60
Drug-Related killings death penalty	June 9, 1988	70–26	60
Great Smoky Mountain Wilderness Act	June 20, 1988	49–35	60
Great Smoky Mountain Wilderness Act	June 21, 1988	54–42	60
Plant-closing notification	June 29, 1988	58–39	60
Plant-closing notification	July 6, 1988	88–5	60
Textile import quotas	September 7, 1988	68–29	60
Minimum wage restoration	September 22, 1988	53–43	60
Minimum wage restoration	September 23, 1988	56–35	60
Parental and medical leave	October 3, 1988	85–6	60
Parental and medical leave	October 7, 1988	50–46	60
Defense authorization, fiscal 1990	August 2, 1989	84–13	60
Airline smoking ban	September 14, 1989	77–21	60
Eastern Airlines strike commission	October 3, 1989	61–36	60
Nicaraguan election aid	October 13, 1989	52–42	60
Nicaraguan election aid	October 17, 1989	74–25	60
Eastern Airlines strike commission	October 26, 1989	62–38	60
Capital gains tax cut	November 14, 1989	51–47	60
Capital gains tax cut	November 15, 1989	51–47	60
Government pay-and-ethics package	November 17, 1989	90–9	60
Armenian genocide day	February 22, 1990	49–49	60
Armenian genocide day	February 27, 1990	48–51	60
Hatch Act revisions	May 1, 1990	70–28	60
AIDS emergency relief	May 15, 1990	95–3	60
Chemical weapons sanctions	May 17, 1990	87–4	60
Omnibus crime package	June 5, 1990	54–37	60
Omnibus crime package	June 7, 1990	57–37	60
Air travel rights for the blind	June 12, 1990	56–44	60
Civil Rights Act of 1990	July 17, 1990	62–38	60
Defense authorization, fiscal1991	August 3, 1990	58–41	60
Motor Vehicle Fuel Efficiency Act	September 14, 1990	68–28	60
Motor Vehicle Fuel Efficiency Act	September 25, 1990	57–42	60
Title X family planning amendments	September 26, 1990	50–46	60
National motor-voter registration	September 26, 1990	55–42	60
Foreign operations funds, fiscal 1991	October 12, 1990	51–38	60
Vertical price fixing	May 7, 1991	61–37	60
Vertical price fixing	May 8, 1991	63–35	60
Crime bill	June 28, 1991	41–58	60

Issue	Date	Vote	Yeas needed
Crime bill	July 10, 1991	56–43	60
Crime bill	July 10, 1991	71–27	60
VA-HUD funds, fiscal 1992	July 18, 1991	57–40	60
National motor-voter registration	July 18, 1991	57–41	60
National motor-voter registration	July 18, 1991	59–40	60
Foreign aid authorization	July 24, 1991	87–10	60
Foreign aid authorization	July 25, 1991	52–44	60
Foreign aid authorization	July 25, 1991	63–33	60
Extended unemployment benefits	July 29, 1991	96–1	60
Defense authorization, fiscal 1992	August 2, 1991	58–40	60
Interior funds, fiscal 1992	September 19, 1991	55–41	60
Federal Facility Compliance Act	October 17, 1991	85–14	60
Civil Rights Act	October 22, 1991	93–4	60
National energy policy	November 1, 1991	50–44	60
Banking reform	November 13, 1991	76–19	60
Iranian hostage release investigation	November 22, 1991	51–43	60
Crime conference report	November 27, 1991	49–38	60
School improvement bill	January 21, 1992	93–0	60
National energy strategy	February 4, 1992	90–5	60
Joint ventures antitrust	February 25, 1992	98–0	60
Lumbee Tribe recognition	February 27, 1992	58–39	60
Public Broadcasting Corp.	March 3, 1992	87–7	60
Crime bill	March 19, 1992	54–43	60
Defense/domestic spending walls	March 26, 1992	50–48	60
Fetal tissue research	March 31, 1992	98–2	60
Motor-voter registration	May 7, 1992	61–38	60
Motor-voter registration	May 12, 1992	58–40	60
Drug abuse mental health	June 9, 1992	84–9	60
Striker replacement	June 11, 1992	55–41	60
Striker replacement	June 16, 1992	57–42	60
Balanced budget amendment	June 30, 1992	56–39	60
Balanced budget amendment	July 1, 1992	56–39	60
National energy strategy	July 23, 1992	58–33	60
National energy strategy	July 28, 1992	93–3	60
Carnes nomination	September 9, 1992	66–30	60
Product liability	September 10, 1992	57–39	60
Product liability	September 10, 1992	58–38	60
School improvement bill	September 15, 1992	85–6	60
Labor, HHS, education funds	September 16, 1992	56–38	60
START treaty	September 29, 1992	87–6	60
Crime bill	October 2, 1992	55–43	60
School improvement bill	October 2, 1992	59–40	60
Fetal tissue research	October 2, 1992	85–12	60
Tax bill	October 8, 1992	80–10	60
National energy strategy	October 8, 1992	84–8	60
Motor-voter registration	March 5, 1993	52–36	60
Motor-voter registration	March 9, 1993	62–38	60
Motor-voter registration	March 16, 1993	59–41	60
Stimulus package	April 2, 1993	55–43	60
Stimulus package	April 3, 1993	52–37	60
Stimulus package	April 5, 1993	49–29	60
Stimulus package	April 21, 1993	56–43	60
Motor-voter registration	May 11, 1993	63–37	60
Campaign finance	June 10, 1993	53–41	60
Campaign finance	June 15, 1993	52–45	60
Campaign finance	June 16, 1993	62–37	60
National service	July 29, 1993	59–41	60
Dellinger nomination	October 7, 1993	59–39	60
Interior funds	October 21, 1993	53–41	60

Issue	Date	Vote	Yeas needed	Issue	Date	Vote	Yeas needed
Interior funds	October 26, 1993	51–45	60	Whitewater committee extension	March 13, 1996	53–47	60
Interior funds	October 28, 1993	54–44	60	Whitewater committee extension	March 14, 1996	51–46	60
State Department nominations	November 3, 1993	58–42	60	Whitewater committee extension	March 20, 1996	53–47	60
Brady bill (gun controls)	November 19, 1993	57–41	60	**Product liability**	March 20, 1996	60–40	60
Brady bill (gun controls)	November 19, 1993	57–42	60	Whitewater committee extension	March 21, 1996	52–46	60
Napolitano nomination	November 19, 1993	72–26	60	Presidio Park management	March 27, 1996	51–49	60
Competitiveness bill	March 15, 1994	56–42	60	Presidio Park management	March 28, 1996	55–45	60
Federal worker retirement buyout	March 24, 1994	58–41	60	Whitewater committee extension	April 16, 1996	51–46	60
Federal worker retirement buyout	March 24, 1994	63–36	60	Term limits constitutional amendment	April 23, 1996	58–42	60
Education goals 2000	March 26, 1994	62–23	60	**Immigration revision**	April 29, 1996	91–0	60
Brown nomination	May 24, 1994	54–44	60	**Immigration revision**	May 2, 1996	100–0	60
Shearer nomination	May 24, 1994	63–35	60	White House Travel Office reimbursement	May 7, 1996	52–44	60
Brown nomination	May 25, 1994	56–42	60	White House Travel Office reimbursement	May 8, 1996	53–45	60
Product liability	June 28, 1994	54–44	60	White House Travel Office reimbursement	May 9, 1996	52–44	60
Product liability	June 29, 1994	57–41	60	White House Travel Office reimbursement	May 14, 1996	54–43	60
Striker replacement	July 12, 1994	53–47	60	Missile defense	June 4, 1996	53–46	60
Striker replacement	July 13, 1994	53–46	60	Campaign finance overhaul	June 25, 1996	54–46	60
Crime bill	August 25, 1994	61–38	60	Defense authorization	June 26, 1996	52–46	60
Campaign finance	September 22, 1994	96–2	60	Defense authorization	June 28, 1996	53–43	60
California desert protection	September 23, 1994	73–20	60	Right-to-work legislation	July 10, 1996	31–68	60
Campaign finance	September 27, 1994	57–43	60	**Nuclear waste storage**	July 16, 1996	65–34	60
Campaign finance	September 30, 1994	52–46	662	**FAA reauthorization**	October 3, 1996	6–31	60
Tigert nomination	October 3, 1994	63–32	65 [3]	Volunteer liability limitation	April 29, 1997	53–46	60
Sarokin nomination	October 4, 1994	85–12	60	Volunteer liability limitation	April 30, 1997	55–44	60
Elementary and secondary education	October 5, 1994	75–24	60	**Supplemental funds**	May 7, 1997	100–0	60
Lobbying disclosure/gift ban	October 6, 1994	52–46	60	Compensatory time, flexible credit	May 15, 1997	53–47	60
Lobbying disclosure/gift ban	October 7, 1994	55–42	60	Compensatory time, flexible credit	June 4, 1997	51–47	60
California desert protection	October 8, 1994	68–23	60	Defense authorization, fiscal 1998	July 8, 1997	46–45	60
Unfunded mandates	January 19, 1995	54–44	60	**Klein nomination**	July 14, 1997	78–11	60
Balanced-budget amendment	February 16, 1995	57–42	60	**FDA overhaul**	September 5, 1997	89–5	60
Striker replacement	March 15, 1995	58–39	60	FDA overhaul	September 16, 1997	94–4	60
Health insurance tax deduction	April 3, 1995	83–0	60	District of Columbia funds, fiscal 1998	September 30, 1997	58–41	60
Supplemental funds and rescissions	April 6, 1995	56–44	60	Campaign finance reform	October 7, 1997	52–48	60
Product liability	May 4, 1995	46–53	60	Campaign finance reform	October 7, 1997	53–47	60
Product liability	May 4, 1995	47–52	60	**District of Columbia funds**	October 7, 1997	99–1	60
Product liability	May 8, 1995	43–49	60	Campaign finance reform	October 8, 1997	52–47	60
Product liability	May 9, 1995	60–38	60	Campaign finance reform	October 9, 1997	51–48	60
Interstate waste	May 12, 1995	50–47	60	Campaign finance reform	October 9, 1997	52–47	60
Telecommunications	June 14, 1995	89–11	60	Highway and Transit reauthorization	October 23, 1997	48–50	60
Foster nomination	June 21, 1995	57–43	60	Highway and Transit reauthorization	October 23, 1997	48–52	60
Foster nomination	June 22, 1995	57–43	60	Highway and Transit reauthorization	October 24, 1997	43–49	60
Regulatory overhaul	July 17, 1995	48–46	60	Highway and Transit reauthorization	October 28, 1997	52–48	60
Regulatory overhaul	July 18, 1995	53–47	60	Education savings accounts	October 31, 1997	56–41	60
Regulatory overhaul	July 20, 1995	58–40	60	**Defense authorization, fiscal 1998**	October 31, 1997	93–2	60
State Department authorization	August 1, 1995	55–45	60	Education savings accounts	November 4, 1997	56–44	60
State Department authorization	August 1, 1995	55–45	60	**Fast track trade procedures**	November 4, 1997	69–31	60
Cuba sanctions	October 12, 1995	56–37	60				
Cuba sanctions	October 17, 1995	59–36	60				
Cuba sanctions	October 18, 1995	98–0	60				
Farm bill	February 1, 1996	53–45	60				
Farm bill	February 6, 1996	59–34	60				
District of Columbia funds	February 27, 1996	54–44	60				
District of Columbia funds	February 29, 1996	52–42	60				
District of Columbia funds	March 5, 1996	53–43	60				
Whitewater committee extension	March 12, 1996	53–47	60				
District of Columbia funds	March 12, 1996	56–44	60				

Issue	Date	Vote	Yeas needed	Issue	Date	Vote	Yeas needed
Satcher confirmation	February 10, 1998	75–23	60	Social Security "lockbox"	June 16, 1999	55–44	60
Human cloning research ban	February 11, 1998	42–54	60	Steel import quotas	June 22, 1999	42–57	60
Restrict political use of union dues	February 26, 1998	45–54	60	Commerce, State, Justice funds, fiscal 2000	June 28, 1999	49–39	60
Restrict political use of union dues	February 26, 1998	51–48	60	Transportation funds, fiscal 2000	June 28, 1999	49–40	60
Highway and mass transit programs	March 11, 1998	96–3	60	Foreign operations funds, fiscal 2000	June 28, 1999	49–41	60
Education savings accounts	March 17, 1998	74–24	60	Agriculture funds, fiscal 2000	June 28, 1999	50–37	60
Expand education savings accounts	March 19, 1998	55–44	60	**Budget procedures**	July 1, 1999	99–1	60
Expand education savings accounts	March 26, 1998	58–42	60	Social Security "lockbox," debt limit	July 16, 1999	52–43	60
U.S. anti-missile defense policy	May 13, 1998	59–41	60	**Intelligence authorization, fiscal 2000**	July 20, 1999	99–0	60
Create nuclear waste storage in Nevada	June 2, 1998	56–39	60	**Juvenile justice programs**	July 28, 1999	77–22	60
Set federal policies to curb smoking	June 9, 1998	42–56	62	Agriculture funds/milk marketing	August 4, 1999	53–47	60
Set federal policies to curb smoking	June 10, 1998	43–55	60	Transportation funds, fiscal 2000	September 9, 1999	49–49	60
Set federal policies to curb smoking	June 11, 1998	43–56	60	Oil royalty valuation system	September 13, 1999	54–40	60
Set federal policies to curb smoking	June 17, 1998	57–42	60	**Puerto Rican nationalists clemency**	September 13, 1999	93–0	60
Limit product liability suits	July 7, 1998	71–24	60	Bankruptcy law revision	September 21, 1999	53–45	60
Limit product liability punitive damages	July 9, 1998	51–47	60	Stewart nomination	September 21, 1999	55–44	60
U.S. court review, local zoning decisions	July 13, 1998	52–42	60	**Oil royalty valuation system**	September 23, 1999	62–39	60
Legislative branch funds, fiscal 1999	July 21, 1998	83–16	60	**Agriculture funds, fiscal 2000**	October 12, 1999	79–20	60
U.S. missile defense policy	September 9, 1998	59–41	60	Campaign finance soft money ban	October 19, 1999	52–48	60
Consumer bankruptcy laws	September 9, 1998	99–1	60	Campaign finance soft money, union dues	October 19, 1999	53–47	60
Campaign finance reform	September 10, 1998	52–48	60	**Trade with Sub-Saharan Africa**	October 26, 1999	91–8	60
Parental consent abortion bill	September 11, 1998	97–0	60	Sub-Saharan African, Caribbean trade	October 29, 1999	45–46	60
Limit union organizing	September 14, 1998	52–42	60	**Sub-Saharan African, Caribbean trade**	November 2, 1999	74–23	60
Evading parental consent abortion laws	September 22, 1998	54–45	60	**Omnibus funds, fiscal 2000**	November 19, 1999	87–9	60
Limit presidential appointment powers	September 24, 1998	96–1	60	**Nuclear waste storage**	February 2, 2000	94–3	60
				Paez nomination	March 8, 2000	85–14	60
Limit presidential appointment powers	September 28, 1998	53–38	60	**Berzon nomination**	March 8, 2000	86–13	60
Internet sales taxes	September 29, 1998	89–6	60	**Flag desecration amendment**	March 29, 2000	100–0	60
Banking regulation revision	October 5, 1998	93–0	60	**Federal gas tax suspension**	March 30, 2000	86–11	60
Ban Internet sales taxes for two years	October 7, 1998	94–4	60	Federal gas tax suspension	April 11, 2000	43–56	60
Waive federal education spending rules	March 8, 1999	54–41	60	Marriage penalty tax	April 13, 2000	53–45	60
Waive federal education spending rules	March 9, 1999	55–39	60	Marriage penalty tax	April 13, 2000	53–45	60
Authorize $11.4 billion for new teachers	March 10, 1999	44–55	60	**Victims' rights**	April 25, 2000	82–12	60
Special education funding	March 10, 1999	55–44	60	Marriage penalty tax	April 27, 2000	51–44	60
U.S. troops in Kosovo	March 23, 1999	55–44	60	**African trade agreement**	May 11, 2000	76–18	60
Social Security "lockbox," debt limit	April 22, 1999	54–45	60	**Estate tax repeal**	July 11, 2000	99–1	60
Y2K liability limits	April 26, 1999	94–0	60	**Intelligence authorization, fiscal 2001**	July 26, 2000	96–1	60
Y2K liability limits	April 29, 1999	52–47	60	**Treasury funds, fiscal 2001**	July 26, 2000	97–0	60
Social Security "lockbox," debt limit	April 30, 1999	49–44	60	**Energy, water funds, fiscal 2001**	July 27, 2000	100–0	60
2K liability limits	May 18, 1999	53–45	60	**Trade with China**	July 27, 2000	86–12	60
Social Security "lockbox" debt limit	June 15, 1999	53–46	60	**High technology visas**	September 19, 2000	97–1	60
				High technology visas	September 26, 2000	94–3	60
Steel, oil, gas loan guarantee	June 15, 1999	70–29	60	**High technology visas**	September 28, 2000	92–3	60
				Interior funds, fiscal 2001	October 5, 2000	89–8	60
				Bankruptcy law revision	November 1, 2000	53–30	60
				Bankruptcy law revision	December 5, 2000	67–31	60
				Bankruptcy law revision	March 14, 2001	80–19	60
				ESEA reauthorization	May 1, 2001	96–3	60

Issue	Date	Vote	Yeas needed	Issue	Date	Vote	Yeas needed
Bankruptcy law revision	July 12, 2001	88–10	60	Interior funds, fiscal 2002/ farm disaster aid	September 23, 2002	49–46	60
Bankruptcy law revision	July 17, 2001	88–10	60	Homeland security department	September 25, 2002	49–49	60
Mexican trucks access to U.S.	July 26, 2001	70–30	60	Interior funds, fiscal 2002/ farm disaster aid	September 25, 2002	51–47	60
Mexican trucks in U.S.	July 27, 2001	57–27	60	Homeland security/worker union rights	September 26, 2002	44–53	60
Supplemental farm funds	July 30, 2001	95–2	60	Homeland security department	September 26, 2002	50–49	60
Transportation/Mexican trucks in U.S.	August 2, 2001	100–0	60	Homeland security/worker union rights	October 1, 2002	45–52	60
Supplemental farm funds	August 3, 2001	49–48	60	**Justice department reauthorization**	October 3, 2002	93–5	60
Defense/energy funds authorization	October 2, 2001	100–0	60	**Use of force against Iraq**	October 3, 2002	95–1	60
Federal airport security	October 9, 2001	97–0	60	**Use of force against Iraq**	October 10, 2002	75–25	60
Aviation workers assistance	October 11, 2001	56–44	60	**Homeland security/worker union rights**	November 13, 2002	89–8	60
Foreign operations funds	October 15, 2001	50–46	60	**Homeland security department**	November 15, 2002	65–29	60
Foreign operations funds	October 23, 2001	50–47	60	**Homeland security department**	November 19, 2002	83–16	60
Safety officers collective bargaining rights	November 6, 2001	56–44	60	**Terrorism insurance**	November 19, 2002	85–12	60
Pension contribution limits	November 29, 2001	96–4	60	Estrada appeals court nomination	March 6, 2003	55–44	60
Energy policies/human cloning	December 3, 2001	1–94	60	Estrada appeals court nomination	March 13, 2003	55–42	60
Railroad retirement pension board	December 3, 2001	81–15	60	Estrada appeals court nomination	March 18, 2003	55–45	60
Farm policy revisions	December 5, 2001	73–26	60	Estrada appeals court nomination	April 2, 2003	55–44	60
Farm policy revisions	December 13, 2001	53–45	60	Owen appeals court nomination	May 1, 2003	52–44	60
Farm policy revisions	December 18, 2001	54–43	60	Estrada appeals court nomination	May 5, 2003	52–39	60
Farm policy revisions	December 19, 2001	54–43	60	Owen appeals court nomination	May 8, 2003	52–45	60
Business tax cut/ unemployment benefits	February 6, 2002	48–47	60	Estrada appeals court nomination	May 8, 2003	54–43	60
Tax bill/unemployment benefits	February 6, 2002	56–39	60	Medical malpractice award caps	July 9, 2003	49–48	60
Election procedures requirements	March 1, 2002	49–39	60	Owen appeals court nomination	July 29, 2003	53–43	60
Election procedures requirements	March 4, 2002	51–44	60	Estrada appeals court nomination	July 30, 2003	55–43	60
Campaign finance revisions	March 20, 2002	68–32	60	Pryor appeals court nomination	July 31, 2003	53–44	60
Energy policy bill	April 10, 2002	48–50	60	Class action lawsuits	October 22, 2003	59–39	60
Energy bill/ANWR drilling	April 18, 2002	36–64	60	Pickering appeals court nomination	October 30, 2003	54–43	60
Energy bill/ANWR drilling	April 18, 2002	46–54	60	Pryor appeals court nomination	November 6, 2003	51–43	60
Energy policy bill	April 23, 2002	86–13	60	Owen appeals court nomination	November 14, 2003	53–42	60
Andean duty-free trade	April 29, 2002	69–21	60	Kuhl appeals court nomination	November 14, 2003	53–43	60
Andean trade/steelworkers health insurance	May 21, 2002	56–40	60	Brown appeals court nomination	November 14, 2003	53–43	60
Andean duty-free trade	May 22, 2002	68–29	60	FAA authorization	November 17, 2003	45–43	60
Supplemental funds, fiscal 2002	June 6, 2002	87–10	60	Dorr agriculture undersecretary nomination	November 18, 2003	57–39	60
Hate crimes definitions	June 11, 2002	54–43	60	Dorr Commodity Credit Corp. nomination	November 18, 2003	57–39	60
Terrorism insurance	June 18, 2002	65–31	60	Energy policy bill conference report	November 21, 2003	57–40	60
Defense authorization, fiscal 2003	June 26, 2002	98–0	60				
Accounting industry reform	July 12, 2002	91–2	60				
Smith appeals court nomination	July 15, 2002	94–3	60				
Drug patents	July 17, 2002	99–0	60				
Clifton appeals court nomination	July 18, 2002	97–1	60				
Carmona surgeon general nomination	July 23, 2002	98–0	60				
Gibbons appeals court nomination	July 26, 2002	89–0	60				
Drug patents	July 31, 2002	66–33	60				
Trade promotion authority	August 1, 2002	64–32	60				
Interior funds, fiscal 2002/ farm disaster aid	September 17, 2002	50–49	60				
Homeland security department	September 19, 2002	50–49	60				

Issue	Date	Vote	Yeas needed
Medicare prescription drug bill	November 24, 2003	70–29	60
Omnibus appropriations, fiscal 2004	January 20, 2004	48–45	60
Omnibus appropriations, fiscal 2004	January 22, 2004	61–32	60
Highway funding	February 2, 2004	75–11	60
Highway funding	February 12, 2004	86–11	60
Medical malpractice lawsuit caps	February 24, 2004	48–45	60
Gun liability lawsuits	February 25, 2004	75–22	60
Corporate tax changes	March 24, 2004	51–47	60
Welfare reauthorization	April 1, 2004	51–47	60
Medical malpractice lawsuit caps	April 7, 2004	49–48	60
Corporate tax changes	April 7, 2004	50–47	60
Asbestos claims fund	April 22, 2004	50–47	60
Internet tax moratorium	April 26, 2004	74–11	60
Internet tax/ethanol	April 29, 2004	40–59	60
Internet tax/energy policy	April 29, 2004	55–43	60
Internet tax moratorium	April 29, 2004	64–34	60
Corporate tax changes	May 11, 2004	90–8	60
Class action lawsuits	July 8, 2004	44–43	60
Same-sex marriage amendment	July 14, 2004	48–50	60
Myers appeals court nomination	July 20, 2004	53–44	60
Saad appeals court nomination	July 22, 2004	52–46	60
McKeague appeals court nomination	July 22, 2004	53–44	60
Griffin appeals court nomination	July 22, 2004	54–44	60
Intelligence operations overhaul	October 5, 2004	85–10	60
Senate intelligence oversight	October 8, 2004	88–3	60
Corporate tax changes	October 10, 2004	66–14	60
Tariffs and trade bill	November 19, 2004	88–5	60
Bankruptcy overhaul	March 8, 2005	69–31	60
Iraq, Afghanistan war funding	April 19, 2005	100–0	60
Foreign workers temporary U.S. status	April 19, 2005	21–77	60
Agricultural workers in U.S. illegally	April 19, 2005	53–45	60
Seasonal workers exemption	April 19, 2005	83–17	60
Surface transportation reauthorization	April 26, 2005	94–6	60
Johnson EPA administrator nomination	April 28, 2005	61–37	60
Surface transportation reauthorization	May 12, 2005	92–7	60
Owen appeals court nomination	May 24, 2005	81–18	60
Bolton United Nations nomination	May 26, 2005	56–42	60
Brown appeals court nomination	June 7, 2005	65–32	60
Pryor appeals court nomination	June 8, 2005	67–32	60
Bolton United Nations nomination	June 20, 2005	54–38	60
Energy policy overhaul	June 23, 2005	92–4	60
Defense authorization	July 26, 2005	50–48	60
Gun liability limitations	July 26, 2005	66–32	60

Issue	Date	Vote	Yeas needed
Defense appropriations	October 5, 2005	95–4	60
Labor–HHS–Education appropriations	October 27, 2005	97–0	60
Patriot Act reauthorization	December 16, 2005	52–47	60
Defense appropriations	December 21, 2005	56–44	60
Alito Supreme Court nomination	January 30, 2006	72–25	60
Asbestos trust fund	February 7, 2006	98–1	60
Patriot Act reauthorization	February 16, 2006	96–3	60
Patriot Act reauthorization	February 28, 2006	69–30	60
Patriot Act reauthorization	March 1, 2006	84–15	60
Low income home energy assistance	March 7, 2006	75–25	60
Lobbying overhaul	March 9, 2006	51–47	60
Lobbying overhaul	March 28, 2006	81–16	60
Immigration overhaul	April 6, 2006	38–60	60
Immigration overhaul	April 6, 2006	39–60	60
Immigration overhaul	April 7, 2006	36–62	60
Flory Defense Department nomination	April 7, 2006	52–41	60
Iraq, Afghanistan war funding	May 2, 2006	92–4	60
Medical malpractice	May 8, 2006	48–42	60
Medical malpractice	May 8, 2006	49–44	60
Small business health plans	May 9, 2006	96–2	60
Small business health plans	May 11, 2006	55–43	60
Immigration overhaul	May 24, 2006	73–25	60
Kavanaugh appeals court nomination	May 25, 2006	67–30	60
Interior secretary nomination	May 26, 2006	85–8	60
Same-sex marriage ban amendment	June 7, 2006	49–48	60
Native Hawaiians policy	June 8, 2006	56–41	60
Estate tax repeal	June 8, 2006	57–41	60
Defense authorization	June 22, 2006	98–1	60
Gulf of Mexico offshore drilling	July 26, 2006	86–12	60
Gulf of Mexico offshore drilling	July 31, 2006	72–23	60
Tax package and minimum wage	August 3, 2006	56–42	60
Port security overhaul	September 14, 2006	98–0	60
U.S.–Mexican border fence	September 20, 2006	94–0	60
U.S.–Mexican border fence	September 28, 2006	71–28	60
Abortion parental notification	September 29, 2006	57–42	60
FDA commissioner nomination	December 7, 2006	89–6	60
Jordan appeals court nomination	December 8, 2006	93–0	60
Tax and trade package	December 9, 2006	78–10	60
Ethics and lobbying overhaul	January 16, 2007	95–2	60
Ethics and lobbying overhaul	January 17, 2007	51–46	60
Minimum wage increase	January 24, 2007	49–48	60
Minimum wage increase	January 24, 2007	54–43	60
Minimum wage increase	January 30, 2007	87–10	60
Minimum wage increase	January 31, 2007	88–8	60
U.S. troop levels in Iraq	February 1, 2007	0–97	60
U.S. troop levels in Iraq	February 5, 2007	49–47	60
Continuing appropriations fiscal 2007	February 13, 2007	71–26	60
Iraq war troop surge	February 17, 2007	56–34	60
September 11 commission recommendations	February 27, 2007	97–0	60

Issue	Date	Vote	Yeas needed
September 11 commission recommendations	March 9, 2007	46–49	60
September 11 commission recommendations	March 9, 2007	69–26	60
Iraq mission	March 14, 2007	89–9	60
Supplemental appropriations fiscal 2007	March 28, 2007	97–0	60
Intelligence authorization fiscal 2007	April 12, 2007	94–3	60
Intelligence authorization fiscal 2007	April 16, 2007	41–40	60
Intelligence authorization fiscal 2007	April 17, 2007	50–45	60
Medicare prescription drug negotiations	April 18, 2007	55–42	60
Court security	April 18, 2007	93–3	60
FDA overhaul	May 3, 2007	63–28	60
FDA overhaul	May 7, 2007	82–8	60
Water projects authorization	May 10, 2007	89–7	60
Iraq troop withdrawal by March 31, 2008	May 16, 2007	29–67	60
Withholding Iraq economic aid	May 16, 2007	52–44	60
Sense of Senate on Iraq funding	May 16, 2007	87–9	60
Sense of Senate on Iraq mission	May 17, 2007	94–1	60
Immigration overhaul	May 21, 2007	69–23	60
Immigration overhaul	June 7, 2007	33–63	60
Immigration overhaul	June 7, 2007	34–61	60
Immigration overhaul	June 7, 2007	45–50	60
No confidence: Attorney General Gonzales	June 11, 2007	53–38	60
Energy policy	June 11, 2007	91–0	60
Energy policy	June 21, 2007	57–36	60
Energy policy	June 21, 2007	61–32	60
Energy policy	June 21, 2007	62–32	60
Employee union formation	June 26, 2007	51–48	60
Immigration overhaul	June 26, 2007	64–35	60
Immigration overhaul	June 28, 2007	46–53	60
Defense authorization fiscal 2008	July 11, 2007	56–41	60
Defense authorization fiscal 2008	July 17, 2007	52–47	60
Small business tax breaks	July 30, 2007	80–0	60
Ethics and lobbying overhaul	August 2, 2007	80–17	60
District of Columbia voting rights	September 18, 2007	57–42	60
Defense authorization fiscal 2008	September 19, 2007	56–43	60
Defense authorization fiscal 2008	September 27, 2007	60–39	60
Children's Health Insurance	September 27, 2007	69–30	60
Defense authorization fiscal 2008	September 27, 2007	89–6	60
Immigrant education	October 24, 2007	52–44	60
Southwick appeals court nomination	October 24, 2007	62–35	60
Amtrak reauthorization	October 30, 2007	79–13	60
Children's health insurance	October 31, 2007	62–33	60
Children's health insurance	November 1, 2007	65–30	60
Iraq war appropriations	November 16, 2007	45–53	60
Iraq war appropriations/troop withdrawal	November 16, 2007	53–45	60
Farm bill reauthorization	November 16, 2007	55–42	60
Alternative minimum tax	December 6, 2007	46–48	60
Energy policy	December 7, 2007	53–42	60
Energy policy/CAFE standards	December 13, 2007	59–40	60
Farm bill reauthorization	December 13, 2007	78–12	60
Foreign intelligence surveillance	December 17, 2007	76–10	60
Omnibus appropriations fiscal 2008	December 18, 2007	44–51	60
Foreign intelligence surveillance	January 28, 2008	48–45	60
Foreign intelligence surveillance	January 28, 2008	48–45	60
Economic stimulus	February 4, 2008	80–4	60
Economic stimulus	February 6, 2008	58–41	60
Foreign intelligence surveillance	February 12, 2008	69–29	60
Intelligence authorization fiscal 2008	February 13, 2008	92–4	60
Indian health care reauthorization	February 25, 2008	85–2	60
U.S. troop deployments in Iraq	February 26, 2008	70–24	60
Report on al Qaeda	February 27, 2008	89–3	60
Renewable energy	February 28, 2008	48–46	60
Consumer Product Safety Commission	March 3, 2008	86–1	60
Renewable energy	April 1, 2008	94–1	60
Renewable energy/mortgage relief	April 8, 2008	92–6	60
Surface Transportation law corrections	April 14, 2008	93–1	60
Surface transportation corrections	April 17, 2008	90–2	60
Veterans benefits expansion	April 22, 2008	94–0	60
Wage discrimination	April 23, 2008	56–42	60
FAA reauthorization	April 28, 2008	88–0	60
FAA reauthorization	May 6, 2008	49–42	60
National flood insurance	May 6, 2008	90–1	60
Public safety workers organizing rights	May 13, 2008	69–29	60
Climate change trading system	June 2, 2008	74–14	60
Climate change trading system	June 6, 2008	48–36	60
Tax reduction extensions	June 10, 2008	50–44	60
Energy and oil company taxes	June 10, 2008	51–43	60
Medicare physician payments	June 12, 2008	54–39	60
Tax reduction extensions	June 17, 2008	52–44	60
Mortgage relief	June 24, 2008	83–9	60
Foreign intelligence surveillance	June 25, 2008	80–15	60
Medicare physician payments	June 26, 2008	58–40	60
Mortgage relief	July 7, 2008	76–10	60
Medicare physician payments	July 9, 2008	69–30	60
Foreign intelligence surveillance	July 9, 2008	72–26	60
Mortgage relief	July 10, 2008	84–12	60
HIV/AIDS program reauthorization	July 11, 2008	65–3	60
Energy futures speculation	July 22, 2008	94–0	60
Energy futures speculation	July 25, 2008	50–43	60
Mortgage relief	July 25, 2008	80–13	60
Low-income energy assistance	July 26, 2008	50–35	60
Omnibus domestic and foreign policy bills	July 28, 2008	52–40	60

Issue	Date	Vote	Yeas needed
Tax cuts extensions	July 29, 2008	53–43	60
Media shield	July 30, 2008	51–43	60
Tax reduction extensions	July 30, 2008	51–43	60
Defense authorization fiscal 2009	July 31, 2008	51–39	60
Defense authorization fiscal 2009	September 8, 2008	83–0	60
Defense authorization fiscal 2009	September 16, 2008	61–32	60
Continuing appropriations	September 27, 2008	83–12	60
Railroad safety/Amtrak authorization	September 29, 2008	69–17	60
Unemployment benefits extension	November 20, 2008	89–6	60
Automobile industry loans	December 11, 2008	52–35	60
Public lands designations	January 11, 2009	66–12	60
Public lands designations	January 14, 2009	68–24	60
Wage discrimination/Lilly Ledbetter	January 15, 2009	72–23	60
Economic stimulus legislation	February 9, 2009	61–36	60
District of Columbia House membership	February 24, 2009	62–34	60
Omnibus appropriations fiscal 2009	March 10, 2009	62–35	60
Public lands historic sites	March 16, 2009	73–21	60
National Service Programs authorization	March 23, 2009	74–14	60
Hill nomination as Iraq ambassador	April 20, 2009	73–17	60
Expand federal fraud laws	April 27, 2009	84–4	60
Hayes nomination as Interior secretary	May 13, 2009	57–39	60
Credit card company regulation	May 19, 2009	92–2	60
Supplemental appropriations fiscal 2009	May 21, 2009	94–1	60
Tobacco regulation by FDA	June 2, 2009	84–11	60
Tobacco regulation by FDA	June 8, 2009	61–30	60
Tobacco regulation by FDA	June 10, 2009	67–30	60
Foreign tourism promotion office	June 16, 2009	53–34	60
Foreign tourism promotion office	June 16, 2009	90–3	60
Koh State Department nomination	June 24, 2009	65–31	60
Groves nomination as Census director	July 13, 2009	76–15	60
Expanding federal hate crime laws	July 16, 2009	63–28	60
Agriculture appropriations fiscal 2010	August 3, 2009	83–11	60
Foreign tourism promotion office	September 8, 2009	80–19	60
Sunstein nomination to OMB office	September 9, 2009	63–35	60
State, Justice, Commerce appropriations fiscal 2010	October 13, 2009	56–38	60
Energy, water appropriations fiscal 2010	October 14, 2009	79–17	60
Medicare doctor reimbursements	October 21, 2009	47–53	60
Defense funding authorization fiscal 2010	October 22, 2009	64–35	60
Unemployment benefits extension	October 27, 2009	87–13	60

Issue	Date	Vote	Yeas needed
Unemployment benefits extension	November 2, 2009	85–2	60
Unemployment benefits extension	November 4, 2009	97–1	60
State, Justice, Commerce appropriations fiscal 2010	November 5, 2009	60–39	60
Hamilton circuit court nomination	November 17, 2009	70–29	60
Health care overhaul, homeowners tax	November 21, 2009	60–39	60
Omnibus appropriations fiscal 2010	December 12, 2009	60–34	60
Defense appropriations fiscal 2010	December 18, 2009	63–33	60
Health care overhaul	December 21, 2009	60–40	60
Health care overhaul	December 22, 2009	60–39	60
Health care overhaul	December 23, 2009	60–39	60
Bernanke Federal Reserve nomination	January 28, 2010	77–23	60
Smith Labor Dept. solicitor nomination	February 1, 2010	60–32	60
Johnson GSA administrator nomination	February 4, 2010	82–16	60
Becker nomination Labor Relations Board	February 9, 2010	52–33	60
Jobs package; payroll tax holiday	February 22, 2010	62–30	60
Travel Promotion, Capitol Police	February 25, 2010	76–20	60
Keenan appeals court nomination	March 2, 2010	99–0	60
Extend tax cut, unemployment benefits	March 9, 2010	66–34	60
Extend tax cuts, unemployment benefits	March 10, 2010	66–33	60
Business taxes, highway extension	March 15, 2010	61–30	60
Short-term program extension	April 12, 2010	60–34	60
Short-term program extensions	April 15, 2010	60–38	60
Brainard Treasury nomination	April 19, 2010	84–10	60
Financial regulatory overhaul	April 26, 2010	57–41	60
Financial regulatory overhaul	April 27, 2010	57–41	60
Financial regulatory overhaul	April 28, 2010	56–42	60
Financial regulatory overhaul	May 19, 2010	57–42	60
Financial regulatory overhaul	May 20, 2010	60–40	60
Supplemental appropriations fiscal 2010	May 27, 2010	69–29	60
Tax cut extension, unemployment benefits	June 17, 2010	56–40	60
Tax cut extension, unemployment benefits	June 24, 2010	57–41	60
Small business taxes and lending fund	June 29, 2010	66–33	60
Tax extension and unemployment benefits	June 30, 2010	58–38	60
Financial regulatory overhaul	July 15, 2010	60–38	60
Unemployment benefits extension	July 20, 2010	60–40	60
Supplemental appropriations fiscal 2010	July 22, 2010	46–51	60

Issue	Date	Vote	Yeas needed	Issue	Date	Vote	Yeas needed
Small business lending fund	July 22, 2010	60–37	60	Myanmar sanctions	September 12, 2011	53–33	60
Campaign finance disclosure	July 27, 2010	57–41	60	**Myanmar sanctions**	September 13, 2011	61–38	60
Small business taxes and lending fund	July 29, 2010	58–42	60	**Trade preferences**	September 19, 2011	84–8	60
Medicaid and education assistance	August 4, 2010	61–38	60	Short-term continuing appropriations	September 26, 2011	54–35	60
Health care overhaul law amendments	September 14, 2010	46–52	60	**Currency misalignment/ China**	October 3, 2011	79–19	60
Health care overhaul law amendments	September 14, 2010	56–42	60	**Currency misalignment/ China**	October 6, 2011	62–38	60
Small business taxes and lending fund	September 14, 2010	61–37	60	Job creation	October 11, 2011	50–49	60
Small business taxes and lending fund	September 16, 2010	61–38	60	Public employee jobs funding	October 20, 2011	50–50	60
"Don't ask, don't tell" policy	September 21, 2010	56–43	60	Tax withholding payments repeal	October 20, 2011	57–43	60
Campaign finance disclosure	September 23, 2010	59–39	60	**Agriculture, CJS, housing appropriations**	October 20, 2011	82–16	60
Social Security tax cut for corporations	September 28, 2010	53–45	60	**Tax withholding payments repeal**	November 7, 2011	94–1	60
Continuing appropriations fiscal 2010 and 2011	September 28, 2010	84–14	60	**Energy, State, Treasury appropriations**	November 10, 2011	81–14	60
Wage discrimination	November 17, 2010	58–4	60	**Defense funding authorization**	November 30, 2011	88–12	60
Food safety overhaul, FDA enforcement	November 17, 2010	74–25	60	Halligan judicial nomination	December 6, 2011	54–45	60
Food safety overhaul, FDA enforcement	November 29, 2010	69–26	60	Cordray consumer agency nomination	December 8, 2011	53–45	60
Tax rate extensions	December 4, 2010	53–36	60	Aponte ambassador nomination	December 12, 2011	49–37	60
Tax rate extensions	December 4, 2010	53–37	60	**Eisen ambassador nomination**	December 12, 2011	70–16	60
Social Security single payment	December 8, 2010	53–45	60	**Congressional insider-trading ban**	January 30, 2012	93–2	60
Public safety workers collective bargaining	December 8, 2010	55–43	60	**Surface transportation reauthorization**	February 9, 2012	85–11	60
"Don't ask, don't tell" policy	December 9, 2010	57–40	60	**Jordan judicial nomination**	February 13, 2012	89–5	60
Health, compensation fund first-responders	December 9, 2010	57–42	60	Surface transportation reauthorization	February 17, 2012	54–42	60
Tax rate extensions	December 13, 2010	83–15	60	Surface transportation reauthorization	March 6, 2012	52–44	60
Immigration policy revisions	December 18, 2010	55–41	60	Small business auditing, SEC oversight	March 20, 2012	54–45	60
"Don't ask, don't tell" policy repeal	December 18, 2010	63–33	60	Small business auditing, SEC oversight	March 20, 2012	55–44	60
New START agreement with Russia	December 21, 2010	67–28	60	**Small business auditing, SEC oversight**	March 21, 2012	76–22	60
Continuing appropriations fiscal 2011	December 21, 2010	82–14	60	**Congressional insider-trading ban**	March 22, 2012	96–3	60
FAA reauthorization	February 17, 2011	96–2	60	**Oil and gas tax breaks repeal**	March 26, 2012	92–4	60
Patent law overhaul	March 7, 2011	87–3	60	Postal Service overhaul	March 27, 2012	51–46	60
Small business research	March 14, 2011	84–12	60	Oil and gas tax breaks repeal	March 29, 2012	51–47	60
Small business research	May 4, 2011	52–44	60	Millionaires minimum tax	April 16, 2012	51–45	60
McConnell judicial nomination	May 4, 2011	63–33	60	**Postal Service overhaul**	April 17, 2012	74–22	60
Cole Justice Department nomination	May 9, 2011	50–40	60	Student loan interest rate extension	May 8, 2012	52–45	60
Liu judicial nomination	May 19, 2011	52–43	60	Outlaw wage discrimination by gender	June 5, 2012	52–47	60
Patriot Act extension	May 23, 2011	74–8	60	**Farm, food, nutrition reauthorizations**	June 7, 2012	90–8	60
Patriot Act extension	May 26, 2011	79–18	60	**Hurwitz judicial nomination**	June 11, 2012	60–31	60
Ethanol tax provisions	June 14, 2011	40–59	60	**Aponte ambassador nomination**	June 14, 2012	62–37	60
Economic development reauthorization	June 21, 2011	49–51	60	**Flood insurance reauthorization**	June 21, 2012	96–2	60
Millionaires taxes sense of Senate	July 7, 2011	74–22	60	**FDA user fees reauthorization**	June 25, 2012	89–3	60
Millionaires taxes sense of Senate	July 13, 2011	51–49	60				
Military constructions, VA funding	July 13, 2011	89–11	60				
Military constructions, VA funding	July 14, 2011	71–26	60				
Debt limit increase	July 31, 2011	50–49	60				
Patent law overhaul	September 6, 2011	93–5	60				

Issue	Date	Vote	Yeas needed	Issue	Date	Vote	Yeas needed
Small business tax cuts	July 10, 2012	80–14	60	**Water Resources Development Act of 2013**	May 6, 2013	UC	60
Small business tax cuts	July 12, 2012	53–44	60	**Water Resources Development Act of 2013**	May 15, 2013	UC	60
Small business tax cuts	July 12, 2012	57–41	60	**Judicial nominee Srikanth Srinivasan**	May 23, 2013	UC	60
Campaign finance disclosure	July 16, 2012	51–44	60	Comprehensive Student Loan Protection Act	June 6, 2013	40–57	60
Campaign finance disclosure	July 17, 2012	53–45	60	Student Loan Affordability Act	June 6, 2013	51–46	60
U.S. jobs outsourcing tax credits	July 19, 2012	56–42	60	**Agriculture Reform, Food, and Jobs Act of 2013**	June 6, 2013	75–22	60
Cybersecurity standards	July 26, 2012	84–11	60	**Border Security, Economic Opportunity, and Immigration Modernization Act**	June 11, 2013	82–15	60
Bacharach judicial nomination	July 30, 2012	56–34	60				
Cybersecurity standards	August 2, 2012	52–46	60	**Border Security, Economic Opportunity, and Immigration Modernization Act**	June 24, 2013	67–27	60
Veterans job trainings	September 11, 2012	95–1	60				
Continuing appropriations fiscal 2013	September 19, 2012	76–22	60	**Border Security, Economic Opportunity, and Immigration Modernization Act**	June 26, 2013	67–31	60
Continuing appropriations fiscal 2013	September 21, 2012	62–30	60				
Hunting access on U.S. lands	September 21, 2012	84–7	60	**Border Security, Economic Opportunity, and Immigration Modernization Act**	June 27, 2013	68–32	60
Cybersecurity standards	November 14, 2012	51–47	60				
Hunting access on U.S. lands	November 15, 2012	84–12	60				
Defense authorization fiscal 2013	December 3, 2012	93–0	60	Keep Student Loans Affordable Act of 2013	July 10, 2013	51–49	60
Extend FDIC insurance	December 11, 2012	76–20	60	**Nominee Richard Cordray**	July 16, 2013	71–29	60
Disaster supplement, Superstorm Sandy	December 21, 2012	91–1	60	**Nominee Richard F. Gri**	July 16, 2013	UC	60
				Nominee Sharon Block	July 16, 2013	UC	60
Nominee Charles Timothy Hagel	February 14, 2013	58–40	60	**Nominee Mark Gaston Pearce**	July 16, 2013	UC	60
Nominee Charles Timothy Hagel Vote No. 21 reconsidered	February 26, 2013	71–27	60	**Nominee Thomas Edward Perez**	July 17, 2013	60–40	60
				Nominee Fred P. Hochberg	July 17, 2013	82–18	60
A bill to provide for a sequester replacement	February 28, 2013	38–62	60	**Nominee Regina McCarthy**	July 18, 2013	69–31	60
Sequestration legislation	February 28, 2013	51–49	60	**Transportation, Housing and Urban Development, and Related Agencies Appropriations**	July 23, 2013	73–26	60
Judicial nominee Caitlin Joan Halligan	March 6, 2013	51–41	60				
Nominee John Owen Brennan	March 7, 2013	81–16	60				
Department of Defense, Military Construction and Veterans Affairs, and Full-Year Continuing Appropriations	March 13, 2013	UC	60	Nominee James B. Comey Jr.	July 29, 2013	UC	60
				Nominee Kent Yoshiho Hirozawa	July 30, 2013	64–34	60
Department of Defense, Military Construction and Veterans Affairs, and Full-Year Continuing Appropriations	March 18, 2013	63–35	60	**Nominee Nancy Jean Schiffer**	July 30, 2013	65–33	60
				Nominee Mark Gaston Pearce	July 30, 2013	69–29	60
Department of Defense, Military Construction and Veterans Affairs, and Full-Year Continuing Appropriations	March 20, 2013	63–36	60	**Nominee Samantha Power**	July 30, 2013	UC	60
				Nominee Byron Todd Jones	July 31, 2013	60–40	60
Safe Communities, Safe Schools Act of 2013	April 11, 2013	68–31	60	Transportation, Housing and Urban Development, and Related Agencies Appropriations	August 1, 2013	54–43	60
Bill to Restore States' Sovereign Rights to Enforce State and Local Sales and Use Tax Laws and for Other Purposes	April 22, 2013	74–20	60				
				Continuing Appropriations Resolution, 2014	September 25, 2013	100–0	60
				Continuing Appropriations Resolution, 2014	September 27, 2013	79–19	60
Bill to Restore States' Sovereign Rights to Enforce State and Local Sales and Use Tax Laws and for Other Purposes	April 25, 2013	63–30	60	Debt Limit bill	October 12, 2013	53–45	60
				Continuing Appropriations Resolution, 2014	October 16, 2013	83–16	60
				Nominee Richard F. Griffin	October 29, 2013	62–37	60

Issue	Date	Vote	Yeas needed	Issue	Date	Vote	Yeas needed
Nominee Thomas Edgar Wheeler	October 29, 2013	no vote	60	**Nominee Jessica Garfola Wright**	December 20, 2013	UC	60
Nominee Katherine Archuleta	October 30, 2013	81–18	60	**Nominee Richard J. Engler**	December 20, 2013	UC	60
Nominee Alan F. Estevez	October 30, 2013	91–8	60	**Emergency Unemployment Compensation Extension Act**	January 7, 2014	60–37	60
Nominee Jacob J. Lew	October 30, 2013	UC	60				
Judicial nominee Patricia Ann Millett	October 31, 2013	55–38	60	Judicial nominee Robert Leon Wilkins Vote No. 235 reconsidered	January 9, 2014	55–38	60
Nominee Melvin L. Watt	October 31, 2013	56–42	60				
Employment Non-Discrimination Act of 2013	November 4, 2013	61–30	60	Emergency Unemployment Compensation Extension Act	January 14, 2014	52–48	60
Employment Non-Discrimination Act of 2013	November 7, 2013	64–34	60	Emergency Unemployment Compensation Extension Act	January 14, 2014	55–45	60
Judicial nominee Cornelia T. L. Pillard	November 12, 2013	56–41	60				
Drug Quality and Security Act	November 12, 2013	97–1	60	**Consolidated Appropriations Act, 2014**	January 16, 2014	72–26	60
Judicial nominee Robert Leon Wilkins	November 18, 2013	53–38	60	**Homeowner Flood Insurance Affordability Act**	January 27, 2014	86–13	60
National Defense Authorization Act for Fiscal Year 2014	November 18, 2013	91–0	60	**Farm Bill**	February 3, 2014	72–22	60
				Emergency Unemployment Compensation Extension Act	February 6, 2014	55–43	60
Drug Quality and Security Act	November 18, 2013	UC	60	Emergency Unemployment Compensation Extension Act	February 6, 2014	58–40	60
National Defense Authorization Act for Fiscal Year 2014	November 21, 2013	51–44	60				
				Bill to Repeal Section 403 of the Bipartisan Budget Act of 2013	February 10, 2014	94–0	60
Judicial nominee Patricia Ann Millett Vote No. 227 reconsidered	November 21, 2013	55–43	60				
				Temporary Debt Limit Extension Act	February 12, 2014	67–31	60
Judicial nominee Cornelia T. L. Pillard Vote No. 233 reconsidered	December 10, 2013	56–42	60	Judicial nominee Jeffrey Alker Meyer	February 24, 2014	55–37	60
Nominee Melvin L. Watt Vote No. 226 reconsidered	December 10, 2013	57–40	60	Judicial nominee James Maxwell Moody Jr.	February 24, 2014	58–34	60
Judicial nominee Elizabeth A. Wolford	December 12, 2013	55–41	60	Judicial nominee James Donato	February 25, 2014	55–42	60
Nominee Chai Rachel Feldblum Reid	December 12, 2013	57–39	60	Judicial nominee Beth Labson Freeman	February 25, 2014	56–42	60
Judicial nominee Brian Morris	December 12, 2013	57–40	60	**Comprehensive Veterans Health and Benefits and Military Retirement Pay Restoration Act of 2014**	February 25, 2014	99–0	60
Nominee Patricia M. Wald	December 12, 2013	57–41	60				
Judicial nominee Susan P. Watters	December 12, 2013	58–39	60				
Nominee Deborah Lee James	December 12, 2013	58–39	60	Comprehensive Veterans Health and Benefits and Military Retirement Pay Restoration Act of 2014	February 27, 2014	no vote	60
Judicial nominee Landya B. McCafferty	December 12, 2013	58–40	60				
Nominee Heather Anne Higginbottom	December 13, 2013	51–34	60	Comprehensive Veterans Health and Benefits and Military Retirement Pay Restoration Act of 2014	February 27, 2014	no vote	60
Nominee Anne W. Patterson	December 13, 2013	54–36	60				
Nominee Jeh Charles Johnson	December 16, 2013	57–37	60	Judicial nominee Debo P. Adegbile	March 5, 2014	47–52	60
Bipartisan Budget Act	December 17, 2013	67–33	60				
Department of Defense Authorization Act, FY2014	December 18, 2013	71–29	60	Nomineee Rose Eilene Gottemoeller	March 5, 2014	55–45	60
				Judicial nominee Pedro A. Delgado Hernandez	March 5, 2014	57–41	60
Nominee Alejandro Nicholas Mayorkas	December 19, 2013	55–45	60	Judicial nominee Vince Girdhari	March 5, 2014	57–43	60
Judicial nominee Brian J. Davis	December 20, 2013	56–36	60	Judicial nominee Timothy L. Brooks	March 5, 2014	59–41	60
Nominee John Andrew Koskinen	December 20, 2013	56–39	60	**Judicial nominee Pamela L. Reeves**	March 5, 2014	62–37	60
Nominee Janet L. Yellen	December 20, 2013	59–34	60				
Nominee Sloan D. Gibson	December 20, 2013	UC	60	**Child Care and Development Block Grant Act of 2013**	March 5, 2014	UC	60
Nominee Sarah Sewall	December 20, 2013	UC	60				
Nominee Michael L. Connor	December 20, 2013	UC	60	**Victims Protection Act of 2014**	March 6, 2014	100–0	60
Nominee Sarah Bloom Raskin	December 20, 2013	UC	60				

Issue	Date	Vote	Yeas needed	Issue	Date	Vote	Yeas needed
Military Justice Improvement Act of 2013	March 6, 2014	55–45	60	Judicial nominee Robin S. Rosenbaum	May 8, 2014	57–37	60
Judicial nominee Carolyn B. McHugh	March 10, 2014	62–34	60	Energy Savings and Industrial Competitiveness Act of 2014	May 12, 2014	55–36	60
Judicial nominee Matthew Frederick Leitman	March 11, 2014	55–43	60	**Legislative vehicle for the tax extenders**	May 13, 2014	96–3	60
Judicial nominee Judith Ellen Levy	March 11, 2014	56–42	60	Judicial nominee Steven Paul Logan	May 14, 2014	58–37	60
Judicial nominee Linda Vivienne Parker	March 11, 2014	56–42	60	**Judicial nominee John Joseph Tuchi**	May 14, 2014	62–35	60
Judicial nominee Laurie J. Michelson	March 11, 2014	56–43	60	**Judicial nominee Diane J. Humetewa**	May 14, 2014	64–34	60
Sovereignty and Democracy in Ukraine Act	March 24, 2014	78–17	60	Legislative vehicle for the tax extenders	May 15, 2014	53–40	60
Judicial nominee Christopher Reid Cooper	March 26, 2014	56–43	60	Judicial nominee Rosemary Marquez	May 15, 2014	58–35	60
Judicial nominee M. Douglas Harpool	March 26, 2014	56–43	60	Judicial nominee Gregg Jeffrey Costa	May 15, 2014	58–36	60
Judicial nominee Gerald Austin McHugh Jr.	March 26, 2014	56–43	60	Judicial nominee Douglas L. Rayes	May 15, 2014	59–35	60
Judicial nominee Edward G. Smith	March 26, 2014	75–23	60	**Judicial nominee James Alan Soto**	May 15, 2014	61–35	60
Judicial nominee John B. Owens	March 27, 2014	54–44	60	**Legislative vehicle for the tax extenders**	May 15, 2014	UC	60
Legislative vehicle for the unemployment insurance extension	March 27, 2014	65–34	60	**Nominee Stanley Fischer**	May 20, 2014	62–35	60
				Judicial nominee David Jeremiah Barron	May 21, 2014	52–43	60
Legislative vehicle for the unemployment insurance extension	April 2, 2014	61–38	60	Nominee Keith M. Harper	June 2, 2014	51–37	60
				Nominee Sharon Y. Bowen	June 3, 2014	50–44	60
Legislative vehicle for the unemployment insurance extension	April 3, 2014	61–35	60	Judicial nominee Tanya S. Chutkan	June 3, 2014	54–40	60
				Judicial nominee Mark G. Mastroianni	June 3, 2014	56–39	60
Paycheck Fairness Act	April 9, 2014	53–44	60	Judicial nominee Bruce Howe Hendricks	June 3, 2014	59–35	60
Judicial nominee Michelle T. Friedland	April 10, 2014	56–41	60	**Nominee Sylvia Mathews Burwell**	June 4, 2014	67–28	60
Nominee David Weil	April 28, 2014	51–42	60	Judicial nominee M. Hannah Lauck	June 9, 2014	52–32	60
Judicial nominee Stanley Allen Bastian	April 29, 2014	55–41	60	Judicial nominee Leo T. Sorokin	June 9, 2014	52–33	60
Judicial nominee Cynthia Ann Bashant	April 29, 2014	56–41	60	Judicial nominee Richard Franklin Boulware II	June 9, 2014	53–34	60
Judicial nominee Daniel D. Crabtree	April 29, 2014	57–39	60	Nominee Stanley Fischer	June 10, 2014	56–38	60
Judicial nominee Manish S. Shah	April 29, 2014	57–40	60	Nominee Jerome H. Powell	June 10, 2014	58–36	60
Judicial nominee Sheryl H. Lipman	April 29, 2014	58–39	60	Nominee Lael Brainard	June 10, 2014	59–35	60
Judicial nominee Jon David Levy	April 29, 2014	63–34	60	Refinancing Federal student loans	June 11, 2014	56–38	60
Minimum Wage Fairness Act	April 30, 2014	54–32	60	Judicial nominee Salvador Mendoza Jr.	June 16, 2014	55–37	60
Judicial nominee Theodore David Chuang	May 1, 2014	54–43	60	Judicial nominee Staci Michelle Yandle	June 16, 2014	55–37	60
Judicial nominee George Jarrod Hazel	May 1, 2014	55–42	60	Judicial nominee Darrin P. Gayles	June 16, 2014	55–37	60
Judicial nominee Nancy L. Moritz	May 1, 2014	60–38	60	Judicial nominee Peter Joseph Kadzik	June 17, 2014	54–43	60
Energy Savings and Industrial Competitiveness Act of 2014	May 6, 2014	79–20	60	**Commerce, Justice, Science, and Related Agencies Appropriations Act, 2015**	June 17, 2014	95–3	60
Judicial nominee Nancy J. Rosenstengel	May 8, 2014	54–42	60	Judicial nominee Geoffrey W. Crawford	June 23, 2014	52–32	60
Judicial nominee Indira Talwani	May 8, 2014	55–41	60	Judicial nominee Paul G. Byron	June 23, 2014	53–30	60
Judicial nominee James D. Peterson	May 8, 2014	56–40	60				

Issue	Date	Vote	Yeas needed	Issue	Date	Vote	Yeas needed
Judicial nominee Carlos Eduardo Mendoza	June 23, 2014	53–31	60	Judicial nominee Brenda K. Sannes	November 19, 2014	55–42	60
Judicial nominee Beth Bloom	June 23, 2014	53–31	60	Judicial nominee Madeline Cox Arleo	November 19, 2014	56–40	60
Nominee Leon Rodriguez	June 24, 2014	52–44	60	Judicial nominee Wendy Beetlestone	November 19, 2014	58–38	60
Judicial nominee Cheryl Ann Krause	June 26, 2014	57–39	60	Judicial nominee Pamela Pepper	November 19, 2014	58–39	60
Bipartisan Sportsmen's Act	July 7, 2014	82–12	60	Nominee Noah Bryson Mamet	December 1, 2014	50–36	60
Bipartisan Sportsmen's Act	July 10, 2014	41–56	60	Nominee Colleen Bradley Bell	December 1, 2014	50–36	60
Nominee Norman C. Bay	July 15, 2014	51–45	60	Nominee Robert S. Adler	December 2, 2014	52–40	60
Nominee Cheryl A. LaFleur	July 15, 2014	85–10	60	Nominee P. David Lopez	December 2, 2014	54–43	60
Judicial nominee Ronnie L. White	July 16, 2014	54–43	60	Nominee Charlotte A. Burrows	December 2, 2014	57–39	60
Protect Women's Health From Corporate Interference	July 16, 2014	56–43	60	Nominee Nani A. Coloretti	December 2, 2014	59–34	60
Judicial nominee Julie E. Carnes	July 17, 2014	68–23	60	**Judicial nominee Mark A. Kearney**	December 3, 2014	60–36	60
Judicial nominee Andre Birotte Jr.	July 22, 2014	56–43	60	**Judicial nominee David J. Hale**	December 3, 2014	65–31	60
Judicial nominee John W. deGravelles	July 22, 2014	57–39	60	**Judicial nominee Gerald J. Pappert**	December 3, 2014	67–28	60
Judicial nominee Robin L. Rosenberg	July 22, 2014	58–42	60	**Nominee Joseph S. Hezir**	December 3, 2014	68–27	60
Bring Jobs Home Act	July 23, 2014	93–7	60	**Nominee Franklin M. Orr Jr.**	December 3, 2014	71–35	60
Judicial nominee Pamela Harris	July 24, 2014	54–41	60	Nominee Lauren McGarity McFerran	December 4, 2014	51–42	60
Bring Jobs Home Act	July 30, 2014	54–42	60	Judicial nominee Lydia Kay Griggsby	December 4, 2014	53–36	60
Emergency Supplemental Appropriations Act, 2014	July 30, 2014	63–33	60	Nominee Jeffery Martin Baran	December 4, 2014	53–40	60
Judicial nominee Jill A. Pryor	July 31, 2014	58–33	60	Nominee Ellen Dudley Williams	December 4, 2014	57–34	60
Emergency Supplemental Appropriations Act, 2014	July 31, 2014	no vote	60	**Judicial nominee Joseph F. Leeson Jr.**	December 4, 2014	66–26	60
Proposing an amendment to the Constitution of the United States relating to contributions and expenditures intended to affect elections	September 8, 2014	79–18	60	**Judicial nominee Gregory N. Stivers**	December 4, 2014	69–24	60
				Nominee Virginia Tyler Lodge	December 9, 2014	63–32	60
Paycheck Fairness Act	September 10, 2014	73–25	60	**Nominee Ronald Anderson Walter**	December 9, 2014	65–31	60
Proposing an amendment to the Constitution of the United States relating to contributions and expenditures intended to affect elections	September 11, 2014	54–42	60	**National Defense Authorization Act for Fiscal Year 2015**	December 12, 2014	89–11	60
				Consolidated and Further Continuing Appropriations Act, 2015	December 13, 2014	77–19	60
Nominee Jeffery Martin Baran	September 15, 2014	52–39	60	**Nominee Carolyn Watts Colvin**	December 13, 2014	UC	60
Paycheck Fairness Act	September 15, 2014	52–40	60	Nominee Frank A. Rose	December 15, 2014	54–39	60
Nominee Stephen G. Burns	September 15, 2014	54–37	60	Nominee Daniel J. Santos	December 15, 2014	54–39	60
Continuing Appropriations Resolution, 2015	September 18, 2014	73–27	60	Judicial nominee Stephen R. Bough	December 16, 2014	51–38	60
Judicial nominee Randolph D. Moss	November 12, 2014	53–45	60	Nominee Vivek Hallegere Murthy	December 16, 2014	51–43	60
Judicial nominee Leigh Martin May	November 12, 2014	67–30	60	Nominee Antony Blinken	December 16, 2014	53–40	60
Child Care and Development Block Grant	November 13, 2014	96–1	60	Nominee Sarah R. Saldana	December 16, 2014	53–41	60
Judicial nominee Eleanor Louise Ross	November 17, 2014	66–29	60	**Nominee Colette Dodson Honorable**	December 16, 2014	65–28	60
Judicial nominee Mark Howard Cohen	November 17, 2014	67–29	60	**Nominee Estevan R. Lopez**	December 16, 2014	UC	60
Judicial nominee Leslie Joyce Abrams	November 17, 2014	68–28	60	**Nominee Marcus Dwayne Jadotte**	December 16, 2014	UC	60
Surveillance Overhaul bill	November 18, 2014	58–42	60	**Nominee Jonathan Nicholas Stivers**	December 16, 2014	UC	60
Judicial nominee Victor Allen Bolden	November 19, 2014	51–44	60	**Nominee John Charles Cruden**	December 16, 2014	UC	60
				Nominee Christopher Smith	December 16, 2014	UC	60

Issue	Date	Vote	Yeas needed	Issue	Date	Vote	Yeas needed
Judicial nominee Jorge Luis Alonso	December 16, 2014	UC	60	**Iran Nuclear Agreement Review Act of 2015**	May 7, 2015	UC	60
Judicial nominee Haywood Stirling Gilliam Jr.	December 16, 2014	UC	60	Legislative vehicle for trade promotion authority	May 12, 2015	52–45	60
Judicial nominee Amit Priyavadan Mehta	December 16, 2014	UC	60	**Legislative vehicle for trade promotion authority**	May 14, 2015	65–33	60
Judicial nominee Allison Dale Burroughs	December 16, 2014	UC	60	**Legislative vehicle for trade promotion authority**	May 21, 2015	62–38	60
Judicial nominee John Robert Blakey	December 16, 2014	UC	60	**Legislative vehicle for trade promotion authority**	May 22, 2015	61–38	60
Judicial nominee Amos L. Mazzant III	December 16, 2014	UC	60	Two month FISA extension	May 23, 2015	45–54	60
Judicial nominee Robert Lee Pitman	December 16, 2014	UC	60	USA Freedom Act of 2015	May 23, 2015	57–42	60
Judicial nominee Robert William Schroeder III	December 16, 2014	UC	60	**USA Freedom Act of 2015**	May 31, 2015	77–17	60
Judicial nominee Joan Marie Azrack	December 16, 2014	UC	60	**USA Freedom Act of 2015**	June 2, 2015	83–14	60
Judicial nominee Elizabeth K. Dillon	December 16, 2014	UC	60	**National Defense Authorization, FY2016**	June 2, 2015	UC	60
Judicial nominee Loretta Copeland Biggs	December 16, 2014	UC	60	National Defense Authorization, FY2016	June 11, 2015	56–40	60
Keystone Pipeline	January 12, 2015	63–32	60	**National Defense Authorization, FY2016**	June 16, 2015	83–15	60
Keystone Pipeline	January 26, 2015	53–39	60	**National Defense Authorization, FY2016**	June 17, 2015	84–14	60
Keystone Pipeline	January 26, 2015	53–39	60	Department of Defense Appropriations, FY2016	June 18, 2015	50–45	60
Keystone Pipeline	January 29, 2015	62–35	60	**Legislative vehicle for trade promotion authority**	June 23, 2015	60–37	60
Department of Homeland Security Appropriations, FY2015	February 3, 2015	51–48	60	**Trade Preferences Extension Act of 2015**	June 24, 2015	76–22	60
Department of Homeland Security Appropriations, FY2015	February 4, 2015	53–47	60	**Trade Facilitation and Trade Enforcement Act of 2015**	June 24, 2015	UC	60
Department of Homeland Security Appropriations, FY2015	February 5, 2015	52–47	60	**National Defense Authorization, FY2016**	July 9, 2015	81–15	60
Department of Homeland Security Appropriations, FY2015	February 23, 2015	47–46	60	**Every Child Achieves Act of 2015**	July 15, 2015	86–12	60
Department of Homeland Security Appropriations, FY2015	February 25, 2015	98–2	60	**Every Child Achieves Act of 2015**	July 16, 2015	79–18	60
Immigration Rule of Law Act	February 27, 2015	57–42	60	Legislative vehicle for highway funding act	July 21, 2015	41–56	60
Department of Homeland Security Appropriations, FY2015	February 27, 2015	68–31	60	**Legislative vehicle for highway funding act**	July 22, 2015	62–36	60
Department of Homeland Security Appropriations, FY2015	March 2, 2015	47–43	60	Legislative vehicle for highway funding act	July 26, 2015	49–43	60
Keystone Pipeline	March 4, 2015	UC	60	**Legislative vehicle for highway funding act**	July 26, 2015	67–26	60
Iran Nuclear Agreement Review Act of 2015	March 9, 2015	UC	60	**Legislative vehicle for highway funding act**	July 27, 2015	62–32	60
Justice for Victims of Trafficking Act 2015	March 17, 2015	55–43	60	**Legislative vehicle for highway funding act**	July 29, 2015	65–35	60
Justice for Victims of Trafficking Act 2015	March 17, 2015	55–43	60	A bill to prohibit Federal funding of Planned Parenthood Federation of America	August 3, 2015	53–46	60
Justice for Victims of Trafficking Act 2015	March 18, 2015	57–41	60	**Cybersecurity Information Sharing Act**	August 5, 2015	UC	60
Justice for Victims of Trafficking Act 2015	March 19, 2015	56–42	60	Legislative vehicle for Iran nuclear agreement resolution of disapproval	September 10, 2015	58–42	60
Justice for Victims of Trafficking Act 2015	March 19, 2015	56–42	60	**Legislative vehicle for Iran nuclear agreement resolution of disapproval**	September 10, 2015	UC	60
Justice for Victims of Trafficking Act 2015	April 16, 2015	UC	60	Legislative vehicle for Iran nuclear agreement resolution of disapproval	September 15, 2015	56–42	60
Nominee Loretta E. Lynch	April 23, 2015	66–34	60	**Legislative vehicle for Iran nuclear agreement resolution of disapproval**	September 15, 2015	UC	60
Iran Nuclear Agreement Review Act of 2015	May 7, 2015	93–6	60				

Issue	Date	Vote	Yeas needed
Legislative vehicle for Iran nuclear agreement resolution of disapproval	September 17, 2015	53–45	60
Legislative vehicle for Iran nuclear agreement resolution of disapproval	September 17, 2015	56–42	60
Legislative vehicle for Iran nuclear agreement resolution of disapproval	September 17, 2015	UC	60
Pain-Capable Unborn Child Protection Act	September 22, 2015	54–42	60
Department of Defense Appropriations, FY2016	September 22, 2015	54–42	60
Legislative vehicle for the continuing resolution, FY 2016	September 24, 2015	47–52	60
TSA Office of Inspection Accountability Act of 2015	September 28, 2015	77–19	60
Military Construction and Veterans Affairs and Related Agencies Appropriations Act	October 1, 2015	50–44	60
National Defense Authorization, FY2016	October 6, 2015	73–26	60
Energy and Water Appropriations Act	October 8, 2015	49–47	60
Sanctuary Jurisdictions	October 20, 2015	54–45	60
Cybersecurity Information Sharing Act	October 22, 2015	83–14	60
Cybersecurity Information Sharing Act	October 27, 2015	UC	60
Bipartisan Budget Act of 2015	October 30, 2015	63–35	60
Federal Water Quality Protection Act	November 3, 2015	57–41	60
Department of Defense Appropriations Act	November 5, 2015	51–44	60
Legislative vehicle for highway funding act	November 10, 2015	82–7	60
Departments of Transportation, Housing and Urban Development, and Related Agencies Appropriations	November 17, 2015	UC	60
Every Child Achieves Act of 2015	November 18, 2015	91–6	60
Departments of Transportation, Housing and Urban Development, and Related Agencies Appropriations	November 19, 2015	UC	60
Departments of Transportation, Housing and Urban Development, and Related Agencies Appropriations	November 19, 2015	UC	60
Every Child Achieves Act of 2015	December 8, 2015	84–12	60
Military Construction and Veterans Affairs and Related Agencies Appropriations Act	December 18, 2015	72–26	60
Federal Reserve Transparency Act of 2015	January 12, 2016	53–44	60
American Security Against Foreign Enemies Act	January 20, 2016	55–43	60
Veto message to accompany S.J.Res.22, the WOTUS rule resolution of disapproval	January 21, 2016	52–40	60
Energy Policy Modernization Act	February 4, 2016	43–54	60
Energy Policy Modernization Act	February 4, 2016	46–50	60
Trade Facilitation and Trade Enforcement Act	February 11, 2016	73–22	60
Nominee Robert McKinnon Cali	February 22, 2016	80–6	60
Comprehensive Addiction and Recovery Act	February 29, 2016	89–0	60
Comprehensive Addiction and Recovery Act	March 7, 2016	86–3	60
Comprehensive Addiction and Recovery Act	March 9, 2016	93–3	60
Defund Planned Parenthood Act	March 16, 2016	48–49	60
Legislative vehicle for FAA Reauthorization Act	April 6, 2016	98–0	60
Legislative vehicle for FAA Reauthorization Act	April 14, 2016	94–4	60
Legislative vehicle for FAA Reauthorization Act	April 18, 2016	89–5	60
Energy and Water Appropriations Act	April 20, 2016	UC	60
Further Continuing Appropriations	April 27, 2016	50–46	60
Departments of Transportation, Housing and Urban Development, and Related Agencies Appropriations	April 27, 2016	UC	60
Further Continuing Appropriations	April 28, 2016	52–43	60
Further Continuing Appropriations	May 9, 2016	50–42	60
Further Continuing Appropriations	May 11, 2016	57–42	60
Further Continuing Appropriations	May 11, 2016	97–2	60
Further Continuing Appropriations	May 12, 2016	UC	60
Departments of Transportation, Housing and Urban Development, and Related Agencies Appropriations	May 17, 2016	50–47	60
Departments of Transportation, Housing and Urban Development, and Related Agencies Appropriations	May 17, 2016	52–45	60
Departments of Transportation, Housing and Urban Development, and Related Agencies Appropriations	May 17, 2016	68–29	60
Departments of Transportation, Housing and Urban Development, and Related Agencies Appropriations	May 19, 2016	88–10	60
Departments of Transportation, Housing and Urban Development, and Related Agencies Appropriations	May 19, 2016	UC	60

Issue	Date	Vote	Yeas needed	Issue	Date	Vote	Yeas needed
National Defense Authorization, FY2017	May 25, 2016	98–0	60	**Water Resources Development Act**	September 12, 2016	90–1	60
Military Construction, Veterans Affairs, and Related Agencies Appropriations FY2017 and Zika Response	June 8, 2016	93–2	60	**Water Resources Development Act**	September 14, 2016	94–3	60
National Defense Authorization, FY2017	June 9, 2016	43–55	60	**Military Construction, Veterans Affairs, and Related Agencies Appropriations FY2017 and Zika Response**	September 20, 2016	89–7	60
National Defense Authorization, FY2017	June 9, 2016	56–42	60	Military Construction, Veterans Affairs, and Related Agencies Appropriations FY2017 and Zika Response	September 27, 2016	40–59	60
National Defense Authorization, FY2017	June 10, 2016	68–23	60	Military Construction, Veterans Affairs, and Related Agencies Appropriations FY2017 and Zika Response	September 27, 2016	45–55	60
Commerce, Justice, Science, and Related Agencies Appropriations, FY2016	June 14, 2016	94–3	60	**Military Construction, Veterans Affairs, and Related Agencies Appropriations FY2017 and Zika Response**	September 28, 2016	77–21	60
Comprehensive Addiction and Recovery Act	June 16, 2016	95–1	60	**Military Construction, Veterans Affairs, and Related Agencies Appropriations FY2017 and Zika Response**	September 28, 2016	77–21	60
Commerce, Justice, Science, and Related Agencies Appropriations, FY2016	June 20, 2016	44–56	60	American Energy and Conservation	November 17, 2016	51–47	60
Commerce, Justice, Science, and Related Agencies Appropriations, FY2016	June 20, 2016	47–53	60	**21st Century Cures Act**	December 5, 2016	85–13	60
Commerce, Justice, Science, and Related Agencies Appropriations, FY2016	June 20, 2016	53–47	60	**National Defense Authorization, FY2017**	December 7, 2016	92–7	60
Commerce, Justice, Science, and Related Agencies Appropriations, FY2016	June 20, 2016	53–47	60	**Further Continuing Appropriations**	December 9, 2016	61–38	60
Commerce, Justice, Science, and Related Agencies Appropriations, FY2016	June 22, 2016	58–38	60	**WINN Act**	December 10, 2016	69–30	60
Military Construction, Veterans Affairs, and Related Agencies Appropriations FY2017 and Zika Response	June 28, 2016	58–48	60	Nominee Rex W. Tillerson	January 24, 2017	56–43	60
Legislative vehicle for PROMESA	June 29, 2016	68–32	60	Nominee Elisabeth Prince DeVos	February 1, 2017	52–48	60
Sanctuary cities	July 6, 2016	53–44	60	Nominee Steven T. Mnuchin	February 2, 2017	53–46	60
Kate's Law	July 6, 2016	55–42	60	Nominee Thomas Price	February 2, 2017	51–48	60
Legislative vehicle for GMO food labeling	July 6, 2016	65–32	60	Nominee Jeff Sessions	February 2, 2017	52–47	60
Department of Defense Appropriations, FY2017	July 7, 2016	50–44	60	**Nominee James Richard Perry**	February 13, 2017	62–37	60
Energy Policy Modernization Act	July 12, 2016	84–3	60	**Nominee Benjamin S. Carson Sr.**	February 13, 2017	62–37	60
Comprehensive Addiction and Recovery Act	July 13, 2016	90–2	60	**Nominee Ryan Zinke**	February 13, 2017	67–31	60
Military Construction, Veterans Affairs, and Related Agencies Appropriations FY2017 and Zika Response	July 14, 2016	52–44	60	**Nominee Wilbur L. Ross Jr.**	February 13, 2017	66–31	60
Department of Defense Appropriations, FY2017	July 14, 2016	55–42	60	Nominee Scott Pruitt	February 13, 2017	54–46	60
National Defense Authorization, FY2017	July 14, 2016	90–7	60	Nominee Mick Mulvaney	February 13, 2017	52–48	60
Military Construction, Veterans Affairs, and Related Agencies Appropriations FY2017 and Zika Response	September 6, 2016	52–46	60	Nominee Seema Verma	March 7, 2017	54–44	60
				Nominee Daniel Coats	March 13, 2017	88–11	60
				Nominee Lt. Gen. Herbert R. McMaster Jr.	March 13, 2017	UC	60
				Nominee David Friedman	March 22, 2017	52–46	60
				NATO Montenegro Treaty	March 23, 2017	97–2	60
				Supreme Court nominee Neil Gorsuch Vote No. 105 reconsidered	April 4, 2017	55–45 No. 105 55–45	60
				Nominee Rod J. Rosenstein	April 7, 2017	92–6	60
				Nominee R. Alexander Acosta	April 24, 2017	61–39	60
				Nominee Jay Clayton	April 28, 2017	60–36	60
Department of Defense Appropriations, FY2017	September 6, 2016	55–43	60	Consolidated Appropriations Act, 2017 motion to concur in the House amendment to the Senate amendment to H.R.244	May 3, 2017	no vote	60

Issue	Date	Vote	Yeas needed
Nominee Scott Gottlieb	May 4, 2017	57–41	60
Nominee Robert Lighthizer	May 9, 2017	81–15	60
Nominee Rachel L. Brand	May 10, 2017	51–47	60
Nominee Jeffrey A. Rosen	May 10, 2017	52–42	60
Nominee Terry Branstad	May 15, 2017	86–12	60
Nominee John J. Sullivan	May 18, 2017	93–6	60
Judicial nominee Amul R. Thapar	May 22, 2017	52–48	60
Nominee Courtney Elwood	May 23, 2017	UC	60
Iran Sanctions motion to proceed	June 5, 2017	91–8	60
Iran Sanctions S.Amdt.232	June 12, 2017	UC	60
Iran Sanctions	June 13, 2017	UC	60
Iran Sanctions committee reported substitute amendment	June 13, 2017	UC	60
Nominee Marshall Billingslea	June 15, 2017	65–34	60
Nominee Sigal Mandelker	June 15, 2017	94–5	60
Nominee Kristine L. Svinicki	June 19, 2017	89–10	60
Nominee Neomi Rao	June 27, 2017	59–36	60
Judicial nominee David C. Nye	June 28, 2017	97–0	60
Nominee William Francis Hagerty IV	June 29, 2017	89–11	60
Nominee Patrick M. Shanahan	July 13, 2017	88–6	60
Nominee David Bernhardt	July 17, 2017	56–39	60
Judicial nominee John Kenneth Bush	July 17, 2017	51–48	60
Judicial nominee Kevin Christopher Newsom	July 28, 2017	68–26	60
Nominee Marvin Kaplan	July 31, 2017	50–48	60
FDA Reauthorization Act motion to proceed	August 1, 2017	96–1	60
Emergency supplemental, continuing resolution and debt limit act motion to concur in the House amendment to the Senate amendment with S. Amdt.808	September 6, 2017	79–18	60
National Defense Authorization Act, Fiscal Year 2018 motion to proceed	September 7, 2017	89–3	60
National Defense Authorization Act, Fiscal Year 2018	September 13, 2017	90–7	60
National Defense Authorization Act, Fiscal Year 2018 S.Amdt.1003	September 13, 2017	84–9	60
Nominee Noel J. Francisco	September 14, 2017	49–47	60
Nominee William J. Emanuel	September 18, 2017	49–44	60
Nominee Ajit Varadaraj Pai	September 26, 2017	55–41	60
Judicial nominee Ralph R. Erickson	September 26, 2017	95–1	60
Nominee Callista L. Gingrich	October 2, 2017	75–20	60
Nominee Randal Quarles	October 2, 2017	62–33	60
Nominee Eric D. Hargan	October 2, 2017	57–38	60
Nominee Lee Francis Cissna	October 2, 2017	54–43	60
Supplemental disaster appropriations motion to concur in the House amendment to the Senate amendment to H.R. 2266 with amendment S.Amdt.1568	October 19, 2017	79–16	60
Judicial nominee Trevor McFadden	October 23, 2017	85–12	60
Judicial nominee Scott Palk	October 23, 2017	79–18	60
Judicial nominee Stephanos Bibas	October 26, 2017	54–43	60
Judicial nominee Allison H. Eid	October 26, 2017	56–42	60
Judicial nominee Joan Louise Larsen	October 26, 2017	60–38	60
Judicial nominee Amy Coney Barrett	October 26, 2017	54–42	60
Nominee Derek Kan	November 2, 2017	87–9	60
Nominee William L. Wehrum	November 2, 2017	49–46	60
Nominee Peter B. Robb	November 2, 2017	51–47	60
Nominee Steven Engel	November 2, 2017	51–47	60
Judicial nominee Dabney Langhorne Friedrich	November 9, 2017	93–4	60
Judicial nominee Donald C. Coggins Jr.	November 9, 2017	96–1	60
Nominee Joseph Otting	November 9, 2017	54–44	60
Nominee David G. Zatezalo	November 9, 2017	52–45	60
Nominee Steven Gill Bradbury	November 9, 2017	50–47	60
Judicial nominee Gregory G. Katsas	November 16, 2017	52–48	60
Nominee Kirstjen Nielsen	December 2, 2017	59–33	60
Judicial nominee James C. Ho	December 7, 2017	53–44	60
Judicial nominee Don R. Willett	December 7, 2017	50–48	60
Judicial nominee Leonard Steven Grasz	December 7, 2017	48–47	60
Judicial nominee Walter David Counts III	January 3, 2018	90–1	60
Judicial nominee Michael Lawrence Brown	January 3, 2018	97–1	60
Judicial nominee Thomas Lee Robinson Parker	January 3, 2018	96–1	60
Judicial nominee William L. Campbell Jr.	January 3, 2018	89–1	60
Legislative vehicle for FISA amendments reauthorization motion to concur in the House amendment to S.139	January 11, 2018	60–38	60
Legislative vehicle for continuing appropriations motion to concur in the House amendment to the Senate amendment to H.R.195	January 18, 2018	50–49	60
Legislative vehicle for continuing appropriations motion to concur in the House amendment to the Senate amendment to H.R.195 with amendment S.Amdt.1917	January 19, 2018	81–18	60
Nominee Samuel Dale Brownback	January 22, 2018	50–49	60
Nominee Alex Michael Azar II	January 22, 2018	54–43	60
Nominee Jerome H. Powell	January 22, 2018	84–12	60
Judicial nominee David Ryan Stras	January 24, 2018	57–41	60
Pain-Capable Unborn Child Protection Act motion to proceed	January 24, 2018	51–46	60
Department of Defense Appropriations, 2018 motion to concur in the House amendment to the Senate amendment to H.R.695	February 6, 2018	55–44	60

Issue	Date	Vote	Yeas needed
Legislative vehicle for Bipartisan Budget Act of 2018 motion to concur in the House amendment to the Senate amendment to H.R. 1892 with amendment S. Amdt.1930	February 7, 2018	73–26	60
Legislative vehicle for immigration motion to proceed	February 9, 2018	97–1	60
legislative vehicle for immigration S.Amdt.1959	February 14, 2018	39–60	60
Legislative vehicle for immigration S.Amdt.1958	February 14, 2018	54–45	60
Legislative vehicle for immigration S.Amdt.1948	February 14, 2018	54–45	60
Legislative vehicle for immigration S.Amdt.1955	February 14, 2018	52–47	60
Judicial nominee Terry A. Doughty	February 15, 2018	94–2	60
Judicial nominee Tilman Eugene Self III	February 15, 2018	85–12	60
Judicial nominee A. Marvin Quattlebaum Jr.	February 15, 2018	96–1	60
Nominee Russell Vought	February 15, 2018	69–29	60
Judicial nominee Elizabeth L. Branch	February 15, 2018	49–48	60
Judicial nominee Karen Gren Scholer	February 15, 2018	72–22	60
Economic Growth, Regulatory Relief, and Consumer Protection Act motion to proceed	March 1, 2018	67–32	60
Nominee Kevin K. McAleenan	March 8, 2018	79–19	60
Economic Growth, Regulatory Relief, and Consumer Protection Act	March 8, 2018	67–31	60
Economic Growth, Regulatory Relief, and Consumer Protection Act S.Amdt.2151	March 8, 2018	66–30	60
Online sex trafficking prevention motion to proceed	March 14, 2018	94–2	60
Consolidated Appropriations Act, 2018 motion to concur in the House amendment to the Senate amendment to H.R.1625	March 22, 2018	67–30	60
Judicial nominee Rebecca Grady Jennings	March 23, 2018	94–2	60
Judicial nominee John W. Broomes	March 23, 2018	74–24	60
Nominee Andrew Wheeler	March 23, 2018	53–45	60
Nominee Patrick Pizzella	March 23, 2018	50–48	60
Nominee John F. Ring	March 23, 2018	50–47	60
Judicial nominee Claria Horn Boom	March 23, 2018	96–2	60
Legislative vehicle for Coast Guard reauthorization motion to concur in the House amendment to S.140	April 12, 2018	55–41	60
Nominee James Bridenstine	April 16, 2018	50–48	60

Issue	Date	Vote	Yeas needed
Legislative vehicle for Coast Guard reauthorization motion to concur in the House amendment to S.140 with amendment S. Amdt.2232	April 16, 2018	56–42	60
Judicial nominee Stuart Kyle Duncan	April 19, 2018	50–44	60
Nominee Richard Grenell	April 24, 2018	UC	60
Nominee Mike Pompeo	April 24, 2018	57–42	60
Judicial nominee Amy J. St. Eve	April 26, 2018	UC	60
Judicial nominee Michael Y. Scudder	April 26, 2018	UC	60
Judicial nominee John B. Nalbandian	April 26, 2018	52–43	60
Judicial nominee Joel M. Carson III	April 26, 2018	71–24	60
Judicial nominee Michael B. Brennan	April 26, 2018	49–47	60
Judicial nominee Kurt D. Engelhardt	April 26, 2018	64–31	60
Nominee James Randolph Evans	May 17, 2018	49–44	60
Nominee Jelena McWilliams	May 17, 2018	73–23	60
Nominee Jelena McWilliams	May 17, 2018	72–25	60
VA MISSION Act motion to concur in the House amendment to S.2372	May 17, 2018	91–4	60
Nominee Dana Baiocco	May 17, 2018	49–45	60
Nominee Gina Haspel	May 17, 2018	54–44	60
Judicial nominee Annemarie Carney Axon	May 24, 2018	84–11	60
Judicial nominee Fernando Rodriguez Jr.	May 24, 2018	94–1	60
Judicial nominee Robert Earl Wier	May 24, 2018	90–1	60
National Defense Authorization Act, Fiscal Year 2019 motion to proceed	June 6, 2018	92–4	60
National Defense Authorization Act, Fiscal Year 2019	June 12, 2018	81–15	60
National Defense Authorization Act, Fiscal Year 2019 S.Amdt.2282	June 12, 2018	83–14	60
National Defense Authorization Act, Fiscal Year 2019 S.Amdt.2700	June 12, 2018	35–62	60
Energy and Water, Legislative Branch, and Military Construction and Veterans Affairs Appropriations, Fiscal Year 2019 motion to proceed	June 14, 2018	92–3	60
Energy and Water, Legislative Branch, and Military Construction and Veterans Affairs Appropriations, Fiscal Year 2019	June 20, 2018	UC	60
Energy and Water, Legislative Branch, and Military Construction and Veterans Affairs Appropriations, Fiscal Year 2019 S. Amdt.2910	June 20, 2018	UC	60
Farm Bill motion to proceed	June 21, 2018	89–3	60

Issue	Date	Vote	Yeas needed	Issue	Date	Vote	Yeas needed
Farm Bill	June 27, 2018	UC	60	Energy and Water, Legislative Branch, and Military Construction and Veterans Affairs Appropriations, Fiscal Year 2019 conference report	September 12, 2018	UC	60
Farm Bill S.Amdt.3224	June 27, 2018	UC	60				
Nominee Paul C. Ney Jr.	June 28, 2018	74–25	60				
Nominee Brian Benczkowski	June 28, 2018	51–48	60				
Judicial nominee Mark Jeremy Bennett	June 28, 2018	72–25	60				
Judicial nominee Ryan Bounds	July 12, 2018	50–49	60	**Defense, Labor, HHS, and Education Appropriations, Fiscal Year 2019 conference report**	September 17, 2018	92–8	60
Judicial nominee Andrew S. Oldham	July 12, 2018	50–49	60				
Nominee Randal Quarles	July 12, 2018	66–33	60				
National Defense Authorization Act, Fiscal Year 2019 conference report	July 26, 2018	UC	60	Nominee Peter A. Feldman	September 18, 2018	50–49	60
				Nominee Peter A. Feldman	September 18, 2018	76–18	60
National Flood Insurance Program motion to concur in the House amendment to S.1182	July 26, 2018	UC	60	**Legislative vehicle for FAA Reauthorization motion to concur in the House amendment to the Senate amendment to H.R. 302**	September 28, 2018	90–7	60
Interior, Environment, Agriculture and Related Agencies Appropriations, Fiscal Year 2019	July 26, 2018	UC	60				
				Supreme Court nominee Brett Kavanaugh	October 3, 2018	51–49	60
Interior, Environment, Agriculture and Related Agencies Appropriations, Fiscal Year 2019 S. Amdt.3399	July 26, 2018	94–4	60	Nominee James N. Stewart	October 6, 2018	UC	60
				Nominee Eric S. Dreiband	October 6, 2018	50–47	60
				Nominee Jeffrey Bossert Clark	October 6, 2018	53–44	60
Judicial nominee Britt Grant	July 26, 2018	52–44	60	**America's Water Infrastructure Act of 2018 motion to concur in the House amendment to S.3021**	October 6, 2018	96–3	60
Judicial nominee Julius Ness Richardson	August 1, 2018	80–10	60				
Judicial nominee A. Marvin Quattlebaum Jr.	August 1, 2018	61–28	60	**Nominee Michelle Bowman**	October 11, 2018	63–36	60
Defense, Labor, HHS, and Education Appropriations, Fiscal Year 2019	August 21, 2018	UC	60	**Legislative vehicle for Coast Guard reauthorization motion to concur in the House amendment to S.140 with amendment S.Amdt.4054**	October 11, 2018	93–5	60
Defense, Labor, HHS, and Education Appropriations, Fiscal Year 2019 S. Amdt.3695	August 21, 2018	90–6	60				
Judicial nominee Alan Albright	August 22, 2018	UC	60	Nominee Kathleen Kraninger	November 15, 2018	50–49	60
Judicial nominee Robert Summerhays	August 22, 2018	UC	60	Judicial nominee Jonathan Kobes	November 15, 2018	50–49	60
Judicial nominee Charles J. Williams	August 22, 2018	UC	60	Judicial nominee Thomas Farr	November 15, 2018	51–50	60
Judicial nominee Dominic Lanza	August 22, 2018	UC	60	**Nominee Karen Kelley**	November 15, 2018	62–37	60
Judicial nominee William Jung	August 22, 2018	UC	60	Nominee Stephen Vaden	November 15, 2018	49–45	60
Judicial nominee Marilyn Horan	August 22, 2018	UC	60	Nominee Bernard McNamee	November 29, 2018	50–49	60
Judicial nominee Susan Baxter	August 22, 2018	UC	60	Nominee Justin Muzinich	December 6, 2018	55–43	60
Judicial nominee James R. Sweeney II	August 22, 2018	UC	60	**Legislative vehicle for the criminal justice reform bill motion to concur in the House amendment to S.756 with amendment S.Amdt.4108**	December 13, 2018	82–12	60
Judicial nominee Barry Ashe	August 22, 2018	UC	60				
Judicial nominee Charles Goodwin	August 22, 2018	UC	60				
Judicial nominee R. Stan Baker	August 22, 2018	UC	60				
Judicial nominee Terry Moorer	August 22, 2018	UC	60	**Nominee Joseph Maguire**	December 17, 2018	95–1	60
Nominee Isabel Patelunas	August 22, 2018	UC	60	**Strengthening America's Security in the Middle East Act motion to proceed Vote No. 1 reconsidered**	January 4, 2019	56–44 / 74–19	60
Nominee Joseph H. Hunt	August 22, 2018	UC	60				
Nominee Richard Clarida	August 22, 2018	UC	60				
Nominee Richard Clarida	August 22, 2018	69–26	60	Strengthening America's Security in the Middle East Act motion to proceed	January 8, 2019	53–43	60
Nominee Lynn A. Johnson	August 22, 2018	60–28	60	Strengthening America's Security in the Middle East Act motion to proceed	January 10, 2019	50–43	60
Nominee Elad L. Roisman	August 28, 2018	83–14	60	Russia sanctions	January 15, 2019	57–42	60
Nominee Charles P. Rettig	September 6, 2018	63–34	60	Prohibiting taxpayer funded abortions motion to proceed	January 16, 2019	48–47	60
				Supplemental Appropriations, Fiscal Year 2019 S.Amdt.6	January 24, 2019	52–44	60
				Supplemental Appropriations, Fiscal Year 2019 S.Amdt.5	January 24, 2019	50–47	60

Issue	Date	Vote	Yeas needed	Issue	Date	Vote	Yeas needed
Strengthening America's Security in the Middle East Act S.Amdt.65	January 29, 2019	68–23	60	Judicial nominee Daniel Desmond Domenico	April 4, 2019	55–42	60
Natural Resources Management Act motion to proceed	January 31, 2019	99–1	60	Nominee David Bernhardt	April 8, 2019	56–41	60
Strengthening America's Security in the Middle East Act	January 31, 2019	72–24	60	**Judicial nominee Joshua Wolson**	April 11, 2019	64–35	60
Nominee William Pelham Barr	February 7, 2019	55–44	60	**Judicial nominee Raul M. Arias-Marxuach**	April 11, 2019	94–5	60
Natural Resources Management Act	February 7, 2019	87–7	60	**Judicial nominee Rodolfo Armando Ruiz II**	April 11, 2019	89–10	60
Legislative vehicle for continuing appropriations motion to proceed	February 11, 2019	no vote	60	Judicial nominee Andrew Lynn Brasher	April 11, 2019	52–47	60
Nominee John L. Ryder	February 14, 2019	UC	60	Judicial nominee J. Campbell Barker	April 11, 2019	52–46	60
Nominee Andrew Wheeler	February 14, 2019	52–46	60	**Nominee Gordon Hartogensis**	April 11, 2019	72–27	60
Nominee Michael J. Desmond	February 14, 2019	84–15	60	**Nominee R. Clarke Cooper**	April 11, 2019	91–8	60
Judicial nominee Eric D. Miller	February 14, 2019	51–46	60	**Nominee William Cooper**	April 11, 2019	63–32	60
Born-Alive Abortion Survivors Protection Act motion to proceed	February 14, 2019	53–44	60	Judicial nominee Michael H. Park	May 2, 2019	51–43	60
Consolidated appropriations, Fiscal Year 2019 conference report	February 14, 2019	84–15	60	Nominee Janet Dhillon	May 2, 2019	52–44	60
Nominee John Fleming	February 28, 2019	UC	60	**Nominee Judith DelZoppo Pryor**	May 2, 2019	79–19	60
Judicial nominee Eric E. Murphy	February 28, 2019	53–46	60	**Nominee Spencer Bachus III**	May 2, 2019	74–24	60
Judicial nominee Chad A. Readler	February 28, 2019	53–45	60	**Nominee Kimberly A. Reed**	May 2, 2019	82–17	60
Judicial nominee Allison Jones Rushing	February 28, 2019	52–43	60	Judicial nominee Joseph F. Bianco	May 2, 2019	51–40	60
Nominee William Beach	March 7, 2019	55–43	60	**Nominee Brian J. Bulatao**	May 9, 2019	90–5	60
Judicial nominee Neomi J. Rao	March 7, 2019	53–46	60	Judicial nominee Wendy Vitter	May 9, 2019	51–45	60
Judicial nominee Paul B. Matey	March 7, 2019	50–44	60	Judicial nominee Kenneth Kiyul Lee	May 9, 2019	50–45	60
Disaster Supplemental Appropriations motion to proceed	March 14, 2019	90–10	60	Judicial nominee Michael J. Truncale	May 9, 2019	49–43	60
Green New Deal motion to proceed	March 14, 2019	0–57	60	Nominee Jeffrey A. Rosen	May 13, 2019	52–44	60
Judicial nominee Bridget S. Bade	March 14, 2019	77–20	60	Judicial nominee Kenneth D. Bell	May 16, 2019	56–42	60
Post-cloture consideration for certain nominations motion to proceed	March 28, 2019	51–48	60	Judicial nominee Carl J. Nichols	May 16, 2019	55–42	60
Disaster Supplemental Appropriations	March 28, 2019	46–48	60	Judicial nominee Stephen R. Clark Sr.	May 16, 2019	53–45	60
Disaster Supplemental Appropriations S.Amdt.201	March 28, 2019	44–49	60	Judicial nominee Howard C. Nielson Jr.	May 16, 2019	52–47	60
Judicial nominee Roy Kalman Altman	April 1, 2019	66–33	60	Judicial nominee Daniel P. Collins	May 16, 2019	51–43	60
Nominee Jeffrey Kessler	April 1, 2019	95–3	60	**Judicial nominee Richard A. Hertling**	May 23, 2019	66–23	60
Nominee Mark Anthony Calabria	April 2, 2019	53–46	60	**Judicial nominee Rossie David Alston Jr.**	May 23, 2019	74–19	60
Judicial nominee David Steven Morales	April 4, 2019	57–41	60	**Judicial nominee Ryan T. Holte**	May 23, 2019	60–33	60
Judicial nominee Holly A. Brady	April 4, 2019	56–43	60	Nominee Susan Combs	May 23, 2019	57–36	60
Nominee John P. Abizaid	April 4, 2019	UC	60	**Nominee Heath P. Tarbert**	May 23, 2019	83–10	60
Nominee Cheryl Marie Stanton	April 4, 2019	53–47	60	**Nominee Heath P. Tarbert**	May 23, 2019	82–9	60
Judicial nominee Patrick R. Wyrick	April 4, 2019	53–46	60	**Nominee David Schenker**	May 23, 2019	83–10	60
				Nominee Andrew M. Saul	May 23, 2019	74–17	60
				A bill to set forth the congressional budget for the U.S. Government, FY2020 motion to proceed	May 23, 2019	22–69	60
				Nominee Edward F. Crawford	June 5, 2019	92–7	60
				Nominee David Stilwell	June 5, 2019	93–4	60
				Judicial nominee Jean-Paul Boulee	June 5, 2019	84–12	60
				Judicial nominee Thomas P. Barber	June 5, 2019	75–21	60

Issue	Date	Vote	Yeas needed	Issue	Date	Vote	Yeas needed
Judicial nominee Rodney Smith	June 5, 2019	77–19	60	Judicial nominee Karin J. Immergut	July 25, 2019	UC	60
Judicial nominee Corey Landon Maze	June 5, 2019	62–34	60	Judicial nominee William Shaw Stickman IV	July 25, 2019	57–31	60
Judicial nominee Pamela A. Barker	June 5, 2019	89–7	60	**Judicial nominee Steven C. Seeger**	July 25, 2019	87–1	60
Judicial nominee Sarah Daggett Morrison	June 5, 2019	89–7	60	**Judicial nominee Martha Maria Pacold**	July 25, 2019	86–2	60
National Defense Authorization Act, Fiscal Year 2020 motion to proceed	June 13, 2019	89–10	60	Judicial nominee Jason K. Pulliam	July 25, 2019	54–34	60
Judicial nominee Greg Gerard Guidry	June 13, 2019	53–43	60	**Judicial nominee Steven D. Grimberg**	July 25, 2019	72–16	60
Judicial nominee James David Cain Jr.	June 13, 2019	76–20	60	**Judicial nominee Ada E. Brown**	July 25, 2019	79–9	60
Judicial nominee Allen Cothrel Winsor	June 13, 2019	54–42	60	**Judicial nominee Stephanie L. Haines**	July 25, 2019	87–1	60
Judicial nominee Matthew J. Kacsmaryk	June 13, 2019	52–44	60	Judicial nominee Brantley Starr	July 25, 2019	51–37	60
Nominee Sean Cairncross	June 13, 2019	59–37	60	Judicial nominee Jeffrey Vincent Brown	July 25, 2019	51–37	60
National Defense Authorization Act, Fiscal Year 2020	June 24, 2019	UC	60	Judicial nominee Mark T. Pittman	July 25, 2019	54–34	60
National Defense Authorization Act, Fiscal Year 2020 S.Amdt.764	June 24, 2019	87–7	60	Judicial nominee Sean D. Jordan	July 25, 2019	54–36	60
Nominee Peter C. Wright	June 27, 2019	53–39	60	**Judicial nominee James Wesley Hendrix**	July 25, 2019	85–5	60
Nominee John P. Pallasch	June 27, 2019	54–41	60	**Judicial nominee Peter D. Welte**	July 25, 2019	66–21	60
Nominee Robert L. King	June 27, 2019	56–39	60	Judicial nominee Michael T. Liburdi	July 25, 2019	51–37	60
Judicial nominee J. Nicholas Ranjan	June 27, 2019	83–15	60	Nominee David L. Norquist	July 29, 2019	UC	60
Judicial nominee Damon Ray Leichty	June 27, 2019	87–11	60	Nominee Kelly Craft	July 29, 2019	57–33	60
Judicial nominee T. Kent Wetherell II	June 27, 2019	82–16	60	Bipartisan Budget Act motion to proceed	July 29, 2019	UC	60
Judicial nominee Daniel Aaron Bress	June 27, 2019	50–42	60	**Nominee Jennifer D. Nordquist**	August 1, 2019	94–0	60
Nominee Donald R. Tapia	July 11, 2019	67–28	60	**Nominee Thomas Peter Feddo**	August 1, 2019	92–1	60
Nominee Lynda Blanchard	July 11, 2019	55–41	60	**Nominee Michelle Bowman**	August 1, 2019	62–31	60
Judicial nominee Clifton L. Corker	July 11, 2019	55–41	60	**Nominee James Byrne**	August 1, 2019	81–13	60
Amending the Tax Convention with Luxembourg	July 11, 2019	UC	60	Nominee Dale Cabaniss	August 1, 2019	53–41	60
Amending the Tax Convention with Japan	July 11, 2019	UC	60	**Nominee Stephen Akard**	August 1, 2019	91–3	60
Amending the Tax Convention with the Swiss Confederation	July 11, 2019	UC	60	Nominee Elizabeth Darling	August 1, 2019	57–37	60
Amending the Tax Convention with Spain	July 11, 2019	94–1	60	Nominee Kelly Craft	August 1, 2019	54–38	60
Judicial nominee Peter Joseph Phipps	July 11, 2019	53–40	60	**Bipartisan Budget Act**	August 1, 2019	67–27	60
Judicial nominee Brian C. Buescher	July 18, 2019	52–39	60	Nominee Brian Callanan	September 12, 2019	55–37 =	60
Judicial nominee Wendy Williams Berger	July 18, 2019	55–37	60	Nominee Brent James McIntosh	September 12, 2019	54–40	60
Nominee Stephen M. Dickson	July 18, 2019	52–45	60	Nominee Robert A. Destro	September 12, 2019	49–44	60
Nominee Mark T. Esper	July 18, 2019	85–6	60	**Nominee Kenneth A. Howery**	September 12, 2019	63–29	60
Judicial nominee Mary M. Rowland	July 25, 2019	UC	60	Nominee John Rakolta Jr.	September 12, 2019	55–27	60
Judicial nominee Stephanie A. Gallagher	July 25, 2019	UC	60	Departments of Labor, HHS, Education, and Related Agencies Appropriations, Fiscal Year 2020 motion to proceed	September 16, 2019	51–44	60
Judicial nominee Mary S. McElroy	July 25, 2019	UC	60	**Nominee Brian McGuire**	September 18, 2019	82–6	60
Judicial nominee John Milton Younge	July 25, 2019	UC	60	**National Defense Authorization Act, Fiscal Year 2020 compound motion to go to conference**	September 18, 2019	87–7	60
				Nominee David Fabian Black	September 19, 2019	66–25	60
				Nominee Daniel Habib Jorjani	September 19, 2019	50–41	60
				Nominee Joseph Cella	September 19, 2019	55–37	60
				Nominee Gen. John E. Hyten	September 24, 2019	73–21	60
				Nominee Eugene Scalia	September 25, 2019	52–42	60
				Judicial nominee Rachel P. Kovner	September 27, 2019	85–3	60

Issue	Date	Vote	Yeas needed
Judicial nominee David John Novak	September 27, 2019	86–4	60
Judicial nominee Charles R. Eskridge III	September 27, 2019	61–29	60
Judicial nominee Frank William Volk	September 27, 2019	90–0	60
Nominee Barbara McConnell Barrett	September 27, 2019	84–7	60
Departments of Labor, HHS, Education, and Related Agencies Appropriations, Fiscal Year 2020 motion to proceed	October 17, 2019		60
Departments of Commerce and Justice, Science, and Related Agencies, Fiscal Year 2020 motion to proceed	October 17, 2019	92–2	60
Nominee Andrew P. Bremberg	October 17, 2019	50–43	60
Protocol to the North Atlantic Treaty of 1949 on the Accession of the Republic of North Macedonia	October 17, 2019	84–2	60
Judicial nominee Justin Reed Walker	October 22, 2019	50–39	60
Departments of Labor, HHS, Education, and Related Agencies Appropriations, Fiscal Year 2020 motion to proceed	October 28, 2019	51–41	60
Departments of Commerce and Justice, Science, and Related Agencies, Fiscal Year 2020	October 28, 2019	UC	60
Departments of Commerce and Justice, Science, and Related Agencies, Fiscal Year 2020 S.Amdt.948	October 28, 2019	88–5	60
Judicial nominee Jennifer Philpott Wilson	October 31, 2019	89–3	60
Judicial nominee Lee Philip Rudofsky	October 31, 2019	51–41	60
Judicial nominee William Joseph Nardini	October 31, 2019	87–3	60
Judicial nominee Danielle J. Hunsaker	October 31, 2019	75–18	60
Judicial nominee David Austin Tapp	October 31, 2019	83–9	60
Judicial nominee Steven J. Menashi	November 7, 2019	51–44	60
Nominee Chad F. Wolf	November 7, 2019	54–40	60
Judicial nominee Adrian Zuckerman	November 14, 2019	65–30	60
Judicial nominee Barbara Lagoa	November 14, 2019	80–15	60
Judicial nominee Robert J. Luck	November 14, 2019	61–30	60
Nominee Dan R. Brouillette	November 20, 2019	74–18	60
Nominee Robert M. Duncan	November 21, 2019	91–1	60
Legislative vehicle for continuing appropriations motion to concur in the House amendment to the Senate amendment to H.R. 3055	November 21, 2019	75–19	60

Issue	Date	Vote	Yeas needed
Judicial nominee Sherri A. Lydon	November 21, 2019	79–14	60
Judicial nominee Richard Ernest Myers II	November 21, 2019	72–22	60
Judicial nominee David B. Barlow	November 21, 2019	88–4	60
Judicial nominee R. Austin Huffaker Jr.	November 21, 2019	88–4	60
Judicial nominee Douglas Russell Cole	November 21, 2019	62–29	60
Judicial nominee Sarah E. Pitlyk	November 21, 2019	50–43	60
Judicial nominee John L. Sinatra Jr.	November 21, 2019	76–16	60
Judicial nominee Eric Ross Komitee	November 21, 2019	81–5	60
Nominee Aurelia Skipwith	December 4, 2019	53–41	60
Nominee Stephen Hahn	December 4, 2019	74–19	60
Nominee John Joseph Sullivan	December 4, 2019	69–25	60
Judicial nominee Lawrence VanDyke	December 4, 2019	53–40	60
Judicial nominee Patrick J. Bumatay	December 4, 2019	47–41	60
National Defense Authorization Act, Fiscal Year 2020 conference report	December 12, 2019	76–6	60
Judicial nominee Stephanie Dawkins Davis	December 16, 2019	90–1	60
Judicial nominee Gary Richard Brown	December 16, 2019	91–2	60
Judicial nominee Lewis J. Liman	December 16, 2019	UC	60
Judicial nominee Robert J. Colville	December 16, 2019	UC	60
Judicial nominee Kea Whetzal Riggs	December 16, 2019	92–1	60
Judicial nominee Mary Kay Vyskocil	December 16, 2019	89–4	60
Judicial nominee Bernard Maurice Jones II	December 16, 2019	88–5	60
Judicial nominee John M. Gallagher	December 16, 2019	82–10	60
Judicial nominee Jodi W. Dishman	December 16, 2019	76–17	60
Judicial nominee Daniel Mack Traynor	December 16, 2019	51–42	60
Judicial nominee Karen Spencer Marston	December 16, 2019	85–7	60
Judicial nominee Anuraag Singhal	December 16, 2019	76–18	60
Judicial nominee Matthew Walden McFarland	December 16, 2019	55–38	60
Consolidated Appropriations, Fiscal Year 2020 motion to concur in the House amendment to the Senate amendment to H.R. 1158	December 17, 2019	77–16	60
Further Consolidated Appropriations, Fiscal Year 2020 motion to concur in the House amendment to the Senate amendment to H.R. 1865	December 17, 2019	71–21	60
Nominee Stephen E. Biegun	December 17, 2019	UC	60

Issue	Date	Vote	Yeas needed
Nominee Jovita Carranza	January 3, 2020	86–5	60
Nominee Michael George DeSombre	January 6, 2020	64–31	60
Judicial nominee Eleni Maria Roumel	January 6, 2020	51–44	60
Judicial nominee Matthew H. Solomson	January 6, 2020	88–7	60
Nominee Paul J. Ray	January 7, 2020	50–45	60
Nominee Peter Gaynor	January 9, 2020	76–8	60
Judicial nominee Philip M. Halpern	February 5, 2020	75–18	60
Judicial nominee John Fitzgerald Kness	February 5, 2020	82–12	60
Judicial nominee Matthew Thomas Schelp	February 5, 2020	72–22	60
Judicial nominee Joshua M. Kindred	February 5, 2020	52–41	60
Judicial nominee Andrew Lynn Brasher	February 5, 2020	46–41	60
Judicial nominee Travis Greaves	February 13, 2020	91–5	60
Nominee Katharine MacGregor	February 13, 2020	59–38	60
Born-Alive Abortion Survivors Protection Act motion to proceed	February 13, 2020	56–41	60
Pain-Capable Unborn Child Protection Act motion to proceed	February 13, 2020	53–44	60
Judicial nominee Silvia Carreno-Coll	February 13, 2020	96–1	60
Judicial nominee Robert Anthony Molloy	February 13, 2020	88–1	60
Legislative vehicle for the Energy bill motion to proceed	February 27, 2020	84–3	60
Legislative vehicle for the Energy bill	March 5, 2020	15–73	60
Legislative vehicle for the Energy bill S.Amdt.1407	March 5, 2020	47–44	60
Nominee James P. Danly	March 10, 2020	54–40	60
USA FREEDOM Reauthorization Act of 2020	March 12, 2020	UC	60
Coronavirus stimulus package motion to proceed Vote No. 77 reconsidered	March 20, 2020	47–4749–46	60
Coronavirus stimulus package motion to proceed	March 23, 2020	UC	60
Nominee William R. Evanina	May 4, 2020	83–7	60
Nominee Troy D. Edgar	May 7, 2020	62–31	60
Nominee Brian D. Montgomery	May 7, 2020	60–29	60
Judicial nominee John Leonard Badalamenti	May 14, 2020	65–28	60
Judicial nominee John F. Heil III	May 14, 2020	76–16	60
Judicial nominee Anna M. Manasco	May 14, 2020	72–20	60
Nominee James E. Trainor III	May 14, 2020	50–43	60
Judicial nominee Scott H. Rash	May 14, 2020	67–21	60
Judicial nominee Drew B. Tipton	May 21, 2020	53–42	60
Nominee James H. Anderson	May 21, 2020	74–18	60
Nominee Brian D. Miller	May 21, 2020	51–40	60
Nominee Victor G. Mercado	May 21, 2020	75–14	60
Nominee Michael Pack	June 2, 2020	53–39	60
legislative vehicle for Great American Outdoors Act motion to proceed	June 4, 2020	80–17	60
Judicial nominee Justin Reed Walker	June 10, 2020	52–46	60
legislative vehicle for Great American Outdoors Act	June 10, 2020	75–23	60
legislative vehicle for Great American Outdoors Act S Amdt.1617	June 10, 2020	65–19	60
Judicial nominee Cory T. Wilson	June 18, 2020	51–43	60
JUSTICE Act motion to proceed	June 22, 2020	55–45	60
National Defense Authorization Act, Fiscal Year 2021 motion to proceed	June 24, 2020	90–7	60
Nominee Russell Vought	June 30, 2020	47–44	60
National Defense Authorization Act, Fiscal Year 2021 S.Amdt.2301	July 2, 2020	87–13	60
National Defense Authorization Act, Fiscal Year 2021	July 6, 2020	86–14	60
Judicial nominee William Scott Hardy	July 21, 2020	60–32	60
Nominee Lauren McGarity McFerran	July 23, 2020	56–41	60
Nominee Marvin Kaplan	July 23, 2020	52–46	60
Nominee Dana T. Wade	July 23, 2020	57–40	60
Judicial nominee David Cleveland Joseph	July 23, 2020	55–42	60
Nominee Derek Kan	July 27, 2020	76–22	60
Nominee Mark Wesley Menezes	July 30, 2020	78–14	60
Judicial nominee John Peter Cronan	August 4, 2020	55–42	60
Judicial nominee Diane Gujarati	August 13, 2020	94–2	60
Judicial nominee Thomas T. Cullen	August 13, 2020	77–18	60
Judicial nominee Hala Y. Jarbou	August 13, 2020	80–15	60
Judicial nominee Christy Criswell Wiegand	August 13, 2020	80–16	60
Judicial nominee Brett H. Ludwig	August 13, 2020	83–6	60
Legislative vehicle for stimulus package motion to concur in the House amendment to S.178 with amendment S.Amdt.2652	September 8, 2020	52–47	60
Judicial nominee Franklin Ulyses Valderrama	September 10, 2020	UC	60
Judicial nominee Iain D. Johnston	September 10, 2020	81–15	60
Judicial nominee Stephen P. McGlynn	September 10, 2020	55–42	60
Judicial nominee David W. Dugan	September 10, 2020	56–40	60
Judicial nominee Todd Wallace Robinson	September 10, 2020	83–13	60

Issue	Date	Vote	Yeas needed
Judicial nominee John W. Holcomb	September 10, 2020	83–13	60
Judicial nominee Stanley Blumenfeld	September 10, 2020	89–6	60
Judicial nominee Mark C. Scarsi	September 10, 2020	77–12	60
Judicial nominee Roderick C. Young	September 17, 2020	93–3	60
Judicial nominee John Charles Hinderaker	September 17, 2020	71–26	60
Nominee Keith E. Sonderling	September 17, 2020	52–41	60
Nominee Jocelyn Samuels	September 17, 2020	UC	60
Nominee Andrea R. Lucas	September 17, 2020	49–44	60
Judicial nominee Edward Hulvey Meyers	September 17, 2020	65–25	60
Continuing Appropriations, Fiscal Year 2021	September 24, 2020	82–6	60
A bill to prevent efforts of the Department of Justice to advocate courts to strike down the Patient Protection and Affordable Care Act.	September 29, 2020	51–43	60
Judicial nominee Michael Jay Newman	September 30, 2020	UC	60
Judicial nominee James Ray Knepp II	September 30, 2020	UC	60
Judicial nominee J. Philip Calabrese	September 30, 2020	UC	60
Judicial nominee Toby Crouse	September 30, 2020	UC	60
Judicial nominee Aileen Mercedes Cannon	September 30, 2020	UC	60
Legislative vehicle for stimulus package motion to concur in the House amendment to S.178 with amendment S.Amdt.2652	October 19, 2020	51–44	60
Judicial nominee Michael Jay Newman	October 20, 2020	66–31	60
Supreme Court nominee Amy Coney Barrett	October 23, 2020	51–48	60
Judicial nominee James Ray Knepp II	October 26, 2020	62–23	60
Judicial nominee Aileen Mercedes Cannon	November 10, 2020	57–21	60
Judicial nominee Taylor B. McNeel	November 12, 2020	52–36	60
Judicial nominee Kathryn Kimball Mizelle	November 12, 2020	49–43	60
Judicial nominee Stephen A. Vaden	November 12, 2020	49–44	60

Issue	Date	Vote	Yeas needed
Judicial nominee Toby Crouse	November 12, 2020	51–44	60
Nominee Judy Shelton	November 12, 2020	47–50	60
Judicial nominee Benjamin Joel Beaton	November 12, 2020	52–44	60
Judicial nominee Kristi Haskins Johnson	November 12, 2020	51–38	60
Judicial nominee Kathryn C. Davis	November 18, 2020	51–44	60
Nominee Kyle Hauptman	November 18, 2020	56–37	60
Judicial nominee J. Philip Calabrese	November 18, 2020	58–35	60
Judicial nominee Liam P. Hardy	November 30, 2020	61–34	60
Nominee Christopher Waller	November 30, 2020	50–45	60
Judicial nominee Nathan A. Simington	December 3, 2020	49–47	60
Judicial nominee Stephen Sidney Schwartz	December 3, 2020	48–46	60
Nominee Sean J. Cooksey	December 7, 2020	UC	60
Nominee Shana M. Broussard	December 7, 2020	UC	60
Nominee Allen Dickerson	December 7, 2020	UC	60
National Defense Authorization Act, Fiscal Year 2021 conference report	December 9, 2020	84–13	60
Judicial nominee Katherine A. Crytzer	December 11, 2020	48–47	60
Judicial nominee Thomas L. Kirsch II	December 11, 2020	51–42	60
Judicial nominee Zachary N. Somers	December 14, 2020	52–42	60
Judicial nominee Charles Edward Atchley Jr.	December 14, 2020	54–41	60
Judicial nominee Joseph Dawson III	December 14, 2020	56–39	60
Judicial nominee Fernando L. Aenlle-Rocha	December 17, 2020	82–7	60
Nominee Charles A. Stones	December 17, 2020	UC	60
Nominee Brian Noland	December 17, 2020	84–5	60
Nominee Beth Harwell	December 17, 2020	61–25	60
Nominee Eric J. Soskin Vote No. 278 reconsidered	December 17, 2020	39–48 48–44	60
Nominee John Chase Johnson	December 17, 2020	39–48	60
Judicial nominee Thompson Michael Dietz	December 17, 2020	50–37	60
Veto message to accompany H.R.6395, National Defense Authorization Act, Fiscal Year 2021	December 30, 2020	80–12	60

115th Congress Special Elections, 2017–2018 Gubernatorial Elections

Special House Elections, 115th Congress

	Vote total	Percent		Vote total	Percent
Kansas 4th CD—April 11, 2017			**Arizona 8th CD—April 24, 2018**		
Ron Estes (R)	64,044	52.2	Debbie Lesko (R)	91,390	52.6
James Thompson (D)	56,435	46.0	Hiral Tipirneni (D)	82,318	47.39
South Carolina AL CD—May 25, 2017			**Texas 27th CD—June 30, 2018**		
Greg Gianforte (R)	1,90,520	50.0	Michael Clouds (R)	19,872	54.8
Rob Quist (D)	1,69,214	44.4	Eric Holguin (D)	11,599	32
California 34th CD—June 6, 2017			**Ohio 12th CD—August 7, 2018**		
Jimmy Gomez (D)	25,569	59.2	Troy Balderson (R)	1,04,328	50.1
Robert Lee Ahn (D)	17,610	40.8	Danny O'Connor (D)	1,02,648	49.3
Georgia 6th CD—June 20, 2017			**Michigan 13th CD—November 6, 2018**		
Karen Handel (R)	1,34,799	51.8	Brenda Jones (D)	1,69,330	86.8
Jon Ossoff (D)	1,25,517	48.2	Marc Joseph Sosnowski (U.S. Taxpayers)	17,302	8.9
South Carolina's 5th CD—June 20, 2017			**New York 25th CD— November 6, 2018**		
Ralph Norman (R)	45,076	51.0	Joseph Morelle (D)	1,41,290	58.3
Archie Parnell (D)	42,341	47.9	James Maxwell (R)	1,01,085	41.7
Utah 3rd CD—November 7, 2017			**Pennsylvania 7th CD—November 6, 2018**		
John Curtis (R)	85,751	58.0	Mary Gay Scanlon (D)	1,73,268	52.3
Kathie Allen (D)	37,801	25.6	Pearl Kim (R)	1,52,503	46
Pennsylvania 18th CD—March 13, 2018			**Pennsylvania 15th CD—November 6, 2018**		
Conor Lamb (D)	1,14,102	49.9	Susan Wild (D)	1,30,353	48.5
Rick Saccone (R)	1,13,347	49.5	Marty Nothstein (R)	1,29,594	48.3

Special Senate Elections, 115th Congress

	Vote total	Percent
Alabama—December 12, 2017		
Doug Jones (D)	6,73,896	50
Roy Moore (R)	6,51,972	48.3
Minnesota—November 6, 2018		
Tina Smith (D)	13,70,540	53
Karin Housley (R)	10,95,777	42.4
Mississippi—November 6, 2018		
Cindy Hyde-Smith (R)	4,86,769	53.6
Mike Espy (D)	4,20,819	46.4

2017 Gubernatorial Elections

	Vote total	Percent		Vote total	Percent
Virginia			**New Jersey**		
Ralph Northam (D)	12,78,932	60.3	Phil Murphy (D)	12,03,110	56.03
Ed Gillespie (R)	8,09,978	38.2	Kim Guadagno (R)	8,99,583	41.89
Cliff Hyra (I)	30,241	1.16	Gina Genovese (I)	12,294	0.57

NOTE: Vote totals are included for all candidates listed on the ballot who received 5 percent or more of the total vote.

House Discharge Petitions since 1931

The discharge petition is a little-used but dramatic House device that enables a majority of representatives to bring to the floor legislation blocked in committee. The following table shows the frequency with which the discharge petition has been used since the present discharge procedure was adopted in 1931 through 2020.

Although the procedure is rarely used and even more rarely successful, it may on occasion indirectly succeed by prompting a legislative committee, the Rules Committee, or the leadership to act on a measure and thereby avoid the discharge.

Congress		Discharge Petitions	Discharge Motion		Underlying Measure [3]		
			Entered [1]	Called Up [2]	Committee Discharged	Passed House	Received Final Approval [4]
72nd	(1931–1933)	12	5	5	1	1	–
73rd	(1933–1935)	31	6	1	1	1	–
74th	(1935–1937)	33	3	2	2	–	–
75th	(1937–1939)	43	4	4	3[5]	2	1
76th	(1939–1941)	37[5]	2	2	2	2	–
77th	(1941–1943)	15	1	1	1	1	–
78th	(1943–1945)	21	3	3	3	3	1[6]
79th	(1945–1947)	35	3	1	1	1	–
80th	(1947–1949)	20	1	1	1	1	–
81st	(1949–1951)	34	3	1	1	1	–
82nd	(1951–1953)	14	–	–	–	–	–
83rd	(1953–1955)	10	1	1	1	1	–
84th	(1955–1957)	6	–	–	–	–	–
85th	(1957–1959)	7	1	1	1	1	–
86th	(1959–1961)	7	1	1	1	1	1
87th	(1961–1963)	6	–	–	–	–	–
88th	(1963–1965)	5	–	–	–	–	–
89th	(1965–1967)	6	1	1	1	1	–
90th	(1967–1969)	4	–	–	–	–	–
91st	(1969–1971)	12	1	1	1	1	–
92nd	(1971–1973)	15	1	1	1	–	–
93rd	(1973–1975)	10	–	–	–	–	–
94th	(1975–1977)	15	–	–	–	–	–
95th	(1977–1979)	11	–	–	–	–	–
96th	(1979–1981)	14	2	1	1	–	–
97th	(1981–1983)	24	1	–	–	–	–
98th	(1983–1985)	13	1	–	–	–	–
99th	(1985–1987)	10	1	–	–	–	–
100th	(1987–1989)	5[8]	–	–	–	–	–
101st	(1989–1991)	8	1	–	–	–	–
102nd	(1991–1993)	8	1[9]	1[9]	1[9]	–	–
103rd	(1993–1995)	26	2[9]	2[9]	2[9]	1	1[6]
104th	(1995–1997)	15	–	–	–	–	–
105th	(1997–1999)	8	–	–	–	–	–
106th	(1999–2001)	11	–	–	–	–	–
107th	(2001–2003)	12	1	–	–	–	–
108th	(2003–2005)	16	–	–	–	–	–
109th	(2005–2007)	18	–	–	–	–	–
110th	(2007–2009)	18	–	–	–	–	–
111th	(2009–2011)	13	–	–	–	–	–
112th	(2011–2013)	6	–	–	–	–	–
113th	(2013–2014)	12	–	–	–	–	–
114th	(2015–2016)	6	–	–	–	–	–
115th	(2017–2018)	11	–	–	–	–	–
116th	(2019–2020)	5	–	–	–	–	–
Totals		652	47	31	26	19	4

SOURCE: Richard S. Beth, "The Discharge Rule in the House: Recent Use in Historical Context," Congressional Research Service, Library of Congress, September 15, 1997; update provided by CRS, September 1999, April 2000, December 2005. Clerk of the House, https://clerk.house.gov/DischargePetition?congressNum=115; https://clerk.house.gov/DischargePetition?Page=1&CongressNum=116

[1] A discharge motion is "entered" when the petition receives a sufficient number of member signatures for it to be entered on the Calendar of Motions to Discharge Committees. This number was 145 in the 72nd and 73rd Congresses, 219 in the 86th and 87th Congresses, and 218 for all other Congresses in the table.

[2] A discharge motion may be offered on the floor on any second or fourth Monday falling at least seven legislative days after the discharge petition is entered. Each day on which the House convenes is usually a legislative day.

[3] A discharge petition may be filed to bring to the floor either a substantive measure in committee or a "special rule" from the Committee on Rules providing for House consideration of such a measure that is either in committee or previously reported. The last two columns of this table reflect action on the underlying, substantive measure, not on the special rule, if any, on which discharge was directly sought.

[4]Includes bills and joint resolutions becoming law; constitutional amendments submitted to the states for ratification; resolutions agreed to by the House; and concurrent resolutions finally agreed to by both chambers.

[5]During this Congress, the Rules Committee was discharged from a special rule for consideration of one measure, and the measure was taken up but then recommitted. Subsequently, the Rules Committee was discharged from a second special rule for consideration of the measure. This measure accordingly appears twice under "Committee discharged" and earlier columns, but only once under "Passed House" and subsequently.

[6]Resolution attempting to change House Rules.

[7]Includes one petition entered with respect to a special rule on a measure and another on the same measure directly.

[8]Includes one petition filed on a special rule for considering two measures.

[9]Includes one measure in the 102nd Congress and two in the 103rd from which the committee was discharged, and which were brought to the floor, by unanimous consent after the discharge petition was entered.

Congressional Reapportionment, 1789–2020

State	Constitution	Year of Census[1]																					
	(1789)[2]	1790	1800	1810	1820	1830	1840	1850	1860	1870	1880	1890	1900	1910	1930[3]	1940	1950	1960	1970	1980	1990	2000	2010	2020
Alabama				1[4]	3	5	7	7	6	8	8	9	9	10	9	9	9	8	7	7	7	7	7	7
Alaska																	1[4]	1	1	1	1	1	1	1
Arizona														1[4]	1	2	2	3	4	5	6	8	9	9
Arkansas						1[4]	1	2	3	4	5	6	7	7	7	7	6	4	4	4	4	4	4	4
California							2[4]	2	3	4	6	7	8	11	20	23	30	38	43	45	52	53	53	52
Colorado										1[4]	1	2	3	4	4	4	4	4	5	6	6	7	7	8
Conn.	5	7	7	7	6	6	4	4	4	4	4	4	5	5	6	6	6	6	6	6	6	5	5	5
Delaware	1	1	1	2	1	1	1	1	1	1	1	1	1	1	1	1	1	1	1	1	1	1	1	1
Florida							1[4]	1	1	2	2	2	3	4	5	6	8	12	15	19	23	25	27	28
Georgia	3	2	4	6	7	9	8	8	7	9	10	11	11	12	10	10	10	10	10	10	11	13	14	14
Hawaii																	1[4]	2	2	2	2	2	2	2
Idaho											1[4]	1	1	2	2	2	2	2	2	2	2	2	2	2
Illinois				1[4]	1	3	7	9	14	19	20	22	25	27	27	26	25	24	24	22	20	19	18	17
Indiana				1[4]	3	7	10	11	11	13	13	13	13	13	12	11	11	11	11	10	10	9	9	9
Iowa							2[4]	2	6	9	11	11	11	11	9	8	8	7	6	6	5	5	4	4
Kansas									1	3	7	8	8	8	7	6	6	5	5	5	4	4	4	4
Kentucky		2	6	10	12	13	10	10	9	10	11	11	11	11	9	9	8	7	7	7	6	6	6	6
Louisiana				1[4]	3	3	4	4	5	6	6	6	7	8	8	8	8	8	8	8	7	7	6	6
Maine				7[4]	7	8	7	6	5	5	4	4	4	4	3	3	3	2	2	2	2	2	2	2
Maryland	6	8	9	9	9	8	6	6	5	6	6	6	6	6	6	6	7	8	8	8	8	8	8	8
Massachusetts	8	14	17	13[5]	13	12	10	11	10	11	12	13	14	16	15	14	14	12	12	11	10	10	9	9
Michigan						1[4]	3	4	6	9	11	12	12	13	17	17	18	19	19	18	16	15	14	13
Minnesota								2[4]	2	3	5	7	9	10	9	9	9	8	8	8	8	8	8	8
Mississippi				1[4]	1	2	4	5	5	6	7	7	8	8	7	7	6	5	5	5	5	4	4	4
Missouri					1	2	5	7	9	13	14	15	16	16	13	13	11	10	10	9	9	9	8	8
Montana											1[4]	1	1	2	2	2	2	2	2	2	1	1	1	2
Nebraska									1[4]	1	3	6	6	6	5	4	4	3	3	3	3	3	3	3
Nevada									1[4]	1	1	1	1	1	1	1	1	1	1	2	2	3	4	4
New Hampshire	3	4	5	6	6	5	4	3	3	3	2	2	2	2	2	2	2	2	2	2	2	2	2	2
New Jersey	4	5	6	6	6	6	5	5	5	7	7	8	10	12	14	14	14	15	15	14	13	13	12	12
New Mexico														1[4]	1	2	2	2	2	3	3	3	3	3
New York	6	10	17	27	34	40	34	33	31	33	34	34	37	43	45	45	43	41	39	34	31	29	27	26
North Carolina	5	10	12	13	13	13	9	8	7	8	9	9	10	10	11	12	12	11	11	11	12	13	13	14
North Dakota											1[4]	1	2	3	2	2	2	2	1	1	1	1	1	1
Ohio			1[4]	6	14	19	21	21	19	20	21	21	21	22	24	23	23	24	23	21	19	18	16	15
Oklahoma													5[4]	8	9	8	6	6	6	6	6	5	5	5
Oregon								1[4]	1	1	1	2	2	3	3	4	4	4	4	5	5	5	5	6
Pennsylvania	8	13	18	23	26	28	24	25	24	27	28	30	32	36	34	33	30	27	25	23	21	19	18	17
Rhode Island	1	2	2	2	2	2	2	2	2	2	2	2	2	3	2	2	2	2	2	2	2	2	2	2
South Carolina	5	6	8	9	9	9	7	6	4	5	7	7	7	7	6	6	6	6	6	6	6	6	7	7
South Dakota											2[4]	2	2	3	2	2	2	2	2	1	1	1	1	1
Tennessee		1[4]	3	6	9	13	11	10	8	10	10	10	10	10	9	10	9	9	9	9	9	9	9	9
Texas							2[4]	2	4	6	11	13	16	18	21	21	22	23	24	27	30	32	36	38
Utah												1[4]	1	2	2	2	2	2	2	3	3	3	4	4
Vermont		2	4	6	5	5	4	3	3	3	2	2	2	2	1	1	1	1	1	1	1	1	1	1
Virginia	10	19	22	23	22	21	15	13	11	9	10	10	10	10	9	9	10	10	10	10	11	11	11	11
Washington											1[4]	2	3	5	6	6	7	7	7	8	9	9	10	10
West Virginia										3	4	4	5	6	6	6	6	5	4	4	3	3	3	2
Wisconsin							2[4]	3	6	8	9	10	11	11	10	10	10	10	9	9	9	8	8	8
Wyoming											1[4]	1	1	1	1	1	1	1	1	1	1	1	1	1
Total	65	106	142	186	213	242	232	237	243	293	332	357	391	435	435	435	435	437[6]	435	435	435	435	435	435

SOURCES: *Biographical Directory of the American Congress* and Bureau of the Census.

[1] Apportionment effective with congressional election two years after census.

[2] Original apportionment made in Constitution, pending first census.

[3] No apportionment was made in 1920.

[4] These figures are not based on any census, but indicate the provisional representation accorded newly admitted states by Congress, pending the next census.

[5] Twenty members were assigned to Massachusetts, but seven of these were credited to Maine when that area became a state.

[6] Normally 435, but temporarily increased two seats by Congress when Alaska and Hawaii became states.

The Presidency

Presidential Vetoes, 2019–2020

President Donald Trump vetoed ten bills during his single presidential term. Half of the bills that he vetoed would have placed various restrictions on U.S. military operations or arms sales. Two of the vetoed bills would have prevented him from transferring federal funds to pay for construction of portions of a wall along the U.S.–Mexico border. Two other bills focused on regulations pertaining to student loan debt and to fishing. The tenth bill that Trump vetoed, and the only one in which Congress overrode his veto, was the fiscal 2021 defense authorization. Trump objected to provisions renaming military installations and ships and to Congress's refusal to remove certain protections from social media platforms.

Trump's ten vetoes were tied with the ten vetoes of President Barack Obama's second term. Obama had vetoed just two bills in his first term.

There has been a total of 2,584 vetoes issued by presidents in U.S. history. Among recent presidents, George W. Bush was notable for having issued no vetoes during his first four years in office, from 2001 through 2004. He was the first president since John Quincy Adams in the 1820s to go through an entire term without issuing a veto. However, he issued twelve vetoes in his second term (2005–2008), with Democrats in control of Congress for two of those four years.

Presidential Vetoes

President	Congress Vetoes	Regular Vetoes	Pocket Vetoes	Total	Overridden
Dwight D. Eisenhower	83rd–86th	73	108	181	2
John F. Kennedy	87th–88th	12	9	21	0
Lyndon B. Johnson	88th–90th	16	14	30	0
Richard M. Nixon	91st–93rd	26	17	43	7
Gerald R. Ford	93rd–94th	48	18	66	12
Jimmy Carter	95th–96th	13	18	31	2
Ronald Reagan	97th–100th	39	39	78	9
George H. W. Bush[1]	101st–102nd	29	15	44	1
Bill Clinton[2]	103rd–106th	36	1	37	2
George W. Bush	107th–108th	12	0	12	4
Barack Obama[3]	109th–110th	2	0	2	0
	111th–114th	10	0	10	3
Donald J. Trump	115th–116th	10	0	10	1

1. President George H. W. Bush attempted to pocket veto two bills during recess periods. Congress considered the two bills enacted into law because of the president's failure to return the legislation. The bills are not counted as pocket vetoes in this table.
2. Does not include line-item vetoes, which were permitted under a 1996 law that was struck down by the Supreme Court.
3. President Barack Obama considered one of his vetoes from 2009, one from 2010, and three from 2015 to be pocket vetoes, but since he returned the parchments to Congress, the Senate considers them regular vetoes.

Following is a list of bills vetoed by President Donald Trump and his messages to Congress about the vetoes.

2019

1. H.J.Res.46 (Relating to a national emergency declared by the president on February 15, 2019)
Vetoed March 15, 2019
The House sustained the veto on March 26 by vote No. 127 (248–181).

2. S.J.Res.7 (Yemen War Powers Resolution)
Vetoed April 16, 2019
The Senate sustained the veto on May 2 by vote No. 94 (53–45).

3. S.J.Res.38 (Saudi Arabia and United Kingdom of Great Britain and Northern Ireland arms sales disapproval resolution)
Vetoed July 24, 2019
The Senate sustained the veto on July 29 by vote No. 233 (46–41).

4. S.J.Res.37 (UAE arms sales disapproval resolution)
Vetoed July 24, 2019
The Senate sustained the veto on July 29 by vote No. 232 (45–39).

5. S.J.Res.36 (Saudi Arabia, United Kingdom of Great Britain and Northern Ireland, Kingdom of Spain, and Italian Republic arms sales disapproval resolution)
Vetoed July 24, 2019
The Senate sustained the veto on July 29 by vote No. 231 (45–40).

6. S.J.Res.54 (Relating to a national emergency declared by the president on February 15, 2019)
Vetoed October 15, 2019
The Senate sustained the veto on October 17 by vote No. 325 (53–36).

2020

1. S.J.Res.68 (Iran War Powers Resolution)
Vetoed May 6, 2020
The Senate sustained the veto on May 7 by vote No. 84 (49–44).

2. H.J.Res.76 (Borrower Defense Institutional Accountability regulation rule)
Vetoed May 29, 2020
The House sustained the veto on June 26 by vote No. 120 (238–173).

3. H.R.6395 (National Defense Authorization Act for Fiscal Year 2021)
Vetoed December 23, 2020
Veto overridden

2021

1. S.906 (Driftnet Modernization and Bycatch Reduction Act)
Vetoed January 1, 2021

President Trump's Veto of Relating to a National Emergency Declared by the President on February 15, 2019

Following is the text of President Trump's March 15, 2019, veto message on H.J.Res.46, which terminates the national emergency related to the U.S.–Mexico border.

To The House of Representatives:

I am returning herewith without my approval H.J. Res. 46, a joint resolution that would terminate the national emergency I declared regarding the crisis on our southern border in

Proclamation 9844 on February 15, 2019, pursuant to the National Emergencies Act.

As demonstrated by recent statistics published by U.S. Customs and Border Protection (CBP) and explained in testimony given by the Secretary of Homeland Security on March 6, 2019, before the House Committee on Homeland Security, our porous southern border continues to be a magnet for lawless migration and criminals and has created a border security and humanitarian crisis that endangers every American. Last month alone, CBP apprehended more than 76,000 aliens improperly attempting to enter the United States along the southern border—the largest monthly total in the last 5 years. In fiscal year 2018, CBP seized more than 820,000 pounds of drugs at our southern border, including 24,000 pounds of cocaine, 64,000 pounds of methamphetamine, 5,000 pounds of heroin, and 1,800 pounds of fentanyl. In fiscal years 2017 and 2018, immigration officers nationwide made 266,000 arrests of aliens previously charged with or convicted of crimes. These crimes included approximately 100,000 assaults, 30,000 sex crimes, and 4,000 killings. In other words, aliens coming across our border have injured or killed thousands of people, while drugs flowing through the border have killed hundreds of thousands of Americans.

The current situation requires our frontline border enforcement personnel to vastly increase their humanitarian efforts. Along their dangerous trek to the United States, 1 in 3 migrant women experiences sexual abuse, and 7 in 10 migrants are victims of violence. Fifty migrants per day are referred for emergency medical care, and CBP rescues 4,300 people per year who are in danger and distress. The efforts to address this humanitarian catastrophe draw resources away from enforcing our Nation's immigration laws and protecting the border, and place border security personnel at increased risk.

As troubling as these statistics are, they reveal only part of the reality. The situation at the southern border is rapidly deteriorating because of who is arriving and how they are arriving. For many years, the majority of individuals who arrived illegally were single adults from Mexico. Under our existing laws, we could detain and quickly remove most of these aliens. More recently, however, illegal migrants have organized into caravans that include large numbers of families and unaccompanied children from Central American countries. Last year, for example, a record number of families crossed the border illegally. If the current trend holds, the number of families crossing in fiscal year 2019 will greatly surpass last year's record total. Criminal organizations are taking advantage of these large flows of families and unaccompanied minors to conduct dangerous illegal activity, including human trafficking, drug smuggling, and brutal killings.

Under current laws, court decisions, and resource constraints, the Government cannot detain families or undocumented alien children from Central American countries in significant numbers or quickly deport them. Instead, the Government is forced to release many of them into the interior of the United States, pending lengthy judicial proceedings. Although many fail ever to establish any legal right to remain in this country, they stay nonetheless.

This situation on our border cannot be described as anything other than a national emergency, and our Armed Forces are needed to help confront it.

My highest obligation as President is to protect the Nation and its people. Every day, the crisis on our border is deepening, and with new surges of migrants expected in the coming months, we are straining our border enforcement personnel and resources to the breaking point.

H.J. Res. 46 ignores these realities. It is a dangerous resolution that would undermine United States sovereignty and threaten the lives and safety of countless Americans. It is, therefore, my duty to return it to the House of Representatives without my approval.

DONALD J. TRUMP.
THE WHITE HOUSE
March 15, 2019

President Trump's Veto of the Yemen War Powers Resolution

Following is the text of President Trump's April 16, 2019, veto message on S.J.Res.7, removing U.S. forces hostilities in Yemen.

To the Senate of the United States:

I am returning herewith without my approval S.J. Res. 7, a joint resolution that purports to direct the President to remove United States Armed Forces from hostilities in or affecting the Republic of Yemen, with certain exceptions. This resolution is an unnecessary, dangerous attempt to weaken my constitutional authorities, endangering the lives of American citizens and brave service members, both today and in the future.

This joint resolution is unnecessary because, apart from counterterrorism operations against al-Qa'ida in the Arabian Peninsula and ISIS, the United States is not engaged in hostilities in or affecting Yemen. For example, there are no United States military personnel in Yemen commanding, participating in, or accompanying military forces of the Saudi-led coalition against the Houthis in hostilities in or affecting Yemen.

Since 2015, the United States has provided limited support to member countries of the Saudi-led coalition, including intelligence sharing, logistics support, and, until recently, in-flight refueling of non-United States aircraft. All of this support is consistent with applicable Arms Export Control Act authorities, statutory authorities that permit the Department of Defense to provide logistics support to foreign countries, and the President's constitutional power as Commander in Chief. None of this support has introduced United States military personnel into hostilities.

We are providing this support for many reasons. First and foremost, it is our duty to protect the safety of the more than 80,000 Americans who reside in certain coalition countries that have been subject to Houthi attacks from Yemen. Houthis, supported by Iran, have used missiles, armed drones, and explosive boats to attack civilian and military targets in those coalition countries, including areas frequented by American citizens, such as the airport in Riyadh, Saudi Arabia. In addition, the conflict in Yemen represents a "cheap" and inexpensive way for Iran to cause trouble for the United States and for our ally, Saudi Arabia.

S.J. Res. 7 is also dangerous. The Congress should not seek to prohibit certain tactical operations, such as in-flight refueling, or require military engagements to adhere to arbitrary timelines. Doing so would interfere with the President's constitutional authority as Commander in Chief of the Armed Forces, and could endanger our service members by impairing their ability to efficiently and effectively conduct military engagements and to withdraw in an orderly manner at the appropriate time.

The joint resolution would also harm the foreign policy of the United States. Its efforts to curtail certain forms of military support would harm our bilateral relationships, negatively affect our ongoing efforts to prevent civilian casualties and prevent the spread of terrorist organizations such as al-Qa'ida in the Arabian Peninsula and ISIS, and embolden Iran's malign activities in Yemen.

We cannot end the conflict in Yemen through political documents like S.J. Res. 7. Peace in Yemen requires a negotiated settlement. Unfortunately, inaction by the Senate has left vacant key diplomatic positions, impeding our ability to engage regional partners in support of the United Nations-led peace process. To help end the conflict, promote humanitarian and commercial access, prevent civilian casualties, enhance efforts to recover American hostages in Yemen, and defeat terrorists that seek to harm the United States, the Senate must act to confirm my nominees for many critical foreign policy positions.

I agree with the Congress about the need to address our engagements in foreign wars. As I said in my State of the Union address in February, great nations do not fight endless wars. My Administration is currently accelerating negotiations to end our military engagement in Afghanistan and drawing down troops in Syria, where we recently succeeded in eliminating 100 percent of the ISIS caliphate. Congressional engagement in those endeavors would be far more productive than expending time and effort trying to enact this unnecessary and dangerous resolution that interferes with our foreign policy with respect to Yemen.

For these reasons, it is my duty to return S.J. Res. 7 to the Senate without my approval.

DONALD J TRUMP.
THE WHITE HOUSE
April 16, 2019

President Trump's Veto of the Saudi Arabia and United Kingdom of Great Britain and Northern Ireland Arms Sales Disapproval Resolution

Following is the text of President Trump's July 24, 2019, veto message on S.J.Res.38, prohibiting the sale of certain defense items to Saudi Arabia and the United Kingdom.

To the Senate of the United States:

I am returning herewith without my approval S.J. Res. 38, a joint resolution that would prohibit the issuance of export licenses for the proposed transfer of defense articles, defense services, and technical data to support the manufacture of the Aurora Fuzing System for the Paveway IV Precision Guided Bomb Program in regard to the Kingdom of Saudi Arabia and the United Kingdom of Great Britain and Northern Ireland. This resolution would weaken America's global competitiveness and damage the important relationships we share with our allies and partners.

In particular, S.J. Res. 38 would prohibit the issuance of export licenses for the proposed transfer of defense articles, defense services, and technical data for the manufacturing of the Aurora Fuzing System for the Paveway IV Precision Guided Bomb

Program. The misguided licensing prohibition in the joint resolution directly conflicts with the foreign policy and national security objectives of the United States, which include strengthening defense alliances with friendly countries throughout the world, deepening partnerships that preserve and extend our global influence, and enhancing our competitiveness in key markets. Apart from negatively affecting our bilateral relationships with Saudi Arabia and the United Kingdom, the joint resolution would hamper the ability of the United States to sustain and shape critical security cooperation activities. S.J. Res. 38 would also damage the credibility of the United States as a reliable partner by signaling that we are willing to abandon our partners and allies at the very moment when threats to them are increasing.

The United States is providing the licenses that the joint resolution seeks to prohibit for many reasons. First and foremost, it is our solemn duty to protect the safety of the more than 80,000 United States citizens who reside in Saudi Arabia and who are imperiled by Houthi attacks from Yemen. The Houthis, supported by Iran, have attacked civilian and military facilities using missiles, armed drones, and explosive boats, including in areas frequented by United States citizens, such as the airport in Riyadh, Saudi Arabia. Second, the joint resolution would degrade Saudi Arabia's military preparedness and ability to protect its sovereignty, directly affecting its ability to defend United States military personnel hosted there. Third, Saudi Arabia is a bulwark against the malign activities of Iran and its proxies in the region, and the licenses the joint resolution would prohibit enhance Saudi Arabia's ability to deter and defend against these threats.

In addition, S.J. Res. 38 would negatively affect our NATO Allies and the transatlantic defense industry. It could, for example, produce unintended consequences for defense procurement and interoperability with and between our partners. It could also create diplomatic and security opportunities for our adversaries to exploit.

Finally, by restricting the ability of our partners to produce and purchase precision-guided munitions, S.J. Res. 38 would likely prolong the conflict in Yemen and deepen the suffering it causes. By undermining bilateral relationships of the United States and impeding our ability to support key partners at a critical time, the joint resolution would harm—not help—efforts to end the conflict in Yemen. And without precision-guided munitions, more—not fewer—civilians are likely to become casualties of the conflict. While I share concerns that certain Members of Congress have expressed about civilian casualties of this conflict, the United States has taken and will continue to take action to minimize such casualties, including training and advising the Saudi-led Coalition forces to improve their targeting processes.

The United States is very concerned about the conflict's toll on innocent civilians and is working to bring the conflict in Yemen to an end. But we cannot end it through ill-conceived and time-consuming resolutions that fail to address its root causes. Rather than expend time and resources on such resolutions, I encourage the Congress to direct its efforts toward supporting our work to achieve peace through a negotiated settlement to the conflict in Yemen.

For these reasons, it is my duty to return S.J. Res. 38 to the Senate without my approval.

DONALD J. TRUMP.
THE WHITE HOUSE
July 24, 2019

President Trump's Veto of the UAE Arms Sales Disapproval Resolution

Following is the text of President Trump's July 24, 2019, veto message on S.J.Res.37, prohibiting the sale of defense items and support services to the United Arab Emirates, the United Kingdom, and France.

To the Senate of the United States:

I am returning herewith without my approval S.J. Res. 37, a joint resolution that would prohibit the issuance of export licenses for certain defense articles, defense services, and technical data to support the transfer of Paveway II kits to the United Arab Emirates (UAE), the United Kingdom of Great Britain and Northern Ireland, and the Republic of France. This resolution would weaken America's global competitiveness and damage the important relationships we share with our allies and partners.

In particular, S.J. Res. 37 would prohibit the issuance of export licenses for Paveway II kits to the UAE, the United Kingdom, and France. The misguided licensing prohibitions in the joint resolution directly conflict with the foreign policy and national security objectives of the United States, which include strengthening defense alliances with friendly countries throughout the world, deepening partnerships that preserve and extend our global influence, and enhancing our competitiveness in key markets. Apart from negatively affecting our bilateral relationships with the UAE, the United Kingdom, and France, the joint resolution would hamper the ability of the United States to sustain and shape critical security cooperation activities with those partners. S.J. Res. 37 would also damage the credibility of the United States as a reliable partner by signaling that we are willing to abandon our partners and allies at the very moment when threats to them are increasing.

The United States is providing the licenses that the joint resolution seeks to prohibit for many reasons. First and foremost, it is our solemn duty to protect the safety of the more than 80,000 United States citizens who reside in Saudi Arabia and are imperiled by Houthis attacking from Yemen using missiles, armed drones, and explosive boats. The UAE is an important part of the Saudi-led Coalition that helps protect Americans from these Iranian-supported Houthi attacks on civilian and military facilities, including those located in areas frequented by United States citizens like the airport in Riyadh, Saudi Arabia. Second, the joint resolution would degrade the UAE's military preparedness and ability to protect its sovereignty, directly affecting its ability to defend the thousands of United States military personnel hosted there. Third, the UAE is a bulwark against the malign activities of Iran and its proxies in the region. It is also an active partner with the United States in combatting terrorism in Yemen and elsewhere. The licenses the joint resolution would prohibit enhance our partner's ability to deter and defend against these threats.

In addition, S.J. Res. 37 would negatively affect our NATO Allies and the transatlantic defense industry. It could, for example, produce unintended consequences for defense procurement and interoperability with and between our partners. It could also create diplomatic and security opportunities for our adversaries to exploit.

Finally, by restricting the ability of our partners to produce and purchase precision-guided munitions, S.J. Res. 37 would likely prolong the conflict in Yemen and deepen the suffering it causes. By undermining bilateral relationships of the United States and impeding our ability to support key partners at a critical time, the joint resolution would harm—not help—efforts to end the conflict in Yemen. And without precision-guided munitions, more—not fewer—civilians are likely to become casualties of the conflict. While I share concerns that certain Members of Congress have expressed about civilian casualties of this conflict, the United States has taken and will continue to take action to minimize such casualties, including training and advising the Saudi-led Coalition forces to improve their targeting processes.

The United States is very concerned about the conflict's toll on innocent civilians and is working to bring the conflict in Yemen to an end. But we cannot end it through ill-conceived and time-consuming resolutions that fail to address its root causes. Rather than expend time and resources on such resolutions, I encourage the Congress to direct its efforts toward supporting our work to achieve peace through a negotiated settlement to the conflict in Yemen.

For these reasons, it is my duty to return S.J. Res. 37 to the Senate without my approval.

DONALD J TRUMP.
THE WHITE HOUSE
July 24, 2019

President Trump's Veto of the Saudi Arabia, United Kingdom of Great Britain and Northern Ireland, Kingdom of Spain, and Italian Republic Arms Sales Disapproval Resolution

Following is the text of President Trump's July 24, 2019, veto message on S.J.Res.36, prohibiting the sale of certain defense articles and support services to Saudi Arabia, the United Kingdom, Spain, and Italy.

To the Senate of the United States:

I am returning herewith without my approval S.J. Res. 36, a joint resolution that would prohibit the issuance of certain licenses with respect to several proposed agreements or transfers to the Kingdom of Saudi Arabia, the United Kingdom of Great Britain and Northern Ireland, the Kingdom of Spain, and the Italian Republic. This resolution would weaken America's global competitiveness and damage the important relationships we share with our allies and partners.

In particular, S.J. Res. 36 would prohibit licensing for manufacturing in Saudi Arabia of Guidance Electronics Detector Assemblies, Computer Control Groups, Airfoil Groups, Aircraft Umbilical Interconnect Systems, Fuses, and other components to support the production of Paveway II, Enhanced Paveway II, and Paveway IV munitions. The misguided licensing prohibitions in the joint resolution directly conflict with the foreign policy and national security objectives of the United States, which include strengthening defense alliances with friendly countries throughout the world, deepening partnerships that preserve and extend

our global influence, and enhancing our competitiveness in key markets. Apart from negatively affecting our bilateral relationships with Saudi Arabia, the United Kingdom, Spain, and Italy, the joint resolution would hamper the ability of the United States to sustain and shape critical security cooperation activities. S.J. Res. 36 would also damage the credibility of the United States as a reliable partner by signaling that we are willing to abandon our partners and allies at the very moment when threats to them are increasing.

The United States is providing the licenses that the joint resolution seeks to prohibit for many reasons. First and foremost, it is our solemn duty to protect the safety of the more than 80,000 United States citizens who reside in Saudi Arabia and who are imperiled by Houthi attacks from Yemen. The Houthis, supported by Iran, have attacked civilian and military facilities using missiles, armed drones, and explosive boats, including in areas frequented by United States citizens, such as the airport in Riyadh, Saudi Arabia. Second, the joint resolution would degrade Saudi Arabia's military preparedness and ability to protect its sovereignty, directly affecting its ability to defend United States military personnel hosted there. Third, Saudi Arabia is a bulwark against the malign activities of Iran and its proxies in the region, and the licenses the joint resolution would prohibit enhance Saudi Arabia's ability to deter and defend against these threats.

In addition, S.J. Res. 36 would negatively affect our NATO Allies and the transatlantic defense industry. It could, for example, produce unintended consequences for defense procurement and interoperability with and between our partners. It could also create diplomatic and security opportunities for our adversaries to exploit.

Finally, by restricting the ability of our partners to produce and purchase precision-guided munitions, S.J. Res. 36 would likely prolong the conflict in Yemen and deepen the suffering it causes. By undermining bilateral relationships of the United States and impeding our ability to support key partners at a critical time, the joint resolution would harm—not help—efforts to end the conflict in Yemen. And without precision-guided munitions, more—not fewer—civilians are likely to become casualties of the conflict. While I share concerns that certain Members of Congress have expressed about civilian casualties of this conflict, the United States has taken and will continue to take action to minimize such casualties, including training and advising Saudi-led Coalition forces to improve their targeting processes.

The United States is very concerned about the conflict's toll on innocent civilians, and is working to bring the conflict in Yemen to an end. But we cannot end it through ill-conceived and time-consuming resolutions that fail to address its root causes. Rather than expend time and resources on such resolutions, I encourage the Congress to direct its efforts toward supporting our work to achieve peace through a negotiated settlement to the conflict in Yemen.

For these reasons, it is my duty to return S.J. Res. 36 to the Senate without my approval.

DONALD J TRUMP.
THE WHITE HOUSE
July 24, 2019

President Trump's Veto of Relating to a National Emergency Declared by the President on February 15, 2019

Following is the text of President Trump's October 15, 2019, veto message on S.J.Res.54, ending the national emergency at the U.S.-Mexico border.

To the Senate of the United States:

I am returning herewith without my approval S.J. Res. 54, a joint resolution that would terminate the national emergency I declared in Proclamation 9844 of February 15, 2019, pursuant to the National Emergencies Act, regarding the ongoing crisis on our southern border. I am doing so for the same reasons I returned an identical resolution, H.J. Res. 46, to the House of Representatives without my approval on March 15, 2019.

Proclamation 9844 has helped the Federal Government address the national emergency on our southern border. It has empowered my Administration's Government-wide strategy to counter large-scale unlawful migration and to respond to corresponding humanitarian challenges through focused application of every Constitutional and statutory authority at our disposal. It has also facilitated the military's ongoing construction of virtually insurmountable physical barriers along hundreds of miles of our southern border.

The southern border, however, continues to be a major entry point for criminals, gang members, and illicit narcotics to come into our country. As explained in Proclamation 9844, in my veto message regarding H.J. Res. 46, and in congressional testimony from multiple Administration officials, the ongoing crisis at the southern border threatens core national security interests. In addition, security challenges at the southern border exacerbate an ongoing humanitarian crisis that threatens the well-being of vulnerable populations, including women and children.

In short, the situation on our southern border remains a national emergency, and our Armed Forces are still needed to help confront it.

Like H.J. Res. 46, S.J. Res. 54 would undermine the Government's ability to address this continuing national emergency. It would, among other things, impair the Government's capacity to secure the Nation's southern borders against unlawful entry and to curb the trafficking and smuggling that fuels the present humanitarian crisis.

S.J. Res. 54 is also inconsistent with other recent congressional actions. For example, the Congress, in an overwhelmingly bipartisan manner, has provided emergency resources to address the crisis at the southern border. Additionally, the Congress has approved a budget framework that expressly preserves the emergency authorities my Administration is using to address the crisis.

Proclamation 9844 was neither a new nor novel application of executive authority. Rather, it is the sixtieth Presidential invocation of the National Emergencies Act of 1976. It relies upon the same statutory authority used by both of the previous two Presidents to undertake more than 18 different military construction projects from 2001 through 2013. And it has withstood judicial challenge in the Supreme Court.

Earlier this year, I vetoed H.J. Res. 46 because it was a dangerous resolution that would undermine United States sovereignty

and threaten the lives and safety of countless Americans. It was, therefore, my duty to return it to the House of Representatives without my approval. It is similarly my duty, in order to protect the safety and security of our Nation, to return S.J. Res. 54 to the Senate without my approval.

DONALD J TRUMP.
THE WHITE HOUSE
October 15, 2019

President Trump's Veto of the Iran War Powers Resolution

Following is the text of President Trump's May 6, 2020, veto message on S.J.Res.68, which directs the President to end the use of U.S. forces against hostilities in Iran unless necessary and authorized by Congress in the event of war or specific military use.

To the Senate of the United States:

I am returning herewith without my approval S.J. Res. 68, a joint resolution that purports to direct the President to terminate the use of United States Armed Forces in hostilities against Iran. This indefinite prohibition is unnecessary and dangerous. It would weaken the President's authority in violation of Article II of the Constitution, and endanger the lives of American citizens and brave service members.

This joint resolution is unnecessary because it rests upon a faulty premise. Due to my decisive actions and effective policies, the United States is not engaged in the use of force against Iran. As Commander in Chief, I will always defend our Nation against threats to our security.

In response to an escalating series of attacks by Iran and Iranian-backed militias on United States forces and interests in the Middle East, on January 2, 2020, United States Armed Forces eliminated Qassem Soleimani, the head of Iran's Islamic Revolutionary Guard Corps-Qods Force as he was traveling in Iraq. The purposes of this strike were to protect United States personnel, deter Iran from conducting or supporting further attacks against United States forces and interests, degrade the ability of Iran and Qods Force-backed militias to conduct attacks, and end Iran's strategic escalation of attacks against and threats to United States interests.

On January 7, 2020, Iran launched 16 ballistic missiles against United States and coalition forces in Iraq. These attacks resulted in no fatalities. The next day, in an address to the Nation, I noted that "Iran appears to be standing down" and emphasized that "the United States is ready to embrace peace with all who seek it."

One day later, this resolution was introduced. Its apparent aim was to prevent an escalation in hostilities between the United States and Iran. Yet no such escalation has occurred over the past 4 months, contrary to the often dire and confident predictions of many.

S.J. Res. 68 is also unnecessary because it incorrectly implies that the military airstrike against Qassem Soleimani in Iraq was conducted without statutory authority. The resolution states that "the 2001 Authorization for Use of Military Force (Public Law 107–40; 50 U.S.C. 1541 note) against the perpetrators of the 9/11 attack and the Authorization for Use of Military Force Against Iraq Resolution of 2002 (Public Law 107–243; 50 U.S.C. 1541 notes) do not serve as a specific statutory authorization for use of force against Iran." The strike against Soleimani, however, was

fully authorized under both the Authorization for Use of Military Force Against Iraq Resolution of 2002 ("2002 AUMF") and the President's constitutional authorities as Commander in Chief and Chief Executive.

The United States has long relied upon the 2002 AUMF to authorize the use of force for the purpose of establishing a stable, democratic Iraq and for addressing terrorist threats emanating from Iraq. Such uses of force need not address only threats from the Iraqi Government apparatus, but may also address threats to the United States posed by militias, terrorist groups, or other armed groups in Iraq. This has been a consistent application of the statute across Administrations, including the last Administration, which relied upon it to conduct operations in response to attacks and threats by Iran-backed militias in Iraq. Moreover, under Article II, the President is empowered to direct the use of military force to protect the Nation from an attack or threat of imminent attack and to protect important national interests.

In addition, S.J. Res. 68 is dangerous because it could hinder the President's ability to protect United States forces, allies, and partners, including Israel, from the continued threat posed by Iran and Iranian-backed militias. The resolution states that it should not "be construed to prevent the United States from defending itself from imminent attack." But this overlooks the President's need to respond to threats beyond imminent attacks on the United States and its forces.

Protecting the national security of the United States involves taking actions to de-escalate threats around the world, including threats posed by Iran and Iranian-backed militias. Iran and Iranian-backed militias have a long history of attacking United States and coalition forces. As demonstrated by the recent indirect fire attacks on January 26, 2020, on the U.S. Embassy in Baghdad and on March 11 and 14, 2020, on Camp Taji, Iraq, Iran and Iranian-backed militias continue to present a threat. This resolution would impede the President's ability to counter adversarial forces by anticipating their next moves and taking swift actions to address them decisively.

For all of these reasons, I cannot support this joint resolution. My Administration has taken strong actions, within statutory authority, to help keep our Nation safe, and I will not approve this resolution, which would undermine my ability to protect American citizens, service members, and interests. Therefore, it is my duty to return S.J. Res. 68 to the Senate without my approval.

DONALD J TRUMP.
THE WHITE HOUSE
May 6, 2020

President Trump's Veto of the Borrower Defense Institutional Accountability Regulation Rule

Following is the text of President Trump's May 29, 2020, veto message on H.J.Res.76, nullifying the Department of Education's rule which required student loan borrowers to apply to ED for a defense to repayment.

To the House of Representatives:

I am returning herewith without my approval H.J. Res. 76, a joint resolution that would undermine the efforts of my

Administration to protect students and taxpayers by nullifying the Borrower Defense Institutional Accountability Regulation, which the Department of Education published in the Federal Register on September 23, 2019, following extensive public hearings and public comment.

The Borrower Defense Institutional Accountability rule sets forth clear standards for borrower defense to repayment, providing needed transparency to both students and schools. Under this rule, a fair process will deliver deserved relief to students harmed by their educational institutions. Whereas the last administration promoted a regulatory environment that produced precipitous school closures and stranded students, this new rule puts the needs of students first, extends the window during which they can qualify for loan discharge, and encourages schools to provide students with opportunities to complete their educations and continue their pursuit of economic success. H.J. Res. 76 would return the country to a regulatory regime in which the Federal Government and State attorneys general, rather than students, determine the kinds of education students need and which schools they should be allowed to attend.

American higher education must transform to better meet the needs of today's students. My Administration stands ready to work with the Congress to foster the development of a more affordable, more flexible, and more innovative system of higher education that is better able to meet the educational needs of our students, and in which schools take on more responsibility for the success of the students who enroll in their programs.

H.J. Res. 76 is a misguided resolution that would increase costs for American students and undermine their ability to make choices about their education in order to best meet their needs. For these reasons, it is my duty to return H.J. Res. 76 to the House of Representatives without my approval.

DONALD J TRUMP.
THE WHITE HOUSE
May 29, 2020

President Trump's Veto of the National Defense Authorization Act for Fiscal Year 2021

Following is the text of President Trump's December 23, 2020, veto message on H.R.6395, authorizing FY2021 appropriations and outlining policies directed to the DOD and other programs.

To the House of Representatives:

I am returning, without my approval, H.R. 6395, the National Defense Authorization Act for Fiscal Year 2021 (the "Act"). My Administration recognizes the importance of the Act to our national security. Unfortunately, the Act fails to include critical national security measures, includes provisions that fail to respect our veterans and our military's history, and contradicts efforts by my Administration to put America first in our national security and foreign policy actions. It is a "gift" to China and Russia.

No one has worked harder, or approved more money for the military, than I have—over $2 trillion. During my 4 years, with the support of many others, we have almost entirely rebuilt the United States military, which was totally depleted when I took office. Your failure to terminate the very dangerous national security risk of Section 230 will make our intelligence virtually impossible to

conduct without everyone knowing what we are doing at every step. The Act fails even to make any meaningful changes to Section 230 of the Communications Decency Act, despite bipartisan calls for repealing that provision. Section 230 facilitates the spread of foreign disinformation online, which is a serious threat to our national security and election integrity. It must be repealed.

Additionally, the Act includes language that would require the renaming of certain military installations. Over the course of United States history, these locations have taken on significance to the American story and those who have helped write it that far transcends their namesakes. My Administration respects the legacy of the millions of American servicemen and women who have served with honor at these military bases, and who, from these locations, have fought, bled, and died for their country. From these facilities, we have won two World Wars. I have been clear in my opposition to politically motivated attempts like this to wash away history and to dishonor the immense progress our country has fought for in realizing our founding principles.

The Act also restricts the President's ability to preserve our Nation's security by arbitrarily limiting the amount of military construction funds that can be used to respond to a national emergency. In a time when adversaries have the means to directly attack the homeland, the President must be able to safeguard the American people without having to wait for congressional authorization. The Act also contains an amendment that would slow down the rollout of nationwide 5G, especially in rural areas.

Numerous provisions of the Act directly contradict my Administration's foreign policy, particularly my efforts to bring our troops home. I oppose endless wars, as does the American public. Over bipartisan objections, however, this Act purports to restrict the President's ability to withdraw troops from Afghanistan, Germany, and South Korea. Not only is this bad policy, but it is unconstitutional.

Article II of the Constitution makes the President the Commander in Chief of the Army and Navy of the United States and vests in him the executive power. Therefore, the decision regarding how many troops to deploy and where, including in Afghanistan, Germany, and South Korea, rests with him. The Congress may not arrogate this authority to itself directly or indirectly as purported spending restrictions.

For all of these reasons, I cannot support this bill. My Administration has taken strong actions to help keep our Nation safe and support our service members. I will not approve this bill, which would put the interests of the Washington, D.C. establishment over those of the American people. It is my duty to return H.R. 6395 to the House of Representatives without my approval.

DONALD J TRUMP.
THE WHITE HOUSE
December 23, 2020

President Trump's Veto of the Driftnet Modernization and Bycatch Reduction Act

Following is the text of President Trump's January 1, 2021, veto message on S.906, seeking to phase out driftnet fishing.

To the Senate of the United States:

I am returning, without my approval, S. 906, the Driftnet Modernization and Bycatch Reduction Act. America's fishermen

have made great sacrifices to ensure that our Nation's marine fisheries are a sustainable economic engine for coastal communities. Under my Administration, the number of United States fish stocks subject to overfishing is at a historic low. This achievement is the result of a transparent and collaborative regulatory process that is supported by regional fishery management councils. At council meetings, fishermen work with Federal Government and State government representatives to meet their statutory obligations under the Magnuson-Stevens Fishery Conservation and Management Act.

In passing S. 906, the Congress has ignored the fact that the regional fishery management process has had strong, bipartisan support since its creation. By forcing the West Coast drift gillnet fishery to use alternative gear that has not been proven to be an economically viable substitute for gillnets, the Congress is effectively terminating the fishery. As a result, an estimated 30 fishing vessels, all of which are operated by family-owned small businesses, will no longer be able to bring their bounty to shore. At a time when our Nation has a seafood trade deficit of nearly $17 billion, S. 906 will exacerbate this imbalance.

Further, S. 906 will not achieve its purported conservation benefits. The West Coast drift gillnet fishery is subject to robust legal and regulatory requirements for environmental protection that equal or exceed the environmental protections that apply to foreign fisheries. Without this fishery, Americans will import more swordfish and other species from foreign sources that frequently have more bycatch than our own fisheries. If the Congress wants to address bycatch, it should insist on a level playing field for imported seafood instead of crushing American fishing families.

My Administration has done more for American fishermen than any President before me. On May 7, 2020, I signed an Executive Order on Promoting American Seafood Competitiveness and Economic Growth to bolster our domestic seafood industry while curbing illegal, unreported, and unregulated fishing abroad. On June 5, 2020, I issued a Proclamation on Modifying the Northeast Canyons and Seamounts Marine National Monument to open it to commercial fishing that is conducted in accordance with the Magnuson-Stevens Act and other applicable laws, regulations, and requirements. And as fishermen struggled to stay on the water during the pandemic, I issued a Memorandum on Protecting the United States Lobster Industry and later made approximately $530 million available, through the U.S. Department of Agriculture's Seafood Trade Relief Program, to support the United States seafood industry and fishermen affected by retaliatory tariffs from foreign governments.

My Administration would support provisions of the enrolled bill, if passed separately, which would authorize fee collection in a different fishery—the Pacific Halibut fishery. This authority is needed to implement a provision of the International Pacific Halibut Commission Convention, to which the United States is a party. However, for the sake of American fishermen nationwide, I will not let the Congress circumvent the fisheries management process by effectively terminating a fishery without appropriate consultation and input from fishery management councils. If this occurred, it would increase our reliance on imported seafood and take away the livelihoods of hard-working Americans and their family businesses. It is my duty to return S. 906 to the Senate without my approval.

DONALD J TRUMP.
THE WHITE HOUSE
January 1, 2021

Political Charts

Summary of Presidential Elections, 1789–2020

Year	No. of States	Candidates	Party	Electoral Vote	Popular Vote
1789[1]	10	**George Washington**	**Fed.**	**69**	—[2]
		John Adams	Fed.	34	
1792[1]	15	**George Washington**	**Fed.**	**132**	—[2]
		John Adams	Fed.	77	
1796[1]	16	**John Adams**	**Fed.**	**71**	—[2]
		Thomas Jefferson	Dem.-Rep.	68	
1800[1]	16	**Thomas Jefferson**	**Dem.-Rep.**	**73**	—[2]
		Aaron Burr	Dem.-Rep.	73	
		John Adams	Fed.	65	
		Charles Cotesworth Pinckney	Fed.	64	
1804	17	**Thomas Jefferson**	**Dem.-Rep.**	**162**	—[2]
		George Clinton			
		Charles Cotesworth Pinckney	Fed.	64	
		Rufus King			
1808	17	**James Madison**	**Dem.-Rep.**	**122**	—[2]
		George Clinton			
		Charles Cotesworth Pinckney	Fed.	64	
		Rufus King			
1812	18	**James Madison**	**Dem.-Rep.**	**128**	—[2]
		Elbridge Gerry			
		George Clinton	Fed.	89	
		Jared Ingersoll			
1816	19	**James Monroe**	**Dem.-Rep.**	**183**	—[2]
		Daniel D. Tompkins			
		Rufus King	Fed.	34	
		John Howard			
1820	24	**James Monroe**	**Dem.-Rep.**	**231**[3]	—[2]
		Daniel D. Tompkins			
1824[4]	24	**John Quincy Adams**	**Dem.-Rep.**	**99**	113,122 (30.9%)
		John C. Calhoun			
		Andrew Jackson	Dem.-Rep.	84	151,271 (41.3%)
		Nathan Sanford			
1828	24	**Andrew Jackson**	**Dem.-Rep.**	**178**	642,553 (56.0%)
		John C. Calhoun			
		John Quincy Adams	Nat.-Rep.	83	500,897 (43.6%)
		Richard Rush			
1832[5]	24	**Andrew Jackson**	**Dem.**	**219**	701,780 (54.2%)
		Martin Van Buren			
		Henry Clay	Nat.-Rep.	49	484,205 (37.4%)
		John Sergeant			
1836[6]	26	**Martin Van Buren**	**Dem.**	**170**	764,176 (50.8%)
		Richard M. Johnson			
		William Henry Harrison	Whig	73	550,816 (36.6%)
		Francis Granger			
1840	26	**William Henry Harrison**	**Whig**	**234**	**1,275,390 (52.9%)**
		John Tyler			
		Martin Van Buren	Dem.	60	1,128,854 (46.8%)
		Richard M. Johnson			
1844	26	**James K. Polk**	**Dem.**	**170**	**1,339,494 (49.5%)**
		George M. Dallas			
		Henry Clay	Whig	105	1,300,004 (48.1%)
		Theodore Frelinghuysen			
1848	30	**Zachary Taylor**	**Whig**	**163**	**1,361,393 (47.3%)**
		Millard Fillmore			
		Lewis Cass	Dem.	127	1,223,460 (42.5%)
		William O. Butler			
1852	31	**Franklin Pierce**	**Dem.**	**254**	**1,607,510 (50.8%)**
		William R. King			
		Winfield Scott	Whig	42	1,386,942 (43.9%)
		William A. Graham			
1856[7]	31	**James Buchanan**	**Dem.**	**174**	**1,836,072 (45.3%)**
		John C. Breckinridge			
		John C. Fremont	Rep.	114	1,342,345 (33.1%)
		William L. Dayton			
1860[8]	33	**Abraham Lincoln**	**Rep.**	**180**	**1,865,908 (39.8%)**
		Hannibal Hamlin			
		Stephen A. Douglas	Dem.	12	1,380,202 (29.5%)
		Herschel V. Johnson			
1864[9]	36	**Abraham Lincoln**	**Rep.**	**212**	**2,218,388 (55.0%)**
		Andrew Johnson			
		George B. McClellan	Dem.	21	1,812,807 (45.0%)
		George H. Pendleton			
1868[10]	37	**Ulysses S. Grant**	**Rep.**	**214**	3,013,650 (52.7%)
		Schuyler Colfax			
		Horatio Seymour	Dem.	80	2,708,744 (47.3%)
		Francis P. Blair Jr.			
1872	37	**Ulysses S. Grant**	**Rep.**	**286**	3,598,235 (55.6%)
		Henry Wilson			
		Horace Greeley	Dem.	—[11]	2,834,761 (43.8%)
		Benjamin Gratz Brown			
1876	38	**Rutherford B. Hayes**	**Rep.**	**185**	4,034,311 (47.9%)
		William A. Wheeler			
		Samuel J. Tilden	Dem.	184	4,288,546 (51.0%)
		Thomas A. Hendricks			
1880	38	**James A. Garfield**	**Rep.**	**214**	4,446,158 (48.3%)
		Chester A. Arthur			
		Winfield S. Hancock	Dem.	155	4,444,260 (48.2%)
		William H. English			
1884	38	**Grover Cleveland**	**Dem.**	**219**	4,874,621 (48.5%)
		Thomas A. Hendricks			
		James G. Blaine	Rep.	182	4,848,936 (48.2%)
		John A. Logan			
1888	38	**Benjamin Harrison**	**Rep.**	**233**	5,443,892 (47.8%)
		Levi P. Morton			
		Grover Cleveland	Dem.	168	5,534,488 (48.6%)
		Allen G. Thurman			
1892[12]	44	**Grover Cleveland**	**Dem.**	**277**	5,551,883 (46.1%)
		Adlai E. Stevenson			
		Benjamin Harrison	Rep.	145	5,179,244 (43.0%)
		Whitelaw Reid			

Year	No. of States	Candidates	Party	Electoral Vote	Popular Vote
1896	45	**William McKinley** *Garret A. Hobart*	**Rep.**	**271**	**7,108,480 (51.0%)**
		William J. Bryan *Arthur Sewall*	Dem.	176	6,511,495 (46.7%)
1900	45	**William McKinley** *Theodore Roosevelt*	**Rep.**	**292**	**7,218,039 (51.7%)**
		William J. Bryan *Adlai E. Stevenson*	Dem.	155	6,358,345 (45.5%)
1904	45	**Theodore Roosevelt** *Charles W. Fairbanks*	**Rep.**	**336**	**7,626,593 (56.4%)**
		Alton B. Parker *Henry G. Davis*	Dem.	140	5,028,898 (37.6%)
1908	46	**William Howard Taft** *James S. Sherman*	**Rep.**	**321**	**7,676,258 (51.6%)**
		William J. Bryan *John W. Kern*	Dem.	162	6,406,801 (43.0%)
1912[13]	48	**Woodrow Wilson** *Thomas R. Marshall*	**Dem.**	**435**	**6,293,152 (41.8%)**
		William Howard Taft *James S. Sherman*	Rep.	8	3,486,333 (23.2%)
1916	48	**Woodrow Wilson** *Thomas R. Marshall*	**Dem.**	**277**	**9,126,300 (49.2%)**
		Charles E. Hughes *Charles W. Fairbanks*	Rep.	254	8,546,789 (46.1%)
1920	48	**Warren G. Harding** *Calvin Coolidge*	**Rep.**	**404**	**16,133,314 (60.3%)**
		James M. Cox *Franklin D. Roosevelt*	Dem.	127	9,140,884 (34.2%)
1924[14]	48	**Calvin Coolidge** *Charles G. Dawes*	**Rep.**	**382**	**15,717,553 (54.1%)**
		John W. Davis *Charles W. Bryan*	Dem.	136	8,386,169 (28.8%)
1928	48	**Herbert C. Hoover** *Charles Curtis*	**Rep.**	**444**	**21,411,991 (58.2%)**
		Alfred E. Smith *Joseph T. Robinson*	Dem.	87	15,000,185 (40.8%)
1932	48	**Franklin D. Roosevelt** *John N. Garner*	**Dem.**	**472**	**22,825,016 (57.4%)**
		Herbert C. Hoover *Charles Curtis*	Rep.	59	15,758,397 (39.6%)
1936	48	**Franklin D. Roosevelt** *John N. Garner*	**Dem.**	**523**	**27,747,636 (60.8%)**
		Alfred M. Landon *Frank Knox*	Rep.	8	16,679,543 (36.5%)
1940	48	**Franklin D. Roosevelt** *Henry A. Wallace*	**Dem.**	**449**	**27,263,448 (54.7%)**
		Wendell L. Willkie *Charles L. McNary*	Rep.	82	22,336,260 (44.8%)
1944	48	**Franklin D. Roosevelt** *Harry S. Truman*	**Dem.**	**432**	**25,611,936 (53.4%)**
		Thomas E. Dewey *John W. Bricker*	Rep.	99	22,013,372 (45.9%)
1948[15]	48	**Harry S. Truman** *Alben W. Barkley*	**Dem.**	**303**	**24,105,587 (49.5%)**
		Thomas E. Dewey *Earl Warren*	Rep.	198	21,970,017 (45.1%)
1952	48	**Dwight D. Eisenhower** *Richard M. Nixon*	**Rep.**	**442**	**33,936,137 (55.1%)**
		Adlai E. Stevenson II *John J. Sparkman*	Dem.	89	27,314,649 (44.4%)
1956[16]	48	**Dwight D. Eisenhower** *Richard M. Nixon*	**Rep.**	**457**	**35,585,245 (57.4%)**
		Adlai E. Stevenson II *Estes Kefauver*	Dem.	73	26,030,172 (42.0%)
1960[17]	50	**John F. Kennedy** *Lyndon B. Johnson*	**Dem.**	**303**	**34,221,344 (49.7%)**
		Richard Nixon *Henry Cabot Lodge*	Rep.	219	34,106,671 (49.5%)
1964	50*	**Lyndon B. Johnson** *Hubert H. Humphrey*	**Dem.**	**486**	**43,126,584 (61.1%)**
		Barry Goldwater *William E. Miller*	Rep.	52	27,177,838 (38.5%)
1968[18]	50*	**Richard Nixon** *Spiro T. Agnew*	**Rep.**	**301**	**31,785,148 (43.4%)**
		Hubert H. Humphrey *Edmund S. Muskie*	Dem.	191	31,274,503 (42.7%)
1972[19]	50*	**Richard Nixon** *Spiro T. Agnew*	**Rep.**	**520**	**47,170,179 (60.7%)**
		George McGovern *Sargent Shriver*	Dem.	17	29,171,791 (37.5%)
1976[20]	50*	**Jimmy Carter** *Walter F. Mondale*	**Dem.**	**297**	**40,830,763 (50.1%)**
		Gerald R. Ford *Robert Dole*	Rep.	240	39,147,793 (48.0%)
1980	50*	**Ronald Reagan** *George Bush*	**Rep.**	**489**	**43,904,153 (50.7%)**
		Jimmy Carter *Walter F. Mondale*	Dem.	49	35,483,883 (41.0%)
1984	50*	**Ronald Reagan** *George Bush*	**Rep.**	**525**	**54,455,074(58.8%)**
		Walter F. Mondale *Geraldine Ferraro*	Dem.	13	37,577,137 (40.6%)
1988[21]	50*	**George Bush** *Dan Quayle*	**Rep.**	**426**	**48,881,278 (53.4%)**
		Michael S. Dukakis *Lloyd Bentsen*	Dem.	111	41,805,374 (45.6%)
1992	50*	**Bill Clinton** *Al Gore*	**Dem.**	**370**	**44,908,233 (43.0%)**
		George Bush *Dan Quayle*	Rep.	168	39,102,282 (37.4%)
1996	50*	**Bill Clinton** *Al Gore*	**Dem.**	**379**	**47,402,357 (49.2%)**
		Bob Dole *Jack Kemp*	Rep.	159	39,198,755 (40.7%)
2000[22]	50*	**George W. Bush** *Richard B. Cheney*	**Rep.**	**271**	**50,455,156 (47.9%)**
		Al Gore *Joseph I. Lieberman*	Dem.	266	50,992,335 (48.4%)
2004[23]	50*	**George W. Bush** *Richard B. Cheney*	**Rep.**	**286**	**62,040,610 (50.7%)**
		John Kerry *John Edwards*	Dem.	251	59,028,439 (48.3%)

Year	No. of States	Candidates	Party	Electoral Vote	Popular Vote	Year	No. of States	Candidates	Party	Electoral Vote	Popular Vote
2008[24]	50*	**Barack Obama** *Joseph R. Biden Jr.*	**Dem.**	**365**	**69,498,516 (52.9%)**	2016[25]	50*	**Donald J. Trump** *Mike Pence*	**Rep.**	**304**	**62,984,828 (46.1%)**
		John McCain *Sarah Palin*	Rep.	173	59,948,323 (45.7%)			Hilary R. Clinton *Tim Kaine*	Dem.	227	65,853,514 (48.2%)
2012	50*	**Barack Obama** *Joseph R. Biden Jr.*	**Dem.**	**332**	**65,915,796 (51.1%)**	2020	50*	**Joseph R. Biden Jr.** *Kamala D. Harris*	**Dem.**	**306**	**81,282,632 (51.3%)**
		Mitt Romney *Paul Ryan*	Rep.	206	60,933,500 (47.2%)			**Donald J. Trump** *Mike Pence*	Rep.	232	74,223,234 (46.9%)

SOURCE: Harold W. Stanley and Richard G. Niemi, *Vital Statistics on American Politics*, 5th ed. (Washington, D.C.: CQ Press, 1995), Table 3-13; Richard M. Scammon, Alice V. McGillivray, and Rhodes Cook, *America Votes 24, 30, 32* (Washington, D.C.: Sage/CQ Press, 2009, 2013, 2016, 2020).

NOTE: Bold indicates victors. In the elections of 1789, 1792, 1796, and 1800, each candidate ran for the office of president. The candidate with the second-highest number of electoral votes became vice president. For elections after 1800, italic indicates vice presidential candidates.

1. Elections of 1789–1800 were held under rules that did not allow separate voting for president and vice president.

2. Popular vote returns are not shown before 1824 because consistent, reliable data are not available.

3. Monroe ran unopposed. One electoral vote was cast for John Adams and Richard Stockton, who were not candidates.

4. 1824: All four candidates represented Democratic-Republican factions. William H. Crawford received 41 electoral votes, and Henry Clay received 37 votes. Since no candidate received a majority, the election was decided (in Adams's favor) by the House of Representatives.

5. 1832: Two electoral votes were not cast.

6. 1836: Other Whig candidates receiving electoral votes were Hugh L. White, who received 26 votes, and Daniel Webster, who received 14 votes.

7. 1856: Millard Fillmore, Whig-American, received 8 electoral votes.

8. 1860: John C. Breckinridge, Southern Democrat, received 72 electoral votes. John Bell, Constitutional Union, received 39 electoral votes.

9. 1864: Because of the Civil War, 81 electoral votes were not cast.

10. 1868: Because of Reconstruction, 23 electoral votes were not cast.

11. 1872: Horace Greeley, Democrat, died after the election. In the electoral college, Democratic electoral votes went to Thomas Hendricks, 42 votes; Benjamin Gratz Brown, 18 votes; Charles J. Jenkins, 2 votes; and David Davis, 1 vote. Seventeen electoral votes were not cast.

12. 1892: James B. Weaver, People's Party, received 22 electoral votes.

13. 1912: Theodore Roosevelt, Progressive Party, received 86 electoral votes.

14. 1924: Robert M. La Follette, Progressive Party, received 13 electoral votes.

15. 1948: J. Strom Thurmond, States' Rights Party, received 39 electoral votes.

16. 1956: Walter B. Jones, Democrat, received 1 electoral vote.

17. 1960: Harry Flood Byrd, Democrat, received 15 electoral votes.

18. 1968: George C. Wallace, American Independent Party, received 46 electoral votes.

19. 1972: John Hospers, Libertarian Party, received 1 electoral vote.

20. 1976: Ronald Reagan, Republican, received 1 electoral vote.

21. 1988: Lloyd Bentsen, the Democratic vice-presidential nominee, received 1 electoral vote for president.

22. 2000: One District of Columbia elector did not vote.

23. 2004: A Democratic elector in Minnesota cast a vote for Edwards rather than Kerry.

24. 2008: Nebraska split its five electoral votes, with four going to John McCain and one to Barack Obama. Nebraska is one of two states, along with Maine, that splits electoral votes between congressional districts. Nebraska has three. The winner of each district receives that district's vote; the statewide winner receives the other two. The 2008 election was the first time that split electoral vote occurred in either state.

25. 2016: Due to faithless electors, the following individuals received electoral votes: Colin Powell (3), Faith Spotted Eagle (1), John Kasich (1), Ron Paul (1), Bernard Sanders (1).

*Fifty states plus the District of Columbia.

Victorious Party in Presidential Races, 1860–2020

State	1860	1864	1868	1872	1876	1880	1884	1888	1892	1896	1900	1904	1908	1912	1916	1920	1924	1928	1932	1936
Alabama	SD	[2]	R	R	D	D	D	D	D	D	D	D	D	D	D	D	D	D	D	D
Alaska																				
Arizona														D	D	R	R	R	D	D
Arkansas	SD	[2]	R	[4]	D	D	D	D	D	D	D	D	D	D	D	D	D	D	D	D
California	R	R	R	R	R	D[6]	R	R	D[7]	R[12]	R	R	R	PR	D	R	R	R	D	D
Colorado					R	R	R	R	PP	D	D	R	D	D	D	R	R	R	D	D
Connecticut	R	R	R	R	D	D	D	D	D	R	R	R	R	D	R	R	R	R	D	D
Delaware	SD	D	D	R	D	D	D	D	D	R	R	R	R	D	R	R	R	R	R	D
Dist. of Columbia																				
Florida	SD	[2]	R	R	R	D	D	D	D	D	D	D	D	D	D	D	D	R	D	D
Georgia	SD	[2]	D	D[5]	D	D	D	D	D	D	D	D	D	D	D	D	D	D	D	D
Hawaii																				
Idaho									PP	D	D	R	R	D	D	R	R	R	D	D
Illinois	R	R	R	R	R	R	R	R	D	R	R	R	R	D	R	R	R	R	D	D
Indiana	R	R	R	R	D	R	D	R	D	R	R	R	R	D	R	R	R	R	D	D
Iowa	R	R	R	R	R	R	R	R	R	R	R	R	R	D	R	R	R	R	D	D
Kansas		R	R	R	R	R	R	R	PP	D	R	R	R	D	D	R	R	R	R	R
Kentucky	CU	D	D	D	D	D	D	D	D	R[13]	D	D	D	D	D	D	R	R	D	D
Louisiana	SD	[2]	D	[4]	R	D	D	D	D	D	D	D	D	D	D	D	D	D	D	D
Maine	R	R	R	R	R	R	R	R	R	R	R	R	R	D	R	R	R	R	R	R
Maryland	SD	R	D	D	D	D	D	D	D	R	R	D[14]	D[15]	D	D	R	R	R	D	D
Massachusetts	R	R	R	R	R	R	R	R	R	R	R	R	R	D	R	R	R	D	D	D
Michigan	R	R	R	R	R	R	R	R	R[8]	R	R	R	R	PR	R	R	R	R	D	D
Minnesota	R	R	R	R	R	R	R	R	R	R	R	R	R	PR	R	R	R	R	D	D
Mississippi	SD	[2]	[3]	R	D	D	D	D	D	D	D	D	D	D	D	D	D	D	D	D
Missouri	D	R	R	D	D	D	D	D	D	D	D	R	D	D	D	R	R	R	D	D
Montana									R	D	D	R	R	D	D	R	R	R	D	D
Nebraska			R	R	R	R	R	R	R	D	R	R	D	D	D	R	R	R	D	D
Nevada		R	R	R	R	D	R	R	PP	D	D	R	D	D	D	R	R	R	D	D
New Hampshire	R	R	R	R	R	R	R	R	R	R	R	R	R	D	R	R	R	R	R	D
New Jersey	R[1]	D	D	R	D	D	D	D	D	R	R	R	R	D	R	R	R	R	D	D
New Mexico														D	D	R	R	R	D	D
New York	R	R	D	R	D	R	D	R	D	R	R	R	R	D	R	R	R	R	D	D
North Carolina	SD	[2]	R	R	D	D	D	D	D	D	D	D	D	D	D	D	D	R	D	D
North Dakota									[9]	R	R	R	R	D	D	R	R	R	D	D
Ohio	R	R	R	R	R	R	R	R	R[10]	R	R	R	R	D	D	R	R	R	D	D
Oklahoma													D	D	D	D	R	R	D	D
Oregon	R	R	D	R	R	R	R	R	R[11]	R	R	R	R	D	R	R	R	R	D	D
Pennsylvania	R	R	R	R	R	R	R	R	R	R	R	R	R	PR	R	R	R	R	R	D
Rhode Island	R	R	R	R	R	R	R	R	R	R	R	R	R	D	R	R	R	D	D	D
South Carolina	SD	[2]	R	R	D	D	D	D	D	D	D	D	D	D	D	D	D	D	D	D
South Dakota									R	D	R	R	R	PR	R	R	R	R	D	D
Tennessee	CU	[2]	R	D	D	D	D	D	D	D	D	D	D	D	D	D	D	R	D	D
Texas	SD	[2]	[3]	D	D	D	D	D	D	D	D	D	D	D	D	D	D	R	D	D
Utah										D	R	R	R	D	D	R	R	R	D	D
Vermont	R	R	R	R	R	R	R	R	R	R	R	R	R	R	R	R	R	R	R	R
Virginia	CU	[2]	[3]	R	D	D	D	D	D	D	D	D	D	D	D	D	D	R	D	D
Washington									R	D	R	R	R	PR	D	R	R	R	D	D
West Virginia		R	R	R	D	D	D	D	D	R	R	R	R	D	R[16]	R	R	R	D	D
Wisconsin	R	R	R	R	R	R	R	R	D	R	R	R	R	D	R	R	PR	R	D	D
Wyoming									R	D	R	R	R	D	D	R	R	R	D	D
Winning Party	R	R	R	R	R	R	D	R	D	R	R	R	R	D	D	R	R	R	D	D

NOTE: With the exception of the District of Columbia, blanks indicate states not yet admitted to the Union. The District of Columbia received the presidential vote in 1961.

KEY: AI–American Independent Party; CU–Constitutional Union Party; D–Democratic Party; PP–People's Party; PR–Progressive (Bull Moose) Party; R–Republican Party; SD–Southern Democratic Party; SR–States' Rights Democratic Party.

1. Four electors voted Republican; three, Democratic.
2. Confederate states did not vote in 1864.
3. Did not vote in 1868.
4. Votes were not counted.
5. Three votes for Greeley not counted.
6. Five electors voted Democratic; one, Republican.
7. Eight electors voted Democratic; one, Republican.
8. Nine electors voted Republican; five, Democratic.
9. One vote each for Democratic, Republican and People's parties.
10. Twenty-two electors voted Republican; one, Democratic.
11. Three electors voted Republican; one, People's Party.
12. Eight electors voted Republican; one, Democratic.

1940	1944	1948	1952	1956	1960	1964	1968	1972	1976	1980	1984	1988	1992	1996	2000	2004	2008	2012	2016	2020	Dems	Reps	Other
D	D	SR	D	D[18]	D[19]	R	AI	R	D	R	R	R	R	R	R	R	R	R	R	R	22	15	0
					R	D	R	R	R	R	R	R	R	R	R	R	R	R	R	R	1	15	0
D	D	D	R	R	R	R	R	R	R	R	R	D	R	R	R	R	R	R	R	D	9	19	0
D	D	D	D	D	D	D	AI	R	R	R	R	D	D	R	R	R	R	R	R	R	25	12	0
D	D	D	R	R	R	D	R	R	R	R	R	D	D	D	D	D	D	D	D	D	17	23	0
R	R	D	R	R	R	D	R	R	R	R	R	D	R	R	R	D	D	D	D	D	14	22	0
D	R	D	R	D	D	R	D	R	D	R	R	R	D	D	D	D	D	D	D	D	19	22	0
D	D	R	R	R	D	D	R	D	R	D	R	R	R	D	D	D	D	D	D	D	22	18	0
					D	D	D	D	D	D	D	D	D	D	D[26]	D	D	D	D	D	15	0	0
D	D	D	R	R	R	D	R	R	D	R	R	R	D	R	D	D	R	R	R	R	22	17	0
D	D	D	D	D	D	R	AI	R	D	D	R	D	R	R	R	R	R	R	R	D	28	10	0
					D	D	D	R	D	D	R	D	D	D	D	D	D	D	D	D	14	2	0
D	D	D	R	R	R	D	R	R	R	R	R	R	R	R	R	R	R	R	R	R	10	22	0
D	D	D	R	R	R	D	R	R	R	R	R	D	D	D	D	D	D	D	D	D	17	24	0
R	R	R	R	R	R	D	R	R	R	R	R	R	R	R	R	D	R	R	R	R	8	33	0
R	R	D	R	R	R	D	R	R	R	R	R	D	D	D	R	D	R	D	R	R	11	30	0
R	R	R	R	R	R	D	R	R	R	R	R	R	R	R	R	R	R	R	R	R	4	35	0
D	D	D	D	R	R	D	R	R	R	R	R	D	D	R	R	R	R	R	R	R	24	16	0
D	D	SR	D	R	D	R	AI	R	D	R	R	R	D	R	R	R	R	R	R	R	23	13	0
R	R	R	R	R	D	R	R	D	R	R	R	D	D	D	D	D	D	D	D	D[29]	11	30	0
D	R	R	R	R	D	D	R	D	R	D	R	D	D	D	D	D	D	D	D	D	28	12	0
D	D	D	D	D	D	D	D	D	R	D	R	R	D	D	D	D	D	D	D	D	21	20	0
R	D	R	R	R	D	D	D	R	R	R	R	D	D	D	D	R	D	D	D	D	13	27	0
D	D	D	R	R	D	D	D	R	D	D	D	D	D	D	D[27]	D	D	D	D	D	20	20	0
D	D	SR	D	D	[20]	R	AI	R	D	R	R	R	R	R	R	R	R	R	R	R	21	14	0
D	D	D	R	D	D	R	D	R	D	R	R	D	R	R	R	R	R	R	R	R	22	19	0
D	D	D	R	R	R	D	R	R	R	R	R	D	R	R	R	R	R	R	R	R	11	22	0
R	R	R	R	R	D	R	R	R	R	R	R	R	R	R	R	R[28]	R	R	R	R[30]	7	32	0
D	D	D	R	R	D	R	R	R	R	R	R	D	D	R	D	R	D	D	D	D	19	20	0
D	D	R	R	R	D	R	R	R	R	R	R	D	D	R	D	R	D	D	D	D	13	28	0
D	D	R	R	R	D	R	R	R	R	R	R	D	D	D	D	D	D	D	D	D	22	19	0
D	D	D	R	R	D	D	R	R	R	R	R	D	D	D	D	D	D	D	D	D	16	12	0
D	D	R	R	R	D	D	D	R	D	R	D	D	D	D	D	D	D	D	D	D	22	19	0
D	D	D	D	D	D	D	R[22]	R	D	R	R	R	R	R	D	R	R	R	R	R	24	15	0
R	R	R	R	R	D	R	R	R	R	R	R	R	R	R	R	R	R	R	R	R	5	27	0
D	R	D	R	R	R	D	R	D	R	R	R	D	D	D	R	D	R	R	R	R	12	29	0
D	D	D	R[21]	R	D	R	R	R	R	R	R	R	R	R	R	R	R	R	R	R	10	19	0
D	D	R	R	R	R	D	R	R	R	R	R	D	D	D	D	D	D	D	R	R	16	25	0
D	D	R	R	R	D	D	D	R	D	R	R	D	D	D	D	D	D	D	R	D	14	26	0
D	D	D	R	R	D	D	D	R	D	D	R	D	D	D	D	D	D	D	D	D	21	20	0
D	D	SR	D	D	D	R	R	D	R	R	R	R	R	R	R	R	R	R	R	R	22	16	0
R	R	R	R	R	R	D	R	R	R	R	R	R	R	R	R	R	R	R	R	R	4	28	0
D	D	D[17]	R	R	R	D	R	D	R	R	R	D	D	R	R	R	R	R	R	R	22	17	0
D	D	D	R	D	D	D	R	D	R	R	R	D	D	R	R	R	R	R	R	R	23	15	0
D	D	D	R	R	R	D	R	R	R	R	R	R	R	R	R	R	R	R	R	R	8	24	0
R	R	R	R	R	D	R	R	R	R	R	D	D	D	D	D	D	D	D	D	D	9	32	0
D	D	D	R	D	D	D	D	R[23]	R	R	R	R	R	R	R	R	D	D	D	D	23	15	0
D	D	D	R	R	R	D	R	R[24]	R	R	D	D	D	D	D	D	D	D	D	D	18	14	0
D	D	D	D	D	R	D	D	R	D	R	D[25]	D	D	R	R	R	R	R	R	R	20	20	0
D	R	D	R	R	D	R	R	R	R	R	R	D	D	D	D	D	D	D	D	R	16	24	0
D	R	D	R	R	R	D	R	R	R	R	R	R	R	R	R	R	R	R	R	R	8	25	0
D	D	D	R	R	D	D	R	R	D	R	R	D	D	R	R	D	R	D	R	D	16	24	0

13. Twelve electors voted Republican; one, Democratic.

14. Seven electors voted Democratic; one, Republican.

15. Six electors voted Democratic; two, Republican.

16. Seven electors voted Republican; one, Democratic.

17. Eleven electors voted Democratic; one, States' Rights.

18. One elector voted for Walter B. Jones.

19. Six of eleven electors voted for Harry F. Byrd.

20. Eight independent electors voted for Byrd.

21. One vote cast for Byrd.

22. Twelve electors voted Republican; one, American Independent.

23. One elector voted Libertarian.

24. One elector voted for Ronald Reagan.

25. One elector voted for Lloyd Bentsen.

26. One elector did not vote.

27. One elector voted for John Edwards.

28. Obama won the vote of one elector.

29. Trump won the vote of one elector.

30. Biden won the vote of one elector.

2020 Presidential Election

State	Total vote	Donald J. Trump (Republican)		Joe R. Biden (Democrat)		Other			Dem.-Rep. Plurality
		Votes	%	Votes	%	Votes	%		
Alabama	23,23,282	14,41,170	62.0%	8,49,624	36.6%	32,488	1.4%	R	5,91,546
Alaska	3,59,530	1,89,951	52.8%	1,53,778	42.8%	15,801	4.4%	R	36,173
Arizona	33,87,326	16,61,686	49.1%	16,72,143	49.4%	53,497	1.6%	D	10,457
Arkansas	12,19,069	7,60,647	62.4%	4,23,932	34.8%	34,490	2.8%	R	3,36,715
California	1,75,00,881	60,06,429	34.3%	1,11,10,250	63.5%	3,84,202	2.2%	D	51,03,821
Colorado	32,56,980	13,64,607	41.9%	18,04,352	55.4%	88,021	2.7%	D	4,39,745
Connecticut	18,23,857	7,14,717	39.2%	10,80,831	59.3%	28,309	1.6%	D	3,66,114
Delaware	5,04,346	2,00,603	39.8%	2,96,268	58.7%	7,475	1.5%	D	95,665
Florida	1,10,67,456	5668731	51.2%	52,97,045	47.9%	1,01,680	0.9%	R	3,71,686
Georgia	49,99,960	2461854	49.2%	24,73,633	49.5%	64,473	1.3%	D	11,779
Hawaii	5,74,469	1,96,864	34.3%	3,66,130	63.7%	11,475	2.0%	D	1,69,266
Idaho	8,67,934	5,54,119	63.8%	2,87,021	33.1%	26,794	3.1%	R	2,67,098
Illinois	60,33,744	24,46,891	40.6%	34,71,915	57.5%	1,14,938	1.9%	D	10,25,024
Indiana	30,33,121	17,29,519	57.0%	12,42,416	41.0%	61,186	2.0%	R	4,87,103
Iowa	16,90,871	8,97,672	53.1%	7,59,061	44.9%	34,138	2.0%	R	1,38,611
Kansas	13,73,986	7,71,406	56.1%	5,70,323	41.5%	32,257	2.3%	R	2,01,083
Kentucky	21,36,768	13,26,646	62.1%	7,72,474	36.2%	37,648	1.8%	R	5,54,172
Louisiana	21,48,062	12,55,776	58.5%	8,56,034	39.9%	36,252	1.7%	R	3,99,742
Maine	8,19,461	3,60,737	44.0%	4,35,072	53.1%	23,652	2.9%	D	74,335
Maryland	30,37,030	9,76,414	32.2%	19,85,023	65.4%	75,593	2.5%	D	10,08,609
Massachusetts	36,31,402	11,67,202	32.1%	23,82,202	65.6%	81,998	2.3%	D	12,15,000
Michigan	55,39,302	26,49,852	47.8%	28,04,040	50.6%	85,410	1.5%	D	1,54,188
Minnesota	32,77,171	14,84,065	45.3%	17,17,077	52.4%	76,029	2.3%	D	2,33,012
Mississippi	13,13,759	7,56,764	57.6%	5,39,398	41.1%	17,597	1.3%	R	2,17,366
Missouri	30,25,962	17,18,736	56.8%	12,53,014	41.4%	54,212	1.8%	R	4,65,722
Montana	6,03,674	3,43,602	56.9%	2,44,786	40.5%	15,286	2.5%	R	98,816
Nebraska	9,56,383	5,56,846	58.2%	3,74,583	39.2%	24,954	2.6%	R	1,82,263
Nevada	14,05,376	6,69,890	47.7%	7,03,486	50.1%	32,000	2.3%	D	33,596
New Hampshire	8,06,205	3,65,660	45.4%	4,24,937	52.7%	15,608	1.9%	D	59,277
New Jersey	45,49,353	18,83,274	41.4%	26,08,335	57.3%	57,744	1.3%	D	7,25,061
New Mexico	9,23,965	4,01,894	43.5%	5,01,614	54.3%	20,457	2.2%	D	99,720
New York	86,16,861	32,51,997	37.7%	52,44,886	60.9%	1,19,978	1.4%	D	19,92,889
North Carolina	55,24,804	27,58,775	49.9%	26,84,292	48.6%	81,737	1.5%	R	74,483
North Dakota	3,62,024	2,35,751	65.1%	1,15,042	31.8%	11,231	3.1%	R	1,20,709
Ohio	59,22,202	31,54,834	53.3%	26,79,165	45.2%	88,203	1.5%	R	4,75,669
Oklahoma	15,60,699	10,20,280	65.4%	5,03,890	32.3%	36,529	2.3%	R	5,16,390
Oregon	23,74,321	9,58,448	40.4%	13,40,383	56.5%	75,490	3.2%	D	3,81,935
Pennsylvania	69,15,283	33,77,674	48.8%	34,58,229	50.0%	79,380	1.1%	D	80,555
Rhode Island	5,17,757	1,99,922	38.6%	3,07,486	59.4%	10,349	2.0%	D	1,07,564
South Carolina	25,13,329	13,85,103	55.1%	10,91,541	43.4%	36,685	1.5%	R	2,93,562
South Dakota	4,22,609	2,61,043	61.8%	1,50,471	35.6%	11,095	2.6%	R	1,10,572
Tennessee	30,53,851	18,52,475	60.7%	11,43,711	37.5%	57,665	1.9%	R	7,08,764
Texas	1,13,15,056	58,90,347	52.1%	52,59,126	46.5%	1,65,583	1.5%	R	6,31,221
Utah	14,88,289	8,65,140	58.1%	5,60,282	37.6%	62,867	4.2%	R	3,04,858
Vermont	3,67,428	1,12,704	30.7%	2,42,820	66.1%	11,904	3.2%	D	1,30,116
Virginia	44,60,524	19,62,430	44.0%	24,13,568	54.1%	84,526	1.9%	D	4,51,138
Washington	40,87,631	15,84,651	48.0%	23,69,612	58.0%	1,33,368	3.3%	D	7,84,961
West Virginia	7,94,731	5,45,382	68.6%	2,35,984	29.7%	13,365	1.7%	R	3,09,398
Wisconsin	32,98,041	16,10,184	48.8%	16,30,866	49.4%	56,991	1.7%	D	20,682
Wyoming	2,76,765	1,93,559	69.9%	73,491	26.6%	9,715	3.5%	R	1,20,068
District of Columbia	3,44,356	18,586	5.4%	3,17,323	92.1%	6,899	2.0%	D	2,98,737
Total	15,84,07,246	7,42,23,509		8,12,82,965		28,99,224			2,30,87,036

NOTE: Percentages are of the total vote.

2020 Electoral Votes and Map

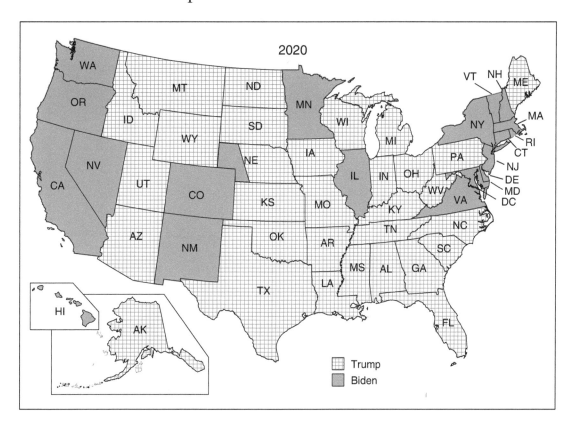

States	Electoral Votes	Trump	Biden	States	Electoral Votes	Trump	Biden
Alabama	9	9	—	Montana	3	3	—
Alaska	3	3	—	Nebraska[2]	5	4	1
Arizona	11	—	11	Nevada	6	—	6
Arkansas	6	6	—	New Hampshire	4	—	4
California	55	—	55	New Jersey	14	—	14
Colorado	9	—	9	New Mexico	5	—	5
Connecticut	7	—	7	New York	29	—	29
Delaware	3	—	3	North Carolina	15	15	—
District of Columbia	3	—	3	North Dakota	3	3	—
Florida	29	29	—	Ohio	18	18	—
Georgia	16	—	16	Oklahoma	7	7	—
Hawaii	4	—	4	Oregon	7	—	7
Idaho	4	4	—	Pennsylvania	20	—	20
Illinois	20	—	20	Rhode Island	4	—	4
Indiana	11	11	—	South Carolina	9	9	—
Iowa	6	6	—	South Dakota	3	3	—
Kansas	6	6	—	Tennessee	11	11	—
Kentucky	8	8	—	Texas	38	38	—
Louisiana	8	8	—	Utah	6	6	—
Maine[1]	4	1	3	Vermont	3	—	3
Maryland	10	—	10	Virginia	13	—	13
Massachusetts	11	—	11	Washington	12	—	12
Michigan	16	—	16	West Virginia	5	5	—
Minnesota	10	—	10	Wisconsin	10	—	10
Mississippi	6	6	—	Wyoming	3	3	—
Missouri	10	10	—	Totals	538	232	306

1. Maine appoints its electors proportionally. Although Biden/Harris won in the First Congressional District and took the state, Trump/Pence won the Second Congressional District. Maine's electoral votes were proportionally awarded accordingly: for Biden 3 and Trump 1.

2. Maine appoints its electors proportionally. Although Trump/Pence won in the First and Third Congressional District and took the state, Biden/Harris won the Second Congressional District. Maine's electoral votes were proportionally awarded accordingly: for Trump 4 and Biden 1.

Distribution of House Seats and Electoral Votes

State	1963–1973	1973 Census changes	1973–1983	1980 Census changes	1983–1993	1990 Census changes	1993–2003	2000 Census changes	2003–2013	2010 Census changes
					US House Seats					
Alabama	8	−1	7	—	7	—	7	—	7	—
Alaska	1	—	1	—	1	—	1	—	1	—
Arizona	3	+ (1)	4	+ (1)	5	+ (1)	6	+ (2)	8	+ (1)
Arkansas	4	—	4	—	4	—	4	—	4	—
California	38	+ (5)	43	+ (2)	45	+ (7)	52	+ (1)	53	—
Colorado	4	+ (1)	5	+ (1)	6	—	6	+ (1)	7	—
Connecticut	6	—	6	—	6	—	6	−1	5	—
Delaware	1	—	1	—	1	—	1	—	1	—
District of Columbia	—	—	—	—	—	—	—	—	—	—
Florida	12	+ (3)	15	+ (4)	19	+ (4)	23	+ (2)	25	+ (2)
Georgia	10	—	10	—	10	+ (1)	11	+ (2)	13	+ (1)
Hawaii	2	—	2	—	2	—	2	—	2	—
Idaho	2	—	2	—	2	—	2	—	2	—
Illinois	24	—	24	−2	22	−2	20	−1	19	−1
Indiana	11	—	11	−1	10	—	10	−1	9	—
Iowa	7	−1	6	—	6	−1	5	—	5	−1
Kansas	5	—	5	—	5	−1	4	—	4	—
Kentucky	7	—	7	—	7	−1	6	—	6	—
Louisiana	8	—	8	—	8	−1	7	—	7	−1
Maine	2	—	2	—	2	—	2	—	2	—
Maryland	8	—	8	—	8	—	8	—	8	—
Massachusetts	12	—	12	−1	11	−1	10	—	10	−1
Michigan	19	—	19	−1	18	−2	16	−1	15	−1
Minnesota	8	—	8	—	8	—	8	—	8	—
Mississippi	5	—	5	—	5	—	5	−1	4	—
Missouri	10	—	10	−1	9	—	9	—	9	−1
Montana	2	—	2	—	2	−1	1	—	1	—
Nebraska	3	—	3	—	3	—	3	—	3	—
Nevada	1	—	1	+ (1)	2	—	2	+ (1)	3	+ (1)
New Hampshire	2	—	2	—	2	—	2	—	2	—
New Jersey	15	—	15	−1	14	−1	13	—	13	−1
New Mexico	2	—	2	1	3	—	3	—	3	—
New York	41	−2	39	+ (5)	34	−3	31	−2	29	−2
North Carolina	11	—	11	—	11	+ (1)	12	+ (1)	13	—
North Dakota	2	−1	1	—	1	—	1	—	1	—
Ohio	24	−1	23	−2	21	−2	19	−1	18	−2
Oklahoma	6	—	6	—	6	—	6	−1	5	—
Oregon	4	—	4	1	5	—	5	—	5	—
Pennsylvania	27	−2	25	−2	23	−2	21	−2	19	−1
Rhode Island	2	—	2	—	2	—	2	—	2	—
South Carolina	6	—	6	—	6	—	6	—	6	+ (1)
South Dakota	2	—	2	−1	1	—	1	—	1	—
Tennessee	9	−1	8	+ (1)	9	—	9	—	9	—
Texas	23	+ (1)	24	+ (3)	27	3	30	+ (2)	32	+ (4)
Utah	2	—	2	+ (1)	3	—	3	—	3	+ (1)
Vermont	1	—	1	—	1	—	1	—	1	—
Virginia	10	—	10	—	10	+ (1)	11	—	11	—
Washington	7	—	7	+ (1)	8	+ (1)	9	—	9	+ (1)
West Virginia	5	−1	4	—	4	+ (1)	3	—	3	—
Wisconsin	10	−1	9	—	9	—	9	−1	8	—
Wyoming	1	—	1	—	1	—	1	—	1	—

NOTE: Table was constructed by CQ Press editors based on the censuses of 1950, 1960, 1970, 1980, 1990, 2000, 2010, and 2020.

			Electoral Votes						
2013–2023	2020 Census changes	2023–2033	1952, 1956, 1960	1964, 1968	1972, 1976, 1980	1984, 1988	1992, 1996, 2000	2004, 2008	2012, 2016, 2020
7	—	7	11	10	9	9	9	9	9
1	—	1	3	3	3	3	3	3	3
9	—	9	4	5	6	7	8	10	11
4	—	4	8	6	6	6	6	6	6
53	−1	52	32	40	45	47	54	55	55
7	+ (1)	8	6	6	7	8	8	9	9
5	—	5	8	8	8	8	8	7	7
1	—	1	3	3	3	3	3	3	3
—	—	—	—	3	3	3	3	3	3
27	+ (1)	28	10	14	17	21	25	27	29
14	—	14	12	12	12	12	13	15	16
2	—	2	3	4	4	4	4	4	4
2	—	2	4	4	4	4	4	4	4
18	−1	17	27	26	26	24	22	21	20
9	—	9	13	13	13	12	12	11	11
4	—	4	10	9	8	8	7	7	6
4	—	4	8	7	7	7	6	6	6
6	—	6	10	9	9	9	8	8	8
6	—	2	10	10	10	10	9	9	8
2	—	2	5	4	4	4	4	4	4
8	—	8	9	10	10	10	10	10	10
9	—	9	16	14	14	13	12	12	11
14	−1	13	20	21	21	20	18	17	16
8	—	8	11	10	10	10	10	10	10
4	—	4	8	7	7	7	7	6	6
8	—	8	13	12	12	11	11	11	10
1	+ (1)	2	4	4	4	4	3	3	3
3	—	3	6	5	5	5	5	5	5
4	—	4	3	3	3	4	4	5	6
2	—	2	4	4	4	4	4	4	4
12	—	12	16	17	17	16	15	15	14
3	—	3	4	4	4	5	5	5	5
27	−1	26	45	43	41	36	33	31	29
13	+ (1)	14	14	13	13	13	14	15	15
1	—	1	4	4	3	3	3	3	3
16	−1	15	25	26	25	23	21	20	18
5	—	5	8	8	8	8	8	7	7
5	+ (1)	6	6	6	6	7	7	7	7
18	−1	17	32	29	27	25	23	21	20
2	—	2	4	4	4	4	4	4	4
7	—	7	8	8	8	8	8	8	9
1	—	1	4	4	4	3	3	3	3
9	—	9	11	11	10	11	11	11	11
36	+ (2)	38	24	25	26	29	32	34	38
4	—	4	4	4	4	5	5	5	6
1	—	1	3	3	3	3	3	3	3
11	—	11	12	12	12	12	13	13	13
10	—	10	9	9	9	10	11	11	12
3	−1	2	8	7	6	6	5	5	5
8	—	8	12	12	11	11	11	10	10
1	—	1	3	3	3	3	3	3	3

Party Affiliations in Congress and the Presidency, 1789–2020

Year	Congress	House Majority party	House Principal minority party	Senate Majority party	Senate Principal minority party	President
1789–1791	1st	AD–38	Op–26	AD–17	Op–9	F (Washington)
1791–1793	2nd	F–37	DR–33	F–16	DR–13	F (Washington)
1793–1795	3rd	DR–57	F–48	F–17	DR–13	F (Washington)
1795–1797	4th	F–54	DR–52	F–19	DR–13	F (Washington)
1797–1799	5th	F–58	DR–48	F–20	DR–12	F (J. Adams)
1799–1801	6th	F–64	DR–42	F–19	DR–13	F (J. Adams)
1801–1803	7th	DR–69	F–36	DR–18	F–13	DR (Jefferson)
1803–1805	8th	DR–102	F–39	DR–25	F–9	DR (Jefferson)
1805–1807	9th	DR–116	F–25	DR–27	F–7	DR (Jefferson)
1807–1809	10th	DR–118	F–24	DR–28	F–6	DR (Jefferson)
1809–1811	11th	DR–94	F–48	DR–28	F–6	DR (Madison)
1811–1813	12th	DR–108	F–36	DR–30	F–6	DR (Madison)
1813–1815	13th	DR–112	F–68	DR–27	F–9	DR (Madison)
1815–1817	14th	DR–117	F–65	DR–25	F–11	DR (Madison)
1817–1819	15th	DR–141	F–42	DR–34	F–10	DR (Monroe)
1819–1821	16th	DR–156	F–27	DR–35	F–7	DR (Monroe)
1821–1823	17th	DR–158	F–25	DR–44	F–4	DR (Monroe)
1823–1825	18th	DR–187	F–26	DR–44	F–4	DR (Monroe)
1825–1827	19th	AD–105	J–97	AD–26	J–20	DR (J. Q. Adams)
1827–1829	20th	J–119	AD–94	J–28	AD–20	DR (J. Q. Adams)
1829–1831	21st	D–139	NR–74	D–26	NR–22	DR (Jackson)
1831–1833	22nd	D–141	NR–58	D–25	NR–21	D (Jackson)
1833–1835	23rd	D–147	AM–53	D–20	NR–20	D (Jackson)
1835–1837	24th	D–145	W–98	D–27	W–25	D (Jackson)
1837–1839	25th	D–108	W–107	D–30	W–18	D (Van Buren)
1839–1841	26th	D–124	W–118	D–28	W–22	D (Van Buren); W (W. Harrison);
1841–1843	27th	W–133	D–102	W–28	D–22	W (Tyler)
1843–1845	28th	D–142	W–79	W–28	D–25	W (Tyler)
1845–1847	29th	D–143	W–77	D–31	W–25	D (Polk)
1847–1849	30th	W–115	D–108	D–36	W–21	D (Polk)
1849–1851	31st	D–112	W–109	D–35	W–25	W (Taylor); W (Fillmore)
1851–1853	32nd	D–140	W–88	D–35	W–24	W (Fillmore)
1853–1855	33rd	D–159	W–71	D–38	W–22	D (Pierce)
1855–1857	34th	R–108	D–83	D–40	R–15	D (Pierce)
1857–1859	35th	D–118	R–92	D–36	R–20	D (Buchanan)
1859–1861	36th	R–114	D–92	D–36	R–26	D (Buchanan)
1861–1863	37th	R–105	D–43	R–31	D–10	R (Lincoln)
1863–1865	38th	R–102	D–75	R–36	D–9	R (Lincoln); R (Lincoln);
1865–1867	39th	U–149	D–42	U–42	D–10	R (A. Johnson)
1867–1869	40th	R–143	D–49	R–42	D–11	R (A. Johnson)
1869–1871	41st	R–149	D–63	R–56	D–11	R (Grant)
1871–1873	42nd	R–134	D–104	R–52	D–17	R (Grant)
1873–1875	43rd	R–194	D–92	R–49	D–19	R (Grant)
1875–1877	44th	D–169	R–109	R–45	D–29	R (Grant)
1877–1879	45th	D–153	R–140	R–39	D–36	R (Hayes)
1879–1881	46th	D–149	R–130	D–42	R–33	R (Hayes)
1881–1883	47th	R–147	D–135	R–37	D–37	R (Garfield); R (Arthur)
1883–1885	48th	D–197	R–118	R–38	D–36	R (Arthur)
1885–1887	49th	D–183	R–140	R–43	D–34	D (Cleveland)
1887–1889	50th	D–169	R–152	R–39	D–37	D (Cleveland)
1889–1891	51st	R–166	D–159	R–39	D–37	R (B. Harrison)
1891–1893	52nd	D–235	R–88	R–47	D–39	R (B. Harrison)
1893–1895	53rd	D–218	R–127	D–44	R–38	D (Cleveland)
1895–1897	54th	R–244	D–105	R–43	D–39	D (Cleveland)
1897–1899	55th	R–204	D–113	R–47	D–34	R (McKinley)
1899–1901	56th	R–185	D–163	R–53	D–26	R (McKinley); R (McKinley);
1901–1903	57th	R–197	D–151	R–55	D–31	R (T. Roosevelt)
1903–1905	58th	R–208	D–178	R–57	D–33	R (T. Roosevelt)
1905–1907	59th	R–250	D–136	R–57	D–33	R (T. Roosevelt)
1907–1909	60th	R–222	D–164	R–61	D–31	R (T. Roosevelt)
1909–1911	61st	R–219	D–172	R–61	D–32	R (Taft)
1911–1913	62nd	D–228	R–161	R–51	D–41	R (Taft)
1913–1915	63rd	D–291	R–127	D–51	R–44	D (Wilson)
1915–1917	64th	D–230	R–196	D–56	R–40	D (Wilson)
1917–1919	65th	D–216	R–210	D–53	R–42	D (Wilson)
1919–1921	66th	R–240	D–190	R–49	D–47	D (Wilson)

Year	Congress	House		Senate		President
		Majority party	Principal minority party	Majority party	Principal minority party	
1921–1923	67th	R–301	D–131	R–59	D–37	R (Harding)
1923–1925	68th	R–225	D–205	R–51	D–43	R (Coolidge)
1925–1927	69th	R–247	D–183	R–56	D–39	R (Coolidge)
1927–1929	70th	R–237	D–195	R–49	D–46	R (Coolidge)
1929–1931	71st	R–267	D–167	R–56	D–39	R (Hoover)
1931–1933	72nd	D–220	R–214	R–48	D–47	R (Hoover)
1933–1935	73rd	D–310	R–117	D–60	R–35	D (F. Roosevelt)
1935–1937	74th	D–319	R–103	D–69	R–25	D (F. Roosevelt)
1937–1939	75th	D–331	R–89	D–76	R–16	D (F. Roosevelt)
1939–1941	76th	D–261	R–164	D–69	R–23	D (F. Roosevelt)
1941–1943	77th	D–268	R–162	D–66	R–28	D (F. Roosevelt)
1943–1945	78th	D–218	R–208	D–58	R–37	D (F. Roosevelt)
						D (F. Roosevelt);
1945–1947	79th	D–242	R–190	D–56	R–38	D (Truman)
1947–1949	80th	R–245	D–188	R–51	D–45	D (Truman)
1949–1951	81st	D–263	R–171	D–54	R–42	D (Truman)
1951–1953	82nd	D–234	R–199	D–49	R–47	D (Truman)
1953–1955	83rd	R–221	D–211	R–48	D–47	R (Eisenhower)
1955–1957	84th	D–232	R–203	D–48	R–47	R (Eisenhower)
1957–1959	85th	D–233	R–200	D–49	R–47	R (Eisenhower)
1959–1961	86th	D–283	R–153	D–64	R–34	R (Eisenhower)
1961–1963	87th	D–263	R–174	D–65	R–35	D (Kennedy)
						D (Kennedy);
1963–1965	88th	D–258	R–177	D–67	R–33	D (L. Johnson)
1965–1967	89th	D–295	R–140	D–68	R–32	D (L. Johnson)
1967–1969	90th	D–247	R–187	D–64	R–36	D (L. Johnson)
1969–1971	91st	D–243	R–192	D–57	R–43	R (Nixon)
1971–1973	92nd	D–254	R–180	D–54	R–44	R (Nixon)
1973–1975	93rd	D–239	R–192	D–56	R–42	R (Nixon); R (Ford)
1975–1977	94th	D–291	R–144	D–60	R–37	R (Ford)
1977–1979	95th	D–292	R–143	D–61	R–38	D (Carter)
1979–1981	96th	D–276	R–157	D–58	R–41	D (Carter)
1981–1983	97th	D–243	R–192	R–53	D–46	R (Reagan)
1983–1985	98th	D–269	R–165	R–54	D–46	R (Reagan)
1985–1987	99th	D–252	R–182	R–53	D–47	R (Reagan)
1987–1989	100th	D–258	R–177	D–55	R–45	R (Reagan)
1989–1991	101st	D–259	R–174	D–55	R–45	R (G. H. W. Bush)
1991–1993	102nd	D–267	R–167	D–56	R–44	R (G. H. W. Bush)
1993–1995	103rd	D–258	R–176	D–57	R–43	D (Clinton)
1995–1997	104th	R–230	D–204	R–53	D–47	D (Clinton)
1997–1999	105th	R–227	D–207	R–55	D–45	D (Clinton)
1999–2001	106th	R–222	D–211	R–55	D–45	D (Clinton)
2001–2003	107th	R–221	D–212	R–50	D–50	R (G. W. Bush)
2003–2005	108th	R–229	D–205	R–51	D–48	R (G. W. Bush)
2005–2007	109th	R–232	D–202	R–55	D–44	R (G. W. Bush)
2007–2009	110th	D–233	R–202	D–49*	R–49	R (G. W. Bush)
2009–2011	111th	D–236	R–199	D–57*	R–41	D (Obama)
2011–2013	112th	R–242	D–193	D–51*	R–47	D (Obama)
2013–2015	113th	R–234	D–201	D–53*	R–45	D (Obama)
2015–2017	114th	R–248	D–192	R–54	D–44*	D (Obama)
2017–2019	115th	R–238	D–197	R–51	D–47	R (Trump)
2019–2021	116th	D–233	R–200	R–52	D–46	R (Trump)

SOURCES: U.S. Bureau of the Census, *Historical Statistics of the United States, Colonial Times to 1970* (Washington, D.C.: Government Printing Office, 1975); and U.S. Congress, Joint Committee on Printing, *Official Congressional Directory* (Washington, D.C.: Government Printing Office, 1967–); and *America Votes 26–31* (Washington, D.C,: CQ Press, 2007, 2009, 2011, 2013, 2015, 2017, 2019, 2020).

NOTE: Figures are for the beginning of the first session of each Congress. Key To Abbreviations: AD—Administration; AM—Anti-Masonic; D—Democratic; DR—Democratic–Republican; F—Federalist; J—Jacksonian; NR—National Republican; Op—Opposition; R—Republican; U—Unionist; W—Whig.

*The 110th Congress had two independent senators who caucused with the Democrats, giving them control of the chamber that otherwise would have been in Republican control because the vice president at the time was Republican, allowing him to cast a deciding vote in case of a tie. The 111th and 112th Congresses, and 113th, and 114th Congresses had two independent senators who caucused with Democrats, thereby increasing their majority in the chamber.

2018 Elections Returns for Governor, Senate, and House

Following are the official vote returns for the gubernatorial, Senate, and House contests based on figures supplied by the fifty state election boards.

Vote totals are included for all candidates listed on the ballot who received 5 percent or more of the total vote. For candidates who received under 5 percent, consult America Votes 33 (2017–2018), published by CQ Press. The percent column shows the percentage of the total vote cast.

An asterisk (*) indicates an incumbent.

An X denotes candidates without major part opposition; no votes were tallied.

KEY: AC—American Constitution; AMI—American Independent; C—Conservative; CNSTP—Constitution; D—Democratic; G—Green; I—Independent; INDC—Independence; L—Liberal; LIBERT—Libertarian; MDE—Moderate; NPA—No Party Affiliation; R—Republican; REF—Reform; WRI—Write-in

An AL indicates an at-large member of Congress in a state with a single congressional district.

		Vote total	Percent
Alabama			
Governor			
	Kay Ivey (D)*	10,22,457	59.5
	Walt Maddox (D)	6,94,495	40.4
House			
1	Bradley Byrne (R)*	1,53,228	63.2
	Robert Kennedy Jr. (D)	89,226	36.8
2	Martha Roby (R)*	1,38,879	61.4
	Tabitha Isner (D)	86,931	38.4
3	Mike Rogers (R)*	1,47,770	63.7
	Mallory Hagan (D)	83,996	36.2
4	Robert Aderholt (R)*	1,84,255	79.8
	Lee Auman (D)	46,492	20.1
5	Mo Brooks (R)*	1,59,063	61.0
	Peter Joffrion (D)	1,01,388	38.9
6	Gary Palmer (R)*	1,92,542	69.2
	Danner Kline (D)	85,644	30.8
7	Terri Sewell (D)*	1,85,010	97.8
Alaska			
Governor			
	Mike Dunleavy (R)	1,45,631	51.4
	Mark Begich (D)	1,25,739	44.4
House			
AL	Don Young (R)*	1,49,779	53.3
	Alyse Galvin (D)	1,31,199	46.7
Arizona			
Governor			
	Doug Ducey (R)*	13,30,863	56.0
	David Garcia (D)	9,94,341	41.8
Senate			
	Kyrsten Sinema (D)	11,91,100	50
	Martha McSally (R)	11,35,200	47.6
House			
1	Tom O'Halleran (D)*	1,43,240	53.8
	Wendy Rogers (R)	1,22,784	46.1
2	Ann Kirkpatrick (D)	1,61,000	54.7
	Lea Marquez Peterson (R)	1,33,083	45.2
3	Raul Grijalva (D)*	1,14,650	63.9
	Nicolas Pierson (R)	64,868	36.1
4	Paul Gosar (R)*	1,88,842	68.2
	David Brill (D)	84,521	30.5
5	Andy Briggs (R)*	1,86,037	59.4
	Joan Greene (D)	1,27,027	40.6
6	David Schweikert (R)*	1,73,140	55.2
	Anita Malik (D)	1,40,559	44.8
7	Ruben Gallego (D)*	1,13,044	85.6
	Gary Swing (Green)	18,706	14.2
8	Debbie Lesko (R)*	1,68,835	55.5
	Hiral Tipirneni (D)	1,35,569	44.5
9	Greg Stanton (D)	1,59,583	61.1
	Stever Ferrara (R)	1,01,662	38.9

		Vote total	Percent
Arkansas			
Governor			
	Asa Hutchinson (R)*	5,82,406	65.3
	Jaren Henderson (D)	2,83,218	31.8
House			
1	Rick Crawford (R)*	1,38,757	68.9
	Chintan Desai (D)	57,907	28.8
2	French Hill (R)*	1,32,125	52.1
	Clarke Tucker (D)	1,16,135	45.8
3	Steve Womack (R)*	1,48,717	64.7
	Joshua Mahony (D)	74,952	32.6
4	Bruce Westerman (R)*	1,36,740	66.7
	Hayden Shamel (D)	63,984	31.2
California			
Governor			
	Gavin Newsom (D)	77,21,410	61.9
	John Cox (R)	47,42,825	38.1
Senate			
	Dianne Feinstein (D)*	60,19,422	54.2
	Kevin de León (D)	50,93,942	45.8
House			
1	Doug LaMalfa (R)*	1,60,046	54.9
	Audrey Denney (D)	1,31,548	45.1
2	Jared Huffman (D)*	2,43,081	77.0
	Dale K. Mensing (R)	72,576	23.0
3	John Garamendi (D)*	1,34,875	58.1
	Charlie Schaupp (R)	97,376	41.9
4	Tom McClintock (R)*	1,84,401	54.1
	Jessica Morse (D)	1,56,253	45.9
5	Mike Thompson (D)*	2,05,860	78.9
	Anthony Mills (I)	55,158	21.1
6	Doris Matsui (D)*	1,62,411	80.4
	Jrmar Jefferson (D)	39,528	19.6
7	Ami Bera (D)*	1,55,016	55.0
	Andrew Grant (R)	1,26,601	45.0
8	Paul Cook (R)*	1,02,415	60.0
	Tim Donnelly (R)	68,370	40.0
9	Jerry McNerney (D)*	1,13,414	56.5
	Marla Livengood (R)	87,349	43.5
10	Josh Harder (D)	1,15,945	52.3
	Jeff Denham (R)*	1,05,955	47.7
11	Mark DeSaulnier (D)*	2,04,369	74.1
	John Fitzgerald (R)	71,312	25.9
12	Nancy Pelosi (D)*	2,75,292	86.8
	Lisa Remmer (R)	41,780	13.2
13	Barbara Lee (D)*	2,60,580	88.4
	Laura Wells (Green)	34,257	11.6
14	Jackie Speier (D)*	2,11,384	79.2
	Christina Osmena (R)	55,439	20.8

		Vote total	Percent
15	Eric Swalwell (D)*	1,77,989	73.0
	Rudy Peters (R)	65,940	27.0
16	Jim Costa (D)*	82,266	57.5
	Elizabeth Heng (R)	60,693	42.5
17	Ro Khanna (D)*	1,59,105	75.3
	Ron Cohen (R)	52,057	24.7
18	Anna Eshoo (D)*	2,25,142	74.5
	Christine Russell (R)	77,096	25.5
19	Zoe Lofgren (D)*	1,62,496	73.8
	Justin Aguilera (R)	57,823	26.2
20	Jimmy Panetta (D)*	1,83,677	81.4
	Ronald Paul Kabat (I)	42,044	18.6
21	TJ Cox (D)	57,239	50.4
	David Valadao (R)*	56,377	49.6
22	Devin Nunes (R)*	1,17,243	52.7
	Andrew Janz (D)	1,05,136	47.3
23	Kevin McCarthy (R)*	1,31,113	63.7
	Tatiana Matta (D)	74,661	36.3
24	Salud Carabajal (D)*	1,66,550	58.6
	Justin Fareed (R)	1,17,881	41.4
25	Katie Hill (D)	1,33,209	54.4
	Steve Knight (R)*	1,11,813	45.6
26	Julia Brownley (D)*	1,58,216	61.9
	Antonio Sabato Jr. (R)	97,210	38.1
27	Judy Chu (D)*	1,60,504	79.2
	Bryan Witt (D)	42,132	20.8
28	Adam Schiff (D)*	1,96,662	78.4
	Johnny Nalbandian (R)	54,272	21.6
29	Tony Cardenas (D)*	1,24,697	80.6
	Benito Bernal (R)	29,995	19.4
30	Brad Sherman (D)*	1,91,573	73.4
	Mark S. Reed (R)	69,420	26.6
31	Pete Aguilar (D)*	1,10,143	58.7
	Sean Flynn (R)	77,352	41.3
32	Grace Napolitano (D)*	1,21,759	68.8
	Joshua Scott (R)	55,272	31.2
33	Ted Lieu (D)*	2,19,091	70.0
	Kenneth Wright (R)	93,769	30.0
34	Jimmy Gomez (D)*	1,10,195	72.5
	Kenneth Mejia (Green)	41,711	27.5
35	Norma Torres (D)*	1,03,420	69.4
	Christian Valiente (R)	45,604	30.6
36	Raul Ruiz (D)*	1,22,169	59.0

		Vote total	Percent
	Kimberlin Brown Pelzer (R)	84,839	41.0
37	Karen Bass (D)*	2,10,555	89.1
	Ron Bassilian (R)	25,823	10.9
38	Linda Sanchez (D)*	1,39,188	68.9
	Ryan Downing (R)	62,968	31.1
39	Gil Cisneros (D)	1,26,002	51.6
	Young Kim (R)	1,18,391	48.4
40	Lucille Roybal-Allard (D)*	93,938	77.3
	Rodolfo Cortes Barragan (Green)	27,511	22.7
41	Mark Takano (D)*	1,08,227	65.1
	Aja Smith (R)	58,021	34.9
42	Ken Calvert (R)*	1,31,040	56.5
	Julia Peacock (D)	1,00,892	43.5
43	Maxine Waters (D)*	1,52,272	77.7
	Omar Navarro (R)	43,780	22.3
44	Nanette Barragan (D)*	97,944	68.3
	Aja Brown (D)	45,378	31.7
45	Katie Porter (D)	1,58,906	52.1
	Mimi Walters (R)*	1,46,383	47.9
46	Lou Correa (D)*	1,02,278	69.1
	Russell Lambert (R)	45,638	30.9
47	Alan Lowenthal (D)*	1,43,354	64.9
	John Briscoe (R)	77,682	35.1
48	Harley Rouda (D)	1,57,837	53.6
	Dana Rohrabacher (R)*	1,36,899	46.4
49	Mike Levin (D)	1,66,453	56.4
	Diane Harkey (R)	1,28,577	43.6
50	Duncan D. Hunter (R)*	1,34,362	51.7
	Ammar Campa-Najjar (D)	1,25,448	48.3
51	Juan Vargas (D)*	1,09,527	71.2
	Juan Hidalgo (R)	44,301	28.8
52	Scott Peters (D)*	1,88,992	63.8
	Omar Qudrat (R)	1,07,015	36.2
53	Susan Davis (D)*	1,85,667	69.1
	Morgan Murtaugh (R)	83,127	30.9

Colorado

Governor

		Vote total	Percent
	Jared Polis (D)	13,48,888	53.4
	Walker Stapleton (R)	10,80,801	42.8

House

		Vote total	Percent
1	Diana DeGette (D)*	2,72,886	73.8
	Casper Stockham (R)	85,207	23.0
2	Joe Neguse (D)	13,48,888	53.4
	Peter Yu (R)	10,80,801	42.8
3	Scott Tipton (R)*	1,73,205	51.5
	Diane Mitsch Bush (D)	1,46,426	43.6
4	Ken Buck (R)*	2,24,038	60.6
	Karen McCormick (D)	1,45,544	39.4
5	Doug Lamborn (R)*	1,84,002	57.0
	Stephany Rose Spaulding (D)	1,26,848	39.3
6	Jason Crow (D)	1,87,639	54.1
	Mike Coffman (R)*	1,48,685	42.9
7	Ed Perlmutter (D)*	2,04,260	60.4
	Mark Barrington (R)	1,19,734	35.4

Connecticut

Governor

		Vote total	Percent
	Ned Lamont (D)	6,94,510	49.4
	Bob Stefanowski (R)	6,50,138	46.2

Senate

		Vote total	Percent
	Chris Murphy (D)*	8,25,579	59.5
	Matthew Corey (R)	5,45,717	39.3

House

		Vote total	Percent
1	John B. Larson (D)*	1,75,087	63.9
	Jennifer Nye (R)	96,024	35.0
2	Joe Courtney (D)*	1,79,731	62.2
	Dan Postemski (R)	1,02,483	35.4
3	Rosa DeLauro (D)*	1,74,572	64.6
	Angel Cadena (R)	95,667	35.4
4	Jim Himes (D)*	1,68,726	61.2
	Harry Arora (R)	1,06,921	38.8
5	Jahanna Hayes (D)	1,51,225	55.9
	Manny Santos (R)	1,19,426	44.1

Delaware

Senate

		Vote total	Percent
	Tom Carper (D)*	2,17,385	60.0
	Robert Arlett (R)	1,37,127	37.8

House

		Vote total	Percent
AL	Lisa Blunt Rochester (D)*	2,27,353	64.5
	Scott Walker (R)	1,25,384	35.5

Florida

Governor

		Vote total	Percent
	Ron DeSantis (R)	40,76,186	49.6
	Andrew Gillum (D)	40,43,723	49.2

Senate

		Vote total	Percent
	Rick Scott (R)	40,99,505	50.1
	Bill Nelson (D)*	40,89,472	49.9

House

		Vote total	Percent
1	Matt Gaetz (R)*	2,16,189	67.1
	Jennifer Zimmerman (D)	1,06,199	32.9
2	Neal Dunn (R)*	1,99,335	67.4
	Bob Rackleff (D)	96,233	32.6
3	Ted Yoho (R)*	1,76,616	57.6
	Yvonne Hayes Hinson (D)	1,29,880	42.4
4	John Rutherford (R)*	2,48,420	65.2
	Ges Selmon (D)	1,23,351	32.4
5	Alfred Lawson (D)*	1,80,527	66.8
	Virginia Fuller (R)	89,799	33.2
6	Michael Waltz (R)	1,87,891	56.3
	Nancy Soderberg (D)	1,45,758	43.7
7	Stephanie Murphy (D)*	1,83,113	57.7
	Mike Miller (R)	1,34,285	42.3
8	Bill Posey (R)*	2,18,112	60.5
	Sanjay Patel (D)	1,42,415	39.5
9	Darren Soto (D)*	1,72,172	58.0
	Wayne Liebnitzky (R)	1,24,565	42.0
10	Val Demings (D)*	X	X
11	Daniel Webster (R)*	2,39,395	65.1
	Dana Cottrell (D)	1,28,053	34.8
12	Gus Bilirakis (R)*	1,94,564	58.1
	Chris Hunter (D)	1,32,844	39.7
13	Charlie Crist (D)*	2,15,405	53.0
	George Buck (R)	1,90,713	47.0
14	Kathy Castor (D)*	X	X
15	Ross Spano (R)	1,51,380	53.0
	Kristen Carlson (D)	1,34,132	47.0
16	Vern Buchanan (R)*	1,97,483	54.6
	David Shapiro (D)	1,64,463	45.4
17	Greg Steube (R)	1,93,326	62.3
	Allen Ellison (D)	1,17,194	37.7
18	Brian Mast (R)*	1,85,905	54.3
	Lauren Baer (D)	1,56,454	45.7
19	Francis Rooney (R)*	2,11,465	62.3
	David Holden (D)	1,28,106	37.7
20	Alcee Hastings (D)*	X	X
21	Lois Frankel (D)*	X	X
22	Ted Deutch (D)*	1,84,634	62.0
	Nicolas Kimaz (R)	1,13,049	38.0
23	Debbie Wasserman Schultz (D)*	1,61,611	58.5
	Joseph "Joe" Kaufman (R)	99,446	36.0
24	Frederica Wilson (D)*	X	X
25	Mario Diaz-Balart (R)*	1,28,672	60.5
	Mary Barzee Flores (D)	84,173	39.5
26	Debbie Mucarsel-Powell (D)*	1,19,797	50.9
	Carlos Curbelo (R)*	1,15,678	49.1
27	Donna Shalala (D)	1,30,743	51.8
	Maria Elvira Salazar (R)	1,15,588	45.8

Georgia

Governor

		Vote total	Percent
	Brian Kemp (R)	19,78,408	50.2
	Stacey Abrams (D)	19,23,685	48.8

House

		Vote total	Percent
1	Earl Carter (R)*	1,89,457	58.3
	Lisa Ring (D)	1,35,238	41.7
2	Sanford Bishop Jr. (D)*	1,36,699	59.6
	Herman West Jr. (R)	92,472	40.4
3	Drew Ferguson (R)*	1,91,996	65.5
	Chuck Enderlin (D)	1,01,010	34.5
4	Hank Johnson (D)*	2,27,717	78.8
	Joe Profit (R)	61,092	21.2
5	John Lewis (D)*	2,75,406	100.0
6	Lucy McBath (D)	1,60,139	50.5
	Karen Handel (R)*	1,56,875	49.5
7	Rob Woodall (R)*	1,40,443	50.1
	Carolyn Bourdeaux (D)	1,40,010	49.9
8	Austin Scott (R)*	1,98,152	99.7
9	Doug Collins (R)*	2,24,661	79.5
	Josh McCall (D)	57,912	20.5
10	Jody Hice (R)*	1,90,396	62.9
	Tabitha Johnson-Green (D)	1,12,339	37.1
11	Barry Loudermilk (R)*	1,91,887	61.8
	Flynn Broady Jr. (D)	1,18,653	38.2
12	Rick Allen (R)*	1,48,986	59.5
	Francys Johnson (D)	1,01,503	40.5
13	David Scott (D)*	2,23,157	76.2
	David Callahan (R)	69,760	23.8
14	Tom Graves (R)*	1,75,743	76.5
	Steven Foster (D)	53,981	23.5

Hawaii

Governor

		Vote total	Percent
	David Ige (D)*	2,44,934	62.7
	Andria Tupola (R)	1,31,719	33.7

Senate

		Vote total	Percent
	Mazie K. Hirono (D)*	2,76,316	71.2
	Ron Curtis (R)	1,12,035	28.8

House

		Vote total	Percent
1	Ed Case (D)	1,34,650	73.1
	Cam Cavasso (R)	42,498	23.1

NOTE: *In Florida in a district where a candidate had no opposition, including write-ins, no vote was taken.*

		Vote total	Percent
2	Tulsi Gabbard (D)*	1,53,271	77.4
	Brian Evans (R)	44,850	22.6

Idaho
Governor

		Vote total	Percent
	Brad Little (R)	3,61,661	59.8
	Paulette E. Jordan (D)	2,31,081	38.2

House

1	Russ Fulcher (R)	1,97,719	62.8
	Cristina McNeil (D)	96,922	30.8
2	Mike Simpson (R)*	1,70,274	60.7
	Aaron Swisher (D)	1,10,381	39.3

Illinois
Governor

	J.B. Pritzker (D)	24,79,746	54.5
	Bruce Rauner (R)*	17,65,751	38.8

House

1	Bobby Rush (D)*	1,89,560	73.5
	Jimmy Lee Tillman (R)	50,960	19.8
2	Robin Kelly (D)*	1,83,816	80.7
	David Merkle (R)	43,875	19.3
3	Dan Lipinski (D)*	1,63,053	73.0
	Arthur Jones (R)	57,885	25.9
4	Jesus Garcia (D)	1,43,895	86.6
	Mark Wayne Lorch (R)	22,294	13.4
5	Mike Quigley (D)*	2,13,992	76.7
	Tom Hanson (R)	65,134	23.3
6	Sean Casten (D)	1,69,001	53.6
	Peter Roskam (R)*	1,46,445	46.4
7	Danny K. Davis (D)*	2,15,746	87.6
	Craig Cameron (R)	30,497	12.4
8	Raja Krishnamoorthi (D)*	1,30,054	66.0
	Jitendra Diganvker (R)	67,073	34.0
9	Jan Schakowsky (D)*	2,13,368	73.5
	John Elleson (R)	76,983	26.5
10	Brad Schneider (D)*	1,51,860	65.4
	Doug Bennett (R)	80,361	34.6
11	Bill Foster (D)*	1,45,407	63.8
	Nick Stella (R)	82,358	36.2
12	Mike Bost (R)*	1,34,884	51.6
	Brendan Kelly (D)	1,18,724	45.4
13	Rodney Davis (R)*	1,36,516	50.4
	Betsy Londrigan (D)	1,34,458	49.6
14	Lauren Underwood (D)	1,56,035	52.5
	Randy Hultgren (R)*	1,41,164	47.5
15	John Shimkus (R)*	1,81,294	70.9
	Kevin Gaither (D)	74,309	29.1
16	Adam Kinzinger (R)*	1,51,254	59.1
	Sara Dady (D)	1,04,569	40.9
17	Cheri Bustos (D)*	1,42,659	62.1
	Bill Fawell (I)	87,090	37.9
18	Darin LaHood (R)*	1,95,927	67.2
	Junius Rodriguez (D)	95,486	32.8

Indiana
Senate

	Mike Braun (R)	11,58,000	50.7
	Joe Donnelly (D)*	10,23,553	44.8

House

1	Pete Visclosky (D)*	1,59,611	65.1
	Mark Leyva (R)	85,594	34.9
2	Jackie Walorski (R)*	1,25,499	54.8
	Mel Hall (D)	1,03,363	45.2
3	Jim Banks (R)*	1,58,927	64.7
	Courtney Tritch (D)	86,610	35.3
4	Jim Baird (R)	1,56,539	64.1
	Tobi Beck (D)	87,824	35.9
5	Susan Brooks (R)*	1,80,035	56.8
	Dee Thornton (D)	1,37,142	43.2
6	Greg Pence (R)*	1,54,260	63.8
	Jeannine Lee Lake (D)	79,430	32.9
7	Andre Carson (D)*	1,41,139	64.9
	Wayne Harmon (R)	76,457	35.1
8	Larry Bucshon (R)*	1,57,396	64.4
	William Tanoos (D)	86,895	35.6
9	Trey Hollingsworth (R)*	1,53,271	56.5
	Liz Watson (D)	1,18,090	43.5

Iowa
Governor

	Kim Reynolds (R)*	6,67,275	50.3
	Fred Hubbell (D)	6,30,986	47.5

House

1	Abby Finkenauer (D)	1,70,342	51.0
	Rod Blum (R)*	1,53,442	45.9
2	Dave Loebsack (D)*	1,71,446	54.8
	Chris Peters (R)	1,33,287	42.6
3	Cindy Axne (D)	1,75,642	49.3
	David Young (R)*	1,67,933	47.1
4	Steve King (R)*	1,57,676	50.3
	J. D. Scholten (D)	1,47,246	47.0

Kansas
Governor

	Laura Kelly (D)	5,06,727	48.0
	Kris Kobach (R)	4,53,645	43.0
	Greg Orman (I)	68,590	6.5

House

1	Roger Marshall (R)*	1,53,082	68.1
	Alan LaPolice (D)	71,558	31.9
2	Steve Watkins (R)	1,26,098	47.6
	Paul Davis (D)	1,23,859	46.8
	Kelly Standley (LIBERT)	14,731	5.6
3	Sharice Davids (D)	1,70,518	53.6
	Kevin Yoder (R)*	1,39,762	43.9
4	Ron Estes (R)*	1,44,248	59.4
	James Thompson (D)	98,445	40.6

Kentucky
House

1	James Comer Jr. (R)	1,72,167	68.6
	Paul Walker (D)	78,849	31.4
2	Brett Guthrie (R)*	1,71,700	66.7
	Hank Linderman (D)	79,964	31.1
3	John Yarmuth (D)*	1,73,002	62.1
	Vickie Yates Glisson (R)	1,01,930	36.6
4	Thomas Massie (R)*	1,62,946	62.2
	Seth Hall (D)	90,584	34.6
5	Hal Rogers (R)*	1,72,093	78.9
	Kenneth Stepp (D)	45,890	21
6	Andy Barr (R)*	1,54,468	51
	Amy McGrath (D)	1,44,736	47.8

Louisiana
House

1	Steve Scalise (R)*	1,92,555	71.5
	Tammy Savoie (D)	44,273	16.4
	Lee A. Dugas (D)	18,560	6.9
2	Cedric Richmond (D)*	1,90,182	80.6
	Jesse Schmidt (I)	20,465	8.7
	Belden Batiste (I)	17,260	7.3
3	Clay Higgins (R)*	1,36,876	55.7
	Mildred Methvin (D)	43,729	17.8
	Josh Guillory (R)	31,387	12.8
	Rob Anderson (D)	13,477	5.5
4	Mike Johnson (R)*	1,39,326	64.2
	Ryan Trundle (D)	72,934	33.6
5	Ralph Abraham (R)*	1,49,018	66.5
	Jessee Carlton Fleenor (D)	67,118	30.0
6	Garret Graves (R)*	1,86,553	69.5
	Justin DeWitt (D)	55,089	20.5
	Andie Saizan (D)	21,627	8.1

Maine
Governor

	Janet T. Mills (D)	3,20,962	50.9
	Shawn Moody (R)	2,72,311	43.2
	Teresea Hayes (I)	37,268	5.9

Senate

	Angus King (I)*	3,44,575	54.3
	Eric Brakey (R)	2,23,502	35.2
	Zak Ringelstein (D)	66,268	10.4

House

1	Chellie Pingree (D)*	2,01,195	58.8
	Mark Holbrook (R)	1,11,188	32.5
	Martin Grohman (I)	29,670	8.7
2	Jared Golden (D)	1,42,440	50.6
	Bruce Poliquin (R)*	1,38,931	49.4

Maryland
Governor

	Larry Hogan (R)*	12,75,644	55.4
	Ben Jealous (D)	10,02,639	43.5

Senate

	Ben Cardin (D)*	14,91,614	64.9
	Tony Campbell (R)	6,97,017	30.3

House

1	Andrew P. Harris (R)*	1,83,662	60
	Jesse Colvin (D)	1,16,631	38.1
2	Dutch Ruppersberger (D)*	1,67,201	66
	Elizabeth Matory (R)	77,782	30.7
3	John Sarbanes (D)*	2,02,407	69.1
	Charles Anthony (R)	82,774	28.3
4	Anthony G. Brown (D)*	2,09,642	78.1
	George McDermott (R)	53,327	19.9
5	Steny Hoyer (D)*	2,13,796	70.3
	William Devine III (R)	82,361	27.1
6	David Trone (D)	1,63,346	59
	Amie Hoeber (R)	1,05,209	38
7	Elijah Cummings (D)*	2,02,345	76.4
	Richmond Davis (R)	56,266	21.3
8	Jamie Raskin (D)*	2,17,679	68.2
	John Walsh (R)	96,525	30.2

Massachusetts
Governor

	Charlie Baker (R)*	17,81,341	64.7
	Jay Gonzalez (D)	8,85,770	32.2

Senate

	Elizabeth Warren (D)*	16,33,371	60.3
	Geoff Diehl (R)	9,79,210	36.2

NOTE: *Iowa's 5th district became obsolete for the 113th Congress in 2013.*

House

	Candidate	Vote total	Percent
1	Richard Neal (D)*	2,11,790	97.6
2	Jim McGovern (D)*	1,91,332	67.2
	Tracy Lovvorn (R)	93,391	32.8
3	Lori Trahan (D)	1,73,175	62.0
	Rick Green (R)	93,445	33.5
4	Joseph P. Kennedy III (D)*	2,45,289	97.7
5	Katherine Clark (D)*	2,36,243	75.9
	John Hugo (R)	74,856	24.0
6	Seth Moulton (D)*	2,17,703	65.2
	Joseph Schneider (R)	1,04,798	31.4
7	Ayanna Pressley (D)	2,16,559	98.3
8	Stephen Lynch (D)*	2,59,159	98.4
9	Bill Keating (D)*	1,92,347	59.4
	Peter Tedeschi (R)	1,31,463	40.6

Michigan

Governor

Candidate	Vote total	Percent
Gretchen Whitmer (D)	22,66,193	53.3
Bill Schuette (R)	18,59,534	43.7

Senate

Candidate	Vote total	Percent
Debbie Stabenow (D)*	22,14,478	52.3
John James (R)	19,38,818	45.8

House

	Candidate	Vote total	Percent
1	Jack Bergman (R)*	1,87,251	56.3
	Matthew Morgan (D)	1,45,246	43.7
2	Bill Huizenga (R)*	1,68,970	55.3
	Rob Davidson (D)	1,31,254	43
3	Justin Amash (R)*	1,69,107	54.4
	Cathy Albro (D)	1,34,185	43.2
4	John Moolenaar (R)*	1,78,510	62.6
	Jerry Hilliard (D)	1,06,540	37.4
5	Dan Kildee (D)*	1,64,502	59.5
	Travis Wines (R)	99,265	35.9
6	Fred Upton (R)*	1,47,436	50.2
	Matt Longjohn (D)	1,34,082	45.7
7	Tim Walberg (R)*	1,58,730	53.8
	Gretchen Driskell (D)	1,36,330	46.2
8	Elissa Slotkin (D)	1,72,880	50.6
	Mike Bishop (R)*	1,59,782	46.8
9	Andy Levin (D)*	1,81,734	59.7
	Candius Stearns (R)	1,12,123	36.8
10	Paul Mitchell (R)*	1,82,808	60.3
	Kimberly Bizon (D)	1,06,061	35
11	Hayley Stevens (D)	1,81,912	51.8
	Lena Epstein (R)	1,58,463	45.2
12	Debbie Dingell (D)*	2,00,588	68.1
	Jeff Jones (R)	85,115	28.9
13	Rashida Tlaib (D)	1,65,355	84.2
14	Brenda Lawrence (D)*	2,14,334	80.9
	Marc Herschfus (R)	45,899	17.3

Minnesota

Governor

Candidate	Vote total	Percent
Tim Walz (D)	13,93,096	53.8
Jeff Johnson (R)	10,97,705	42.4

Senate

Candidate	Vote total	Percent
Amy Klobuchar (D)*	15,66,174	60.3
Jim Newberger (R)	9,40,437	36.2
Special Tina Smith (D)*	13,70,540	53.0
Karin Housley (R)	10,95,777	42.4

House

	Candidate	Vote total	Percent
1	Jim Hagedorn (R)	1,46,200	50.1
	Dan Feehan (D)	1,44,885	49.7
2	Angie Craig (D)	1,77,958	52.7
3	Dean Phillips (D)	2,02,404	55.6
	Erik Paulsen (R)*	1,60,839	44.2
4	Betty McCollum (D)*	2,16,865	66.0
	Greg Ryan (R)	97,747	29.8
5	Ilhan Omar (D)	2,67,703	78.0
	Jennifer Zielinski (R)	74,440	21.7
6	Tom Emmer (R)*	1,92,931	61.1
	Ian Todd (D)	1,22,332	38.8
7	Collin Peterson (D)*	1,46,672	52.1
	Dave Hughes (R)	1,34,668	47.8
8	Pete Stauber (R)	1,59,364	50.7
	Joe Radinovich (D)	1,41,950	45.2

Mississippi

Senate

	Candidate	Vote total	Percent
	Roger Wicker (R)*	5,47,619	58.5
	David Baria (D)	3,69,567	39.5
Special	Cindy Hyde-Smith (R)*	4,86,769	53.6
	Mike Espy (D)	4,20,819	46.4

House

	Candidate	Vote total	Percent
1	Trent Kelly (R)*	1,58,245	66.9
	Randy Wadkins (D)	76,601	32.4
2	Bennie Thompson (D)*	1,58,921	71.8
	Troy Ray (I)	48,104	21.7
	Irving Harris (REF)	14,354	6.5
3	Michael Guest (R)	1,60,284	62.3
	Michael Evans (D)	94,461	36.7
4	Steven Palazzo (R)*	1,52,633	68.2
	Jeramey Anderson (D)	68,787	30.8

Missouri

Senate

Candidate	Vote total	Percent
Josh Hawley (R)	12,54,927	51.4
Claire McCaskill (D)*	11,12,935	45.6

House

	Candidate	Vote total	Percent
1	Lacy Clay (D)*	2,19,781	80.1
	Robert Vroman (R)	45,867	16.7
2	Ann Wagner (R)*	1,92,477	51.2
	Cort VanOstran (D)	1,77,611	47.2
3	Blaine Luetkemeyer (R)*	2,11,243	65.1
	Katy Geppert (D)	1,06,589	32.8
4	Vicky Hartzler (R)*	1,90,138	64.8
	Renee Hoagenson (D)	95,968	32.7
5	Emanuel Cleaver II (D)*	1,75,019	61.7
	Jacob Turk (R)	1,01,069	35.6
6	Sam Graves (R)*	1,99,796	65.4
	Henry Martin (D)	97,660	32.0
7	Billy Long (R)*	1,96,343	66.2
	Jamie Schoolcraft (D)	89,190	30.1
8	Jason Smith (R)*	1,94,042	73.4
	Kathy Ellis (D)	66,151	25.0

Montana

Senate

Candidate	Vote total	Percent
Jon Tester (D)*	2,53,876	50.3
Matt Rosendale (R)	2,35,963	46.8

House

	Candidate	Vote total	Percent
AL	Greg Gianforte (R)*	2,56,661	50.9
	Kathleen Williams (D)	2,33,284	46.2

Nebraska

Governor

Candidate	Vote total	Percent
Pete Ricketts (R)*	4,11,812	59.0
Bob Krist (D)	2,86,169	41.0

Senate

Candidate	Vote total	Percent
Deb Fischer (R)*	4,03,151	57.7
Jane Raybould (D)	2,69,917	38.6

House

	Candidate	Vote total	Percent
1	Jeff Fortenberry (R)*	1,41,712	60.4
	Jessica McClure (D)	93,069	39.6
2	Don Bacon (R)*	1,26,715	51.0
	Kara Eastman (D)	1,21,770	49.0
3	Adrian Smith (R)*	1,63,650	76.7
	Paul Theobald (D)	49,654	23.3

Nevada

Governor

Candidate	Vote total	Percent
Steve Sisolak (D)	4,80,007	49.4
Adam Laxalt (R)	4,40,320	45.3

Senate

Candidate	Vote total	Percent
Jacky Rosen (D)	4,90,071	50.4
Dean Heller (R)*	4,41,202	45.4

House

	Candidate	Vote total	Percent
1	Dina Titus (D)*	1,00,707	66.2
	Joyce Bentley (R)	46,978	30.9
2	Mark Amodei (R)*	1,67,435	58.2
	Clint Koble (D)	1,20,102	41.8
3	Susie Lee (D)	1,48,501	51.9
	Danny Tarkanian (R)	1,22,566	42.8
4	Steven Horsford (D)	1,21,962	51.9
	Cresent Hardy (R)	1,02,748	43.8

New Hampshire

Governor

Candidate	Vote total	Percent
Chris Sununu (R)*	3,02,764	52.8
Molly Kelly (D)	2,62,359	45.8

House

	Candidate	Vote total	Percent
1	Chris Pappas (D)	1,55,884	53.6
	Eddie Edwards (R)	1,30,996	45.0
2	Ann McLane Kuster (D)*	1,55,358	55.5
	Steve Negron (R)	1,17,990	42.2

New Jersey

Senate

Candidate	Vote total	Percent
Bob Menendez (D)*	17,11,654	54.0
Bob Hugin (R)	13,57,355	42.8

House

	Candidate	Vote total	Percent
1	Donald Norcross (D)*	1,69,628	64.4
	Paul Dilks (R)	87,617	33.3
2	Jeff Van Drew (D)	1,36,685	52.9
	Seth Grossman (R)	1,16,866	45.2
3	Andrew Kim (D)	1,53,473	50.0
	Tom MacArthur (R)*	1,49,500	48.7
4	Chris Smith (R)*	1,63,065	55.4
	Josh Welle (D)	1,26,766	43.1
5	Josh Gottheimer (D)*	1,69,546	56.2
	John McCann (R)	1,28,255	42.5
6	Frank Pallone (D)*	1,40,752	63.6
	Rich Pezzullo (R)	80,443	36.4
7	Tom Malinowski (D)	1,66,985	51.7
	Leonard Lance (R)*	1,50,785	46.7
8	Albio Sires (D)*	1,19,881	78.1
	John Muniz (R)	28,725	18.7
9	Bill Pascrell (D)*	1,40,832	70.3
	Eric Fisher (R)	57,854	28.9
10	Donald Payne, Jr. (D)*	1,75,253	87.6
	Agha Khan (R)	20,191	10.1
11	Mikie Sherrill (D)	1,83,684	56.8
	Jay Webber (R)	1,36,322	42.1
12	Bonnie Watson Coleman (D)*	1,73,334	68.7
	Daryl Kipnis (R)	79,041	31.3

	Vote total	Percent
New Mexico		
Governor		
Michelle Lujan		
Grisham (D)	3,98,368	57.2
Steve Pearce (R)	2,98,091	42.8
Senate		
Martin Heinrich (D)	3,76,998	54.1
Mick Rich (R)	2,12,813	30.5
Gary Johnson		
(LIBERT)	1,07,201	15.4
House		
1 Debra Haaland (D)	1,47,336	59.1
Janice Arnold-		
Jones (R)	90,507	36.3
2 Xochitl Torres		
Small (D)	1,01,489	50.9
Yvette Herrell (R)	97,767	49.1
3 Ben R. Lujan (D)*	1,55,201	63.4
Jerald Steve		
McFall (R)	76,427	31.2
Christopher Manning		
(LIBERT)	13,265	5.4
New York		
Governor		
Andrew Cuomo		
(D)*	36,35,340	59.6
Marcus		
Molinaro (R)	22,07,602	36.2
Senate		
Kirsten		
Gillibrand (D)*	40,56,931	67.0
Chele Farley (R)	19,98,220	33.0
House		
1 Lee Zeldin (R)*	1,39,027	51.5
Perry Gershon (D)	1,27,991	47.4
2 Peter T. King (R)*	1,28,078	53.1
Liuba Grechen		
Shirley (D)	1,13,074	46.9
3 Tom Suozzi (D)*	1,57,456	59.0
Dan DeBono (R)	1,09,514	41.0
4 Kathleen Rice (D)*	1,59,535	61.3
Ameer Benno (R)	1,00,571	38.7
5 Gregory W.		
Meeks (D)*	1,60,500	99.4
6 Grace Meng (D)*	1,11,646	90.9
Tom Hillgardner		
(Green)	11,209	9.1
7 Nydia Velazquez (D)*	1,46,687	93.4
Joseph Lieberman		
(C)	8,670	5.5
8 Hakeem		
Jeffries (D)*	1,80,376	94.2
Ernest Johnson (C)	9,997	5.2
9 Yvette Clarke (D)*	1,81,455	89.2
Lutchi Gayot (R)	20,901	10.3
10 Jerrold Nadler (D)*	1,73,095	82.1
Namoi Levin (R)	37,619	17.8
11 Max Rose (D)	1,01,823	53
Daniel Donovan		
(R)*	89,441	46.6
12 Carolyn		
Maloney (D)*	2,17,430	86.4
Eliot Rabin (R)	30,446	12.1
13 Andriano Espaillat		
(D)*	1,80,035	94.6
Jineea Butler (R)	10,268	5.4
14 Alexandria Ocasio-		
Cortez (D)	1,10,318	78.2
Anthony Pappas (R)	19,202	13.6
Joseph Crowley		
(WFP)*	9,348	6.6

	Vote total	Percent
15 Jose E. Serrano (D)*	1,24,469	96.0
Jason Gonzalez (R)	5,205	4.0
16 Eliot Engel (D)*	1,82,044	100.0
17 Nita Lowey (D)*	1,70,168	88.0
Joseph Ciardullo		
(REF)	23,150	12.0
Sean Patrick		
18 Maloney (D)*	1,39,564	55.5
James O'Donnell		
(R)	1,12,035	45.5
19 Antonio Delgado		
(D)	1,47,873	51.4
John Faso (R)*	1,32,873	46.2
20 Paul D. Tonko (D)*	1,76,811	66.5
Joe Vitollo (R)	89,058	33.5
21 Elise M. Stefanik		
(R)*	1,31,981	56.1
Tedra Cobb (D)	99,791	42.4
22 Anthony Brindisi		
(D)	1,27,715	50.9
Claudia Tenney		
(R)*	1,23,242	49.1
23 Thomas W. Reed		
II (R)*	1,30,323	54.2
Tracy Mitrano (D)	1,09,932	45.8
24 John M. Katko (R)*	1,36,920	52.6
Dana Balter (D)	1,23,226	47.4
25 Joseph Morelle		
(D)*	1,41,290	58.3
James Maxwell (R)	1,01,085	41.7
26 Brian Higgins (D)*	1,69,166	73.3
Renee Zeno (R)	61,488	26.7
27 Chris Collins (R)*	1,40,146	49.1
Nate McMurray (D)	1,39,059	48.8
North Carolina		
House		
1 G. K. Butterfield		
(D)*	1,90,457	69.8
Roger Allison (R)	82,218	30.2
2 George E.B.		
Holding (R)*	1,70,072	51.3
Linda Coleman (D)	1,51,977	45.8
3 Walter B. Jones Jr.		
(R)*	1,87,901	100.0
4 David Price (D)*	2,47,067	72.4
Steve Von Loor (R)	82,052	24.0
5 Virginia Foxx (R)*	1,59,917	57.0
Denise Adams (D)	1,20,468	43.0
6 Mark Walker (R)*	1,60,709	56.5
Ryan Watts (D)	1,23,651	43.5
7 David Rouzer (R)*	1,56,809	55.5
Kyle Horton (D)	1,20,838	42.8
8 Richard Hudson		
(R)*	1,41,402	55.3
Frank McNeill (D)	1,14,119	44.7
9 Dan McCready (D)	1,38,341	48.9
Mark Harris (R)	1,39,246	49.3
10 Patrick McHenry		
(R)*	1,64,969	59.3
David Wilson		
Brown (D)	1,13,259	40.7
11 Mark Meadows (R)*	1,78,012	59.2
Phillip Price (D)	1,16,508	38.7
12 Alma Adams (D)*	2,03,974	73.1
Paul Wright (R)	75,164	26.9
13 Ted Budd (R)*	1,47,570	51.5
Kathy Manning (D)	1,30,402	45.5
North Dakota		
Senate		
Kevin Cramer (R)	1,79,720	55.1
Heidi Heitkamp		
(D)*	1,44,376	44.3

	Vote total	Percent
House		
AL Kelly Armstrong (R)	1,93,568	60.2
Mac Schneider (D)	1,14,377	35.6
Ohio		
Governor		
Richard Michael		
DeWine (R)	22,31,917	50.4
Ed FitzGerald (D)	20,67,847	46.7
Senate		
Sherrod Brown		
(D)*	23,55,923	53.4
Jim Renacci (R)	20,53,963	46.4
House		
1 Steve Chabot (R)*	1,54,409	51.3
Aftab Pureval (D)	1,41,118	46.9
2 Brad Wenstrup (R)*	1,66,714	57.6
Jill Schiller (D)	1,19,333	41.2
3 Joyce Beatty (D)*	1,81,575	73.6
Jim Burgess (R)	65,040	26.4
4 Jim Jordan (R)*	1,67,993	65.3
Janet Garrett (D)	89,412	34.7
5 Bob Latta (R)*	1,76,569	62.3
John Michael		
Galbraith (D)	99,655	35.1
6 Bill Johnson (R)*	1,72,774	69.3
Shawna Roberts (D)	76,716	30.7
7 Bob Gibbs (R)*	1,53,117	58.7
Ken Harbaugh (D)	1,07,536	41.3
8 Warren Davidson		
(R)*	1,77,892	66.5
Vanessa Enoch (D)	89,451	33.5
9 Marcy Kaptur (D)*	1,57,219	67.8
Steven Kraus (R)	74,670	32.2
10 Mike Turner (R)*	1,57,554	55.9
Theresa Gasper (D)	1,18,785	42.2
11 Marcia Fudge (D)*	2,06,138	82.2
Beverly Goldstein		
(R)	44,486	17.7
12 Troy Balderson (R)*	1,75,677	51.4
Danny O'Connor (D)	1,61,251	47.2
13 Tim Ryan (D)*	1,53,323	61.0
Christopher		
DePizzo (R)	98,047	39.0
14 David Joyce (R)*	1,69,809	55.2
Betsy Rader (D)	1,37,549	44.8
15 Steve Stivers (R)*	1,70,593	58.3
Rick Neal (D)	1,16,112	39.7
16 Anthony Gonzalez		
(R)	1,70,029	56.7
Susan Moran		
Palmer (D)	1,29,681	43.3
Oklahoma		
Governor		
Kevin Stitt (R)	6,44,579	54.3
Drew		
Edmondson (D)	5,00,973	42.2
House		
1 Kevin Hern (R)	1,50,129	59.3
Tim Gilpin (D)	1,03,042	40.7
2 Markwayne Mullin		
(R)*	1,40,451	65.0
Jason Nichols (D)	65,021	30.1
3 Frank Lucas (R)*	1,72,913	73.9
Frankie Robbins (D)	61,152	26.1
4 Tom Cole (R)*	1,49,227	63.1
Mary Brannon (D)	78,088	33.0
5 Kendra Horn (D)	1,21,149	50.7
Steve Russell (R)*	1,17,811	49.3
Oregon		
Governor		
Kate Brown (D)*	9,34,498	50.1
Knute Buehler (R)	8,14,988	43.7

		Vote total	Percent

House

		Vote total	Percent
	Suzanne Bonamici		
1	(D)*	2,31,198	63.6
	John Verbeek (R)	1,16,446	32.1
2	Greg Walden (R)*	2,07,597	56.3
	Jamie McLeod-Skinner (D)	1,45,298	39.4
	Earl Blumenauer		
3	(D)*	2,79,019	72.6
	Tom Harrison (R)	76,187	19.8
4	Peter DeFazio (D)*	2,08,710	56.0
	Art Robinson (R)	1,52,414	40.9
5	Kurt Schrader (D)*	1,97,187	55.0
	Mark Callahan (R)	1,49,887	41.8

Pennsylvania

Governor

		Vote total	Percent
	Tom Wolf (D)*	28,95,652	57.8
	Scott Wagner (R)	20,39,882	40.7

Senate

		Vote total	Percent
	Bob Casey Jr. (D)*	27,92,437	55.7
	Lou Barletta (R)	21,34,848	42.6

House

		Vote total	Percent
1	Brian Fitzpatrick (R)*	1,69,053	51.2
	Scott Wallace (D)	1,60,745	48.7
2	Brendan F. Boyle (D)*	1,59,600	79.0
	David Torres (R)	42,382	21.0
3	Dwight Evans (D)*	2,87,610	93.4
	Bryan Leib (R)	20,387	6.6
4	Madeleine Dean (D)	2,11,524	63.5
	Dan David (R)	1,21,467	36.5
5	Mary Gay Scanlon (D)	1,98,639	65.2
	Pearl Kim (R)	1,06,075	34.8
6	Chrissy Houlahan (D)	1,77,704	58.8
	Greg McCauley (R)	1,24,124	41.1
7	Susan Wild (D)	1,40,813	53.5
	Marty Nothstein (R)	1,14,437	43.5
8	Matt Cartwright (D)*	1,35,603	54.6
	John Chrin (R)	1,12,563	45.3
9	Dan Meuser (R)	1,48,723	59.7
	Denny Wolff (D)	1,00,204	40.2
10	Scott Perry (R)*	1,49,365	51.3
	George Scott (D)	1,41,668	48.6
11	Lloyd Smucker (R)*	1,63,708	58.9
	Jessica King (D)	1,13,876	41.0
12	Tom Marino (R)*	1,61,047	66.0
	Marc Friedenberg (D)	82,825	33.9
13	John Joyce (R)	1,78,533	70.4
	Brent Ottaway (D)	74,733	29.5
14	Guy Reschenthaler (R)	1,51,386	57.9
	Bibiana Boerio (D)	1,10,051	42.1
15	Glenn Thompson (R)*	1,65,245	67.8
	Susan Boser (D)	78,327	32.1
16	Mike Kelly (R)*	1,35,348	51.5
	Ronald DiNicola (D)	1,24,109	47.3
17	Conor Lamb (D)*	1,83,162	56.2
	Keith Rothfus (R)*	1,42,417	43.7
18	Michael Doyle (D)*	2,31,472	96.1

Rhode Island

Governor

		Vote total	Percent
	Gina Raimondo (D)*	1,98,122	52.6
	Allan Fung (R)	1,39,932	37.2

Senate

		Vote total	Percent
	Sheldon Whitehouse (D)*	2,31,477	61.4
	Robert Flanders Jr. (R)	1,44,421	38.3

House

		Vote total	Percent
1	David Cicilline (D)*	1,16,099	66.7
	Patrick Donovan (R)	57,567	33.1
2	James Langevin (D)*	1,26,476	63.5
	Salvatore Caiozzo (R)	72,271	36.3

South Carolina

Governor

		Vote total	Percent
	Henry McMaster (R)*	9,21,342	54
	James Smith Jr. (D)	7,84,182	45.9

House

		Vote total	Percent
1	Joe Cunningham (D)	1,45,455	50.6
	Katie Arrington (R)	1,41,473	49.2
2	Joe Wilson (R)*	1,44,642	56.3
	Sean Carrigan (D)	1,09,199	42.5
3	Jeff Duncan (R)*	1,53,338	67.8
	Mary Geren (D)	70,046	31.0
4	William Timmons (R)	1,45,321	59.6
	Brandon Brown (D)	89,182	36.6
5	Ralph Norman (R)*	1,41,757	57.0
	Archie Parnell (D)	1,03,129	41.5
6	James Clyburn (D)*	1,44,765	70.1
	Gerhard Gressmann (R)	58,282	28.2
7	Tom Rice (R)*	1,42,681	59.6
	Robert Williams (D)	96,564	40.3

South Dakota

Governor

		Vote total	Percent
	Kristi L. Noem (R)	1,72,912	51
	Billie Sutton (D)	1,61,454	47.6

House

		Vote total	Percent
AL	Dusty Johnson (R)	2,02,695	60.3
	Timothy Bjorkman (D)	1,21,033	36

Tennessee

Governor

		Vote total	Percent
	Bill Lee (R)	13,36,106	59.6
	Karl Dean (D)	8,64,863	38.6

Senate

		Vote total	Percent
	Marsha Blackburn (R)	12,27,483	54.7
	Phil Bredesen (D)	9,85,450	43.9

House

		Vote total	Percent
1	Phil Roe (R)*	1,72,835	77.1
	Marty Olsen (D)	47,138	21.0
2	Tim Burchett (R)	1,72,856	65.9
	Renee Hoyos (D)	86,668	33.1
	Chuck Fleischmann		
3	(R)	1,56,512	63.7
	Danielle Mitchell (D)	84,731	34.5
4	Scott DesJarlais (R)*	1,47,323	63.4
	Mariah Phillips (D)	78,065	33.6
5	Jim Cooper (D)*	1,77,923	67.8
	Jody Ball (R)	84,317	32.2
6	John Rose (R)	1,72,810	69.5
	Dawn Barlow (D)	70,370	28.3
7	Mark Green (R)	1,70,071	66.9
	Justin Kanew (D)	81,661	32.1
8	David Kustoff (R)*	1,68,030	67.7

		Vote total	Percent
	Erika Stotts Pearson (D)	74,755	30.1
9	Steve Cohen (D)*	1,45,139	80.0
	Charlotte Bergmann (R)	34,901	19.2

Texas

Governor

		Vote total	Percent
	Greg Abbott (R)*	46,56,196	55.8
	Lupe Valdez (D)	35,46,615	24.5

Senate

		Vote total	Percent
	Ted Cruz (R)*	42,60,553	50.9
	Beto O'Rourke (D)	40,45,632	48.3

House

		Vote total	Percent
1	Louis Gohmert (R)*	1,68,165	72.3
	Shirley McKellar (D)	61,263	26.3
	Daniel Crenshaw		
2	(R)	1,39,188	52.8
	Todd Litton (D)	1,19,992	45.6
3	Van Taylor (R)	1,69,520	54.2
	Lorie Burch (D)	1,38,234	44.2
4	John Ratcliffe (R)*	1,88,667	75.7
	Catherine Krantz (D)	57,400	23.0
5	Lance Gooden (R)	1,30,617	62.3
	Dan Wood (D)	78,666	37.5
6	Ronald Wright (R)	1,35,961	53.1
	Jana Lynne Sanchez (D)	1,16,350	45.4
7	Lizzie Pannill Fletcher (D)	1,27,959	52.5
	John Culberson (R)*	1,15,642	47.5
8	Kevin Brady (R)*	2,00,619	73.4
	Steven David (D)	67,930	24.9
9	Al Green (D)*	1,36,256	89.1
	Phil Kurtz (LIBERT)	5,940	3.9
10	Michael McCaul (R)*	1,57,166	51.1
	Mike Siegel (D)	1,44,034	46.8
11	Mike Conaway (R)*	1,76,603	80.1
	Jennie Lou Leeder (D)	40,631	18.4
12	Kay Granger (R)*	1,72,557	64.3
	Vanessa Adia (D)	90,994	33.9
13	Mac Thornberry (R)*	1,69,027	81.5
	Greg Sagan (D)	35,083	16.9
14	Randy Weber (R)*	1,38,942	59.2
	Adrienne Bell (R)	92,212	39.3
	Vicente Gonzalez		
15	Jr. (D)*	98,333	59.7
	Tim Westley (R)	63,862	38.8
	Veronica Escobar		
16	(D)	1,24,437	68.5
	Rick Seeberger (R)	49,127	27.0
17	Bill Flores (R)*	1,34,841	56.8
	Rick Kennedy (D)	98,070	41.3
18	Sheila Jackson Lee (D)*	1,38,704	75.2
	Ava Pate (R)	38,368	20.8
19	Jodey Arrington (R)*	1,51,946	75.2
	Miguel Levario (D)	50,039	24.8
20	Joaquin Castro (D)*	1,39,038	80.9
	Jeffrey C. Blunt (LIBERT)	32,925	19.1
21	Chip Roy (R)	1,77,654	50.2
	Joseph Kopser (D)	1,68,421	47.6
22	Pete Olson (R)*	1,52,750	51.4

	Candidate	Vote total	Percent
	Sri Preston Kulkarni (D)	1,38,153	46.5
23	Will Hurd (R)*	1,03,285	49.2
	Gina Ortiz Jones (D)	1,02,359	48.7
24	Kenny Marchant (R)*	1,33,317	50.6
	Jan McDowell (D)	1,25,231	47.5
25	Roger Williams (R)*	1,63,023	53.5
	Julie Oliver (D)	1,36,385	44.8
26	Michael Burgess (R)*	1,85,551	59.4
	Linsey Fagan (D)	1,21,938	39.0
27	Michael Cloud (R)*	1,25,118	60.3
	Eric Holguin (D)	75,929	36.6
28	Henry Cuellar (D)*	1,17,494	84.4
	Arthur Thomas IV (LIBERT)	21,732	15.6
29	Sylvia Garcia (D)	88,188	75.1
	Phillip Arnold Aronoff (R)	28,098	23.9
30	Eddie Bernice Johnson (D)*	1,66,784	91.1
	Shawn Jones (LIBERT)	16,390	8.9
31	John Carter (R)*	1,44,680	50.6
	Mary Jennings Hegar (D)	1,36,362	47.7
32	Colin Allred (D)	1,44,067	52.3
	Pete Sessions (R)*	1,26,101	45.8
33	Marc Veasey (D)*	90,805	76.2
	Willie Billips (R)	26,120	21.9
34	Filemon Vela (D)*	85,825	60.0
	Rey Gonzalez Jr. (R)	57,243	40.0
35	Lloyd Doggett (D)*	1,38,278	71.3
	David Smalling (D)	50,553	26.0
36	Brian Babin (R)*	1,61,048	72.6
	Dayna Steele (D)	60,908	27.4

Utah

Senate
	Candidate	Vote total	Percent
	Mitt Romney (R)	6,65,215	62.6
	Jenny Wilson (D)	3,28,541	30.9

House
	Candidate	Vote total	Percent
1	Rob Bishop (R)*	1,56,692	61.6
	Lee Castillo (D)	63,308	24.9
2	Chris Stewart (R)*	1,51,489	56.1
	Shireen Ghorbani (D)	1,05,051	38.9
3	John Curtis (R)*	1,74,856	67.5
	James Singer (D)	70,686	27.3
4	Ben McAdams (D)	1,34,964	50.1
	Mia Love (R)*	1,34,270	49.9

Vermont

Governor
Candidate	Vote total	Percent
Phil Scott (R)*	1,51,261	55.2
Christine Hallquist (D)	1,10,335	40.3

Senate
Candidate	Vote total	Percent
Bernie Sanders (I)*	1,83,649	67.3
Lawrence Zupan (R)	74,663	27.4

House
	Candidate	Vote total	Percent
AL	Peter Welch (D)*	1,88,547	69.2
	Anya Tynio (R)	70,705	26.0

Virginia

Senate
Candidate	Vote total	Percent
Tim Kaine (D)*	19,10,370	57
Corey Stewart (R)	13,74,313	41

House
	Candidate	Vote total	Percent
1	Rob Wittman (R)*	1,83,250	55.2
	Vangie Williams (D)	1,48,464	44.7
2	Elaine Luria (D)	1,39,571	51.0
	Scott Taylor (R)*	1,33,458	48.8
3	Bobby Scott (D)*	1,98,615	91.2
4	Aston Donald McEachin (D)*	1,87,642	62.6
	Ryan McAdams (R)	1,07,706	35.9
5	Denver Lee Riggleman III (R)	1,65,339	53.2
	Leslie Cockburn (D)	1,45,040	46.6
6	Benjamin Lee Cline (R)	1,67,957	59.7
	Jennifer Lewis (D)	1,13,133	40.2
7	Abigail Spanberger (D)	1,76,079	50.3
	Dave Brat (R)*	1,69,295	48.4
8	Don Beyer (D)*	2,47,137	76.1
	Thomas Oh (R)	76,899	23.7
9	Morgan Griffith (R)*	1,60,933	65.2
	Anthony Flaccavento (D)	85,833	34.8
10	Jennifer Wexton (D)	2,06,356	56.1
	Barbara Comstock (R)*	1,60,841	43.7
11	Gerry Connolly (D)*	2,19,191	71.1
	Jeffery Anthony Dove Jr. (R)	83,023	26.9

Washington

Senate
Candidate	Vote total	Percent
Maria Cantwell (D)*	18,03,364	58.4
Susan Hutchison (R)	12,82,804	41.6

House
	Candidate	Vote total	Percent
1	Suzan DelBene (D)*	1,97,209	59.3
	Jeffrey Beeler (R)	1,35,534	40.7
2	Rick Larsen (D)*	2,10,187	71.3
	Brian Luke (LIBERT)	84,646	28.7
3	Jaime Herrera Beutler (R)*	1,61,819	52.7
	Carolyn Long (D)	1,45,407	47.3
4	Dan Newhouse (R)*	1,41,551	62.8
	Christine Brown (D)	83,785	37.2
5	Cathy McMorris Rodgers (R)*	1,75,422	54.8
	Lisa Brown (D)	1,44,925	45.2
6	Derek Kilmer (D)*	2,06,409	63.9
	Douglas Dightman (R)	1,16,677	36.1
7	Pramila Jayapal (D)*	3,29,800	83.6
	Craig Keller (R)	64,881	16.4
8	Kim Schrier (D)	1,64,089	52.4
	Dino Rossi (R)	1,48,968	47.6
9	Adam Smith (D)*	1,63,345	67.9
	Sarah Smith (D)	77,222	32.1
10	Denny Heck (D)*	1,66,215	61.5
	Joseph Brumbles (R)	1,03,860	38.5

West Virginia

Senate
Candidate	Vote total	Percent
Joe Manchin III (D)*	2,90,510	49.6
Patrick Morrisey (R)	2,71,113	46.3

House
	Candidate	Vote total	Percent
1	David McKinley (R)*	1,27,997	64.6
	Kendra Fershee (D)	70,217	35.4
2	Alex Mooney (R)*	1,10,504	54.0
	Talley Sergent (D)	88,011	43.0
3	Carol Miller (R)	98,645	56.4
	Richard Ojeda (D)	76,340	43.6

Wisconsin

Governor
Candidate	Vote total	Percent
Tony Evers (D)	13,24,307	49.5
Scott Walker (R)*	12,95,080	58.4

Senate
Candidate	Vote total	Percent
Tammy Baldwin (D)*	14,72,914	55.4
Leah Vukmir (R)	11,84,885	44.6

House
	Candidate	Vote total	Percent
1	Bryan Steil (R)	1,77,492	54.6
	Randy Bryce (D)	1,37,508	42.3
2	Mark Pocan (D)*	3,09,116	97.4
3	Ron Kind (D)*	1,87,888	59.6
	Steve Toft (R)	1,26,980	40.3
4	Gwen Moore (D)*	2,06,487	75.6
	Robert Raymond (I)	59,091	21.6
5	Jim Sensenbrenner (R)*	2,25,619	61.9
	Tom Palzewicz (D)	1,38,385	38.0
6	Glenn Grothman (R)*	1,80,311	55.5
	Dan Kohl (R)	1,44,536	44.5
7	Sean Duffy (R)*	1,94,061	60.1
	Margaret Engebretson (R)	1,24,307	38.5
8	Mike Gallagher (R)*	2,09,410	63.7
	Beau Liegeois (D)	1,19,265	36.3

Wyoming

Governor
Candidate	Vote total	Percent
Mark Gordon (R)	1,36,412	67.1
Mary Throne (D)	55,965	27.5

Senate
Candidate	Vote total	Percent
John Barrasso (R)*	1,36,210	67.0
Gary Trauner (D)	61,227	30.1

House
	Candidate	Vote total	Percent
AL	Liz Cheney (R)*	1,27,963	63.6
	Greg Hunter (D)	59,903	29.8

116th Congress Special Elections, 2019 Gubernatorial Elections

Special House Elections, 116th Congress

	Vote total	Percent		Vote total	Percent
Pennsylvania 12th CD—May 21, 2019			**California 25th CD—May 12, 2020**		
Marc Friedenberg (D)	42,195	31.9	Christy Smith (D)	78,721	45.1
North Carolina 3rd CD—September 10, 2019			**Wisconsin 7th CD—May 12, 2020**		
Gregory Murphy (R)	70,407	61.7	Tom Tiffany (R)	1,09,498	57.1
Allen Thomas (D)	42,738	37.5	Tricia Zunker (D)	82,135	42.9
North Carolina 9th CD—September 10, 2019			**New York 27th CD—June 23, 2020**		
Dan Bishop (R)	96,573	50.7	Christopher Jacobs (R/I)	81,085	51.8
Dan McCready (D)	92,785	48.7	Nate McMurray (D /Working Families Party)	72,998	46.6
Maryland 7th CD—April 28, 2020			**Georgia 5th CD—December 1, 2020**		
Kweisi Mfume (D)	1,11,955	73.8	Kwanza Hall (D)	12,094	54
Kim Klacik (R)	38,102	25.1	Robert Franklin (D)	10,300	46
Illinois 18th CD—September 10, 2015					
Darin LaHood (R)	33,319	68.8			
Robert Mellon (D)	15,127	31.2			

Special Senate Elections, 116th Congress

	Vote total	Percent
Arizona—November 3, 2020		
Mark Kelly (D)	17,16,467	51.2
Roy Moore (R)	16,37,661	48.8
Minnesota—November 6, 2018		
Tina Smith (D)	13,70,540	53
Karin Housley (R)	10,95,777	42.4
Mississippi—November 6, 2018		
Cindy Hyde-Smith (R)	4,86,769	53.6
Mike Espy (D)	4,20,819	46.4

2019 Gubernatorial Elections

	Vote total	Percent		Vote total	Percent
Kentucky			**Mississippi**		
Andy Beshear (D)	7,09,890	49.2	Tate Reeves (R)	4,59,396	51.9
Matt Bevin (R)	7,04,754	48.8	Jim Hood (D)	4,14,368	46.8
Louisiana					
John Bel Edwards (D)	7,74,498	51.3			
Eddie Rispone (R)	7,34,286	48.7			

NOTE: Vote totals are included for all candidates listed on the ballot who received 5 percent or more of the total vote.

2020 Election Returns for Governor, Senate, and House

Following are the official vote returns for the gubernatorial, Senate, and House contests based on figures supplied by the fifty state election boards.

Vote totals are included for all candidates listed on the ballot who received 5 percent or more of the total vote. For candidates who received under 5 percent, consult *America Votes 34 (2019–2020)*, published by CQ Press. The percent column shows the percentage of the total vote cast.

An asterisk (*) indicates an incumbent.

An *X* denotes candidates without major part opposition; no votes were tallied.

KEY: AC—American Constitution; AMI—American Independent; C—Conservative; CNSTP—Constitution; D—Democratic; G—Green; GLCM—Grassroots-Legalize Cannabis Party of Minnesota; HES—Healthcare Environment Stability; I—Independent; INDC—Independence; L—Liberal; LIBERT—Libertarian; LMN—Legal Marijuana Now Party; MDE—Moderate; NPA—No Party Affiliation; SAMP—Save America Freedom Party; SOCP—Save Our City Party; R—Republican; REF—Reform; WFP—Working Families Party; WRI—Write-in

An AL indicates an at-large member of Congress in a state with a single congressional district.

Alabama

		Vote total	Percent
Senate			
	Tommy Tuberville (R)	13,92,076	60.1
	Doug Jones (D)*	9,20,478	39.7
House			
1	Jerry Carl (R)	2,11,825	64.4
	James Averhart (D)	1,16,949	35.5
2	Barry Moore (R)	1,97,996	65.2
	Phyllis Harvey-Hall (D)	1,05,286	34.7
3	Mike Rogers (R)*	2,17,384	67.5
	Adia Winfrey (D)	1,04,595	32.5
4	Robert Aderholt (R)*	2,61,553	82.2
	Rick Neighbors (D)	56,237	17.7
5	Mo Brooks (R)*	2,53,094	95.8
6	Gary Palmer (R)*	2,74,160	97.1
7	Terri Sewell (D)*	2,25,742	97.2

Alaska

		Vote total	Percent
Senate			
	Daniel S. Sullivan (R)*	1,91,112	53.9
	Al Gross (NPA)	1,46,068	41.2
House			
AL	Don Young (R)*	1,92,126	54.4
	Alyse Galvin (D)	1,59,856	45.3

Arizona

		Vote total	Percent
Senate			
	Mark Kelly (D)	17,16,467	51.2
	Martha McSally (R)*	16,37,661	48.8
House			
1	Tom O'Halleran (D)*	1,88,469	51.6
	Tiffany Shedd (R)	1,76,709	48.4
2	Ann Kirkpatrick (D)*	2,09,945	55.1
	Brandon Martin (R)	1,70,975	44.9
3	Raul Grijalva (D)*	1,74,243	64.6
	Daniel Wood (R)	95,594	35.4
4	Paul Gosar (R)*	2,78,002	69.7
	Delina DiSanto (D)	1,20,484	30.2
5	Andy Briggs (R)*	2,62,414	58.9
	Joan Greene (D)	1,83,171	41.1
6	David Schweikert (R)*	2,17,783	52.2
	Hiral Tipirneni (D)	1,99,644	47.8
7	Ruben Gallego (D)*	1,65,452	76.7
	Josh Barnett (R)	50,226	23.3
8	Debbie Lesko (R)*	2,51,633	59.6
	Hiral Tipirneni (D)	1,70,816	40.4
9	Greg Stanton (D)*	2,17,094	61.6
	Dave Giles (R)	1,35,180	38.4

Arkansas

		Vote total	Percent
Senate			
	Tom Cotton (R)*	7,93,871	66.5
	Ricky Dale Harrington Jr. (LIBERT)	3,99,390	33.5
House			
1	Rick Crawford (R)*	2,37,596	100.0
2	French Hill (R)*	1,84,093	55.4
	Joyce Elliott (D)	1,48,410	44.6
3	Steve Womack (R)*	2,14,960	64.3
	Celeste Williams (D)	1,06,325	31.8
4	Bruce Westerman (R)*	1,91,617	69.7
	William Hanson (D)	75,750	27.5

California

		Vote total	Percent
House			
1	Doug LaMalfa (R)*	2,04,190	57.0
	Audrey Denney (D)	1,54,073	43.0
2	Jared Huffman (D)*	2,94,435	75.7
	Dale K. Mensing (R)	94,320	24.3
3	John Garamendi (D)*	1,76,043	54.7
	Tamika Hamilton (R)	1,45,945	45.3
4	Tom McClintock (R)*	2,47,291	55.9
	Brynne Kennedy (D)	1,94,731	44.1
5	Mike Thompson (D)*	2,71,233	76.1
	Scott Giblin (R)	85,227	23.9
6	Doris Matsui (D)*	2,29,648	73.3
	Chris Bish (R)	83,466	26.7
7	Ami Bera (D)*	2,17,416	56.6
	Buzz Patterson (R)	1,66,549	43.4
8	Jay Obernolte (R)	1,58,711	56.1
	Chris Bubser (D)	1,24,400	43.9
9	Jerry McNerney (D)*	1,74,252	57.6
	Antonio Amador (R)	1,28,358	42.4
10	Josh Harder (D)*	1,66,865	55.2
	Ted Howze (R)	1,35,629	44.8
11	Mark DeSaulnier (D)*	2,71,063	73.0
	Nisha Sharma (R)	1,00,293	27.0
12	Nancy Pelosi (D)*	2,81,776	77.6
	Shahid Buttar (D)	81,174	22.4
13	Barbara Lee (D)*	3,27,863	90.4
	Nikka Piterman (R)	34,955	9.6
14	Jackie Speier (D)*	2,78,300	79.3
	Ran Petel (R)	72,705	20.7
15	Eric Swalwell (D)*	2,42,991	70.9
	Alison Hayden (R)	99,710	29.1
16	Jim Costa (D)*	1,28,690	59.4
	Kevin Cookingham (R)	88,039	40.6
17	Ro Khanna (D)*	2,12,137	71.3
	Ritesh Tandon (R)	85,199	28.7
18	Anna Eshoo (D)*	2,17,388	63.2
	Rishi Kumar (D)	1,26,751	36.8
19	Zoe Lofgren (D)*	2,24,385	71.7
	Justin Aguilera (R)	88,642	28.3
20	Jimmy Panetta (D)*	2,36,896	76.8
	Jeff Gorman (R)	71,658	23.2
21	David Valadao (R)	85,928	50.4
	TJ Cox (D)*	84,406	49.6
22	Devin Nunes (R)*	1,70,888	54.2
	Phil Arballo (D)	1,44,251	45.8
23	Kevin McCarthy (R)*	1,90,222	62.1
	Kim Mangone (D)	1,15,896	37.9
24	Salud Carabajal (D)*	2,12,564	58.7
	Andy Caldwell (R)	1,49,781	41.3
25	Mike Garcia (R)*	1,69,638	50.0
	Christy Smith (D)	1,69,305	50.0
26	Julia Brownley (D)*	2,08,856	60.6
	Ronda Kennedy (R)	1,35,877	39.4
27	Judy Chu (D)*	2,21,411	69.8
	Johnny Nalbandian (R)	95,907	30.2
28	Adam Schiff (D)*	2,44,271	72.7
	Eric Early (R)	91,928	27.3
29	Tony Cardenas (D)*	1,19,420	56.6
	Angélica María Dueñas (D)	91,524	43.4
30	Brad Sherman (D)*	2,40,038	69.5
	Mark S. Reed (R)	1,05,426	30.5
31	Pete Aguilar (D)*	1,75,315	61.3

		Vote total	Percent
	Agnes Gibboney (R)	1,10,735	38.7
32	Grace Napolitano (D)*	1,72,942	66.6
	Joshua Scott (R)	86,818	33.4
33	Ted Lieu (D)*	2,57,094	67.6
	James P. Bradley (R)	1,23,334	32.4
34	Jimmy Gomez (D)*	1,08,792	53.0
	David Kim (D)	96,554	47.0
35	Norma Torres (D)*	1,69,405	69.3
	Mike Cargile (R)	74,941	30.7
36	Raul Ruiz (D)*	1,85,151	60.3
	Erin Cruz (R)	1,21,698	39.7
37	Karen Bass (D)*	2,54,916	85.9
	Errol Webber (R)	41,705	14.1
38	Linda Sanchez (D)*	1,90,467	74.3
	Michael Tolar (D)	65,739	25.7
39	Young Kim (R)	1,73,946	50.6
	Gil Cisneros (D)*	1,69,837	49.4
40	Lucille Roybal-Allard (D)*	1,35,572	72.7
	C. Antonio Delgado (R)	50,809	27.3
41	Mark Takano (D)*	1,68,126	64.0
	Aja Smith (R)	94,447	36.0
42	Ken Calvert (R)*	2,10,274	57.1
	William O'Mara (D)	1,57,773	42.9
43	Maxine Waters (D)*	1,99,210	71.7
	Joe Collins (R)	78,688	28.3
44	Nanette Barragan (D)*	1,39,661	67.8
	Analilia Joya (D)	66,375	32.2
45	Katie Porter (D)*	2,21,843	53.5
	Greg Raths (R)	1,93,096	46.5
46	Lou Correa (D)*	1,57,803	68.8
	James Waters (R)	71,716	31.2
47	Alan Lowenthal (D)*	1,97,028	63.3
	John Briscoe (R)	1,14,371	36.7
48	Michelle Steel (R)	2,01,738	51.1
	Harley Rouda (D)*	1,93,362	48.9
49	Mike Levin (D)*	2,05,349	53.1
	Brian Maryott (R)	1,81,157	46.9
50	Darrell Issa (R)	1,95,521	54.0
	Ammar Campa-Najjar (D)	1,66,869	46.0
51	Juan Vargas (D)*	1,65,596	68.3
	Juan Hidalgo (R)	76,841	31.7
52	Scott Peters (D)*	2,44,145	61.6
	Jim DeBello (R)	1,52,350	38.4
53	Sara Jacobs (D)	1,99,244	59.5
	Georgette Gómez (D)	1,35,614	40.5

Colorado

Senate

		Vote total	Percent
	John Hickenlooper (D)	17,31,114	53.5
	Cory Gardner (R)*	14,29,492	44.2

House

		Vote total	Percent
1	Diana DeGette (D)*	3,31,621	73.6
	Shane Bolling (R)	1,05,955	23.5
2	Joe Neguse (D)*	3,16,925	61.5
	Charles Winn (R)	1,82,547	35.4
3	Lauren Boebert (R)	2,20,634	51.4
	Diane Mitsch Bush (D)	1,94,122	45.2
4	Ken Buck (R)*	2,85,606	60.1
	Isaac McCorkle (D)	1,73,945	36.6
5	Doug Lamborn (R)*	2,49,013	57.6

		Vote total	Percent
	Jillian Freeland (D)	1,61,600	37.4
6	Jason Crow (D)*	2,50,314	57.1
	Steve House (R)	1,75,192	40.0
7	Ed Perlmutter (D)*	2,50,525	59.1
	Casper Stockham (R)	1,59,301	37.6

Connecticut

House

		Vote total	Percent
1	John B. Larson (D)*	2,22,668	63.8
	Mary Fay (R)	1,22,111	35.0
2	Joe Courtney (D)*	2,17,982	59.4
	Justin Anderson (R)	1,40,340	38.2
3	Rosa DeLauro (D)*	2,03,265	58.7
	Margaret Streicker (R/I)	1,37,596	39.8
4	Jim Himes (D)*	2,24,432	62.2
	Jonathan Riddle (R)	1,30,627	36.2
5	Jahanna Hayes (D)	1,92,484	55.1
	David Xavier Sullivan (R)	1,51,988	43.5

Delaware

Governor

		Vote total	Percent
	John C. Carney Jr. (D)*	2,92,903	59.5
	Julianne Murray (R)	1,90,312	38.6

Senate

		Vote total	Percent
	Chris Coons (D)*	2,91,804	59.4
	Lauren Witzke (R)	1,86,054	37.9

House

		Vote total	Percent
AL	Lisa Blunt Rochester (D)*	2,81,382	57.6
	Lee Murphy (R)	1,96,392	40.2

Florida

House

		Vote total	Percent
1	Matt Gaetz (R)*	2,83,352	64.6
	Phil Ehr (D)	1,49,172	34.0
2	Neal Dunn (R)*	3,05,337	97.9
3	Kat Cammack (R)	2,23,075	57.1
	Adam Christensen (D)	1,67,326	42.9
4	John Rutherford (R)*	3,08,497	61.1
	Donna Deegan (D)	1,96,423	38.9
5	Alfred Lawson (D)*	2,19,463	65.1
	Gary Adler (R)	1,17,510	34.9
6	Michael Waltz (R)*	2,65,393	60.6
	Clinton Curtis (D)	1,72,305	39.4
7	Stephanie Murphy (D)*	2,24,946	55.3
	Leo Valentin (R)	1,75,750	43.2
8	Bill Posey (R)*	2,82,093	61.4
	Jim Kennedy (D)	1,77,695	38.6
9	Darren Soto (D)*	2,40,724	56.0
	Bill Olson (R)	1,88,889	44.0
10	Val Demings (D)*	2,39,434	63.6
	Vennia Francois (R)	1,36,889	36.4
11	Daniel Webster (R)*	3,16,979	66.7
	Dana Cottrell (D)	1,58,094	33.3
12	Gus Bilirakis (R)*	2,84,941	62.9
	Kimberly Walker (D)	1,68,194	37.1
13	Charlie Crist (D)*	2,15,405	53.0
	Anna Paulina Luna (R)	1,90,713	47.0
14	Kathy Castor (D)*	2,24,240	60.3
	Christine Quinn (R)	1,47,896	39.7

		Vote total	Percent
15	Scott Franklin (R)	2,16,374	55.4
	Alan Cohn (D)	1,74,297	44.6
16	Vern Buchanan (R)*	2,69,001	55.5
	Margaret Good (D)	2,15,683	44.5
17	Greg Steube (R)*	2,66,514	64.6
	Allen Ellison (D)	1,40,487	34.1
18	Brian Mast (R)*	2,53,286	56.3
	Pam Keith (D)	1,86,674	41.5
19	Byron Donalds (R)	2,72,440	61.3
	Cindy Banyai (D)	1,72,146	38.7
20	Alcee Hastings (D)*	2,53,661	78.7
	Greg Musselwhite (R)	68,748	21.3
21	Lois Frankel (D)*	2,37,925	59.0
	Laura Loomer (R)	1,57,612	39.1
22	Ted Deutch (D)*	2,35,764	58.6
	James Pruden (R)	1,66,553	41.4
23	Debbie Wasserman Schultz (D)*	2,21,239	58.2
	Carla Spalding (R)	1,58,874	41.8
24	Frederica Wilson (D)*	2,18,825	75.6
	Lavern Spicer (R)	59,084	20.4
25	Mario Diaz-Balart (R)*	X	X
26	Carlos Gimenez (R)	1,77,223	51.7
	Debbie Mucarsel-Powell (D)*	1,65,407	48.3
27	Maria Elvira Salazar (R)	1,76,141	51.4
	Donna Shalala (D)*	1,66,758	48.6

Georgia

Senate

		Vote total	Percent
	Jon Ossoff (D)	22,69,923	50.6
	David Perdue (R)*	22,14,979	49.4
Special	Raphael Warnock (D)	22,89,113	51.0
	Kelly Loeffler (R)*	21,95,841	49.0

House

		Vote total	Percent
1	Earl Carter (R)*	1,89,457	58.3
	Joyce Marie Griggs (D)	1,35,238	41.7
2	Sanford Bishop Jr. (D)*	1,61,397	59.1
	Donald Cole (R)	1,11,620	40.9
3	Drew Ferguson (R)*	2,41,526	65.0
	Val Almonord (D)	1,29,792	35.0
4	Hank Johnson (D)*	2,78,906	80.1
	Johsie Cruz (R)	69,393	19.9
5	Nikema Williams (D)	3,01,857	85.1
	Angela Stanton King (R)	52,646	14.9
6	Lucy McBath (D)*	2,16,775	54.6
	Karen Handel (R)	1,80,329	45.4
7	Carolyn Bourdeaux (D)	1,90,900	51.4
	Rich McCormick (R)	1,80,564	48.6
8	Austin Scott (R)*	1,98,701	64.5
	Lindsay Holliday (D)	1,09,264	35.5
9	Andrew Clyde (R)	2,92,750	78.6
	Devin Pandy (D)	79,797	21.4
10	Jody Hice (R)*	2,35,810	62.3
	Tabitha Johnson-Green (D)	1,42,636	37.7

NOTE: *In Florida in a district where a candidate had no opposition, including write-ins, no vote was taken.*

		Vote total	Percent
11	Barry Loudermilk (R)*	2,45,259	60.4
	Dana Barrett (D)	1,60,623	39.6
12	Rick Allen (R)*	1,81,038	58.4
	Liz Johnson (D)	1,29,061	41.6
13	David Scott (D)*	2,79,045	77.4
	Becky E. Hites (R)	81,476	22.6
14	Marjorie Taylor Greene (R)	2,29,827	74.7
	Kevin Van Ausdal (D)	77,798	25.3

Hawaii

House

		Vote total	Percent
1	Ed Case (D)*	1,83,245	72.0
	Ron Curtis (R)	71,188	28.0
2	Kaiali'i Kahele (D)	1,71,517	63.0
	Joseph Akana (R)	84,027	30.9

Idaho

Senate

		Vote total	Percent
	Jim Risch (R)*	5,38,446	62.6
	Paulette E. Jordan (D)	2,85,864	33.2

House

		Vote total	Percent
1	Russ Fulcher (R)*	3,10,736	67.8
	Rudy Soto (D)	1,31,380	28.6
2	Mike Simpson (R)*	2,50,669	64.1
	Aaron Swisher (D)	1,24,151	31.7

Illinois

Senate

		Vote total	Percent
	Dick Durbin (D)*	32,78,930	54.9
	Mark Curran (R)	23,19,870	38.9

House

		Vote total	Percent
1	Bobby Rush (D)*	2,39,943	73.8
	Philanise White (R)	85,027	26.2
2	Robin Kelly (D)*	2,34,896	78.8
	Theresa Raborn (R)	63,142	21.2
3	Marie Newman (D)	1,72,997	56.4
	Mike Fricilone (R)	1,33,851	43.6
4	Jesus Garcia (D)*	1,87,219	84.1
	Jesus Solorio (R)	35,518	15.9
5	Mike Quigley (D)*	2,55,661	70.8
	Tom Hanson (R)	96,200	26.6
6	Sean Casten (D)*	2,13,777	52.8
	Jeanne M. Ives (R)	1,83,891	45.4
7	Danny K. Davis (D)*	2,49,383	80.4
	Craig Cameron (R)	41,390	13.3
	Tracy Jennings (I)	19,355	6.2
8	Raja Krishnamoorthi (D)*	1,86,251	73.2
	Preston Nelson (LIBERT)	68,327	26.8
9	Jan Schakowsky (D)*	2,62,045	71.0
	Sargis Sangari (R)	1,07,125	29.0
10	Brad Schneider (D)*	2,02,402	63.9
	Valerie Ramirez Mukherjee (R)	1,14,442	36.1
11	Bill Foster (D)*	1,94,557	63.3
	Rick Laib (R)	1,12,807	36.7
12	Mike Bost (R)*	1,94,839	60.4
	Ray Lenzi (D)	1,27,577	39.6
13	Rodney Davis (R)*	1,81,373	54.5
	Betsy Londrigan (D)	1,51,648	45.5
14	Lauren Underwood (D)*	2,03,209	50.7
	Jim Oberweis (R)	1,97,835	49.3
15	Mary Miller (R)	2,44,947	73.4
	Erika Weaver (D)	88,559	26.6
16	Adam Kinzinger (R)*	2,18,839	64.7
	Dani Brzozowski (D)	1,19,313	35.3
17	Cheri Bustos (D)*	1,56,011	52.0
	Esther Joy King (R)	1,43,863	48.0
18	Darin LaHood (R)*	2,61,840	70.4
	George Petrilli (D)	1,10,039	29.6

Indiana

Governor

		Vote total	Percent
	Eric Holcomb (R)*	17,06,724	56.5
	Woody Myers (D)	9,68,092	32.1
	Donald Rainwater (LIBERT)	3,45,567	11.4

House

		Vote total	Percent
1	Frank Mrvan (D)	1,85,180	56.6
	Mark Leyva (R)	1,32,247	40.4
2	Jackie Walorski (R)*	1,83,601	61.5
	Pat Hackett (D)	1,14,967	38.5
3	Jim Banks (R)*	2,20,989	67.8
	Chip Coldiron (D)	1,04,762	32.2
4	Jim Baird (R)*	2,25,531	66.6
	Joe Mackey (D)	1,12,984	33.4
5	Victoria Spartz (R)	2,08,212	50.0
	Christina Hale (D)	1,91,226	45.9
6	Greg Pence (R)*	2,25,318	68.7
	Jeannine Lee Lake (D)	91,103	27.8
7	Andre Carson (D)*	1,76,422	62.4
	Susan Marie Smith (R)	1,06,146	37.6
8	Larry Bucshon (R)*	2,14,643	66.9
	Thomasina Marsili (D)	95,691	29.8
9	Trey Hollingsworth (R)*	2,18,606	60.9
	Andy Ruff (D)	1,24,826	34.8

Iowa

Senate

		Vote total	Percent
	Joni Ernst (R)*	8,64,997	51.7
	Theresa Greenfield (D)	7,54,859	45.2

House

		Vote total	Percent
1	Ashley Hinson (R)	2,12,088	51.2
	Abby Finkenauer (D)*	2,01,347	48.6
2	Mariannette Miller-Meeks (R)	1,96,964	49.9
	Rita Hart (D)	1,96,958	49.9
3	Cindy Axne (D)*	2,19,205	48.9
	David Young (R)	2,12,997	47.5
4	Randy Feenstra (R)	2,37,369	62.0
	J.D. Scholten (D)	1,44,761	37.8

Kansas

Senate

		Vote total	Percent
	Roger Marshall (R)	7,27,962	53.2
	Barbara Bollier (D)	5,71,530	41.8
	Jason Buckley (LIBERT)	68,263	5.0

House

		Vote total	Percent
1	Tracey Mann (R)	2,08,229	71.2
	Kali Barnett (D)	84,393	28.8
2	Jacob LaTurner (R)	1,85,464	55.1
	Michelle De La Isla (D)	1,36,650	40.6
3	Sharice Davids (D)*	2,20,049	53.6
	Amanda Adkins (R)	1,78,773	43.6
4	Ron Estes (R)*	2,03,432	63.7
	Laura Lombard (D)	1,16,166	36.3

Kentucky

Senate

		Vote total	Percent
	Mitch McConnell (R)*	12,33,315	57.8
	Amy McGrath (D)	8,16,257	38.2

House

		Vote total	Percent
1	James Comer Jr. (R)*	2,46,329	75.0
	James Rhodes (D)	82,141	25.0
2	Brett Guthrie (R)*	2,55,735	71.0
	Hank Linderman (D)	94,643	26.3
3	John Yarmuth (D)*	2,30,672	62.7
	Rhonda Palazzo (R)	1,37,425	37.3
4	Thomas Massie (R)*	2,56,613	67.1
	Alexandra Owensby (D)	1,25,896	32.9
5	Hal Rogers (R)*	2,50,914	84.2
	Matthew Ryan Best (D)	47,056	15.8
6	Andy Barr (R)*	2,16,948	57.3
	Josh Hicks (D)	1,55,011	41.0

Louisiana

Senate

		Vote total	Percent
	Bill Cassidy (R)*	12,28,908	59.3
	Adrian Perkins (D)	3,94,049	19.0
	Derrick Edwards (D)	2,29,814	11.1

House

		Vote total	Percent
1	Steve Scalise (R)*	2,70,330	72.2
	Lee A. Dugas (D)	94,730	25.3
2	Cedric Richmond (D)*	2,01,636	63.6
	David Schilling (R)	47,575	15.0
	Glenn Harris (D)	33,684	10.6
3	Clay Higgins (R)*	2,30,480	67.8
	Braylon Harris (D)	60,852	17.9
	Rob Anderson (D)	39,423	11.6
4	Mike Johnson (R)*	1,85,265	60.4
	Kenny Houston (D)	78,157	25.5
	Ryan Trundle (D)	23,813	7.8
	Ben Gibson (R)	19,343	6.3
5	Luke Letlow (R)	49,183	62.0
	Lance Harris (R)	30,124	38.0
6	Garret Graves (R)*	2,65,706	71.0
	Dartanyon Williams (D)	95,541	25.5

Maine

Senate

		Vote total	Percent
	Susan Collins (R)*	4,17,645	51.0
	Sara Gideon (D)	3,47,223	42.4
	Lisa Savage (I)	40,579	5.0

House

		Vote total	Percent
1	Chellie Pingree (D)*	2,71,004	62.2
	Jay Allen (R)	1,65,008	37.8
2	Jared Golden (D)*	1,97,974	53.0
	Dale Crafts (R)	1,75,228	47.0

Maryland

House

		Vote total	Percent
1	Andrew P. Harris (R)*	2,50,901	63.4
	Mia Mason (D)	1,43,877	36.4

NOTE: *Iowa's 5th district became obsolete for the 113th Congress in 2013.*

		Vote total	Percent
2	Dutch Ruppersberger (D)*	2,24,836	67.7
	Johnny Ray Salling (R)	1,06,355	32.0
3	John Sarbanes (D)*	2,60,358	69.8
	Charles Anthony (R)	1,12,117	30.0
4	Anthony G. Brown (D)*	2,82,119	79.6
	George McDermott (R)	71,671	20.2
5	Steny Hoyer (D)*	2,74,210	68.8
	Chris Palombi (R)	1,23,525	31.0
6	David Trone (D)*	2,15,540	58.8
	Neil Parrott (R)	1,43,599	39.2
7	Kweisi Mfume (D)*	2,37,084	71.6
	Kim Klacik (R)	92,825	28.0
8	Jamie Raskin (D)*	2,74,716	68.2
	Gregory Coll (R)	1,27,157	31.6

Massachusetts

Senate

		Vote total	Percent
	Edward J. Markey (D)*	23,57,809	66.2
	Kevin O'Connor (R)	11,77,765	33.0

House

		Vote total	Percent
1	Richard Neal (D)*	2,75,376	96.5
2	Jim McGovern (D)*	2,49,854	65.3
	Tracy Lovvorn (R)	1,32,220	34.6
3	Lori Trahan (D)*	2,86,896	97.7
4	Jake Auchincloss (D)	2,51,102	60.8
	Julie Hall (R)	1,60,474	38.9
5	Katherine Clark (D)*	2,94,427	74.3
	Caroline Colarusso (R)	1,01,351	25.6
6	Seth Moulton (D)*	2,86,377	65.4
	John Paul Moran (R)	1,50,695	34.4
7	Ayanna Pressley (D)*	2,67,362	86.6
	Roy Owens (I)	38,675	12.5
8	Stephen Lynch (D)*	3,10,940	80.7
	Jonathan D. Lott (HES)	72,060	18.7
9	Bill Keating (D)*	2,60,262	61.3
	Helen Brady (R)	1,54,261	36.3

Michigan

Senate

		Vote total	Percent
	Gary Peters (D)*	27,34,568	49.9
	John James (R)	26,42,233	48.2

House

		Vote total	Percent
1	Jack Bergman (R)*	2,56,581	61.6
	Dana Alan Ferguson (D)	1,53,328	36.8
2	Bill Huizenga (R)*	2,38,711	59.2
	Bryan Berghoef (D)	1,54,122	38.2
3	Peter Meijer (R)	2,13,649	53.0
	Hillary Scholten (D)	1,89,769	47.0
4	John Moolenaar (R)*	2,42,621	65.0
	Jerry Hilliard (D)	1,20,802	32.4
5	Dan Kildee (D)*	1,96,599	54.5
	Tim Kelly (R)	1,50,772	41.8
6	Fred Upton (R)*	2,11,496	55.8
	Jon Hoadley (D)	1,52,085	40.1
7	Tim Walberg (R)*	2,27,524	58.8
	Gretchen Driskell (D)	1,59,743	41.2
8	Elissa Slotkin (D)*	2,17,922	50.9
	Paul Junge (R)	2,02,525	47.3
9	Andy Levin (D)*	2,30,318	57.7

		Vote total	Percent
	Charles Langworthy (R)	1,53,296	38.4
10	Lisa McClain (R)	2,71,607	66.3
	Kimberly Bizon (D)	1,38,179	33.7
11	Hayley Stevens (D)*	2,26,128	50.2
	Eric Esshaki (R)	2,15,405	47.8
12	Debbie Dingell (D)*	2,54,957	66.4
	Jeff Jones (R)	1,17,719	30.7
13	Rashida Tlaib (D)*	2,23,205	78.1
	David Dudenhoefer (R)	53,311	18.6
14	Brenda Lawrence (D)*	2,71,370	79.3
	Robert Vance Patrick (R)	62,664	18.3

Minnesota

Senate

		Vote total	Percent
	Tina Smith (D)*	15,66,522	48.8
	Jason Lewis (R)	13,98,145	43.6
	Kevin O'Connor (LMN)	1,85,064	5.8

House

		Vote total	Percent
1	Jim Hagedorn (R)*	1,79,234	48.6
	Dan Feehan (D)	1,67,890	45.5
	Bill Rood (GLCM)	21,448	5.8
2	Angie Craig (D)*	2,04,534	48.2
	Tyler Kistner (R)	1,94,954	45.9
	Adam Weeks (LMN)	24,751	5.8
3	Dean Phillips (D)*	2,46,666	55.6
	Kendall Qualls (R)	1,96,625	44.3
4	Betty McCollum (D)*	2,45,813	63.2
	Gene Rechtzigel (R)	1,12,730	29.0
	Susan Pendergast Sindt (GLCM)	29,537	7.6
5	Ilhan Omar (D)*	2,55,924	64.3
	Lacy Johnson (R)	1,02,878	25.8
	Mickey Moore (LMN)	37,979	9.5
6	Tom Emmer (R)*	2,70,901	65.7
	Tawnja Zahradka (D)	1,40,853	34.2
7	Michelle Fischbach (R)	1,94,066	53.4
	Collin Peterson (D)*	1,44,840	39.8
8	Pete Stauber (R)*	2,23,432	56.8
	Quinn Nystrom (D)	1,47,853	37.6
	Judith Schwartzbacker (GLCM)	22,190	5.6

Mississippi

Senate

		Vote total	Percent
	Cindy Hyde-Smith (R)*	7,09,511	54.1
	Mike Espy (D)	5,78,691	44.1

House

		Vote total	Percent
1	Trent Kelly (R)*	2,28,787	68.7
	Antonia Eliason (D)	1,04,008	31.3
2	Bennie Thompson (D)*	1,96,224	66.0
	Brian Flowers (R)	1,01,010	34.0
3	Michael Guest (R)*	2,21,064	64.7
	Dorothy Benford (D)	1,20,782	35.3
4	Steven Palazzo (R)*	2,55,971	100.0

Missouri

Governor

		Vote total	Percent
	Mike Parson (R)*	17,20,202	57.1
	Nicole Galloway (D)	12,25,771	40.7

House

		Vote total	Percent
1	Cori Bush (D)	2,49,087	78.8
	Anthony Rogers (R)	59,940	19.0
2	Ann Wagner (R)*	2,33,157	51.9
	Jill Schupp (D)	2,04,540	45.5
3	Blaine Luetkemeyer (R)*	2,82,866	69.4
	Megan Rezabek (D)	1,16,095	28.5
4	Vicky Hartzler (R)*	2,45,247	67.6
	Lindsey Simmons (D)	1,07,635	29.7
5	Emanuel Cleaver II (D)*	2,07,180	58.8
	Ryan Derks (R)	1,35,934	38.6
6	Sam Graves (R)*	2,58,709	67.1
	Gena Ross (D)	1,18,926	30.8
7	Billy Long (R)*	2,54,318	68.9
	Teresa Montseny (D)	98,111	26.6
8	Jason Smith (R)*	2,53,811	76.9
	Kathy Ellis (D)	70,561	21.4

Montana

Governor

		Vote total	Percent
	Greg Gianforte (R)	3,28,548	54.4
	Mike Cooney (D)	2,50,860	41.6

Senate

		Vote total	Percent
	Steve Daines (R)*	3,33,174	55.0
	Steve Bullock (D)	2,72,463	45.0

House

		Vote total	Percent
AL	Matt Rosendale (R)	3,39,169	56.4
	Kathleen Williams (D)	2,62,340	43.6

Nebraska

Senate

		Vote total	Percent
	Ben Sasse (R)*	5,83,507	62.7
	Chris Janicek (D)	2,27,191	24.4
	Preston Love Jr. (D/WRI)	58,411	6.3
	Gene Siadek (LIBERT)	55,115	5.9

House

		Vote total	Percent
1	Jeff Fortenberry (R)*	1,89,006	59.5
	Kate Bolz (D)	1,19,622	37.7
2	Don Bacon (R)*	1,71,071	50.8
	Kara Eastman (D)	1,55,706	46.2
3	Adrian Smith (R)*	2,25,157	78.5
	Mark Elworth Jr. (D)	50,690	17.7

Nevada

House

		Vote total	Percent
1	Dina Titus (D)*	1,37,868	61.8
	Joyce Bentley (R)	74,490	33.4
2	Mark Amodei (R)*	2,16,078	56.5
	Patricia Ackerman (D)	1,55,780	40.7
3	Susie Lee (D)*	2,03,421	48.8
	Daniel Rodimer (R)	1,90,975	45.8
4	Steven Horsford (D)*	1,68,457	50.7
	Jim Marchant (R)	1,52,284	45.8

New Hampshire

Governor

		Vote total	Percent
	Chris Sununu (R)*	5,16,609	65.1
	Dan Feltes (D)	2,64,639	33.4

Senate

		Vote total	Percent
	Jeanne Shaheen (D)*	4,50,778	56.6
	Bryant Messner (R)	3,26,229	41.0

House

		Vote total	Percent
1	Chris Pappas (D)*	2,05,606	51.3

	Vote total	Percent
Matt Mowers (R)	1,85,159	46.2
2 Ann McLane Kuster (D)*	2,08,289	53.9
Steve Negron (R)	1,68,886	43.7

New Jersey

Senate

	Vote total	Percent
Cory Booker (D)*	25,41,178	57.2
Rik Mehta (R)	18,17,052	40.9

House

	Vote total	Percent
1 Donald Norcross (D)*	2,40,567	62.5
Claire Gustafson (R)	1,44,463	37.5
2 Jeff Van Drew (D)*	1,95,526	51.9
Amy Kennedy (D)	1,73,849	46.2
3 Andrew Kim (D)*	2,29,840	53.2
David Richter (R)	1,96,327	45.5
4 Chris Smith (R)*	2,54,103	59.9
Stephanie Schmid (D)	1,62,420	38.3
5 Josh Gottheimer (D)*	2,25,175	53.2
Frank Pallotta (R)	1,93,333	45.6
6 Frank Pallone (D)*	1,99,648	61.2
Christian Onuoha (R)	1,26,760	38.8
7 Tom Malinowski (D)*	2,19,629	50.6
Thomas Kean Jr. (R)	2,14,318	49.4
8 Albio Sires (D)*	1,76,758	74.0
Jason Mushnick (R)	58,686	24.6
9 Bill Pascrell (D)*	2,03,674	65.8
Billy Prempeh (R)	98,629	31.9
10 Donald Payne, Jr. (D)*	2,41,522	83.3
Jennifer Zinone (R)	40,298	13.9
11 Mikie Sherrill (D)*	2,35,163	53.3
Rosemary Becchi (R)	2,06,013	46.7
12 Bonnie Watson Coleman (D)*	2,30,883	65.6
Mark Razzoli (R)	1,14,591	32.6

New Mexico

Senate

	Vote total	Percent
Ben Ray Luján (D)	4,74,483	51.7
Mark Ronchetti (R)	4,18,483	45.6

House

	Vote total	Percent
1 Debra Haaland (D)*	1,86,953	58.2
Michelle Garcia Holmes (R)	1,34,337	41.8
2 Yvette Herrell (R)	1,42,283	53.7
Xochitl Torres Small (D)*	1,22,546	46.3
3 Teresa Leger Fernandez (D)	1,86,282	58.7
Alexis Martinez Johnson (R)	1,31,166	41.3

New York

House

	Vote total	Percent
1 Lee Zeldin (R/C/I)*	1,99,763	55.9
Nancy Goroff (D/WFP)	1,57,484	44.1
2 Andrew Garbarino (R/C/L/SAMP)	1,77,353	52.9
Jackie Gordon (D/WFP/I)	1,54,123	46.0
3 Tom Suozzi (D/WFP/I)*	2,08,412	55.9
George Devolder-Santos (R/C)	1,61,907	43.5
4 Kathleen Rice (D)*	1,99,762	56.1
Douglas Tuman (R/C)	1,53,007	43.0
5 Gregory W. Meeks (D)*	2,29,125	99.3
6 Grace Meng (D/WFP)*	1,58,862	67.9
Thomas Zmich (R/LIBERT/C/SOCP)	74,829	32.0
7 Nydia Velazquez (D/WFP)*	1,91,073	84.8
Brian Kelly (R/C)	32,520	14.4
8 Hakeem Jeffries (D/WFP)*	2,34,933	84.8
Garfield Wallace (R/C)	42,007	15.2
9 Yvette Clarke (D/WFP)*	2,30,221	83.0
Constantine Jean-Pierre (R/C)	43,950	15.9
10 Jerrold Nadler (WFP/D)*	2,06,310	74.5
Cathy Bernstein (R/C)	66,889	24.1
11 Nicole Malliotakis (R/C)	1,55,608	53.1
Max Rose (D/I)*	1,37,198	46.8
12 Carolyn Maloney (D)*	2,65,172	82.1
Carlos Santiago-Cano (R/C)	53,061	16.4
13 Andriano Espaillat (D/WFP)*	2,31,841	90.8
Lovelynn Gwinn (R)	19,829	7.8
14 Alexandria Ocasio-Cortez (D)*	1,52,661	71.6
John Cummings (R/C)	58,440	27.4
15 Ritchie Torres (D)	1,69,533	88.7
Patrick Delices (R/C)	21,221	11.1
16 Jamaal Bowman (D)	2,18,471	84.0
Patrick McManus (C)	41,085	15.8
17 Mondaire Jones (D/WFP)	1,97,353	59.3
Maureen McArdle Schulman (R)	1,17,307	35.2
18 Sean Patrick Maloney (D/WFP/I)*	1,87,169	55.8
Chele Farley (R/C)	1,45,098	43.2
19 Antonio Delgado (D/WFP/SAMP)*	1,92,100	54.5
Kyle Van De Water (R)	1,51,475	42.9
20 Paul D. Tonko (D/WFP/I)*	2,19,705	61.1
Elizabeth Joy (R/C/SAMP)	1,39,446	38.8
21 Elise M. Stefanik (R/C/I)*	1,88,649	58.8
Tedra Cobb (D/WFP)	1,31,992	41.1
22 Claudia Tenney (R/C)	1,56,098	48.8
Anthony Brindisi (D/WFP/I)*	1,55,989	48.8
23 Thomas W. Reed, II (R/C/I)*	1,81,060	57.7
Tracy Mitrano (D/WFP)	1,29,014	41.1
24 John M. Katko (R/C/I)*	1,82,567	53.1
Dana Balter (D)	1,47,638	43.0
25 Joseph Morelle (D/WFP/I)*	2,06,396	59.3
James Maxwell (R/C)	1,36,198	39.1
26 Brian Higgins (D/WFP/SAMP)*	2,23,276	69.8
Ricky Donovan, Sr. (R)	91,687	28.7
27 Chris Jacobs (R/C/I)*	2,29,044	59.7
Nate McMurray (D/WFP)	1,49,559	39.0

North Carolina

Governor

	Vote total	Percent
Roy Cooper (D)*	28,34,790	51.5
Dan Forest (R)	25,86,605	47.0

Senate

	Vote total	Percent
Thom Tillis (R)*	26,65,598	48.7
Cal Cunningham (D)	25,69,965	46.9

House

	Vote total	Percent
1 G. K. Butterfield (D)*	1,88,870	54.2
Sandy Smith (R)	1,59,748	45.8
2 Deborah Ross (D)	3,11,887	63.0
Alan Swain (R)	1,72,544	34.8
3 Gregory Murphy (R)*	2,29,800	63.4
Daryl Farrow (D)	1,32,752	36.6
4 David Price (D)*	3,32,421	67.3
Robert Thomas (R)	1,61,298	32.7
5 Virginia Foxx (R)*	2,57,843	66.9
David Wilson Brown (D)	1,19,846	31.1
6 Kathy Manning (D)	2,53,531	62.3
Joseph Lee Haywood (R)	1,53,598	37.7
7 David Rouzer (R)*	2,72,443	60.2
Christopher Ward (D)	1,79,045	39.6
8 Richard Hudson (R)*	2,02,774	53.3
Patricia Timmons-Goodson (D)	1,77,781	46.7
9 Dan Bishop (R)*	2,24,661	55.6
Cynthia Wallace (D)	1,79,463	44.4
10 Patrick McHenry (R)*	2,84,095	68.9
David Parker (D)	1,28,189	31.1
11 Madison Cawthorn (R)	2,45,351	54.5
Morris Davis (D)	1,90,609	42.3
12 Alma Adams (D)*	3,41,457	100.0
13 Ted Budd (R)*	2,67,181	68.2
Scott Huffman (D)	1,24,684	31.8

	Vote total	Percent

North Dakota

Governor

		Vote total	Percent
	Doug Burgum (R)*	2,35,629	65.8
	Shelley Lenz (D)	90,925	25.4

House

	Kelly Armstrong		
AL	(R)*	2,45,229	69.0
	Zach Raknerud (D)	97,970	27.6

Ohio

House

1	Steve Chabot (R)*	1,99,560	51.8
	Kate Schroder (D)	1,72,022	44.6
2	Brad Wenstrup (R)*	2,30,430	61.1
	Jaime Castle (D)	1,46,781	38.9
3	Joyce Beatty (D)*	2,27,420	70.8
	Mark Richardson (R)	93,569	29.1
4	Jim Jordan (R)*	2,35,875	67.9
	Shannon		
	Freshour (D)	1,01,897	29.3
5	Bob Latta (R)*	2,57,019	68.0
	Nick Rubando (D)	1,20,962	32.0
6	Bill Johnson (R)*	2,49,130	74.4
	Shawna Roberts (D)	85,661	25.6
7	Bob Gibbs (R)*	2,36,607	67.5
	Quentin Potter (D)	1,02,271	29.2
8	Warren Davidson		
	(R)*	2,46,277	69.0
	Vanessa Enoch (D)	1,10,766	31.0
9	Marcy Kaptur (D)*	1,90,328	63.1
	Rob Weber (R)	1,11,385	36.9
10	Mike Turner (R)*	2,12,972	58.4
	Desiree Tims (D)	1,51,976	41.6
	Marcia Fudge		
11	(D)*	2,42,098	80.1
	Laverne Gore (R)	60,323	19.9
12	Troy Balderson (R)*	2,41,790	55.2
	Alaina Shearer (D)	1,82,847	41.8
13	Tim Ryan (D)*	1,73,631	52.5
	Christina Hagan (R)	1,48,648	44.9
14	David Joyce (R)*	2,38,864	60.1
	Hillary O'Connor		
	Mueri (D)	1,58,586	39.9
15	Steve Stivers (R)*	2,43,103	63.4
	Joel Newby (D)	1,40,183	36.6
16	Anthony Gonzalez		
	(R)*	2,47,335	63.2
	Aaron Godfrey (D)	1,44,071	36.8

Oklahoma

Senate

	Jim Inhofe (R)*	9,79,140	62.9
	Abby Broyles (D)	5,09,763	32.8

House

1	Kevin Hern (R)*	2,13,700	63.7
	Kojo Asamoa-		
	Caesar (D)	1,09,641	32.7
2	Markwayne Mullin		
	(R)*	2,16,511	75.0
	Danyell Lanier (D)	63,472	22.0
3	Frank Lucas (R)*	2,42,677	78.5
	Zoe Ann		
	Midyett (D)	66,501	21.5
4	Tom Cole (R)*	2,13,096	67.8
	Mary Brannon (D)	90,459	28.8
5	Stephanie Bice (R)	1,58,191	52.1
	Kendra Horn (D)*	1,45,658	47.9

	Vote total	Percent

Oregon

Senate

	Jeff Merkley (D/I/		
	WFP)*	13,21,047	56.9
	Jo Rae Perkins (R)	9,12,814	39.3

House

1	Suzanne Bonamici		
	(D/WFP)*	2,97,071	64.6
	Christopher		
	Christensen (R)	1,61,928	35.2
2	Cliff Bentz (R)	2,73,835	59.9
	Alex Spenser (D)	1,68,881	36.9
3	Earl Blumenauer (D/		
	WFP)*	3,43,574	73.0
	Joanna Harbour (R)	1,10,570	23.5
4	Peter DeFazio (D/		
	WFP/I)*	2,40,950	51.5
	Alek Skarlatos (R)	2,16,081	46.2
5	Kurt Schrader (D)*	2,34,683	51.9
	Amy Ryan Courser		
	(R)	2,04,372	45.2

Pennsylvania

House

1	Brian Fitzpatrick		
	(R)*	2,49,804	56.6
	Christina Finello (D)	1,91,875	43.4
2	Brendan F. Boyle		
	(D)*	1,98,140	72.5
	David Torres (R)	75,022	27.5
3	Dwight Evans (D)*	3,41,708	91.0
	Michael Harvey (R)	33,671	9.0
	Madeleine Dean		
4	(D)*	2,64,637	59.5
	Kathy Barnette (R)	1,79,926	40.5
	Mary Gay Scanlon		
5	(D)*	2,55,743	64.7
	Dasha Pruett (R)	1,39,552	35.3
	Chrissy Houlahan		
6	(D)*	2,26,440	56.1
	John Emmons (R)	1,77,526	43.9
7	Susan Wild (D)*	1,95,475	51.9
	Lisa Scheller (R)	1,81,407	48.1
8	Matt Cartwright		
	(D)*	1,78,004	51.8
	Jim Bognet (R)	1,65,783	48.2
9	Dan Meuser (R)*	2,32,988	66.3
	Gary Wegman (D)	1,18,266	33.7
10	Scott Perry (R)*	2,08,896	53.3
	Eugene		
	DePasquale (D)	1,82,938	46.7
11	Lloyd Smucker (R)*	2,41,915	63.1
	Sarah Hammond (D)	1,41,325	36.9
12	Fred Keller (R)*	2,41,035	70.8
	Lee Griffin (D)	99,199	29.2
13	John Joyce (R)*	2,67,789	73.5
	Todd Rowley (D)	96,612	26.5
14	Guy Reschenthaler		
	(R)*	2,41,688	64.7
	William Marx (D)	1,31,895	35.3
15	Glenn Thompson		
	(R)*	2,55,058	73.5
	Robert Williams (D)	92,156	26.5
16	Mike Kelly (R)*	2,10,088	59.3
	Kristy Gnibus (D)	1,43,962	40.7
17	Conor Lamb (D)*	2,22,253	51.1
	Sean Parnell (R)	2,12,284	48.9

		Vote total	Percent
18	Michael Doyle (D)*	2,66,084	69.2
	Luke Negron (R)	1,18,163	30.8

Rhode Island

Senate

	Jack Reed (D)*	3,28,574	66.5
	Allen Waters (R)	1,64,855	33.4

House

1	David Cicilline (D)*	1,58,550	70.8
	Frederick Wysocki		
	(I)	35,457	15.8
	Jeffrey Lemire (I)	28,300	12.6
2	James Langevin		
	(D)*	1,54,086	58.2
	Robert Lancia (R)	1,09,894	41.5

South Carolina

Senate

	Lindsey Graham		
	(R)*	13,69,137	54.4
	Jaime Harrison (D)	11,10,828	44.2

House

1	Nancy Mace (R)	2,16,042	50.6
	Joe Cunningham		
	(D)*	2,10,627	49.3
2	Joe Wilson (R)*	2,02,715	55.7
	Adair Ford		
	Boroughs (D)	1,55,118	42.6
3	Jeff Duncan (R)*	2,37,544	71.2
	Hosea Cleveland (D)	2,37,544	28.7
4	William Timmons		
	(R)*	2,22,126	61.6
	Kim Nelson (D)	1,33,023	36.9
5	Ralph Norman (R)*	2,20,006	60.1
	Moe Brown (D)	1,45,979	39.9
6	James Clyburn (D)*	1,97,477	68.2
	John McCollum (R)	89,258	30.8
7	Tom Rice (R)*	2,24,993	61.8
	Melissa Watson (D)	1,38,863	38.1

South Dakota

Senate

	Mike Rounds (R)*	2,76,232	65.7
	Dan Ahlers (D)	1,43,987	34.3

House

AL	Dusty Johnson (R)*	3,21,984	81.0
	Randy Luallin		
	(LIBERT)	75,748	19.0

Tennessee

Senate

	Bill Hagerty (R)	18,40,926	62.2
	Marquita		
	Bradshaw (D)	10,40,691	35.2

House

1	Diana		
	Harshbarger (R)	2,28,181	74.7
	Blair		
	Walsingham (D)	68,617	22.5
2	Tim Burchett (R)*	2,38,907	67.6
	Renee Hoyos (D)	1,09,684	31.1
	Chuck Fleischmann		
3	(R)*	2,15,571	67.3
	Meg Gorman (D)	97,687	30.5
4	Scott DesJarlais (R)*	2,23,802	66.7
	Christopher		
	Hale (D)	1,11,908	33.3
5	Jim Cooper (D)*	2,52,155	100.0
6	John Rose (R)*	2,57,572	73.7

		Vote total	Percent
	Christopher Finley (D)	83,852	24.0
7	Mark Green (R)*	2,45,188	69.9
	Kiran Sreepada (D)	95,839	27.3
8	David Kustoff (R)*	2,27,216	68.5
	Erika Stotts Pearson (D)	97,890	29.5
9	Steve Cohen (D)*	1,87,905	77.4
	Charlotte Bergmann (R)	48,818	20.1

Texas

Senate

		Vote total	Percent
	John Cornyn (R)*	59,62,983	53.5
	Mary Jennings Hegar (D)	48,88,764	43.9

House

		Vote total	Percent
1	Louis Gohmert (R)*	2,19,726	72.6
	Hank Gilbert (D)	83,016	27.4
2	Daniel Crenshaw (R)*	1,92,828	55.6
	Sima Ladjevardian (D)	1,48,374	42.8
3	Van Taylor (R)*	2,30,512	55.1
	Lulu Seikaly (D)	1,79,458	42.9
4	Pat Fallon (R)	2,53,837	75.1
	Russell Foster (D)	76,326	22.6
5	Lance Gooden (R)*	1,73,836	62.0
	Carolyn Salter (D)	1,00,743	35.9
6	Ronald Wright (R)*	1,79,507	52.8
	Stephen Daniel (D)	1,49,530	44.0
7	Lizzie Pannill Fletcher (D)*	1,59,529	50.8
	Wesley Hunt (R)	1,49,054	47.5
8	Kevin Brady (R)*	2,77,327	72.5
	Elizabeth Hernandez (D)	97,409	25.5
9	Al Green (D)*	1,72,938	75.5
	Johnny Teague (R)	49,575	21.6
10	Michael McCaul (R)*	2,17,216	52.5
	Mike Siegel (D)	1,87,686	45.3
11	August Pfluger (R)	2,32,568	79.7
	Jon Mark Hogg (D)	53,394	18.3
12	Kay Granger (R)*	2,33,853	63.7
	Lisa Welch (D)	1,21,250	33.0
13	Ronny L. Jackson (R)	2,17,124	79.4
	Gus Trujillo (D)	50,477	18.5
14	Randy Weber (R)*	1,90,541	61.6
	Adrienne Bell (R)	1,18,574	38.4
15	Vicente Gonzalez Jr. (D)*	1,15,605	50.5
	Monica De La Cruz (R)	1,09,017	47.6
16	Veronica Escobar (D)*	1,54,108	64.7
	Irene Armendariz-Jackson (R)	84,006	35.3
17	Pete Sessions (R)	1,71,390	55.9
	Rick Kennedy (D)	1,25,565	40.9
18	Sheila Jackson Lee (D)*	1,80,952	73.3
	Wendell Champion (R)	58,033	23.5
19	Jodey Arrington (R)*	1,98,198	74.8
	Tom Watson (D)	60,583	22.9

		Vote total	Percent
20	Joaquin Castro (D)*	1,75,078	64.7
	Mauro Garza (R)	89,628	33.1
21	Chip Roy (R)*	2,35,740	52.0
	Wendy Davis (D)	2,05,780	45.4
22	Troy Nehls (R)	2,10,259	51.5
	Sri Preston Kulkarni (D)	1,81,998	44.6
23	Tony Gonzales (R)	1,49,395	50.6
	Gina Ortiz Jones (D)	1,37,693	46.6
24	Beth Van Duyne (R)	1,67,910	48.8
	Candace Valenzuela (D)	1,63,326	47.5
25	Roger Williams (R)*	2,20,088	55.9
	Julie Oliver (D)	1,65,697	42.1
26	Michael Burgess (R)*	2,61,963	60.6
	Carol Iannuzzi (D)	1,61,099	37.3
27	Michael Cloud (R)*	1,72,305	63.1
	Ricardo De La Fuente (D)	95,466	34.9
28	Henry Cuellar (D)*	1,37,494	58.3
	Sandra Whitten (R)	91,925	39.0
29	Sylvia Garcia (D)*	1,11,305	71.4
	Jaimy Annette Zoboulikos-Blanco (R)	42,840	27.5
30	Eddie Bernice Johnson (D)*	2,04,928	77.5
	Tre Pennie (R)	48,685	18.4
31	John Carter (R)*	2,12,695	53.4
	Donna Imam (D)	1,76,293	44.3
32	Colin Allred (D)*	1,78,542	51.9
	Genevieve Collins (R)	1,57,867	45.9
33	Marc Veasey (D)*	1,05,317	66.8
	Fabian Cordova Vasquez (R)	39,638	25.2
34	Filemon Vela (D)*	1,11,439	55.4
	Rey Gonzalez Jr. (R)	84,119	41.8
35	Lloyd Doggett (D)*	1,76,373	65.4
	Jenny Garcia Sharon (R)	80,795	29.9
36	Brian Babin (R)*	2,22,712	73.6
	Rashad Lewis (D)	73,418	24.3

Utah

Governor

		Vote total	Percent
	Spencer Cox (R)	9,18,754	63.0
	Chris Peterson (D)	4,42,754	30.3

House

		Vote total	Percent
1	Blake Moore (R)	2,37,988	69.5
	Darren Parry (D)	1,04,194	30.4
2	Chris Stewart (R)*	2,08,997	59.0
	Kael Weston (D)	1,29,762	36.6
3	John Curtis (R)*	2,46,674	68.7
	Devin Thorpe (D)	96,067	26.8
4	Burgess Owens (R)	1,79,688	47.7
	Ben McAdams (D)*	1,75,923	46.7

Vermont

Governor

		Vote total	Percent
	Phil Scott (R)*	2,48,412	68.5
	David Zuckerman (VT Progressive Party/D)	99,214	27.4

House

		Vote total	Percent
AL	Peter Welch (D)*	2,38,827	67.3
	Miriam Berry (R)	95,830	27.0

Virginia

Senate

		Vote total	Percent
	Mark Warner (D)*	24,66,500	56.0
	Daniel Gade (R)	19,34,199	43.9

House

		Vote total	Percent
1	Rob Wittman (R)*	2,60,614	58.1
	Qasim Rashid (D)	1,86,923	41.7
2	Elaine Luria (D)*	1,85,733	51.6
	Scott Taylor (R)	1,65,031	45.8
3	Bobby Scott (D)*	2,33,326	68.4
	John Collick (R)	1,07,299	31.4
4	Aston Donald McEachin (D)*	2,41,142	61.6
	Leon Benjamin Sr. (R)	1,49,625	38.2
5	Bob Good (R)	2,10,988	52.4
	Cameron Webb (D)	1,90,315	47.3
6	Benjamin Lee Cline (R)*	2,46,606	64.6
	Nicholas Betts (D)	1,34,729	35.3
7	Abigail Spanberger (D)*	2,30,893	50.8
	Nick Freitas (R)	2,22,623	49.0
8	Don Beyer (D)*	3,01,454	75.8
	Jeff Jordan (R)	95,365	24.0
9	Morgan Griffith (R)*	2,71,851	94.0
10	Jennifer Wexton (D)*	2,68,734	56.5
	Aliscia Andrews (R)	2,06,253	43.4
11	Gerry Connolly (D)*	2,80,725	71.4
	Manga Anantatmula (R)	1,11,380	28.3

Washington

Governor

		Vote total	Percent
	Jay Inslee (D)*	22,94,243	56.6
	Loren Culp (R)	17,49,066	43.1

House

		Vote total	Percent
1	Suzan DelBene (D)*	2,49,944	58.6
	Jeffrey Beeler (R)	1,76,407	41.3
2	Rick Larsen (D)*	2,55,252	63.1
	Timothy Hazelo (R)	1,48,384	36.7
3	Jaime Herrera Beutler (R)*	2,35,579	56.4
	Carolyn Long (D)	1,81,347	43.4
4	Dan Newhouse (R)*	2,02,108	66.2
	Doug McKinley (D)	1,02,667	33.6
5	Cathy McMorris Rodgers (R)*	2,47,815	61.3
	Dave Wilson (D)	1,55,737	38.5
6	Derek Kilmer (D)*	2,47,429	59.3
	Elizabeth Kreiselmaier (R)	1,68,783	40.5
7	Pramila Jayapal (D)*	3,87,109	83.0
	Craig Keller (R)	78,240	16.8
8	Kim Schrier (D)*	2,13,123	51.7
	Jesse Jensen (R)	1,98,423	48.1
9	Adam Smith (D)*	2,58,771	74.1
	Douglas Michael Basler (R)	89,697	25.7
10	Marilyn Strickland (D)	1,67,937	49.3
	Beth Doglio (D)	1,21,040	35.6

		Vote total	Percent
	West Virginia		
Governor			
	Jim Justice (R)*	4,97,944	63.5
	Ben Salango (D)	2,37,024	30.2
Senate			
	Shelley Moore Capito (R)*	5,47,454	70.3
	Paula Jean Swearengin (D)	2,10,309	27.0
House			
1	David McKinley (R)*	1,80,488	69.0
	Natalie Cline (D)	81,177	31.0
2	Alex Mooney (R)*	1,72,195	63.1
	Cathy Kunkel (D)	1,00,799	36.9

		Vote total	Percent
3	Carol Miller (R)*	1,61,585	71.3
	Hilary Turner (D)	64,927	28.7
	Wisconsin		
House			
1	Bryan Steil (R)*	2,38,271	59.3
	Roger Polack (D)	1,63,170	40.6
2	Mark Pocan (D)*	3,18,523	69.7
	Peter Theron (R)	1,38,306	30.3
3	Ron Kind (D)*	1,99,870	51.3
	Derrick Van Orden (R)	1,89,524	48.6
4	Gwen Moore (D)*	2,32,668	74.6
	Tim Rogers (R)	70,769	22.7
5	Scott Fitzgerald (R)	2,65,434	60.1
	Tom Palzewicz (D)	1,75,902	39.8

		Vote total	Percent
6	Glenn Grothman (R)*	2,38,874	59.2
	Jessica King (D)	1,64,239	40.7
7	Tom Tiffany (R)*	2,52,048	60.7
	Tricia Zunker (D)	1,62,741	39.2
8	Mike Gallagher (R)*	2,68,173	64.2
	Amanda Stuck (D)	1,49,558	35.8
	Wyoming		
Senate			
	Cynthia Lummis (R)	1,98,100	72.8
	Merav Ben-David (D)	72,766	26.8
House			
AL	Liz Cheney (R)*	1,85,732	68.6
	Lynnette Grey Bull (D)	66,576	24.6

Results of House Elections, 1928–2020

	1928	1930	1932	1934	1936	1938	1940	1942	1944	1946	1948	1950	1952	1954	1956	1958	1960	1962	1964	1966	1968	1970
Totals																						
Democrats	165	217	313	322	334	262	268	222	242	188	263	235	213	232	234	283	263	259	295	248	243	255
Republicans	269	217	117	103	88	169	162	209	191	246	171	199	221	203	201	153	174	176	140	187	192	180
Independents/																						
Libertarians																						
Alabama																						
Democrats	10	10	9[1]	9	9	9	9	9	9	9	9	9	9	9	9	9	9	8[1]	3	5	5	5
Republicans	0	0	0	0	0	0	0	0	0	0	0	0	0	0	0	0	0	0	5	3	3	3
Alaska																						
Democrats	—	—	—	—	—	—	—	—	—	—	—	—	—	—	—	1	1	1	1	0	0	1
Republicans	—	—	—	—	—	—	—	—	—	—	—	—	—	—	—	0	0	0	0	1	1	0
Arizona																						
Democrats	1	1	1	1	1	1	1	2[2]	2	2	2	2	1	1	1	1	1	2[2]	2	1	1	1
Republicans	0	0	0	0	0	0	0	0	0	0	0	0	1	1	1	1	1	1	1	2	2	2
Arkansas																						
Democrats	7	7	7	7	7	7	7	7	7	7	7	7	6[1]	6	6	6	6	4[1]	4	3	3	3
Republicans	0	0	0	0	0	0	0	0	0	0	0	0	0	0	0	0	0	0	0	1	1	1
California																						
Democrats	1	1	11[2]	13	15	12	11	12[2]	16	9	10	10	11[2]	11	13	16	16	25[2,3]	23	21	21	20
Republicans	10	10	9	7	4	8	9	11	7	14	13	13	19	19	17	14	14	13	15	17	17	18
Colorado																						
Democrats	1	1	4	4	4	4	2	1	0	1	3	2	2	2	2	3	2	2	4	3	3	2
Republicans	3	3	0	0	0	0	2	3	4	3	1	2	2	2	2	1	2	2	0	1	1	2
Connecticut																						
Democrats	0	2	2[2]	4	6	2	6	0	4	0	3	2	1	1	0	6	4	5	6	5	4	3
Republicans	5	3	4	2	0	4	0	6	2	6	3	4	5	5	6	0	2	1	0	1	2	2
Delaware																						
Democrats	0	0	1	0	1	0	1	0	1	0	0	0	0	1	0	1	1	1	1	0	0	0
Republicans	1	1	0	1	0	1	0	1	0	1	1	0	1	0	0	0	0	0	0	1	1	1
Florida																						
Democrats	4	4	5[2]	5	5	5	5	6[2]	6	6	6	6	8[2]	7	7	7	7	10[2]	10	9	9	9
Republicans	0	0	0	0	0	0	0	0	0	0	0	0	0	1	1	1	1	2	2	3	3	3
Georgia																						
Democrats	12	12	10[1]	10	10	10	10	10	10	10	10	10	10	10	10	10	10	10	9	8	8	8
Republicans	0	0	0	0	0	0	0	0	0	0	0	0	0	0	0	0	0	0	1	2	2	2
Hawaii																						
Democrats	—	—	—	—	—	—	—	—	—	—	—	—	—	—	—	1	2[2]	2	2	2	2	2
Republicans	—	—	—	—	—	—	—	—	—	—	—	—	—	—	—	0	0	0	0	0	0	0
Idaho																						
Democrats	0	0	2	2	2	1	1	1	1	0	1	0	1	1	1	1	2	2	1	0	0	0
Republicans	2	2	0	0	0	1	1	1	1	2	1	2	1	1	1	1	0	0	1	2	2	2
Illinois																						
Democrats	6	13[4]	19	21	21	17	11	71	11	6	12	8	9[1]	12	11	14	14	12[1]	13	12	12	12
Republicans	21	14	8	6	6	10	16	19	15	20	14	18	16	13	14	11	11	12	11	12	12	12
Indiana																						
Democrats	3	9	12[1]	11	11	5	4	2[1]	2	2	7	2	1	2	2	8	4[4]	4	6	5	4	5
Republicans	10	4	0	1	1	7	8	9	9	9	4	9	10	9	9	3	7	7	5	6	7	6
Iowa																						
Democrats	0	1	6[1]	6	5	2	2	1	0	0	0	0	0	0	1	4	2	1[1]	6	2	2	2
Republicans	11	10	3	3	4	7	7	8	8	8	8	8	8	8	7	4	6	6	1	5	5	5
Kansas																						
Democrats	1	1	3[1]	3	2	1	1	1	0	0	0	0	1	0	1	3	1	1	0	0	0	1
Republicans	7	7	4	4	5	6	6	6	6	6	6	6	5	6	5	3	5	5	5	5	5	4
Kentucky																						
Democrats	2	9	9[1]	8	8	8	8	8	8	6	7	7	6[1]	6	6	7	7	5[1]	6	4	4	5
Republicans	9	2	0	1	1	1	1	1	1	3	2	2	2	2	2	1	1	2	1	3	3	2
Louisiana																						
Democrats	8	8	8	8	8	8	8	8	8	8	8	8	8	8	8	8	8	8	8	8	8	8
Republicans	0	0	0	0	0	0	0	0	0	0	0	0	0	0	0	0	0	0	0	0	0	0
Maine																						
Democrats	0	0	2[1]	2	0	0	0	0	0	0	0	0	0	0	1	2	0	1	1	2	2	2
Republicans	4	4	1	1	3	3	3	3	3	3	3	3	3	3	2	1	3	2	1	0	0	0

1972	1974	1976	1978	1980	1982	1984	1986	1988	1990	1992	1994	1996	1998	2000	2002	2004	2006	2008	2010	2012	2014	2016	2018	2020
243	291	292	277	243	269	253	258	260	267	258	204	207	211	212	205	202	233	255	193	201	188	194	197	233
192	144	143	158	192	166	182	177	175	167	176	230	227	223	221	229	232	202	180	242	234	247	241	238	200
																								2
4[1]	4	4	4	4	5	5	5	5	5	4	4	2	2	2	2	2	2	3	1	1	1	1	1	1
3	3	3	3	3	2	2	2	2	2	3	3	5	5	5	5	5	5	4	6	6	6	6	6	6
1[3]	0	0	0	0	0	0	0	0	0	0	0	0	0	0	0	0	0	0	0	0	0	0	0	0
0	1	1	1	1	1	1	1	1	1	1	1	1	1	1	1	1	1	1	1	1	1	1	1	1
1[2]	1	2	2	2	2[2]	1	1	1	1	3[2]	1	1	1	1	2	2	4	3	3	5[2]	4	4	4	5
3	3	2	2	2	3	4	4	4	4	3	5	5	5	5	6	6	4	5	5	4	5	5	5	4
3	3	3	2	2	2	3	3	3	3	2	2	2	2	3	3	3	3	3	1	0	0	0	0	0
1	1	1	2	2	2	1	1	1	1	2	2	2	2	1	1	1	1	1	3	4	4	4	4	4
23[2]	28	29	26	22	28[2]	27	27	27	26	30[2]	27	29	28	32	33	33	34	34	34	38	39	39	39	45
20	15	14	17	21	17	18	18	18	19	22	25	23	24	20	20	20	19	19	19	15	14	14	14	8
2[2]	3	3	3	3	3[2]	2	3	3	3	2	2	2	2	2	2	3	4	5	3	3	3	3	3	4
3	2	2	2	2	3	4	3	3	3	4	4	4	4	4	5	4	3	2	4	4	4	4	4	3
										3														
3	4	4	5	4	4	3	3	3	3	3	3	4	4	3	2	2	4	5	5	5	5	5	5	5
3	2	2	1	2	2	3	3	3	3	3	3	2	2	3	3	3	1	0	0	0	0	0	0	0
0	0	0	0	0	1	1	1	1	1	0	0	0	0	0	0	0	0	0	1	1	1	1	1	1
1	1	1	1	1	0	0	0	0	0	0	1	1	1	1	1	1	1	1	0	0	0	0	0	0
11[2]	10	10	12	11	13[2]	12	12	10	9	10[2]	8	8	8	8	7	7	9	10	6	10[2]	10	11	11	13
4	5	5	3	4	6	7	7	9	10	13	15	15	15	15	18	18	16	15	19	17	17	16	16	14
9	10	10	9	9	9	8	8	9	9	7[2]	4	3	3	3	5	6	7	6	5	5[2]	4	4	4	5
1	0	0	1	1	1	2	2	1	1	4	7	8	8	8	8	7	6	7	8	9	10	10	10	9
2	2	2	2	2	2	2	1	1	2	2	2	2	2	2	2	2	2	2	2	2	2	2	2	2
0	0	0	0	0	0	0	1	1	0	0	0	0	0	0	0	0	0	0	0	0	0	0	0	0
0	0	0	0	0	0	1	1	1	2	1	0	0	0	0	0	0	2	1	0	0	0	0	0	0
2	2	2	2	2	2	1	1	1	0	1	2	2	2	2	2	2	0	1	2	2	2	2	2	2
10	13	12	11	10	12[1]	13	13	14	15	12[1]	10	10	10	10	9	10	10	12	8	12[1]	10	11	11	13
14	11	12	13	14	10	9	9	8	7	8	10	10	10	10	10	9	9	7	11	6[8]	8	7	7	5
4	9	8	7	6	5[1]	5[4]	6	6	8	7	4	4	4	4	3	2	5	5	3	2	2	2	2	2
7	2	3	4	5	5	5	4	4	2	3	6	6	6	6	6	7	4	4	6	7	7	7	7	7
3[1]	5	4	3	3	3	2	2	2	2	1[1]	0	1	1	1	1	1	3	3	3	2[1]	1	1	1	3
3	1	2	3	3	3	4	4	4	4	4	5	4	4	4	4	4	2	2	2	2	3	3	3	1
1	1	2	1	1	2	2	2	2	2	2[1]	0	0	1	1	1	1	2	1	0	0	0	0	0	1
4	4	3	4	4	3	3	3	3	3	2	4	4	3	3	3	3	2	3	4	4	4	4	4	3
5	5	5	4	4	4	4	4	4	4	4[1]	2	1	1	1	1	1	2	2	2	1	1	1	1	1
2	2	2	3	3	3	3	3	3	3	2	4	5	5	5	5	5	4	4	4	5	5	5	5	5
7[3]	6[5]	6	5	6	6	6	5	4	4	4[1]	4	2	2	2	3	2	2	1	1	1[1]	1	1	1	1
1	2	2	3	2	2	2	3	4	4	3	3	5	5	5	4	5	5	6	6	5	5	5	5	5
1	0	0	0	0	0	0	1	1	1	1	1	2	2	2	2	2	2	2	2	2	1	1	1	2
1	2	2	2	2	2	2	1	1	1	1	1	1	0	0	0	0	0	0	0	0	0	1	1	0

	1928	1930	1932	1934	1936	1938	1940	1942	1944	1946	1948	1950	1952	1954	1956	1958	1960	1962	1964	1966	1968	1970
Maryland																						
Democrats	4	6	6	6	6	6	6	4	5	4	4	3	3²	4	4	7	6	6²	6	5	4	5
Republicans	2	0	0	0	0	0	0	2	1	2	2	3	4	3	3	0	1	2	2	3	4	3
Massachusetts																						
Democrats	3	4	5¹	7	5	5	6	4¹	4	5	4	6	6	7	7	8	8	7¹	7	7	7	8
Republicans	13	12	10	8	10	10	9	10	10	9	8	8	8	7	7	6	6	5	5	5	5	4
Michigan																						
Democrats	0	0	10²	6	8	5	6	5	6	3	5	5	5²	7	6	7	7	8²	12	7	7	7
Republicans	13	13	7	11	9	12	11	12	11	14	12	12	13	11	12	11	11	11	7	12	12	12
Independents/																						
Libertarians																						
Minnesota																						
Democrats	0	0	1¹	1	1	1	0	0	2	1	4	4	4	5	5	4	3	4¹	4	3	3	4
Republicans	9	9	3	5	3	7	8	8	7	8	5	5	5	4	4	5	6	4	4	5	5	4
Mississippi																						
Democrats	8	8	7¹	7	7	7	7	7	7	7	7	7	6¹	6	6	6	6	5¹	4	5	5	5
Republicans	0	0	0	0	0	0	0	0	0	0	0	0	0	0	0	0	0	0	1	0	0	0
Missouri																						
Democrats	6	12	13¹	12	12	12	10	5	7	4	12	10	7	9	10	10	9	8¹	8	8	9	9
Republicans	10	4	0	1	1	1	3	8	6	9	1	3	4	2	1	1	2	2	2	2	1	1
Montana																						
Democrats	1	1	2	2	2	1	1	2	1	1	1	1	1	1	2	2	1	1	1	1	1	1
Republicans	1	1	0	0	0	1	1	0	1	1	1	1	1	1	0	0	1	1	1	1	1	1
Nebraska																						
Democrats	2	4	5¹	4	4	2	2	1	0	0	1	0	0	0	0	2	0	1	1	0	0	0
Republicans	4	2	0	1	1	3	3	4	4	4	3	4	4	4	4	2	4	3	2	3	3	3
Nevada																						
Democrats	0	0	1	1	1	1	1	1	1	0	1	1	0	0	1	1	1	1	1	1	1	1
Republicans	1	1	0	0	0	0	0	0	0	1	0	0	1	1	0	0	0	0	0	0	0	0
New Hampshire																						
Democrats	0	0	1	1	1⁴	0	0	0	0	0	0	0	0	0	0	0	0	0	1	0	0	0
Republicans	2	2	1	1	1	2	2	2	2	2	2	2	2	2	2	2	2	2	1	2	2	2
New Jersey																						
Democrats	2	3	4²	4	7	3	4	3	2	2	5	5	5	6	4	5	6	7²	11	9	9	9
Republicans	10	9	10	10	7	11	10	11	12	12	9	9	9	8	10	9	8	8	4	6	6	6
New Mexico																						
Democrats	0	1	1	1	1	1	1	2²	2	2	2	2	2	2	2	2	2	2	2	2	0	1
Republicans	1	0	0	0	0	0	0	0	0	0	0	0	0	0	0	0	0	0	0	0	2	1
New York																						
Democrats	23	23	29²	29	29	25	25	23	22	16	24	23	16¹	17	17	19	22	20¹	27	26	26	24
Republicans	20	20	16	16	16	19	19	21	22	28	20	22	27	26	26	24	21	21	14	15	15	17
North Carolina																						
Democrats	8	10	11²	11	11	11	11	12²	12	12	12	12	11	11	11	11	11	9¹	9	8	7	7
Republicans	2	0	0	0	0	0	0	0	0	0	0	0	1	1	1	1	1	2	2	3	4	4
North Dakota																						
Democrats	0	0	1	0	0	0	0	0	0	0	0	0	0	0	0	1	0	0	1	0	0	1
Republicans	3	3	2	2	2	2	2	2	2	2	2	2	2	2	2	1	2	2	1	2	2	1
Ohio																						
Democrats	3	9	18²	18	22	9	12	3¹	6	4	12	7	6	6	6	9	7	6²	10	5	6	7
Republicans	19	13	6	6	2	15	12	20	17	19	11	15	16	17	17	14	16	18	14	19	18	17
Oklahoma																						
Democrats	5	7	9²	9	9	9	8	7¹	6	6	8	6	5¹	5	5	5	5	5	5	4	4	4
Republicans	3	1	0	0	0	0	1	1	2	2	0	2	1	1	1	1	1	1	1	2	2	2
Oregon																						
Democrats	0	1	2	1	2	1	1	2	0	0	0	0	0	1	3	3	2	3	3	2	2	2
Republicans	3	2	1	2	1	2	2	4	4	4	4	4	4	3	1	1	2	1	1	2	2	2
Pennsylvania																						
Democrats	1	3	11¹	23	27	15	19	14¹	15	5	16	13	11¹	14	13	16	14	13¹	15	14	14	14
Republicans	35	33	23	11	7	9	15	19	18	28	19	20	19	16	17	14	16	14	12	13	13	13
Rhode Island																						
Democrats	1	1	2¹	2	2	0	2	2	2	2	2	2	2	2	2	2	2	2	2	2	2	2
Republicans	2	2	0	0	0	2	0	0	0	0	0	0	0	0	0	0	0	0	0	0	0	0
South Carolina																						
Democrats	7	7	6¹	6	6	6	6	6	6	6	6	6	6	6	6	6	6	6	6	6	5	5
Republicans	0	0	0	0	0	0	0	0	0	0	0	0	0	0	0	0	0	0	0	0	1	1

1972	1974	1976	1978	1980	1982	1984	1986	1988	1990	1992	1994	1996	1998	2000	2002	2004	2006	2008	2010	2012	2014	2016	2018	2020
4	5	5	6	7	7	6	6	6	5	4	4	4	4	4	6	6	6	7	6	7	7	7	7	7
4	3	3	2	1	1	2	2	2	3	4	4	4	4	4	2	2	2	1	2	1	1	1	1	1
9[6]	10	10	10	10	10[1]	10	10	10	10	8[1]	8	10	10	10	10	10	10	10	10	9	9	9	9	9
3	2	2	2	2	1	1	1	1	1	2	2	0	0	0	0	0	0	0	0	0	0	0	0	0
7	12	11	13	12	12[1]	11	11	11	11	10[1]	9	10	10	9	6	6	6	8	6	5[1]	5	5	5	7
12	7	8	6	7	6	7	7	7	7	6	7	6	6	7	9	9	9	7	9	9	9	9	9	5
																								2
4	5	5	4	3	5	5	5	5	6	6	6	6	6	5	4	4	5	5	4	5	5	5	5	5
4	3	3	4	5	3	3	3	3	2	2	2	2	2	3	4	4	3	3	4	3	3	3	3	3
3	3	3	3	3	3	3	4	4	5	5	4	2	3	3	2	2	2	3	1	1	1	1	1	1
2	2	2	2	2	2	2	1	1	0	0	1	3	2	2	2	2	2	1	3	3	3	3	3	3
9	9	8	8	6	6[1]	6	5	5	6	6	6	5	5	4	4	4	4	4	3	2[1]	2	2	2	2
1	1	2	2	4	3	3	4	4	3	3	3	4	4	5	5	5	5	5	6	6	6	6	6	6
1	2	1	1	1	1	1	1	1	1	1[1]	1	1	0	0	0	0	0	0	0	0	0	0	0	0
1	0	1	1	1	1	1	1	1	1	0	0	0	1	1	1	1	1	1	1	1	1	1	1	1
0	0	1	1	0	0	0	0	1	1	1	0	0	0	0	0	0	0	0	0	0	1	0	0	0
3	3	2	2	3	3	3	3	2	2	2	3	3	3	3	3	3	3	3	3	3	2	3	3	3
0	1	1	1	1	1[2]	1	1	1	1	1	0	0	1	1	1	1	1	2	1	2	1	3	3	3
1	0	0	0	0	1	1	1	1	1	1	2	2	1	1	2	2	2	1	2	2	3	1	1	1
0	1	1	1	1	1	0	0	0	1	1	0	0	0	0	0	0	2	2	0	2	1	2	2	2
2	1	1	1	1	1	2	2	2	1	1	2	2	2	2	2	2	0	0	2	0	1	0	0	0
8	12	11	10	8	9[1]	8	8	8	8	7[1]	5	6	7	7	7	7	7	8	7	6[1]	6	7	7	10
7	3	4	5	7	5	6	6	6	6	6	8	7	6	6	6	6	6	5	6	6	6	5	5	2
1	1	1	1	0	1[2]	1	1	1	1	1	1	1	1	1	1	1	1	3	2	2	2	2	2	3
1	1	1	1	2	2	2	2	2	2	2	2	2	2	2	2	2	2	0	1	1	1	1	1	0
22[1]	27	28	26	22	20[1]	19	20	21	21	18[1]	17	18	18	19	19	20	23	26	21	21[1]	18	18	18	21
17	12	11	13	17	14	15	14	13	13	13	14	13	13	12	10	9	6	3	8	6	9	9	9	6
7	9	9	9	7	9	6	8	8	7	8[2]	4	6	5	5	6	6	7	8	7	4	3	3	3	3
4	2	2	2	4	2	5	3	3	4	4	8	6	7	7	7	7	6	5	6	9	10	10	10	10
1	0	0	0	1	1	1	1	1	1	1	1	1	1	1	1	1	1	0	0	0	0	0	0	0
1	1	1	1	0	0	0	0	0	0	0	0	0	0	0	0	0	0	0	1	1	1	1	1	1
7[1]	8	10	10	11	10[1]	11	11	11	11	10[1]	6	8	8	8	6	6	7	10	5	41	4	4	4	4
16	15	13	13	12	11	10	10	10	10	9	13	11	11	11	12	12	11	8	13	12	12	12	12	12
5	6	5	5	5	5	5	4	4	4	4	1	0	0	1	1	1	1	1	1	0	0	0	0	1
1	0	1	1	1	1	1	2	2	2	2	5	6	6	5	4	4	4	4	4	5	5	5	5	4
2	4	4	4	3	3[2]	3	3	3	4	4	3	4	4	4	4	4	4	4	4	4	4	4	4	4
2	0	0	0	1	2	2	2	2	1	1	2	1	1	1	1	1	1	1	1	1	1	1	1	1
13[1]	14	17	15	13[6]	13[1]	13	12	12	11	11[1]	11	11	11	10	7	7	11	12	7	5[1]	5	5	8	9
12	11	8	10	12	10	10	11	11	12	10	10	10	10	11	12	12	8	7	12	13	13	13	10	9
2	2	2	2	1	1	1	1	0	1	1	2	2	2	2	2	2	2	2	2	2	2	2	2	2
0	0	0	0	1	1	1	1	1	2	1	1	0	0	0	0	0	0	0	0	0	0	0	0	0
4	5	5	4	2	3	3	4	4	4	3	2	2	2	2	2	2	2	2	1	1[2]	1	1	1	2
2	1	1	2	4	3	3	2	2	2	2	3	4	4	4	4	4	4	4	5	6	6	6	6	5

	1928	1930	1932	1934	1936	1938	1940	1942	1944	1946	1948	1950	1952	1954	1956	1958	1960	1962	1964	1966	1968	1970
South Dakota																						
Democrats	0	0	2[1]	2	1	0	0	0	0	0	0	0	0	0	1	1	0	0	0	0	0	2
Republicans	3	3	0	0	1	2	2	2	2	2	2	2	2	2	1	1	2	2	2	2	2	0
Tennessee																						
Democrats	8	8	7[1]	7	7	7	7	8[2]	8	8	8	8	71	7	7	7	7	6	6	5	5	5
Republicans	2	2	2	2	2	2	2	2	2	2	2	2	2	2	2	2	2	3	3	4	4	4
Texas																						
Democrats	17	17	21[2]	21	21	21	21	21	21	21	21	21	22[2]	21	21	21	21	21[2]	23	21	20	20
Republicans	17	1	0	0	0	0	0	0	0	0	0	0	0	0	1	1	1	1	2	0	2	3
Utah																						
Democrats	0	0	2	2	2	2	2	2	2	1	2	2	0	0	0	1	2	0	1	0	0	1
Republicans	2	2	0	0	0	0	0	0	0	1	0	0	2	2	2	1	0	2	1	2	2	1
Vermont																						
Democrats	0	0	1	0	0	0	0	0	0	0	0	0	0	0	0	1	0	0	0	0	0	0
Republicans	2	2	1	1	1	1	1	1	1	1	1	1	1	1	1	0	1	1	1	1	1	1
Virginia																						
Democrats	8	9	9[1]	9	9	9	9	9	9	9	9	9	7[2]	8	8	8	8	8	8	6	5	4
Republicans	2	1	0	0	0	0	0	0	0	0	0	0	3	2	2	2	2	2	2	4	5	6
Washington																						
Democrats	1	1	6[2]	6	6	6	6	3	4	1	2	2	1[2]	1	1	1	2	1	5	5	5	6
Republicans	4	4	0	0	0	0	0	3	2	5	4	4	6	6	6	6	5	6	2	2	2	1
West Virginia																						
Democrats	1	2	6	6	6	5	6	3	5	2	6	6	5	6	4	5	5	4[1]	4	4	5	5
Republicans	5	4	0	0	0	1	0	3	1	4	0	0	1	0	2	1	1	1	1	1	0	0
Wisconsin																						
Democrats	0	1	5[1]	3	3	0	1	3	2	0	2	1	1	3	3	5	4	4	5	3	3	5
Republicans	11	10	5	0	0	8	6	5	7	10	8	9	9	7	7	5	6	6	5	7	7	5
Wyoming																						
Democrats	0	0	0	1	1	0	1	0	0	0	0	0	0	0	0	0	0	1	0	0	1	1
Republicans	1	1	1	0	0	1	0	1	1	1	1	1	1	1	1	1	1	0	1	1	0	0

1. State lost seats due to reapportionment.

2. State gained seats due to reapportionment.

3. Alaska 1972, California 1962, and Louisiana 1972: national and state totals reflect the reelection of a Democrat who died before the election but whose name remained on the ballot.

4. Illinois 1930, Indiana 1960 and 1984, and New Hampshire 1936: national and state totals reflect the final outcome of a contested election in which a Republican was first certified the winner, but the House decided to seat the Democrat.

5. Louisiana 1974: national and state totals reflect the final outcome of a contested election in which no winner was declared, followed by a special election won by the Republican.

6. Massachusetts 1972 and Pennsylvania 1980: national and state Democratic totals reflect the election of an Independent candidate who previously announced he would serve as a Democrat.

7. Texas 1928: national and state totals reflect the final outcome of a contested election in which a Democrat was at first certified the winner, but the House decided to seat the Republican.

8. At the time of the 2012 elections, Illinois had 18 House seats divided between 12 Democrats and 6 Republicans. However, in following the election one Democrat—Jesse Jackson Jr.—resigned his seat, citing health and other issues. A special election to fill the vacancy was scheduled in 2013. For purposes of this table, that contest has been assigned to Democrats because Jackson's seat in Chicago is one of the safest Democratic seats in the nation. If a Democrat wins, as expected, the Illinois ratio of Democrats to Republicans will be 12 to 6.

NOTES: State totals reflect the number of Democrats and Republicans in each House delegation at the start of each Congress. The above totals do not include "other" representatives elected as independent or third-party candidates. Those numbers are California: Progressive 1936 (1). (No formal party. The representative became a Democrat in 1938.) Minnesota: Farmer-Labor 1928–1930 (1), 1932 (5), 1934 (3), 1936 (5), 1938–1942 (1). (Merged with D in 1944.) New York: American Labor 1938–1948 (1). (Party disbanded after 1954.) Ohio: Independent 1950–1952 (1). (Defeated by Democrat in 1954.) Wisconsin: Progressive 1934 (7), 1936–1938 (2), 1940 (3), 1942 (2) and 1944 (1). (Disbanded after 1944. The last Progressive became a Republican in 1946.) Vermont: Independent 1990–2000 (1). Virginia: Independent 2000 (1). National totals: 1928–1930 (1), 1932 (5), 1934 (10), 1936 (13), 1938 (4), 1940 (5), 1942 (4), 1944 (2), 1946–1952 (1), 1990–1998 (1), and 2000 (2).

1972	1974	1976	1978	1980	1982	1984	1986	1988	1990	1992	1994	1996	1998	2000	2002	2004	2006	2008	2010	2012	2014	2016	2018	2020
1	0	0	1	1	1[1]	1	1	1	1	1	1	0	0	0	0	1	1	1	0	0	0	0	0	0
1	2	2	1	1	0	0	0	0	0	0	0	1	1	1	1	0	0	0	1	1	1	1	1	1
31	5	5	5	5	6[2]	6	6	6	6	6	4	4	4	4	5	5	5	5	2	2	2	2	2	2
5	3	3	3	3	3	3	3	3	3	3	5	5	5	5	4	4	4	4	7	7	7	7	7	7
20[2]	21	22	20	19	22[2]	17	17	19	19	21[2]	19	17	17	17	17	11	13	12	9	12[2]	11	11	11	13
4	3	2	4	5	5	10	10	8	8	9	11	13	13	13	15	21	19	20	23	24	25	25	25	23
2	2	1	1	0	2	0	1	1	2	2	1	0	0	1	1	1	1	1	1	12	0	0	0	1
0	0	1	1	2	3	3	2	2	1	1	2	3	3	2	2	2	2	2	2	3	4	4	4	3
0	0	0	0	0	0	0	0	0	0	0	0	0	0	0	0	0	1	1	1	1	1	1	1	1
1	1	1	1	1	1	1	1	1	0	0	0	0	0	0	0	0	0	0	0	0	0	0	0	0
3	5	4	4	1	4	4	5	5	6	7[2]	6	6	6	4	3	3	3	6	3	3	3	4	4	7
7	5	6	6	9	6	6	5	5	4	4	5	5	5	6	8	8	8	5	8	8	8	7	7	4
6	6	6	6	5	5[2]	5	5	5	5	8[2]	2	3	5	6	6	6	6	6	5	6[2]	6	6	6	7
1	1	1	1	2	3	3	3	3	3	1	7	6	4	3	3	3	3	3	4	4	4	4	4	3
4[1]	4	4	4	2	4	4	4	4	4	3[1]	3	3	3	2	2	2	2	2	1	1	0	0	0	0
0	0	0	0	2	0	0	0	0	0	0	0	0	0	0	1	1	1	1	1	2	2	3	3	3
5[1]	7	7	6	5	5	5	5	5	4	4	3	5	4	5	4	4	5	5	3	3	3	3	3	3
4	2	2	3	4	4	4	4	4	5	5	6	4	5	4	4	4	3	3	5	5	5	5	5	5
1	1	0	0	0	0	0	0	0	0	0	0	0	0	0	0	0	0	0	0	0	0	0	0	0
0	0	0	1	1	1	1	1	1	1	1	1	1	1	1	1	1	1	1	1	1	1	1	1	1

Governors, 2018–2021

Following is a list of governors who served during the period of President Donald Trumps's first term, 2017–2021; multiple governors who began their service in 2022 are also listed. All governors serve four-year terms except those who served as acting governors or those representing New Hampshire and Vermont; they serve two-year terms. Party designations appear in parentheses following the governor's name. The following abbreviations were used: (D) Democrat; (R) Republican.

	Dates of Service		*Dates of Service*
Alabama		**Kansas**	
Kay Ivey (R)	April 10, 2017–	Jeff Colyer (R)	January 31, 2018–January 14, 2019
Alaska		Laura Kelly (D)	January 14, 2019–
Bill Walker (R)	December 1, 2014–December 3, 2018	**Kentucky**	
Mike Dunleavy (R)	December 3, 2018–	Matt Bevin (D)	December 8, 2015–December 9, 2019
Arizona		Andy Beshear (D)	December 10, 2019–
Doug Ducey (R)	January 5, 2015–	**Louisiana**	
Arkansas		John Bel Edwards (D)	January 11, 2016–
Asa Hutchinson (R)	January 13, 2015–	**Maine**	
California		Paul R. LePage (R)	January 5, 2011–January 1, 2019
Jerry Brown (D)	January 3, 2011–January 7, 2019	Janet Mills (D)	January 2, 2019–
Gavin Newsom (D)	January 7, 2019–	**Maryland**	
Colorado		Larry Hogan (R)	January 21, 2015–
John W. Hickenlooper (D)	January 11, 2011–January 9, 2019	**Massachusetts**	
Jared Polis (D)	January 9, 2019–	Charlie Baker (D)	January 8, 2015–
Connecticut		**Michigan**	
Dannel P. Malloy (D)	January 5, 2011–January 9, 2019	Rick Synder (R)	January 1, 2011–January 1, 2019
Ned Lamont (D)	January 9, 2019–	Gretchen Whitmer (D)	January 1, 2019–
Delaware		**Minnesota**	
John Carney (D)	January 17, 2017–	Mark Dayton (D)	January 3, 2011–January 7, 2019
Florida		Tim Walz (D)	January 7, 2019–
Rick Scott (R)	January 4, 2011–January 7, 2019	**Mississippi**	
Ron DeSantis (R)	January 8, 2019–	Phil Bryant (R)	January 10, 2012 – January 13, 2020
Georgia		Tate Reeves (R)	January 14, 2020 –
Nathan Deal (R)	January 10, 2011–January 13, 2019	**Missouri**	
Brian Kemp (R)	January 14, 2019–	Mike Parson (R)	June 1, 2018–
Hawaii		**Montana**	
David Ige (D)	December 1, 2014–January 7, 2019	Steve Bullock (D)	January 7, 2013–January 3, 2021
Idaho		Greg Gianforte (R)	January 4, 2021–
C.L. "Butch" Otter (R)	January 1, 2007 –January 7, 2019	**Nebraska**	
Brad Little (R)	January 7, 2019–	Pete Ricketts (R)	January 8, 2015–
Illinois		**Nevada**	
Bruce Rauner (R)	January 12, 2015–January 14, 2019	Brian Sandoval (R)	January 3, 2011–January 7, 2019
J.B. Pritzker (D)	January 14, 2019–	Steve Sisolak (D)	January 7, 2019–
Indiana		**New Hampshire**	
Eric Holcomb (R)	January 9, 2017–	Chris Sununu (R)	January 5, 2017–
Iowa		**New Jersey**	
Terry E. Branstad (R)	January 14, 2011–May 24, 2017	Phil Murphy (D)	January 16, 2018–
Kim Reynolds (R)	May 24, 2017–		

Dates of Service

New Mexico

Susana Martinez (R)	January 1, 2011–January 1, 2019
Michelle Lujan Grisham (D)	January 1, 2019–

New York

Andrew M. Cuomo (D)	January 1, 2011–August 23, 2021
Kathy Hochul (D)	August 24, 2019–

North Carolina

Roy Cooper (D)	January 1, 2017–

North Dakota

Doug Burgum (R)	December 15, 2016–

Ohio

John R. Kasich (R)	January 10, 2011–January 14, 2019
Mike DeWine (R)	January 14, 2019–

Oklahoma

Mary Fallin (R)	January 10, 2011–January 14, 2019
Kevin Stitt (R)	January 14, 2019–

Oregon

Kate Brown (D)	February 18, 2015–

Pennsylvania

Tom Wolf (D)	January 20, 2015–

Rhode Island

Gina Raimondo (D)	January 6, 2015–March 2, 2021
Dan McKee (D)	March 2, 2021–

South Carolina

Henry McMaster (R)	January 24, 2017–

Dates of Service

South Dakota

Dennis Daugaard (R)	January 8, 2011–January 5, 2019
Kristi Noem (R)	January 8, 2019–

Tennessee

Bill Haslam (R)	January 15, 2011–January 8, 2019
Bill Lee (R)	January 19, 2019–

Texas

Greg Abbott (R)	January 20, 2015–

Utah

Gary R. Herbert (R)	August 11, 2009–January 3, 2021
Spencer Cox (R)	January 4, 2021–

Vermont

Phil Scott (R)	January 5, 2017 –

Virginia

Ralph Northam (D)	January 13, 2018–January 15, 2022
Glenn Youngkin (R)	January 15, 2022–

Washington

Jay Inslee (D)	January 16, 2013–

West Virginia

Jim Justice (R)	January 16, 2017–

Wisconsin

Scott Walker (R)	January 3, 2011–January 7, 2019
Tony Evers (D)	January 7, 2019–

Wyoming

Matt Mead (R)	January 3, 2011–January 7, 2019
Mark Gordon (R)	January 7, 2019–

Index

Note: Page references with (fig.) or (table) refer to figures and tables, respectively.